THE NEW BEACON BOOK OF

# Quotations by Women

*Other books by Rosalie Maggio*

The Nonsexist Word Finder

The Music Box Christmas

How to Say It

The Bias-Free Word Finder

Marie Marvingt:
La Femme d'un Siècle

The Beacon Book of
Quotations by Women

The New Beacon Book of

# Quotations
# by Women

Rosalie Maggio

BEACON PRESS · BOSTON

Beacon Press
25 Beacon Street
Boston, Massachusetts 02108-2892

Beacon Press books are published under the auspices of
the Unitarian Universalist Association of Congregations.

99 98   8 7 6 5 4 3 2

Text design by Boskydell Studio

*Library of Congress Cataloging-in-Publication Data*

The New Beacon book of quotations by
women / [compiled by] Rosalie Maggio.
p.    cm.
ISBN 0-8070-6782-2 (cloth)
ISBN 0-8070-6783-0 (paper)
1. Quotations, English.  2. Women—Quotations.
I. Maggio, Rosalie.
PN6081.5.N48    1996
082'.082—dc20    96-19641

To DAVID

*Liz, Katie, Matt*

*"A book which hath been culled from the flowers of all books."*

George Eliot, *The Spanish Gypsy* (1868)

# Contents

# Acknowledgments

The first debt to be acknowledged in a book such as this must be to the gifted, perceptive, and acutely alive writers, speakers, thinkers, and doers who have by their words given us new ways of looking at ourselves and our world.

Appreciation and special thanks are due Liz Koskenmaki, Daniel Willms, Mary Maggio, Tom Pliner, Katie Koskenmaki, and Jayne Lindesmith for their careful research work. Matt Koskenmaki provided irreplaceable technical support and suggestions that greatly simplified the handling of so much material.

For their contributions of quotations and support, I'm grateful to Sandy Berman, Jan DeSirey, Chris Dodge, Michelle Edwards, Mary Kaye Medinger, the late Grace Nash, O.S.F., the Reverend Thomas C. Nash, Carol Andrus, Daniel A. Mastry, Dorothy Wightman, Bonnie Z. Goldsmith, Diane Burns, Esther Lilley, Joyce Koskenmaki, Anne E. Patrick, Alexandra Robbin, Laura Gregg, and Heidi Eschenbacher.

The expert reference librarians at the St. Paul Public Library made it possible for me to visit libraries throughout the country without ever leaving home, while the cheerful and helpful librarians at the Lexington branch make it a model of what is best in such critically important neighborhood libraries.

Susan Worst is the editor every writer fantasizes about finding. Her keen vision, common sense, and good humor have been critical to the book and have led to a writer-editor relationship that I feel is a model for trust and friendship as well as for effective business practices.

"Call it a clan, call it a network, call it a tribe, call it a family. Whatever you call it, whoever you are, you need one" (Jane Howard). A broad thank you to my parents, Irene Nash Maggio and Paul Joseph Maggio, and to my siblings, Frank Maggio, Patrick J. Maggio, Kevin Michael Maggio, Mary Maggio, Paul T. Maggio, Mark E. Maggio, and Matthew J. Maggio.

And the finest blessing of them all: a congenial family—husband David, adult children Liz, Katie, and Matt, who respect, support, and encourage each person's work and choices. What they have put up with in the way of my absentmindedness and in being followed around and quoted at they are much too nice to tell.

# Notes to the Reader

"Traversing a slow page, to come upon
a lode of the pure shining metal
is to exult inwardly for greedy hours."

Kathleen Norris, "Beauty in Letters,"
*These I Like Best* (1941)

## User's Guide

You, the reader, have been very much a part of my life for all the years I've been reading and collecting these quotations. I have often imagined your delight, your shock, your burst of laughter, your "aha!" or your sigh as you found words that you yourself would have said had you just thought of them in time. If you find only half as much pleasure here as I have imagined for you, you will have a very good time indeed.

You can enter this collection of ideas, feelings, and brilliantly worked words in three ways. If you are looking for a quotation by a specific woman, use the name index in the back of the book. If you need a quotation on a specific subject, the subject and key line index in the back of the book or the alphabetically arranged topic headings and numerous cross-references in the body of the book will help you find what you need. If you are the third seeker, the browser, you need no further help. However, with you in mind, quotations have been arranged under topic headings in essay-like fashion for your reading pleasure.

Quotations were selected for their memorability, their original use of language, their brevity, their ability to shatter conventional patterns of speech or thought, and their potential usefulness to readers needing quotations for speaking and writing. Although some quotations are included because they belong to the canon of the familiar, others bring you unfamiliar words by familiar women (and vice versa), while thousands of others appear for the first time in a collection of quotations (approximately eighty percent of the quotations in this book appear in no other collection).

The date that follows a book title is generally the date of first publication; in some cases this occurred years or even centuries after the quoted words were said or written. Whenever possible, the original date of the material is included in parentheses after the name. For consistency, spellings have been Americanized.

### It's Good, But Did a Woman Say It?

Every person included in this book is really a woman, despite such names as Lawrence L. Lynch, James Tiptree, Jr., Ralph Iron, Anthony Gilbert, Joseph Shearing, Roman Doubleday, Lawrence Hope, Miles Franklin, and others. Any entry by "anonymous" or nonspecific name ("actor," "telephone operator") has been ascertained to be a woman.

### Can You Depend on It?

In order to assure myself and guarantee you of accuracy, I have examined the original source of almost every quotation. Approximately three percent of the quotations were unfindable in the original—by me at this time, at any rate. When I was unable to locate the original quotation, I credited the earliest publication of it in a secondary source.

In the section on misquotations (located between "misfortune" and "mistakes"), you will find popular quotations that have been attributed to the wrong person or that contain some other error of fact.

### A Nice Book, But So Many Typos!

When you see a name like bell hooks or BarbaraNeely, a book title like *The Young Visiters,* or a quote like this: "A Famous Film Star who is left alone is more alone than any other person has ever been in the whole Histry of the World, because of the contrast to our normal enviromint," know that bell hooks and BarbaraNeely spell their names that way, nine-year-old Daisy Ashford misspells the title of her book, and Anita Loos deliberately used idiosyncratic spelling and capitalization. Carolyn Wells wrote "Maxioms," Audrey Hepburn's name was originally Andry, and it is Virgilia, not Virginia, Peterson.

Putting "[sic]" after each unusual usage would have looked, in the end, like a book with the hiccups. There is an astonishing variety of expression and nonstandard usage in these quotations—all forms of language that supported good ideas have seemed valuable to me. There may, of course, be typographical errors in the book, but it is much more likely that you are looking at the intended form.

### Quotations With Sexist Language

Given the grammatical conventions and social mores of their times, many women quoted here use language that is today considered sexist and inaccurate (for example, the pseudogeneric "he," "man," and "mankind"). Just as you may see "thee" or "thou" or "wouldst" in some of the quotations, so too you will see language that is obsolete by today's inclusive standards.

Quotations with sexist language are reproduced here as they were originally written—out of respect for the writers, out of a feeling for reality that says "this is what was," and from a belief that one does not rewrite history or literature. Reinterpret, add to, discover lost pieces of, evaluate with new eyes—yes. Rewrite—no. However, I strongly urge anyone who uses quotations containing sexist language to adapt them so as not to perpetuate the sexism. This can be done in a number of ways.

- Put only part of the quotation in quotation marks, rewriting the rest. Agnes Repplier: "The vanity of man revolts from the serene indifference of the cat." Suggested adaptation: Agnes Repplier tells us that our vanity "revolts from the serene indifference of the cat." Jane Austen: "One man's way may be as good as another's, but we all like our own best." Suggested adaptation: When Jane Austen says that one person's way may be as good as another's she adds, "but we all like our own best."
- Use brackets or ellipsis dots to replace or omit sexist material. Vita Sackville-West: "Ambition, old as mankind, the immemorial weakness of the strong." Suggested adaptation: "Ambition, old as [creation], the immemorial weakness of the strong." Or: "Ambition . . . the immemorial weakness of the strong."
- In certain cases, you may want to use "[sic]" to indicate that the material was sexist in the original and to draw your audience's attention to the inaccuracy. Helen Rowland: "The dollar sign is the only sign in which the modern man appears to have any real faith." Suggested adaptation: "The dollar sign is the only sign in which the modern man [sic] appears to have any real faith."
- When a quotation is tightly woven with sexist words, credit the writer for the idea, omitting the quotation marks and rephrasing the words. Mary Renault: "In all men is evil sleeping; the good man is he who will not awaken it, in himself or in other men." Suggested adaptation: Mary Renault says that evil sleeps in all of us. The good among us will not awaken it, in ourselves or in others.

## Your Help Wanted

If you have corrections, additions, or suggestions—or can supply the original source for a quotation credited to a secondary source—I would very much appreciate hearing from you: Rosalie Maggio, c/o Beacon Press, 25 Beacon Street, Boston, MA 02108-2892.

# A

## ⑨ ABILITY

1 In the first grade, I already knew the pattern of my life. I didn't know the living of it, but I knew the line. . . . From the first day in school until the day I graduated, everyone gave me one hundred plus in art. Well, where do you go in life? You go to the place where you got one hundred plus.

Louise Nevelson, *Dawns + Dusks* (1976)

2 When a workman knows the use of his tools, he can make a door as well as a window.

George Eliot, *The Mill on the Floss* (1860)

3 Nature distributes her favors unequally.

George Sand (1837), in Marie Jenny Howe, ed., *The Intimate Journal of George Sand* (1929)

4 There is only one proof of ability: action.

Marie von Ebner-Eschenbach, *Aphorisms* (1893)

See also Sales Ability, Talent.

## ⑨ ABORTION

5 Abortion, for many women, is more than an experience of suffering beyond anything most men will ever know, it is an act of mercy, and an act of self-defense.

Alice Walker, "The Right to Life: What Can the White Man Say to the Black Woman?" *Her Blue Body Everything We Know* (1991)

6 nobody really wants to get up on that table! / nobody really wants to kill a part of themselves. / nobody wants to meet their ancestors with blood on / their hands/but when a woman knows she CANT / handle bringing new life into fullness/she

more than / has the right, to beg that life's forgiveness / and send it back to the spirit world.

Laini Mataka, "Just Becuz U Believe in Abortion Doesn't Mean U're Not Pro-Life," *Restoring the Queen* (1994)

7 There is tremendous sadness, loneliness, in the cry, "A woman's right to choose." No one wants an abortion as she wants an ice-cream cone or a Porsche. She wants an abortion as an animal, caught in a trap, wants to gnaw off its own leg. Abortion is a tragic attempt to escape a desperate situation by an act of violence and self-loss.

Frederica Mathewes-Green, "Unplanned Parenthood," in *Policy Review* (1991)

8 Abortions will not let you forget. / You remember the children you got that you did not get.

Gwendolyn Brooks, "the mother," *A Street in Bronzeville* (1945)

9 they say the wrath of God will visit anyone who has / an abortion/but i got news for them—most women / punish themselves more severely than God ever cld / or wld and any God that cant forgive, needs to / be replaced.

Laini Mataka, "Just Becuz U Believe in Abortion Doesn't Mean U're Not Pro-Life," *Restoring the Queen* (1994)

10 I believe that in a contest between the living and the almost living, the latter must, if necessary, give way to the will of the former.

Anna Quindlen, "Some Thoughts About Abortion," *Living Out Loud* (1988)

11 In nature, creatures never ended the lives of others except to survive. To women, abortion was self-defense and preservation of the species. Abortion was not a fancy born out of the female mind. Abortion was instinct beyond ideas.

Ana Castillo, *Sapogonia* (1990)

1 I belong to that enormous group, very likely a majority, in fact, who are both pro-choice and anti-abortion.

Nancy Mairs, *Ordinary Time* (1993)

2 Abortion does not belong in the Constitution, presidential politics, or back alleys.

Alida Brill, *Nobody's Business* (1990)

3 In front of the clinic, holding the bullhorn, was a thin hyperthyroid man. . . . His supporters included a number of college-age young men, all fervently committed to carrying their own pregnancies to term.

Sara Paretsky, *Bitter Medicine* (1987)

4 If men could get pregnant, abortion would be a sacrament.

Anonymous Boston cabdriver, to Florynce R. Kennedy (1960s)

See also Birth Control, Childbirth, Pregnancy.

## ❧ ABSENCE

5 when you're away i feel like / i'm only wearing one shoe.

Alta, *i am not a practicing angel* (1975)

6 Where you used to be, there is a hole in the world, which I find myself constantly walking around in the day-time, and falling into at night. I miss you like hell.

Edna St. Vincent Millay (1920), in Allan Ross Macdougall, ed., *Letters of Edna St. Vincent Millay* (1952)

7 Absence on Love effects the same / As winds oppos'd to fire / Extinguishes a feeble Flame / And blows a great one higher.

Anne Finch, "On Absence," *Miscellany Poems, Written by a Lady* (1713)

8 How long time is when one is sad! Is it three years or three days since you went away. . . ?

Eugénie de Guérin (1831), in Guillaume S. Trébutien, ed., *Letters of Eugénie de Guérin* (1865)

9 It takes time for the absent to assume their true shape in our thoughts.

Colette, *Sido* (1929)

10 Absence becomes the greatest Presence.

May Sarton, "Difficult Scene," *The Lion and the Rose* (1948)

11 It is only love that has already fallen sick that is killed by absence.

Diane de Poitiers (1550), in Winifred Gordon, *A Book of Days* (1910)

12 All along, one of my major complaints was his absence from home, and even worse, his absence when he *was* home.

Sonia Johnson, *From Housewife to Heretic* (1981)

13 Absence is one of the most useful ingredients of family life, and to dose it rightly is an art like any other.

Freya Stark, *The Coast of Incense* (1953)

14 Fond as we are of our loved ones, there comes at times during their absence an unexplained peace.

Anne Shaw, *But Such Is Life* (1931)

15 The heart may think it knows better: the senses know that absence blots people out. We have really no absent friends.

Elizabeth Bowen, *The Death of the Heart* (1938)

16 Absence makes the heart grow fonder, / And presents make it fonder still.

Rose Henniker Heaton, *The Perfect Hostess* (1931)

See also Farewells, Parting, Reunions.

## ❧ ABSENTMINDEDNESS

17 If you didn't sit with your head in the clouds so perpetually you wouldn't get so many shocks.

Ethel M. Dell, *The Unknown Quantity* (1924)

18 In the family it is said Gabe "doesn't notice much—his head is in the clouds." He accepts this criticism as complimentary: "In the clouds? Oh, thank you. I try."

Laura Cunningham, *Sleeping Arrangements* (1989)

## ❧ ABSOLUTES

19 In this unbelievable universe in which we live, there are no absolutes. Even parallel lines, reaching into infinity, meet somewhere yonder.

Pearl S. Buck, *A Bridge for Passing* (1962)

20 I was seized again with a desperate longing for the absolute.

Caryl Churchill, *Top Girls* (1984)

1 Absolutes are absolutely dangerous.
> James Tiptree, Jr., *Up the Walls of the World* (1978)

See also Dogma.

## ❦ ABUNDANCE

2 Abundance is, in large part, an attitude.
> Sue Patton Thoele, *The Woman's Book of Confidence* (1992)

## ❦ ABUSE

3 If spanking worked, we'd only have to do it once.
> Nancy Samalin, with Catherine Whitney, *Love and Anger* (1991)

4 The unsuccessful bully can always become the father of a family.
> Rebecca West, in *The Freewoman* (1912)

5 Few people who are hit once by someone they love respond in the way they might to a singular physical assault by a stranger.
> bell hooks, *Talking Back* (1989)

6 I labored to obtain protection for unhappy wives, beaten, mangled, mutilated, or trampled on by brutal husbands. . . . I came to the conclusion that in spite of all the authority in favor of flogging the delinquents it was *not* expedient on the women's behalf that they should be so punished, since after they had undergone such chastisement, however well merited, the ruffians would inevitably return more brutalized and infuriated than ever; and again have their wives at their mercy. The only thing really effective, I considered, was to give the wife the power of separating herself and her children from her tyrant.
> Frances Power Cobbe, *Life of Frances Power Cobbe*, vol. 2 (1894)

## ❦ ACCEPTANCE

7 I accept the universe!
> Margaret Fuller, to Thomas Carlyle (1846), in Perry Miller, ed., *Margaret Fuller* (1963)

8 I can accept the world, the plan / Allotted to the race of man. / But Margaret Fuller's brag was worse. / She could accept the universe. / Carlyle said, "By Gad, she'd better!" / And so did everyone who met her.
> Helen Bevington, "Margaret Fuller in Chelsea," *Nineteen Million Elephants* (1950)

9 Learning to live with what you're born with / is the process, / the involvement, / the making of a life.
> Diane Wakoski, "I Have Had to Learn to Live With My Face," *The Motorcycle Betrayal Poems* (1971)

10 If Fate should say, "Thy course is run," / It would not make me sad; / All that I wished to do is done, / All that I would have, had.
> Laurence Hope, "The Court of Pomegranates," *Stars of the Desert* (1903)

11 I love my past. I love my present. I'm not ashamed of what I've had, and I'm not sad because I have it no longer.
> Colette, *The Last of Cheri* (1926)

12 There are people who live lives little different than the beasts, and I don't mean that badly. I mean that they accept whatever happens day to day without struggle or question or regret. To them things just are, like the earth and sky and seasons.
> Celeste De Blasis, *Wild Swan* (1984)

13 Whatever is—is best.
> Ella Wheeler Wilcox, poem title, *Poems of Pleasure* (1888)

14 Everything in life that we really accept undergoes a change.
> Katherine Mansfield (1920), *Journal of Katherine Mansfield* (1927)

See also Resignation, Self-Acceptance, Tolerance.

## ❦ ACCIDENTS

15 Don't go into Mr. McGregor's garden: your Father had an accident there; he was put in a pie by Mrs. McGregor.
> Beatrix Potter, *The Tale of Peter Rabbit* (1901)

16 Harry is walking with a cane these days. . . . What necessitated the cane was the fact of Young Cat scampering among Harry's ankles at a moment

when Harry happened to be walking among them himself.

Margaret Halsey, *This Demi-Paradise* (1960)

1 I suffered two grave accidents in my life. One in which a streetcar knocked me down. . . . The other accident is Diego.

Frida Kahlo, on her husband, Diego Rivera, in Hayden Herrera, *Frida* (1983)

2 Accident is veiled necessity.

Marie von Ebner-Eschenbach, *Aphorisms* (1893)

# ❦ ACCOMPLISHMENT

3 Out of the strain of the Doing, / Into the peace of the Done.

Julia Louise Woodruff, "Harvest Home," in *Sunday at Home* (1910)

4 I don't like the sound of all those lists he's making—it's like taking too many notes at school; you feel you've achieved something when you haven't.

Dodie Smith, *I Capture the Castle* (1948)

5 Accomplishments have no color.

Leontyne Price, in Brian Lanker, *I Dream a World* (1989)

See also Success.

# ❦ ACTING

6 Acting is standing up naked and turning around very slowly.

Rosalind Russell, with Chris Chase, *Life Is a Banquet* (1977)

7 Acting is a form of confession.

Tallulah Bankhead, *Tallulah* (1952)

8 Acting for me was the gospel, the love of the spoken word.

Jeanne Moreau, in Oriana Fallaci, *Limelighters* (1963)

9 Without wonder and insight, acting is just a trade. With it, it becomes creation.

Bette Davis, *The Lonely Life* (1962)

10 Imagination, industry, and intelligence—"the three I's"—are all indispensable to the actress, but of these three the greatest is, without any doubt, imagination.

Ellen Terry, *The Story of My Life* (1908)

11 An actor is exactly as big as his imagination.

Minnie Maddern Fiske, in Alexander Woollcott, *Mrs. Fiske* (1917)

12 For an actress to be a success, she must have the face of a Venus, the brains of a Minerva, the grace of Terpsichore, the memory of a Macaulay, the figure of Juno, and the hide of a rhinoceros.

Ethel Barrymore, in George Jean Nathan, *The Theatre in the Fifties* (1953)

13 Oh, those wonder-filled evenings when acting enables me for a short moment to have more life.

Liv Ullmann, *Choices* (1984)

14 Acting requires absorption, but not self-absorption and, in the actor's mind, the question must always be "Why am I doing this?", not "How am I doing it?"

Maureen Lipman, *How Was It for You?* (1985)

15 The actor must know that since he, himself, is the instrument, he must play on it to serve the character with the same effortless dexterity with which the violinist makes music on his. Just because he doesn't look like a violin is no reason to assume his techniques should be thought of as less difficult.

Uta Hagen, *A Challenge for the Actor* (1991)

16 Actors are cave dwellers in a rich darkness which they love and hate.

Iris Murdoch, *The Sea, The Sea* (1978)

17 All the things that are negative in me as a person—the incompetence and despair and weakness and pain—are like a gift from God in a performer. If you don't hide them and if you stop lying to yourself about what you are and are not, there is a ring or a tent or a stage where you can take them and use them to make something beautiful.

Elizabeth Ashley, with Ross Firestone, *Actress: Postcards From the Road* (1978)

18 Movie actors are just ordinary, mixed-up people—with agents.

Jean Kerr, *Mary, Mary* (1963)

19 At one time I thought he wanted to be an actor. He had certain qualifications, including no money and a total lack of responsibility.

Hedda Hopper, *From Under My Hat* (1952)

1 He told me that I couldn't act. I said, "Well, that's no news to me. You didn't hire me because I could act, you know. They hired me because I'm Dolly Parton and I'm a personality—and if you're any kind of a director, then you'll make it look like I'm acting."

Dolly Parton, to "Steel Magnolias" director Herbert Ross, news item (1994)

2 If there wasn't something called acting, they would probably hospitalize people like me.

Whoopi Goldberg, in Dotson Rader, "'I Knew What I Wanted to Be,'" *Parade* (1992)

3 If I weren't doing what I'm doing now, the actress thing, the star business, if you want to call it that, whatever it is, I'd be in an asylum. I'm sure of it.

Mia Farrow, in John Robert Colombo, *Popcorn in Paradise* (1979)

4 I found out that acting was hell. You spend all your time trying to do what they put people in asylums for.

Jane Fonda, in John Robert Colombo, *Popcorn in Paradise* (1979)

5 I detest acting because it is sheer drudgery.

Tallulah Bankhead, *Tallulah* (1952)

6 The question actors most often get asked is how they can bear saying the same things over and over again night after night, but God knows the answer to *that* is, don't we all *anyway*; might as well get paid for it.

Elaine Dundy, *The Dud Avocado* (1958)

7 We're harmless megalomaniacs, fanatic in our devotion to a profession which rarely rewards us with a livelihood. Since we court public display we're the foes of privacy. The glass house is our favorite residence.

Tallulah Bankhead, *Tallulah* (1952)

8 An actor can remember his briefest notice well into senescence and long after he has forgotten his phone number and where he lives.

Jean Kerr, "One Half of Two on the Aisle," *Please Don't Eat the Daisies* (1957)

9 Every actor has a natural animosity toward every other actor, present or absent, living or dead.

Louise Brooks, *Lulu in Hollywood* (1982)

10 I want only dead actors. That way there'll be no jealousy.

Simone Signoret, *Adieu, Volodya* (1986)

11 I do not regret one professional enemy I have made. Any actor who doesn't dare to make an enemy should get out of the business.

Bette Davis, *The Lonely Life* (1962)

12 I have yet to see one completely unspoiled star, except for the animals—like Lassie.

Edith Head, in C. Robert Jennings, "Body by MacLaine—in Originals by Edith Head," *The Saturday Evening Post* (1963)

13 Actors may know how to act, but a lot of them don't know how to behave.

Carrie Fisher, *Postcards From the Edge* (1987)

14 We were worse name-droppers than people who dropped our names. Another actor was a "best friend," "know him very well," "died in my arms."

Mary Astor, *A Life on Film* (1967)

15 Other artists—poets, painters, sculptors, musicians—produce something which lives after them and enshrines their memories in positive evidences of their divine mission; but we,—we strut and fret our hour upon the stage, and then the curtain falls and all is darkness and silence.

Charlotte Cushman, in Emma Stebbins, *Charlotte Cushman* (1878)

16 Every other species of talent carries with it its eternity; we enjoy the work of the poet, the painter, the sculptor, only as thousands will do after us; but the actor—his memory is with his generation, and that passes away.

L.E. Landon, *Romance and Reality* (1831)

17 You're only as good as your last picture.

Marie Dressler, in Hedda Hopper and James Brough, *The Whole Truth and Nothing But* (1963)

18 If THIS is the way to fame and fortune, movies and TV, it's a fate worse than debt.

Carolyn Kenmore, on the casting couch, *Mannequin* (1969)

19 An actor is supposed to be a sensitive instrument. Isaac Stern takes good care of his violin. What if everybody jumped on his violin?

Marilyn Monroe (1962), in Bob Chieger, *Was It Good for You, Too?* (1983)

20 A painter paints, a musician plays, a writer writes—but a movie actor waits.

Mary Astor, *A Life on Film* (1967)

1  The rehearsals began just as all rehearsals begin. Not at all. The participants stood around sniffing each other.

   Hildegard Knef, *The Verdict* (1975)

2  Without discipline and detachment, an actor is an emotional slob, spilling his insides out. This abandonment is having an unfortunate vogue. It is tasteless, formless, absurd. Without containment there is no art. All this vomiting and wheezing and bursting at the seams is no more great acting than the convulsions of raving maniacs.

   Bette Davis, *The Lonely Life* (1962)

3  Even her eyelashes acted.

   Virginia Woolf, "Ellen Terry," *The Moment* (1947)

4  Imported actors, like certain wines, sometimes do not stand the ocean trip.

   Edna Ferber, *A Kind of Magic* (1963)

5  Five stages in the life of an actor. . . . 1. Who's Mary Astor? 2. Get me Mary Astor. 3. Get me a Mary Astor type. 4. Get me a young Mary Astor. 5. Who's Mary Astor?

   Mary Astor, *A Life on Film* (1967)

See also Celebrity, Comebacks, Comedy, Fame, Films, Hollywood, Performance, Posing, Stage and Screen, Theater.

## § ACTION

6  Action is the antidote to despair.

   Joan Baez, in *Rolling Stone* (1983)

7  What you will do matters. All you need is to do it.

   Judy Grahn, *Another Mother Tongue* (1984)

8  It is better to wear out than to rust out.

   Frances E. Willard (1880), in Ray Strachey, *Frances Willard* (1912)

9  When you're frightened don't sit still, keep on doing something. The act of doing will give you back your courage.

   Grace Ogot, *The Promised Land* (1966)

10  Being told to sit still and enjoy myself is logically incompatible.

   Leslie Glendower Peabody, "The Canoe and the Woman," in *Outing* (1901)

11  It is in vain to say human beings ought to be satisfied with tranquillity: they must have action; and they will make it if they cannot find it.

   Charlotte Brontë, *Jane Eyre* (1847)

12  God is ACTION—let us be like God.

   Frances E. Willard, in Anna A. Gordon, ed., *What Frances E. Willard Said* (1905)

13  I don't waste time thinking, "Am I doing it right?" I say, "Am I doing it?"

   Georgette Mosbacher, *Feminine Force* (1993)

14  For those of us who have a ground of knowledge which we cannot transmit to outsiders, it is perhaps more profitable to act fearlessly than to argue.

   Olive Schreiner, *Woman and Labor* (1911)

15  We do not need, and indeed never will have, all the answers before we act. . . . It is often only through taking action that we can discover some of them.

   Charlotte Bunch, "Not by Degrees," *Passionate Politics* (1987)

16  There is a saying, "To think is to act." . . . Too often, action which should be the result of thought, becomes the substitute for it. Presently, "to act is to think" seems an excellent precept, and by and by merely to act seems all that is necessary. Then the wrong mountains may get moved.

   Bertha Damon, *Grandma Called It Carnal* (1938)

17  To leap is not only to leap, it is to hit the ground somewhere.

   Elizabeth Bowen, *The House in Paris* (1935)

18  "Men of action," whose minds are too busy with the day's work to see beyond it . . . are essential men, we cannot do without them, and yet we must not allow all our vision to be bound by the limitations of "men of action."

   Pearl S. Buck, *What America Means to Me* (1943)

19  It will never rain roses: when we want / To have more roses we must plant more trees.

   George Eliot, *The Spanish Gypsy* (1868)

See also Actions, Behavior, Effort.

## ❦ ACTIONS

1 Sow an act and you reap a habit; sow a habit and you reap a character; sow a character and you reap a destiny.

> Frances E. Willard, in Anna A. Gordon, ed., *What Frances E. Willard Said* (1905)

2 I've arrived at this outermost edge of my life by my own actions. Where I am is thoroughly unacceptable. Therefore, I must stop doing what I've been doing.

> Alice Koller, *An Unknown Woman* (1982)

3 I think one's feelings waste themselves in words; they ought all to be distilled into actions which bring results.

> Florence Nightingale, in Ray Strachey, *"The Cause"* (1928)

4 We should do only those righteous actions which we cannot stop ourselves from doing.

> Simone Weil, *Gravity and Grace* (1947)

5 One never notices what has been done; one can only see what remains to be done.

> Marie Curie (1894), in Eve Curie, *Madame Curie* (1938)

6 One sad thing about this world is that the acts that take the most out of you are usually the ones that other people will never know about.

> Anne Tyler, *Celestial Navigation* (1974)

7 I have long since come to believe that people never mean half of what they say, and that it is best to disregard their talk and judge only their actions.

> Dorothy Day, *The Long Loneliness* (1952)

8 We have too many high sounding words, and too few actions that correspond with them.

> Abigail Adams, to her husband, John Adams (1774), *Letters of Mrs. Adams* (1848)

9 Our high resolves / Look down upon our slumbering acts.

> L.E. Landon, "A History of the Lyre," *The Venetian Bracelet* (1829)

10 There can be no happiness if the things we believe in are different from the things we do.

> Freya Stark, *The Lycian Shore* (1956)

11 Actions lie louder than words.

> Carolyn Wells, "More Mixed Maxims," *Folly for the Wise* (1904)

12 If you could make a pudding wi' thinking o' the batter, it 'ud be easy getting dinner.

> George Eliot, *Adam Bede* (1859)

See also Action, Behavior, Deeds.

## ❦ ACTIVISM

13 All progressive legislation has always had its genesis in the mind of one person. . . . One can do much. And one and one and one can move mountains.

> Joan Ward-Harris, *Creature Comforts* (1979)

14 A small group of thoughtful people could change the world. Indeed, it's the only thing that ever has.

> Margaret Mead, in *The Utne Reader* (1992)

15 The ocean is made of drops.

> Mother Teresa, in Daphne Rae, *Love Until It Hurts* (1980)

16 In the unceasing ebb and flow of justice and oppression we must all dig channels as best we may, that at the propitious moment somewhat of the swelling tide may be conducted to the barren places of life.

> Jane Addams, *Twenty Years at Hull House* (1910)

17 Battling racism and battling heterosexism and battling apartheid share the same urgency inside me as battling cancer.

> Audre Lorde, title essay, *A Burst of Light* (1988)

18 As citizens, we must prevent wrong-doing because the world in which we all live, wrong-doer, wrong-sufferer, and spectator, is at stake; the City has been wronged.

> Hannah Arendt, *The Life of the Mind*, vol. 1 (1978)

19 Even if I do not see the fruits, the struggle has been worthwhile. If my life has taught me anything, it is that one must fight.

> Ella Winter, *And Not to Yield* (1963)

20 It is so much easier sometimes to sit down and be resigned than to rise up and be indignant.

> Nellie L. McClung, *In Times Like These* (1915)

21 If you're not living on the edge, you're taking up too much room.

> Lorraine Teel, in *Minnesota Women's Press* (1996)

1 The role of the Do-Gooder is not what actors call a fat part.
     Margaret Halsey, *The Folks at Home* (1952)

See also Leadership, Reform, Service, Social Change, Volunteers.

## ❧ ADAPTABILITY

2 It is wonderful how quickly you get used to things, even the most astonishing.
     Edith Nesbitt, *Five Children and It* (1902)

3 We shall hardly notice in a year or two. / You can get accustomed to anything.
     Edna St. Vincent Millay, "Spring Song," *The Harp-Weaver* (1923)

4 Adaptable as human beings are and have to be, I sometimes sympathize with the chameleon who had a nervous breakdown on a patchwork quilt.
     John Stephen Strange, *Unquiet Grave* (1949)

See also Change, Resilience.

## ❧ ADDICTION

5 Strange! that what is enjoyed without pleasure cannot be discontinued without pain!
     Hannah More, "On Habits," *Christian Morals* (1812)

6 The problem with addicted people, communities, corporations, or countries is that they tend to lie, cheat, or steal to get their "fix." Corporations are addicted to profit and governments to power.
     Helen Caldicott, *If You Love This Planet* (1992)

See also Alcoholism, Codependence, Drinking, Drug Abuse, Smoking, Tobacco.

## ❧ ADMIRATION

7 No soul is desolate as long as there is a human being for whom it can feel trust and reverence.
     George Eliot, *Romola* (1862)

8 The modern world is not given to uncritical admiration. It expects its idols to have feet of clay, and can be reasonably sure that press and camera will report their exact dimensions.
     Barbara Ward, "First Lady, First Person," in *The Saturday Review* (1961)

9 You can't ever be really free if you admire somebody too much.
     Tove Jansson, *Tales From Moominvalley* (1963)

See also Appreciation, Hero-Worship, Respect.

## ❧ ADOLESCENCE

10 Caron is fifteen, to put it mildly.
     Joan Hess, *A Really Cute Corpse* (1988)

11 I remember adolescence, the years of having the impulse control of a mousetrap, of being as private as a safe-deposit box.
     Anna Quindlen, "Mom, Dad, and Abortion," *Thinking Out Loud* (1993)

12 A shrewd observer has significantly characterized the period as the time when the boy wishes he were dead, and everybody else wishes so too.
     Harriet Beecher Stowe, *The Pearl of Orr's Island* (1862)

13 Adolescence is like cactus.
     Anaïs Nin, *A Spy in the House of Love* (1954)

14 In no order of things is adolescence a time of the simple life.
     Janet Erskine Stuart, in Maud Monahan, *Life and Letters of Janet Erskine Stuart* (1922)

15 A normal adolescent isn't a normal adolescent if he acts normal.
     Judith Viorst, *Necessary Losses* (1986)

16 Mope—hope—grope.
     Maxine Davis, *The Lost Generation* (1936)

17 Show Miss Manners a grown-up who has happy memories of teenage years, with their endless round of merry-making and dancing the night away, and Miss Manners will show you a person who has either no heart or no memory.
     Judith Martin, *Miss Manners' Guide to Rearing Perfect Children* (1984)

1 I couldn't remember how to forget myself. I didn't want to think about myself, to reckon myself in, to deal with myself every livelong minute on top of everything else—but swerve as I might, I couldn't avoid it. I was a boulder blocking my own path. I was a dog barking between my own ears, a barking dog who wouldn't hush. So this was adolescence.

Annie Dillard, *An American Childhood* (1987)

2 At fourteen you don't need sickness or death for tragedy.

Jessamyn West, *Cress Delahanty* (1948)

3 You've got to wish for something the whole time when you're seventeen. You've got to, or there's nothing to live for. However impossible you've got to *think* you want it. . . . When I couldn't think of a thing I wanted I nearly died.

Charlotte Bingham, *Coronet Among the Weeds* (1963)

4 Growing up is like taking down the sides of your house and letting strangers walk in.

Maureen Daly, *Seventeenth Summer* (1942)

5 Friends aren't any more important than breath or blood to a high school senior.

Betty Ford, with Chris Chase, *The Times of My Life* (1978)

6 Adolescence is to life what baking powder is to cake. (And it's better to have too much than too little.)

Marcelene Cox, in *Ladies' Home Journal* (1946)

7 We become adolescents when the words that adults exchange with one another become intelligible to us.

Natalia Ginzburg, *The Little Virtues* (1962)

8 No man knows his true character until he has run out of gas, purchased something on the installment plan, and raised an adolescent.

Marcelene Cox, in *Ladies' Home Journal* (1955)

9 With any child entering adolescence, one hunts for signs of health, is desperate for the smallest indication that the child's problems will never be important enough for a television movie.

Delia Ephron, *Funny Sauce* (1986)

10 Bringing up teenagers is like sweeping back ocean waves with a frazzled broom—the inundation of outside influences never stops. Whatever the lure —cars, easy money, cigarettes, drugs, booze, sex, crime—much that glitters along the shore has a thousand times the appeal of a parent's lecture.

Mary Ellen Snodgrass, "Motherhood or Bust," in *On the Issues* (1990)

11 The difficulty between parents and adolescents is not always caused by the fact that parents fail to remember what growing up was like, but that they do.

Marcelene Cox, in *Ladies' Home Journal* (1954)

12 Adolescence is a twentieth-century invention most parents approach with dread and look back on with the relief of survivors.

Faye Moskowitz, *A Leak in the Heart* (1985)

13 A teen-ager out of sight is like a kite in the clouds; even though you can't see it you feel the tug on the string.

Marcelene Cox, in *Ladies' Home Journal* (1948)

14 The invention of the teenager was a mistake, in Miss Manners' opinion. . . . Once you identify a period of life in which people have few restrictions and, at the same time, few responsibilities—they get to stay out late but don't have to pay taxes— naturally, nobody wants to live any other way.

Judith Martin, *Miss Manners' Guide for the Turn-of-the-Millennium* (1989)

See also Childhood, Children, Youth.

# ❦ ADULTHOOD

15 We thought we were running away from the grownups, and now we are the grownups.

Margaret Atwood, *Cat's Eye* (1988)

16 Was I the only woman in the world who, at my age—and after a lifetime of quite rampant independence—still did not quite feel grown up?

Dodie Smith, *The Town in Bloom* (1965)

17 Another belief of mine: that everyone else my age is an adult, whereas I am merely in disguise.

Margaret Atwood, *Cat's Eye* (1988)

18 Maybe I'm an adult because my friends are. Could that be the way you tell? My friends are tall and drink coffee and have sex. They also eat strawberry ice cream straight from the box and hide notes from their dentists . . . and play card games and

sulk when their names are left off memos. Maybe no one actually turns into an adult. Maybe you just get to be an older and older kid. Maybe the whole world is being run by old kids.

Adair Lara, *Welcome to Earth, Mom* (1992)

1 If this was adulthood, the only improvement she could detect in her situation was that now she could eat dessert without eating her vegetables.

Lisa Alther, *Kinflicks* (1975)

2 When we were children, we used to think that when we were grown-up we would no longer be vulnerable. But to grow up is to accept vulnerability.

Madeleine L'Engle, *Walking on Water* (1980)

3 One of the signs of passing youth is the birth of a sense of fellowship with other human beings as we take our place among them.

Virginia Woolf, in *The London Times Literary Supplement* (1916)

4 Every human being on this earth is born with a tragedy, and it isn't original sin. He's born with the tragedy that he has to grow up. . . . He has to lose everything that is lovely and fight for a new loveliness of his own making, and it's a tragedy. A lot of people don't have the courage to do it.

Helen Hayes, in Roy Newquist, *Showcase* (1966)

5 By the bye, as I must leave off being young, I find many douceurs in being a sort of chaperon for I am put on the sofa near the fire and can drink as much wine as I like.

Jane Austen, to her sister Cassandra (1813), in R.W. Chapman, ed., *Jane Austen's Letters*, vol. 2 (1932)

See also Age, Maturity, Middle Age.

## & ADVENTURE

6 Adventure can be an end in itself. Self-discovery is the secret ingredient that fuels daring.

Grace Lichtenstein, *Machisma* (1981)

7 Nobody is ever met at the airport when beginning a new adventure. It's just not done.

Elizabeth Warnock Fernea, *A View of the Nile* (1970)

8 He's going for the adventure of it. They always have, no matter what excuse they've given, from the Holy Grail to the California gold fields. The difference in America is that the women have always gone along.

Edna Ferber, *Cimarron* (1930)

9 Send me out into another life. But get me back for supper.

Faith Popcorn, *The Popcorn Report* (1991)

See also Travel, Wanderlust.

## & ADVERSITY

10 If we had no winter the spring would not be so pleasant: if we did not sometimes taste of adversity, prosperity would not be so welcome.

Anne Bradstreet, "Meditations Divine and Moral" (1664), in John Harvard Ellis, ed., *The Works of Anne Bradstreet in Prose and Verse* (1867)

11 It is not given to everyone to shine in adversity.

Jane Aiken Hodge, *Marry in Haste* (1961)

See also Misfortune, Suffering, Trouble.

## & ADVERTISING

12 Advertise, or go under.

Dorothy L. Sayers, *Murder Must Advertise* (1933)

13 We grew up founding our dreams on the infinite promise of American advertising. I *still* believe that one can learn to play the piano by mail and that mud will give you a perfect complexion.

Zelda Fitzgerald, *Save Me the Waltz* (1932)

14 All our advertising is propaganda, of course, but it has become so much a part of our life, is so pervasive, that we just don't know what it is propaganda *for.*

Pauline Kael, *I Lost It at the Movies* (1965)

15 In Europe, a product must be good, or it will not sell in competition with other products; with you, it is enough to *say* that it is good, often enough and sufficiently loudly. The keenest competition is not in the making of things but in the advertising of them!

Ann Bridge, *Singing Waters* (1946)

1 A good ad should be like a good sermon: It must not only comfort the afflicted—it also must *afflict the comfortable*!

Bernice Fitz-Gibbon, *Macy's, Gimbels, and Me* (1967)

2 The advertising agency, as it stands today, is a peculiar manifestation of American business life of the twentieth century—glossy, brash, and insecure.

Ilka Chase, *Past Imperfect* (1942)

3 Copywriters may struggle to distill their messages of enthusiasm in bright prose and snappy slogans, but the one word favored by advertisers over the years, is still the old word *new*.

Judith Groch, *The Right to Create* (1969)

4 Know the difference between Giant and Jumbo? Between two-ounce and a *big* two-ounce? Between a quart and a *full* quart? What's a *tall* 24-inch? What does Extra Long mean? Who's kidding who?

Marya Mannes, "Packaged Deception," *But Will It Sell?* (1964)

5 When the Florida Department of Citrus promotes orange juice as "cholesterol-free," it's depending on and fostering a thudding dullness of mind. This is like saying, "Fly Eastern—it's dandruff-free!"

Leslie Savan, *The Sponsored Life* (1994)

6 The art of advertisement—untruthfulness combined with repetition.

Freya Stark, *East Is West* (1945)

7 All advertising tells lies, but there are little lies and there are big lies. Little lie: This beer tastes great. Big lie: this beer makes *you* great.

Leslie Savan, *The Sponsored Life* (1994)

8 Truth in advertising is like leaven. . . . It provides a suitable quantity of gas, with which to blow out a mass of crude misrepresentation into a form that the public can swallow.

Dorothy L. Sayers, *Murder Must Advertise* (1933)

9 Advertisement . . . has brought our disregard for truth into the open without even a figleaf to cover it.

Freya Stark, *A Peak in Darien* (1976)

10 No, I most certainly do not think advertising people are wonderful. I think they are horrible, and the worst menace to mankind, next to war; perhaps ahead of war. They stand for the material viewpoint, for the importance of possessions, of desire, of envy, of greed. And war comes from these things.

Marjorie Kinnan Rawlings, letter to Maxwell E. Perkins (1945), *Selected Letters of Marjorie Kinnan Rawlings* (1982)

11 Advertising . . . is a parasitic activity; it forces goods for which there is no real need or demand on a foolish or even a reluctant public, always by appealing to their lower instincts.

Ann Bridge, *Singing Waters* (1946)

12 Its total message seems to be: "Use more things, want more things, other people have more things so why not you, because on the multiplicity of your material wants and your success in satisfying them depends your happiness and the greatness of your nation."

Mary Stocks, *My Commonplace Book* (1970)

13 What I find most injurious to mankind in modern advertising is the constant appeal to material standards and values, the elevating of material things into an end in themselves, a virtue.

Ann Bridge, *Singing Waters* (1946)

14 Of course advertising creates wants. Of course it makes people discontented, dissatisfied. Satisfaction with things as they are would defeat the American dream.

Bernice Fitz-Gibbon, *Macy's, Gimbels, and Me* (1967)

15 The advertising media in this country continuously informs the American male of his need for indispensable signs of his virility.

Frances M. Beal, "Double Jeopardy: To Be Black and Female," in Robin Morgan, ed., *Sisterhood Is Powerful* (1970)

16 Most admakers understand that in order to sell to you they have to know your desires and dreams better than you may know them yourself.

Leslie Savan, *The Sponsored Life* (1994)

See also Media, Persuasian, Publicity, Repetition.

## ❧ ADVICE

17 Advice is what we ask for when we already know the answer but wish we didn't.

Erica Jong, *How to Save Your Own Life* (1977)

1 I give my self sometimes admirable advice but I am incapable of taking it.

> Lady Mary Wortley Montagu (1725), in Robert Halsband, ed., *The Complete Letters of Lady Mary Wortley Montagu* (1965)

2 No vice is so bad as advice.

> Marie Dressler, in Martha Lupton, *The Speaker's Desk Book* (1937)

3 It is not advisable, James, to venture unsolicited opinions. You should spare yourself the embarrassing discovery of their exact value to your listener.

> Ayn Rand, *Atlas Shrugged* (1957)

4 Advice is one of those things it is far more blessed to give than to receive.

> Carolyn Wells, *The Rest of My Life* (1937)

5 Advice . . . is a habit-forming drug. You give a dear friend a bit of advice today, and next week you find yourself advising two or three friends, and the week after, a dozen, and the week following, crowds!

> Carolyn Wells, *The Rest of My Life* (1937)

6 It is very difficult to live among people you love and hold back from offering them advice.

> Anne Tyler, *Celestial Navigation* (1974)

7 Among the most disheartening and dangerous of . . . advisors, you will often find those closest to you, your dearest friends, members of your own family, perhaps, loving, anxious, and knowing nothing whatever.

> Minnie Maddern Fiske, letter (1908), in Alexander Woollcott, *Mrs. Fiske* (1917)

8 There is nothing so easy as to be wise for others; a species of prodigality, by-the-by—for such wisdom is wholly wasted.

> L.E. Landon, *Romance and Reality* (1831)

9 The true secret of giving advice is, after you have honestly given it, to be perfectly indifferent whether it is taken or not, and never persist in trying to set people right.

> Hannah Whitall Smith (1902), in Logan Pearsall Smith, ed., *Philadelphia Quaker* (1950)

10 A woman in love never takes advice.

> Rosamond Marshall, *Kitty* (1943)

11 I am very handy with my advice and then when anybody appears to be following it, I get frantic.

> Flannery O'Connor, in Sally Fitzgerald, ed., *The Habit of Being* (1979)

12 Please give me some good advice in your next letter. I promise not to follow it.

> Edna St. Vincent Millay (1913), in Allan Ross Macdougall, ed., *Letters of Edna St. Vincent Millay* (1952)

13 Strange, when you ask anyone's advice you see yourself what is right.

> Selma Lagerlöf, *Jerusalem* (1915)

14 Something occurred while they were at Hartfield, to make Emma want their advice; and, which was still more lucky, she wanted exactly the advice they gave.

> Jane Austen, *Emma* (1816)

15 The wanting of advice is the sign that the Spirit in you has not yet spoken with the compelling voice that you ought to obey.

> Annie Besant, *Theosophy and Life's Deeper Problems* (1916)

16 "For your own good" is a persuasive argument that will eventually make man agree to his own destruction.

> Janet Frame, *Faces in the Water* (1961)

17 The strongest possible piece of advice I would give to any young woman is: Don't screw around, and don't smoke.

> Edwina Currie, in *The Observer* (1988)

18 "Pull yourself together" is seldom said to anyone who can.

> Mignon McLaughlin, *The Neurotic's Notebook* (1963)

19 Be plain in dress, and sober in your diet, / In short, my deary, kiss me! and be quiet.

> Lady Mary Wortley Montagu, "A Summary of Lord Lyttleton's Advice to a Lady" (1768), *The Works of the Right Honorable Lady Mary Wortley Montagu*, vol. 5 (1803)

## ❧ AFFECTION

20 Trust in my affection for you. Tho' I may not display it exactly in the way you like and expect it, it is not therefore less deep and sincere.

> Anna Jameson (1833), in G.H. Needler, *Letters of Anna Jameson to Ottilie Von Goethe* (1939)

1 One is apt to think of people's affection as a fixed quantity, instead of a sort of moving sea with tide always going out or coming in but still fundamentally *there*.

  Freya Stark, *The Coast of Incense* (1953)

2 Affection is a habit.

  L.E. Landon, *Ethel Churchill* (1837)

3 Affection! Affection is false.

  Elizabeth I (1600), in J.E. Neale, *Queen Elizabeth I* (1934)

See also Friendship, Love.

## ᕦ AFRICA

4 All that you have given me Africa / Makes me walk / With a step that is like no other.

  Anoma Kanié, "All That You Have Given Me Africa," in Kathleen Weaver, tr., and Carol Cosman et al., eds., *Penguin Book of Women Poets* (1978)

5 Africa is mystic; it is wild; it is a sweltering inferno; it is a photographer's paradise, a hunter's Valhalla, an escapist's Utopia. It is what you will, and it withstands all interpretations. It is the last vestige of a dead world or the cradle of a shiny new one. To a lot of people, as to myself, it is just "home." It is all these things but one thing—it is never dull.

  Beryl Markham, *West With the Night* (1942)

6 The breezes of the West African night were intimate and shy, licking the hair, sweeping through cotton dresses with unseemly intimacy, then disappearing into the utter blackness.

  Maya Angelou, *All God's Children Need Traveling Shoes* (1986)

7 In Africa people learn to serve each other. They live on credit balances of little favors that they give and may, one day, ask to have returned.

  Beryl Markham, *West With the Night* (1942)

8 We were Black Americans in West Africa, where for the first time in our lives the color of our skin was accepted as correct and normal.

  Maya Angelou, *All God's Children Need Traveling Shoes* (1986)

9 It is a cruel country that will take the heart out of your breast and grind it into powder, powdered stone. And no one will mind, that is the worst of it. No one will mind.

  Elspeth Huxley, *The Flame Trees of Thika* (1959)

10 In the family of continents, Africa is the silent, the brooding sister, courted for centuries by knight-errant empires—rejecting them one by one and severally, because she is too sage and a little bored with the importunity of it all.

  Beryl Markham, *West With the Night* (1942)

11 Africa is less a wilderness than a repository of primary and fundamental values, and less a barbaric land than an unfamiliar voice.

  Beryl Markham, *West With the Night* (1942)

12 Africa is never the same to anyone who leaves it and returns again. It is not a land of change, but it is a land of moods and its moods are numberless. It is not fickle, but because it has mothered not only men, but races, and cradles not only cities, but civilizations—and seen them die, and seen new ones born again—Africa can be dispassionate, indifferent, warm, or cynical, replete with the weariness of too much wisdom.

  Beryl Markham, *West With the Night* (1942)

13 Writers brought up in Africa have many advantages—being at the center of a modern battlefield; part of a society in rapid, dramatic change. But in the long run it can also be a handicap: to wake up every morning with one's eyes on a fresh evidence of inhumanity; to be reminded twenty times a day of injustice, and always the same brand of it, can be limiting.

  Doris Lessing, *African Stories* (1965)

14 There are many Africas.

  Beryl Markham, *West With the Night* (1942)

See also Egypt, South Africa.

## ᕦ AFRICAN AMERICANS

See Blacks.

## ᕦ AGE

15 For years I wanted to be older, and now I am.

  Margaret Atwood, *Cat's Eye* (1988)

16 Age seldom arrives smoothly or quickly. It's more often a succession of jerks.

  Jean Rhys, in *The Observer* (1975)

1 I'd like to grow very old as slowly as possible.
   Irene Mayer Selznick, *A Private View* (1983)

2 The aging aren't only the old; the aging are all of us.
   Alexandra Robbin, *Aging: A New Look* (1982)

3 Do not deprive me of my age. I have earned it.
   May Sarton, *The Poet and the Donkey* (1969)

4 I am luminous with age.
   Meridel Le Sueur, title poem, *Rites of Ancient Ripening* (1975)

5 I'm just the same age I've always been.
   Carolyn Wells, *The Rest of My Life* (1937)

6 The great thing about getting older is that you don't lose all the other ages you've been.
   Madeleine L'Engle, in *The New York Times* (1985)

7 There is no old age. There is, as there always was, just you.
   Carol Matthau, *Among the Porcupines* (1992)

8 We did not change as we grew older; we just became more clearly ourselves.
   Lynn Hall, *Where Have All the Tigers Gone?* (1989)

9 My childhood is very vivid to me, and I don't feel very different now from the way I felt then. It would appear I am the very same person, only with wrinkles.
   Natalie Babbitt, in *The Horn Book* (1993)

10 I'm the same person I was back then, / A little less hair, a little less chin, / A lot less lungs and much less wind, / But ain't I lucky I can still breathe in.
   Maya Angelou, "On Aging," *And Still I Rise* (1978)

11 We turn not older with years, but newer every day.
   Emily Dickinson (1874), in Mabel Loomis Todd, ed., *Letters of Emily Dickinson*, vol. 2 (1894)

12 Her grandmother, as she gets older, is not fading but rather becoming more concentrated.
   Paulette Bates Alden, "Legacies," *Feeding the Eagles* (1988)

13 Old age is somewhat like dieting. Every day there is less of us to be observed.
   Doris Grumbach, *Fifty Days of Solitude* (1994)

14 About the only thing that comes to us without effort is old age.
   Gloria Pitzer, in *Reader's Digest* (1979)

15 Old age is perhaps life's decision about us.
   Christina Stead, *The Man Who Loved Children* (1940)

16 Old age is the verdict of life.
   Amelia E. Barr, *All the Days of My Life* (1913)

17 Age transfigures, or petrifies.
   Marie von Ebner-Eschenbach, *Aphorisms* (1893)

18 Old age makes caricatures of us all.
   P.D. James, *A Taste for Death* (1986)

19 In youth we learn, in age we understand.
   Marie von Ebner-Eschenbach, *Aphorisms* (1893)

20 Growing old was simply a process of drawing closer to that ultimate independence called death.
   Martha Ostenso, *The White Reef* (1934)

21 Growing old is partly an inescapable process of accommodation and adjustment.
   Käthe Kollwitz (1910), in Hans Kollwitz, ed., *The Diaries and Letters of Käthe Kollwitz* (1955)

22 I must be getting old. . . . People are beginning to tell me I *look so young.*
   L.M. Montgomery, *Rilla of Ingleside* (1921)

23 The first time you are reconciled to the terrible unfairness of disappointment, you are getting old.
   Mary Lee Settle, *The Love Eaters* (1954)

24 The real evidence of growing older is that things level off in importance. . . . Days are no longer jagged peaks to climb; time is a meadow, and we move over it with level steps.
   Gladys Taber, *The Book of Stillmeadow* (1948)

25 If you don't want to get old, don't mellow.
   Linda Ellerbee, *Move On* (1991)

26 I suppose real old age begins when one looks backward rather than forward.
   May Sarton, *At Seventy* (1984)

27 When one begins to think of oneself as growing old, one is already old.
   Elsie de Wolfe, *After All* (1935)

28 And just here let me advise thee not to talk of thyself as being *old.* There *is* something in Mind Cure, after all, and, if thee continually talks of thyself as being old, thee may perhaps bring on some

of the infirmities of age. At least I would not risk it if I were thee.

Hannah Whitall Smith (1907), in Logan Pearsall Smith, ed., *Philadelphia Quaker* (1950)

1 We are not old unless we desire to be.

Taylor Caldwell, *Great Lion of God* (1970)

2 You stay young as long as you can learn, acquire new habits and suffer contradiction.

Marie von Ebner-Eschenbach, *Aphorisms* (1893)

3 Tis a Maxim with me to be young as long as one can. There is nothing can pay one for that invaluable ignorance which is the companion of youth, those sanguine groundless Hopes, and that lively vanity which makes all the Happiness of Life. To my extreme Mortification I grow wiser every day.

Lady Mary Wortley Montagu (1712), in Robert Halsband, ed., *The Complete Letters of Lady Mary Wortley Montagu* (1965)

4 Oh, the soul keeps its youth!

Amelia E. Barr, *The Belle of Bowling Green* (1904)

5 Age doesn't protect you from love. But love, to some extent, protects you from age.

Jeanne Moreau, in John Robert Colombo, *Popcorn in Paradise* (1979)

6 The gold that was my hair has turned / silently to gray. Don't pity me! / Everything's been realized, / in my breast all's blended and attuned.

Marina Tsvetaeva (1922), Paul Graves, tr., in Jane Hirshfield, ed., *Women in Praise of the Sacred* (1994)

7 With a triumphant smile, / I confront time / as its edged diamond / sculpts my features.

Nina Cassian, "Poets," *Cheerleader for a Funeral* (1992)

8 I have still the best comforts of life—books and friendships—and I trust never to lose my relish for either.

Mary Russell Mitford (1851), in Henry Chorley, ed., *Letters of Mary Russell Mitford*, 2nd series, vol. 2 (1872)

9 Come what may, / I have had my day!

Julia C.R. Dorr, "Come What May," *Poems* (1892)

10 She had settled down to age as if she found it very pleasant company.

Phyllis Bottome, "That for an Hermitage," *Innocence and Experience* (1934)

11 Time deals gently with me; and though I feel that I descend, the slope is easy.

Anna Laetitia Barbauld (1813), *The Works of Anna Laetitia Barbauld*, vol. 2 (1825)

12 It is a mistake to regard age as a downhill grade toward dissolution. The reverse is true. As one grows older one climbs with surprising strides.

George Sand (1868), in Marie Jenny Howe, ed., *The Intimate Journal of George Sand* (1929)

13 Old age is not an illness, it is a timeless ascent. As power diminishes, we grow toward the light.

May Sarton, in "The Family of Woman: Growing Toward the Light," *Ms.* (1982)

14 She had accomplished what according to builders is only possible to wood and stone of the very finest grain; she had *weathered*, as they call it, with beauty.

Ethel Smyth (1920), on the Empress Eugénie at age 95, in Christopher St. John, *Ethel Smyth* (1959)

15 Grey-haired old ladies of few words . . . are old age's flowers to mortals.

Erinna, "Beauty of Old Age" (4th cent. B.C.), in Marion Mills Miller, tr., *The Songs of Sappho* (1925)

16 So much has been said and sung of beautiful young girls, why doesn't somebody wake up to the beauty of old women?

Harriet Beecher Stowe, *Uncle Tom's Cabin* (1852)

17 With age comes the inner, the higher life. Who would be forever young, to dwell always in externals?

Elizabeth Cady Stanton (1853), in Theodore Stanton and Harriot Stanton Blatch, eds., *Elizabeth Cady Stanton As Revealed in Her Letters Diary and Reminiscences*, vol. 2 (1922)

18 Old age is not one of the beauties of creation, but it is one of its harmonies.

Anne-Sophie Swetchine, in Count de Falloux, ed., *The Writings of Madame Swetchine* (1869)

19 I never feel age. . . . If you have creative work, you don't have age or time.

Louise Nevelson (1980), in Alexandra Robbin, *Aging: A New Look* (1982)

20 Every time I think that I'm getting old, and gradually going to the grave, something else happens.

Lillian Carter, in *Ms.* (1976)

21 There is something to be said for growing old. Not much, but something.

Laura Black, *Strathgallant* (1981)

1 The nearer I come to the end of my days, the more I am enabled to see that strange thing, a life, and to see it whole.

    Simone de Beauvoir, *All Said and Done* (1972)

2 That's the purpose of old age. . . . To give us a breathing space before we die, in which to see why we did what we did.

    Colleen McCullough, *The Thorn Birds* (1977)

3 I am enjoying to the full that period of reflection which is the happiest conclusion to a life of action.

    Willa Cather, *Death Comes for the Archbishop* (1927)

4 Ripe old age, cheerful, useful, and understanding, is one of the finest influences in the world.

    Ida Tarbell, *The Business of Being a Woman* (1912)

5 It seems to me nowadays that the most important task for someone who is aging is to spread love and warmth wherever possible.

    Käthe Kollwitz (1916), in Hans Kollwitz, ed., *The Diaries and Letters of Käthe Kollwitz* (1955)

6 The body keeps an accurate count of years. / . . . / But the bold spirit / pays little heed to time. If it grow weary / it is through sorrow, not through age.

    Elizabeth Coatsworth, "Body and Spirit," *Down Half the World* (1968)

7 The birds sing louder when you grow old.

    Rose Chernin, in Kim Chernin, *In My Mother's House* (1983)

8 If old age in the shape of waning strength says to me often, "Thou shalt not!" so do my years smile upon me and say to me, "Thou needst not."

    Mary Heaton Vorse, *Autobiography of an Elderly Woman* (1911)

9 I dread no more the first white in my hair, / Or even age itself, the easy shoe, / The cane, the wrinkled hands, the special chair: / Time, doing this to me, may alter too / My sorrow, into something I can bear.

    Edna St. Vincent Millay, "Time," *Wine From These Grapes* (1934)

10 I've got everything I always had. Only it's six inches lower.

    Gypsy Rose Lee, in Barbara McDowell and Hana Umlauf, *Woman's Almanac* (1977)

11 I'm not to blame for an old body, but I would be to blame for an old soul. An old soul is a shameful thing.

    Margaret Deland, *Dr. Lavendar's People* (1903)

12 Though drab outside—wreckage to the eye, mirrors a mortification—inside we flame with a wild life that is almost incommunicable.

    Florida Scott-Maxwell, *The Measure of My Days* (1968)

13 Wisdom doesn't automatically come with old age. Nothing does—except wrinkles.

    Abigail Van Buren, syndicated column "Dear Abby" (1978)

14 The problem of aging is the problem of living. There is no simple solution.

    Coco Chanel, in Joseph Barry, "An Interview With Chanel," *McCall's* (1965)

15 There are days of oldness, and then one gets young again. It goes backward and forward, not in one direction.

    Katharine Butler Hathaway (1930), *The Journals and Letters of the Little Locksmith* (1946)

16 They will not be so long from dawn to dark, / The few,—the golden-few days that remain! / . . . / How I do prize the few days that remain!

    Edith M. Thomas, "The Days That Remain," *Selected Poems* (1926)

17 The nearer she came to death, the more, by some perversity of nature, did she enjoy living.

    Ellen Glasgow, *Barren Ground* (1925)

18 Old age is not synonymous with being "glad to die."

    Elisabeth Kübler-Ross, *Questions and Answers On Death and Dying* (1974)

19 An old earthen pipe like myself is dry and thirsty and so a most voracious drinker of life at its source; I'm no more to be split by the vital stream than if I were stone or steel.

    Elinor Wylie, *Jennifer Lorn* (1923)

20 There's that "You're only as old as you feel" business, which is true to a point, but you can't be Shirley Temple on the Good Ship Lollipop forever. Sooner or later, dammit, you're *old.*

    Joan Crawford, in Roy Newquist, *Conversations With Joan Crawford* (1980)

21 Growing old is like riding a train: we seem to sit still while the landscape moves by.

    Marcelene Cox, in *Ladies' Home Journal* (1949)

22 The trouble was, she could not see the justice of her state. She was not old: she was a girl hidden behind a mask. Now that she had realized she was no

longer young, she did not know how she should behave. She had become a stranger in her own life.

Olivia Manning, *The Doves of Venus* (1955)

1 Old age would be the most happy of the stages of life, if only it did not know it was the last.

Comtesse Diane, *Les Glanes de la Vie* (1898)

2 Old age was growing inside me. It kept catching my eye from the depths of the mirror. I was paralyzed sometimes as I saw it making its way toward me so steadily when nothing inside me was ready for it.

Simone de Beauvoir, *Force of Circumstance* (1963)

3 Having watched herself in the speckled mirror . . . she was already shocked beyond surprise at what the flat hand of age could do.

Mary Lee Settle, *The Love Eaters* (1954)

4 The years seem to *rush* by now, and I think of death as a fast approaching end of a journey—double and treble reasons for loving as well as working while it is day.

George Eliot (1861), in J.W. Cross, ed., *George Eliot's Life As Related in Her Letters and Journals* (1885)

5 One day you're racing about the business of life, harried but vital, a part of its machinery. Then gradually but inexorably you are left out, until one day you find the machinery tearing along without you—and nobody even notices.

Marjorie Holmes, *Love and Laughter* (1967)

6 How short the road has suddenly become, / The end of which seemed out of sight before!

Anna Akhmatova, "Why Wonder" (1958), *Poems* (1988)

7 My age I will not once lament, / But sing, my time so near is spent.

Anne Bradstreet, "I Had Eight Birds" (1656), in Jeannine Hensley, ed., *Works of Anne Bradstreet* (1967)

8 Just as you began to feel that you could make good use of time, there was no time left to you.

Lisa Alther, *Kinflicks* (1975)

9 Now I am capable of youth, but not capable of few years—that is the pitiful thing.

Helen Westley (1917), in Djuna Barnes, *I Could Never Be Lonely Without a Husband* (1985)

10 I find that age is not good for much, that one becomes deafer and less sensitive. Also, the higher up the mountain you climb, the less of a view you get. A mist closes in and cheats you of the hoped-for and expected opportunity to see far and wide.

Käthe Kollwitz, in Hans Kollwitz, ed., *The Diaries and Letters of Käthe Kollwitz* (1955)

11 It's true, some wines improve with age. But only if the grapes were good in the first place.

Abigail Van Buren, syndicated column "Dear Abby" (1978)

12 To grow old is to have taken away, one by one, all gifts of life, the food and wine, the music and the company. . . . The gods unloose, one by one, the mortal fingers that cling to the edge of the table.

Storm Jameson, *Three Kingdoms* (1926)

13 The last steps of life are ever slow and difficult.

Madame de Staël, *Corinne* (1807)

14 It is old age, rather than death, that is to be contrasted with life. Old age is life's parody, whereas death transforms life into a destiny.

Simone de Beauvoir, *The Coming of Age* (1970)

15 There's no such thing as old age; there is only sorrow.

Edith Wharton, *A Backward Glance* (1934)

16 Wrecked on the lee shore of age.

Sarah Orne Jewett, *The Country of the Pointed Firs* (1896)

17 I wore old age like a tunic / too heavy for my shoulders.

Rosario Castellanos, "Hecuba's Testament" (1969), in Julian Palley, tr., *Meditation on the Threshold* (1988)

18 Years are only garments, and you either wear them with style all your life, or else you go dowdy to the grave.

Dorothy Parker, "The Middle or Blue Period" (1944), *The Portable Dorothy Parker*, rev. ed. (1973)

19 We are old—it must be so, / Oft they say it—they must know.

Edith M. Thomas, "We Are Old," *Selected Poems* (1926)

20 How old am I? / As days are told, / The earth is younger / than I am old.

Sister M. Madeleva, "You Ask My Age," *Collected Poems* (1947)

21 The fact was I didn't want to look my age, but I didn't want to act the age I wanted to look either. I also wanted to grow old enough to understand that sentence.

Erma Bombeck, *Aunt Irma's Cope Book* (1979)

1 "When I was your age—." "No one," said Viki, "is ever anyone else's age, except physically."

    Faith Baldwin, *One More Time* (1972)

2 Years do not always make age.

    George Sand, *The Haunted Pool* (1851)

3 Age has extremely little to do with anything that matters. The difference between one age and another is, as a rule, enormously exaggerated.

    Rose Macaulay, *Dangerous Ages* (1921)

4 It is not mere chance that makes families speak of a child who is "extraordinary for his age" and also of an old man who is "extraordinary for his age"; the extraordinariness lies in their behaving like human beings when they are either not yet or no longer men.

    Simone de Beauvoir, *The Coming of Age* (1970)

5 There are no old people nowadays; they are either "wonderful for their age" or dead.

    Mary Pettibone Poole, *A Glass Eye at a Keyhole* (1938)

6 Our days glide gently and imperceptibly along, like the motion of the hour-hand, which we cannot discover. . . . We advance gradually; we are the same to-day as yesterday, and to-morrow as to-day: thus we go on, without perceiving it, which is a miracle of the Providence I adore.

    Marie de Rabutin-Chantal, Marquise de Sévigné (1687), *Letters of Madame de Sévigné to Her Daughter and Her Friends*, vol. 7 (1811)

7 It was formerly a terrifying view to me that I should one day be an old woman. I now find that Nature has provided pleasures for every state.

    Lady Mary Wortley Montagu (1747), in Octave Thanet, ed., *The Best Letters of Lady Mary Wortley Montagu* (1901)

8 I used to dread getting older because I thought I would not be able to do all the things I wanted to do, but now that I am older I find that I don't want to do them.

    Nancy Astor (1959), in Michèle Brown and Ann O'Connor, *Hammer and Tongues* (1986)

9 Nothing makes people crosser than being considered too old for love.

    Nancy Mitford, *Love in a Cold Climate* (1949)

10 How unnatural the imposed view, imposed by a puritanical ethos, that passionate love belongs only to the young, that people are dead from the neck down by the time they are forty, and that any deep feeling, any passion after that age, is either ludicrous or revolting!

    May Sarton, *Journal of a Solitude* (1973)

11 A woman who will tell her age will tell anything.

    Rita Mae Brown, *Southern Discomfort* (1982)

12 The years that a woman subtracts from her age are not lost: they are added to the ages of other women.

    Comtesse Diane, *Les Glanes de la Vie* (1898)

13 When I am an old woman I shall wear purple.

    Jenny Joseph, "Warning," in Sandra Martz, ed., *When I Am an Old Woman I Shall Wear Purple* (1987)

14 It's time for us old women to rip to shreds the veil of invisibility that has encased us. We have to fight the societal stereotype that keeps us on the periphery, outside the mainstream. We have experience to offer, judgment, wisdom, balance and charm.

    Miriam Reibold, news item (1991)

15 Women may be the one group that grows more radical with age.

    Gloria Steinem, *Outrageous Acts and Everyday Rebellions* (1983)

16 An old woman . . . is a person who has no sense of decency; if once she takes to living, the devil himself can't get rid of her.

    Fanny Burney, *Cecilia* (1782)

17 Time and trouble will tame an advanced young woman, but an advanced old woman is uncontrollable by any earthly force.

    Dorothy L. Sayers, *Clouds of Witness* (1926)

18 We have a lot to do. . . . People don't understand this. They think we're sitting around in rocking chairs, which isn't at all true. Why, we don't even own a rocking chair.

    Sadie Delany, age 103, on her 101-year-old sister and herself, in Sarah and A. Elizabeth Delany, with Amy Hill Hearth, *Having Our Say* (1993)

19 I have never wanted to live to be old, so old I'd run out of friends or money.

    Margot Fonteyn, in *Parade* (1991)

20 I have, alas! outlived almost every one of my contemporaries. One pays dear for living long.

    Hannah More (1826), in Arthur Roberts, ed., *Letters of Hannah More to Zachary Macaulay* (1860)

1 The loss of friends is a tax on age!

Ninon de Lenclos, in Mrs. Griffith, tr., *The Memoirs of Ninon de L'Enclos*, vol. 1 (1761)

2 I can think of nothing sadder / Than to feel, when days are few, / There's nobody left to lean on, / Nobody older than you!

Florence Smith, "Song," in Hazel Felleman, ed., *The Best Loved Poems of the American People* (1936)

3 When you get to be my age, all your friends have either died or moved to Florida.

Helen Van Slyke, *No Love Lost* (1980)

4 Old age is like a plane flying through a storm. Once you're aboard, there's nothing you can do.

Golda Meir, in Oriana Fallaci, *L'Europeo* (1973)

5 One keeps forgetting old age up to the very brink of the grave.

Colette, *My Mother's House* (1922)

6 The country of the aged is a land few people think very hard and seriously about before the time of life when they sense that they're *arriving* there. Somehow, throughout much of life, being old seems to be something that happens to other people.

Maggie Scarf, *Unfinished Business* (1980)

7 Science has salvaged scrap metal and even found vitamins and valuable oils in refuse, but old people are extravagantly wasted.

Anzia Yezierska, "One Thousand Pages of Research," *Commentary* (1963)

8 Society turns away from the aged worker as though he belonged to another species. . . . Old age exposes the failure of our entire civilization.

Simone de Beauvoir, *The Coming of Age* (1970)

9 Never lose sight of the fact that old age needs so little but needs that little so much.

Margaret Willour, in *Reader's Digest* (1982)

10 Of all the self-fulfilling prophecies in our culture, the assumption that aging means decline and poor health is probably the deadliest.

Marilyn Ferguson, *The Aquarian Conspiracy* (1980)

11 Seal my lips on aches and pains. They are increasing, and love of rehearsing them is becoming sweeter as the years go by.

Rosalind Russell, with Chris Chase, *Life Is a Banquet* (1977)

12 Egoism is in general the malady of the aged; . . . we become occupied with our own existence in proportion as it ceases to be interesting to others.

Countess of Blessington, *Journal of Conversations With Lord Byron* (1834)

13 The crucial task of age is balance, a veritable tightrope of balance; keeping just well enough, just brave enough, just gay and interested and starkly honest enough to remain a sentient human being.

Florida Scott-Maxwell, *The Measure of My Days* (1968)

14 I'm at an age when my back goes out more than I do.

Phyllis Diller, *The Joys of Aging—And How to Avoid Them* (1981)

15 "I'm falling into disrepair," she told the children. "I've outlived myself."

Anne Tyler, *Dinner at the Homesick Restaurant* (1982)

16 She had finally reached the age where she was more afraid of getting old than dying.

Julia Phillips, *You'll Never Eat Lunch in This Town Again* (1991)

17 The fear of aging, a commonplace neurosis, does not usually wait for age and spares neither sex.

Colette, "Beauties" (1928), *Journey for Myself* (1972)

18 Dread of one's own aging leads to fear and dislike of old people, and the fear feeds upon itself. In Western society this cycle of dread has been going on a long, long time.

Alexandra Robbin, *Aging: A New Look* (1982)

19 Growing old is not a thing to watch. It cannot be forgiven in others. Alone, it can be borne. Even indulged.

Jennifer Stone, *Telegraph Avenue Then* (1992)

20 She was an old woman now, and her life had become memories.

Leslie Marmon Silko, "Lullaby," *Storyteller* (1981)

21 Old men's eyes are like old men's memories; they are strongest for things a long way off.

George Eliot, *Romola* (1862)

22 The old creep out at the churchyard gate, while the young bound in at the front door.

Elizabeth Rundle Charles, *Chronicles of the Schönberg-Cotta Family* (1863)

1 Paradoxical as it may seem, to believe in youth is to look backward; to look forward, we must believe in age.
   Dorothy L. Sayers, "Strong Meat," *Creed or Chaos?* (1949)

2 It is easier to counterfeit old age than youth.
   Elizabeth Peters, *The Snake, the Crocodile and the Dog* (1992)

3 Perhaps one has to be very old before one learns how to be amused rather than shocked.
   Pearl S. Buck, *China, Past and Present* (1972)

4 I've always thought that very few people grow old as admirably as academics. At least books never let them down.
   Margaret Drabble, *A Summer Bird-Cage* (1962)

5 It's wonderful to be married to an archaeologist— the older you get the more interested he is in you.
   Agatha Christie, quoting an unidentified woman (although the quote is always attributed to Christie), in Jeffrey Feinman, *The Mysterious World of Agatha Christie* (1975)

6 I'm in my anecdotage.
   Clare Boothe Luce, in *Town and Country* (1981)

7 Old age is a great trial, John. One has to be so damned *good*!
   May Sarton, *Kinds of Love* (1970)

8 One cannot be honest even at the end of one's life, for no one is wholly alone. We are bound to those we love, or to those who love us, and to those who need us to be brave, or content, or even happy enough to allow them not to worry about us. So we must refrain from giving pain, as our last gift to our fellows.
   Florida Scott-Maxwell, *The Measure of My Days* (1968)

9 I want to get leaner and meaner / Sharp edged / Color of the ground / Till I discorporate / From sheer joy.
   Julia Kooken, "Outrageous Old Woman," in Jeanne Tetrault and Sherry Thomas, eds., *Country Women* (1976)

10 Twenty-three is said to be the prime of life by those who have reached so far and no farther. It shares this distinction with every age, from ten to three-score and ten.
   Stella Benson, *I Pose* (1915)

11 Never trust a woman who will not lie about her age after thirty. She is unwomanly and unhuman and there is no knowing what crimes she will commit.
   Gertrude Atherton, *The Aristocrats* (1901)

12 "Nan is thirty-three." "A dangerous age." "All Nan's ages have been dangerous. Nan is like that."
   Rose Macaulay, *Dangerous Ages* (1921)

13 After thirty, a body has a mind of its own.
   Bette Midler, in *Reader's Digest* (1982)

14 Life begins at forty.
   Sophie Tucker, title of song by Jack Yellen associated with her, in Sophie Tucker, *Some of These Days* (1945)

15 The forties are when you start trading your psychological problems for physical ones.
   Marilyn vos Savant, in *Parade* (1992)

16 I was grown up at ten, and first began to grow young at forty.
   Madge Kendal, in Mrs. Alec-Tweedie, *Behind the Footlights* (1904)

17 Forty is . . . an age at which people have histories and options. At thirty, they had perhaps less history. At fifty, perhaps fewer options.
   Ellen Goodman, *At Large* (1981)

18 I have enjoyed greatly the second blooming that comes when you finish the life of the emotions and of personal relations; and suddenly find—at the age of fifty, say—that a whole new life has opened before you, filled with things you can think about, study, or read about. . . . It is as if a fresh sap of ideas and thoughts was rising in you.
   Agatha Christie, *An Autobiography* (1977)

19 At fifty, the madwoman in the attic breaks loose, stomps down the stairs, and sets fire to the house. She won't be imprisoned anymore.
   Erica Jong, *Fear of Fifty* (1994)

20 Upon becoming fifty the one thing you can't afford is habit.
   Carolyn Heilbrun, *Writing Women's Lives* (1994)

21 I have a problem about being nearly sixty: I keep waking up in the morning and thinking I'm thirty-one.
   Elizabeth Janeway, *Between Myth and Morning* (1974)

22 I can't actually see myself putting make-up on my face at the age of sixty. But I can see myself going on a camel train to Samarkand.
   Glenda Jackson, in John Robert Colombo, *Popcorn in Paradise* (1979)

1  I do the things I like to do, / And leave undone the things I don't— / Because I'm sixty!
   Mrs. C.B.F., in Hazel Felleman, ed., *The Best Loved Poems of the American People* (1936)

2  Though it sounds absurd, it is true to say I felt younger at sixty than I had felt at twenty.
   Ellen Glasgow, *The Woman Within* (1954)

3  It is not a sin to be seventy but it is also no joke.
   Golda Meir, *My Life* (1975)

4  Davey and Aunt Emily . . . sat there, smugly thinking that they had always looked exactly the same. Quite useless to discuss questions of age with old people, they have such peculiar ideas on the subject. "Not really old at all, only seventy," you hear them saying.
   Nancy Mitford, *Love in a Cold Climate* (1949)

5  Being over seventy is like being engaged in a war. All our friends are going or gone and we survive amongst the dead and the dying as on a battlefield.
   Muriel Spark, *Memento Mori* (1959)

6  You don't realize what fine fighting material there is in age. . . . You show me any one who's lived to over seventy and you show me a fighter—some one who's got the will to live.
   Agatha Christie, *Dumb Witness* (1937)

7  When you're fifty, you're neither young nor old; you're just uninteresting. When you are sixty, and still dancing, you become something of a curiosity. And boy! if you hit seventy and can still get a foot off the ground, you're phenomenal!
   Ruth St. Denis, in Elizabeth Anticaglia, *Twelve American Women* (1975)

8  Age puzzles me. I thought it was a quiet time. My seventies were interesting, and fairly serene, but my eighties are passionate. I grow more intense as I age.
   Florida Scott-Maxwell, *The Measure of My Days* (1968)

9  In a dream you are never eighty.
   Anne Sexton, "Old," *All My Pretty Ones* (1961)

10  Eighty's a landmark and people treat you differently than they do when you're seventy-nine. At seventy-nine, if you drop something it just lies there. At eighty, people pick it up for you.
   Helen Van Slyke, *No Love Lost* (1980)

11  I am eighty years old. There seems to be nothing to add to this statement. I have reached the age of undecorated facts—facts that refuse to be softened by sentiment, or confused by nobility of phrase.
   Agnes Repplier, title essay, *Eight Decades* (1937)

12  I find Lady Ponsonby, the wise judge, the firm Liberal, more and more delightful; at last one feels she is getting old—she is eighty-two. She is like a fine flame kindled by sea-logs and sandalwood—good to watch and good to warm the mind at, and the heart too.
   Edith Sichell (1914), in Ethel Smyth, *Impressions That Remained* (1919)

13  It is so comic to hear one's self called old; even at ninety, I suppose!
   Alice James (1889), in Anna Robeson Burr, *Alice James* (1934)

14  There is nothing inherently wrong with a brain in your nineties. If you keep it fed and interested, you'll find it lasts you very well.
   Mary Stoneman Douglas, *Voices of the River* (1987)

15  I have always felt that a woman has the right to treat the subject of her age with ambiguity until, perhaps, she passes into the realm beyond ninety. Then it is better that she be candid with herself and with the world.
   Helena Rubinstein, *My Life for Beauty* (1966)

16  I'm a hundred-and-one years old and at my age, honey, I can say what I want!
   Bessie Delany, in Sarah and A. Elizabeth Delany, with Amy Hill Hearth, *Having Our Say* (1993)

See also Adolescence, Adulthood, Childhood, Middle Age, Retirement, Time, Years, Youth.

## ◊ AGGRESSION

17  Frankie [Avalon] . . . was interested in eating everything so it didn't eat him first.
   Rona Barrett, *Miss Rona* (1977)

18  Historically, it appears that society has capitalized on what is at most a degree of difference between the sexes in order to institutionalize the polarization of aggression.
   Freda Adler, *Sisters in Crime* (1975)

## ❧ AIDS

1 Over and over, these men cry out against the weight of so many losses—not just a lover dead, but friends and friends of friends, dozens of them, until it seems that AIDS is all there is and all there ever will be.

Jane Gross, in *The New York Times* (1987)

2 Like the effects of industrial pollution and the new system of global financial markets, the AIDS crisis is evidence of a world in which nothing important is regional, local, limited; in which everything that can circulate does, and every problem is, or is destined to become, worldwide.

Susan Sontag, *AIDS and Its Metaphors* (1989)

3 The only good thing about the AIDS epidemic is that as much as it's brought forth all sorts of fear and hatred from people, it's also taught people how to love in a new way.

Jane Redmont, in Jim Castelli, *How I Pray* (1994)

4 I think the Reagan and Bush administrations will be remembered one hundred years hence as the people who could have stopped the plague but chose not to because the right people were dying.

Rita Mae Brown, *Venus Envy* (1993)

See also Illness.

## ❧ AIR

5 The soul is a breath of living spirit, that with excellent sensitivity, permeates the entire body to give it life. Just so, the breath of the air makes the earth fruitful. Thus the air is the soul of the earth, moistening it, greening it.

Hildegard of Bingen (1150), in Gabriele Uhlein, ed., *Meditations With Hildegard of Bingen* (1983)

6 Air is a much kinder magician than fire, altering without destroying.

Virginia Moore, *Virginia Is a State of Mind* (1942)

## ❧ ALARM

7 A little alarm now and then keeps life from stagnation.

Fanny Burney, *Camilla* (1796)

8 If you look at life one way, there is always cause for alarm.

Elizabeth Bowen, *The Death of the Heart* (1938)

9 Nervous alarms should always be communicated, that they may be dissipated.

Charlotte Brontë, *Shirley* (1849)

See also Fear, Stress, Worry.

## ❧ ALASKA

10 Someday . . . this part of the world is going to be so important that just to say you're an Alaskan will be bragging.

Edna Ferber, *Ice Palace* (1958)

11 The whole town looks as if it had been left out in the rain too long and by mistake.

Linda Ellerbee, on Juneau, *Move On* (1991)

12 This city is made of stone, of blood, and fish.

Joy Harjo, "Anchorage," in Joseph Bruchac, ed., *Songs From This Earth on Turtle's Back* (1983)

## ❧ ALCOHOL

13 Alcohol is a good preservative for everything but brains.

Mary Pettibone Poole, *A Glass Eye at a Keyhole* (1938)

14 Employed as I had been employing it, liquor is a fixative of old patterns.

Margaret Halsey, *No Laughing Matter* (1977)

15 Almost anything can be preserved in alcohol, except health, happiness, and money.

Mary Wilson Little, *A Paragrapher's Reveries* (1904)

16 Alcohol is an allergy of the body and an obsession of the mind.

Rita Mae Brown, *Starting From Scratch* (1988)

17 Alcohol doesn't console, it doesn't fill up anyone's psychological gaps, all it replaces is the lack of God.

Marguerite Duras, *Practicalities* (1987)

1 Drink was the most fearsome of deceivers . . . for it promised one thing and came through with quite another.

    Kay Boyle, in Robert McAlmon, *Being Geniuses Together* (1968)

2 Liquor is such a nice substitute for facing adult life.

    Dorothy B. Hughes, *In a Lonely Place* (1947)

3 Alcoholic drinks introduce added friction into the machinery of body and mind; by their use the individual is handicapped in the race toward a higher and more perfect individuality, and what hinders one in this race hinders us all.

    Frances E. Willard, in Anna A. Gordon, ed., *What Frances E. Willard Said* (1905)

4 Alcohol flings back, almost illimitably, the boundaries of humor so that we can find uproarious things which our poor sober friends miss altogether. It is necessary, if the joke is really good and really should be shared, to repeat it time and again until finally it penetrates those solemn skulls.

    Jean Stafford, *Boston Adventure* (1944)

5 Someone is putting brandy in your bonbons, Grand Marnier in your breakfast jam, Kahlua in your ice cream, Scotch in your mustard and Wild Turkey in your cake. Americans may be drinking fewer alcoholic beverages, but they are certainly eating more of them than ever before. Wittingly or un.

    Marian Burros, "Alcohol, the Ultimate Additive," in *The New York Times* (1986)

6 The reward for total abstinence from alcohol seems, illogically enough, to be the capacity for becoming intoxicated without it.

    Rebecca West, *Black Lamb and Grey Falcon* (1941)

See also Addiction, Alcoholism, Drinking, Prohibition, Sobriety, Temperance, Wine.

## & ALCOHOLISM

7 Your medicine is your poison is your medicine is your poison and there is no end but madness.

    Lillian Roth, with Mike Connolly and Gerold Frank, *I'll Cry Tomorrow* (1954)

8 He who has once taken to drink can seldom be said to be guilty of one sin only.

    Hannah More, "The History of Hester Wilmot," *The Works of Hannah More*, vol. 1 (1841)

9 The true alcoholic takes the first drink for the person, or situation, or insult, that upsets him. He takes the rest of the drinks for himself.

    Lillian Roth, with Mike Connolly and Gerold Frank, *I'll Cry Tomorrow* (1954)

10 There are plenty of alcoholics who can be magnificent when drunk: it does not make them any less alcoholic.

    Ingrid Bengis, "Monroe According to Mailer," in *Ms.* (1973)

11 Anybody who drinks seriously is poor: so poor, poor, extra poor, me.

    Caitlin Thomas, *Leftover Life to Kill* (1957)

12 The true evil of drink lies in the disillusion: that the initial pleasure very soon evaporates, leaving a demoralizing craving for more, which is not even temporarily pleasurable. Which then leads to deterioration of the faculties of both body and mind; plus a bewildering lack of co-operation between the two.

    Caitlin Thomas, *Not Quite Posthumous Letter to My Daughter* (1963)

13 You cannot live with active alcoholism without being profoundly affected.

    Janet Geringer Woititz, in *Co-Dependency* (1984)

14 I'm the child of an alcoholic. I know about promises.

    Sandra Scoppettone, *I'll Be Leaving You Always* (1993)

15 Alcoholism isn't a spectator sport. Eventually the whole family gets to play.

    Joyce Rebeta-Burditt, *The Cracker Factory* (1977)

16 If a man be discreet enough to take to hard drinking in his youth, before his general emptiness is ascertained, his friends invariably credit him with a host of shining qualities, which, we are given to understand, lie balked and frustrated by his one unfortunate weakness.

    Agnes Repplier, "A Plea for Humor," *Points of View* (1891)

See also Addiction, Alcohol, Codependence, Drinking, Sobriety, Temperance.

## ❦ ALIENATION

1 Alienation produces eccentrics or revolutionaries.
  Jenny Holzer, *Truisms* (1979)

2 Idealization of a group is a natural consequence of separation from the group; in other words, it is a by-product of alienation.
  Paula Gunn Allen, *The Sacred Hoop* (1986)

See also Outsiders.

## ❦ ALONE

3 Tonight as always / There is no one to share my thoughts.
  Chu Shu-Chen, "Alone" (1182), in Aliki Barnstone and Willis Barnstone, eds., *A Book of Women Poets From Antiquity to Now* (1980)

4 The Moon and Pleiades have set, / Midnight is nigh, / The time is passing, passing, yet / Alone I lie.
  Sappho (6th cent. B.C.), in C.R. Gaines, ed., *Sappho: The Poems and Fragments* (1926)

5 I want to be alone. . . . I just want to be alone.
  Greta Garbo, in William A. Drake, scriptwriter, *Grand Hotel* (1932)

6 I never said, "I want to be alone." I only said, "I want to be *let* alone." There is all the difference.
  Greta Garbo, in John Bainbridge, *Garbo* (1955)

7 Once you have lived with another it is a great torture to have to live alone.
  Carson McCullers, *The Ballad of the Sad Café* (1953)

8 You come into the world alone and you go out of the world alone yet it seems to me you are more alone while living than even going and coming.
  Emily Carr, *Hundreds and Thousands* (1966)

9 And a Famous Film Star who is left alone is more alone than any other person has ever been in the whole Histry of the World, because of the contrast to our normal enviromint.
  Anita Loos, *A Mouse Is Born* (1951)

10 No matter how lonely you get or how many birth announcements you receive, the trick is not to get frightened. There's nothing wrong with being alone.
  Wendy Wasserstein, *Isn't It Romantic* (1983)

11 Anything we fully do is an alone journey.
  Natalie Goldberg, *Writing Down the Bones* (1986)

12 He travels fastest who travels alone, and that goes double for she.
  Florence King, *With Charity Toward None* (1992)

13 Being alone and liking it is, for a woman, an act of treachery, an infidelity far more threatening than adultery.
  Molly Haskell, *Love and Other Infectious Diseases* (1990)

14 I wonder if living alone makes one more alive. No precious energy goes in disagreement or compromise. No need to augment others, there is just yourself, just truth—a morsel—and you.
  Florida Scott-Maxwell, *The Measure of My Days* (1968)

15 When you live alone, you can be sure that the person who squeezed the toothpaste tube in the middle wasn't committing a hostile act.
  Ellen Goodman, *Close to Home* (1979)

16 My kitchen linoleum is so black and shiny that I waltz while I wait for the kettle to boil. This pleasure is for the old who live alone.
  Florida Scott-Maxwell, *The Measure of My Days* (1968)

17 It's true that living alone for years makes you eccentric. I talk to my cat. Why lie? Over the years I've developed the habit of *actually answering myself, in the cat's voice* (or what I imagine her voice to be).
  Stephanie Brush, in *McCall's* (1993)

18 To be alone is to be different, to be different is to be alone.
  Suzanne Gordon, *Lonely in America* (1976)

19 Nobody, but nobody / Can make it out here alone.
  Maya Angelou, "Alone," *Oh Pray My Wings Are Gonna Fit Me Well* (1975)

See also Celibacy, Loneliness, Self-Sufficiency, Single, Solitude, Widowhood.

## ❦ ALTRUISM

20 Maybe selflessness was only selfishness on another level.
  Margaret Landon, *Anna and the King of Siam* (1944)

1 Every major horror of history was committed in the name of an altruistic motive. Has any act of selfishness ever equaled the carnage perpetrated by disciples of altruism?

Ayn Rand, *The Fountainhead* (1943)

See also Idealism, Unselfishness.

## ♦ ALZHEIMER'S

2 This disease is a maniac. It goes through the life of the victim, ransacking the order of learning— dropping precious things it took years to acquire, forcing horrible new habits on its way.

Marion Roach, *Another Name for Madness* (1985)

3 The brain's asleep before its time. / I would that thou hadst died outright, / And I had seen thee, in thy prime, / Go half to darkness, half to light!

Mary Coleridge, "Horror" (1888), in Theresa Whistler, ed., *The Collected Poems of Mary Coleridge* (1954)

4 There is no more terrible woe upon earth than the woe of the stricken brain, which remembers the days of its strength, the living light of its reason, the sunrise of its proud intelligence, and knows that these have passed away like a tale that is told.

Ouida, *Wisdom, Wit and Pathos* (1884)

5 The one who knows best—the victim—about what is happening, loses the ability to tell us, the family, how to help. The ability to panic leaves the victim; it swarms over the family. As the victim forgets what is wrong, the family sees how it is, all very wrong.

Marion Roach, *Another Name for Madness* (1985)

6 Seven years I watched the next-door / Lady stroll her empty mate.

Louise Glück, "Late Snow," *Firstborn* (1968)

7 Ann finds it hard to judge the placement of her chair. At one time she tried to sit on Noelle's lap. Neither one could solve the problem. In fact Noelle was content to serve as a chair.

Judith Stoughton, *One Woman's Pascal Journey* (1991)

8 She is losing her mind in handfuls.

Marion Roach, *Another Name for Madness* (1985)

See also Mind.

## ♦ AMBIGUITY

9 Everything is ambiguous. It's exciting, in a way, if you can tolerate ambiguity. I can't, but I'm taking a course where it's taught, in the hope of acquiring the skill. It's called Modern Living, and you get no credit.

Sheila Ballantyne, *Norma Jean the Termite Queen* (1975)

See also Ambivalence, Indecision, Paradox.

## ♦ AMBITION

10 Mama exhorted her children at every opportunity to "jump at de sun." We might not land on the sun, but at least we would get off the ground.

Zora Neale Hurston, *Dust Tracks on a Road* (1942)

11 My passions were all gathered together like fingers that made a fist. Drive is considered aggression today; I knew it then as purpose.

Bette Davis, *The Lonely Life* (1962)

12 This fire in me, it's not just the hunger of a woman for a man—it's the hunger of all my people back of me, from all ages, for light, for the life higher!

Anzia Yezierska, "Hunger," *Hungry Hearts* (1920)

13 She had learned the self-deprecating ways of the woman who does not want to be thought hard and grasping, but her artifices could not always cover the nakedness of her need to excel.

Faith Sullivan, *The Cape Ann* (1988)

14 Ambition, old as mankind, the immemorial weakness of the strong.

Vita Sackville-West, *No Signposts in the Sea* (1961)

15 Ambition is peculiarly the passion of great minds. It is the aspiration after a sphere of those who feel within them the capability of filling one.

Lady Wilde, "Charles Kean as King Richard," *Notes on Men, Women, and Books* (1891)

16 To gain that which is worth having, it may be necessary to lose everything else.

Bernadette Devlin, *The Price of My Soul* (1969)

17 If ambition doesn't hurt you, you haven't got it.

Kathleen Norris, *Hands Full of Living* (1931)

1 Ambition, if it were to be savored, let alone achieved, had to be rooted in possibility.

    P.D. James, *A Taste for Death* (1986)

2 Ambition if it feeds at all, does so on the ambition of others.

    Susan Sontag, *The Benefactor* (1963)

3 On what strange stuff Ambition feeds!

    Eliza Cook, "Poor Hood," *New Echoes* (1864)

4 Here's a riddle for Our Age: when the sky's the limit, / how can you tell you've gone too far?

    Rita Dove, "And Counting," *Grace Notes* (1989)

5 Because we are always staring at the stars, we learn the shortness of our arms.

    Mary Roberts Rinehart, *The Red Lamp* (1925)

6 I used to think I had ambition . . . but now I'm not so sure. It may have been only discontent. They're easily confused.

    Rachel Field, *All This and Heaven Too* (1939)

7 Nobody in our family is smitten with ambition. Daddy is smitten with religion, Mama is smitten with love for her family, Kevy is smitten with Ronnie, Arlie is smitten with shame, and I love to sing.

    Ruth Wolff, *A Crack in the Sidewalk* (1965)

8 There are no persons capable of stooping so low as those who desire to rise in the world.

    Countess of Blessington, *Desultory Thoughts and Reflections* (1839)

9 Beware of the man who denounces ambition; / his fingers itch under his gloves.

    Erica Jong, "Seventeen Warnings in Search of a Feminist Poem," *Half-Lives* (1971)

## ॐ AMBIVALENCE

10 I felt a Cleaving in my Mind — / As if my Brain had split — / I tried to match it — Seam by Seam — / But could not make them fit.

    Emily Dickinson (1864), in Mabel Loomis Todd, ed., *Poems by Emily Dickinson*, 3rd series (1896)

11 I am and am not; freeze, and yet I burn, / Since from myself my other self I turn.

    Elizabeth I (1582), in Gwen John, *Queen Elizabeth* (1924)

12 Ambivalence is a wonderful tune to dance to. It has a rhythm all its own.

    Erica Jong, *Fear of Flying* (1973)

13 I happen to feel that the degree of a person's intelligence is directly reflected by the number of conflicting attitudes she can bring to bear on the same topic.

    Lisa Alther, *Kinflicks* (1975)

14 The human soul is hospitable, and will entertain conflicting sentiments and contradictory opinions with much impartiality.

    George Eliot, *Romola* (1862)

15 The older you grow, the more you realize that one half of you can firmly believe what the other half equally firmly refuses.

    Constance Holme, *He-Who-Came?* (1930)

16 It is human nature to stand in the middle of a thing.

    Marianne Moore, "A Grave" (1924), *Selected Poems* (1935)

17 He had felt like a man rushing to catch a train he was anxious to miss.

    Helen Hudson, *Meyer Meyer* (1967)

See also Ambiguity, Conflict, Indecision, Paradox.

## ॐ AMERICA

See United States.

## ॐ AMERICAN INDIANS

18 No, I don't know where you can get peyote. / No, I don't know where you can get Navajo rugs real cheap. / No, I didn't make this. I bought it at Bloomingdales. / Thank you. I like your hair too. / . . . / This ain't no stoic look. / This is my face.

    Diane Burns, "Sure You Can Ask Me a Personal Question," in Joseph Bruchac, ed., *Songs From This Earth on Turtle's Back* (1983)

19 I am visible—see this Indian face—yet I am invisible. I both blind them with my beak nose and am their blind spot. But I exist, we exist. They'd like to

think I have melted in the pot. But I haven't, we haven't.

Gloria Anzaldúa, *Borderlands/La Frontera* (1987)

1 You have to understand an Indian / to see he isn't there.

Diane Glancy, "Portrait of Lone Dog," *Lone Dog's Winter Count* (1991)

2 She realized that white people rarely concerned themselves with Indian matters, that Indians were the shadow people, living almost invisibly on the fringes around them, and that this shadowy world allowed for a strange kind of freedom.

Linda Hogan, *Mean Spirit* (1990)

3 What hurts Indians most is that our costumes are considered beautiful, but it's as if the person wearing it didn't exist.

Rigoberta Menchú, in Elisabeth Burgos-Debray, ed., *I, Rigoberta Menchú* (1983)

4 They liked to romanticize the earlier days when they believed the Indians lived in a simple way and wore more colorful clothing than the complicated Indians who lived alongside them in the modern world. They believed the Indians used to have power. In the older, better times, that is, before the people had lost their land and their sacred places on earth to the very people who wished the Indians were as they had been in the past.

Linda Hogan, *Mean Spirit* (1990)

5 Our sacred beliefs have been made pencils / names of cities gas stations / My knee is wounded so badly that I limp constantly / Anger is my crutch  I hold myself upright with it / My knee is wounded / see / How I Am Still Walking.

Chrystos, "I Walk in the History of My People," *Not Vanishing* (1988)

6 Our religion and ceremonies have become fads, and a fashionable pastime among many whites seeking for something that they hope will give meaning to their empty lives. . . . After macrobiotics, Zen, and channeling, the "poor Vanishing Indian" is once more the subject of "deep and meaningful conversation" in the high rises.

Mary Brave Bird, with Richard Erdoes, *Ohitika Woman* (1993)

7 It has seemed so strange to me that the larger culture, with its own absence of spirit and lack of attachment for the land, respects these very things about Indian traditions, without adopting those respected ways themselves.

Linda Hogan, "The Sacred Seed of the Medicine Tree," *Northern Lights* (1990)

8 They have our bundles split open in museums / our dresses & shirts at auctions / our languages on tape / our stories in locked rare book libraries / our dances on film / The only part of us they can't steal / is what we know.

Chrystos, "Vision: Bundle," *Not Vanishing* (1988)

9 Not even anthropologists or intellectuals, no matter how many books they have, can find out all our secrets.

Rigoberta Menchú, in Elisabeth Burgos-Debray, ed., *I, Rigoberta Menchú* (1983)

10 The joke used to be that in every Indian home, there is the mother, father, children, grandparents, and the anthropologist.

Elizabeth Cook-Lynn, *From the River's Edge* (1991)

11 An odd thing occurs in the minds of Americans when Indian civilization is mentioned: little or nothing.

Paula Gunn Allen, *The Sacred Hoop* (1986)

12 If you were going to compete successfully in a white man's world, you had to learn to play the white man's game. It was not enough that an Indian be *as good as*; an Indian had to be *better than*.

Janet Campbell Hale, *The Jailing of Cecelia Capture* (1985)

13 It's only a matter of time, Indian / you can't sleep with the river forever.

Leslie Marmon Silko, "Indian Song: Survival," *Storyteller* (1981)

14 When I look back on reservation life it seems that I spent a great deal of time attending the funerals of my relatives or friends of my family. . . . Death was so common on the reservation that I did not understand the implications of the high death rate until after I moved away and was surprised to learn that I've seen more dead bodies than my friends will probably ever see in their lifetime.

Barbara Cameron, in Cherríe Moraga and Gloria Anzaldúa, eds., *This Bridge Called My Back* (1983)

15 Our tribe unraveled like a coarse rope, frayed at either end as the old and new among us were taken.

Louise Erdrich, *Tracks* (1988)

1 By the time I was done with the car it looked worse than any typical Indian car that has been driven all its life on reservation roads, which they always say are like government promises—full of holes.

   Louise Erdrich, *Love Medicine* (1984)

2 The white man had come with the Bible in one hand, the bottle in the other.

   E. Pauline Johnson, *The Moccasin Maker* (1913)

3 "Coffin-nails" are of the white man's inception, along with his multitudinous diseased adjuncts of civilization: whiskey, beer, wine and opium with attending crimes and ills. And to cap the irony of it all, he brings the "glad tidings" of an endlessly burning hell where we are roasted for emulating his "superior" example.

   Mourning Dove, *Cogewea* (1927)

4 America does not seem to remember that it derived its wealth, its values, its food, much of its medicine, and a large part of its "dream" from Native America.

   Paula Gunn Allen, *The Sacred Hoop* (1986)

5 The Indians of North America are, perhaps, the only race of men of whom it may be said, that though conquered, they were never enslaved. They could not submit, and live.

   C.M. Sedgwick, *Hope Leslie* (1827)

6 Being Indian is an attitude, a state of mind, a way of being in harmony with all things and all beings. It is allowing the heart to be the distributor of energy on this planet: to allow feelings and sensitivities to determine where energy goes; bringing aliveness up from the Earth and down from the Sky, putting it in and giving it out from the heart.

   Brooke Medicine Eagle, in Joan Halifax, *Shamanic Voices* (1979)

7 We are the land. To the best of my understanding, that is the fundamental idea that permeates American Indian life.

   Paula Gunn Allen, *The Sacred Hoop* (1986)

8 They seemed to have none of the European's desire to "master" nature, to arrange and re-create. They spent their ingenuity in the other direction; in accommodating themselves to the scene in which they found themselves. . . . It was as if the great country were asleep, and they wished to carry on their lives without awakening it.

   Willa Cather, *Death Comes for the Archbishop* (1927)

9 For the American Indian, the ability of all creatures to share in the process of ongoing creation makes all things sacred.

   Paula Gunn Allen, *The Sacred Hoop* (1986)

10 It is impossible to come into contact with Native American spirituality and not be struck with the immensity of the gratitude expressed.

   Anne Wilson Schaef, *Meditations for Women Who Do Too Much* (1990)

11 Indians think it is important to remember, while Americans believe it is important to forget.

   Paula Gunn Allen, *The Sacred Hoop* (1986)

See also Minorities, Oppression, Racism, Time.

## ✿ ANCESTORS

12 We all grow up with the weight of history on us. Our ancestors dwell in the attics of our brains as they do in the spiraling chains of knowledge hidden in every cell of our bodies.

   Shirley Abbott, *Womenfolks: Growing Up Down South* (1983)

13 Our mothers and grandmothers, some of them: moving to music not yet written.

   Alice Walker, title essay (1974), *In Search of Our Mothers' Gardens* (1983)

14 Ancestral habits of mind can be constricting; they also confer one's individuality.

   Bharati Mukherjee, in Janet Sternburg, ed., *The Writer on Her Work*, vol. 2 (1991)

See also Family, Genealogy, Grandparents, Roots.

## ✿ ANDROGYNY

15 Male and female represent the two sides of the great radical dualism. But, in fact, they are perpetually passing into one another. Fluid hardens to solid, solid rushes to fluid. There is no wholly masculine man, no purely feminine woman.

   Margaret Fuller, *Woman in the Nineteenth Century* (1845)

16 Perhaps a mind that is purely masculine cannot create, any more than a mind that is purely feminine. . . . It is fatal to be a man or woman pure and

simple; one must be woman-manly or man-womanly.

Virginia Woolf, *A Room of One's Own* (1929)

1 I had reached the conclusion myself that sex was not a division but a continuum, that almost nobody was altogether of one sex or another, and that the infinite subtlety of the shading from one extreme to the other was one of the most beautiful of nature's phenomena.

Jan Morris, *Conundrum* (1974)

2 What is most beautiful in virile men is something feminine; what is most beautiful in feminine women is something masculine.

Susan Sontag, "Notes on 'Camp'" (1964), *Against Interpretation* (1966)

3 The feminine in the man is the sugar in the whisky. The masculine in the woman is the yeast in the bread. Without these ingredients the result is flat, without tang or flavor.

Edna Ferber, *A Kind of Magic* (1963)

4 The term "androgyny" . . . defines a condition under which the characteristics of the sexes, and the human impulses expressed by men and women, are not rigidly assigned. Androgyny seeks to liberate the individual from the confines of the appropriate.

Carolyn Heilbrun, *Toward a Recognition of Androgyny* (1973)

5 Androgyny suggests a spirit of reconciliation between the sexes.

Carolyn Heilbrun, *Toward a Recognition of Androgyny* (1973)

6 As to sex, the original pleasure, I cannot recommend too highly the advantages of androgyny.

Jan Morris, *Pleasures of a Tangled Life* (1989)

7 Thou large-brained woman and large-hearted man.

Elizabeth Barrett Browning, "To George Sand—A Desire," *Poems* (1844)

8 The word [androgyny] is misbegotten—conveying something like "John Travolta and Farrah Fawcett-Majors scotch-taped together."

Mary Daly, *Gyn/Ecology* (1978)

9 Androgyne, you're a funny valentine.

Helen Lawrenson, *Latins Are Still Lousy Lovers* (1968)

See also Gender, Sex Roles, Women and Men.

## ❧ ANECDOTES

10 Anecdotes, / The poor man's history.

Rita Dove, "The Gorge," *Grace Notes* (1989)

## ❧ ANGELS

11 Imagine them as they were first conceived: / part musical instrument and part daisy.

P.K. Page, "Images of Angels," *The Metal and the Flower* (1954)

12 Angels are pure thoughts from God, winged with Truth and Love.

Mary Baker Eddy, *Science and Health* (1875)

13 I was talking to angels long before they got fashionable. . . . So maybe you don't believe in angels, that's all right, they don't care. They're not like Tinkerbell, you know, they don't depend on your faith to exist. A lot of people didn't believe the earth was round either, but that didn't make it any flatter.

Nancy Pickard, *Confession* (1994)

14 No one who has seen an angel ever mistakes it for a ghost. Angels are remarkable for their warmth and light, and all who see them speak in awe of their iridescent and refulgent light, of brilliant colors, or else of the unbearable whiteness of their being. You are flooded with laughter, happiness.

Sophy Burnham, *A Book of Angels* (1990)

15 Angels come in all sizes and shapes and colors, visible and invisible to the physical eye. But always you are changed from having seen one.

Sophy Burnham, *A Book of Angels* (1990)

## ❧ ANGER

16 Anger is a signal, and one worth listening to.

Harriet Lerner, *The Dance of Anger* (1985)

17 Anger is loaded with information and energy.

Audre Lorde, "The Uses of Anger" (1981), *Sister Outsider* (1984)

1  The first step in claiming yourself is anger.

> Jamaica Kincaid, in Donna Perry, ed., *Backtalk* (1993)

2  At least if I can stay mad I can stay alive.

> Magdalena Gomez, "Solo Palabras," in Faythe Turner, ed., *Puerto Rican Writers at Home in the USA* (1991)

3  Anger is protest.

> Lillian Hellman, *Watch on the Rhine* (1941)

4  I have a right to my anger, and I don't want anybody telling me I shouldn't be, that it's not nice to be, and that something's wrong with me because I get angry.

> Maxine Waters, in Brian Lanker, *I Dream a World* (1989)

5  Anger is its own excuse and its own reward.

> Anne Rivers Siddons, *Outer Banks* (1991)

6  I have suckled the wolf's lip of anger and I have used it for illumination, laughter, protection, fire in places where there was no light, no food, no sisters, no quarter.

> Audre Lorde, "The Uses of Anger" (1981), *Sister Outsider* (1984)

7  Grab the broom of anger and drive off the beast of fear.

> Zora Neale Hurston, *Dust Tracks on a Road* (1942)

8  Anger as well as love casts out fear.

> Margaret Deland, *Small Things* (1919)

9  Through anger, the truth looks simple.

> Jane McCabe, in Carolyn Heilbrun, *Writing a Woman's Life* (1988)

10  People in a temper often say a lot of silly, terrible things they mean.

> Penelope Gilliatt, in Katharine Whitehorn, *View From a Column* (1981)

11  He was really very fond of his temper, and rather enjoyed referring to it with tolerant regret as being a bad one and beyond his control—with a manner which suggested that the attribute was the inevitable result of strength of character and masculine spirit.

> Frances Hodgson Burnett, *The Shuttle* (1907)

12  We wish to make rage into a fire that cooks things rather than a fire of conflagration.

> Clarissa Pinkola Estés, *Women Who Run With the Wolves* (1992)

13  The anger she felt within her acted like yeast on bread dough. She felt its rapid rising, flowing into every last recess of her body; like yeast in a small bowl, it spilled over to the outside, escaping in the form of steam through her ears, nose, and all her pores.

> Laura Esquivel, *Like Water for Chocolate* (1992)

14  I don't know if fury can compete with necessity as the mother of invention, but I recommend it.

> Gloria Steinem, *Moving Beyond Words* (1994)

15  Many of our problems with anger occur when we choose between having a relationship and having a self.

> Harriet Lerner, *The Dance of Anger* (1985)

16  Anger is a tool for change when it challenges us to become more of an expert on the self and less of an expert on others.

> Harriet Lerner, *The Dance of Anger* (1985)

17  I am no longer afraid of anger. I find it to be a creative, transforming force; anger is a stage I must go through if I am ever to get to what lies beyond.

> Mary Kaye Medinger (1987), in Kay Vander Vort et al., *Walking in Two Worlds* (1992)

18  Anger stirs and wakes in her; it opens its mouth, and like a hot-mouthed puppy, laps up the dredges of her shame. Anger is better. There is a sense of being in anger. A reality and presence. An awareness of worth.

> Toni Morrison, *The Bluest Eye* (1970)

19  Anger, used, does not destroy. Hatred does.

> Audre Lorde, "Eye to Eye," *Sister Outsider* (1984)

20  Anger as soon as fed is dead — / 'Tis starving makes it fat.

> Emily Dickinson (1881), in T.W. Higginson and Mabel Loomis Todd, eds., *Poems by Emily Dickinson*, 2nd series (1891)

21  Anger is like milk, it should not be kept too long.

> Phyllis Bottome, "The Home-Coming," *Innocence and Experience* (1934)

22  Bad temper is its own safety valve. He who can bark does not bite.

> Agatha Christie, title story, *The Under Dog* (1951)

23  I was so mad you could have boiled a pot of water on my head.

> Alice Childress, *Like One of the Family* (1956)

1 She wouldn't talk to him at all. She just swelled up like a toad-fish and sat and looked at the fire without cracking her teeth.

Julia Peterkin, *Scarlet Sister Mary* (1928)

2 Then there was no end to the rage and disappointment of Tom Thumb and Hunca Munca.

Beatrix Potter, *The Tale of Two Bad Mice* (1904)

3 Their anger dug out for itself a deep channel, so that future angers might more easily follow.

Radclyffe Hall, *The Well of Loneliness* (1928)

4 There are so many roots to the tree of anger / that sometimes the branches shatter / before they bear.

Audre Lorde, "Who Said It Was Simple" (1970), *Undersong* (1992)

5 When the habitually even-tempered suddenly fly into a passion, that explosion is apt to be more impressive than the outburst of the most violent amongst us.

Margery Allingham, *Death of a Ghost* (1934)

6 In anger, you look ten years older.

Hedda Hopper, *From Under My Hat* (1952)

7 Beware of anger. It is the most difficult to remove of all the hindrances. But it is the alcohol of the body, you know, and the devil of it is that it deadens the perceptions.

Margery Allingham, *The Tiger in the Smoke* (1952)

8 Anger is the common refuge of insignificance. People who feel their character to be slight, hope to give it weight by inflation: but the blown bladder at its fullest distention is still empty.

Hannah More, "On the Comparatively Small Faults and Virtues," *Practical Piety* (1811)

9 The devil-ache of loneliness seldom deserts the bones of the angry.

Lucy Freeman, *Before I Kill More* (1955)

10 Anger makes us all stupid.

Johanna Spyri, *Heidi* (1881)

11 Anger makes dull men witty, but it keeps them poor.

Elizabeth I, in Francis Bacon, *Apophthegms* (1625)

See also Indignation, Outrage, Resentment.

## ✿ ANIMAL RIGHTS

12 A sense of the Rights of Animals has slowly been awakened, and is becoming, by not imperceptible degrees, a new principle of ethics.

Frances Power Cobbe, *Life of Frances Power Cobbe*, vol. 1 (1894)

13 We all love animals, but why do we call some "pets" and some "dinner"?

k.d. lang, PETA-sponsored anti-meat commercial, in Mark Bego, *Country Gals* (1994)

14 I ask people why they have deer heads on their walls, and they say, "Because it's such a beautiful animal." There you go. Well, I think my mother's attractive, but I have *photographs* of her.

Ellen DeGeneres, *My Point . . . And I Do Have One* (1995)

15 Making animals perform for the amusement of human beings is / Utterly disgraceful and abominable. / Animals are animals and have their nature / And that's enough, it is enough, leave it alone.

Stevie Smith, "This Is Disgraceful and Abominable," *Not Waving But Drowning* (1957)

16 People who let their dogs and cats have litters in order to show their children the "miracle of birth" should come witness the "miracle of death" performed in the back rooms of animal shelters all over the country.

Phyllis Wright, in Ingrid Newkirk, *Save the Animals!* (1990)

17 Fur used to turn heads, now it turns stomachs.

Rue McClanahan, in Ingrid Newkirk, *Save the Animals!* (1990)

18 Since we humans have the better brain, isn't it our responsibility to protect our fellow creatures from, oddly enough, ourselves?

Joy Adamson, in Barbara McDowell and Hana Umlauf, *Woman's Almanac* (1977)

19 I am the voice of the voiceless; / . . . / And I am my brother's keeper, / And I will fight his fight, / And speak the word for beast and bird, / Till the world shall set things right.

Ella Wheeler Wilcox, "The Voice of the Voiceless," *Poems of Experience* (1910)

20 Hurt no living thing: / Ladybird, nor butterfly, / Nor moth with dusty wing, / Nor cricket chirping cheerily.

Christina Rossetti, "Hurt No Living Thing," *Sing-Song* (1872)

See also Animals, Vegetarianism, Vivisection.

## ❧ ANIMALS

1 Animals are such agreeable friends—they ask no questions, they pass no criticisms.

> George Eliot, "Mr. Gilfil's Love Story," *Scenes of Clerical Life* (1857)

2 Animals do not betray; they do not exploit; they do not oppress; they do not enslave; they do not sin. They have their being, and their being is honest, and who can say this of man?

> Taylor Caldwell, *Great Lion of God* (1970)

3 Animals give us their constant, unjaded faces and we burden them with our bodies and civilized ordeals.

> Gretel Ehrlich, *The Solace of Open Spaces* (1985)

4 We humans should never forget our capacity to connect with the collective spirit of animals. Their energy is essential to our future growth.

> Shirley MacLaine, *Dancing in the Light* (1985)

5 There is not one world for man and one for animals, they are part of the same one and lead parallel lives.

> Rigoberta Menchú, in Elisabeth Burgos-Debray, ed., *I, Rigoberta Menchú* (1983)

6 Birds and beasts have in fact our own nature, flattened a semi-tone.

> Lydia Maria Child, *Letters From New York*, 2nd series (1845)

7 Animals were once, for all of us, teachers. They instructed us in ways of being and perceiving that extended our imaginations, that were models for additional possibilities.

> Joan McIntyre, *Mind in the Waters* (1974)

8 Animals are so much quicker in picking up our thoughts than we are in picking up theirs. I believe they must have a very poor opinion of the human race.

> Barbara Woodhouse, in *The Telegraph Sunday Magazine* (1984)

9 "Talking to animals" isn't a matter of words used, it is a matter of your thoughts, your expression, and above all the tone of your voice. A harsh voice from me can make my cows jump in terror. I shouted at old Queenie once and she got such a shock that she fell down just as if she'd been shot.

> Barbara Woodhouse, *Talking to Animals* (1954)

10 We call them dumb animals, and so they are, for they cannot tell us how they feel, but they do not suffer less because they have no words.

> Anna Sewell, *Black Beauty* (1877)

11 Nature is not silent, and never was a name more derisively inappropriate than when we speak of these non-human creatures who hoot and crow and bray as the *dumb* animals.

> Winifred Holtby, in Vera Brittain, *Testament of Friendship* (1940)

12 I believe that animals have been talking to human beings ever since we were all made and put into this world.

> Barbara Woodhouse, *Talking to Animals* (1954)

13 Children feel what their elders forget, our touching kinship with animals. To me a chipmunk was a far more real personality than Great-Uncle Aaron, and the mousehole gnawed in the lower left corner of the door to down cellar a more delightful habitation for the mind to contemplate than the parsonage.

> Bertha Damon, *Grandma Called It Carnal* (1938)

14 My mother thought it would make us feel better to know animals had no souls and thus their deaths were not to be taken seriously. But it didn't help and when I think of some of the animals I have known, I wonder. The only really "soulful" eyes in the world belong to the dog or cat who sits on your lap or at your feet commiserating when you cry.

> Liz Smith, *The Mother Book* (1978)

15 Some animals, like some men, leave a trail of glory behind them. They give their spirit to the place where they have lived, and remain forever a part of the rocks and streams and the wind and sky.

> Marguerite Henry, *Brighty of the Grand Canyon* (1953)

16 Animals in different countries have different expressions just as the people in different countries differ in expression.

> Gertrude Stein, *Everybody's Autobiography* (1937)

17 The dog opened one eye, cocked it at me, and rolled it up before her lids closed. People should not feed moralistic animals. If they're so holy, where are their books?

> Annie Dillard, *The Writing Life* (1989)

1 I like handling newborn animals. Fallen into life from an unmappable world, they are the ultimate immigrants, full of wonder and confusion.

Diane Ackerman, *The Moon by Whale Light* (1991)

2 Few know the ways of this rapt eremite / By civilization he is not impressed; / Lost in the spiral of his conscience, he / Detachedly takes rest.

Laura Benét, "The Snail," *Noah's Dove* (1929)

3 Signs of mice were in the kitchen. Sometimes they dropped in for warmth and charity.

Helen Bevington, *The House Was Quiet and the World Was Calm* (1971)

4 I found some of the most minute mouse tracks this morning, like little necklaces in the snow.

Tasha Tudor, with Richard Brown, *The Private World of Tasha Tudor* (1992)

5 I think mice / Are rather nice.

Rose Fyleman, "Mice" (1920), in Jack Prelutsky, ed., *Read-Aloud Rhymes for the Very Young* (1986)

6 Adult bats don't weigh much. They're mainly fur and appetite.

Diane Ackerman, *The Moon by Whale Light* (1991)

7 "He is well behaved, señora," the old man said when he sold it to me. "He is not vulgar. He will never embarrass you." The parrot eyed me slyly and malevolently, like a wrongdoer who hears his lawyer praising him in court.

Gertrude Diamant, *The Days of Ofelia* (1942)

8 Short, potbellied penguins, whose necks wobbled with baby fat, huddled together like Russian businessmen in fur coats.

Diane Ackerman, *The Moon by Whale Light* (1991)

9 Penguins mate for life. Which doesn't exactly surprise me that much 'cause they all look alike—it's not like they're gonna meet a better-looking penguin someday.

Ellen DeGeneres, in *Mirabella* (1992)

10 Still and silent and inimitably grave, were two baby owls taking an airing. . . . The four eyes were focused like cameras in a certain direction, and anything that came within the line of vision was necessarily taken in by them. One waited with the concentrated longing of the photographed for the little click of release. It never came, and I realized that this was to be an endless exposure.

Mary Webb, *The Spring of Joy* (1917)

11 I met a baby owl in a wood, when it fell over dead, apparently from sheer temper, because I dared to approach it. It defied me first, and then died. I have never forgotten the horror and shame I experienced when that soft fluffy thing (towards which I had nothing but the most humanitarian motives) fell dead from rage at my feet.

Vita Sackville-West, "Owls," *Country Notes* (1940)

12 There is nothing in nature quite so joyful as the very young and silly lamb—odd that it should develop into that dull and sober animal the sheep.

Esther Meynell, *A Woman Talking* (1940)

13 The foolish square calves pretend to be frightened of our train. Bluffers! Haven't they seen it every day since they were born? It's just an excuse to shake the joy out of their heels.

Emily Carr (1933), *Hundreds and Thousands* (1966)

14 I went through the fields, and sat for an hour afraid to pass a cow. The cow looked at me, and I looked at the cow, and whenever I stirred the cow gave over eating.

Dorothy Wordsworth (1802), in William Knight, ed., *Journals of Dorothy Wordsworth*, vol. 1 (1897)

15 How agreeable to watch, from the other side of the high stile, this mighty creature, this fat bull of Bashan, snorting, champing, pawing the earth, lashing the tail, breathing defiance at heaven and at me . . . his heart hot with hate, unable to climb a stile.

Rose Macaulay, *Personal Pleasures* (1936)

16 We would see a long line of cattle like black lace against the sunset sky.

Georgia O'Keeffe, *Georgia O'Keeffe* (1976)

17 On the way down we met a few yaks puffing and steaming in their progress uphill. . . . They reminded me of overstuffed ottomans, with fringes of long black hair rather in the shape of loose covers.

Antonia Deacock, *No Purdah in Padam* (1960)

18 I had seen a herd of buffalo, one hundred and twenty-nine of them, come out of the morning mist under a copper sky, one by one, as if the dark and massive, iron-like animals with the mighty horizontally swung horns were not approaching, but were being created before my eyes and sent out as they were finished.

Isak Dinesen, *Out of Africa* (1937)

1 [The lion] began to contemplate me with a kind of quiet premeditation, like that of a slow-witted man fondling an unaccustomed thought.

Beryl Markham, *West With the Night* (1942)

2 This little panther wears a coat of soot, / Well-suited so. Stretched out along his shelf, / Still as one brooding storm, the sultry brute / Looks soft as darkness folded on itself.

Babette Deutsch, "Creatures in the Zoo," *The Collected Poems of Babette Deutsch* (1969)

3 The African leopard is an audacious animal, although it is ungrateful of me to say a word against him, after the way he has let me off personally. . . . Taken as a whole, he is the most lovely animal I have ever seen; only seeing him, in the one way you can gain a full idea of his beauty, namely in his native forest, is not an unmixed joy to a person, like myself, of a nervous disposition.

Mary H. Kingsley, *Travels in West Africa* (1897)

4 A big leopard . . . was crouching on the ground, with his magnificent head thrown back and his eyes shut. His fore-paws were spread out in front of him and he lashed the ground with his tail, and I grieve to say, in face of that awful danger—I don't mean me, but the tornado—that depraved creature swore, softly, but repeatedly and profoundly.

Mary H. Kingsley, *Travels in West Africa* (1897)

5 Did you ever see a giraffe? . . . It is like seeing something from between the regions of truth and fiction.

Geraldine Jewsbury (1844), in Mrs. Alexander Ireland, ed., *Selections From the Letters of Geraldine Endsor Jewsbury to Jane Welsh Carlyle* (1892)

6 I . . . watched the progression across the plain of the giraffe, in their queer, inimitable, vegetative gracefulness, as if it were not a herd of animals but a family of rare, long-stemmed, speckled gigantic flowers slowly advancing.

Isak Dinesen, *Out of Africa* (1937)

7 If you ever, ever, ever meet a grizzly bear, / You must never, never, never ask him *where* / He is going, / Or *what* he is doing; / For if you ever, ever dare / To stop a grizzly bear, / You will never meet *another* grizzly bear.

Mary Austin, "Grizzly Bear," *The Children Sing in the Far West* (1928)

8 The white bears, all in a dim blue world / Mumbling their meals by twilight.

Jean Ingelow, "Gladys and Her Island," *A Story of Doom* (1867)

9 A gorilla is a stupendous creature, very up and coming. He seems to belong to the dawn of his time, the origin, not the end, the elemental stuff packed with compressed vitality from whom everything is still to come.

L.M. Boston, *A Stranger at Green Knowe* (1961)

10 If we don't exterminate the gorillas before we exterminate ourselves, the gorilla will have his chance. He's one of the really great ones of the earth, and he's not specialized, he's versatile. It's the versatile who survive.

L.M. Boston, *A Stranger at Green Knowe* (1961)

11 Peanuts . . . suddenly stopped and turned to stare directly at me. The expression in his eyes was unfathomable. Spellbound, I returned his gaze—a gaze that seemed to combine elements of inquiry and acceptance. . . . I returned to camp and cabled Dr. Leaky, "I've finally been accepted by a gorilla."

Dian Fossey, *Gorillas in the Mist* (1983)

12 One immense old lady has a family of lively young crocodiles running over her, evidently playing like a lot of kittens. The heavy musky smell they give off is most repulsive, but we do not rise up and make a row about this, because we feel hopelessly in the wrong in intruding into these family scenes uninvited.

Mary H. Kingsley, *Travels in West Africa* (1897)

13 Not much is known about alligators. They don't train well. And they're unwieldy and rowdy to work with in laboratories.

Diane Ackerman, *The Moon by Whale Light* (1991)

14 I startled a weasel who startled me, and we exchanged a long glance. . . . Our eyes locked, and someone threw away the key.

Annie Dillard, *Teaching a Stone to Talk* (1982)

15 A beaver does not, as legend would have it, know which direction the tree will fall when he cuts it, but counts on alacrity to make up for lack of engineering expertise.

Ann Zwinger, *Beyond the Aspen Grove* (1970)

16 The self-assured porcupine, endearingly grotesque, waddles up the road in broad daylight. He looks as

if he had slept in his rumpled spiky clothes, and he probably has.

Bertha Damon, *A Sense of Humus* (1943)

1 I know animals more gallant than the African warthog, but none more courageous. He is the peasant of the plains—the drab and dowdy digger in the earth. He is the uncomely but intrepid defender of family, home, and bourgeois convention, and he will fight anything of any size that intrudes upon his smug existence. . . . His eyes are small and lightless and capable of but one expression—suspicion. What he does not understand, he suspects, and what he suspects, he fights.

Beryl Markham, *West With the Night* (1942)

See also Animal Rights, Birds, Camels, Cats, Cats and Dogs, Dogs, Elephants, Horses, Pets, Rabbits, Veterinary Medicine, Vivisection, Wildlife, Wolves, Zoos.

# ❧ ANONYMOUS

2 I would venture to guess that Anon, who wrote so many poems without signing them, was often a woman.

Virginia Woolf, *A Room of One's Own* (1929)

3 Anonymous: Prolific female author. Has written hundreds of thousands of books, articles, poems, essays, memos, broadsides, and treatises. Under this name many women for centuries have written, published, or produced art, either deliberately to avoid the problems and punishments awaiting the woman artist or by default because their names were lost or forgotten.

Cheris Kramarae and Paula A. Treichler, *A Feminist Dictionary* (1985)

# ❧ ANSWERS

4 Our whole life consists of despairing of an answer and seeking an answer.

Dorothee Sölle, *The Truth Is Concrete* (1967)

5 The only interesting answers are those which destroy the questions.

Susan Sontag, in *Esquire* (1968)

6 There have been so many answers / they have all been right.

Deborah Keenan, "Dialogue," *Household Wounds* (1981)

7 There are answers which, in turning away wrath, only send it to the other end of the room.

George Eliot, *Middlemarch* (1871)

8 Great evil has been done on earth by people who think they have all the answers.

Ruby Plenty Chiefs, in Lynn V. Andrews, *Crystal Woman* (1987)

9 He had a way of meeting a simple question with a compound answer—you could take the part you wanted, and leave the rest.

Eva Lathbury, *Mr. Meyer's Pupil* (1907)

10 What is the answer? . . . Then, what is the question?

Gertrude Stein, last words (1946), in Elizabeth Sprigge, *Gertrude Stein* (1957)

See also Explanations, Questions.

# ❧ ANTHOLOGIES

11 Oh, shun, lad, the life of an author. / It's nothing but worry and waste. / Avoid that utensil, / The laboring pencil, / And pick up the scissors and paste.

Phyllis McGinley, "A Ballad of Anthologies," *Stones From a Glass House* (1946)

12 As long as mixed grills and combination salads are popular, anthologies will undoubtedly continue in favor.

Elizabeth Janeway, in Helen R. Hull, ed., *The Writer's Book* (1950)

13 There is surely no more unselfish person than the anthologist. For while all we others are striving to ensure our own immortality with eagerness, beguilements, buffooneries, loud voices, "the sound of battle and garments rolled in blood," the anthologist is quietly ensuring the immortality of somebody else.

Mary Webb, in *The Bookman* (1926)

14 There is usually no dreamer so unworldly as the anthologist. He wanders in a vast garden, lost in wonder, unable to decide often between flowers of equal loveliness. . . . The true anthologist has the

greatest difficulty in finishing his book. There is always just one more, a new, delicious discovery.

Mary Webb, in *The Bookman* (1926)

## ❧ ANTICIPATION

1 Anticipation was the soul of enjoyment.

Elizabeth Gaskell, "The Cage at Cranford," in *All the Year Round* (1863)

2 Looking forward to things is half the pleasure of them.

L.M. Montgomery, *Anne of Green Gables* (1908)

3 Anticipation of pleasure is a pleasure in itself.

Sylvia Townsend Warner (1960), in William Maxwell, ed., *Letters: Sylvia Townsend Warner* (1982)

4 'T ain't worth while to wear a day all out before it comes.

Sarah Orne Jewett, *The Country of the Pointed Firs* (1896)

See also Expectations, Hope.

## ❧ ANTI-FEMINISM

5 The Queen is most anxious to enlist everyone who can speak or write to join in checking this mad, wicked folly of "Woman's Rights," with all its attendant horrors.... It is a subject which makes the Queen so furious that she cannot contain herself.

Queen Victoria, letter to Sir Theodore Martin (1870), in Lytton Strachey, *Queen Victoria* (1921)

6 I have not, in general, much belief in the ability of woman as a creative artist. Unwritten lyrics, as Emerson said once when we conversed on this subject, should be her forte.

Fredrika Bremer (1850), *America of the Fifties* (1924)

7 If civilization had been left in female hands, we would still be living in grass huts.

Camille Paglia, *Sexual Personae* (1990)

8 Every year, feminists provide more and more evidence for the old charge that women can neither think nor write.

Camille Paglia, "Junk Bonds and Corporate Raiders: Academe in the Hour of the Wolf," *Sex, Art, and American Culture* (1992)

9 Her secret feeling was, I expect, that of many anti-suffragist women I have known, who, for some reason or other on the pinnacle of man's favor themselves, had no objection to the rest of womenkind being held in contempt.

Ethel Smyth, *Impressions That Remained* (1919)

See also Backlash, Sexism.

## ❧ ANTI-INTELLECTUALISM

10 There is at present in the United States a powerful activist movement that is anti-intellectual, anti-science, and anti-technology. If we are to have faith that mankind will survive and thrive on the face of the Earth, we must depend on the continued revolutions brought about by science.

Rosalyn Yalow, in Sharon Bertsch McGrayne, *Nobel Prize Women in Science* (1993)

11 One of the frightening things about our time is the number of people who think it is a form of intellectual audacity to be stupid. A whole generation seems to be taking on an easy distrust of thought.

Renata Adler, *A Year in the Dark* (1969)

12 Too many of our countrymen rejoice in stupidity, look upon ignorance as a badge of honor. They condemn everything they don't understand.

Tallulah Bankhead, *Tallulah* (1952)

13 As towards most other things of which we have but little personal experience (foreigners, or socialists, or aristocrats, as the case may be), there is a degree of vague ill-will towards what is called *Thinking*.

Vernon Lee, "Against Talking," *Hortus Vitae* (1904)

14 In our society to admit inferiority is to be a fool, and to admit superiority is to be an outcast. Those who are in reality superior in intelligence can be accepted by their fellows only if they pretend they are not.

Marya Mannes, *More in Anger* (1958)

15 The sad truth is that excellence makes people nervous.

Shana Alexander, "Neglected Kids—the Bright Ones," in *Life* (1966)

## ❧ ANTI-SEMITISM

1 No yellow armband, no marked park bench, no Gestapo. Just here a flick and there another.... But day by day the little thump of insult. Day by day the tapping on the nerves, the delicate assault on the proud stuff of a man's identity.

　　Laura Z. Hobson, *Gentleman's Agreement* (1947)

2 That a Jew is despised or persecuted is bad for him, of course—but far worse for the Christian who does it—for although persecuted he can remain a good Jew—whereas no Christian who persecutes can possibly remain—if he ever was one—a good Christian.

　　Phyllis Bottome, *The Mortal Storm* (1938)

3 It came to me ... that for extremely stupid people anti-Semitism was a form of intellectuality, the sole form of intellectuality of which they were capable. It represented, in a rudimentary way, the ability to make categories, to generalize.

　　Mary McCarthy, "Artists in Uniform" (1953), *On the Contrary* (1961)

4 "I'm no antisemite. Why, some of my best—" "I know, dear," Anne put in, "and some of your other best friends are Methodists, but you never bother saying it."

　　Laura Z. Hobson, *Gentleman's Agreement* (1947)

See also Discrimination, Exclusion, Intolerance, Oppression, Prejudice.

## ❧ ANXIETY

5 Love looks forward, hate looks back, anxiety has eyes all over its head.

　　Mignon McLaughlin, *The Neurotic's Notebook* (1963)

6 Anxiety is love's greatest killer, because it is like the stranglehold of the drowning.

　　Anaïs Nin (1948), *The Diary of Anaïs Nin*, vol. 5 (1974)

7 If I knew what I was so anxious about, I wouldn't be so anxious.

　　Mignon McLaughlin, *The Second Neurotic's Notebook* (1966)

8 I'm a firm believer in anxiety and the power of negative thinking.

　　Gertrude Berg, *Molly and Me* (1961)

9 The opposite of anxiety is not happiness. The opposite of anxiety is death.

　　Susan Ohanian, *Ask Ms. Class* (1996)

10 Why is life speeded up so? Why are things so terribly, unbearably precious that you can't enjoy them but can only wait breathless in dread of their going?

　　Anne Morrow Lindbergh, *Hour of Gold, Hour of Lead* (1973)

11 His heart was behaving in that strange way again, like a madly bouncing ball, beating the breath out of his body.

　　Helen Hudson, "An Appointment With Armstrong," *The Listener* (1968)

12 What's the use of watching? A watched pot never boils.

　　Elizabeth Gaskell, *Mary Barton* (1848)

See also Insecurity, Nerves, Panic, Stress, Worry.

## ❧ APATHY

13 Science may have found a cure for most evils; but it has found no remedy for the worst of them all— the apathy of human beings.

　　Helen Keller, *My Religion* (1927)

See also Boredom, Indifference.

## ❧ APHORISMS

14 An aphorism is the last link in a long chain of thought.

　　Marie von Ebner-Eschenbach, *Aphorisms* (1893)

15 The aphorisms of one generation become the clichés of the next.

　　Lillian Day, *Ninon* (1957)

16 If, with the literate, I am / Impelled to try an epigram, / I never seek to take the credit; / We all assume that Oscar said it.

　　Dorothy Parker, "A Pig's-Eye View of Literature: Oscar Wilde," *Sunset Gun* (1928)

See also Proverbs, Quotations, Slogans.

## ❧ APOLOGIES

1 Apology is a lovely perfume; it can transform the clumsiest moment into a gracious gift.

> Margaret Lee Runbeck, *Time for Each Other* (1944)

2 A general rule of etiquette is that one apologizes for the unfortunate occurrence, but the unthinkable is unmentionable.

> Judith Martin, *Miss Manners' Guide to Excruciatingly Correct Behavior* (1982)

See also Repentance.

## ❧ APPEARANCE

3 If I did not wear torn pants, orthopedic shoes, frantic disheveled hair, that is to say, if I did not tone down my beauty, people would go mad. Married men would run amuck.

> Brenda Ueland, *Strength to Your Sword Arm* (1993)

4 I just can't stand to look plain, 'cause that don't fit my personality. I may be a very artificial-looking person, but the good news is, I'm very real on the inside.

> Dolly Parton, in Mark Bego, *Country Gals* (1994)

5 Lots of women buy just as many wigs and makeup things as I do. . . . They just don't wear them all at the same time.

> Dolly Parton, in *Ms.* (1979)

6 You have no idea how much it costs to make a person look this cheap.

> Dolly Parton, in *USA Today* (1986)

7 You don't have to be dowdy to be a Christian.

> Tammy Faye Bakker, in *Newsweek* (1987)

8 I embarked on a risky course of plastic surgery and silicone injections, major dental realignments and gruesome medical procedures. I pray that young dancers, those who imitate me at their peril, will avoid this blind alley. It is more than a dead end; it is a dead beginning.

> Gelsey Kirkland, *Dancing on My Grave* (1986)

9 Anybody who is anybody seems to be getting a lift—by plastic surgery these days. It's the new world wide craze that combines the satisfactions of psychoanalysis, massage, and a trip to the beauty salon.

> Eugenia Sheppard, in *The New York Herald Tribune* (1958)

10 I've found two gray hairs in my head the week before last, and an impertinent crow has planted a delicate impression of his foot under my right eye.

> Mary Elizabeth Braddon, *Lady Audley's Secret* (1862)

11 If God had to give a woman wrinkles, he might at least have put them on the soles of her feet.

> Ninon de Lenclos (1665), in Lillian Day, *Ninon* (1957)

12 Why not be one's self? That is the whole secret of a successful appearance. If one is a greyhound, why try to look like a Pekingese?

> Edith Sitwell, "Why I Look As I Do," in Elizabeth Salter and Allanah Harper, eds., *Edith Sitwell* (1976)

13 If you go through life trading on your good looks, there'll come a time when no one wants to trade.

> Lynne Alpern and Esther Blumenfeld, *Oh, Lord, I Sound Just Like Mama* (1986)

14 The tragedy of our time is not that we are so eye centered, so appearance besotted. The tragedy is that we do not know what we like until we are told by our advertisers and entertainers.

> Jessamyn West, *Love Is Not What You Think* (1959)

15 Men seldom makes passes / At girls who wear glasses.

> Dorothy Parker, "News Item," *Enough Rope* (1926)

16 My sort of looks are of the kind that bore me when I see them on other people.

> Margot Asquith, *More or Less About Myself* (1934)

17 She had a creditable collection of features, but one had to take an inventory of them to find out that she was good-looking. The fusing grace had been omitted.

> Edith Wharton, "The Mission of Jane," *The Descent of Man* (1904)

18 He hated himself for being bald and middle-aged in a culture that was all youth and hair.

> Helen Hudson, *Meyer Meyer* (1967)

19 People on horses look better than they are. People in cars look worse than they are.

> Marya Mannes, *More in Anger* (1958)

1 I think I'm a bit better-looking than she is.

> Princess Anne, on being told by a horse show spectator that she looked like Princess Anne, in Clifton Fadiman, ed., *The Little, Brown Book of Anecdotes* (1985)

2 Her frame and features when moving, talking, feeling were like the pebbles at the bottom of the branch: not worth a glance without the living water that flowed over them.

> Jessamyn West, *Leafy Rivers* (1967)

3 Women looked like great sea snails—the corded wood, babies, and laundry they carried were the whorls on their backs.

> Maxine Hong Kingston, *The Woman Warrior* (1976)

4 With her skin deeply tanned by constant exposure to the sun, she had the shriveled appearance of a wind-dried shrimp.

> Li Ang, *The Butcher's Wife* (1983)

5 She looked like a woman who was being sent to a mental institution, but did not know it.

> Edna O'Brien, "Cords," *The Love Object* (1968)

6 Mrs. Carey looked as if she were mentally holding on to hanging straps that weren't there.

> Richard Shattuck, *The Half-Haunted Saloon* (1945)

7 General de Gaulle is very pituitary these days, to judge by his increased appearance at his recent, and important, press conference. . . . Time, weight, and, evidently, the General's glands are giving his visage a heavy, royal outline; he looks more like a man of dynasty than of destiny.

> Janet Flanner ("Genêt"), *Paris Journal 1944-1965* (1965)

8 General de Gaulle is again pictured in our newspapers, looking as usual like an embattled codfish.

> Sylvia Townsend Warner (1948), in William Maxwell, ed., *Letters: Sylvia Townsend Warner* (1982)

9 Quite early in life they had acquired rolls of flesh at the back of their necks and round their hips, and middle age brought them a lumpish look as if they had been stuffed by an unskillful upholsterer.

> Rebecca West, "On a Form of Nagging," in *Time and Tide* (1924)

10 He somehow managed to look both stately and overworked.

> Patricia Hampl, in *The New York Times Book Review* (1992)

11 She had . . . the over-alert look of a ventriloquist's dummy.

> Elizabeth Taylor, "The Letter-Writers," *The Blush* (1959)

12 The dark-haired man stood observing her steadily, with his arms crossed protectively in front of him, wearing an expression only a cello could play.

> Carrie Fisher, *Surrender the Pink* (1990)

13 She looked as new as a peeled egg.

> Dorothy Parker, "Here We Are," *The Collected Stories of Dorothy Parker* (1942)

14 In the short distance between the two houses he had somehow managed to acquire the ragged, spent look of a man who had crossed a continent on horseback.

> Lucille Kallen, *The Tanglewood Murder* (1980)

15 He looked home-made, as though his wife had self-consciously knitted or somehow contrived a husband when she sat alone at night.

> Eudora Welty, "The Key," *A Curtain of Green* (1941)

16 Judge Taylor was on the bench, looking like a sleepy old shark, his pilot fish writing rapidly below in front of him.

> Harper Lee, *To Kill a Mockingbird* (1960)

17 Chaperons dozed in their corsets like jellies left overnight in their molds.

> Rebecca West, *Harriet Hume* (1929)

18 The rehearsal had not been over for more than ten minutes and he could not have been standing there for more than six, but the look of exhaustion and reproach in his eyes suggested I had kept him waiting for days in some remote and shelterless mountain pass.

> Lucille Kallen, *The Tanglewood Murder* (1980)

19 He reminded one of a bottle with the cork driven in too far. One longed to get hold of his head and pull it out sharply so as to give him a bit more neck.

> Christianna Brand, *Green for Danger* (1944)

20 To superficial observers his chin had too vanishing an aspect, looking as if it were being gradually reabsorbed. And it did indeed cause him some difficulty about the fit of his satin stocks, for which chins were at that time useful.

> George Eliot, *Middlemarch* (1871)

21 All God's children are not beautiful. Most of God's children are, in fact, barely presentable.

> Fran Lebowitz, *Metropolitan Life* (1978)

See also Beauty, Body, Clothes, Dress, Ears, Eyes, Face.

## ♦ APPEARANCES

1 [We] talked on about household forms and ceremonies, as if we all believed that our hostess had a
regular servants' hall . . . instead of the one little
charity-school maiden, whose short ruddy arms
could never have been strong enough to carry the
tray up-stairs, if she had not been assisted in private
by her mistress, who now sat in state, pretending
not to know what cakes were sent up; though she
knew, and we knew, and she knew that we knew,
and we knew that she knew that we knew, she had
been busy all the morning making tea-bread and
sponge cakes.
  Elizabeth Gaskell, *Cranford* (1853)

2 The majority cares little for ideals or integrity.
What it craves is display.
  Emma Goldman, "Minorities Versus Majorities,"
  *Anarchism* (1910)

3 I know you! Your motto is "Silk socks and dubious
feet."
  Colette, *The Other One* (1929)

4 By our moral code, my dear, an appearance of
error is punished more severely than error itself.
  Ellen Glasgow, *Vein of Iron* (1935)

5 The sweat of hard work is not to be displayed. It is
much more graceful to appear favored by the gods.
  Maxine Hong Kingston, *The Woman Warrior* (1976)

6 There is more here than meets the eye.
  Lady Murasaki, *The Tale of Genji* (c. 1008)

7 Things never seem as bad as they are.
  Craig Rice, *The Big Midget Murders* (1942)

## ♦ APPETITE

8 When one has an honest appetite all food tastes
good: shrimps Newburg with hot rolls and alligator
pear salad, or black bread and sour cheese.
  Kathleen Norris, *Hands Full of Living* (1931)

9 The appetite grows for what it feeds on.
  Ida B. Wells (1889), in Alfreda M. Duster, ed., *Crusade for
  Justice* (1970)

10 Food, sex, and liquor create their own appetite.
  Sheilah Graham, *A State of Heat* (1972)

See also Eating, Food, Gastronomy, Hunger.

## ♦ APPLAUSE

11 Anybody's applause is better than nobody's.
  L.E. Landon, *Francesca Carrara* (1834)

12 I beat my brains out, and I like to hear the echo.
  Mary Martin, in Hedda Hopper and James Brough, *The
  Whole Truth and Nothing But* (1963)

13 Laughter is much more important than applause.
Applause is almost a duty. Laughter is a reward.
  Carol Channing, in John Robert Colombo, *Popcorn in
  Paradise* (1979)

14 Applause is nothing compared with laughter. Anyone can clap hands, and the mind be miles away. A
laugh comes right from the center. No wonder
comedians love their audiences.
  Jessamyn West, *A Matter of Time* (1966)

15 There is no applause that so flatters a man as that
which he wrings from unwilling throats.
  Ouida, title story, *Pipistrello* (1881)

See also Audience, Performance.

## ♦ APPRECIATION

16 Next to genius, is the power / Of feeling where true
genius lies.
  Sarah Josepha Hale, *The Ladies' Wreath* (1837)

17 All the goodness, beauty and perfection of a human
being belong to the one who knows how to recognize these qualities.
  Georgette Leblanc (1898), in Janet Flanner, tr., *Souvenirs*
  (1932)

See also Admiration.

## ♦ APPROVAL

18 Material things aside, we need not advice but approval.
  Coco Chanel, in Marcel Haedrich, *Coco Chanel* (1972)

19 I need no warrant for being, and no word of sanction upon my being. I am the warrant and the
sanction.
  Ayn Rand, *Anthem* (1946)

1 You can't break the mold and also be consoled for breaking it, old fool!

    May Sarton, *Mrs. Stevens Hears the Mermaids Singing* (1965)

2 Patrick Henry, Thomas Jefferson, and John Adams.

    Mother Jones, reply to judge asking who issued her a permit to speak on the streets, in Linda Atkinson, *Mother Jones* (1978)

## ᕥ APRIL

3 Sweet was April, sweet was April!

    Katharine Tynan Hinkson, "Cuckoo Song," *Ballads and Lyrics* (1891)

4 April the angel of the months, the young / Love of the year.

    Vita Sackville-West, "Spring," *The Garden* (1946)

5 April is hope.

    Gladys Taber, *The Book of Stillmeadow* (1948)

6 April's rare capricious loveliness.

    Julia C.R. Dorr, "November," *Poems* (1913)

7 April hath a fickle mind.

    Ellen Mackay Hutchinson Cortissoz, "April Fantasie," in Edmund Clarence Stedman, ed., *An American Anthology 1787-1900* (1900)

8 That enchantment that I lightly took / Out of the lovely April is for ever.

    Léonie Adams, "An Old Spell," *Those Not Elect* (1925)

9 April / Comes like an idiot, babbling and strewing flowers.

    Edna St. Vincent Millay, "Spring," *Second April* (1921)

See also Seasons, Spring.

## ᕥ ARCHITECTURE

10 Architecture is frozen music.

    Madame de Staël, in Ralph Waldo Emerson, *Letters and Social Aims* (1876)

11 A perfect piece of architecture kindles that aimless reverie, which bears the soul we know not whither.

    Madame de Staël, *Corinne* (1807)

12 Architecture is the purest of the plastic arts, for it does not reproduce scenes from nature and it does not borrow any literary interest by representing subjects. It stands by itself on its own ground.

    C. Anstruther-Thomson, *Art and Man* (1923)

13 Architecture is both a matter of utility and a matter of art, its complexities exceeding our expectations for the merely useful or merely artistic.

    Dora P. Crouch, *History of Architecture* (1985)

14 When the process of building is so carefully thought out that the product is thereby raised above the utilitarian, we call the product architecture.

    Dora P. Crouch, *History of Architecture* (1985)

15 Architecture is the printing-press of all ages, and gives a history of the state of the society in which it was erected.

    Sydney, Lady Morgan, *Passages From My Autobiography* (1859)

16 Either a building is part of a place, or it is not. Once that kinship is there, time will only make it stronger.

    Willa Cather, *Death Comes for the Archbishop* (1927)

17 Every builder builds somewhat for unknown purposes, and is in a measure a prophet.

    Mary E. Wilkins Freeman, "The Revolt of 'Mother'," *A New England Nun* (1891)

18 Simplicity of heart is just as necessary to an architect as for a farmer or a minister if the architect is going to build great buildings.

    Anna Wright, to her son Frank Lloyd Wright, in Frank Lloyd Wright, *An Autobiography* (1943)

19 Architecture should be working on improving the environment of people in their homes, in their places of work, and their places of recreation. It should be functional and pleasant, not just in the image of the architect's ego.

    Norma Merrick Sklarek, in Brian Lanker, *I Dream a World* (1989)

20 I realized that architecture was made for people who go about on their feet, that that is what architecture is made for.

    Gertrude Stein, "Raoul Dufy" (1946), in *Harper's Bazaar* (1949)

1 We have no sociology of architecture. Architects are unaccustomed to social analysis and mistrust it; sociologists have fatter fish to fry.

> Denise Scott Brown, "Room at the Top" (1975), in Ellen Perry Berkeley and Matilda McQuaid, eds., *Architecture: A Place for Women* (1989)

2 A Gothic building engenders true religion. . . . The light, falling through colored glass, the singular forms of the architecture, unite to give a silent image of that infinite mystery which the soul for ever feels, and never comprehends.

> Madame de Staël, *Corinne* (1807)

3 The Greek temple is the creation, *par excellence*, of mind and spirit in equilibrium.

> Edith Hamilton, *The Greek Way* (1930)

4 The sight of such a building is like a ceaseless, changeless melody.

> Madame de Staël, *Corinne* (1807)

5 The building is a national tragedy . . . a cross between a concrete candy box and a marble sarcophagus in which the art of architecture lies buried.

> Ada Louise Huxtable, on the John F. Kennedy Center for the Performing Arts in Washington, D.C., in *The New York Times* (1971)

6 The Frink National Bank Building displayed the entire history of Roman art. . . . It offered so many columns, pediments, friezes, tripods, gladiators, urns and volutes that it looked as if it had not been built of white marble, but squeezed out of a pastry tube.

> Ayn Rand, *The Fountainhead* (1943)

7 The builder had lacked an architect's eye. He had used the idiom of the time, but it had apparently not been native to him.

> Josephine Tey, *The Franchise Affair* (1948)

See also Houses.

## ❧ ARGUMENTS

8 Her arguments are like elephants. They squash you flat.

> Rumer Godden, *The Battle at the Villa Fiorita* (1963)

9 Arguing with Lucy was like trying to sew with no knot in your thread.

> Margaret Deland, "Mr. Horace Shields," *Old Chester Tales* (1898)

10 She had a point and Aragon guessed that she would cling to it even if it impaled her.

> Margaret Millar, *Ask for Me Tomorrow* (1976)

11 She bombarded the soft underbelly of his mind.

> Alice Tisdale Hobart, *The Serpent-Wreathed Staff* (1951)

12 Arguing with Owen was like fencing with a bag of wool.

> Julia O'Faolain, *No Country for Young Men* (1980)

13 He asked no better revenge than a reply—and arrayed in his own mind a whole battalion of arguments, and a light armed troop of sneers.

> L.E. Landon, *Romance and Reality* (1831)

14 Rarely an hour passed that they didn't argue about something. They had lived together for so many years that they mistook their arguments for conversations.

> Marjorie Kellogg, *Tell Me That You Love Me, Junie Moon* (1968)

15 Elinor agreed to it all, for she did not think he deserved the compliment of rational opposition.

> Jane Austen, *Sense and Sensibility* (1811)

16 He is dead: I am eighty. There's no arguing with either of us.

> Enid Bagnold, *Enid Bagnold's Autobiography* (1969)

17 When one person's mad and the other isn't, the mad one always wins.

> Mary O'Hara, *Green Grass of Wyoming* (1946)

18 Much waste of words and of thought too would be avoided if disputants would always begin with a clear statement of the question, and not proceed to argue till they had agreed upon what it was that they were arguing about.

> Sara Coleridge (1848), *Memoir and Letters*, vol. 2 (1873)

19 Who is not apt, on occasion, to assign a multitude of reasons when one will do? This is a sure sign of weakness in argument.

> Harriet Martineau, "On the Art of Thinking" (1829), *Miscellanies*, vol. 1 (1836)

See also Conflict, Quarrels.

## ❧ ARISTOCRACY

1 Aristocracies are erected on the work of other people, in whatever manner secured.
  Sarah Tarleton Colvin, *A Rebel in Thought* (1944)

2 The aristocrat, when he wants to, has very good manners. The Scottish upper classes, in particular, have that shell-shocked look that probably comes from banging their heads on low beams leaping to their feet whenever a woman comes into the room.
  Jilly Cooper, *Class* (1979)

3 An aristocracy in a republic is like a chicken whose head has been cut off: it may run about in a lively way, but in fact it is dead.
  Nancy Mitford, *Noblesse Oblige* (1956)

See also Class.

## ❧ ARROGANCE

4 The scornful nostril and the high head gather not the odors that lie on the track of truth.
  George Eliot, *Felix Holt, the Radical* (1866)

5 Nobody who is Somebody looks down on anybody.
  Margaret Deland, *Captain Archer's Daughter* (1932)

6 People in big empty places are likely to behave very much as the gods did on Olympus.
  Edna Ferber, *Giant* (1952)

7 It seems odd / That whenever man chooses / To play God— / God loses.
  Felicia Lamport, "Historical Survey," *Cultural Slag* (1966)

8 If arrogance is the heady wine of youth, then humility must be its eternal hangover.
  Helen Van Slyke, *Always Is Not Forever* (1977)

9 I do not want Miss Mannin's feelings to be hurt by the fact that I have never heard of her. . . . At the moment I am debarred from the pleasure of putting her in her place by the fact that she has not got one.
  Edith Sitwell (1930), in John Pearson, *Façades* (1978)

10 The entire crew were working like dogs to make the star look good in her first picture, and she treated them like ants trying to get into her lunch.
  Carolyn Kenmore, *Mannequin* (1969)

11 "I am Melba. I shall sing when and where I like and I shall sing in my own way." It may sound arrogant, but arrogance of that sort is not a bad way to get things done.
  Nellie Melba, *Melodies and Memories* (1925)

See also Conceit, Egocentrism, Self-Importance, Vanity.

## ❧ ART

12 Art is not a luxury, but a necessity.
  Rebecca West, title essay, *The Strange Necessity* (1928)

13 Art is the signature of civilizations.
  Beverly Sills, interview (1985)

14 Art is how a culture records its life, how it poses questions for the next generation and how it will be remembered.
  Marsha Norman, speech (1995)

15 Nothing reveals more about the inner life of a people than their arts.
  Diane Ackerman, *A Natural History of Love* (1994)

16 Art is the only way to run away without leaving home.
  Twyla Tharp, *Push Comes to Shove* (1992)

17 Art is the only thing that can go on mattering once it has stopped hurting.
  Elizabeth Bowen, *The Heat of the Day* (1949)

18 I cannot see that art is anything less than a way of making joys perpetual.
  Rebecca West, title essay, *The Strange Necessity* (1928)

19 True revolutions in art restore more than they destroy.
  Louise Bogan, "Reading Contemporary Poetry," in *College English* (1953)

20 Art is at least in part a way of collecting information about the universe.
  Rebecca West, title essay, *The Strange Necessity* (1928)

1 Art is an artificial organization of experience.
  Sara Maitland, in Zoë Fairbairns et al., *Tales I Tell My Mother* (1978)

2 The difference between writing a story and simply relating past events is that a story, in order to be acceptable, must have shape and meaning. It is the old idea that art is the bringing of order out of chaos.
  Katherine Paterson, *The Spying Heart* (1989)

3 The arts are life accelerated and concentrated.
  Edith Sitwell, *Taken Care Of* (1965)

4 Art is not for the cultivated taste. It is to cultivate a taste.
  Nikki Giovanni, with Margaret Walker, *A Poetic Equation* (1974)

5 What was any art but an effort to make a sheath, a mold in which to imprison for a moment the shining, elusive element which is life itself,—life hurrying past us and running away, too strong to stop, too sweet to lose?
  Willa Cather, *The Song of the Lark* (1915)

6 Art is so much more real than life. Some art is much more real than some life, I mean.
  Rebecca West, *The Fountain Overflows* (1956)

7 Always Art is Art, only by presenting an adequate outward symbol of some fact in the interior life.
  Margaret Fuller, in *The New-York Daily Tribune* (1847)

8 Art is a kind of artificial memory and the pain which attends all serious art is a sense of that factitiousness.
  Iris Murdoch, *The Black Prince* (1973)

9 All great art contains an element of the irrational.
  Edith Sitwell (1929), in Elizabeth Salter and Allanah Harper, eds., *Edith Sitwell* (1976)

10 All art deals with the absurd and aims at the simple.
  Iris Murdoch, *The Black Prince* (1973)

11 A masterpiece doesn't so much transcend its time as perpetuate it; it keeps its moment alive.
  Arlene Croce, *Afterimages* (1976)

12 Real art has the capacity to make us nervous.
  Susan Sontag, title essay, *Against Interpretation* (1966)

13 All art requires courage.
  Anne Tucker, *The Woman's Eye* (1973)

14 To create one's own world in any of the arts takes courage.
  Georgia O'Keeffe, *Georgia O'Keeffe* (1976)

15 This is what art is all about. It is weaving fabric from the feathers you have plucked from your own breast. But no one must ever see the process—only the finished bolt of goods. They must never suspect that that crimson thread running through the pattern is blood.
  Katherine Paterson, *The Spying Heart* (1989)

16 Art does the same things dreams do. We have a hunger for dreams and art fulfills that hunger. So much of real life is a disappointment. That's why we have art.
  Joyce Carol Oates, in *Newsweek* (1970)

17 Art is a framework, a kind of living trellis, on which public dreaming can shape itself.
  Elizabeth Janeway, *Powers of the Weak* (1980)

18 Art can excite, titillate, please, entertain, and sometimes shock; but its ultimate function is to ennoble.
  Marya Mannes, *More in Anger* (1958)

19 Art must take reality by surprise.
  Françoise Sagan, in Malcolm Cowley, ed., *Writers at Work* (1958)

20 Belief of some sort is the lifeblood of Art.
  Ouida, *Wisdom, Wit and Pathos* (1884)

21 All truly great art is propaganda.
  Ann Petry, in Helen Hull, ed., *The Writer's Book* (1950)

22 Art is the objectification of feeling, and the subjectification of nature.
  Susanne K. Langer, *Mind*, vol. 1 (1967)

23 The arts objectify subjective reality, and subjectify outward experience of nature. Art education is the education of feeling, and a society that neglects it gives itself up to formless emotion. Bad art is corruption of feeling.
  Susanne K. Langer, *Philosophical Sketches* (1962)

24 Without a strong cup to carry the emotion, it is only a curiosity. Great art can come to us only in strong cups. Without emotion, there is nothing to carry.
  Nadia Boulanger, in Don G. Campbell, *Reflections of Boulanger* (1982)

1 The basic unit for contemporary art is not the idea, but the analysis of and extension of sensations.

Susan Sontag, "One Culture and the New Sensibility," *Against Interpretation* (1966)

2 Art is not emotion. Art is the medium in which emotion is expressed.

Nadia Boulanger, in Don G. Campbell, *Reflections of Boulanger* (1982)

3 We need emotional outlets in this country, and the more artistic people we develop the better it will be for us as a nation.

Eleanor Roosevelt, *My Days* (1938)

4 A part of all art is to make silence speak. The things left out in painting, the note withheld in music, the void in architecture—all are as necessary and as active as the utterance itself.

Freya Stark, "On Silence," in *The Cornhill Magazine* (1966)

5 Good art speaks truth, indeed *is* truth, perhaps the only truth.

Iris Murdoch, *The Black Prince* (1973)

6 Art is not cozy and it is not mocked. Art tells the only truth that ultimately matters. It is the light by which human things can be mended. And after art there is, let me assure you all, nothing.

Iris Murdoch, *The Black Prince* (1973)

7 Art is the expression of a man's life, of his mode of being, of his relations with the universe, since it is, in fact, man's inarticulate answer to the universe's unspoken message.

Vernon Lee, *Renaissance Fancies and Studies* (1895)

8 Art, true art, is the desire of a man to express himself, to record the reactions of his personality to the world he lives in.

Amy Lowell, *Tendencies in Modern American Poetry* (1917)

9 Art being so much greater than ourselves, it will not give up once it has taken hold.

Emily Carr, *The House of All Sorts* (1944)

10 Art isn't something you do or are. It's where you aim, the target you shoot at.

Elizabeth Ashley, with Ross Firestone, *Actress* (1978)

11 Artistic growth is, more than it is anything else, a refining of the sense of truthfulness. The stupid believe that to be truthful is easy; only the artist, the great artist, knows how difficult it is.

Willa Cather, *The Song of the Lark* (1915)

12 If nothing will finally survive of life besides what artists report of it, we have no right to report what we know to be lies.

Alison Lurie, *Real People* (1969)

13 Real art is religion, a search for the beauty of God deep in all things.

Emily Carr (1935), *Hundreds and Thousands* (1966)

14 Religion and art spring from the same root and are close kin. Economics and art are strangers.

Willa Cather, *On Writing* (1949)

15 If it's bad art, it's bad religion, no matter how pious the subject.

Madeleine L'Engle, *Walking on Water* (1980)

16 Great art is cathartic; it is always moral.

Joyce Carol Oates, in Sandra M. Gilbert and Susan Gubar, eds., *The Norton Anthology of Literature by Women* (1985)

17 By getting us used to what, formerly, we could not bear to see or hear, because it was too shocking, painful, or embarrassing, art changes morals.

Susan Sontag, *On Photography* (1977)

18 Art is the indispensable medium for the communication of a moral ideal.

Ayn Rand, *The Romantic Manifesto* (1969)

19 The moral pleasure in art, as well as the moral service that art performs, consists in the intelligent gratification of consciousness.

Susan Sontag, "On Style," *Against Interpretation* (1966)

20 Moralists have no place in an art gallery.

Han Suyin, *A Many-Splendored Thing* (1952)

21 Many artists have said that when life itself becomes fully conscious, art as we know it will vanish. Art is only a stopgap, an imperfect effort to wrest meaning from an environment where nearly everyone is sleepwalking.

Marilyn Ferguson, *The Aquarian Conspiracy* (1980)

22 In art the past particular transmutes itself into the present universal.

Blanche H. Dow, "Roads and Vistas," in Jean Beaven Abernethy, ed., *Meditations for Women* (1947)

23 What society requires from art . . . is that it function as an early warning system.

Elizabeth Janeway, *Between Myth and Morning* (1974)

24 Art is in the process of redefining our relationships to each other. . . . The creative minds are bubbling,

bubbling, and I know the soup that's coming up next time is going to feed a lot more of us.

Ruby Dee, in *Teaching Tolerance* (1992)

1 There is art and there is official art, there always has been and there always will be.

Gertrude Stein, *The Autobiography of Alice B. Toklas* (1933)

2 Minority art, vernacular art, is marginal art. Only on the margins does growth occur.

Joanna Russ, *How to Suppress Women's Writing* (1983)

3 The attribute of all true art, the highest and the lowest, is this—that it says more than it says, and takes you away from itself. It is a little door that opens into an infinite hall where you may find what you please. Men, thinking to detract, say, "People read more in this or that work of genius than was ever written in it," not perceiving that they pay the highest compliment.

Ralph Iron, *The Story of an African Farm* (1883)

4 Art doesn't come in measured quantities: it's got to be too much or it's not enough.

Pauline Kael (1965), in *Newsweek* (1991)

5 The only real rival of love is Art, for that in itself is a deep personal passion, its function an act of creation, fed by some mysterious perversion of sex, and demanding all the imagination's activities.

Gertrude Atherton, *Julia France and Her Times* (1912)

6 The best work is a fusion of love and praise.

Barbara Grizzuti Harrison, *The Astonishing World* (1992)

7 The arts are good and providential in that they allow the soul to imitate the movements of love, and to feel love without its being returned—which, perhaps, is the only way of feeling it permanently.

Princess Marthe Bibesco, *Catherine-Paris* (1928)

8 In every art the desire to practice it precedes both the full ability to do so and the possession of something worthwhile to express by its means.

Phyllis Bentley, "*O Dreams, O Destinations*" (1962)

9 A great work of Art demands a great thought or a thought of beauty adequately expressed.—Neither in Art nor Literature more than in Life can an ordinary thought be made interesting because well-dressed.

Margaret Fuller, in *The New-York Daily Tribune* (1847)

10 Great art is the expression of a solution of the conflict between the demands of the world without and that within.

Edith Hamilton, *The Greek Way* (1930)

11 Any authentic work of art must start an argument between the artist and his audience.

Rebecca West, *The Court and the Castle* (1957)

12 A work of art may be simple, though that is not necessary. There is no logical reason why the camel of great art should pass through the needle of mob intelligence.

Rebecca West, "Battlefield and Sky," *The Strange Necessity* (1928)

13 Art, it seems to me, should simplify. That, indeed, is very nearly the whole of the higher artistic process; finding what conventions of form and what detail one can do without and yet preserve the spirit of the whole—so that all that one has suppressed and cut away is there to the reader's consciousness as much as if it were in type on the page.

Willa Cather, "On the Art of Fiction" (1920), *On Writing* (1949)

14 One thing living in Japan did for me was to make me feel that what is left out of a work of art is as important as, if not more important than, what is put in.

Katherine Paterson, *The Spying Heart* (1989)

15 Art is collective. Always, it has a tradition behind it.

Joanna Russ, in Donna Perry, ed., *Backtalk* (1993)

16 Masterpieces are not single and solitary births; they are the outcome of many years of thinking in common, of thinking by the body of the people, so that the experience of the mass is behind the single voice.

Virginia Woolf, *A Room of One's Own* (1929)

17 A work of art has an author and yet, when it is perfect, it has something which is essentially anonymous about it.

Simone Weil, *Gravity and Grace* (1947)

18 All craftsmen share a knowledge. They have held / Reality down fluttering to a bench.

Vita Sackville-West, "Summer," *The Land* (1927)

19 When art finds no temple open, it takes refuge in the workshop.

Marie von Ebner-Eschenbach, *Aphorisms* (1893)

1 Art is a profession, not a shrine.

> Elizabeth Hardwick, "Memoirs, Conversations and Diaries"
> (1953), *A View of My Own* (1962)

2 Art . . . is as much a source of happiness for the beginner as for the master. One forgets everything in one's work.

> Marie Bashkirtseff (1877), in Mary J. Serrano, tr., *The Journal of a Young Artist* (1919)

3 No form of art repeats or imitates successfully all that can be said by another; the writer conveys his experience of life along a channel of communication closed to painter, mathematician, musician, film-maker.

> Storm Jameson, *Parthian Words* (1970)

4 Art is not national. It is international. Music is not written in red, white and blue; it is written with the heart's blood of the composer.

> Nellie Melba, *Melodies and Memories* (1925)

5 Art belongs to all times and to all countries; its special benefit is precisely to be still living when everything else seems dying; that is why Providence shields it from too personal or too general passions, and grants it a patient and persevering organization, durable sensibility, and the contemplative sense in which lies invincible faith.

> George Sand (1863), in Raphaël Ledos de Beaufort, ed.,
> *Letters of George Sand* (1886)

6 It is well known that studying art is best done in almost any country than that in which one happens to be born.

> Mary Pakenham, *Brought Up and Brought Out* (1938)

7 Most works of art, like most wines, ought to be consumed in the district of their fabrication.

> Rebecca West, "'Journey's End' Again," *Ending in Earnest*
> (1931)

8 Grievance does not make for great art.

> Eva Figes, *Patriarchal Attitudes* (1970)

9 Precepts, conventions—above all traditions—have no value in art.

> Eleonora Duse, in Eva Le Gallienne, *The Mystic in the Theater* (1965)

10 Perfectionism is the enemy of art. Since art is essentially divine play, not dogged work, it often happens that as one becomes more professionally driven one also becomes less capriciously playful.

> Erica Jong, *Parachutes & Kisses* (1984)

11 By reducing the work of art to its content and then interpreting *that*, one tames the work of art. Interpretation makes art manageable, conformable.

> Susan Sontag, title essay, *Against Interpretation* (1966)

12 Interpretation is the revenge of the intellect upon art.

> Susan Sontag, title essay, *Against Interpretation* (1966)

13 I believe in art that conceals art.

> Rita Mae Brown, *Starting From Scratch* (1988)

14 One cannot demand of art that it pay you in any other way than in the satisfaction of the work itself.

> Uta Hagen, *A Challenge for the Actor* (1991)

15 The reward of art is not fame or success, but intoxication; that is why so many bad artists are unable to live without it.

> Eileen Walkenstein (1984), in Donna Ward La Cour, ed.,
> *Artists in Quotation* (1989)

16 The artist's relation to money is always queer because the production of art is not *for* money; one would do it even if one got paid nothing at all.

> Erica Jong, *Parachutes & Kisses* (1984)

17 Great art likes chains. The greatest artists have created art within bounds. Or else they have created their own chains.

> Nadia Boulanger (1939), in Léonie Rosenstiel, *Nadia Boulanger* (1982)

18 Composition limits the size of the subject to that which our eye can take in as a whole and our lungs can breathe in one long breath, for we are finite beings and cannot live up to overpowering strength for more than a fraction of time. Art must, for the main part, keep well within what we can manage on pain of breaking us.

> C. Anstruther-Thomson, *Art and Man* (1923)

19 Science, far from being the enemy of Art, is the only way to hand Art on, to make it a tradition. It is *apathy* which is really the enemy of Art.

> C. Anstruther-Thomson, *Art and Man* (1923)

20 Art isn't a fringe on life, it is one of life's great vital forces. . . . But to get on such terms we must get very close, take a great deal of trouble, put off natural apathy. Just walking through a gallery glancing at the works of Art won't do it, any more than leaving cards on neighbors will turn them into life-long friends.

> C. Anstruther-Thomson, *Art and Man* (1923)

1 Everybody's an art critic.
   Judith Martin, *Style and Substance* (1986)

2 Nobody can foresee what will please the critics. Every artistic activity is, and always will be, a poker game.
   Marlene Dietrich, *Marlene* (1989)

3 "Organic" is a word I'll stick by. It means the work is an extension of your blood and body; it has the rhythm of nature. This is something artists don't talk about much and it's not even well understood: the fact that there exists a state of feeling and that when you reach it, when you hit it, you can't go wrong.
   Nell Blaine, in Eleanor Munro, *Originals: American Women Artists* (1979)

4 Allowing for exceptions, there is still one basic difference between the traditional arts and the mass-media arts: in the traditional arts, the artist grows; in a mass medium, the artist decays profitably.
   Pauline Kael, *Deeper Into Movies* (1973)

5 Art and Entertainment are the same thing, in that the more deeply and genuinely entertaining a work is, the better art it is. To imply that Art is something heavy and solemn and dull, and Entertainment is modest but jolly and popular, is neo-Victorian idiocy at its worst.
   Ursula K. Le Guin, "The Stone Ax and the Muskoxen" (1975), *Language of the Night* (1979)

6 The reiterated insinuation that formal art is fraudulent because it is difficult to understand and makes no effort to appeal to the majority . . . is a typical bourgeois notion that has been around for a long time. . . . The fact remains that no civilization has ever produced a literature out of folk (either current or revived) alone. The formal artist cannot be outlawed.
   Louise Bogan, "Some Notes on Popular and Unpopular Art" (1943), *Selected Criticism* (1955)

7 Genius can probably run on ahead and seek out new ways. But the good artists who follow after genius—and I count myself among these—have to restore the lost connection once more. A pure studio art is unfruitful and frail, for anything that does not form living roots—why should it exist at all?
   Käthe Kollwitz (1916), in Hans Kollwitz, ed., *The Diaries and Letters of Käthe Kollwitz* (1955)

8 Another unsettling element in modern art is that common symptom of immaturity, the dread of doing what has been done before.
   Edith Wharton, *The Writing of Fiction* (1925)

9 Clay. It's rain, dead leaves, dust, all my dead ancestors. Stones that have been ground into sand. Mud. The whole cycle of life and death.
   Martine Vermeulen, on her pottery, in *The New York Times* (1975)

10 Abstract art: a construction site for high fashion, for advertising, for furniture.
   Adrienne Monnier (1939), in Richard McDougall, tr., *The Very Rich Hours of Adrienne Monnier* (1976)

11 The United States has always had an uneasy relationship with its art and artists; as a nation, we regard art as something "other." Visual images are not viewed as a necessary part of our existence.
   Carolyn McMaster, in *The San Francisco Review of Books* (1993)

12 We should not have a tin cup out for something as important as the arts in this country, the richest in the world. Creative artists are always begging, but always being used when it's time to show us at our best.
   Leontyne Price, in Brian Lanker, *I Dream a World* (1989)

13 Art in America has always been regarded as a luxury.
   Hallie Flanagan, *Arena* (1940)

See also Artists, Creation, Creativity, Originality, Painting, Photography, Sculpture, Writing.


❦ ARTISTS

14 What an artist is for is to tell us what we see but do not know that we see.
   Edith Sitwell (1929), in Elizabeth Salter and Allanah Harper, eds., *Edith Sitwell* (1976)

15 Great artists are people who find the way to be themselves in their art. Any sort of pretension induces mediocrity in art and life alike.
   Margot Fonteyn, *Margot Fonteyn* (1975)

16 The artist must / create himself or be born again.
   Denise Levertov, "In Memory of Boris Pasternak," *The Jacob's Ladder* (1961)

1 One must be born an artist in order to do the work of becoming one.

Comtesse Diane, *Les Glanes de la Vie* (1898)

2 The wretched Artist himself is alternatively the lowest worm that ever crawled when no fire is in him: or the loftiest God that ever sang when the fire is going.

Caitlin Thomas, *Not Quite Posthumous Letter to My Daughter* (1963)

3 I think perhaps I've learned to be myself. I have a theory that all artists who would be important . . . must learn to be themselves. It takes a very long time.

Margot Fonteyn, in *Newsweek* (1967)

4 I believe that each work of art, whether it is a work of great genius, or something very small, comes to the artist and says, "Here I am. Enflesh me. Give birth to me."

Madeleine L'Engle, *Walking on Water* (1980)

5 The work of art which I do not make, none other will ever make it.

Simone Weil, *The Notebooks of Simone Weil* (1951)

6 The most potent and sacred command which can be laid upon any artist is the command: wait.

Iris Murdoch, *The Black Prince* (1973)

7 To rebel or revolt against the status quo is in the very nature of an artist.

Uta Hagen, with Haskel Frankel, *Respect for Acting* (1973)

8 No artist is ahead of his time. He *is* his time; it is just that others are behind the times.

Martha Graham, in John Heilpern, "The Amazing Martha," *The Observer Magazine* (1979)

9 No one is ahead of his time, it is only that the particular variety of creating his time is the one that his contemporaries who also are creating their own time refuse to accept.

Gertrude Stein, "Composition As Explanation" (1926), *What Are Masterpieces* (1940)

10 In art one is usually totally alone with oneself.

Paula Modersohn-Becker (1906), in Gillian Perry, *Paula Modersohn-Becker* (1979)

11 Off fall the wife, the mother, the lover, the teacher, and the violent artist takes over. I am I alone. I belong to no one but myself. I mate with no one but the spirit. I own no land, have no kin, no friend or enemy. I have no road but this one.

Sylvia Ashton-Warner (1942), *Myself* (1967)

12 Art is an affirmation of life, a rebuttal of death. And here we blunder into paradox again, for during the creation of any form of art, which affirms the value and the holiness of life, the artist must die. To serve a work of art, great or small, is to die, to die to self.

Madeleine L'Engle, *Walking on Water* (1980)

13 The more visible my work became, the less visible I grew to myself.

Anne Truitt, *Daybook* (1982)

14 The key is what is within the artist. The artist can only paint what she or he is about.

Lee Krasner, in Eleanor Munro, *Originals: American Women Artists* (1979)

15 I think that one's art is a growth inside one. I do not think one can explain growth. It is silent and subtle. One does not keep digging up a plant to see how it grew.

Emily Carr (1936), *Hundreds and Thousands* (1966)

16 The most demanding part of living a lifetime as an artist is the strict discipline of forcing oneself to work steadfastly along the nerve of one's own most intimate sensitivity.

Anne Truitt, *Daybook* (1982)

17 When you make any kind of artwork, you have to serve it. You could easily call the artist a servant.

M.B. Goffstein, in *The Five Owls* (1991)

18 The untutored child possesses two qualities which are always preserved in the mature artist: imagination, and the ability to encounter his own feelings.

Judith Groch, *The Right to Create* (1969)

19 Every artist is an unhappy lover.

Iris Murdoch, *The Black Prince* (1973)

20 No artist is pleased. . . . There is only a queer divine dissatisfaction, a blessed unrest that keeps us marching and makes us more alive than the others.

Martha Graham, in Agnes de Mille, *Dance to the Piper* (1952)

21 There is nothing harder for an Artist than to retain his Artistic integrity in the tomb of success. A tomb, nevertheless, which nearly every Artist:

whether he admits it or not; naturally wants to get into.

Caitlin Thomas, *Not Quite Posthumous Letter to My Daughter* (1963)

1 Media saturation is probably very destructive to art. New movements get overexposed and exhausted before they have a chance to grow, and they turn to ashes in a short time. Some degree of time and obscurity is often very necessary to artists.

Joyce Johnson, in Sybil Steinberg, ed., *Writing for Your Life* (1992)

2 The communal mental picture of the artist starving in a garret seems to me to have a grain of truth in it. . . . The artist starves in his garret because he must have the resistance of the garret and the starvation but these privations can take many forms.

Jane Duncan, *Letter From Reachfar* (1975)

3 It is the nature of the artist to mind excessively what is said about him. Literature is strewn with the wreckage of men who have minded beyond reason the opinions of others.

Virginia Woolf, *A Room of One's Own* (1929)

4 The first prerogative of an artist in any medium is to make a fool of himself.

Pauline Kael, *I Lost It at the Movies* (1965)

5 In all the arts abundance seems to be one of the surest signs of vocation.

Edith Wharton, *The Writing of Fiction* (1925)

6 Real artists, it seems to me, are those who don't repeat themselves.

Joanna Russ, in Donna Perry, ed., *Backtalk* (1993)

7 The important thing is to keep producing. All artists have that quality. You have to be tenacious.

Mary Frank, in Eleanor Munro, *Originals: American Women Artists* (1979)

8 I . . . found myself saying to myself—I can't live where I want to—I can't go where I want to—I can't do what I want to—I can't even say what I want to. . . . I decided I was a very stupid fool not to at least paint as I wanted to and say what I wanted to when I painted as that seemed to be the only thing I could do that didn't concern anybody but myself.

Georgia O'Keeffe (1923), *Georgia O'Keeffe* (1976)

9 Through poverty, godhunger, the family debacle, I kept a sense of worth. I could limn and paint like

no-one else in this human-wounded land: I was worth the while of living. Now my skill is dead. I should be.

Keri Hulme, *The Bone People* (1983)

10 Trouble is said to be good for an artist's soul but almost never is.

Rita Mae Brown, *In Her Day* (1976)

11 It is the artists who make the true value of the world, though at times they may have to starve to do it. They are like earthworms, turning up the soil so things can grow, eating dirt so that the rest of us may eat green shoots.

Erica Jong, *Serenissima* (1987)

12 One has to have a bit of neurosis to go on being an artist. A balanced human seldom produces art. It's that imbalance which impels us.

Beverly Pepper, in Eleanor Munro, *Originals: American Women Artists* (1979)

13 The successful artist is one who, among other things, finds by luck, labor, instinct, or whatever a form and image to reflect in power (never in literal representation) the original sensory experiences that were received by the [child's] innocent mind. And by contrast, a failed or weak artist would then be one for whom, among other things, the way back is lost or confused or the reflecting image a counterfeit one or mechanically imitative.

Eleanor Munro, *Originals: American Women Artists* (1979)

14 Artists are exposed to great temptations: their eyes see paradise before their souls have reached it, and that is a great danger.

Phyllis Bottome, "Brother Leo," *Innocence and Experience* (1934)

15 The independence of the artist is one of the great safeguards of the freedom of the human spirit.

C.V. Wedgwood, *Velvet Studies* (1946)

16 There is a vitality, a life-force, an energy, a quickening that is translated through you into action and because there is only one of you in all of time, this expression is unique. And if you block it, it will never exist through any other medium and be lost. The world will not have it. It is not your business to determine how good it is nor how valuable nor how it compares with other expressions. It is your business to keep it yours clearly and directly, to keep the channel open.

Martha Graham, in Agnes de Mille, *Dance to the Piper* (1952)

1 I am always watching for fear of getting feeble and *passé* in my work. I don't want to trickle out. I want to pour till the pail is empty, the last bit going out in a gush, not in drops.

    Emily Carr (1936), *Hundreds and Thousands* (1966)

2 Never strive, O artist, to create what you are not irresistibly impelled to create!

    Marie von Ebner-Eschenbach, *Aphorisms* (1893)

3 Another real thing! I am not dead yet! I can still call forth a piece of soul and set it down in color, fixed forever.

    Keri Hulme, *The Bone People* (1983)

4 In order to be an artist, one must be deeply rooted in the society.

    Simone de Beauvoir, *The Second Sex* (1949)

5 Life, religion and art all converge in Bali. They have no word in their language for "artist" or "art." Everyone is an artist.

    Anaïs Nin (1974), *The Diary of Anaïs Nin*, vol. 7 (1980)

6 All art is one art. In the man or woman, thoroughly in love with his or her chosen art, there must be struck a sympathetic chord for the sister branches.

    Olive Beatrice Muir, *With Malice Toward None* (1900)

7 The artist is not separate from the work and therefore cannot judge it.

    Madeleine L'Engle, *Two-Part Invention* (1988)

8 As long as critics have been around, they have insisted that the artist's life and art are inextricably linked.

    Claudia Tate, *Black Women Writers at Work* (1983)

9 Deliver me from writers who say the way they live doesn't matter. I'm not sure a bad person can write a good book. If art doesn't make us better, then what on earth is it for?

    Alice Walker, in Evelyn L. Beilenson and Ann Tenenbaum, eds., *Wit and Wisdom of Famous American Women* (1986)

10 People . . . take their literature and art from the past. They are not interested in what the present generation is thinking or painting or doing if it doesn't fit the enclosure of their personal apprehension. Present day geniuses can no more help doing what they are doing than you can help not understanding it, but if you think we do it for effect, and to make a sensation, you're crazy.

    Gertrude Stein, in John Malcolm Brinnin, *The Third Rose* (1959)

11 Dead artists always bring out an older, richer crowd.

    Elizabeth Shaw, in *The New York Times* (1976)

12 Artists often think they are going to die before their time. They seem to possess a heightened sense of the passing of the hours.

    Catherine Drinker Bowen, in *The Atlantic* (1961)

13 Art is the only thing you cannot punch a button for. You must do it the old-fashioned way. Stay up and really burn the midnight oil. There are no compromises.

    Leontyne Price, in Brian Lanker, *I Dream a World* (1989)

14 Their [artists'] essential effort is to catapult themselves wholly, without holding back one bit, into a course of action without having any idea where they will end up. They are like riders who gallop into the night, eagerly leaning on their horse's neck, peering into a blinding rain. And they have to do it over and over again.

    Anne Truitt, *Daybook* (1982)

15 I murmured to Picasso that I liked his portrait of Gertrude Stein. Yes, he said, everybody said that she does not look like it but that does not make any difference, she will, he said.

    Gertrude Stein, *The Autobiography of Alice B. Toklas* (1933)

16 Very few people possess true artistic ability. It is therefore both unseemly and unproductive to irritate the situation by making an effort. If you have a burning, restless urge to write or paint, simply eat something sweet and the feeling will pass.

    Fran Lebowitz, *Metropolitan Life* (1978)

See also Art, Dance, Poets, Singing, Writers.

## ❧ ASIA

See China, Hong Kong, India, Iran, Israel, Japan, the Philippines, Russia, Turkey.

## ❧ ASIAN AMERICANS

17 born into the / skin of yellow women / we are born / into the armor of warriors.

    Kitty Tsui, "Chinatown Talking Story," *The Words of a Woman Who Breathes Fire* (1983)

1 We are not afraid to rock the boat. Making waves. This is what Asian American women have done and will continue to do.

> Asian Women United of California, eds., *Making Waves* (1989)

2 As a first-generation "Asian American woman," for one thing, I knew there was no such thing as an "Asian American woman." Within this homogenizing labeling of an exotica, I knew there were entire racial/national/cultural/sexual-preferenced groups, many of whom find each other as alien as mainstream America apparently finds us.

> Shirley Geok-lin Lim, "A Dazzling Quilt," in Shirley Geok-lin Lim, Mayumi Tsutakawa, and Margarita Donnelly, eds., *The Forbidden Stitch* (1989)

3 My race is a line that stretches across ocean and time to link me to the shrine where my grandmother was raised.

> Kesaya E. Noda, "Growing Up Asian in America," in Asian Women United of California, eds., *Making Waves* (1989)

See also Bigotry, Discrimination, Minorities, Oppression.

## ❦ ASSERTIVENESS

4 Although I may not be a lioness, I am a lion's cub, and inherit many of his qualities; and as long as the King of France treats me gently he will find me as gentle and tractable as he can desire; but if he be rough, I shall take the trouble to be just as troublesome and offensive to him as I can.

> Queen Elizabeth I (1574), in Frederick Chamberlin, *The Sayings of Queen Elizabeth* (1923)

See also Chutzpah.

## ❦ ASSUMPTIONS

5 Assumptions are dangerous things.

> Agatha Christie, "The Herb of Death," *Thirteen Problems* (1932)

6 Until we can understand the assumptions in which we are drenched we cannot know ourselves.

> Adrienne Rich, "When We Dead Awaken: Writing As Re-Vision," *On Lies, Secrets, and Silence* (1979)

7 I suppose one gets to know men quickest by the things they take for granted.

> Mary Stewart, *My Brother Michael* (1959)

8 Some people become so expert at reading between the lines they don't read the lines.

> Margaret Millar, *The Soft Talkers* (1957)

See also Stereotypes.

## ❦ ATHEISM

9 Ah, the bitter, hopeless heart-hunger of godlessness none but an atheist can understand!

> Miles Franklin, *My Brilliant Career* (1901)

## ❦ ATHLETES

10 It's really impossible for athletes to grow up. As long as you're playing, no one will let you. On the one hand, you're a child, still playing a game. And everybody around you acts like a kid, too. But on the other hand, you're a superhuman hero that everyone dreams of being. No wonder we have such a hard time understanding who we are.

> Billie Jean King, with Frank Deford, *Billie Jean* (1982)

11 Men sometimes seem more ready to accept women as brain surgeons than as athletes.

> Janice Kaplan, *Women and Sports* (1979)

12 I don't think being an athlete is unfeminine. I think of it as a kind of grace.

> Jackie Joyner-Kersee, in *Time* (1988)

13 You'd definitely think of me more as a good sport than as an athlete.

> Gabrielle Burton, "Running for Our Lives," in *Ms.* (1993)

See also Sports.

## ❦ ATTENTION

14 Most people would far rather be seen through than not be seen at all.

> Ada Leverson, *Tenterhooks* (1912)

1 It is better to be looked over than overlooked.
> Mae West, *Belle of the Nineties* (1934)

2 Attention is a silent and perpetual flattery.
> Anne-Sophie Swetchine, in Count de Falloux, ed., *The Writings of Madame Swetchine* (1869)

3 Those who are unhappy have no need for anything in this world but people capable of giving them their attention.
> Simone Weil, *Waiting for God* (1950)

4 [She is] like a bear you have to keep throwing buns at.
> Elizabeth Bowen, *To the North* (1933)

See also Listening.

## ❧ ATTITUDE

5 A willing heart adds feather to the heel.
> Joanna Baillie, *De Montfort* (1798)

See also Enthusiasm, Motives, Purpose.

## ❧ AUDIENCE

6 As half of a poem lies with the reader, so half of an actor's effects lies with his audience, and often the best half.
> Mary Anderson, *A Few Memories* (1896)

7 Your audience gives you everything you need. They tell you. There is no director who can direct you like an audience.
> Fanny Brice, in Norman Katkov, *The Fabulous Fanny* (1952)

8 I can never remember being afraid of an audience. If the audience could do better, they'd be up here on stage and I'd be out there watching them.
> Ethel Merman, in Barbara McDowell and Hana Umlauf, *Woman's Almanac* (1977)

9 You cannot fool an audience.
> Marian Anderson, *My Lord, What a Morning* (1956)

10 The audience . . . is practically infallible, since there is no appeal from its verdict. It is a little like a supreme court composed of irresponsible minors.
> Agnes Repplier, "Actor and Audience," *Times and Tendencies* (1931)

11 The theater audience is the ultimate teacher, instructing the actor on the degree to which he has executed both the author's and the director's intent.
> Joan Fontaine, *No Bed of Roses* (1978)

12 A musical audience is at best uninspiring, at worst definitely drab. . . . Respectability hangs like a pall over the orchestra and the boxes; a sort of sterile sobriety ill-fitted to the passionate geometry of music.
> Marya Mannes, *Message From a Stranger* (1948)

13 Nothing is so calculated to lose you audience sympathy as too many tears. Move your listeners all you can but let them do the crying.
> Ilka Chase, *Elephants Arrive at Half-Past Five* (1963)

14 If *you* cry, honey, they don't!
> Fanny Brice, in Helen Hayes, with Sandford Dody, *On Reflection* (1968)

15 In the theater, I've found that, in general, reaction and laughter come easier at an evening performance, when the audience is more inclined to forget its troubles. Matinee customers must enter the theater in a more matter-of-fact frame of mind, hanging on tightly before they let themselves go.
> Beatrice Lillie, *Every Other Inch a Lady* (1972)

16 At last it was over, and the theater rang and rang with the grateful applause of the released.
> Edith Wharton, *The Gods Arrive* (1932)

See also Applause, Performance, Spectators.

## ❧ AUGUST

17 August is a wicked month.
> Edna O'Brien, book title (1965)

18 August is a month when if it is hot weather it is really very hot.
> Gertrude Stein, *Ida* (1941)

1 The August day came out at them like a parched and coated tongue.

> Fannie Hurst, "Seven Candles," in *Cosmopolitan* (1923)

2 Oh, these damp, sultry days of August! how oppressive they are to mind and body!

> Lydia Maria Child, *Letters From New York*, 1st series (1842)

3 August is motionless, and hot. It is curiously silent, too, with blank white dawns and glaring noons, and sunsets smeared with too much color. . . . These are strange and breathless days, the dog days, when people are led to do things they are sure to be sorry for.

> Natalie Babbit, *Tuck Everlasting* (1975)

4 August is the mute month, / In a doze, / Leaf-laden and lackluster, / Comatose.

> Helen Bevington, "August Is the Mute Month," *Nineteen Million Elephants* (1950)

See also Summer.

## ❧ AUNTS

5 Aunts are discreet, a little shy / By instinct. They forbear to pry.

> Phyllis McGinley, "Girl's-Eye View of Relatives," *Times Three* (1960)

6 The good aunt always gives to any kind of nieces and nephews the something extra, the something unexpected, the something which comes from outside the limits of their habitual world. She is an aviator from another country who drops leaflets out of the sky. She does not intend to start a revolution, she only wants them to learn that there are other countries besides their own.

> Katharine Butler Hathaway, *The Little Locksmith* (1942)

7 She is the Buffer of civilization.

> Margaret Deland, "Aunts," *The Common Way* (1904)

8 Every man should have aunts. They illustrate the triumph of guesswork over logic.

> Agatha Christie, *Murder Is Easy* (1939)

9 Sometimes a child has a great urge to talk what its mother calls nonsense. Sometimes even a child's worry about death and about the beginning and the end of the universe seems like nonsense to the busy mother when she knows by taking one quick animal sniff of him that there is nothing wrong with him. This is where the good maiden aunt comes in.

> Katharine Butler Hathaway, *The Little Locksmith* (1942)

## ❧ AUSTRALIA

10 I love a sunburnt country, / . . . / An opal-hearted country, / A willful, lavish land.

> Dorothea Mackellar, "My Country," *The Closed Door* (1911)

11 Australia is a country not so much of fulfillment as of theatrical expectation.

> Jan Morris, "Nothing If Not Australian," *Locations* (1992)

12 Sydney . . . was confusion surrounded on three sides by water and on the fourth by the hospital.

> Kylie Tennant, *Ride On Stranger* (1943)

## ❧ AUTHORITY

13 All progress in knowledge takes place through the correction of that which has been received on authority . . . without the huge body of traditional knowledge, accurate and inaccurate together, there would be nothing even to correct. Progress is not made in spite of authority, but by means of it.

> Margaret Benson, *The Venture of Rational Faith* (1908)

14 Authority without wisdom is like a heavy axe without an edge, fitter to bruise than polish.

> Anne Bradstreet, "Meditations Divine and Moral" (1664), in John Harvard Ellis, ed, *The Works of Anne Bradstreet in Prose and Verse* (1867)

15 I believe in a lively disrespect for most forms of authority.

> Rita Mae Brown, *Starting From Scratch* (1988)

See also Power.

## ❧ AUTOBIOGRAPHY

16 Writing the story of your own life, I now know, is an agonizing experience, a bit like drilling your own teeth.

> Gloria Swanson, *Swanson on Swanson* (1980)

1 The urge to write one's autobiography, so I have been told, overtakes everyone sooner or later.

Agatha Christie, *An Autobiography* (1977)

2 Autobiography at least saves a man or woman that the world is curious about from the publication of a string of mistakes called "Memoirs."

George Eliot (1876), in J.W. Cross, ed., *George Eliot's Life As Related in Her Letters and Journals* (1884)

3 Few books are more thrilling than certain confessions, but they must be honest, and the author must have something to confess.

Simone de Beauvoir, *The Second Sex* (1949)

4 Writing an autobiography, usually thought of as a looking back, can just as well be a looking *across* or *through*, with the passing of time giving an X-ray quality to the eye.

Janet Frame, *An Angel at My Table* (1984)

5 The autobiography is at one and the same time a single element in the series of the writer's created works and an interpretation of the whole series.

Dorothy L. Sayers, *The Mind of the Maker* (1941)

6 A third volume of Memoirs is really a bold undertaking. . . . I cannot, like a certain female writer, say, I hope if I have done nothing to please, I have done nothing to offend; for truly I mean to give both pleasure and offense.

Letitia Pilkington, *Memoirs of Mrs. Letitia Pilkington Written by Herself*, vol. 3 (1754)

7 You have to take pains in a memoir not to hang on the reader's arm, like a drunk, and say, "And then I did this and it was so interesting."

Annie Dillard, in William Zinsser, ed., *Inventing the Truth* (1989)

8 I am constantly writing autobiography, but I have to turn it into fiction in order to give it credibility.

Katherine Paterson, *The Spying Heart* (1989)

9 I'll be eighty this month. Age, if nothing else, entitles me to set the record straight before I dissolve. I've given my memoirs far more thought than any of my marriages. You can't divorce a book.

Gloria Swanson, in *The New York Times* (1979)

10 Some censuring Readers will scornfully say, why hath this Lady writ her own Life? since none cares to know whose daughter she was or whose wife she is, or how she was bred, or what fortunes she had, or how she lived, or what humor or disposition she was of? I answer that it is true, that 'tis to no purpose to the Readers, but it is to the Authoress, because I write it for my own sake, not theirs.

Margaret Cavendish, Duchess of Newcastle (1655), in Mary Ellen Chase, *A Goodly Heritage* (1932)

11 Hiring someone to write your autobiography is like hiring someone to take a bath for you.

Mae West, in *Bookviews* (1977)

12 All autobiography is self-indulgent.

Daphne du Maurier, *Myself When Young* (1977)

13 Your life story would not make a good book. Do not even try.

Fran Lebowitz, *Metropolitan Life* (1978)

See also Biography.


## ❧ AUTUMN

14 Autumn begins to decorate the ground / with its fragile bits of loosened gold.

Teresita Fernández, "Every Day That I Love You," in Margaret Randall, ed., *Twentieth Century Poetry by Cuban Women* (1982)

15 Autumn burned brightly, a running flame through the mountains, a torch flung to the trees.

Faith Baldwin, *American Family* (1935)

16 Autumn in felted slipper shuffles on, / Muted yet fiery.

Vita Sackville-West, "Autumn," *The Garden* (1946)

17 Delicious autumn! My very soul is wedded to it, and if I were a bird I would fly about the earth seeking the successive autumns.

George Eliot (1840), in J.W. Cross, ed., *George Eliot's Life As Related in Her Letters and Journals* (1884)

18 The spirit of the year, like bacchant crowned, / With lighted torch goes careless on his way; / And soon bursts into flame the maple's spray, / And vines are running fire along the ground.

Edith M. Thomas, "Autumn," *Lyrics and Sonnets* (1887)

19 As dyed in blood the streaming vines appear, / While long and low the wind about them grieves: /

The heart of Autumn must have broken here, / And poured its treasure out upon the leaves.

> Charlotte Fiske Bates, "Woodbines in October," in Edmund Clarence Stedman, ed., *An American Anthology 1787-1900* (1900)

1 One only leaf upon the top of a tree—the sole remaining leaf—danced round and round like a rag blown by the wind.

> Dorothy Wordsworth (1798), in William Knight, ed., *Journals of Dorothy Wordsworth*, vol. 1 (1897)

2 All those golden autumn days the sky was full of wings. Wings beating low over the blue water of Silver Lake, wings beating high in the blue air far above it. Wings of geese, of brant, of ducks and pelicans and cranes and heron and swans and gulls, bearing them all away to green fields in the South.

> Laura Ingalls Wilder, *On the Shores of Silver Lake* (1939)

3 Autumn is full of leave-taking. In September the swallows are chattering of destination and departure like a crowd of tourists.

> Mary Webb, *The Spring of Joy* (1917)

4 Autumn is the best season in which to sniff, and to sniff for pleasure, for this is the season of universal pungency.

> Bertha Damon, *A Sense of Humus* (1943)

5 Autumn . . . makes a double demand. It asks that we prepare for the future—that we be wise in the ways of garnering and keeping. But it also asks that we learn to let go—to acknowledge the beauty of sparseness.

> Bonaro W. Overstreet, "Mists and Mellow Fruitfulness," in Jean Beaven Abernethy, *Meditations for Women* (1947)

6 The red leaves take the green leaves' place, and the landscape yields. We go to sleep with the peach in our hands and wake with the stone, but the stone is the pledge of summers to come.

> Emily Dickinson (1874), in Mabel Loomis Todd, ed., *Letters of Emily Dickinson*, vol. 2 (1894)

7 When autumn shadows throw their patterns across the land, they are not the images of fragile, dying leaves, not the bared arms of lofty elms, not shadows of a fading summer; but swinging shapes as of books upon a strap, of round and square boxes held under an arm, of hurrying little people heading toward the nearest school.

> Djuna Barnes, "Our School's Open Again; We're Glad to Get Back," in *The Brooklyn Daily Eagle* (1913)

8 I've never known anyone yet who doesn't suffer a certain restlessness when autumn rolls around. . . . We're all eight years old again and anything is possible.

> Sue Grafton, "Long Gone," in Marilyn Wallace, ed., *Sisters in Crime 4* (1991)

9 Autumn is an unkindly thing / In a town.

> Sylvia Townsend Warner, "Country Thought From a Town," *The Espalier* (1925)

10 Autumn comes to the sea with a fresh blaze of phosphorescence, when every wave crest is aflame. Here and there the whole surface may glow with sheets of cold fire, while below schools of fish pour through the water like molten metal.

> Rachel Carson, *The Sea Around Us* (1950)

11 Autumn is a hound that shrills, my heart is for her gnawing, / The quarry goes to Autumn, let Spring die.

> Babette Deutsch, "The Hound," in Burton E. Stevenson, ed., *The Home Book of Modern Verse* (1925)

See also November, October, Seasons, September.

## ❧ AVARICE

12 Avarice breeds envy, a worm that is always gnawing, letting the avaricious enjoy neither their own nor anyone else's good.

> St. Catherine of Siena, in Suzanne Noffke, tr., *Dialogue* (1378)

13 Avarice is especially, I suppose, a disease of the imagination.

> Sara Coleridge (1848), *Memoir and Letters*, vol. 2 (1873)

14 Avarice, with all its black attendants, is confessedly a crime of old age, and seldom arrives at maturity till accompanied with gray hairs.

> Mary Collyer, *Felicia to Charlotte* (1744)

15 Avarice is rarely the vice of youth.

> Sophia Lee, *The Recess* (1785)

See also Greed, Miserliness.

## ❧ AVERAGES

16 Averages . . . seduce us away from minute observation.

> Florence Nightingale, *Notes on Nursing* (1859)

1 Things in this world are very roughly averaged; and although averaging is a useful, rapid way of dispatching business, it does undoubtedly waste a great deal which is too good for wasting.

Vernon Lee, *Renaissance Fancies and Studies* (1895)

2 We've taken disturbances and fluctuations and averaged them together to give us comfortable statistics. Our training has been to look for big numbers, important trends, major variances. Yet it is the slight variations—soft-spoken, even whispered at first—that we need to encourage.

Margaret J. Wheatley, *Leadership and the New Science* (1992)

## ❧ AWARENESS

3 I break up through the skin of awareness a thousand times a day, as dolphins burst through seas, and dive again, and rise, and dive.

Annie Dillard, *An American Childhood* (1987)

4 It was as if I had worked for years on the wrong side of a tapestry, learning accurately all its lines and figures, yet always missing its color and sheen.

Anna Louise Strong, *I Change Worlds* (1935)

5 Sometimes I think we're all tightrope walkers suspended on a wire two thousand feet in the air, and so long as we never look down we're okay, but some of us lose momentum and look down for a second and are never quite the same again: we *know*.

Dorothy Gilman, *The Tightrope Walker* (1979)

6 Eden is that old-fashioned House / We dwell in every day / Without suspecting our abode / Until we drive away.

Emily Dickinson, in Martha Dickinson Bianchi, ed., *The Single Hound* (1914)

7 Every dog has its day, but it's not every dog that knows when he's having it.

Winifred Gordon, *A Book of Days* (1910)

8 When you don't know when you have been spit on, it does not matter too much what else you think you know.

Ruth Shays, in John Langston Gwaltney, *Drylongso* (1980)

9 It's so easy to be wicked without knowing it, isn't it?

L.M. Montgomery, *Anne of Green Gables* (1908)

10 It's exhilarating to be alive in a time of awakening consciousness; it can also be confusing, disorienting, and painful.

Adrienne Rich, "When We Dead Awaken: Writing As Re-Vision," *On Lies, Secrets, and Silence* (1979)

See also Knowledge, Self-Knowledge, Sensitivity.

# B

## ❦ BABIES

1 It sometimes happens, even in the best families, that a baby is born. This is not necessarily cause for alarm. The important thing is to keep your wits about you and borrow some money.

Elinor Goulding Smith, *The Complete Book of Absolutely Perfect Baby and Child Care* (1957)

2 Now the thing about having a baby—and I can't be the first person to have noticed this—is that thereafter you *have* it.

Jean Kerr, *Please Don't Eat the Daisies* (1957)

3 Keeping a baby requires a good deal of time, effort, thought and equipment, so unless you are prepared for this, we recommend that you start with a hamster, whose wants are far simpler.

Elinor Goulding Smith, *The Complete Book of Absolutely Perfect Baby and Child Care* (1957)

4 In came . . . a baby, eloquent as infancy usually is, and like most youthful orators, more easily heard than understood.

L.E. Landon, *Romance and Reality* (1831)

5 I just can't get over how much babies cry. I really had no idea what I was getting into. To tell you the truth, I thought it would be more like getting a cat.

Anne Lamott, *Operating Instructions* (1993)

6 Having a baby is like suddenly getting the world's worst roommate, like having Janis Joplin with a bad hangover and PMS come to stay with you.

Anne Lamott, *Bird by Bird* (1994)

7 They lie flat on their noses at first in what appears to be a drunken slumber, then flat on their backs kicking and screaming, demanding impossibilities in a foreign language.

Katherine Anne Porter, "'Marriage Is Belonging,'" *The Days Before* (1952)

8 Home alone with a wakeful newborn, I could shower so quickly that the mirror didn't fog and the backs of my knees stayed dry.

Marni Jackson, *The Mother Zone* (1992)

9 A man finds out what is meant by a spitting image when he tries to feed cereal to his infant.

Imogene Fey, in Jilly Cooper and Tom Hartman, *Violets and Vinegar* (1982)

10 You were courted and got married in the magic world, but you had your baby in the real one.

Bess Streeter Aldrich, *Song of Years* (1939)

11 Sometimes we think a *ménage à trois* would be easier than an old marriage and a new baby.

Marguerite Kelly and Elia Parsons, *The Mother's Almanac* (1975)

12 For years we have given scientific attention to the care and rearing of plants and animals, but we have allowed babies to be raised chiefly by tradition.

Edith Belle Lowry, *False Modesty* (1912)

13 I feel sure that unborn babies pick their parents.

Gloria Swanson, *Swanson on Swanson* (1980)

14 Little wild baby, that knowest not where thou art going, / Lie still! lie still! Thy mother will do the rowing.

Margaret Thomson Janvier, "Little Wild Baby," in Edmund Clarence Stedman, ed., *An American Anthology 1787-1900* (1900)

15 Like a round loaf . . . / I kneaded you, patted you, / greased you smooth, floured you.

Judit Tóth, "To the Newborn," in Joanna Bankier and Deirdre Lashgari, eds., *Women Poets of the World* (1983)

16 [He] resumed contemplation of his toes. These, to his never-failing and delighted surprise, continued to be ten in number, no matter how suddenly and without warning he descended upon them; his

startled cataloguing of the suspicious members constituted at present his chief employment, and the subsequent deep breath of relief on finding that all was well and not one of them had escaped his vigilance was one of the joys of his parents.

Josephine Daskam, *The Memoirs of a Baby* (1904)

1  Infants, I note with envy, are receptive to enjoyment in a degree not attained by adults this side of the new Jerusalem.

Margaret Halsey, *Some of My Best Friends Are Soldiers* (1944)

2  Don't forget that compared to a grownup person every baby is a genius. Think of the capacity to learn! The freshness, the temperament, the will of a baby a few months old!

May Sarton, *Mrs. Stevens Hears the Mermaids Singing* (1965)

3  If you want a baby, have a new one. Don't baby the old one.

Jessamyn West, *To See the Dream* (1957)

See also Childbirth, Children, Pregnancy.


## ❦ BACHELORS

4  A bachelor never quite gets over the idea that he is a thing of beauty and a boy forever!

Helen Rowland, *A Guide to Men* (1922)

5  A bachelor is a man who can take a nap on top of a bedspread.

Marcelene Cox, in *Ladies' Home Journal* (1949)

6  In Mexico a bachelor is a man who can't play the guitar.

Lillian Day, *Kiss and Tell* (1931)


## ❦ BACKLASH

7  Though differences in attitudes between men and women still form a favorite topic of drawing-room conversation . . . women's abilities are no longer seriously in doubt. These discussions rather seem to be a kind of rearguard action carried on after the main battle has been decided.

Alva Myrdal and Viola Klein, *Women's Two Roles* (1956)

8  We end up with the contradictory picture of a society that appears to throw its doors wide open to women, but translates her every step towards success as having been damaging.

Margaret Mead, *Male and Female* (1949)

9  The last decade has seen a powerful counterassault on women's rights, a backlash, an attempt to retract the handful of small and hard-won victories that the feminist movement did manage to win for women. This counterassault is largely insidious: in a kind of pop-culture version of the Big Lie, it stands the truth boldly on its head and proclaims that the very steps that have elevated women's position have actually led to their downfall.

Susan Faludi, *Backlash* (1991)

10  The progress of women's rights in our culture, unlike other types of "progress," has always been strangely reversible.

Ann Douglas, *The Feminization of American Culture* (1977)

11  They used to give us a day—it was called International Women's Day. In 1975 they gave us a year, the Year of the Woman. Then from 1975 to 1985 they gave us a decade, the Decade of the Woman. I said at the time, who knows, if we behave they may let us into the whole thing. Well, we didn't behave and here we are.

Bella Abzug, speech, Fourth World Conference on Women, Beijing (1995)

12  The central argument of the backlash [is] that women's equality is responsible for women's unhappiness.

Susan Faludi, *Backlash* (1991)

See also Anti-Feminism, Sexism.


## ❦ BALANCE

13  There is no such thing as balance. How I long for that sense of repose after a good day's work. Does anyone have it?

Naomi Thornton, in Sara Ruddick and Pamela Daniels, eds., *Working It Out* (1977)


## ❦ BALDNESS

14  He . . . had gone completely bald very young as though to get *that* over with as soon as possible.

Helen Hudson, *Meyer Meyer* (1967)

1 This head has risen above its hair in a moment of abandon known only to men who have drawn their feet out of their boots to walk awhile in the corridors of the mind.

> Djuna Barnes, "Who Is This Tom Scarlett?" (1916), *Smoke* (1982)

2 He wore baldness like an expensive hat, as if it were out of the question for him to have hair like other men.

> Gloria Swanson, on Cecil B. DeMille, in Celebrity Research Group, *The Bedside Book of Celebrity Gossip* (1984)

## ❦ BALLET

3 Ballet's image of perfection is fashioned amid a milieu of wracked bodies, fevered imaginations, Balkan intrigue, and sulfurous hatreds where anything is likely, and dancers know it.

> Shana Alexander, *Nutcracker* (1985)

4 Ballet technique is arbitrary and very difficult. It never becomes easy; it becomes possible.

> Agnes de Mille, *Dance to the Piper* (1952)

5 Ballet is a riddle of means and ends.

> Gelsey Kirkland, *Dancing on My Grave* (1986)

6 A toe shoe is as eccentric as the ballerina who wears it: their marriage is a commitment.

> Toni Bentley, in *Smithsonian* (1984)

7 A brand-new pair of toe shoes presents itself to us as an enemy with a will of its own that must be tamed.

> Toni Bentley, in *Smithsonian* (1984)

See also Artists, Dance.

## ❦ BARGAINS

8 Bargaining is essential to the life of the world; but nobody has ever claimed that it is an ennobling process.

> Agnes Repplier, "Allies," *Under Dispute* (1924)

9 The wealthy had a passion for bargains as lively as it was pointless.

> Françoise Sagan, *The Painted Lady* (1983)

10 The less I pay for something, the more it is worth to me. I have a dress that I paid so little for that I am afraid to wear it. I could spill something on it, and then how would I replace it for that amount of money? Tell me that.

> Rita Rudner, *Naked Beneath My Clothes* (1992)

11 There is nothing so costly as bargains.

> Margaret Oliphant, in Mrs. Harry Coghill, ed., *The Autobiography and Letters of Mrs. M.O.W. Oliphant* (1899)

See also Consumerism, Finances, Money.

## ❦ BAR MITZVAHS

12 I suppose the nearest equivalent to a Bar Mitzvah in terms of emotional build-up would probably not even be one's wedding day, but one's coronation.

> Maureen Lipman, *Thank You for Having Me* (1990)

## ❦ BASEBALL

13 Watching a ball game is one of the sweetest pleasures in the world.

> Silvia Tennenbaum, *Rachel, the Rabbi's Wife* (1978)

14 It's about / the ball, / the bat, / the mitt, / the bases / and the fans. / It's done / on a diamond, / and for fun. / It's about / home, and it's about run.

> May Swenson, "Analysis of Baseball," *More Poems to Solve* (1971)

15 Baseball is played on the fields of the imagination as much as on the diamond.

> Elinor Nauen, in Elinor Nauen, ed., *Diamonds Are a Girl's Best Friend* (1994)

16 Baseball lasts as long as it takes. Like life, like love, baseball exists in real time.

> Carol Tavris, "Why I Love Baseball," in Elinor Nauen, ed., *Diamonds Are a Girl's Best Friend* (1994)

17 I oiled my glove yesterday. / Half the season is over. / When will I be ready?

> Lynn Rigney Schott, "Spring Training," in *The New Yorker* (1984)

18 That crack of the bat against a ball has been my mantra, a sound I hear in desperate moments, at

times when I crave total satisfaction, a sound I hear over and over when I want something very badly but can't express what it is.

> Lucy Jane Bledsoe, "State of Grace," in Naomi Holoch and Joan Nestle, eds., *Women on Women 2* (1993)

1 Pitching was about fooling people, manipulating them, making them believe in something that ultimately wasn't there. Great pitching was great lying.

> Linda Ellerbee, *Move On* (1991)

2 In a neighborhood where most children grew up Lutheran or Methodist, we grew up Baseball.

> Molly O'Neill, "Coming to the Plate," in Elinor Nauen, ed., *Diamonds Are a Girl's Best Friend* (1994)

3 All through my childhood, my father kept from me the knowledge that the daily papers printed daily box scores, allowing me to believe that without my personal renderings of all those games he missed while he was at work, he would be unable to follow our team in the only proper way a team should be followed, day by day, inning by inning. In other words, without me, his love for baseball would be forever incomplete.

> Doris Kearns Goodwin, *Diamonds Are Forever* (1987)

4 Baseball is where boys practice being boys and / men practice being boys, and / they get real good at it.

> Mary Cecile Leary, "Why I Love It," in Elinor Nauen, ed., *Diamonds Are a Girl's Best Friend* (1994)

5 For every man with a baseball story—a memory of a moment at the plate or in the field—there is a woman with a couldn't-play-baseball story.

> Mariah Burton Nelson, *Are We Winning Yet?* (1991)

6 Baseball is . . . the world's most tranquil sport. It is probably the only active sport where you are not seriously required to be alive to play.

> Nikki Giovanni, "A Patriotic Plea for Poetry Justice," *Sacred Cows . . . And Other Edibles* (1988)

7 A fan without a team is like a hog without truffles—she has nothing to root for.

> Carol Tavris, "Why I Love Baseball," in Elinor Nauen, ed., *Diamonds Are a Girl's Best Friend* (1994)

8 Being a Cubs fan prepares you for life—and Washington.

> Hillary Rodham Clinton, in *Newsweek* (1994)

9 "Does one eat peanuts at a ball game?" "It ain't hardly legal if you don't."

> Edna Ferber, *Buttered Side Down* (1912)

See also Athletes, Softball, Sports.

♦ BASKETBALL

10 In basketball, you need to snatch a rebound as if you own the ball, as if you're starving and it's the last coconut on the tree.

> Mariah Burton Nelson, *The Stronger Women Get, the More Men Love Football* (1994)

See also Sports.

♦ BATH

11 A hot bath! How exquisite a vespertine pleasure, how luxurious, fervid and flagrant a consolation for the rigors, the austerities, the renunciations of the day.

> Rose Macaulay, *Personal Pleasures* (1936)

12 There must be quite a few things a hot bath won't cure, but I don't know many of them.

> Sylvia Plath, *The Bell Jar* (1963)

13 I can't think of any sorrow in the world that a hot bath wouldn't help, just a little bit.

> Susan Glaspell, *The Visioning* (1911)

14 Noble deeds and hot baths are the best cures for depression.

> Dodie Smith, *I Capture the Castle* (1948)

15 Shunning the upstart shower, / The cold and cursory scrub, / I celebrate the power / That lies within the Tub.

> Phyllis McGinley, "Ode to the Bath," *A Pocketful of Wry* (1940)

♦ BEAUTY

16 Beauty is everlasting / and dust is for a time.

> Marianne Moore, "In Distrust of Merits," *Nevertheless* (1944)

17 Oh who can tell the range of joy / Or set the bounds of beauty?

> Sara Teasdale, "A Winter Bluejay," *Rivers to the Sea* (1915)

18 Art should be Truth; and Truth unadorned, unsentimentalized, is Beauty.

> Elizabeth Borton de Treviño, *I, Juan de Pareja* (1965)

1 Perhaps all this modern ferment of what's known as "social conscience" or "civic responsibility" isn't a result of the sense of duty, but of the old, old craving for beauty.

Dorothy Canfield Fisher, *The Bent Twig* (1915)

2 I will hold beauty as a shield against despair.

Elsie Robinson, "Beauty As a Shield," in Hazel Felleman, ed., *The Best Loved Poems of the American People* (1936)

3 Think of all the beauty that's still left in and around you and be happy!

Anne Frank, *The Diary of a Young Girl* (1952)

4 What delights us in visible beauty is the invisible.

Marie von Ebner-Eschenbach, *Aphorisms* (1893)

5 Restraint is the better part of beauty.

Frances Gray Patton, *Good Morning, Miss Dove* (1955)

6 All things are perceived in the light of charity, and hence under the aspect of beauty: for beauty is simply Reality seen with the eyes of love.

Evelyn Underhill, *Mysticism* (1955)

7 By its very nature the beautiful is isolated from everything else. From beauty no road leads to reality.

Hannah Arendt, *Rahel Varnhagen* (1957)

8 Beauty more than bitterness / Makes the heart break.

Sara Teasdale, "Vignettes Overseas," *Rivers to the Sea* (1915)

9 Beauty that dies the soonest has the longest life. Because it cannot keep itself for a day, we keep it forever. Because it can have existence only in memory, we give it immortality there.

Bertha Damon, *A Sense of Humus* (1943)

10 The beauty of the world . . . has two edges, one of laughter, one of anguish, cutting the heart asunder.

Virginia Woolf, *A Room of One's Own* (1929)

11 The most deeply moving element in the contemplation of beauty is the element of loss. We desire to hold; but the sunset melts into the night, and the secret of the painting on the wall can never be the secret of the buyer.

Pamela Hansford Johnson, *Catherine Carter* (1958)

12 O, beauty, are you not enough? / Why am I crying after love?

Sara Teasdale, "Spring Night," *Rivers to the Sea* (1915)

13 To die would have been beautiful. But I belong to those who do not die for the sake of beauty.

Agnes Smedley, *Daughter of Earth* (1929)

14 You agree—I'm sure you agree, that beauty is the only thing worth living for.

Agatha Christie, *The Moving Finger* (1942)

15 To seek after beauty as an end, is a wild goose chase, a will-o'-the-wisp, because it is to misunderstand the very nature of beauty, which is the normal condition of a thing being as it should be.

Ade Bethune, in Judith Stoughton, *Proud Donkey of Schaerbeek* (1988)

16 Beauty without grace, is a hook without bait.

Ninon de Lenclos, in Mrs. Griffith, tr., *The Memoirs of Ninon de L'Enclos*, vol. 1 (1761)

17 All ugliness passes, and beauty endures, excepting of the skin.

Edith Sitwell (1941), in John Lehmann and Derek Parker, eds., *Selected Letters* (1970)

18 I'm tired of all this nonsense about beauty being only skin-deep. That's deep enough. What do you want—an adorable pancreas?

Jean Kerr, *The Snake Has All the Lines* (1960)

19 Beauty is a simple passion, / but, oh my friends, in the end / you will dance the fire dance in iron shoes.

Anne Sexton, "Snow White and the Seven Dwarfs," *Transformations* (1971)

20 Oh, grieve not, ladies, if at night / Ye wake to feel your beauty going. / It was a web of frail delight, / Inconstant as an April snowing.

Anna Hempstead Branch, "Grieve Not, Ladies," *The Shoes That Danced* (1905)

21 Beauty is in the eye of the beholder.

The Duchess, *Molly Bawn* (1878)

See also Appearance.

## ❦ BECOMING

22 The idea came to me that I *was, am,* and *will be,* but perhaps will not *become.* This did not scare me. There was for me in *being* an intensity I did not feel in *becoming.*

Nina Berberova, *The Italics Are Mine* (1969)

## ❧ BED

1 My bed is the place where it all comes together. Here is where I think naked thoughts, daydream, make love, worry, plot, argue, get my back scratched, speculate, talk about growing old, and, finally, cut the mooring ties and drift out with the dream tide. The bed, the place where we are born and die, is our primeval place.

Laura Green, *Reinventing Home* (1991)

2 There is hardly any one in the civilized world—particularly of those who do just a little more every day than they really have strength to perform—who has not at some time regarded bed as a refuge.

J.E. Buckrose, "Bed As a Refuge," *What I Have Gathered* (1923)

3 It is in bed that we learn to bear the inevitable. We are learning this all the time while we lie with our face turned to the wall thinking we are doing nothing.

J.E. Buckrose, "Bed As a Refuge," *What I Have Gathered* (1923)

4 My bed is my best friend. . . . I type in it, telephone in it, think in it, and stare at the wall from it. Some morning, a long time from now, I hope I will be found peacefully dead in it, lying in a narrow but cozy space between old manuscripts, lost books, empty teacups, misplaced nightgowns, and unsharpened pencils.

Jane O'Reilly, *The Girl I Left Behind* (1980)

## ❧ BEGINNING

5 Nourish beginnings, let us nourish beginnings. / Not all things are blest, but the / seeds of all things are blest. / The blessing is in the seed.

Muriel Rukeyser, "Elegy in Joy," *The Green Wave* (1948)

6 It is only the first step that is difficult.

Marie de Vichy-Chamrond, Marquise du Deffand, on the legend that after being beheaded St. Denis walked six miles with his head in his hands, letter to Jean le Rond D'Alembert (1763)

7 Beginnings are apt to be shadowy.

Rachel Carson, *The Sea Around Us* (1950)

8 The beginning of things, of a world especially, is necessarily vague, tangled, chaotic, and exceedingly disturbing.

Kate Chopin, *The Awakening* (1899)

9 No first step can be really great; it must of necessity possess more of prophecy than of achievement; nevertheless it is by the first step that a man marks the value, not only of his cause, but of himself.

Katherine Cecil Thurston, *The Masquerader* (1904)

10 We are always afraid to start something that we want to make very good, true, and serious.

Brenda Ueland (1938), *Me* (1983)

11 The way to achieve a difficult thing was to set it in motion.

Kate O'Brien, *The Last of Summer* (1943)

12 The fresh start is always an illusion but a necessary one.

Eleanor Clark, *Eyes, Etc.* (1977)

13 Nothing, of course, begins at the time you think it did.

Lillian Hellman, *An Unfinished Woman* (1969)

14 Almost anything is easier to get into than to get out of.

Agnes Allen, in *Omni* (1979)

15 The world is round and the place which may seem like the end may also be only the beginning.

Ivy Baker Priest, in *Parade* (1958)

16 In my end is my beginning.

Mary Stuart, Queen of Scots, motto (1568), in Francis de Zulueta, *Embroideries by Mary Stuart and Elizabeth Talbot* (1923)

17 *In my end is my beginning*—that's what people are always saying. But what does it mean?

Agatha Christie, *Endless Night* (1968)

See also Slippery Slope.

## ❧ BEHAVIOR

18 He was a rather commonplace youth at bottom, with more behavior than brains.

Ellen Glasgow, *Vein of Iron* (1935)

1 Life with Mary was like being in a telephone booth with an open umbrella—no matter which way you turned, you got it in the eye.

    Jean Kerr, *Mary, Mary* (1963)

2 They were drinking ginger ale on her front porch and she kept rattling the ice in her glass, rattling her beads, rattling her bracelet like an impatient pony jingling its harness.

    Flannery O'Connor, "The Displaced Person," *A Good Man Is Hard to Find* (1953)

3 Her incessant movements were not the result of shyness: she thought it the correct thing to be animated in society, and noise and restlessness were her only notion of vivacity.

    Edith Wharton, *The Custom of the Country* (1913)

4 [He drove] at a stately thirty miles an hour, triumphant but alert, eyes flicking left and right, like an Allied general entering a newly liberated town.

    Lucille Kallen, *Introducing C.B. Greenfield* (1979)

5 He's as finicky as the five-times-table, and about as lively.

    Mary Stewart, *Nine Coaches Waiting* (1958)

6 Stanley never answered a doorbell naturally and innocently as other people do. He always debated whether it was wise to answer it at all.

    Ruth Rendell, *One Across, Two Down* (1971)

7 His wife was thin as a splinter and as annoying.

    Faith Baldwin, *Thursday's Child* (1976)

8 He used his hands as though they were feet.

    Rae Foley, *The Hundredth Door* (1950)

9 He smelled submission in Quoyle, guessed he was butter of fair spreading consistency.

    E. Annie Proulx, *The Shipping News* (1993)

10 Mrs. Gollie came into Luke's office as if she was hastening to the scene of some terrible personal disaster, or perhaps merely going on the stage.

    Margery Allingham, *The Tiger in the Smoke* (1952)

11 Marcia was incredibly organized, obsessively neat. . . . She folded her underwear like origami.

    Linda Barnes, "Lucky Penny," in Marilyn Wallace, ed., *Sisters in Crime* (1989)

12 "Ah," said Mrs. Peniston, shutting her lips with the snap of a purse closing against a beggar.

    Edith Wharton, *The House of Mirth* (1905)

13 Her mouth dropped open to let this thought come in and nourish her brain.

    Amy Tan, *The Kitchen God's Wife* (1991)

14 She had a curiously intense stare, like a greedy child waiting for sweets.

    Beryl Bainbridge, *A Quiet Life* (1976)

15 He gazed on her thoughtfully, like a cook who has been brought an unfamiliar kind of game and wonders if she ought to prepare it like quail or like plover.

    Rebecca West, *The Thinking Reed* (1936)

16 His tone was about as informative, and as welcoming, as a blank wall with broken glass on the top.

    Mary Stewart, *This Rough Magic* (1964)

17 When she raises her eyelids it's as if she were taking off her clothes.

    Colette, *Claudine and Annie* (1903)

18 Our humanity rests upon a series of learned behaviors, woven together into patterns that are infinitely fragile and never directly inherited.

    Margaret Mead, *Male and Female* (1949)

See also Actions, Character, Deeds, Personality.

## ֍ BELIEF

19 There is only one history of any importance, and it is the history of what you once believed in, and the history of what you came to believe in.

    Kay Boyle, "White As Snow," *The White Horses of Vienna* (1936)

20 "What I believe" is a process rather than a finality. Finalities are for gods and governments, not for the human intellect.

    Emma Goldman, "What I Believe," in *The New York World* (1908)

21 They were so strong in their beliefs that there came a time when it hardly mattered what exactly those beliefs were; they all fused into a single stubbornness.

    Louise Erdrich, *Love Medicine* (1984)

1 To believe in something not yet proved and to underwrite it with our lives: it is the only way we can leave the future open.

 Lillian Smith, *The Journey* (1954)

2 You can make an audience see nearly anything, if you yourself believe in it.

 Mary Renault, *The Mask of Apollo* (1966)

3 One can only believe entirely, perhaps, in what one cannot see.

 Virginia Woolf, *Orlando* (1928)

4 Not seeing is half-believing.

 Vita Sackville-West, *The Edwardians* (1930)

5 We do not believe until we want a thing and feel that we shall die if 'tis not granted to us, and then we kneel and kneel and believe.

 Frances Hodgson Burnett, *A Lady of Quality* (1896)

6 I am always easy of belief when the creed pleases me.

 Charlotte Brontë, *Shirley* (1849)

7 I've never been one for religion, but yet I've never been what ye could call an unbeliever. What I say is, nothin' don't seem impossible once you've clapped eyes on a whale.

 Elizabeth Goudge, *Green Dolphin Street* (1944)

8 There are no atheists on turbulent airplanes.

 Erica Jong, *Fear of Flying* (1973)

9 He was paralyzed with the impossibility of either belief or disbelief.

 L.M. Boston, *A Stranger at Green Knowe* (1961)

10 Better a false belief than no belief at all.

 George Eliot, *Daniel Deronda* (1874)

See also Convictions, Credulity, Doctrine, Dogma, Faith, Ideals, Opinion, Philosophy, Superstition.

## ∮ BELLS

11 Brief, on a flying night, / From the shaken tower / A flock of bells take flight, / And go with the hour.

 Alice Meynell, "Chimes," *Poems* (1913)

12 I have known some grim bells, with not a single joyous note in the whole peal, so forced to hurry for a human festival, with their harshness made light of, as though the Bishop of Hereford had again been forced to dance in his boots by a merry highwayman.

 Alice Meynell, "Bells," *The Spirit of Place* (1898)

## ∮ BEREAVEMENT

13 Bereavement is waiting, waiting for / a known death to be undone.

 Janet Frame, "Some Thoughts on Bereavement," *The Pocket Mirror* (1967)

See also Grief, Loss, Mourning, Sorrow, Suffering.

## ∮ BETRAYAL

14 The one who deals the mortal blow / Receives the mortal wound.

 Maude Parker, "I Do Hereby Bequeath. . .," in William Nichols, ed., *Words to Live By* (1962)

15 I saw this thing turn, like a flower, once picked, turning petals into bright knives in your hand. And it was so much desired, so lovely, that your fingers will not loosen, and you have only disbelief that this, of all you have ever known, should have the possibility of pain.

 Nadine Gordimer, *The Lying Days* (1953)

16 To a generous mind few circumstances are more afflicting than a discovery of perfidy in those whom we have trusted.

 Ann Radcliffe, *The Romance of the Forest* (1791)

See also Infidelity, Treachery.

## ∮ BIBLE

17 He who would be well-traveled should journey through the Bible's books, / For the whole world can be seen there.

 Sibylle Schwarz (1650), in Katharina M. Wilson and Frank J. Warnke, *Women Writers of the Seventeenth Century* (1989)

18 Amid ancient lore the Word of God stands unique and pre-eminent. Wonderful in its construction,

admirable in its adaptation, it contains truths that a child may comprehend, and mysteries into which angels desire to look.

Frances Ellen Watkins Harper, "Christianity," in *Christian Recorder* (1853)

1 The Bible writers didn't care that they were bunching together sequences some of which were historical, some preposterous, and some downright manipulative. Faithful recording was not their business; faith was.

Jeanette Winterson, *Boating for Beginners* (1985)

2 In my opinion what distinguishes the Bible from the other books is its sense of time. Its first concern is to establish a calendar. Then it traces a genealogy. It imposes rhythms, it orders, it operates, it does not abandon the earth where its destiny must be fulfilled and whose own destiny must be fulfilled by it.

Adrienne Monnier (1938), in Richard McDougall, tr., *The Very Rich Hours of Adrienne Monnier* (1976)

3 People who quoted the Scriptures in criticism of others were terrible bores and usually they misapplied the text. One could prove anything against anyone from the Bible.

Muriel Spark, *The Mandelbaum Gate* (1965)

4 Cowards always drag in the Bible to back theirselves up far more than proper people does.

Miles Franklin, *Some Everyday Folk and Dawn* (1909)

5 When he hed a p'int to prove, he'd jest go through the Bible, and drive all the texts ahead o' him like a flock o' sheep; and then, if there was a text that seemed agin him, why, he'd come out with his Greek and Hebrew, and kind o' chase it round a spell . . . and make him jump the fence arter the rest. I tell you, there wa'n't no text in the Bible that could stand agin the doctor when his blood was up.

Harriet Beecher Stowe, "The Minister's Housekeeper," *Sam Lawson's Oldtown Fireside Stories* (1871)

6 Bible texts are best read with a pair of glasses made out of today's newspaper.

Dorothee Sölle, in Karen Lebacqz, *Justice in an Unjust World* (1987)

7 The Bible has been used as a way of making us accept our situation, and not to bring enlightenment to the poor.

Rigoberta Menchú, in Elisabeth Burgos-Debray, ed., *I, Rigoberta Menchú* (1983)

8 People have founded vast schemes upon a very few words.

Florence Nightingale (1860), in Mary Poovey, ed., *Cassandra and Other Selections From Suggestions for Thought* (1992)

9 The consensus appears to be that as it is presented and practiced in our churches the gospel is not *Good News* for women.

Elaine Storkey, *What's Right With Feminism* (1985)

10 The Bible is used as a means of reinforcing . . . [women's] subordination to men through divine sanction.

Letty Russell, *The Liberating Word* (1976)

11 The Old Testament is the record of men's conviction that God speaks directly to men.

Edith Hamilton, *Spokesmen for God* (1949)

12 Kindly inform the Church of England they have loused up the most beautiful prose ever written, whoever told them to tinker with the Vulgate Latin? They'll burn for it, you mark my words.

Helene Hanff, *84, Charing Cross Road* (1970)

See also Torah.

## ❧ BICYCLES

13 The bicycle is the steed that never tires, and is "mettlesome" in the fullest sense of the word. It is full of tricks and capers, and to hold his head steady and make him prance to suit you is no small accomplishment.

Frances E. Willard, *A Wheel Within a Wheel* (1895)

14 As a temperance reformer I always felt a strong attraction toward the bicycle, because it is the vehicle of so much harmless pleasure, and because the skill required in handling it obliges those who mount to keep clear heads and steady hands.

Frances E. Willard, *A Wheel Within a Wheel* (1895)

See also Sports.

## ❧ BIGOTRY

15 More people have died from bigotry than any other disease.

Lynne Alpern and Esther Blumenfeld, *Oh, Lord, I Sound Just Like Mama* (1986)

1 Bigotry is ever the child of ignorance, and the cultivation of the understanding is the only radical cure for it.

Mary Hays, *Letters and Essays, Moral and Miscellaneous* (1793)

2 Fashions in bigotry come and go. The right thing lasts.

Anna Quindlen, in *The New York Times* (1993)

3 Religious bigotry is a dull fire—hot enough to roast an ox, but with no lambent, luminous flame shooting up from it.

Sara Coleridge (1842), *Memoir and Letters*, vol. 1 (1873)

4 Every bigot was once a child free of prejudice.

Sister Mary de Lourdes, in *Reader's Digest* (1983)

See also Discrimination, Oppression, Prejudice, Racism.

## ❧ BIOGRAPHY

5 The best biographies leave their readers with a sense of having all but entered into a second life, and of having come to know another human being in some ways better than he knew himself.

Mary Cable, "Saint-Gaudens and the Gilded Era," in *The New York Times Book Review* (1969)

6 The pleasure of reading biography, like that of reading letters, derives from the universal hunger to penetrate other lives.

Patricia Meyer Spacks, *Gossip* (1985)

7 A biography is considered complete if it merely accounts for six or seven selves, whereas a person may well have as many as a thousand.

Virginia Woolf, *Orlando* (1928)

8 Biography is a dangerous undertaking— / Like building love's mansion from blueprints, / Or testing the blood-stream for germs of truth.

Minna Gellert, "To Biographers," *Flesh of the Furies* (1947)

9 Just how difficult it is to write biography can be reckoned by anybody who sits down and considers just how many people know the real truth about his or her love affairs.

Rebecca West, "The Art of Scepticism," in *Vogue* (1952)

10 Writing biography is a paradoxical enterprise, at once solitary and communal.

Penelope Niven, *Carl Sandburg* (1991)

11 To the biographer all lives bar none are dramatic constructions.

Katherine Anthony, in Helen Hull, ed., *The Writer's Book* (1950)

12 A woman's biography—with about eight famous historical exceptions—so often turns out to be the story of a man and the woman who helped his career.

Catherine Drinker Bowen, in Barbara Sicherman and Carol Hurd Green, eds., *Notable American Women* (1980)

13 Nobody should be authorized to describe the dissolution of a man, still less to do so for money or sensationalism. In the name of human dignity, there should be a prohibition against baring the private lives of others.

Mary Hemingway, in Oriana Fallaci, *Gli Antipatici* (1963)

See also Autobiography, Writing.

## ❧ BIOLOGY

14 We are a sad lot, the cell biologists; like the furtive collectors of stolen art, we are forced to be lonely admirers of spectacular architecture, exquisite symmetry, dramas of violence and death, nobility, self-sacrifice and, yes, rococo sex.

L.L. Larison Cudmore, *The Center of Life* (1977)

15 All cell biologists are condemned to suffer from an incurable secret sorrow: the size of the objects of their passion. Almost anyone with an obsession can share it with someone else. . . . But those of us enamored of the cell must resign ourselves to the perverse, lonely fascination of a human being for things invisible to the naked human eye.

L.L. Larison Cudmore, *The Center of Life* (1977)

16 A single cell can have everything except fire, and intellectually I like that thought a lot. Emotionally, I feel that cells have done too much. They seem to have accomplished everything we pride ourselves on, but they did it two billion years ago. Granted, their pexicysts are not exactly SAMs or ICBMs, but they're not bad at all for something without a brain

and without hands, and they do what is needed without contaminating the environment.

L.L. Larison Cudmore, *The Center of Life* (1977)

1 Man is the only mammal whose normal method of locomotion is to walk on two legs. A pattern of mammal behavior that emerges only once in the whole history of life on earth takes a great deal of explaining.

Elaine Morgan, *The Aquatic Ape* (1982)

2 I am convinced that biology should be taught as a course in human-animal relationships—not as a study of dead bodies or caged victims.

Dorothy Richards, with Hope Sawyer Buyukmihci, *Beaversprite* (1977)

3 Considering the very close genetic relationship that has been established by comparison of biochemical properties of blood proteins, protein structure and DNA, and immunological responses, the differences between a man and a chimpanzee are more astonishing than the resemblances.

Elaine Morgan, *The Aquatic Ape* (1982)

4 Ah, the architecture of this world. Amoebas may not have backbones, brains, automobiles, plastic, television, Valium or any other of the blessings of a technologically advanced civilization; but their architecture is two billion years ahead of its time. The amoeba had the architectural ideas of R. Buckminster Fuller before there was anyone around capable of having an idea.

L.L. Larison Cudmore, *The Center of Life* (1977)

5 Biology transcends society.

Jessie Fauset, *The Chinaberry Tree* (1931)

See also Science.

## ♪ BIRDS

6 There are more birds about than usual.

Daphne du Maurier, "The Birds," *Kiss Me Again, Stranger* (1952)

7 I hope you love birds, too. It is economical. It saves going to Heaven.

Emily Dickinson (1885), in Mabel Loomis Todd, ed., *Letters of Emily Dickinson*, vol. 2 (1894)

8 Few forms of life are so engaging as birds.

Ellen Glasgow, *Letters of Ellen Glasgow* (1958)

9 Birds! birds! ye are beautiful things, / With your earth-treading feet and your cloud-cleaving wings!

Eliza Cook, "Birds," *The Poetical Works of Eliza Cook* (1848)

10 Sweet was the hour, when Nature gave / Her loveliest treasures birth, / And sent these artless choristers / To bless the smiling earth.

Cynthia Taggart, "The Happy Birds," *Poems* (1832)

11 How pleasant the lives of the birds must be, / Living in love in a leafy tree!

Mary Howitt, "Birds in Summer," *Ballads and Other Poems* (1847)

12 For most bird-watchers, the coming of the warblers has the same effect as catnip on a cat.

Arline Thomas, in *Audubon's Birds* (1992)

13 For many birds May is the most important month of the year, for it is their time of nesting. Their song now approaches its greatest perfection. Early in the month it expresses the rapture of courtship, later the joy of possession.

Mrs. William Starr Dana, *According to Season* (1894)

14 A bird arranges / two notes at right angles.

Elizabeth Bishop, "Sunday, 4 a.m.," *Questions of Travel* (1965)

15 Sweet poet of the woods.

Charlotte Smith, "On the Departure of the Nightingale," *Elegiac Sonnets* (1784)

16 Swamp sparrows, catbird, bluebird, rose-breasted grosbeak, Baltimore oriole, brown thrasher, bobolink, marsh wren, scarlet tanager, indigo bunting hold matins and vespers in the leafy aisles along the brook.

Eloise Butler, in Martha E. Hellender, *The Wild Gardener* (1992)

17 A prompt — executive Bird is the Jay — / Bold as a Bailiff's Hymn.

Emily Dickinson (1865), in Martha Dickinson Bianchi, ed., *The Single Hound* (1914)

18 Shoot all the bluejays you want, if you can hit 'em, but remember it's a sin to kill a mockingbird. . . . Mockingbirds don't do one thing but make music for us to enjoy. They don't eat up people's gardens, don't nest in corncribs, they don't do one thing but sing their hearts out for us.

Harper Lee, *To Kill a Mockingbird* (1960)

19 List to that bird! His song—what poet pens it? / Brigand of birds, he's stolen every note! / Prince

though of thieves—hark! how the rascal spends it! / Pours the whole forest from one tiny throat!

Ednah Proctor Hayes, "The Mocking-Bird," in Edmund Clarence Stedman, ed., *An American Anthology 1787-1900* (1900)

1 A certain red cardinal sounded like a little bottle being filled up, up, up with some clear liquid.

Elizabeth Enright, *Gone-Away Lake* (1957)

2 The flamingoes are the most delicately colored of all the African birds, pink and red like a flying twig of an oleander bush.

Isak Dinesen, *Out of Africa* (1937)

3 The wild geese were passing over. . . . There was an infinite cold passion in their flight, like the passion of the universe, a proud mystery never to be solved.

Martha Ostenso, *Wild Geese* (1925)

4 The silence and the solitude were touched by wild music, thin as air, the faraway gabbling of geese flying at night. Presently I caught sight of them as they streamed across the face of the moon, the high, excited clamor of their voices tingling through the night, and suddenly I saw, in one of those rare moments of insight, what it means to be wild and free.

Martha Reben, *A Sharing of Joy* (1963)

5 No sadder sound salutes you than the clear, / Wild laughter of the loon.

Celia Thaxter, "Seaward," *Poems* (1872)

6 Over increasingly large areas of the United States, spring now comes unheralded by the return of the birds, and the early mornings are strangely silent where once they were filled with the beauty of bird song.

Rachel Carson, *Silent Spring* (1962)

See also Pets.

## ❦ BIRTH

7 I was so surprised at being born that I didn't speak for a year and a half.

Gracie Allen (1932), in George Burns, *Gracie* (1988)

8 I think of birth as the search for a larger apartment.

Rita Mae Brown, *Starting From Scratch* (1988)

9 To be born is to start the journey towards death.

Madeleine L'Engle, *Walking on Water* (1980)

10 I/woman give birth: / and this time to / myself.

Alma Villanueva, "I Sing to Myself," in *Third Chicano Literary Prize* (1977)

See also Beginning, Childbirth.

## ❦ BIRTH CONTROL

11 Birth control is the means by which woman attains basic freedom.

Margaret Sanger, *Woman and the New Race* (1920)

12 If women cannot plan their pregnancies, they can plan little else in their lives.

Alice S. Rossi, "The Right to One's Body," *The Feminist Papers* (1973)

13 We want better reasons for having children than not knowing how to prevent them.

Dora Russell, *Hypatia* (1925)

14 A modern and humane civilization *must* control conception or sink into barbaric cruelty to individuals.

Marie Stopes, *Contraception* (1923)

15 No woman can call herself free who does not own and control her body. No woman can call herself free until she can choose consciously whether she will or will not be a mother.

Margaret H. Sanger, *Woman and the New Race* (1920)

16 The greatest issue is to raise the question of birth control out of the gutter of obscenity . . . into the light of intelligence and human understanding.

Margaret H. Sanger (1915), in Hope Stoddard, *Famous American Women* (1970)

17 Biological *possibility* and desire are not the same as biological *need*. Women have child-bearing equipment. To choose not to use the equipment is no more blocking what is instinctive than it is for a man who, muscles or no, chooses not to be a weight lifter.

Betty Rollin, "Motherhood: Who Needs It?" in *Look* (1970)

18 Through its prohibition on birth control, the Church has suggested that the only right way to have children is . . . a kind of forced labor culminating in the production of another soul for God.

What kind of a God stands like Lee Iacocca at the end of an assembly line, driving his workers with a greedy "More! More!" while the automobiles pile up in showrooms and on freeways and in used-car lots and finally junkyards, his only satisfaction the gross production figures at the end of every quarter?

Nancy Mairs, *Ordinary Time* (1993)

1 The greatest of all contraceptives is affluence.

Indira Gandhi, *Freedom Is the Starting Point* (1976)

2 If one is willing to have children, Rhythm is probably the best method of contraception.

Elizabeth Hawes, *Anything But Love* (1948)

3 Joan . . . had five kids in the '60s before she became a recovering Catholic ("We used the rhythm method for the last three").

Mary Kay Blakely, *American Mom* (1994)

4 Sex is still the leading cause of pregnancy.

Frederica Mathewes-Green, "Unplanned Parenthood," in *Policy Review* (1991)

See also Condoms.

## ❧ BIRTHDAY

5 Happy birthday to you.

Patty Smith Hill and Mildred J. Hill, song originally titled "Good Morning All," in *Song Stories for the Kindergarten* (1893)

6 It is lovely, when I forget all birthdays, including my own, to find that somebody remembers me.

Ellen Glasgow, *Letters of Ellen Glasgow* (1958)

7 Yours is the year that counts no season; / I can never be sure what age you are.

Vita Sackville-West, *The Garden* (1946)

## ❧ BISEXUALS

8 The time has come, I think, when we must recognize bisexuality as a normal form of human behavior.

Margaret Mead, in *Redbook* (1975)

9 The bisexual experience calls into question traditional definitions of the nature of sexual identity development. Fluid, ambiguous, subversive, multifarious, bisexuality can no longer be denied.

Rebecca Shuster (1987), in Loraine Hutchins and Lani Kaahumanu, *Bi Any Other Name* (1991)

10 Bisexuality invalidates either/or formulation, either/or analysis. . . . If you are free, you are not predictable and you are not controllable. To my mind, that is the keenly positive, politicizing significance of bisexual affirmation: To insist upon complexity, to insist upon the equal validity of all of the components of social/sexual complexity.

June Jordan, "A New Politics of Sexuality," *Technical Difficulties* (1992)

11 Homosexuality was invented by a straight world dealing with its own bisexuality.

Kate Millett, *Flying* (1990)

12 Because our society is so polarized between homosexuals and heterosexuals, the bisexual closet has two doors.

Loraine Hutchins and Lani Kaahumanu, *Bi Any Other Name* (1991)

13 There is one thing new in sexual mores and that is today's bisexual chic. . . . If you can't truthfully claim to be bisexual yourself, the next best thing is to reveal that one, or both, of your parents was.

Helen Lawrenson, *Whistling Girl* (1978)

14 What is new is not bisexuality, but rather the widening of our awareness and acceptance of human capacities for sexual love.

Margaret Mead, in *Redbook* (1975)

15 Bisexuality is not so much a cop-out as a fearful compromise.

Jill Johnston, *Lesbian Nation* (1973)

16 We're here to talk today about everybodyexceptyou. We're working for the rights of everybodyexceptyou. The oppression of everybodyexceptyou has got to end.

Susan Carlton, "This poem can be put off no longer," in Loraine Hutchins and Lani Kaahumanu, *Bi Any Other Name* (1991)

See also Gay Men, Lesbians, Lesbians and Gay Men, Love, Relationships, Sex, Transsexuals.

## ❧ BITTERNESS

1 My bitterness is not an abstract substance, it is as solid as a Christmas cake; I can cut it in slices and hand it round and there is still plenty left, for tomorrow.
  Caitlin Thomas, *Leftover Life to Kill* (1957)

2 If bitterness were a whetstone, I could be sharp as grief.
  Audre Lorde, *The Cancer Journals* (1980)

3 Bitterness hardly cares what food it eats.
  Leslie Ford, *Invitation to Murder* (1954)

4 Vinegar he poured on me all his life; I am well marinated; how can I be honey now?
  Tillie Olsen, title story, *Tell Me a Riddle* (1956)

5 Bitterness had become a habit between them.
  Edna O'Brien, "A Woman by the Seaside," *Mrs. Reinhardt* (1978)

6 Bitterness . . . is the eternal cul-de-sac.
  Agatha Christie, *Murder in Three Acts* (1934)

7 One may have been a fool, but there's no foolishness like being bitter.
  Kathleen Norris, *Bread Into Roses* (1936)

8 I have loved, and bitterness left me for that hour. But there are times when love itself is bitter.
  Agnes Smedley, *Daughter of Earth* (1929)

See also Anger, Resentment.

## ❧ BLACKS

9 Who / can be born / black / and not exult!
  Mari E. Evans, "My Father's Passage," *I Am a Black Woman* (1970)

10 The way I was taught, being black was a plus, always. Being a human being, being in America, and being black, all three were the greatest things that could happen to you. The combination was unbeatable.
  Leontyne Price, in Brian Lanker, *I Dream a World* (1989)

11 we have always loved each other / children  all ways / pass it on.
  Lucille Clifton, "listen children," *Good News About the Earth* (1972)

12 Anything I have ever learned of any consequence, I have learned from Black people. I have never been bored by *any* Black person, ever.
  Toni Morrison, in Roseann P. Bell, Bettye J. Parker, and Beverly Guy-Sheftall, eds., *Sturdy Black Bridges* (1979)

13 I am here, and you will know that I am the best and will hear me. The color of my skin or the kink of my hair or the spread of my mouth has nothing to do with what you are listening to.
  Leontyne Price, in *Time* (1985)

14 For though I'm black, yet am I also fair / and in my mortal form, Thine doth appear.
  Sor Juana Inés de la Cruz, "The Divine Narcissus" (1690), in Irene Nicholson, *A Guide to Mexican Poetry* (1968)

15 I am dark but fair, / Black but fair.
  Alice Meynell, "The Moon to the Sun!" *Poems* (1893)

16 I adore my black skin and my kinky hair. The Negro hair is more educated than the white man's hair. Because with Negro hair, where you put it, it stays. It's obedient. The hair of the white, just give one quick movement, and it's out of place. It won't obey. If reincarnation exists I want to come back black.
  Carolina Maria de Jesus (1958), *Child of the Dark* (1962)

17 Black people are nature, they possess the secret of joy.
  Mirella Ricciardi, *African Saga* (1982)

18 I really hope no white person ever has cause / to write about me / because they never understand / Black love is Black wealth and they'll / probably talk about my hard childhood / and never understand that / all the while I was quite happy.
  Nikki Giovanni, "Nikki-Rosa," *Black Judgement* (1968)

19 There is an incredible amount of magic and feistiness in black men that nobody has been able to wipe out. But everybody has tried.
  Toni Morrison, in Dexter Fisher, ed., *The Third Woman* (1980)

20 I tell you, Joe, little Willie said, / Black is as tired as it is beautiful.
  Carolyn M. Rodgers, "The Revolution Is Resting," *how i got ovah* (1975)

21 When you get up in the morning, you merely put on your clothes. When a colored man gets up in the morning, he puts on his armor.
  Kristin Hunter, *The Landlord* (1966)

1 It is utterly exhausting being Black in America—physically, mentally, and emotionally. While many minority groups and women feel similar stress, there is no respite or escape from your badge of color.

    Marian Wright Edelman, *The Measure of Our Success* (1992)

2 The most fundamental truth to be told in any art form, as far as Blacks are concerned, is that America is killing us.

    Sonia Sanchez, in Mari E. Evans, ed., *Black Women Writers (1950-1980)* (1984)

3 "Crisis" seems to be too mild a word to describe conditions in countless African-American communities. It is beyond crisis when in the richest nation in the world, African Americans in Harlem live shorter lives than the people of Bangladesh, one of the poorest nations of the world.

    Johnnetta B. Cole, speech (1990)

4 To be a colored man in America . . . and enjoy it, you must be greatly daring, greatly stolid, greatly humorous and greatly sensitive. And at all times a philosopher.

    Jessie Fauset, *Comedy American Style* (1933)

5 Raising Black children—female and male—in the mouth of a racist, sexist, suicidal dragon is perilous and chancy. If they cannot love and resist at the same time, they will probably not survive.

    Audre Lorde, "Man Child," in *Conditions* (1979)

6 To me the phrase, "Act like you have some sense," probably spoken by at least one Black woman to every Black child who ever lived, is a cryptic warning that says volumes about keeping your feet on the ground and your ass covered.

    Barbara Smith, *Home Girls* (1983)

7 As a blackwoman / the bearing of my child / is a political act.

    Maud Sulter, title poem, *As a Blackwoman* (1985)

8 The drums of Africa still beat in my heart. They will not let me rest while there is a single Negro boy or girl without a chance to prove his worth.

    Mary McLeod Bethune, in *Who, the Magazine About People* (1941)

9 I am a child of America / a step child / raised in the back room.

    Pat Parker, *Movement in Black* (1978)

10 It is not healthy when a nation lives within a nation, as colored Americans are living inside America. A nation cannot live confident of its tomorrow if its refugees are among its own citizens.

    Pearl S. Buck, *What America Means to Me* (1943)

11 Black people cannot and will not become integrated into American society on any terms but those of self-determination and autonomy.

    Gerda Lerner, *Black Women in White America* (1972)

12 The first thing you do is to forget that i'm Black. / Second, you must never forget that i'm Black.

    Pat Parker, "For the White Person Who Wants to Know How to Be My Friend," *Movement in Black* (1978)

13 Take us generally as a people, we are neither lazy nor idle . . . although I acknowledge, with extreme sorrow, that there are some who never were and never will be serviceable to society. And have you not a similar class among yourselves?

    Maria W. Stewart (1832), in Dorothy Porter, ed., *Early Negro Writing 1760-1837* (1971)

14 Black people are the only segment in American society that is defined by its weakest elements. Every other segment is defined by its highest achievement. We have to turn that around.

    Jewell Jackson McCabe, in Brian Lanker, *I Dream a World* (1989)

15 The various and varied complexions in our group . . . range from the deep black to the fairest white with all the colors of the rainbow thrown in for good measure. When twenty or thirty of us meet, it is as hard to find three or four with the same complexion as it would be catch greased lightning in a bottle.

    Mary Church Terrell, in *The Washington Post* (1949)

16 It is an incontrovertible truth that there is no such thing as an unmixed black on the American continent.

    Pauline E. Hopkins, *Contending Forces* (1900)

17 Even today it is erroneously believed that all racial development among colored people has taken place since emancipation. It is impossible of belief for some, that little circles of educated men and women of color have existed since the Revolutionary War.

    Pauline E. Hopkins, *Contending Forces* (1900)

18 We live surrounded by white images, and white in this world is synonymous with the good, light,

beauty, success, so that, despite ourselves sometimes, we run after that whiteness and deny our
darkness, which has been made into the symbol of
all that is evil and inferior.

Paule Marshall, title story, *Reena* (1983)

1 she never wanted / no never once / did she wanna
/ be white/to pass / dreamed only of bein darker.

Mary Hope Lee, "on not bein," in Cherríe Moraga and
Gloria Anzaldúa, eds., *This Bridge Called My Back* (1983)

2 To be black and female, in a society which is both
racist and sexist, is to be in a unique position of
having nowhere to go but up.

Rosemary Brown, in John Robert Colombo, *Colombo's
Concise Canadian Quotations* (1976)

3 Any woman who has a great deal to offer the world
is in trouble. And if she's a black woman, she's in
deep trouble.

Hazel Scott, in Margo Jefferson, "Great (Hazel) Scott!" *Ms.*
(1974)

4 Let me state here and now that the black woman in
America can justly be described as a "slave of a
slave."

Frances M. Beal, "Double Jeopardy: To Be Black and
Female," in Robin Morgan, ed., *Sisterhood Is Powerful* (1970)

5 No other group in America has so had their identity socialized out of existence as have black
women. . . . When black people are talked about
the focus tends to be on black *men*; and when
women are talked about the focus tends to be on
*white* women.

bell hooks, *Ain't I a Woman?* (1981)

6 And she had nothing to fall back on; not maleness,
not whiteness, not ladyhood, not anything. And
out of the profound desolation of her reality she
may very well have invented herself.

Toni Morrison, "What the Black Women Think About
Women's Lib," in *The New York Times Magazine* (1971)

7 The colored woman of today occupies, one may
say, a unique position in this country. In a period
of itself transitional and unsettled, her status seems
one of the least ascertainable and definitive of all
the forces which make for our civilization. She is
confronted by both a woman question and a race
problem.

Anna Julia Cooper, *A Voice From the South* (1892)

8 Only the BLACK WOMAN can say "when and
where I enter, in the quiet, undisputed dignity of

my womanhood, without violence and without su-
ing or special patronage, then and there the whole
. . . race enters with me."

Anna Julia Cooper, *A Voice From the South* (1892)

9 Usually, when people talk about the "strength" of
black women they are referring to the way in which
they perceive black women coping with oppression. They ignore the reality that to be strong in the
face of oppression is not the same as overcoming
oppression, that endurance is not to be confused
with transformation. . . . The tendency to romanticize the black female experience that began in the
feminist movement was reflected in the culture as
a whole.

bell hooks, *Ain't I a Woman?* (1981)

10 On the road to equality there is no better place for
blacks to detour around American values than in
foregoing its example in the treatment of its
women and the organization of its family life.

Eleanor Holmes Norton, "For Sadie and Maude," in Robin
Morgan, ed., *Sisterhood Is Powerful* (1970)

11 The Black emphasis must be not *against white* but
*FOR Black*.

Gwendolyn Brooks, in Mari E. Evans, ed., *Black Women
Writers (1950-1980)* (1984)

12 Black ice is the smoothest naturally occurring ice
there is, as if nature were condescending to art. . . .
Black ice is an act of nature as elusive as grace, and
far more rare. . . . I have never skated on black ice,
but perhaps my children will. They'll know it, at
least, when it appears: that the earth can stretch
smooth and unbroken like grace, and they'll know
as they know my voice that they were meant to
have their share.

Lorene Cary, *Black Ice* (1991)

See also Bigotry, Blacks and Whites, Discrimination, Oppression, Prejudice, Racism.

## ❦ BLACKS AND WHITES

13 White folks needs what black folks got just as much
as black folks needs what white folks got, and we's
all got to stay here mongst each other and git along,
that's what.

Margaret Walker, *Jubilee* (1966)

1 Far as I'm concerned, friendship between black and white don't mean that much 'cause it usually ain't on a equal basis. . . . Maybe one day whites and blacks can be real friends, but right now the country ain't built that way.

> Mildred D. Taylor, *Roll of Thunder, Hear My Cry* (1976)

2 One very important difference between white people and black people is that white people think that you *are* your work. . . . Now, black people think that my work is just what I have to do to get what I want.

> May Anna Madison, in *Drylongso* (1980)

3 It is not the destiny of Black America to repeat white America's mistakes. But we will, if we mistake the trappings of success in a sick society for the signs of a meaningful life.

> Audre Lorde, in Mari E. Evans, ed., *Black Women Writers (1950-1980)* (1984)

See also Bigotry, Blacks, Discrimination, Oppression, Prejudice, Racism, Whites.

## ॐ BLAME

4 There's folks 'ud stand on their heads and then say the fault was i' their boots.

> George Eliot, *Adam Bede* (1859)

5 My parents . . . had decided early on that all of the problems in my family had somehow to do with me. All roads led to Roseyville, a messy, chaotic town where, as parents, they were required to visit, but could never get out of quick enough or find a decent parking place.

> Roseanne Arnold, *My Lives* (1994)

See also Responsibility.

## ॐ BLESSINGS

6 Stretch out your hand!—let no human soul wait for a benediction.

> Marie Corelli, *The Master Christian* (1900)

7 All the great blessings of my life / Are present in my thoughts to-day.

> Phoebe Cary, "My Blessings," *Poems and Parodies* (1853)

## ॐ BOATS

8 The only thing a canoe really demands of you is a nice sense of poise, and a getting back to those antique laws of equilibrium, laws that get lost in the hurrying world of today.

> Leslie Glendower Peabody, "The Canoe and the Woman," in *Outing* (1901)

9 Boats, like pet dogs, were leashed to the docks, and one little tug looking like a spitz growled at our side, sticking its nose out of the green, loose water as though it were trying to bite.

> Djuna Barnes, "The Hem of Manhattan," in *The New York Morning Telegraph Sunday Magazine* (1917)

See also Ships.

## ॐ BODY

10 The body is a sacred garment.

> Martha Graham, *Blood Memory* (1991)

11 I believe that the physical is the geography of the being.

> Louise Nevelson, *Dawns + Dusks* (1976)

12 The body is shaped, disciplined, honored, and in time, trusted.

> Martha Graham, *Blood Memory* (1991)

13 Over the years our bodies become walking autobiographies, telling friends and strangers alike of the minor and major stresses of our lives.

> Marilyn Ferguson, *The Aquarian Conspiracy* (1980)

14 The body says what words cannot.

> Martha Graham, in "Martha Graham Reflects on Her Art and a Life in Dance," *The New York Times* (1985)

15 The body is wiser than its inhabitants. The body *is* the soul. We ignore its aches, its pains, its eruptions, because we fear the truth. The body is God's messenger.

> Erica Jong, *Fear of Fifty* (1994)

16 The body has its own way of knowing, a knowing that has little to do with logic, and much to do with truth, little to do with control, and much to do with acceptance, little to do with division and analysis, and much to do with union.

> Marilyn Sewell, *Cries of the Spirit* (1991)

1 Body my house / my horse my hound / what will I do / when you are fallen.

  May Swenson, "Question," *To Mix With Time* (1963)

2 This morning it occurred to me for the first time that my body, my faithful companion and friend, truer and better known to me than my own soul, may be after all only a sly beast who will end by devouring his master.

  Marguerite Yourcenar, *Memoirs of Hadrian* (1951)

3 We think in youth that our bodies are identical with ourselves and have the same interests, but discover later that they are heartless companions who have been accidentally yoked with us, and who are as likely as not, in our extreme sickness or old age, to treat us with less mercy than we would have received at the hands of the worst bandits.

  Rebecca West, *Black Lamb and Grey Falcon* (1941)

4 This body is the seat of all good and bad.

  Yeshe Tsogyel (8th cent.), in Keith Dowman, *Sky Dancer* (1984)

5 We should be provided with a new body about the age of thirty or so when we have learnt to attend to it with consideration.

  Freya Stark (1927), *Letters From Syria* (1942)

6 At my age the bones are water in the morning until food is given them.

  Pearl S. Buck, *The Good Earth* (1931)

7 We have so many words for states of mind, and so few words for the states of the body.

  Jeanne Moreau, in *The New York Times* (1976)

8 The body is simple as a turtle / and straight as a dog: / the body cannot lie.

  Marge Piercy, "A shadow play for guilt," *To Be of Use* (1973)

9 Movement never lies.

  Martha Graham, *Blood Memory* (1991)

10 The gesture is the thing truly expressive of the individual—as we think so will we act.

  Martha Graham, in John Heilpern, "The Amazing Martha," *The Observer Magazine* (1979)

11 The mind has great advantages over the body; however the body often furnishes little treats . . . which offer the mind relief from sad thoughts.

  Ninon de Lenclos (1698), in Edgar H. Cohen, *Mademoiselle Libertine* (1970)

12 I will be good to my stomach, / Tomorrow; listen, and believe it / For a while.

  Kathleen Norris, "Stomach," *Falling Off* (1971)

13 Ro doesn't stand like Brent or Dad. His hands hang kind of stiffly from the shoulder joints, and when he moves, his palms are tucked tight against his thighs, his stomach sticks out like a slightly pregnant woman's. Each culture establishes its own manly posture, different ways of claiming space.

  Bharati Mukherjee, "Orbiting," *The Middleman* (1988)

14 Mr. Richards is a tall man with what must have been a magnificent build before his stomach went in for a career of its own.

  Margaret Halsey, *Some of My Best Friends Are Soldiers* (1944)

15 His main problem was apparently whether to wear his belt above or below his paunch. Above was said to indicate optimism, below a sign of depression.

  P.D. James, *Devices and Desires* (1989)

16 I've got a stomach now as well as a behind. And I mean—well, you can't pull it in both ways, can you? . . . I've made it a rule to pull in my stomach and let my behind look after itself.

  Agatha Christie, "The Dressmaker's Doll," *Double Sin* (1960)

17 I had to face the facts, I was pear-shaped. I was a bit depressed because I hate pears. 'Specially their shape.

  Charlotte Bingham, *Coronet Among the Weeds* (1963)

18 Her large hips fluttered as if a bird imprisoned in her pelvis was attempting flight.

  Maya Angelou, *The Heart of a Woman* (1981)

19 these hips are big hips / . . . / they don't like to be held back. / these hips have never been enslaved, / they go where they want to go / they do what they want to do. / these hips are mighty hips. / these hips are magic hips.

  Lucille Clifton, *Two-Headed Woman* (1980)

20 You washed those parts quickly, without looking at them. They had no names. Good people were required to refer to them with prepositions, rather than straightforwardly with nouns, as with decent things like tables and chairs. "Down there." "In between." "Behind."

  Shirley Abbott, *The Bookmaker's Daughter* (1991)

1 Ava was young and slender and proud. And she had It. It, hell; she had Those.

> Dorothy Parker, "Madame Glyn Lectures on 'It'," in *The New Yorker* (1927)

2 So the legs are a little short, the knees maybe knock a little but who listens?

> Gertrude Berg, *Molly and Me* (1961)

See also Appearance, Beauty, Bodybuilding, Ears, Eyes, Face, Feet, Hair, Hands, Nudity, Teeth.

## ❧ BODYBUILDING

3 Bodybuilding is about making oneself seem larger than life.

> Mariah Burton Nelson, *Are We Winning Yet?* (1991)

See also Body, Sports.

## ❧ BOOKS

4 There is no Frigate like a Book / To take us Lands away.

> Emily Dickinson (1873), in Mabel Loomis Todd, ed., *Letters of Emily Dickinson*, vol. 1 (1894)

5 Books are the carriers of civilization. Without books, history is silent, literature dumb, science crippled, thought and speculation at a standstill.

> Barbara W. Tuchman, in *Authors' League Bulletin* (1979)

6 We are made whole / By books, as by great spaces and the stars.

> Mary Carolyn Davies, "Books," *The Skyline Trail* (1924)

7 Just the knowledge that a good book is awaiting one at the end of a long day makes that day happier.

> Kathleen Norris, *Hands Full of Living* (1931)

8 My home is where my books are.

> Ellen Thompson, *A Book of Hours* (1909)

9 I hoard books. They are people who do not leave.

> Anne Sexton (1962), in Linda Gray Sexton and Lois Ames, eds., *Anne Sexton* (1977)

10 I do love secondhand books that open to the page some previous owner read oftenest.

> Helene Hanff, *84, Charing Cross Road* (1970)

11 I only really love a book when I have read it at least four times.

> Nancy Spain, *A Funny Thing Happened on the Way* (1964)

12 Books, *books*, BOOKS kept / Insanely breeding. / De Quincey wept, / And went on reading.

> Helen Bevington, "De Quincey Wept," *Nineteen Million Elephants* (1950)

13 It was clear that the books owned the shop rather than the other way about. Everywhere they had run wild and taken possession of their habitat, breeding and multiplying and clearly lacking any strong hand to keep them down.

> Agatha Christie, *The Clocks* (1963)

14 It is a generally received opinion that there are too many books in the world already. I cannot, however, subscribe to any Institution that proposes to alter this state of affairs, because I find no consensus of opinion as to which are the superfluous books.

> Mary H. Kingsley, *West African Studies* (1899)

15 If I read a book that impresses me, I have to take myself firmly in hand, before I mix with other people; otherwise they would think my mind rather queer.

> Anne Frank, *The Diary of a Young Girl* (1952)

16 She is too fond of books, and it has turned her brain.

> Louisa May Alcott, *Work* (1873)

17 Books . . . are like lobster shells, we surround ourselves with 'em, then we grow out of 'em and leave 'em behind, as evidence of our earlier stages of development.

> Dorothy L. Sayers, *The Unpleasantness at the Bellona Club* (1928)

18 There are books that one needs maturity to enjoy just as there are books an adult can come on too late to savor.

> Phyllis McGinley, "The Consolations of Illiteracy," *The Province of the Heart* (1959)

19 Fitting people with books is about as difficult as fitting them with shoes.

> Sylvia Beach, *Shakespeare and Company* (1956)

1 I was born with the impression that what happened in books was much more reasonable, and interesting, and *real*, in some ways, than what happened in life.

Anne Tyler, in Janet Sternburg, ed., *The Writer on Her Work*, vol. 1 (1980)

2 I had a perfect confidence, still unshaken, in books. If you read enough you would reach the point of no return. You would cross over and arrive on the safe side. There you would drink the strong waters and become addicted, perhaps demented—but a Reader.

Helen Bevington, *The House Was Quiet and the World Was Calm* (1971)

3 He felt about books as doctors feel about medicines, or managers about plays—cynical but hopeful.

Rose Macaulay, *Crewe Train* (1926)

4 Which is to say that I can easily do without people (there are days when I could easily do without myself), and that in the country of books where I dwell, the dead can count entirely as much as the living.

Adrienne Monnier, in Richard McDougall, tr., *The Very Rich Hours of Adrienne Monnier* (1976)

5 The wonderful thing about books is that they allow us to enter imaginatively into someone else's life. And when we do that, we learn to sympathize with other people. But the real surprise is that we also learn truths about ourselves, about our own lives, that somehow we hadn't been able to see before.

Katherine Paterson, in *The Horn Book* (1991)

6 The lover of books is a miner, searching for gold all his life long. He finds his nuggets, his heart leaps in his breast; he cannot believe in his good fortune. Traversing a slow page, to come upon a lode of the pure shining metal is to exult inwardly for greedy hours. It belongs to no one else; it is not interchangeable.

Kathleen Norris, "Beauty in Letters," *These I Like Best* (1941)

7 I believe I belong to the last literary generation, the last generation, that is, for whom books are a religion.

Erica Jong, *The Devil at Large* (1993)

8 Let us secure not such books as people want, but books just above their wants, and they will reach up to take what is put out for them.

Maria Mitchell (1887), in Phebe Mitchell Kendall, ed., *Maria Mitchell* (1896)

9 Books, to the reading child, are so much more than books—they are dreams and knowledge, they are a future, and a past.

Esther Meynell, *A Woman Talking* (1940)

10 There is no substitute for books in the life of a child.

Mary Ellen Chase, *Recipe for a Magic Childhood* (1952)

11 The memory of having been read to is a solace one carries through adulthood. It can wash over a multitude of parental sins.

Kathleen Rockwell Lawrence, *The Boys I Didn't Kiss* (1990)

12 When I was about eight, I decided that the most wonderful thing, next to a human being, was a book.

Margaret Walker, in Brian Lanker, *I Dream a World* (1989)

13 We raked books off the shelves by the dozen and hauled them along on picnics, to haylofts, up oak trees, to bath and to bed. The one terrifying possibility was to find oneself without a book.

Kathleen Norris, *These I Like Best* (1941)

14 It had been startling and disappointing to me to find out that story books had been written by *people*, that books were not natural wonders, coming up of themselves like grass.

Eudora Welty, *One Writer's Beginnings* (1984)

15 I would be most content if my children grew up to be the kind of people who think decorating consists mostly of building enough bookshelves.

Anna Quindlen, "Bookshelves," *Thinking Out Loud* (1993)

16 Critics: people who make monuments out of books. Biographers: people who make books out of monuments. Poets: people who raze monuments. Publishers: people who sell rubble. Readers: people who buy it.

Cynthia Ozick, *Trust* (1966)

17 A book cannot easily be too bad for the general public, but may easily be too good.

Marie von Ebner-Eschenbach, *Aphorisms* (1893)

18 Once a book is published, it no longer belongs to me. My creative task is done. The work now belongs to the creative mind of my readers. I had my turn to make of it what I would, now it is their turn.

Katherine Paterson, *Gates of Excellence* (1981)

19 *I* don't think four thousand copies such a wretched sale. You should try to take a longer view of it. If

you had sold four thousand female tortoiseshell kittens, for instance, you would think you had done marvels.

Sylvia Townsend Warner (1956), in William Maxwell, ed., *Letters: Sylvia Townsend Warner* (1982)

1 There is a secret and wholesome conviction in the heart of every man or woman who has written a book that it should be no easy matter for an intelligent reader to lay down that book unfinished. There is a pardonable impression among reviewers that half an hour in its company is sufficient.

Agnes Repplier, "Reviewers and Reviewed," *In the Dozy Hours* (1894)

2 Like all former thinkers, I'm writing a book.

Lillian Hellman, *The Searching Wind* (1944)

3 I sat staring up at a shelf in my workroom from which thirty-one books identically dressed in neat dark green leather stared back at me with a sort of cold hostility like children who resent their parents. Don't stare at us like that! they said. Don't blame us if we didn't turn out to be the perfection you expected. We didn't ask to be brought into the world.

Edna Ferber, *A Kind of Magic* (1963)

4 I suppose anyone who has ever written a travel book has had the experience of being accosted by a reader with blood in his eye and a lawsuit in his voice.

Ilka Chase, *Elephants Arrive at Half-Past Five* (1963)

5 If we are told, for example, that "The Raj Quartet" is a four-volume epic about the end of British rule in India, we're apt to smile and say, "How interesting." Meaning we feel a certain duty to read such a tome, but never will unless we have both legs in traction.

Martha Bayles, in *The Wall Street Journal* (1984)

6 I asked how long it was. "Eight hundred and ninety-seven pages," he said. Then he added, earnestly, "You don't suppose they'll think I wrote it in a fit of pique."

Renata Adler, *Speedboat* (1986)

7 Reading it is . . . a sort of permanent occupation.

Katherine Anne Porter, on Gertrude Stein's *Making of Americans* (1927), *The Days Before* (1952)

8 This is a book lined with hard facts and stitched up with strong opinions.

Suzy Menkes, book review, in *The London Times* (1984)

9 I can imagine now that a time will come, that it is almost upon us, when no one will love books. . . . It is no accident, I think, that books and nature (as we know it) may disappear simultaneously from human experience. There is no mind-body split.

Andrea Dworkin, "First Love," in Julia Wolf Mazow, ed., *The Woman Who Lost Her Names* (1980)

See also Anthologies, Borrowing, Libraries, Prefaces, Publishing, Reading, Self-Help Books, Titles, Writing.

## ❦ BORDERS

10 Living on borders and in margins, keeping intact one's shifting and multiple identity and integrity, is like trying to swim in a new element, an "alien" element.

Gloria Anzaldúa, *Borderlands/La Frontera* (1987)

11 I'm sick of seeing and touching / Both sides of things / Sick of being the damn bridge for everybody.

Kate Rushin, "The Bridge Poem," in Cherríe Moraga and Gloria Anzaldúa, eds., *This Bridge Called My Back* (1983)

12 The U.S.-Mexican border *es una herida abierta* where the Third World grates against the first and bleeds. And before a scab forms it hemorrhages again, the lifeblood of two worlds merging to form a third country—a border culture.

Gloria Anzaldúa, *Borderlands/La Frontera* (1987)

13 It is hopeless to try to convert some borders into seams.

Jane Jacobs, *The Death and Life of Great American Cities* (1961)

See also Immigrants, Outsiders, Refugees.

## ❦ BOREDOM

14 Boredom is the fear of self.

Comtesse Diane, *Les Glanes de la Vie* (1898)

15 Were it not for the amusement of our books, we should be moped to death for want of occupation.

It rains incessantly.... We tickle ourselves in order to laugh; to so low an ebb are we reduced.

> Marie de Rabutin-Chantal, Marquise de Sévigné (1671), *Letters of Madame de Sévigné to Her Daughter and Her Friends*, vol. 1 (1811)

1 I am tired to death! tired of everything! I would give the universe for a disposition less difficult to please. Yet, after all, what is there to give pleasure? When one has seen one thing, one has seen everything.

> Fanny Burney, *Cecilia* (1782)

2 She wanted something to happen—something, anything; she did not know what.

> Kate Chopin, *The Awakening* (1899)

3 Every time I think I've touched bottom as far as boredom is concerned, new vistas of ennui open up.

> Margaret Halsey, *No Laughing Matter* (1977)

4 One of the dreariest spots on life's road is the point of conviction that nothing will ever again happen to you.

> Faith Baldwin, *The West Wind* (1962)

5 I feel monotony and death to be almost the same.

> Charlotte Brontë, *Shirley* (1849)

6 Ennui is the disease of hearts without feeling, and of minds without resources.

> Marie-Jeanne Roland (1793), in Lydia Maria Child, *Memoirs of Madame de Staël and of Madame Roland* (1847)

7 Bored people, unless they sleep a lot, are cruel.

> Renata Adler, *Speedboat* (1976)

8 It was a fête worse than death.

> Barbara Stanwyck, in Reader's Digest editors, *Fun Fare* (1949)

9 Peel me a grape, Beulah!

> Mae West, *I'm No Angel* (1933)

See also Bores, Dullness, Restlessness.


## ❧ BORES

10 A bore is a person not interested in you.

> Mary Pettibone Poole, *A Glass Eye at a Keyhole* (1938)

11 Bores: People who talk of themselves, when you are thinking only of yourself.

> Countess of Blessington, *Desultory Thoughts and Reflections* (1839)

12 [A bore is] a vacuum cleaner of society, sucking up everything and giving nothing.

> Elsa Maxwell, *How to Do It* (1957)

13 He's the kind of bore who's here today and here tomorrow.

> Binnie Barnes, in *The Wisdom of Women* (1971)

14 Under pressure people admit to murder, setting fire to the village church, or robbing a bank, but never to being bores.

> Elsa Maxwell, *How to Do It* (1957)

15 The bore is usually considered a harmless creature, or of that class of irrational bipeds who hurt only themselves.

> Maria Edgeworth, *Thoughts on Bores* (1826)

16 The bore is good for promoting sleep; but though he causeth sleep in others, it is uncertain whether he ever sleeps himself; as few can keep awake in his company long enough to see. It is supposed that when he sleeps it is with his mouth open.

> Maria Edgeworth, *Thoughts on Bores* (1826)

17 It is always your heaviest bore who is astonished at the tameness of modern celebrities: naturally; for a little of his company has reduced them to a state of flaccid fatigue.

> George Eliot, *Impressions of Theophrastus Such* (1879)

18 A cardinal rule was that you never sat interesting people with bores. You put all the bores at one table. They didn't know they were bores, and they had a marvelous time.

> Joyce Haber, *The Users* (1976)

19 I am one of those unhappy persons who inspire bores to the highest flights of their art.

> Edith Sitwell, in Elizabeth Salter, *The Last Years of a Rebel* (1967)

20 Definitely a dreary woman. Rather like an earwig. She's a devoted mother. So are earwigs, I believe.

> Agatha Christie, *Dumb Witness* (1937)

21 If you have once thoroughly bored somebody it is next to impossible to unbore him.

> Elizabeth von Arnim, *The Enchanted April* (1922)

1 Tallulah [Bankhead] never bored anyone, and I consider that humanitarianism of a very high order indeed.

    Anita Loos, in *The New York Times* (1968)

See also Boredom.


## ❧ BORROWING

2 Have you got De Tocqueville's *Journey to America*? Somebody borrowed mine and never gave it back. Why is it that people who wouldn't dream of stealing anything else think it's perfectly all right to steal books?

    Helene Hanff, *84, Charing Cross Road* (1970)

3 They borrow books they will not buy, / They have no ethics or religions; / I wish some kind Burbankian guy / Would cross my books with homing pigeons.

    Carolyn Wells, "Book Borrowers" (1900)

4 My brother was what he is now; I never had a cent that he didn't borrow. He calls it borrowing.

    Kathleen Norris, *Woman in Love* (1935)

5 Everything they had was borrowed; they had nothing of their own at all.

    Mary Norton, *The Borrowers* (1952)


## ❧ BOSTON

6 Boston—wrinkled, spindly-legged, depleted of nearly all her spiritual and cutaneous oils, provincial, self-esteeming—has gone on spending and spending her inflated bills of pure reputation, decade after decade.

    Elizabeth Hardwick, "Boston" (1959), *A View of My Own* (1962)

7 Harvard (across the river in Cambridge) and Boston are two ends of one mustache. . . . Without the faculty, the visitors, the events that Harvard brings to the life here, Boston would be intolerable to anyone except genealogists, antique dealers, and those who find repletion in a closed local society.

    Elizabeth Hardwick, "Boston" (1959), *A View of My Own* (1962)

8 A profit is not without honor save in Boston.

    Carolyn Wells, "Inexpensive Cynicisms," *Folly for the Wise* (1904)

See also New England.


## ❧ BRAIN

9 The brain is a muscle / of busy hills, the struggle / of unthought things with things / eternally thought.

    Joyce Carol Oates, "The Grave Dwellers," *Love and Its Derangements* (1970)

10 The softest, freest, most pliable and changeful living substance is the brain—the hardest and most iron-bound as well.

    Charlotte Perkins Gilman, *The Home* (1903)

11 The brain is only three pounds of blood, dream, and electricity, and yet from that mortal stew come Beethoven's sonatas. Dizzie Gillespie's jazz. Audrey Hepburn's wish to spend the last month of her life in Somalia, saving children.

    Diane Ackerman, *A Natural History of Love* (1994)

12 I like going from one lighted room to another, such is my brain to me; lighted rooms.

    Virginia Woolf (1924), in Leonard Woolf, ed., *A Writer's Diary* (1953)

13 I feel like a baited bull and look a wreck, and as for my unfortunate brain well I saw it neatly described yesterday on an automatic thing in the tube: This machine is EMPTY till further notice.

    Jean Rhys, *Letters 1931-1966* (1984)

14 There is no female mind. The brain is not an organ of sex. As well speak of a female liver.

    Charlotte Perkins Gilman, *Women and Economics* (1898)

15 Nature is perfectly impartial. Brain has no sex!

    Margaret Deland, *The Rising Tide* (1916)

16 The grim possibility is that she who "hides her brains" will, more than likely, end up with a mate who is only equal to a woman with "hidden brains" or none at all.

    Lorraine Hansberry, "In Defense of the Equality of Men," in Sandra M. Gilbert and Susan Gubar, eds., *The Norton Anthology of Literature by Women* (1985)

1 He's very clever, but sometimes his brains go to his head.

> Margot Asquith, *The Autobiography of Margot Asquith* (1936)

2 She had one of those small, summery brains, that flower early and run to seed.

> Dorothy L. Sayers, *Gaudy Night* (1935)

3 "What was her name again?" asked the old lady, whose brain was like a worn-out strainer, very fine in places but with big holes in others.

> Vicki Baum, *Mortgage on Life* (1946)

See also Intelligence, Mind, Thinking.

## ⟡ BREVITY

4 Brevity is the soul of lingerie.

> Dorothy Parker (1916), in Marion Meade, *Dorothy Parker: What Fresh Hell Is This?* (1988)

5 The brightest light burns the quickest.

> Olive Beatrice Muir, *With Malice Toward None* (1900)

## ⟡ BRIDGE

6 When the human passions are ebbing, bridge takes their place.

> Anne Shaw, *But Such Is Life* (1931)

7 Bridge is a social but not a very sociable game—that is, if you take it seriously, as most bridge players do.

> Ruth Mills Teague, "Conversation Piece," in *Ladies' Home Journal* (1947)

8 One of the first things a bridge player learns is to take it on the shin.

> Kay Ingram, in *The Saturday Evening Post* (1950)

See also Hobbies.

## ⟡ BRIDGES

9 The bridge is the most trodden part of the road.

> Emily Taylor, *Hither and Thither* (1938)

10 Bridges are places where two ways meet, yet never meet. They provide safe conduct but are not built for sanctuary.

> Emily Taylor, *Hither and Thither* (1938)

## ⟡ BROKEN HEART

11 While nearly every way of falling in love is kind, every way of getting out of love is cruel.

> J.E. Buckrose, "Broken Engagements," *What I Have Gathered* (1923)

12 There were many ways of breaking a heart. Stories were full of hearts being broken by love, but what really broke a heart was taking away its dream—whatever the dream might be.

> Pearl S. Buck, *The Patriot* (1939)

13 'Tis not love's going hurts my days, / But that it went in little ways.

> Edna St. Vincent Millay, "The Spring and the Fall," *The Harp-Weaver* (1923)

14 Love dies because its birth was an error.

> Susan Sontag, "The Artist As Exemplary Sufferer," *Against Interpretation* (1966)

15 where have you gone / with your confident / walk your / crooked smile the / rent money / in one pocket and / my heart / in another.

> Mari E. Evans, "Where Have You Gone," in Dudley Randall, ed., *The Black Poets* (1971)

16 In any triangle, who is the betrayer, who the unseen rival, and who the humiliated lover? Oneself, oneself, and no one but oneself!

> Erica Jong, *How to Save Your Own Life* (1977)

17 The best remedy for a bruised heart is not, as so many people seem to think, repose upon a manly bosom. Much more efficacious are honest work, physical activity, and the sudden acquisition of wealth.

> Dorothy L. Sayers, *Have His Carcase* (1932)

18 The time you spend grieving over a man should never exceed the amount of time you actually spent with him.

> Rita Rudner, *Naked Beneath My Clothes* (1992)

19 A broken heart is what makes life so wonderful five years later, when you see the guy in an elevator and he is fat and smoking a cigar and saying long-time-

no-see. If he hadn't broken your heart, you couldn't have that glorious feeling of relief!

Phyllis Battelle, in *The New York Journal-American* (1962)

1 It is only the happy who are hard, Gilles. I think perhaps it is better for the world if—if one has a broken heart. One is quick to recognize it, elsewhere. And one has time to think about other people, if there is nothing left to hope for any more.

Helen Waddell, *Peter Abelard* (1933)

2 Pain / Rusts into beauty, too. / I know full well that this is so: / I had a heartbreak long ago.

Mary Carolyn Davies, "Rust," *Youth Riding* (1919)

3 If you can't live without me, why aren't you dead yet?

Cynthia Heimel, book title (1991)

See also Divorce, Estrangement, Heart, Love, Relationships, Sorrow.

## ❧ BROTHERS

4 Blessings on that brother of mine!

Dorothy Wordsworth (1802), in William Knight, ed., *Journals of Dorothy Wordsworth*, vol. 1 (1897)

5 if i cud ever write a poem as beautiful / as u, little 2/yr/old/brotha, / poetry wud go out of bizness.

Sonia Sanchez, "to P.J. (2 yrs old who sed write a poem for me in Portland, Oregon)," *It's a New Day* (1971)

6 What strange creatures brothers are! You would not write to each other but upon the most urgent necessity in the world; and when obliged to take up the pen to say that such a horse is ill, or such a relation dead, it is done in the fewest possible words. You have but one style among you. . . . "Dear Mary, I am just arrived. Bath seems full, and every thing as usual. Yours sincerely." That is the true manly style; that is a complete brother's letter.

Jane Austen, *Mansfield Park* (1814)

7 My brothers, the dragon slayers, capable and strong.

Patricia Penton Leimbach, *All My Meadows* (1977)

See also Siblings.

## ❧ BRUGES

8 When I am far from here, / Bruges, / little city of love, / keep my heart / in the measured beauty / of bells, / ringing their carillon / in the grey steeple.

Caryll Houselander, "Bruges," *The Flowering Tree* (1945)

9 Life is long since asleep in Bruges; fantastic dreams alone breathe over tower and medieval house front, enchanting the eye, inspiring the soul and filling the mind with the great beauty of contemplation.

Katherine Mansfield, "A Truthful Adventure" (1910), *Something Childish* (1924)

## ❧ BULLIES

10 A bully is not reasonable—he is persuaded only by threats.

Marie de France (12th cent.), in Jeanette Beer, tr., *Medieval Fables of Marie de France* (1981)

11 A placated bully is a hand-fed bully.

Edna Ferber, *A Kind of Magic* (1963)

12 The Argument from Intimidation is a confession of intellectual impotence.

Ayn Rand, *The Virtue of Selfishness* (1964)

13 He couldn't see a belt without hitting below it.

Margot Asquith, on David Lloyd George, in Mark Bonham Carter, ed., *The Autobiography of Margot Asquith* (1963)

See also Violence.

## ❧ BUREAUCRACY

14 Of all the 'cracies—Democracy, Plutocracy, Autocracy, Aristocracy, and Bureaucracy—it is the last one at whose door must lie the largest portion of the harm done in our day.

Lady Norah Bentinck, *My Wanderings and Memories* (1924)

15 Bureaucracy, safely repeating today what it did yesterday, rolls on as ineluctably as some vast computer, which, once penetrated by error, duplicates it forever.

Barbara W. Tuchman, *The March of Folly* (1984)

1 Once a policy, like a set of steel rails, had been laid down for him by his superiors, his obedience ran along it unswerving.

Kylie Tennant, *Ride On Stranger* (1943)

2 The civil servant is primarily the master of the short-term solution.

Indira Gandhi, *Freedom Is the Starting Point* (1976)

3 Bureaucracy, the rule of nobody.

Hannah Arendt, *The Human Condition* (1958)

4 Bureaucracy, the rule of no one, has become the modern form of despotism.

Mary McCarthy, "The *Vita Activa*" (1958), *On the Contrary* (1961)

5 Power is sweet, and when you are a little clerk you love its sweetness quite as much as if you were an emperor, and maybe you love it a good deal more.

Ouida, *Wisdom, Wit and Pathos* (1884)

6 People without authority will often simply stand there, reciting the rules like mynah birds. Having no power, they also seem to take a vicious satisfaction in forcing others to comply.

Sue Grafton, "Long Gone," in Marilyn Wallace, ed., *Sisters in Crime 4* (1991)

7 What gets me is you work all your life like a dog, you pay into these government programs. But still, when you need help, the people that's paid to help you they act like it's coming out of their own pocket.

Artie Chandler, in Kathy Kahn, ed., *Hillbilly Women* (1973)

8 The whole evolution of present-day society tends to develop the various forms of bureaucratic oppression and to give them a sort of autonomy in regard to capitalism as such.

Simone Weil (1933), *Oppression and Liberty* (1955)

9 Incompetence is a heavy contender with greed as prime motivator of the bureaucracy. . . . Any time there's money to be had, every manner of opportunist crawls out for a piece. Combined, these fundamentals form the basis of public policy.

Theresa Funiciello, *Tyranny of Kindness* (1993)

10 The speed with which bureaucracy has invaded almost every branch of human activity is something astounding once one thinks about it.

Simone Weil (1933), *Oppression and Liberty* (1955)

11 I had received my first establishment grants in response to applications filed the year before. To the pages of baffling forms I had simply attached a handwritten note saying, "I make dances, not applications. Send the money. Love, Twyla."

Twyla Tharp, *Push Comes to Shove* (1992)

12 It never pays to deal with the flyweights of the world. They take far too much pleasure in thwarting you at every turn.

Sue Grafton, "*H*" *Is for Homicide* (1991)

13 Batista wondered at the purpose of a bureaucracy which could not be subverted.

Karen Tei Yamashita, *Through the Arc of the Rain Forest* (1990)

14 I'm sorry that government involves filling out a lot of forms. . . . I'm sorry myself that we're not still on the frontier, where we could all tote guns, shoot anything that moved and spit to our hearts' content. But we live in a diverse and crowded country, and with civilization comes regulation.

Molly Ivins, in *The Fort Worth Star-Telegram* (1995)

See also Government, Institutions.

## & BUSINESS

15 Business before pleasure.

L.E. Landon, *Francesca Carrara* (1834)

16 Business is other people's money.

Delphine de Girardin, *Marguerite* (1852)

17 One of the first things to be noted in business life is its imperialism. Business is exacting, engrossing, and inelastic.

Margaret E. Sangster, *Winsome Womanhood* (1900)

18 Our Republic is not a pastoral, not a military, not an agricultural, not a nomadic, not a clerical, but a business civilization. Nor is there anything random, casual or accidental about the United States as a business society. It is thoroughly well integrated—organized from top to bottom for the maximum efficiency of commerce and industry, for the maximum efficiency of making money.

Margaret Halsey, *The Folks at Home* (1952)

19 There are . . . other business societies—England, Holland, Belgium and France, for instance. But

ours [the United States] is the only culture now extant in which business so completely dominates the national scene that sports, crime, sex, death, philanthropy and Easter Sunday are money-making propositions.

Margaret Halsey, *The Folks at Home* (1952)

1 In a business society, the role of sex can be summed up in five pitiful little words. There is money in it.

Margaret Halsey, *The Folks at Home* (1952)

2 The military influence on business is morphologic; it relates to the form and structure of organization, considered apart from function. The functions of private industry—the everyday operations—are governed by another formula which has its genesis in a more familiar though not unrelated activity—team sports.

Betty Lehan Harragan, *Games Mother Never Taught You* (1977)

3 Humans must breathe, but corporations must make money.

Alice Embree, "Media Images I: Madison Avenue Brainwashing—the Facts," in Robin Morgan, ed., *Sisterhood Is Powerful* (1970)

4 A business set up just to make money is rarely efficient, because it is not often intended to create wealth; it is only expected to make a fortune for certain people who occupy executive positions.

Sarah Tarleton Colvin, *A Rebel in Thought* (1944)

5 You may break any written law in America with impunity. There is an unwritten law that you break at your peril. It is: Do not attack the profit system.

Mary Heaton Vorse, *A Footnote to Folly* (1935)

6 The business society is interested in training its citizens to make money, and, in this objective, it is often successful. Many of them do make money, and the ones who do not obligingly regard themselves as failures who have wasted the precious gift of life.

Margaret Halsey, *The Folks at Home* (1952)

7 Contrary to popular opinion, the hustle is not a new dance step—it is an old business procedure.

Fran Lebowitz, in *The Observer* (1979)

8 A corporation does seem like a family. Not necessarily that one big happy family they like to boast about when they're hiring you, but, just like every family, a hotbed of passion, rivalry, and dreams that build or destroy careers.

Paula Bernstein, *Family Ties, Corporate Bonds* (1985)

9 Today's corporate family is headed by a "father" who finds the child he never had, the child he always wanted, at the office and guides him (sometimes her) up the ladder.

Paula Bernstein, *Family Ties, Corporate Bonds* (1985)

10 The trouble in corporate America is that too many people with too much power live in a box (their home), then travel the same road every day to another box (their office).

Faith Popcorn, *The Popcorn Report* (1991)

11 It's easy to make money. You put up the sign *Bank* and someone walks in and hands you his money. The façade is everything.

Christina Stead, *House of All Nations* (1938)

12 The single most dangerous word to be spoken in business is "no." The second most dangerous word is "yes." It is possible to avoid saying either.

Lois Wyse, *Company Manners* (1987)

13 You start by saying no to requests. Then if you have to go to yes, OK. But if you start with yes, you can't go to no.

Mildred Perlman, in *The New York Times* (1975)

14 If the word *frankly* or *sincerely* is not uttered in the first ten minutes—or *let us speak openly*—then you are not in the presence of a genuine businessman, and he will certainly go bankrupt: take care.

Françoise Mallet-Joris, *A Letter to Myself* (1963)

15 In a business society, the emotional economy is an economy of scarcity.

Margaret Halsey, *The Folks at Home* (1952)

16 Advertising prods people into wanting more and better things. Of course advertising makes people dissatisfied with what they have—makes them raise their sights. Mighty good thing it does. Nothing could be worse for the United States than 200,000,000 satisfied Americans.

Bernice Fitz-Gibbon, *Macy's, Gimbels, and Me* (1967)

17 An assumption deeply integral to capitalism . . . [is] not enough to go around: not enough love, not enough time, not enough appointments at the food stamps office, not enough food stamps, not enough money, not enough seats on the subway. It's perva-

sive. We learn mistrust of each other, bone deep: everything is skin off somebody's nose.

> Melanie Kaye/Kantrowitz, "To Be a Radical Jew in the Late Twentieth Century," in Christian McEwen and Sue O'Sullivan, eds., *Out the Other Side* (1988)

1 If it is good and I want it, they don't make it anymore.

> Elizabeth C. Finegan (1968), in Harold Faber, *The Book of Laws* (1979)

2 Customers must be delicately angled for at a safe distance—show yourself too much, and, like trout, they flashed away.

> Mrs. Humphry Ward, *The History of David Grieve* (1891)

3 American business, while it does not frown on helping the human race, frowns on people who start right in helping the human race without first proving that they can sell things to it.

> Margaret Halsey, *The Folks at Home* (1952)

4 The great majority of successful business men and women have been and are possessors of strong personalities of the right sort, and by analyzing their climb to success it is amazing to discover how large a part good manners, good breeding and correct behavior have had in helping them to win the goal.

> Ida White Parker, *Office Etiquette for Business Women* (1924)

5 Women have been in business such a long time now, they have for so many years been accepted on the same terms with men, that it seems almost archaic to caution them about expecting special courtesies and favors because of their sex.

> Ida White Parker, *Office Etiquette for Business Women* (1924)

6 Oh, and what color car does *your* company give *you*?

> Shirley Hutton, responding to ridicule of pink cars given by Mary Kay Cosmetics to top salespeople, in *The Minneapolis Star Tribune* (1994)

7 Mamma was a crackerjack of a business woman. The kind that'd make money if you let her down a well.

> Dorothy Canfield Fisher, *Bonfire* (1933)

8 I ran the wrong kind of business, but I did it with integrity.

> Sydney Biddle Barrows, in Marian Christy, "'Mayflower Madam' Tells All," *The Boston Globe* (1986)

9 He has an edifice complex. Buying buildings is his sex life.

> Caroline Llewellyn, *Life Blood* (1993)

10 Many people called him a wizard of finance—which is not the same thing as a wizard of magic, though sometimes fairly similar.

> Dodie Smith, *One Hundred and One Dalmatians* (1956)

11 Dear, never forget one little point. It's my business. You just work there.

> Elizabeth Arden, to her husband, in Alfred Allan Lewis and Constance Woodworth, *Miss Elizabeth Arden* (1972)

See also Economics, Entrepreneurs, Industrialism, Labor, Management, Money, Organizations, Politics and Business, Profit, Scarcity, Stock Market, Work.

## ♦ BUSYNESS

12 In a society that judges self-worth on productivity, it's no wonder we fall prey to the misconception that the more we do, the more we're worth.

> Ellen Sue Stern, *The Indispensable Woman* (1988)

13 Too many people, too many demands, too much to do; competent, busy, hurrying people—It just isn't living at all.

> Anne Morrow Lindbergh, *Bring Me a Unicorn* (1971)

14 Life comes in clusters, clusters of solitude, then a cluster when there is hardly time to breathe.

> May Sarton, *Journal of a Solitude* (1973)

15 People who are genuinely involved in life, not just living a routine they've contrived to protect them from disaster, always seem to have more demanded of them than they can easily take on.

> Amanda Cross, *No Word From Winifred* (1986)

16 Time is always wanting to me, and I cannot meet with a single day when I am not hurried along, driven to my wits'-end by urgent work, business to attend to, or some service to render.

> George Sand (1863), in Raphaël Ledos de Beaufort, ed., *Letters of George Sand* (1886)

17 Medicine is such a jealous lover that lately the only exercise I get is putting my foot down. For social life, I climb into the front seats of taxicabs on my way to work and talk to the drivers. Very interesting fellows.

> Elizabeth Kenny, in Victor Cohn, *Sister Kenny* (1975)

1 I am furious at all the letters to answer, when all I
want to do is think and write poems. . . . I long for
open time, with no obligations except toward the
inner world and what is going on there.

    May Sarton, *Journal of a Solitude* (1973)

2 Women aren't trying to do too much. Women
*have* too much to do.

    Mary Kay Blakely, *American Mom* (1994)

3 Women never have an half-hour in all their lives
(excepting before or after anybody is up in the
house) that they can call their own, without fear of
offending or of hurting someone. Why do people
sit up so late, or, more rarely, get up so early? Not
because the day is not long enough, but because
they have "no time in the day to themselves."

    Florence Nightingale, "Cassandra" (1852), in Ray Strachey,
    *"The Cause"* (1928)

4 My piano playing again falls completely by the
wayside, as is always the case when Robert composes. Not a single little hour can be found for me
the entire day!

    Clara Schumann (1841), in Gerd Nauhaus, ed., *The
    Marriage Diaries of Robert and Clara Schumann* (1993)

5 Like all energetic people, the more he had to do the
more time he seemed to find.

    Elizabeth Gaskell, *Mary Barton* (1848)

6 Busy people are never busybodies.

    Ethel Watts Mumford, in Oliver Herford, Ethel Watts
    Mumford, and Addison Mizner, *The Complete Cynic* (1902)

7 I am convinced that there are times in everybody's
experience when there is so much to be done, that
the only way to do it is to sit down and do nothing.

    Fanny Fern, *Folly As It Flies* (1868)

See also Action, Interruptions, Leisure, Time.

## ❦ BUTTERFLIES

8 Yellow butterflies / look like flowers flying through
/ the warm summer air.

    Andrea Willis, "Yellow Butterflies," in Louis M. Savary, S.J.,
    and Thomas J. O'Connor, *The Heart Has Its Seasons* (1970)

# C

## CALIFORNIA

1 Californians try everything once.

    T.J. MacGregor, *Kill Flash* (1987)

2 California is a state peculiarly addicted to swift enthusiasms. It is a seed-bed of all manner of cults and theories, taken up, and dropped, with equal speed.

    Charlotte Perkins Gilman, *The Living of Charlotte Perkins Gilman* (1935)

3 California is once-and-future America, and much that is newest and biggest in this country, both its best and worst, is concentrated along our western edge. . . . What is liveliest in America, most energetic, most dissatisfied with things-as-they-are, more ardent for things-as-they-might-be has always tended to pile up along our Pacific shore.

    Shana Alexander, *Talking Woman* (1976)

4 California is a place in which a boom mentality and a sense of Chekhovian loss meet in uneasy suspension; in which the mind is troubled by some buried but ineradicable suspicion that things had better work here, because here, beneath that immense bleached sky, is where we run out of continent.

    Joan Didion, "Notes From a Native Daughter," *Slouching Towards Bethlehem* (1968)

5 Did California cause any of this? No, though it does seem to draw to it people with unusual inclinations.

    Jessamyn West, *The Life I Really Lived* (1979)

6 All creative people should be required to leave California for three months every year.

    Gloria Swanson, in K. Madsen Roth, ed., *Hollywood Wits* (1995)

7 Always there is a sort of dream of air between you and the hills of California, a veil of unreality in the intervening air. It gives the hills the bloom that peaches have, or grapes in the dew.

    Stella Benson, *Poor Man* (1923)

8 I am a Californian, and we have twice the individuality and originality of any people in the United States. We always get quite huffy when we are spoken of as merely Americans.

    Gertrude Atherton, *Transplanted* (1919)

9 What does a Californian make for dinner? Reservations.

    Maureen Lipman, *How Was It for You?* (1985)

10 Californians are good at planning for the earthquake, while simultaneously denying it will happen.

    Sheila Ballantyne, "Letter to John Lennon," *Life on Earth* (1988)

11 Nobody can tell about this California climate. One minit its hot and the next minit its cold, so a person never knows what to hock.

    Anita Loos, *A Mouse Is Born* (1951)

12 He was wearing a hat and a necktie so he couldn't have been in California long.

    Dorothy B. Hughes, *Dread Journey* (1945)

13 Nearly everybody in San Francisco writes poetry. Few San Franciscans would admit this, but most of them would rather like to have their productions accidentally discovered.

    Stella Benson, *Poor Man* (1923)

14 What was the use of my having come from Oakland it was not natural to have come from there yes write about it if I like or anything if I like but not there, there is no there there.

    Gertrude Stein, *Everybody's Autobiography* (1937)

1 In California death is one of the most successfully kept secrets there is. If you doubt this, try to find a cemetery.

Sheila Ballantyne, *Norma Jean the Termite Queen* (1975)

See also Los Angeles.

## ❧ CALM

2 The spirit of man should be like a lake unruffled by wind or storm. Under such conditions a lake will reflect perfectly the mountains which are around it and the sky above it. . . . If the spirit is ruffled, then the Divine Image cannot mirror itself thereon.

Annie Besant, in *The Metaphysical Magazine* (1895)

3 Like water which can clearly mirror the sky and the trees only so long as its surface is undisturbed, the mind can only reflect the true image of the Self when it is tranquil and wholly relaxed.

Indra Devi, *Renewing Your Life Through Yoga* (1963)

4 I begin to think, that a calm is not desirable in any situation in life. . . . Man was made for action and for bustle too, I believe.

Abigail Adams (1784), *Letters of Mrs. Adams* (1848)

5 They sicken of the calm, who knew the storm.

Dorothy Parker, "Fair Weather," *Sunset Gun* (1928)

See also Peace, Silence.

## ❧ CAMELS

6 The red Sahara . . . across its hollows trailed / Long strings of camels, gloomy-eyed and slow.

Jean Ingelow, "The Four Bridges," *The Poetical Works of Jean Ingelow* (1863)

7 Uncouth as dreams may be, sluggish as far-off ships,— / What bring ye me, O camels?

Josephine Preston Peabody, "Caravans," in Edmund Clarence Stedman, ed., *An American Anthology 1787-1900* (1900)

8 Eight of them came padding past our door at dusk as we came up the steps; rolling along like waves in the half light.

Freya Stark (1928), *Letters From Syria* (1942)

9 The camels stand in all their vague beauty— / at night they fold up like pale accordions.

Rita Dove, "Notes From a Tunisian Journal," *The Yellow House on the Corner* (1980)

10 The camel is an ugly animal, seen from above. Its shoulders slope formless like a sack, its silly little ears and fluff of bleached curls behind them have a respectable, boarding-house look, like some faded neatness that dresses for propriety but never dressed for love.

Freya Stark, *A Winter in Arabia* (1940)

11 The camel carries on his dreary circular task with his usual slow and pompous step and head poised superciliously, as if it were a ritual affair above the comprehension of the vulgar; and no doubt he comforts himself for the dullness of life by a sense of virtue, like many other formalists beside him.

Freya Stark, *The Southern Gates of Arabia* (1936)

12 It is a curious fact that camels walk more quickly and straighter to the sound of singing.

Rosita Forbes, *The Secret of the Sahara* (1921)

13 Ah, the camel of Cairo! . . . He went quietly and comfortably through the narrowest lanes and the densest crowds by the mere force of his personality. He was the most impressive living thing we saw in Egypt, not excepting two Pashas and a Bey. He was engaged with large philosophies, one could see that.

Sara Jeannette Duncan, *A Social Departure* (1890)

14 His skin is the most interesting thing about him, to a lover of the antique. It seems to have been in constant use since the original camel took it out of the ark with him, it is so battered and tattered, so seamy and patched, so disreputably parchment-colored.

Sara Jeannette Duncan, *A Social Departure* (1890)

15 There are camels which have the quality which in humans is called the revolutionary spirit, and the caravan leader fears to keep one of these in his ranks, because its instinct is always toward revolt against authority. One such camel will sometimes break up the discipline of a whole train, for, owing to the mass mentality of the herd, even peaceful beasts are suddenly infected with the spirit of revolt and in a few minutes the whole caravan is in utter disorder.

Mildred Cable, with Francesca French, *The Gobi Desert* (1942)

1 The camel has his virtues—so much at least must be admitted; but they do not lie upon the surface.

    Amelia B. Edwards, *One Thousand Miles Up the Nile* (1877)

2 Irreproachable as a beast of burden, he is open to many objections as a steed. It is unpleasant, in the first place, to ride an animal which not only objects to being ridden, but cherishes a strong personal antipathy to his rider.

    Amelia B. Edwards, *One Thousand Miles Up the Nile* (1877)

3 I looked at our eighteen camels with much anxiety. . . . One of them was a living picture of all that a camel should *not* be. He might have been used successfully by the Khartoum Camel Corps as an example to enthusiastic young officers of what *not* to buy.

    Rosita Forbes, *The Secret of the Sahara* (1921)

4 Many of us have been bitten by his long front teeth, trampled over by his noiseless feet, deafened by his angry roar, and insulted by the protrusion of his contemptuous upper lip. No one who thus knows him at home retains a spark of belief in the beast's patience, amiability, fidelity, or any other virtue.

    Frances B. Cobbe, *False Beasts and True* (1876)

## ⚜ CAMPING

5 That was, I think, the most magical dawn I have ever attended. But when I remarked to Rachel that one wet night was a small price to pay for such an experience she merely grunted and went on wringing out her flea-bag. Perhaps at fourteen one's aesthetic sensibilities are still latent.

    Dervla Murphy, *Muddling Through in Madagascar* (1985)

## ⚜ CANADA

6 The air and the sky seem to have been freshly washed and polished, and the people too.

    Marlene Dietrich, *Marlene Dietrich's ABC* (1962)

7 Canada is bounded on the north by gold; on the west by the East; on the east by history; and on the south by friends.

    Frances Shelley Wees, "Geography Lesson" (1937), in John Robert Colombo, *Colombo's Concise Canadian Quotations* (1976)

8 The personality of St. John's, Newfoundland, hits you like a smack in the face with a dried cod, enthusiastically administered by its citizenry.

    Jan Morris, "Thwack!" *Locations* (1992)

9 If the national mental illness of the United States is megalomania, that of Canada is paranoid schizophrenia.

    Margaret Atwood, *The Journals of Susanna Moodie* (1970)

## ⚜ CANCER

10 An individual doesn't get cancer, a family does.

    Terry Tempest Williams, *Refuge* (1991)

11 The goal is to live a full, productive life even with all that ambiguity. No matter what happens, whether the cancer never flares up again or whether you die, the important thing is that the days that you have had you will have *lived*.

    Gilda Radner, *It's Always Something* (1989)

12 Cancer is a demonic pregnancy.

    Susan Sontag, *Illness As Metaphor* (1978)

See also Illness.

## ⚜ CAPITALISM

13 I am going to fight capitalism even if it kills me. It is wrong that people like you should be comfortable and well fed while all around you people are starving.

    Sylvia Pankhurst, speech (1921), in David Mitchell, *The Fighting Pankhursts* (1967)

14 Capitalism and altruism are incompatible; they are philosophical opposites; they cannot co-exist in the same man or in the same society.

    Ayn Rand, *For the New Intellectual* (1961)

15 Capitalism with near-full employment was an impressive spectacle.

    Joan Robinson, title essay, in Rendigs Fels, ed., *The Second Crisis of Economic Theory* (1972)

See also Economics.

## ❧ CAPITAL PUNISHMENT

1 Why do we kill people who are killing people / To show that killing people is wrong.

> Holly Near, "Foolish Notion" (1980), in Holly Near with Derk Richardson, *Fire in the Rain . . . Singer in the Storm* (1990)

2 We don't cut off the hands of thieves or castrate rapists. Why must we murder murderers?

> Wendy Kaminer, in *Redbook* (1994)

3 Many of us do not believe in capital punishment, because thus society takes from a man what society cannot give.

> Katharine Fullerton Gerould, *Modes and Morals* (1920)

4 Executions, far from being useful examples to the survivors, have, I am persuaded, a quite contrary effect, by hardening the heart they ought to terrify. Besides the fear of an ignominious death, I believe, never deterred anyone from the commission of a crime, because, in committing it, the mind is roused to activity about present circumstances.

> Mary Wollstonecraft, *Letters Written During a Short Residence in Sweden, Norway, and Denmark* (1796)

5 The people doin' the thinkin' and the people doin' the murderin' are two separate sets of people.

> Sister Helen Prejean, on capital punishment as a deterrent to crime, news item (1995)

## ❧ CARS

6 The car, by bisecting the human outline, diminishes it, producing a race of half-people in a motion not of their own making.

> Marya Mannes, *More in Anger* (1958)

7 A car is just a moving, giant handbag! You never have actually to carry groceries, or dry cleaning, or anything! You can have five pairs of shoes with you at all times!

> Cynthia Heimel, *Get Your Tongue Out of My Mouth, I'm Kissing You Good-Bye!* (1993)

8 I bought Henry a beautiful Daimler coupé, the first new car we have ever had, a tender antelope of a car.

> Rebecca West, in Victoria Glendinning, *Rebecca West* (1987)

See also Drivers.

## ❧ CATS

9 I alone am free—I am THE CAT.

> Leila Usher, "I Am the Cat," in Hazel Felleman, ed., *The Best Loved Poems of the American People* (1936)

10 Nothing makes a house cozier than cats.

> Gladys Taber, *The Book of Stillmeadow* (1948)

11 This is the sphinx of the hearthstone, the little god of domesticity, whose presence turns a house into a home.

> Agnes Repplier, "Agrippina," *Essays in Idleness* (1893)

12 Nobody keeps a cat. They condescend to live with you is all.

> Dell Shannon, *Case Pending* (1960)

13 The Cat was a creature of absolute convictions, and his faith in his deductions never varied.

> Mary E. Wilkins Freeman, "The Cat," in Roger Caras, ed., *Treasury of Great Cat Stories* (1987)

14 A cat is, by and large, sophisticated and complex, and capable of creating three-act plays around any single piece of action.

> Gladys Taber, *The Book of Stillmeadow* (1948)

15 Cats think about three things: food, sex, and nothing.

> Adair Lara, *Welcome to Earth, Mom* (1992)

16 One reason cats are happier than people / is that they have no newspapers.

> Gwendolyn Brooks, title poem, *In the Mecca* (1968)

17 There are three basic personality factors in cats: The kind who run up when you say hello and rub against you in cheap romance; the kind who run away certain that you mean to ravish them; and the kind who just look back and don't move a muscle. I love all three kinds.

> Eve Babitz, *Eve's Hollywood* (1974)

18 The way to get on with a cat is to treat it as an equal—or even better, as the superior it knows itself to be.

> Elizabeth Peters, *The Snake, the Crocodile and the Dog* (1992)

19 My cat does not talk as respectfully to me as I do to her.

> Colette, *Prisons and Paradise* (1932)

1 Who can tell what just criticisms Murr the Cat may be passing on us beings of wider speculation?

George Eliot, *Middlemarch* (1871)

2 Oh, the cats in this town have their secrets.

Mary Virginia Micka, "Small Things Tell Us," *Letter to My Landlady* (1986)

3 The vanity of man revolts from the serene indifference of the cat.

Agnes Repplier, "The Grocer's Cat," *Americans and Others* (1912)

4 That cat is in love with me, but to say that it's "mutual" doesn't begin to describe *anything*. I'm totally irrational about her. She and I are a *scandal*.

Helen Gurley Brown, in Judy Fireman, ed., *Cat Catalog* (1976)

5 Is it enough to know that one creature likes what you do and the way you do it and that that creature is your cat?

Naomi Thornton, in Sara Ruddick and Pamela Daniels, eds., *Working It Out* (1977)

6 Cats sleep / Anywhere, / Any table, / Any chair, / Top of piano, / Window-ledge, / In the middle, / On the edge.

Eleanor Farjeon, "Cats," *The Children's Bells* (1960)

7 Cats sleep fat and walk thin.

Rosalie Moore, "Catalog," in *The New Yorker* (1940)

8 Oh cat; I'd say, or pray: Be-*ooo*tiful cat! Delicious cat! Exquisite cat! Satiny cat! Cat like a soft owl, cat with paws like moths, jeweled cat, miraculous cat! Cat, cat, cat, cat.

Doris Lessing, *Particularly Cats . . . and Rufus* (1967)

9 A black cat dropped soundlessly from a high wall, like a spoonful of dark treacle, and melted under a gate.

Elizabeth Lemarchand, *Alibi for a Corpse* (1969)

10 If a fish is the movement of water embodied, given shape, then cat is a diagram and pattern of subtle air.

Doris Lessing, *Particularly Cats . . . and Rufus* (1967)

11 People are always commenting that you never know what cats are thinking. The observation tells us a little about cats and a lot more about people. It implies that people *ought* to know what other beings are thinking, and that cats violate this norm in some strange way. Why?

Anne Mendelson, "Cats Are Not People," in Judy Fireman, ed., *Cat Catalog* (1976)

12 Yesterday . . . was a very queer and alarming day: classically still and brooding, and both our cats with staring coats, and slinking about at my heels in the most woe-begone way. They have a wonderful talent for being Cassandras, only unfortunately they cannot prophesy with any explicit detail, so we never know whether to expect floods, lightning, or visitors.

Sylvia Townsend Warner (1957), in William Maxwell, ed., *Letters: Sylvia Townsend Warner* (1982)

13 The more you talk to cats . . . the smarter they become. An occasional "nice kitty" will have no measurable effect; intelligent conversation is required.

Lilian Jackson Braun, *The Cat Who Knew Shakespeare* (1988)

14 She is a gray cat, but around her eyes the fur is black, so that she looks a little like those fifteen-year-olds who believe that being Cleopatra is mostly a matter of mascara.

Jessamyn West, *A Matter of Time* (1966)

15 Round, gray, plump-jowled like a grandmother, she washed, ate, and saw to it that she and her offspring went outside for calls of nature as regularly as any privy-bound housewife. With a recipe written in cat language, she could have baked cookies or fried a chicken.

Jessamyn West, *The Life I Really Lived* (1979)

16 I have just been given a very engaging Persian kitten . . . and his opinion is that *I* have been given to *him*.

Evelyn Underhill (1933), in Charles Williams, ed., *The Letters of Evelyn Underhill* (1943)

17 I have three cats, all so loving and insistent that they play cat's-cradle with every train of thought. They drove me distracted while I was having influenza, gazing at me with large eyes and saying: O Sylvia, you are so ill, you'll soon be dead. And who will feed us then? FEED US NOW!

Sylvia Townsend Warner (1977), in William Maxwell, ed., *Letters: Sylvia Townsend Warner* (1982)

18 Mr. Cat knows that a whisker spied is not a whole mouse.

Marguerite Henry, *San Domingo, the Medicine Hat Stallion* (1972)

1 [Charles Dickens] was reading at a small table, on which a lighted candle was placed. Suddenly the candle went out. My father, who was much interested in his book, relighted the candle, stroked the cat, who was looking at him pathetically he noticed, and continued his reading. A few minutes later, as the light became dim, he looked up just in time to see puss deliberately put out the candle with his paw, and then look appealingly toward him.

Mamie Dickens, *My Father As I Recall Him* (1898)

2 The two cats, drowsing side by side in a Victorian nursing chair, their paws, their ears, their tails complementarily adjusted, their blue eyes blinking open on a single thought of when I shall remember it's their suppertime . . . might have been composed by Bach for two flutes.

Sylvia Townsend Warner (1965), in William Maxwell, ed., *Letters: Sylvia Townsend Warner* (1982)

See also Animals, Cats and Dogs, Pets.

## ❧ CATS AND DOGS

3 It's funny how dogs and cats know the inside of folks better than other folks do, isn't it?

Eleanor H. Porter, *Pollyanna* (1912)

4 I love both the way a dog looks up to me and a cat condescends to me.

Gladys Taber, *Stillmeadow Daybook* (1955)

5 A good recipe for a human reducing breakfast is a lot of good things to eat, and three spaniels and two cats to eat with.

Gladys Taber, *The Book of Stillmeadow* (1948)

6 Dogs . . . can be made to feel guilty about anything, including the sins of their owners. Cats refuse to take the blame for anything—including their own sins.

Elizabeth Peters, *Trojan Gold* (1987)

7 A man who owns a dog is, in every sense of the words, its master; the term expresses accurately their mutual relations. But it is ridiculous when applied to the limited possession of a cat.

Agnes Repplier, "Agrippina," *Essays in Idleness* (1893)

8 Dogs will come when called. Cats will take a message and get back to you.

Missy Dizick and Mary Bly, *Dogs Are Better Than Cats* (1985)

9 I cannot imagine a cat in an Obedience ring, running around in the hot sun and doing things on command. For it would not make sense. Whereas a dog is tolerant of your not making sense and only wants to fix things so you are happy.

Gladys Taber, *Stillmeadow Daybook* (1955)

10 Dogs are high on life. Cats need catnip.

Missy Dizick and Mary Bly, *Dogs Are Better Than Cats* (1985)

See also Animals, Cats, Dogs, Pets.

## ❧ CAUSES

11 It is often interesting, in retrospect, to consider the trifling causes that lead to great events. A chance encounter, a thoughtless remark—and the tortuous chain reaction of coincidence is set in motion, leading with devious inevitability to some resounding climax.

Patricia Moyes, *Down Among the Dead Men* (1961)

12 Causes are often disproportioned to effects.

Hannah Farnham Lee, *The Log-Cabin* (1844)

## ❧ CAUTION

13 One should not run on a new road.

Amelia E. Barr, *The Bow of Orange Ribbon* (1886)

14 Everybody knows if you are too careful you are so occupied in being careful that you are sure to stumble over something.

Gertrude Stein, *Everybody's Autobiography* (1937)

15 Sometimes I wonder what the difference is between being cautious and being dead.

Sue Grafton, *"D" Is for Deadbeat* (1987)

16 Caution is the instinct of the weaker animals.

C.M. Sedgwick, *Hope Leslie* (1827)

See also Fastidiousness, Fear.

## ❦ CELEBRITY

1 Alas, how wretched is the being who depends on the stability of public favor!

> Sarah Siddons, *The Reminiscences of Sarah Kemble Siddons 1773-1785* (1942)

2 Nobody mentions how it feels to become a freak / because you have talent and how / no one gives a damn how you feel.

> Nikki Giovanni, "Poem for Aretha," *Re:Creation* (1970)

3 If I'm such a legend, then why am I so lonely? If I'm such a legend, then why do I sit at home for hours staring at the damned telephone, hoping it's out of order, even calling the operator asking her if she's *sure* it's not out of order?

> Judy Garland, in John Gruen, *Close-Up* (1968)

4 If so many people love me, how come I'm alone?

> Doris Day, in A.E. Hotchner, *Doris Day* (1975)

5 The easiest kind of relationship for me is with ten thousand people. The hardest is with one.

> Joan Baez, in Joan Didion, "Just Folks at a School for Non-Violence," *The New York Times Magazine* (1966)

6 I suck my thumb a lot.

> Julie Andrews, on being asked how it feels to be a star, in Roy Newquist, *Showcase* (1966)

7 A celebrity is someone who no longer does the things that made him a celebrity.

> Peg Bracken, *But I Wouldn't Have Missed It for the World!* (1973)

8 Someone who . . . is famous for being famous.

> Erica Jong, *Parachutes & Kisses* (1984)

9 A celebrity is one who works all his life to become well-known and then goes through back streets wearing dark glasses so he won't be recognized.

> Jane Powell, in Lester Gordon, *Let's Go to the Movies!* (1992)

10 The press frequently sneers at the hype devoted to a superstar, but the press itself is responsible for all the hype.

> Beverly Sills, with Lawrence Linderman, *Beverly* (1987)

11 Go back to that wonderful Alan Jay Lerner song in *Camelot*, the one about "I wonder what the king is doing tonight." We really want to know what the king is up to. It must be something bred into us from peasantry.

> Liz Smith, on celebrity journalism, in James Brady, "In Step with Liz Smith," *Parade* (1991)

12 Poring over fragments of other people's lives, peering into their bedrooms when they don't know we're there, we thrill to the glamour and the power of secret knowledge, partly detoxified but also heightened by being shared.

> Patricia Meyer Spacks, *Gossip* (1985)

13 I'm sure that people all over the world got awfully tired of reading about us. I know I did.

> Princess Grace of Monaco, on the press coverage of her marriage to Prince Rainier III, news item (1956)

14 Unless an artist or public celebrity is wary and firm, the disaster of success will deliver him into the public embrace, devour his time, corrupt his values, and addle his talent.

> Judith Groch, *The Right to Create* (1969)

15 It is all the question of identity. . . . As long as the outside does not put a value on you it remains outside but when it does put a value on you then it gets inside or rather if the outside puts a value on you then all your inside gets to be outside.

> Gertrude Stein, *Everybody's Autobiography* (1937)

16 A writer is hoisted up onto a pedestal only to scrutinize him more closely and conclude that it was a mistake to put him up there in the first place.

> Simone de Beauvoir, *Force of Circumstance* (1963)

17 We like to know the weakness of eminent persons; it consoles us for our inferiority.

> Madame de Lambert, in Kate Sanborn, *The Wit of Women* (1885)

18 Whoso appears before the public should expect no consideration and demand none.

> Marie von Ebner-Eschenbach, *Aphorisms* (1893)

19 Performers and their public should never meet. Once the curtain comes down, the performer should fly away like a magician's dove.

> Edith Piaf, in Simone Berteaut, *Piaf* (1969)

20 As a general rule, fans and idols should always be kept at arm's length, the length of the arm to be proportionate to the degree of sheer idolatry involved. Don't take a Beatle to lunch. Don't wait up to see if the Easter Bunny is real. Just enjoy the egg hunt.

> Shana Alexander, "A Big Mistake in London," in *Life* (1966)

1 Mountains appear more lofty, the nearer they are approached; but great men, to retain their altitude, must only be viewed from a distance.

    Countess of Blessington, *Desultory Thoughts and Reflections* (1839)

2 Celebrities used to be found in clusters, like oysters—and with much the same defensive mechanisms.

    Barbara Walters, *How to Talk With Practically Anybody About Practically Anything* (1970)

3 In common with many other people he cherished the secret conviction that a celebrity should look peculiar, at the very least, and had hitherto been happy to note that a great number did.

    Margery Allingham, *The Fashion in Shrouds* (1938)

4 All the famous people had had an awful time. One of them had a drunken father. Another had a stammer. Another had to wash hundreds of dirty bottles. They had all had what was called a difficult childhood. Clearly you had to have one if you wanted to become famous.

    Judith Kerr, *When Hitler Stole Pink Rabbit* (1971)

5 You ought to try eating raw oysters in a restaurant with every eye focused upon you—it makes you feel as if the creatures were whales, your fork a derrick and your mouth Mammoth Cave.

    Lillian Russell, in Marie Dressler, *The Life Story of an Ugly Duckling* (1924)

6 In a nation of celebrity worshipers, amid followers of the cult of personality, individual modesty becomes a heroic quality. I find heroism in the acceptance of anonymity, in the studied resistance to the normal American tropism toward the limelight.

    Shana Alexander, *Talking Woman* (1976)

7 It is strange what society will endure from its idols.

    L.E. Landon, *Ethel Churchill* (1837)

8 It is not enough to become admired, one must also be forgiven for it.

    Comtesse Diane, *Les Glanes de la Vie* (1898)

9 A star is only as good as her last picture.

    Barbara Stanwyck (1930), in Al DiOrio, *Barbara Stanwyck* (1984)

10 *The Night Porter* is said . . . to have made a big star of Charlotte Rampling, but surely one twinkle doesn't make a star.

    Pauline Kael, *Reeling* (1976)

11 Any star can be devoured by human adoration, sparkle by sparkle.

    Shirley Temple Black, in Heidi Yorkshire, "Shirley Temple Black Sets the Record Straight," *McCall's* (1989)

12 Authentic stardom . . . is a gift which, if it is to have any permanent significance, must be bestowed by a public rather than a manager.

    Katharine Cornell, *I Wanted to Be an Actress* (1939)

13 To be a star is to own the world and all the people in it.

    Hedy Lamarr, *Ecstasy and Me* (1966)

14 Long life will sometimes obscure the star of fame.

    Marie de Rabutin-Chantal, Marquise de Sévigné (1675), *Letters of Madame de Sévigné to Her Daughter and Her Friends*, vol. 3 (1811)

15 Once you start you can't stop; you've got to go on doing things to keep famous because an ex-famous person is better off dead. . . . My Dad told me that. He was a hurdler in his youth, and then someone jumped higher than he did and people acted funny toward him all his life. They couldn't forget and he couldn't jump any higher.

    Richard Shattuck, *The Half-Haunted Saloon* (1945)

16 After a taste of stardom, everything else is poverty.

    Hedy Lamarr, *Ecstasy and Me* (1966)

17 For some people life outside the spotlight is death.

    Nadia Comaneci, in Barbara Grizzuti Harrison, *The Astonishing World* (1992)

See also Admiration, Comebacks, Fame, Glamour, "Somebody."

# ❦ CELIBACY

18 In its most beautiful expression and sublimest manifestations, the celibate ideal has proclaimed a world-wide love, in place of the narrower human love of home and children.

    Marie Stopes, *Married Love* (1918)

See also Chastity, Virginity.

# ❦ CEMETERIES

19 I do like Italian graves; they look so much more lived in.

    Elizabeth Bowen, *The Hotel* (1928)

1 The straight sunny tombstones looked sociable, fresh wreaths were laid on the breasts of the graves. You could almost see the dead sitting up holding their flowers, like invalids on a visiting-day, waiting to hear the music. Only the very new dead, under raw earth with no tombstones, lay flat in despair.

Elizabeth Bowen, *To the North* (1933)

See also Funerals.

## ❧ CENSORSHIP

2 I disapprove of what you say, but will defend to the death your right to say it.

S.G. Tallentyre, *The Friends of Voltaire* (1906)

3 The case against censoring anything is absolute: . . . nothing that could be censored can be so bad in its effects, *in the long run*, as censorship itself.

Katharine Whitehorn, *Roundabout* (1962)

4 The free expression of the hopes and aspirations of a people is the greatest and only safety in a sane society.

Emma Goldman, *Living My Life* (1931)

5 There is no danger is letting people have their say. . . . There is a danger when you try to stop them from saying it.

Helen Gahagan Douglas (1946), *A Full Life* (1982)

6 Censorship, like charity, should begin at home; but unlike charity, it should end there.

Clare Boothe Luce, in Evelyn L. Beilenson and Ann Tenenbaum, eds., *Wit and Wisdom of Famous American Women* (1986)

7 It would be nice to think that a censor could allow a genuine work of artistic seriousness and ban a titillating piece of sadism, but it would take a miracle to make such a distinction stick.

Katharine Whitehorn, *Roundabout* (1962)

8 To admit authorities, however heavily furred and gowned, into our libraries and let them tell us how to read, what to read, what value to place upon what we read, is to destroy the spirit of freedom which is the breath of those sanctuaries. Everywhere else we may be bound by laws and conventions—there we have none.

Virginia Woolf, "How Should One Read a Book?" *The Common Reader*, 2nd series (1932)

9 Crankish attacks on the freedom to read are common at present. When backed and coordinated by organized groups, they become sinister.

Ursula K. Le Guin, *Dancing at the Edge of the World* (1989)

10 Censorship is the height of vanity.

Martha Graham, *Blood Memory* (1991)

11 The heaviest restriction upon the freedom of public opinion is not the official censorship *of* the Press, but the unofficial censorship *by* a Press which exists not so much to express opinion as to manufacture it.

Dorothy L. Sayers, "How Free Is the Press?" (1941), *Unpopular Opinions* (1947)

12 "Censorship" is a term pertaining only to governmental action. No private action is censorship. No private individual or agency can silence a man or suppress a publication; only the government can do so. The freedom of speech of private individuals includes the right not to agree, not to listen and not to finance one's own antagonists.

Ayn Rand, *The Virtue of Selfishness* (1964)

13 There seems to be an assumption that if you're offended by movie brutality, you are somehow playing into the hands of the people who want censorship. But this would deny those of us who don't believe in censorship the use of the only counter-balance: the freedom of the press to say that there's anything conceivably damaging in these films—the freedom to analyze their implications. . . . How can people go on talking about the dazzling brilliance of movies and not notice that the directors are sucking up to the thugs in the audience?

Pauline Kael, *Deeper Into Movies* (1973)

14 Is it really beyond our wits to devise some form of censorship which would trap only the crudely sadistic?

Storm Jameson, *Parthian Words* (1970)

15 Censorship may have to do with literature; but literature has nothing whatever to do with censorship.

Nadine Gordimer, *The Essential Gesture* (1988)

16 Perhaps these men in the House Caucus Room [Committee on Un-American Activities] are determined to spread silence: to frighten those voices which will shout no, and ask questions, defend the few, attack cruelty and proclaim the rights and dig-

nity of man. . . . America is going to look very strange to Americans and they will not be at home here, for the air will slowly become unbreathable to all forms of life except sheep.

Martha Gellhorn, "Cry Shame," in *The New Republic* (1947)

## ❧ CERTAINTY

1 One certainty we all accept is the condition of being uncertain and insecure.

Doris Lessing, title essay (1957), in Paul Schlueter, ed., *A Small Personal Voice* (1974)

2 Certainty always produces questions, uncertainty statements. It is a balancing law of nature.

Djuna Barnes, "A Visit to the Favored Haunt of the I.W.W.'s," in *The New York Press* (1915)

3 The minute one utters a certainty, the opposite comes to mind.

May Sarton, *Mrs. Stevens Hears the Mermaids Singing* (1965)

4 It is wise to be sure, but otherwise to be too sure.

Sophie Irene Loeb, *Epigrams of Eve* (1913)

5 People like definite decisions, / Tidy answers, all the little ravelings / Snipped off, the lint removed, they / Hop happily among their roughs / Calling what they can't clutch insanity / Or saintliness.

Gwendolyn Brooks, "Memorial to Ed Bland," *Annie Allen* (1949)

6 I'm often wrong, but never in doubt.

Ivy Baker Priest, *Green Grows Ivy* (1958)

7 "Certainly." He beamed uncertainly. "Certainly."

Holly Roth, *Button, Button* (1966)

See also Ambivalence, Doubt, Exceptions, Security.

## ❧ CHALLENGE

8 To be tested is good. The challenged life may be the best therapist.

Gail Sheehy, *Spirit of Survival* (1986)

9 Providence has hidden a charm in difficult undertakings, which is appreciated only by those who dare to grapple with them.

Anne-Sophie Swetchine, in Count de Falloux, ed., *The Writings of Madame Swetchine* (1869)

10 You must do the thing you think you cannot do.

Eleanor Roosevelt, *You Learn by Living* (1960)

11 When people keep telling you that you can't do a thing, you kind of like to try it.

Margaret Chase Smith, in *Time* (1964)

12 The fruit that can fall without shaking, / Indeed is too mellow for me.

Lady Mary Wortley Montagu, "Answer, for Lord William Hamilton" (1768), *The Works of the Right Honorable Lady Mary Wortley Montagu*, vol. 5 (1803)

13 One sank into the ancient sin of anomie when challenges failed.

Amanda Cross, *Death in a Tenured Position* (1981)

See also Opportunity, Opposition.

## ❧ CHANGE

14 Autumn to winter, winter into spring, / Spring into summer, summer into fall— / So rolls the changing year, and so we change; / Motion so swift, we know not that we move.

Dinah Maria Mulock Craik, "Immutable," *Mulock's Poems, New and Old* (1880)

15 Change is the constant, the signal for rebirth, the egg of the phoenix.

Christina Baldwin, *One to One* (1977)

16 Fluidity and discontinuity are central to the reality in which we live.

Mary Catherine Bateson, *Composing a Life* (1989)

17 When you're stuck in a spiral, to change all aspects of the spin you need only to change one thing.

Christina Baldwin, "Solo Dancing on the Spiral Quest," in Kay Vander Vort, Joan H. Timmerman, and Eleanor Lincoln, eds., *Walking in Two Worlds* (1992)

18 The need for change bulldozed a road down the center of my mind.

Maya Angelou, *I Know Why the Caged Bird Sings* (1970)

1 You start out with one thing, end / up with another, and nothing's / like it used to be, not even
the future.

Rita Dove, "Ö," *The Yellow House on the Corner* (1980)

2 Neither situations nor people can be altered by the
interference of an outsider. If they are to be altered,
that alteration must come from within.

Phyllis Bottome, *Survival* (1943)

3 Some women wait for something / to change and
nothing / does change / so they change / themselves.

Audre Lorde, "Stations," *Our Dead Behind Us* (1986)

4 A person can run for years but sooner or later he
has to take a stand in the place which, for better or
worse, he calls home, do what he can to change
things there.

Paule Marshall, *The Chosen Place, The Timeless People* (1969)

5 I, like a river, / Have been turned aside by this harsh
age. / I am a substitute. My life has flowed / Into
another channel / And I do not recognize my
shores.

Anna Akhmatova, "Northern Elegies" (1945), in D.M.
Thomas, tr., *You Will Hear Thunder* (1985)

6 A person needs at intervals to separate himself
from family and companions and go to new places.
He must go without his familiars in order to be
open to influences, to change.

Katharine Butler Hathaway, *The Journals and Letters of the
Little Locksmith* (1946)

7 I knew here could never be as sweet as there; going
was a question, staying was an answer.

Linda Ellerbee, *Move On* (1991)

8 I'm doing well, especially since / I moved away
from here.

Judy Grahn, *The Queen of Swords* (1987)

9 I am full of the sorrow that goes with changes in
surroundings, those successive stages of annihilation that slowly lead to the great and final void.

Isabelle Eberhardt (1900), in Nina de Voogd, tr., *The
Passionate Nomad* (1988)

10 It is not the conscious changes made in their lives
by men and women—a new job, a new town, a
divorce—which really shape them, like the chapter
headings in a biography, but a long, slow mutation
of emotion, hidden, all-penetrative; something by
which they may be so taken up that the practical
outward changes of their lives in the world, noted
with surprise, scandal or envy by others, pass almost unnoticed by themselves. This gives a shifting
quality to the whole surface of life; decisions made
with reason and the tongue may never be made
valid by the heart.

Nadine Gordimer, *The Lying Days* (1953)

11 People change and forget to tell each other.

Lillian Hellman, *Toys in the Attic* (1960)

12 The tragedy of life is that people do not change.

Agatha Christie, *There Is a Tide* (1948)

13 People don't alter. They may with enormous difficulty modify themselves, but they never really
change.

Margery Allingham, *Safer Than Love* (1962)

14 It is only in romances that people undergo a sudden metamorphosis. In real life, even after the most
terrible experiences, the main character remains
exactly the same.

Isadora Duncan, *My Life* (1942)

15 Once an old woman at my church said the secret is
that God loves us *exactly* the way we are *and* that he
loves us too much to let us stay like this, and I'm
just trying to trust that.

Anne Lamott, *Operating Instructions* (1993)

16 Youth is always sure that change must mean something better.

Amelia E. Barr, *All the Days of My Life* (1913)

17 So often I heard people paying blind obeisance to
change—as though it had some virtue of its own.
Change or we will die. Change or we will stagnate.
Evergreens don't stagnate.

Judith Rossner, *Nine Months in the Life of an Old Maid*
(1969)

18 Better never means better for everyone, he says. It
always means worse, for some.

Margaret Atwood, *The Handmaid's Tale* (1985)

19 You must not change one thing, one pebble, one
grain of sand, until you know what good and evil
will follow on that act.

Ursula K. Le Guin, *A Wizard of Earthsea* (1968)

20 He acted too often without counting the cost, from
some dazzling conception,—one could not say
from impulse, for impulses are from the heart. He
liked to reorganize and change things for the sake

of change, to make a fine gesture. He destroyed the old before he had clearly thought out the new.

Willa Cather, *Shadows on the Rock* (1931)

1 The difference between transformation by accident and transformation by a system is like the difference between lightning and a lamp. Both give illumination, but one is dangerous and unreliable, while the other is relatively safe, directed, available.

Marilyn Ferguson, *The Aquarian Conspiracy* (1980)

2 There is no sin punished more implacably by nature than the sin of resistance to change.

Anne Morrow Lindbergh, *The Wave of the Future* (1940)

3 Things good in themselves . . . perfectly valid in the integrity of their origins, become fetters if they cannot alter.

Freya Stark, *The Lycian Shore* (1956)

4 It's unbelievable the primitive feelings that are aroused by rapid change.

Sheila Ballantyne, *Norma Jean the Termite Queen* (1975)

5 All birth is unwilling.

Pearl S. Buck, *What America Means to Me* (1943)

6 Every new fad or fashion at once has its denouncers from the pulpit, platform, professor's chair.

Alice Dunbar-Nelson (1926), in Gloria T. Hull, ed., *The Works of Alice Dunbar-Nelson*, vol. 2 (1988)

7 It's the most unhappy people who most fear change.

Mignon McLaughlin, *The Second Neurotic's Notebook* (1966)

8 Come, come, my conservative friend, wipe the dew off your spectacles, and see that the world is moving.

Elizabeth Cady Stanton, *The Woman's Bible* (1895)

9 Yesterday people were permitted to change things. They will be permitted to advocate changing them tomorrow. It is only dangerous to think of changing anything today.

Elizabeth Hawes, *Men Can Take It* (1939)

See also Adaptability, Growth, Impermanence, Moving, Social Change.

## ❦ CHANGEABLE

10 I never wanted what I thought I wanted / But always something else / Which changed again as soon as I had found it.

Mary Carolyn Davies, "Autobiography," *The Skyline Trail* (1924)

## ❦ CHAOS

11 Whenever there is chaos, it creates wonderful thinking. I consider chaos a gift.

Septima Poinsette Clark, in Brian Lanker, *I Dream a World* (1989)

12 The splendid discontent of God / With chaos, made the world.

Ella Wheeler Wilcox, "Discontent," *Poems of Pleasure* (1888)

13 Chaos is not brought about by rebellion; it is brought about by the absence of political struggle.

Susan Sherman, "Women and Process," in Charlotte Bunch and Sandra Pollack, eds., *Learning Our Way* (1983)

See also Disorder, Order.

## ❦ CHARACTER

14 It is not in the still calm of life, or the repose of a pacific station, that great characters are formed. . . . The habits of a vigorous mind are formed in contending with difficulties. All history will convince you of this, and that wisdom and penetration are the fruit of experience, not the lessons of retirement and leisure. Great necessities call out great virtues.

Abigail Adams, letter to her son, John Quincy Adams (1780), *Letters of Mrs. Adams* (1848)

15 Character cannot be developed in ease and quiet. Only through experiences of trial and suffering can the soul be strengthened, vision cleared, ambition inspired and success achieved.

Helen Keller, *Helen Keller's Journal* (1938)

16 'Tis true that tho' People can transcend their Characters in Times of Tranquillity, they can ne'er do so in Times of Tumult.

Erica Jong, *Fanny: Being the True History of the Adventures of Fanny Hackabout-Jones* (1980)

1 I never like anyone till I've seen him at his worst.

    Ethel M. Dell, *The Keeper of the Door* (1915)

2 Character builds slowly, but it can be torn down with incredible swiftness.

    Faith Baldwin, "July," *Harvest of Hope* (1962)

3 The world may take your reputation from you, but it cannot take your character.

    Emma Dunham Kelley, *Megda* (1891)

4 Character demonstrates itself in trifles.

    Louise Imogen Guiney, *Goose-Quill Papers* (1885)

5 The best index to a person's character is (a) how he treats people who can't do him any good, and (b) how he treats people who can't fight back.

    Abigail Van Buren, syndicated column "Dear Abby" (1974)

6 Some people are molded by their admirations, others by their hostilities.

    Elizabeth Bowen, *The Death of the Heart* (1938)

7 Why can't people be both flexible *and* efficient?

    Margaret Drabble, *The Middle Ground* (1980)

8 The shell is America's most active contribution to the formation of character. A tough hide. Grow it early.

    Anaïs Nin (1946), *The Diary of Anaïs Nin*, vol. 4 (1971)

9 Everybody in Maycomb, it seemed, had a streak: a Drinking Streak, a Gambling Streak, a Mean Streak, a Funny Streak.

    Harper Lee, *To Kill a Mockingbird* (1960)

See also Behavior, Essence, Faults, Fictional Characters, Human Differences, Identity, Personality, Self, Temperament.

## ❦ CHARISMA

10 There are some men who possess a quality which goes way beyond romantic or even sexual appeal, a quality which literally enslaves. It has very little to do with looks and nothing at all to do with youth, because there are some quite mature and unathletic specimens who have it. It's an expression in the eyes, or an aura of being in control, and responsible, or something easy and powerful in the stance, or who knows.

    Lucille Kallen, *Introducing C.B. Greenfield* (1979)

11 Lack of charisma can be fatal.

    Jenny Holzer, *Truisms* (1991)

See also Charm, Popularity, Sex Appeal.

## ❦ CHARITY

12 To have and not to give is often worse than to steal.

    Marie von Ebner-Eschenbach, *Aphorisms* (1893)

13 Charity is a calm, severe duty. . . . It is a strange mistake that it should ever be considered a merit; its fulfillment is only what we owe to each other, and is a debt never paid to its full extent.

    L.E. Landon, *Ethel Churchill* (1837)

14 Do not let the bread of the hungry mildew in your larder! Do not let moths eat the poor man's cloak. Do not store the shoes of the barefoot. Do not hoard the money of the needy. Things you possess in too great abundance belong to the poor and not to you.

    Christine de Pisan, "Le livre des trois vertus" (1405), in Charity Cannon Willard, tr., and Madeleine Pelner Cosman, ed., *A Medieval Woman's Mirror of Honor* (1989)

15 There is an ordinary proverb for this: "Stinginess does not enrich; charity does not impoverish."

    Glückel of Hameln, *Memoirs of Glückel of Hameln* (1724)

16 The charity that begins at home cannot rest there but draws one inexorably over the threshold and off the porch and down the street and so out and out and out and out into the world which becomes the home wherein charity begins until it becomes possible, in theory at least, to love the whole of creation with the same patience, affection, and amusement one first practiced, in between the pouts and tantrums, with parents, siblings, spouse, and children.

    Nancy Mairs, *Ordinary Time* (1993)

17 The results of philanthropy are always beyond calculation.

    Miriam Beard, *A History of Business* (1938)

18 The feeding of those that are hungry is a form of contemplation.

    Simone Weil, *The Notebooks of Simone Weil* (1951)

1 What is this Charity, this clinking of money between strangers. . . . The real Love knows her
neighbor face to face, and laughs with him and
weeps with him, and eats and drinks with him, so
that at last, when his black day dawns, she may
share with him, not what she can spare, but all that
she has.

    Stella Benson, *Living Alone* (1919)

2 I don't want you to give me your surplus. I want
you to give with personal deprivation.

    Mother Teresa (1977), *Heart of Joy* (1987)

3 Lots of people think they are charitable if they give
away their old clothes and things they don't want.

    Myrtle Reed, *Old Rose and Silver* (1909)

4 Charity has always been a expression of the guilty
consciences of a ruling class.

    Doris Lessing, *Children of Violence: A Proper Marriage* (1954)

5 Pity and charity may be at root an attempt to pro-
pitiate the dark powers that have not touched us
yet.

    Marilynne Robinson, *Housekeeping* (1980)

6 Charity is an ugly trick. It is a virtue grown by the
rich on the graves of the poor. Unless it is accompanied by sincere revolt against the present social
system, it is cheap moral swagger. In former times
it was used as fire insurance by the rich, but now
that the fear of Hell has gone along with the rest of
revealed religion, it is used either to gild mean lives
with nobility or as a political instrument.

    Rebecca West, in *The Clarion* (1912)

7 All philanthropy . . . is only a savory fumigation
burning at the mouth of a sewer.

    Ellen Key, *The Century of the Child* (1909)

8 Charity separates the rich from the poor; aid raises
the needy and sets him on the same level with the
rich. . . . Almsgiving tends to perpetuate poverty;
aid does away with it once and for all.

    Eva Perón, speech (1949)

9 Private beneficence is totally inadequate to deal
with the vast numbers of the city's disinherited.

    Jane Addams, *Twenty Years at Hull House* (1910)

10 Some [charities] may have been started with truly
beneficent intentions, but even these finally give
way to a pragmatism that shifts focus away from
"helping the poor" and toward sustaining the institutions. These dual objectives come increasingly to
be at odds.

    Theresa Funiciello, *Tyranny of Kindness* (1993)

11 Blest are the poor, whose needs enable / The rich
but timely charitable / To take the Kingdom of
Heaven by force. / The poor are also saved, of
course.

    Sylvia Townsend Warner, "Grace and Good Works," *The Espalier* (1925)

12 The nonprofit service sector has never been richer
(in terms of share of the gross national product and
jobs), more powerful, or less accountable. It is the
only significant power bloc that is essentially un-
regulated, in spite of the fact that most of its money
comes from the government, through either direct
service contracts or tax expenditures. . . . Taxpay-
ers foot the bill. Poor people suffer the consequences.

    Theresa Funiciello, *Tyranny of Kindness* (1993)

13 Charity degrades those who receive it and hardens
those who dispense it.

    George Sand, *Consuelo* (1842)

14 For those who are not hungry, it is easy to palaver
about the degradation of charity.

    Charlotte Brontë, *Shirley* (1849)

15 You have no idea, sir, how difficult it is to be the
victim of benevolence.

    Jane Aiken Hodge, *Marry in Haste* (1961)

16 To a haughty belly, kindness is hard to swallow and
harder to digest.

    Zora Neale Hurston, *Moses: Man of the Mountain* (1939)

17 One applauds the industry of professional philanthropy. But it has its dangers. After a while the
private heart begins to harden. We fling letters into
the wastebasket, are abrupt to telephoned solicita-
tions. Charity withers in the incessant gale.

    Phyllis McGinley, "Aspects of Sanctity," *Saint-Watching* (1969)

18 The contents of his pockets were often emptied
into the hands of small, ragged little boys, nor
could he understand how so much wealth should
go brushing by, unmindful of the poor.

    Annie Oakley, on Sitting Bull, in Courtney Ryley Cooper, *Annie Oakley* (1927)

1 She . . . kind o' heaves benefits at your head, same's she would bricks; but they're benefits just the same.

Kate Douglas Wiggin, *Rebecca of Sunnybrook Farm* (1903)

2 A giver of the shirt from someone else's back.

Rae Foley, *Curtain Call* (1961)

3 The little entourage of friends and relatives whom she completely dominated was fond of saying, "Becky would give you the shirt off her back." And it was true. The only trouble was that she neglected to take it off first, and what you found on your back was not only Becky's shirt but Becky too.

Margaret Halsey, *No Laughing Matter* (1977)

See also Generosity, Giving, Poverty, The Rich and the Poor, Virtue, Welfare.

## ♦ CHARM

4 Charm is the ability to make someone else think that both of you are pretty wonderful.

Kathleen Winsor, *Star Money* (1950)

5 People were not charmed with Eglantine because she herself was charming, but because she was charmed.

Ada Leverson, *Love at Second Sight* (1916)

6 To enjoy yourself is the easy method to give enjoyment to others.

L.E. Landon, "The Talisman," *The Book of Beauty* (1833)

7 It is not enough to be wise, one must be engaging.

Ninon de Lenclos (1699), in Edgar H. Cohen, *Mademoiselle Libertine* (1970)

8 Charm is a cunning self-forgetfulness.

Christina Stead, *House of All Nations* (1938)

9 No one has it who isn't capable of genuinely liking others, at least at the actual moment of meeting and speaking. Charm is always genuine; it may be superficial but it isn't false.

P.D. James, *The Children of Men* (1992)

10 I realized he would not make the first move to leave; it was instinctive with him to make a woman feel she was too important to be treated lightly—an instinct totally unrelated to the degree of his inter-

est, but it had the effect of a pint of vodka, taken neat.

Lucille Kallen, *Introducing C.B. Greenfield* (1979)

11 His charm, like type O+ blood, suits everyone.

Jane Howard, "The Power That Didn't Corrupt," in *Ms.* (1974)

12 Dad could charm a dog off a meat wagon.

Rita Mae Brown, *Bingo* (1988)

13 When people say you're charming you are in deep trouble.

Jamaica Kincaid, in Donna Perry, ed., *Backtalk* (1993)

14 There is entirely too much charm around, and something must be done to stop it.

Dorothy Parker, "These Much Too Charming People," in *The New Yorker* (1928)

See also Charisma.

## ♦ CHASTITY

15 Chastity is not given once and for all like a wedding ring that is put on never to be taken off, but is a garden which each day must be weeded, watered, and trimmed anew, or soon there will be only brambles and wilderness.

Joanna Russ, *Souls* (1982)

See also Celibacy, Virginity.

## ♦ CHAUVINISM

16 In men this blunder still you find, / All think their little set—mankind.

Hannah More, "Florio" (1786), *The Works of Hannah More*, vol. 1 (1841)

17 When man, Apollo man, rockets into space, it isn't in order to find his brother, I'm quite sure of that. It's to confirm that he hasn't any brothers.

Françoise Sagan, *Scars on the Soul* (1972)

18 We can never give up the belief that the good guys always win. And that we are the good guys.

Faith Popcorn, *The Popcorn Report* (1991)

See also Discrimination, Prejudice.

## ❦ CHEERFULNESS

1 It is easy enough to be pleasant / When life flows by like a song, / But the man worth while is the one who will smile / When everything goes dead wrong.

    Ella Wheeler Wilcox, "Worth While," *An Erring Woman's Love* (1892)

2 A happy woman is one who has no cares at all; a cheerful woman is one who has cares but doesn't let them get her down.

    Beverly Sills, interview (1975)

3 Cheerfulness, it would appear, is a matter which depends fully as much on the state of things within, as on the state of things without and around us.

    Charlotte Brontë, *Shirley* (1849)

4 Good humor, like the jaundice, makes every one of its own complexion.

    Elizabeth Inchbald, *A Simple Story* (1791)

5 We have no more right to steal the brightness out of the day for our own family than we have to steal the purse of a stranger.

    Laura Ingalls Wilder (1917), in Stephen W. Hines, ed., *Little House in the Ozarks* (1991)

See also Optimism.

## ❦ CHESS

6 The laws of chess are as beautiful as those governing the universe—and as deadly.

    Katherine Neville, *A Calculated Risk* (1992)

## ❦ CHICAGO

7 Chicago's downtown seems to me to constitute, all in all, the best-looking twentieth-century city, the city where contemporary technique has best been matched by artistry, intelligence, and comparatively moderated greed. No doubt about it, if style were the one gauge, Chicago would be among the greatest of all the cities of the world.

    Jan Morris, "Boss No More," *Locations* (1992)

8 Was there ever a name more full of purpose than Chicago's? . . . Spoken as Chicagoans themselves speak it, with a bit of a spit to give heft to its slither, it is gloriously onomatopoeic.

    Jan Morris, "Boss No More," *Locations* (1992)

## ❦ CHILDBIRTH

9 Having a baby can be a scream.

    Joan Rivers, book title (1974)

10 [It's] like pushing a piano through a transom.

    Fanny Brice, in Norman Katkov, *The Fabulous Fanny* (1952)

11 Hard labor: A redundancy, like "working mother."

    Joyce Armor, *The Dictionary According to Mommy* (1990)

12 Everybody was bustling about in a very annoying way, plumping pillows, chattering away about centimeters of dilation and how strong the baby's heartbeat sounded. Nobody seemed to have any interest in my heartbeat, and nobody, but nobody, was getting the picture here. I was not having a good time.

    Adair Lara, *Welcome to Earth, Mom* (1992)

13 My cousin Shirley, who never complains, screamed and screamed when she was having her baby. True, this was just during *conception*.

    Joan Rivers, *Having a Baby Can Be a Scream* (1974)

14 I'll bet you one thing, if the man had to have the first baby there wouldn't be but two in the family. Yes sir, let him have the first one and the woman the next one, and his time wouldn't come around no more.

    Josephine Riley Matthews, in Brian Lanker, *I Dream a World* (1989)

15 If men had to have babies they would only ever have one each.

    Diana, Princess of Wales, in *The Observer* (1984)

16 If God were a woman, She would have installed one of those turkey thermometers in our belly buttons. When we were done, the thermometer pops up, the doctor reaches for the zipper conveniently located beneath our bikini lines and out comes a smiling, fully diapered baby.

    Candice Bergen, in *Woman's Day* (1992)

17 The revolting details of childbirth had been hidden from me with such care that I was as surprised as I was horrified, and I cannot help thinking that the

vows most women are made to take are very fool-hardy. I doubt whether they would willingly go to the altar to swear that they will allow themselves to be broken on the wheel every nine months.

Suzanne Curchod Necker (1766), in J. Christopher Herold, *Mistress to an Age* (1958)

1 One pain like this should be enough to save / the world forever.

Toi Derricotte, title poem, *Natural Birth* (1983)

2 The burning embers within me burst into flame / My body becomes a fire-lit torch. / Ho someone! Send for the mid-wife.

Amrita Pritam, "The Annunciation," in Joanna Bankier and Deirdre Lashgari, eds., *Women Poets of the World* (1983)

3 Nature's sharpest pangs . . . free thee living from thy living tomb.

Anna Laetitia Barbauld, "To a Little Invisible Being Who Is Expected Soon to Become Visible" (1773), *The Works of Anna Laetitia Barbauld*, vol. 1 (1825)

4 All night I have suffered; all night my flesh has trembled to bring forth its gift. The sweat of death is on my forehead; but it is not death, it is life!

Gabriela Mistral, "Dawn," *Desolación* (1922)

5 My head rang like a fiery piston / my legs were towers between which / A new world was passing.

Audre Lorde, "Now That I Am Forever With Child," in Arnold Adoff, ed., *The Poetry of Black America* (1973)

6 Dancer / woman in childbirth / you alone / carry on the hidden navel-string / of your body / the identical god-given jewels / of death and birth.

Nelly Sachs, "Dancer," *O the Chimneys* (1967)

7 My babies tore out of me / like poems.

Audre Lorde, "Change of Season" (1969), *Undersong* (1992)

8 nine months passed and my body / heavy with the knowledge of gods / turned landward, came to rest.

Sonia Sanchez, "Rebirth," *A Blues Book for Blue Black Magical Women* (1974)

9 Before I had children I always wondered whether their births would be, for me, like the ultimate in my gym class failures. And discovered, instead . . . that I'd finally found my sport.

Joyce Maynard, in Nancy R. Newhouse, ed., *Hers* (1986)

10 When you were born I held you wet and unfolding, like a butterfly newly born from the chrysalis of my body.

Joy Harjo, "Rainy Dawn," *In Mad Love and War* (1990)

11 I have never heard two firsthand reports of child-birth that sounded remotely alike. The only thing that all women seem to have in common on this subject is a kindly desire to reassure you, the nov-ice, and a natural tendency to discuss it over and over again.

Emily Hahn, *China to Me* (1944)

12 As often as I have witnessed the miracle, held the perfect creature with its tiny hands and feet, each time I have felt as though I were entering a cathe-dral with prayer in my heart.

Margaret Sanger, *Margaret Sanger* (1938)

13 Having a baby is definitely a labor of love.

Joan Rivers, *Having a Baby Can Be a Scream* (1974)

14 Good work, Mary. We all knew you had it in you.

Dorothy Parker, telegram sent (collect) after an ostentatious pregnancy (1915), in Marion Meade, *Dorothy Parker: What Fresh Hell Is This?* (1988)

15 I lost everything in the post-natal depression.

Erma Bombeck, book title (1970)

16 Amnesia: The condition that enables a woman who has gone through labor to have sex again.

Joyce Armor, *The Dictionary According to Mommy* (1990)

See also Babies, Birth, Midwifery, Pregnancy.

## ❧ CHILDHOOD

17 Childhood is the kingdom where nobody dies.

Edna St. Vincent Millay, poem title, *Wine From These Grapes* (1934)

18 Childhood is but change made gay and visible.

Alice Meynell, "That Pretty Person," *Essays* (1914)

19 The sun never again shone as in the first days / of my existence.

Noémia da Sousa, "Poem of Distant Childhood," in Kathleen Weaver, ed., *Penguin Book of Women Poets* (1978)

20 The older I grow the more earnestly I feel that the few intense joys of childhood are the best that life has to give.

Ellen Glasgow, *Letters of Ellen Glasgow* (1958)

21 What one loves in childhood stays in the heart forever.

Mary Jo Putney, *Silk and Secrets* (1992)

1 One of the luckiest things that can happen to you in life is, I think, to have a happy childhood.

Agatha Christie, *An Autobiography* (1977)

2 Childhood has no forebodings; but then, it is soothed by no memories of outlived sorrow.

George Eliot, *The Mill on the Floss* (1860)

3 Oh! to be a child again. My only treasures, bits of shell and stone and glass. To love nothing but maple sugar. To fear nothing but a big dog. To go to sleep without dreading the morrow. To wake up with a shout. Not to have seen a dead face. Not to dread a living one. To be able to *believe*.

Fanny Fern, *Ginger-Snaps* (1870)

4 Childhood is the fiery furnace in which we are melted down to essentials and that essential shaped for good.

Katherine Anne Porter, "Reflections on Willa Cather," *The Days Before* (1952)

5 Childhood was not a time in a person's life, but a country, a country under siege, from which certain individuals were taken too soon and never allowed to return. All people were exiled eventually, but whatever happened to them there marked them all their days.

Kate Green, *Black Dreams* (1993)

6 The child gathers the food on which the adult feeds to the end.

Ralph Iron, *The Story of an African Farm* (1883)

7 When we talk of leaving our childhood behind us, we might as well say that the river flowing onward to the sea had left the fountain behind.

Anna Jameson, *A Commonplace Book* (1855)

8 Adults are always telling young people, "These are the best years of your life." Are they? I don't know. Sometimes when adults say this to children I look into their faces. They look like someone on the top seat of the Ferris wheel who has had too much cotton candy and barbecue. They'd like to get off and be sick but everyone keeps telling them what a good time they're having.

Erma Bombeck, *At Wit's End* (1965)

9 The myth of childhood happiness flourishes so wildly not because it satisfies the needs of children but because it satisfies the needs of adults. In a culture of alienated people, the belief that everyone has at least one good period in life free of care and drudgery dies hard. And obviously you can't expect it in your old age. So it must be you've already had it.

Shulamith Firestone, *The Dialectic of Sex* (1970)

10 To children childhood holds no particular advantage.

Kathleen Norris, *Hands Full of Living* (1931)

11 Childhood is only the beautiful and happy time in contemplation and retrospect: to the child it is full of deep sorrows, the meaning of which is unknown.

George Eliot (1844), in J.W. Cross, ed., *George Eliot's Life As Related in Her Letters and Journals* (1884)

12 Childhood is the one prison from which there's no escape, the one sentence from which there's no appeal. We all serve our time.

P.D. James, *Innocent Blood* (1980)

13 Childhood is long and narrow like a coffin, and you can't get out of it on your own.

Tove Ditlevsen (1967), in Tiina Nunnally, tr., *Early Spring* (1985)

14 My childhood grew thin and flat, paperlike. It was tired and threadbare, and in low moments it didn't look like it would last until I was grown up.

Tove Ditlevsen (1967), in Tiina Nunnally, tr., *Early Spring* (1985)

15 The actual American childhood is less Norman Rockwell and Walt Disney than Nathaniel Hawthorne and Edgar Allan Poe.

Susan Cheever, *A Woman's Life* (1994)

16 Two things are terrible in childhood: helplessness (being in other people's power) and apprehension—the apprehension that something is being concealed from us because it was too bad to be told.

Elizabeth Bowen, *Collected Impressions* (1950)

17 Being a child is largely a flux of bold and furtive guesswork, fixed ideas continually dislodged by scrambling and tentative revision. . . . All our energy and cunning go into getting our bearings without letting on that we are ignorant and lost.

Fernanda Eberstadt, *Isaac and His Demons* (1991)

18 A child's business is an open yard, into which any passer-by may peer curiously. It is no house, not even a glass house. A child's reticence is a little white fence around her business, with a swinging,

helpless gate through which grown-ups come in or go out, for there are no locks on your privacy.

· Margaret Lee Runbeck, *Our Miss Boo* (1942)

1 Perhaps there is something more than courtesy behind the dissembling reticence of childhood. . . . Most artists dislike having their incomplete work considered and discussed and this analogy, I think, is valid. The child is incomplete, too, and is constantly experimenting as he seeks his own style of thought and feeling.

Dervla Murphy, *Wheels Within Wheels* (1979)

2 So much of growing up is an unbearable waiting. A constant longing for another time. Another season.

Sonia Sanchez, *Under a Soprano Sky* (1987)

3 I never meet anyone nowadays who admits to having had a happy childhood.

Jessamyn West, *The Life I Really Lived* (1979)

4 Childhood is less clear to me than to many people: when it ended I turned my face away from it for no reason that I know about, certainly without the usual reason of unhappy memories. For many years that worried me, but then I discovered that the tales of former children are seldom to be trusted. Some people supply too many past victories or pleasures with which to comfort themselves, and other people cling to pains, real and imagined, to excuse what they have become.

Lillian Hellman, *Pentimento* (1973)

5 A childhood is what anyone wants to remember of it. It leaves behind no fossils, except perhaps in fiction.

Carol Shields, *The Stone Diaries* (1994)

6 Some veil between childhood and the present is necessary. If the veil is withdrawn, the artistic imagination sickens and dies, the prophet looks in the mirror with a disillusioned and cynical sneer, the scientist goes fishing.

Margaret Mead, *Male and Female* (1949)

7 The illusions of childhood are necessary experiences: a child should not be denied a balloon just because an adult knows that sooner or later it will burst.

Marcelene Cox, in *Ladies' Home Journal* (1948)

8 I do not believe in a child world. It is a fantasy world. I believe the child should be taught from the very first that the whole world is his world, that

adult and child share one world, that all generations are needed.

Pearl S. Buck, *To My Daughters, With Love* (1967)

9 Growing up is the best revenge.

Judith Martin, *Miss Manners' Guide to Excruciatingly Correct Behavior* (1982)

See also Adolescence, Babies, Children, Youth.

## ❧ CHILDREN

10 When they were wild / When they were not yet human / When they could have been anything, / I was on the other side ready with milk to lure them, / And their father, too, each name a net in his hands.

Louise Erdrich, "Birth," *Baptism of Desire* (1989)

11 To heir is human.

Marcelene Cox, in *Ladies' Home Journal* (1953)

12 The reason most people have kids is because they get pregnant.

Barbara Kingsolver, *The Bean Trees* (1989)

13 There's a time when you have to explain to your children why they're born, and it's a marvelous thing if you know the reason by then.

Hazel Scott, in Margo Jefferson, "Great (Hazel) Scott!" *Ms.* (1974)

14 If you don't have children the longing for them will kill you, and if you do, the worrying over them will kill you.

Buchi Emecheta, *The Joys of Motherhood* (1979)

15 Making the decision to have a child—it's momentous. It is to decide forever to have your heart go walking around outside your body.

Elizabeth Stone, in Ellen Cantarow, "No Kids," *The Village Voice* (1985)

16 The children were there, unannounced, unapologized for; young children, still fresh from the impropriety of birth.

Elizabeth Bowen, "Mrs. Moysey," *Joining Charles* (1929)

17 As the most recently arrived to earthly life, children can seem in lingering possession of some heavenly lidless eye.

Lorrie Moore, *I Know Some Things* (1992)

1 Yes, the race of children possesses magically saga-
cious powers!

    Gail Godwin, title story, *Dream Children* (1976)

2 That most sensitive, most delicate of instruments
—the mind of a little child!

    Henry Handel Richardson, *The Fortunes of Richard
Mahoney: Ultima Thule* (1929)

3 The hearts of small children are delicate organs. A
cruel beginning in this world can twist them into
curious shapes.

    Carson McCullers, *The Ballad of the Sad Café* (1953)

4 A child is fed with milk and praise.

    Mary Lamb, "The First Tooth," *Poetry for Children* (1809)

5 A child with an intense capacity for feeling can
suffer to a degree that is beyond any degree of adult
suffering, because imagination, ignorance, and the
conviction of utter helplessness are untempered
either by reason or by experience.

    E.M. Delafield, *Humbug* (1922)

6 The grief of a child is always terrible. It is bottom-
less, without hope. A child has no past and no
future. It just lives in the present moment—wholeheartedly. If the present moment spells disaster, the
child suffers it with his whole heart, his whole soul,
his whole strength, his whole little being.

    Maria von Trapp, *Yesterday, Today, and Forever* (1952)

7 Very young people are true but not resounding
instruments.

    Elizabeth Bowen, *The Death of the Heart* (1938)

8 No one has yet fully realized the wealth of sympathy, kindness, and generosity hidden in the soul of
a child. The effort of every true educator should be
to unlock that treasure.

    Emma Goldman, *Living My Life* (1931)

9 Children have two visions, the inner and the outer.
Of the two the inner vision is brighter.

    Sylvia Ashton-Warner, *Teacher* (1963)

10 What a difference it makes to come home to a
child!

    Margaret Fuller, letter (1849), in Alice S. Rossi, ed., *The
Feminist Papers* (1973)

11 Few things are more rewarding than a child's open
uncalculating devotion.

    Vera Brittain, *Testament of Friendship* (1940)

12 What feeling in all the world is so nice as that of a
child's hand in yours? It is soft. It is small and
warm. It is as innocent and guileless as a rabbit or
a puppy or a kitten huddling in the shelter of your
clasp.

    Marjorie Holmes, *Love and Laughter* (1967)

13 What are so mysterious as the eyes of a child?

    Phyllis Bottome, "Brother Leo," *Innocence and Experience*
(1934)

14 Children are unaccountable little creatures.

    Katherine Mansfield, "Sixpence" (1921), *Something Childish*
(1924)

15 In their sympathies, children feel nearer animals
than adults.

    Jessamyn West, *The Life I Really Lived* (1979)

16 A Child of Happiness always seems like an old soul
living in a new body, and her face is very serious
until she smiles, and then the sun lights up the
world. . . . Children of Happiness always look not
quite the same as other children. They have strong,
straight legs and walk with purpose. They laugh as
do all children, and they play as do all children,
they talk child talk as do all children, but they are
different, they are blessed, they are special, they are
sacred.

    Anne Cameron, *Daughters of Copper Woman* (1981)

17 They weary and restore me.

    Marita Golden, *A Woman's Place* (1986)

18 My children . . . have been a constant joy to me
(except on the days when they weren't).

    Evelyn Fairbanks, *The Days of Rondo* (1990)

19 Being constantly with the children was like wearing
a pair of shoes that were expensive and too small.
She couldn't bear to throw them out, but they gave
her blisters.

    Beryl Bainbridge, *Injury Time* (1977)

20 One hour with a child is like a ten-mile run.

    Joan Benoit Samuelson, in *The New York Times* (1991)

21 Every minute in the presence of a child takes seven
minutes off your life.

    Barbara Kingsolver, *Animal Dreams* (1990)

22 It seems to me that since I've had children, I've
grown richer and deeper. They may have slowed

down my writing for a while, but when I did write, I had more of a self to speak from.

Anne Tyler, in Janet Sternburg, ed., *The Writer on Her Work*, vol. 1 (1980)

1 [Children] use up the same part of my head as poetry does. To deal with children is a matter of terrific imaginative identification. And the children have to come first. It's no use putting off their evening meal for two months.

Libby Houston, in Cheris Kramarae and Paula A. Treichler, *A Feminist Dictionary* (1985)

2 Children can't be a center of life and a reason for being. They can be a thousand things that are delightful, interesting, satisfying, but they can't be a well-spring to live from. Or they shouldn't be.

Doris Lessing, "To Room Nineteen," *A Man and Two Women* (1963)

3 Ours is the first society in history in which parents expect to learn from their children, rather than the other way around. Such a topsy-turvy situation has come about at least in part because, unlike the rest of the world, we are an immigrant society, and for immigrants the only hope is in the kids.

Shana Alexander (1972), *Talking Woman* (1976)

4 Once they all stop drinking your blood, and start functioning on their own systems, they become galaxies, spinning away from you, covering greater distances with every passing year.

Sheila Ballantyne, *Norma Jean the Termite Queen* (1975)

5 A blossom must break the sheath it has been sheltered by.

Phyllis Bottome, *The Mortal Storm* (1938)

6 It kills you to see them grow up. But I guess it would kill you quicker if they didn't.

Barbara Kingsolver, *Animal Dreams* (1990)

7 There is a certain melancholy in having to tell oneself that one has said good-bye—unless of course one is a grandmother—to the age and the circumstances that enable one to observe young children closely and passionately.

Colette, *Paris From My Window* (1944)

8 Indians still consider the whites a brutal people who treat their children like enemies—playthings, too, coddling them like pampered pets or fragile toys, but underneath always like enemies, enemies that must be restrained, bribed, spied upon, and punished. They believe that children so treated will grow up as dependent and immature as pets and toys, and as angry and dangerous as enemies within the family circle, to be appeased and fought.

Mari Sandoz, *Sandhill Sundays and Other Recollections* (1970)

9 What its children become, that will the community become.

Suzanne La Follette, "Woman and Marriage," *Concerning Women* (1926)

10 In the last analysis civilization itself is measured by the way in which children will live and what chance they will have in the world.

Mary Heaton Vorse, *A Footnote to Folly* (1935)

11 Children are an embarrassment to a business civilization. A business society needs children for the same reason that a nomadic or a pastoral society needs them—to perpetuate itself. Unfortunately, however, children are of no use to a business society until they have almost reached physical maturity.

Margaret Halsey, *The Folks at Home* (1952)

12 A business society . . . always has in its children a large group of individuals who cannot make money and who do not understand (or want to understand) the profit motive. In short, they are subversives.

Margaret Halsey, *The Folks at Home* (1952)

13 If our American way of life fails the child, it fails us all.

Pearl S. Buck, *Children for Adoption* (1964)

14 When a species fails to care for its progeny, the species is doomed.

Georgia Savage, in Mary Ann Grossmann, "Readers Get 'Gobstuck' Over Kindly Savage," *St. Paul Pioneer Press* (1991)

15 The society that destroys its children is eating its own tail, committing suicide in the most perverse way.

Jennifer Stone, in *Mama Bears News & Notes* (1996)

16 The young, young children, O my brothers, / They are weeping bitterly! / They are weeping in the playtime of the others, / In the country of the free.

Elizabeth Barrett Browning, "The Cry of the Children," *Poems* (1844)

17 All adults stand accused . . . the society responsible for the welfare of children has been put on trial. There is something apocalyptic about this startling

accusation; it is mysterious and terrible like the voice of the Last Judgment: "What have you done to the children I entrusted to you?"

Maria Montessori, *The Secret of Childhood* (1936)

1 The truly beneficent mind looks upon every child of sorrow as their relation, and entitled to their assistance.

Eliza Parsons, *Castle of Wolfenbach* (1793)

2 The mother's battle for her child—with sickness, with poverty, with war, with all the forces of exploitation and callousness that cheapen human life— needs to become a common human battle, waged in love and in the passion for survival.

Adrienne Rich, *Of Woman Born* (1976)

3 We are willing to spend the least amount of money to keep a kid at home, more to put him in a foster home, and the most to institutionalize him.

Marian Wright Edelman, in Margie Casady, "Society's Pushed-Out Children," *Psychology Today* (1975)

4 Children's talent to endure stems from their ignorance of alternatives.

Maya Angelou, *I Know Why the Caged Bird Sings* (1970)

5 Children cannot eat rhetoric and they cannot be sheltered by commissions. I don't want to see another commission that studies the needs of kids. We need to help them.

Marian Wright Edelman, in Brian Lanker, *I Dream a World* (1989)

6 Everywhere, everywhere, children are the scorned people of the earth.

Toni Morrison, in Charles Ruas, *Conversations With American Writers* (1984)

7 Oh dear, dark boy. There was such promise of happiness balanced there. But your mama never rocked you when you were a baby, you say, and your daddy died when you were seventeen. And all the rest of us can never make it up to you.

Sonia Johnson, *From Housewife to Heretic* (1981)

8 There are no illegitimate children, only illegitimate parents—if the term is to be used at all.

Bernadette Devlin, in *The Irish Times* (1971)

9 The children are always the chief victims of social chaos.

Agnes E. Meyer, *Out of These Roots* (1953)

10 The crisis of children having children has been eclipsed by the greater crisis of children killing children.

Marian Wright Edelman, news item (1994)

11 Children whose problems aren't recognized become problem children.

Marcelene Cox, in *Ladies' Home Journal* (1944)

12 So long as little children are allowed to suffer, there is no true love in this world.

Isadora Duncan, "Memoirs," in *This Quarter* (1929)

13 I suppose we make kids the repository of our highest ideals because children are powerless. In that way we can have ideals and ignore them at the same time.

Ellen Goodman, *At Large* (1981)

14 If responsibility for the upbringing of children is to continue to be vested in the family, then the rights of children will be secured only when parents are able to make a living for their families with so little difficulty that they may give their best thought and energy to the child's development and the problem of helping it adjust itself to the complexities of the modern environment.

Suzanne La Follette, "Institutional Marriage and Its Economic Aspects," *Concerning Women* (1926)

15 Having a baby . . . brought home to me with real force the hopelessly unbalanced nature of a society which is organized solely for the needs of people without responsibility for children.

Angela Phillips, "Two Steps Forward, One Step Back?" in Michelene Wandor, ed., *On Gender and Writing* (1983)

16 It's clear that most American children suffer too much mother and too little father.

Gloria Steinem, in *The New York Times* (1971)

17 The American child, driven to school by bus and stupefied by television, is losing contact with reality. There is an enormous gap between the sheer weight of the textbooks that he carries home from school and his capacity to interpret what is in them.

Marguerite Yourcenar, *With Open Eyes* (1980)

18 In this era of affluence and of permissiveness, we have, in all but cultural areas, bred a nation of overprivileged youngsters, saturated with vitamins, television and plastic toys. But they are nurtured from infancy on a Dick-and-Jane literary and artistic level; and the cultural drought, as far as enter-

tainment is concerned, sets in when they are between six and eight.

Judith Crist, *The Private Eye, the Cowboy and the Very Naked Girl* (1968)

1 The finest inheritance you can give to a child is to allow it to make its own way, completely on its own feet.

Isadora Duncan, *My Life* (1942)

2 At every step the child should be allowed to meet the real experiences of life; the thorns should never be plucked from his roses.

Ellen Key, *The Century of the Child* (1909)

3 Our children . . . are not treated with sufficient respect as human beings, and yet from the moment they are born they have this right to respect. We keep them children for too long, their world separate from the real world of life.

Pearl S. Buck, *My Several Worlds* (1954)

4 I . . . protest against the efforts, so often made, to shield children and young people from all that has to do with death and sorrow, to give them a good time at all hazards on the assumption that the ills of life will come soon enough. Young people themselves . . . feel set aside and belittled as if they were denied the common human experiences.

Jane Addams, *Twenty Years at Hull House* (1910)

5 When we want to infuse new ideas, to modify or better the habits and customs of a people, to breathe new vigor into its national traits, we must use the child as our vehicle; for little can be accomplished with adults.

Maria Montessori, *The Absorbent Mind* (1949)

6 Children are not born knowing the many opportunities that are theirs for the taking. Someone who does know must tell them.

Ruth Hill Viguers, in Joan Peterson, "Ruth Hill Viguers," *The Horn Book* (1991)

7 Parents of young children should realize that few people, and maybe no one, will find their children as enchanting as they do.

Barbara Walters, *How to Talk With Practically Anybody About Practically Anything* (1970)

8 Adorable children are considered to be the general property of the human race. (Rude children belong to their mothers.)

Judith Martin, *Miss Manners' Guide to Rearing Perfect Children* (1984)

9 Was it possible that not so many months ago they had waited for his words as for pearls and rubies? Was this the child whose uncanny silence had stricken them with shame in the presence of other young parents? His voice was high and clear; no door could shut out its intonations. He chanted with a steadily rising inflection the saga of his past day interwoven with irrelevant excerpts from the pig-telephone story and one other, his longest, which dealt mysteriously with a cup and saucer, a lady and a pianola.

Josephine Daskam, *The Memoirs of a Baby* (1904)

10 Children . . . will put up with nothing that is unpleasant to them, without at least making a noise, which I do detest and dread; though I know mothers ought to "get used to such things." I have heard that eels get accustomed to being skinned, but I doubt the fact.

Mrs. Mary Clavers, *A New Home* (1839)

11 Children always take the line of most persistence.

Marcelene Cox, in *Ladies' Home Journal* (1947)

12 We love those we feed, not vice versa; in caring for others we nourish our own self esteem. Children are dependent upon adults. It's a craven role for a child. It's very natural to want to bite the hand that feeds you.

Jessamyn West, *The Life I Really Lived* (1979)

13 It is not a bad thing that children should occasionally, and politely, put parents in their place.

Colette, "The Priest on the Wall," *My Mother's House* (1922)

14 There is such a rebound from parental influence that it generally seems that the child makes use of the directions given by the parent only to avoid the prescribed path.

Margaret Fuller, in *The Dial* (1841)

15 The character and history of each child may be a new and poetic experience to the parent, if he will let it.

Margaret Fuller, *Summer on the Lakes* (1844)

16 The temperaments of children are often as oddly unsuited to parents as if capricious fairies had been filling cradles with changelings.

Harriet Beecher Stowe, *The Pearl of Orr's Island* (1862)

17 Hedda was queasily phobic of children and, by extension, of short people in general. They were too condensed, like undiluted cans of soup—too in-

tensely human and, therefore, too intensely not to be trusted. The mistakes in the basic ingredients—the stupidity, the cruelty—were overpoweringly present.

Rebecca Goldstein, *The Dark Sister* (1991)

1 I wasn't used to children and they were getting on my nerves. Worse, it appeared that I was a child, too. I hadn't known that before; I thought I was just short.

Florence King, on her first day in kindergarten, *Confessions of a Failed Southern Lady* (1985)

2 I was a very ancient twelve; my views at that age would have done credit to a Civil War veteran. I am much younger now than I was at twelve or anyway, less burdened. The weight of the centuries lies on children, I'm sure of it.

Flannery O'Connor, in Sally Fitzgerald, ed., *The Habit of Being* (1979)

3 There are children born to be children, and others who must mark time till they can take their natural places as adults.

Mignon McLaughlin, *The Neurotic's Notebook* (1963)

4 He is not like other children, not cruel, or savage. For this very reason he is called "strange." A child who is mature, in the sense that the heart is mature, is always, I have observed, called deficient.

Djuna Barnes, *Nightwood* (1937)

5 Too much indulgence has ruined thousands of children; too much *Love* not one.

Fanny Fern, *Caper Sauce* (1872)

6 Children robbed of love will dwell on magic.

Barbara Kingsolver, *Animal Dreams* (1990)

7 A child who constantly hears "Don't," "Be careful," "Stop" will eventually be overtaken by schoolmates, business associates, and rival suitors.

Marcelene Cox, in *Ladies' Home Journal* (1943)

8 A child does not thrive on what he is prevented from doing, but on what he actually does.

Marcelene Cox, in *Ladies' Home Journal* (1947)

9 Two important things to teach a child: to do and to do without.

Marcelene Cox, in *Ladies' Home Journal* (1957)

10 It is a mystery why adults expect perfection from children. Few grownups can get through a whole day without making a mistake.

Marcelene Cox, in *Ladies' Home Journal* (1943)

11 A child can never be better than what his parents think of him.

Marcelene Cox, in *Ladies' Home Journal* (1945)

12 Children in a family are like flowers in a bouquet: there's always one determined to face in an opposite direction from the way the arranger desires.

Marcelene Cox, in *Ladies' Home Journal* (1956)

13 Likely as not, the child you can do the least with will do the most to make you proud.

Mignon McLaughlin, *The Second Neurotic's Notebook* (1966)

14 Play is not for every hour of the day, or for any hour taken at random. There is a tide in the affairs of children. Civilization is cruel in sending them to bed at the most stimulating time of dusk.

Alice Meynell, "Under the Early Stars," *The Children* (1897)

15 As the youngsters grow attached to their teachers and classmates . . . they can finally say good-bye to their mothers without re-enacting the death scene from *Camille*.

Sue Mittenthal, in *The New York Times* (1984)

16 I love children, especially when they cry, because then somebody takes them away.

Nancy Mitford, "The Tourist" (1959), *The Water Beetle* (1962)

17 Where there's a will there's a way, and where there's a child there's a will.

Marcelene Cox, in *Ladies' Home Journal* (1950)

18 All encounters with children are touched with social embarrassment.

Sylvia Townsend Warner, "View Halloo," *The Museum of Cheats* (1947)

19 Anybody who thinks there is any vague chance of adult exchange with a child is up the spout; and would be much less disappointed if they recognized the chasm unbridgeably dividing them.

Caitlin Thomas, *Leftover Life to Kill* (1957)

20 Notoriously insensitive to subtle shifts in mood, children will persist in discussing the color of a recently sighted cement-mixer long after one's own interest in the topic has waned.

Fran Lebowitz, *Metropolitan Life* (1978)

1 A child's attitude toward everything is an artist's attitude.

> Willa Cather, *The Song of the Lark* (1915)

2 All children are artists, and it is an indictment of our culture that so many of them lose their creativity, their unfettered imaginations, as they grow older.

> Madeleine L'Engle, *Walking on Water* (1980)

3 I see the mind of the five-year-old as a volcano with two vents: destructiveness and creativeness.

> Sylvia Ashton-Warner, *Teacher* (1963)

4 A child motivated by competitive ideals will grow into a man without conscience, shame, or true dignity.

> George Sand (1837), in Marie Jenny Howe, ed., *The Intimate Journal of George Sand* (1929)

5 The easiest way for your children to learn about money is for you not to have any.

> Katharine Whitehorn, *How to Survive Children* (1975)

6 To give children everything is often worse than giving them nothing.

> Marcelene Cox, in *Ladies' Home Journal* (1947)

7 It is frequently said that children do not know the value of money. This is only partially true. They do not know the value of *your* money. *Their* money, they know the value of.

> Judy Markey, *You Only Get Married for the First Time Once* (1988)

8 One should, I think, always give children money, for they will spend it for themselves far more profitably than we can ever spend it for them.

> Rose Macaulay, "Christmas Presents," *A Casual Commentary* (1926)

9 Children are rarely in the position to lend one a truly interesting sum of money. There are, however, exceptions, and such children are an excellent addition to any party.

> Fran Lebowitz, *Metropolitan Life* (1978)

10 Ask your child what he wants for dinner only if he's buying.

> Fran Lebowitz, *Social Studies* (1977)

11 The best way to keep children at home is to make the home atmosphere pleasant, and let the air out of the tires.

> Dorothy Parker, in Frank Muir, *Frank Muir on Children* (1980)

12 Give the neighbors' kids an inch and they'll take the whole yard.

> Helen Castle, in *The Saturday Evening Post* (1950)

13 Even when freshly washed and relieved of all obvious confections, children tend to be sticky.

> Fran Lebowitz, *Metropolitan Life* (1978)

14 Never allow your child to call you by your first name. He hasn't known you long enough.

> Fran Lebowitz, *Social Studies* (1977)

15 One of the things I've discovered in general about raising kids is that they really don't give a damn if you walked five miles to school.

> Patty Duke, with Kenneth Turan, *Call Me Anna* (1987)

See also Adolescence, Babies, Childhood, Daughters, Discipline, Family, Generations, Grandparents, Orphans, Parenthood, Parents, Sons, Youth.

## ❦ CHILDREN'S LITERATURE

16 A child's own story is a dream, but a good story is a dream that is true for more than one child.

> Margaret Wise Brown, in Leonard S. Marcus, *Margaret Wise Brown* (1992)

17 Only as we give the children the truth about life can we expect any improvement in it.

> Mabel Louise Robinson, in Helen Hull, ed., *The Writer's Book* (1950)

18 There is nothing more important than writing well for the young, if literature is to have a continuance. . . . They will inherit the earth; and nothing that we value will endure in the world unless they can be persuaded to value it too.

> Jill Paton Walsh, in Eleanor Cameron, *The Seed and the Vision* (1993)

19 Books that children read but once are of scant service to them; those that have really helped to warm our imaginations and to train our faculties are the few old friends we know so well that they have become a portion of our thinking selves.

> Agnes Repplier, "What Children Read," *Books and Men* (1888)

20 He seemed to share the view of many intelligent, well-educated, well-meaning people that, while adult literature may aim to be art, the object of

children's books is to whip the little rascals into shape.

Katherine Paterson, *Gates of Excellence* (1981)

1 When I am grappling with ideas which are radical enough to upset grown-ups, then I am likely to put these ideas into a story which will be marketed for children, because children understand what their parents have rejected and forgotten.

Madeleine L'Engle, *Walking on Water* (1980)

2 The children's writer not only makes a satisfactory connection between his present maturity and his past childhood, he also does the same for his child-characters in reverse—makes the connection between their present childhood and their future maturity. That their maturity is never visibly achieved makes no difference; the promise of it is there.

Philippa Pearce, "The Writer's View of Childhood," in *The Horn Book* (1962)

3 By providing cheap and wholesome reading for the young, we have partly succeeded in driving from the field that which was positively bad; yet nothing is easier than to overdo a reformation, and, through the characteristic indulgence of American parents, children are drugged with a literature whose chief merit is its harmlessness.

Agnes Repplier, "What Children Read," *Books and Men* (1888)

4 Children's books are looked on as a sideline of literature. A special smile.... I was determined not to have this label of sentimentality put on me so I signed by my initials, hoping people wouldn't bother to wonder if the books were written by a man, woman or kangaroo.

P.L. Travers, in Haskel Frankel, "A Rose for Mary Poppins," *Saturday Review* (1964)

5 Over and over again women and men ... come to me saying, I don't know enough to write a book for adults, and so I'd like to try a book for children. And I tell them that when they have learned enough to write for an adult perhaps a child will listen to them.

Mabel Louise Robinson, in Helen Hull, ed., *The Writer's Book* (1950)

6 Sure it's simple, writing for kids. Just as simple as bringing them up.

Ursula K. Le Guin, "Dreams Must Explain Themselves" (1973), *Language of the Night* (1979)

See also Literature, Nursery Rhymes, Writing.

## ❦ CHINA

7 China is a long caravan, longer and stronger than the Wall.

Genevieve Taggard, "Turn to the East," *Collected Poems* (1938)

8 In yielding we are like the water, by nature placid, conforming to the hollow of the smallest hand; in time, shaping even the mountains to its will. Thus we keep duty and honor. We cherish clan and civilization. We are Chinese.

Bette Bao Lord, *Spring Moon* (1981)

9 Nothing and no one can destroy the Chinese people. They are relentless survivors. They are the oldest civilized people on earth. . . . They yield, they bend to the wind, but they never break.

Pearl S. Buck, *China Past and Present* (1972)

10 Like most Chinese, I am basically a fatalist—too sophisticated for religion and too superstitious to deny the gods.

Bette Bao Lord, *Spring Moon* (1981)

## ❦ CHIVALRY

11 There is no country in the world where there is so much boasting of the "chivalrous" treatment she [woman] enjoys. . . . In short, indulgence is given her as a substitute for justice.

Harriet Martineau, *Society in America* (1837)

12 Chivalry is a poor substitute for justice, if one cannot have both. Chivalry is something like the icing on the cake, sweet but not nourishing.

Nellie L. McClung, *In Times Like These* (1915)

13 A pedestal is as much a prison as any other small space.

Anonymous woman, in Gloria Steinem, *Moving Beyond Words* (1994)

14 Opening the door is a political act. The door-opening ceremony represents a non-obtrusive measure of authority. The hand that holds the door-knob rules the world.

Laurel Richardson Walum, in *The Observer* (1973)

1 I admit it is better fun to punt than to be punted, and that a desire to have all the fun is nine-tenths of the law of chivalry.

   Dorothy L. Sayers, *Gaudy Night* (1935)

2 Chivalry, I don't abuse you, / Not at all—the only rub / Is that those who praise you, use you / Very often as a club.

   Alice Duer Miller, "To Chivalry," *Women Are People!* (1917)

3 If the bird *does* like its cage, and *does* like its sugar, and will not leave it, why keep the door so very carefully shut?

   Ralph Iron, *The Story of an African Farm* (1883)

4 Beware of the man who wants to protect you; / he will protect you from everything but himself.

   Erica Jong, "Seventeen Warnings in Search of a Feminist Poem," *Half-Lives* (1971)

5 You are not our protectors. . . . If you were, who would there be to protect us from?

   Mary Walker (1871), addressing her male readers, in Charles McCool Snyder, *Dr. Mary Walker* (1962)

6 Protectiveness has often muffled the sound of doors closing against women.

   Betty Friedan, *The Feminine Mystique* (1963)

## ❦ CHOCOLATE

7 Chocolate is no ordinary food. It is not something you can take or leave, something you like only moderately. You don't *like* chocolate. You don't even *love* chocolate. Chocolate is something you have an *affair* with.

   Geneen Roth, *Feeding the Hungry Heart* (1982)

8 Research tells us that fourteen out of any ten individuals like chocolate.

   Sandra Boynton, *Chocolate: The Consuming Passion* (1982)

9 Much serious thought has been devoted to the subject of chocolate: What does chocolate *mean*? Is the pursuit of chocolate a right or a privilege? Does the notion of chocolate preclude the concept of free will?

   Sandra Boynton, *Chocolate: The Consuming Passion* (1982)

10 Britt ate lots of chocolate but never got fat—a sure sign of demonic possession.

   Erica Jong, *How to Save Your Own Life* (1977)

11 As with most fine things, chocolate has its season. There is a simple memory aid that you can use to determine whether it is the correct time to order chocolate dishes: Any month whose name contains the letter a, e, or u is the proper time for chocolate.

   Sandra Boynton, *Chocolate: The Consuming Passion* (1982)

12 Cocoa. Damn miserable puny stuff, fit for kittens and unwashed boys. Did *Shakespeare* drink cocoa?

   Shirley Jackson, *The Bird's Nest* (1954)

13 I advise nobody to drown sorrow in cocoa. It is bad for the figure and it does not alleviate the sorrow.

   Winifred Holtby, "The Right Side of Thirty" (1930), *Pavements at Anderby* (1937)

See also Food.

## ❦ CHOICE

14 The strongest principle of growth lies in human choice.

   George Eliot, *Daniel Deronda* (1874)

15 Choice is the essence of what I believe it is to be human.

   Liv Ullmann, *Choices* (1984)

16 It is the ability to choose which makes us human.

   Madeleine L'Engle, *Walking on Water* (1980)

17 It's when we're given choice that we sit with the gods and design ourselves.

   Dorothy Gilman, *Caravan* (1992)

18 We cannot freely and wisely choose the right way for ourselves unless we know both good and evil.

   Helen Keller, *My Religion* (1927)

19 Choose well: your choice is brief and yet endless.

   Ella Winter, *And Not to Yield* (1963)

20 You cannot choose your battlefield, / The gods do that for you, / But you can plant a standard / Where a standard never flew.

   Nathalia Crane, "The Colors," *The Singing Crow* (1926)

21 The most painful moral struggles are not those between good and evil, but between the good and the lesser good.

   Barbara Grizzuti Harrison, "Moral Ambiguity," *Off Center* (1980)

1 There are no signposts in the sea.
   Vita Sackville-West, *No Signposts in the Sea* (1961)

2 To choose is also to begin.
   Starhawk, *Dreaming the Dark* (1982)

3 Long afterwards, she was to remember that moment when her life changed its direction. It was not predestined; she had a choice. Or it seemed that she had. To accept or refuse. To take one turning down the crossroads to the future or another. But this would be hindsight, and time always mocked truth.
   Evelyn Anthony, *The Avenue of the Dead* (1982)

4 Choice has always been a privilege of those who could afford to pay for it.
   Ellen Frankfort, in Michèle Brown and Ann O'Connor, *Woman Talk*, vol. 1 (1984)

5 Bread sets free; but does not necessarily set free for good ends—that dear illusion of so many generous hearts. It sets a man free to choose: it often sets free for the bad, but man has a right to that choice and to that evil, without which he is no longer a man.
   Françoise Mallet-Joris, *A Letter to Myself* (1963)

6 I have a theory that every time you make an important choice, the part of you left behind continues the other life you could have had.
   Jeanette Winterson, *Oranges Are Not the Only Fruit* (1985)

See also Decision, Priorities, Variety.

# ❦ CHRIST

7 Jesus loves me—this I know, / For the Bible tells me so.
   Anna Bartlett Warner, "The Love of Jesus" (1858)

8 I am amazed by the sayings of Christ. They seem truer than anything I have ever read. And they certainly turn the world upside down.
   Katharine Butler Hathaway, *The Journals and Letters of the Little Locksmith* (1946)

9 The people who hanged Christ . . . thought Him too dynamic to be safe. It has been left for later generations to muffle up that shattering personality and surround Him with an atmosphere of tedium.
   Dorothy L. Sayers, "The Greatest Drama Ever Staged," *Creed or Chaos?* (1949)

10 God was executed by people painfully like us, in a society very similar to our own . . . by a corrupt church, a timid politician, and a fickle proletariat led by professional agitators.
   Dorothy L. Sayers, *The Man Born to Be King* (1943)

11 I am not sure that Christ would have been very satisfied to foresee that He would be looked upon principally as a *redeemer* and nailed forever upon the cross by human ignorance. It seems to me that He above all desired to bring men a message of truth, that He wanted to heal them of their faults by making an appeal to all their energy; He shook them as much as He could, He did not seek to spare them the trouble.
   Adrienne Monnier (1938), in Richard McDougall, tr., *The Very Rich Hours of Adrienne Monnier* (1976)

12 Christ must be rediscovered perpetually.
   Edith Hamilton, *Witness to the Truth* (1948)

13 The feet of Christ are set in human places.
   Sister M. Madeleva, "Post-Communion," *Collected Poems* (1947)

14 Whar did your Christ come from? From God and a woman! Man had nothing to do with Him.
   Sojourner Truth, speech (1851), in Olive Gilbert, *Narrative of Sojourner Truth* (1878)

15 It is part of the amazing originality of Christ that there is to be found in his teaching no word whatever which suggests a difference in the spiritual ideals, the spheres, or the potentialities of men and women.
   Maude Royden, *The Church and Women* (1924)

16 As we know, our own mother bore us only into pain and dying. But our true mother, Jesus, who is all love, bears us into joy and endless living.
   Julian of Norwich, *Revelations of Divine Love* (1373)

17 Jesus would be framed and in jail if he was living today.
   Carson McCullers, *The Heart Is a Lonely Hunter* (1940)

See also Christianity, God.

# ❦ CHRISTIANITY

18 The Christian tradition was passed on to me as a great rich mixture, a bouillabaisse of human imagi-

nation and wonder brewed from the richness of individual lives.

Mary Catherine Bateson, *With a Daughter's Eye* (1984)

1 There are two kinds of Christian experience, one of which is an experience of bondage, and the other an experience of liberty.

Hannah Whitall Smith, *The Christian's Secret of a Happy Life* (1870)

2 Authentic Christianity never destroys what is good. It makes it grow, transfigures it and enriches itself from it.

Claire Huchet Bishop, *France Alive* (1947)

3 Does being born into a Christian family make one a Christian? No! God has no grandchildren.

Corrie ten Boom, *Each New Day* (1977)

4 The philosophy of love and peace strangely overlooked who was in possession of the guns. There had been love and peace for some time on the continent of Africa because for all this time black men had been captivated by the doctrines of Christianity. It took them centuries to realize its contradictions. . . . Perhaps there was no greater crime as yet than all the lies Western civilization had told in the name of Jesus Christ.

Bessie Head, *When Rain Clouds Gather* (1969)

5 Christian ideology has contributed no little to the oppression of woman.

Simone de Beauvoir, *The Second Sex* (1949)

6 It is not Christianity but priestcraft that has subjected woman as we find her.

Lucretia Mott (1853), in Dana Greene, ed., *Lucretia Mott* (1980)

7 Christianity, which has ever sought to moderate the profit-seeking of the business man, has assisted him to develop finance and industry. It was the curious destiny of this greatest spiritual force in the Western world to prepare mankind for materialism and mechanization. Yet it has exerted ceaseless pressure on the money-makers to consider the effects of their activities upon society and their own souls.

Miriam Beard, *A History of Business* (1938)

8 What about Christianity? Are we right in the face of so long a record of its poverty in international achievement, to keep invoking it as a standard, almost synonymous with civilization?

Rose Macaulay (1948), in Jane Emery, *Rose Macaulay* (1991)

9 The arrogance of some Christians would close heaven to them if, to their misfortune, it existed.

Simone de Beauvoir, *All Said and Done* (1972)

10 Persons who would never think of announcing boldly to the world, "I am a scholar," "I am a great artist," "I am a beautiful woman," nevertheless seem to think it wholly within the bounds of good taste to announce that they are Christians!

Georgia Harkness, *The Resources of Religion* (1936)

11 I'm startled or taken aback when people walk up to me and tell me they are Christians. My first response is the question "Already?"

Maya Angelou, *Wouldn't Take Nothing for My Journey Now* (1993)

See also Christ, Church, Clergy, Episcopalians, God, Religion, Spirituality, Theology.

# ❧ CHRISTMAS

12 Welcome Christmas! heel and toe, / Come and fill us ere you go!

Mary Mapes Dodge, "Stocking Song on Christmas Eve," *Rhymes and Jingles* (1904)

13 God rest ye, merry gentlemen, let nothing you dismay, / For Jesus Christ, our Saviour, was born on Christmas-day.

Dinah Maria Mulock Craik, "Christmas Carol," *Poems* (1859)

14 When Christmas bells are swinging above the fields of snow, / We hear sweet voices ringing from lands of long ago, / And etched on vacant places / Are half-forgotten faces / Of friends we used to cherish, and loves we used to know.

Ella Wheeler Wilcox, "Christmas Fancies," *Poems of Power* (1910)

15 Christmas is a kindling of new fires.

Gladys Taber, *Stillmeadow Daybook* (1955)

16 Christmas isn't a season. It's a feeling.

Edna Ferber, *Roast Beef Medium* (1913)

17 Christmas is a season of convergence.

Lilly Golden, *A Literary Christmas* (1992)

18 Christmas is a bridge. We need bridges as the river of time flows past. Today's Christmas should mean

creating happy hours for tomorrow and reliving those of yesterday.

Gladys Taber, *Still Cove Journal* (1981)

1 Christmas . . . is not an external event at all, but a piece of one's home that one carries in one's heart: like a nursery story, its validity rests on exact repetition, so that it comes around every time as the evocation of one's whole life and particularly of the most distant bits of it in childhood.

Freya Stark, "The Wise Men," in *Time and Tide* (1953)

2 Christmas Eve was a night of song that wrapped itself about you like a shawl. But it warmed more than your body. It warmed your heart . . . filled it, too, with melody that would last forever.

Bess Streeter Aldrich, *Song of Years* (1939)

3 I do hope your Christmas has had a little touch of Eternity in among the rush and pitter patter and all. It always seems such a mixing of this world and the next—but that after all *is* the idea!

Evelyn Underhill (1936), in Charles Williams, ed., *The Letters of Evelyn Underhill* (1943)

4 There is nothing sadder in this world than to awake Christmas morning and not be a child. . . . Time, self-pity, apathy, bitterness, and exhaustion can take the Christmas out of the child, but you cannot take the child out of Christmas.

Erma Bombeck, *I Lost Everything in the Post-Natal Depression* (1970)

5 "It's better'n a Christmas," they told their mother, "to get ready for it!"

Margaret Sidney, *Five Little Peppers and How They Grew* (1881)

6 Christmas won't be Christmas without any presents.

Louisa May Alcott, *Little Women* (1868)

7 Our children await Christmas presents like politicians getting in election returns: there's the Uncle Fred precinct and the Aunt Ruth district still to come in.

Marcelene Cox, in *Ladies' Home Journal* (1950)

8 No matter how many Christmas presents you give your child, there's always that terrible moment when he's opened the very last one. That's when he expects you to say, "Oh yes, I almost forgot," and take him out and show him the pony.

Mignon McLaughlin, *The Second Neurotic's Notebook* (1966)

9 'Tis blessed to bestow, and yet, / Could we bestow the gifts we get, / And keep the ones we give away, / How happy were our Christmas Day!

Carolyn Wells, "A Christmas Thought," *Folly for the Wise* (1904)

10 Twenty-five years ago, Christmas was not the burden that it is now; there was less haggling and weighing, less *quid pro quo*, less fatigue of body, less weariness of soul; and, most of all, there was less loading up with trash.

Margaret Deland, "Concerning Christmas Giving," *The Common Way* (1904)

11 Like everyone in his right mind, I feared Santa Claus.

Annie Dillard, *Teaching a Stone to Talk* (1982)

12 For months they have lain in wait, dim shapes lurking in the forgotten corners of houses and factories all over the country and now they are upon us, sodden with alcohol, their massive bodies bulging with strange green protuberances, attacking us in our homes, at our friends' homes, at our offices— there is no escape, it is the hour of the fruitcake.

Deborah Papier, in *Insight* (1985)

13 The juggernaut of Christmas will not be stopped.

Marni Jackson, *The Mother Zone* (1992)

14 Every year, in the deep midwinter, there descends upon this world a terrible fortnight. . . . Every shop is a choked mass of humanity . . . nerves are jangled and frayed, purses emptied to no purposes, all amusements and all occupations suspended in favor of frightful businesses with brown paper, string, letters, cards, stamps, and crammed post offices. This period is doubtless a foretaste of whatever purgatory lies in store for human creatures.

Rose Macaulay, *Crewe Train* (1926)

15 A perfectly managed Christmas correct in every detail is, like basted inside seams and letters answered by return, a sure sign of someone who hasn't enough to do.

Katharine Whitehorn, "Keeping Cool," *Sunday Best* (1976)

16 I hate, loathe, and despise Christmas. It's a time when single people have to take cover or get out of town.

Kristin Hunter, *The Landlord* (1966)

17 Evidently Christmas was an unmitigated joy only for the people who inhabited department-store brochures and seasonal television specials. For eve-

ryone else the day seemed to be a trip across a mine field seeded with resurrected family feuds, exacerbated loneliness, emotional excess, and the inevitable disappointments that arise when expectations fall far short of reality.

Joyce Rebeta-Burditt, *The Cracker Factory* (1977)

1 There are few sensations more painful, than, in the midst of deep grief, to know that the season which we have always associated with mirth and rejoicing is at hand.

Mrs. Sarah J. Hale, *Traits of American Life* (1835)

2 I can understand people simply fleeing the mountainous effort Christmas has become. . . . But there are always a few saving graces and finally they make up for all the bother and distress.

May Sarton, *Journal of a Solitude* (1973)

3 Christmas was a miserable time for a Jewish child in those days. . . . Decades later, I still feel left out at Christmas, but I sing the carols anyway. You might recognize me if you ever heard me. I'm the one who sings, "La-la, the la-la is born."

Faye Moskowitz, *A Leak in the Heart* (1985)

## § CHURCH

4 She say, Celie, tell the truth, have you ever found God in church? I never did. I just found a bunch of folks hoping for him to show. Any God I ever felt in church I brought in with me. And I think all the other folks did too. They come to church to *share* God, not find God.

Alice Walker, *The Color Purple* (1982)

5 If we go to church we are confronted with a system of begging so complicated and so resolute that all other demands sink into insignificance by its side.

Agnes Repplier, in Emma Repplier, *Agnes Repplier* (1957)

6 I make a distinction between the doctrines of the Church, which matter, and the structure invented by half a dozen Italians who got to be pope and which is of very little use to anybody.

Bernadette Devlin, *The Price of My Soul* (1969)

7 When one loves God better than the Church is one called a heretic?

Marie Corelli, *The Master Christian* (1900)

8 It is a very rare church indeed that encourages its members to think for themselves in religious matters, or even tolerates this, and in most of them the clergy are quite ready to lay down the law in other fields too.

Anne Roe, *The Making of a Scientist* (1952)

9 Everybody knows that really intimate conversation is only possible between two or three. As soon as there are six or seven, collective language begins to dominate. That is why it is a complete misinterpretation to apply to the Church the words "Wheresoever two or three are gathered together in my name, there am I in the midst of them." Christ did not say two hundred, or fifty, or ten. He said two or three.

Simone Weil, *Waiting for God* (1950)

10 Our Lord said, "Feed my sheep"; He did not say, "Count them."

Dora P. Chaplin, on numbers as a measuring stick for religion, *The Privilege of Teaching* (1962)

11 Churches, like all the rest of our major institutions, are rooted in capitalism. For a church to attack capitalism is to "bite the hand that feeds it."

Georgia Harkness, *The Resources of Religion* (1936)

12 Most sermons sound to me like commercials—but I can't make out whether God is the Sponsor or the Product.

Mignon McLaughlin, *The Second Neurotic's Notebook* (1966)

13 The Nurse knew why she disliked church services, for as she raised her head, she observed that the Curate, and the Rector and the Archbishop were all men. The vergers were men; the organist was a man; the choir boys, the sidesmen and soloist and church wardens, all were men. The architects who had built the church, the composers of the music, the translators of the psalms, the compilers of the liturgy, all these too, the Nurse pondered, had been men.

Winifred Holtby, "Nurse to the Archbishop" (1931), *Truth Is Not Sober* (1934)

14 The church belongs to its hierarchy, which is men in power. Those outside the hierarchy, and especially women, are at best only renters and at worst squatters in religious territory.

Sonia Johnson, *From Housewife to Heretic* (1981)

15 The Church will go on being a Royal Academy of Males.

Dorothy M. Richardson, *Pilgrimage: Revolving Lights* (1923)

1 Most churches on either side of the ocean see women as playing only a "supportive," if any, role in their congregations. Men preach, women listen. Men pray, women say "Amen." Men form the clergy, the diaconate or the oversight, women abide by their leadership. Men study theology, women sew for the bazaar. Men make decisions, women make the tea.

Elaine Storkey, *What's Right With Feminism* (1985)

2 Again, as I had often met it in my own church, I was confronted with the Impurity of Women doctrine that seemed to preoccupy all clergymen.

Harper Lee, *To Kill a Mockingbird* (1960)

3 The Bible and Church have been the greatest stumbling blocks in the way of woman's emancipation.

Elizabeth Cady Stanton, in *Free Thought Magazine* (1896)

4 He would do the thing thoroughly. He would enter once more into that great ark of refuge from perplexing thoughts, the Roman branch of the Catholic Church.

Rose Macaulay, *Told by an Idiot* (1923)

5 A vast Church, whose shadow has been the graveyard of religious thought for a thousand years.

Frances B. Cobbe, on Roman Catholicism, *Italics* (1864)

See also Christianity, Clergy, God, Religion, Sermons, Spirituality, Theology, Worship.

❦ CHUTZPAH

6 "Chutzpah" is best defined as a small boy peeing through someone's letter box, then ringing the doorbell to ask how far it went.

Maureen Lipman, *How Was It for You?* (1985)

See also Assertiveness.

❦ CIRCUS

7 The circus is perhaps the most vital of all spectacles. . . . These bodily acts, these attractions that are daughters of universal Attraction take place with great ceremony. What is so moving as the roll of the drum that precedes the most perilous moment of the number and the total silence that follows it?

Shall we hesitate to think of the Elevation of the Mass? And what is so noble as the hand of the gymnast, who stands up absolutely straight after his stunt, with his palm open like the very symbol of work and its fulfillment?

Adrienne Monnier (1935), in Richard McDougall, tr., *The Very Rich Hours of Adrienne Monnier* (1976)

❦ CITIES

8 The seeds of civilization are in every culture, but it is city life that brings them to fruition.

Susanne K. Langer, *Philosophical Sketches* (1962)

9 In great cities where people of ability abound, there is always a feverish urge to keep ahead, to set the pace, to adopt each new fashion in thought and theory as well as in dress—or undress.

Charlotte Perkins Gilman, *The Living of Charlotte Perkins Gilman* (1935)

10 Great cities are not like towns, only larger. They are not like suburbs, only denser. They differ from towns and suburbs in basic ways, and one of these is that cities are, by definition, full of strangers.

Jane Jacobs, *The Death and Life of Great American Cities* (1961)

11 To approach a city, or even a city neighborhood, as if it were a larger architectural problem, capable of being given order by converting it into a disciplined work of art, is to make the mistake of attempting to substitute art for life. The results of such profound confusion between art and life are neither life nor art. They are taxidermy.

Jane Jacobs, *The Death and Life of Great American Cities* (1961)

12 In our big cities there is nothing at all not made by ourselves except the air. We are our own context and live by picking each other's brains.

L.M. Boston, *A Stranger at Green Knowe* (1961)

13 When we deal with cities we are dealing with life at its most complex and intense. Because this is so, there is a basic aesthetic limitation on what can be done with cities: A city cannot be a work of art.

Jane Jacobs, *The Death and Life of Great American Cities* (1961)

1 Does anybody really want to attend to cities other than to flee, fleece, privatize, butcher or decimate them?

    Jane Holtz Kay, in *The New York Times Book Review* (1992)

2 Today barbarism has taken over many city streets, or people fear it has, which comes to much the same thing in the end.

    Jane Jacobs, *The Death and Life of Great American Cities* (1961)

3 There is no solitude in the world like that of the big city.

    Kathleen Norris, *Hands Full of Living* (1931)

4 In a few hours one could cover that incalculable distance; from the winter country and homely neighbors, to the city where the air trembled like a tuning-fork with unimaginable possibilities.

    Willa Cather, *Lucy Gayheart* (1935)

5 No rural community, no suburban community, can ever possess the distinctive qualities that city dwellers have for centuries given to the world.

    Agnes Repplier, "Town and Suburb," *Times and Tendencies* (1931)

6 People in towns are always preoccupied. "Have I missed the bus? Have I forgotten the potatoes? Can I get across the road?"

    Nancy Mitford, "Diary of a Visit to Russia," *The Water Beetle* (1962)

7 New Orleans is one of the two most ingrown, self-obsessed little cities in the United States. (The other is San Francisco.)

    Nora Ephron, *Scribble Scribble* (1978)

8 Detroit is really the most perfectly laid out city one could imagine, and such an enchanting park and lake,—infinitely better than any town I know in Europe. It ought to be a paradise in about fifty years when it has all matured.

    Elinor Glyn, *Elizabeth Visits America* (1909)

9 One always, sooner or later, comes upon a city which is an image of one's inner cities. Fez is an image of my inner self. . . . The layers of the city of Fez are like the layers and secrecies of the inner life. One needs a guide. . . . There were in Fez, as in my life, streets which led nowhere, impasses which remained a mystery.

    Anaïs Nin (1936), *The Diary of Anaïs Nin*, vol. 2 (1967)

10 In the '70s Prague was pewter gray in spirit, broken and oddly adrift in the middle of Europe. The most golden thing about it then was its silence. Loneliness was its chief allure, radiating a sullen romance bred of cigarette smoke and satire.

    Patricia Hampl, in *The New York Times Magazine* (1993)

11 Celia soon grew to love Havana, its crooked streets and the balconies like elegant chariots in the air.

    Cristina Garcia, *Dreaming in Cuban* (1992)

12 Most gay, conversational, careless, lovely city . . . where one drinks golden Tokay until one feels most beautiful, and warm and loved—oh, Budapest!

    Winifred Holtby (1924), in Alice Holtby and Jean McWilliam, eds., *Letters to a Friend* (1937)

13 If there is a heartache Vienna cannot cure I hope never to feel it.

    Storm Jameson, "Delicate Monster," *Women Against Men* (1933)

See also Boston, Bruges, Chicago, Hollywood, London, Los Angeles, New York, Paris, Rome, Venice, Washington, D.C.


❦ CIVILIZATION

14 We are all born charming, frank, and spontaneous and must be civilized before we are fit to participate in society.

    Judith Martin, *Miss Manners' Guide to Excruciatingly Correct Behavior* (1982)

15 It is a matter of civilizing *everyone* or not being civilized at all: the decay has always come from a *partial* civilization.

    Freya Stark (1945), in Caroline Moorehead, ed., *Over the Rim of the World* (1988)

16 Civilization has developed executive powers far beyond its creative understanding.

    Maude Meagher, *Fantastic Traveler* (1931)

17 Civilization is only the advance from shoeless toes to toeless shoes.

    Marcelene Cox, in *Ladies' Home Journal* (1943)

18 Civilization in certain respects is as inadequate as it was a thousand years ago.

    Gertrude Atherton, *The Living Present* (1917)

1 The age in which we live can only be characterized as one of barbarism. Our civilization is in the process not only of being militarized, but also being brutalized.

Alva Myrdal, in Barbara Shiels, *Women and the Nobel Prize* (1985)

2 For the first time ever in the history of mankind, the wilderness is safer than "civilization."

Faith Popcorn, *The Popcorn Report* (1991)

3 Whatever your color or creed may be, when you get too close to civilization, you can probably expect to be done in.

Shirley Abbott, *Womenfolks: Growing Up Down South* (1983)

4 The test of a civilization is in the way that it cares for its helpless members.

Pearl S. Buck, *My Several Worlds* (1954)

5 Civilization, let me tell you what it is. First the soldier, then the merchant, then the priest, then the lawyer. The merchant hires the soldier and priest to conquer the country for him. First the soldier, he is a murderer; then the priest, he is a liar; then the merchant, he is a thief; and they all bring in the lawyer to make their laws and defend their deeds, and there you have your civilization!

Katherine Anne Porter, *Ship of Fools* (1962)

6 To certain temperaments civilization in general is a bore.

Abby B. Longstreet, *Social Etiquette of New York* (1888)

7 Civilization is a perishable commodity.

Helen MacInnes, *The Venetian Affair* (1963)

See also Culture, Society.

# ❧ CLASS

8 All new money is made through the shifting of social classes and the dispossession of old classes.

Christina Stead, *House of All Nations* (1938)

9 The class struggle is precisely that which resolves the contradictions between two opposed classes by abolishing them at the same time that it constitutes and reveals them as classes.

Monique Wittig, "The Category of Sex" (1972), *The Straight Mind* (1992)

10 Classism and greed are making insignificant all other kinds of isms.

Ruby Dee, in Brian Lanker, *I Dream a World* (1989)

11 It is impossible for one class to appreciate the wrongs of another.

Elizabeth Cady Stanton, Susan B. Anthony, and Matilda J. Gage, eds., *The History of Woman Suffrage*, vol. 1 (1881)

12 You who have read the history of nations, from Moses down to our last election, where have you ever seen one class looking after the interests of another?

Elizabeth Cady Stanton, speech (1860)

13 I can assure you that the class system is alive and well and living in people's minds in England.

Jilly Cooper, *Class* (1979)

14 There were few if any Englishmen, even to the lowliest subject, who did not possess an inborn reverence for the next man above him and a corresponding contempt for the other one, just down the line.

Dr. (Mrs.) F.L.S. Aldrich, *The One Man* (1910)

15 I classify São Paolo this way: The Governor's Palace is the living room. The mayor's office is the dining room and the city is the garden. And the favela is the back yard where they throw the garbage.

Carolina Maria de Jesus, *Child of the Dark* (1962)

16 Upper class means a certainty of belonging, an assumption of one's importance in the world. . . . Take away black studies, women's studies, ethnic studies, Jewish studies, labor history, Chicano studies, Native American studies: what is left is what has passed for "history" with no qualifying adjective, the story of those whose belonging was never disputed.

Susanna J. Sturgis, "Class/Act," in Christian McEwen and Sue O'Sullivan, eds., *Out the Other Side* (1988)

17 Planning ahead is a measure of class. The rich and even the middle class plan for future generations, but the poor can plan ahead only a few weeks or days.

Gloria Steinem, *Outrageous Acts and Everyday Rebellions* (1983)

18 The upper classes are merely a nation's past; the middle class is its future.

Ayn Rand, in *The Ayn Rand Letter* (1971)

1 To fear the bourgeois is bourgeois.
   Maureen Howard, *Facts of Life* (1978)

2 Being in the middle class is a feeling as well as an income level.
   Margaret Halsey, *The Folks at Home* (1952)

3 The last boat to the middle class was leaving and we'd better get on it.
   Ellen Goodman, *Close to Home* (1979)

4 While he himself derived from the hardworking poor, he greatly mistrusted the ragtag and bobtail who lived in the shacks south of the junkyard, suspecting them of the criminality and moral decay to which he might sink, were he in their place.
   Faith Sullivan, *The Cape Ann* (1988)

See also Aristocracy, Poverty, The Rich and the Poor.

## ❧ CLERGY

5 People are as severe toward the clergy as toward women; they want to see absolute devotion to duty from both.
   Madame de Staël, *Considerations* (1818)

6 Vicars were not vicarious enough. Most of them expected you to worship God in them.
   Ruth Rendell, *Sins of the Fathers* (1967)

7 Highly concentrated clericalism is always autocratic.
   Norah Bentinck, *My Wanderings and Memories* (1924)

8 We are apt to attribute to them all the virtues they preach.
   Barbara Pym, *Crampton Hodnet* (1985)

9 It is clearly absurd that it should be possible for a woman to qualify as a saint with direct access to the Almighty, while she may not qualify as a curate.
   Mary Stocks, *Still More Commonplace* (1973)

10 It has always seemed very odd to me that this particular sphere of activity should remain a male closed shop, seeing that, to judge from church attendance, women are the more religious sex— while our criminal statistics make quite clear that they are the least wicked.
   Mary Stocks, *Still More Commonplace* (1973)

11 There comes a time in every rabbi's life when he thinks he's Moses.
   Silvia Tennenbaum, *Rachel, the Rabbi's Wife* (1978)

See also Church, Religion.

## ❧ CLEVERNESS

12 If all the good people were clever, / And all clever people were good, / The world would be nicer than ever / We thought that it possibly could. / But somehow 'tis seldom or never / The two hit it off as they should, / The good are so harsh to the clever, / The clever, so rude to the good!
   Elizabeth Wordsworth, "Good and Clever" (1890), *Poems and Plays* (1931)

13 I'm accused of cleverness as if it were a sin. She is merely clever, they say.
   Jennifer Stone, *Telegraph Avenue Then* (1992)

See also Insights, Intelligence.

## ❧ CLICHÉS

14 The clichés of a culture sometimes tell the deepest truths.
   Faith Popcorn, *The Popcorn Report* (1991)

15 Clichés are like a cat's fleas. The work in progress is the cat, a living, beautiful creature, but the fleas hop automatically onto its body, and there must be a constant warfare against them. Nothing less than a catlike biting hunt can rid a piece of my writing of its clichés.
   Katharine Butler Hathaway, *The Journals and Letters of the Little Locksmith* (1946)

16 Your soul needs to be lonely so that its strangest elements can moil about, curl and growl and jump, fail and get triumphant, all inside you. Sociable people have the most trouble hearing their unconscious. They have trouble getting rid of clichés because clichés are sociable.
   Carol Bly, *The Passionate, Accurate Story* (1990)

See also Aphorisms, Language, Platitudes, Words.

§ CLOTHES

1 Your clothes speak even before you do.

   Jacqueline Murray, with Toni Nebel, *The Power of Dress* (1989)

2 We can lie in the language of dress, or try to tell the truth; but unless we are naked and bald it is impossible to be silent.

   Alison Lurie, *The Language of Clothes* (1981)

3 Even when we say nothing our clothes are talking noisily to everyone who sees us, telling them who we are, where we come from, what we like to do in bed and a dozen other intimate things.

   Alison Lurie, *The Language of Clothes* (1981)

4 Who said that clothes make a statement? What an understatement that was. Clothes never shut up.

   Susan Brownmiller, *Femininity* (1984)

5 On the subject of dress almost no one, for one or another reason, feels truly indifferent: if their own clothes do not concern them, somebody else's do.

   Elizabeth Bowen, *Collected Impressions* (1950)

6 It is almost as stupid to let your clothes betray that you know you are ugly as to have them proclaim that you think you are beautiful.

   Edith Wharton, *The House of Mirth* (1905)

7 Any garment that makes you feel bad will make you look bad.

   Victoria Billings, *The Womansbook* (1974)

8 Clothes and courage have so much to do with each other.

   Sara Jeannette Duncan, *An American Girl in London* (1900)

9 Exhibitionism and a nervous wish for concealment, for anonymity . . . battle inside the buyer of any piece of clothing.

   Elizabeth Bowen, *Collected Impressions* (1950)

10 If you want to move up in the organization, you go along with the culture. If you don't care, well, you can wear anything.

   Cora Rose, in Jacqueline Murray with Toni Nebel, *The Power of Dress* (1989)

11 Here I am a woman attorney being told I can't practice law in slacks by a judge dressed in drag.

   Florynce R. Kennedy, in Sidney Abbott and Barbara Love, *Sappho Was a Right-On Woman* (1972)

12 He had always been sartorially unlucky. . . . A conspiracy of tailors and outfitters, as it seemed to him, caused him always to be nipped at the armpits by waistcoats, irked across the back by coats, deserted by studs, tortured by shoes, blistered by socks, betrayed by sock-suspenders and braces.

   Stella Benson, *Pipers and a Dancer* (1924)

13 No Westerner ever sees an Albanian for the first time without thinking that the poor man's trousers are just about to drop off. They are cut in a straight line across the loins, well below the hip-bone, and have no visible means of support; and to make matters psychologically worse they are of white or biscuit homespun heavily embroidered with black wool in designs that make a stately reference to the essential points of male anatomy.

   Rebecca West, *Black Lamb and Grey Falcon* (1941)

14 Why don't men . . . leave off those detestable stiff collars, stocks, and things, that make them all look like choked chickens, and which hide so many handsomely-turned throats, that a body never sees, unless a body is married, or unless a body happens to see a body's brothers while they are shaving.

   Fanny Fern, *Fresh Leaves* (1857)

15 She spotted an Adolfo suit in that shade of tan that comes from mixing brown with a great deal of money.

   Judith Kelman, *Hush Little Darlings* (1989)

16 She all dressed up so till it would take a doctor to tell her how near she is dressed to death.

   Zora Neale Hurston, *Moses: Man of the Mountain* (1939)

17 You can say what you like about long dresses, but they cover a multitude of shins.

   Mae West, in Joseph Weintraub, ed., *The Wit and Wisdom of Mae West* (1967)

18 Marlene Dietrich and Roy Rogers are the only two living humans who should be allowed to wear black leather pants.

   Edith Head, in C. Robert Jennings, "Body by MacLaine—in Originals by Edith Head," *The Saturday Evening Post* (1963)

19 You know, don't you, that the bikini is only the most important thing since the atom bomb?

   Diana Vreeland, in Helen Lawrenson, "Androgyne, You're a Funny Valentine," *Latins Are Still Lousy Lovers* (1968)

20 Wet beige knee-highs hang in my hands like wilted skins.

   Christina Baldwin, *One to One* (1977)

1 Wool, cotton, and the odd bits of silk and cashmere are the only acceptable materials for Prep clothes. They look better. They require professional maintenance. They are more expensive.

Lisa Birnbach, *The Official Preppy Handbook* (1980)

2 Designer clothes worn by children are like snowsuits worn by adults. Few can carry it off successfully.

Fran Lebowitz, *Social Studies* (1977)

3 While clothes with pictures and/or writing on them are not entirely an invention of the modern age, they are an unpleasant indication of the general state of things. . . . I mean, be realistic. If people don't want to listen to *you* what makes you think they want to hear from your sweater?

Fran Lebowitz, *Metropolitan Life* (1978)

4 There are two times in a woman's life when clothes are important: when she is young and when she is old.

Marcelene Cox, in *Ladies' Home Journal* (1944)

5 Friendship is not possible between two women one of whom is very well dressed.

Laurie Colwin, *Happy All the Time* (1978)

6 She knew someday she would find the exact right outfit that would make her life work. Maybe not her whole life, she thought, as she got back in bed, but at least the parts she had to dress for.

Carrie Fisher, *Postcards From the Edge* (1987)

See also Appearance, Dress, Hats.

# ❧ CLOUDS

7 The cloud controls the light. . . . It is the cloud that, holding the sun's rays in a sheaf as a giant holds a handful of spears, strikes the horizon, touches the extreme edge with a delicate revelation of light, or suddenly puts it out and makes the foreground shine.

Alice Meynell, "Cloud," *Essays* (1914)

8 The clouds hung above the mountains like puffs of white smoke left in the wake of a giant old-fashioned choo-choo train.

Sue Grafton, *"B" Is for Burglar* (1985)

9 We talk of sunshine and moonshine, but not of cloud-shine, which is yet one of the illuminations of our skies. A shining cloud is one of the most majestic of all secondary lights.

Alice Meynell, "Cloud," *Essays* (1914)

10 Clouds were piled up like heads of cauliflower in a roadside stand.

Sue Grafton, *"B" Is for Burglar* (1985)

11 Spring and autumn are inconsiderable events in a landscape compared with the shadows of a cloud.

Alice Meynell, "Cloud," *Essays* (1914)

See also Sky.

# ❧ CODEPENDENCE

12 It is easier to live through someone else than to become complete yourself.

Betty Friedan, *The Feminine Mystique* (1963)

13 How much of my true self I camouflage and choke in order to commend myself to him, denying the fullness of me. . . . How I've toned myself down, diluted myself to maintain his approval.

Sylvia Ashton-Warner (1943), *Myself* (1967)

14 Nora robbed herself for everyone; incapable of giving herself warning, she was continually turning about to find herself diminished. Wandering people the world over found her profitable in that she could be sold for a price forever, for she carried her betrayal money in her own pocket.

Djuna Barnes, *Nightwood* (1937)

15 She had become a kind of emotional tapeworm hanging cosily in the mid-gut of other people's affairs and digesting any entertainment to be derived therefrom.

Kylie Tennant, *Ride On Stranger* (1943)

16 When, like me, one has nothing in oneself one hopes for everything from another.

Colette, *Claudine and Annie* (1903)

17 I looked always outside of myself to see what I could make the world give me instead of looking within myself to see what was there.

Belle Livingstone, *Belle of Bohemia* (1927)

1 Some women have to cling to somethin', no matter if they have to support it themselves.

    Julie M. Lippmann, *Martha By-the-Day* (1912)

2 Calvin had got the habit of takin' care of somebody, and it growed on him like drink.

    Laura E. Richards, *Up to Calvin's* (1910)

3 People who let the weak or greedy drink their blood sometimes have a need to play God.

    Helen Van Slyke, *A Necessary Woman* (1979)

4 People who are always thinking of the feelings of others can be very destructive because they are hiding so much from themselves.

    May Sarton, *Crucial Conversations* (1975)

5 Those who make some other person their job . . . are dangerous.

    Dorothy L. Sayers, *Gaudy Night* (1935)

6 There are people, who the more you do for them, the less they will do for themselves.

    Jane Austen, *Emma* (1816)

7 Our love relationships have been based on the pathological model that two persons who pair will become one. Because this model does not allow for separateness in relationships, it has fostered dependency.

    Marilyn Mason, in *Co-Dependency* (1984)

8 We stay in the house so much because I am waiting for the telephone. I seem to be back in my teens, a period I thought I would never have to endure again: my life is spent hoping for things that only someone else can bring about.

    Anne Tyler, *Celestial Navigation* (1974)

9 Co-dependence [is] . . .taking someone else's temperature to see how you feel.

    Linda Ellerbee, *Move On* (1991)

10 When death approaches the co-dependent sees someone else's life flash before her eyes.

    Anne Carolyn Klein, *Meeting the Great Bliss Queen* (1994)

11 A codependent person is one who has let another person's behavior affect him or her, and who is obsessed with controlling that person's behavior.

    Melody Beattie, *Codependent No More* (1987)

12 There are almost as many definitions of codependency as there are experiences that represent it.

    Melody Beattie, *Codependent No More* (1987)

13 There are only two states of being in the world of codependency—recovery and denial.

    Wendy Kaminer, *I'm Dysfunctional, You're Dysfunctional* (1992)

14 I struggled with Mac. . . . Talked to his family, his church, AA, hid the bottles, threatened the liquor man, left a good job to play nurse, mistress, kitten, buddy. But then he stopped calling me Dahlin and started calling me Mama. I don't play that. I'm my daughter's mama. So I split.

    Toni Cade Bambara, "Medley," *The Sea Birds Are Still Alive* (1982)

See also Addiction, Alcoholism, Dependence, Drug Abuse, Interference.

# ❦ COFFEE

15 I found myself face to face with a long line of people resembling extras off the set of *Night of the Living Dead*: shuffling along, pale and twitching, empty cups in hand—murderous. Miserable. No matter that the air was rich with vapors of fresh-ground beans and warm muffins; no matter that the soft piped-in Vivaldi poured over us like steamed milk. These angry zombies were rushing to work, and their eyes flashed fair warning: *Don't mess with us. We haven't had our coffee.*

    Joan Frank, "Achieving Legal Liftoff," in *The San Francisco Examiner Image* (1991)

16 Coffee, according to the women of Denmark, is to the body what the word of the Lord is to the soul.

    Isak Dinesen, "The Supper at Elsinore," *Seven Gothic Tales* (1934)

17 Coffee was a food in that house, not a drink.

    Patricia Hampl, *A Romantic Education* (1981)

18 For a writer, it's more essential than food.

    Joan Frank, "Achieving Legal Liftoff," in *The San Francisco Examiner Image* (1991)

19 Coffee: We can get it anywhere, and get as loaded as we like on it, until such teeth-chattering, eye-bulging, nonsense-gibbering time as we may be classified unable to operate heavy machinery.

    Joan Frank, "Achieving Legal Liftoff," in *The San Francisco Examiner* (1991)

1 There was a tiny range within which coffee was effective, short of which it was useless, and beyond which, fatal.

  Annie Dillard, *The Writing Life* (1989)

2 Never drink black coffee at lunch; it will keep you awake in the afternoon.

  Jilly Cooper, *How to Survive From Nine to Five* (1970)

3 The coffee was so strong it snarled as it lurched out of the pot.

  Betty MacDonald, *The Egg and I* (1945)

4 The coffee was strong enough to trot a mouse across.

  Diane Ackerman, *The Moon by Whale Light* (1991)

5 Coffee is not as necessary to ministers of the reformed faith as to Catholic priests. The latter are not allowed to marry, and coffee is said to induce chastity.

  Charlotte-Elisabeth, Duchesse d'Orléans (1706), *The Letters of Madame*, vol. 1 (1924)

6 I am grieved to learn, dear Louise, that you have taken to coffee; nothing is so unhealthy, and I see many here who have had to give it up because of the diseases it has brought upon them.

  Charlotte-Elisabeth, Duchesse d'Orléans (1710), *Life and Letters of Charlotte Elizabeth* (1889)

See also Tea.

## ❦ COINCIDENCE

7 I know coincidence has a long arm, but it's not an octopus.

  Anthony Gilbert, *The Wrong Body* (1950)

See also Accidents.

## ❦ COLLABORATION

8 When you collaborate with other people, you tend to regard your own individual contribution as the most important.

  Yang Jiang, *A Cadre School Life* (1980)

9 Where two people are writing the same book, each believes he gets all the worries and only half the royalties.

  Agatha Christie (1955), in James Beasley Simpson, *Best Quotes of '54, '55, '56* (1957)

See also Committees, Cooperation.

## ❦ COLLECTING

10 The collector walks with blinders on; he sees nothing but the prize. In fact, the acquisitive instinct is incompatible with true appreciation of beauty.

  Anne Morrow Lindbergh, *Gift From the Sea* (1955)

11 Collections are amusing only in the making; afterwards they are like sporting prints without the sport. The sons of collectors inherit only the corpse of their fathers' satisfied passion.

  Princess Marthe Bibesco, *Catherine-Paris* (1928)

12 One cannot collect all the beautiful shells on the beach. One can collect only a few, and they are more beautiful if they are few.

  Anne Morrow Lindbergh, *Gift From the Sea* (1955)

See also Hobbies.

## ❦ COLONIALISM

13 He was one of those staunch patriotic Britons who, having made a portion of a foreign country their own, strongly resent the original inhabitants of it.

  Agatha Christie, *The Mystery of the Blue Train* (1928)

14 The talk at the table was full of expanding British power.... They discussed campaigns and victories, and spoke contemptuously of the "natives," who everyone agreed had to be put in their place periodically. "Their place?" Anna Harriette pondered, strangely troubled. "And what is their place in their own country?"

  Margaret Landon, *Anna and the King of Siam* (1944)

15 It is more than their land that you take away from the people, whose native land you take. It is their past as well, their roots and their identity. If you take away the things that they have been used to

see, and will be expecting to see, you may, in a way, as well take their eyes.

     Isak Dinesen, *Out of Africa* (1937)

See also Imperialism.

## ❧ COLORS

1 Green is the fresh emblem of well-founded hopes. In blue the spirit can wander, but in green it can rest.

     Mary Webb, *The Spring of Joy* (1917)

2 Red has been praised for its nobility of the color of life. But the true color of life is not red. Red is the color of violence, or of life broken open, edited, and published.

     Alice Meynell, title essay, *The Color of Life* (1896)

3 I had forgotten what mustard fields looked like. . . . Sheet upon sheet of blazing yellow, half-way between sulphur and celandine, with hot golden sunshine pouring down upon them out of a dazzling June sky. It thrilled me like music.

     Monica Baldwin, *I Leap Over the Wall* (1950)

4 It's beige! My color!

     Elsie de Wolfe, at first sight of the Acropolis, in Jane S. Smith, *Elsie de Wolfe* (1982)

5 Of all colors, brown is the most satisfying. It is the deep, fertile tint of the earth itself; it lies hidden beneath every field and garden; it is the garment of multitudes of earth's children, from the mouse to the eagle.

     Mary Webb, *The Spring of Joy* (1917)

6 Black was bestlooking. . . . Ebony was the best wood, the hardest wood; it was black. Virginia ham was the best ham. It was black on the outside. Tuxedos and tail coats were black and they were a man's finest, most expensive clothes. You had to use pepper to make most meats and vegetables fit to eat. The most flavorsome pepper was black. The best caviar was black. The rarest jewels were black: black opals, black pearls.

     Ann Petry, *The Narrows* (1953)

7 When I fell in love with black, it contained all color. It wasn't a negation of color. It was an acceptance. Because black encompasses all colors. Black is the most aristocratic color of all. The only aristocratic color. . . . There is no color that will give you the feeling of totality. Of peace. Of greatness. Of quietness. Of excitement. I have *seen things* that were transformed into black, that took on just greatness.

     Louise Nevelson, *Dawns + Dusks* (1976)

8 You think dark is just one color, but it ain't. There're five or six kinds of black. Some silky, some woolly. Some just empty. Some like fingers. And it don't stay still. It moves and changes from one kind of black to another. Saying something is pitch black is like saying something is green. What kind of green? Green like my bottles? Green like a grasshopper? Green like a cucumber, lettuce, or green like the sky is just before it breaks loose to storm? Well, night black is the same way. Might as well be a rainbow.

     Toni Morrison, *Song of Solomon* (1977)

## ❧ COMEBACKS

9 You people book me so seldom that every time I work it's called a comeback.

     Lillian Roth, to her agent, with Mike Connolly and Gerold Frank, *I'll Cry Tomorrow* (1954)

10 Some damn body is always trying to embalm me. I'm always making a comeback, but nobody ever tells me where I've been.

     Billie Holiday, with William Dufty, *Lady Sings the Blues* (1956)

See also Acting, Celebrity, Fame, Resilience.

## ❧ COMEDY

11 Great comedy calls large matters into question.

     Penelope Gilliatt, *To Wit* (1990)

12 A comedian is not funny unless he is taking his demons out for a walk.

     Cynthia Heimel, *But Enough About You* (1986)

13 The masters of the comic spirit are often our prophets.

     Penelope Gilliatt, *To Wit* (1990)

1 Comedians on the stage are invariably suicidal when they get home.

Elsa Lanchester, *Charles Laughton and I* (1938)

2 Being a funny person does an awful lot of things to you. You feel that you mustn't get serious with people. They don't expect it from you, and they don't want to see it. You're not entitled to be serious, you're a clown, and they only want you to make them laugh.

Fanny Brice, in Norman Katkov, *The Fabulous Fanny* (1952)

3 Comedy is very controlling—you are making people laugh. It is there in the phrase "*making* people laugh." You feel completely in control when you hear a wave of laughter coming back at you that you have caused.

Gilda Radner, *It's Always Something* (1989)

4 We never respect those who amuse us, however we may smile at their comic powers.

Countess of Blessington, *Desultory Thoughts and Reflections* (1839)

See also Humor.

## ❦ COMFORT

5 I love it—I love it; and who shall dare / To chide me for loving that old arm-chair?

Eliza Cook, "The Old Arm-Chair," *The Poetical Works of Eliza Cook* (1848)

6 Comfort me with apples! / For lo! I am sick; I am sad and opprest; / I come back to the place where, a child, I was blest. / Hope is false, love is vain, for the old things I sigh; / And if these cannot comfort me, then I must die!

Phoebe Cary, "Homesick," *Poems of Faith, Hope, and Love* (1874)

7 Give me a well-cooked, well-served meal, a bouquet, and a sunset, and I can do more for a man's soul than all the cant ever preached. I can even do it without a sunset!

Anne Ellis, *The Life of an Ordinary Woman* (1929)

8 I simply cannot understand the passion that some people have for making themselves thoroughly uncomfortable and then boasting about it afterwards.

Patricia Moyes, *Down Among the Dead Men* (1961)

9 One sits uncomfortably on a too comfortable cushion.

Lillian Hellman, *Scoundrel Time* (1976)

10 You cannot settle a new country without suffering, exposure, and danger. Cheerful endurance of hardships and contempt of surroundings become a virtue in a pioneer. Comfort is a comparatively new thing in the United States.

Ida Tarbell, *New Ideals in Business* (1914)

11 Comfort . . . easily merges into license.

Miriam Beard, *A History of Business* (1938)

See also Consolation, Contentment, Satisfaction.

## ❦ COMMITTEES

12 The best committee's a committee of one!

Naomi Mitchison, *Lobsters on the Agenda* (1952)

13 The more committees you belong to, the less of ordinary life you will understand. When your daily round becomes nothing more than a daily round of committees you might as well be dead.

Stella Benson, *Living Alone* (1919)

14 A committee, of course, exists for the purpose of damping enthusiasms.

Stella Benson, *Living Alone* (1919)

15 Any committee is only as good as the most knowledgeable, determined and vigorous person on it. There must be somebody who provides the flame.

Lady Bird Johnson, *A White House Diary* (1970)

16 The mind is an attribute of the individual. There is no such thing as a collective brain. There is no such thing as a collective thought. An agreement reached by a group of men is only a compromise or an average drawn upon many individual thoughts.

Ayn Rand, *The Fountainhead* (1943)

17 The only good thing ever done by a committee was the King James version.

Rita Mae Brown, *Bingo* (1988)

See also Collaboration, Meetings.

## ❦ COMMON SENSE

1 I'm not one o' those as can see the cat i' the dairy, an' wonder what she's come after.
George Eliot, *Adam Bede* (1859)

2 Why are the umpires, the only two people on the field who aren't going to get grass stains on their knees, the only ones allowed to wear dark trousers?
Katharine Whitehorn, "If It's Agony, It Must Be Cricket," *View From a Column* (1981)

3 If the cat has kittens in the oven, that don't make 'em biscuits.
Elisabeth Ogilvie, *The Summer of the Osprey* (1987)

4 Common sense is a very tricky instrument; it is as deceptive as it is indispensable.
Susanne K. Langer, *Philosophical Sketches* (1962)

5 Common-sense knowledge is prompt, categorical, and inexact.
Susanne K. Langer, *Philosophy in a New Key* (1942)

See also Knowledge, Self-Evident, Sensible, Wisdom.

## ❦ COMMUNICATION

6 Once a human being has arrived on this earth, communication is the largest single factor determining what kinds of relationships he makes with others and what happens to him in the world about him.
Virginia Satir, *Peoplemaking* (1972)

7 Self-expression must pass into communication for its fulfillment.
Pearl S. Buck, in Helen R. Hull, ed., *The Writer's Book* (1950)

8 Letters are venerable; and the telephone valiant, for the journey is a lonely one, and if bound together by notes and telephones we went in company, perhaps—who knows?—we might talk by the way.
Virginia Woolf, *Jacob's Room* (1922)

9 Good communication is stimulating as black coffee, and just as hard to sleep after.
Anne Morrow Lindbergh, *Gift From the Sea* (1955)

10 The more people are reached by mass communications, the less they communicate with each other.
Marya Mannes, "The Carriers," *But Will It Sell?* (1964)

11 To be a bestseller is not necessarily a measure of quality, but it *is* a measure of communication.
Barbara W. Tuchman, speech (1966)

12 Sometimes there is greater lack of communication in facile talking than in silence.
Faith Baldwin, "Communication," *Face Toward the Spring* (1956)

13 There can be too much communication between people.
Ann Beattie, "Weekend," *Secrets and Surprises* (1978)

14 A good message will always find a messenger.
Amelia E. Barr, *All the Days of My Life* (1913)

See also Conversation, Letters, Speech, Talking, Telephone, Writing.

## ❦ COMMUNISM

15 The . . . irrational fear of communism is being deliberately used in many quarters to blind us to our real problems.
Helen Gahagan Douglas (1946), *A Full Life* (1982)

16 I am not so repelled by communism: an element of communism in politics is necessary and inevitable. In any involved society there must be a feeling that something must be done about poverty—which is the basis of communism.
Rebecca West, in Victoria Glendinning, "Talk With Rebecca West," *The New York Times Book Review* (1977)

17 The word *Communist*, of course, has become a rallying cry for certain people here just as the word Jew was in Hitler's Germany, a way of arousing emotion without engendering thought.
Eleanor Roosevelt, *Tomorrow Is Now* (1963)

18 Such pip-squeaks as Nixon and McCarthy are trying to get us so frightened of Communism that we'll be afraid to turn out the lights at night.
Helen Gahagan Douglas, speech (1950), in Lee Israel, "Helen Gahagan Douglas," *Ms.* (1973)

19 The word "Communist" is like the word "bastard." It started out as a specific label for a definite thing, but it's grown into a term of general abuse. If I get

into a fight with a taxi driver and he calls me a bastard, he doesn't mean I'm illegitimate. He doesn't know whether I am or not. He just means he thoroughly disapproves of me.

Margaret Halsey, *Some of My Best Friends Are Soldiers* (1944)

1 The American Communist Party was notoriously infiltrated by informers . . . it used to be said that spies practically kept the Party going with their dues and contributions.

Helen Lawrenson, *Whistling Girl* (1978)

## § COMMUNITY

2 A community can never be created: not through hard work or in any other way. It must simply be recognized and respected.

Sigrid Nielsen, "Strange Days," in Christian McEwen and Sue O'Sullivan, eds., *Out the Other Side* (1988)

3 People had changed—or rather fridges had changed them. Mrs. Munde felt that being able to store food for longer periods had broken down the community spirit. There was no need to share now, no need to meet every day, gathering your veg or killing a few rabbits.

Jeanette Winterson, *Boating for Beginners* (1985)

See also Human Family, Society.

## § COMPASSION

4 It's compassion that makes gods of us.

Dorothy Gilman, *The Tightrope Walker* (1979)

5 Spiritual energy brings compassion into the real world. With compassion, we see benevolently our own human condition and the condition of our fellow beings. We drop prejudice. We withhold judgment.

Christina Baldwin, *Life's Companion* (1990)

6 The love of our neighbor in all its fullness simply means being able to say to him, "What are you going through?"

Simone Weil, *Waiting for God* (1950)

7 Here and there the lantern of compassion / can be shown to the fish, / where the fishhook is swallowed / or suffocation practiced.

Nelly Sachs, "Here and there the lantern of compassion," *O the Chimneys* (1967)

8 In its sentimental mode, compassion is an exercise in moral indignation, in feeling good rather than doing good. . . . In its unsentimental mode, compassion seeks above all to *do* good.

Gertrude Himmelfarb, *Poverty and Compassion* (1991)

9 Even the little pigs grunt when the old boar suffers.

Selma Lagerlöf, *The General's Ring* (1928)

10 I've got 's much feelin' as the next one, but when folks drives in their spiggits and wants to draw a bucketful o' compassion every day right straight along, there does come times when it seems as if the bar'l was getting low.

Sarah Orne Jewett, in Kate Sanborn, *The Wit of Women* (1885)

See also Charity, Concern, Empathy, Kindness, Service, Sympathy, Virtue.

## § COMPETENCE

11 There's one thing I've always known: You can let people suspect anything else about you, but you must *never* let them suspect you of knowing what you're doing.

Kathleen Winsor, *Star Money* (1950)

12 The code of competence is the only system of morality that's on a gold standard.

Ayn Rand, *Atlas Shrugged* (1957)

## § COMPETITION

13 Competition is about passion for perfection, and passion for other people who join in this impossible quest.

Mariah Burton Nelson, "My Mother, My Rival," in Ron Rapoport, ed., *A Kind of Grace* (1994)

14 To be my best I need you / swimming beside me.

Mariah Burton Nelson, "Competition," *Are We Winning Yet?* (1991)

1 I don't have to be enemies with someone to be competitors with them.

> Jackie Joyner-Kersee, in Mariah Burton Nelson, *Are We Winning Yet?* (1991)

2 Your opponent, in the end, is never really the player on the other side of the net, or the swimmer in the next lane, or the team on the other side of the field, or even the bar you must high-jump. Your opponent is yourself, your negative internal voices, your level of determination.

> Grace Lichtenstein, "Competition in Women's Athletics," in Valerie Miner and Helen E. Longino, eds., *Competition* (1987)

3 Even in misery we love to be foremost, to have the bitter in our cup acknowledged as more bitter than that of others.

> Mrs. Oliphant, *A House in Bloomsbury* (1894)

4 Never compete. Never. Watching the other guy is what kills all forms of energy.

> Diana Vreeland, in Nancy Collins, *Hard to Get* (1990)

5 The great disadvantage of being in a rat race is that it is humiliating. The competitors in a rat race are, by definition, rodents.

> Margaret Halsey, *The Folks at Home* (1952)

## ❧ COMPLACENCY

6 He found that the spirits can be raised by self-complacency even more agreeably than by burgundy.

> Maria Edgeworth, *Belinda* (1811)

7 The gain isn't counted to the recluse and inactive that, having nothing to measure themselves by and never being tested by failure, they simmer and soak perpetually in conscious complacency.

> Alice James (1891), in Anna Robeson Burr, *Alice James* (1934)

8 Self complacency is fatal to progress.

> Margaret E. Sangster, *Winsome Womanhood* (1900)

9 Unhurt people are not much good in the world.

> Enid Starkie, in Joanna Richardson, *Enid Starkie* (1973)

10 No, one couldn't make a revolution, one couldn't even start a riot, with sheep that asked only for better browsing.

> Ellen Glasgow, *Vein of Iron* (1935)

See also Contentment, Easygoing, Self-Satisfaction.

## ❧ COMPLAINTS

11 This world is a sad, sad place I know; / And what soul living can doubt it. / But it will not lessen the want and woe, / To be always singing about it.

> Ella Wheeler Wilcox, "This World," *Shells* (1873)

12 To be reasonable one should never complain but when one hopes redress.

> Lady Mary Wortley Montagu (1712), in Octave Thanet, ed., *The Best Letters of Lady Mary Wortley Montagu* (1901)

13 I mustn't bother you with this. One should consume one's own smoke.

> Rose Macaulay (1950), in Constance Babington-Smith, ed., *Letters to a Friend 1950-1952* (1961)

14 Those who do not complain are never pitied.

> Jane Austen, *Pride and Prejudice* (1813)

15 She knitted a loud woolen cap of her recriminations and yanked it over his head.

> Karen Elizabeth Gordon, *Intimate Apparel* (1989)

See also Grievances.

## ❧ COMPLIMENTS

16 That is one great difference between us. Compliments always take *you* by surprise, and *me* never.

> Jane Austen, *Pride and Prejudice* (1813)

17 Bing Crosby sings like all people *think* they sing in the shower.

> Dinah Shore, in Leslie Halliwell, *The Filmgoer's Book of Quotes* (1973)

See also Flattery, Praise.

## ❧ COMPROMISE

18 I've a theory that one can always get anything one wants if one will pay the price. And do you know what the price is, nine times out of ten? Compromise.

> Agatha Christie, *The Secret of Chimneys* (1925)

19 Compromise, if not the spice of life, is its solidity.

> Phyllis McGinley, "Suburbia: Of Thee I Sing," in *Harper's Magazine* (1949)

1 Don't compromise yourself. You are all you've got.
   Janis Joplin, in *Reader's Digest* (1973)

2 *Compromise* is something people write about. It does not work well in real life.
   Judy Markey, *You Only Get Married for the First Time Once* (1988)

See also Consensus, Moderation, Neutrality.


## ❦ CONCEALMENT

3 Show me one who boasts continually of his "openness," and I will show you one who conceals much.
   Minna Thomas Antrim, *At the Sign of the Golden Calf* (1905)

4 The gates of my happy childhood had clanged shut behind me; I had become adult enough to recognize the need to conceal unbearable emotions for the sake of others.
   Eva Figes, *Little Eden* (1978)

5 There is nothing that gives more assurance than a mask.
   Colette, *My Apprenticeships* (1936)

See also Discretion, Hiding, Lying, Privacy, Secrets.


## ❦ CONCEIT

6 I've never any pity for conceited people, because I think they carry their comfort about with them.
   George Eliot, *The Mill on the Floss* (1860)

7 Self-love, so sensitive in its own cause, has rarely any sympathy to spare for others.
   Madame de Staël, *Corinne* (1807)

8 Conceit is the devil's horse, and reformers generally ride it when they are in a hurry.
   Margaret Deland, *The Kays* (1924)

See also Arrogance, Egocentrism, Self-Importance, Vanity.


## ❦ CONCEPTS

9 Concepts antedate facts.
   Charlotte Perkins Gilman, *Human Work* (1904)

See also Ideas, Theories, Thoughts.


## ❦ CONCERN

10 Friends worry about me and are upset that somehow / I might tumble into bed with a nobody.
   Sulpicia (1st cent. B.C.), in Aliki Barnstone and Willis Barnstone, eds., *A Book of Women Poets From Antiquity to Now* (1980)

11 We may feel genuinely concerned about world conditions, though such a concern should drive us into action and not into a depression.
   Karen Horney, *Self-Analysis* (1942)

See also Anxiety, Compassion, Empathy, Kindness, Sympathy, Worry.


## ❦ CONCLUSION

12 I have come to the conclusion, after many years of sometimes sad experience, that you cannot come to any conclusion at all.
   Vita Sackville-West, "May," *In Your Garden Again* (1953)

13 You'd have done fine at track meets. Especially if they'd had an event called Jumping to Conclusions.
   Kristin Hunter, *The Landlord* (1966)

See also Decision.


## ❦ CONDOMS

14 If he ain't willin' to strap on the rubber bridle, then I ain't willin' to ride.
   Calamity Wronsky and Belle Bendall, *Dear Calamity . . . Love, Belle* (1994)

15 "This damned thing," he said. . . . "You're speaking of the sixteenth of an inch between me and the Home for Unwed Mothers."
   Rona Jaffe, *The Best of Everything* (1958)

See also Birth Control.


## ❦ CONFESSION

16 True confession consists in telling our deed in such a way that our soul is changed in the telling of it.
   Maude Petre, "Devotional Essays," in *The Method of Theology* (1902)

1 If you can tell anyone about it, it's not the worst thing you ever did.

> Mignon McLaughlin, *The Neurotic's Notebook* (1963)

2 Most wrong-doing works, on the whole, less mischief than its useless confession.

> Edith Wharton, *The Reef* (1912)

3 There must be reserves—except with God. The human soul is solitary. But for confession that is different; justice and reparation sometimes demand it; but, again, justice and courage sometimes forbid it.

> Margaret Deland, *The Wisdom of Fools* (1897)

4 Many think that when they have confessed a fault there is no need of correcting it.

> Marie von Ebner-Eschenbach, *Aphorisms* (1893)

5 Confession often prompts a response of confession.

> George Eliot, "Janet's Repentance," *Scenes of Clerical Life* (1857)

## ❦ CONFIDENCE

6 Confidence is a plant of slow growth.

> Anna Leonowens, *The Romance of the Harem* (1872)

7 I felt so young, so strong, so sure of God.

> Elizabeth Barrett Browning, *Aurora Leigh* (1856)

8 If you think you can, you can. And if you think you can't, you're right.

> Mary Kay Ash, in *The New York Times Book Review* (1985)

9 I was thought to be "stuck up." I wasn't. I was just sure of myself. This is and always has been an unforgivable quality to the unsure.

> Bette Davis, *The Lonely Life* (1962)

10 Self-trust, we know, is the first secret of success.

> Lady Wilde, "Miss Martineau," *Notes on Men, Women, and Books* (1891)

11 If one burdens the future with one's worries, it cannot grow organically. I am filled with confidence, not that I shall succeed in worldly things, but that even when things go badly for me I shall still find life good and worth living.

> Etty Hillesum (1942), *An Interrupted Life* (1983)

12 Putting the World to Rights.

> Margaret Thatcher, chapter title, *The Downing Street Years* (1993)

13 My parents . . . always told me I could do anything but never told me how long it would take.

> Rita Rudner, *Naked Beneath My Clothes* (1992)

See also Self-Esteem, Self-Respect.

## ❦ CONFIDENCES

14 She liked to receive confidences if these were conferred prettily, with some suggestion of her own specialness, not dropped on her toes all anyhow, like a bulky valise someone is anxious to put down.

> Elizabeth Bowen, *To the North* (1933)

See also Confession, Emotions, Secrets.

## ❦ CONFLICT

15 Conflict begins at the moment of birth.

> Jean Baker Miller, *Toward a New Psychology of Women* (1986)

16 He was dizzy with conflict; he had two souls, and not to save them both could he have disentangled the soul of light from the soul of shadow.

> Elinor Wylie, *The Orphan Angel* (1926)

17 To be desperate is to discover strength. / We die of comfort and by conflict live.

> May Sarton, "Take Anguish for Companion," *The Land of Silence* (1953)

18 Unlike lions and dogs, we are a dissenting animal. We need to dissent in the same way that we need to travel, to make money, to keep a record of our time on earth and in dream, and to leave a permanent mark. Dissension is a drive, like those drives.

> Carol Bly, "Extended vs. Nuclear Families," *Letter From the Country* (1981)

19 There can be no reconciliation where there is no open warfare. There must be a battle, a brave, boisterous battle, with pennants waving and cannon roaring, before there can be peaceful treaties and enthusiastic shaking of hands.

> Mary Elizabeth Braddon, *Lady Audley's Secret* (1862)

1 One person who wants something is a hundred times stronger than a hundred who want to be left alone.

Barbara Ward, "The First International Nation" (1968), in William Kilbourn, ed., *Canada: A Guide to the Peaceable Kingdom* (1970)

2 Those who attack always do so with greater fervor than those who defend.

Eleanor Roosevelt, *My Days* (1938)

3 I do not love strife, because I have always found that in the end each remains of the same opinion.

Catherine the Great (1770), in Katharine Anthony, *Catherine the Great* (1926)

4 There's no use throwing down the gauntlet in front of me and daring me to pick it up. "Pick it up yourself," I'd say.

Helen Lawrenson, *Stranger at the Party* (1975)

5 The world is wide, and I will not waste my life in friction when it could be turned into momentum.

Frances Willard (1874), in Ray Strachey, *Frances Willard* (1912)

6 People who fight fire with fire usually end up with ashes.

Abigail Van Buren, syndicated column "Dear Abby" (1974)

7 The moral absolute should be: if and when, in any dispute, one side *initiates* the use of physical force, *that side is wrong*—and no consideration or discussion of the issues is necessary or appropriate.

Ayn Rand, in *The Objectivist* (1969)

8 The children worked on each other like two indestructible pieces of sand-paper.

Elizabeth Bowen, "The Inherited Clock," *Ivy Gripped the Steps* (1946)

9 Even when you think people are wrong, it is easy to tell when they are right. When they are right about something you are trying very hard to hide from others and yourself, you know they are right because you want to kill them.

Candice Bergen, *Knock Wood* (1984)

See also Ambivalence, Arguments, Enemies, Quarrels, War.

## ⸱ CONFORMITY

10 Only dead fish swim with the stream.

Linda Ellerbee, *Move On* (1991)

11 Every society honors its live conformists and its dead troublemakers.

Mignon McLaughlin, *The Neurotic's Notebook* (1963)

12 Miss Ogilvy had found as her life went on that in this world it is better to be one with the herd, that the world has no wish to understand those who cannot conform to its stereotyped pattern.

Radclyffe Hall, *Miss Ogilvy Finds Herself* (1926)

13 Honey, try harder to be like th rest—tu run with th rest—it's easier, an you'll be happier in th end—I guess.

Harriette Arnow, *The Dollmaker* (1954)

14 Nothing is more restful than conformity.

Elizabeth Bowen, *Collected Impressions* (1950)

15 Once conform, once do what other people do because they do it, and a lethargy steals over all the finer nerves and faculties of the soul.

Virginia Woolf, "Montaigne," *The Common Reader*, 1st series (1925)

16 The more a soul conforms to the sanity of others, the more does it become insane.

Mary Webb, *The House in Dormer Forest* (1920)

17 She had for so many years been trying to be like other people, that she was now like nothing in heaven or earth.

Mary Webb, *The House in Dormer Forest* (1920)

18 I think the reward for conformity is that everyone likes you except yourself.

Rita Mae Brown, *Bingo* (1988)

See also Conventionality, Conventions, Traditions.

## ⸱ CONFUSION

19 It is while trying to get everything straight in my head that I get confused.

Mary Virginia Micka, *Fiction, Oddly Enough* (1990)

20 Whenever anything contained the merest hint of a double meaning, Timmy always pounced on the wrong one.

Margaret Merrill, *Bears in My Kitchen* (1956)

1 One learns in life to keep silent and draw one's own confusions.

> Cornelia Otis Skinner, in Evelyn Oppenheimer, *The Articulate Woman* (1968)

See also Puzzlement, Uncertainty.

## ❦ CONGRESS

2 Congress—these, for the most part, illiterate hacks whose fancy vests are spotted with gravy, and whose speeches, hypocritical, unctuous, and slovenly, are spotted also with the gravy of political patronage.

> Mary McCarthy, "America the Beautiful: The Humanist in the Bathtub" (1947), *On the Contrary* (1961)

3 It was ... mortifying to see this splendid hall, fitted up in so stately and sumptuous a manner, filled with men sitting in the most unseemly attitudes, a large majority with their hats on, and nearly all spitting to an excess that decency forbids me to describe.

> Mrs. Trollope, *Domestic Manners of the Americans* (1832)

4 We have not been impressed with any attribute of the Senate other than its appearance and manners. ... The speeches are constantly degenerating into empty rhetoric; they abound in quotations from well-known authors or from their *own* former speeches.

> Beatrice Webb (1898), in David A. Shannon, ed., *Beatrice Webb's American Diary* (1963)

5 I do strive to think well of my fellow man, but no amount of striving can give me confidence in the wisdom of a congressional vote.

> Agnes Repplier, in Emma Repplier, *Agnes Repplier* (1957)

6 The inside operation of Congress—the deals, the compromises, the selling out, the co-opting, the unprincipled manipulating, the self-serving career-building—is a story of such monumental decadence that I believe if people find out about it they will demand an end to it.

> Bella Abzug, *Bella!* (1972)

7 Congress seems drugged and inert most of the time.

> Shirley Chisholm, *Unbought and Unbossed* (1970)

8 Sport has been called the last bastion of male domination. Unfortunately, there are others—Congress, for instance.

> Mariah Burton Nelson, *The Stronger Women Get, the More Men Love Football* (1994)

9 Both houses are dominated by a male, white, middle-aged, middle- and upper-middle-class power elite that stand with their backs turned to the needs and demands of our people for realistic change.

> Bella Abzug, in *Time* (1971)

10 It's really funny if two women stand on the House floor. There are usually at least two men who go by and say, "What is this, a coup?" They're almost afraid to see us in public together.

> Patricia Schroeder, in Mary Kay Blakely, *American Mom* (1994)

11 We favor putting Congress on a commission basis. Pay them for results. If they do a good job and the country prospers, they get 10% of the extra take.

> Gracie Allen, *How to Become President* (1940)

12 The Senate is the only show in the world where the cash customers have to sit in the balcony.

> Gracie Allen, *How to Become President* (1940)

See also Government, Politicians, Politics.

## ❦ CONNECTIONS

13 Connections are made slowly, sometimes they grow underground.

> Marge Piercy, "The Seven of Pentacles," *Circles on the Water* (1982)

14 Making mental connections is our most crucial learning tool, the essence of human intelligence: to forge links; to go beyond the given; to see patterns, relationship, context.

> Marilyn Ferguson, *The Aquarian Conspiracy* (1980)

## ❦ CONSCIENCE

15 The needle of our conscience is as good a compass as any.

> Ruth Wolff, *I, Keturah* (1963)

1 Conscience is the anticipation of the fellow who awaits you if and when you come home.

Hannah Arendt, *The Life of the Mind*, vol. 1 (1978)

2 That's what a conscience is made of, scar tissue. . . . Little strips and pieces of remorse sewn together year by year until they formed a distinctive pattern, a design for living.

Margaret Millar, *Do Evil in Return* (1950)

3 The private conscience is the last and only protection of the civilized world.

Martha Gellhorn, "Eichmann and the Private Conscience," in *The Atlantic* (1962)

4 I cannot and will not cut my conscience to fit this year's fashions.

Lillian Hellman, letter to the U.S. House of Representatives Committee on Un-American Activities (1952), in Lillian Hellman, *Scoundrel Time* (1976)

5 The one thing that doesn't abide by majority rule is a person's conscience.

Harper Lee, *To Kill a Mockingbird* (1960)

6 Conscience that isn't hitched up to common sense is a mighty dangerous thing.

Margaret Deland, *The Promises of Alice* (1919)

7 Conscientious people are apt to see their duty in that which is the most painful course.

George Eliot, *The Mill on the Floss* (1860)

8 Some laborers have hard hands, and old sinners have brawny consciences.

Anne Bradstreet, "Meditations Divine and Moral" (1664), in John Harvard Ellis, ed., *The Works of Anne Bradstreet in Prose and Verse* (1867)

9 Each wrong act brings with it its own anesthetic, dulling the conscience and blinding it against further light, and sometimes for years.

Rose Macaulay (1951), in Constance Babington-Smith, ed., *Letters to a Friend 1950-1952* (1961)

10 Conscience, like a child, is soon lulled to sleep.

L.E. Landon, "Rebecca," *The Book of Beauty* (1833)

11 It wasn't so much that he'd smothered his conscience as that he couldn't spell the word.

Anthony Gilbert, *A Spy for Mr. Crook* (1944)

12 I've got just as much conscience as any man in business can afford to keep,—just a little, you know, to swear by, as 'twere.

Harriet Beecher Stowe, *Uncle Tom's Cabin* (1852)

13 Conscience is a treacherous thing, and mine behaves badly whenever there is a serious danger of being found out.

Margaret Lane, *A Calabash of Diamonds* (1961)

14 Altogether his conscience pricked him a good deal; and when people's consciences prick them, sometimes they get angry with other people, which is very silly, and only makes matters worse.

Dinah Maria Mulock Craik, *The Adventures of a Brownie* (1872)

15 A guilty conscience is the mother of invention.

Carolyn Wells, "Maxims," *Folly for the Wise* (1904)

16 Conscience represents a fetish to which good people sacrifice their own happiness, bad people their neighbors'.

Ellen Glasgow, *The Descendant* (1897)

See also Judgment, Morality.

## & CONSENSUS

17 To me consensus seems to be: the process of abandoning all beliefs, principles, values and policies in search of something in which no one believes, but to which no one objects.

Margaret Thatcher, speech (1980), *The Downing Street Years* (1993)

See also Compromise.

## & CONSEQUENCES

18 No doing without some ruing.

Sigrid Undset, *Kristin Lavransdatter: The Bridal Wreath* (1920)

19 Consequences are unpitying.

George Eliot, *Adam Bede* (1859)

20 Their mothers had finally caught up to them and been proven right. There were consequences after all; but they were the consequences to things you didn't even know you'd done.

Margaret Atwood, "The Age of Lead," *Wilderness Tips* (1991)

## ♦ CONSERVATIVES

1 There is a strong conservative instinct in the average man or woman, born of the hereditary fear of life, that prompts them to cling to old standards, or, if too intelligent to look inhospitably upon progress, to move very slowly. Both types are the brakes and wheelhorses necessary to a stable civilization, but history . . . would be dull reading if there were no adventurous spirits willing to do battle for new ideas.

Gertrude Atherton, *The Living Present* (1917)

2 The development of society and culture depends upon a changing balance, maintained between those who innovate and those who conserve the status quo. Relentless, unchecked, and untested innovation would be a nightmare. . . . If repetition and rigidity are the dark side of the conservative coin, loyalty and stability are its bright side.

Judith Groch, *The Right to Create* (1969)

See also Constancy, Conventionality, Status Quo.

## ♦ CONSISTENCY

3 Life hath its phases manifold, / Yet still the new repeats the old; / There is no truer truth than this: / What was, is still the thing that is.

Julia C.R. Dorr, "The First Fire," *Poems* (1892)

4 The dense and godly wear consistency as a flower, the imaginative fling it joyfully behind them.

Stella Benson, *I Pose* (1915)

5 Consistency is a human word, but it certainly expresses nothing human.

L.E. Landon, *Francesca Carrara* (1834)

See also Constancy, Steadfastness.

## ♦ CONSOLATION

6 Let nothing disturb thee; / Let nothing dismay thee: / All things pass; / God never changes.

St. Teresa of Avila (c. 1550), in E. Allison Peers, tr., *The Complete Works of St. Teresa of Jesus* (1946)

7 All shall be well, and all shall be well, and all manner of thing shall be well.

Julian of Norwich, *Revelations of Divine Love* (1373)

8 He [Jesus] did not say, "You will never have a rough passage, you will never be over-strained, you will never feel uncomfortable," but he *did* say, "You will never be overcome."

Julian of Norwich, *Revelations of Divine Love* (1373)

9 I can understand the things that afflict mankind, but I often marvel at those which console.

Anne-Sophie Swetchine, in Count de Falloux, ed., *The Writings of Madame Swetchine* (1869)

10 The reminder that there are people who have worse troubles than you is not an effective pain-killer.

Mary Astor, *A Place Called Saturday* (1968)

See also Comfort, Sympathy.

## ♦ CONSTANCY

11 Constancy, far from being a virtue, seems often to be the besetting sin of the human race, daughter of laziness and self-sufficiency, sister of sleep, the cause of most wars and practically all persecutions.

Freya Stark, *Perseus in the Wind* (1948)

See also Conservatives, Consistency, Steadfastness.

## ♦ CONSUMERISM

12 Consumerism is our national religion.

Jennifer Stone, "Epilogue," *Mind Over Media* (1988)

13 In the comparatively short time between my childhood and my daughter's, the business society has ceased urging people to produce and is now exerting its very considerable influence to get them to consume.

Margaret Halsey, *The Folks at Home* (1952)

14 Necessity need not be the mother of invention, but today invention becomes the mother of necessity. Our affluent society is preoccupied with the production and compulsive consumption of material goods we have been taught to want.

Judith Groch, *The Right to Create* (1969)

1 The metabolism of a consumer society requires it continually to eat and excrete, every day throwing itself away in plastic bags.

    Shana Alexander (1971), *Talking Woman* (1976)

2 America is a consumer culture, and when we change what we buy—and how we buy it—we'll change who we are.

    Faith Popcorn, *The Popcorn Report* (1991)

3 We get a deal o' useless things about us, only because we've got the money to spend.

    George Eliot, *The Mill on the Floss* (1860)

4 He who buys what he does not want ends in wanting what he cannot buy.

    Mrs. Alec-Tweedie, *Behind the Footlights* (1904)

5 An honest man is one who knows that he can't consume more than he has produced.

    Ayn Rand, *Atlas Shrugged* (1957)

6 The pyramids were built for pharaohs on the happy theory that they could take their stuff with them. Versailles was built for kings on the theory that they should live surrounded by the finest stuff. The Mall of America is built on the premise that we should all be able to afford this stuff. It may be a shallow culture, but it's by-God democratic. Sneer if you dare; this is something new in world history.

    Molly Ivins, in *The Fort Worth Star-Telegram* (1994)

7 In department stores, so much kitchen equipment is bought indiscriminately by people who just come in for men's underwear.

    Julia Child, interview (1973)

8 I'm not just buying a car—I'm buying a lifestyle!

    Lynn Johnston, *Pushing 40* (1988)

9 One quarter of what you buy will turn out to be mistakes.

    Delia Ephron, *Funny Sauce* (1986)

See also Advertising, Business, Materialism, Possessions.

## ❦ CONTENTMENT

10 Although I have no fish, / I do not want any frog; / Or any elderberries either, / Instead of a bunch of grapes: / Although I have no love, / I do not want anything else, / Whether Love is gracious to me or hostile.

    Hadewijch, "No Frog, No Elderberries" (13th cent.), in Mother Columba Hart, *Hadewijch* (1980)

11 No one is contented is this world, I believe. There is always something left to desire, and the last thing longed for always seems the most necessary to happiness.

    Marie Corelli, *A Romance of Two Worlds* (1886)

12 When you are unhappy or dissatisfied, is there anything in the world more maddening than to be told that you should be contented with your lot?

    Kathleen Norris, *Hands Full of Living* (1931)

13 I have guarded myself more carefully against contented people than against contagious diseases.

    Victoria Wolff, *Spell of Egypt* (1943)

14 It's not a very big step from contentment to complacency.

    Simone de Beauvoir, *Memoirs of a Dutiful Daughter* (1958)

15 Content is not the pathway to great deeds.

    Ella Wheeler Wilcox, "The Choosing of Esther," *Poems of Progress* (1909)

16 Contentment is the result of a limited imagination.

    Carolyn Wells, "Wiseacreage," *Folly for the Wise* (1904)

See also Complacency, Enough, Happiness, Joy, Satisfaction, Self-Satisfaction.

## ❦ CONTRADICTION

17 Contradiction itself, far from always being a criterion of error, is sometimes a sign of truth.

    Simone Weil (1943), *Oppression and Liberty* (1955)

See also Paradox.

## ❦ CONTRARINESS

18 There are some people who don't conform to the signals. An ordinary well-regulated locomotive slows down or pulls up when it sees the red light hoisted against it. Perhaps I was born color blind. When I see the red signal—I can't help forging

ahead. And in the end, you know, that spells disaster.

Agatha Christie, *The Secret of Chimneys* (1925)

1 I never would just open a door and walk through, I had to bust it down for the hell of it. I just naturally liked doing things the hard way.

Edna Ferber, *Saratoga Trunk* (1941)

2 When anybody talks to me as if I hadn't good sense, I'm immediately tempted to act as if I hadn't. Like sticking beans up your nose.

Helen Eustis, *The Horizontal Man* (1962)

3 That was Felicitas. Ask her to pour oil on troubled waters and she'd light a match.

Mary Gordon, *The Company of Women* (1980)

4 You must not use wood to put out the fire.

Bette Bao Lord, *Spring Moon* (1981)

See also Troublemaker.

## ✦ CONTROL

5 We are most deeply asleep at the switch when we fancy we control any switches at all.

Annie Dillard, *Holy the Firm* (1977)

See also Force, Interference, Order, Power.

## ✦ CONTROVERSY

6 I am not afraid the book will be controversial, I'm afraid it will not be controversial.

Flannery O'Connor, in Sally Fitzgerald, ed., *The Habit of Being* (1979)

## ✦ CONVENTIONALITY

7 I have tried and failed to lead a conventional life. When I try to be like other people, I fall out of bed.

Marian Engel, *The Tattooed Woman* (1985)

8 The truth was, she was becoming more and more uncomfortably conscious not only that the things she said, and a good many of the things she thought, had been taken down off a rack and put on, but that what she really felt was something else again.

Doris Lessing, *The Summer Before the Dark* (1973)

9 Outwardly she differed from the rest of the teaching staff in that she was still in a state of fluctuating development, whereas they had only too understandably not trusted themselves to change their minds, particularly on ethical questions, after the age of twenty.

Muriel Spark, *The Prime of Miss Jean Brodie* (1962)

10 And so is the world put back by the death of every one who has to sacrifice the development of his or her peculiar gifts (which were meant, not for selfish gratification, but for the improvement of that world) to conventionality.

Florence Nightingale, "Cassandra" (1852), in Ray Strachey, *"The Cause"* (1928)

11 Ah, beware, Susan, lest as you become "respectable," you become conservative.

Elizabeth Cady Stanton, letter to Susan B. Anthony (1880), in Theodore Stanton and Harriot Stanton Blatch, eds., *Elizabeth Cady Stanton As Revealed in Her Letters Diary and Reminiscences*, vol. 2 (1922)

12 It saves trouble to be conventional, for you're not always explaining things.

Myrtle Reed, *Old Rose and Silver* (1909)

13 An ounce of convention is worth a pound of explanation.

Ethel Watts Mumford, in Oliver Herford, Ethel Watts Mumford, and Addison Mizner, *The Complete Cynic* (1902)

14 It's terrible to allow conventional habits to gain a hold on a whole household; to eat, sleep and live by clock ticks.

Zelda Fitzgerald (1923), in Nancy Milford, *Zelda* (1970)

15 Orthodoxy is a fixed habit of mind. The average man and woman hug their orthodoxies and spit their venom on those that outrage them.

Gertrude Atherton, *Black Oxen* (1923)

16 Society's the mother of convention.

Carolyn Wells, "More Maxioms," *Folly for the Wise* (1904)

17 The suitable is the last thing we ever want.

Ellen Glasgow, *The Romantic Comedians* (1926)

1 If you are way ahead with your head, you naturally are old fashioned and regular in your daily life.

    Gertrude Stein, in John Malcolm Brinnin, *The Third Rose* (1959)

2 I cannot write too much upon how necessary it is to be completely conservative that is particularly traditional in order to be free.

    Gertrude Stein, *Paris France* (1940)

See also Conformity, Conventions, Normalcy, Ordinariness, Uniformity.

## ❦ CONVENTIONS

3 Today's shocks are tomorrow's conventions.

    Carolyn Heilbrun, *Toward a Recognition of Androgyny* (1973)

4 Conventions, like clichés, have a way of surviving their own usefulness.

    Jane Rule, *The Desert of the Heart* (1965)

5 Human beings tend to regard the conventions of their own societies as natural, often as sacred.

    Mary Catherine Bateson, *Composing a Life* (1989)

6 Conventions are like coins, an easy way of dealing with the commerce of relations.

    Freya Stark, *Beyond Euphrates* (1951)

7 Society, by insisting on conventions, has merely insisted on certain convenient signs by which we may know that a man is considering, in daily life, the comfort of other people.

    Katharine Fullerton Gerould, *Modes and Morals* (1920)

8 Convention was our safeguard: could one have stronger?

    Elizabeth Bowen, "A Day in the Dark," in *Mademoiselle* (1957)

9 Convention, so often a mask for injustice.

    Edith Hamilton, *The Greek Way* (1930)

10 They clung like barnacles to the sunken keel of the style and tastes of the 'Nineties.

    Vicki Baum, *I Know What I'm Worth* (1964)

11 No written law has ever been more binding than unwritten custom supported by popular opinion.

    Carrie Chapman Catt, speech (1900), in Susan B. Anthony and Ida Husted, eds., *The History of Woman Suffrage*, vol. 4 (1902)

See also Conformity, Conventionality, Custom, Traditions, Uniformity.

## ❦ CONVERSATION

12 Most conversations are simply monologues delivered in the presence of a witness.

    Margaret Millar, *The Weak-Eyed Bat* (1942)

13 There is no such thing as conversation. It is an illusion. There are intersecting monologues, that is all.

    Rebecca West, "There Is No Conversation," *The Harsh Voice* (1935)

14 To talk easily with people, you must firmly believe that either you or they are interesting. And even then it's not easy.

    Mignon McLaughlin, *The Second Neurotic's Notebook* (1966)

15 Their civil discussions weren't interesting, and their interesting discussions weren't civil.

    Lisa Alther, *Kinflicks* (1975)

16 Polite conversation is rarely either.

    Fran Lebowitz, *Social Studies* (1977)

17 It is not the correct thing to invite many people who like to monopolize conversation; one of this kind will be found amply sufficient.

    Florence Howe Hall, *The Correct Thing* (1902)

18 A gossip is one who talks to you about others; a bore is one who talks to you about himself; and a brilliant conversationalist is one who talks to you about yourself.

    Lisa Kirk, in *The New York Journal-American* (1954)

19 There is no arena in which vanity displays itself under such a variety of forms as in conversation.

    Madame de Staël, in R.R. Madden, *The Literary Life and Correspondence of the Countess of Blessington*, vol. 1 (1855)

20 It is not hard to converse for a short space of time on subjects about which one knows little, and it is indeed often amusing to see how cunningly one can steer the conversational barque, hoisting and lowering her sails, tacking this way and that to avoid reefs, and finally racing feverishly for home with the outboard engine making a loud and cheerful noise.

    Virginia Graham, *Say Please* (1949)

1 Click, clack, click, clack, went their conversation, like so many knitting-needles, purl, plain, purl, plain, achieving a complex pattern of references, cross-references, Christian names, nicknames, and fleeting allusions.

 Vita Sackville-West, *The Edwardians* (1930)

2 This wasn't conversation. This was oral death.

 Edna Ferber, "Old Man Minick," *Gigolo* (1922)

3 Each person's life is lived as a series of conversations.

 Deborah Tannen, *You Just Don't Understand* (1990)

4 Conversation is like a dear little baby that is brought in to be handed round. You must rock it, nurse it, keep it on the move if you want it to keep smiling.

 Katherine Mansfield, title story, *The Doves' Nest* (1923)

5 Your conversation is a spring that never fails, never overflows.

 Mary Russell Mitford (1854), in Henry Chorley, ed., *Letters of Mary Russell Mitford*, 2nd series, vol. 2 (1872)

6 The conversation of two people remembering, if the memory is enjoyable to both, rocks on like music or lovemaking. There is a rhythm and a predictability to it that each anticipates and relishes.

 Jessamyn West, *The State of Stony Lonesome* (1984)

7 Generous with ideas that he had not yet written, apparently as much a dilettante as I, our conversations became our works, outlines on the tablets of bright midnights.

 Natalie Clifford Barney, on Paul Valéry, *Adventures of the Mind* (1929)

8 Remember my unalterable maxim, where we love, we have always something to say.

 Lady Mary Wortley Montagu (1755), in Octave Thanet, ed., *The Best Letters of Lady Mary Wortley Montagu* (1901)

9 "My idea of good company, Mr. Elliot, is the company of clever, well-informed people, who have a great deal of conversation; that is what I call good company." "You are mistaken," said he gently, "that is not good company, that is the best."

 Jane Austen, *Persuasion* (1818)

10 If one talks to more than four people, it is an audience; and one cannot really think or exchange thoughts with an audience.

 Anne Morrow Lindbergh, *North to the Orient* (1935)

11 A group of three isn't such a good idea. Two can be honest with each other. Two can mutually prove what they are made of. The third is the beginning of a crowd. He brings convention to the other two, deprecation of individual worth. His presence makes each of the others lose something of their personality.

 Victoria Wolff, *Spell of Egypt* (1943)

12 It is not restful, it is not *possible* to talk wholeheartedly to more than one person at a time. You can't really talk with a person unless you surrender to them, for the moment (all other talk is futile). You can't surrender to more than one person a moment.

 Anne Morrow Lindbergh, *Bring Me a Unicorn* (1971)

13 While games and other amusements may serve for a temporary variety (always excepting games known as "kissing-games," which should be promptly tabooed and denounced, and ever will be in truly refined society), yet animated and intelligent conversation must always hold the first place in the list of the pleasures of any refined society circle.

 Helen Ekin Starrett, *The Charm of Fine Manners* (1907)

14 Humans abhor a vacuum. The immediate filling of a vacuum is one of the basic functions of speech. Meaningless conversations are no less important in our lives than meaningful ones.

 Lidia Ginzburg, "The Siege of Leningrad," in *Soviet Women Writing* (1990)

15 The real art of conversation is not only to say the right thing in the right place, but, far more difficult still, to leave unsaid the wrong thing at the tempting moment.

 Dorothy Nevill, *Under Five Reigns* (1910)

16 Silence is one of the great arts of conversation.

 Hannah More, "Thoughts on Conversation," *Essays on Various Subjects* (1777)

17 Conversation is the wall we build between ourselves and other people, too often with tired words like used and broken bottles which, catching the sunlight as they lie embedded in the wall, are mistaken for jewels.

 Janet Frame, *Faces in the Water* (1961)

18 One has to grow up with good talk in order to form the habit of it.

 Helen Hayes, with Lewis Funke, *A Gift of Joy* (1965)

1 Too much brilliance has its disadvantages, and misplaced wit may raise a laugh, but often beheads a topic of profound interest.

Margot Asquith, *More or Less About Myself* (1934)

2 It is . . . owing to the preponderance of the commercial element in Society that conversation has sunk to its present dull level of conventional chatter. The commercial class has always mistrusted verbal brilliancy and wit, deeming such qualities, perhaps with some justice, frivolous and unprofitable.

Dorothy Nevill, *The Reminiscences of Lady Dorothy Nevill* (1906)

3 Up here in the hills you hardly ever get down to business right off. First you say your howdys and then you talk about anything else but what you come for, and finally, when the mosquitoes start to bite, you say what's on your mind. But you always edge into it, not to offend.

Phyllis Reynolds Naylor, *Shiloh* (1991)

4 In no time the conversation was leaping like canoes with the tide.

Sylvia Ashton-Warner, *Teacher* (1963)

5 The conversation whipped gaily around the table like rags in a high wind.

Margaret Halsey, *With Malice Toward Some* (1938)

6 Anything that begins "I don't know how to tell you this" is never good news.

Ruth Gordon, in John Robert Colombo, *Popcorn in Paradise* (1979)

7 "It's like anything else," Mrs. Moone said, largely. She said it quite often, I noticed, one of those fat, loose remarks that seem to settle down over everything, like a collapsing tent.

Peg Bracken, *But I Wouldn't Have Missed It for the World!* (1973)

8 From politics it was an easy step to silence.

Jane Austen, *Northanger Abbey* (1818)

9 A self-taught conversationalist, his style with new acquaintances had the immediate warmth of an investigative journalist tracking down discrepancies in a municipal budget.

Mary Kay Blakely, *Wake Me When It's Over* (1989)

10 Lord Beaconsfield in his later years talked little when in society—men of his stamp, although they possess the gold of conversation, seldom have its small change.

Dorothy Nevill, *Under Five Reigns* (1910)

11 He was, conversationally, a born elephant.

Eleanor Dark, *Return to Coolami* (1936)

12 She never lets ideas interrupt the easy flow of her conversation.

Jean Webster, *Daddy-Long-Legs* (1912)

13 When it came to chit-chat, he made Silas Marner look like Arsenio Hall.

Roseanne Arnold, *My Lives* (1994)

14 I never saw so intelligent a man have so much trouble in getting out a connected sentence. . . . It is like getting congealed liquid from a demijohn; you know the jug is large and full, but getting the contents out is the problem.

Elizabeth Cady Stanton (1880), in Theodore Stanton and Harriot Stanton Blatch, eds., *Elizabeth Cady Stanton As Revealed in Her Letters Diary and Reminiscences*, vol. 2 (1922)

15 [Samuel] Johnson's conversation was by much too strong for a person accustomed to obsequiousness and flattery; it was *mustard in a young child's mouth!*

Hester Lynch Piozzi (1781), in *Boswell's Life of Johnson* (1791)

16 It was possible to talk to Agatha and read simultaneously.

Martha Grimes, *Help the Poor Struggler* (1985)

17 With Mrs. Fairford conversation seemed to be a concert and not a solo. She kept drawing in the others, giving each a turn, beating time for them with her smile, and somehow harmonizing and linking together what they said.

Edith Wharton, *The Custom of the Country* (1913)

18 Beatrice cut her conversation as an inspired dressmaker cuts expensive materials without the need of a pattern. The shape was in her mind; and it was sometimes a little alarming to watch the ruthless decision with which Beatrice wielded her conversational shears.

Phyllis Bottome, *Windlestraws* (1929)

19 Her conversation was like a very light champagne, sparkling but not mounting to the brain.

Gertrude Atherton, *Transplanted* (1919)

20 He loved to talk better than to hear, and to dispute better than to please. . . . People generally left the

room with a high opinion of that gentleman's parts and a confirmed resolution to avoid his society.

Hester Lynch Piozzi (1776), *Thraliana* (1942)

1 Miss Bart had the gift of following an undercurrent of thought while she appeared to be sailing on the surface of conversation.

Edith Wharton, *The House of Mirth* (1905)

2 She will not be interrupted. Break into her train of thought, and she simply starts over. From the top. It is like trying to hold a conversation with a cassette.

Shana Alexander, *Nutcracker* (1985)

3 She was like a recorded telephone message—she didn't listen, she only spoke.

Silvia Tennenbaum, *Rachel, the Rabbi's Wife* (1978)

4 Jeering seemed to be a conversational tic with him.

Liza Cody, *Dupe* (1981)

5 Miss Corby's rôle was jocularity: she always entered the conversation with a handspring.

Edith Wharton, *The House of Mirth* (1905)

6 Once someone like her got a leg in the conversation, she would be all over it.

Flannery O'Connor, "Revelation," *Everything That Rises Must Converge* (1965)

7 Craddock thinks a conversation consists of him talking and everybody else nodding.

Caroline Llewellyn, *Life Blood* (1993)

8 He's seen so many plays he uses dialogue instead of conversation.

Ruth Gordon, *The Leading Lady* (1948)

9 She wanted to get away from herself, and conversation was the only means of escape that she knew.

Edith Wharton, *The House of Mirth* (1905)

See also Arguments, Communication, Listening, Speech, Talking.

## ⑤ CONVERSION

10 A conversion is a lonely experience.

Dorothy Day, *From Union Square to Rome* (1938)

See also Religion, Spirituality.

## ⑤ CONVICTIONS

11 There is a certain strong sense of inner conviction that strikes, with a pang as that of birth, through the very soul, and which is experienced but once or twice in a lifetime.

E.M. Delafield, *The Heel of Achilles* (1921)

12 Convictions do not imply reasons.

Margaret Deland, "The Promises of Dorothea," *Old Chester Tales* (1898)

13 Conviction without experience makes for harshness.

Flannery O'Connor, in Sally Fitzgerald, ed., *The Habit of Being* (1979)

See also Beliefs, Ideals, Principles.

## ⑤ COOKING

14 Cooking may be as much a means of self-expression as any of the arts.

Fannie Merritt Farmer, *The Boston Cooking-School Cook Book* (1896)

15 If you're interested in cooking, you're also just naturally interested in art, in love and in culture.

Madame Jehane Benoît, in *The Canadian* (1974)

16 To cook, and to do it well, every talent must be used; the strength of a prize-fighter, the imagination of a poet, the brain of an empire builder, the patience of Job, the eye and the touch of an artist, and, to turn your mistakes into edible assets, the cleverness of a politician.

Anne Ellis, *Plain Anne Ellis* (1931)

17 Cooking is like love. It should be entered into with abandon or not at all.

Harriet Van Horne, in *Vogue* (1956)

18 Cooking should never be frantic or angry or rushed because the most important ingredient is the spirit.

Alice May Brock, *Alice's Restaurant Cookbook* (1969)

19 What I love about cooking is that after a hard day, there is something comforting about the fact that if you melt butter and add flour and then hot stock, *it will get thick!*

Nora Ephron, *Heartburn* (1983)

1 Neither knowledge nor diligence can create a great chef. Of what use is conscientiousness as a substitute for inspiration?

  Colette, *Prisons and Paradise* (1932)

2 I feel a recipe is only a theme, which an intelligent cook can play each time with a variation.

  Jehane Benoît, *Enjoying the Art of Canadian Cooking* (1974)

3 I do not like people that are hungry. Hungry people eat any thing: I would have my dishes create, of themselves, an appetite; I do not wish them to be wanted till they are tasted, and then to eat is a compliment.

  L.E. Landon, *Romance and Reality* (1831)

4 She was a natural-born cook. . . . People gnawed their fingers and bit their tongues just to smell the steam when she lifted the pot lids.

  Julia Peterkin, *Black April* (1927)

5 Artur has his piano. I play my sonatas on the stove.

  Nella Rubinstein, in Elsa Maxwell, *How to Do It* (1957)

6 She has got on to the right side of the baking powder, and her cakes and things are so light they fly down your throat of themselves.

  Susan Hale (1907), in Caroline P. Atkinson, ed., *Letters of Susan Hale* (1918)

7 What is sauce for the goose may be sauce for the gander but is not necessarily sauce for the chicken, the duck, the turkey or the guinea hen.

  Alice B. Toklas, *The Alice B. Toklas Cook Book* (1954)

8 The carp was dead, killed, assassinated, murdered in the first, second and third degree. Limp, I fell into a chair, with my hands still unwashed reached for a cigarette, lighted it and waited for the police to come and take me into custody.

  Alice B. Toklas, *The Alice B. Toklas Cook Book* (1954)

9 "Correct the seasoning"—how that time-tested direction stimulates the born cook!

  Irma S. Rombauer and Marion Rombauer Becker, *The Joy of Cooking* (1931)

10 Some people *pretend* to like capers, but the truth is that any dish that tastes good with capers in it tastes even better with capers not in it.

  Nora Ephron, *Heartburn* (1983)

11 Dried peas and beans, being rather on the dull side, much like dull people respond readily to the right contacts.

  Irma S. Rombauer and Marion Rombauer Becker, *The Joy of Cooking* (1931)

12 "May your rice never burn," is the New Year's greeting of the Chinese. "May it never be gummy," is ours.

  Irma S. Rombauer and Marion Rombauer Becker, *The Joy of Cooking* (1931)

13 Life is too short to stuff a mushroom.

  Shirley Conran, *Superwoman* (1975)

14 The French use cooking as a means of self-expression, and this meal perfectly represented the personality of a cook who had spent the morning resting her unwashed chin on the edge of a tureen, pondering whether she should end her life immediately by plunging her head into her abominable soup.

  Rebecca West, "Increase and Multiply," *Ending in Earnest* (1931)

See also Eating, Food.

## & COOPERATION

15 Cooperation is an intelligent functioning of the concept of *laissez faire*—a thorough conviction that nobody can get there unless everybody gets there.

  Virginia Burden Tower, *The Process of Intuition* (1975)

See also Collaboration.

## & COSMETICS

16 Wearing makeup is an apology for our actual faces.

  Cynthia Heimel, *Get Your Tongue Out of My Mouth, I'm Kissing You Good-Bye!* (1993)

17 I can't see how any woman can find time to do to herself all the things that must apparently be done to make herself beautiful and, having once done them, how anyone without the strength of mind of a foreign missionary can keep up such a regime.

  Cornelia Otis Skinner, "The Skin-Game," *Dithers and Jitters* (1938)

1 Great parts of our economy are directly dependent upon women having a weak self-concept. A multi-billion dollar fashion-cosmetic industry testifies to the validity of this approach. A woman who does not know who she is can be sold anything.

> Gabrielle Burton, *I'm Running Away From Home, But I'm Not Allowed to Cross the Street* (1972)

2 There is a sound reason why one and a half billion dollars are spent for cosmetics in your country every year, and only half that sum for education: There are no naturally pretty girls in the United States.

> Elizabeth Hawes, *Anything But Love* (1948)

## ✿ COSMOPOLITAN

3 cosmopolitan: / look like you don't really look; / act like you don't really act; / sit like you wouldn't sit if you were home alone.

> Alta, *Letters to Women* (1970)

See also Worldliness.

## ✿ COUGHING

4 We cough because we can't help it, but others do it on purpose.

> Mignon McLaughlin, *The Neurotic's Notebook* (1963)

## ✿ THE COUNTRY

5 The country washes to my door / Green miles on miles in soft uproar, / The thunder of the woods, and then / The backwash of green surf again.

> Katharine Tynan Hinkson, "The Old Love," *Collected Poems* (1930)

6 Country things are the necessary root of our life—and that remains true even of a rootless and tragically urban civilization. To live permanently away from the country is a form of slow death.

> Esther Meynell, *A Woman Talking* (1940)

7 I suppose the pleasure of country life lies really in the eternally renewed evidences of the determination to live.

> Vita Sackville-West, "A Country Life," *Country Notes* (1940)

8 Farmers are philosophical; they have learned that it is less wearing to shrug than to beat their breasts. But there is another angle to their attitude. Things happen rapidly in the country; something new always comes along to divert them and it isn't necessarily another calamity.

> Ruth Stout, *How to Have a Green Thumb Without an Aching Back* (1955)

9 We have our own front page, as all people do who live in the country. It is the sky and the earth, with headlines new every morning. We wake to take in its news as city dwellers reach across thresholds for their newspapers.

> Margaret Lee Runbeck, *Our Miss Boo* (1942)

10 I believed, like many others, that country life is simple. Now I know that the only thing simple about it is the person who thinks it is going to be.

> Bertha Damon, *A Sense of Humus* (1943)

See also Farming, Land.

## ✿ COURAGE

11 Courage is the price that Life exacts for granting peace. / The soul that knows it not, knows no release / From little things: / Knows not the livid loneliness of fear, / Nor mountain heights where bitter joy can hear / The sound of wings.

> Amelia Earhart, in Helen Ferris, ed., *Five Girls Who Dared* (1931)

12 Courage can't see around corners, but goes around them anyway.

> Mignon McLaughlin, *The Neurotic's Notebook* (1963)

13 How cool, how quiet is true courage!

> Fanny Burney, *Evelina* (1778)

14 Courage is the only Magick worth having.

> Erica Jong, *Fanny: Being the True History of the Adventures of Fanny Hackabout-Jones* (1980)

15 Your courage was a small coal / that you kept swallowing.

> Anne Sexton, "Courage," *The Awful Rowing Toward God* (1975)

1 With courage a human being is safe enough. And without it—he is never for one instant safe!

Phyllis Bottome, *The Mortal Storm* (1938)

2 No coward soul is mine.

Emily Brontë (1846), in Charlotte Brontë, ed., "Selections From the Literary Remains of Ellis and Acton Bell," memorial edition of *Wuthering Heights* and *Agnes Grey* (1850)

3 Life shrinks or expands in proportion to one's courage.

Anaïs Nin (1941), *The Diary of Anaïs Nin*, vol. 3 (1969)

4 The only courage that matters is the kind that gets you from one moment to the next.

Mignon McLaughlin, *The Second Neurotic's Notebook* (1966)

5 You become courageous by doing courageous acts. . . . Courage is a habit.

Mary Daly, in *Minnesota Women's Press* (1993)

6 Like a muscle, it is strengthened by use.

Ruth Gordon, in *L'Officiel* (1980)

7 Courage is the ladder on which all the other virtues mount.

Clare Boothe Luce, in *Reader's Digest* (1979)

8 It isn't for the moment you are struck that you need courage but for the long uphill climb back to sanity and faith and security.

Anne Morrow Lindbergh (1932), *Hour of Gold, Hour of Lead* (1973)

9 In true courage there is always an element of choice, of an ethical choice, and of anguish, and also of action and deed. There is always a flame of spirit in it, a vision of some necessity higher than oneself.

Brenda Ueland, *Strength to Your Sword Arm* (1993)

10 I wanted you to see what real courage is, instead of getting the idea that courage is a man with a gun in his hand. It's when you know you're licked before you begin but you begin anyway and you see it through no matter what.

Harper Lee, *To Kill a Mockingbird* (1960)

11 Courage is as often the outcome of despair as hope; in the one case we have nothing to lose, in the other all to gain.

Diane de Poitiers (1550), in Winifred Gordon, *A Book of Days* (1910)

12 People sometimes believed that it was safer to live with complaints, was necessary to cooperate with grief, was all right to become an accomplice in self-ambush. . . . Took heart to flat out decide to be well and stride into the future sane and whole.

Toni Cade Bambara, *The Salt Eaters* (1980)

13 It takes far less courage to kill yourself than it takes to make yourself wake up one more time.

Judith Rossner, *Nine Months in the Life of an Old Maid* (1969)

14 Anyone who has gumption knows what it is, and any one who hasn't can never know what it is. So there is no need of defining it.

L.M. Montgomery, *Anne of the Island* (1915)

15 Only yield when you must; / Never "give up the ship," / But fight on to the last / "With a stiff upper lip!"

Phoebe Cary, "Keep a Stiff Upper Lip," *The Poetical Works of Alice and Phoebe Cary* (1876)

16 It is only in his head that man is heroic; in the pit of his stomach he is always a coward.

Mary Roberts Rinehart, *The Red Lamp* (1925)

17 I'm not brave. When a thing is certain, there's nothing to be brave about. All you can do is to find your consolation.

Agatha Christie, *Endless Night* (1967)

18 Courage is a word for others to use about us, not something we can seek for ourselves.

Lillian Smith, *The Journey* (1954)

19 The truly fearless think of themselves as normal.

Margaret Atwood, "The Whirlpool Rapids," *Bluebeard's Egg* (1986)

20 There are some women who seem to be born without fear, just as there are people who are born without the ability to feel pain. The painless ones go around putting their hands on hot stoves, freezing their feet to the point of gangrene, scalding the lining of their throats with boiling coffee, because there is no warning anguish. . . . Providence appears to protect such women, maybe out of astonishment.

Margaret Atwood, "The Whirlpool Rapids," *Bluebeard's Egg* (1986)

21 Courage and clemency are equal virtues.

Mary Delarivière Manley, *The Royal Mischief* (1696)

1 There is plenty of courage among us for the abstract but not enough for the concrete.

    Helen Keller, *Let Us Have Faith* (1940)

2 The executioner is, I hear, very expert; and my neck is very slender.

    Anne Boleyn (1536), in Willis John Abbot, *Notable Women in History* (1913)

3 Courage! I have shown it for years; think you I shall lose it at the moment when my sufferings are to end?

    Marie Antoinette, on the way to the guillotine (1793)

See also Adventure, Chutzpah, Cowardice, Danger, Daring, Honor, Risk, Virtue.

## ❧ COURTSHIP

4 There is too little courtship in the world. . . . For courtship means a wish to stand well in the other person's eyes, and, what is more, a readiness to be pleased with the other's ways; a sense on each side of having had the better of the bargain; an undercurrent of surprise and thankfulness at one's good luck.

    Vernon Lee, "In Praise of Courtship," *Hortus Vitae* (1904)

See also Dating, Love, Relationships, Romance.

## ❧ COWARDICE

5 Cowardice conserves strength.

    Victoria Wolff, *Spell of Egypt* (1943)

See also Courage, Fear.

## ❧ COWBOYS AND COWGIRLS

6 A few cowboys are still around, old men now, hanging half in, half out, of a legend they helped to make. . . . Their world was one of silver moonlit silence, of lonesome yips from the coyote pack, of thousands of bawling cattle, of uninterrupted prairies, rivers, canyons, and mountains. A world of freedom of infinity. A world of sweat and discomfort.

    Katie Lee, *Ten Thousand Goddam Cattle* (1976)

7 The cowboy's brash, rebellious years were short. Two small decades made him immortal. He was America's last paladin, the idol of an age turned to legend.

    Katie Lee, *Ten Thousand Goddam Cattle* (1976)

8 While the cow*boy* is our favorite American hero—the quintessential man—most of us see the cow*girl* as a child who will grow up someday and be something else. The cowboy's female counterpart—who can ride and rope and wrangle, who understands land and stock and confronts the elements on a daily basis—is somehow missing from our folklore.

    Teresa Jordan, *Cowgirls* (1984)

## ❧ CRANKS

9 It is legitimate to have one's own point of view and political philosophy. But there are people who make anger, rather than a deeply held belief, the basis of their actions. They do not seem to mind harming society as a whole in the pursuit of their immediate objective. No society can survive if it yields to the demands of frenzy, whether of the few or the many.

    Indira Gandhi, *Freedom Is the Starting Point* (1976)

10 A sure sign of a crisis is the prevalence of cranks. It is characteristic of a crisis in theory that cranks get a hearing from the public which orthodoxy is failing to satisfy.

    Joan Robinson, title essay, in Rendigs Fels, ed., *The Second Crisis of Economic Theory* (1972)

See also Extremes, Fanaticism, Radio.

## ❧ CREATION

11 mitch had convinced sassafras that everything waz an art / so nothin in life cd be approached lightly / creation waz inherent in every thing anybody ever did right / that waz one of the mottos of the house.

    Ntozake Shange, *Sassafras* (1976)

1 The world is the work of a single thought, expressed in a thousand different ways.

> Madame de Staël, *Corinne* (1807)

2 Creations, whether they are children, poems, or organizations, take on a life of their own.

> Starhawk, *The Spiral Dance* (1979)

3 The universe was not made in jest but in solemn incomprehensible earnest. By a power that is unfathomably secret, and holy, and fleet.

> Annie Dillard, *Pilgrim at Tinker Creek* (1974)

4 The best thing about being God would be making the heads.

> Iris Murdoch, *A Severed Head* (1961)

5 Fido and Rover are partaking of a mystery of which, further up the table, Cézanne and Beethoven are participants also.

> Rebecca West, title essay, *The Strange Necessity* (1928)

6 I beheld the wretch—the miserable monster whom I had created.

> Mary Shelley, *Frankenstein* (1818)

7 All things bright and beautiful, / All creatures great and small, / All things wise and wonderful, / The Lord God made them all.

> Mrs. Cecil Frances Alexander, *All Things Bright and Beautiful* (1848)

See also Art, Creativity, Invention, Newness.


## ❦ CREATIVITY

8 Creativity is like a great receptive womb.

> Lynn V. Andrews, *Crystal Woman* (1987)

9 Creativity comes from trust. Trust your instincts. And never hope more than you work.

> Rita Mae Brown, *Starting From Scratch* (1988)

10 Creation is a better means of self-expression than possession; it is through creating, not possessing, that life is revealed.

> Vida D. Scudder, *The Privilege of Age* (1939)

11 It is the creative potential itself in human beings that is the image of God.

> Mary Daly, *Beyond God the Father* (1973)

12 Creation lives alone in a small temple. Only one may worship at a time.

> Nancy Hale, *Prodigal Women* (1942)

13 Creative minds always have been known to survive any kind of bad training.

> Anna Freud, speech (1968)

14 Creativity can be described as letting go of certainties.

> Gail Sheehy, *Pathfinders* (1981)

15 Creativity comes by breaking the rules, by saying you're in love with the anarchist.

> Anita Roddick, in Daniel Goleman, Paul Kaufman, and Michael Ray, *The Creative Spirit* (1992)

16 The core of creation is to summon an image and the power to work with the image.

> Anaïs Nin, *The Novel of the Future* (1968)

17 Many people are inventive, sometimes cleverly so. But real creativity begins with the drive to work on and on and on.

> Margueritte Harmon Bro, *Sarah* (1949)

18 The richest source of creation is feeling, followed by a vision of its meaning.

> Anaïs Nin, *Realism and Reality* (1946)

19 Living in a state of psychic unrest, in a Borderland, is what makes poets write and artists create.

> Gloria Anzaldúa, *Borderlands/La Frontera* (1987)

20 I can always be distracted by love, but eventually I get horny for my creativity.

> Gilda Radner, *It's Always Something* (1989)

21 I invented this rule for myself to be applied to every decision I might have to make in the future. I would sort out all the arguments and see which belonged to fear and which to creativeness, and other things being equal I would make the decision which had the larger number of creative reasons on its side. I think it must be a rule something like this that makes jonquils and crocuses come pushing through cold mud.

> Katharine Butler Hathaway, *The Little Locksmith* (1942)

22 When we are writing, or painting, or composing, we are, during the time of creativity, freed from normal restrictions, and are opened to a wider world, where colors are brighter, sounds clearer,

and people more wondrously complex than we normally realize.

Madeleine L'Engle, *Walking on Water* (1980)

1 The process of writing, any form of creativity, is a power intensifying life.

Rita Mae Brown, *Starting From Scratch* (1988)

2 Self-forgetfulness in creativity can lead to self-transcendence.

Sylvia Ashton-Warner (1945), *Myself* (1967)

3 The most important thing any person can do is to get out of the light. Get out of his own light, I mean. Most of the time we let our shadows block off the sun. It takes so much not-doing to accomplish anything.

Margueritte Harmon Bro, *Sarah* (1949)

4 The mystics are the only ones who have gained a glimpse into what is possible when this same capacity is used primarily in the service of the individual himself instead of for the creation of art.

Beatrice Hinkle, "The Psychology of the Artist," *The Re-Creating of the Individual* (1923)

5 I do believe it is possible to create, even without ever writing a word or painting a picture, by simply molding one's inner life. And that too is a deed.

Etty Hillesum (1942), *An Interrupted Life* (1983)

6 I think most artists create out of despair. . . . If labor pain is for physical birth, then there is a psychic and spiritual pain for creation. . . . The very nature of creation is not a performing glory on the outside, it's a painful, difficult search within.

Louise Nevelson, *Dawns + Dusks* (1976)

7 To fulfill a dream, to be allowed to sweat over lonely labor, to be given the chance to create, is the meat and potatoes of life. The money is the gravy. As everyone else, I love to dunk my crust in it. But alone, it is not a diet designed to keep body and soul together.

Bette Davis, *The Lonely Life* (1962)

8 Creative endeavor requires physical and mental space; without privacy, solitude, and time it suffocates. . . . It is impossible to pursue original thought in the scattered remnants of a day or of a lifetime.

Judith Groch, *The Right to Create* (1969)

9 Perhaps the best thing we can do for the creative person is to stay out of his way.

Judith Groch, *The Right to Create* (1969)

10 When I can no longer create anything, I'll be done for.

Coco Chanel, in Marcel Haedrich, *Coco Chanel* (1972)

11 In this country we encourage "creativity" among the mediocre, but real bursting creativity appalls us. We put it down as undisciplined, as somehow "too much."

Pauline Kael, *Kiss Kiss Bang Bang* (1968)

12 Those who create are rare; those who cannot are numerous. Therefore, the latter are stronger.

Coco Chanel, in *This Week* (1961)

13 Americans worship creativity the way they worship physical beauty—as a way of enjoying elitism without guilt: God did it.

Florence King, *Reflections in a Jaundiced Eye* (1989)

14 After each creative act one has to be sustained by one's strength of character, by a moral sense, by I don't know what, lest one tumble.

Etty Hillesum (1942), *An Interrupted Life* (1983)

15 One must also accept that one has "uncreative" moments. The more honestly one can accept that, the quicker these moments will pass. One must have the courage to call a halt, to feel empty and discouraged.

Etty Hillesum (1942), *An Interrupted Life* (1983)

16 Creativity varies inversely with the number of cooks involved with the broth.

Bernice Fitz-Gibbon, *Macy's, Gimbels, and Me* (1967)

17 Under all the superficial praise of the "creative" is the desire to kill. It is the old war between the mystic and the nonmystic, a war to the death.

May Sarton, *Mrs. Stevens Hears the Mermaids Singing* (1965)

18 My husband's family was terribly refined. Within their circle you could know Beethoven, but God forbid if you were Beethoven.

Louise Nevelson, in Arnold B. Glimcher, *Louise Nevelson* (1972)

See also Art, Creation, Genius, Imagination, Improvisation.

## & CREDULITY

1 The age of credulity is every age the world has ever known. Men have always turned from the ascertained, which is limited and discouraging, to the dubious, which is unlimited and full of hope for everybody.

Agnes Repplier, "The Public Looks at Pills," *Times and Tendencies* (1931)

2 Credulity and the Want of Foresight, are Imperfections in the human Character, that no Politician can sufficiently guard against.

Abigail Adams, to her husband, John Adams (1776), in L.H. Butterfield et al., eds., *The Book of Abigail and John* (1975)

3 Credulity is always a ridiculous, often a dangerous failing: it has made of many a clever man, a fool; and of many a good man, a knave.

Frances Wright, *A Few Days in Athens* (1822)

4 What one heart finds hard to believe, a hundred find easy.

Nancy Willard, *Things Invisible to See* (1984)

5 A little credulity helps one on through life very smoothly.

Elizabeth Gaskell, *Cranford* (1853)

See also Belief, Innocence.

## & CRIME

6 Crime is naught but misdirected energy.

Emma Goldman, title essay, *Anarchism* (1910)

7 There is hardly any deviancy, no matter how reprehensible in one context, which is not extolled as a virtue in another. There are no natural crimes, only legal ones.

Freda Adler, *Sisters in Crime* (1975)

8 We make our own criminals, and their crimes are congruent with the national culture we all share. It has been said that a people get the kind of political leadership they deserve. I think they also get the kinds of crime and criminals they themselves bring into being.

Margaret Mead, in *Redbook* (1978)

9 Stripped of ethical rationalizations and philosophical pretensions, a crime is anything that a group in power chooses to prohibit.

Freda Adler, *Sisters in Crime* (1975)

10 Crime . . . can be a way of establishing identity or acquiring security—at least the magistrate addresses you by name.

Diana Norman, *Road From Singapore* (1970)

11 He'd forgotten just how addictive crime can be. Repeat offenders are motivated more by withdrawal symptoms than necessity.

Sue Grafton, *"H" Is for Homicide* (1991)

12 Lawlessness is a self-perpetuating, ever-expanding habit.

Dorothy Thompson, *The Courage to Be Happy* (1957)

13 The scope of his crimes is biblical.

Julia O'Faolain, *Women in the Wall* (1975)

See also Evil, Lawlessness, Murder, Rape, Sexual Harassment, Sin, Theft, Vice.

## & CRISES

14 We don't get offered crises, they arrive.

Elizabeth Janeway, *Cross Sections* (1982)

15 The great crises of life are not, I think, necessarily those which are in themselves the hardest to bear, but those for which we are least prepared.

Mary Adams, *Confessions of a Wife* (1902)

16 He was about as useful in a crisis as a sheep.

Dorothy Eden, *The Laughing Ghost* (1968)

See also Disaster, Problems, Stress, Tragedy, Trouble.

## & CRITICISM

17 People fed on sugared praises cannot be expected to feel an appetite for the black broth of honest criticism.

Agnes Repplier, "Curiosities of Criticism," *Books and Men* (1888)

1 You cannot do good work if you take your mind off the work to see how the community is taking it.

> Dorothy L. Sayers, "Why Work?" *Creed or Chaos?* (1949)

2 It is a happy and easy way of filling a book that the present race of authors have arrived at—that of criticizing the works of some eminent poet, with monstrous extracts and short remarks. It is a species of cookery that I begin to grow tired of: they cut up their authors in chops, and by adding a little crumbled bread of their own, and tossing it up a little, they present it as a fresh dish: you are to dine upon the poet; the critic supplies the garnish, yet has the credit as well as the profit of the whole entertainment.

> Hannah More (1775), in Mrs. Helen C. Knight, *Hannah More or Life in Hall and Cottage* (1862)

3 If the novel is dying, I see no chance that dismembering it will revive it.

> Storm Jameson, *Parthian Words* (1970)

See also Books, Criticisms, Critics, Literature, Theater.

## ᛃ CRITICISMS

4 This book of essays . . . has all the depth and glitter of a worn dime.

> Dorothy Parker, "Re-Enter Margot Asquith," in *The New Yorker* (1927)

5 The affair between Margot Asquith and Margot Asquith will live as one of the prettiest love stories in all literature.

> Dorothy Parker, "Re-Enter Margot Asquith," in *The New Yorker* (1927)

6 Never before or since has any book been so much relished by its author.

> Agnes Repplier, on Margot Asquith's autobiography, "Writing an Autobiography," *Under Dispute* (1924)

7 It may be that this autobiography [Aimee Semple McPherson's] is set down in sincerity, frankness, and simple effort. It may be, too, that the Statue of Liberty is situated in Lake Ontario.

> Dorothy Parker, "Our Lady of the Loudspeaker," in *The New Yorker* (1928)

8 At the end, Schwarzenegger makes his ritual preparations for the climactic showdown, decking himself out in leather, packing up an arsenal of guns, and, as he leaves his apartment, copping a quick look of satisfaction in the mirror. It's his only love scene.

> Pauline Kael, *Hooked* (1989)

9 It [*The Fraud of Feminism* by Belfort Bax] is written in "the hope that honest, straightforward men who have been bitten by feminist wiles"—probably a misprint for wives—"will take a pause and reconsider their position," and it is one of the most distressing books I have yet endured. It is like answering a call on the telephone and hearing no words but distant shrieks and groans and thuds.

> Rebecca West, in *The Clarion* (1913)

10 Every word she writes is a lie, including "and" and "the."

> Mary McCarthy, on Lillian Hellman, in televised interview with Dick Cavett (1980), in Carol Gelderman, *Conversations With Mary McCarthy* (1991)

11 Updike's style is an exquisite blend of Melville and Austen: reading him is like cutting through whale blubber with embroidery scissors.

> Florence King, *Reflections in a Jaundiced Eye* (1989)

12 She . . . actually perpetrated a sonnet to the moon, which sonnet, contrary to the well-known recipe of Boileau and the ordinary practice of all nations, contained eighteen lines, four quatrains and a couplet; a prodigality of words which the fair poetess endeavored to counterbalance by a corresponding sparingness of idea.

> Mary Russell Mitford, *Our Village* (1848)

13 Surely, if Mr. Lewis in outlining his plot to some friend, had only said, "Stop me if you've heard this," more than two hundred pages of *Dodsworth* need never have been written.

> Dorothy Parker, "And Again, Mr. Sinclair Lewis," in *The New Yorker* (1929)

14 He thinks he was knocked off his horse by God, like St. Paul on the road to Damascus. His critics think he simply fell off it from old age.

> Katharine Whitehorn, on Malcolm Muggeridge, *View From a Column* (1981)

15 Your two friends, Prudence and Reflection, I am informed, have lately ventured to pay you a visit; for which I heartily congratulate you, as nothing can possibly be more joyous to the heart than the

return of absent friends, after a long and painful peregrination.

Charlotte Charke, *A Narrative of the Life of Mrs. Charlotte Charke* (1755)

1 I wonder by what accident Miss Seward came by her fame. Setting aside her pedantry and presumption, there is no poet male or female who ever clothed so few ideas in so many words.

Mary Russell Mitford (1818), in Henry Chorley, ed., *Letters of Mary Russell Mitford,* 2nd series, vol. 1 (1872)

2 Stravinsky's Cantata for mezzo-soprano, tenor, women's choir and five instruments, based on Tudor verses, is a mercilessly dull, wholly unleavened essay in boredom.... The most invigorating sound I heard was a restive neighbor winding his watch.

Mildred Norton, in Nicolas Slonimsky, *Lexicon of Musical Invective* (1953)

3 Too many notes!

Nadia Boulanger (c. 1927), on the music of Richard Strauss, in Léonie Rosenstiel, *Nadia Boulanger* (1982)

4 As the great Brahms recently proclaimed: / "A clever woman is a thing of naught!" / So let us diligently cultivate stupidity, / That being the only quality demanded / Of a female Brahms-admirer!

Ethel Smyth, *Impressions That Remained* (1919)

5 Writers on the subject of August Strindberg have hitherto omitted to mention that he could not write.... Strindberg, who was neither a good nor a wise man, had a stroke of luck. He went mad. He lost the power of inhibition. Everything down to the pettiest suspicion that the dog had been given the leanest mutton chop, poured out of his lips. Men of his weakness and sensuality are usually, from their sheer brutishness, unable to express themselves. But Strindberg was mad and articulate. That is what makes him immortal.

Rebecca West, in *The Freewoman* (1912)

6 The Government should prohibit the import of literary pulp as well as wood pulp from Sweden. From that country comes the erotopriggery of Miss Ellen Key, which exhorts women to abandon all personality and creative effort and be but the damp towel to bind round the heated temples of intellectual man. And from that country comes August Strindberg, that unattractive person who was never at his ease except when he was suffering from persecution mania, and who regarded three wives and a few delusions as adequate material for hundreds

of plays. And from that country Strindberg constantly comes, and continues to come.

Rebecca West, in *The New York Daily News* (1916)

7 I do not think very highly of Madame D'Arblay's books. The style is so strutting. She does so stalk about on Dr. Johnson's old stilts.

Mary Russell Mitford (1819), in the Reverend A.G. L'Estrange, ed., *The Life of Mary Russell Mitford,* vol. 2 (1870)

8 Ibsen cried out for ideas for the same reason that men call out for water, because he had not got any.

Rebecca West, *Black Lamb and Grey Falcon* (1941)

9 Miss Heilgers belongs to that school of fiction... who imagine that by cataloging stimuli one can produce a feeling of stimulation; as though one could convey the joys and miseries of drunkenness by enumerating the public-houses in the Harrow Road.

Rebecca West, in *The Freewoman* (1912)

10 [Henry James] chaws more than he bites off.

Marian Hooper Adams (1882), in Eugenia Kaledin, *The Education of Mrs. Henry Adams* (1981)

11 His book... makes nice reading for people. But what's the use? Except, of course, to kill time for those who prefer it dead.

Rose Macaulay, *Potterism* (1920)

12 This is not a novel to be tossed aside lightly. It should be thrown with great force.

Dorothy Parker (1930), in Robert E. Drennan, *The Algonquin Wits* (1968)

13 The central theme of the novel is that they were glad to see each other.

Gertrude Stein, in John Malcolm Brinnin, *The Third Rose* (1959)

14 The book [Edna Ferber's *Ice Palace*], which is going to be a movie, has the plot and characters of a book which is going to be a movie.

Dorothy Parker, *Esquire* (1958)

15 It [William Lyon Phelps's *Happiness*] is second only to a rubber duck as the ideal bathtub companion. It may be held in the hand without causing muscular fatigue... and it may be read through before the water has cooled. And if it slips down the drain pipe, all right, it slips down the drain pipe.

Dorothy Parker, "The Professor Goes in for Sweetness and Light," in *The New Yorker* (1927)

1 Mr. Theodore Dreiser's book about himself sounds like nothing but a loud, human purr.

Agnes Repplier, in Emma Repplier, *Agnes Repplier* (1957)

2 Me no Leica.

Caroline Lejeune, reviewing the film *I Am a Camera*, in *The Observer* (1955)

3 It [scene in *The Killing of Sister George*] is the longest, most unerotic, cash-conscious scene between a person and a breast there has ever been, on screen and outside a surgeon's office.

Renata Adler, *A Year in the Dark* (1969)

4 *Rain Man* is Dustin Hoffman humping one note on a piano for two hours and eleven minutes.

Pauline Kael, *Movie Love* (1991)

5 There's less in this than meets the eye.

Tallulah Bankhead (1922), *Tallulah* (1952)

6 He [Van Wyck Brooks] fails from sheer excess of the housewifely qualities. He is saving: just as in happier circumstances he would have put every scrap into the stockpot, so now he refuses to throw away the very driest bone of thought, and insists on boiling it up into his mental soup. He is hospitable: the deadest idea does not get turned away from his doorstep. He is cleanly: his bleached, scentless style suggests that he hung out the English language on the line in the dry, pure breezes of Boston before he used it.

Rebecca West, in *The New York Daily News* (1915)

7 There is a curious film of dirtiness over the whole book, which one can't explain. I am sure as a boy he never washed his hands, but drank ink and kept mice in his pockets.

Edith Sitwell, on John Cowper Powys' *Wolf Solent* (1935), in John Lehmann and Derek Parker, eds., *Selected Letters* (1970)

8 "The Way We Were" is a fluke—a torpedoed ship full of gaping holes which comes snugly into port.

Pauline Kael, *Reeling* (1976)

9 As a singer you're a great dancer.

Amy Leslie, to George Primrose, in Edward B. Marks, *They All Sang* (1934)

10 I've always told him he should give up writing and take up singing.

Nora Joyce, on her husband James, in Brenda Maddox, *Nora: The Real Life of Molly Bloom* (1988)

11 It's an ugly, stupid instant movie ["You Are What You Eat"] made by people who substitute promotion for talent and technique. It's the aesthetic equivalent of mugging the audience.

Pauline Kael, *Going Steady* (1970)

12 One of Mr. [Thomas] Hardy's ancestors must have married a weeping willow. There are pages and pages in his collected poems which are simply plain narratives in ballad form of how an unenjoyable time was had by all.

Rebecca West, "Two Kinds of Memory," *The Strange Necessity* (1928)

13 The vacuity of the Ross Hunter-George Seaton ten-million-dollar *Airport* has the dull innocence of an accounting error.

Pauline Kael, *Deeper Into Movies* (1973)

14 The movie [*Song of Norway*] is of an unbelievable badness; it brings back clichés you didn't know you knew—they're practically from the unconscious of moviegoers. You can't get angry at something this stupefying; it seems to have been made by trolls.

Pauline Kael, *Deeper Into Movies* (1973)

15 To lambaste a Ross Hunter production is like flogging a sponge.

Pauline Kael, *Reeling* (1976)

16 Mr. [Aldous] Huxley has been the alarming young man for a long time, a sort of perpetual clever nephew who can be relied on to flutter the lunch party. Whatever will he say next? How does he think of those things? He has been deplored once or twice, but feeling is in his favor: he is steadily read. He is at once the truly clever person and the stupid person's idea of the clever person.

Elizabeth Bowen, *Collected Impressions* (1950)

17 Alan Parker has technique to burn in *Angel Heart*, and that's what he should do with it.

Pauline Kael, *Hooked* (1989)

18 Meryl Streep just about always seems miscast. (She makes a career out of seeming to overcome being miscast.)

Pauline Kael, *Movie Love* (1991)

19 *The House Beautiful* is the play lousy.

Dorothy Parker, in *The New Yorker* (1933)

20 She ran the whole gamut of emotions, from A to B.

Dorothy Parker, on Katharine Hepburn (1933), in Robert E. Drennan, *The Algonquin Wits* (1968)

1 Upton Sinclair is his own King Charles' head. He cannot keep himself out of his writings, try though he may; or, by this time, try though he doesn't.

Dorothy Parker, "The Socialist Looks at Literature," in *The New Yorker* (1927)

2 The book [Lou Tellegen's *Women Have Been Kind*] . . . has all the elegance of a quirked little finger and all the glitter of a pair of new rubbers.

Dorothy Parker, "Kiss and Tellegen," in *The New Yorker* (1931)

3 This play [John Drinkwater's *Abraham Lincoln*] holds the season's record, thus far, with a run of four evening performances and one matinee. By an odd coincidence, it ran just five performances too many.

Dorothy Parker, in *Vanity Fair* (1920)

4 Tonstant Weader fwowed up.

Dorothy Parker ("Constant Reader"), "Far From Well," review of *The House at Pooh Corner*, in *The New Yorker* (1928)

See also Criticism, Critics, Insults.

## & CRITICS

5 They never raised a statue to a critic.

Martha Graham, in Agnes de Mille, *Dance to the Piper* (1952)

6 There is a great supply of amateur undertakers in show business.

Ethel Waters, with Charles Samuels, *His Eye Is on the Sparrow* (1951)

7 To be a critic, you have to have maybe three percent education, five percent intelligence, two percent style, and ninety percent gall and egomania in equal parts.

Judith Crist, in John Robert Colombo, *Popcorn in Paradise* (1979)

8 While in some quarters it is felt that the critic is just a necessary evil, most serious-minded, decent, talented theater people agree that the critic is an unnecessary evil.

Jean Kerr, "One Half of Two on the Aisle," *Please Don't Eat the Daisies* (1957)

9 It is as hard to find a neutral critic as it is a neutral country in time of war. I suppose if a critic were neutral, he wouldn't trouble to write anything.

Katherine Anne Porter (1948), *The Collected Essays and Occasional Writings of Katherine Anne Porter* (1970)

10 Too often do reviewers remind us of the mob of Astrologers, Chaldeans, and Soothsayers gathered before "the writing on the wall," and unable to read the characters or make known the interpretation.

Charlotte Brontë, biographical note (1850) to Emily Brontë's *Wuthering Heights* (1847)

11 One would think that an unsuccessful volume was like a degree in the school of reviewing. . . . The severity of "the ungentle craft" originates in its own want of success: they cannot forgive the popularity which has passed them over.

L.E. Landon, *Romance and Reality* (1831)

12 What a pity when editors review a woman's book, that they so often fall into the error of reviewing the *woman* instead.

Fanny Fern, *Ginger-Snaps* (1870)

13 Rex Reed is either at your feet or at your throat.

Ava Gardner, in John Robert Colombo, *Popcorn in Paradise* (1979)

14 Poets are lovers. Critics are / mean, solitary masturbators.

Gwen Harwood, "Critic's Nightwatch," *Poems* (1963)

15 A critic . . . is a mental eunuch; he can criticize, but he cannot create.

Mary Austin, in T.M. Pearce, *The Beloved House* (1940)

16 Critics and reviewers do not use / Their precious ammunition to abuse / A worthless work. That, left alone, they know / Will find its proper level; and they aim / Their batteries at rising works which claim / Too much of public notice.

Ella Wheeler Wilcox, *Maurine* (1901)

17 An intelligent man or woman willing to make a career of reviewing fiction is hard to come by. . . . And the temporaries do the work cheaply. Moreover, continuity may be got at the expense of intellectual arthritis; a reviewer who has been at his grisly task for half a lifetime may stiffen into prejudices of every sort, and become too anchylosed to do better than turn his back to a new wave when it rushes down on him.

Storm Jameson, *Parthian Words* (1970)

1 What tongue could speak but to an intelligent ear, and every noble work demands its critic. . . . The critic is not a base caviller, but the younger brother of genius. . . . The critic, then, should be not merely a poet, nor merely a philosopher, not merely an observer, but tempered of all three.

Margaret Fuller, in *The Dial* (1840)

2 Every eye can detect the grains of gold, but it is only the philosopher can prove to us how much dross the ore contains.

Lady Wilde, "Miss Martineau," *Notes on Men, Women, and Books* (1891)

3 If you think it so easy to be a critic, so difficult to be a poet or a painter or film experimenter, may I suggest you try both? You may discover why there are so few critics, so many poets.

Pauline Kael, *I Lost It at the Movies* (1965)

4 The labors of the true critic are more essential to the author, even, than to the reader.

Agnes Repplier, "Curiosities of Criticism," *Books and Men* (1888)

5 You don't have to lay an egg to know if it tastes good.

Pauline Kael, *I Lost It at the Movies* (1965)

6 More in anger than sorrow.

Hester Lynch Piozzi, on the way she viewed her critics, in Alice Meynell, "Hester," in *Pall Mall Gazette* (1893)

See also Criticism, Criticisms.

## § CRUELTY

7 Cruelty is the only sin.

Ellen Glasgow, *The Woman Within* (1954)

8 Cruelty is the only thing that strikes me as completely unforgivable. The unpardonable sin.

Rae Foley, *The Last Gamble* (1956)

9 Cruelty, like every other vice, requires no motive outside itself; it only requires opportunity.

George Eliot, "Janet's Repentance," *Scenes of Clerical Life* (1857)

10 An animal is not cruel; it lives wholly in the instant leap on its prey, in the present taste of marrow or blood. Cruelty begins with the memory, and the pleasures of the memory are impure; they draw their strength along levels where no sun has reached.

Storm Jameson, *The Journal of Mary Hervey Russell* (1945)

11 I think that the desire to be cruel and to hurt (with words because any other way might be dangerous to ourself) is part of human nature. Parties are battles (most parties), a conversation is a duel (often). Everybody's trying to hurt first, to get in the dig that will make him or her feel superior, feel triumph.

Jean Rhys, *Letters, 1931-1966* (1984)

12 Cruelty is contagious in uncivilized communities.

Harriet A. Jacobs, *Incidents in the Life of a Slave Girl, Written by Herself* (1861)

13 A hurtful act is the transference to others of the degradation which we bear in ourselves.

Simone Weil, *Gravity and Grace* (1947)

14 Unkindness almost always stands for the displeasure that one has in oneself.

Adrienne Monnier (1939), in Richard McDougall, tr., *The Very Rich Hours of Adrienne Monnier* (1976)

15 Experience has taught me that the only cruelties people condemn are those with which they do not happen to be familiar.

Ellen Glasgow, *Letters of Ellen Glasgow* (1958)

16 My doctrine is this, that if we see cruelty or wrong that we have the power to stop, and do nothing, we make ourselves sharers in the guilt.

Anna Sewell, *Black Beauty* (1877)

See also Evil, Heartlessness, Ruthlessness, Vice.

## § CRYING

17 To hide your own crying was the Griswold way of feeling grief. To ignore another's crying, the Griswold way of curing it.

Bertha Damon, *Grandma Called It Carnal* (1938)

See also Tears.

## § CULTS

18 Persecution always acts as a jell for members of cults; it proves to them, in the absence of history,

liturgy, tradition, and doctrine, that they are God's chosen.

Barbara Grizzuti Harrison, "Horror at Island Pond" (1984), *The Astonishing World* (1992)

1 I didn't mind giving up carnality, jewelry and red meat in return for comradeship and an afterlife.

Margaret Millar, *Ask for Me Tomorrow* (1976)

## ❦ CULTURE

2 Culture is both an intellectual phenomenon and a moral one.

Raisa M. Gorbachev, *I Hope* (1991)

3 Most people . . . are plastic to the molding force of the society into which they are born. It does not matter whether, with the Northwest Coast, it requires delusions of self-reference, or with our own civilization the amassing of possessions. In any case the great mass of individuals take quite readily the form that is presented to them.

Ruth Benedict, *Patterns of Culture* (1934)

4 Cultural constraints condition and limit our choices, shaping our characters with their imperatives.

Jeane J. Kirkpatrick, speech (1981)

5 Culture is not a biologically transmitted complex.

Ruth Benedict, *Patterns of Culture* (1934)

6 Culture—as we know it—is an instrument manipulated by teachers for manufacturing more teachers, who, in their turn, will manufacture still more teachers.

Simone Weil, *The Need for Roots* (1949)

7 Culture is what your butcher would have if he were a surgeon.

Mary Pettibone Poole, *A Glass Eye at a Keyhole* (1938)

8 Mrs. Ballinger is one of the ladies who pursue Culture in bands, as though it were dangerous to meet alone.

Edith Wharton, title story, *Xingu* (1916)

See also Civilization, Society.

## ❦ CURIOSITY

9 Curiosity is the one thing invincible in Nature.

Freya Stark (1940), in Caroline Moorehead, ed., *Over the Rim of the World* (1988)

10 Curiosity is one of those insatiable passions that grow by gratification.

Sarah Scott, *A Description of Millenium Hall* (1762)

11 Curiosity needs food as much as any of us, and dies soon if denied it.

Stella Benson, *I Pose* (1915)

12 There is nothing so carking as the pangs of unsatisfied curiosity.

Gertrude Atherton, *Sleeping Fires* (1922)

13 He was overwhelmingly curious. He had a mind like a child's, or a puppy's, or an old-fashioned novelist's, prying into everything and weaving stories around whatever caught his attention.

Emily Hahn, *China to Me* (1944)

14 Curiosity ran unchecked through him, like the wind outside through the deserted streets, along the canal, around the little wooden houses, everywhere, as far as the mountain.

Gabrielle Roy, *The Tin Flute* (1947)

15 Some men and women are inquisitive about everything, they are always asking, if they see any one with anything they ask what is that thing, what is it you are carrying, what are you going to be doing with that thing, why have you that thing, where did you get that thing, how long will you have that thing, there are very many men and women who want to know about anything about everything.

Gertrude Stein, *The Making of Americans* (1925)

16 It is inconceivable that anything should be existing. It is not inconceivable that a lot of people should also be existing who are not interested in the fact that they exist. But it is certainly very odd.

Celia Green, *The Decline and Fall of Science* (1976)

17 I think, at a child's birth, if a mother could ask a fairy godmother to endow it with the most useful gift, that gift should be curiosity.

Eleanor Roosevelt, in *Reader's Digest* (1983)

18 Worlds can be found by a child and an adult bending down and looking together under the grass stems or at the skittering crabs in a tidal pool.

Mary Catherine Bateson, *With a Daughter's Eye* (1984)

1 It doesn't do to be curious at Jamaica Inn, and I'll
have you remember that.
   Daphne du Maurier, *Jamaica Inn* (1935)

2 The curious are always in some danger. If you are
curious you might never come home.
   Jeanette Winterson, *Oranges Are Not the Only Fruit* (1985)

3 Curiosity is its own suicide.
   L.E. Landon, *Romance and Reality* (1831)

4 Try curiosity.
   Dorothy Parker, to a friend whose sick cat needed to be put
   to sleep, in Robert E. Drennan, *The Algonquin Wits* (1968)

See also Nosiness, Questions.


## ❦ CUSTOM

5 There is nothing more innately human than the
tendency to transmute what has become customary into what has been divinely ordained.
   Suzanne La Follette, "The Beginnings of Emancipation,"
   *Concerning Women* (1926)

6 Custom is never, by her nature, the handmaid of
freedom.
   Maria W. Chapman, *Right and Wrong in Massachusetts*
   (1839)

7 Custom, that merciless torrent that carries all before it.
   Mary Astell, *A Serious Proposal to the Ladies* (1694)

8 What custom hath endear'd / We part with sadly,
though we prize it not.
   Joanna Baillie, *Basil* (1798)

See also Conventions, Habit, Ritual, Traditions.


## ❦ CYNICISM

9 Cynicism's always a pose.
   Grace S. Richmond, *Red of the Redfields* (1924)

10 Cynicism is more than a pose; it's also a handy time
saver. By deflating your companion's enthusiasm,
you can cut conversations in half.
   Lisa Birnbach, *The Official Preppy Handbook* (1980)

11 The cynic is a coward. He foresees all barrenness so
that barrenness can never surprise him.
   Anaïs Nin (1926), *Linotie, the Early Diary of Anaïs Nin,*
   vol. 3 (1983)

12 Cynicism is an unpleasant way of saying the truth.
   Lillian Hellman, *The Little Foxes* (1939)

13 Cynicism is a sure sign of youth.
   Ellen Glasgow, *The Descendant* (1897)

14 A cynical young person is almost the saddest sight
to see, because it means that he or she has gone
from knowing nothing to believing in nothing.
   Maya Angelou, in Brian Lanker, *I Dream a World* (1989)

15 Cynicism . . . is the trade-mark of failure.
   Katherine Cecil Thurston, *The Masquerader* (1904)

16 "Cynic" is the sentimentalist's name for the realist.
   Amanda Cross, *The Question of Max* (1976)

17 Cynical speech is characterized by a lengthening of
vowel sounds in the syllable that is normally ac-
cented, i.e., "Woooonderful." Derivation of this
attitude can be traced to the manufacture of the
first synthetic fabrics. "That sweater's proooobably
acryyyylic."
   Lisa Birnbach, *The Official Preppy Handbook* (1980)

18 I worry no matter how cynical you become, it's
never enough to keep up.
   Jane Wagner, *The Search for Signs of Intelligent Life in the
   Universe* (1985)

See also Pessimism.

# D

## ❦ DANCE

1 Dance is the hidden language of the soul.
  Martha Graham, in "Martha Graham Reflects on Her Art and a Life in Dance," *The New York Times* (1985)

2 The truest expression of a people is in its dances and its music.
  Agnes de Mille, in *The New York Times Magazine* (1975)

3 Dancing is just discovery, discovery, discovery.
  Martha Graham, in "Martha Graham Reflects on Her Art and a Life in Dance," *The New York Times* (1985)

4 Every dance is a kind of fever chart, a graph of the heart.
  Martha Graham, *Blood Memory* (1991)

5 Man learned to resort to the dance when he felt helpless or fragmentary, when he felt dislocated in his universe.
  Mary Austin, *The American Rhythm* (1923)

6 You can't lie when you dance. It's so direct. You do what is in you. You can't dance out of the side of your mouth.
  Shirley MacLaine, in James Spada, *Shirley and Warren* (1985)

7 My Art is just an effort to express the truth of my Being in gesture and movement. It has taken me long years to find even one absolutely true movement.
  Isadora Duncan, *My Life* (1927)

8 I have *performed* for thousands when they found me exotic, the vogue, daring, but I have *danced*, at any given time, for about ten people. . . . They were the ones that left the theater forever different from the way they were when they came in. All of my long, long life, I have danced for those ten.
  Ruth St. Denis, in Elizabeth Anticaglia, *Twelve American Women* (1975)

9 Good choreography fuses eye, ear, and mind.
  Arlene Croce, *Afterimages* (1976)

10 The choreographic process is exhausting. It happens on one's feet after hours of work, and the energy required is roughly the equivalent of writing a novel and winning a tennis match simultaneously.
  Agnes de Mille, *Dance to the Piper* (1952)

11 Dancing is like bank robbery. It takes split-second timing.
  Twyla Tharp, in *Ms.* (1976)

12 Dancers are both athletes and artists.
  Margot Fonteyn, *A Dancer's World* (1979)

13 Being a dancer meant you nearly always thought about food.
  Shirley MacLaine, *Dance While You Can* (1991)

14 Every dancer lives on the threshold of chucking it.
  Judith Jamison, in *The New York Times Magazine* (1976)

15 The nature of my compulsion was such that I danced in my sleep. The entire household was sometimes awakened by loud thumping sounds coming from my room.
  Gelsey Kirkland, *Dancing on My Grave* (1986)

16 [Fred Astaire] does his longest and most absorbing solo of the series so far, full of stork-legged steps on toe, wheeling pirouettes in which he seems to be winding one leg around the other, and those ratcheting tap clusters that fall like loose change from his pockets.
  Arlene Croce, *The Fred Astaire & Ginger Rogers Book* (1972)

17 You leap like living music thru the air.
  Babette Deutsch, "The Dancers," *Banners* (1919)

1 I danced with a passion to spite the music.

Gelsey Kirkland, *Dancing on My Grave* (1986)

2 Even the ears must dance.

Natalia Makarova, in *Newsweek* (1975)

3 Think of the magic of that foot, comparatively small, upon which your whole weight rests. It's a miracle, and the dance . . . is a celebration of that miracle.

Martha Graham, speech (1965)

4 A good education is usually harmful to a dancer. A good calf is better than a good head.

Agnes de Mille, news item (1954)

5 There are short-cuts to happiness, and dancing is one of them.

Vicki Baum, *I Know What I'm Worth* (1964)

6 Part of the joy of dancing is conversation. Trouble is, some men can't talk and dance at the same time.

Ginger Rogers, *Ginger* (1991)

7 It may be possible to do without dancing entirely. Instances have been known of young people passing many, many months successively, without being at any ball of any description, and no material injury accrue either to body or mind;—but when a beginning is made—when the felicities of rapid motion have once been, though slightly, felt—it must be a very heavy set that does not ask for more.

Jane Austen, *Emma* (1816)

8 I loved dancing with a delirious "I wish I could die" passion . . . but alas! only one in ten partners had any notion of time, and what made it worse, the nine were always behind, never before the beat. . . . Sometimes I would firmly seize smaller, lighter partners by the scruff of the neck, so to speak, and whirl them along in the way they should go, but I saw they were not enjoying themselves.

Ethel Smyth, *Impressions That Remained* (1919)

9 Fine dancing, I believe, like virtue, must be its own reward. Those who are standing by are usually thinking of something very different.

Jane Austen, *Emma* (1816)

10 We waltzed Lisztlessly.

Karen Elizabeth Gordon, *The Transitive Vampire* (1984)

See also Artists, Ballet.

## ❦ DANGER

11 Avoiding danger is no safer in the long run than outright exposure. The fearful are caught as often as the bold.

Helen Keller, *Let Us Have Faith* (1940)

12 Considering how dangerous everything is nothing is really very frightening.

Gertrude Stein, *Everybody's Autobiography* (1937)

13 Without imagination, nothing is dangerous.

Georgette Leblanc (1898), in Janet Flanner, tr., *Souvenirs* (1932)

14 In danger there is great power.

Agnes Whistling Elk, in Lynn V. Andrews, *Crystal Woman* (1987)

15 The more hidden the venom, the more dangerous it is.

Marguerite de Valois, in *French Wit and Wisdom* (1950)

16 To assess the damage is a dangerous act.

Cherríe Moraga, "La Guëra," in Cherríe Moraga and Gloria Anzaldúa, eds., *This Bridge Called My Back* (1983)

See also Courage, Daring, Risk.

## ❦ DARING

17 I am a writer who came of a sheltered life. A sheltered life can be a daring life as well. For all serious daring starts from within.

Eudora Welty, "Finding a Voice," *One Writer's Beginnings* (1984)

See also Courage, Danger, Risk.

## ❦ DARKNESS

18 Darkness began to drink up the last cold light upon the mountainside.

Phyllis Bottome, *The Mortal Storm* (1938)

19 The darkness grew thinner and thinner like the walls of a bubble, before it breaks.

Phyllis Bottome, "The Gate," *Innocence and Experience* (1934)

1 I'm not frightened of the darkness outside. It's the darkness inside houses I don't like.
  Shelagh Delaney, *A Taste of Honey* (1958)

2 And I saw *darkness* for weeks. It never dawned on me that I could come out of it, but you heal. Nature heals you, and you do come out of it. All of a sudden I saw a crack of light . . . then all of a sudden I saw another crack of light. Then I saw *forms* in the light. And I recognized that there was no darkness, that in darkness there'll always be light.
  Louise Nevelson, *Dawns + Dusks* (1976)

3 The dark has to be contained in the light or the light will be contained in the dark.
  Nancy Hale, *Heaven and Hardpan Farm* (1957)

See also Evening, Night, Sunset, Twilight.

## ✷ DATA

4 Everything is data. But data isn't everything.
  Pauline Bart, in Cheris Kramarae and Paula A. Treichler, *A Feminist Dictionary* (1985)

See also Facts, Information, Statistics.

## ✷ DATING

5 I will not go out with a man who wears more jewelry than me, and I'll never, ever go to bed with a guy who calls me Babe. Other than that, however, I'm real flexible.
  Linda Sunshine, *Women Who Date Too Much (And Those Who Should Be So Lucky)* (1988)

6 I've figured out why first dates don't work any better than they do. It's because they take place in restaurants. Women are weird and confused and unhappy about food, and men are weird and confused and unhappy about money, yet off they go, the minute they meet, to where you use money to buy food.
  Adair Lara, *Welcome to Earth, Mom* (1992)

7 The man she had was kind and clean / And well enough for every day, / But, oh, dear friends, you should have seen / The one that got away!
  Dorothy Parker, "Tombstones in the Starlight: The Fisherwoman," *Death and Taxes* (1931)

8 If you're willing to travel, or just super-desperate, the best place in the world to meet unattached men is on the Alaska pipeline. I'm told that the trek through the frozen tundra is well worth the effort for any woman who wants to know what it feels like to be Victoria Principal.
  Linda Sunshine, *Women Who Date Too Much (And Those Who Should Be So Lucky)* (1988)

9 I've got a heart like a college prom. Each one I dance with seems the best of all.
  Ilka Chase, *In Bed We Cry* (1943)

10 A girl can have two beaus to her string, can't she?
  Richard Shattuck, *Said the Spider to the Fly* (1944)

11 Plenty of guys are good at sex, but conversation, now there's an art.
  Linda Barnes, *A Trouble of Fools* (1987)

12 It's surely one of the strange phenomena of this decade that the most thoughtful gift you can bring a date is not flowers, chocolates, or ankle-length pearls, but a note from your doctor.
  Linda Sunshine, *Women Who Date Too Much (And Those Who Should Be So Lucky)* (1988)

13 When someone asks, "Why do you think he's not calling me?" there's always one answer—"He's not interested." There's not ever any other answer.
  Fran Lebowitz, in *Mirabella* (1992)

14 If you never want to see a man again, say, "I love you, I want to marry you, I want to have children"—they leave skid marks.
  Rita Rudner, in *The New York Times* (1985)

15 I waited / For the phone to ring / And when at last / It didn't, / I knew it was you.
  Eleanor Bron, "No Answer," *The Pillow Book of Eleanor Bron* (1985)

16 My boyfriend and I broke up. He wanted to get married, and I didn't want him to.
  Rita Rudner, in Julia Klein, "The New Stand-Up Comics," *Ms.* (1984)

17 She'll throw herself at his head until he loses consciousness, and then she'll marry him.
  Ruth Sawyer, *The Primrose Ring* (1915)

18 Platonic friendship:—The interval between the introduction and the first kiss.
  Sophie Irene Loeb, *Epigrams of Eve* (1913)

1 Let this serve as an axiom to every lover: A woman who refuses lunch refuses everything.

Enid Bagnold, *A Diary Without Dates* (1918)

2 Nothing is more maddening than being questioned by the object of one's interest about the object of hers, should that object not be you.

Iris Murdoch, *Under the Net* (1954)

3 I have honorable intentions towards no man.

Maxine Elliott (1911), on a rumored engagement, in Diana Forbes Robertson, *My Aunt Maxine* (1964)

See also Courtship, Love, Relationships, Romance, Sex.

## ❧ DAUGHTERS

4 I *shall* be glad to see thee back, daughter, for I miss thee dreadfully. I wish I did not! I was taking a nap in my chair today, and I thought I heard thee rustling thy papers, and I looked over at thy table expecting to see thee, and alas! thee was not there, and it was dreadful.

Hannah Whitall Smith (1905), in Logan Pearsall Smith, ed., *Philadelphia Quaker* (1950)

5 Our mythology tells us so much about fathers and sons. . . . What do we know about mothers and daughters? . . . Our power is so oblique, so hidden, so ethereal a matter, that we rarely struggle with our daughters over actual kingdoms or corporate shares. On the other hand, our attractiveness dries as theirs blooms, our journey shortens just as theirs begins. We too must be afraid and awed and amazed that we cannot live forever and that our replacements are eager for their turn, indifferent to our wishes, ready to leave us behind.

Anne Roiphe, *Lovingkindness* (1987)

6 All daughters, even when most aggravated by their mothers, have a secret respect for them. They believe perhaps that they can do everything better than their mothers can, and many things they *can* do better, but they have not yet lived long enough to be sure how successfully they will meet the major emergencies of life, which lie, sometimes quite creditably, *behind* their mothers.

Phyllis Bottome, *Survival* (1943)

7 Being a daughter is only half the equation; bearing one is the other.

Erica Jong, *Parachutes & Kisses* (1984)

8 "Daughter" is not a lifelong assignment.

Shirley Abbott, *The Bookmaker's Daughter* (1991)

See also Family, Fathers, Mothers, Parents.

## ❧ DAYDREAMS

9 To make a prairie it takes a clover and one bee, / One clover, and a bee, / And revery. / The revery alone will do, / If bees are few.

Emily Dickinson, in Mabel Loomis Todd, ed., *Poems by Emily Dickinson*, 3rd series (1896)

10 A daydreamer is prepared for most things.

Joyce Carol Oates, "Accomplished Desires," *The Wheel of Love* (1969)

11 A dreamer—you know—it's a mind that looks over the edges of things.

Mary O'Hara, *My Friend Flicka* (1941)

12 Leisure for reverie, gay or somber, does much to enrich life.

Miriam Beard, *Realism in Romantic Japan* (1930)

See also Dreams, Fantasy, Visions.

## ❧ DAYS

13 A day so soft you could wrap a baby in it.

Marcelene Cox, in *Ladies' Home Journal* (1948)

14 Noon — is the Hinge of Day.

Emily Dickinson (1864), in Mabel Loomis Todd and Millicent Todd Bingham, eds., *Bolts of Melody* (1945)

15 The afternoon sways like an elephant. . . / . . . / This elephant afternoon / Winks at the glory of which it is part, / And bears itself with patience. Soon / It will be trumpeting.

Babette Deutsch, "July Day," *The Collected Poems of Babette Deutsch* (1969)

See also Monday, Sunday.

## ❦ DEAFNESS

1 Deafness has left me acutely aware of both the duplicity that language is capable of and the many expressions the body cannot hide.

Terry Galloway, "I'm Listening As Hard As I Can," in Marsha Saxton and Florence Howe, eds., *With Wings* (1987)

2 I tried the plan of talking incessantly myself, so as to hide the fact I didn't hear anything they said, the result was nobody paid the slightest attention to my (doubtless brilliant) remarks.

Susan Hale (1907), in Caroline P. Atkinson, ed., *Letters of Susan Hale* (1918)

3 The problems of deafness are deeper and more complex, if not more important, than the problems of blindness. Deafness is a much worse misfortune. For it means the loss of the most vital stimulus— the sound of the voice that brings language, sets thoughts astir and keeps us in the intellectual company of man.

Helen Keller (1910), in Brian Grant, ed., *The Quiet Ear* (1987)

4 The inability to hear is a nuisance; the inability to communicate is the tragedy.

Lou Ann Walker, *A Loss for Words* (1986)

5 I do prefer "stone deaf"; stones may be mute, but they are warm in the sun, they feel soothing in the palm. It is a piece of the earth, attached to God. I do not know what the pedants mean when they write "profoundly deaf" to describe the person who has never heard a sound. Deaf is deaf and silence is forever.

Ruth Sidransky, *In Silence* (1990)

6 I need to know what is being said. Always. Anywhere. Not just a word now and then.

Eleanore Devine, "Brotherhood," *You're Standing in My Light* (1990)

See also Disabilities.

## ❦ DEATH

7 The one inexorable thing!

Louise Imogen Guiney, "A Friend's Song for Simoisius," *A Roadside Harp* (1893)

8 All your lovely words are spoken. / Once the ivory box is broken, / Beats the golden bird no more.

Edna St. Vincent Millay, "Memorial to D.C.," *Second April* (1921)

9 Into the darkness they go, the wise and the lovely.

Edna St. Vincent Millay, "Dirge Without Music," *The Buck in the Snow* (1928)

10 Like a bird out of our hand, / Like a light out of our heart, / You are gone.

H.D., "Hymen," *Collected Poems* (1925)

11 Death is the last fact of which we can be certain.

Geraldine Jewsbury, *Zoë*, vol. 2 (1845)

12 Death is the last / Secret implicit within you, the hidden, the deepest / Knowledge of all you will ever unfold / In this body of earth.

Kathleen Raine, "Introspection," *The Year One* (1953)

13 Death was but the unfolding of a long bud-bound flower; the bursting forth of a rock-hampered fountain.

Mourning Dove, *Cogewea* (1927)

14 Knowledge by suffering entereth, / And life is perfected by death.

Elizabeth Barrett Browning, "A Vision of Poets," *Poems* (1844)

15 Death is the ultimate disappearing act.

Kate Green, *Night Angel* (1989)

16 Death's not a separation or alteration or parting it's just a one-handled door.

Stevie Smith, "Mrs. Simpkins," *A Good Time Was Had by All* (1937)

17 Death is the opening—and the closing—of a Door.

Ethel M. Dell, *The Keeper of the Door* (1915)

18 Death is a door life opens.

Adela Rogers St. Johns, *Love, Laughter and Tears* (1978)

19 Death is only an old door / Set in a garden wall.

Nancy Byrd Turner, "Death Is a Door," *Star in a Well* (1935)

20 There is no Death, / What seems so is transition.

Marie Corelli, *The Life Everlasting* (1911)

21 A human being does *not* cease to exist at death. It is change, not destruction, which takes place.

Florence Nightingale (1860), in Michael D. Calabria and Janet A. Macrae, eds., *Suggestions for Thought* (1994)

1 There is no death to those who perfectly love,—
only disappearance, which in time may be borne.

> Harriet Martineau (1840), in Elisabeth Sanders Arbuckle,
> *Harriet Martineau's Letters to Fanny Wedgwood* (1983)

2 Death is the gentlest of the world's replies.

> Rose Hawthorne Lathrop, "Give Me Not Tears," in
> Edmund Clarence Stedman, ed., *An American Anthology
> 1787-1900* (1900)

3 Mortality is the essential characteristic of humanity.

> Yeshe Tsogyel (8th cent.), in Keith Dowman, *Sky Dancer*
> (1984)

4 O Death, the loveliness that is in thee, / Could the
world know, the world would cease to be.

> Mary Emily Bradley, "In Death," in Edmund Clarence
> Stedman, ed., *An American Anthology 1787-1900* (1900)

5 I hope the exit is joyful—and I hope never to come
back.

> Frida Kahlo (1954), in Hayden Herrera, *Frida* (1983)

6 Death does not exaggerate.

> Elsa Triolet, *Proverbes d'Elsa* (1971)

7 Death, however long expected, is sudden at the last.

> Mrs. Mary J. Holmes, *Dora Deane* (1870)

8 Death makes us all equal.

> Marie de Rabutin-Chantal, Marquise de Sévigné (1690),
> *Letters of Madame de Sévigné to Her Daughter and Her
> Friends*, vol. 9 (1811)

9 Death is a slave's freedom.

> Nikki Giovanni, speech at Martin Luther King, Jr.'s funeral
> (1968)

10 Death! It is rest to the aged, it is oblivion to the
atheist, it is immortality to the poet!

> Ouida, *Wisdom, Wit and Pathos* (1884)

11 It is not *dying*, but *living*, that is a preparation for
Death.

> Margot Asquith, *More or Less About Myself* (1934)

12 Death sanctifies. It's solemn enough to make its
own shrine, where it happens.

> Charlotte Armstrong, *The Chocolate Cobweb* (1948)

13 Death is the perfect knowing.

> Marjorie Holmes, *I've Got to Talk to Somebody, God* (1969)

14 Who dares to be intellectual in the presence of
death?

> Freya Stark, *Perseus in the Wind* (1948)

15 Death cannot alter facts—only feelings.

> Frances Noyes Hart, *The Crooked Lane* (1933)

16 An absolute condition of all successful living,
whether for an individual or a nation, is the acceptance of death.

> Freya Stark, *The Journey's Echo* (1988)

17 I rebel against death, yet I know that it is how I
respond to death's inevitability that is going to
make me less or more fully alive.

> Madeleine L'Engle, *The Summer of the Great-Grandmother*
> (1974)

18 I knew the facts of death before I knew the facts of
life. There never was a time when I didn't see the
skull beneath the skin.

> P.D. James, *The Skull Beneath the Skin* (1982)

19 I am not ready to die, / But I am learning to trust
death / As I have trusted life.

> May Sarton, "Gestalt at Sixty," *Selected Poems of May Sarton*
> (1978)

20 By "coming to terms with life" I mean: the reality
of death has become a definite part of my life; my
life has, so to speak, been extended by death, by my
looking death in the eye and accepting it, by accepting destruction as part of life and no longer wasting
my energies on fear of death or the refusal to acknowledge its inevitability.

> Etty Hillesum (1942), *An Interrupted Life* (1983)

21 The child who enters life comes not with knowledge or intent, / So those who enter death must go
as little children sent. / . . . as life is to the living, so
death is to the dead.

> Mary Mapes Dodge, "The Two Mysteries," in Edmund
> Clarence Stedman, ed., *An American Anthology 1787-1900*
> (1900)

22 If I knew for certain that I should die next week, I
would still be able to sit at my desk all week and
study with perfect equanimity, for I know now that
life and death make a meaningful whole.

> Etty Hillesum (1942), *An Interrupted Life* (1983)

23 You never realize death until you realize love.

> Katharine Butler Hathaway (1928), *The Journals and Letters
> of the Little Locksmith* (1946)

24 Death pays all debts.

> Amelia E. Barr, *All the Days of My Life* (1913)

1 Death in its way comes just as much of a surprise as birth.

Edna O'Brien, "A Rose in the Heart," *Mrs. Reinhardt* (1978)

2 As subjects, we all live in suspense, from day to day, from hour to hour; in other words, we are the hero of our own story. We cannot believe that it is finished, that we are "finished," even though we may say so; we expect another chapter, another installment, tomorrow or next week.

Mary McCarthy, "Characters in Fiction," *On the Contrary* (1961)

3 Death,—a passage outside the range of imagination, but within the range of experience.

Isak Dinesen, *Out of Africa* (1937)

4 Death is terrifying because it is so ordinary. It happens all the time.

Susan Cheever, *Home Before Dark* (1984)

5 Everyone eventually dies. Why shouldn't I accomplish it as well as the next one? Why not, indeed? I relax. It is all an experience to be experienced; I shall do it as well as the next one.

Violet Weingarten, *Intimations of Mortality* (1978)

6 One thing about death— / it's hereditary.

Diane Ackerman, *Wife of Light* (1978)

7 Surprise will be my last emotion, not fear.

Storm Jameson, *Journey From the North*, vol. 2 (1970)

8 It's only another adventure, after all.

Dorothy Eden, *The Laughing Ghost* (1968)

9 Let us try, if we can, to enter into death with open eyes.

Marguerite Yourcenar, *Memoirs of Hadrian* (1951)

10 Down, down, down into the darkness of the grave / Gently they go, the beautiful, the tender, the kind; / Quietly they go, the intelligent, the witty, the brave. / I know. But I do not approve. And I am not resigned.

Edna St. Vincent Millay, "Dirge Without Music," *The Buck in the Snow* (1928)

11 Against you I will fling myself, unvanquished and unyielding, O Death!

Virginia Woolf, *The Waves* (1931)

12 Death is an ill; 'tis thus the Gods decide: / For had death been a boon, the Gods had died.

Sappho (6th cent. B.C.), in C.R. Haines, ed., *Sappho: The Poems and Fragments* (1926)

13 I shall die, but that is all that I shall do for Death; I am not on his pay-roll.

Edna St. Vincent Millay, "Conscientious Objector" (1917), *Wine From These Grapes* (1934)

14 Death is too much to ask of the living.

Dodie Smith, *The Town in Bloom* (1965)

15 Death's a cruel note, / Set in a mortal throat.

Léonie Adams, "Every Bird of Nature," *High Falcon* (1929)

16 Death . . . is so inevitable, so lasting, so unexpected, so imminent.

Ellen O'Grady, in Djuna Barnes, "Woman Police Deputy Is Writer of Poetry," *The New York Sun Magazine* (1918)

17 There is no solution to death. There is no means whatever whereby you or I, by taking thought, can solve this difficulty in such a manner that it no longer exists.

Dorothy L. Sayers, *The Mind of the Maker* (1941)

18 Death must be got through as life had been, just somehow.

Dorothy M. Richardson, "Death," in *Weekly Westminster* (1924)

19 Although he had painted a wondrous heaven to sufferers whose life on earth was a hell, rarely had he found anyone eager for release. Not even the old; sometimes they were the most frightened and clung like birds to the bars of their cage.

Frances Marion, *Westward the Dream* (1948)

20 It's never been my experience that men part with life any more readily at eighty than they do at eighteen.

Anthony Gilbert, *The Mouse Who Wouldn't Play Ball* (1943)

21 Yesterday, at Andillac, a little child went to heaven. If I were a little child I should like to follow it, but when one gets old, if one could help it, one would never die. Then it is that the threads that once attached us to earth become cables.

Eugénie de Guérin (1831), in Guillaume S. Trébutien, ed., *Letters of Eugénie de Guérin* (1865)

22 Nobody fought death so hard as a mother did, who left children behind her to root-pig-or-die-pore in a hard old world.

Caroline Miller, *Lamb in His Bosom* (1933)

23 There is no sound so terrible as a man's sorrow for his own death.

Sue Grafton, *"H" Is for Homicide* (1991)

1 Oh, dark, inevitable and awful day, / When one of us will go, and one must stay.

> Ella Wheeler Wilcox, "That Day," *The Collected Poems of Ella Wheeler Wilcox* (1917)

2 There will be a time you bury me / Or I bury you in the garden.

> Tomioka Taeko, "Living Together," in Joanna Bankier and Deirdre Lashgari, eds., *Women Poets of the World* (1983)

3 One of us two must sometime face existence / Alone with memories that but sharpen pain. / . . . / One of us two shall find all life, all beauty, / All joy on earth, a tale forever done; / Shall know henceforth that life means only duty. / O God! O God! have pity on that one!

> Ella Wheeler Wilcox, "One of Us Two," *Poems of Pleasure* (1888)

4 One pities most those who loved, and still died. Only those who love, dread death.

> Craig Rice, *Telefair* (1942)

5 Life, struck sharp on death, / Makes awful lightning.

> Elizabeth Barrett Browning, *Aurora Leigh* (1857)

6 It's so unfair that we should die, just because we are born.

> Anna Magnani, in Oriana Fallaci, *Limelighters* (1963)

7 I don't want to die. I think death is a greatly overrated experience.

> Rita Mae Brown, *Bingo* (1988)

8 Because I could not stop for Death — / He kindly stopped for me — / The Carriage held but just Ourselves — / And Immortality.

> Emily Dickinson (1863), in Mabel Loomis Todd and T.W. Higginson, eds., *Poems by Emily Dickinson* (1890)

9 I have faced Death. I have been caught in the wild weed tangles of her hair, seen the gleam of her jade eyes. I will go when it is time—no choice!—but now I *want* life.

> Keri Hulme, *The Bone People* (1983)

10 Just then, Death finished his prowling through the house on his padded feet and entered the room. He bowed to Mama in his way, and she made her manners and left us to act out our ceremonies over unimportant things.

> Zora Neale Hurston, *Dust Tracks on a Road* (1942)

11 Eternal death has worked like a warrior rat, with diabolical sense of duty, to gnaw my bottom. Everything is finished now.

> Ama Ata Aidoo, "The Message," *No Sweetness Here* (1970)

12 Death clutches me by the ear.

> Josephine Herbst, *Pity Is Not Enough* (1933)

13 It is the denial of death that is partially responsible for people living empty, purposeless lives; for when you live as if you'll live forever, it becomes too easy to postpone the things you know that you must do.

> Elisabeth Kübler-Ross, *Death: The Final Stage of Growth* (1975)

14 Death is dancing me ragged.

> Linda Hogan, "The Women Are Grieving," *Eclipse* (1983)

15 I thought death would be a final leap out of the old tire swing into shimmering Bald Eagle Lake after a final push from long-dead Aunt Ethel, godmother and childhood pal.

> Judith Stoughton, *One Woman's Pascal Journey* (1991)

16 Death was not to be a leap: it was to be a long descent under thickening shadows.

> George Eliot, *The Mill on the Floss* (1860)

17 I have only one curiosity left: death.

> Coco Chanel, in Marcel Haedrich, *Coco Chanel* (1972)

18 I am old and years are peeling / petal-wise, undone. / I am old, and feeling / presses dry and feversprung. / Bless me now, Earth, warm me deep. / I am old, would sleep.

> Sheila Pritchard, "Old Woman in the Sun," *In Rainwater Evening* (1958)

19 If I must go, let it be easy, slow / The curve complete, and a sure swerve / To the goal.

> Dorothy Livesay, "Improvisation on an Old Theme," *Poems for People* (1947)

20 "Come close! Look at mother! Is she better—or is she dead?" . . . "She is better!" he said gently, "and she is dead."

> Kate Douglas Wiggin, *New Chronicles of Rebecca* (1907)

21 Oh, write of me, not "Died in bitter pains," / But "Emigrated to another star!"

> Helen Hunt Jackson, "Emigravit" (1876), in Edmund Clarence Stedman, ed., *An American Anthology 1787-1900* (1900)

22 What we call death was to him only emigration.

> Amelia E. Barr, *All the Days of My Life* (1913)

1 I know for sure / that at the end, / the playful stranger who appears / is not death / but love.

Kathleen Norris, "Three Small Songs for the Muse," in Marilyn Sewell, ed., *Cries of the Spirit* (1991)

2 Watching a peaceful death of a human being reminds us of a falling star; one of the million lights in a vast sky that flares up for a brief moment only to disappear into the endless night forever.

Elisabeth Kübler-Ross, *On Death and Dying* (1969)

3 I would like to believe when I die that I have given myself away like a tree that sows seed every spring and never counts the loss, because it is not loss, it is adding to future life. It is the tree's way of being. Strongly rooted perhaps, but spilling out its treasure on the wind.

May Sarton, *Recovering* (1980)

4 I have scattered seed / Shall ripen at the end; / Old Age holds more than I shall need, / Death more than I can spend.

Lizette Woodworth Reese, "Growth," *A Quiet Road* (1896)

5 Death still celebrates / the life in you.

Nelly Sachs, "Death still celebrates," *O the Chimneys* (1967)

6 Her mother was no longer there. Susanna did not think of it as a death, but as a fading away, like a pattern on washed cloth. It was the continuation of something that had been happening all her life anyway.

Margaret Atwood, "Uncles," *Wilderness Tips* (1991)

7 Death transfigured her. In a matter of minutes I saw the beauty of her young days reassert itself on her blurred careworn face. It was like something in music, the re-establishment of the original key, the return of the theme.

Sylvia Townsend Warner (1969), in William Maxwell, ed., *Letters: Sylvia Townsend Warner* (1982)

8 When I am dead and over me bright April / Shakes out her rain-drenched hair, / Tho' you should lean above me broken-hearted, / I shall not care.

Sara Teasdale, "I Shall Not Care," *Rivers to the Sea* (1915)

9 Death is sometimes not the worst situation you can be in.

Nancy Cruzan, as reported by her sister in the Supreme Court brief to allow Cruzan to die after being in a coma for years, in Alida Brill, *Nobody's Business* (1990)

10 Death? Why this fuss about death. Use your imagination, try to visualize a world *without* death!

Charlotte Perkins Gilman, *The Living of Charlotte Perkins Gilman* (1935)

11 Most people are dead, and none of them seem to mind it. One hears a great many complaints about life, doesn't one? And there are people I know who would certainly grumble—however dead they were—if there were anything to grumble at.

Phyllis Bottome, *Windlestraws* (1929)

12 If there wasn't death I think you couldn't go on.

Stevie Smith, in *The Observer* (1969)

13 Life would be as insupportable without the prospect of death, as it would be without sleep.

Countess of Blessington, *Desultory Thoughts and Reflections* (1839)

14 Her course was run . . . she would not have wished to outlive herself.

Edith Wharton, *The Gods Arrive* (1932)

15 Is death the great healing? Is our life on earth partially a wound that death finally heals?

Macrina Wiederkehr, *A Tree Full of Angels* (1988)

16 One of the uncovenanted benefits of living for a long time is that, having so many more dead than living friends, death can appear as a step backwards into the joyous past.

Storm Jameson, *Journey From the North*, vol. 2 (1970)

17 It is better to die young than to outlive *all* one loved, and *all* that rendered one lovable.

Lady Marguerite Blessington, *The Confessions of an Elderly Gentleman* (1836)

18 I hoped for, and expected early death till it was too late to die early.

Harriet Martineau (1839), *Autobiography*, vol. 2 (1877)

19 It is necessary that we should all have a little of the will to die, because otherwise we would find the performance of our biological duty of death too difficult.

Rebecca West, in Victoria Glendinning, *Rebecca West* (1987)

20 Say not Good night, but in some brighter clime / Bid me Good morning.

Anna Laetitia Barbauld, "Life" (1773), *The Works of Anna Laetitia Barbauld*, vol. 1 (1825)

21 The world, with all its beauty and adventure, its richness and variety, is darkened by cruelty. Death,

if it ends the loveliness, the adventure, ends also that. Death balances the picture.

Winifred Holtby, *Virginia Woolf* (1978)

1 When I am dead, my dearest, / Sing no sad songs for me; / Plant thou no roses at my head, / Nor shady cypress tree: / Be the green grass above me / With showers and dewdrops wet; / And if thou wilt, remember, / And if thou wilt, forget.

Christina Rossetti, "Song" (1848), *Goblin Market* (1862)

2 Death . . . is not a great affair! Think—it happens once only—to each of us—as birth does. What do you know about being born? that—and no more—will you know about the act of death.

Phyllis Bottome, *The Mortal Storm* (1938)

3 Death persecutes before it executes.

Cynthia Ozick, *Trust* (1966)

4 It is a pity we do not die when our lives are finished.

Mary Borden, *Jane—Our Stranger* (1923)

5 We never know how dead we are until we come to die.

Lavinia Dickinson, in Carolyn Wells, *The Rest of My Life* (1937)

6 How can they tell?

Dorothy Parker, on being told that President Coolidge was dead (1933), in J. Bryan III, *Merry Gentlemen (and One Lady)* (1985)

7 Possibly everyone now dead considered his own death as a freak accident, a mistake. Some bad luck caused it. Every enterprising man jack of them, and every sunlit vigorous woman and child, too, who had seemed so alive and pleased, was cold as a meat hook, and new chattering people trampled their bones unregarding, and rubbed their hands together and got to work improving their prospects till their own feet slipped and they went under themselves. . . . Every place was a tilting edge.

Annie Dillard, *The Living* (1992)

8 You do not die from being born, nor from having lived, nor from old age. You die from *something*. . . . There is no such thing as a natural death: nothing that happens to a man is ever natural, since his presence calls the world into question. All men must die: but for every man his death is an accident and, even if he knows it and consents to it, an unjustifiable violation.

Simone de Beauvoir, *A Very Easy Death* (1966)

9 My grandmother refused to concede that any member of the family died of natural causes. An uncle's cancer in middle age occurred because all the suitcases fell off the luggage rack onto him when he was in his teens, and so forth. Death was an acquired characteristic.

Renata Adler, *Speedboat* (1976)

10 There is much precedent in the family for pretending that the dead have not died but are living in other cities. Practicing a form of emotional etiquette, it is considered good form to spare elderly relatives sad news. . . . When a cousin actually did move to California, no one believed it—the other cousins all believed this was a euphemism for the much-longer journey.

Laura Cunningham, *Sleeping Arrangements* (1989)

11 He is not dead! he only left / A precious robe of clay behind, / To draw a robe of love and light / Around his disembodied mind.

Frances Ellen Watkins Harper, "Obituary for J. Edwards Barnes," in *National Anti-Slavery Standard* (1858)

12 The body was so little a part of him that its final stillness seemed nothing of importance. He was half out of it anyway and death was only a slipping out of it altogether and being at last what he always was, a spirit. We buried the pearly shell upon the mountain top.

Pearl S. Buck, *Fighting Angel* (1936)

13 You walked over death / like a bird in snow.

Nelly Sachs, "Glowing Enigma III," *O the Chimneys* (1967)

14 coming to the end of spring / my grandmother kicks off her shoes / steps out of her faltering body.

Betsy Sholl, "Spring Fragments," *Rooms Overhead* (1986)

15 Do you suppose that / when grandma dies / more of her stays than goes?

Paula Gunn Allen, "Grandma's Dying Poem," *Skins and Bones* (1988)

16 All that is buried is not dead.

Ralph Iron, *The Story of an African Farm* (1883)

17 Death did not come to my mother / Like an old friend. / She was a mother, and she must / Conceive him.

Josephine Miles, "Conception," *To All Appearances* (1974)

18 How strange—a daughter watching the mother who had given her life lose her own. Is that what it's all about?

Lauren Bacall, *Lauren Bacall by Myself* (1979)

1 Every time a man dies, a child dies too, and an adolescent and a young man as well; everyone weeps for the one who was dear to him.

Simone de Beauvoir, *Force of Circumstance* (1963)

2 I am unable, mentally incapable, of relating the dead thing, the broken body refusing to divulge why or where the occupant has gone, to the thing that was alive.

Caitlin Thomas, *Leftover Life to Kill* (1957)

3 I never get used to it, the unknowable mystery of a person so suddenly, totally closed, snapped shut like a half-read novel.

Linda Barnes, *Steel Guitar* (1991)

4 Looking at Death, is Dying.

Emily Dickinson (1861), in Martha Dickinson Bianchi and Alfred Leete Hampson, eds., *Unpublished Poems of Emily Dickinson* (1935)

5 If death becomes cheap it is the watcher, not the dying, who is poisoned.

Enid Bagnold, *A Diary Without Dates* (1918)

6 Life flows on over death as water closes over a stone dropped into a pool.

Winifred Holtby, in Vera Brittain, *Testament of Friendship* (1940)

7 For rain it hath a friendly sound / To one who's six feet under ground; / And scarce the friendly voice or face, / A grave is such a quiet place.

Edna St. Vincent Millay, title poem, *Renascence* (1917)

8 Heap not on this mound / Roses that she loved so well; / Why bewilder her with roses, / That she cannot see or smell?

Edna St. Vincent Millay, "Epitaph," *Second April* (1921)

9 'Tis sweet to know that stocks will stand / When we with Daisies lie — / That Commerce will continue — / And Trades as briskly fly.

Emily Dickinson (1858), in T.W. Higginson and Mabel Loomis Todd, eds., *Poems by Emily Dickinson*, 2nd series (1891)

10 When I die, people will say it is the best thing for me. It is because they know it is the worst. They want to avoid the feeling of pity. As though they were the people most concerned!

Ivy Compton-Burnett, *The Mighty and Their Fall* (1962)

11 There is something disorderly about the death of a young person. In a universe disturbed by so much over which we have no control, an untimely trag-edy rattles the teeth of our already shaken confidence. We want to domesticate death, fight it on our own turf, in familiar rooms with shades drawn evenly, top sheets turned back, and a circle of hushed voices closing in.

Faye Moskowitz, *A Leak in the Heart* (1985)

12 God have mercy, that such a young man should have to chew the black earth!

Glückel of Hameln, *Memoirs of Glückel of Hameln* (1724)

13 When a child dies, it breaks the pattern, the most fundamental pattern in life.

Jane Stanton Hitchcock, *Trick of the Eye* (1992)

14 With our parents we bury our past, with our children our future.

Marie von Ebner-Eschenbach, *Aphorisms* (1893)

15 Why shouldn't we be as angry about not having always been alive as about having to stop being alive?

Madame de Staël, *Reflections on Suicide* (1813)

16 Why is it harder to think of his going to nothing than to think of his coming from nothing? One direction is just as dark as the other.

Anne Morrow Lindbergh, *Hour of Gold, Hour of Lead* (1973)

17 I am not afraid of death, but would not want to die in some obscure or pointless way.

Isabelle Eberhardt (1901), *The Passionate Nomad* (1987)

18 The timing of death, like the ending of a story, gives a changed meaning to what preceded it.

Mary Catherine Bateson, *With a Daughter's Eye* (1984)

19 The company you keep at death is, of all things, most dependent on chance.

Keri Hulme, *The Bone People* (1983)

20 O Earth! art thou not weary of thy graves? / Dear, patient mother Earth, upon thy breast / How are they heaped from farthest east to west!

Julia C.R. Dorr, "O Earth! Art Thou Not Weary?" *Poems* (1892)

21 Curious, how each one of us secretly carries his private cemetery around with him and watches it filling up with ever new graves. The last one to be our own.

Vicki Baum, *I Know What I'm Worth* (1964)

1 Death sits with his key in my lock. / Not one day is taken for granted.

> Anne Sexton (1971), in Linda Gray Sexton, ed., *Words for Dr. Y.* (1978)

2 The dead make rules, and I obey. / I, too, shall be dead some day.

> Mary Carolyn Davies, "The Dead Make Rules," *Youth Riding* (1919)

3 The dead don't bear a grudge nor seek a blessing. The dead don't rest uneasy. Only the living.

> Margaret Laurence, *The Stone Angel* (1964)

4 There is nothing sadder than the cheerful letters of the dead, expressing hopes that were never fulfilled, ambitions that were never achieved, dreams cut off before they could come to fruition.

> Elizabeth Peters, *Naked Once More* (1989)

5 University students are rarely able to cope with universals and death is the most embarrassing universal.

> Kate Cruise O'Brien, "Henry Died," *A Gift Horse* (1978)

6 Joggers die. Health-food addicts die, and so do people who have spent their entire lives in lounge chairs eating corn curls. Don't muddy it all up feeling guilty. If you've been told you're going to die soon, the only word that should bother you is "soon."

> Kathleen MacInnes, in *American Journal of Nursing* (1992)

7 It costs me never a stab nor squirm / To tread by chance upon a worm. / "Aha, my little dear," I say, / "Your clan will pay me back one day."

> Dorothy Parker, "Thought for a Sunshiny Morning," *Sunset Gun* (1928)

8 It'll be with me like it was with Uncle Ned's ole ox, I reckon; he kep' a-goin' an' a-goin' till he died a-standin' up, an' even then they had to push him over.

> Alice Caldwell Rice, *Mrs. Wiggs of the Cabbage Patch* (1901)

9 But it's so unlike her!

> Anonymous Elizabeth Arden employee upon hearing that the energetic and vociferous Miss Arden had died (1966), in Alfred Allan Lewis and Constance Woodworth, *Miss Elizabeth Arden* (1972)

See also Bereavement, Capital Punishment, Dying, Euthanasia, Funerals, Grief, Life and Death, Lifelessness, Mourning, Murder, Suicide, Widowhood.

## ❦ DEBTS

10 Let us run up debts. One is nobody without debts.

> Muriel Spark, "The Fathers' Daughters," *Voices at Play* (1961)

11 I've often known people more shocked because you are not bankrupt than because you are.

> Margaret Baillie-Saunders, *A Shepherd of Kensington* (1907)

12 Debt is the sort of Bedfellow who is forever pulling all the Covers his way.

> Minna Thomas Antrim, *Don'ts for Bachelors and Old Maids* (1908)

13 A man was lost if he went to a usurer, for the interest ran faster than a tiger upon him.

> Pearl S. Buck, "The Frill," *The First Wife* (1933)

14 The payment of debts is necessary for social order. The non-payment is quite equally necessary for social order. For centuries humanity has oscillated, serenely unaware, between these two contradictory necessities.

> Simone Weil (1937), *Selected Essays 1934-1943* (1962)

See also Economics, Finances, Money.

## ❦ DECEPTION

15 Deception and "con games" are a way of life in all species and throughout nature. Organisms that do not improve their ability to deceive—and to detect deception—are less apt to survive.

> Harriet Lerner, *The Dance of Deception* (1993)

16 The practice of deception was so constant with her that it got to be a kind of truth.

> Louise Erdrich, *Tracks* (1988)

17 The old fellow seemed to spot deceit as if it reeked like a goat.

> Margery Allingham, *The Tiger in the Smoke* (1952)

See also Dishonesty.

## ❦ DECISION

18 God send us power to make decision / With muscular, clean, fierce precision. / In life and song.

> Anna Wickham, "Choice," *The Contemplative Quarry* (1915)

1 A peacefulness follows any decision, even the wrong one.

Rita Mae Brown, *Sudden Death* (1983)

2 What is living about? It is the decisions you must make between two rights, hard and costly decisions because always you can do one right thing, but sometimes not two.

Willa Gibbs, *Seed of Mischief* (1953)

3 Only those who must bear the consequences of a decision have the right to make it.

Starhawk, *Dreaming the Dark* (1982)

4 No trumpets sound when the important decisions of our life are made. Destiny is made known silently.

Agnes de Mille, *Dance to the Piper* (1952)

5 Once again she decided not to decide. She preferred being compelled into her decisions.

Lisa Alther, *Kinflicks* (1975)

6 All decisions are made on insufficient evidence.

Rita Mae Brown, *In Her Day* (1976)

7 Like other potentates with a long habit of arbitrary authority, she covered her perplexity with a smart show of decision.

Dorothy Canfield Fisher, *The Bent Twig* (1915)

8 If I eat lobster, and if I don't eat lobster, I shall regret it.

Ellen Glasgow, *The Descendant* (1897)

See also Choice, Conclusion.

## ❦ DEEDS

9 Our deeds still travel with us from afar, / And what we have been makes us what we are.

George Eliot, *Middlemarch* (1871)

10 Our deeds determine us, as much as we determine our deeds.

George Eliot, *Adam Bede* (1859)

11 Our deeds have even less substance than we ourselves.

Craig Rice, *Telefair* (1942)

12 No good deed will go unpunished.

Clare Boothe Luce, attributed (also sometimes attributed to Walter Annenberg), in Harold Faber, *The Book of Laws* (1979)

See also Actions, Behavior.

## ❦ DEFEAT

13 We may encounter many defeats but we must not be defeated.

Maya Angelou, in Devinia Sookia, "Singing, Swinging, and Still Living Life to the Full," *Caribbean Times* (1987)

14 No man is defeated without until he has first been defeated within.

Eleanor Roosevelt, *You Learn by Living* (1960)

15 A faint endeavor ends in a sure defeat.

Hannah More, "On Habits," *Christian Morals* (1812)

16 Victory fades so quickly that it is scarcely apparent and it is always the face of defeat that we are able to see.

Jane Bowles, *Two Serious Ladies* (1943)

17 In some circumstances, the refusal to be defeated is a refusal to be educated.

Margaret Halsey, *No Laughing Matter* (1977)

See also Failure, Victory.

## ❦ DEFINITIONS

18 If we are to reclaim our culture, we cannot afford narrow definitions.

Starhawk, *The Spiral Dance* (1979)

19 It's the frames which make some things important and some things forgotten. It's all only frames from which the content rises.

Eve Babitz, *Eve's Hollywood* (1974)

20 We expect definitions to tell us not only what is, but what to do about it. . . . A label is the first step toward action.

Elizabeth Janeway, *Improper Behavior* (1987)

See also Labels, Names, Naming.

## ❧ DELEGATING

1 I don't keep a dog and bark myself.

> Elizabeth I (c. 1590), in Frederick Chamberlin, *The Sayings of Queen Elizabeth* (1923)

## ❧ DELUSION

2 Our ability to delude ourselves may be an important survival tool.

> Jane Wagner, *The Search for Signs of Intelligent Life in the Universe* (1985)

See also Illusions.

## ❧ DEMOCRACY

3 Democracy forever teases us with the contrast between its ideals and its realities, between its heroic possibilities and its sorry achievements.

> Agnes Repplier, "Americanism," *Counter-Currents* (1916)

4 Democracy is not an easy form of government, because it is never final; it is a living, changing organism, with a continuous shifting and adjusting of balance between individual freedom and general order.

> Ilka Chase, *Past Imperfect* (1942)

5 Democracy must be conceived as a process, not a goal.

> M.P. Follett, *The New State* (1918)

6 When we define democracy now it must still be as a thing hoped for but not seen.

> Pearl S. Buck, speech (1941)

7 Democracy . . . is never won but always to be won.

> Hallie Flanagan, *Arena* (1940)

8 In an autocracy, one person has his way; in an aristocracy, a few people have their way; in a democracy, no one has his way.

> Celia Green, *The Decline and Fall of Science* (1976)

9 Despotism subjects a nation to one tyrant; democracy, to many.

> Countess of Blessington, *Desultory Thoughts and Reflections* (1839)

10 What keeps the democracy alive at all but the hatred of excellence; the desire of the base to see no head higher than their own?

> Mary Renault, *The Last of the Wine* (1956)

11 Democracy is the fig leaf of elitism.

> Florence King, *Reflections in a Jaundiced Eye* (1989)

12 With the people, for the people, by the people, I crack up when I hear it; I say, with the handful, for the handful, by the handful, 'cause that's really what happens.

> Fannie Lou Hamer (1965), in Kay Mills, *This Little Light of Mine* (1993)

13 A democratic state is not proven by the welfare of the strong but by the welfare of the weak.

> June Jordan, "For the Sake of a People's Poetry," *Passion* (1980)

14 Democracy always makes for materialism, because the only kind of equality that you can guarantee to a whole people is, broadly speaking, physical.

> Katharine Fullerton Gerould, *Modes and Morals* (1920)

15 Democracy, like the human organism, carries within it the seed of its own destruction.

> C.V. Wedgwood, *Velvet Studies* (1946)

16 A fatal defect in majority rule is that by its very nature it abolishes itself. Majority rule must inevitably become minority rule: the majority is too big to handle itself; it organizes itself into committees . . . which in their turn resolve themselves into a committee of one.

> M.P. Follett, *The New State* (1918)

17 Although most governments in the world are, as they always have been, autocracies of one kind or another, no idea holds greater sway in the mind of educated Americans than the belief that it is possible to democratize governments, anytime, anywhere, under any circumstances.

> Jeane J. Kirkpatrick, "Dictatorship and Double Standards," in *Commentary* (1979)

18 Every democratic system evolves its own conventions. It is not only the water but the banks which make the river.

> Indira Gandhi (1967), *Speeches and Writings* (1975)

19 Democracy, like any noncoercive relationship, rests on a shared understanding of limits.

> Elizabeth Drew, in *Washington Journal* (1975)

1 A democratic form of government, a democratic way of life, presupposes free public education over a long period; it presupposes also an education for personal responsibility that too often is neglected.

> Eleanor Roosevelt, "Let Us Have Faith in Democracy," in Department of Agriculture, *Land Policy Review* (1942)

2 Democracy is not a spectator sport.

> Marian Wright Edelman, *Families in Peril* (1987)

3 Trusting each other is the beginning of a certain secular faith, a faith that allows us to live in families and communities and nations. Democracy, above all other forms of government, requires this faith.

> Sue Halpern, *Migrations to Solitude* (1993)

4 A democracy without faith is just a machine without power. Nothing can make it function except faith in itself, in the ordinary man and woman.

> Eleanor Dark, *The Little Company* (1945)

5 We have forgotten that democracy must live as it thinks and think as it lives.

> Agnes E. Meyer, *Journey Through Chaos* (1944)

6 The capacity to combine commitment with skepticism is essential to democracy.

> Mary Catherine Bateson, *Composing a Life* (1989)

7 Democracy is an interesting, even laudable, notion and there is no question but that when compared to Communism, which is too dull, or Fascism, which is too exciting, it emerges as the most palatable form of government.

> Fran Lebowitz, *Social Studies* (1977)

8 In a true democracy everyone can be upper class and live in Connecticut.

> Lisa Birnbach, *The Official Preppy Handbook* (1980)

See also Equality, Government, United States.

## 🖠 DENMARK

9 That little country of cottage cheese and courage.

> Bette Midler, *A View From a Broad* (1980)

## 🖠 DENTISTS

10 He got into my mouth along with a pickaxe and telescope, battering-ram and other instruments, and drove a lawn-cutting machine up and down my jaws for a couple of hours. When he came out he said he meant wonderful improvements, and it seems I'm to have a bridge and a mill-wheel and summit and crown of gold, and harps, and Lord knows what.

> Susan Hale (1907), in Caroline P. Atkinson, ed., *Letters of Susan Hale* (1918)

See also Teeth.

## 🖠 DEPENDENCE

11 There are no words more obscene than "I can't live without you."

> Sally Miller Gearhart, *The Wanderground* (1979)

12 Oh, the bitter, bitter bread of dependence!

> Fanny Fern, *Fern Leaves*, 2nd series (1853)

13 In all the world there are no people so piteous and forlorn as those who are forced to eat the bitter bread of dependence in their old age, and find how steep are the stairs of another man's house.

> Dorothy Dix, *Dorothy Dix—Her Book* (1926)

14 No crust so tough as the grudged bread of dependence.

> Fanny Fern, *Folly As It Flies* (1868)

15 I did not want / to be the dead star / that absorbs borrowed light to revive itself.

> Rosario Castellanos, "Foreign Woman," in Joanna Bankier and Deirdre Lashgari, eds., *Women Poets of the World* (1983)

16 There is *no* power greater than the power of passive dependency.

> Marilyn French, *The Bleeding Heart* (1980)

See also Codependence, Independence.

## 🖠 DEPRESSION

17 I was much too far out all my life / And not waving but drowning.

> Stevie Smith, title poem, *Not Waving But Drowning* (1957)

1 Tired of the daily round, / And tired of all my being; / My ears are tired with sound, / And mine eyes with seeing.

> Mary Coleridge, untitled (1887), in Theresa Whistler, ed., *The Collected Poems of Mary Coleridge* (1954)

2 I cannot remember the time when I have not longed for death. . . . for years and years I used to watch for death as no sick man ever watched for the morning.

> Florence Nightingale (1881), in Cecil Woodham-Smith, *Florence Nightingale* (1950)

3 Depression sits on my chest like a sumo wrestler.

> Sandra Scoppettone, *I'll Be Leaving You Always* (1993)

4 There is this difference between depression and sorrow—sorrowful, you are in great trouble because something matters so much; depressed, you are miserable because nothing really matters.

> J.E. Buckrose, "Depression," *What I Have Gathered* (1923)

5 Sadness is more or less like a head cold—with patience, it passes. Depression is like cancer.

> Barbara Kingsolver, *The Bean Trees* (1989)

6 Depression was a very active state really. Even if you appeared to an observer to be immobilized, your mind was in a frenzy of paralysis. You were unable to function, but were actively despising yourself for it.

> Lisa Alther, *Kinflicks* (1975)

7 Depression—that is what we all hate. We the afflicted. Whereas the relatives and shrinks, the tribal ring, they rather welcome it: you are quiet and you suffer.

> Kate Millett, *The Loony-Bin Trip* (1990)

8 Depression is a very sensible reaction to just about everything we live in now.

> Chrystos, "Perhaps," in Christian McEwen and Sue O'Sullivan, eds., *Out the Other Side* (1988)

9 Sometimes one has simply to endure a period of depression for what it may hold of illumination if one can live through it, attentive to what it exposes or demands.

> May Sarton, *Journal of a Solitude* (1973)

10 Cecily was not likely to be cheerful, and Cecily depressed had the art of clawing all the emotional stuffing out of people.

> E.X. Ferrars, *Cheat the Hangman* (1946)

11 If life is a bowl of cherries, what am I doing in the pits?

> Erma Bombeck, book title (1971)

See also Despair, Melancholy, Mental Illness.

## &#10087; DESERT

12 The Desert proclaiming itself, speaks gently.

> Idah Meacham Strobridge, *In Miners' Mirage-Land* (1904)

13 The Sahara was a spectacle as alive as the sea. The tints of the dunes changed according to the time of day and the angle of the light: golden as apricots from far off, when we drove close to them they turned to freshly made butter; behind us they grew pink; from sand to rock, the materials of which the desert was made varied as much as its tints.

> Simone de Beauvoir, *Force of Circumstance* (1963)

14 The desert floras shame us with their cheerful adaptations to the seasonal limitations. Their whole duty is to flower and fruit, and they do it hardly, or with tropical luxuriance, as the rain admits. . . . One hopes the land may breed like qualities in her human offspring, not tritely to "try," but to do.

> Mary Austin, *The Land of Little Rain* (1904)

15 I saw the desert, it grew upon me. There are times, when I have sorrows, that I hunger and thirst for it.

> Isabel Burton, *The Inner Life of Syria, Palestine, and the Holy Land* (1884)

16 For all the toll the desert takes of a man it gives compensations, deep breaths, deep sleep, and the communion of the stars.

> Mary Austin, *The Land of Little Rain* (1904)

17 In the desert the detachment of life from all normal intercourse imparts a sense of gravity to every rencontre, and each touch with human beings is fraught with a significance lacking in the too hurried intercourse of ordinary everyday life. On the desert track, there is no such thing as a casual meeting.

> Mildred Cable, with Francesca French, *The Gobi Desert* (1942)

18 This is one of the charms of the desert, that removing as it does nearly all the accessories of life, we see

the thin thread of necessities on which our human existence is suspended.

   Freya Stark, *Baghdad Sketches* (1929)

1  The desert is a nun, for no man's wooing, / Vowed to eternal silence through the years, / Serene, unchangeable, past all pursuing, / And all neglect. The desert knows no tears.

   Mary Carolyn Davies, "The Desert," *The Skyline Trail* (1924)

2  To wake in that desert dawn was like waking in the heart of an opal. . . . See the desert on a fine morning and die—if you can!

   Gertrude Bell, in Janet E. Courtney, *An Oxford Portrait Gallery* (1931)

3  Night comes to the desert all at once, as if someone turned off a light.

   Joyce Carol Oates, "Interior Monologue," *The Wheel of Love* (1969)

4  Summer on the desert dies like a snake. You think it's done for, dead as a doornail, then there comes another fierce burst of life.

   Jessamyn West, *A Matter of Time* (1966)

5  A wind came up and ran along the rock base lifting the sand like the edge of a carpet.

   Olivia Manning, *The Danger Tree* (1977)

6  The palpable sense of mystery in the desert air breeds fables, chiefly of lost treasure. . . . It is a question whether it is not better to be bitten by the little horned snake of the desert that goes sidewise and strikes without coiling, than by the tradition of a lost mine.

   Mary Austin, *The Land of Little Rain* (1904)

7  Things grew and lived in constant adversity, ingenious in solving problems of existence.

   Mary Astor, *A Place Called Saturday* (1968)

8  The desert breeds reserve. It is so big that one's own plans and projects seem too little to be talked about. Also, there is so much time to say anything that one continually puts it off and ends by never saying it at all.

   Rosita Forbes, *The Secret of the Sahara* (1921)

9  Without water the desert is nothing but a grave.

   Mildred Cable, with Francesca French, *The Gobi Desert* (1942)

10  Much has been written about the beauty, the stillness, the terror of the desert but little about its flies.

   Belle Livingstone, *Belle Out of Order* (1959)

See also Camels, Nature.

## ❧ DESERTION

11  But mayn't desertion be a brave thing? A fine thing? To desert a thing we've gone beyond—to have the courage to desert it and walk right off from the dead thing to the live thing—?

   Susan Glaspell, *The Visioning* (1911)

See also Parting, Quitting, Renunciation, Running Away.

## ❧ DESIRE

12  How helpless we are, like netted birds, when we are caught by desire!

   Belva Plain, *Evergreen* (1978)

13  There is only one big thing—desire. And before it, when it is big, all is little.

   Willa Cather, *The Song of the Lark* (1915)

14  In my experience, there is only one motivation, and that is desire. No reasons or principles contain it or stand against it.

   Jane Smiley, *Ordinary Love* (1989)

15  One must desire something, to be alive: perhaps absolute satisfaction is only another name for Death.

   Margaret Deland, *Florida Days* (1889)

16  To want is more than to attain.

   Georgiana Goddard King, *The Way of Perfect Love* (1909)

17  Desire creates its own object.

   Barbara Grizzuti Harrison, *Foreign Bodies* (1984)

18  Desire is a renewable commodity.

   Christine Brückner, in Eleanor Bron, tr., *Desdemona—If You Had Only Spoken* (1992)

19  Our visions begin with our desires.

   Audre Lorde, in Claudia Tate, ed., *Black Women Writers at Work* (1983)

1 The things that one most wants to do are the things that are probably most worth doing.

  Winifred Holtby (1927), in Alice Holtby and Jean McWilliam, eds., *Letters to a Friend* (1937)

2 Desire is prayer.

  Terry McMillan, *Mama* (1987)

3 Nothing's far when one wants to get there.

  Queen Marie of Rumania, *Masks* (1937)

4 What was the desire of the flesh beside the desire of the mind?

  Helen Waddell, *Peter Abelard* (1933)

5 Compared to my heart's desire / the sea is a drop.

  Adélia Prado, "Denouement," in Ellen Watson, tr., *The Alphabet in the Park* (1990)

6 Desire can blind us to the hazards of our enterprises.

  Marie de France (12th cent.), in Jeanette Beer, tr., *Medieval Fables of Marie de France* (1981)

7 It is possible to wish so greatly for the unattained that in time you believe it has been won—indeed, you can even remember the winning of it.

  Craig Rice, *Telefair* (1942)

8 I suppose you can't have everything, though my instinctive response to this sentiment is always, "Why not?"

  Margaret Halsey, *Some of My Best Friends Are Soldiers* (1944)

9 Unfulfilled desires are dangerous forces.

  Sarah Tarleton Colvin, *A Rebel in Thought* (1944)

10 It is human nature to overestimate the thing you've never had.

  Ellen Glasgow, *The Romantic Comedians* (1926)

11 You can have anything you want if you want it desperately enough. You must want it with an inner exuberance that erupts through the skin and joins the energy that created the world.

  Sheilah Graham, *The Rest of the Story* (1964)

12 Our desire must be like a slow and stately ship, sailing across endless oceans, never in search of safe anchorage. Then suddenly, unexpectedly, it will find mooring for a moment.

  Etty Hillesum (1942), *An Interrupted Life* (1983)

13 The more anybody wants a thing, the more they do think others want it.

  Mary Webb, *Precious Bane* (1924)

14 Protect me from what I want.

  Jenny Holzer, *Survival Series* (1987)

See also Longing, Passion.

## ֍ DESPAIR

15 Perhaps despair is the only human sin.

  Gretel Ehrlich, *Islands, the Universe, Home* (1991)

16 Those who despair of life are not long for it.

  Elizabeth Janeway, *Powers of the Weak* (1980)

17 There is no despair so absolute as that which comes with the first moments of our first great sorrow, when we have not yet known what it is to have suffered and be healed, to have despaired and recovered hope.

  George Eliot, *Adam Bede* (1859)

18 Despair is anger with no place to go.

  Mignon McLaughlin, *The Neurotic's Notebook* (1963)

19 To live is often only to have a choice of several despairs.

  Georgette Leblanc (1914), in Janet Flanner, tr., *Souvenirs* (1932)

20 No one has a right to sit down and feel hopeless. There's too much work to do.

  Dorothy Day (1940), in *The Catholic Worker* (1994)

21 I'll have to, as you say, take a stand, do something toward shaking up that system. . . . Despair . . . is too easy an out.

  Paule Marshall, *The Chosen Place, The Timeless People* (1969)

22 Despair makes us serve evil as much as good.

  Hadewijch, "The Nature of Love" (13th cent.), in Mother Columba Hart, *Hadewijch* (1980)

23 If, every day, I dare to remember that I am here on loan, that this house, this hillside, these minutes are all leased to me, not given, I will never despair. Despair is for those who expect to live forever. I no longer do.

  Erica Jong, *Fear of Fifty* (1994)

See also Depression, Discouragement, Hope, Lifelessness.

## ❧ DESTINY

1 Everyone has a Destiny who knows what kind of destiny he has.

    Rahel Varnhagen (1810), in Hannah Arendt, *Rahel Varnhagen* (1957)

2 Men heap together the mistakes of their lives and create a monster which they call Destiny.

    John Oliver Hobbes, *The Sinner's Comedy* (1892)

3 How rash to assert that man shapes his own destiny. All he can do is determine his inner responses.

    Etty Hillesum (1942), *An Interrupted Life* (1983)

4 There is no creature whose inward being is so strong that it is not greatly determined by what lies outside it.

    George Eliot, *Middlemarch* (1871)

5 Destiny's bank is inexorable, all accounts must balance.

    Dorothy Fuldheim, *A Thousand Friends* (1974)

6 She felt again that small shiver that occurred to her when events hinted at a destiny being played out, of unseen forces intervening.

    Dorothy Gilman, *Mrs. Pollifax and the Whirling Dervish* (1990)

7 I am not afraid. . . . I was born to do this.

    Joan of Arc (1429), in Edward Lucie-Smith, *Joan of Arc* (1976)

8 The portion of some is to have their afflictions by drops, now one drop and then another; but the dregs of the cup, the wine of astonishment, like a sweeping rain that leaveth no food, did the Lord prepare to be my portion.

    Mary Rowlandson, *A Narrative of the Captivity and Restoration of Mrs. Mary Rowlandson* (1682)

9 In that time and by God's will there died my mother, who was a great hindrance unto me in following the way of God; my husband died likewise, and in a short time there also died all my children. And because I had commenced to follow the aforesaid way and had prayed God that He would rid me of them, I had great consolation of their deaths, albeit I did also feel some grief.

    Blessed Angela of Foligno, *The Book of Divine Consolation* (1536)

10 Far rather would I sit and sew beside my poor mother, for this thing is not of my condition. But I must go, and I must do this thing, because my Lord will have it so. Rather now than tomorrow, and tomorrow than the day after!

    Joan of Arc (1430), in Willard Trask, tr., *Joan of Arc* (1936)

11 When a laborer sweats his sweat of blood and weeps his tears of blood a remedy is thrust upon the world. I am remedy.

    Mother Jones (1915), in Djuna Barnes, *Interviews* (1985)

12 All I was doing was trying to get home from work.

    Rosa Parks, on refusing to move to the back of the bus, televised interview (1985)

See also Fate.

## ❧ DESTRUCTION

13 Destruction is ultimately self-destruction.

    Anaïs Nin (1961), *The Diary of Anaïs Nin*, vol. 6 (1976)

14 There is only one answer to destructiveness and that is creativity.

    Sylvia Ashton-Warner, *Teacher* (1963)

15 If you can't create, you destroy.

    Anaïs Nin (1959), *The Diary of Anaïs Nin*, vol. 6 (1976)

16 Those who cannot live fully often become destroyers of life.

    Anaïs Nin, *The Diary of Anaïs Nin*, vol. 4 (1967)

17 Abel was a dog poisoner. It sometimes works out that way. A man wants to have some direct connection with life. If he can't bring life into being, he'll put an end to it. In that way he's not completely powerless. Some men can start it. Others can end it.

    Jessamyn West, *The Life I Really Lived* (1979)

See also Evil.

## ❧ DETACHMENT

18 Attachment is a manufacturer of illusions and whoever wants reality ought to be detached.

    Simone Weil, *Gravity and Grace* (1947)

1 We are able to laugh when we achieve detachment, if only for a moment.

    May Sarton, *Journal of a Solitude* (1973)

2 Only an indirect method is effective. We do nothing if we have not first drawn back.

    Simone Weil, *Gravity and Grace* (1947)

3 The average reader can contemplate with considerable fortitude the sorrows and disappointments of someone else.

    Nellie L. McClung, *The Stream Runs Fast* (1945)

See also Objectivity.

## ❧ DETECTION

4 Society punishes not the vices of its members, but their detection.

    Countess of Blessington, *Desultory Thoughts and Reflections* (1839)

5 I could never have survived being "found out." . . . That eleventh commandment is the only one that it is vitally important to keep in these days.

    Bertha H. Buxton, *Jenny of "The Prince's"* (1876)

6 Terror of being found out is not always a preservative, it sometimes hurries on the act which it ought to prevent.

    Mrs. Oliphant, *A House in Bloomsbury* (1894)

7 We are more prone to murmur at the punishment of our faults than to lament them.

    Countess of Blessington, *Desultory Thoughts and Reflections* (1839)

8 No one is more trustworthy than the repentant sinner who has been found out.

    Ethel Smyth, *What Happened Next* (1940)

See also Guilt, Wrongdoing.

## ❧ DETERMINATION

9 I am the initial Fish / rejected on the beach / but determined to live.

    Etel Adnan, "The Beirut-Hell Express," in Joanna Bankier and Deirdre Lashgari, eds., *Women Poets of the World* (1983)

10 If enough people think of a thing and work hard enough at it, I guess it's pretty nearly bound to happen, wind and weather permitting.

    Laura Ingalls Wilder, *On the Shores of Silver Lake* (1939)

11 "The doctor says I'm going blind," she told the children, but privately, she'd intended to do no such thing.

    Anne Tyler, *Dinner at the Homesick Restaurant* (1982)

12 I would . . . be so exhausted by my determination that I had no strength left to do the actual work.

    Etty Hillesum (1942), *An Interrupted Life* (1983)

13 I might have been born in a hovel but I determined to travel with the wind and the stars.

    Jacqueline Cochran, *The Stars at Noon* (1954)

14 I . . . resolved to take Fate by the throat and shake a living out of her.

    Louisa May Alcott (1858), in Ednah D. Cheney, ed., *Louisa May Alcott* (1889)

15 Then I will speak upon the ashes.

    Sojourner Truth, when told of a threat to burn down the hall where she was to speak (1862), in Olive Gilbert, *Narrative of Sojourner Truth* (1878)

See also Perseverance, Stubbornness.

## ❧ DEVIL

16 The devil never sleeps.

    St. Catherine of Siena (c. 1375), in Vida D. Scudder, ed., *St. Catherine of Siena As Seen in Her Letters* (1905)

17 The devil never seems so busy as where the saints are.

    Elizabeth Rundle Charles, *Chronicles of the Schönberg-Cotta Family* (1863)

18 All that the Devil asks is acquiescence.

    Suzanne Massie, in Robert and Suzanne Massie, *Journey* (1975)

19 The devil's most devilish when respectable.

    Elizabeth Barrett Browning, *Aurora Leigh* (1857)

20 Does the devil know he is a devil?

    Elizabeth Madox Roberts, *Black Is My Truelove's Hair* (1938)

1 What's devil to some is good to some others.

> Elizabeth Madox Roberts, *Black Is My Truelove's Hair* (1938)

2 Where there is no faith, devils are a necessity.

> Rita Mae Brown, *Bingo* (1988)

3 Under all the different systems of religion that have guided or misguided the world for the last six thousand years, the Devil has been the grand scapegoat. . . . All the evil that gets committed is laid to his door, and he has, besides, the credit of hindering all the good that has never got done at all. If mankind were not thus one and all victims to the Devil, what an irredeemable set of scoundrels they would be obliged to confess themselves!

> Geraldine Jewsbury, *Zoë*, vol. 2 (1845)

4 The Christians were the first to make the existence of Satan a dogma of the Church. . . . What is the use in a Pope, if there is no Devil?

> H.P. Blavatsky, *Isis Unveiled*, vol. 2 (1877)

5 It is wonderful how much time good people spend fighting the devil. If they would only expend the same amount of energy loving their fellow men, the devil would die in his own tracks of ennui.

> Helen Keller, *The Story of My Life* (1902)

See also Evil, Sin, Villains.

## &#10022; DEVOTION

6 That's the worst of devotion—its trade-mark is anxiety.

> Phyllis Bottome, "The Battle-Field," *Innocence and Experience* (1934)

See also Affection, Love, Loyalty.

## &#10022; DIAMONDS

7 Diamonds are the tears of the poor.

> Helen McCloy, *A Change of Heart* (1973)

8 Men would wither and custom stale them, but diamonds! Ah, they were crystalized immortality!

> Mae West, *Diamond Lil* (1932)

9 Ah, the feeling you get holding a diamond in your hand! . . . It's like holding a bit of the moon.

> Anna Magnani, in Oriana Fallaci, *Limelighters* (1963)

10 Diamonds talk, and I can stand listenin' to 'em often.

> Mae West, *Diamond Lil* (1932)

11 Kissing your hand may make you feel very good but a diamond bracelet lasts forever.

> Anita Loos, *Gentlemen Prefer Blondes* (1925)

See also Jewels.

## &#10022; DIARIES

12 Writing a journal means that facing your ocean you are afraid to swim across it, so you attempt to drink it drop by drop.

> George Sand (1837), in Marie Jenny Howe, ed., *The Intimate Journal of George Sand* (1929)

13 A journal is a leap of faith. You write without knowing what the next day's entry will be—or when the last.

> Violet Weingarten, *Intimations of Mortality* (1978)

14 People who keep journals have life twice.

> Jessamyn West, *To See the Dream* (1957)

15 Journal writing is a voyage to the interior.

> Christina Baldwin, *One to One* (1977)

16 What fun it is to generalize in the privacy of a note book. It is as I imagine waltzing on ice might be. A great delicious sweep in one direction, taking you your full strength, and then with no trouble at all, an equally delicious sweep in the opposite direction. My note book does not help me think, but it eases my crabbed heart.

> Florida Scott-Maxwell, *The Measure of My Days* (1968)

17 My diary seems to keep me whole.

> Anaïs Nin (1936), *The Diary of Anaïs Nin*, vol. 2 (1967)

18 Rather than calling this diary a record of my life, it's more accurate to regard it as the sum of all my tears.

> Ding Ling, "Miss Sophia's Diary" (1927), *I Myself Am a Woman* (1989)

1 I think this journal will be disadvantageous for me, for I spend my time now like a spider spinning my own entrails.

  Mary Boykin Chesnut (1861), *A Diary From Dixie* (1905)

2 Recording happiness made it last longer, we felt, and recording sorrow dramatized it and took away its bitterness; and often we settled some problem which beset us even while we wrote about it.

  Dorothy Day, *From Union Square to Rome* (1940)

3 My diaries were written primarily, I think, not to preserve the experience but to savor it, to make it even more real, more visible and palpable, than in actual life. For in our family an experience was not finished, not truly experienced, unless written down or shared with another.

  Anne Morrow Lindbergh, *Bring Me a Unicorn* (1971)

4 I got out this diary and read, as one always does read one's own writing, with a kind of guilty intensity.

  Virginia Woolf (1919), in Leonard Woolf, ed., *A Writer's Diary* (1953)

5 It's been a rare year, o paper soul, and against all the preceding bitterness and bile, this one shining scrawl. . . . Maybe I should fold you away to pull you out again in a decade, see whether the flowering that now seems promised, came; see whether it was untimely frostbit, or died without fruit, because you chart the real deeps of me. No: I hold you a pelorus, a flexing mirror, strange quarters for the wind of God.

  Keri Hulme, *The Bone People* (1983)

6 I think that if I get into the habit of writing a bit about what happens, or rather doesn't happen, I may lose a little of the sense of isolation and desolation which abides with me. My circumstances allowing of nothing but the ejaculation of one-syllabled reflections, a written monologue by that most interesting being, myself, may have its yet to be discovered consolations.

  Alice James (1889), in Anna Robeson Burr, *Alice James* (1934)

7 To Nobody, then, will I write my Journal! since to Nobody can I be wholly unreserved, to Nobody can I reveal every thought, every wish of my heart, with the most unlimited confidence, the most unremitting sincerity, to the end of my life!

  Fanny Burney (1768), in Charlotte Barrett, ed., *Diary and Letters of Madame D'Arblay*, vol. 1 (1842)

8 To one who has enjoyed the full life of any scene, of any hour, what thoughts can be recorded about it seem like the commas and semicolons in the paragraph—mere stops.

  Margaret Fuller, *Summer on the Lakes* (1844)

9 What is a diary as a rule? A document useful to the person who keeps it, dull to the contemporary who reads it, invaluable to the student, centuries afterwards, who treasures it!

  Ellen Terry, *The Story of My Life* (1908)

10 None but the lonely heart, they say, keeps a diary. None but a lonelier heart, perhaps, reads one. The diary keeper has no one to speak to; the diary reader has no one who speaks to him. The diary writer is at least talking to himself. The diary reader is listening to a man talking to himself.

  Jessamyn West, *A Matter of Time* (1966)

11 In those happy days when leisure was held to be no sin, men and women wrote journals whose copiousness both delights and dismays us.

  Agnes Repplier, "The Deathless Diary," *Varia* (1897)

12 So many people, you know, hit the White House with their dictaphone running. I never even kept a journal. I thought, "I want to live my life, not record it."

  Jacqueline Kennedy Onassis (1981), in Laurence Leamer, *The Kennedy Women* (1994)

13 That all my dreams might not prove empty, I have been writing this useless account—though I doubt it will long survive me.

  Lady Nijo (1306), in Karen Brazell, tr., *Confessions of Lady Nijo* (1950)

14 It's an odd idea for someone like me to keep a diary; not only because I have never done so before, but because it seems to me that neither I—nor for that matter anyone else—will be interested in the unbosomings of a thirteen-year-old schoolgirl.

  Anne Frank (1942), *The Diary of a Young Girl* (1952)

See also Writing.

## ﴾ DICTATORS

1 It is an illusion to suppose that a Dictator makes himself; at most he seizes an opportunity made for him by passive, stupid, incompetent, and above all, unsatisfied and fearful men.

    L. Susan Stebbing, *Ideas and Illusions* (1941)

2 There is an interesting resemblance in the speeches of dictators, no matter what country they may hail from or what language they may speak.

    Edna Ferber, *A Kind of Magic* (1963)

See also Leadership, Tyranny.

## ﴾ DIETING

3 I've been on a diet for two weeks and all I lost is two weeks.

    Totie Fields, in Joe Franklin, *Joe Franklin's Encyclopedia of Comedians* (1979)

4 The first thing I did when I made the decision to kill myself was to stop dieting. Let them dig a wider hole.

    Gail Parent, *Sheila Levine Is Dead and Living in New York* (1972)

5 If you have formed the habit of checking on every new diet that comes along, you will find that, mercifully, they all blur together, leaving you with only one definite piece of information: french-fried potatoes are out.

    Jean Kerr, "Aunt Jean's Marshmallow Fudge Diet," *Please Don't Eat the Daisies* (1957)

6 If one doesn't have a character like Abraham Lincoln or Joan of Arc, a diet simply disintegrates into eating exactly what you want to eat, but with a bad conscience.

    Maria Augusta Trapp, *The Story of the Trapp Family Singers* (1949)

7 As she is a woman, and as she is an American, she was dieting.

    Katharine Whitehorn, "Meeting Mary McCarthy," in *The Observer* (1965)

See also Food, Nutrition, Weight.

## ﴾ DIFFERENCE

8 Fear of difference is fear of life itself.

    M.P. Follett, *Creative Experience* (1924)

9 Differences challenge assumptions.

    Anne Wilson Schaef, *Women's Reality* (1981)

See also Diversity, Human Differences.

## ﴾ DINNER

10 The dinner table is the center for the teaching and practicing not just of table manners but of conversation, consideration, tolerance, family feeling, and just about all the other accomplishments of polite society except the minuet.

    Judith Martin, *Miss Manners' Guide for the Turn-of-the-Millennium* (1989)

11 When does the mind put forth its powers? when are the stores of memory unlocked? when does wit "flash from fluent lips?"—when but after a good dinner? Who will deny its influence on the affections? Half our friends are born of turbots and truffles.

    L.E. Landon, *Romance and Reality* (1831)

12 When one is too old for love, one finds great comfort in good dinners.

    Zora Neale Hurston, *Moses: Man of the Mountain* (1939)

13 When my mother had to get dinner for eight she'd just make enough for sixteen and only serve half.

    Gracie Allen, in Liz Smith, *The Mother Book* (1978)

14 My grandmother, when she served dinner, was a virtuoso hanging on the edge of her own ecstatic performance. . . . She was a little power crazed: she had us and, by God, we were going to eat. . . . The futility of saying no was supreme, and no one ever tried it. How could a son-in-law, already weakened near the point of imbecility by the once, twice, thrice charge to the barricades of pork and mashed potato, be expected to gather his feeble wit long enough to ignore the final call of his old commander when she sounded the alarm: "Pie, Fred?"

    Patricia Hampl, *A Romantic Education* (1981)

See also Cooking, Eating.

## ❧ DIPLOMACY

1 If a diplomat says *yes*, he means *perhaps*. If he says *perhaps* he means *no*. And if he says *no*, he's the hell of a diplomat.

> Agnes Sligh Turnbull, *The Golden Journey* (1955)

See also Discretion.

## ❧ DIRT

2 Where there is dirt there is system. Dirt is the byproduct of a systematic ordering and classification of matter.

> Mary Douglas, *Purity and Danger* (1969)

3 I make desperate attempts to turn 7G into House Beautiful in time for the home visit. I take more Clorox and wipe at the fingerprints that surround every light switch. Why, I wonder as I wipe, were we clawing at these light switches? It looks as if coal miners were trying to escape.

> Laura Cunningham, *Sleeping Arrangements* (1989)

4 There are two types of dirt: the dark kind, which is attracted to light objects, and the light kind, which is attracted to dark objects.

> Ely Slick, in *Omni* (1979)

See also Housework.

## ❧ DISABILITIES

5 Our disabilities may impose limitations, but physical, economic, and political barriers impede us far more.

> Laura Hershey, "False Advertising," in *Ms.* (1995)

6 To admit that disability and illness are hard doesn't mean that they are wholly negative experiences, meaningless.

> Anne Finger, *Past Due* (1990)

7 Physical disability looms pretty large in one's life. But it doesn't devour one wholly. I'm not, for instance, Ms. MS, a walking, talking embodiment of a chronic incurable degenerative disease.

> Nancy Mairs, *Carnal Acts* (1990)

8 The fact is that ours is the only minority you can join involuntarily, without warning, at any time. And if you live long enough, as you're increasingly likely to do, you may well join it.

> Nancy Mairs, *Carnal Acts* (1990)

9 Though we [people with disabilities] have become more vocal in recent years, we still constitute a very small minority. Yet the Beautiful People—the slender, fair and perfect ones—form a minority that may be even smaller.

> Debra Kent, "In Search of Liberation," in Marsha Saxton and Florence Howe, eds., *With Wings* (1987)

10 Ours is a culture that emphasizes cure, or, short of that, immediate relief from symptoms, so that we can carry on with our busy lives. Unfortunately, in our cultural denial of the reality of chronic illness and disability, we frequently silence the voices of those who cannot deny it.

> Marsha Saxton and Florence Howe, *With Wings* (1987)

11 With the rise of industrialism, words like "normal" and "defective," words that had once only been used to refer to things, began to be used to refer to people. . . . In the industrial age, a new degree of uniformity was expected of people.

> Anne Finger, *Past Due* (1990)

12 People used to say to my friend Mary, a quadriplegic, "You still have your mind." She would say, "I still have my body." The world tells me to divorce myself from my flesh, to live in my head. . . . I didn't want to be fleshless.

> Anne Finger, *Past Due* (1990)

13 Like children in a schoolyard, they want to know what was my accident, how much did it hurt, and what did I look like afterward. . . . I am not the only person I have known who has encountered emotional sightseers.

> Natalie Kusz, *Road Song* (1990)

See also Deafness, Illness.

## ❧ DISAPPOINTMENT

14 How Disappointment tracks / The steps of Hope.

> L.E. Landon, "A History of the Lyre," *The Venetian Bracelet* (1829)

1 My life is a perfect graveyard of buried hopes. That's a sentence I read in a book once, and I say it over to comfort myself whenever I'm disappointed in anything.

    L.M. Montgomery, *Anne of Green Gables* (1908)

2 Disappointment tears the bearable film off life.

    Elizabeth Bowen, *The House in Paris* (1935)

3 What we never have had, remains; / It is the things we have that go.

    Sara Teasdale, "Wisdom," *Dark of the Moon* (1926)

4 People are only "disappointing" when one makes a wrong diagnosis.

    Charlotte Mew (1917), in Penelope Fitzgerald, *Charlotte Mew and Her Friends* (1984)

5 Let me ask you, my friend, whether you do not think, that many of our disappointments and much of our unhappiness arise from our forming false notions of things and persons.

    Abigail Adams (1761), *Letters of Mrs. Adams* (1848)

6 It is unfair to hold people responsible for our illusions about them.

    Comtesse Diane, *Les Glanes de la Vie* (1898)

7 The reality has displaced from my mind an illusion much more magnificent than itself. . . . I am an ass's head, a clod, a wooden spoon, a fat weed growing on Lethe's brink, a stock, a stone, a petrifaction. For have I not seen Niagara, the wonder of wonders, and felt—no words can tell *what*—disappointment?

    Anna Jameson (1836), in Geraldine Macpherson, *Memoirs of the Life of Anna Jameson* (1878)

See also Discouragement, Disillusionment, Pouting.

## ⟡ DISAPPROVAL

8 It was a pity he couldna be hatched o'er again, an' hatched different.

    George Eliot, *Adam Bede* (1859)

9 I can make him feel so low he'll be able to sit on a dime and swing his feet.

    Helen Eustis, *The Horizontal Man* (1962)

10 He went to work on my character with the unstoppable fury of Oliver Cromwell putting dents in the church plate.

    Margaret Halsey, *No Laughing Matter* (1977)

11 The silence of a man who loves to praise, is a censure sufficiently severe.

    Charlotte Lennox, *The Female Quixote* (1752)

12 Next to the joy of the egotist is the joy of the detractor.

    Agnes Repplier, "Writing an Autobiography," *Under Dispute* (1924)

13 I would prefer a thousand times to receive reproofs than to give them to others.

    St. Thérèse of Lisieux (1897), in John Clarke, tr., *Story of a Soul* (1972)

14 The man who slurs / Some other man is guiltier / Of just the same misdeed, I'm sure, / That he maintains the other is.

    Christine de Pisan, "Tale of the Rose" (1402), in Thelma S. Fenster and Mary Carpenter Erler, eds., *Poems of Cupid, God of Love* (1990)

15 Someone has said that it requires less mental effort to condemn than to think.

    Emma Goldman, title essay, *Anarchism* (1910)

See also Criticism, Criticisms, Disillusionment, Insults, Nagging.

## ⟡ DISASTER

16 We like to talk over our disasters, because they are ours; and others like to listen, because they are not theirs.

    L.E. Landon, *Francesca Carrara* (1834)

17 I always thought it mattered, to know what is the worst possible thing that can happen to you, to know how you can avoid it, to not be drawn by the magic of the unspeakable.

    Amy Tan, *The Joy Luck Club* (1989)

18 No one ever understood disaster until it came.

    Josephine Herbst, *Nothing Is Sacred* (1928)

19 She suddenly felt quite safe. It was a very strange feeling, and she found it indescribably nice. But

what was there to worry over? The disaster had come at last.

    Tove Jansson, *Tales From Moominvalley* (1963)

1 On ruins one can begin to build. Anyhow, looking out from ruins one clearly sees; there are no obstructing walls.

    Rose Macaulay, *The Valley Captives* (1911)

See also Crises, Tragedy, Trouble.

## ❧ DISCIPLINE

2 When you were quite a little boy somebody ought to have said "hush" just once!

    Mrs. Patrick Campbell, letter to George Bernard Shaw (1912), in Alan Dent, ed., *Bernard Shaw and Mrs. Patrick Campbell* (1952)

3 The ultimate mistake in discipline is the ultimatum.

    Marcelene Cox, in *Ladies' Home Journal* (1950)

See also Parenthood.

## ❧ DISCONTENT

4 Were there none who were discontented with what they have, the world would never reach anything better.

    Florence Nightingale, "Cassandra" (1852), in Ray Strachey, *"The Cause"* (1928)

5 This struggle of people against their conditions, this is where you find the meaning in life.

    Rose Chernin, in Kim Chernin, *In My Mother's House* (1983)

6 Discontent and disorder were signs of energy and hope, not of despair.

    C.V. Wedgwood, *The Great Rebellion* (1958)

7 Happiness makes us older, less romantic, less in need of dreams. Discontent, not happiness, is the food of youth and poetry.

    Nan Fairbrother, *An English Year* (1954)

8 She would not measure living by the many who had less but always by the few who had more than she had.

    Faith Baldwin, *The Clever Sister* (1947)

9 No matter what you achieve in life, you're always wondering, "Is there something I should be doing? Is there something I'm missing?"

    Reba McEntire, in Mark Bego, *Country Gals* (1994)

See also Restlessness, Unhappiness.

## ❧ DISCOURAGEMENT

10 When we yield to discouragement it is usually because we give too much thought to the past and to the future.

    St. Therese of Lisieux (1897), in *Peacemaking* (1989)

11 Discouragement seizes us only when we can no longer rely on chance.

    George Sand, *Handsome Lawrence* (1872)

12 I'm sick and tired of being sick and tired.

    Fannie Lou Hamer, in Jerry DeMuth, "'Tired of Being Sick and Tired,'" *The Nation* (1964)

See also Despair, Disappointment, Disillusionment, Melancholy.

## ❧ DISCOVERY

13 Most new discoveries are suddenly-seen things that were always there.

    Susanne K. Langer, *Philosophy in a New Key* (1942)

14 The poverty of our imagination is no measure of the world's resources. Our posterity will no doubt get fuel in ways that we are unable to devise for them.

    George Eliot, *Impressions of Theophrastus Such* (1879)

15 The world is equally astonished—and resentful—at every new discovery, but it in a short time accepts it as a commonplace.

    Gertrude Atherton, *Black Oxen* (1923)

See also Innovation, Invention, Newness, Progress.

## ⬧ DISCRETION

1 The less said the better.

  Jane Austen, *Sense and Sensibility* (1911)

2 Well, I aren't like a bird-clapper, forced to make a rattle when the wind blows on me. I can keep my own counsel when there's no good i' speaking.

  George Eliot, *Adam Bede* (1859)

3 She had seen enough of the world to know that in few people is discretion stronger than the desire to tell a good story.

  Lady Murasaki, *The Tale of Genji* (c. 1008)

4 The danger lies not in the big ears of little pitchers, but in the large mouths.

  Ethel Watts Mumford, in Oliver Herford, Ethel Watts Mumford, and Addison Mizner, *The Complete Cynic* (1902)

5 There is such a thing as tempting the gods. Talking too much, too soon and with too much self-satisfaction has always seemed to me a sure way to court disaster. . . . The forces of retribution are always listening. They never sleep.

  Meg Greenfield, in *Newsweek* (1991)

6 Wiggins was about to answer, and seeing he might be divulging privileged information, shut up like a drawer.

  Martha Grimes, *The Man With a Load of Mischief* (1981)

See also Concealment, Diplomacy, Reticence, Secrets.

## ⬧ DISCRIMINATION

7 We need every human gift and cannot afford to neglect any gift because of artificial barriers of sex or race or class or national origin.

  Margaret Mead, *Male and Female* (1949)

8 Exclusions and devaluations of whole groups of people on the scale and of the range, tenacity, and depth of racism and sexism and classism are systemic and shape the world within which we all struggle to live and find meaning.

  Elizabeth Kamarck Minnick, *Transforming Knowledge* (1990)

9 What a child does not know and does not want to know of race and color and class, he learns soon enough as he grows to see each man flipped inexorably into some predestined groove like a penny or a sovereign in a banker's rack.

  Beryl Markham, *West With the Night* (1942)

10 Once any group in society stands in a relatively deprived position in relation to other groups, it is genuinely deprived.

  Margaret Mead, *Twentieth Century Faith* (1972)

11 If threatened by law that either they welcome the outsiders into their midst or be punished for failure to do so, the insiders can make their system work so as to avoid either outcome entirely. . . . Saying that a person cannot be kept out doesn't ensure that that person can get in, and more important, stay in.

  Margaret Hennig and Anne Jardim, *The Managerial Woman* (1976)

12 Sometimes, I feel discriminated against, but it does not make me angry. It merely astonishes me. How *can* any deny themselves the pleasure of my company? It's beyond me.

  Zora Neale Hurston, "How It Feels to Be Colored Me" (1928), in Alice Walker, ed., *I Love Myself When I Am Laughing . . . And Then Again When I Am Looking Mean and Impressive* (1979)

13 The paradox is here: when cultivated people do stay away from a certain portion of the population, when all social advantages are persistently withheld, it may be for years, the result itself is pointed to as a reason and is used as an argument for the continued withholding.

  Jane Addams (1890), *Twenty Years at Hull House* (1910)

14 As a society emphasizes and values some aspects of the total range of human potentials more than others, the valued aspects are associated closely with, and limited to, the dominant group's domain.

  Jean Baker Miller, *Toward a New Psychology of Women* (1986)

15 Racism and oppression have traditionally been synonymous with good business practice for America.

  Beverly J. Hawkins, *Woman Is Not Just a Female* (1973)

1 In the end, antiblack, antifemale, and all forms of discrimination are equivalent to the same thing—antihumanism.

    Shirley Chisholm, *Unbought and Unbossed* (1970)

See also Anti-Semitism, Bigotry, Class, Exclusion, Injustice, Oppression, Persecution, Prejudice, Racism, Rights, Sexism.

## ❧ DISEASES

2 Diseases have no eyes. They pick with a dizzy finger anyone, just anyone.

    Sandra Cisneros, *The House on Mango Street* (1989)

3 Diseases, as all experience shows, are adjectives, not noun substantives.

    Florence Nightingale, *Notes on Nursing* (1859)

4 Disease is an experience of so-called mortal mind. It is fear made manifest on the body.

    Mary Baker Eddy, *Science and Health* (1875)

5 Mother has lupus. / She says it's a disease / of self-attack. / It's like a mugger broke into your home / and you called the police / and when they came they beat up on you / instead of on your attackers, / she says.

    Paula Gunn Allen, "Dear World," *Skins and Bones* (1988)

See also AIDS, Alzheimer's, Cancer, Doctors, Health, Hospitals, Illness, Medicine, Nurses, Pain, Surgery.

## ❧ DISHONESTY

6 Those who have two strings to their bow may shoot stronger, but they rarely shoot straight.

    Elizabeth I (1568), in J.E. Neale, *Queen Elizabeth I* (1934)

7 There's a strong aroma of sawn lady about this.

    Josephine Tey, *To Love and Be Wise* (1950)

8 She could carry off anything; and some people said that she did.

    Ada Leverson, *Love at Second Sight* (1916)

9 Nothing he did was ever illegal—but as soon as he'd got on to it, you had to have a law about it, if you know what I mean.

    Agatha Christie, *Crooked House* (1949)

10 He was so crooked, you could have used his spine for a safety-pin.

    Dorothy L. Sayers, *The Nine Tailors* (1934)

11 It is better in the long run to be cheated than to cheat. I have learned that there is no middle way.

    Phyllis Bottome, *Old Wine* (1925)

12 No one is ever warmed by wool pulled over his eyes.

    Marcelene Cox, in *Ladies' Home Journal* (1948)

13 The tendrils of graft and corruption have become mighty interlacing roots so that even men who would like to be honest are tripped and trapped by them.

    Agnes Sligh Turnbull, *The Golden Journey* (1955)

See also Betrayal, Deception, Lying, Treachery.

## ❧ DISILLUSIONMENT

14 Disillusion comes only to the illusioned. One cannot be disillusioned of what one never put faith in.

    Dorothy Thompson, *The Courage to Be Happy* (1957)

15 This is then complete disillusionment in living, the complete realization that no one can believe as you do about anything.

    Gertrude Stein, *The Making of Americans* (1925)

16 Disillusions all come from within . . . from the failure of some dear and secret hope. The *world* makes no promises; we only dream it does; and when we wake, we cry!

    John Oliver Hobbes, *The Ambassador* (1898)

17 Death from disillusion is not instantaneous, and there are no mercy killers for the disillusioned.

    Anaïs Nin (1946), *The Diary of Anaïs Nin*, vol. 4 (1971)

18 The *disillusioner* is seldom forgiven.

    Frances Little, *The Lady and Sada San* (1912)

19 Only my dogs will not betray me.

    Maria Callas, in Arianna Stassinopoulos, *Maria Callas* (1981)

1 Miss Findlater spoke with the air of a disillusioned rake, who has sucked life's orange and found it dead sea fruit.
Dorothy L. Sayers, *Unnatural Death* (1927)

See also Disappointment, Illusions.

## ❧ DISORDER

2 There is no disorder but the heart's.
Mona Van Duyn, "The Gardener to His God," *A Time of Bees* (1964)

See also Chaos.

## ❧ DISTRUST

3 Distrust . . . is the beginning of hatred.
Marguerite de Valois, *Memoirs* (1628)

4 Set the foot down with distrust upon the crust of the world—it is thin.
Edna St. Vincent Millay, "Underground System," *Huntsman, What Quarry?* (1939)

5 Hers was one of those inconvenient natures which trust blindly or not at all: once worked on by a doubt or a suspicion, they are never able to shake themselves free of it again.
Henry Handel Richardson, *The Fortunes of Richard Mahoney: Australia Felix* (1917)

6 I wouldn't mind being your partner if there were two of me.
Christina Stead, *House of All Nations* (1938)

7 What loneliness is more lonely than distrust?
George Eliot, *Middlemarch* (1871)

See also Doubt, Misanthropy, Suspicion, Trust.

## ❧ DIVERSITY

8 The music of difference, all alive. / The founders and this people, who set in diversity / The base of our living.
Muriel Rukeyser, "Young," *One Life* (1957)

9 Mankind will endure when the world appreciates the logic of diversity.
Indira Gandhi, *Freedom Is the Starting Point* (1976)

10 Diversity is the most basic principle of creation. No two snowflakes, blades of grass or people are alike.
Lynn Maria Laitala, "In the Aftermath of Empire," in *The Finnish American Reporter* (1992)

11 What people often mean by getting rid of conflict is getting rid of diversity, and it is of the utmost importance that these should not be considered the same.
M.P. Follett, *Creative Experience* (1924)

12 The idea of diversity becomes our strength, sacred to us. / The range broadening, the potential becoming a way and a song. / Many have fought this reality. We know the wounds.
Muriel Rukeyser, "Young," *One Life* (1957)

See also Difference, Human Differences, Human Family.

## ❧ DIVINITY

13 Maybe the tragedy of the human race was that we had forgotten we were each Divine.
Shirley MacLaine, *Out on a Limb* (1983)

14 In my opinion, the Divine is revealed to all men once at least in their lives.
Marie Corelli, *The Master Christian* (1900)

15 The veil between us and the divine is more permeable than we imagine.
Sue Patton Thoele, *The Woman's Book of Courage* (1991)

16 Divinity is in its omniscience and omnipotence like a wheel, a circle, a whole, that can neither be understood, nor divided, nor begun nor ended.
Hildegard of Bingen (1150), in Gabriele Uhlein, ed., *Meditations With Hildegard of Bingen* (1983)

See also God, Holiness, The Sacred, Spirituality.

## ❧ DIVORCE

17 Divorce is only less painful than the need for divorce.
Jane O'Reilly, *The Girl I Left Behind* (1980)

1 A divorce is like an amputation; you survive, but there's less of you.

　　Margaret Atwood, in *Time* (1973)

2 Being divorced is like being hit by a Mack truck. If you live through it, you start looking very carefully to the right and to the left.

　　Jean Kerr, *Mary, Mary* (1963)

3 Divorce is the psychological equivalent of a triple coronary by-pass. After such a monumental assault on the heart, it can take a whole decade to amend all the habits and attitudes that led up to it.

　　Mary Kay Blakely, *American Mom* (1994)

4 Divorce is one of the loneliest of modern rituals. Before, during, and after the actual culmination of the legal process it is an ordeal that rips people away from their roots, their important relationships, and a part of themselves. There is really nothing like it—except perhaps war.

　　Suzanne Gordon, *Lonely in America* (1976)

5 My marriage . . . sprang a leak and had to be towed into court.

　　Sophie Tucker, *Some of These Days* (1945)

6 I smother in the house in the valley below, / Let me out to the dark, let me go, let me go.

　　Anna Wickham, "Divorce," *Songs of John Oland* (1911)

7 Such is the nature of the marriage relation that a breach once made cannot be healed, and it is the height of folly to waste one's life in vain efforts to make a binary compound of two diverse elements. What would we think of the chemist who should sit twenty years trying to mix oil and water, and insist upon it that his happiness depended upon the result of the experiment?

　　Elizabeth Cady Stanton (1860), in Theodore Stanton and Harriot Stanton Blatch, eds., *Elizabeth Cady Stanton As Revealed in Her Letters Diary and Reminiscences*, vol. 2 (1922)

8 When two people decide to get a divorce, it isn't a sign that they "don't understand" one another, but a sign that they have, at last, begun to.

　　Helen Rowland, *A Guide to Men* (1922)

9 Divorce is the one human tragedy that reduces everything to cash.

　　Rita Mae Brown, *Sudden Death* (1983)

10 I know one husband and wife who, whatever the official reasons given to the court for the breakup of their marriage, were really divorced because the husband believed that nobody ought to read while he was talking and the wife that nobody ought to talk while she was reading.

　　Vera Brittain, in Jilly Cooper and Tom Hartman, *Violets and Vinegar* (1980)

11 I'm not upset about my divorce. I'm only upset that I'm not a widow.

　　Roseanne Barr, in *Life* (1995)

12 I find to my astonishment that an unhappy marriage goes on being unhappy when it is over.

　　Rebecca West, in Victoria Glendinning, *Rebecca West* (1987)

13 So many persons think divorce a panacea for every ill, who find out, when they try it, that the remedy is worse than the disease.

　　Dorothy Dix, *Dorothy Dix—Her Book* (1926)

14 However often marriage is dissolved, it remains indissoluble. Real divorce, the divorce of heart and nerve and fiber, does not exist, since there is no divorce from memory.

　　Virgilia Peterson, *A Matter of Life and Death* (1961)

See also Broken Heart, Desertion, Estrangement, Marriage.

## ❧ DOCTORS

15 The Doctor's Motto: Have patients.

　　Ethel Watts Mumford, in Oliver Herford, Ethel Watts Mumford, and Addison Mizner, *The Complete Cynic* (1902)

16 Good doctors get a mechanic's pleasure in making you tick over.

　　Margery Allingham, in Nancy Spain, *Why I'm Not a Millionaire* (1956)

17 Some people think that doctors and nurses can put scrambled eggs back into the shell.

　　Dorothy Canfield Fisher, in Martha Lupton, *The Speaker's Desk Book* (1937)

18 He will persist in laboring under the delusion that patients want commonsense instead of magic.

　　Rae Foley, *The Last Gamble* (1956)

1 A physician can sometimes parry the scythe of death, but has no power over the sand in the hourglass.

    Hester Lynch Piozzi, to Fanny Burney (1781), in R. Brimley Johnson, ed., *The Letters of Mrs. Thrale* (1926)

2 You can argue with a theologian or a politician, but doctors are sacrosanct. They *know*, you do not.

    Brenda Ueland, *Strength to Your Sword Arm* (1993)

3 Patients did not usually interrupt his rounds and any delay in his progress caused as much concern among the staff as if an important train carrying bullion had been held up by bandits.

    Janet Frame, *Faces in the Water* (1961)

4 The real trouble with the doctor image in America is that it has been grayed by the image of the doctor-as-businessman, the doctor-as-bureaucrat, the doctor-as-medical-robot, and the doctor-as-terrified-victim-of-malpractice-suits.

    Shana Alexander, "An Ordeal to Choke a Sword-Swallower," in *Life* (1966)

5 He bore the stamp of the unforgivable sin in a physician—uncertainty.

    Rae Foley, *The Sleeping Wolf* (1952)

6 Heart surgeons do not have the world's smallest egos: when you ask them to name the world's three leading practitioners, they never can remember the names of the other two.

    Sara Paretsky, "The Case of the Pietro Andromache," in Marilyn Wallace, ed., *Sisters in Crime* (1989)

7 I would never go to see a male gynecologist. That would be like having your car worked on by a garage mechanic who never owned a car.

    Carrie Snow (1981), in Bob Chieger, *Was It Good for You, Too?* (1983)

8 Other books have been written by men physicians. . . . One would suppose in reading them that women possessed but one class of physical organs, and that these are always diseased. Such teaching is pestiferous, and tends to cause and perpetuate the very evils it professes to remedy.

    Mary A. Livermore, *What Shall We Do With Our Daughters?* (1883)

9 I had never gone to a doctor in my adult life, feeling instinctively that doctors meant either cutting or, just as bad, diet.

    Carson McCullers, *Clock Without Hands* (1961)

10 Ah, what a grudge I owe physicians! what mummery is their art!

    Marie de Rabutin-Chantal, Marquise de Sévigné (1676), *Letters of Madame de Sévigné to Her Daughter and Her Friends*, vol. 4 (1811)

11 You know doctors. For every one thing they tell you, there are two things hidden under the tongue.

    Rose Chernin, in Kim Chernin, *In My Mother's House* (1983)

12 Doctors always think anybody doing something they aren't is a quack; also they think all patients are idiots.

    Flannery O'Connor, in Sally Fitzgerald, ed., *The Habit of Being* (1979)

13 "Somebody that's not busy call for the ambulance," said the doctor in the off-hand voice young doctors adopt for terrible occasions.

    Flannery O'Connor, "Revelation," *Everything That Rises Must Converge* (1965)

14 Ethel's husband stayed in his office or walked through the halls carrying his little black bag like a small sample cut from the shadow of death.

    Helen Hudson, *Meyer Meyer* (1967)

15 Historically speaking, it has generally been deemed far more appropriate for ladies to marry M.D.s than to earn them.

    Autumn Stephens, *Wild Women* (1992)

See also Diseases, Health Care, Hospitals, Illness, Medicine, Nurses, Surgery.

## ✦ DOCTRINE

16 The best doctrine may become the worst, if imperfectly understood, erroneously interpreted, or superstitiously followed.

    Anna Leonowens, *The English Governess at the Siamese Court* (1870)

See also Belief, Dogma, Religion, Theology.

## ✦ DOGMA

17 You can't teach an old dogma new tricks.

    Dorothy Parker, in Robert E. Drennan, *The Algonquin Wits* (1968)

1 Every dogma must have its day.

> Carolyn Wells, "Inexpensive Cynicisms," *Folly for the Wise* (1904)

2 Dogmas are the toys that amuse and can satisfy but unreasoning children. They are the offspring of human speculation and prejudiced fancy.

> H.P. Blavatsky, in *The Spiritualist* (1878)

3 Creeds grow so thick along the way, / Their boughs hide God; I cannot pray.

> Lizette Woodworth Reese, "Doubt," *Selected Poems* (1927)

4 Dogma can in no way limit a limitless God.

> Flannery O'Connor, in Sally Fitzgerald, ed., *The Habit of Being* (1979)

5 The incidence of violent brand-loyalty to one's own current dogma has risen.

> Marge Piercy, "The Grand Coolie Damn," in Robin Morgan, ed., *Sisterhood Is Powerful* (1970)

See also Absolutes, Belief, Doctrine, Religion, Theology.

## ❧ DOGS

6 Pastrasche was their alpha and omega; their treasury and granary; their store of gold and wand of wealth; their bread-winner and minister; their only friend and comforter. . . . Pastrasche was their dog.

> Louise de la Ramée, *A Dog of Flanders* (1872)

7 My little old dog: / A heart-beat at my feet.

> Edith Wharton, "A Lyrical Epigram," *Artemis to Actaeon* (1909)

8 Dogs are the most amazing creatures; they give unconditional love. For me they are the role model for being alive.

> Gilda Radner, *It's Always Something* (1989)

9 If there is no God for thee / Then there is no God for me.

> Anna Hempstead Branch, "To a Dog," *Sonnets From a Lock Box* (1929)

10 May all dogs that I have ever loved / carry my coffin, / howl at the moonless sky, / & lie down with me sleeping / when I die.

> Erica Jong, "Best Friends," *At the Edge of the Body* (1979)

11 Let us love dogs; let us love only dogs! Men and cats are unworthy creatures.

> Maria Bashkirtseff (1874), in Mary J. Serrano, tr., *The Journal of a Young Artist* (1919)

12 Our dogs will love and admire the meanest of us, and feed our colossal vanity with their uncritical homage.

> Agnes Repplier, "The Idolatrous Dog," *Under Dispute* (1923)

13 Dogs' lives are too short. Their only fault, really.

> Agnes Sligh Turnbull, *The Flowering* (1972)

14 Like many other much-loved humans, they believed that they owned their dogs, instead of realizing that their dogs owned them.

> Dodie Smith, *One Hundred and One Dalmatians* (1956)

15 Dogs are a habit, I think.

> Elizabeth Bowen, "Aunt Tatty," *Joining Charles* (1929)

16 When I hear tell of the character and the loyalty and devotion of dogs, I remain unmoved. All of my dogs have been scamps and thieves and troublemakers and I've adored them all.

> Helen Hayes, with Sandford Dody, *On Reflection* (1968)

17 There is no doubt about it. Dog loving is closely related to the pounding-yourself-on-the-head-with-a-hammer-because-it-is-so-pleasant-when-you-stop school of masochism.

> Betty MacDonald, *Onions in the Stew* (1955)

18 Our house was always filled with dogs. . . . They helped make our house a kennel, it is true, but the constant patter of their filthy paws and the dreadful results of their brainless activities have warmed me throughout the years.

> Helen Hayes, with Sandford Dody, *On Reflection* (1968)

19 When you feel really lousy, puppy therapy is indicated.

> Sara Paretsky, *Burn Marks* (1990)

20 A puppy is but a dog, plus high spirits, and minus common sense.

> Agnes Repplier, "A Kitten," *In the Dozy Hours* (1894)

21 He had let out the dogs and they were jumping around him frantic with joy, as if they were afraid, every night, there would never be another letting out or another morning.

> Mary O'Hara, *My Friend Flicka* (1941)

1 Dogs act exactly the way we would act if we had no shame.

> Cynthia Heimel, *Get Your Tongue Out of My Mouth, I'm Kissing You Good-Bye!* (1993)

2 An animal on a leash is not tamed by the owner. The owner is extending himself through the leash to that part of his personality which is pure dog, that part of him which just wants to eat, sleep, bark, hump chairs, wet the floor in joy, and drink out of a toilet bowl.

> Diane Ackerman, *A Natural History of Love* (1994)

3 No animal should ever jump up on the dining-room furniture unless absolutely certain that he can hold his own in the conversation.

> Fran Lebowitz, *Social Studies* (1977)

4 Dogs who chase cars evidently see them as large, unruly ungulates badly in need of discipline and shepherding.

> Elizabeth Marshall Thomas, *The Hidden Life of Dogs* (1993)

5 Bonny isn't ordinary. She has a liquid, intellectual gaze, as if she's not a dog but a Democrat, interested, like Gabe and Len, in civil liberties.

> Laura Cunningham, *Sleeping Arrangements* (1989)

6 Arnold was a dog's dog. Whenever he shuffled along walks and through alleyways, he always gave the impression of being onto something big.

> Martha Grimes, *The Old Fox Deceiv'd* (1982)

7 I'm a lean dog, a keen dog, a wild dog, and alone; / I'm a rough dog, a tough dog, hunting on my own; / I'm a bad dog, a mad dog, teasing silly sheep; / I love to sit and bay at the moon, to keep fat souls from sleep.

> Irene Macleod, "Lone Dog," *Songs to Save a Soul* (1915)

8 Why, that dog is practically a Phi Beta Kappa. She can sit up and beg, and she can give her paw—I don't say she will but she can.

> Dorothy Parker, "Toward the Dog Days," in *McCall's* (1928)

9 While he has not, in my hearing, spoken the English language, he makes it perfectly plain that he understands it. And he uses his ears, tail, eyebrows, various rumbles and grumbles, the slant of his head, a nudge from his huge paw, a thrust of his great, cold nose or a succession of heartrending sighs to get his meaning across.

> Jean Little, *Stars Come Out Within* (1990)

10 Though he had very little Latin beyond "Cave canem," he had, as a young dog, devoured Shakespeare (in a tasty leather binding).

> Dodie Smith, *One Hundred and One Dalmatians* (1956)

11 I sometimes look into the face of my dog Stan and see wistful sadness and existential angst, when all he is actually doing is slowly scanning the ceiling for flies.

> Merrill Markoe, *What the Dogs Have Taught Me* (1992)

12 The only food he has ever stolen has been down on a coffee table. He claims that he genuinely believed it to be a table meant for dogs.

> Jean Little, *Stars Come Out Within* (1990)

13 Many dogs can understand almost every word humans say, while humans seldom learn to recognize more than half a dozen barks, if that. And barks are only a small part of the dog language. A wagging tail can mean so many things. Humans know that it means a dog is pleased, but not what a dog is saying about his pleasedness. (Really, it is very clever of humans to understand a wagging tail at all, as they have no tails of their own.)

> Dodie Smith, *One Hundred and One Dalmatians* (1956)

14 I am simply delighted that you have a Springer spaniel. That is the perfect final touch to our friendship. Do you know there is always a barrier between me and any man or woman who does not like dogs.

> Ellen Glasgow, *Letters of Ellen Glasgow* (1958)

15 You should see my corgis at sunset in the snow. It's their finest hour. About five o'clock they glow like copper. Then they come in and lie in front of the fire like a string of sausages.

> Tasha Tudor, with Richard Brown, *The Private World of Tasha Tudor* (1992)

16 There is no such thing as a difficult dog, only an inexperienced owner.

> Barbara Woodhouse, *No Bad Dogs* (1978)

17 A dog needs God. It lives by your glances, your wishes. It even shares your humor. This happens about the fifth year. If it doesn't happen you are only keeping an animal.

> Enid Bagnold, *Enid Bagnold's Autobiography* (1969)

1 A real dog, beloved and therefore pampered by his mistress, is a lamentable spectacle. He suffers from fatty degeneration of his moral being.

Agnes Repplier, "The Idolatrous Dog," *Under Dispute* (1924)

2 Dog lovers are a good breed themselves.

Gladys Taber, *The Book of Stillmeadow* (1948)

See also Animal Rights, Animals, Cats and Dogs, Pets, Vivisection.

## ✥ DOLLS

3 To this crib I always took my doll. . . . It puzzles me now to remember with what absurd sincerity I doted on this little toy, half fancying it alive and capable of sensation. I could not sleep unless it was folded in my night-gown; and when it lay there safe and warm, I was comparatively happy, believing it to be happy likewise.

Charlotte Brontë, *Jane Eyre* (1847)

## ✥ DOMESTICITY

4 She had learnt the fundamental art of domestic happiness: that of creating appetites which she was able to satisfy.

Princess Marthe Bibesco, *Catherine-Paris* (1928)

5 I feel domesticity just slipping off me. . . . Either one can let it go or one can intensify it. The people who intensify it seem to get quite a lot of interest out of that, too, and are as preoccupied as pirates.

Sylvia Townsend Warner (1942), in William Maxwell, ed., *Letters: Sylvia Townsend Warner* (1982)

6 I have led a free, wandering life for so long now that I should find myself quite incapable of settling down. . . . Women like myself can neither bring happiness into a domestic life, nor (even under the most desirable circumstances), find it there.

Margaret Fountaine (1904), in W.F. Cater, ed., *Love Among the Butterflies* (1980)

7 Domesticity is essentially drama, for drama is conflict, and the home compels conflict by its con-

centration of active personalities in a small area. The real objection to domesticity is that it is too exciting.

Rebecca West (1912), in Jane Marcus, ed., *The Young Rebecca* (1982)

8 Fang, my husband, says the only thing domestic about me is that I was born in this country.

Phyllis Diller, *Phyllis Diller's Housekeeping Hints* (1966)

See also Housewife, Housework.

## ✥ DOUBT

9 To Death I yield, but not to Doubt, who slays before!

Edith M. Thomas, "Doubt," *A Winter Swallow* (1896)

10 Faith and doubt both are needed—not as antagonists but working side by side—to take us around the unknown curve.

Lillian Smith, *The Journey* (1954)

11 The believer who has never doubted will hardly convert a doubter.

Marie von Ebner-Eschenbach, *Aphorisms* (1893)

12 Doubt remains a luxury I won't do without.

Eleanor Clark, *Eyes, Etc.* (1977)

13 I think there is no suffering greater than what is caused by the doubts of those who want to believe.

Flannery O'Connor, in Sally Fitzgerald, ed., *The Habit of Being* (1979)

14 Doubts, like facts, are stubborn things.

L.E. Landon, *Romance and Reality* (1831)

15 Where so many hours have been spent in convincing myself that I am right, is there not some reason to fear I may be wrong?

Jane Austen, *Sense and Sensibility* (1811)

16 Four be the things I'd been better without: / Love, curiosity, freckles, and doubt.

Dorothy Parker, "Inventory," *Enough Rope* (1926)

17 Her doubts are her sop to conscience. Like the person who takes a third helping and says with shining eyes, "This is sheer greed!"

Gordon Daviot, *The Laughing Woman* (1934)

1 A doubt would suddenly dart out of her, like a mouse from its hole.

    Mary McCarthy, *The Groves of Academe* (1952)

See also Distrust, Faith, Indecision, Suspicion, Uncertainty.

## ❧ DRAMATICS

2 Valentine's tiresome sister has lost her job. And created over this as if she had lost her hair, her teeth, her legs, her good name, and her latchkey.

    Sylvia Townsend Warner (1961), in William Maxwell, ed., *Letters: Sylvia Townsend Warner* (1982)

3 To hear Alice [Keppel] talk about her escape from France, one would have thought that she had swum the Channel with her maid between her teeth.

    Mrs. Greville (1939), in Jilly Cooper and Tom Hartman, *Violets and Vinegar* (1980)

4 In politics, arts / no issue's dramatic / nor will "play" till its heart's / simplified to fanatic.

    Mona Van Duyn, "Minimalist Sonnet Translations," *Firefall* (1993)

See also Exaggeration.

## ❧ DREAMS

5 Last night I dreamt I went to Manderley again.

    Daphne du Maurier, *Rebecca* (1938)

6 Hold fast—hold fast your dreams!

    Louise Driscoll, "Hold Fast Your Dreams," in Hazel Felleman, ed., *The Best Loved Poems of the American People* (1936)

7 At the armed borders of sleep / my dreams stand waving.

    Linda Pastan, "At the Armed Borders of Sleep," *Aspects of Eve* (1975)

8 in the middle of the night / people tell their dreams / and it is important, even / though there is never much / of an audience.

    Michelene Wandor, untitled, *Gardens of Eden* (1990)

9 Dreams are the subtle Dower / That make us rich an Hour — / Then fling us poor / Out of the purple Door.

    Emily Dickinson (1876), in Mabel Loomis Todd and Millicent Todd Bingham, eds., *Bolts of Melody* (1945)

10 I've dreamt in my life dreams that have stayed with me ever after, and changed my ideas: they've gone through and through me, like wine through water, and altered the color of my mind.

    Emily Brontë, *Wuthering Heights* (1847)

11 Dreams are . . . illustrations from the book your soul is writing about you.

    Marsha Norman, *The Fortune Teller* (1987)

12 Dreaming is the well-mannered people's way of committing suicide.

    Isak Dinesen, "The Dreamers," *Seven Gothic Tales* (1934)

13 Dreams the sources of action, the meeting and the end, / a resting-place among the flight of things.

    Muriel Rukeyser, "Easter Eve 1945," *The Green Wave* (1948)

14 Dreams are . . . an expansion of life, an enlightenment, and a discipline. I thank God for my dream life; my daily life would be far poorer, if it wanted the second sight of dreams.

    Amelia E. Barr, *All the Days of My Life* (1913)

15 our dreams draw blood from old sores.

    Ntozake Shange, *spell # 7: geechee jibara quik magic trance manual for technologically stressed third world people* (1981)

16 During the day, our souls gather their . . . impressions of us, how our lives feel. . . . Our spirits collect these impressions, keep them together, like wisps of smoke in a bag. Then, when we're asleep, our brains open up these bags of smoke . . . and take a look.

    Marsha Norman, *The Fortune Teller* (1987)

17 People's dreams are made out of what they do all day. The same way a dog that runs after rabbits will dream of rabbits. It's what you do that makes your soul, not the other way around.

    Barbara Kingsolver, *Animal Dreams* (1990)

18 When you dream, you dialogue with aspects of yourself that normally are not with you in the day-

time and you discover that you know a great deal more than you thought you did.

Toni Cade Bambara, in Roseann P. Bell, Bettye J. Parker, and Beverly Guy-Sheftall, eds., *Sturdy Black Bridges* (1979)

1 Dreams are only the image of outward things shown on an inward mirror. But the mirror is the soul's enclosing darkness.

Maude Meagher, *Fantastic Traveler* (1931)

2 Dreams are the only / afterlife we know; / the place where the children / we were / rock in the arms of the children / we have become.

Linda Pastan, "Dreams," *PM/AM* (1982)

3 Hopes are what your waking mind can imagine. Like prayers. Like bridges you can cross to a better place. And however wild these hopes may be, they are still basically thinkable things. But dreams . . . dreams are the unthinkable, the unsayable.

Marsha Norman, *The Fortune Teller* (1987)

4 Dreams pass into the reality of action. From the action stems the dream again; and this interdependence produces the highest form of living.

Anaïs Nin (1946), *The Diary of Anaïs Nin*, vol. 4 (1971)

5 Dreams grow holy, put in action.

Adelaide Anne Procter, "Philip and Mildred," *Legends and Lyrics* (1858)

6 She . . . marveled at the strangeness and mystery of dreams, in which the dreamer is at the same time both inventor and surprised spectator.

Susan Ertz, *The Story of Julian* (1931)

7 You know that there's a whole underground system that you call "dreams," having nothing better to call them, and that this system is not like roads or tunnels but more like a live body network, all coiling and stretching, unpredictable but finally familiar—where you are now, where you've always been.

Alice Munro, *Friend of My Youth* (1990)

8 Only the dreamer shall understand realities, though in truth his dreaming must be not out of proportion to his waking.

Margaret Fuller, *Summer on the Lakes* (1844)

9 I was not looking for my dreams to interpret my life, but rather for my life to interpret my dreams.

Susan Sontag, *The Benefactor* (1963)

10 There are some wiser in their sleeping than in their waking.

Ralph Iron, *The Story of an African Farm* (1883)

11 In forming a bridge between body and mind, dreams may be used as a springboard from which man can leap to new realms of experience lying outside his normal state of consciousness and enlarge his vision not only of himself, but also of the universe in which he lives.

Ann Faraday, *Dream Power* (1972)

12 People need dreams, there's as much nourishment in 'em as food.

Dorothy Gilman, *Caravan* (1992)

13 Like all people who have nothing, I lived on dreams.

Anzia Yezierska, "The Miracle," *Hungry Hearts* (1920)

14 When I dream / I am always ageless.

Elizabeth Coatsworth, *Personal Geography* (1976)

15 Dreams are, by definition, cursed with short life-spans.

Candice Bergen, *Knock Wood* (1984)

16 Dreams can be relentless tyrants.

Morgan Llywelyn, *Bard* (1984)

17 Saddle your dreams afore you ride 'em.

Mary Webb, *Precious Bane* (1924)

18 Our dreams are never realized and as soon as we see them betrayed we realize that the intensest joys of our life have nothing to do with reality. No sooner do we see them betrayed than we are consumed with regret for the time when they glowed within us. And in this succession of hopes and regrets our life slips by.

Natalia Ginzburg, *The Little Virtues* (1962)

19 For most of us, dreams come true only after they do not matter. Only in childhood do we ever have the chance of making dreams come true when they mean everything.

Lois Wyse, *Far From Innocence* (1979)

20 It's a risky thing to talk about one's most secret dreams a bit too early.

Tove Jansson, *Tales From Moominvalley* (1963)

21 I dream, therefore I become.

Cheryl Grossman, button (1989)

See also Daydreams, Fantasy, Visions.

## ♠ DRESS

1 Their dress is very independent of fashion; as they observe, "What does it signify how we dress here at Cranford, where everybody knows us?" And if they go from home, their reason is equally cogent: "What does it signify how we dress here, where nobody knows us?"
Elizabeth Gaskell, *Cranford* (1853)

2 If you can dress for a different party (i.e., wear black tie to a cocktail party, or tennis clothes for lunch), so much the better. You give the impression of being much in demand.
Lisa Birnbach, *The Official Preppy Handbook* (1980)

3 Even if they've never been near a duck blind or gone beagling, Preppies are dressed for it.
Lisa Birnbach, *The Official Preppy Handbook* (1980)

4 If you can't dress for success, at least dress for trying.
Lynne Alpern and Esther Blumenfeld, *Oh, Lord, I Sound Just Like Mama* (1986)

See also Appearance, Clothes, Fashion.

## ♠ DRINKING

5 I drank at every vine. / The last was like the first. / I came upon no wine / So wonderful as thirst.
Edna St. Vincent Millay, "Feast," *The Harp-Weaver* (1923)

6 Nobody ever stops drinking until the cost of drinking becomes higher than the cost of not drinking.
Isabelle Holland, *The Long Search* (1990)

7 Even though a number of people have tried, no one has yet found a way to drink for a living.
Jean Kerr, *Poor Richard* (1965)

8 One reason I don't drink is that I want to know when I am having a good time.
Nancy Astor, in *Reader's Digest* (1960)

9 Almost all [Americans] are at odds with themselves; drink offers a remedy for this inner malady of which boredom is the most usual sign: as drinking is accepted by society, it does not appear as a sign of their inability to adapt themselves; it is rather the adapted form of inadaptability.
Simone de Beauvoir, *America Day by Day* (1948)

10 Drinking isn't necessarily the same as wanting to die. But you can't drink without thinking you're killing yourself.
Marguerite Duras, *Practicalities* (1987)

11 What stops you killing yourself when you're intoxicated out of your mind is the thought that once you're dead you won't be able to drink any more.
Marguerite Duras, *Practicalities* (1987)

12 I acquired that drinker's face before I drank. Drink only confirmed it. The space for it existed in me.
Marguerite Duras, *The Lover* (1984)

13 He'd got a thirst on him all wool and a yard wide.
Anthony Gilbert, *The Fingerprint* (1964)

14 Ain't nobody as drinks but wants a heap o' t'others to keep 'em company. 'Pears like it's lonesome kind of work.
Mary Nelson Carter, *North Carolina Sketches* (1900)

15 When I spoke of having *a* drink, it was a euphemism for having a whole flock of them.
Margaret Halsey, *No Laughing Matter* (1977)

16 One more drink and I'd have been under the host.
Dorothy Parker (1930), in Howard Teichmann, *George S. Kaufman* (1972)

17 When she reached the bar, she ordered the equivalent of a small safe to be dropped on her head.
Carrie Fisher, *Surrender the Pink* (1990)

18 I was sitting before my third or fourth Jellybean— which is anisette, grain alcohol, a lit match, and a small, wet explosion in the brain.
Louise Erdrich, "Scales," in Rayna Green, ed., *That's What She Said* (1984)

19 You can't drown your troubles . . . because troubles can swim.
Margaret Millar, *Ask for Me Tomorrow* (1976)

20 I drank, because I wanted to drown my sorrows, but now the damned things have learned to swim.
Frida Kahlo (1938), in Hayden Herrera, *Frida* (1983)

1 The sharp odor of gin hit me. Charlie was drowning his sorrows, and they apparently were dying hard.

    Marcia Muller, *Edwin of the Iron Shoes* (1977)

2 The wages of Gin is Debt.

    Ethel Watts Mumford, in Oliver Herford, Ethel Watts Mumford, and Addison Mizner, *The Complete Cynic* (1902)

3 Now a double scotch is about the size of a small scotch before the war, and a single scotch is nothing more than a dirty glass.

    Lora Dundee, in *The Observer* (1960)

4 Absinthe makes the heart grow fonder.

    Ethel Watts Mumford, in Oliver Herford, Ethel Watts Mumford, and Addison Mizner, *The Complete Cynic* (1902)

5 No matter what ailed you, a small glass of schnapps would take care of it at once. This particular remedy was so good my grandfather would frequently take the cure even before there was anything wrong with him.

    Molly Picon, *So Laugh a Little* (1962)

6 Do not allow your children to mix drinks. It is unseemly and they use too much vermouth.

    Fran Lebowitz, *Social Studies* (1977)

7 Why is it that one has to drink? / Why is it that one's hosts should think / It queer these days if guests prefer / A respite? Doesn't it occur / To anyone that no offense / Is meant by harmless abstinence?

    Margaret Fishback, "Slow Down Rounding Curve," *I Take It Back* (1935)

See also Alcohol, Alcoholism, Temperance, Wine.

## ❦ DRIVERS

8 For a driver to be driven by somebody else is an ordeal, for there are only three types of drivers: the too fast, the timid and oneself.

    Virginia Graham, *Say Please* (1949)

9 Everybody I know grows claws and fur behind the wheel. . . . It is only here, in your very own castle of rubber and steel, that you can for a short but blissful time throw off the cloak of civilization and be the raging Hun you always wanted to be.

    Adair Lara, *Welcome to Earth, Mom* (1992)

10 Natives who beat drums to drive off evil spirits are objects of scorn to smart Americans who blow horns to break up traffic jams.

    Mary Ellen Kelly, in Michèle Brown and Ann O'Connor, *Woman Talk*, vol. 1 (1984)

See also Cars, Highways.

## ❦ DRUG ABUSE

11 Of all the tyrannies which have usurped power over humanity, few have been able to enslave the mind and body as imperiously as drug addiction.

    Freda Adler, *Sisters in Crime* (1975)

12 The only merciful thing about drug abuse is the speed with which it devastates you. Alcoholics can take decades to destroy themselves and everyone they touch. The drug addict can accomplish this in a year or two. Of course, suicide is even more efficient.

    Rita Mae Brown, *Starting From Scratch* (1988)

13 Druggies don't keep their looks any longer than they keep their promises.

    Liza Cody, "Lucky Dip," in Sara Paretsky, ed., *A Woman's Eye* (1991)

14 Cocaine habit-forming? Of course not. I ought to know. I've been using it for years.

    Tallulah Bankhead, *Tallulah* (1952)

15 Just say no.

    Nancy Reagan, slogan (1983)

See also Addiction, Codependence, Drugs.

## ❦ DRUGS

16 One pill makes you larger / and one pill makes you small / And the ones that mother gives you / don't do anything at all. / Go ask Alice / when she's ten feet tall.

    Grace Slick, "White Rabbit" (1967)

17 The era of psychopharmacology has dawned and with it the offer of the "chemical vacation," not however without the hazards of the road.

    Judith Groch, *The Right to Create* (1969)

1 Drugs are a carnival in hell.

Edith Piaf, in Simone Berteaut, *Piaf* (1969)

2 When you're doing drugs, today is yesterday, tomorrow never comes.

Mary Daheim, *The Alpine Decoy* (1994)

3 I was into pain reduction and mind expansion, but what I've ended up with is pain expansion and mind reduction.

Carrie Fisher, *Postcards From the Edge* (1987)

See also Addiction, Codependence, Drug Abuse, Medicine.

## 🙵 DUALISM

4 Spirit is the real and eternal; matter is the unreal and temporal.

Mary Baker Eddy, *Science and Health* (1875)

5 You are an indivisible entity of matter and consciousness. Renounce your consciousness and you become a brute. Renounce your body and you become a fake. Renounce the material world and you surrender it to evil.

Ayn Rand, *Atlas Shrugged* (1957)

## 🙵 DULLNESS

6 Dullness is a kind of luxury.

Bharati Mukherjee, *Jasmine* (1989)

7 Let dullness have its due: and remember that if life and conversation are happily compared to a bowl of punch, there must be more water in it than spirit, acid, or sugar.

Hester Lynch Piozzi (1817), in A. Hayward, ed., *Autobiography, Letters, and Literary Remains of Mrs. Piozzi (Thrale)*, vol. 2 (1861)

8 You could, without arousing a storm of protest, have described us as rather a dull couple.

Margaret Halsey, *No Laughing Matter* (1977)

9 They lived a comfortable humdrum life, conscious of no higher existence. Doubtless they were quite happy—and so are oysters!

Dinah Maria Mulock Craik, *The Ogilvies* (1898)

10 In all private quarrels the duller nature is triumphant by reason of dullness.

George Eliot, *Felix Holt, the Radical* (1866)

See also Boredom.

## 🙵 DUTY

11 The boy stood on the burning deck / Whence all but he had fled.

Felicia Hemans, "Casabianca," *The Poetical Works of Felicia Dorothea Hemans* (1914)

12 I slept and dreamed that life was Beauty,— / I woke, and found that life was Duty.

Ellen H. Hooper, untitled poem (1840), *A Collection of Poems* (1848)

13 We need to restore the full meaning of that old word, duty. It is the other side of rights.

Pearl S. Buck, *To My Daughters, With Love* (1967)

14 Duties are what make life most worth the living. Lacking them, you are not necessary to anyone.

Marlene Dietrich, in Steven Bach, *Marlene Dietrich* (1992)

15 Do your duty until it becomes your joy.

Marie von Ebner-Eschenbach, *Aphorisms* (1893)

16 There is nothing in the universe that I fear, but that I shall not know all my duty or fail to do it.

Mary Lyon (1849), in Constance Jones, ed., *Great Thoughts of Great Americans* (1951)

17 The one predominant duty is to find one's work and do it.

Charlotte Perkins Gilman, *The Living of Charlotte Perkins Gilman* (1935)

18 Duty is ours and events are God's.

Angelina Grimké, *Appeal to the Christian Women of the South* (1836)

19 We cannot hope to scale great moral heights by ignoring petty obligations.

Agnes Repplier, *Americans and Others* (1912)

20 When two duties jostle each other, one of 'em isn't a duty.

Margaret Deland, *The Promises of Alice* (1919)

1 One of the most destructive anti-concepts in the history of moral philosophy is the term "duty."

  Ayn Rand, *Philosophy: Who Needs It?* (1982)

2 The worst of doing one's duty was that it apparently unfitted one for doing anything else.

  Edith Wharton, *The Age of Innocence* (1920)

3 You look as if you had lived on duty and it hadn't agreed with you.

  Ellen Glasgow, *The Romantic Comedians* (1926)

4 Oh! Duty is an icy shadow.

  Augusta J. Evans, *Beulah* (1859)

See also "Ought," Responsibility.

## § DYING

5 My body, eh? Friend Death, how now? / Why all this tedious pomp of writ? / Thou has reclaimed it sure and slow / For half a century, bit by bit.

  Helen Hunt Jackson, "Habeas Corpus" (1885), five days before her death, in Edmund Clarence Stedman, ed., *An American Anthology 1787–1900* (1900)

6 But I'm gettin' ready to go. How am I doin' it? I'm layin' aside every weight and a sin that does so easily beset me and I'm gettin' light for the flight.

  Willie Mae Ford Smith, in Brian Lanker, *I Dream a World* (1989)

7 Dying / Is an art, like everything else. / I do it exceptionally well.

  Sylvia Plath, "Lady Lazarus," *Ariel* (1965)

8 'Tis dying — I am doing — but / I'm not afraid to know.

  Emily Dickinson (1863), in Mabel Loomis Todd and T.W. Higginson, eds., *Poems by Emily Dickinson* (1890)

9 Death deceives relations often, and doctors sometimes, but the patient—never.

  Phyllis Bottome, "The Wonder-Child," *Strange Fruit* (1928)

10 The Heart asks Pleasure — first — / And then — Excuse from Pain— / And then — those little Anodynes / That deaden suffering — / And then — to go to sleep — / And then — if it should be / The will of its Inquisitor / The privilege to die.

  Emily Dickinson (1862), in Mabel Loomis Todd and T.W. Higginson, eds., *Poems by Emily Dickinson* (1890)

11 When one gets near the grave . . . there is a little light from beyond, and many things are seen not seen before.

  Amelia E. Barr, *Jan Vedder's Wife* (1885)

12 I fall and burst beneath the sacred human tree. / Release my seed and let me fall.

  Meridel Le Sueur, title poem, *Rites of Ancient Ripening* (1975)

13 My breath hovers over the river of God— / Softly I set my foot / On the path to my long home.

  Else Lasker-Schüler, "I Know That I Must Die Soon," in Nathan and Marynn Ausubel, eds., *A Treasury of Jewish Poetry* (1957)

14 One sweetly solemn thought / Comes to me o'er and o'er; / I am nearer home to-day / Than I ever have been before.

  Phoebe Cary, "Nearer Home," *Poems of Faith, Hope, and Love* (1874)

15 I think that the dying pray at the last not "please," but "thank you," as a guest thanks his host at the door. Falling from airplanes the people are crying thank you, thank you, all down the air; and the cold carriages draw up for them on the rocks.

  Annie Dillard, *Pilgrim at Tinker Creek* (1974)

16 Glad was the living—blessed be the dying. / Let the leaves fall.

  Harriet Monroe, "A Farewell," *You and I* (1914)

17 Such hard work it is to die? Such hard work?

  Tillie Olsen, title story, *Tell Me a Riddle* (1956)

18 The leaves move in the garden, the sky is pale, and I catch myself weeping. It is hard—it is hard to make a good death.

  Katherine Mansfield (1920), *Journal of Katherine Mansfield* (1927)

19 I'm not afraid of life and I'm not afraid of death: Dying's the bore.

  Katherine Anne Porter, in *The New York Times* (1970)

20 I'm afraid of dying, she admitted, but not of death.

  Faith Baldwin, *One More Time* (1972)

21 Dying doesn't cause suffering. Resistance to dying does.

  Terry Tempest Williams, *Refuge* (1991)

22 The dying must often feel this way—steaming along just fine, while on ahead someone has torn up the rails.

  Annie Dillard, *The Living* (1992)

1 You will wake up and search, and you will find no one. You will remember that you once could remember, but you will not be afraid. The words will be blotted out, but the rhythm will persist. You will remember that death is one of the adventures that were promised to you, and that immensity bears you and enfolds you as softly as the down of a bird's nest.

Julia Brewster, "Via Lucis," in Ethel Smyth, *What Happened Next* (1940)

2 In all dying our ages are the same.

Maureen Duffy, "Der Rosenkavalier," *The Venus Touch* (1971)

3 One had to listen very intently to catch the words that she labored to breathe out; words whose mystery made them as disturbing as those of an oracle. Her memories, her desires, her anxieties were floating somewhere outside time, turned into unreal and poignant dreams by her childlike voice and the imminence of death.

Simone de Beauvoir, *A Very Easy Death* (1966)

4 She had supposed that on her deathbed, she would have something final to tell her children when they gathered round. But nothing was final. She didn't have anything to tell them. She felt a kind of shyness; she felt inadequate.

Anne Tyler, *Dinner at the Homesick Restaurant* (1982)

5 I still grieve for the words unsaid. Something terrible happens when we stop the mouths of the dying before they are dead. A silence grows up between us then, profounder than the grave. If we force the dying to go speechless, the stone dropped into the well will fall forever before the answering splash is heard.

Faye Moskowitz, *A Leak in the Heart* (1985)

6 That is what they call being reconciled to die. They call it reconciled when pain has strummed a symphony of suffering back and forth across you, up and down, round and round you until each little fiber is worn tissue-thin with aching. And when you are lying beaten, and buffeted, battered and broken—pain goes out, joins hands with Death and comes back to dance, dance, dance, stamp, stamp, stamp down on you until you give up.

Marita Bonner, "A Possible Triad on Black Notes" (1933), *Frye Street and Environs* (1987)

7 Feelings are dulled these days, as though life is already going, slowly leaking out and ebbing away. Maybe it will make my dying that much easier . . .

when I come to die, there will be little left to die. I'm already a ghost with set wings, stalking tombstone territory.

Keri Hulme, *The Bone People* (1983)

8 The night is darkening around me.

Emily Brontë (1837), in Clement Shorter, ed., *The Complete Poems of Emily Brontë* (1910)

9 Dying was apparently a weaning process; all the attachments to familiar people and objects had to be undone.

Lisa Alther, *Kinflicks* (1975)

10 His grasp on life fanned shallow as poplar roots.

Yvette Nelson, *We'll Come When It Rains* (1982)

11 As the day grew brighter, he grew dimmer, and more of his friends gathered around his bed. They took up their oars and rowed with him as far as they could.

Carrie Fisher, *Delusions of Grandma* (1994)

12 He moved, she noticed, frail as trailing smoke on soft autumn days, and she feared she would soon lose him, like smoke rising through the trees, not as a ripping flash of summer lightning, but softly one evening.

Yvette Nelson, *We'll Come When It Rains* (1982)

13 In life, periods of solitude were blessings. Dying alone was a bitter curse.

Faye Kellerman, *The Quality of Mercy* (1989)

14 Dying nowadays is more gruesome in many ways, namely, more lonely, mechanical, and dehumanized; at times it is even difficult to determine technically when the time of death has occurred.

Elisabeth Kübler-Ross, *On Death and Dying* (1969)

15 He had been up until three with an old woman who thought she was sick, and he had been routed out of bed again at five because she told her family that she was going to die. William King was not given to sarcasm, but he longed to say to the waiting relatives, "There is no hope!—she'll live."

Margaret Deland, *Dr. Lavendar's People* (1903)

16 We look on those approaching the banks of a river all must cross, with ten times the interest they excited when dancing in the meadow.

Hester Lynch Piozzi (1817), in A. Hayward, ed., *Autobiography, Letters, and Literary Remains of Mrs. Piozzi (Thrale)*, vol. 2 (1861)

1 She'd been preoccupied with death for several years now; but one aspect had never before crossed her mind: dying, you don't get to see how it all turns out.

    Anne Tyler, *Dinner at the Homesick Restaurant* (1982)

2 Her cheeks flushed at the indecency of being seen, dying and then dead. If only she could get it over and lay herself out decent before anyone came in to see and meddle.

    Dorothy M. Richardson, "Death," in *Weekly Westminster* (1924)

3 Through the pitchy darkness that was coming she saw the glimmer of another, milder sun, she smelt the scent of the herbs in the garden at the world's end.

    Sigrid Undset, *Kristin Lavransdatter: The Mistress of Husaby* (1921)

See also Death, Grief, Last Words, Mourning.

# E

## ♪ EARS

1 Thank goodness he hasn't got ears like his father.

> Diana, Princess of Wales, after the birth of her son William (1982), in Andrew Morton, *Diana* (1992)

## ♪ EARTH

2 We have a beautiful / mother / Her green lap / immense / Her brown embrace / eternal / Her blue body / everything / we know.

> Alice Walker, "We Have a Beautiful Mother," *Her Blue Body Everything We Know* (1991)

3 Tread softly! all the earth is holy ground.

> Christina Rossetti, "Later Life," *A Pageant* (1881)

4 How shall I / celebrate the planet / that, even now, carries me / in its fruited womb?

> Diane Ackerman, *The Planets* (1976)

5 The world turns softly / Not to spill its lakes and rivers.

> Hilda Conkling, "Water," *Poems by a Little Girl* (1920)

6 If dead things love, if earth and water distinguish friends from enemies, I should like to possess their love. I should like the green earth not to feel my step as a heavy burden. I should like her to forgive that she for my sake is wounded by plow and harrow, and willingly to open for my dead body.

> Selma Lagerlöf, *The Story of Gösta Berling* (1891)

7 You must bind up any wounds you give the earth and you must feed her to replace what you take from her. Every gift she gives, every tree, every stalk of grain, costs her. Only if you repay your debts will she continue to provide.

> Morgan Llywelyn, *Bard* (1984)

8 We are earth of this earth, and we are bone of its bone. / This is a prayer I sing, for we have forgotten this and so / The earth is perishing.

> Barbara Deming, "Spirit of Love" (1973), *We Are All Part of One Another* (1984)

9 We are of the earth, made of the same stuff; there is no other, no division between us and "lower" or "higher" forms of being.

> Estella Lauder, *Women As Mythmakers* (1984)

10 Unless the gentle inherit the earth, / There will be no earth.

> May Sarton, "New Year Poem," *The Silence Now* (1988)

11 This earth is my sister; I love her daily grace, her silent daring, and how loved I am, *how we admire this strength in each other, all that we have lost, all that we have suffered, all that we know: we are stunned by this beauty*, and I do not forget: what she is to me, what I am to her.

> Susan Griffin, *Woman and Nature* (1978)

12 Earth-songs come up from the ground through the plants; and in their flowering, and in the days before these days are come, they do tell the earth-songs to the wind. And the wind in her goings does whisper them to folks to print for other folks, so other folks do have knowing of earth's songs. When I grow up, I am going to write for children—and grownups that haven't grown up too much—all the earth-songs I now do hear.

> Opal Whiteley (1920), in Benjamin Hoff, ed., *The Singing Creek Where the Willows Grow* (1986)

13 Earth, old man of the planets, you suck at my foot / which wants to fly.

> Nelly Sachs, "Earth, Old Man of the Planets, You Suck at My Foot," *O the Chimneys* (1967)

See also Environment, Land, Nature, Stones, Trees.

## ✥ EASTER

1 It is Easter morning. / Children who are still / as gentle as milk / wake to its wonder.

    Caryll Houselander, "Soeur Marie Emilie," *The Flowering Tree* (1945)

2 Upon an Easter Morning, / So early in the day, / The bird raised up his whistle / To tune the night away.

    Eleanor Farjeon, "Upon an Easter Morning," *The Children's Bells* (1960)

## ✥ EASYGOING

3 Show me an "easy person," and I will show you a selfish one. Good-natured he may be; why not? since the disastrous consequences of his "easiness" are generally shouldered by other people.

    Fanny Fern, *Ginger-Snaps* (1870)

See also Complacency.

## ✥ EATING

4 Eating is never so simple as hunger.

    Erica Jong, "The Catch," *Becoming Light* (1991)

5 The interest in good meals is universal.

    Louise M. Neuschutz, *A Job for Every Woman* (1948)

6 When we eat / we are like / everyone else.

    Patricia Hampl, "Asceticism," *Woman Before an Aquarium* (1978)

7 Eating without conversation is only stoking.

    Marcelene Cox, in *Ladies' Home Journal* (1943)

8 I would, if I could, always feed to music. The singularly graceless action of thus filling one's body with roots and dead animals and powdered grain is given some significance then.

    Winifred Holtby (1924), in Alice Holtby and Jean McWilliam, eds., *Letters to a Friend* (1937)

9 I feel now that gastronomical perfection can be reached in these combinations: one person dining alone, usually upon a couch or a hill side; two people, of no matter what sex or age, dining in a good restaurant; six people, of no matter what sex or age, dining in a good home.

    M.F.K. Fisher, "From A to Z," *An Alphabet for Gourmets* (1949)

10 I'm inclined to think that eating is a private thing and should be done alone, like other bodily functions.

    Sylvia Ashton-Warner (1942), *Myself* (1967)

11 The family ate hugely, they were like a school of voracious fish feeding under the sea of chatter.

    Marjorie Kinnan Rawlings, *The Sojourner* (1953)

12 We arrive eager, we stuff ourselves and we go away depressed and disappointed and probably feeling a bit queasy into the bargain. It's an image of the *déçu* in human existence. A greedy start and a stupefied finish. Waiters, who are constantly observing this cycle, must be the most disillusioned of men.

    Iris Murdoch, *A Fairly Honorable Defeat* (1970)

13 That's something I've noticed about food: whenever there's a crisis if you can get people to eating normally things get better.

    Madeleine L'Engle, *The Moon by Night* (1963)

14 The business of eating, which in common with a crisis or danger brings heterogeneous incompatibles comfortably together, was over and now suddenly we were all fallen apart.

    Nadine Gordimer, *The Lying Days* (1953)

15 We use eating as a medium for social relationships: satisfaction of the most individual of needs becomes a means of creating community.

    Margaret Visser, *The Rituals of Dinner* (1991)

16 There are many ways of eating, for some eating is living for some eating is dying, for some thinking about ways of eating gives to them the feeling that they have it in them to be alive and to be going on living, to some to think about eating makes them know that death is always waiting that dying is in them.

    Gertrude Stein, *The Making of Americans* (1925)

17 Intemperance in eating is one of the most fruitful of all causes of disease and death.

    Catharine E. Beecher and Harriet Beecher Stowe, *American Woman's Home* (1869)

1 There is small danger of being starved in our land of plenty; but the danger of being stuffed is imminent.

Mrs. Sarah J. Hale, *Traits of American Life* (1835)

2 Many tender, delicate mothers, seem to think that to make their children *eat*, is all that is requisite to make them *great*.

Mrs. Sarah J. Hale, *Traits of American Life* (1835)

3 She could still taste the plump fine oysters from Zeeland that he had ordered for her last meal in the world, the dry sparkle of the vintage Rudesheimer which had cost him the fees of at least five visits to patients, and the ice cream richly sauced with crushed glazed chestnuts which she loved.

Kathryn Hulme, *The Nun's Story* (1956)

4 Parson Legg crunched away at the venison and corn bread,—doing this with more gusto than was pleasant for either eye or ear.

Mary Devereux, *From Kingdom to Colony* (1900)

5 He was the delight of fine cooks, who took his absent-minded capacity for appreciation.

Marjorie Kinnan Rawlings, *The Sojourner* (1953)

6 They sat at a corner table in the little restaurant, eating with gusto and noise after the manner of simple-hearted people who like their neighbors to see and know their pleasures.

Jean Rhys, *The Left Bank* (1927)

7 The waitress intoned the specialties of the day. "Chicken Cordon Bleu, Sole Amandine, Veal Marsala." She might have been a train conductor in a foreign country, calling out the strange names of the stations.

Hilma Wolitzer, *Hearts* (1980)

8 My stomach is of many minds; / It believes everything it eats.

Kathleen Norris, "Stomach," *Falling Off* (1971)

See also Appetite, Cooking, Dieting, Dinner, Etiquette, Food, Gastronomy, Nutrition, Vegetarianism, Weight.

## ❦ ECCENTRICITY

9 I am not an eccentric. It's just that I am more alive than most people. I am an unpopular electric eel in a pool of catfish.

Edith Sitwell, in *Life* (1963)

10 It is to the eccentrics that the world owes most of its knowledge.

Rose Macaulay (1955), in Constance Babington-Smith, ed., *Last Letters to a Friend* (1962)

11 It made me feel good. To know the nuts still have a chance to take over the world.

Judith Guest, *Ordinary People* (1976)

See also Human Differences, Individuality, Uniqueness.

## ❦ ECONOMICS

12 A sound economy is a sound understanding brought into action: it is calculation realized; it is the doctrine of proportion reduced to practice; it is foreseeing consequences, and guarding against them; it is expecting contingencies and being prepared for them.

Hannah More, "The Practical Use of Female Knowledge," *Strictures on the Modern System of Female Education* (1799)

13 Economics is not a science, in the sense that a policy can be repeatedly applied under similar conditions and will repeatedly produce similar results.

Millicent Fenwick, *Speaking Up* (1982)

14 I learned that economics was not an exact science and that the most erudite men would analyze the economic ills of the world and derive a totally different conclusion.

Edith Summerskill, *A Woman's World* (1967)

15 Economics limps along with one foot in untested hypotheses and the other in untestable slogans.

Joan Robinson, "Metaphysics, Morals and Science," *Economic Philosophy* (1962)

16 As a pure subject it [economics] is too difficult to be a rewarding object of study; the beauty of mathematics and the satisfaction of discoveries in the natural sciences are denied to the practitioners of this scrappy, uncertain, ill-disciplined subject.

Joan Robinson, "What Are the Rules of the Game?" *Economic Philosophy* (1962)

17 Observation of realities has never, to put it mildly, been one of the strengths of economic development theory.

Jane Jacobs, *Cities and the Wealth of Nations* (1984)

1 [Economists' advice] is something like patent medicine—people know it is largely manufactured by quacks and that a good percentage of the time it won't work, but they continue to buy the brand whose flavor they like.

    Barbara Bergmann (1974), in Michael Jackman, *The Macmillan Book of Business and Economic Quotations* (1984)

2 Most economists, like doctors, are reluctant to make predictions, and those who make them are seldom accurate. The economy, like the human body, is a highly complex system whose workings are not thoroughly understood.

    Alice M. Rivlin, *Reviving the American Dream* (1992)

3 Normality is a fiction of economic textbooks.

    Joan Robinson, title essay, in Rendigs Fels, ed., *The Second Crisis of Economic Theory* (1972)

4 In the field of economics we maintain to this day some of the most primitive ideas, some of the most radically false ideas, some of the most absurd ideas a brain can hold. . . . This gives no uneasiness to the average brain. That long-suffering organ has been trained for more thousands of years than history can uncover to hold in unquestioning patience great blocks of irrelevant idiocy and large active lies.

    Charlotte Perkins Gilman, *Human Work* (1904)

5 Economic systems are not value-free columns of numbers based on rules of reason, but ways of expressing what varying societies believe is important.

    Gloria Steinem, *Moving Beyond Words* (1994)

6 The first essential for economists . . . is to . . . combat, not foster, the ideology which pretends that values which can be measured in terms of money are the only ones that ought to count.

    Joan Robinson, "What Are the Rules of the Game?" *Economic Philosophy* (1962)

7 Economics lie at the very root of practical morality.

    Josephine Butler (1870), in Ray Strachey, *"The Cause"* (1928)

8 Economics and ethics have little in common.

    Agnes Repplier, "Conservative's Consolations," *Points of Friction* (1920)

9 The principal sources of human misery may fairly be said to lie in the over-possession, under-possession, and the unwise use of economic goods.

    Georgia Harkness, *Conflicts in Religious Thought* (1929)

10 Economic growth may one day turn out to be a curse rather than a good, and under no conditions can it either lead into freedom or constitute a proof for its existence.

    Hannah Arendt, *On Revolution* (1963)

11 Economics has not yet had a Thales, an Archimedes, or a Lavoisier.

    Simone Weil (1937), *Selected Essays 1934-1943* (1962)

12 We think of the experiments of particle physicists and space explorers as being extraordinarily expensive, and so they are. But the costs are as nothing compared with the incomprehensibly huge resources that banks, industries, governments and international institutions . . . have poured into tests of macro-economic theory. Never has a science, or supposed science, been so generously indulged. And never have experiments left in their wakes more wreckage, unpleasant surprises, blasted hopes and confusion, to the point that the question seriously arises whether the wreckage is reparable.

    Jane Jacobs, *Cities and the Wealth of Nations* (1984)

13 Unless we do change our whole way of thought about work, I do not think we shall ever escape from the appalling squirrel-cage of economic confusion in which we have been madly turning for the last three centuries or so, the cage in which we landed ourselves by acquiescing in a social system based upon Envy and Avarice.

    Dorothy L. Sayers, "Why Work?" *Creed or Chaos?* (1949)

14 What a country calls its vital economic interests are not the things which enable its citizens to live, but the things which enable it to make war; petrol is much more likely than wheat to be a cause of international conflict.

    Simone Weil, "The Power of Words," *The Simone Weil Reader* (1977)

15 Only by transforming our own economy to one of peace can we make possible economic democracy in the Third World or our own country. The present economy generates wars to protect its profits and its short-term interests, while squandering the future. Unless we transform the economy, we cannot end war.

    Starhawk, *Truth or Dare* (1987)

16 If the present economic structure can change only by collapsing, then it had better collapse as soon as possible.

    Germaine Greer, *The Female Eunuch* (1971)

1 A society in which consumption has to be artificially stimulated in order to keep production going is a society founded on trash and waste.

Dorothy L. Sayers, "Why Work?" *Creed or Chaos?* (1949)

2 Where is the pricing system that offers the consumer a fair choice between air to breathe and motor cars to drive about in?

Joan Robinson, title essay, in Rendigs Fels, ed., *The Second Crisis of Economic Theory* (1972)

3 A depression is a situation of self-fulfilling pessimism.

Joan Robinson, "The Short Period," *Economic Heresies* (1970)

4 With the slow menace of a glacier, depression came on. No one had any measure of its progress; no one had any plan for stopping it. Everyone tried to get out of its way.

Frances Perkins, *People at Work* (1934)

5 Owning capital is not a productive activity.

Joan Robinson, *An Essay on Marxian Economics* (1942)

6 The other man's money is *capital*; getting it is *labor*.

Mary Pettibone Poole, *A Glass Eye at a Keyhole* (1938)

7 Capital is the result of saving, and not of spending. The spendthrift who wastes his substance in riotous living decreases the capital of the country, and therefore the excuse often made for extravagance, that it is good for trade, is based upon false notions respecting capital.

Millicent Garrett Fawcett, *Political Economy for Beginners* (1870)

8 Unequal distribution of income is an excessively uneconomic method of getting the necessary saving done.

Joan Robinson, *An Essay on Marxian Economics* (1942)

9 Innovating economies expand and develop. Economies that do not add new kinds of goods and services, but continue only to repeat old work, do not expand much nor do they, by definition, develop.

Jane Jacobs, *The Economy of Cities* (1969)

10 Contrary to economists' beliefs, the informal sectors of the world's economies, in total, are predominant, and the institutionalized, monetized sectors grow out of them and rest upon them, rather than the reverse.

Hazel Henderson, *The Politics of the Solar Age* (1981)

11 One of the main effects (I will not say purposes) of orthodox traditional economics was . . . a plan for explaining to the privileged class that their position was morally right and was necessary for the welfare of society.

Joan Robinson, "An Economist's Sermon," *Essays in the Theory of Employment* (1937)

12 The primary conflict, I think, is between people whose interests are with already well-established economic activities, and those whose interests are with the emergence of new economic activities.

Jane Jacobs, *The Economy of Cities* (1969)

13 A "mixed economy" is a society in the process of committing suicide.

Ayn Rand, in *The Los Angeles Times* (1962)

14 Until economic freedom is attained for everybody, there can be no real freedom for anybody.

Suzanne La Follette, "What Is to Be Done," *Concerning Women* (1926)

15 This used to be a government of checks and balances. Now it's all checks and no balances.

Gracie Allen, *How to Become President* (1940)

See also Business, Capitalism, Debts, Inflation, Money, Utility.

## ❧ ECSTASY

16 Ecstasy cannot be constant, or it would kill.

Eleanor Farjeon, *Portrait of a Family* (1936)

17 Ecstasies inspire and awaken the soul; they convince the mind absolutely of the existence of another form of living.

Anonymous mystic, in Sir Francis Younghusband, *Modern Mystics* (1935)

18 Ecstasy is what everyone craves—not love or sex, but a hot-blooded, soaring intensity, in which being alive is a joy and a thrill. That enravishment doesn't give meaning to life, and yet without it life seems meaningless.

Diane Ackerman, *A Natural History of Love* (1994)

See also Joy, Pleasure.

## ⑤ EDITORS

1 I dare say you will try to make me believe that Editors are human. Now I deny that, for I myself have, in past days, had evidence to the contrary.

Fanny Fern, *Caper Sauce* (1872)

2 I was born to be an editor. . . . I can't make things. I can only revise what has been made. And it is this eternal revising that has given me my nervous face.

Margaret Anderson, *My Thirty Years' War* (1930)

3 The copyeditor I drew was a brachycephalic, web-footed cretin who should have been in an institution learning how to make brooms.

Florence King, *Reflections in a Jaundiced Eye* (1989)

See also Journalism, Publishing.

## ⑤ EDUCATION

4 If there's a single message passed down from each generation of American parents to their children, it is a two-word line: Better Yourself. And if there's a temple of self-betterment in each town, it is the local school. We have worshiped there for some time.

Ellen Goodman, *At Large* (1981)

5 It made me gladsome to be getting some education, it being like a big window opening.

Mary Webb, *Precious Bane* (1924)

6 To be able to be caught up into the world of thought—that is to be educated.

Edith Hamilton, in Richard Thruelsen and John Kobler, eds., *Adventures of the Mind*, 1st series (1959)

7 Education, fundamentally, is the increase of the percentage of the conscious in relation to the unconscious.

Sylvia Ashton-Warner, *Teacher* (1963)

8 An educated man should know everything about something, and something about everything.

C.V. Wedgwood, speech (1963)

9 Our fundamental task as human beings is to seek out connections—to exercise our imaginations. It follows, then, that the basic task of education is the care and feeding of the imagination.

Katherine Paterson, *The Spying Heart* (1989)

10 Our belief in education is unbounded, our reverence for it is unfaltering, our loyalty to it is unshaken by reverses. Our passionate desire, not so much to acquire it as to bestow it, is the most animated of American traits.

Agnes Repplier, "The American Credo," *Times and Tendencies* (1931)

11 Education must have an end in view, for it is not an end in itself.

Sybil Marshall, *An Experiment in Education* (1963)

12 As soon as you start asking what education is *for*, what the use of it is, you're abandoning the basic assumption of any true culture, that education is worth while for its own sake.

Ann Bridge, *Singing Waters* (1946)

13 Education strays from reality when it divides its knowledge into separate compartments without due regard to the connection between them.

Frances Wosmek, *Acknowledge the Wonder* (1988)

14 Education is a private matter between the person and the world of knowledge and experience and has only a little to do with school or college.

Lillian Smith, "Bridges to Other People" (1959), in *Redbook* (1969)

15 I am my own University, I my own Professor.

Sylvia Ashton-Warner (1941), *Myself* (1967)

16 The advantage of an enlightened, nay, even a common education, was denied me, lest Knowledge should only serve to foster Poetry, and make "a sentimental fool" of me. I was left like a wild colt on the fresh and boundless common of Nature, to pick up a mouthful of Truth where I could.

Eliza Cook, *The Poetical Works of Eliza Cook* (1848)

17 It is as impossible to withhold education from the receptive mind, as it is impossible to force it upon the unreasoning.

Agnes Repplier, "The American Credo," *Times and Tendencies* (1931)

18 As educators, we live in a fool's paradise, or worse in a knave's, if we are unaware that when we are teaching *something* to anyone we are also teaching *everything* to that same anyone.

Florence Howe, *Myths of Coeducation* (1984)

19 The educational system is regarded simultaneously as the nation's scapegoat and savior.

Judith Groch, *The Right to Create* (1969)

1 If education is always to be conceived along the same antiquated lines of a mere transmission of knowledge, there is little to be hoped from it in the bettering of man's future.

Maria Montessori, *The Absorbent Mind* (1949)

2 Men and women must be educated, in a great degree, by the opinions and manners of the society they live in. In every age there has been a stream of popular opinion that has carried all before it, and given a family character, as it were, to the century. It may then fairly be inferred, that, till society be differently constituted, much cannot be expected from education.

Mary Wollstonecraft, *A Vindication of the Rights of Woman* (1792)

3 The process of education is not generally a process of teaching people to think and ask questions. It . . . is mostly one of teaching the young what *is* and getting them into a mood where they will go on keeping it that way.

Elizabeth Hawes, *Men Can Take It* (1939)

4 Most higher education is devoted to affirming the traditions and origins of an existing elite and transmitting them to new members.

Mary Catherine Bateson, *Composing a Life* (1989)

5 "Predigested food" should be inscribed over every hall of learning as a warning to all who do not wish to lose their own personalities and their original sense of judgment.

Emma Goldman, "The Child and Its Enemies," in *Mother Earth* (1906)

6 Education! Is it education to teach the young that their chances of happiness depend on being richer than their neighbors? Yet that is what it all tends to. Get on!—be successful!

Marie Corelli, *A Romance of Two Worlds* (1886)

7 It is in and through education that a culture, and polity, not only tries to perpetuate but enacts the kinds of thinking it welcomes, and discards and/or discredits the kinds it fears.

Elizabeth Kamarck Minnick, *Transforming Knowledge* (1990)

8 Schooling, instead of encouraging the asking of questions, too often discourages it.

Madeleine L'Engle, *Walking on Water* (1980)

9 To repeat what others have said, requires education; to challenge it, requires brains.

Mary Pettibone Poole, *A Glass Eye at a Keyhole* (1938)

10 Children must be taught how to think, not what to think.

Margaret Mead, *Coming of Age in Samoa* (1928)

11 Children . . . come to school with their heads crammed with prejudices, and their memories with words, which it should be part of the work of school to reduce to truth and clearness, by substituting principles for the one, and annexing ideas to the other.

Harriet Martineau, *Society in America*, vol. 3 (1837)

12 Those who have been required to memorize the world as it is will never create the world as it might be.

Judith Groch, *The Right to Create* (1969)

13 Education has chosen to emphasize decoding and computation rather than the cultivation of the imagination. We like, you see, what we can manage . . . for we know instinctively that the imagination is a wild, hardly tamable commodity. There is no way to measure it objectively, so anything in the curriculum that has to do with the growth of the inner life of a child we tend to classify as a frill and either shove it to the periphery or eliminate it from the curriculum altogether.

Katherine Paterson, *The Spying Heart* (1989)

14 The first rule of education is that if somebody will fund it, somebody will do it. The second rule of education is that once something is funded, workbooks will follow.

Susan Ohanian, *Ask Ms. Class* (1996)

15 A workbook should be carefully structured, analyzed for appropriate reading level, matched to every student's individual learning styles, and then thrown out the window.

Susan Ohanian, *Ask Ms. Class* (1996)

16 It is the function of a liberal university not to give right answers, but to ask right questions.

Cynthia Ozick, "Women and Creativity," in *Motive* (1969)

17 Ignorance, arrogance, and racism have bloomed as Superior Knowledge in all too many universities.

Alice Walker (1972), *In Search of Our Mothers' Gardens* (1983)

18 Both class and race survived education, and neither should. What is education then? If it doesn't help a human being to recognize that humanity is hu-

manity, what is it for? So you can make a bigger salary than other people?

Beah Richards, in Brian Lanker, *I Dream a World* (1989)

1 The highest result of education is tolerance.

Helen Keller, *Optimism* (1903)

2 Theories and goals of education don't matter a whit if you don't consider your students to be human beings.

Lou Ann Walker, *A Loss for Words* (1986)

3 The common stock of intellectual enjoyment should not be difficult of access because of the economic position of him who would approach it.

Jane Addams, *Twenty Years at Hull House* (1910)

4 Equality! Where is it, if not in education? Equal rights! They cannot exist without equality of instruction.

Frances Wright, "Of Free Enquiry," *Course of Popular Lectures* (1829)

5 The content of the curriculum should never exclude the realities of the very students who must intellectually wrestle with it. When students study all worlds except their own, they are miseducated.

Johnnetta B. Cole, *Conversations* (1993)

6 Ignorance, far more than idleness, is the mother of all the vices. . . . The destinies of the future lie in judicious education; an education that must be universal, to be beneficial.

L.E. Landon, *Ethel Churchill* (1837)

7 To me education is a leading out of what is already there in the pupil's soul. To Miss Mackay it is a putting in of something that is not there, and that is not what I call education, I call it intrusion.

Muriel Spark, *The Prime of Miss Jean Brodie* (1962)

8 Those who cannot remember clearly their own childhood are poor educators.

Marie von Ebner-Eschenbach, *Aphorisms* (1893)

9 It is always easier . . . to manipulate the child to fit the theory than to adjust the theory to suit the child—provided, of course, one is very careful not to look at the child.

Judith Groch, *The Right to Create* (1969)

10 In our mechanized society where thoughts as well as automobiles may be assembled in an automated factory, it is also, by some narrow logic, expedient to reduce children to those yes-no codes most eas-

ily processed by such a system. . . . When life becomes one giant data-processing system, the winners are those with the greatest aptitude for being data.

Judith Groch, *The Right to Create* (1969)

11 One might say that the American trend of education is to reduce the senses almost to nil.

Isadora Duncan, *My Life* (1927)

12 We already have so much pressure towards sameness through radio, film and comic outside the school, that we can't afford to do a thing inside that is not toward individual development.

Sylvia Ashton-Warner, *Teacher* (1963)

13 So far, we do not seem appalled at the prospect of exactly the same kind of education being applied to all the school children from the Atlantic to the Pacific, but there is an uneasiness in the air, a realization that the individual is growing less easy to find; an idea, perhaps, of what standardization might become when the units are not machines, but human beings.

Edith Hamilton, in Richard Thruelsen and John Kobler, eds., *Adventures of the Mind*, 1st series (1959)

14 Equalizing opportunity through universal higher education subjects the whole population to the intellectual mode natural only to a few. It violates the fundamental egalitarian principle of respect for the differences between people.

Caroline Bird, *The Case Against College* (1975)

15 Intellectual freedom, of course, implies intellectual diversity.

Frances FitzGerald, *Fire in the Lake* (1972)

16 Nowadays it seems that moral education is no longer considered necessary. Attention is wholly centered on intelligence, while the heart life is ignored.

George Sand (1837), in Marie Jenny Howe, ed., *The Intimate Journal of George Sand* (1929)

17 The instruction furnished is not good enough for the youth of such a country. . . . There is not even any systematic instruction given on political morals: an enormous deficiency in a republic.

Harriet Martineau, *Society in America*, vol. 3 (1837)

18 If the study to which you apply yourself has a tendency to weaken your affections, and to destroy your taste for those simple pleasures in which no alloy can possibly mix, then that study is certainly

unlawful, that is to say, not befitting the human mind.

Mary Shelley, *Frankenstein* (1818)

1 Education, as conceived today, is something separated both from biological and social life.

Maria Montessori, *The Absorbent Mind* (1949)

2 The world of education is like an island where people, cut off from the world, are prepared for life by exclusion from it.

Maria Montessori, *The Absorbent Mind* (1949)

3 Education has become a prisoner of contemporaneity.

Camille Paglia, *Sex, Art, and American Culture* (1992)

4 The American school system has, to some extent, simply "happened." . . . It has not been carefully planned. It has not been based on a study, either of children on the one hand, or of society's needs on the other.

Agnes E. Benedict, *Progress to Freedom* (1942)

5 All schoolchildren are hostages to red tape and fiscal insufficiency.

Rosellen Brown, *Civil Wars* (1984)

6 Helping children to face up to a certain amount of drudgery, cheerfully and energetically, is one of the biggest problems that teachers, in these days of ubiquitous entertainment, have to face in our schools.

Miss Read, *Village Diary* (1957)

7 The trouble with education is that we always read everything when we're too young to know what it means. And the trouble with life is that we're always too busy to re-read it later.

Margaret Barnes, *Years of Grace* (1930)

8 I realized with grief that purposeless activities in language arts are probably the burial grounds of language development and that coffins can be found in most classrooms, including mine.

Mem Fox, *Radical Reflections* (1993)

9 Everywhere I go I'm asked if I think the university stifles writers. My opinion is that they don't stifle enough of them. There's many a best-seller that could have been prevented by a good teacher.

Flannery O'Connor, "The Nature and Aim of Fiction," in Sally and Robert Fitzgerald, eds., *Mystery and Manners* (1969)

10 She passed in only two subjects . . . intending to let the stream of education play gently over her mental surfaces and not get any wetter than she could help.

Kate Douglas Wiggin, *Rebecca of Sunnybrook Farm* (1903)

11 As I inched sluggishly along the treadmill of the Maycomb County school system, I could not help receiving the impression that I was being cheated out of something. Out of what I knew not, yet I did not believe that twelve years of unrelieved boredom was exactly what the state had in mind for me.

Harper Lee, *To Kill a Mockingbird* (1960)

12 The first idea that the child must acquire, in order to be actively disciplined, is that of the difference between *good* and *evil*; and the task of the educator lies in seeing that the child does not confound *good* with *immobility*, and *evil* with *activity*.

Maria Montessori, *The Montessori Method* (1912)

13 We have what I would call educational genocide . . . when I see more black students in the laboratories than I see on the football field, I'll be happy.

Jewel Plummer Cobb, in Brian Lanker, *I Dream a World* (1989)

14 The ladder was there from "the gutter to the university," and for those stalwart enough to ascend it, the schools were a boon and a path out of poverty.

Diane Ravitch, *The Great School Wars* (1974)

15 At last I came to college. I rushed for it with the outstretched arms of youth's aching hunger to give and take of life's deepest, and highest, and I came against the solid wall of the well-fed, well-dressed world—the frigid whitewashed wall of cleanliness. . . . How I pinched, and scraped, and starved myself, to save enough to come to college! Every cent of the tuition fee I paid was drops of sweat and blood from underpaid laundry work. And what did I get for it? A crushed spirit, a broken heart, a stinging sense of poverty that I never felt before.

Anzia Yezierska, "Soap and Water," *Hungry Hearts* (1920)

16 I learned three important things in college—to use a library, to memorize quickly and visually, to drop asleep at any time given a horizontal surface and fifteen minutes. What I could not learn was to think creatively on schedule.

Agnes de Mille, *Dance to the Piper* (1952)

17 Mistrust of godless higher education is a constant theme of the evangelicals. "You can educate yourself right out of a relationship with God."

Tammy Faye Bakker, in *The Observer* (1988)

1 Education is a wonderful thing. If you couldn't sign your name you'd have to pay cash.
   Rita Mae Brown, *Starting From Scratch* (1988)

2 It's the educated barbarian who is the worst: he knows what to destroy.
   Helen MacInnes, *The Venetian Affair* (1963)

3 The only thing better than education is more education.
   Agnes E. Benedict, *Progress to Freedom* (1942)

See also Knowledge, Learning, School, Sex Education, Students, Teaching.

## § EFFECTIVENESS

4 The knife flaying the elephant does not have to be large, only sharp!
   Andre Norton, *Wraiths of Time* (1976)

5 It is better to arm and strengthen your hero, than to disarm and enfeeble the foe.
   Anne Brontë, *The Tenant of Wildfell Hall* (1848)

## § EFFORT

6 I try. I am trying. I was trying. I will try. I shall in the meantime try. I sometimes have tried. I shall still by that time be trying.
   Diane Glancy, "Portrait of the Lone Survivor," *Lone Dog's Winter Count* (1991)

7 To know that one has never really tried—that is the only death.
   Marie Dressler, with Mildred Harrington, *My Own Story* (1934)

8 We do what we can. The results are none of our business.
   Jennifer Stone, *Telegraph Avenue Then* (1992)

9 To try to be better is to be better.
   Charlotte Cushman, in Emma Stebbins, *Charlotte Cushman* (1878)

10 Babies are a nuisance, of course. But so does everything seem to be that is worth while—husbands and books and committees and being loved and everything. We have to choose between barren ease and rich unrest.
   Winifred Holtby, in Vera Brittain, *Testament of Friendship* (1940)

11 I'm glad you like my Catherine. I like her too. She ruled thirty million people and had three thousand lovers. I do the best I can in two hours.
   Mae West, on her show, "Catherine Was Great," in Joseph Weintraub, ed., *The Wit and Wisdom of Mae West* (1967)

12 And when I lie in the green kirkyard, / With the mold upon my breast, / Say not that "She did well—or ill," / Only, "She did her best!"
   Dinah Maria Mulock Craik, "Headings of Chapters," *Mulock's Poems, New and Old* (1880)

See also Action, Actions, Determination.

## § EGGS

13 Consider the egg. / . . . / It's boilable, poachable, fryable; / It scrambles, it makes a sauce thicken. / It's also the only reliable / Device for producing a chicken.
   Felicia Lamport, "Eggomania," *Light Metres* (1982)

14 Nothing stimulates the practiced cook's imagination like an egg.
   Irma S. Rombauer and Marion Rombauer Becker, *The Joy of Cooking* (1931)

## § EGOCENTRISM

15 We do not want to think. We do not want to hear. We do not care about anything. Only give us a good dinner and plenty of money, and let us outshine our neighbors. There is the Nineteenth Century Gospel.
   Ouida, *Wisdom, Wit and Pathos* (1884)

16 Hurry, drive and bustle. . . . Everybody looking out for number one, and caring little who jostled past, if their rights were not infringed.
   Fanny Fern, *Fern Leaves*, 1st series (1853)

17 Modern neurosis began with the discoveries of Copernicus. Science made man feel small by show-

ing him that the earth was not the center of the universe.

Mary McCarthy, "Tyranny of the Orgasm," *On the Contrary* (1961)

1 He who cries, "What do I care about universality? I only know what is in *me*," does not know even that.

Cynthia Ozick, *Trust* (1966)

2 Only a very small percentage can regard conditions from any but a selfish point of view or conceive of any but their own shoe-pinch.

Miles Franklin, *Some Everyday Folk and Dawn* (1909)

3 The recognition of personal separateness—of others having their own concepts, different from his, because they see things from their position and condition as individuals and not from his own—is not ordinarily possible before a child is seven. Immaturity in adults reveals itself clearly in the retention of this infantile orientation.

Miriam Lindstrom, *Children's Art* (1962)

4 We were like a lot of clocks, he thought, all striking different hours, all convinced we were telling the right time.

Susan Ertz, *The Story of Julian* (1931)

5 The only people whose mainspring is not egotism are the dead.

Miles Franklin, *My Career Goes Bung* (1946)

6 Egotism—usually just a case of mistaken nonentity.

Barbara Stanwyck, in Reader's Digest Editors, *Fun Fare* (1949)

See also Arrogance, Chauvinism, Conceit, Point of View, Self-Importance, Vanity.

❦ EGYPT

7 Egypt is full of dreams, mysteries, memories.

Janet Erskine Stuart, in Maud Monahan, *Life and Letters of Janet Erskine Stuart* (1922)

❦ ELECTIONS

8 An election is coming. Universal peace is declared, and the foxes have a sincere interest in prolonging the lives of the poultry.

George Eliot, *Felix Holt, the Radical* (1866)

9 Though in Paradise the lion will lie down with the lamb, in Paradise they will not have to submit their rival political views to general elections.

Amelia E. Barr, *The Belle of Bowling Green* (1904)

10 No candidate too pallid, / No issue too remote, / But it can snare / A questionnaire / To analyze our vote.

Phyllis McGinley, "Ballad of the Preëlection Vote," *A Pocketful of Wry* (1940)

11 A platform is something a candidate stands for and the voters fall for.

Gracie Allen, *How to Become President* (1940)

12 All the other candidates are making speeches about how much they have done for their country, which is ridiculous. I haven't done anything yet, and I think it's just common sense to send me to Washington and make me do my share.

Gracie Allen, *How to Become President* (1940)

See also Political Campaigns, Politicians, Politics, Suffrage.

❦ ELEGANCE

13 The only real elegance is in the mind; if you've got that, the rest really comes from it.

Diana Vreeland, in *Newsweek* (1962)

14 Elegance has a bad effect on my constitution.

Louisa May Alcott, *Little Women* (1868)

See also Fashion, Glamour, Poise, Style.

❦ ELEPHANTS

15 Once there was an elephant, / Who tried to use the telephant— / No! no! I mean an elephone / Who tried to use the telephone.

Laura E. Richards, "Eletelephony" (1890), *Tirra Lirra* (1932)

16 They come / from the east, trunk to tail, / clumsy ballerinas.

Rita Dove, "Five Elephants," *The Yellow House on the Corner* (1980)

1 I had seen a herd of elephant traveling through dense native forest . . . pacing along as if they had an appointment at the end of the world.

    Isak Dinesen, *Out of Africa* (1937)

## ❧ EMBARRASSMENT

2 I was so embarrassed I could feel my nerves curling like bacon over a hot fire.

    Margaret Halsey, *Some of My Best Friends Are Soldiers* (1944)

3 They were women of the world, and so dreaded an embarrassment more than they did sin.

    Grace King, "The Old Lady's Restoration," *Balcony Stories* (1892)

4 If a young dog strays up the aisle during church no one says anything, no one does anything, but, none the less, he soon becomes aware that something is wrong. Even so, as the distance between myself and the hearthrug diminished, did I become aware that something was very wrong indeed.

    Ethel Smyth, *Streaks of Life* (1922)

See also Humiliation.

## ❧ EMOTIONS

5 Life without emotion was like an engine without fuel.

    Mary Astor, *A Place Called Saturday* (1968)

6 A belief which does not spring from a conviction in the emotions is no belief at all.

    Evelyn Scott, *Escapade* (1923)

7 If facts are the seeds that later produce knowledge and wisdom, then the emotions and the impressions of the senses are the fertile soil in which the seeds must grow. . . . Once the emotions have been aroused—a sense of the beautiful, the excitement of the new and the unknown, a feeling of sympathy, pity, admiration or love—then we wish for knowledge about the object of our emotional response.

    Rachel Carson, *The Sense of Wonder* (1965)

8 Emotion seemed more valid than experience, for I had so much of the former and so little of the latter.

    Helen Van Slyke, *Always Is Not Forever* (1977)

9 We are not, most of us, capable of exalted emotion, save rarely.

    Dorothy Day, *From Union Square to Rome* (1940)

10 Emotion doesn't travel in a straight line. Like water, our feelings trickle down through cracks and crevices, seeking out the little pockets of neediness and neglect, the hairline fractures in our character usually hidden from public view.

    Sue Grafton, *"I" Is for Innocence* (1992)

11 I'm committed to the idea that one of the few things human beings have to offer is the richness of unconscious and conscious emotional responses to being alive. . . . The kind of esteem that's given to brightness/smartness obliterates average people or slow learners from participating fully in human life, particularly technical and intellectual life. But you cannot exclude any human being from emotional participation.

    Ntozake Shange, in Claudia Tate, ed., *Black Women Writers at Work* (1983)

12 One loses the capacity to grieve as a child grieves, or to rage as a child rages: hotly, despairingly, with tears of passion. One grows up, one becomes civilized, one learns one's manners, and consequently can no longer manage these two functions—sorrow and anger—adequately.

    Anita Brookner, *Brief Lives* (1990)

13 He liked to observe emotions; they were like red lanterns strung along the dark unknown of another's personality, marking vulnerable points.

    Ayn Rand, *Atlas Shrugged* (1957)

14 They are emotional gluttons, both of them. They gobbled up every sensation they could extract from marriage, and now they are seeing if separation won't provide them with a few more.

    Margaret Kennedy, *Lucy Carmichael* (1951)

15 He . . . treats his emotions like mice that infest our basement or the rats in the garage, as vermin to be crushed in traps or poisoned with bait.

    Marge Piercy, *Braided Lives* (1982)

16 When she fell in love it was with a perfect fury of accumulated dishonesty; she became instantly a

dealer in second-hand and therefore incalculable emotions.

Djuna Barnes, *Nightwood* (1937)

1  Anger and jealousy can no more bear to lose sight of their objects than love.

George Eliot, *The Mill on the Floss* (1860)

2  He who is sorrowful can force himself to smile, but he who is glad cannot weep.

Selma Lagerlöf, *The Story of Gösta Berling* (1891)

3  Those who don't know how to weep with their whole heart don't know how to laugh either.

Golda Meir, in *Ms.* (1973)

4  I hate people doing an emotional striptease. It's never genuine or they wouldn't drag outsiders in.

Evelyn Anthony, *The Avenue of the Dead* (1982)

5  He hated people who reeled off their thoughts and feelings to you, who took it for granted that you wanted to know all their inner mechanism. Reserve was always more interesting.

Agatha Christie, *Sad Cypress* (1939)

6  Spilling your guts is just exactly as charming as it sounds.

Fran Lebowitz, *Social Studies* (1977)

7  It is very bizarre to watch total strangers stand up and tell a TV camera things that are almost too personal to hear from your best friend.

Judy Markey, *You Only Get Married for the First Time Once* (1988)

8  Unwonted circumstances may make us all rather unlike ourselves: there are conditions under which the most majestic person is obliged to sneeze, and our emotions are liable to be acted on in the same incongruous manner.

George Eliot, *Middlemarch* (1871)

9  No emotion is the final one.

Jeanette Winterson, *Oranges Are Not the Only Fruit* (1985)

See also Feelings.

## ❧ EMPATHY

10  Empathy, the least comfortable of human emotions.

Frances Gray Patton, *Good Morning, Miss Dove* (1955)

11  We want people to feel with us more than to act for us.

George Eliot (1856), in J.W. Cross, ed., *George Eliot's Life As Related in Her Letters and Journals* (1884)

12  She did not talk to people as if they were strange hard shells she had to crack open to get inside. She talked as if she were already in the shell. In their very shell.

Marita Bonner, "Nothing New" (1926), *Frye Street and Environs* (1987)

13  Unto a broken heart / No other one may go / Without the high prerogative / Itself hath suffered too.

Emily Dickinson (1955), in Thomas H. Johnson, ed., *The Complete Poems of Emily Dickinson* (1960)

14  For the first time she had dimly realized that only the hopeless are starkly sincere and that only the unhappy can either give or take sympathy—even some of the bitter and dangerous voluptuousness of misery.

Jean Rhys, *The Left Bank* (1927)

15  Her back ached with the burdens other people were carrying.

Hilda Lawrence, *The House* (1947)

See also Compassion, Concern, Understanding.

## ❧ END

16  The weariest nights, the longest days, sooner or later must perforce come to an end.

Baroness Orczy, *The Scarlet Pimpernel* (1905)

17  The adventure is over. Everything gets over, and nothing is ever enough. Except the part you carry with you.

E.L. Konigsburg, *From the Mixed-Up Files of Mrs. Basil E. Frankweiler* (1967)

18  The last time you're doing something—knowing you're doing it for the last—makes it even more alive than the first.

Gloria Naylor, *Mama Day* (1988)

19  The completion of an important project has every right to be dignified by a natural grieving process.

Something that required the best of us has ended. We will miss it.

> Anne Wilson Schaef, *Meditations for Women Who Do Too Much* (1990)

1 That's all there is, there isn't any more.

> Ethel Barrymore, curtain call (1904)

2 I have had enough.

> Golda Meir, upon resigning (1974)

3 The end of a thing, / is never the end, / something is always being born like / a year or a baby.

> Lucille Clifton, "December," *Everett Anderson's Year* (1971)

4 Never think you've seen the last of anything.

> Eudora Welty, *The Optimist's Daughter* (1968)

See also Beginning, Farewells, Impermanence, Parting, Quitting.

## ❦ ENDURANCE

5 If she does not like it, she can lump it.

> Mrs. Henry Wood, *East Lynne* (1861)

6 Some things persist by suffering change, others / Endure.

> Babette Deutsch, "Homage to the Philosopher," *The Collected Poems of Babette Deutsch* (1969)

7 The thought that we are enduring the unendurable is one of the things that keep us going.

> Molly Haskell, *Love and Other Infectious Diseases* (1990)

8 Folks differs, dearie. They differs a lot. Some can stand things that others can't. There's never no way of knowin' how much they can stand.

> Ann Petry, *The Street* (1946)

9 People have to learn sometimes not only how much the heart, but how much the head, can bear.

> Maria Mitchell (1853), in Phebe Mitchell Kendall, ed., *Maria Mitchell, Life, Letters, and Journals* (1896)

10 Endurance can be a harsh and bitter root in one's life, bearing poisonous and gloomy fruit, destroying other lives. Endurance is only the beginning. There must be acceptance.

> Pearl S. Buck, *The Child Who Never Grew* (1950)

11 The stoicism that comes of endurance has something of death in it.

> Mary Catherwood, *Lazarre* (1901)

12 Nothing is won by endurance / but endurance.

> Marge Piercy, "When a friend dies," *The Moon Is Always Female* (1980)

See also Perseverance, Stubbornness, Survival.

## ❦ ENEMIES

13 People wish their enemies dead—but I do not; I say give them the gout, give them the stone!

> Lady Mary Wortley Montagu, in Horace Walpole (1778), *Horace Walpole's Correspondence*, vol. 35 (1973)

14 I don't have a warm personal enemy left. They've all died off. I miss them terribly because they helped define me.

> Clare Boothe Luce, interview (1981)

15 I make enemies deliberately. They are the *sauce piquante* to my dish of life.

> Elsa Maxwell, in *The New York Journal-American* (1963)

16 Lifelong enemies are, I think, as hard to make and as important to one's well-being as lifelong friends.

> Jessica Mitford, "The Best of Frenemies," *The Making of a Muckraker* (1979)

17 We no more forget the faces of our enemies than of those we love.

> Ruth Rendell, *Talking to Strange Men* (1987)

18 Prudence advises us to use our enemies as if one day they might be friends.

> Marguerite de Valois, *Memoirs* (1628)

19 It is hard to fight an enemy who has outposts in your head.

> Sally Kempton, "Cutting Loose," in *Esquire* (1970)

20 When my enemies stop hissing, I shall know I'm slipping.

> Maria Callas, in Arianna Stassinopoulos, *Maria Callas* (1981)

21 Scratch a lover, and find a foe.

> Dorothy Parker, "Ballade of a Great Weariness," *Enough Rope* (1926)

See also Conflict, Opposition.

## ❧ ENERGY

1 Life engenders life. Energy creates energy. It is by
spending oneself that one becomes rich.
  Sarah Bernhardt, in Cornelia Otis Skinner, *Madame Sarah*
  (1966)

2 Energy is the power that drives every human being.
It is not lost by exertion but maintained by it, for it
is a faculty of the psyche.
  Germaine Greer, *The Female Eunuch* (1971)

3 The human organism has only so much energy at
its disposal. If you divert a great deal of it into any
one channel, you can expect the others to collapse
or atrophy. If you squander your vital energies on
your emotional life . . . plan to be physically and
mentally bankrupt, as it were.
  Lisa Alther, *Kinflicks* (1975)

4 Whatever is not an energy source, is an energy sink.
  Marge Piercy, "Laying Down the Tower," *To Be of Use*
  (1973)

5 Energy had fastened upon her like a disease.
  Ellen Glasgow, *Vein of Iron* (1935)

See also Vitality.

## ❧ ENGLAND

6 Whoever considers England will find it no small
favor of God to have been made one of its natives.
  Lucy Hutchinson, *Memoirs of the Life of Colonel Hutchinson*
  (1806)

7 England is the only civilized country in the world
where it is etiquette to fall on the food like a wolf
the moment it is served. Elsewhere it is *comme il
faut* to wait until everybody has helped himself to
everything and until everything on everybody's
plate is stone cold.
  Virginia Graham, *Say Please* (1949)

8 It is possible to eat English piecrust, whatever you
may think at first. The English eat it, and when they
stand up and walk away, they are hardly bent over
at all.
  Margaret Halsey, *With Malice Toward Some* (1938)

9 I always felt that the boiled potato, not the Tudor
rose, should be the national emblem.
  Ilka Chase, *Past Imperfect* (1942)

10 I was well warned about English food, so it did not
surprise me, but I do wonder, sometimes, how they
ever manage to prise it up long enough to get a
plate under it.
  Margaret Halsey, *With Malice Toward Some* (1938)

11 Listening to Britons dining out is like watching
people play first-class tennis with imaginary balls.
  Margaret Halsey, *With Malice Towards Some* (1938)

12 The stately Homes of England, / How beautiful
they stand!
  Felicia Hemans, "The Homes of England," *The Poetical
  Works of Felicia Dorothea Hemans* (1914)

13 Those comfortably padded lunatic asylums which
are known, euphemistically, as the stately homes of
England.
  Virginia Woolf, "Outlines: Lady Dorothy Nevill," *The
  Common Reader* (1925)

14 Suicide and antipathy to fires in a bedroom seem to
be among the national characteristics. Perhaps the
same moral cause may originate both.
  L.E. Landon, *Romance and Reality* (1831)

15 In this country there are only two seasons, winter
and winter.
  Shelagh Delaney, *A Taste of Honey* (1958)

16 Rain is one thing the British do better than anybody else.
  Marilyn French, *The Bleeding Heart* (1980)

17 England is an aquarium, not a nation.
  Rita Mae Brown, *Southern Discomfort* (1982)

18 I begin to suspect that England is the most melancholy country in the world.
  Natalia Ginzburg, *The Little Virtues* (1962)

19 England that little gray island in the clouds where
governments don't fall overnight and children
don't sell themselves in the street and my money is
safe.
  Caryl Churchill, *Serious Money* (1987)

20 Wonderful, mysterious, grand, clever old England,
who keeps the Ritz Hotel front-door closed on
Sundays and the side-door open!
  Lady Norah Bentinck, *My Wanderings and Memories* (1924)

1 Oxford is overpowering, being so replete with architecture and history and anecdote that the visitor's mind feels dribbling and helpless, as with an over-large mouthful of nougat.

Margaret Halsey, *With Malice Toward Some* (1938)

2 It takes a great deal to produce ennui in an Englishman and if you do, he only takes it as convincing proof that you are well-bred.

Margaret Halsey, *With Malice Toward Some* (1938)

3 The English don't go in for imagination: imagination is considered to be improper if not downright alarmist.

Martha Gellhorn, "The Lord Will Provide for England," in *Collier's* (1938)

4 [The English] find ill-health not only interesting but respectable and often experience death in the effort to avoid a fuss.

Pamela Frankau, *Pen to Paper* (1961)

5 True Brits loathe newness, and display a profound fear of change. . . . (Britain is the heartland of "We've Always Done It This Way.") Conclusion: change nothing unless forced. Remember that God usually gets it right the first time.

Jane Walmsley, *Brit-Think, Ameri-Think* (1986)

6 England is a country where people stay exactly as they are. The soul does not receive the slightest jolt.

Natalia Ginzburg, *The Little Virtues* (1962)

7 English people . . . never speak, excepting in cases of fire or murder, unless they are introduced.

L.E. Landon, "Experiments," *The Book of Beauty* (1833)

8 Cecilia's lunch party, having heard through the open door the first phrase of the interlude, had exchanged less than a glance and, all raising their voices, maintained a strenuous conversation till she came back. They were not English for nothing.

Elizabeth Bowen, *To the North* (1933)

9 England, where nobody ever says what they mean: and by denying feeling, kill it off stone-cold at the roots.

Caitlin Thomas, *Leftover Life to Kill* (1957)

10 Slow to understand a new joke, they are equally slow to part with one that has been mastered.

Mrs. Pennell, in Agnes Repplier, "Humor: English and American," *In the Dozy Hours* (1894)

11 This Englishwoman is so refined / She has no bosom and no behind.

Stevie Smith, "This Englishwoman," *A Good Time Was Had by All* (1937)

12 The English never smash in a face. They merely refrain from asking it to dinner.

Margaret Halsey, *With Malice Toward Some* (1938)

13 An enraged Briton does not paw the ground, he writes to the papers.

Emily Hahn, *Times and Places* (1970)

14 The trouble about most Englishwomen is that they *will* dress as if they had been a mouse in a previous incarnation, or hope to be one in the next.

Edith Sitwell, "How to Wear Dramatic Clothes," in Elizabeth Salter and Allanah Harper, eds., *Edith Sitwell* (1976)

15 Englishwomen's shoes look as if they had been made by someone who had often heard shoes described, but had never seen any.

Margaret Halsey, *With Malice Toward Some* (1938)

16 Contrary to popular belief, English women do not wear tweed nightgowns.

Hermione Gingold, in *Saturday Review* (1955)

17 She respected Americans: they were not like the English, who, under a surface of annoying moroseness of manner, were notoriously timid and easy to turn round your finger.

Jean Rhys, *The Left Bank* (1927)

18 The English possess too many agreeable traits to permit them to be as much disliked as they think and hope they are.

Agnes Repplier, "The Estranging Sea," *Americans and Others* (1912)

See also Europe, London.

# ❦ ENOUGH

19 I do not like new things of any kind . . . far less a new acquaintance, therefore make as few as possible; one can but have one's heart and hands full, and mine are. I have love and work enough to last me the rest of my life.

Anna Jameson (1841), in Geraldine Macpherson, *Memoirs of the Life of Anna Jameson* (1878)

1 One man's enough is another's privation.
  Jessamyn West, *Hide and Seek* (1973)

2 Enough is as good as a feast.
  Katharine Tynan, *The Years of the Shadow* (1919)

See also Contentment, Satisfaction.


## ✋ ENTERTAINING

3 Entertaining is one method of avoiding people. It is very often the negation of hospitality.
  Elizabeth Bibesco, *The Fir and the Palm* (1924)

See also Guests, Hospitality, Invitation, Parties.


## ✋ ENTERTAINMENT

4 All entertainment is education in some way, many times more effective than schools because of the appeal to the emotions rather than to the intellect.
  Hortense Powdermaker, *Hollywood, The Dream Factory* (1950)

5 Entertainment for entertainment's sake is the most expensive form of death.
  John Oliver Hobbes, *The Ambassador* (1898)

6 We live in an age which *must* be amused, though genius, feeling, trust, and principle be the sacrifice.
  Hannah More, "Address to Women of Rank and Fortune," *Strictures on the Modern System of Female Education* (1799)

7 The so-called selfishness of moderns is partly due to the tremendous amount of stimulation received. They are aroused and drawn into experience by theaters, books, automobiles, great cities. The current is quick and strong.
  Katharine Butler Hathaway, *The Journals and Letters of the Little Locksmith* (1946)

See also Comedy, Films, Hollywood, Show Business, Spectators, Stage and Screen, Television.


## ✋ ENTHUSIASM

8 Enthusiasm is a divine possession.
  Margaret E. Sangster, *Winsome Womanhood* (1900)

9 Enthusiasm is the divine particle in our composition: with it we are great, generous, and true; without it, we are little, false, and mean.
  L.E. Landon, *Ethel Churchill* (1837)

10 Enthusiasm raises the artist above himself . . . in an ordinary mood one would not have been able to accomplish many of the things for which enthusiasm lends one everything, energy, fire.
  Clara Schumann (1841), in Gerd Nauhaus, ed., *The Marriage Diaries of Robert and Clara Schumann* (1993)

11 Enthusiasm is contagious. Be a carrier.
  Susan Rabin, with Barbara Lagowski, *How to Attract Anyone, Anytime, Anyplace* (1993)

12 Enthusiasm, though the seed / Of every high heroic deed, / Each pious sacrifice—its lot / Is scorn, from those who feel it not.
  Madame de Staël, *Corinne* (1807)

13 You will do foolish things, but do them with enthusiasm.
  Colette, in *The New York World-Telegram & Sun* (1961)

14 Latins are tenderly enthusiastic. In Brazil they throw flowers at you. In Argentina they throw themselves.
  Marlene Dietrich, in *Newsweek* (1959)

15 Like simplicity, and candor, and other much-commended qualities, enthusiasm is charming until we meet it face to face, and cannot escape from its charm.
  Agnes Repplier, "The Chill of Enthusiasm," *Americans and Others* (1912)

16 When you appreciate a thing best—and you are a great appreciator, dear Ethel—you rather hug the life out of it.
  Vernon Lee (1893), in Ethel Smyth, *As Time Went On. . .* (1936)

17 It is so much easier to be enthusiastic than to reason!
  Eleanor Roosevelt, *My Days* (1938)

18 A mediocre idea that generates enthusiasm will go further than a great idea that inspires no one.
  Mary Kay Ash, *On People Management* (1984)

See also Passion.

## ❧ ENTREPRENEURS

1 I don't think I'm a risk-taker. I don't think any entrepreneur is. I think that's one of those myths of commerce. The new entrepreneur is more values-led: you do what looks risky to other people because that's what your convictions tell you to do. Other companies would say I'm taking risks, but that's my path—it doesn't feel like risk to me.

   Anita Roddick, in Daniel Goleman, Paul Kaufman, and Michael Ray, *The Creative Spirit* (1992)

## ❧ ENVIRONMENT

2 Something has gone unspeakably wrong . . . we human beings have made a terminal mess of this earth.

   Lise Weil, in Christina Thürmer-Rohr, *Vagabonding* (1991)

3 We have become as poisoned as the eagle's eggshell.

   Chrystos, "No Rock Scorns Me As Whore," in Cherríe Moraga and Gloria Anzaldúa, eds., *This Bridge Called My Back* (1983)

4 No enemy action had silenced the rebirth of new life in this stricken world. The people had done it themselves.

   Rachel Carson, *Silent Spring* (1962)

5 Under the philosophy that now seems to guide our destinies, nothing must get in the way of the man with the spray gun.

   Rachel Carson, *Silent Spring* (1962)

6 In terms of the biology of the planet, *development* is a euphemism for *destruction*.

   Helen Caldicott, *If You Love This Planet* (1992)

7 For the first time in the history of the world, every human being is now subjected to contact with dangerous chemicals, from the moment of conception until death.

   Rachel Carson, *Silent Spring* (1962)

8 As crude a weapon as the cave man's club, the chemical barrage has been hurled against the fabric of life—a fabric on the one hand delicate and destructible, on the other miraculously tough and resilient, and capable of striking back in unexpected ways.

   Rachel Carson, *Silent Spring* (1962)

9 The aboriginal peoples of Australia illustrate the conflict between technology and the natural world succinctly, by asking, "What will you do when the clever men destroy your water?" That, in truth, is what the world is coming to.

   Winona LaDuke, in Beth Brant, ed., *A Gathering of Spirit* (1984)

10 To people who think of themselves as God's houseguests, American enterprise must seem arrogant beyond belief. Or stupid. A nation of amnesiacs, proceeding as if there were no other day but today. Assuming the land could also forget what had been done to it.

   Barbara Kingsolver, *Animal Dreams* (1990)

11 Today everyone can see the full extent of the past and present atrocities on this earth. No one can any longer claim she or he didn't know anything.

   Christina Thürmer-Rohr, *Vagabonding* (1991)

12 Feeling that morality has nothing to do with the way you use the resources of the world is an idea that can't persist much longer. If it does, then we won't.

   Barbara Kingsolver, in Donna Perry, ed., *Backtalk* (1993)

13 I have become an environmentalist, because it is over the environment that the last of the Indian Wars will be fought.

   Mary Brave Bird, with Richard Erdoes, *Ohitika Woman* (1993)

14 As a physician I examine the dying planet as I do a dying patient. The earth has a natural system of interacting homeostatic mechanisms similar to the human body's. If one system is diseased, like the ozone layer, then other systems develop abnormalities in function—the crops will die, the plankton will be damaged, and the eyes of all creatures on the planet will become diseased and vision impaired.

   Helen Caldicott, *If You Love This Planet* (1992)

15 The maltreatment of the natural world and its impoverishment leads to the impoverishment of the human soul. It is related to the outburst of violence in human society. To save the natural world today means to save what is human in humanity.

   Raisa M. Gorbachev, *I Hope* (1991)

16 I had assumed that the Earth, the spirit of the Earth, noticed exceptions—those who wantonly damage it and those who do not. But the Earth is

wise. It has given itself into the keeping of all, and all are therefore accountable.

> Alice Walker, "Everything Is a Human Being," *Living by the Word* (1988)

1 Slowly the wasters and despoilers are impoverishing our land, our nature, and our beauty, so that there will not be one beach, one hill, one lane, one meadow, one forest free from the debris of man and the stigma of his improvidence.

> Marya Mannes, *More in Anger* (1958)

2 Those hills hold nothing now   Mostly leveled Without deer, without puma, without pheasant, without blue-bellied lizards, without quail, without ancient oaks   Lawns instead   Deeply disgusted by lawns   Stupid flat green crew cuts   Nothing for anybody to eat.

> Chrystos, "No Rock Scorns Me As Whore," in Cherríe Moraga and Gloria Anzaldúa, eds., *This Bridge Called My Back* (1983)

3 Ahh, my heart fell down when I began to see dead buffalo scattered all over our beautiful country, killed and skinned, and left to rot by white men, many, many hundreds of buffalo. . . . Our hearts were like stones. And yet nobody believed, even then, that the white man could kill *all* the buffalo. Since the beginning of things there had always been so many!

> Pretty-shield, in Frank Bird Linderman, *Pretty-Shield, Medicine Woman of the Crows* (1932)

4 Man is a great blunderer going about in the woods, and there is no other except the bear that makes so much noise. . . . The cunningest hunter is hunted in turn, and what he leaves of his kill is meat for some other. That is the economy of nature, but with it all there is not sufficient account taken of the works of man. There is no scavenger that eats tin cans, and no wild thing leaves a like disfigurement on the forest floor.

> Mary Austin, *The Land of Little Rain* (1904)

5 Every person who builds a second home on a pristine lake or in a secluded area of woods, or who invests in urban-sprawl development, is part of the same global pattern of encroachment that displaces wildlife and decreases the wild space our own species needs for its survival.

> Deane Morrison, *Of Kinkajous, Capybaras, Seladangs, Horned-Beetles* (1991)

6 Man . . . thinks of himself as a creator instead of a user, and this delusion is robbing him, not only of his natural heritage, but perhaps of his future.

> Helen Hoover, "The Waiting Hills," *The Long-Shadowed Forest* (1963)

7 The "control of nature" is a phrase conceived in arrogance, born of the Neanderthal age of biology and philosophy, when it was supposed that nature exists for the convenience of man.

> Rachel Carson, *Silent Spring* (1962)

8 Only within the moment of time represented by the present century has one species—man—acquired significant power to alter the nature of his world.

> Rachel Carson, *Silent Spring* (1962)

See also Earth, Land, Nature, Wilderness.

# ❧ ENVY

9 Some folk are always thirsting for water from other people's wells.

> Jessamyn West, *Leafy Rivers* (1967)

10 If one has one cow, it is always better not to be too familiar with those who have seven.

> Phyllis Bottome, *Old Wine* (1925)

11 How Envy dogs success.

> L.E. Landon, "A History of the Lyre," *The Venetian Bracelet* (1829)

12 People only threw stones at the tree that was loaded with fruit.

> Rachel Field, *All This and Heaven Too* (1939)

13 Nobody pushed him uphill, but everybody was willing to lend a hand on the downward shove.

> Zora Neale Hurston, *Jonah's Gourd Vine* (1934)

14 The happiness of others is never bearable for very long.

> Françoise Sagan, *A Reluctant Hero* (1985)

15 Do we want laurels for ourselves most, / Or most that no one else shall have any?

> Amy Lowell, "La Ronde du Diable," *What's O'Clock* (1925)

16 She wished all the faculties she did not share to be looked on as diseases.

> Madame de Staël, *Corinne* (1807)

1 An envious heart makes a treacherous ear.

    Zora Neale Hurston, *Their Eyes Were Watching God* (1937)

2 Spite is never lonely; envy always tags along.

    Mignon McLaughlin, *The Neurotic's Notebook* (1963)

3 Envy is one of the scorpions of the mind, often having little to do with the objective, external world.

    Bonnie Friedman, *Writing Past Dark* (1993)

4 Not the bite of a serpent, nor the blow of a sword, nor any other sharp thrust was ever as dangerous as the tongue of an envious person.

    Christine de Pisan, "Le livre des trois vertus" (1405), in Charity Cannon Willard, tr., and Madeleine Pelner Cosman, ed., *A Medieval Woman's Mirror of Honor* (1989)

See also Jealousy.

# ❦ EPISCOPALIANS

5 [There are] three kinds of services you generally find in the Episcopal churches. I call them either low-and-lazy, broad-and-hazy, or high-and-crazy.

    Willa Gibbs, "The Dean," in Michèle Brown and Ann O'Connor, *Woman Talk*, vol. 1 (1984)

6 Episcopalians have always preferred the flying buttress to the pillar of the church.

    Florence King, *When Sisterhood Was in Flower* (1982)

7 Her Episcopalian friends were persuading her to their wishy-washy way of worship. They really believed you could get to heaven without any shouting.

    Dorothy West, *The Living Is Easy* (1948)

See also Church, Religion.

# ❦ EQUALITY

8 All men are free and equal *in the grave*, if it comes to that.

    Harriet Beecher Stowe, *Uncle Tom's Cabin* (1852)

9 We cannot legislate equality but we can legislate . . . equal opportunity for all.

    Helen Gahagan Douglas (1945), *A Full Life* (1982)

10 Equality . . . is the result of human organization insofar as it is guided by the principle of justice. . . . We are not born equal.

    Hannah Arendt, *Origins of Totalitarianism* (1951)

11 I have come to the conclusion that the modern interpretation of the Declaration of Independence is something like this: *I am as good as those that think themselves better and a long sight better than those who only think themselves as good.*

    Gertrude Atherton, *The Aristocrats* (1901)

12 We hold these truths to be self-evident: that all men and women are created equal.

    "Declaration of Sentiments and Resolutions," The First Woman's Rights Convention (1848), in Elizabeth Cady Stanton, Susan B. Anthony, and Matilda J. Gage, eds., *The History of Woman Suffrage*, vol. 1 (1881)

13 We were equals once when we lay new-born babes on our nurse's knees. We will be equals again when they tie up our jaws for the last sleep.

    Ralph Iron, *The Story of an African Farm* (1883)

14 The woman's bill of rights is, unhappily, long overdue. It should have run along with the rights of man in the eighteenth century. Its drag as to time of official proclamation is a drag as to social vision. And even if equal rights were now written into the law of our land, it would be so inadequate today as a means to food, clothing and shelter for women at large that what they would still be enjoying would be equality in disaster rather than in realistic privilege.

    Mary Ritter Beard (1937), in Nancy F. Cott, *A Woman Making History* (1991)

15 Equity speaks softly and wins in the end. But it is expedience, with its loud voice, that sets the time of victory.

    Caroline Bird, *Born Female* (1968)

16 I am working for the time when unqualified blacks, browns and women join the unqualified men in running our government.

    Sissy Farenthold (1974), in Daniel B. Baker, *Power Quotes* (1992)

17 We don't so much want to see a female Einstein become an assistant professor. We want a woman

schlemiel to get promoted as quickly as a male schlemiel.

Bella Abzug (1977), in Lois Gordon and Alan Gordon, *American Chronicle* (1987)

1 What I'm working for is the day when a mediocre woman can get as far as a mediocre man.

Anonymous public relations executive, in Caroline Bird, *Born Female* (1968)

2 "Men always say there is no female Shakespeare." "Humph! You study the fellows who say that, and you'll see they are a long way from being Shakespeares themselves. Why shouldn't women have the same privilege?"

Miles Franklin, *My Career Goes Bung* (1946)

3 I took Josiah out to one side, and says I, "Josiah Allen, if Tirzah Ann is to be brought up to think that marriage is the chief aim of her life, Thomas J. shall be brought up to think that marriage is his chief aim." Says I, "It looks just as flat in a woman, as it does in a man."

Josiah Allen's Wife, *My Opinions and Betsey Bobbet's* (1872)

4 Who ever walked behind anyone to freedom? If we can't go hand in hand, I don't want to go.

Hazel Scott, in Margo Jefferson, "Great (Hazel) Scott!" *Ms.* (1974)

5 I tasted the bread and wine of equality.

Anzia Yezierska, *Red Ribbon on a White Horse* (1950)

See also Discrimination, Human Differences, Justice, Racism, Sexism.

## ❧ EQUIVOCATION

6 I will not say that your mulberry trees are dead, but I am afraid they are not alive.

Jane Austen, to her sister Cassandra (1811), in R.W. Chapman, ed., *Jane Austen's Letters*, vol. 2 (1932)

7 Do not fear those who argue, but rather those who are evasive.

Marie von Ebner-Eschenbach, *Aphorisms* (1893)

See also Euphemisms.

## ❧ ERAS

8 The ages are but baubles hung upon / The thread of some strong lives—and one slight wrist / May lift a century above the dust.

Edith Wharton, "A Torchbearer," *Artemis to Actaeon* (1909)

9 Decades have a delusive edge to them. They are not, of course, really periods at all, except as any other ten years would be. But we, looking at them, are caught by the different name each bears, and give them different attributes, and tie labels on them, as if they were flowers in a border.

Rose Macaulay, *Told by an Idiot* (1923)

See also The Sixties, Time, Years.

## ❧ THE EROTIC

10 What is erotic? The acrobatic play of the imagination. The sea of memories in which we bathe. The way we caress and worship things with our eyes. Our willingness to be stirred by the sight of the voluptuous. What is erotic is our passion for the liveliness of life.

Diane Ackerman, *A Natural History of Love* (1994)

11 We tend to think of the erotic as an easy, tantalizing sexual arousal. I speak of the erotic as the deepest life force, a force which moves us toward living in a fundamental way.

Audre Lorde, in Claudia Tate, ed., *Black Women Writers at Work* (1983)

12 American eroticism has always been of a different provenance and complexion than the European variety, an enjoyment both furtive and bland that is closer to a blushing cartoon than a sensual celebration.

Molly Haskell, *From Reverence to Rape* (1974)

See also Seduction, Sex.

## ❧ ERROR

13 By our errors we see deeper into life.

Ralph Iron, *The Story of an African Farm* (1883)

1 Many a truth is the result of an error.
   Marie von Ebner-Eschenbach, *Aphorisms* (1893)

2 To see a shadow and think it is a tree—that is a pity, but to see a tree and think it is a shadow can be fatal.
   Phyllis Bottome, *Against Whom?* (1954)

3 Who thinks it just to be judged by a single error?
   Beryl Markham, *West With the Night* (1942)

4 I was no pope—I could not boast infallibility.
   Charlotte Brontë, *The Professor* (1846)

5 We are living in the Age of Human Error. . . . Since we're all human, since anybody can make mistakes, since nobody's perfect, and since everybody is "equal," a human error is Democracy in Action.
   Florence King, *Reflections in a Jaundiced Eye* (1989)

See also Delusions, Mistakes.

## ❧ ERUDITION

6 Erudition, like a bloodhound, is a charming thing when held firmly in leash, but it is not so attractive when turned loose upon a defenseless, unerudite public.
   Agnes Repplier, *Points of View* (1891)

See also Jargon, Knowledge.

## ❧ ESSAYS

7 A good essay must have this permanent quality about it; it must draw its curtain round us, but it must be a curtain that shuts us in, not out.
   Virginia Woolf, "The Modern Essay," *The Common Reader*, 1st series (1925)

8 An essay is a work of literary art which has a minimum of one anecdote and one universal idea.
   Carol Bly, *The Passionate, Accurate Story* (1990)

9 There is no room for the impurities of literature in an essay.
   Virginia Woolf, "The Modern Essay," *The Common Reader*, 1st series (1925)

See also Literature, Writing.

## ❧ ESSENCE

10 Rose is a rose is a rose is a rose.
   Gertrude Stein, *Sacred Emily* (1913)

11 A snake will always be a snake, even if you put a chain around its neck and try to make it walk upright.
   Lisa Alther, *Kinflicks* (1975)

12 Wood may remain twenty years in the water, but it is still not a fish.
   Jane Yolen, *Sister Light, Sister Dark* (1988)

13 The Arabian horse will not plow well, nor can the plowhorse be rode to play the jereed.
   Margaret Fuller, *Summer on the Lakes* (1844)

14 Runners are poor walkers.
   Marie von Ebner-Eschenbach, *Aphorisms* (1893)

15 You can't get tender shoots from a rotten bamboo stalk.
   Li Ang, *The Butcher's Wife* (1983)

16 She was the same through and through. You could go on cutting slice after slice and you knew you would never light upon a plum or a cherry or even a piece of peel.
   Katherine Mansfield (1918), *Journal of Katherine Mansfield* (1927)

17 I think character never changes; the Acorn becomes an Oak, which is very little like an Acorn to be sure, but it never becomes an Ash.
   Hester Lynch Piozzi (1797), in Oswald G. Knapp, ed., *The Intimate Letters of Hester Piozzi and Penelope Pennington 1788-1821* (1914)

18 Any one seed may be too old to sprout or inferior in some way, but it will never try to be something it isn't fitted to be. A man may study to be a surgeon when he should have been a shoemaker, a talented painter may spend his life trying to convince himself and his fellows that he is a lawyer, but a turnip seed will never attempt to grow into an ear of corn. If you plant a good turnip seed properly a turnip is what you will get every single time.
   Ruth Stout, *How to Have a Green Thumb Without an Aching Back* (1955)

19 With him for a sire and her for a dam, / What should I be but just what I am?
   Edna St. Vincent Millay, "The Singing-Woman From the Wood's Edge," *A Few Figs From Thistles* (1920)

1 My theory is that when we come on this earth, many of us are ready-made. Some of us—most of us—have genes that are ready for certain performances. Nature gives you these gifts. There's no denying that Caruso came with a voice, there's no denying that Beethoven came with music in his soul. Picasso was drawing like an angel in the crib. You're born with it.

Louise Nevelson, *Dawns + Dusks* (1976)

2 One ship drives east and another drives west / With the selfsame winds that blow. / 'Tis the set of sails and not the gales / Which tells us the way to go.

Ella Wheeler Wilcox, "Winds of Fate," in Hazel Felleman, ed., *The Best Loved Poems of the American People* (1936)

3 I was raised the Chinese way: I was taught to desire nothing, to swallow other people's misery, to eat my own bitterness. And even though I taught my daughter the opposite, still she came out the same way! Maybe it is because she was born to me and she was born a girl. And I was born to my mother and I was born a girl. All of us are like stairs, one step after another, going up and down, but all going the same way.

Amy Tan, *The Joy Luck Club* (1989)

See also Character, Heredity, Identity, Nature.

## ❦ ESTRANGEMENT

4 My mother and father and I now lived in the intimacy of estrangement that exists between married couples who have nothing left in common but their incompatibility.

Nadine Gordimer, *The Lying Days* (1953)

5 Sleep on, I sit and watch your tent in silence, / White as a sail upon this sandy sea, / And know the Desert's self is not more boundless / Than is the distance 'twixt yourself and me.

Laurence Hope, title poem, *Stars of the Desert* (1903)

6 If you leave me, can I come too?

Cynthia Heimel, book title (1995)

See also Broken Heart, Divorce.

## ❦ ETERNITY

7 The hunger of the spirit for eternity—as fierce as a starving man's for bread—is much less a craving to go on living than a craving for redemption. Oh, and a protest against absurdity.

Storm Jameson, *Journey From the North*, vol. 2 (1970)

8 Our deepest mature conviction is that . . . time and eternity interpenetrate, and our problems must be solved in the light of that conviction.

Lily Dougall, "The Undiscovered Country," in B.H. Streeter et al., *Immortality* (1917)

9 Eternity is not something that begins after you are dead. It is going on all the time. We are in it now.

Charlotte Perkins Gilman, in *The Forerunner* (1909)

10 Stars and blossoming fruit trees: Utter permanence and extreme fragility give an equal sense of eternity.

Simone Weil, *Gravity and Grace* (1947)

See also Immortality, Time.

## ❦ ETHICS

11 Since when do grown men and women, who presume to hold high government office and exercise what they think of as "moral leadership," require ethics officers to tell them whether it is or isn't permissible to grab the secretary's behind or redirect public funds to their own personal advantage?

Meg Greenfield, in *Newsweek* (1995)

12 The stress laid on upward social mobility in the United States has tended to obscure the fact that there can be more than one kind of mobility and more than one direction in which it can go. There can be ethical mobility as well as financial, and it can go down as well as up.

Margaret Halsey, *No Laughing Matter* (1977)

13 Today we live in a society suffering from ethical rickets.

Rita Mae Brown, *In Her Day* (1976)

14 It is no wonder we behave badly, we are literally ignorant of the laws of ethics, which is the simplest of sciences, the most necessary, the most continuously needed. The childish misconduct of our "revolted youth" is quite equaled by that of older people, and neither young nor old seem to have any

understanding of the reasons why conduct is "good" or "bad."

Charlotte Perkins Gilman, *The Living of Charlotte Perkins Gilman* (1935)

1 Action is indeed the sole medium of expression for ethics.

Jane Addams, "Political Reform," *Democracy and Social Ethics* (1902)

2 The real nature of an ethic is that it does not become an ethic *unless and until it goes into action.*

Margaret Halsey, *The Folks at Home* (1952)

See also Evil, Morality, Religion, Sin.

## ❧ ETIQUETTE

3 Etiquette is what you are doing and saying when people are looking and listening. What you are thinking is your business.

Virginia Cary Hudson, *O Ye Jigs and Juleps* (1962)

4 Etiquette—a fancy word for simple kindness.

Elsa Maxwell, *Elsa Maxwell's Etiquette Book* (1951)

5 Etiquette is based on tradition, and yet it can change. Its ramifications are trivialities, but its roots are in great principles.

Millicent Fenwick, *Vogue's Book of Etiquette* (1948)

6 Etiquette may be despotic, but its cruelty is inspired by intelligent kindness.

Abby B. Longstreet, *Social Etiquette of New York* (1888)

7 Animals are murdered to produce meat; vegetables are torn up, peeled, and chopped; most of what we eat is treated with fire; and chewing is designed remorselessly to finish what killing and cooking began. People naturally prefer that none of this should happen to them. Behind every rule of table etiquette lurks the determination of each person present to be a diner, not a dish.

Margaret Visser, *The Rituals of Dinner* (1991)

8 In society it is etiquette for ladies to have the best chairs and get handed things. In the home the reverse is the case. That is why ladies are more sociable than gentlemen.

Virginia Graham, *Say Please* (1949)

9 There is no harm in eating corn off the cob; the impoliteness consists in looking at the person who is doing it.

Mary Wilson Little, *A Paragrapher's Reveries* (1904)

10 When you see persons slip down on the ice, do not laugh at them. . . . It is more feminine on witnessing such a sight, to utter an involuntary scream.

Eliza Leslie, *Miss Leslie's Behavior Book* (1859)

See also Manners, Politeness, Protocol, Rudeness.

## ❧ EUPHEMISMS

11 The trouble with this country is the national passion for euphemisms.

E.S. Liddon, *The Riddle of the Florentine Folio* (1935)

12 I know uh secret code. I ain' crazy, I got uh 'motional disorder; I ain' got fits, I got uh convulsive disorder; an' I ain' ugly, I plain; an' I ain' black, I dusky; an' my children ain' bastards, they—they *love-flowers!*

Joanne Greenberg, *The Monday Voices* (1965)

13 There are new words now that excuse everybody. Give me the good old days of heroes and villains. The people you can bravo or hiss. There was a truth to them that all the slick credulity of today cannot touch.

Bette Davis, *The Lonely Life* (1962)

14 The empty forms of social behavior survive inappropriately in business situations. We all know that when a business sends its customers "friendly reminders," it really means business.

Judith Martin, *Common Courtesy* (1985)

15 Euphemisms, like fashions, have their day and pass, perhaps to return at another time. Like the guests at a masquerade ball, they enjoy social approval only so long as they retain the capacity for deception.

Freda Adler, *Sisters in Crime* (1975)

16 The practice of hinting by single letters those expletives with which profane and violent persons are wont to garnish their discourse, strikes me as a proceeding which, however well meant, is weak

and futile. I cannot tell what good it does—what feeling it spares—what horror it conceals.

> Charlotte Brontë, editor's preface to Emily Brontë, *Wuthering Heights* (1847)

1 Excuse me, everybody, I have to go to the bathroom. I really have to telephone, but I'm too embarrassed to say so.

> Dorothy Parker, in Robert E. Drennan, *The Algonquin Wits* (1968)

See also Equivocation, Optimism, Words.

## ❧ EUROPE

2 Oh, lovely Europe, your flowers and your wine, your bread, your music.

> Belva Plain, *Evergreen* (1978)

3 That is what is so marvelous about Europe; the people long ago learned that space and beauty and quiet refuges in a great city, where children may play and old people sit in the sun, are of far more value to the inhabitants than real estate taxes and contractors' greed.

> Ilka Chase, *Fresh From the Laundry* (1967)

See also Cities, Denmark, England, France, Greece, Holland, Ireland, Italy, Portugal, Russia, Scandinavians, Spain, Turkey.

## ❧ EUTHANASIA

4 Euthanasia . . . is simply to be able to die with dignity at a moment when life is devoid of it.

> Marya Mannes, *Last Rights* (1974)

5 The time is approaching when we shall consider it abhorrent to our civilization to allow a human being to die in prolonged agony which we should mercifully end in any other creature.

> Charlotte Perkins Gilman, *The Living of Charlotte Perkins Gilman* (1935)

6 I wonder how often not the intention but the desire springs up in a doctor's mind: "Can I let this human being out of the trap of Life?"

> Phyllis Bottome, *Survival* (1943)

7 Euthanasia is a long, smooth-sounding word, and it conceals its danger as long, smooth words do, but the danger is there, nevertheless.

> Pearl S. Buck, *The Child Who Never Grew* (1950)

See also Death, Suicide.

## ❧ EVENING

8 In the evening / my griefs come to me / one by one.

> Linda Pastan, "Old Woman," *The Five Stages of Grief* (1978)

9 The evening was like some great black cow standing there beside her panting softly, so that she could feel its sides breathe. Sweet-smelling darkness with a give to it like a cow's flank.

> Fannie Hurst, *Lummox* (1923)

See also Night, Twilight.

## ❧ EVIL

10 There is evil everywhere under the sun.

> Agatha Christie, *Evil Under the Sun* (1940)

11 The arrogance of men, indeed, / comes full equipped with evil, / in promise and insistency, / the world, the flesh, the Devil.

> Sor Juana Inés de la Cruz (1690), in Irene Nicholson, *A Guide to Mexican Poetry* (1968)

12 Evil is not something superhuman, it's something *less* than human.

> Agatha Christie, *The Pale Horse* (1961)

13 Can spirit from the tomb, or fiend from hell, / More hateful, more malignant be than man— / Than villainous man?

> Joanna Baillie, *Orra* (1812)

14 In all men is evil sleeping; the good man is he who will not awaken it, in himself or in other men.

> Mary Renault, *The Praise Singer* (1978)

15 The evil of the world is made possible by nothing but the sanction you give it.

> Ayn Rand, *Atlas Shrugged* (1957)

16 The spread of evil is the symptom of a vacuum. Whenever evil wins, it is only by default: by the

moral failure of those who evade the fact that there can be no compromise on basic principles.

Ayn Rand, *Capitalism: The Unknown Ideal* (1966)

1 The sad truth of the matter is that most evil is done by people who never made up their minds to be or do either evil or good.

Hannah Arendt, *The Life of the Mind,* vol. 1 (1978)

2 No man chooses evil because it is evil; he only mistakes it for happiness, the good he seeks.

Mary Wollstonecraft, *A Vindication of the Rights of Men* (1790)

3 The lesser evil is also evil.

Naomi Mitchison, *Lobsters on the Agenda* (1952)

4 It may be necessary temporarily to accept a lesser evil, but one must never label a necessary evil as good.

Margaret Mead, in *Redbook* (1978)

5 We *may* draw good out of evil: we *must not* do evil, that good may come.

Maria Chapman, speech (1855)

6 Little evil would be done in the world if evil never could be done in the name of good.

Marie von Ebner-Eschenbach, *Aphorisms* (1893)

7 Evil when we are in its power is not felt as evil but as a necessity, or even a duty.

Simone Weil, *Gravity and Grace* (1947)

8 Evil is obvious only in retrospect.

Gloria Steinem, *Outrageous Acts and Everyday Rebellions* (1983)

9 An evil discovered is half healed.

Jane de Chantal (1632), in Péronne Marie Thibert, tr., *Francis de Sales, Jane de Chantal: Letters of Spiritual Direction* (1988)

10 Evils we have never experienced, we are unprepared to resist.

Mrs. M. Harley, *St. Bernard's Priory* (1786)

11 Aye, have you not heard that all evil drags a long tail behind it?

Sigrid Undset, *Kristin Lavransdatter: The Bridal Wreath* (1920)

12 To hate the devil and all his works is one thing, but to say who is the devil and which are his works is another.

Miss Thackeray, *Old Kensington,* vol. 1 (1873)

13 It is a pity but what bad men could be turned inside out sometimes: to put others on their guard.

Mrs. Henry Wood, *East Lynne* (1861)

14 I will never be able to hate any human being for his so-called "wickedness." . . . I shall only hate the evil that is within me, though hate is perhaps putting it too strongly even then. In any case, we cannot be lax enough in what we demand of others and strict enough in what we demand of ourselves.

Etty Hillesum (1942), *An Interrupted Life* (1983)

15 A towering intellect, grand in its achievements, and glorious in its possibilities, may, with the moral and spiritual faculties held in abeyance, be one of the most dangerous and mischievous forces in the world.

Frances Ellen Watkins Harper, "A Factor in Human Progress," in *African Methodist Episcopal Church Review* (1885)

16 It is bitter to lose a friend to evil, before one loses him to death.

Mary Renault, *The Praise Singer* (1978)

17 Stupidity always accompanies evil. Or evil, stupidity.

Louise Bogan (1935), in Ruth Limmer, ed., *Journey Around My Room* (1980)

18 There's too much tendency to attribute to God the evils that man does of his own free will.

Agatha Christie, *The Moving Finger* (1942)

19 Only if, deep inside, we rebel against every kind of evil, will we be able to put a stop to it. . . . While everything within us does not yet scream out in protest, so long will we find ways of adapting ourselves, and the horrors will continue.

Etty Hillesum (1942), *An Interrupted Life* (1983)

20 In any compromise between food and poison, it is only death that can win. In any compromise between good and evil, it is only evil that can profit.

Ayn Rand, *Atlas Shrugged* (1957)

21 It is right noble to fight with wickedness and wrong; the mistake is in supposing that spiritual evil can be overcome by physical means.

Lydia Maria Child, *Letters From New York,* 1st series (1842)

22 Faced with two evils, I picked one every time.

Loretta Gage, with Nancy Gage, *If Wishes Were Horses* (1992)

1 Between two evils, I always pick the one I never tried before.

Mae West, in *Klondike Annie* (1936)

See also Crime, Cruelty, Devil, Good and Evil, Sin, Vice, Villains, Wickedness, Wrongdoing.

## ❧ EVOLUTION

2 I worry that humanity has been "advanced" to its present level of incompetency because evolution works on the Peter Principle.

Jane Wagner, *The Search for Signs of Intelligent Life in the Universe* (1985)

## ❧ EXAGGERATION

3 Every man is bound to leave a story better than he found it.

Mrs. Humphry Ward, *Robert Elsmere* (1888)

4 The gardener was one of those who are never surprised without being thunderstruck.

Stella Benson, *I Pose* (1915)

5 I know exaggerators of both kinds: people whose lies are only picturesque adjectives, and people whose picturesque adjectives are only lies.

Katharine Fullerton Gerould, *Modes and Morals* (1920)

6 Her own excited feelings had magnified it in length, and breadth, and height—had made a molehill into a mountain.

Mrs. Henry Wood, *East Lynne* (1861)

See also Dramatics.

## ❧ EXCELLENCE

7 The secret of joy in work is contained in one word—excellence. To know how to do something well is to enjoy it.

Pearl S. Buck, *The Joy of Children* (1964)

8 We only do well the things we like doing.

Colette, *Prisons and Paradise* (1932)

9 Excellence is not an act but a habit. The things you do the most are the things you will do best.

Marva Collins, in "Marva Collins: Teaching Success in the City," *Message* (1987)

10 When we do the best that we can, we never know what miracle is wrought in our life, or in the life of another.

Helen Keller, *Out of the Dark* (1914)

11 Excellence in any pursuit is the late, ripe fruit of toil.

W.M.L. Jay, *Shiloh* (1872)

12 The good is the greatest rival of the best.

Nellie L. McClung, *In Times Like These* (1915)

13 It is more to my personal happiness and advantage to indulge the love and admiration of excellence, than to cherish a secret envy of it.

Elizabeth Montagu, letter (1774), in Anna Letitia Le Breton, *Memoir of Mrs. Barbauld* (1874)

14 Excellence costs a great deal.

May Sarton, *The Small Room* (1961)

See also Mediocrity, Perfectionism.

## ❧ EXCEPTIONS

15 Experience shows that exceptions are as true as rules.

Edith Ronald Mirrielees, *Story Writing* (1947)

16 People always make mistakes when they fancy themselves exceptions.

Geraldine Jewsbury, *Zoë*, vol. 1 (1845)

See also Rules.

## ❧ EXCESS

17 She believed in excess. How can you tell whether or not you have had enough until you've had a little too much?

Jessamyn West, *Hide and Seek* (1973)

1 Something is always born of excess: great art was born of great terrors, great loneliness, great inhibitions, instabilities, and it always balances them.

    Anaïs Nin (1945), *The Diary of Anaïs Nin*, vol. 4 (1971)

2 I'm the foe of moderation, the champion of excess. If I may lift a line from a die-hard whose identity is lost in the shuffle, "I'd rather be strongly wrong than weakly right."

    Tallulah Bankhead, *Tallulah* (1952)

3 Modern life is given over to immoderation. Immoderation invades everything: actions and thought, public and private life.

    Simone Weil, *Gravity and Grace* (1947)

4 Perhaps too much of everything is as bad as too little.

    Edna Ferber, *Giant* (1952)

See also Extremes, Luxury.

## ❦ EXCLUSION

5 No loose fish enters our quiet bay.

    Gertrude Atherton, *Sleeping Fires* (1922)

6 It [James Gould Cozzens' *By Love Possessed*] is a vast enterprise encompassing all sorts of love, except, naturally, those branches which extend to Jews, Negroes, and people who have lost track of their great-grandparents.

    Dorothy Parker, in *Esquire* (1957)

7 I was strong and tough enough and charming. / How else is a fat Jew lesbian poet gonna get by? / Listening to the radio, staying home, staying alone, like / they mean us to. / Who means you to be left out? / Who don't?

    Elana Dykewomon, "Traveling Fat," in Christian McEwen and Sue O'Sullivan, eds., *Out the Other Side* (1988)

8 Exclusion is always dangerous. Inclusion is the only safety if we are to have a peaceful world.

    Pearl S. Buck, *A Bridge for Passing* (1962)

9 Blessed are the inclusive for they shall be included. . . . Cursed are the exclusive for they shall be excluded.

    Frances E. Willard, in Anna A. Gordon, ed., *What Frances E. Willard Said* (1905)

10 Omissions are not accidents.

    Marianne Moore, *The Complete Poems of Marianne Moore* (1958)

See also Discrimination, Oppression, Outsiders, Racism, Segregation, Sexism.

## ❦ EXCUSES

11 There are reasons, and then there are excuses.

    Julia Child, *Julia Child & Company* (1978)

12 When someone gives me three reasons instead of one, I'm inclined not to believe any of them.

    Margaret Millar, *The Fiend* (1964)

13 I can't help it . . . that's what we all say when we don't want to exert ourselves.

    Eva Lathbury, *Mr. Meyer's Pupil* (1907)

14 There is always a *but* in this imperfect world.

    Anne Brontë, *The Tenant of Wildfell Hall* (1848)

15 I attribute my success to this. I never gave or took an excuse.

    Florence Nightingale, in Cecil Woodham-Smith, *Florence Nightingale* (1950)

See also Explanations, Rationalizations.

## ❦ EXERCISE

16 There's no such thing as excess eating, only inadequate activity.

    Dorothy Harris, in Janice Kaplan, *Women and Sports* (1979)

17 I am persuaded that the greater part of our complaints arise from want of exercise.

    Marie de Rabutin-Chantal, Marquise de Sévigné (1671), *Letters of Madame de Sévigné to Her Daughter and Her Friends*, vol. 1 (1811)

18 Running is the right thing to do! I am free, healthy with a good complexion. It is that automobile addict who should be ashamed: driving in a sealed car in warmed-over carbon monoxide and smoking a seegar. I am the Goddess! He is a bug in a monkey nut!

    Brenda Ueland, *Strength to Your Sword Arm* (1993)

1 Getting fit is a political act—you are taking charge of your life.

  Jane Fonda, in Thomas Kiernan, *Jane Fonda* (1982)

2 We are rich earthy cooks / both of us and the flesh we are working / off was put on with grave pleasure.

  Marge Piercy, "Morning Athletes," *The Moon Is Always Female* (1980)

3 It takes six months to get into shape and two weeks to get out of shape. Once you know this you can stop being angry about other things in life and only be angry about this.

  Rita Rudner, *Naked Beneath My Clothes* (1992)

4 I think anyone who comes upon a Nautilus machine suddenly will agree with me that its prototype was clearly invented at some time in history when torture was considered a reasonable alternative to diplomacy.

  Anna Quindlen, "Stretch Marks," *Living Out Loud* (1988)

5 Aerobics has to be the least appealing activity. I don't even know how this word came into being: "aerobics." I guess gym instructors got together and said, "If we're going to charge ten dollars an hour, we can't call it 'jumping up and down.'"

  Rita Rudner, *Naked Beneath My Clothes* (1992)

6 My grandmother started walking five miles a day when she was sixty—she's ninety-seven today and we don't know where the hell she is.

  Ellen DeGeneres, in *Mirabella* (1992)

See also Sports.

## ❧ EXILES

7 Doesn't everyone feel rather exiled? . . . The mere passage of time makes us all exiles.

  Joyce Carol Oates, in Robert Phillips, "Joyce Carol Oates: The Art of Fiction LXXII," *The Paris Review* (1978)

8 For the exile, as for ailing / Or jailed folk, always have I bled. / Deep shadows are your lone path veiling / And ever sour is alien bread.

  Anna Akhmatova, "I Am Not One of Those Abdicators," *Anno Domini* (1922)

9 Exile: A tomb in which you can get mail.

  Madame de Staël (1812), in J. Christopher Herold, *Mistress to an Age* (1958)

See also Homeland, Immigrants, Outsiders.

## ❧ EXPECTATIONS

10 It's expectation that differentiates you from the dead. The dead, so low in their stone rows, making no demands, without desire.

  Sheila Ballantyne, *Norma Jean the Termite Queen* (1975)

11 Talk about the joys of the unexpected, can they compare with the joys of the expected, of finding everything delightfully and completely what you knew it was going to be?

  Elizabeth Bibesco, *Balloons* (1922)

12 Expectation . . . quickens desire, while possession deadens it.

  Hannah More, *Coelebs in Search of a Wife* (1808)

13 Hope for forces which you do not yet have. That is what is most impossible, and nevertheless possible.

  Rahel Varnhagen, letter (1805), in Hannah Arendt, *Rahel Varnhagen* (1957)

14 There is no such thing as expecting too much.

  Susan Cheever, *Looking for Work* (1979)

15 We always attract into our lives whatever we think about most, believe in most strongly, expect on the deepest level, and imagine most vividly.

  Shakti Gawain, *Reflections in the Light* (1988)

16 He who demands little gets it.

  Ellen Glasgow, *The Voice of the People* (1900)

17 In some extremely important ways, people are what you expect them to be, or at least they behave as you expect them to behave.

  Naomi Weisstein, "Psychology Constructs the Female," in Vivian Gornick and Barbara K. Moran, eds., *Woman in Sexist Society* (1971)

18 Women run on expectations, the way a car is fueled by gas. And it doesn't matter whose: unspoken assignments from parents, bosses, clients, children, and lovers crowd our calendars' borders, in ink only we can see.

  Amy Lindgren, in *SCAN* (1993)

19 Our wishes never seem so little desirable as when on the verge of accomplishment; we draw back instinctively, they look so different from what we expected.

  Geraldine Jewsbury, *Zoë*, vol. 1 (1845)

1 My expectations—which I extended whenever I came close to accomplishing my goals—made it impossible ever to feel satisfied with my success.
   Ellen Sue Stern, *The Indispensable Woman* (1988)

2 How extraordinary people are, that they get themselves into such situations where they go on doing what they dislike doing, and have no need or obligation to do, simply because it seems to be expected.
   Margaret Drabble, *The Middle Ground* (1980)

3 Nothing is so good as it seems beforehand.
   George Eliot, *Silas Marner* (1861)

4 Nothing is ever so good or so bad in reality as it is in the anticipation.
   Marie Bashkirtseff (1883), in Mary J. Serrano, tr., *The Journal of a Young Artist* (1919)

5 Events never arrive as we fear they will, nor as we hope they will.
   Comtesse Diane, *Les Glanes de la Vie* (1898)

6 How tedious is time, when his wings are loaded with expectation!
   Mary Collyer, *Felicia to Charlotte* (1744)

7 Expectations are the most perilous form of dream, and when dreams do realize themselves it is in the waking world: the difference is subtly but often painfully felt.
   Elizabeth Bowen, *The Death of the Heart* (1938)

8 No pleasure or success in life quite meets the capacity of our hearts. We take in our good things with enthusiasm, and think ourselves happy and satisfied; but afterward, when the froth and foam have subsided, we discover that the goblet is not more than half-filled with the golden liquid that was poured into it.
   Louise Imogen Guiney, *Goose-Quill Papers* (1885)

9 We generally get the evil we expect.
   Amelia E. Barr, *The Belle of Bowling Green* (1904)

10 The expectation of an unpleasantness is more terrible than the thing itself.
   Marie Bashkirtseff (1873), in Mary J. Serrano, tr., *The Journal of a Young Artist* (1919)

11 What is destructive is impatience, haste, expecting too much too fast.
   May Sarton, *Journal of a Solitude* (1973)

12 The wise expect nothing, hope for nothing, thus avoiding all disappointment and anxiety.
   Alexandra David-Neel (1889), *La Lampe de Sagesse* (1986)

13 We survive day by day on this planet by adjusting down, adjusting down. Little by little, imperceptibly, we adjust to increasingly deadly conditions, and come to accept them as "natural" or inevitable.
   Sonia Johnson, *Going Out of Our Minds* (1987)

14 Expect nothing. Live frugally / On surprise.
   Alice Walker, "Expect Nothing," *Revolutionary Petunias* (1971)

15 Life's under no obligation to give us what we expect.
   Margaret Mitchell, *Gone With the Wind* (1936)

See also Anticipation, Hope, Unexpected.

## ❧ EXPEDIENCE

16 The immediate is often the enemy of the ultimate.
   Indira Gandhi, *Freedom Is the Starting Point* (1976)

17 Perhaps it is the expediency in the political eye that blinds it.
   Virgilia Peterson, *A Matter of Life and Death* (1961)

18 Wars come and wars go but the world does not change: it will always forget an indebtedness which it thinks it expedient not to remember.
   Radclyffe Hall, *Miss Ogilvy Finds Herself* (1926)

19 I do not believe / our wants / have made our lies / holy.
   Audre Lorde, "Between Ourselves," in Joanna Bankier and Deirdre Lashgari, eds., *Women Poets of the World* (1983)

20 Lips say "God be pitiful," / Who ne'er said "God be praisèd."
   Elizabeth Barrett Browning, "Cry of the Human," *Poems* (1844)

21 Sometimes you have to deal / Devilishly with drowning men in order to swim them to shore.
   Gwendolyn Brooks, "Negro Hero," *A Street in Bronzeville* (1945)

1 That woman . . . would use the third-rising of a corpse for her ends.

Djuna Barnes, *Nightwood* (1937)

See also Self-Interest.

## ❧ EXPERIENCE

2 Experience is what really happens to you in the long run; the truth that finally overtakes you.

Katherine Anne Porter, "St. Augustine and the Bullfight" (1955), *The Collected Essays and Occasional Writings of Katherine Anne Porter* (1970)

3 Experience is what you get looking for something else.

Mary Pettibone Poole, *A Glass Eye at a Keyhole* (1938)

4 The fruit of life is experience, not happiness.

Amelia E. Barr, *All the Days of My Life* (1913)

5 Everything you experience is what constitutes *you* as a human being, but the experience passes away and the person's left. The person is the residue.

Ilka Chase, *New York 22* (1951)

6 Experience has no text books nor proxies. She demands that her pupils answer to her roll-call personally.

Minna Thomas Antrim, *Naked Truth and Veiled Illusions* (1901)

7 The real stuff of life was experience, in which sorrow and fear and disaster had as important a part to play as beauty and joy.

Sheila Kaye-Smith, *A Challenge to Sirius* (1917)

8 It is better to take experience, to suffer, to love, and to remember than to walk unscathed between the fires. . . . The two fires of poverty and passion have . . . never burned me, and I am a lesser person for my safety.

Winifred Holtby (1926), in Alice Holtby and Jean McWilliam, eds., *Letters to a Friend* (1937)

9 Our experiences tend to support our belief systems.

T.J. MacGregor, *Death Sweet* (1988)

10 One never believes other people's experience, and one is only very gradually convinced by one's own.

Vita Sackville-West, *The Edwardians* (1930)

11 There is a large stock on hand; but somehow or other, nobody's experience ever suits us except our own.

L.E. Landon, *Romance and Reality* (1831)

12 I long to put the experience of fifty years at once into your young lives, to give you at once the key to that treasure chamber every gem of which has cost me tears and struggles and prayers, but you must work for these inward treasures yourselves.

Harriet Beecher Stowe, letter to her twin daughters (1861)

13 What is it which is bought dearly, offered for nothing, and then most often refused?—Experience, old people's experience.

Isak Dinesen, "The Monkey," *Seven Gothic Tales* (1934)

14 A rattlesnake that doesn't bite teaches you nothing.

Jessamyn West, *The Life I Really Lived* (1979)

15 Experience may be hard but we claim its gifts because they are real, even though our feet bleed on its stones.

M.P. Follett, *Creative Experience* (1924)

16 Experience is never at bargain price.

Alice B. Toklas, *The Alice B. Toklas Cook Book* (1954)

17 Experience is a good teacher, but she sends in terrific bills.

Minna Thomas Antrim, *Naked Truth and Veiled Illusions* (1902)

18 Experience teaches, it is true; but she never teaches in time.

L.E. Landon, *Romance and Reality* (1831)

19 Experience—A comb life gives you after you lose your hair.

Judith Stern, in Bennett Cerf, *The Laugh's on Me* (1959)

20 Experience isn't interesting till it begins to repeat itself—in fact, till it does that, it hardly *is* experience.

Elizabeth Bowen, *The Death of the Heart* (1938)

21 None are so eager to gain new experience as those who don't know how to make use of the old ones.

Marie von Ebner-Eschenbach, *Aphorisms* (1893)

22 Unless the knowledge gained from experience is reconditioned in each new situation, it is a rigid and a dangerous guide.

Blanche H. Dow, "Roads and Vistas," in Jean Beaven Abernethy, ed., *Meditations for Women* (1947)

1 There are roughly two sorts of informed people, aren't there? People who start off right by observing the pitfalls and mistakes and going round them, and the people who fall into them and get out and know they're there because of that. They both come to the same conclusions but they don't have quite the same point of view.

Margery Allingham, *Dancers in Mourning* (1937)

2 All writers, musicians, artists, choreographers/dancers, etc., work with the stuff of their experiences. It's the translation of it, the conversion of it, the shaping of it that makes for the drama.

Toni Cade Bambara, in Claudia Tate, ed., *Black Women Writers at Work* (1983)

3 Over the airways, in movies, experiences have come to be dogmatized to certain kinds of experience at the cost of all others.

Josephine Herbst, *New Green World* (1954)

See also Life.

## § EXPERTS

4 I wish we could understand the word expert as expressing an attitude of mind which we can all acquire rather than the collecting of information by a special caste. . . . Many of us are calling for experts because, acutely conscious of the mess we are in, we want someone to pull us out.

M.P. Follett, *Creative Experience* (1924)

5 It is a rare expert who clearly realizes how inexpert someone else can be.

Peg Bracken, *I Didn't Come Here to Argue* (1969)

6 An expert is anyone from out of town.

Mem Fox, *Radical Reflections* (1993)

7 Don't ever accept an expert's opinion if it violates your own, because the experts can change their minds.

Mary Kay Blakely, *Wake Me When It's Over* (1989)

8 If you take passionate interest in a subject, it is hard not to believe yourself specially equipped for it.

Ethel Smyth, *Streaks of Life* (1922)

See also Specialization.

## § EXPLANATIONS

9 I warned you / Don't ask for explanations / When you walk with me.

Lami'a Abbas al-'Imarah, "The Path of Silence," in Elizabeth Warnock Fernea, *Women and the Family in the Middle East* (1985)

10 Let the wise be warned against too great readiness to explanation: it multiplies the sources of mistake, lengthening the sum for reckoners sure to go wrong.

George Eliot, *Middlemarch* (1871)

11 To rush into explanations and excuses is always a sign of weakness.

Agatha Christie, *The Seven Dials Mystery* (1929)

12 The simplest explanation is always the most likely.

Agatha Christie, *The Mysterious Affair at Styles* (1920)

13 When driven to the necessity of explaining, I found that I did not myself understand what I meant.

Maria Edgeworth, "To-Morrow," *Popular Tales* (1804)

14 Nothing annoys me more than having the most trivial action analyzed and explained.

Zelda Fitzgerald, in Nancy Milford, *Zelda* (1970)

15 A writer should give direct certainty; explanations are so much water poured into the wine.

Virginia Woolf, "Addison," *The Common Reader*, 1st series (1925)

16 Holly conducted herself like a bird of paradise that had flown through the window of a house in Des Moines and settled down; she explained very little.

Laurie Colwin, *Happy All the Time* (1978)

17 [The play] "Yang Zen Froggs" is so rambunctious and odd it's like trying to describe Man Ray to your dog.

Jayne M. Blanchard, in *St. Paul Pioneer Press* (1995)

See also Answers, Excuses, Reason, Why.

## § EXTRAVAGANCE

18 I like extravagance. Letters which give the postman a stiff back to carry, books which overflow from

their covers, sexuality which bursts the thermometers.

Anaïs Nin (1933), *The Diary of Anaïs Nin*, vol. 1 (1966)

1 We owe something to extravagance, for thrift and
adventure seldom go hand in hand.

Jennie Jerome Churchill, "Extravagance," in *Pearson's* (1915)

2 Spending money is my only extravagance.

Lillian Day, *Kiss and Tell* (1931)

3 All right, so I spend money. Can you name one
other extravagance I have?

Cindy Adams, in Joey Adams, *Cindy and I* (1957)

4 We both deplore extravagance. He deplores mine,
and I deplore his.

Jane Goodsell, "Wedlock Deadlock," in the Editors of
Reader's Digest, *Laughter, the Best Medicine* (1981)

See also Excess, Luxury, Self-Indulgence.


❦ EXTREMES

5 Only by pursuing the extremes in one's nature,
with all its contradictions, appetites, aversions,
rages, can one hope to understand a little—oh, I
admit only a very little—of what life is about.

Françoise Sagan, *Scars on the Soul* (1972)

6 Impassioned characters never attain their mark till
they have overshot it.

Anne-Sophie Swetchine, in Count de Falloux, ed., *The
Writings of Madame Swetchine* (1869)

7 One cannot be too extreme in dealing with social
ills; besides, the extreme thing is generally the true
thing.

Emma Goldman, *Anarchism* (1910)

8 All extremes are dangerous.

Virginia Woolf, "Montaigne," *The Common Reader*, 1st
series (1925)

9 Every political good carried to the extreme must be
productive of evil.

Mary Wollstonecraft, *An Historical and Moral View of the
Origin and Progress of the French Revolution* (1794)

10 Almost anything carried to its logical extreme becomes depressing, if not carcinogenic.

Ursula K. Le Guin, *The Left Hand of Darkness* (1969)

See also Cranks, Excess, Fanaticism.


❦ EXTROVERTS AND INTROVERTS

11 I have seen faces age and sag under the onslaught
of amiable extroversion.

Kate O'Brien, *Farewell Spain* (1987)

12 One day I shall write a little book of conduct myself, and I shall call it *Social Problems of the Unso-
ciable*. And the root problem, beneath a hundred
varying manifestations, is How to Escape. How to
escape, that is, at those times, be they few or frequent, when you want to keep yourself to yourself.

Rose Macaulay, "Problems of Social Life," *A Casual
Commentary* (1926)

13 Extraverts . . . cannot understand life until they
have lived it. Introverts . . . cannot live life until
they understand it.

Isabel Briggs Myers, with Peter B. Myers, *Gifts Differing*
(1980)

14 Present Western civilization . . . is dominated by
the extravert viewpoint. There are plenty of reasons
for this domination: extraverts are more vocal than
introverts; they are more numerous, apparently in
the ratio of three to one; and they are accessible and
understandable, whereas the introverts are not
readily understandable, even to each other, and are
likely to be thoroughly incomprehensible to the
extraverts.

Isabel Briggs Myers, with Peter B. Myers, *Gifts Differing*
(1980)

See also Inner Life, Introspection, Social Skills.


❦ EYES

15 Eyes, what are they? Colored glass, / Where reflections come and pass. / Open windows—by them sit
/ Beauty, Learning, Love, and Wit.

Mary Coleridge, "Eyes" (1890), in Theresa Whistler, ed.,
*The Collected Poems of Mary Coleridge* (1954)

16 The eye is complicated. It mixes the colors [it sees]
for you. . . . The painter must unmix them and lay
them on again shade by shade, and then the eye of
the beholder takes over and mixes them again.

Elizabeth Borton de Treviño, *I, Juan de Pareja* (1965)

17 Look in the mirror. The face that pins you with its
double gaze reveals a chastening secret. You are
looking into a predator's eyes. Most predators have

eyes set right on the front of their heads, so they can use binocular vision to sight and track their prey. . . . Prey, on the other hand, have eyes at the sides of their heads, because what they really need is peripheral vision, so they can tell when something is sneaking up behind them. Something like us.

Diane Ackerman, *A Natural History of the Senses* (1990)

1 You need eyes like an archerfish, able to see what happens on two planes at once. One set for watching the hands [signing], and the other for watching whatever it is he mouths.

Keri Hulme, *The Bone People* (1983)

2 The eyelids . . . express so much by seeming to hide or to reveal that which indeed expresses nothing. For there is no message from the eye. It has direction, it moves, in the service of the sense of sight; it receives the messages of the world. But expression is outward, and the eye has it not. There are no windows of the soul, there are only curtains.

Alice Meynell, "Eyes," *The Color of Life* (1896)

3 Her eyes were like two thumbtacks, trying to pin me to the wall.

Susan Isaacs, *Shining Through* (1988)

4 The woman's eyes were alive as oysters.

Marian Engel, *Bear* (1976)

5 Her eyes were so brown they appeared to have no pupils, giving her the smoldering look of a burning tire.

Laurie Colwin, "Imelda," *Passion and Affect* (1974)

6 They told me later my eyes were sticking out like organ stops.

Anne Worboys, "The Last Cog in the Law Machine," in Dilys Winn, *Murder Ink* (1977)

7 One woman . . . claimed that with her eyes alone she could bring a man to the verge of climax. She did it by looking directly into his eyes and concentrating, like Uri Geller bending a fork. (In fact, I don't know why I'm being so coy about it. It was me.)

Helen Lawrenson, *Whistling Girl* (1978)

8 His eyes . . . not only undressed you unblinkingly, but shaved your head, called your parents, and refused to refinance your house.

Carrie Fisher, *Surrender the Pink* (1990)

9 Her dull mushroom eyes seemed to have grown smaller, as though they had been sautéed too long.

Helen Hudson, *Meyer Meyer* (1967)

See also Face.

# F

§ FACE

1 The mind, the tongue, soon learn to dissemble, to guard a secret well, but the human face is a window.

  Lawrence L. Lynch, *Shadowed by Three* (1883)

2 I carry my unwritten poems in cipher on my face!

  George Eliot, *Romola* (1862)

3 I have not learned happily / to live with my face.

  Diane Wakoski, "I Have Had to Learn to Live With My Face," *The Motorcycle Betrayal Poems* (1971)

4 The face of a woman is always a help or a hindrance in her life story, whatever the strength or range of her mind, however important the things which concern her. Men have wanted it to be this way.

  Madame de Staël, "Vanity," *The Influence of the Passions* (1796)

5 Nature gives you the face you have at twenty; it is up to you to merit the face you have at fifty.

  Coco Chanel, in *Ladies' Home Journal* (1956)

6 The facial contours of youth were deceptive. . . . It was only when age began to write on the face that the signature could no longer be forged.

  Marjorie Carleton, *Vanished* (1955)

7 Nothing ruins a face so fast as double-dealing. Your face telling one story to the world. Your heart yanking your face to pieces, trying to let the truth be known.

  Jessamyn West, *The Life I Really Lived* (1979)

8 A face that has the marks of having lived intensely, that expresses some phase of life, some dominant quality or intellectual power, constitutes for me an interesting face. For this reason, the face of an older person, perhaps not beautiful in the strictest sense, is usually more appealing than the face of a younger person who has scarcely been touched by life.

  Doris Ulmann, in Dale Warren, "Doris Ulmann: Photographer-in-Waiting," *The Bookman* (1930)

9 Her face is closed as a nut, / closed as a careful snail / or a thousand-year-old seed.

  Elizabeth Bishop, "House Guest," *The Complete Poems* (1969)

10 Dalloway's face tightened like a fist.

  Margaret Millar, *Rose's Last Summer* (1952)

11 Her face worked and broke into strained, hardening lines, as if there had been a death—that too-explicit evidence of agony in the desire to communicate.

  Eudora Welty, "The Key," *A Curtain of Green* (1941)

12 Orin was pacing the floor with a face as long as the moral law.

  Kathleen Moore Knight, *Akin to Murder* (1953)

13 Una's face was an unbroken block of calculation, saving where, upon her upper lip, a little down of hair fluttered. Yet it gave one an uncanny feeling. It made one think of a tassel on a hammer.

  Djuna Barnes, "The Earth" (1916), *Smoke* (1982)

14 His face looked as if it had rotted when it should have matured.

  Liza Cody, *Dupe* (1981)

15 She could imagine his expression . . . anxiety and annoyance chasing each other like the hands of a clock around his wide, flat face.

  Helen Hudson, *Meyer Meyer* (1967)

16 [He had a] face like a buttered scone, dripping complacency.

  Helen Hudson, "After Cortés," *The Listener* (1968)

1 She drooped her eyelids and put on an expression that made her face look like an unmade bed.

Rebecca West, *The Thinking Reed* (1936)

See also Body, Ears, Eyes, Mouth, Smile, Teeth.

## ❧ FACTS

2 Fact explains nothing. On the contrary, it is fact that requires explanation.

Marilynne Robinson, *Housekeeping* (1980)

3 There is nothing so uncertain and slippery as *fact*.

Sara Coleridge (1849), *Memoir and Letters*, vol. 2 (1873)

4 When we know what we want to prove, we go out and find our facts. They are always there.

Pearl S. Buck, *God's Men* (1951)

5 If there is an opinion, facts will be found to support it.

Judy Sproles, in *Omni* (1979)

6 There's a world of difference between truth and facts. Facts can obscure the truth.

Maya Angelou, in Brian Lanker, *I Dream a World* (1989)

7 People who mistake facts for ideas are incomplete thinkers; they are gossips.

Cynthia Ozick, "We Are the Crazy Lady and Other Feisty Feminist Fables," in Francine Klagsbrun, ed., *The First Ms. Reader* (1972)

8 Facts don't lie—not if you've got enough of 'em.

John Stephen Strange, *Silent Witnesses* (1938)

9 She always says, my lord, that facts are like cows. If you look them in the face hard enough they generally run away.

Dorothy L. Sayers, *Clouds of Witness* (1926)

10 We cannot alter facts, but we can alter our ways of looking at them.

Phyllis Bottome, *Under the Skin* (1950)

11 Facts—all facts—explain and confirm each other. They are only partially true until you link them together.

Willa Gibbs, *Tell Your Sons* (1946)

12 The most familiar facts are often hardest to understand.

Charlotte Perkins Gilman, *Human Work* (1904)

13 Every fact is a clod, from which may grow an amaranth or a palm.

Margaret Fuller, *Summer on the Lakes* (1844)

14 Facts are only tools to gain control over yourself and other people.

Nikki Giovanni, *Gemini* (1971)

15 The human race's favorite method for being in control of facts is to ignore them.

Celia Green, *The Decline and Fall of Science* (1976)

16 No facts however indubitably detected, no effort of reason however magnificently maintained, can prove that Bach's music is beautiful.

Edith Hamilton, *Witness to the Truth* (1948)

17 In science, all facts, no matter how trivial or banal, enjoy democratic equality.

Mary McCarthy, "The Fact in Fiction," *On the Contrary* (1961)

See also Data, Information, Knowledge.

## ❧ FAILURE

18 Failure? / I'm not ashamed to tell it, / I never learned to spell it. / Not Failure.

Maya Angelou, *Wouldn't Take Nothing for My Journey Now* (1993)

19 Failure is just another way to learn how to do something right.

Marian Wright Edelman, *Families in Peril* (1987)

20 A series of failures may culminate in the best possible result.

Gisela M.A. Richter, *My Memoirs: Recollections of an Archaeologist's Life* (1972)

21 Sometimes what you want to do *has* to fail so you won't.

Margueritte Harmon Bro, *Sarah* (1949)

22 People fail forward to success.

Mary Kay Ash, *On People Management* (1984)

23 Some of the biggest failures I ever had were successes.

Pearl Bailey, *Talking to Myself* (1971)

24 Nothing succeeds like failure.

Rebecca West, in Agnes de Mille, *Dance to the Piper* (1952)

1 Apparent failure may hold in its rough shell the germs of a success that will blossom in time, and bear fruit throughout eternity.

Frances Ellen Watkins Harper (1875), in Frances Smith Foster, ed., *A Brighter Coming Day* (1990)

2 In a total work, the failures have their not unimportant place.

May Sarton, *Mrs. Stevens Hears the Mermaids Singing* (1965)

3 No honest work of man or woman "fails"; / It feeds the sum of all human action.

Michelene Wandor, *Aurora Leigh* (1979)

4 Flops are a part of life's menu and I've never been a girl to miss out on any of the courses.

Rosalind Russell, in *The New York Herald Tribune* (1957)

5 If you have made mistakes, even serious ones, there is always another chance for you. What we call failure is not the falling down, but the staying down.

Mary Pickford, in *Reader's Digest* (1979)

6 When I strike the earth, like the giant of old, I rise more violently than ever.

Wanda Gág, *Growing Pains* (1940)

7 Best to have failure happen early. It wakes up the phoenix bird in you.

Anne Baxter, in John Robert Colombo, *Popcorn in Paradise* (1979)

8 Mine was a life of failure—one thing after another—like most lives . . . but that is all right, it is universal, it is the great human experience to fail.

Katharine Butler Hathaway, *The Journals and Letters of the Little Locksmith* (1946)

9 If at first you don't succeed, destroy all evidence that you tried.

Susan Ohanian, *Ask Ms. Class* (1996)

10 Three failures denote uncommon strength. A weakling has not enough grit to fail thrice.

Minna Thomas Antrim, *At the Sign of the Golden Calf* (1905)

11 The sheer rebelliousness in giving ourselves permission to fail frees a childlike awareness and clarity. . . . When we give ourselves permission to fail, we at the same time give ourselves permission to excel.

Eloise Ristad, *A Soprano on Her Head* (1982)

12 When we can begin to take our failures non-seriously, it means we are ceasing to be afraid of them.

It is of immense importance to learn to *laugh at ourselves*.

Katherine Mansfield (1922), *Journal of Katherine Mansfield* (1927)

13 Failure must be but a challenge to others.

Amelia Earhart, *Last Flight* (1937)

14 Is it age, or was it always my nature, to take a bad time, block out the good times, until any success became an accident and failure seemed the only truth?

Lillian Hellman, *An Unfinished Woman* (1969)

15 Close only counts in horseshoes.

Joan Hess, *A Really Cute Corpse* (1988)

16 To think of losing is to lose already.

Sylvia Townsend Warner (1951), in William Maxwell, ed., *Letters: Sylvia Townsend Warner* (1982)

17 Victory is fleeting, but losing is forever.

Billie Jean King, with Kim Chapin, *Billie Jean* (1974)

18 The art of losing isn't hard to master.

Elizabeth Bishop, "One Art," *Geography III* (1976)

19 In all failures, the beginning is certainly the half of the whole.

George Eliot, *Middlemarch* (1871)

20 Failure can get to be a rather comfortable old friend.

Mignon McLaughlin, *The Second Neurotic's Notebook* (1966)

21 Success and failure are both greatly overrated but failure gives you a whole lot more to talk about.

Hildegard Knef, *The Gift Horse* (1970)

See also Defeat, Error, Mistakes, Success and Failure.

## ✦ FAINTING

22 Birdeen fainted the way other people took a nap. She wouldn't take a rest of her own free will. Nature gave her a rest by letting her lie down unconscious for a few minutes.

Jessamyn West, *The State of Stony Lonesome* (1984)

## ❦ FAIRNESS

1 Fair and unfair are among the most influential words in English and must be delicately used.
Freya Stark, *A Peak in Darien* (1976)

2 Nothing is satisfactory that is one-sided.
Charles Egbert Craddock, *The Story of Old Fort Loudon* (1889)

3 Fair play is less characteristic of groups than of individuals.
Agnes Repplier, "Are Americans Timid?" *Under Dispute* (1924)

4 Lack of fairness to an opponent is essentially a sign of weakness.
Emma Goldman, *Living My Life* (1931)

See also Justice.

## ❦ FAITH

5 Faith hasn't got no eyes, but she' long-legged.
Zora Neale Hurston, *Jonah's Gourd Vine* (1934)

6 Faith is that quality or power by which the things desired become the things possessed.
Kathryn Kuhlman, *I Believe in Miracles* (1962)

7 Faith is not *being sure*. It is *not being sure*, but betting with your last cent.
Mary Jean Irion, *Yes, World* (1970)

8 When faith is supported by facts or by logic it ceases to be faith.
Edith Hamilton, *Witness to the Truth* (1948)

9 If it can be verified, we don't need faith. . . . Faith is for that which lies on the *other* side of reason. Faith is what makes life bearable, with all its tragedies and ambiguities and sudden, startling joys.
Madeleine L'Engle, *Walking on Water* (1980)

10 Faith is not belief. Belief is passive. Faith is active.
Edith Hamilton, *Witness to the Truth* (1948)

11 Faith walks simply, childlike, between the darkness of human life and the hope of what is to come.
Catherine de Hueck Doherty, *Poustinia* (1975)

12 Faith is the centerpiece of a connected life. It allows us to live by the grace of invisible strands. It is a belief in a wisdom superior to our own. Faith becomes a teacher in the absence of fact.
Terry Tempest Williams, *Refuge* (1991)

13 Faith is an excitement and an enthusiasm, a state of intellectual magnificence which we must . . . not squander on our way through life in the small coin of empty words and inexact, pedantic arguments.
George Sand, *Correspondance de George Sand*, vol. 5 (1884)

14 Faith . . . is nothing at all tangible. It is simply believing God; and, like sight, it is nothing apart from its object. You might as well shut your eyes and look inside, and see whether you have sight, as to look inside to discover whether you have faith.
Hannah Whitall Smith, *The Christian's Secret of a Happy Life* (1870)

15 Who has seen the wind? / Neither you nor I: / But when the trees bow down their heads / The wind is passing by.
Christina Rossetti, "Who Has Seen the Wind?" *The Poetical Works of Christina Georgina Rossetti* (1904)

16 Doubt is a necessity of the mind, faith of the heart.
Comtesse Diane, *Les Glanes de la Vie* (1898)

17 Faith, it seems to me, is not the holding of certain dogmas; it is simply openness and readiness of heart to believe any truth which God may show.
Margaret Deland, *John Ward, Preacher* (1888)

18 The prayer that reforms the sinner and heals the sick is an absolute faith that all things are possible to God.
Mary Baker Eddy, *Science and Health* (1875)

19 It seems to me that in our time faith in God is the same thing as faith in good and the ultimate triumph of good over evil.
Svetlana Alliluyeva, *Twenty Letters to a Friend* (1967)

20 The world is full of people who have lost faith: politicians who have lost faith in politics, social workers who have lost faith in social work, schoolteachers who have lost faith in teaching and, for all I know, policemen who have lost faith in policing and poets who have lost faith in poetry. It's a condition of faith that it gets lost from time to time, or at least mislaid.
P.D. James, *A Taste for Death* (1986)

21 Possessing faith is not convenient. You still have to live it.
Françoise Mallet-Joris, *A Letter to Myself* (1963)

1 Faith is not making religious-sounding noises in the daytime. It is asking your inmost self questions at night—and then getting up and going to work.

> Mary Jean Irion, *Yes, World* (1970)

2 Faith is a curious thing. It must be renewed; it has its own spring.

> Gladys Taber, *The Book of Stillmeadow* (1948)

3 It is the virtue of the storm, just as happiness is the virtue of the sunshine.

> Ruth Benedict, in Margaret Mead, *An Anthropologist at Work* (1959)

4 If there be a faith that can remove mountains, it is faith in one's own power.

> Marie von Ebner-Eschenbach, *Aphorisms* (1893)

5 Kill the snake of doubt in your soul, crush the worms of fear in your heart and mountains will move out of your way.

> Kate Seredy, *The White Stag* (1937)

6 Faith is not a series of gilt-edged propositions that you sit down to figure out, and if you follow all the logic and accept all the conclusions, then you have it. It is crumpling and throwing away everything, proposition by proposition, until nothing is left, and then writing a new proposition, your very own, to throw in the teeth of despair.

> Mary Jean Irion, *Yes, World* (1970)

7 Without faith, nothing is possible. With it, nothing is impossible.

> Mary McLeod Bethune, in Mary Alice Warner and Dayna Beilenson, eds., *Women of Faith and Spirit* (1987)

8 Faith is fundamentally a kind of folly.

> Catherine de Hueck Doherty, *Poustinia* (1975)

9 "Faith" is a fine invention / When Gentlemen can *see* — / But *Microscopes* are prudent / In an Emergency.

> Emily Dickinson (1860), *Poems by Emily Dickinson*, 2nd series (1891)

See also Belief, Doubt, Religion, Spirituality, Trust.

## ♦ FAITHFULNESS

10 God has not called me to be successful; he has called me to be faithful.

> Mother Teresa, in *The New York Times* (1980)

11 And Ruth said, Entreat me not to leave thee, or to return from following after thee: for whither thou goest, I will go; and where thou lodgest, I will lodge; thy people shall be my people, and thy God, my God. Where thou diest, will I die, and there will I be buried: the Lord do so to me, and more also, if aught but death part thee and me.

> Ruth, Ruth 1:16-17 (c. 1100 B.C.)

12 Oh! when thy heart and home were glad, / I freely shared thy joyous lot; / And now that heart is lone and sad, / Cease to entreat—I'll leave thee not.

> Frances Ellen Watkins Harper, "Ruth and Naomi," *Poems on Miscellaneous Subjects* (1857)

13 My faithfulness is but fidelity / Since I am never faithful, but to you.

> Laurence Hope, "To Aziz: Song of Mahomed Akram," *Stars of the Desert* (1903)

14 Old love, old love, / How can I be true? / Shall I be faithless to myself / Or to you?

> Sara Teasdale, "New Love and Old," *Rivers to the Sea* (1915)

15 It is better to be unfaithful than faithful without wanting to be.

> Brigitte Bardot, in *The Observer* (1968)

See also Constancy, Loyalty, Virtue.

## ♦ FAME

16 Fame is a fickle food / Upon a shifting plate.

> Emily Dickinson, in Martha Dickinson Bianchi, ed., *The Single Hound* (1914)

17 Fame is a bee. / It has a song — / It has a sting — / Ah, too, it has a wing.

> Emily Dickinson (1898), in Thomas H. Johnson, ed., *The Complete Poems of Emily Dickinson* (1960)

18 Fame is a pearl many dive for and only a few bring up. Even when they do, it is not perfect, and they sigh for more, and lose better things in struggling for them.

> Louisa May Alcott, *Jo's Boys* (1886)

19 Fame is a boomerang.

> Maria Callas, in Arianna Stassinopoulos, *Maria Callas* (1981)

20 It's such a corrosive chemical: fame.

> Candice Bergen, in David Bailey and Peter Evans, *Goodbye Baby and Amen* (1969)

1 So this was fame at last! Nothing but a vast debt to be paid to the world in energy, blood, and time.

    May Sarton, *Mrs. Stevens Hears the Mermaids Singing* (1965)

2 That's what fame is: solitude.

    Coco Chanel, in Marcel Haedrich, *Coco Chanel* (1972)

3 Fame always brings loneliness. Success is as ice cold and as lonely as the north pole.

    Vicki Baum, *Grand Hotel* (1929)

4 Fame separates you from life.

    Anne Morrow Lindbergh, in Julie Nixon Eisenhower, *Special People* (1977)

5 Fame is bought by happiness.

    L.E. Landon, *Ethel Churchill* (1837)

6 Fame compensates for a column of wants.

    Gertrude Atherton, *Los Cerritos* (1890)

7 I am not famous for anything in particular. I am just famous.

    Iris Murdoch, *The Flight From the Enchanter* (1956)

8 You don't get to choose what you get famous for and you don't get to control which of your life's many struggles gets to stand for you.

    Erica Jong, *Fear of Fifty* (1994)

9 Do not confound noise with fame. The man who is remembered, is not always honored.

    Frances Wright, *A Few Days in Athens* (1822)

10 It takes very little fire to make a great deal of smoke nowadays, and notoriety is not real glory.

    Louisa May Alcott, *Jo's Boys* (1886)

11 People feel fame gives them some kind of privilege to walk up to you and say anything to you, of any kind of nature—and it won't hurt your feelings—like it's happening to your clothing.

    Marilyn Monroe, in Gloria Steinem, "Marilyn: The Woman Who Died Too Soon," *Ms.* (1972)

12 The Press blew, the public stared, hands flew out like a million little fishes after bread.

    Enid Bagnold, *National Velvet* (1935)

13 He had managed to get himself so much publicity that he was even better than well-known; he had enemies.

    Lucille Kallen, *Out There, Somewhere* (1964)

14 There may be wonder in money, but, dear God, there is money in wonder.

    Enid Bagnold, *National Velvet* (1935)

15 Americans respect talent only insofar as it leads to fame, and we reserve our most fervent admiration for famous people who destroy their lives as well as their talent. The fatal flaws of Elvis, Judy, and Marilyn register much higher on our national applause meter than their living achievements. In America, talent is merely a tool for becoming famous in life so you can become more famous in death—where all are equal.

    Florence King, *Lump It or Leave It* (1990)

16 Legend adheres to artists whose deaths seem the corollaries of their works.

    Joyce Johnson, *Minor Characters* (1983)

17 That's the trouble with hitching your wagon to a star—nothing happens when you say, "Giddyap!"

    Margaret Halsey, *Some of My Best Friends Are Soldiers* (1944)

See also Celebrity, Comebacks, Notoriety, "Somebody."

## ❧ FAMILIARITY

18 Fish are not the best authority on water.

    Jane Yolen, *Sister Light, Sister Dark* (1988)

19 You do not notice changes in what is always before you.

    Colette, *My Apprenticeships* (1936)

20 I like familiarity. In me it does not breed contempt. Only more familiarity.

    Gertrude Stein, in *Reader's Digest* (1935)

21 Familiarity doesn't breed contempt, it *is* contempt.

    Florence King, *With Charity Toward None* (1992)

22 Familiarity breeds consent.

    Rita Mae Brown, *In Her Day* (1976)

23 People who live at a distance are naturally less faulty than those immediately under our own eyes.

    George Eliot, *The Mill on the Floss* (1860)

1 She was the crow of the reservation, she lived off our scraps, and she knew us best because the scraps told our story.

> Louise Erdrich, *Tracks* (1988)

# ❦ FAMILY

2 The family—that dear octopus from whose tentacles we never quite escape, nor, in our inmost hearts, ever quite wish to.

> Dodie Smith, *Dear Octopus* (1938)

3 Call it a clan, call it a network, call it a tribe, call it a family. Whatever you call it, whoever you are, you need one.

> Jane Howard, *Families* (1978)

4 Families will not be broken. Curse and expel them, send their children wandering, drown them in floods and fires, and old women will make songs out of all these sorrows and sit in the porches and sing them on mild evenings.

> Marilynne Robinson, *Housekeeping* (1980)

5 We cannot destroy kindred: our chains stretch a little sometimes, but they never break.

> Marie de Rabutin-Chantal, Marquise de Sévigné (1670), *Letters of Madame de Sévigné to Her Daughter and Her Friends*, vol. 1 (1811)

6 Healthy families are our greatest national resource.

> Dolores Curran, *Traits of a Healthy Family* (1983)

7 Our family never had any hard luck, because nothing seemed hard luck to it, nor was it ever disgraced for there was nothing which it would acknowledge as disgrace.

> Box-Car Bertha, *Sister of the Road* (1937)

8 What families have in common the world around is that they are the place where people learn who they are and how to be that way.

> Jean Illsley Clarke, *Self-Esteem* (1978)

9 Every family is a "normal" family—no matter whether it has one parent, two or no children at all. A family can be made up of any combination of people, heterosexual or homosexual, who share their lives in an intimate (not necessarily sexual) way. . . . Wherever there is lasting love, there is a family.

> Shere Hite, *The Hite Report on the Family* (1994)

10 The family. We were a strange little band of characters trudging through life sharing diseases and toothpaste, coveting one another's desserts, hiding shampoo, borrowing money, locking each other out of our rooms, inflicting pain and kissing to heal it in the same instant, loving, laughing, defending, and trying to figure out the common thread that bound us all together.

> Erma Bombeck, *Family—The Ties That Bind . . . And Gag!* (1987)

11 They none of them threw themselves into the interests of the rest, but each plowed his or her own furrow. Their thoughts, their little passions and hopes and desires, all ran along separate lines. Family life is like this—animated, but collateral.

> Rose Macaulay, *Daisy and Daphne* (1928)

12 Within our family there was no such thing as a person who did not matter. Second cousins thrice removed mattered. We knew—and thriftily made use of—everybody's middle name. We knew who was buried where. We all mattered, and the dead most of all.

> Shirley Abbott, *Womenfolks: Growing Up Down South* (1983)

13 The particular human chain we're part of is central to our individual identity. Even if we loathe our families, in order to know ourselves, we seem to need to know about them, just as prologue. Not to know is to live with some of the disorientation and anxiety of the amnesiac.

> Elizabeth Stone, *Black Sheep and Kissing Cousins* (1988)

14 Pluck from under the family all the props which religion and morality have given it, strip it of the glamour, true or false, cast round it by romance, it will still remain a prosaic, indisputable fact, that the whole business of begetting, bearing and rearing children, is the most essential of all the nation's businesses.

> Eleanor F. Rathbone, *The Disinherited Family* (1924)

15 When all of us had time to be together we didn't want to share it with outsiders. As a result the Kennedy children became natives of the Kennedy family, first and foremost, before any city or any country.

> Rose Kennedy (1939), in Laurence Leamer, *The Kennedy Women* (1994)

16 Large families are apt to get into a state of savage exclusiveness.

> Charlotte M. Yonge, *The Pillars of the House*, vol. 1 (1889)

1 The great advantage of living in a large family is that early lesson of life's essential unfairness.
Nancy Mitford, *The Pursuit of Love* (1945)

2 Family is just accident. . . . They don't mean to get on your nerves. They don't even mean to be your family, they just are.
Marsha Norman, *'Night, Mother* (1983)

3 Blacks concede that hurrawing, jibing, jiving, signifying, disrespecting, cursing, even outright insults might be acceptable under particular conditions, but aspersions cast against one's family call for immediate attack.
Maya Angelou, *All God's Children Need Traveling Shoes* (1986)

4 The first world we find ourselves in is a family that is not of our choosing.
Harriet Lerner, *The Dance of Deception* (1993)

5 There's something stubborn about families, unhappy ones in particular: they outlive themselves, and then they live on.
Daphne Merkin, *Enchantment* (1986)

6 Family jokes, though rightly cursed by strangers, are the bond that keeps most families alive.
Stella Benson, *Pipers and a Dancer* (1924)

7 Heirlooms we don't have in our family. But stories we've got.
Rose Chernin, in Kim Chernin, *In My Mother's House* (1983)

8 Like all cultures, one of the family's first jobs is to persuade its members they're special, more wonderful than the neighboring barbarians. The persuasion consists of stories showing family members demonstrating admirable traits, which it claims are family traits. Attention to the stories' actual truth is never the family's most compelling consideration. Encouraging belief is.
Elizabeth Stone, *Black Sheep and Kissing Cousins* (1988)

9 It will be a beautiful family talk, mean and worried and full of sorrow and spite and excitement.
Ivy Compton-Burnett, *A Family and a Fortune* (1939)

10 Family traits, like murder, will out. Nature has but so many molds.
Louise Imogen Guiney, *Goose-Quill Papers* (1885)

11 A group of closely related persons living under one roof; it is a convenience, often a necessity, sometimes a pleasure, sometimes the reverse; but who first exalted it as admirable, an almost religious ideal?
Rose Macaulay, *The World My Wilderness* (1950)

12 Family life! The United Nations is child's play compared to the tugs and splits and need to understand and forgive in any family.
May Sarton, *Kinds of Love* (1970)

13 Marry orphans or immigrants.
Elizabeth Stone, *Black Sheep and Kissing Cousins* (1988)

14 If there's anythin' on earth that can be more tryin' than any kind of relative, I don't know what it is, but relatives by marriage comes first—easy.
Myrtle Reed, *A Weaver of Dreams* (1911)

15 In the traditional family structure of Persia . . . one simply cannot discard close relatives just because one does not like them; rather one has to accommodate them, make allowances and accept them, like misfortune.
Shusha Guppy, *The Blindfold Horse* (1988)

16 With relatives, long distance is even better than being there.
Lynne Alpern and Esther Blumenfeld, *Oh, Lord, I Sound Just Like Mama* (1986)

17 You think you have a handle on God, the Universe, and the Great White Light until you go home for Thanksgiving. In an hour, you realize how far you've got to go and who is the real turkey.
Shirley MacLaine, *Dance While You Can* (1991)

18 Nobody, who has not been in the interior of a family, can say what the difficulties of any individual of that family may be.
Jane Austen, *Emma* (1816)

19 This family was a raw onion. Peel off one tear-inducing layer of deception, and you found another.
Judith Van Gieson, *The Lies That Bind* (1993)

20 In some families, *please* is described as the magic word. In our house, however, it was *sorry*.
Margaret Laurence, *A Bird in the House* (1963)

21 We had codes / In our house.
Louise Glück, "Scraps," *Firstborn* (1968)

22 In families there are frequently matters of which no one speaks, nor even alludes. There are no words for these matters. As the binding skeleton beneath

the flesh is never acknowledged by us and, when at last it defines itself, is after all an obscenity.

Joyce Carol Oates, *I Lock My Door Upon Myself* (1990)

1 One may have staunch friends in one's own family, but one seldom has admirers.

Willa Cather, *The Song of the Lark* (1915)

2 Personal hatred and family affection are not incompatible; they often flourish and grow strong together.

Willa Cather, *Lucy Gayheart* (1935)

3 We do not discuss the members of our family to their faces.

Ivy Compton-Burnett, *A House and Its Head* (1935)

4 Family life in America is a minefield, an economic trap for women, a study in disappointment for both sexes.

Anne Roiphe, *Lovingkindness* (1987)

5 Unkindness is death to the home. One unkind, unsocial, critical, eternally dissatisfied member can destroy any family.

Kathleen Norris, *Hands Full of Living* (1931)

6 Family relationships have made me so *ill*!

Sophia Tolstoy (1897), in O.A. Golinenko et al., eds., *The Diaries of Sophia Tolstoy* (1985)

7 It was the old psychosomatic side-step. Everyone in my family dances it at every opportunity. You've given me a splitting headache! You've given me indigestion! You've given me crotch rot! You've given me auditory hallucinations! You've given me a heart attack! You've given me cancer!

Erica Jong, *Fear of Flying* (1973)

8 The psychological attitudes which are indispensable in the American market place are disastrous to family life. Family life . . . requires yieldingness, generosity, sympathy, altruism, tenderness—all the qualities, in fact, which lead straight to bankruptcy. . . . The American family is tragically out of gear with the profit structure which has mushroomed up around it.

Margaret Halsey, *The Folks at Home* (1952)

9 The family as an institution is *both* oppressive and protective and, depending on the issue, is experienced sometimes one way, sometimes the other—often in some mix of the two—by most people who live in families.

Lillian Breslow Rubin, *Worlds of Pain* (1976)

10 One never knows how much a family may grow; and when a hive is too full, and it is necessary to form a new swarm, each one thinks of carrying away his own honey.

George Sand, *The Haunted Pool* (1851)

11 The men in this family seemed like garden flowers, sweet and colorful and quick to fade. . . . The women, by contrast, were like weeds—there were so many of them, and they lasted on and on with a minimal flowering, able to subsist on altogether less in the way of space, nourishment and hope.

Judith Grossman, *Her Own Terms* (1988)

12 Families composed of rugged individualists have to do things obliquely.

Florence King, *Confessions of a Failed Southern Lady* (1985)

See also Ancestors, Aunts, Brothers, Childhood, Children, Daughters, "Family Values," Fathers, Grandparents, Heredity, Husbands, Marriage, Mothers, Parenthood, Parents, Relationships, Roots, Siblings, Sisters, Sons, Television, Uncles, Wives.

## ❧ "FAMILY VALUES"

13 Though it is fairly easy to describe what constitutes a bad home, there is no simple definition of a good one. Conformity with the traditional pattern certainly is no guarantee of the happiest results.

Alva Myrdal and Viola Klein, *Women's Two Roles* (1956)

14 The capacity of the human mind to resist knowledge is nowhere more painfully illustrated than in the postulate laid down by average minds that home is always to be just what it is now—forgetting that in no two consecutive generations has it remained the same.

Frances E. Willard, in Anna A. Gordon, ed., *What Frances E. Willard Said* (1905)

15 The home is a human institution. All human institutions are open to improvement.

Charlotte Gilman, *The Home* (1903)

16 Fortunately the family is a human institution: humans made it and humans can change it.

Shere Hite, *The Hite Report on the Family* (1994)

## ❦ FANATICISM

1 Without fanaticism one cannot accomplish anything.

> Eva Perón, in *Time* (1951)

2 Hell hath no fury like a fanatic asked to find a reason for what he's doing. He simply wants to do it, and generally he wants to do it because he observes, often unconsciously, that something new is coming into existence and he doesn't like it, and he's going out with fire and sword to hold it back.

> Gwen Bristow, *Tomorrow Is Forever* (1943)

3 Every believer is an anarchist at heart. True believers would rather see governments topple and history rewritten than scuff the cover of their faith.

> Jeanette Winterson, *Boating for Beginners* (1985)

4 There is no fanatic like a religious fanatic.

> Agatha Christie, "The Chocolate Box," *Poirot Investigates* (1925)

5 Fanatics are, for one thing, boring and, for another, unreliable. They tend to burn out just when you need them.

> Nikki Giovanni, in Mari E. Evans, ed., *Black Women Writers (1950-1980)* (1984)

See also Cranks, Extremes.

## ❦ FANTASY

6 If one is lucky a solitary fantasy can totally transform one million realities.

> Maya Angelou, *The Heart of a Woman* (1981)

7 If you have enough fantasies, you're ready, in the event that something happens.

> Sheila Ballantyne, *Norma Jean the Termite Queen* (1975)

See also Daydreams, Dreams, Imagination.

## ❦ FANTASY FICTION

8 Dragons are more dangerous, and a good deal commoner, than bears. Fantasy is nearer to poetry, to mysticism, and to insanity than naturalistic fiction is. It is a real wilderness, and those who go there should not feel too safe.

> Ursula K. Le Guin, "From Elfland to Poughkeepsie" (1973), *Language of the Night* (1979)

9 Those who refuse to listen to dragons are probably doomed to spend their lives acting out the nightmares of politicians. We like to think we live in daylight, but half the world is always dark; and fantasy, like poetry, speaks the language of the night.

> Ursula K. Le Guin, *Language of the Night* (1979)

## ❦ FAREWELLS

10 Farewell to thee, farewell to thee . . . / Until we meet again.

> Lydia Kamekeha Liliuokalani, "Aloha Oe" (1878)

11 Farewell's a bitter word to say.

> L.E. Landon, *Ethel Churchill* (1837)

12 Nothing is so dear as what you're about to leave.

> Jessamyn West, *The Life I Really Lived* (1979)

13 We never know the good we have till constant friends depart / And leave us just with half a life and half a heart.

> Katharine Tynan Hinkson, "The Mist That's Over Ireland," *Irish Poems* (1914)

14 In thoughts one keeps a reserve of hope, in spite of everything. You cannot say good-bye in imagination. That is something you can only do in actuality.

> Shirley Hazzard, *The Transit of Venus* (1980)

15 Every arrival foretells a leave-taking: every birth a death. Yet each death and departure comes to us as a surprise, a sorrow never anticipated. Life is a long series of farewells; only the circumstances should surprise us.

> Jessamyn West, *The Life I Really Lived* (1979)

16 In all separations there are the elements of eternity; and in every farewell to the being we love we set foot upon an undug grave.

> Mary Adams, *Confessions of a Wife* (1902)

17 Every day I shall put my papers in order and every day I shall say farewell. And the real farewell, when it comes, will only be a small outward confirmation

of what has been accomplished within me from day to day.

Etty Hillesum (1942), *An Interrupted Life* (1983)

1 Good-byes breed a sort of distaste for whomever you say good-bye to; this hurts, you feel, this must not happen again.

Elizabeth Bowen, *The House in Paris* (1935)

2 Mayo was anxious to leave and like so many enthusiasts seemed liable to turn a social escape into a jail break if anything threatened to hinder him.

Margery Allingham, *The Mind Readers* (1965)

3 It is a widespread and firm belief among guests that their departure is always a matter of distress to their hosts, and that in order to indicate that they have been pleasantly entertained, they must demonstrate an extreme unwillingness to allow the entertainment to conclude. This is not necessarily true.

Judith Martin, *Miss Manners' Guide for the Turn-of-the-Millennium* (1989)

4 It is never any good dwelling on good-byes. It is not the being together that it prolongs, it is the parting.

Elizabeth Bibesco, *The Fir and the Palm* (1924)

5 It was typical of him that he lacked the taste to make a final exit. He spent too long at his farewells, chatting in the doorway, letting in the cold.

Anne Tyler, *Dinner at the Homesick Restaurant* (1982)

6 He turned back from the door. Apparently, like adolescents, he thought he had gone when he had said good-bye.

Rae Foley, *The Brownstone House* (1974)

7 You have delighted us long enough.

Jane Austen, *Pride and Prejudice* (1813)

See also End, Parting.

## ❧ FARMING

8 For all-around, everyday, all-season wear, farmers can't be beat. They are inclined to chafe under the burden of leisure (a minor vexation on the farm), but they thrive on neglect and adversity.

Patricia Penton Leimbach, *All My Meadows* (1977)

9 A farmer is dependent on too many things outside his control; it makes for modesty.

Bharati Mukherjee, *Jasmine* (1989)

10 How will you know a good farmer when you meet him? He will not ask you for any favors.

Jane Smiley, *A Thousand Acres* (1991)

11 The only difference between a pigeon and a farmer today is a pigeon can still make a deposit on a John Deere tractor.

M.E. Kerr, *Deliver Us From Evie* (1994)

12 Farming isn't what it was, and when I come to think on, it never has been.

Winifred Holtby, "Mr. Harper Larns 'Em" (1928), *Truth Is Not Sober* (1934)

13 It's a pleasanter way of losing money than most.

Josephine W. Johnson, *Now in November* (1934)

14 The truth is I've got the land on my back, an' it's drivin' me. Land is a hard driver.

Ellen Glasgow, *Barren Ground* (1925)

15 There's no beginning to the farmer's year, / Only recurrent patterns on a scroll / Unwinding.

Vita Sackville-West, "Spring," *The Land* (1927)

16 Once a man had thrust his hands into the soil and knew the grit of it between his teeth, he felt something rise within him that was not of his day or generation, but had persisted through birth and death from a time beyond recall.

Martha Ostenso, *The Stone Field* (1937)

17 Raise less corn and more hell.

Mary Elizabeth Lease (1892), advice to Kansas farmers, attributed, in Edward T. James, *Notable American Women 1607-1950*, vol. 2 (1971)

See also The Country.

## ❧ FASHION

18 Does fashion matter? Always—though not quite as much after death.

Joan Rivers, in *The New York Times Magazine* (1993)

19 As a lifelong fashion dropout, I have still read enough fashion mags while waiting at the dentist's to know that the object of fashion is to make A Statement—all I've achieved, statement-wise, is

"Woman Who Wears Clothes So She Won't Be Naked."

Molly Ivins, in *The Fort Worth Star-Telegram* (1992)

1 My mother insisted that I had to try things on to make sure they were becoming. Becoming what, I always asked.

Edith Konecky, *Allegra Maud Goldman* (1976)

2 I base most of my fashion taste on what doesn't itch.

Gilda Radner, *It's Always Something* (1989)

3 When people tell you a coat or dress is cut on classic lines it means it's something that isn't smart now and won't be smart ten years hence.

Anthony Gilbert, *A Case for Mr. Crook* (1952)

4 With issues like our country's teen-age pregnancy rate, fashion's importance ranks right up there with cleaning your ears. Except right before going on television to talk about teen-age pregnancy rates, when all I can think of is what I'm going to wear.

Jane Pratt, in *The New York Times Magazine* (1993)

5 Fashion, the constant and needless change of things, is fast becoming one of the greater ills of our time.

Elizabeth Hawes, *Men Can Take It* (1939)

6 Fashion is made to become unfashionable.

Coco Chanel, in *Life* (1957)

7 So soon as a fashion is universal, it is out of date.

Marie von Ebner-Eschenbach, *Aphorisms* (1893)

8 Fashion absolutely matters, but it doesn't matter absolutely.

Claudia Shear, in *The New York Times Magazine* (1993)

9 Fashion is architecture: it is a matter of proportions.

Coco Chanel, in Marcel Haedrich, *Coco Chanel* (1972)

10 It is not chic to be too chic.

Elsie de Wolfe, *After All* (1935)

11 No fashion has ever been created expressly for the lean purse or for the fat woman: the dressmaker's ideal is the thin millionairess.

Katharine Fullerton Gerould, *Modes and Morals* (1920)

12 Fashion seems to exist for an abstract person who is not you or me.

Elizabeth Bowen, *Collected Impressions* (1950)

13 To call a fashion wearable is the kiss of death. No new fashion worth its salt is ever wearable.

Eugenia Sheppard, in *The New York Herald Tribune* (1960)

14 Fashion, as we knew it, is over; people wear now exactly what they feel like wearing.

Mary Quant, in David Bailey and Peter Evans, *Goodbye Baby and Amen* (1969)

See also Appearance, Clothes, Dress, Elegance, Glamour, Style, Trends.

## ❦ FASTIDIOUSNESS

15 There is a great amount of poetry in unconscious fastidiousness.

Marianne Moore, "Critics and Connoisseurs," *Selected Poems* (1935)

## ❦ FAT

16 Women should try to increase their size rather than decrease it, because I believe the bigger we are, the more space we'll take up, and the more we'll have to be reckoned with. I think every woman should be fat like me.

Roseanne Barr, in *The Utne Reader* (1991)

17 She was fat and comfortable, both in mind and body.

L.T. Meade, *The Honorable Miss* (1900)

18 Mary first met us in the avenue. She looked so fat and well that we were made very happy by the sight of her.

Dorothy Wordsworth (1802), in William Knight, ed., *Journals of Dorothy Wordsworth*, vol. 1 (1897)

19 I'm tired of being regarded as less-than because of my more-than size. When are we going to understand that fat is an adjective, not an epithet?

Denise Rubin, in Leslie Lampert, "Fat Like Me," *St. Paul Pioneer Press* (1993)

20 The awful thing about being fat is you can't get away from it. Everywhere you go, there it is; all

round you; hanging and swinging, yards and yards of it, under your arms, everywhere. And everyone else is so thin.

Charlotte Bingham, *Coronet Among the Weeds* (1963)

1 All fat people are "outed" by their appearance.

Jennifer A. Coleman, in *Newsweek* (1993)

2 Fat is the last preserve for unexamined bigotry.

Jennifer A. Coleman, in *Newsweek* (1993)

3 Fat is a feminist issue.

Susie Orbach, book title (1978)

4 Fat people aren't really jolly. Sometimes we act that way so you will leave us alone. We pay a price for this. But at least we get to hang on to what self-respect we smuggled out of grade school and adolescence.

Jennifer A. Coleman, in *Newsweek* (1993)

5 He's got so many love handles he needs a bookmark to find his shorts.

Cynthia Heimel, *Get Your Tongue Out of My Mouth, I'm Kissing You Good-Bye!* (1993)

6 Nobody, but nobody, is as fat as she thinks she is.

Cynthia Heimel, *Sex Tips for Girls* (1983)

See also Dieting, Weight.

## ❦ FATE

7 Fate keeps on happening.

Anita Loos, *Gentlemen Prefer Blondes* (1925)

8 Fate is not an eagle, it creeps like a rat.

Elizabeth Bowen, *The House in Paris* (1935)

9 You strain like a hooked fish against this fate, then slowly weaken. Your silver scales dim.

Sheila Ballantyne, "Letters to the Darkness," *Life on Earth* (1988)

10 People so reasonable, so devoted, so strongly loving and hard working should have been exempt, one feels, from the vagaries of a malicious fate.

Janet Lewis, *The Wife of Martin Guerre* (1941)

11 Oh, how unconstantly our fortune turns. / One hour in joy, the next with sorrow mourns.

Mary Delarivière Manley, *The Royal Mischief* (1696)

12 These great turning-days of life cast no shadow before, slip by unconsciously. Only a trifle, a little turn of the rudder, and the ship goes to heaven or hell.

Rebecca Harding Davis, "Life in the Iron-Mills," in *The Atlantic Monthly* (1861)

13 Lives that flash in sunshine, and lives that are born in tears, receive their hue from circumstances.

Harriet A. Jacobs, *Incidents in the Life of a Slave Girl, Written by Herself* (1861)

14 Thus strangely are our souls constructed and by such slight ligaments are we bound to prosperity or ruin.

Mary Shelley, *Frankenstein* (1818)

15 All our footsteps, set to make / Metric advance, / Lapse into arcs in deference / To circumstance.

Josephine Miles, "On Inhabiting an Orange," *Poems (1930-1960)* (1960)

See also Coincidence, Destiny, Free Will, Luck.

## ❦ FATHERS

16 Father! blessed word.

Maria S. Cummins, *The Lamplighter* (1934)

17 To her the name of father was another name for love.

Fanny Fern, *Fresh Leaves* (1857)

18 No music is so pleasant to my ears as that word—father.

Lydia Maria Child, *Philothea* (1836)

19 Old as she was, she still missed her daddy sometimes.

Gloria Naylor, *Mama Day* (1988)

20 The sound of his father's voice was a necessity. He longed for the sight of his stooped shoulders as he had never, in the sharpest of his hunger, longed for food.

Marjorie Kinnan Rawlings, *The Yearling* (1938)

21 Every day I grieve / for your great heart broken and you gone.

Elaine Feinstein, "Dad," *Some Unease and Angels* (1977)

1  How I miss my father. / I wish he had not been / so tired / when I was / born.

> Alice Walker, "Poem at Thirty-Nine," *Horses Make a Landscape Look More Beautiful* (1979)

2  He was generous with his affection, given to great, awkward, engulfing hugs, and I can remember so clearly the smell of his hugs, all starched shirt, tobacco, Old Spice and Cutty Sark. Sometimes I think I've never been properly hugged since.

> Linda Ellerbee, *Move On* (1991)

3  My dear father! When I remember him, it is always with his arms open wide to love and comfort me.

> Isobel Field, *This Life I've Lived* (1937)

4  All the feeling which my father could not put into words was in his hand—any dog, child or horse would recognize the kindness of it.

> Freya Stark, *Traveler's Prelude* (1950)

5  He wrapt his little daughter in his large / Man's doublet, careless did it fit or no.

> Elizabeth Barrett Browning, *Aurora Leigh* (1857)

6  Whenever I try to recall that long-ago first day at school only one memory shines through: my father held my hand.

> Marcelene Cox, in *Ladies' Home Journal* (1954).

7  Beaming like a lesser god, / He bounced upon the earth he trod.

> May Sarton, "A Celebration for George Sarton," *In Time Like Air* (1958)

8  He can snare / The future in his net of deeds that bite / Reality.

> Mary O'Connor, "Man of Stature," in Katie May Gill, ed., *Father* (1957)

9  My father . . . lived as if he were poured from iron, and loved his family with a vulnerability that was touching.

> Mari E. Evans, in Mari E. Evans, ed., *Black Women Writers* (1984)

10  It was my father's hand that opened wide / The door to poetry, where printed line / Became alive.

> Helen Bean Byerly, "Father's Hand," in Katie May Gill, ed., *Father* (1957)

11  My heart is happy, my mind is free / I had a father who talked with me.

> Hilda Bigelow, in Abigail Van Buren, syndicated column "Dear Abby" (1993)

12  He opened the jar of pickles when no one else could. He was the only one in the house who wasn't afraid to go into the basement by himself. He cut himself shaving, but no one kissed it or got excited about it. It was understood when it rained, he got the car and brought it around to the door. When anyone was sick, he went out to get the prescription filled. He took lots of pictures . . . but he was never in them.

> Erma Bombeck, *Family—The Ties That Bind . . . And Gag!* (1987)

13  The history, the root, the strength of my father is the strength we / now rest on.

> Carolyn M. Rodgers, "For Our Fathers," *how i got ovah* (1975)

14  Down in the bottom of my childhood my father stands laughing.

> Tove Ditlevsen (1967), in Tiina Nunnally, tr., *Early Spring* (1985)

15  I laughed once in my father's face, / and he laughed, and the two laughters / locked like bumpers / that still rust away between us.

> Linda Pastan, "Between Generations," *A Perfect Circle of Sun* (1971)

16  One day I found in my hands the manuscript of a poem in my father's handwriting. He had died when I was only fifteen. We had been in love with each other ever since I could remember, but he had died while our minds were still separated by my immaturity.

> Katharine Butler Hathaway, *The Journals and Letters of the Little Locksmith* (1946)

17  It's a wise father that knows his own child—hood.

> Marcelene Cox, in *Ladies' Home Journal* (1945)

18  "I never could suffer infants, but this kid is different to all I've seen," is an expression often heard from proud young fathers.

> Miles Franklin, *Some Everyday Folk and Dawn* (1909)

19  Into the father's grave the daughter, sometimes a gray-haired woman, lays away forever the little pet names and memories which to all the rest of the world are but foolishness.

> Constance Fenimore Woolson, *Anne* (1882)

20  The mature, forty-five-year-old woman, quite experienced in matters of life and death, knows that it was "for the best," but Daddy's girl, who hung onto his belt and danced fox trots on the tops of his

shoes, cannot accept that Daddy is not here any-more.

Mary-Lou Weisman (1983), in Nancy R. Newhouse, ed., *Hers* (1986)

1 Like all children I had taken my father for granted. Now that I had lost him, I felt an emptiness that could never be filled. But I did not let myself cry, believing as a Muslim that tears pull a spirit earth-ward and won't let it be free.

Benazir Bhutto, *Daughter of Destiny* (1989)

2 My father walked with me, and still does walk, / Yet now, he reckons neither time nor space.

Mary Salinda Foster, "My Father Walked With Me" (1941), in Katie May Gill, ed., *Father* (1957)

3 Every father knows at once too much and too little about his own son.

Fanny Fern, *Fern Leaves*, 2nd series (1853)

4 My father, dead so long now, looms up as unex-plored landscape, the mountains of the moon, a text that has lain in a drawer, undeciphered, for which I have had no Rosetta Stone.

Shirley Abbott, *The Bookmaker's Daughter* (1991)

5 It doesn't matter who my father was; it matters who I *remember* he was.

Anne Sexton, "All God's Children Need Radios," in *Ms.* (1973)

6 My father is dead and I cannot turn him into a white rose, though I try.

Deborah Keenan, "Grace," *The Only Window That Counts* (1985)

7 I wanted him to cherish and approve of me, not as he had when I was a child, but as the woman I was, who had her own mind and had made her own choices.

Adrienne Rich, "Split at the Root," *Blood, Bread, and Poetry* (1986)

8 I want something from Daddy that he is not able to give me. . . . It is only that I long for Daddy's real love: not only as his child, but for me—Anne, my-self.

Anne Frank (1942), *The Diary of a Young Girl* (1952)

9 Oh my gloomy father, / why were you always so silent then.

Ingeborg Bachmann, "Curriculum Vitae," in Aliki Barnstone and Willis Barnstone, eds., *A Book of Women Poets From Antiquity to Now* (1980)

10 In my dreams / my father is always kind.

Paula Gunn Allen, "Paternity," *Shadow Country* (1982)

11 Father. I write all my poems so I may bury you more kindly. / Father. I write all my poems to keep you alive.

Deborah Keenan, "July Twenty-Seventh, Nineteen-Seventy Nine," *Household Wounds* (1981)

12 Early on, my abandoning father had set the pattern of my love life on the loom of my subconscious.

Jane Stanton Hitchcock, *Trick of the Eye* (1992)

13 The human father has to be confronted and recog-nized as human, as a man who created a child and then, by his absence, left the child fatherless and then Godless.

Anaïs Nin (1933), *The Diary of Anaïs Nin*, vol. 1 (1966)

14 Finding out about fathers is not easy. It's only in the last twenty years that they have been considered by the psychological community as much more than the "other" parent, taking a very distant sec-ond place to Mom.

Victoria Secunda, *Women and Their Fathers* (1992)

15 How many of the people I know—sons and daugh-ters—have intricate abstract expressionist paint-ings of their mothers, created out of their own emotions, attitudes, hands. And how many have only Polaroid pictures of their fathers.

Ellen Goodman, *At Large* (1981)

16 We criticize mothers for closeness. We criticize fa-thers for distance. How many of us have expected less from our fathers and appreciated what they gave us more? How many of us always let them off the hook?

Ellen Goodman, *At Large* (1981)

17 A father had to work only half as hard as any mother to be considered twice as good.

Mary Kay Blakely, *American Mom* (1994)

18 Four people, four lives that boiled down to one life and that was my father's. What occupied him was what occupied us.

Irene Mayer Selznick, *A Private View* (1983)

19 They didn't believe their father had ever been young; surely even in the cradle he had been a very, very small man in a gray suit, with a little dark mustache and flat, incurious eyes.

Richard Shattuck, *The Half-Haunted Saloon* (1945)

1 Josephine had had a moment of absolute terror at the cemetery, while the coffin was lowered, to think that she and Constantia had done this thing without asking his permission. What would father say when he found out? For he was bound to find out sooner or later. He always did. "Buried. You two girls had me *buried*!"

    Katherine Mansfield, "The Daughters of the Late Colonel," *The Garden Party* (1922)

See also Parents.

## ✶ FATIGUE

2 I am worn to a raveling.

    Beatrix Potter, *The Tailor of Gloucester* (1901)

3 Dog-tiredness is such a lovely prayer, really, if only we would recognize it as such.

    Mother Maribel of Wantage, in Sister Janet, CSMV, *Mother Maribel of Wantage* (1972)

4 At last, deathly tiredness drained him of all apprehension; so might a man fall asleep half-an-hour before he was to be woken by a firing squad.

    Nadine Gordimer, *July's People* (1981)

5 There is fatigue so great that the body cries, even in its sleep.

    Martha Graham, *Blood Memory* (1991)

See also Sleep.

## ✶ FAULTFINDING

6 Most people are so hard to please that if they met God, they'd probably say yes, she's great, but. . .

    Diana Ross, in *Essence* (1989)

7 What they need is a little immorality in their lives. Then they wouldn't be so busy looking for it in other people's.

    Agatha Christie, *Murder at the Vicarage* (1930)

8 When you talk yourself, you think how witty, how original, how acute you are; but when another does so, you are very apt to think only—What a crib from Rochefoucauld!

    Ouida, *Wisdom, Wit and Pathos* (1884)

9 There's nothing kills a man so soon as having nobody to find fault with but himself.

    George Eliot, *Silas Marner* (1861)

10 Heavens! whatever possesses us, here below, that we mutually torment ourselves, sourly reproach our mutual faults, and mercilessly condemn all that is not cut according to our pattern?

    George Sand (1831), in Raphaël Ledos de Beaufort, ed., *Letters of George Sand,* vol. 1 (1886)

See also Criticism, Disapproval, Judgmental.

## ✶ FAULTS

11 Faults! I *adore* faults! I can never find too many in any creature.

    John Oliver Hobbes, *The Ambassador* (1898)

12 Your thorns are the best part of you.

    Marianne Moore, *Selected Poems* (1935)

13 Faults often talk louder than virtues.

    Florence Crannell Means, *A Candle in the Mist* (1931)

14 My instinct has always been to turn drawbacks into drawing cards.

    Marie Dressler, *The Life Story of an Ugly Duckling* (1924)

15 If you are being run out of town, get in front of the crowd and make it look like a parade.

    Sally Stanford, in Bob Chieger, *Was It Good for You, Too?* (1983)

16 Only those faults which we encounter in ourselves are insufferable to us in others.

    Anne-Sophie Swetchine, in Count de Falloux, ed., *The Writings of Madame Swetchine* (1869)

17 We don't ask others to be faultless, we only ask that their faults should not incommode our own.

    Gyp, in J.R. Solly, *A Cynic's Breviary* (1925)

18 It would have been a fault in her, not to have been faulty.

    Mary Delarivière Manley, *The Adventures of Rivella* (1714)

19 The fault no child ever loses is the one he was most punished for.

    Mignon McLaughlin, *The Neurotic's Notebook* (1963)

1 Mrs. Hopewell had no bad qualities of her own but she was able to use other people's in such a constructive way that she never felt the lack.

Flannery O'Connor, "Good Country People," *A Good Man Is Hard to Find* (1953)

See also Imperfection.

## ❧ FAVORS

2 There are many ways of asking a favor; but to assume that you are granting the favor that you ask shows spirit and invention.

Agnes Repplier, "The Literary Lady," *A Happy Half-Century* (1908)

## ❧ FEAR

3 Fear is the beginning of wisdom.

Eugénie de Guérin (1838), in Guillaume S. Trébutien, ed., *Letters of Eugénie de Guérin* (1865)

4 Fear is an emotion indispensable for survival.

Hannah Arendt, in *The New Yorker* (1977)

5 Fear is a slinking cat I find / Beneath the lilacs of my mind.

Sophie Tunnell, "Fear," in Martha Lupton, *The Speaker's Desk Book* (1937)

6 Fear is a sign—usually a sign that I'm doing something *right*.

Erica Jong, *The Devil at Large* (1993)

7 When fear seizes, change what you are doing. You are doing something wrong.

Jean Craighead George, *Julie of the Wolves* (1972)

8 Fear is born in uncertainty and nourished by pessimism.

Lois Wyse, *The Rosemary Touch* (1974)

9 Fear is a question: What are you afraid of, and why? Just as the seed of health is in illness, because illness contains information, our fears are a treasure house of self-knowledge if we explore them.

Marilyn Ferguson, *The Aquarian Conspiracy* (1980)

10 What makes us so afraid is the thing we half see, or half hear, as in a wood at dusk, when a tree stump becomes an animal and a sound becomes a siren. And most of that fear is the fear of not knowing, of not actually seeing correctly.

Edna O'Brien, in Joseph McCulloch, *Under Bow Bells* (1974)

11 It's like the smarter you are, the more things can scare you.

Katherine Paterson, *Bridge to Terabithia* (1977)

12 They that know nothing fear nothing.

Frances E. Willard, *A Wheel Within a Wheel* (1895)

13 The sight of a cage is only frightening to the bird that has once been caught.

Rachel Field, *All This and Heaven Too* (1939)

14 Fear has a smell, as love does.

Margaret Atwood, *Surfacing* (1972)

15 Fear is for the old. Lack of it is one of the joys of youth.

Helen Van Slyke, *No Love Lost* (1980)

16 I have not ceased being fearful, but I have ceased to let fear control me. I have accepted fear as a part of life, specifically the fear of change, the fear of the unknown, and I have gone ahead despite the pounding in the heart that says: turn back, turn back, you'll die if you venture too far.

Erica Jong, in Janet Sternburg, ed., *The Writer on Her Work*, vol. 1 (1980)

17 I shall never be afraid / Even of life; / And who that does not fear life can fear Death / Which is so much a lesser thing?

Mary Carolyn Davies, "A Mining Town," *The Skyline Trail* (1924)

18 To fear is one thing. To let fear grab you by the tail and swing you around is another.

Katherine Paterson, *Jacob Have I Loved* (1980)

19 Nothing in life is to be feared. It is only to be understood.

Marie Curie, in Donald O. Bolander et al., *Instant Quotation Dictionary* (1969)

20 I realize that if I wait until I am no longer afraid to act, write, speak, be, I'll be sending messages on a ouija board, cryptic complaints from the other side.

Audre Lorde, *The Cancer Journals* (1980)

21 There are those who have discovered that fear is death in life, and have willingly risked physical

death and loss of all that is considered valuable in order to live in freedom.

Virginia Burden Tower, *The Process of Intuition* (1975)

1 Proust has pointed out that the predisposition to love creates its own objects: is this not true of fear?

Elizabeth Bowen, *Collected Impressions* (1950)

2 What difference do it make if the thing you scared of is real or not?

Toni Morrison, *Song of Solomon* (1977)

3 In spite of what the child has been told he knows that a room in the dark is not the same as one seen earlier in bright daylight.

Hallie Burnett, *The Brain Pickers* (1957)

4 A wild beast has no need to leap in order to promote fear.

Colette, *Cheri* (1930)

5 Afraid is a country with no exit visas.

Audre Lorde, "Diaspora," *Our Dead Behind Us* (1986)

6 Was there no one over thirty-five who had not some secret agony, some white-faced fear? Half one's life one walked carelessly, certain that some day one would have one's heart's desire: and for the rest of it, one either goes empty, or walks carrying a full cup, afraid of every step.

Helen Waddell, *Peter Abelard* (1933)

7 The most destructive element in the human mind is fear. Fear creates aggressiveness; aggressiveness engenders hostility; hostility engenders fear—a disastrous circle.

Dorothy Thompson, *The Courage to Be Happy* (1957)

8 In every mind where there is a strong tendency to fear, there is a strong capacity to hate. Those who dwell in fear dwell next door to hate.

Anna Jameson, *A Commonplace Book* (1855)

9 Great self-destruction follows upon unfounded fear.

Ursula K. Le Guin, *The Lathe of Heaven* (1971)

10 Oh! how many times we die before death!

Julie de Lespinasse (1773), in Katharine Prescott Wormeley, tr., *Letters of Mlle. de Lespinasse* (1901)

11 That fear of missing out on things makes you miss out on everything.

Etty Hillesum (1941), *An Interrupted Life* (1983)

12 My knees could have been stirred with a spoon.

Margaret Halsey, *With Malice Toward Some* (1938)

13 She was always the kid who had to back down the ladder of the high dive.

Paulette Bates Alden, "Ladies Luncheon," *Feeding the Eagles* (1988)

14 A man from hell is not afraid of hot ashes.

Dorothy Gilman, *Incident at Badamyâ* (1989)

15 He who is in the grasp of the cobra can smile at the lightning's forked tongue.

Alice Tilton, *Cold Steal* (1939)

16 To everything there is an end—except fear.

Phyllis Bottome, "The Vocation," *Innocence and Experience* (1934)

See also Anxiety, Panic, Phobias, Superstition, Worry.

## ❦ FEBRUARY

17 The reason God made February short a few days was because he knew that by the time people came to the end of it they would die if they had to stand one more blasted day.

Katherine Paterson, *Jacob Have I Loved* (1980)

18 February was like a snake with a broken back. It could still bite.

Jessamyn West, *The Massacre at Fall Creek* (1975)

19 February's the worst month, you get so tired of everything and everybody, you seem to have done everything before.

Mary Stewart Cutting, "On the Ridge," *The Suburban Whirl* (1907)

20 February is just plain malicious. It knows your defenses are down.

Katherine Paterson, *Jacob Have I Loved* (1980)

21 February, when the days of winter seem endless and no amount of wistful recollecting can bring back any air of summer.

Shirley Jackson, *Raising Demons* (1956)

See also Winter.

## ❧ FEELINGS

1 i move on feeling and have learned to distrust those who don't.

    Nikki Giovanni, *Poem of Angela Yvonne Davis* (1970)

2 Better to be without logic than without feeling.

    Charlotte Brontë, *The Professor* (1846)

3 The wide discrepancy between reason and feeling may be unreal; it is not improbable that intellect is a high form of feeling—a specialized, intensive feeling about intuitions.

    Susanne K. Langer, *Mind*, vol. 1 (1967)

4 We reason deeply when we forcibly feel.

    Mary Wollstonecraft, *Letters Written During a Short Residence in Sweden, Norway, and Denmark* (1796)

5 Our feelings are our most genuine paths to knowledge.

    Audre Lorde, in Claudia Tate, ed., *Black Women Writers at Work* (1983)

6 You cannot know what you do not feel.

    Marya Mannes, *They* (1968)

7 Only that which is deeply felt can change us. Rational arguments alone cannot penetrate the layers of fear and conditioning that comprise our crippling belief system.

    Marilyn Ferguson, *The Aquarian Conspiracy* (1980)

8 An astonishing observation: it is precisely for feeling that one needs time, and not for thought. . . . Feeling is apparently more demanding than thought.

    Anna Tsetsaeyva (1927), in Tillie Olsen, *Silences* (1978)

9 Feelings change facts.

    Phyllis Bottome, *The Life Line* (1946)

10 Human relations are built on feeling, not on reason or knowledge. And feeling is not an exact science; like all spiritual qualities, it has the vagueness of greatness about it.

    Amelia E. Barr, *The Belle of Bowling Green* (1904)

11 The truth is that we can overhaul our surroundings, renovate our environment, talk a new game, join a new club, far more easily than we can change the way we respond emotionally. It is easier to change behavior than feelings about that behavior.

    Ellen Goodman, *Turning Points* (1979)

12 There is so little feeling in the world that even when it takes the wrong method of expressing itself it is something that the world cannot do without.

    Ellen O'Grady, in Djuna Barnes, "Woman Police Deputy Is Writer of Poetry," *The New York Sun Magazine* (1918)

13 Like the one-tenth of our brain that we currently use, I think now that most if not all of us have access to about one-tenth of our possible feelings.

    Sonia Johnson, *The Ship That Sailed Into the Living Room* (1991)

14 Our society allows people to be absolutely neurotic and totally out of touch with their feelings and everyone else's feelings, and yet be very respectable.

    Ntozake Shange, in Claudia Tate, ed., *Black Women Writers at Work* (1983)

15 It is unwise to feel too much if we think too little.

    Agnes Repplier, in Emma Repplier, *Agnes Repplier* (1957)

16 You cannot make yourself feel something you do not feel, but you can make yourself do right in spite of your feelings.

    Pearl S. Buck, *To My Daughters, With Love* (1967)

17 It was one of those dangerous moments when speech is at once sincere and deceptive—when feeling, rising high above its average depth, leaves flood-marks which are never reached again.

    George Eliot, *The Mill on the Floss* (1860)

18 Men and women make sad mistakes about their own symptoms, taking their vague uneasy longings, sometimes for genius, sometimes for religion, and oftener still for a mighty love.

    George Eliot, *Middlemarch* (1871)

19 The best way of forgetting how you think you feel is to concentrate on what you know you know.

    Mary Stewart, *This Rough Magic* (1964)

20 Atrophy of feeling creates criminals.

    Anaïs Nin (1940), *The Diary of Anaïs Nin*, vol. 3 (1969)

21 One of the quickest ways to become exhausted is by suppressing your feelings.

    Sue Patton Thoele, *The Courage to Be Yourself* (1988)

22 Why is it that people who cannot show feeling presume that that is a strength and not a weakness?

    May Sarton, *At Seventy* (1982)

23 People who cannot feel punish those who do.

    May Sarton, *Mrs. Stevens Hears the Mermaids Singing* (1965)

1 Feelings are untidy.

     Esther Hautzig, *The Endless Steppe* (1968)

2 To have felt too much is to end in feeling nothing.

     Dorothy Thompson (1942), in Vincent Sheean, *Dorothy and Red* (1963)

3 Even when her husband died it . . . was . . . not that Mrs. Marston did not feel it. She did, as deeply as her nature could. But she felt it, as a well-padded boy feels a whacking, through layers of convention.

     Mary Webb, *Gone to Earth* (1917)

See also Emotions.

## § FEET

4 Tiny feet . . . crept, mice-like, in and out from under the sweeping folds of her silken robe.

     Fanny Fern, *Fern Leaves*, 1st series (1853)

5 The feet should have more of the acquaintance of earth, and know more of flowers, freshness, cool brooks, wild thyme, and salt sand than does anything else about us. . . . It is only the entirely unshod that have lively feet.

     Alice Meynell, "The Foot," *Essays* (1914)

## § "FEMININITY"

6 You may know more about vintage wine than the wine steward, but if you're smart you'll let your man do the choosing and be ecstatic over his selection, even if it tastes like shampoo.

     Arlene Dahl, *Always Ask a Man: Arlene Dahl's Key to Femininity* (1965)

7 NEVER upstage a man. Don't top his joke, even if you have to bite your tongue to keep from doing it. Never launch loudly into your own opinions on a subject—whether it's petunias or politics. Instead, draw out his ideas to which you can gracefully add your footnotes from time to time.

     Arlene Dahl, *Always Ask a Man: Arlene Dahl's Key to Femininity* (1965)

## § FEMINISM

8 For many people, feminism is one of those words of which, as St. Augustine said about time, they know the meaning as long as no one is asking.

     Katha Pollitt, *Reasonable Creatures* (1994)

9 Feminism is not being ashamed of being a woman and not using woman as a swear word. It also means not hating women you don't approve of simply because you don't approve of them.

     Alta, in Jennifer Stone, *Stone's Throw* (1988)

10 Feminism is the most revolutionary idea there has ever been. Equality for women demands a change in the human psyche more profound than anything Marx dreamed of. It means valuing parenthood as much as we value banking.

     Polly Toynbee, in *The Guardian* (1987)

11 Feminism is not a patch; it is a whole new pattern which can only be realized by weaving a new garment, seamless from top to bottom and multicolored from the beginning.

     Sandra M. Schneiders, *Beyond Patching* (1991)

12 The point of feminism . . . is to win women a wider range of experience. Feminism remains a pretty simple concept, despite repeated—and enormously effective—efforts to dress it up in greasepaint and turn its proponents into gargoyles.

     Susan Faludi, *Backlash* (1991)

13 Feminism is to sexism what black nationalism is to racism; the most rational response to the problem.

     Pearl Cleage, "Basic Training: The Beginnings of Wisdom," *Deals With the Devil* (1993)

14 An indigenous feminism has been present in every culture in the world and in every period of history since the suppression of women began.

     Robin Morgan, *Sisterhood Is Global* (1984)

15 People call me a feminist whenever I express sentiments that differentiate me from a doormat or a prostitute.

     Rebecca West, in *The Clarion* (1913)

16 She specialized in feminism, and in her eyes to be a woman was in itself a good argument.

     Stella Benson, *I Pose* (1915)

17 For me, to be a feminist is to answer the question "Are women human?" with a yes.

     Katha Pollitt, *Reasonable Creatures* (1994)

1 I became a feminist as an alternative to becoming a masochist.

Sally Kempton, "Cutting Loose," in *Esquire* (1970)

2 "I'm not a feminist," some women say sternly as they march off to work where equal opportunity legislation protects them. . . . Women who say they are not feminists and act like individuals with basic human rights have just got their terminology wrong.

Kaz Cooke, *The Modern Girl's Guide to Everything* (1989)

3 Most women preface their support of the women's movement with "I'm not a feminist, but. . ." But? But, what? You think God is going to get you if you say, "I am for women's liberation and. . ." Right? Well, She is not.

Victoria Billings, *The Womansbook* (1974)

4 Modern young women . . . show a strong hostility to the word "feminism," and all which they imagine it to connote. They are, nevertheless, themselves the products of the women's movement.

Ray Strachey, *Our Freedom and Its Results* (1936)

5 All women are feminists, whether they know it or not.

Isabelle Holland, *The Long Search* (1990)

6 Like Broadway, the novel, and God, feminism has been declared dead many times.

Katha Pollitt, *Reasonable Creatures* (1994)

See also Anti-Feminism, Discrimination, Sexism, Sex Roles, Women, Women's Movement.

# ❦ FICTION

7 Fortunately, there is more to life than death. There is for one thing, fiction. A thousand thousand characters to be sent marching out into the world to divert time from its forward gallop to the terrible horizon.

Fay Weldon, *Down Among the Women* (1971)

8 Fiction reveals truths that reality obscures.

Jessamyn West, *To See the Dream* (1957)

9 Fiction supplies the only philosophy that many readers know; it establishes their ethical, social, and material standards; it confirms them in their prejudices or opens their minds to a wider world.

Dorothea Brande, *Becoming a Writer* (1934)

10 Fiction is the great repository of the moral sense. The wicked get punished.

Anita Brookner, in Sybil Steinberg, ed., *Writing for Your Life* (1992)

11 Fiction is not only the historian of life but its apologist.

Gertrude Atherton, *The Living Present* (1917)

12 Fiction keeps its audience by retaining the world as its subject matter. People like the world. Many people actually prefer it to art and spend their days by choice in the thick of it.

Annie Dillard, *Living by Fiction* (1983)

13 Fiction is like a spider's web, attached ever so lightly perhaps, but still attached to life at all four corners.

Virginia Woolf, *A Room of One's Own* (1929)

14 For my own purpose, I defined the art of fiction as experience illuminated.

Ellen Glasgow, *A Certain Measure* (1943)

15 Fiction is about everything human and we are made out of dust, and if you scorn getting yourself dusty, then you shouldn't write fiction. It isn't grand enough for you.

Flannery O'Connor, "The Nature and Aim of Fiction," in Sally and Robert Fitzgerald, eds., *Mystery and Manners* (1969)

16 "The proper stuff of fiction" does not exist; everything is the proper stuff of fiction, every feeling, every thought; every quality of brain and spirit is drawn upon; no perception comes amiss.

Virginia Woolf, "Modern Fiction" *The Common Reader*, 1st series (1925)

17 Nothing, except the weather report or a general maxim of conduct, is so unsafe to rely upon as a theory of fiction.

Ellen Glasgow, *A Certain Measure* (1943)

18 The fact, and the intuition or logic about the fact, are severe coordinates in fiction. In the short story they must cross with hair-line precision.

Louise Bogan, "Flowering Judas" (1930), *Selected Criticism* (1955)

19 Fiction is not a dream. Nor is it guesswork. It is imagining based on facts, and the facts must be

accurate or the work of imagining will not stand up.

Margaret Culkin Banning, in *The Writer* (1960)

1 If fiction does not show us a better life than reality, what is the good of it?

Amelia E. Barr, *All the Days of My Life* (1913)

2 The two worst sins of bad taste in fiction are pornography and sentimentality. One is too much sex and the other too much sentiment.

Flannery O'Connor, in Sally Fitzgerald, ed., *The Habit of Being* (1979)

See also Fantasy Fiction, Fictional Characters, Literature, Mysteries, Novels, Science Fiction, Stories, Writers, Writing.

## & FICTIONAL CHARACTERS

3 One of the strangest quirks of the human mind is its capacity for being moved to tears, laughter, anger, anxiety, joy by a "person" who exists nowhere except in imagination!

Jane Fitz-Randolph, *How to Write for Children and Young Adults* (1980)

4 When the writer looks back upon her own childhood, it seems to her that she lived in company with a delightful host of little playmates, bright, busy, clever children, whose cheerful presence remains more vividly in her mind than that of many of the real little boys and girls who used to appear and disappear disconnectedly as children do in childhood.

Miss Thackeray, *A Book of Sibyls* (1883)

5 Knowing few children of my age with whom to compare notes, I envied the children of literature to whom interesting things were always happening.

Jessica Mitford, *Daughters and Rebels* (1960)

6 Fictional characters, he had lately found, were generally more interesting dinner companions than flesh-and-blood ones.

Martha Grimes, *The Old Silent* (1989)

7 For the last six weeks I have found myself pestered by some characters in search of an author.

Sylvia Townsend Warner (1941), in William Maxwell, ed., *Letters: Sylvia Townsend Warner* (1982)

8 I live with the people I create and it has always made my essential loneliness less keen.

Carson McCullers, *The Square Root of Wonderful* (1958)

9 I don't think I ever relinquish a person I have known, and surely not my fictional characters. I see them, I hear them, with a clarity that I would call hallucinatory if hallucination didn't mean something else. . . . A character whom we create can never die, any more than a friend can die. . . . Through [my characters] I've lived many parallel lives.

Marguerite Yourcenar, *With Open Eyes* (1980)

10 It is hard to make your adversaries real people unless you recognize yourself in them—in which case, if you don't watch out, they cease to be adversaries.

Flannery O'Connor, in Sally Fitzgerald, ed., *The Habit of Being* (1979)

11 The ability to pursue a course, whether it is a popular one or not, is measured in courage. The greater the courage, the greater the possibility we will act for change. I build my characters around the dynamics of choice, courage, and change.

Mildred Pitts Walter, in *The Horn Book* (1991)

12 I remember how surprised I was when my first novel was about to be published and I was informed that I could be sued for anything any one of my characters said. "But I often don't agree with what they say," I protested. The lawyer was not interested in the clear distinction I make between my own voice and the voices of my characters. Neither, I have found, are many of my readers.

Jane Rule, "Sexuality in Literature," *Outlander* (1981)

13 As a creator of character his peculiarity is that he creates wherever his eyes rest. . . . With such a power at his command Dickens made his books blaze up, not by tightening the plot or sharpening the wit, but by throwing another handful of people upon the fire.

Virginia Woolf, "David Copperfield" (1925), *The Moment* (1947)

See also Fiction.

## & FILMS

14 Cinema is a kind of pan-art. It can use, incorporate, engulf virtually any other art: the novel, poetry,

theater, painting, sculpture, dance, music, architecture. Unlike opera, which is a (virtually) frozen art form, the cinema is and has been a fruitfully conservative medium of ideas and styles of emotions.

Susan Sontag, "A Note on Novels and Films" (1961), *Against Interpretation* (1966)

1 Movies have mirrored our moods and myths since the century began. They have taken on some of the work of religion.

Jennifer Stone, "Epilogue," *Mind Over Media* (1988)

2 For a while in the twenties and thirties, art was talked about as a substitute for religion; now B movies are a substitute for religion.

Pauline Kael, *Movie Love* (1991)

3 Other than life experience, nothing left a deeper imprint on my formative self than the movies.

Letty Cottin Pogrebin, *Deborah, Golda, and Me* (1991)

4 The motion picture is the people's Art.

Adela Rogers St. Johns, *Love, Laughter and Tears* (1978)

5 There are two cinemas: the films we have actually seen and the memories we have of them.

Molly Haskell, in John Robert Colombo, *Popcorn in Paradise* (1979)

6 Perhaps making movies is a step toward being able to move backward and forward and in and out of linear time.

Eleanor Coppola, *Notes* (1979)

7 The words "Kiss Kiss Bang Bang," which I saw on an Italian movie poster, are perhaps the briefest statement imaginable of the basic appeal of movies.

Pauline Kael, *Kiss Kiss Bang Bang* (1968)

8 South Sea natives who have been exposed to American movies classify them into two types, "kiss-kiss" and "bang-bang."

Hortense Powdermaker, *Hollywood, The Dream Factory* (1950)

9 If you're afraid of movies that excite your senses, you're afraid of movies.

Pauline Kael (1978), in *Newsweek* (1991)

10 Entertainment must be a satisfying emotional experience, a stirring of the heart. We need all kinds of young men and women. Those people with an artist's eye and an executive's brain that we term directors. Those wrestlers with their souls and

typewriters known as authors. The beggars on horseback called actors and actresses.

Hedda Hopper, with James Brough, *The Whole Truth and Nothing But* (1963)

11 Movies have been doing so much of the same thing—in slightly different ways—for so long that few of the possibilities of this great hybrid art have yet been explored.

Pauline Kael, *Going Steady* (1970)

12 People have been modeling their lives after films for years, but the medium is somehow unsuited to moral lessons, cautionary tales, or polemics of any kind.

Renata Adler, *A Year in the Dark* (1969)

13 The motion picture . . . confers celebrity. Not just on people—on acts, and objects, and places, and ways of life. The camera brings a kind of stardom to them all. I therefore doubt that film can ever argue effectively against its own material: that a genuine antiwar film, say, can be made on the basis of even the ugliest battle scenes. . . . No matter what filmmakers intend, film always argues yes.

Renata Adler, *A Year in the Dark* (1969)

14 We are all actors now. . . . Everyone in America now explains a moment in their lives by saying, "It was like a scene out of. . ."

Peggy Noonan, *What I Saw at the Revolution* (1990)

15 In my films I always wanted to make people see deeply. I don't want to show things, but to give people the desire to see.

Agnès Varda, in John Robert Colombo, *Popcorn in Paradise* (1979)

16 The geniuses who conduct the motion-picture business killed glamour when they decided that what the public wanted was not dream stuff, from which movies used to be made, but realism.

Hedda Hopper, with James Brough, *The Whole Truth and Nothing But* (1963)

17 Hollywood reflected, if it did not actually produce, the sexual climate of our land.

Anita Loos, *Kiss Hollywood Good-by* (1974)

18 Just as violence is the last refuge of the inarticulate, so it is also the first resort of the incompetent, the easy out for the man who is capable of expressing himself only in the most primitive and vulgar of dramatic terms. He leaves us with only the obscenity of violence per se—and the pornographer

thereof will always be with us, in film as in any other medium. And so will his audience.

Judith Crist, *The Private Eye, the Cowboy and the Very Naked Girl* (1968)

1 We always knew there were such things as sewers, but never before have audiences had their noses pushed over so many gratings.

Hedda Hopper, with James Brough, *The Whole Truth and Nothing But* (1963)

2 His [Roger Vadim's] announced messianic urge is to eliminate all sense of guilt about the human body and all erotic complexes, a not unlaudable aim which possibly would be more attainable if he made better pictures.

Helen Lawrenson, "Jane Fonda: All You Need Is Love, Love, Love," *Latins Are Still Lousy Lovers* (1968)

3 Audiences will get just as tired of people wrestling on a bed as they did of Tom Mix kissing his horse.

Mary Astor, *A Life on Film* (1967)

4 The film was so typically American that it left nothing to thought.

Simone de Beauvoir, *America Day by Day* (1948)

5 Movies are so rarely great art, that if we cannot appreciate great *trash*, we have very little reason to be interested in them.

Pauline Kael, *Going Steady* (1970)

6 Most movies are not very good. Most people know it and like to see them anyway.

Renata Adler, *A Year in the Dark* (1969)

7 Tasteful and colossal are—in movies, at least—basically antipathetic.

Pauline Kael, *Deeper Into Movies* (1973)

8 We learn to settle for so little, we moviegoers.

Pauline Kael, *Going Steady* (1970)

9 Economy, speed, nervousness, and desperation produce the final wasteful, semi-incoherent movies we see.

Pauline Kael, *Kiss Kiss Bang Bang* (1968)

10 Movies are our cheap and easy expression, the sullen art of displaced persons.

Pauline Kael, *Going Steady* (1970)

11 Black and white are the most ravishing colors of all in film.

Penelope Gilliatt, *Three-Quarter Face* (1980)

12 The rich will always be with us. Especially on our movie screens.

Kathi Maio, *Feminist in the Dark* (1988)

13 Every sacred cow in the business has to do with economics.

Gena Rowlands, in Judith Crist, *Take 22* (1984)

14 I used to be prejudiced against directors, but now I'm bigoted against them.

Isobel Lennart, in John Robert Colombo, *Popcorn in Paradise* (1979)

15 I wouldn't say when you've seen one Western you've seen the lot; but when you've seen the lot you get the feeling you've seen one.

Katharine Whitehorn, "Decoding the West," *Sunday Best* (1976)

16 When I see those ads with the quote "You'll have to see this picture twice," I know it's the kind of picture I don't want to see once.

Pauline Kael, *Deeper Into Movies* (1973)

See also Acting, Entertainment, Hollywood, Show Business, Stage and Screen.

## § FINANCES

17 A man who accustoms himself to buy superfluities, is often in want of necessaries.

Hannah Farnham Lee, *The Log-Cabin* (1844)

18 I believe that one's basic financial attitudes are—like a tendency toward fat knees—probably formed *in utero*, or, at the very latest, *in cribbo*.

Peg Bracken, *I Didn't Come Here to Argue* (1969)

19 The average family exists only on paper and its average budget is a fiction, invented by statisticians for the convenience of statisticians.

Sylvia Porter, *Sylvia Porter's Money Book* (1975)

20 I want to ask thee a solemn question. Did thee ever one single time have thy Bank book balance and thy own check book balance agree exactly? Do not tell, but *I* never did.

Hannah Whitall Smith, letter to her sister (1885), in Logan Pearsall Smith, ed., *Philadelphia Quaker* (1950)

21 The bailiffs were at the door. . . . Two large bailiffs, they were, who visited frequently and smiled like grand pianos, the only really reliable men in my

life. They told me what they were going to do and they did it, woe was me.

Jill Tweedie, "Strange Places," in Michelene Wandor, ed., *On Gender and Writing* (1983)

1 People keep telling us about their love affairs, when what we really want to know is how much money they make and how they manage on it.

Mignon McLaughlin, *The Neurotic's Notebook* (1963)

2 Women don't get the credit they deserve—in more ways than one.

Paula Nelson, *The Joy of Money* (1975)

See also Economics, Money, Poverty.

## ❦ FIRE

3 Fire is a natural symbol of life and passion, though it is the one element in which nothing can actually live.

Susanne K. Langer, *Philosophy in a New Key* (1942)

4 Fire is a good companion for the mind.

May Sarton, "Reflections by a Fire," *Cloud, Stone, Sun, Vine* (1961)

5 There is much wisdom that may be learned before a peat fire.

Ellen Thompson, *A Book of Hours* (1909)

6 A house with no fireplace is a house without a heart.

Gladys Taber, *The Book of Stillmeadow* (1948)

7 People who light fires on the slightest provocation are always the nicest.

Jane England, in *The New York Times* (1948)

8 Burning logs can carry on quite a conversation! . . . Have you ever heard apple wood talking? It's the most loquacious of all. You really can't get a word in edgeways.

Agnes Sligh Turnbull, *The Golden Journey* (1955)

9 Nothing smelled so good or danced so well as a birch fire.

Katherine Paterson, *Lyddie* (1991)

10 The fire rose in two branched flames like the golden antlers of some enchanted stag.

Katherine Mansfield (1919), *Journal of Katherine Mansfield* (1927)

11 Fire destroys that which feeds it.

Simone Weil, *The Notebooks of Simone Weil* (1951)

## ❦ FIRST LADY

12 The first lady is, and always has been, an unpaid public servant elected by one person, her husband.

Lady Bird Johnson, in *U.S. News and World Report* (1987)

13 No matter how different our First Ladies have been—and as individual women they have ranged from recluses to vibrant hostesses to political manipulators on a par with Machiavelli—they have all shared the unnerving experience of facing a job they did not choose.

Margaret Truman, *First Ladies* (1995)

14 First ladies are doing a lot. But the job remains undefined, frequently misunderstood, and subject to political attacks far nastier in some ways than those any President has ever faced.

Margaret Truman, *First Ladies* (1995)

15 First ladies throughout our history have been expected to be adoring wives and perfect mothers.

Rosalynn Carter, *First Lady From Plains* (1984)

16 The one thing I do not want to be called is "First Lady." It sounds like a saddle horse.

Jacqueline Kennedy (1961), in Ralph G. Martin, *A Hero for Our Time* (1983)

17 She's intrepid; she's the biggest bargain America ever got, bigger than that Louisiana Purchase from my French friends.

Jacqueline Kennedy Onassis, on Hillary Rodham Clinton, quoted by Raymond Marriner Schwartz, in *The New York Times Magazine* (1994)

18 Someday, someone will follow in my footsteps and preside over the White House as the President's spouse. And I wish him well.

Barbara Bush, speech (1990)

## ❦ FISHING

19 Something between a sport and a religion.

Josephine Tey, *The Singing Sands* (1952)

1 Mama went fishing every time the spirit moved her to go, and the spirit moved her every time Brother Tiffin offered to take her.

Evelyn Fairbanks, *The Days of Rondo* (1990)

2 We go down to the mouth of our brook with flashlights and catch the fish in our hands, very silvery and mysterious, like a poem by W.B. Yeats.

Katharine Butler Hathaway (1936), *The Journals and Letters of the Little Locksmith* (1946)

3 I really fished mainly because I wanted to be alone on the middle of the lake. . . . Sometimes a fish jumped nearby, as though it knew it was safe.

Susan Allen Toth, *Blooming* (1978)

4 One can no more have trout than fame or riches without some accompanying disadvantages.

C.R.C., "Woman's Hour Has Struck" (1890), in Holly Morris, ed., *Uncommon Waters* (1991)

5 The difficult art I was attempting had . . . a powerful fascination, before which the past faded, the future receded, and the whole of experience narrowed down to this stretch of glancing, glimmering water, and the fly I was trying to cast across it.

Mary Stewart, *Wildfire at Midnight* (1956)

6 The truth is, fly fishing is folly: useless, unreasonable, irrational, and without purpose. Fly fishing is folly precisely because it makes survival harder than it already is, and by doing so, turns survival into art.

Ailm Travler, "Fly Fishing Folly," in Holly Morris, ed., *Uncommon Waters* (1991)

7 The bass failed to rally around him with the unanimity he had hoped for, and his spirits were not raised by his son's cheerful comments on that fact.

Josephine Daskam, *The Memoirs of a Baby* (1904)

8 It is remarkable how generous fishermen are. When you meet a man who has returned from a fishing trip he always tells you that he gave his share to the other fellow.

Mary Wilson Little, *A Paragrapher's Reveries* (1904)

9 There is one distinctive charm about fishing—its fascinations will stand any climate. You may sit crouching on ice over a hole inside the arctic circle, or on a Windsor chair by the side of the River Lea in the so-called temperate zone, or you may squat in a canoe on an equatorial river, with the surrounding atmosphere forty-five percent mosquito, and if you are fishing you will enjoy yourself.

Mary H. Kingsley, *West African Studies* (1899)

10 The curious thing about fishing is that you never want to go home. If you catch something, you can't stop. If you don't catch anything, you hate to leave in case something might bite.

Gladys Taber, *The Book of Stillmeadow* (1948)

11 People who fish know that life is a morality play in which you are sometimes the victor, sometimes vanquished. It is all of life's lessons in the space of a morning. Only an extraordinary person would purposely risk being outsmarted by a creature often less than twelve inches long, over and over again.

Janna Bialek, "Thoughts From a Fishing Past," in Holly Morris, ed., *Uncommon Waters* (1991)

12 Catching something is purely a by-product of our fishing. It is the act of fishing that wipes away all grief, lightens all worry, dissolves fear and anxiety.

Gladys Taber, *The Book of Stillmeadow* (1948)

13 The man who goes fishing gets something more than the fish he catches.

Mary Astor, *A Life on Film* (1967)

14 The profound difference that divides the human race is a question of bait—whether to fish with worms or not.

Virginia Woolf, "Fishing," *The Moment* (1947)

See also Hobbies.

## ❧ FLATTERY

15 Flattery is praise without foundation.

Eliza Leslie, *Miss Leslie's Behavior Book* (1859)

16 Flattery affects a man like any other sort of "dope." It stimulates and exhilarates him for the moment, but usually ends by going to his head and making him act foolish.

Helen Rowland, *A Guide to Men* (1922)

17 The aim of flattery is to soothe and encourage us by assuring us of the truth of an opinion we have already formed about ourselves.

Edith Sitwell, in Elizabeth Salter, *The Last Years of a Rebel* (1967)

1 Flattery, if judiciously administered, is always acceptable, however much we may despise the flatterer.

> Countess of Blessington, *Desultory Thoughts and Reflections* (1839)

2 "You are like me!" The deepest flattery one creature pays its fellow.

> Enid Bagnold, *A Diary Without Dates* (1918)

3 I struck the usual bargain, paying for flattery by calling it insight.

> Patricia Hampl, *Virgin Time* (1992)

4 The most flattering words are not those which we devise, but those which escape us unthinkingly.

> Ninon de Lenclos (1660), *Lettres de Ninon de Lenclos* (1870)

5 No adulation; 'tis the death of virtue; / Who flatters is of all mankind the lowest, / Save he who courts flattery.

> Hannah More, "Daniel," *Sacred Dramas* (1782)

6 It is happy for you that you possess the talent of flattering with delicacy. May I ask whether these pleasing attentions proceed from the impulse of the moment, or are the result of previous study?

> Jane Austen, *Pride and Prejudice* (1813)

See also Praise, Speech.

## ❧ FLIRTATION

7 Flirtation is merely an expression of considered desire coupled with an admission of its impracticability.

> Marya Mannes, "A Plea for Flirtation," *But Will It Sell?* (1964)

8 Flirtation . . . is a graceful salute to sex, a small impermanent spark between one human being and another, between a man and a woman not in need of fire.

> Marya Mannes, "A Plea for Flirtation," *But Will It Sell?* (1964)

9 Flirtation envies Love, and Love envies Flirtation.

> Carolyn Wells, "Wiseacreage," *Folly for the Wise* (1904)

See also Seduction.

## ❧ FLORIDA

10 Here in Florida the seasons move in and out like nuns in soft clothing, making no rustle in their passing.

> Marjorie Kinnan Rawlings, *Cross Creek* (1942)

11 Perhaps the spirit of the Everglades was most evident in the unseen, the hidden, the implied.

> T.J. MacGregor, *Kin Dread* (1990)

12 The whole peninsula of Florida was weighted down with regret. Everyone had left behind a real life.

> Cynthia Ozick, "Rosa," *The Shawl* (1989)

13 Miami lacks the history, the roots, and the traditions of other major metropolitan areas. Everybody here is from someplace else.

> Edna Buchanan, *The Corpse Had a Familiar Face* (1987)

14 We were part of the first wave of Cubans in Miami. When my mother first went to look for an apartment, it was a case of "No children, no pets, no Cubans."

> Gloria Estefan, in Grace Catalano, *Gloria Estefan* (1991)

## ❧ FLOWERS

15 Have you ever looked into the heart of a flower? . . . I love their delicacy, their disarming innocence, and their defiance of life itself.

> Princess Grace of Monaco, with Gwen Robyns, *My Book of Flowers* (1980)

16 I've always thought my flowers had souls.

> Myrtle Reed, *Lavender and Old Lace* (1902)

17 Flowers and plants are silent presences; they nourish every sense except the ear.

> May Sarton, *Plant Dreaming Deep* (1968)

18 The career of flowers differs from ours only in inaudibleness.

> Emily Dickinson (1874), in Mabel Loomis Todd, ed., *Letters of Emily Dickinson*, vol. 2 (1894)

19 People from a planet without flowers would think we must be mad with joy the whole time to have such things about us.

> Iris Murdoch, *A Fairly Honorable Defeat* (1970)

1 I am inclined to think that the flowers we most love are those we knew when we were very young, when our senses were most acute to color and to smell, and our natures most lyrical.

Dorothy Thompson, *The Courage to Be Happy* (1957)

2 Arranging a bowl of flowers in the morning can give a sense of quiet in a crowded day—like writing a poem, or saying a prayer.

Anne Morrow Lindbergh, *Gift From the Sea* (1955)

3 I like to see flowers growing, but when they are gathered, they cease to please. I look on them as things rootless and perishable; their likeness to life makes me sad. I never offer flowers to those I love; I never wish to receive them from hands dear to me.

Charlotte Brontë, *Villette* (1853)

4 Azaleas were his special passion, and one of his most dreadful crimes was that on several occasions he had gone down with a trowel to the Botanic Gardens, and with the help of a fellow azalea-lover, a priest with a big umbrella, he had pinned down several azalea shoots with hairpins until they rooted; and again, with the help of his ally and the big umbrella, had dug these furtive treasures from the ground and carried them away under his coat.

Kylie Tennant, *Ride On Stranger* (1943)

5 See the last orange roses, how they blow / Deeper and heavier than in their prime, / In one defiant flame before they go.

Vita Sackville-West, "Autumn," *The Garden* (1946)

6 One of the buds on the rosebush opened into a blossom, white and silky as a baby's fist.

Natalie Babbitt, *The Devil's Storybook* (1974)

7 Do you think amethysts can be the souls of good violets?

L.M. Montgomery, *Anne of Green Gables* (1908)

8 One violet is as sweet as an acre of them.

Mary Webb, *The Spring of Joy* (1917)

9 I had not thought of violets of late, / The wild, shy kind that springs beneath your feet / In wistful April days.

Alice Dunbar-Nelson, "Violets," in *The Crisis* (1917)

10 Forsythia is pure joy. There is not an ounce, not a glimmer of sadness or even *knowledge* in forsythia. Pure, undiluted, untouched joy.

Anne Morrow Lindbergh, *Bring Me a Unicorn* (1971)

11 Cowslips in water . . . I found them wading / Up to their little green knees.

Hilda Conkling, "May Basket," *Shoes of the Wind* (1922)

12 No garden can really be too small to hold a peony. Had I but four square feet of ground at my disposal, I would plant a peony in the center and proceed to worship.

Mrs. Edward Harding, *Peonies in the Little Garden* (1923)

13 Daffodils . . . grew among the mossy stones about and above them; some rested their heads upon these stones, as on a pillow, for weariness.

Dorothy Wordsworth (1802), in William Knight, ed., *Journals of Dorothy Wordsworth*, vol. 1 (1897)

14 The first dandelions touch the heart-strings in much the same way as do the early notes of the robin, their blessed familiarity impressing us like a happy surprise.

Mrs. William Starr Dana, *According to Season* (1894)

15 Dandelions were what she chiefly saw. Yellow jewels for everyday, studding the patched green dress of her back yard.

Gwendolyn Brooks, *Maud Martha* (1953)

16 Dandelions meet me wherever I am they overrun Germany's railway embankments dusty corners fields seize even well-trimmed gardens through hedges leaves like fine saws new flowers every day have the wind to carry them over rivers walled boundaries stick my fingers together when I try to fend them off.

Sarah Kirsch, "Dandelions for Chains," in Joanna Bankier and Deirdre Lashgari, eds., *Women Poets of the World* (1983)

17 Give dandelions an inch and they'll take a yard.

Edith A. Van Sant, in Reader's Digest editors, *Fun Fare* (1949)

See also Gardening, Nature, Plants.

# ❦ FLYING

18 Aviation is poetry. . . . It's the finest kind of moving around, you know, just as poetry is the finest way of using words.

Jessie Fauset, *Comedy American Style* (1933)

19 Flight is nothing but an attitude in motion.

Diane Ackerman, *On Extended Wings* (1985)

1 This new sport is comparable to no other. It is, in my opinion, one of the most intoxicating forms of sport, and will, I am sure, become one of the most popular. Many of us will perish before then, but that prospect will not dismay the braver spirits. . . . How delicious to fly like a bird!

    Marie Marvingt, in "The Sky Women," *Collier's* (1911)

2 There are no signposts in the sky to show a man has passed that way before. There are no channels marked. The flier breaks each second into new uncharted seas.

    Anne Morrow Lindbergh, *North to the Orient* (1935)

3 [Flying] may not be all plain sailing. . . . But the fun of it is worth the price.

    Amelia Earhart, *The Fun of It* (1932)

4 Landing a Tomcat [on an aircraft carrier] is sort of like dancing with an elephant—you can kind of nudge it over to the right and ease it over to the left, but when it decides it's going to sit down, there's not a thing you can do about it.

    Kara S. Hultgreen, in *McCall's* (1994)

5 When one commits one's self to an airborne craft and the door is fastened against earth and home, there is no escape even by running away. The result is a strange sense of peace—desperate, perhaps, but peace.

    Pearl S. Buck, *A Bridge for Passing* (1962)

6 I feel about airplanes the way I feel about diets. It seems to me that they are wonderful things for other people to go on.

    Jean Kerr, *The Snake Has All the Lines* (1960)

7 One did not "hop" a plane. One took a long slow ride to an airport, and argued for hours with ticket agents who seemed to have been hired five minutes ago for what they supposed to be another job; and if one survived that, one got to Chicago only to join a "stack" over the airfield there, and then either died of boredom or crashed into a plane that thought it was in the stack over Newark.

    Amanda Cross, *In the Last Analysis* (1964)

8 If God had meant us to travel tourist class, he would have made us narrower.

    Martha Zimmerman, in *The Wall Street Journal* (1977)

9 I don't think they have to go that high. That is not necessary, to be that high in the air. I think they're showing off, those pilots. I think we could just go really fast just a few feet off the ground. Just high enough to miss the animals.

    Ellen DeGeneres, in *Mirabella* (1992)

See also Travel.

## ❧ FOLKLORE

10 Folklore is a collection of ridiculous notions held by other people, but not by you and me.

    Margaret Halsey, *The Folks at Home* (1952)

11 Folklore is the boiled-down juice, or pot-likker, of human living.

    Zora Neale Hurston, *Folklore Field Notes* (1925)

See also Legends, Myths, Stories.

## ❧ FOOD

12 Food is an important part of a balanced diet.

    Fran Lebowitz, *Metropolitan Life* (1978)

13 If we mammals don't get something to eat every day or two, our temperature drops, all our signs fall off, and we begin to starve. Living at biological red alert, it's not surprising how obsessed we are with food; I'm just amazed we don't pace and fret about it all the time.

    Diane Ackerman, *The Moon by Whale Light* (1991)

14 Food for all is a necessity. Food should not be a merchandise, to be bought and sold as jewels are bought and sold by those who have the money to buy. Food is a human necessity, like water and air, and it should be as available.

    Pearl S. Buck, *To My Daughters, with Love* (1967)

15 The straightest road to a man's heart is through his palate.

    Fanny Fern, *Fern Leaves*, 2nd series (1853)

16 Food has the dubious advantage of being legitimate, and one's customers somehow manage to live longer without sex than food, if you call that living.

    Sally Stanford, ex-madam entering the restaurant business, *The Lady of the House* (1966)

1 Food is the most primitive form of comfort.

Sheilah Graham, *A State of Heat* (1972)

2 The seat of the greatest patriotic loyalties is in the stomach. Long after giving up all attachment to the land of his birth, the naturalized American citizen holds fast to the food of his parents.

Vicki Baum, *I Know What I'm Worth* (1964)

3 The best foods are the products of infinite and wearying trouble. The trouble need not be taken by the consumer, but someone, ever since the Fall, has had to take it.

Rose Macaulay, *Personal Pleasures* (1936)

4 To lift off the cover of a tomato-y mixture and let it bubble up mushroom and basil under my nose does a lot to counteract the many subtle efforts a part of me makes to punish myself for all those worst of my shortcomings—those I can neither name nor find a shape for. Terrible brown ghosts with sinews like bedsprings.

Mary Virginia Micka, *The Cazenovia Journal* (1986)

5 With steamed clams, we like only hot buttered toast and adults. It takes an almost fanatical affection for children or clams to put up with the "What's this little green thing, Mommy? Do we eat this ugly black part? Do you think this is a worm?" that always accompanies any child's eating of clams.

Betty MacDonald, *Onions in the Stew* (1955)

6 We do not desecrate the dish by serving any other, neither salad nor dessert. We just eat crab Newburg. My friends rise from the table, wring my hand with deep feeling, and slip quietly and reverently away. I sit alone and weep for the misery of a world that does not have blue crabs and a Jersey cow.

Marjorie Kinnan Rawlings, *Cross Creek* (1942)

7 Bread that must be sliced with an ax is bread that is too nourishing.

Fran Lebowitz, *Metropolitan Life* (1978)

8 An omelet so light we had to lay our knives across it and even then it struggled.

Margaret Halsey, *With Malice Toward Some* (1938)

9 As for butter versus margarine, I trust cows more than chemists.

Joan Gussow, in *The New York Times* (1986)

10 I came from a family that considered gravy a beverage.

Erma Bombeck, *A Marriage Made in Heaven . . . or Too Tired for an Affair* (1993)

11 Soup not only warms you and is easy to swallow and to digest, it also creates the illusion in the back of your mind that Mother is there.

Marlene Dietrich, *Marlene Dietrich's ABC* (1962)

12 Cold soup is a very tricky thing and it is a rare hostess who can carry it off. More often than not the dinner guest is left with the impression that had he only come a little earlier he could have gotten it while it was still hot.

Fran Lebowitz, *Metropolitan Life* (1978)

13 The soup, thin and dark and utterly savorless, tasted as if it had been drained out of the umbrella stand.

Margaret Halsey, *With Malice Toward Some* (1938)

14 Everything you see I owe to spaghetti.

Sophia Loren, in John Robert Colombo, *Popcorn in Paradise* (1979)

15 Noodles are not only amusing but delicious.

Julia Child, *Julia Child & Company* (1978)

16 At a sidewalk table outside a crummy café facing the station, I gulped down a patch of lasagna. It was clammy-cold and looked like something that should be bandaged.

Patricia Hampl, *Virgin Time* (1992)

17 All food starting with *p* is comfort food . . . pasta, potato chips, pretzels, peanut butter, pastrami, pizza, pastry.

Sara Paretsky, *Killing Orders* (1985)

18 We recommend that no one eat more than two tons of turkey—that's what it would take to poison someone.

Elizabeth Whelan, on the levels of toxins and carcinogens in holiday meals, in *U.S. News & World Report* (1986)

19 Roast Beef, Medium, is not only a food. It is a philosophy. . . . Roast Beef, Medium, is safe, and sane, and sure.

Edna Ferber, *Roast Beef Medium* (1913)

20 There were twelve dishes of lamb cooked in different rich sauces, with a monster bowl of strange

oddments, which I imagine also belonged to the private life of a sheep.

Rosita Forbes, *The Secret of the Sahara* (1921)

1 While it is undeniably true that people love a surprise, it is equally true that they are seldom pleased to suddenly and without warning happen upon a series of prunes in what they took to be a normal loin of pork.

Fran Lebowitz, *Metropolitan Life* (1978)

2 Molded salads are best served in situations where they have little or no competition. . . . Like television, gelatin is too often a vehicle for limp leftovers that couldn't make it anywhere else.

Peg Bracken, *Appendix to the I Hate to Cook Book* (1966)

3 These [recipes] are very nice ways to cook string beans but they interfere with the poor vegetable's leading a life of its own.

Alice B. Toklas, *The Alice B. Toklas Cook Book* (1954)

4 The tomato hides its griefs. Internal damage is hard to spot.

Julia Child, *Julia Child & Company* (1978)

5 The effect of eating too much lettuce is "soporific."

Beatrix Potter, *Flopsy Bunnies* (1902)

6 Vegetables are interesting but lack a sense of purpose when unaccompanied by a good cut of meat.

Fran Lebowitz, *Metropolitan Life* (1978)

7 [They] hunted mushrooms with Moravian cunning and passion.

Patricia Hampl, *A Romantic Education* (1981)

8 Your truffles must come to the table in their own stock. . . . And as you break open this jewel sprung from a poverty-stricken soil, imagine—if you have never visited it—the desolate kingdom where it rules.

Colette, *Prisons and Paradise* (1932)

9 Pistachio nuts, the red ones, cure any problem.

Paula Danziger, *The Pistachio Prescription* (1978)

10 Cherry cobbler is shortcake with a soul.

Edna Ferber, "Afternoon of a Faun," *Gigolo* (1922)

11 Piecrust is like a wild animal; when it sees fear in the eyes of its tamer it goes out of control.

Marcelene Cox, in *Ladies' Home Journal* (1947)

12 Fancy cream puffs so soon after breakfast. The very idea made one shudder. All the same, two minutes later Jose and Laura were licking their fingers with that absorbed inward look that only comes from whipped cream.

Katherine Mansfield, title story, *The Garden Party* (1922)

13 He said I was the most sensitive person he'd ever seen—that I belonged to the hyper-hyper type and we *rarely* survive! Of course, I was examined, and so was the éclair, and they found that the éclair contains *every*thing my system lacks. So I take three a day and I feel like a new woman!

Ruth Draper, "Doctors and Diets," *The Art of Ruth Draper* (1960)

14 This was the dawn of plastic eating in America. . . . We doted on Velveeta. Spam. Canned ravioli. Instant puddings. Instant anything. The further a thing was from the texture, flavor, and terrifying unpredictability of real food, the better.

Shirley Abbott, *The Bookmaker's Daughter* (1991)

15 Cheese that is required by law to append the word *food* to its title does not go well with red wine or fruit.

Fran Lebowitz, *Metropolitan Life* (1978)

16 Fake food—I mean those patented substances chemically flavored and mechanically bulked out to kill the appetite and deceive the gut—is unnatural, almost immoral, a bane to good eating and good cooking.

Julia Child, *Julia Child & Company* (1978)

17 Some children like to make castles out of their rice pudding, or faces with raisins for eyes. It is forbidden—so sternly that, when they grow up, they take a horrid revenge by dying meringues pale blue or baking birthday cakes in the form of horseshoes or lyres or whatnot.

Julia Child, *Julia Child & Company* (1978)

18 Lunch was not good. . . . There was trout beside which I felt young and innocent; veal the condition of which was inexplicable unless it had spent its lifetime competing in six-day bicycle races; the spinach was a dark offense. Apart from the culinary malpractices, there was that in the restaurant which gave me a temporary dislike for life.

Rebecca West, "Increase and Multiply," *Ending in Earnest* (1931)

19 Japanese food is very pretty and undoubtedly a suitable cuisine in Japan, which is largely populated

by people of below average size. Hostesses hell-bent on serving such food to occidentals would be well advised to supplement it with something more substantial and to keep in mind that almost everybody likes french fries.

Fran Lebowitz, *Metropolitan Life* (1978)

1 Tomatoes and oregano make it Italian; wine and tarragon make it French. Sour cream makes it Russian; lemon and cinnamon make it Greek. Soy sauce makes it Chinese; garlic makes it good.

Alice May Brock, *Alice's Restaurant Cookbook* (1969)

See also Appetite, Chocolate, Coffee, Cooking, Dieting, Eating, Eggs, Fruit, Gastronomy, Kosher, Lobster, Nutrition, Oysters, Tea, Weight, Wine, Zucchini.

## ✣ FOOLS

2 Fools are more to be feared than the wicked.

Queen Christina (1680), in Mrs. Jameson, *Memoirs of Celebrated Female Sovereigns* (1831)

3 The fool shouts loudly, thinking to impress the world.

Marie de France (12th cent.), in Jeanette Beer, tr., *Medieval Fables of Marie de France* (1981)

4 It is in the nature of foolish reasonings to seem good to the foolish reasoner.

George Eliot, *Impressions of Theophrastus Such* (1879)

5 Why is it that fools always have the instinct to hunt out the unpleasant secrets of life, and the hardiness to mention them?

Emily Eden, *The Semi-Attached Couple* (1860)

6 People do not wish to appear foolish; to avoid the appearance of foolishness, they were willing to remain actually fools.

Alice Walker (1978), in Gloria T. Hull, Patricia Bell Scott, and Barbara Smith, eds., *All the Women Are White, All the Blacks Are Men, But Some of Us Are Brave* (1982)

7 When in doubt, make a fool of yourself. There is a microscopically thin line between being brilliantly creative and acting like the most gigantic idiot on earth. So what the hell, leap.

Cynthia Heimel, "Lower Manhattan Survival Tactics," in *Village Voice* (1983)

8 The greatest fools, when active, may blunder into the right sometimes.

Sophia, A Person of Quality, *Woman Not Inferior to Man* (1739)

9 When he said we were trying to make a fool of him, I could only murmur that the Creator had beaten us to it.

Ilka Chase, in Jilly Cooper and Tom Hartman, *Violets and Vinegar* (1980)

## ✣ FOOTBALL

10 The stronger women get, the more men love football.

Mariah Burton Nelson, book title (1994)

11 There can be no etiquette prescribed for the players in a football game. . . . But the people who are watching the game must observe a certain good conduct, if they wish to be considered entirely cultured. For instance, even though the game becomes very exciting, it is bad form to stand up on the seats and shout words of encouragement to the players. Yet how many, who claim to be entirely well-bred, do this very thing!

Lillian Eichler, *Book of Etiquette* (1921)

See also Sports.

## ✣ FORCE

12 Beware of trying to accomplish anything by force.

Sister Angela Merici (1540), in Sigrid Undset, *Stages on the Road* (1934)

13 Nothing fruitful ever comes when plants are forced to flower in the wrong season.

Bette Bao Lord, *Spring Moon* (1981)

14 We must not force events, but rather make / The heart soil ready for their coming, as / The earth spreads carpets for the feet of Spring.

Ella Wheeler Wilcox, "Protest," *Poems of Problems* (1914)

15 How pure are those who have never forced anything open!

Colette, *La naissance du jour* (1928)

1 Who is to decide between "Let it be" and "Force it"?

> Katherine Mansfield (1914), *Journal of Katherine Mansfield* (1927)

2 You can't push a wave onto the shore any faster than the ocean brings it in.

> Susan Strasberg, *Bittersweet* (1980)

See also Control, Violence.

## ❦ FOREIGN AFFAIRS

3 A respect for the rights of other peoples to determine their forms of government and their economy will not weaken our democracy. It will inevitably strengthen it.

> Eleanor Roosevelt, *Tomorrow Is Now* (1963)

4 The western world today . . . is supremely wealthy and, on the whole, supremely confident. A deep instinct is to let the rest of the world go hang.

> Barbara Ward, in Richard Thruelsen and John Kobler, eds., *Adventures of the Mind*, 2nd series (1961)

5 The question before the advanced nations is not whether they can afford to help the developing nations, but whether they can afford not to do so.

> Indira Gandhi (1968), *Speeches and Writings* (1975)

6 Casually, unconsciously, but with deadly effectiveness, western man all round the globe destroyed the traditional gods and the ancient societies with his commerce and his science. . . . Does it mean nothing to him if great areas of the world, where western influence has been predominant, emerge from this tutelage unable to return to the old life, yet unfitted for the new? It is hard to believe that the future could ever belong to men demonstrating irresponsibility on so vast a scale.

> Barbara Ward, in Richard Thruelsen and John Kobler, eds., *Adventures of the Mind*, 2nd series (1961)

7 I've always had a weakness for foreign affairs.

> Mae West, in Joseph Weintraub, ed., *The Wit and Wisdom of Mae West* (1967)

## ❦ FORENSICS

8 Forensics is eloquence and reduction.

> Gertrude Stein, "Forensics," *How to Write* (1931)

See also Speeches.

## ❦ FORESIGHT

9 Forethought spares afterthought.

> Amelia E. Barr, *Jan Vedder's Wife* (1885)

10 Oh, if at every moment of our lives we could know the consequences of some of the utterings, thoughts and deeds that seem so trivial and unimportant at the time! And should we not conclude from such examples that there is no such thing in life as unimportant moments devoid of meaning for the future?

> Isabelle Eberhardt (1901), in Nina de Voogd, tr., *The Passionate Nomad* (1988)

11 It is seldom in life that one knows that a coming event is to be of crucial importance.

> Anya Seton, *The Turquoise* (1946)

12 In various and different circumstances certain objects and individuals are going to turn out to be vital. The wager of survival cannot, by its nature, reveal which, in advance of events.

> Nadine Gordimer, *July's People* (1981)

See also Preparedness, Thinking.

## ❦ FORESTS

13 There is no woe the forest can not heal, nor any grief.

> Mary Carolyn Davies, "Trails," *The Skyline Trail* (1924)

14 The woods seemed all answer and healing and more than enough to live for.

> Josephine W. Johnson, *Now in November* (1934)

15 There is memory in the forest.

> Margaret Widdemer, "Remembrance: Greek Folk-Song," *The Factories* (1915)

16 The woods, tall as waves, sang in mixed / tongues that loosened the scalp.

> Sonia Sanchez, *Under a Soprano Sky* (1987)

17 What a noble gift to man are the forests! What a debt of gratitude and admiration we owe for their utility and their beauty!

> Susan Fenimore Cooper, *Rural Hours* (1887)

18 The grim, grand African forests are like a great library, in which, so far, I can do little more than look at the pictures, although I am now busily

learning the alphabet of their language, so that I may some day read what these pictures mean.

Mary H. Kingsley, *Travels in West Africa* (1897)

1 The woods is gray in winter, when come cold days. And gray shadows walk among the trees. They touch one's face with velvet fingers, when one goes walking there in the woods. In the winter, old gray leaves grow to look like lace.

Opal Whiteley (1920), in Benjamin Hoff, ed., *The Singing Creek Where the Willows Grow* (1986)

2 It is the peculiar nature of the forest, that life and death may ever be found within its bounds, in immediate presence of each other; both with ceaseless, noiseless advances, aiming at the mastery; and if the influences of the first be most general, those of the last are the most striking.

Susan Fenimore Cooper, *Rural Hours* (1887)

See also Nature, Plants, Trees, Wilderness.

## ❧ FORGETTING

3 Forgetting is the cost / Of living cheerfully.

Zoë Akins, title poem, *The Hills Grow Smaller* (1937)

4 I shall go the way of the open sea, / To the lands I knew before you came, / And the cool clean breezes shall blow from me / The memory of your name.

Laurence Hope, "The End," *Stars of the Desert* (1903)

5 If we were always to continue in the same mind we are in at the end of a journey, we should never stir from the place we were then in: but Providence in kindness to us causes us to forget it. It is much the same with lying-in women. Heaven permits this forgetfulness that the world may be peopled, and that folks may take journeys to Provence.

Marie de Rabutin-Chantal, Marquise de Sévigné (1671), *Letters of Madame de Sévigné to Her Daughter and Her Friends*, vol. 1 (1811)

See also Memory, Remembrance.

## ❧ FORGIVENESS

6 Forgiveness is the economy of the heart. . . . Forgiveness saves expense of anger, the cost of hatred, the waste of spirits.

Hannah More, "Christianity a Practical Principle," *Practical Piety* (1811)

7 As long as you don't forgive, who and whatever it is will occupy rent-free space in your mind.

Isabelle Holland, *The Long Search* (1990)

8 Forgiveness is the act of admitting we are like other people.

Christina Baldwin, *Life's Companion* (1990)

9 True forgiveness includes total acceptance.

Catherine Marshall, *Christy* (1967)

10 If you haven't forgiven yourself something, how can you forgive others?

Dolores Huerta, in Barbara L. Baer, "Stopping Traffic: One Woman's Cause," *The Progressive* (1975)

11 Surely it is much more generous to forgive and remember, than to forgive and forget.

Maria Edgeworth, "An Essay on the Noble Science of Self-Justification" (1787), *Letters for Literary Ladies* (1795)

12 I think one should forgive and remember. . . . If you forgive and forget in the usual sense, you're just driving what you remember into the subconscious; it stays there and festers. But to look, even regularly, upon what you remember and *know* you've forgiven is achievement.

Faith Baldwin, *The West Wind* (1962)

13 Who understands much, forgives much.

Madame de Staël, *Corinne* (1807)

14 If you understand something, you don't forgive it, you are the thing itself: forgiveness is for what you *don't* understand.

Doris Lessing, "To Room Nineteen," *A Man and Two Women* (1963)

15 The unforgivable was usually the most easily forgiven.

P.D. James, *Death of an Expert Witness* (1977)

16 We can forgive anything as long as it isn't done to us.

P.D. James, *Innocent Blood* (1980)

17 Many people believe in turning the other cheek, especially when it is your cheek.

Anne Ellis, *The Life of an Ordinary Woman* (1929)

18 I shall be an autocrat: that's my trade. And the good Lord will forgive me: that's his.

Catherine the Great, attributed (1762), in *Who Said What When* (1988)

1 If we forgive God for his crime against us, which is to have made us finite creatures, He will forgive our crime against him, which is that we are finite creatures.

Simone Weil, *First and Last Notebooks* (1970)

2 I know now that patriotism is not enough; I must have no hatred and bitterness toward anyone.

Edith Cavell, the night before her execution, in *The London Times* (1915)

3 I have resigned myself to the fact that Rick is always going to hate me because he has committed a grave offense against me, for which he will never forgive me.

Sonia Johnson, *From Housewife to Heretic* (1981)

4 It is very easy to forgive others their mistakes; it takes more grit and gumption to forgive them for having witnessed your own.

Jessamyn West, *To See the Dream* (1957)

5 You could have forgiven my committing a sin if you hadn't feared that I had committed a pleasure as well.

Ellen Glasgow, *The Romantic Comedians* (1926)

6 Forgiveness should be an act, but this is a state with him.

Elizabeth Bowen, *The House in Paris* (1935)

7 It makes you feel very virtuous when you forgive people, doesn't it?

L.M. Montgomery, *Anne of Green Gables* (1908)

8 Forgiveness is the one unpardonable sin.

Dorothy L. Sayers, *The Five Red Herrings* (1931)

See also Mercy.

## ❦ 1492

9 Thou two-faced year, Mother of Change and Fate.

Emma Lazarus, "1492" (1882), in H.E. Jacob, *The World of Emma Lazarus* (1949)

10 The "discovery" of poverty at the beginning of the 1960s was something like the "discovery" of America almost five hundred years earlier. In the case of each of these exotic terrains, plenty of people were on the site before the discoverers ever arrived.

Barbara Ehrenreich, *Fear of Falling* (1989)

## ❦ FRANCE

11 You have two countries, your own and France.

Grace Moore, *You're Only Human Once* (1944)

12 The universe is in France; outside it, there is nothing.

Madame de Staël (1796), in J. Christopher Herold, *Mistress to an Age* (1958)

13 It is nice in France they adapt themselves to everything slowly they change completely but all the time they know that they are as they were.

Gertrude Stein, *Paris France* (1940)

14 France is the genius among nations.

Gertrude Atherton, *The Living Present* (1917)

15 Passion here is virtue.

Ann Radcliffe, *The Romance of the Forest* (1791)

16 It may be the only country in the world where the rich are sometimes brilliant.

Lillian Hellman, *An Unfinished Woman* (1969)

17 France eats more consciously, more intelligently, than any other nation.

M.F.K. Fisher, *Serve It Forth* (1937)

18 In France, cooking is a serious art form and a national sport.

Julia Child, in *The New York Times* (1986)

19 Really, Emma, you're like so many Americans—if the French baked a gopher and stuck sprigs of parsley in its ears, you'd think it was delicious.

Mary Daheim, *The Alpine Decoy* (1994)

20 The French have taste the way other people have gods or despots. The fact of an authorized, official good taste reassures them. They would be anxious without it, because their articles of taste are like articles of faith—not meant for improvisation but firm and aggressive, like good haircuts or well-cut suits or the right flowers on the table.

Jane Kramer, "Prisoners of Taste" (1989), in Steven Barclay, ed., *A Place in the World Called Paris* (1994)

21 The French are a race of individuals. There is no type.

Gertrude Atherton, *The Living Present* (1917)

22 Stoicism is the fundamental characteristic of the French.

Gertrude Atherton, *The Living Present* (1917)

1 They never stop taking exams. They start when they're five, then just never stop. And they spend the whole time asking each other about them: when they're going to take them, how they're going to do them, whether they passed, why they failed, when the next one is. It's a sort of social game really.

    Charlotte Bingham, *Coronet Among the Weeds* (1963)

2 I always hotly defend the French against the charge that they are grasping materialists only interested in money. A nation of shopkeepers whose motto is obviously "The customer is always wrong," simply cannot care that much about money.

    Alice Furlaud, *Air Fair* (1989)

See also Europe, Paris.

## ❧ FRANKNESS

3 When one is frank, one's very presence is a compliment.

    Marianne Moore, "Peter" (1924), *Selected Poems* (1935)

4 It's important to our friends to believe that we are unreservedly frank with them, and important to friendship that we are not.

    Mignon McLaughlin, *The Neurotic's Notebook* (1963)

5 Frankness is usually a euphemism for rudeness.

    Muriel Spark, *Loitering With Intent* (1981)

6 A world of vested interests is not a world which welcomes the disruptive force of candor.

    Agnes Repplier, "Are Americans Timid?" *Under Dispute* (1924)

See also Sincerity, Truth.

## ❧ FREEDOM

7 Freedom breeds freedom. Nothing else does.

    Anne Roe, *The Making of a Scientist* (1952)

8 In every human breast, God has implanted a principle, which we call love of freedom; it is impatient of oppression and pants for deliverance.

    Phillis Wheatley, in *The Boston Post-Boy* (1774)

9 Freedom / Is dearer than bread or joy.

    Jessie E. Sampter, "The Sabbath at Merchaviah," *The Emek* (1927)

10 Freedom works.

    Jeane J. Kirkpatrick, in *Time* (1985)

11 Men would rather be starving and free than fed in bonds.

    Pearl S. Buck, *What America Means to Me* (1943)

12 Nobody's free until everybody's free.

    Fannie Lou Hamer (1971), in Kay Mills, *This Little Light of Mine* (1993)

13 That is the truly beautiful and encouraging aspect of freedom; no one struggles for it just for himself.

    Fanny Lewald, in Hanna Ballin Lewis, tr., *The Education of Fanny Lewald* (1871)

14 To be free you must afford freedom to your neighbor, regardless of race, color, creed or national origin, and that, sometimes, for some, is very difficult.

    Helen Gahagan Douglas (1945), *A Full Life* (1982)

15 Real freedom is not a matter of the shifting of advantage from one sex to the other or from one class to another. Real freedom means the disappearance of advantage, and primarily of economic advantage.

    Suzanne La Follette, *Concerning Women* (1926)

16 Freedom comes in individual packages.

    Shirley Boone, *One Woman's Liberation* (1972)

17 It is by the exercise of political freedom men become qualified to use it.

    Frances B. Cobbe, *Italics* (1864)

18 While any one is base, none can be entirely free and noble.

    Margaret Fuller, *Woman in the Nineteenth Century* (1845)

19 Freedom was born in Greece because there men limited their own freedom. . . . The limits to action established by law were a mere nothing compared to the limits established by a man's free choice.

    Edith Hamilton, *The Echo of Greece* (1957)

20 Total freedom is never what one imagines and, in fact, hardly exists. It comes as a shock in life to learn that we usually only exchange one set of restrictions for another. The second set, however, is self-chosen, and therefore easier to accept.

    Anne Morrow Lindbergh, *Hour of Gold, Hour of Lead* (1973)

1 Too much freedom is its own kind of cage.
  Patricia MacDonald, *Secret Admirer* (1995)

2 Freedom is a dangerous intoxicant and very few people can tolerate it in any quantity.
  Katherine Anne Porter, *The Never-Ending Wrong* (1977)

3 Absolute freedom is absolute responsibility.
  Ursula K. Le Guin, "Talking About Writing," *Language of the Night* (1979)

4 When the freedom they wished most for was freedom from responsibility, then Athens ceased to be free and was never free again.
  Edith Hamilton, "The Lessons of the Past," in Richard Thruelsen and John Kobler, eds., *Adventures of the Mind*, 1st series (1959)

5 Freedom is fragile and must be protected. To sacrifice it, even as a temporary measure, is to betray it.
  Germaine Greer, *The Female Eunuch* (1970)

6 There is nothing inevitable. The actions of the past operate at every instant and so, at every instant, does freedom.
  Nan Shin, *Diary of a Zen Nun* (1986)

7 None who have always been free can understand the terrible fascinating power of the hope of freedom to those who are not free.
  Pearl S. Buck, *What America Means to Me* (1943)

8 Golden fetters hurt as cruelly as iron ones.
  Minna Thomas Antrim, *Naked Truth and Veiled Allusions* (1901)

9 There's one thing about freedom . . . each generation of people begins by thinking they've got it for the first time in history, and ends by being sure the generation younger than themselves have too much of it. It can't really always have been increasing at the rate people suppose, or there would be more of it by now.
  Rose Macaulay, *Told by an Idiot* (1923)

10 Freedom is not won on the battlefields. The chance for freedom is won there. The final battle is won or lost in our hearts and minds.
  Helen Gahagan Douglas (1945), *A Full Life* (1982)

11 Freedom is always and exclusively freedom for the one who thinks differently. Not because of any fanatical concept of "justice" but because all that is instructive, wholesome and purifying in political freedom depends on this essential characteristic, and its effectiveness vanishes when "freedom" becomes a special privilege.
  Rosa Luxemburg, *The Russian Revolution* (1922)

12 There are only two kinds of freedom in the world: the freedom of the rich and powerful, and the freedom of the artist and the monk who renounce possessions.
  Anaïs Nin (1940), *The Diary of Anaïs Nin*, vol. 3 (1969)

13 Only on the surface of things have I ever trod the beaten path. So long as I could keep from hurting anyone else, I have lived, as completely as it was possible, the life of my choice. I have been free. . . . I have done the work I wished to do for the sake of that work alone.
  Ellen Glasgow, *The Woman Within* (1954)

14 Miss Gavin was emancipated, or believed herself to be, which amounts to the same thing.
  Ellen Glasgow, *The Descendant* (1897)

See also Independence, Liberation, Liberty, Self-Determination.

## ❧ FREE WILL

15 Those who believe in freedom of the will have never loved and never hated.
  Marie von Ebner-Eschenbach, *Aphorisms* (1893)

See also Destiny, Fate.

## ❧ FRIENDLINESS

16 I'm not against friendliness, she said, I'm not even against Americans.
  Grace Paley, *Enormous Changes at the Last Minute* (1974)

17 You can't always be friendly. It's impossible, there isn't the time.
  Tove Jansson, *Tales From Moominvalley* (1963)

See also Friendship.

## ❧ FRIENDSHIP

18 Friendship's a noble name, 'tis love refined.
  Susannah Centlivre, *The Stolen Heiress* (1703)

1 Oh, the comfort—the inexpressible comfort of feeling *safe* with a person—having neither to weigh thoughts nor measure words, but pouring them all right out, just as they are, chaff and grain together; certain that a faithful hand will take and sift them, keep what is worth keeping, and then with the breath of kindness blow the rest away.

   Dinah Maria Mulock Craik, *A Life for a Life* (1866)

2 True friends are those who really know you but love you anyway.

   Edna Buchanan, *Suitable for Framing* (1995)

3 Friendship is the bread of the heart.

   Mary Russell Mitford (1853), in the Reverend A.G. L'Estrange, ed., *The Life of Mary Russell Mitford*, vol. 3 (1870)

4 My friends are my estate.

   Emily Dickinson (1858), in Mabel Loomis Todd, ed., *Letters of Emily Dickinson*, vol. 1 (1894)

5 Prosperity provideth, but adversity proveth friends.

   Queen Elizabeth I (1580), in Frederick Chamberlin, *The Sayings of Queen Elizabeth* (1923)

6 Friends make good furniture and easy windows.

   Constance Nivelle, in John Marvin, ed., *You're My Friend So I Brought You This Book* (1970)

7 There are people whom one loves immediately and for ever. Even to know they are alive in the world with one is quite enough.

   Nancy Spain, *Why I'm Not a Millionaire* (1956)

8 I felt it shelter to speak to you.

   Emily Dickinson (1878), in Mabel Loomis Todd, ed., *Letters of Emily Dickinson*, vol. 2 (1894)

9 I suppose there is one friend in the life of each of us who seems not a separate person, however dear and beloved, but an expansion, an interpretation, of one's self, the very meaning of one's soul.

   Edith Wharton, *A Backward Glance* (1934)

10 She is a friend of my mind. She gather me, man. The pieces I am, she gather them and give them back to me in all the right order.

   Toni Morrison, *Beloved* (1987)

11 Each friend represents a world in us, a world possibly not born until they arrive, and it is only by this meeting that a new world is born.

   Anaïs Nin (1937), *The Diary of Anaïs Nin*, vol. 2 (1967)

12 Only solitary men know the full joys of friendship. Others have their family; but to a solitary and an exile his friends are everything.

   Willa Cather, *Shadows on the Rock* (1931)

13 It's the ones you can call up at 4:00 a.m. that matter.

   Marlene Dietrich, in John Robert Colombo, *Popcorn in Paradise* (1979)

14 I always feel that the great high privilege, relief and comfort of friendship was that one had to explain nothing.

   Katherine Mansfield, in Antony Alpers, *Katherine Mansfield* (1954)

15 Parents are friends that life gives us; friends are parents that the heart chooses.

   Comtesse Diane, *Les Glanes de la Vie* (1898)

16 Friends are the family we choose for ourselves.

   Edna Buchanan, *Suitable for Framing* (1995)

17 In real friendship the judgment, the genius, the prudence of each party become the common property of both.

   Maria Edgeworth, *Letters of Julia and Caroline* (1795)

18 A friend in need is a friend indeed.

   Susan Ferrier, *The Inheritance*, vol. 1 (1824)

19 There's no friend like someone who has known you since you were five.

   Anne Stevenson, *Coil of Serpents* (1977)

20 Even where the affections are not strongly moved by any superior excellence, the companions of our childhood always possess a certain power over our minds which hardly any later friend can obtain.

   Mary Shelley, *Frankenstein* (1818)

21 Yes'm, old friends is always best, 'less you can catch a new one that's fit to make an old one out of.

   Sarah Orne Jewett, *The Country of the Pointed Firs* (1896)

22 I have come to esteem history as a component of friendships. In my case at least friendships are not igneous but sedimentary.

   Jane Howard, *Please Touch* (1970)

23 Two may talk together under the same roof for many years, yet never really meet; and two others at first speech are old friends.

   Mary H. Catherwood, "Marianson," *Mackinac and Lake Stories* (1899)

1 She found to her surprise that an old friend is not always the person whom it is easiest to make a confidant of: there was the barrier of remembered communication under other circumstances—there was the dislike of being pitied and informed by one who had been long wont to allow her the superiority.

George Eliot, *Middlemarch* (1871)

2 However deep our devotion may be to parents, or to children, it is our contemporaries alone with whom understanding is instinctive and entire.

Vera Brittain, *Testament of Youth* (1933)

3 In a world more and more polluted by the lying of politicians and the illusions of the media, I occasionally crave to hear and tell the truth. . . . Friendship is by its very nature freer of deceit than any other relationship we can know because it is the bond least affected by striving for power, physical pleasure, or material profit, most liberated from any oath of duty or of constancy.

Francine du Plessix Gray, in Adelaide Bry, *Friendship* (1979)

4 Funny, you don't look like a friend—ah, but they never do.

Grace Metalious, in John Marvin, ed., *You're My Friend So I Brought You This Book* (1970)

5 It seems to me that trying to live without friends is like milking a bear to get cream for your morning coffee. It is a whole lot of trouble, and then not worth much after you get it.

Zora Neale Hurston, *Dust Tracks on a Road* (1942)

6 Life without a friend is death without a witness.

Rose Macaulay, *Daisy and Daphne* (1928)

7 The hearts that never lean, must fall.

Emily Dickinson (1881), in Mabel Loomis Todd, ed., *Letters of Emily Dickinson*, vol. 1 (1894)

8 None but the unhappy are worthy of friends; if your soul had never suffered never could you have entered mine.

Julie de Lespinasse (1773), in Katharine Prescott Wormeley, tr., *Letters of Mlle. de Lespinasse* (1901)

9 In meeting again after a separation, acquaintances ask after our outward life, friends after our inner life.

Marie von Ebner-Eschenbach, *Aphorisms* (1893)

10 A friend can tell you things you don't want to tell yourself.

Frances Ward Weller, *Boat Song* (1987)

11 A friend is one who withholds judgment no matter how long you have his unanswered letter.

Sophie Irene Loeb, *Epigrams of Eve* (1913)

12 What I cannot love, I overlook. Is that real friendship?

Anaïs Nin (1953), *The Diary of Anaïs Nin*, vol. 5 (1974)

13 Though friendship is not quick to burn, / It is explosive stuff.

May Sarton, "Friendship: The Storms," *A Grain of Mustard Seed* (1971)

14 True friendship is never tranquil.

Marie de Rabutin-Chantal, Marquise de Sévigné (1671), in M. Monmerqué, ed., *Lettres de Madame de Sévigné de sa famille et de ses amis*, vol. 2 (1862)

15 Relations are errors that Nature makes. / Your spouse you can put on the shelf. / But your friends, dear friends, are the quaint mistakes / You always commit, yourself.

Phyllis McGinley, "Marginal Notes," *On the Contrary* (1934)

16 It is the greatest mistake, both in life and in literature, to suppose that love is the difficult, the complicated thing. It is not love, it is friendship, which is the great problem of civilized society. The other is quite elemental beside it.

Mary Adams, *Confessions of a Wife* (1902)

17 Friendship has splendors that love knows not. It grows stronger when crossed, whereas obstacles kill love. Friendship resists time, which wearies and severs couples. It has heights unknown to love.

Mariama Bâ, *So Long a Letter* (1980)

18 Friendship is far more delicate than love. Quarrels and fretful complaints are attractive in the last, offensive in the first. And the very things which heap fuel on the fire of ardent passion, choke and extinguish sober and true regard. On the other hand, time, which is sure to *destroy* that love of which half certainly depends on *desire*, is as sure to increase a friendship founded on talents, warm with esteem, and ambitious of success for the object of it.

Hester Lynch Piozzi (1820), in Oswald G. Knapp, ed., *The Intimate Letters of Hester Piozzi and Penelope Pennington 1788-1821* (1914)

1 Friendship, which is of its nature a delicate thing, fastidious, slow of growth, is easily checked, will hesitate, demur, recoil where love, good old blustering love, bowls ahead and blunders through every obstacle.

Colette, *My Apprenticeships* (1936)

2 Friendships begin with liking or gratitude—roots that can be pulled up.

George Eliot, *Daniel Deronda* (1874)

3 Friendship is a difficult, dangerous job. It is also (though we rarely admit it) extremely exhausting.

Elizabeth Bibesco, *Balloons* (1922)

4 Friendship is an art, and very few persons are born with a natural gift for it.

Kathleen Norris, *Hands Full of Living* (1931)

5 Really, one has some friends, and when one comes to think about it it is impossible to tell how one ever became friendly with them.

Françoise Mallet-Joris, *A Letter to Myself* (1963)

6 You can keep your friends by not giving them away.

Mary Pettibone Poole, *A Glass Eye at a Keyhole* (1938)

7 It is wise to apply the oil of refined politeness to the mechanism of friendship.

Colette, *The Pure and the Impure* (1932)

8 Friendship with oneself is all-important, because without it one cannot be friends with anyone else in the world.

Eleanor Roosevelt, "How to Take Criticism," in *Ladies' Home Journal* (1944)

9 She didn't know how to be friends with more than one person at a time.

Mary Calhoun, *Julie's Tree* (1988)

10 There was a definite process by which one made people into friends, and it involved talking to them and listening to them for hours at a time.

Rebecca West, *The Thinking Reed* (1936)

11 It is the steady and merciless increase of occupations, the augmented speed at which we are always trying to live, the crowding of each day with more work and amusement than it can profitably hold, which has cost us, among other good things, the undisturbed enjoyment of friends. Friendship takes time, and we have no time to give it.

Agnes Repplier, "Guests," *In the Dozy Hours* (1894)

12 The pleasures of intimacy in friendship depend far more on external circumstances than people of a sentimental turn of mind are willing to concede; and when constant companionship ceases to suit the convenience of both parties, the chances are that it will be dropped on the first favorable opportunity.

Hester Lynch Piozzi (1783), in A. Hayward, ed., *Autobiography, Letters, and Literary Remains of Mrs. Piozzi (Thrale)*, vol. 1 (1861)

13 Friendship has no civil, and few emotional, rights in our society.

Christina Baldwin, *One to One* (1977)

14 Business, you know, may bring money, but friendship hardly ever does.

Jane Austen, *Emma* (1816)

15 We may generally conclude the Marriage of a Friend to be the Funeral of a Friendship.

Katherine Philips (1662), in Philip Webster Souers, *The Matchless Orinda* (1931)

16 Constant use had not worn ragged the fabric of their friendship.

Dorothy Parker, "The Standard of Living," *The Portable Dorothy Parker* (1944)

17 No two men saw less eye to eye and the result was unexpected harmony, as if a dog and a fish had mysteriously become friends and were proud each of the other's remarkable dissimilarity to himself.

Margery Allingham, *The Tiger in the Smoke* (1952)

18 There seems to be a peculiar and particular tie between men who have been drunk together.

Anne Ellis, *The Life of an Ordinary Woman* (1929)

19 Female friendships that work are relationships in which women help each other belong to themselves.

Louise Bernikow, *Among Women* (1980)

20 Often intimacies between women go backwards, beginning with revelations and ending up in small talk without loss of esteem.

Elizabeth Bowen, *The Death of the Heart* (1938)

21 [Friendships] are easy to get out of compared to love affairs, but they are not easy to get out of compared to, say, jail.

Fran Lebowitz, in *Mirabella* (1992)

22 It's very important when making a friend to check and see if they have a private plane. People think a

good personality trait in a friend is kindness or a sense of humor. No, in a friend a good personality trait is a Gulfstream.

Fran Lebowitz, in *Travel & Leisure* (1994)

See also Affection, Friendliness, Intimacy, Lovers, Relationships.

## ❧ FRUIT

1 Deep from her blue apron pocket / she drew a ripe orange to slice / and squirt light / —your mouth was stained with sun.

Janet Frame, "Summer," *The Pocket Mirror* (1967)

2 Gooseberry virtues / take some getting / used to.

Amy Clampitt, "Gooseberry Fool," *What the Light Was Like* (1985)

3 If peaches had arms / surely they would hold one another / in their peach sleep.

Sandra Cisneros, "Peaches—Six in a Tin Bowl, Sarajevo," *My Wicked Wicked Ways* (1987)

4 For the first time I tasted this tropical fruit, which people here are so fond of. . . . I could have fancied I was biting into soap. I have a notion that we shall not become very good friends, the banana and I.

Fredrika Bremer (1850), *America of the Fifties* (1924)

## ❧ FUNCTION

5 Recognition of function always precedes recognition of being.

Rita Mae Brown, *Starting From Scratch* (1988)

See also Purpose.

## ❧ FUNERALS

6 Alas, poor Yorick! How surprised he would be to see how his counterpart of today is whisked off to a funeral parlor and is in short order sprayed, sliced, pierced, pickled, trussed, trimmed, creamed, waxed, painted, rouged and neatly dressed—transformed from a common corpse into a Beautiful Memory Picture.

Jessica Mitford, *The American Way of Death* (1963)

7 O death, where is thy sting? O grave, where is thy victory? Where, indeed. Many a badly stung survivor, faced with the aftermath of some relative's funeral, has ruefully concluded that the victory has been won hands down by a funeral establishment—in disastrously unequal battle.

Jessica Mitford, *The American Way of Death* (1963)

8 We managed to arrive at San Lorenzo fuori le Mura at the same moment as a funeral. . . . A fat priest in his vestments came out of the first coach like an overgrown dahlia, and roared his way through the service with a speed only to be matched by the speed of the organist, who kept on tripping him over with the first chord of the responses, like a rugby tackle.

Sylvia Townsend Warner (1955), in William Maxwell, ed., *Letters: Sylvia Townsend Warner* (1982)

See also Cemeteries, Death.

## ❧ FUTILITY

9 An ass may bray a good while before he shakes the stars down.

George Eliot, *Romola* (1862)

10 It's but little good you'll do a-watering the last year's crop.

George Eliot, *Adam Bede* (1859)

11 You can't make soufflé rise twice.

Alice Roosevelt Longworth (1948), in James T. Patterson, *Mr. Republican* (1972)

12 There is no irritant as painful as an ace up your sleeve that you can never use; it's the kind of thing that causes oysters to produce pearls.

Sheila Ballantyne, *Imaginary Crimes* (1982)

13 I, who have been a net spread in the deep, / return to the surface without a fish.

Rosario Castellanos, "The Useless Day," in Magda Bogin, tr., *The Selected Poems of Rosario Castellanos* (1988)

14 He saw lying behind him the whole futility of his life; it seemed to him now like a mumbled string of

meaningless prayers, a foolish litany which ended in the priest falling asleep.

Sheila Kaye-Smith, *A Challenge to Sirius* (1917)

1 People have been marrying and bringing up children for centuries now. Nothing has ever come of it.

Celia Green, *The Decline and Fall of Science* (1976)

2 It was one of the late Conservative Government's gestures towards agriculture—graceful as a kiss, and of about as much use.

Sheila Kaye-Smith, *Gipsy Waggon* (1933)

3 Art is a form of catharsis, / And love is a permanent flop, / And work is the province of cattle, / And rest's for a clam in a shell, / So I'm thinking of throwing the battle— / Would you kindly direct me to hell?

Dorothy Parker, "Coda," *Sunset Gun* (1928)

## ❧ FUTURE

4 The future: A consolation for those who have no other.

Countess of Blessington, *Desultory Thoughts and Reflections* (1839)

5 The future bears a great resemblance to the past, only more so.

Faith Popcorn, *The Popcorn Report* (1991)

6 The future is made of the same stuff as the present.

Simone Weil, *On Science, Necessity, and the Love of God* (1968)

7 Our faith in the present dies out long before our faith in the future.

Ruth Benedict (1913), in Margaret Mead, *An Anthropologist at Work* (1959)

8 The future was plump with promise.

Maya Angelou, *All God's Children Need Traveling Shoes* (1986)

9 My future is a secret. / It is as shy as a mole.

Anne Sexton (1964), in Linda Gray Sexton, ed., *Words for Dr. Y.* (1978)

10 Nobody can take away your future. Nobody can take away something you don't have yet.

Dorothy B. Hughes, *Dread Journey* (1945)

11 We grow in time to trust the future for our answers.

Ruth Benedict (1915), in Margaret Mead, *An Anthropologist at Work* (1959)

12 The future is a fog that is still hanging out over the sea, a boat that floats home or does not. The trade winds blow me, and I do not know where the land is; the waves fold over each other; they are in love with themselves; sleeping in their own skin; and I float over them and I do not know about tomorrow.

Anne Sexton (1958), in Linda Gray Sexton and Lois Ames, eds., *Anne Sexton: A Self-Portrait in Letters* (1977)

13 I never was able to believe in the existence of next year except as in a metaphysical notion.

Madame de Staël, in J. Christopher Herold, *Mistress to an Age* (1958)

14 While to live in the past and think of what was good and beautiful about it amounts to a sort of *seasoning* of the present, the perennial wait for tomorrow is bound to result in chronic discontent that poisons one's entire outlook.

Isabelle Eberhardt (1900), in Nina de Voogd, tr., *The Passionate Nomad* (1988)

15 If we can recognize that change and uncertainty are basic principles, we can greet the future and the transformation we are undergoing with the understanding that *we do not know enough to be pessimistic.*

Hazel Henderson, *The Politics of the Solar Age* (1981)

16 Children of yesterday, / Heirs of to-morrow, / What are you weaving? / Labor and sorrow? / Look to your looms again. / Faster and faster / Fly the great shuttles / Prepared by the Master, / Life's in the loom, / Room for it— / Room!

Mary Artemisia Lathbury, "Song of Hope," *Poems of Mary Artemisia Lathbury* (1915)

17 The wave of the future is coming and there is no fighting it.

Anne Morrow Lindbergh, *The Wave of the Future* (1940)

18 "What about her Future?" Future, as she pronounced it, was spelled with a capital F and was a thin disguise for the word husband.

Edna Ferber, *Show Boat* (1926)

See also Past, Present, Time, Tomorrow.

# G

## ⟡ GAIETY

1 There is nothing more tedious than a constant
round of gaiety.

   Margery Sharp, *The Rescuers* (1959)

See also Parties.

## ⟡ GAMBLING

2 Time spent in a casino is time given to death, a
foretaste of the hour when one's flesh will be diverted to the purposes of the worm and not of the
will.

   Rebecca West, *The Thinking Reed* (1936)

3 Casino owners spoke more loudly than any of the
other kings of industry to defend their contribution to society. They could speak more loudly because theirs was the purest activity of civilized man.
They had transcended the need for a product. They
could maintain and advance life with machines
that made nothing but money.

   Jane Rule, *The Desert of the Heart* (1965)

4 I've been writing a book for years. It's called *Horses
That Owe Me Money*, and I haven't come to the end
of it yet.

   Sophie Tucker, *Some of These Days* (1945)

5 I figure you have the same chance of winning the
lottery whether you play or not.

   Fran Lebowitz, in Roz Warren, ed., *Glibquips* (1994)

See also Lotteries.

## ⟡ GARDENING

6 O the green things growing, the green things growing, / The faint sweet smell of the green things
growing!

   Dinah Maria Mulock Craik, "Green Things Growing,"
   *Mulock's Poems, New and Old* (1880)

7 The kiss of sun for pardon, / The song of the birds
for mirth,— / One is nearer God's heart in a garden
/ Than anywhere else on earth.

   Dorothy Frances Gurney, "God's Garden," in Burton E.
   Stevenson, ed., *The Home Book of Modern Verse* (1925)

8 I love spring anywhere, but if I could choose I
would always greet it in a garden.

   Ruth Stout, *How to Have a Green Thumb Without an
   Aching Back* (1955)

9 I am weary of swords and courts and kings. Let us
go into the garden and watch the minister's bees.

   Mary Johnston, *To Have and to Hold* (1900)

10 Gardening is not a rational act.

   Margaret Atwood, "Unearthing Suite," *Bluebeard's Egg*
   (1986)

11 Gardening has compensations out of all proportion to its goals. It is creation in the pure sense.

   Phyllis McGinley, "Against Gardens," *The Province of the
   Heart* (1959)

12 Gardening is an exercise in optimism. Sometimes,
it is the triumph of hope over experience.

   Marina Schinz, *Visions of Paradise* (1985)

13 The trouble with gardening . . . is that it does not
remain an avocation. It becomes an obsession.

   Phyllis McGinley, "Against Gardens," *The Province of the
   Heart* (1959)

1 Gardening is a madness, a folly that does not go away with age. Quite the contrary.

May Sarton, *At Seventy* (1984)

2 A garden isn't meant to be useful. It's for joy.

Rumer Godden, *China Court* (1961)

3 I think this is what hooks one on gardening: it is the closest one can come to being present at the Creation.

Phyllis Theroux, in *Reader's Digest* (1979)

4 Gardens are the result of a collaboration between art and nature.

Penelope Hobhouse, *Garden Style* (1988)

5 There is a kind of immortality in every garden.

Gladys Taber, *Stillmeadow Daybook* (1955)

6 A garden is always a series of losses set against a few triumphs, like life itself.

May Sarton, *At Seventy* (1984)

7 Neither a garden nor a gardener can be made in one year, nor in one generation even.

The Gardener, *The Garden of a Commuter's Wife* (1905)

8 Working in the garden . . . gives me a profound feeling of inner peace. Nothing here is in a hurry. There is no rush toward accomplishment, no blowing of trumpets. Here is the great mystery of life and growth. Everything is changing, growing, aiming at something, but silently, unboastfully, taking its time.

Ruth Stout, *How to Have a Green Thumb Without an Aching Back* (1955)

9 To create a garden is to search for a better world. In our effort to improve on nature, we are guided by a vision of paradise. Whether the result is a horticultural masterpiece or only a modest vegetable patch, it is based on the expectation of a glorious future. This hope for the future is at the heart of all gardening.

Marina Schinz, *Visions of Paradise* (1985)

10 To garden is a solitary act.

Michelle Cliff, *Claiming an Identity They Taught Me to Despise* (1980)

11 True gardeners cannot bear a glove / Between the sure touch and the tender root.

May Sarton, "An Observation," *As Does New Hampshire* (1967)

12 In what other job can a person be inventor, scientist, landscape gardener, ditch digger, researcher, problem solver, artist, exorcist, and on top of all that eat one's successes at dinner?

Dorothy Gilman, *A New Kind of Country* (1978)

13 The successful truck gardener can never go out to dinner in the summer or spend a weekend away, because his conscience tells him he has to be at home eating up his corn or packaging his beans for the freezer.

Phyllis McGinley, "Against Gardens," *The Province of the Heart* (1959)

14 Huldy was one o' them that has the gift, so that ef you jist give 'em the leastest sprig of anything they make a great bush out of it right away.

Harriet Beecher Stowe, "The Minister's Housekeeper," *Sam Lawson's Oldtown Fireside Stories* (1871)

15 Grandma spent much time "working in the garden." She called it that, but it wasn't like work. It was a kind of formative being present, intensely aware—that combination of willing and of gloating, simultaneously, that is creation.

Bertha Damon, *Grandma Called It Carnal* (1938)

16 Lyda was an exuberant, even a dramatic gardener. . . . She was always holding up a lettuce or a bunch of radishes, with an air of resolute courage, as though she had shot them herself.

Renata Adler, *Speedboat* (1976)

17 Walter would not tolerate an unhealthy or badly grown plant and if he saw anything that wasn't looking happy he pulled it up. Often I would go out and find a row of sick looking plants laid out like a lot of dead rats.

Margery Fish, *We Made a Garden* (1956)

18 I wanted no one lifting a finger in that garden unless he loved doing it. What if Fred had hired a man to dig those trenches and it had turned out that he didn't love to dig? Who could eat that kind of asparagus?

Ruth Stout, *How to Have a Green Thumb Without an Aching Back* (1955)

19 People in England who do not like gardening are very few, and of the few there are, many do not own to it, knowing that they might just as well own to having been in prison, or got drunk at Buckingham Palace.

E.M. Delafield, *General Impressions* (1933)

1 Firmness in all aspects is a most important quality when gardening, not only in planting but in pruning, dividing and tying up. Plants are like babies, they know when an amateur is handling them.

  Margery Fish, *We Made a Garden* (1956)

2 There's little risk in becoming overly proud of one's garden because gardening by its very nature is humbling. It has a way of keeping you on your knees.

  JoAnn R. Barwick, in *Reader's Digest* (1993)

3 The process of weeding can be as beneficial to the gardener as to the garden. It gives scope to the aggressive instinct—what a satisfaction to pull up an enemy by the roots and throw him into a heap! And yet, paradoxically, weeding is the most peaceful of any outdoor task.

  Bertha Damon, *A Sense of Humus* (1943)

4 Nature soon takes over if the gardener is absent.

  Penelope Hobhouse, *The Country Gardener* (1989)

5 Each garden has its own surprise.

  Susan Allen Toth, *My Love Affair With England* (1992)

6 Every flower holds the whole mystery in its short cycle, and in the garden we are never far away from death, the fertilizing, good, *creative* death.

  May Sarton, *Journal of a Solitude* (1973)

7 We have descended into the garden and caught three hundred slugs. How I love the mixture of the beautiful and the squalid in gardening. It makes it so lifelike.

  Evelyn Underhill (1912), in Charles Williams, ed., *The Letters of Evelyn Underhill* (1943)

8 What impressed me most about English gardens was their generosity of spirit, an exuberant lavishness that could not always be contained within strict squares or rectangles. . . . I discovered cultivated flowers that soared on trellises, curved along winding paths, tumbled over walls, popped up between stones on a terrace, clustered in hidden corners like gossiping friends at a tea party, and crowded each other to show off their colors in mixed borders.

  Susan Allen Toth, *My Love Affair With England* (1992)

9 The eighteenth-century view of the garden was that it should lead the observer to the enjoyment of the aesthetic sentiments of regularity and order, proportion, color and utility, and, furthermore, be capable of arousing feelings of grandeur, gaiety, sadness, wildness, domesticity, surprise and secrecy.

  Penelope Hobhouse, *The Country Gardener* (1989)

10 You mustn't rely on your flowers to make your garden attractive. A good bone structure must come first, with an intelligent use of evergreen plants so that the garden is always clothed, no matter what time of year. Flowers are an added delight, but a good garden is the garden you enjoy looking at even in the depths of winter.

  Margery Fish, *We Made a Garden* (1956)

11 The garden . . . was like a blossoming meadow; from the house it suggested a many-colored sea of petals floating above the ground. Over the surface of this sea there were always butterflies dancing, rather like flowers detached from their stems.

  Janet Gillespie, *The Joy of a Small Garden* (1963)

12 If "heartache" sounds exaggerated then surely you have never gone to your garden one rare morning in June to find that the frost, without any perceptible motive, any hope of personal gain, has quietly killed your strawberry blossoms, tomatoes, lima and green beans, corn, squash, cucumbers. A brilliant sun is now smiling at this disaster with an insensitive cheerfulness as out of place as a funny story would be if someone you loved had just died.

  Ruth Stout, *How to Have a Green Thumb Without an Aching Back* (1955)

13 Weather means more when you have a garden: there's nothing like listening to a shower and thinking how it is soaking in around your lettuce and green beans.

  Marcelene Cox, in *Ladies' Home Journal* (1944)

14 [Radishes] are the one amateur crop to be relied on. Many are sowed, but few are eaten, except those first prompt miraculous test cases which the gardener wipes on the seat of his overalls and eats on the spot, with no condiment but grit.

  Bertha Damon, *A Sense of Humus* (1943)

15 In the spring, at the end of the day, you should smell like dirt.

  Margaret Atwood, "Unearthing Suite," *Bluebeard's Egg* (1986)

16 A garden has a curious innocent way of consuming cash while all the time you are under the illusion that you are spending nothing.

  Esther Meynell, *A Woman Talking* (1940)

1 You must remember garden catalogues are as big liars as house-agents.

Rumer Godden, *China Court* (1961)

2 May you have a good sowing / And a gallant crop; / May your weeds never begin, / Your flowers never stop; / May your radishes be bright, / Your new potatoes succulent, / Your leeks all gentleness, / Your roses truculent.

Marie de L. Welch, "Rhymes to Hang in Bertha's Barn," in Bertha Damon, *A Sense of Humus* (1943)

See also Flowers, Plants, Zucchini.

## ❧ GASTRONOMY

3 Unlike music or poetry or painting, food rouses no response in passionate and emotional youth. Only when the surge of the blood is quieted does gastronomy come into its own with philosophy and theology and the sterner delights of the mind.

Dorothy L. Sayers, *The Documents in the Case* (1930)

See also Cooking, Eating, Food.

## ❧ GAY MEN

4 We know that priorities are amiss in the world when a man gets a military medal of honor for killing another man and a dishonorable discharge for loving one.

Charlotte Bunch, "Speaking Out, Reaching Out," *Passionate Politics* (1987)

5 He was the wren and the rain, he was the wind and the trees bending under the wind. He was split in two, the mover and the moved, the male and the female.

Margaret Millar, *Beast in View* (1955)

See also Lesbians and Gay Men, Men.

## ❧ GENDER

6 To me gender is not physical at all, but is altogether insubstantial. It is soul, perhaps, it is talent, it is taste, it is environment, it is how one feels, it is light and shade, it is inner music. . . . It is the essentialness of oneself.

Jan Morris, *Conundrum* (1974)

See also Androgyny, Sex Roles.

## ❧ GENEALOGY

7 The craze for genealogy . . . is connected with the epidemic for divorce. . . . If we can't figure out who our living relatives are, then maybe we'll have more luck with the dead ones.

Jane Howard, *Families* (1978)

8 Of all the trees that have ever been cultivated by man, the genealogical tree is the driest. It is one, we may be sure, that had no place in the garden of Eden.

Amelia B. Edwards, *Half a Million of Money* (1866)

## ❧ GENERALIZATIONS

9 All sweeping assertions are erroneous.

L.E. Landon, *Romance and Reality* (1831)

10 Generalizations, one is told, are dangerous. So is life, for that matter, and it is built up on generalization—from the earliest effort of the adventurer who dared to eat a second berry because the first had not killed him.

Freya Stark, *The Lycian Shore* (1956)

11 We always are thinking of a woman when we generalize about women.

Roman Doubleday, *The Hemlock Avenue Mystery* (1908)

12 These people are a specimen of how people talk, the wide world over. . . . You see how they argue upon the vast interests of vast bodies from the temporary aspect of their own little affairs.

Harriet Martineau, *Illustrations of Taxation* (1834)

13 Generalizations are merely conveniences, an attempt to oil the wheels of such civilization as we have. It is exhausting to come newly to everything,

to have the same decisions to make over and over again.

Elizabeth Taylor, *At Mrs. Lippincote's* (1945)

See also Stereotypes.

## ❦ GENERATIONS

1 She said there were two people you had to be true to—those people who came before you and those people who came after you.

Gayl Jones, *Eva's Man* (1976)

2 We didn't have a generation gap, we had a generation Grand Canyon.

Mary Crow Dog, with Richard Erdoes, *Lakota Woman* (1990)

3 The dead might as well try to speak to the living as the old to the young.

Willa Cather, *One of Ours* (1922)

4 Today age segregation has passed all sane limits. Not only are fifteen-year-olds isolated from seventy-year-olds but social groups divide those in high school from those in junior high, and those who are twenty from those who are twenty-five. There are middle-middle-age groups, late-middle-age groups, and old-age groups—as though people with five years between them could not possibly have anything in common.

Suzanne Gordon, *Lonely in America* (1976)

5 There are two barriers that often prevent communication between the young and their elders. The first is middle-aged forgetfulness of the fact that they themselves are no longer young. The second is youthful ignorance of the fact that the middle aged are still alive.

Jessamyn West, *To See the Dream* (1957)

6 It is so easy for a middle-aged person, in the presence of youth, to be deluded about his own age. The young faces are so exactly like the one he saw in his own mirror—only day before yesterday, it seems.

Jessamyn West, *To See the Dream* (1957)

7 As long as any adult thinks that he, like the parents and teachers of old, can become introspective, in-

voking his own youth to understand the youth before him, he is lost.

Margaret Mead, *Culture and Commitment* (1970)

8 Parents and children cannot be to each other, as husbands with wives and wives with husbands. Nature has separated them by an almost impassable barrier of time; the mind and the heart are in quite a different state at fifteen and forty.

Sara Coleridge (1846), *Memoir and Letters*, vol. 2 (1873)

9 You, that have toiled during youth, to set your son upon higher ground, and to enable him to begin where you left off, do not expect that son to be what you were,—diligent, modest, active, simple in his tastes, fertile in resources. . . . Poverty educated you; wealth will educate him. You cannot suppose the result will be the same.

Anna Laetitia Barbauld, "On Education," *The Works of Anna Laetitia Barbauld*, vol. 2 (1825)

10 Even very recently, the elders could say: "You know, I have been young and *you* never have been old." But today's young people can reply: "You never have been young in the world I am young in, and you never can be." . . . The older generation will never see repeated in the lives of young people their own unprecedented experience of sequentially emerging change. This break between generations is wholly new: it is planetary and universal.

Margaret Mead, *Culture and Commitment* (1970)

11 When we are young our parents run our life; when we get older, our children do.

Vicki Baum, *I Know What I'm Worth* (1964)

12 We have no patriotism toward posterity; and the selfish amusement of the present always has, and always will, outweigh the important interests of the future.

L.E. Landon, *Romance and Reality* (1831)

13 The desire to enforce our own moral and spiritual criteria upon posterity is quite as strong as the desire to enforce them upon contemporaries.

Suzanne La Follette, "Institutional Marriage and Its Economic Aspects," *Concerning Women* (1926)

14 My Mamá Grande, a tiny Mayan woman, took me aside when I was an adolescent and told me several things that didn't make a bit of sense to my young and inattentive ears, and as young people tend to waste all attempts of our elders to relay to us wis-

dom accumulated over the decades, I thought my Mamá Grande had a few mice in the attic.

Ana Castillo, *Sapagonia* (1990)

1 Women who outlive their daughters are orphans, Abuela tells me. Only their granddaughters can save them, guard their knowledge like the first fire.

Cristina Garcia, *Dreaming in Cuban* (1992)

2 What mother and daughter understand each other, or even have the sympathy for each other's lack of understanding?

Maya Angelou, *I Know Why the Caged Bird Sings* (1970)

3 Total separation between parents and [adult] children is one of the great tragedies of our culture. Both generations really need the sustenance the other has to give and both are impoverished when the relationship does not continue.

Adelaide Bry, *Friendship* (1979)

4 Once an angry man dragged his father along the ground through his own orchard. "Stop!" cried the groaning old man at last, "Stop! I did not drag my father beyond this tree."

Gertrude Stein, *The Making of Americans* (1925)

5 The heterodoxy of one generation is the orthodoxy of the next.

Edith Hamilton, *The Greek Way* (1930)

6 The heresy of one age becomes the orthodoxy of the next.

Helen Keller, *Optimism* (1903)

7 The minority of one generation is usually the majority of the next.

Gertrude Atherton, *The Aristocrats* (1901)

8 When three generations are present in a family, one of them is bound to be revolutionary.

Elise Boulding, *The Family As a Way Into the Future* (1978)

9 We are a people without tears. The things that moved our parents do not move us at all.

Natalia Ginzburg, *The Little Virtues* (1962)

10 They're grown up and moved to Minneapolis. Every generation goes someplace bigger.

Faith Sullivan, *The Cape Ann* (1988)

11 Each generation supposes that the world was simpler for the one before it.

Eleanor Roosevelt, *You Learn by Living* (1960)

12 Every generation must go further than the last or what's the use in it?

Meridel Le Sueur, "The Dead in Steel," *Salute to Spring* (1940)

13 Perhaps every generation thinks of itself as a lost generation and perhaps every generation is right.

Erica Jong, *Fear of Fifty* (1994)

14 You are all a lost generation.

Gertrude Stein, in Ernest Hemingway, *The Sun Also Rises* (1926)

15 It was this hotel keeper who said what it is said I said that the war generation was a lost generation. And he said it this way. He said that every man becomes civilized between the ages of eighteen and twenty-five. If he does not go through a civilizing experience at that time in his life he will not be a civilized man. And men who went to the war at eighteen missed the period of civilizing, and they could never be civilized. They were a lost generation.

Gertrude Stein, *Everybody's Autobiography* (1937)

See also Ancestors, Children, Grandparents, Parents.

## ❦ GENEROSITY

16 It was dangerous to praise or even to approve of any thing belonging to herself in her hearing; if it had been the carpet under her feet or the shawl on her shoulders, either would instantly have been stripped off to offer.

Mary Russell Mitford, *Our Village* (1848)

17 It is better not to say lend. There is no lending in that house. There is only giving.

Pearl S. Buck, *The Good Earth* (1931)

18 That's what I consider true generosity. You give your all and yet you always feel as if it costs you nothing.

Simone de Beauvoir, *All Men Are Mortal* (1955)

19 About generosity Freya did not think at all—for those who practice it never weigh it.

Phyllis Bottome, *The Mortal Storm* (1938)

1 Generosity with strings is not generosity: it is a deal.

Marya Mannes, "The Handsome Heart," *But Will It Sell?* (1964)

2 'Tis a curious fact that a generous act / Brings leisure and luck to a day.

Ella Wheeler Wilcox, "Time Enough," *Poems of Progress* (1909)

3 The spirit, I think, is a stream, a fountain, and must be continually poured out, for only if it is poured out will more and clearer streams come.

Brenda Ueland (1939), *Me* (1983)

4 We'd all like a reputation for generosity and we'd all like to buy it cheap.

Mignon McLaughlin, *The Neurotic's Notebook* (1963)

See also Charity, Giving, Kindness, Unselfishness, Virtue.

## § GENIUS

5 Genius is the talent for seeing things straight . . . seeing them as they are, without any warping of vision. Flawless mental sight! That is genius!

Maude Adams, in Ada Patterson, *Maude Adams* (1907)

6 They talk of genius—it is nothing but this, that a man knows what he can do best, and does it, and nothing else.

Ralph Iron, *The Story of an African Farm* (1883)

7 Genius is expansive, irresistible, and irresistibly expansive. If it is in you, no cords can confine it.

Gail Hamilton, *Country Living and Country Thinking* (1862)

8 True genius doesn't fulfill expectations, it shatters them.

Arlene Croce, *Afterimages* (1976)

9 You cannot create genius. All you can do is nurture it.

Ninette de Valois, in *Time* (1960)

10 There is no balking Genius. Only death / Can silence it, or hinder.

Ella Wheeler Wilcox, *Maurine* (1901)

11 Genius may be for an hour or a thousand years; its indispensable quality is continuity with the life-push.

Mary Austin, *Everyman's Genius* (1925)

12 Genius will live and thrive without training, but it does not the less reward the watering-pot and pruning knife.

Margaret Fuller, in Thomas Wentworth Higginson, *Margaret Fuller Ossoli* (1890)

13 The meaning of genius is that it doesn't have to work to attain what people without it must labor for—and not attain.

Margaret Anderson, *My Thirty Years' War* (1930)

14 You can't have genius without patience.

Margaret Deland, *The Awakening of Helena Richie* (1906)

15 When you think you've got hold of a genius . . . you can't be sure whether it's a spark of the divine fire or a mere flash in the pan.

May Sinclair, *The Divine Fire* (1904)

16 It takes people a long time to learn the difference between talent and genius, especially ambitious young men and women.

Louisa May Alcott, *Little Women* (1868)

17 The distinction between talent and genius is definite. Talent combines and uses; genius combines and creates.

Anna Jameson, *A Commonplace Book* (1855)

18 Genius is the gold in the mine, talent is the miner who works and brings it out.

Lady Marguerite Blessington, in R.R. Madden, *The Literary Life and Correspondence of the Countess of Blessington*, vol. 1 (1855)

19 There are some people that you cannot change, you must either swallow them whole, or leave them alone. . . . You can do something with talent, but nothing with genius.

Margot Asquith, *More or Less About Myself* (1934)

20 It is quite hard at times to distinguish a genius from a lunatic.

Dorothy Thompson, *The Courage to Be Happy* (1957)

21 Genius must ever be imperfect. Life is not long enough nor slow enough for both brain and character to grow side by side to superhuman proportions.

Gertrude Atherton, *The Conqueror* (1902)

22 Even the people who have it do not definitely know what genius is.

Mary Austin, *Everyman's Genius* (1925)

1 Human nature is a mystic duality, half animal, half angel; a worm, a God; and the contrast and strife between the two natures is never so marked as in the gifted.

> Lady Wilde, "Miss Martineau," *Notes on Men, Women, and Books* (1891)

2 I am sick of the jargon about the idleness of genius. All the greatest geniuses have worked hard at everything—energetic, persevering, and laborious. . . . It is the energy that gives what we call "genius"; that leaves its impression on all it touches.

> Sydney, Lady Morgan (1828), *Lady Morgan's Memoir*, vol. 2 (1862)

3 The only genius that's worth anything is the genius for hard work.

> Kathleen Winsor, *Star Money* (1950)

4 Does it not appear to you that versatility is the true and rare characteristic of that rare thing called genius—versatility and playfulness? In my mind they are both essential.

> Mary Russell Mitford (1813), in the Reverend A.G. L'Estrange, ed., *The Life of Mary Russell Mitford*, vol. 1 (1870)

5 One of the marks of true genius is a quality of abundance. A rich, rollicking abundance, enough to give indigestion to ordinary people. Great artists turn it out in rolls, in swatches. They cover whole ceilings with paintings, they chip out a mountainside in stone, they write not one novel but a shelf full. It follows that some of their work is better than other. As much as a third of it may be pretty bad. Shall we say this unevenness is the mark of their humanity—of their proud mortality as well as of their immortality?

> Catherine Drinker Bowen, in *The Atlantic* (1961)

6 It is characteristic of genius to be hopeful and aspiring. It is characteristic of genius to break up the artificial arrangements of conventionalism, and to view mankind in true perspective, in their gradations of inherent rather than of adventitious worth. Genius is therefore essentially democratic, and has always been so.

> Harriet Martineau, *Society in America*, vol. 1 (1837)

7 Genius has no sex!

> Madame de Staël (1798), in J. Christopher Herold, *Mistress to an Age* (1958)

8 Society expresses its sympathy for the geniuses of the past to distract attention from the fact that it has no intention of being sympathetic to the geniuses of the present.

> Celia Green, *The Decline and Fall of Science* (1976)

9 Geniuses should always be given dinners when they are struggling; it gives them encouragement. If you wait till they are recognized it only gives them indigestion.

> Charlotte Mansfield, *The Girl and the Gods* (1907)

10 It takes a lot of time to be a genius, you have to sit around so much doing nothing, really doing nothing.

> Gertrude Stein, *Everybody's Autobiography* (1937)

11 Genius . . . is necessarily intolerant of fetters.

> George Eliot, *Middlemarch* (1871)

12 The real wonder is not that one man should be a genius, but that every man should not be.

> Mary Austin, *Everyman's Genius* (1925)

13 Since when was genius found respectable?

> Elizabeth Barrett Browning, *Aurora Leigh* (1857)

See also Intelligence, Precocity, Talent.

## ❦ GENTLENESS

14 There is nothing stronger in the world than gentleness.

> Han Suyin, *A Many-Splendored Thing* (1952)

15 Remember / the bread you meet each day / is still rising / Don't scare the dough.

> Macrina Wiederkehr, *Seasons of Your Heart* (1979)

16 Never take anything in life but flowers, and from flowers, only the perfume.

> Émilie Carles, *A Life of Her Own* (1977)

See also Tenderness.

## ❦ GEOGRAPHY

17 In our changing world nothing changes more than geography.

> Pearl S. Buck, *A Bridge for Passing* (1962)

## GHETTO

1 One day you find yourself entangled—enmeshed—pinioned in the seaweed of a Black Ghetto. . . . Milling around like live fish in a basket. Those at the bottom crushed into a sort of stupid apathy by the weight of those on top. Those on top leaping, leaping; leaping to scale the sides; to get out.

Marita Bonner, "On Being Young—A Woman—and Colored" (1925), *Frye Street and Environs* (1987)

See also Poverty.

## GHOSTS

2 The ass of Balaam had at least the faculty of perceiving spirits, while some of those who bray in our academies and hospitals show no evidence of its possession. Sad degeneration of species!

H.P. Blavatsky, in *Banner of Light* (1876)

3 Obviously, not everybody who dies becomes a ghost, otherwise those who are psychic would be aware of shouldering through deep crowds of assorted shades every time they moved.

Diana Norman, *The Stately Ghosts of England* (1963)

4 Ghosts cannot be put on the witness stand, or have their fingerprints taken. They are completely proof against proof.

Diana Norman, *The Stately Ghosts of England* (1963)

5 Does one ever see any ghost that is not oneself?

Joseph Shearing, *Mignonette* (1948)

See also Supernatural.

## GIFTS

6 A *gift*—be it a present, a kind word or a job done with care and love—*explains itself!* . . . and if receivin' it embarrasses you it's because your "thanks box" is warped.

Alice Childress, *Like One of the Family* (1956)

7 It is tragic that some gifts have to be made so costly, so damaging to the giver that there remains no small part of the giver to go with the gift.

Bertha Damon, *Grandma Called It Carnal* (1938)

8 Why is it no one ever sent me yet / One perfect limousine, do you suppose? / Ah no, it's always just my luck to get / One perfect rose.

Dorothy Parker, "One Perfect Rose," *Enough Rope* (1926)

9 The only suitable gift for the man who has everything is your deepest sympathy.

Imogene Fey, in *The Reader's Digest Dictionary of Quotations* (1968)

10 No sensitive person can walk round the tables set out at a big wedding without feeling that queer chill which is generated in the atmosphere by a large number of lifeless gifts which never had a soul.

J.E. Buckrose, "On Giving," *What I Have Gathered* (1923)

See also Generosity, Giving.

## GIVING

11 The fragrance always remains in the hand that gives the rose.

Heda Bejar, in *Peacemaking: Day by Day*, vol. 2 (1989)

12 A cheerful giver does not count the cost of what he gives. His heart is set on pleasing and cheering him to whom the gift is given.

Julian of Norwich, *Revelations of Divine Love* (1373)

13 I have come to believe that giving and receiving are really the same. Giving and *receiving*—not giving and taking.

Joyce Grenfell, *Joyce Grenfell Requests the Pleasure* (1976)

14 We are rich only through what we give, and poor only through what we refuse.

Anne-Sophie Swetchine, in Count de Falloux, ed., *The Writings of Madame Swetchine* (1869)

15 Let me give freely lest my giving take / With it freedom. Not the frailest strand / Of obligation must go with my gift.

Joyce Grenfell, "Sonnet" (1940), in Reggie Grenfell and Richard Garnett, eds., *Joyce by Herself and Her Friends* (1980)

1 If my hands are fully occupied in holding on to something, I can neither give nor receive.

> Dorothee Sölle, in Mary Alice Warner and Dayna Beilenson, eds., *Women of Faith and Spirit* (1987)

2 A cup that is already full cannot have more added to it. In order to receive the further good to which we are entitled, we must give of that which we have.

> Margaret Becker, "There Is But One Source," in Jacob Braude, *Second Encyclopedia of Stories, Quotations, and Anecdotes* (1957)

3 You cannot give to people what they are incapable of receiving.

> Agatha Christie, *Funerals Are Fatal* (1953)

4 Giving is a necessity sometimes . . . more urgent, indeed, than having.

> Margaret Lee Runbeck, *Our Miss Boo* (1942)

5 One must be poor to know the luxury of giving!

> George Eliot, *Middlemarch* (1871)

6 There is only one real deprivation, I decided this morning, and that is not to be able to give one's gifts to those one loves most.

> May Sarton, *Journal of a Solitude* (1973)

7 It may be more blessed to give than to receive, but there is more grace in receiving than giving. When you receive, whom do you love and praise? The giver. When you give, the same holds true.

> Jessamyn West, *The Woman Said Yes* (1976)

8 Nothing is more pleasing and engaging than the sense of having conferred benefits. Not even the gratification of receiving them.

> Ellis Peters, *The Hermit of Eyton Forest* (1987)

See also Charity, Generosity, Gifts, Receiving, Sacrifice, Sharing.

## ♪ GLADNESS

9 "Oh, I'm so glad," exulted Pollyanna.

> Eleanor H. Porter, *Pollyanna* (1912)

10 The game was to just find something about everything to be glad about—no matter what 'twas. . . . You see, when you're hunting for the glad things, you sort of forget the other kind.

> Eleanor H. Porter, *Pollyanna* (1912)

See also Contentment, Happiness, Joy.

## ♪ GLAMOUR

11 There are always those who cannot distinguish between glitter and glamour. . . . The glamour of Isadora Duncan came from her great, torn, bewildered, foolhardy soul.

> Dorothy Parker, "Poor, Immortal Isadora," in *The New Yorker* (1928)

See also Celebrities, Elegance, Fame, Fashion, Style.

## ♪ GOALS

12 I want a busy life, a just mind and a timely death.

> Zora Neale Hurston, *Dust Tracks on a Road* (1942)

13 An ignorance of means may minister / To greatness, but an ignorance of aims / Makes it impossible to be great at all.

> Elizabeth Barrett Browning, *Casa Guidi Windows* (1851)

14 To save the mind from preying inwardly upon itself, it must be encouraged to some outward pursuit. There is no other way to elude apathy, or escape discontent; none other to guard the temper from that quarrel with itself, which ultimately ends in quarreling with all mankind.

> Fanny Burney, *Camilla* (1796)

15 What we truly and earnestly aspire *to be*, that in some sense we *are*. The mere aspiration, by changing the frame of the mind, for the moment realizes itself.

> Anna Jameson, *A Commonplace Book* (1855)

16 Goals too clearly defined can become blinkers.

> Mary Catherine Bateson, *Composing a Life* (1989)

See also Ambition, Journeys, Means, Purpose.

## ♪ GOD

17 Earth's crammed with heaven, / And every common bush afire with God.

> Elizabeth Barrett Browning, *Aurora Leigh* (1857)

18 God is universal; confined to no spot, defined by no dogma, appropriated by no sect.

> Mary Baker Eddy, *Miscellaneous Writings: 1883-1896* (1896)

1 This whole world is full of God!

   Blessed Angela of Foligno, *The Book of Divine Consolation* (1536)

2 God, I can push the grass apart / And lay my finger on Thy heart!

   Edna St. Vincent Millay, title poem, *Renascence* (1917)

3 i found god in myself / & i loved her / i loved her fiercely.

   Ntozake Shange, *For Colored Girls Who Have Considered Suicide/When the Rainbow Is Enuf* (1975)

4 Why believe we'll realize God years from now, after many years of spiritual practice, after many more lifetimes of practice? She's right here, right now! We don't have to wait another second.

   Linda Johnsen, "The Shadow of the Goddess," in Theresa King, ed., *The Divine Mosaic* (1994)

5 The soul is kissed by God in its innermost regions.

   Hildegard of Bingen, *Scivias* (1150), in Gabriele Uhlein, ed., *Meditations With Hildegard of Bingen* (1983)

6 Nearer, my God, to Thee, / Nearer to Thee.

   Sarah Flower Adams, "Nearer My God to Thee" (1876)

7 *God is enough*! All religion is enfolded for me now in these three words.

   Hannah Whitall Smith (1901), in Logan Pearsall Smith, ed., *Philadelphia Quaker* (1950)

8 Gd is a Gd of Lovingkindness.

   Anne Roiphe, *Lovingkindness* (1987)

9 It is easier to gaze into the sun, than into the face of the mystery of God. Such is its beauty and its radiance.

   Hildegard of Bingen, *Scivias* (1150), in Gabriele Uhlein, ed., *Meditations With Hildegard of Bingen* (1983)

10 god is not / the voice in the whirlwind / god is the whirlwind.

   Margaret Atwood, "Resurrection," *The Journals of Susanna Moodie* (1970)

11 It is madness to wear ladies' . . . hats to church; we should all be wearing crash helmets. Ushers should issue life preservers and signal flares; they should lash us to our pews. For the sleeping God may wake someday and take offense, or the waking God may draw us out to where we can never return.

   Annie Dillard, *Teaching a Stone to Talk* (1982)

12 Why indeed must "God" be a noun? Why not a verb—the most active and dynamic of all?

   Mary Daly, *Beyond God the Father* (1973)

13 My soul was always so full of aspirations, that a God was a necessity to me. I was like a bird with an instinct of migration upon me, and a country to migrate to was as essential as it is to the bird.

   Hannah Whitall Smith (1902), in Logan Pearsall Smith, ed., *Philadelphia Quaker* (1950)

14 How much did I hear of religion as a child? Very little, and yet my heart leaped when I heard the name of God. I do believe every soul has a tendency toward God.

   Dorothy Day, *The Long Loneliness* (1952)

15 Until I am essentially united with God, I can never have full rest or real happiness.

   Julian of Norwich, *Revelations of Divine Love* (1373)

16 O my Lord, the stars are shining and the eyes of men are closed, and kings have shut their doors and every lover is alone with his beloved, and here am I alone with Thee.

   Rabi'a the Mystic (8th cent.), in Margaret Smith, *Rabi'a the Mystic* (1928)

17 I cannot walk an inch / without trying to walk to God.

   Anne Sexton, "Not So. Not So," *The Awful Rowing Toward God* (1975)

18 Destiny doesn't exist. It's God we need, and fast.

   Adélia Prado, "Dysrhythmia," in Ellen Watson, tr., *The Alphabet in the Park* (1990)

19 I met God. "What," he said, "you already?" "What," I said, "you still?"

   Laura Riding, in Michèle Brown and Ann O'Connor, *Hammer and Tongues* (1986)

20 You can never prove God; you can only find Him.

   Kate Douglas Wiggin, *New Chronicles of Rebecca* (1907)

21 Science conducts us, step by step, through the whole range of creation, until we arrive, at length, at God.

   Marguerite de Valois, *Memoirs* (1628)

22 God is not in the vastness of greatness. He is hid in the vastness of smallness. He is not in the general. He is in the particular.

   Pearl S. Buck, *God's Men* (1951)

1 Anyone who . . . thinks that, through her own words and actions, she initiates and controls the connections between herself and God—mustn't have much experience of God's boundless affection for even the grudgingest of creatures.

   Nancy Mairs, *Ordinary Time* (1993)

2 In God's sight we do not fall: in our own we do not stand.

   Julian of Norwich, *Revelations of Divine Love* (1373)

3 I believe that God is in me as the sun is in the color and fragrance of a flower—the Light in my darkness, the Voice in my silence.

   Helen Keller, *Midstream* (1930)

4 God is our clothing, that wraps, clasps and encloses us so as to never leave us.

   Julian of Norwich, *Revelations of Divine Love* (1373)

5 Just as a circle embraces all that is within it, so does the God-head embrace all. No one has the power to divide this circle, to surpass it, or to limit it.

   Hildegard of Bingen (1150), in Gabriele Uhlein, ed., *Meditations With Hildegard of Bingen* (1983)

6 We must be as satisfied to be powerless, idle and still before God, and dried up and barren when He permits it, as to be full of life, enjoying His presence with ease and devotion. The whole matter of our union with God consists in being content either way.

   Jane de Chantal (1640), in Péronne Marie Thibert, V.H.M., tr., *Francis de Sales, Jane de Chantal: Letters of Spiritual Direction* (1988)

7 God is not indifferent to your need. / You have a thousand prayers, / but God has one.

   Anne Sexton, "Not So. Not So," *The Awful Rowing Toward God* (1975)

8 Home is the definition of God.

   Emily Dickinson (1870), in Mabel Loomis Todd, ed., *Letters of Emily Dickinson*, vol. 2 (1894)

9 There is neither father, nor mother, nor son, nor any other person whatsoever who can embrace the object beloved with so great a love as that wherewith God embraceth the soul.

   Blessed Angela of Foligno, *The Book of Divine Consolation* (1536)

10 For god is nothing other than the eternally creative source of our relational power, our common strength, a god whose movement is to empower, bringing us into our own together, a god whose name in history is love.

   Carter Heyward, *Our Passion for Justice* (1984)

11 Sickness, sin, and death, being inharmonious, do not originate in God nor belong to His government.

   Mary Baker Eddy, *Science and Health* (1875)

12 Does God sing?

   Mary Virginia Micka, "These and Like Questions," *All Rounds Returning* (1986)

13 Because I believe in a God with a sense of humor (and not only because he created ducks), I believe he is lovingly amused at my impertinence—like parents with very small bumptious children—, not angry about it.

   Elsie Chamberlain, in Rupert E. Davies, *We Believe in God* (1968)

14 Listen, God love everything you love—and a mess of stuff you don't. But more than anything else, God love admiration. . . . I think it pisses God off if you walk by the color purple in a field somewhere and don't notice it.

   Alice Walker, *The Color Purple* (1982)

15 God's gifts put man's best dreams to shame.

   Elizabeth Barrett Browning, *Sonnets From the Portuguese* (1850)

16 if there has to be a god can she be a committee of women dedicated to wiping out earthly oppression.

   hattie gossett, "womanmansion to my sister mourning her mother," *presenting . . . sister noblues* (1988)

17 A priest friend of mine has cautioned me away from the standard God of our childhoods, who loves and guides you and then, if you are bad, roasts you: God as high school principal in a gray suit who never remembered your name but is always leafing unhappily through your files.

   Anne Lamott, *Bird by Bird* (1994)

18 Before I was ten I became critical of the anthropomorphic God as interpreted in the churches. I did not warm to One thus revealed as the semblance of a bullying and mean old man who must have all his own way, be praised all the time and for attributes which were deplorable in us.

   Miles Franklin, *Childhood at Brindabella* (1963)

1 God is inside you and inside everybody else. You come into the world with God. But only them that search for it inside find it. And sometimes it just manifest itself even if you not looking, or don't know what you looking for. Trouble do it for most folks, I think. . . . Yeah, It. God ain't a he or a she, but a It.

Alice Walker, *The Color Purple* (1982)

2 Were we [women] to express our conceptions of God, it would never enter into the head of any one of us to describe him as a venerable old man.

Sophia, A Person of Quality, *Woman Not Inferior to Man* (1739)

3 As truly as God is our Father, so truly is God our Mother.

Julian of Norwich, *Revelations of Divine Love* (1373)

4 God has always been to me not so much like a father as like a dear and tender mother.

Harriet Beecher Stowe, *The Pearl of Orr's Island* (1862)

5 Certain ancient cavilers have gone so far as to deny that the female sex, as opposed to the male sex, is made in the likeness of God, which likeness they must have taken to be, as far as I can tell, in the beard.

Marie de Gournay, *The Equality of Men and Women* (1622)

6 When we choose a god we choose one as much like ourselves as possible, or even more so!

Rebecca West, in Crystal Eastman, *Equal Rights* (1925)

7 The gender of God, God's presumed masculinity, has functioned as the ultimate religious legitimization of the unjust social structures which victimize women.

Sandra M. Schneiders, *Women and the Word* (1986)

8 Though language about God cannot really tell us about the nature of God, because of the limitations of language and the nature of God, it can tell us a great deal about those who create and use the God-language.

Rita M. Gross, in Susan Weidman Schneider, *Jewish and Female* (1984)

9 Metaphors for God drawn from human experience can easily be literalized. While we are immediately aware that the personal God is not really a rock or a mother eagle, it is easy enough to imagine that God is really a king or a father.

Sandra M. Schneiders, *Women and the Word* (1986)

10 Many now veer away from the time-honored use of the term Father as applied to the Christian God. . . . This difficulty rests mainly, I believe, on failure to distinguish between a symbol and a definition.

Georgia Harkness, *The Resources of Religion* (1936)

11 While officially it is rightly and consistently said that God is spirit and so beyond identification with either male or female sex, yet the daily language of preaching, worship, catechesis, and instruction conveys a different message: God is male, or at least more like a man than a woman, or at least more fittingly addressed as male than as female.

Elizabeth A. Johnson, *She Who Is* (1993)

12 Jewish, Christian, and Islamic theologians today are quick to point out that God is not to be considered in sexual terms at all. Yet the actual language they use in daily worship and prayer conveys a different message: who, growing up with Jewish or Christian tradition, has escaped the distinct impression that God is *masculine*?

Elaine Pagels, *The Gnostic Gospels* (1979)

13 If God is male, then the male is God. The divine patriarch castrates women as long as he is allowed to live on in the human imagination.

Mary Daly, *Beyond God the Father* (1973)

14 God is always more unlike what we say than like it.

Denise Lardner Carmody, *Virtuous Woman* (1992)

15 No matter how entrenched in the imagination of the average Christian the image of a male God might be, theological tradition has never assigned sex to God.

Sandra M. Schneiders, *Women and the Word* (1986)

16 Whoever is so stupid as to imagine God to be either masculine or feminine openly shows that he is as bad a philosopher as a theologian.

Marie de Gournay, *The Equality of Men and Women* (1622)

17 Ain't no way to read the bible and not think God white, she say. Then she sigh. When I found out I thought God was white, and a man, I lost interest.

Alice Walker, *The Color Purple* (1982)

18 I saw God last night. Really? What's he like? Well, *he's* a *woman* and she's *Black*!

Anonymous woman, in Constance M. Carroll, "Three's a Crowd," in Gloria T. Hull, Patricia Bell Scott, and Barbara Smith, eds., *All the Women Are White, All the Blacks Are Men, But Some of Us Are Brave* (1982)

1 The Passion that one Soul hath for God cannot be judged by another.

Erica Jong, *Fanny: Being the True History of the Adventures of Fanny Hackabout-Jones* (1980)

2 Those who turn to God for comfort may find comfort but I do not think they will find God.

Mignon McLaughlin, *The Neurotic's Notebook* (1963)

3 God is no White Knight who charges into the world to pluck us like distressed damsels from the jaws of dragons, or diseases. God chooses to become present to and through us. It is up to us to rescue one another.

Nancy Mairs, *Ordinary Time* (1993)

4 Act, and God will act.

Joan of Arc (1430), in Edward Lucie-Smith, *Joan of Arc* (1976)

5 How can God direct our steps if we're not taking any?

Sarah Leah Grafstein, in Sherry Ruth Anderson and Patricia Hopkins, *The Feminine Face of God* (1991)

6 She makes everything possible.

Helen Reddy, in Barbara McDowell and Hana Umlauf, *Woman's Almanac* (1977)

7 Call on God, my dear. She will help you.

Mrs. O.H.P. Belmont, to a discouraged young suffragist (1920), in Carol McPhee and Ann FitzGerald, *Feminist Quotations* (1979)

8 God very seldom succeeds. He has very nearly everything against him, of course.

Rose Macaulay, *Told by an Idiot* (1923)

9 My parents professed to believe in God, but I rarely heard his name mentioned unattached to "damn" or "sakes" or "willing."

Edith Konecky, *Allegra Maud Goldman* (1976)

10 One cannot expect to be conscious of God's presence when one has only a bowing acquaintance with Him.

Madame Chiang Kai-shek, *I Confess My Faith* (1943)

11 One may take many liberties with God which one cannot take with men.

Isak Dinesen, "Echoes," *Last Tales* (1957)

12 To be without God is to be a snake / who wants to swallow an elephant.

Anne Sexton, "The Play," *The Awful Rowing Toward God* (1975)

13 There is nothing like despair to make one throw oneself upon the gods.

Mary Renault, *The Praise Singer* (1978)

14 New gods arise when they are needed.

Josephine W. Johnson, "On a Winter Morning," in *Ohio* (1990)

15 When souls before Thee reverently bow, / Oh, carest Thou what name the lips breathe low / Jove, or Osiris, or the God Unknown . . . ?

Julia C.R. Dorr, "Thy Name," *Poems* (1892)

16 In the native world, major gods come in trios, duos, and groups. It is the habit of non-natives to discover the supreme being, the one and only head god, a habit lent to them by monotheism.

Paula Gunn Allen, *Grandmothers of the Light* (1991)

17 I tell you the gods are still alive / And they are not consoling.

May Sarton, "At Delphi," *Selected Poems of May Sarton* (1978)

18 They treated their God like a desk clerk with whom they lodged requests and complaints.

Helen Hudson, "After Cortés," *The Listener* (1968)

19 I'll bet when you get down on them rusty knees and get to worrying God, He just goes in His privyhouse and slams the door. That's what He thinks about *you* and *your* prayers.

Zora Neale Hurston, *Seraph on the Suwanee* (1948)

20 But who walks with Him?—dares to take His arm, / To slap Him on the shoulder, tweak His ear, / Buy Him a Coca-Cola or a beer, / Pooh-pooh His politics, call Him a fool?

Gwendolyn Brooks, "the preacher: ruminates behind the sermon," *A Street in Bronzeville* (1945)

21 Sophia wished that Florence would not talk about the Almighty as if his real name was Godfrey, and God was just Florence's nickname for him.

Nancy Mitford, *Pigeon Pie* (1940)

22 If I wanted a new belief system, I'd choose to believe in God—He's been in business longer than Werner [Erhard, founder of est], and He has better music.

Barbara Grizzuti Harrison, "Invasion of the Mind-Stealers," *Off Center* (1980)

23 I'd begun to think you were a bit like God—you make things happen but you don't exist.

Caryl Churchill, *Serious Money* (1987)

1 Of two men who have no experience of God, he who denies him is perhaps nearer to him than the other.

    Simone Weil, *Gravity and Grace* (1947)

2 I read the book of Job last night—I don't think God comes well out of it.

    Virginia Woolf (1922), in Nigel Nicolson, ed., *The Letters of Virginia Woolf* (1976)

3 Lord, how Thou dost afflict Thy lovers!

    St. Teresa of Avila (1577), in E. Allison Peers, tr., *Interior Castle* (1961)

4 Very few of us are capable of being Free Thinkers, needing neither to adore nor to insult God, the insult often being an act of faith more profound than adoration.

    Alexandra David-Neel (1914), *La Lampe de Sagesse* (1986)

5 Those who've never rebelled against God or at some point in their lives shaken their fists in the face of heaven, have never encountered God at all.

    Catherine Marshall, *Christy* (1967)

6 It isn't that I believe God is dead, but God is so silent, has been for so long, and is so hidden, I take it as a sign I must watch in other places or simply tend my small fires until the end.

    Mary Virginia Micka, *The Cazenovia Journal* (1986)

7 God's been going deaf. . . . Here God used to raineth bread from clouds, smite the Phillipines, sling fire down on red-light districts where people got stabbed. He even appeared in person every once in a while. God used to pay attention, is what I'm saying.

    Louise Erdrich, *Love Medicine* (1984)

8 I would rather believe that God did not exist than believe that he was indifferent.

    George Sand, *Impressions et Souvenirs* (1873)

9 One thing I have no worry about is whether God exists. But it has occurred to me that God has Alzheimer's and has forgotten we exist.

    Jane Wagner, *The Search for Signs of Intelligent Life in the Universe* (1985)

See also Atheism, Christ, Devil, Divinity, Providence, Religion, The Sacred, Spirituality, Theology, Worship.

## ❦ GOLD

10 Gold has no name, it licks the hand of anyone who has it: good dog!

    Christina Stead, *House of All Nations* (1938)

11 When people are collecting gold they aren't doing business. . . . Gold is constipation: even bankruptcy is more fluid. Gold isn't wealth: positions in markets are wealth.

    Christina Stead, *House of All Nations* (1938)

See also Money, Wealth.

## ❦ GOLF

12 One of the most distressing defects of civilization.

    Winifred Holtby, *Mandoa, Mandoa!* (1933)

13 Night after night I went to sleep murmuring, "Tomorrow I will be easy, strong, quick, supple, accurate, dashing and self-controlled all at once!" For not less than this is necessary in the Game of Life called Golf.

    Ethel Smyth, *What Happened Next* (1940)

14 Golf is a particularly severe strain upon the amiability of the average person's temper, and in no other game, except bridge, is serenity of disposition so essential.

    Emily Post, *Etiquette* (1922)

## ❦ GOOD

15 I did and still do find a serious error in the emphasis of spiritual masters and hagiographers of all faiths on self-denial and austerity as an end in itself, instead of a means. L'art pour l'art. We must do the good because it is good, not because it is difficult.

    Ade Bethune, in Judith Stoughton, *Proud Donkey of Schaerbeek* (1988)

16 There is a haphazard sort of doing good, which is nothing but temperamental pleasure-seeking.

    Fanny Lewald, *Emotions and Thoughts* (1900)

17 Good works may only be beautiful sins, if they are not done in a true spirit.

    Margaret Oliphant, *The Perpetual Curate* (1870)

1 When I'm good I'm very good, but when I'm bad I'm better.

   Mae West, in *I'm No Angel* (1933)

2 Too much of a good thing can be wonderful.

   Mae West, *Goodness Had Nothing to Do With It!* (1959)

See also Good and Evil, Goodness, Virtue.

## ✎ GOOD AND EVIL

3 There are times when it would seem as if God fished with a line, and the devil with a net.

   Anne-Sophie Swetchine, in Count de Falloux, ed., *The Writings of Madame Swetchine* (1869)

4 As I get older there is nothing more constantly astonishing to me than the goodness of the Bad;— unless it is the badness of the Good.

   Margaret Deland, *Dr. Lavendar's People* (1903)

5 There is much said about the wickedness of doing evil that good may come. Alas! there is such a thing as doing good that evil may come.

   Amelia E. Barr, *Jan Vedder's Wife* (1885)

6 Good and evil travel on the same road, but they leave different impressions.

   Marie de Rabutin-Chantal, Marquise de Sévigné (1675), *Letters of Madame de Sévigné to Her Daughter and Her Friends*, vol. 3 (1811)

7 Good and evil, as we term them, are not antagonistic; they are ever found hand in hand. Humanity has never achieved a single conquest without the aid of both. Indeed how can she? What adds to moral strength, but a grappling with temptation?

   Sarah M. Grimké, "The Education of Women" (1852), in Elizabeth Ann Bartlett, ed., *Letters on the Equality of the Sexes and Other Essays* (1988)

8 A good oyster cannot please the palate as acutely as a bad one can revolt it, and a good oyster cannot make him who eats it live for ever though a bad one can make him dead for ever.

   Rebecca West, *Black Lamb and Grey Falcon* (1941)

9 The bad is more easily perceived than the good. A fresh lobster does not give such pleasure to the consumer as a stale one will give him pain.

   Rebecca West, in Victoria Glendinning, *Rebecca West* (1987)

10 It is the modern nature of goodness to exert itself quietly, while a few characters of the opposite cast seem, by the rumor of their exploits, to fill the world; and by their noise to multiply their numbers.

   Hannah More, *Strictures on the Modern System of Female Education* (1799)

11 Vice is always in the active, virtue often in the passive.

   Frances E. Willard (1876), *Woman and Temperance* (1883)

12 Good is too often allied with vulnerability and evil with power.

   James Tiptree, Jr., *Up the Walls of the World* (1978)

13 We do good by ourselves, but we seldom do wrong alone.

   Phyllis Bottome, "The Home-Coming," *Innocence and Experience* (1934)

See also Evil, Good, Goodness.

## ✎ GOODNESS

14 Only the young die good.

   Ethel Watts Mumford, in Oliver Herford, Ethel Watts Mumford, and Addison Mizner, *The Complete Cynic* (1902)

15 She tended to be impatient with that sort of intellectual who, for all his brilliance, has never been able to arrive at the simple conclusion that to be reasonably happy you have to be reasonably good.

   Carolyn Kizer, "A Slight Mechanical Failure," in Howard Moss, ed., *The Poet's Story* (1973)

16 The first condition of human goodness is something to love; the second, something to reverence.

   George Eliot, "Janet's Repentance," *Scenes of Clerical Life* (1857)

17 Frances's goodness was the worst part of her.

   Margaret Deland, *Philip and His Wife* (1894)

18 I know what kind of people would have the hottest corner in my conception of hell. It would be those who have helped to give goodness a bad name.

   J.E. Buckrose, "On Giving Goodness a Bad Name," *What I Have Gathered* (1923)

19 It is not *badness*, it is the absence of *goodness*, which, in Art as in Life, is so depressing.

   Freya Stark, *Baghdad Sketches* (1929)

1 Goodness had nothing to do with it, dearie.

> Mae West, replying to the remark, "Goodness, what beautiful diamonds!" in *Night After Night* (1932)

See also Good, Morality, Saints, Virtue, Wisdom.


# ❦ GOSSIP

2 Gossip is just news running ahead of itself in a red satin dress.

> Liz Smith, in *The Dallas Times-Herald* (1978)

3 Gossip is a news story with a lot of leeway.

> Liz Smith, in *Modern Maturity* (1994)

4 Gossip . . . is only fiction produced by non-professionals.

> Dorothy Canfield Fisher, in Elizabeth Yates, *Pebble in a Pool* (1958)

5 Good gossip approximates art.

> Rachel M. Brownstein, *Becoming a Heroine* (1982)

6 The right sort of gossip is a charming and stimulating thing. The *Odyssey* itself is simply glorious gossip, and the same may be said of nearly every tale of mingled fact and legend which has been handed down to us through the ages.

> J.E. Buckrose, "Gossip," *What I Have Gathered* (1923)

7 Professional psychologists seem to think that they are the only people who make sense out of human actions. The rest of us know that everybody tries to do just this. What else is gossip?

> Dorothy Canfield, "The Moran Scandal," *Four-Square* (1949)

8 Gossip is theology translated into experience. In it we hear great stories of conversion, like the drunk who turns his or her life around, as well as stories of failure. We can see that pride really does go before a fall, and that hope is essential. We watch closely those who retire, or who lose a spouse, lest they lose interest in living. When we gossip we are also praying, not only for them but for ourselves.

> Kathleen Norris, *Dakota* (1993)

9 I don't call it gossip, I call it "emotional speculation."

> Laurie Colwin, *Happy All the Time* (1978)

10 Gossip is the opiate of the oppressed.

> Erica Jong, *Fear of Flying* (1973)

11 Never . . . use the word *gossip* in a pejorative sense. It's the very stuff of biography and has to be woven in. To suggest that the personal life is not an essential element in the creative life is absurd.

> Joan Peyser, in *Publishers Weekly* (1987)

12 By some mysterious method, Susan Carr's gossip gave the listener a gentler feeling towards his kind. When she spoke of her neighbors' faults, one knew that somehow they were simply virtues gone to seed.

> Margaret Deland, *Philip and His Wife* (1894)

13 Bad gossip drives out good gossip.

> Liz Smith, in *Modern Maturity* (1994)

14 I minded my own business, and, unfortunately, so did everyone else.

> Frances Farmer, *Will There Really Be a Morning?* (1972)

15 "Ah," said that gentleman, ever ready to discuss one friend with another—in fact, it was chiefly for this pleasure that he made them.

> John Oliver Hobbes, *The Sinner's Comedy* (1892)

16 You're shocked, Mr. Burton, at hearing what our gossiping little town thinks. I can tell you this—they always think the worst!

> Agatha Christie, *The Moving Finger* (1942)

17 Nobody's interested in sweetness and light.

> Hedda Hopper, in John Robert Colombo, *Popcorn in Paradise* (1979)

18 If you haven't got anything good to say about anyone come and sit by me.

> Alice Roosevelt Longworth, maxim embroidered on a velvet cushion, in Michael Teague, *Mrs. L.* (1981)

19 By the general love of scandal and detraction in Dublin, one might reasonably imagine they were all to feed themselves through the holes which they had made in the characters of others.

> Letitia Pilkington, *Memoirs of Mrs. Letitia Pilkington Written by Herself*, vol. 3 (1754)

20 Their tongues are like chicken feet. Scratching at everything.

> Carolina Maria de Jesus (1955), *Child of the Dark* (1962)

21 She brought back gossip like a bird adding string and twigs to a growing nest.

> Hallie Burnett, *The Brain Pickers* (1957)

1 Gossip is a sort of smoke that comes from the dirty tobacco-pipes of those who diffuse it; it proves nothing but the bad taste of the smoker.

George Eliot, *Daniel Deronda* (1874)

2 It is almost impossible to throw dirt on someone without getting a little on yourself.

Abigail Van Buren, syndicated column "Dear Abby" (1991)

3 Gossip is irresponsible communication.

Rita Mae Brown, *A Plain Brown Rapper* (1976)

4 Malicious gossip . . . takes the place of creation in noncreative lives.

Nancy Hale, in Richard Thruelsen and John Kobler, eds., *Adventures of the Mind*, 2nd series (1961)

5 Gossip, even when it avoids the sexual, bears about it a faint flavor of the erotic.

Patricia Meyer Spacks, *Gossip* (1985)

6 I'm enormously less interested in whom you sleep with than I am in with whom you're prepared to die.

Ti-Grace Atkinson, "Strategy and Tactics," *Amazon Odyssey* (1974)

7 As I grow older and older / And totter towards the tomb, / I find that I care less and less / Who goes to bed with whom.

Dorothy L. Sayers (1953), in Janet Hitchman, *Such a Strange Lady* (1975)

See also Celebrity, Nosiness, Rumor, Small Towns, Talking, "They."

## ❧ GOVERNMENT

8 We must have government, but we must watch them like a hawk.

Millicent Fenwick, in *Reader's Digest* (1983)

9 Government is a tool, like a hammer. You can use a hammer to build with or you can use a hammer to destroy with.

Molly Ivins, in *The Fort Worth Star-Telegram* (1992)

10 The government's like a mule, it's slow and it's sure; it's slow to turn, and it's sure to turn the way you don't want it.

Ellen Glasgow, *The Voice of the People* (1900)

11 A government is not legitimate merely because it exists.

Jeane J. Kirkpatrick, in *Time* (1985)

12 There is no such thing as a good government.

Emma Goldman, in Katherine Anne Porter, *The Never-Ending Wrong* (1977)

13 Every government whatever its form, character or color—be it absolute or constitutional, monarchy or republic, Fascist, Nazi or bolshevik—is by its very nature conservative, static, intolerant of change and opposed to it.

Emma Goldman, *My Further Disillusionment in Russia* (1924)

14 The most appalling cruelties are committed by apparently virtuous governments in expectation of a great good to come, never learning that the evil done now is the sure destroyer of the expected good.

Katherine Anne Porter, *The Never-Ending Wrong* (1977)

15 A phenomenon noticeable throughout history regardless of place or period is the pursuit by governments of policies contrary to their own interests.

Barbara W. Tuchman, *The March of Folly* (1984)

16 Wooden-headedness, the source of self-deception, is a factor that plays a remarkably large role in government. It consists in assessing a situation in terms of preconceived fixed notions while ignoring or rejecting any contrary signs. It is acting according to wish while not allowing oneself to be deflected by the facts.

Barbara W. Tuchman, *The March of Folly* (1984)

17 There is only one institution that can arrogate to itself the power legally to trade by means of rubber checks: the government. And it is the only institution that can mortgage your future without your knowledge or consent: government securities (and paper money) are promissory notes on future tax receipts, i.e., on your future production.

Ayn Rand, *Philosophy: Who Needs It?* (1982)

18 Generosity is a virtue for individuals, not governments. When governments are generous it is with other people's money, other people's safety, other people's future.

P.D. James, *The Children of Men* (1992)

1 Government remains the paramount area of folly because it is there that men seek power over others—only to lose it over themselves.

Barbara W. Tuchman, *The March of Folly* (1984)

2 Statutory regulations, legislative enactments, constitutional provisions, are invasive. They never yet induced man to do anything he could and would not do by virtue of his intellect or temperament, nor prevented anything that man was impelled to do by the same dictates.

Emma Goldman, "What I Believe," in *The New York World* (1908)

3 Till I see money spent on the betterment of man instead of on his idleness and destruction, I shall not believe in any perfect form of government.

Margot Asquith, *More or Less About Myself* (1934)

4 I believe—indeed, I know—that whatever is fine and beautiful in the human expresses and asserts itself in spite of government, and not because of it.

Emma Goldman, "What I Believe," in *The New York World* (1908)

5 A government which can protect and defend its citizens from wrong and outrage and does not is vicious.

Frances Ellen Watkins Harper, in Rachel F. Avery, ed., *Transactions of the National Council of Women of the United States* (1891)

6 There is something that governments care far more for than human life, and that is the security of property.

Emmeline Pankhurst, *My Own Story* (1914)

7 Under a Labor government, there's virtually nowhere you can put your savings where they would be safe from the state. . . . If you put money in a sock they'd probably nationalize socks.

Margaret Thatcher, speech (1983), *The Downing Street Years* (1993)

8 There is hardly a facet of life that is now free of some sort of federal action.

Millicent Fenwick, *Speaking Up* (1982)

9 It's all very well to run around saying regulation is bad, get the government off our backs, etc. Of course our lives are regulated. When you come to a stop sign, you stop; if you want to go fishing, you get a license; if you want to shoot ducks, you can shoot only three ducks. The alternative is dead bodies at the intersections, no fish and no ducks. OK?

Molly Ivins, in *The Fort Worth Star-Telegram* (1995)

10 In a democracy such as ours the leading minds seldom achieve a place of permanent influence. And the men who sit in Congress or even in the White House are usually not our leading minds. They are not the thinkers. Still less have they time for reflection.

Pearl S. Buck, *My Several Worlds* (1954)

11 If there is one thing the past years have taught us, it is the importance of a keen and high sense of honor in those who handle our governmental affairs.

Millicent Fenwick, in *The New York Times* (1976)

12 The difference between government and leadership is that leadership has a soul.

Anna Quindlen, "No There There," *Thinking Out Loud* (1993)

13 The only people who should be in government are those who care more about people than they do about power.

Millicent Fenwick, *Speaking Up* (1982)

14 Ah! that Senate is a world of ice and darkness! It votes the destruction of peoples as the simplest and wisest thing; for its members themselves are moribund.

George Sand (1863), in Raphaël Ledos de Beaufort, ed., *Letters of George Sand*, vol. 2 (1886)

15 We put up with a lot to be saved from chaos. We always have.

Elizabeth Janeway, *Improper Behavior* (1987)

16 Cynics about government find much to be cynical about.

Alice M. Rivlin, *Reviving the American Dream* (1992)

17 We've got to bring the government up to date. It's insane to try to live under the same governmental structures set up nearly two hundred years ago.

Bella Abzug, *Bella!* (1972)

18 The government cannot do everything all at once. It can't wave a magic wand and meet everyone's demands simultaneously.

Corazon C. Aquino, in Isabelo T. Crisostomo, *Cory* (1987)

1 The stakes . . . are too high for government to be a spectator sport.

   Barbara Jordan, speech (1977)

2 No government can act in advance of the moral will of the people.

   P.D. James, *The Children of Men* (1992)

3 For a considerable price, it relieves us of responsibilities, performing acts that would be as unsavory for most of us as butchering our own beef. As our agent, the government can bomb and tax. As our agent, it can relieve us of the responsibilities once borne face to face by the community: caring for the young, the war-wounded, the aged, the handicapped. It extends our impersonal benevolence to the world's needy, relieving our collective conscience without uncomfortable first-hand involvement. It takes our power, our responsibility, *our consciousness.*

   Marilyn Ferguson, *The Aquarian Conspiracy* (1980)

4 Everyone in America seems to be joining an organization of some kind, and in Congress one hears from them all.

   Millicent Fenwick (1975), *Speaking Up* (1982)

5 Every program develops a constituency. That's why it's such perfect hell trying to cut anything, not just good programs, but also dopey ones, spectacularly cost-ineffective ones and some that are, by any known measure, at least three quarters of a century out of date.

   Meg Greenfield, in *Newsweek* (1995)

6 The advance planning and sense stimuli employed to capture a $10 million cigarette or soap market are nothing compared to the brainwashing and propaganda blitzes used to insure control of the largest cash market in the world: the Executive Branch of the United States Government.

   Phyllis Schlafly, *A Choice Not an Echo* (1964)

7 Everyone else is represented in Washington by a rich and powerful lobby, it seems. But there is no lobby for the people.

   Shirley Chisholm, *Unbought and Unbossed* (1970)

8 The State is a term for the legislative and administrative machinery whereby certain business of the people is transacted, and badly so.

   Emma Goldman, "The Individual, Society and the State" (1940), in Alix Kates Shulman, ed., *Red Emma Speaks* (1983)

9 The business of government should be business-like.

   Dorcas Hardy, in Deborah Churchman, "Dorcas Hardy's Stamp on Social Security," *Christian Science Monitor* (1987)

10 If you were starting from scratch to invent an instrument that could impose fiscal discipline, the last one on earth you would come up with is the United States government.

   Meg Greenfield, in *Newsweek* (1995)

11 It is not that the U.S. government is an entirely comic matter; but to deal in power, ambition, and the people driven by both, a fine madness and sense of humor are handy things to have.

   Barbara Howar, *Laughing All the Way* (1973)

12 Sure, now ivery child knows what's guvermint. It's half a dozen gintlemen an' the loike maybe, that meets an' thinks what's best fer thimsilves, an' thin says that's best fer us—an' that's guvermint.

   Civil War widow, in Gerald F. Lieberman, *3,500 Good Quotes for Speakers* (1983)

13 Government! Government! What do I get for all I give, I'd like to know! Potholes and bombs!

   Cecil Dawkins, *Charleyhorse* (1985)

See also Bureaucracy, Congress, Democracy, Leadership, Politicians, Politics, Social Security, Taxes.

## ❦ GRACE

14 Grace fills empty spaces, but it can only enter where there is a void to receive it, and it is grace itself which makes this void.

   Simone Weil, *Gravity and Grace* (1947)

15 All is waiting and all is work; all is change and all is permanence. All is grace.

   Barbara Grizzuti Harrison, *Foreign Bodies* (1984)

16 If I am not, may it please God to bring me into it; if I am, may He preserve me in it.

   Joan of Arc (1431), responding to trick question about whether she believed herself in a state of grace, in Jules Michelet, *Joan of Arc* (1853)

See also Mercy.

## ❧ GRACIOUSNESS

1 Blessed are those who can give without remembering, and take without forgetting.

Elizabeth Bibesco, in Jacob Braude, *Second Encyclopedia of Stories, Quotations, and Anecdotes* (1957)

2 It's a rare thing, graciousness. The shape of it can be acquired, but not, I think, the substance.

Gertrude Schweitzer, *Shadows on the Left Bank* (1973)

3 Be pretty if you can, be witty if you must, but be gracious if it *kills* you.

Elsie de Wolfe, in Mrs. Falk Feeley, *A Swarm of Wasps* (1983)

See also Kindness, Politeness, Tact.


## ❧ GRANDPARENTS

4 No one . . . who has not known the inestimable privilege can possibly realize what good fortune it is to grow up in a home where there are grandparents.

Suzanne LaFollette, in Alice S. Rossi, ed., *The Feminist Papers* (1973)

5 The closest friends I have made all through life have been people who also grew up close to a loved and loving grandmother or grandfather.

Margaret Mead, *Blackberry Winter* (1972)

6 I loved their home. Everything smelled older, worn but safe; the food aroma had baked itself into the furniture.

Susan Strasberg, *Bittersweet* (1980)

7 A house needs a grandma in it.

Louisa May Alcott (1857), in Ednah D. Cheney, ed., *Louisa May Alcott* (1889)

8 A home without a grandmother is like an egg without salt.

Florence King, *Reflections in a Jaundiced Eye* (1989)

9 I'm a flower, *poa*, a flower opening and reaching for the sun. You are the sun, grandma, you are the sun in my life.

Kitty Tsui, "Poa Poa Is Living Breathing Light," *The Words of a Woman Who Breathes Fire* (1983)

10 Uncles, and aunts, and cousins, are all very well, and fathers and mothers are not to be despised; but a *grandmother*, at holiday time, is worth them all.

Fanny Fern, *Folly As It Flies* (1868)

11 Grandpa . . . was ever ready to cheer and help me, ever sure that I was a remarkable specimen. He was a dear old man who asked little from life and got less.

Miles Franklin, *Childhood at Brindabella* (1963)

12 Hindered characters / seldom have mothers / in Irish stories, but they all have grandmothers.

Marianne Moore, "Spenser's Ireland," *What Are Years?* (1941)

13 Grandma . . . had a great deal to do with the education of her granddaughters. In general she not so much trained as just shed herself upon us.

Bertha Damon, *Grandma Called It Carnal* (1938)

14 My grandmothers are full of memories / Smelling of soap and onions and wet clay / With veins rolling roughly over quick hands / They have many clean words to say.

Margaret Walker, "Lineage," *For My People* (1942)

15 I cultivate / Being Uppity / It's something / My Gramom taught me.

Kate Rushin, "Family Tree," in Patricia Bell-Scott et al., eds., *Double Stitch* (1991)

16 One could not live without delicacy, but when / I think of love I think of the big, clumsy-looking / hands of my grandmother, each knuckle a knob.

Mona Van Duyn, "A Bouquet of Zinnias," *Near Changes* (1990)

17 My grandmothers were strong. / Why am I not as they?

Margaret Walker, "Lineage," *For My People* (1942)

18 Grandma was a kind of first-aid station, or a Red Cross nurse, who took up where the battle ended, accepting us and our little sobbing sins, gathering the whole of us into her lap, restoring us to health and confidence by her amazing faith in life and in a mortal's strength to meet it.

Lillian Smith, in Tillie Olsen, *Mother to Daughter, Daughter to Mother* (1984)

19 It had not occurred to me that she would sleep in my room: I am eight and she is nearly eighty. . . . I've acquired not the doting Nana of my dreams,

but an aged kid sister. Within hours, the theft and rivalry begin.

> Laura Cunningham, *Sleeping Arrangements* (1989)

1 Helped grandma with the weekend shopping. She was dead fierce in the grocer's; she watched the scales like a hawk watching a fieldmouse. Then she pounced and accused the shop assistant of giving her underweight bacon. The shop assistant was dead scared of her and put another slice on.

> Sue Townsend, *The Secret Diary of Adrian Mole Aged 13-3/4* (1982)

2 So long and so slow had been her descent into poverty that a grandmother was needed to remember her setting out upon the road to it.

> Grace King, "The Old Lady's Restoration," *Balcony Stories* (1892)

3 As I do not live in an age when rustling black skirts billow about me, and I do not carry an ebony stick to strike the floor in sharp rebuke, as this is denied me, I rap out a sentence in my note book and feel better. If a grandmother wants to put her foot down, the only safe place to do it these days is in a note book.

> Florida Scott-Maxwell, *The Measure of My Days* (1968)

4 I wish to ask you how you find yourself, on being a grandfather. . . . The prospect is worse than the reality.

> Marie de Rabutin-Chantal, Marquise de Sévigné (1687), *Letters of Madame de Sévigné to Her Daughter and Her Friends*, vol. 7 (1811)

See also Family, Generations.

## ❦ GRATIFICATION

5 Deferring gratification is a good definition of being civilized.

> Bernice Fitz-Gibbon, *Macy's, Gimbels, and Me* (1967)

6 Instant gratification takes too long.

> Carrie Fisher, *Postcards From the Edge* (1987)

See also Satisfaction.

## ❦ GRATITUDE

7 There shall be / Eternal summer in the grateful heart.

> Celia Thaxter, "A Grateful Heart," *Poems* (1872)

8 It was easier to do a friendly thing than it was to stay and be thanked for it.

> Louisa May Alcott, *Little Women* (1868)

9 Like most people who felt they owed a debt they could never repay, she was vaguely uncomfortable in my presence.

> Marcia Muller, *Pennies on a Dead Woman's Eyes* (1992)

10 It needs a great nature to bear the weight of a great gratitude.

> Ouida, *Wisdom, Wit and Pathos* (1884)

11 Gratitude weighs heavily on us only when we no longer feel it.

> Comtesse Diane, *Les Glanes de la Vie* (1898)

12 For what I have received may the Lord make me truly thankful. And more truly for what I have not received.

> Storm Jameson, *Journey From the North*, vol. 2 (1970)

See also Ingratitude, Receiving.

## ❦ GREECE

13 Greece is not a country of happy mediums: everything there seems to be either wonderful or horrible.

> Nancy Mitford, "Wicked Thoughts in Greece" (1955), *The Water Beetle* (1962)

14 Greece is a good place for rebirths.

> Judith Martin, *Style and Substance* (1986)

## ❦ GREED

15 Only the dead fail to reach out with both hands.

> Christine de Pisan, "Le livre des trois vertus" (1405), in Charity Cannon Willard, tr., and Madeleine Pelner Cosman, ed., *A Medieval Woman's Mirror of Honor* (1989)

16 Greed stains our culture, soaks our sensibilities and has replaced grace as a sign of our intimacy with the divine.

> Jennifer Stone, "Epilogue," *Mind Over Media* (1988)

17 It was left for the present age to endow Covetousness with glamour on a big scale, and to give it a title which it could carry like a flag. It occurred to

somebody to call it Enterprise. From the moment of that happy inspiration, Covetousness has gone forward and never looked back.

Dorothy L. Sayers, "The Other Six Deadly Sins," *Creed or Chaos?* (1949)

1 We're all born brave, trusting, and greedy, and most of us remain greedy.

Mignon McLaughlin, *The Second Neurotic's Notebook* (1966)

2 Greed probably figures in my intellectual life as well, as I attempt to absorb a massive amount of information with consequent mental indigestion.

Etty Hillesum (1941), *An Interrupted Life* (1983)

3 The trouble with Clare was not only that she wanted to have her cake and eat it too but that she wanted to nibble at the cakes of other folk as well.

Nella Larsen, "Passing" (1929), *An Intimation of Things Distant* (1992)

See also Avarice, Miserliness, Selfishness.

# ❧ GRIEF

4 After great pain, a formal feeling comes — / . . . / This is the Hour of Lead — / Remembered, if outlived, / As Freezing persons, recollect the Snow — / First — Chill — then Stupor — then the letting go.

Emily Dickinson (1862), in Martha Dickinson Bianchi and Alfred Leete Hampson, eds., *Further Poems of Emily Dickinson* (1929)

5 Grief is a circular staircase.

Linda Pastan, title poem, *The Five Stages of Grief* (1978)

6 Part of getting over it is knowing that you will never get over it.

Anne Finger, *Past Due* (1990)

7 You don't get over it because "it" is the person you loved.

Jeanette Winterson, *Written on the Body* (1992)

8 What was so terrible about grief was not grief itself, but that one got over it.

P.D. James, *Innocent Blood* (1980)

9 Oh! grief is fantastic . . . as light, it fills all things, and, like light, it gives its own colors to all.

Mary Shelley, *The Last Man* (1826)

10 Grief-stricken. Stricken is right; it is as though you had been felled. Knocked to the ground; pitched out of life and into something else.

Penelope Lively, *Moon Tiger* (1987)

11 Grief is an illness I can't recover from.

Sue Grafton, *"C" Is for Corpse* (1986)

12 What's grief but the after-blindness / of the spirit's dazzle of love?

Gwen Harwood, "Past and Present," *Poems, Volume Two* (1968)

13 Grief means not being able to read more than two sentences at a time. It is walking into rooms with intention that suddenly vanishes.

Stephanie Ericsson, *Companion Through the Darkness* (1993)

14 Grief is a mute sense of panic.

Marion Roach, *Another Name for Madness* (1985)

15 This is the way of grief: / spinning in the rhythm of memories / that will not let you up / or down, / but keeps you grinding through / a granite air.

Gloria C. Oden, "The Carousel," in Arnold Adoff, ed., *The Poetry of Black America* (1973)

16 There are some griefs so loud / They could bring down the sky, / And there are griefs so still / None knows how deep they lie.

May Sarton, "Of Grief," *A Durable Fire* (1972)

17 Grief is, of all the passions, the one that is the most ingenious and indefatigable in finding food for its own subsistence.

Lady Marguerite Blessington, *The Governess* (1840)

18 My bowl is full of grief / and the wind is up.

Meridel Le Sueur, "Let the Bird of Earth Fly!" *Rites of Ancient Ripening* (1975)

19 I find the weight of air / Almost too great to bear.

Anne Morrow Lindbergh, "Mountain," *The Unicorn* (1956)

20 The sun has set in your life; it is getting cold. The hundreds of people around you cannot console you for the loss of the one.

Maria Augusta Trapp, *The Story of the Trapp Family Singers* (1949)

21 The Bustle in a House / The Morning after Death / Is solemnest of industries / Enacted upon earth — / The Sweeping up the Heart / And putting Love

away / We shall not want to use again / Until Eternity.

> Emily Dickinson (1866), in Mabel Loomis Todd and T.W. Higginson, eds., *Poems by Emily Dickinson* (1890)

1 Nothing on earth can make up for the loss of one who has loved you.

> Selma Lagerlöf, *Jerusalem* (1915)

2 You take a handful of rocks and put them in a jar. Then once a week, you take one tiny pebble out of the jar and throw it away. When the jar is empty, why, you'll just about be over your grief. . . . Time alone will do if you're short on rocks.

> Sharyn McCrumb, *Lovely in Her Bones* (1985)

3 Mine enemy is Grief! . . . And one of us must die!

> Adelaide Anne Procter, "Grief," *Legends and Lyrics* (1858)

4 Since every death diminishes us a little, we grieve—not so much for the death as for ourselves.

> Lynn Caine, *Widow* (1974)

5 All my life's bliss is in the grave with thee.

> Emily Brontë, "Remembrance," *Poems by Currer, Ellis, and Acton Bell* (1846)

6 I have lost the one who makes me own / the memory of pain with which I am obsessed. / Gone are the days of joy I once possessed. / With poison herbs my hard terrain is sewn. / I am a widow, robed in black, alone.

> Christine de Pisan (1390), in Aliki Barnstone and Willis Barnstone, eds., *A Book of Women Poets From Antiquity to Now* (1980)

7 She must face her grief where the struggle is always hardest—in the place where each trivial object is attended by pleasant memories.

> Ellen Glasgow, *The Battle-Ground* (1902)

8 Hundreds of times you start to put on their place at the table, or plan for clothes . . . but the keenest of all is when it is stormy, and you think this one is safe here or there, for a moment it flashes in your mind—that she isn't in yet.

> Anne Ellis, on the death of her nine-year-old, *The Life of an Ordinary Woman* (1929)

9 Emptied with weeping / my eyes are / two buckets of the waterman / as he walks among orchard trees.

> Safiya bint Musafir, "At the Badr Trench" (7th cent.), in Joanna Bankier and Deirdre Lashgari, eds., *Women Poets of the World* (1983)

10 Griefs, when divided become less poignant.

> Eliza Parsons, *Castle of Wolfenbach* (1793)

11 He shared their sorrow, and they became a part of his, and the sharing spread their grief a little, by thinning it.

> Marjorie Kinnan Rawlings, *The Sojourner* (1953)

12 Grief can't be shared. Everyone carries it alone, his own burden, his own way.

> Anne Morrow Lindbergh, *Dearly Beloved* (1962)

13 I measure every Grief I meet / With narrow, probing, Eyes — / I wonder if It weighs like Mine — / Or has an Easier size.

> Emily Dickinson (1862), in Mabel Loomis Todd, ed., *Poems by Emily Dickinson*, 3rd series (1896)

14 There is no aristocracy of grief. Grief is a great leveler.

> Anne Morrow Lindbergh, *Hour of Gold, Hour of Lead* (1973)

15 Time has its due influence over visible grief, that which is expressed by visible emotions—it softens sighs and dries tears . . . but the loss of that which is, or *was*, part of yourself, remains for ever.

> Sydney, Lady Morgan (1844), *Lady Morgan's Memoir*, vol. 2 (1862)

16 How futile are words in the ears of those who mourn.

> Helen Keller, *We Bereaved* (1929)

17 My dear mother, sisters and brothers comforted me, but their comfort only increased my sorrow and poured more oil on the fire, so that the flames grew ever higher.

> Glückel of Hameln, *Memoirs of Glückel of Hameln* (1724)

18 My own grief was a boulder that I carried everywhere. . . . Introductions stated our names, perhaps where we came from, but never, "and we are grieving for our child." The stranger would look and smile, and not see the most important thing, would offer a hand to shake thinking I could spare one of mine and still hold the invisible burden.

> Margaret Todd Maitland, "The Dome of Creation," in *The Hungry Mind Review* (1994)

19 She had borne about with her for years like an arrow sticking in her heart the grief, the anguish.

> Virginia Woolf, *Mrs. Dalloway* (1925)

1 Grief sooner may distract than kill, / And the Unhappy often prove / Death is as coy a thing as Love.

    Katherine Philips, "To My Antenor" (1661), *Poems* (1678)

2 Have you ever thought, when something dreadful happens, "a moment ago things were not like this; let it be *then*, not *now*, anything but *now*"? And you try and try to remake *then*, but you know you can't. So you try to hold the moment quite still and not let it move on and show itself.

    Mary Stewart, *Nine Coaches Waiting* (1958)

3 There are griefs which grow with years.

    Harriet Beecher Stowe, *The Pearl of Orr's Island* (1862)

4 Memory is the only friend of grief.

    Rumer Godden, *China Court* (1961)

5 Sleep brings no joy to me, / Remembrance never dies.

    Emily Brontë (1837), in Clement Shorter, ed., *The Complete Poems of Emily Brontë* (1910)

6 Beware the easy griefs / that fool and fuel nothing.

    Gwendolyn Brooks, "Boys. Black," *Beckonings* (1975)

7 How cold to the living hour grief could make you!

    Eudora Welty, "Music From Spain," *The Golden Apples* (1949)

8 I tell you, hopeless grief is passionless.

    Elizabeth Barrett Browning, "Grief," *Poems* (1844)

9 There is an indolence in grief / Which will not even seek relief.

    L.E. Landon, title poem, *The Troubadour* (1825)

10 Grief, I have cursed thee often—now at last / To hate thy name I am no longer free; / Caught in thy bony arms and prisoned fast, / I love no love but thee.

    Mary Coleridge, "My True Love Hath My Heart and I Have His" (1887), in Theresa Whistler, ed., *The Collected Poems of Mary Coleridge* (1954)

11 Grief is not graceful.

    Mariette Hartley, in Joan Rivers, with Richard Meryman, *Still Talking* (1991)

12 Grief may be joy misunderstood; / Only the Good discerns the good.

    Elizabeth Barrett Browning, "De Profundis" (1840), *Last Poems* (1862)

13 Life must go on; / I forget just why.

    Edna St. Vincent Millay, "Lament," *Second April* (1921)

14 Grass grows at last above all graves.

    Julia C.R. Dorr, "Grass-Grown," *Poems* (1892)

See also Bereavement, Death, Loss, Misfortune, Mourning, Sorrow, Suffering.

## & GRIEVANCES

15 This, it seemed, was one of those angry natures that feeds on grievance; nothing would madden her more than to know that what she complained of had been put right.

    Mary Stewart, *Airs Above the Ground* (1965)

16 The stems of grievance put down their heavy roots / And by the end of summer crack the pavement.

    Josephine Miles, "Grievances," *Kinds of Affection* (1967)

17 A woman of the world should always be the mistress of sorrow and not its servant. She may have a grief but never a grievance.

    Elsie de Wolfe, *After All* (1935)

See also Complaints, Indignation.

## & GROUPS

18 In crowds we have unison, in groups harmony. We want the single voice but not the single note; that is the secret of the group.

    M.P. Follett, *The New State* (1918)

19 Crowd action is the outcome of agreement based on concurrence of emotion rather than of thought.

    M.P. Follett, *The New State* (1918)

20 The collective intelligence of any group of people who are thinking as a "herd" rather than individually is no higher than the intelligence of the stupidest members.

    Mary Day Winn, *Adam's Rib* (1931)

21 As every authoritarian regime knows, association can be a dangerous thing. From discussion it is only a few steps to action.

    Anne Firor Scott, "The 'New Woman' in the New South," *South Atlantic Quarterly* (1962)

See also Committees, Meetings, Organizations.

## ❧ GROWING UP

See Adolescence, Adulthood, Age, Growth, Maturity.

## ❧ GROWTH

1 Buds will be roses, and kittens, cats,—more's the pity!

   Louisa May Alcott, *Little Women* (1868)

2 Our consciousness rarely registers the beginning of a growth within us any more than without us: there have been many circulations of the sap before we detect the smallest sign of the bud.

   George Eliot, *Silas Marner* (1861)

3 Growth itself contains the germ of happiness.

   Pearl S. Buck, *To My Daughters, With Love* (1967)

4 We do not grow absolutely, chronologically. We grow sometimes in one dimension, and not in another, unevenly. We grow partially. We are relative. We are mature in one realm, childish in another. The past, present, and future mingle and pull us backward, forward, or fix us in the present. We are made up of layers, cells, constellations.

   Anaïs Nin (1946), *The Diary of Anaïs Nin*, vol. 4 (1971)

5 A finished person is a boring person.

   Anna Quindlen, in *Writer's Digest* (1993)

6 We are not unlike a particularly hardy crustacean. . . . With each passage from one stage of human growth to the next we, too, must shed a protective structure. We are left exposed and vulnerable—but also yeasty and embryonic again, capable of stretching in ways we hadn't known before. These sheddings may take several years or more. Coming out of each passage, though, we enter a longer and more stable period in which we can expect relative tranquillity and a sense of equilibrium regained.

   Gail Sheehy, *Passages* (1976)

7 Growth is not concerned with itself.

   Meridel Le Sueur, "Formal 'Education' in Writing" (1935), *Harvest Song* (1990)

See also Adulthood, Change, Maturity, Self-Actualization.

## ❧ GUESTS

8 Guests are the delight of leisure, and the solace of ennui.

   Agnes Repplier, "Guests," *In the Dozy Hours* (1894)

9 A guest should be permitted to graze, as it were, in the pastures of his host's kindness, left even to his own devices, like a rational being, and handsomely neglected.

   Louise Imogen Guiney, *Goose-Quill Papers* (1885)

10 My father used to say, / "Superior people never make long visits."

   Marianne Moore, "Silence" (1921), *Selected Poems* (1935)

11 Emily was feeling the elation of conscientious hosts when they can temporarily escape a ubiquitous houseguest.

   Carol Bly, "Talk of Heroes," *Backbone* (1982)

12 Dear visitors, what largesse have you given, not only in departing, but in coming, that we might learn to prize your absence, wallow the more exquisitely in the leisure of your not-being. To-night we shall sleep deep. We need no more hope that you "have everything you want"; we know that you have, for you are safely home, and can get it from your kitchen if you haven't.

   Rose Macaulay, *Personal Pleasures* (1936)

See also Farewells, Hospitality, Invitation, Visits.

## ❧ GUILT

13 Guilt is . . . the next best thing to being there.

   Ellen Sue Stern, *The Indispensable Woman* (1988)

14 Guilt: the gift that keeps on giving.

   Erma Bombeck, in *Time* (1984)

15 There smiles no Paradise on earth so fair, / But guilt will raise avenging phantoms there.

   Felicia Hemans, "The Abencerrage," *The Poetical Works of Felicia Dorothea Hemans* (1914)

16 Guilt is a Jewish invention improved upon by Christians for the last two thousand years.

   Rita Mae Brown, *In Her Day* (1976)

1 Show me a woman who doesn't feel guilty and I'll show you a man.

　　Erica Jong, *Fear of Flying* (1973)

2 Among women, guilt spreads with the rampant fury of bubonic plague. . . . I used to feel guilty if the cat had matted fur.

　　Sue Patton Thoele, *The Courage to Be Yourself* (1988)

3 She felt that old generic guilt, the kind you feel even when you can't think of what in the world you are supposed to have done.

　　Meg Wolitzer, *This Is My Life* (1988)

4 Could she conceive an environment which had never allowed one to forget guilt? In which, if one were not actually guilty of anything at the moment the chances were that one would be shortly?

　　Eleanor Dark, *The Little Company* (1945)

5 My mother could make anybody feel guilty—she used to get letters of apology from people she didn't even know.

　　Joan Rivers, with Richard Meryman, *Still Talking* (1991)

6 No-fault guilt: This is when, instead of trying to figure out who's to blame, everyone pays.

　　Judith Viorst, *Love and Guilt and the Meaning of Life, Etc.* (1979)

7 I believe in guilt. There's not enough guilt around these days for my taste.

　　Joy Williams, in Janet Sternburg, ed., *The Writer on Her Work*, vol. 2 (1991)

8 Guilt is an emotion that has periodically served me well.

　　Barbara E. Mraz, *Sacred Strands* (1991)

9 Guilt is the major motivating force in my life.

　　Linda Barnes, *Steel Guitar* (1991)

10 Guilt didn't put any butter on the bread of life.

　　Leonore Fleischer, *The Fisher King* (1991)

11 I cannot keep feeling guilty about that which guilt will not change.

　　Barbara A. Robinson, *And Still I Cry* (1992)

12 Guilt is a rope that wears thin.

　　Ayn Rand, *Atlas Shrugged* (1957)

13 Guilt is unfelt pain.

　　Alice Molloy, *In Other Words* (1973)

14 Ah! it is well for the unfortunate to be resigned, but for the guilty there is no peace.

　　Mary Shelley, *Frankenstein* (1818)

15 Guilt is the one burden human beings can't bear alone.

　　Anaïs Nin, *A Spy in the House of Love* (1954)

16 We all want to be guilty, because guilt is power.

　　Alison Lurie, *Love and Friendship* (1962)

17 Guilt is often an excuse for not thinking.

　　Lillian Hellman, *Pentimento* (1973)

18 I have no creative use for guilt, yours or my own. Guilt is only another way of avoiding informed action, of buying time out of the pressing need to make clear choices, out of the approaching storm that can feed the earth as well as bend the trees.

　　Audre Lorde, "The Uses of Anger" (1981), *Sister Outsider* (1984)

19 The ultimate egocentricity of guilt.

　　Nancy Hale, *Prodigal Women* (1942)

20 Where all are guilty, no one is.

　　Hannah Arendt, "On Violence," *Crises of the Republic* (1972)

21 Guilt is the teacher, love is the lesson.

　　Joan Borysenko, book title (1990)

22 If love begets love, guilt begets guilt. . . . If Mom and Dad behaved toward each other as though they had been partners in some unspoken misdeed in bringing us into the world, we were drenched with a sense of having sinned from the hour of our birth. The thought was drummed into us that the discord in which the family lived much of the time was all of our doing. . . . We could be dutiful, obedient, hard-working, but how could that possibly erase the crime of our existence?

　　Annette, Cécile, Marie, and Yvonne Dionne, with James Brough, *"We Were Five"* (1965)

See also Remorse, Shame.

## ❦ GUNS

23 Guns know no policy except destruction.

　　Clare Boothe, *Europe in the Spring* (1940)

1 Men are not killed because they get mad at each other. They're killed because one of them has a gun.

> Jeannette Rankin (1966), in Hannah Josephson, *Jeannette Rankin* (1974)

2 No country that permits firearms to be widely and randomly distributed among its population—especially firearms that are capable of wounding and killing human beings—can expect to escape violence, and a great deal of violence.

> Margaret Mead, in *Redbook* (1972)

See also Violence.

# H

## ❧ HABIT

1 Habit has a kind of poetry.
   Simone de Beauvoir, *The Coming of Age* (1970)

2 Habit is our idea of eternity.
   L.E. Landon, "Rebecca," *The Book of Beauty* (1833)

3 Habits are the shorthand of behavior.
   Julie Henderson, *The Lover Within* (1986)

4 Things start as hopes and end up as habits.
   Lillian Hellman, *Days to Come* (1936)

5 Rigid, the skeleton of habit alone upholds the human frame.
   Virginia Woolf, *Mrs. Dalloway* (1925)

6 Old habits are strong and jealous.
   Dorothea Brande, *Becoming a Writer* (1934)

7 Habit, a particularly insidious thug who chokes passion and smothers love. Habit puts us on autopilot.
   Diane Ackerman, *A Natural History of Love* (1994)

8 Nothing in life is more corroding than habit.
   Gertrude Atherton, *Black Oxen* (1923)

9 Habit, you know, blunts the moral sense.
   Elizabeth Elton Smith, *The Three Eras of Woman's Life* (1836)

10 Small habits well pursu'd betimes, / May reach the dignity of crimes.
   Hannah More, "Florio" (1786), *The Works of Hannah More*, vol. 1 (1841)

11 Curious things, habits. People themselves never knew they had them.
   Agatha Christie, "Witness for the Prosecution," *The Hound of Death* (1933)

12 I have no faith in a human critter who hasn't one or two bad habits.
   Margaret Deland, *Captain Archer's Daughter* (1932)

13 It's just like magic. When you live by yourself, all your annoying habits are *gone*!!
   Merrill Markoe, *What the Dogs Have Taught Me* (1992)

14 Looking back at a repetition of empty days, one sees that monuments have sprung up. Habit is not mere subjugation, it is a tender tie: when one remembers habit it seems to have been happiness.
   Elizabeth Bowen, *The Death of the Heart* (1938)

15 Everything was leveled, there were no extremes of joy or sorrow any more but only habit, routine, ancient family names and rites and customs, slow careful old people moving cautiously around furniture that had sat in the same positions for fifty years.
   Anne Tyler, *Searching for Caleb* (1975)

16 We each have a litany of holiday rituals and everyday habits that we hold on to, and we often greet radical innovation with the enthusiasm of a baby meeting a new sitter. We defend against it and—not always, but often enough—reject it. Slowly we adjust, but only if we have to.
   Ellen Goodman, *Turning Points* (1979)

17 Habit is necessary; it is the habit of having habits, of turning a trail into a rut, that must be incessantly fought against if one is to remain alive.
   Edith Wharton, *A Backward Glance* (1934)

See also Custom, Routine, Traditions.

## ❧ HAIR

1 I have always believed that hair is a very sure index of character.

    Katharine Tynan, *Twenty-Five Years* (1913)

2 Hair brings one's self-image into focus; it is vanity's proving ground. . . . Hair is terribly personal, a tangle of mysterious prejudices.

    Shana Alexander, "Hair Is Terribly Personal," in *Life* (1966)

3 I've discovered over the years that if my hair is all right, then generally speaking, so am I.

    Maureen Lipman, *Thank You for Having Me* (1990)

4 Gorgeous hair is the best revenge.

    Ivana Trump, in hair product commercial (1992)

5 The three most important things to a Southern girl are God, family and hair, almost never in that order.

    Lucinda Ebersole, in *The New York Times Magazine* (1993)

6 Ladies with curly hair / Have time to spare.

    Phyllis McGinley, "The Bonus," *Times Three* (1960)

7 Gentlemen prefer blondes.

    Anita Loos, book title (1925)

8 Is it true. . . . Blondes have more fun?

    Shirley Polykoff, Clairol slogan (1957), *Does She . . . or Doesn't She?* (1975)

9 Does she . . . or doesn't she? Only her hairdresser knows for sure.

    Shirley Polykoff, Clairol slogan (1955), *Does She . . . or Doesn't She?* (1975)

10 [Long hair] is considered bohemian, which may be why I grew it, but I keep it long because I love the way it feels, part cloak, part fan, part mane, part security blanket.

    Marge Piercy, *Braided Lives* (1982)

11 Ethel patted her hair and looked very sneery.

    Daisy Ashford (aged 9), *The Young Visiters* (1919)

12 To Crystal, hair was the most important thing on earth. She would never get married because you couldn't wear curlers in bed then.

    Edna O'Brien, "Irish Revel," *The Love Object* (1968)

13 Her locks had been so frequently and drastically brightened and curled that to caress them, one felt,

would be rather like running one's fingers through julienne potatoes.

    Dorothy Parker, "Lolita," *The Portable Dorothy Parker*, rev. ed. (1973)

14 She had hard gray hair pressed into waves that grasped her scalp like a migraine.

    Susanna Kaysen, *Girl, Interrupted* (1993)

15 The owner of Mojo's was a suicide blonde, dyed by her own hand.

    Rita Mae Brown, *Bingo* (1988)

## ❧ HANDS

16 How to paint your lovely hands, fluttering over the silks like two dark birds?

    Elizabeth Borton de Treviño, *I, Juan de Pareja* (1965)

17 Nervous hands as if the fingers were dripping from them like icicles.

    Fannie Hurst, *Lummox* (1923)

18 She inspected her finger nails of so thick and glistening a red that it seemed as if she but recently had completed tearing an ox apart with her naked hands.

    Dorothy Parker, "Cousin Larry," *The Portable Dorothy Parker* (1944)

19 Her handshake ought not to be used except as a tourniquet.

    Margaret Halsey, *With Malice Toward Some* (1938)

## ❧ HANDWRITING

20 It is remarkable what fine hands men of genius write, even when they are as awkward in all other uses of the hand as a cow with a musket.

    Sara Coleridge (1850), *Memoir and Letters*, vol. 2 (1873)

21 Gerald's straight, round writing had, to her imagination, a queer totter, like someone running for life in tight shoes.

    Elizabeth Bowen, *The Last September* (1929)

22 When Mr. Wiggs traveled to eternity by the alcohol route, she buried his faults with him, and for want

of better virtues to extol she always laid stress on the fine hand he wrote.

Alice Caldwell Rice, *Mrs. Wiggs of the Cabbage Patch* (1901)

## ❧ HAPPINESS

1 Happiness is nothing but everyday living seen through a veil.

Zora Neale Hurston, *Moses: Man of the Mountain* (1939)

2 Each moment in time we have it all, even when we think we don't.

Melody Beattie, *The Lessons of Love* (1994)

3 Happiness consists not in having much, but in being content with little.

Countess of Blessington, *Desultory Thoughts and Reflections* (1839)

4 The bliss e'en of a moment still is bliss.

Joanna Baillie, *The Beacon* (1802)

5 When, a small child, . . . I thought that success spelled happiness. I was wrong. Happiness is like a butterfly which appears and delights us for one brief moment, but soon flits away.

Anna Pavlova, "Pages of My Life," in A.H. Franks, ed., *Pavlova* (1956)

6 Happiness hangs by a hair.

Mary O'Hara, *Thunderhead* (1943)

7 Getting what you go after is success; but liking it while you are getting it is happiness.

Bertha Damon, *A Sense of Humus* (1943)

8 Happiness lies in the consciousness we have of it.

George Sand, *Handsome Lawrence* (1872)

9 Happiness is the ability to recognize it.

Carolyn Wells, "Wiseacreage," *Folly for the Wise* (1904)

10 The genius for happiness is still so rare, is indeed on the whole the rarest genius. To possess it means to approach life with the humility of a beggar, but to treat it with the proud generosity of a prince; to bring to its totality the deep understanding of a great poet and to each of its moments the abandonment and ingenuousness of a child.

Ellen Key, title essay, *The Morality of Women* (1911)

11 It is not easy to find happiness in ourselves, and it is not possible to find it elsewhere.

Agnes Repplier, in Emma Repplier, *Agnes Repplier* (1957)

12 Happiness is not a station you arrive at, but a manner of traveling.

Margaret Lee Runbeck, *Time for Each Other* (1944)

13 Happiness is a tide: it carries you only a little way at a time; but you have covered a vast space before you know that you are moving at all.

Mary Adams, *Confessions of a Wife* (1902)

14 Happiness is a change of trouble.

Malvina Hoffman, slogan of her "Trouble Bureau" for needy artists and musicians, *Yesterday Is Tomorrow* (1965)

15 All happiness is a form of innocence.

Marguerite Yourcenar, *Alexis* (1929)

16 Happiness consists in the full employment of our faculties in some pursuit.

Harriet Martineau, "On the Art of Thinking" (1829), *Miscellanies*, vol. 1 (1836)

17 Happiness is not something you get, but something you do.

Marcelene Cox, in *Ladies' Home Journal* (1947)

18 That is happiness; to be dissolved into something complete and great.

Willa Cather, *My Antonia* (1918)

19 Happiness is that state of consciousness which proceeds from the achievement of one's values.

Ayn Rand, *Atlas Shrugged* (1957)

20 Many persons have a wrong idea of what constitutes real happiness. It is not obtained through self-gratification but through fidelity to a worthy purpose.

Helen Keller, *Helen Keller's Journal* (1938)

21 Happiness is to take up the struggle in the midst of the raging storm and not to pluck the lute in the moonlight or recite poetry among the blossoms.

Ding Ling, "Thoughts on March 8" (1942), *I Myself Am a Woman* (1989)

22 The way to achieve happiness is to have a high standard for yourself and a medium one for everyone else.

Marcelene Cox, in *Ladies' Home Journal* (1954)

1 There is only one happiness in life, to love and be loved.

George Sand (1862), *Correspondance de George Sand*, vol. 16 (1981)

2 Too much good fortune can make you smug and unaware. Happiness should be like an oasis, the greener for the desert that surrounds it.

Rachel Field, *And Now Tomorrow* (1942)

3 Happiness is not a possession to be prized, it is a quality of thought, a state of mind.

Daphne du Maurier, *Rebecca* (1938)

4 Happiness is excitement that has found a settling down place, but there is always a little corner that keeps flapping around.

E.L. Konigsburg, *From the Mixed-Up Files of Mrs. Basil E. Frankweiler* (1967)

5 How little has situation to do with happiness!

Fanny Burney, *Evelina* (1778)

6 Happiness for the average person may be said to flow largely from common sense—adapting oneself to circumstances—*and* a sense of humor.

Beatrice Lillie, *Every Other Inch a Lady* (1972)

7 Happiness, to some, elation; / Is, to others, mere stagnation.

Amy Lowell, "Happiness," *Sword Blades and Poppy Seed* (1914)

8 He loved being happy! He loved happiness like I love tea.

Eudora Welty, *The Ponder Heart* (1954)

9 No stair is steep to happy feet!

Mary F. Robinson, "A Word in Counsel," *Retrospect* (1893)

10 We all of us deserve happiness or none of us does.

Mary Gordon, *The Company of Women* (1980)

11 Fill the cup of happiness for others, and there will be enough overflowing to fill yours to the brim.

Rose Pastor Stokes (1901), in Herbert Shapiro and David L. Sterling, eds., *"I Belong to the Working Class"* (1992)

12 No one has a right to consume happiness without producing it.

Helen Keller, *The Open Door* (1957)

13 It is not swinish to be happy unless one is happy in swinish ways.

L. Susan Stebbing, *Ideas and Illusions* (1941)

14 A sure way to lose happiness, I found, is to want it at the expense of everything else.

Bette Davis, *This 'N That* (1987)

15 The surest way to get a thing in this life is to be prepared for doing without it, to the exclusion even of hope.

Jane Welsh Carlyle (1849), in Alan and Mary McQueen Simpson, eds., *I Too Am Here* (1977)

16 It may be that true happiness lies in the conviction that one has irremediably lost happiness. Then we can begin to move through life without hope or fear, capable of finally enjoying all the small pleasures, which are the most lasting.

Maria-Luisa Bombal, "The Tree," in Zoila Nelken and Rosalie Torres-Rioseco, eds., *Short Stories of Latin America* (1963)

17 We cannot make bargains for blisses, / Nor catch them like fishes in nets; / And sometimes the thing our life misses, / Helps more than the thing which it gets.

Alice Cary, "Nobility," *The Poetical Works of Alice and Phoebe Cary* (1876)

18 Stop running around after happiness. If you make up your mind not to be happy there's no reason why you shouldn't have a fairly good time.

Edith Wharton, "The Last Asset," *The Hermit and the Wild Woman* (1908)

19 One of the greatest hindrances to happiness in the present day is our tendency to standardize our conception of it.

J.E. Buckrose, "Happiness," *What I Have Gathered* (1923)

20 Life may take away happiness. But it can't take away having had it.

Ellen Glasgow, *Vein of Iron* (1935)

21 One cannot divine nor forecast the conditions that will make happiness; one only stumbles upon them by chance, in a lucky hour, at the world's end somewhere, and holds fast to the days, as to fortune or fame.

Willa Cather, *Willa Cather in Europe* (1956)

22 Happiness isn't like unhappiness. You recover from it!

Simone Berteaut, *Piaf* (1969)

23 The happiest women, like the happiest nations, have no history.

George Eliot, *The Mill on the Floss* (1860)

1 Happiness puts on as many shapes as discontent, and there is nothing odder than the satisfactions of one's neighbor.

Phyllis McGinley, "Pipeline and Sinker," *The Province of the Heart* (1959)

2 When one door of happiness closes, another opens; but often we look so long at the closed door that we do not see the one which has been opened for us.

Helen Keller, *We Bereaved* (1929)

3 Recurrence is sure. What the mind suffered last week, or last year, it does not suffer now; but it will suffer again next week or next year. Happiness is not a matter of events; it depends upon the tides of the mind.

Alice Meynell, "The Rhythm of Life," *Essays* (1914)

4 If you haven't been happy very young, you can still be happy later on, but it's much harder. You need more luck.

Simone de Beauvoir, in *The Observer* (1975)

5 New happiness too must be learned to bear.

Marie von Ebner-Eschenbach, *Aphorisms* (1893)

6 The only people who are truly happy are the people we do not know very well.

Susan Isaacs, *After All These Years* (1993)

See also Contentment, Gladness, Joy, Pleasure.

## ❧ HATE

7 Hatred is like fire—it makes even light rubbish deadly.

George Eliot, "Janet's Repentance," *Scenes of Clerical Life* (1857)

8 There was too much hatred in the world; it was manifestly as dangerous as gunpowder, yet people let it lie about, in the way of ignition.

Rebecca West, *The Thinking Reed* (1936)

9 Hate is all a lie, there is no truth in hate.

Kathleen Norris, *Hands Full of Living* (1931)

10 God . . . cannot occupy the human soul at the same time that it is occupied by hatred.

Ann Fairbairn, *Five Smooth Stones* (1966)

11 Hate is not a good counselor.

Victoria Wolff, *Spell of Egypt* (1943)

12 Now when you hates you shrinks up inside and gets littler and you squeezes your heart tight and you stays so mad with peoples you feels sick all the time like you needs the doctor.

Margaret Walker, *Jubilee* (1966)

13 The enslaver is / enslaved; the hater, harmed.

Marianne Moore, "In Distrust of Merits," *Nevertheless* (1944)

14 Hate smolders and eventually destroys, not the hated but the hater.

Dorothy Thompson, "On Hate," in *Ladies' Home Journal* (1943)

15 You cannot hate other people without hating yourself.

Oprah Winfrey, in Brian Lanker, *I Dream a World* (1989)

16 In hatred as in love, we grow like the thing we brood upon. What we loathe, we graft into our very soul.

Mary Renault, *The Mask of Apollo* (1966)

17 You can't be beautiful and hate because hate is a corroding disease and affects the way you look. . . . You can't hide it—ever. It shows in your eyes.

Bess Myerson (1945), in Shana Alexander, *When She Was Bad* (1990)

18 The intensest form of hatred is that rooted in fear.

George Eliot, *Daniel Deronda* (1874)

19 People hate what they don't understand.

Eva Le Gallienne (1934), in Robert A. Schanke, *Shattered Applause* (1992)

20 Nothing is more common than for persons to hate those whom they have injured.

Charlotte Lennox, *Sophia* (1762)

21 None do we hate so heartily as those who try to use us, unless it may be those whom we try in vain to use.

Minna Thomas Antrim, *At the Sign of the Golden Calf* (1905)

22 Didn't you ever notice how it's always people who wish they had somethin' or had done somethin' that hate the hardest?

Grace Metalious, *Peyton Place* (1956)

23 Hatred is a deathwish for the hated, not a lifewish for anything else.

Audre Lorde, "Eye to Eye," *Sister Outsider* (1984)

1 They say that oppression engenders hate. They are heard on all sides crying hate hate.

    Monique Wittig, *Les Guérillères* (1969)

2 Misery generates hate.

    Charlotte Brontë, *Shirley* (1849)

3 Only ways you can keep folks hating is to keep them apart and separated from each other.

    Margaret Walker, *Jubilee* (1966)

4 I tell you, there is such a thing as creative hate!

    Willa Cather, *The Song of the Lark* (1915)

5 Hatred is a passion requiring one hundred times the energy of love. Keep it for a cause, not an individual. Keep it for intolerance, injustice, stupidity. For hatred is the strength of the sensitive. Its power and its greatness depend on the selflessness of its use.

    Olive Moore, *Collected Writings* (1992)

6 When all that hate energy was focused on me, it was transformed into a fantastic energy. It was supporting me. If you are centered and you can transform all this energy that comes in, it will help you. If you believe it is going to kill you, it will kill you.

    Yoko Ono, in Jerry Hopkins, *Yoko Ono* (1986)

7 It's a sign of your own worth sometimes if you are hated by the right people.

    Miles Franklin, *My Career Goes Bung* (1946)

8 One should hate very little, because it's extremely fatiguing. One should despise much, forgive often and never forget. Pardon does not bring with it forgetfulness; at least not for me.

    Sarah Bernhardt, in Cornelia Otis Skinner, *Madame Sarah* (1966)

9 I don't hate anyone. I dislike. But my dislike is the equivalent of anyone else's hate.

    Elsa Maxwell, in *Time* (1963)

10 It was hate at first sight, clean, pure and strong as grain alcohol.

    Elizabeth Peters, *Naked Once More* (1989)

11 Hate seemed to crackle out of him in little flashes, like electricity in a cat's fur.

    M.F.K. Fisher, *The Gastronomical Me* (1943)

See also Love and Hate, Misanthropy.

## ❧ HATS

12 She had a passion for hats, none of which returned her affection.

    Storm Jameson, *The Intruder* (1956)

13 Communists all seem to wear small caps, a look I consider better suited to tubes of toothpaste than to people.

    Fran Lebowitz, *Metropolitan Life* (1978)

## ❧ HAWAII

14 For all I know, Eden still exists on this planet. If so, Hawaii is a place to look.

    Helen Bevington, *The Journey Is Everything* (1983)

## ❧ HEAD AND HEART

15 Never till Time is done / Will the fire of the heart and the fire of the mind be one.

    Edith Sitwell, in Elizabeth Salter and Allanah Harper, eds., *Edith Sitwell* (1976)

16 I think that "intellectuals" cause a great deal of trouble trying to do it all with the mind. It is the heart that counts.

    Louise Bogan (1955), in Ruth Limmer, ed., *What the Woman Lived* (1973)

17 Very rare, the intelligence of the heart. The intelligence of the whimsical brain is less rare, less attaching, sometimes tedious.

    Storm Jameson, *Parthian Words* (1970)

18 I am all for people having their heart in the right place; but the right place for a heart is not inside the head.

    Katharine Whitehorn, *Roundabout* (1962)

19 Pity me that the heart is slow to learn / What the swift mind beholds at every turn.

    Edna St. Vincent Millay, "Pity Me Not," *The Harp-Weaver* (1923)

See also Heart, Mind.

## ✿ HEALTH

1 Thousands upon thousands of persons have studied disease. Almost no one has studied health.

Adelle Davis, *Let's Eat Right to Keep Fit* (1954)

2 Health is not simply the absence of sickness.

Hannah Green, *I Never Promised You a Rose Garden* (1964)

3 Health is not a condition of matter, but of Mind.

Mary Baker Eddy, *Science and Health* (1875)

4 As I see it, every day you do one of two things: build health or produce disease in yourself.

Adelle Davis, *Let's Eat Right to Keep Fit* (1954)

5 Talk health. The dreary, never-ending tale / Of mortal maladies is worn and stale; / You cannot charm or interest or please / By harping on that minor chord disease. / Say you are well, or all is well with you, / And God shall hear your words and make them true.

Ella Wheeler Wilcox, "Speech," *Poems of Pleasure* (1888)

6 I consider myself an expert on love, sex, and health. Without health you can have very little of the other two.

Barbara Cartland, in Gwen Robyns, *Barbara Cartland* (1984)

7 The longer I live, the more I am certified that men, in all that relates to their own health, have not common sense! . . . Either by their wild impatience of bodily suffering, and the exaggerated moan they make over it, or else by their reckless defiance of it, and neglect of every dictate of prudence!

Jane Welsh Carlyle (1862), in James Anthony Froude, ed., *Letters and Memorials of Jane Welsh Carlyle*, vol. 2 (1883)

8 You cannot keep up a nightlife and amount to anything in the day. You cannot indulge in those foods and liquors that destroy the physique and still hope to have a physique that functions with the minimum of destruction to itself. A candle burnt at both ends may shed a brighter light, but the darkness that follows is for a longer time.

Coco Chanel, in Djuna Barnes, *I Could Never Be Lonely Without a Husband* (1985)

9 It is strange indeed that the more we learn about how to build health, the less healthy Americans become.

Adelle Davis, *Let's Have Healthy Children* (1951)

10 I got well by talking. Death could not get a word in edgewise, grew discouraged, and traveled on.

Louise Erdrich, *Tracks* (1988)

See also Diseases, Doctors, Exercise, Health Care, Hospitals, Illness, Medicine, Nurses, Sanity, Surgery.

## ✿ HEALTH CARE

11 We are gradually learning that under our economic system of "free enterprise," adequate medical service can never be paid for as a private cost.

Sarah Tarleton Colvin, *A Rebel in Thought* (1944)

12 The more efficient we become in eliminating disease, the more our services are out of reach of the people.

Alice Tisdale Hobart, *The Serpent-Wreathed Staff* (1951)

13 Health care delivery is one of the tragedies still in America.

Jewel Plummer Cobb, in Brian Lanker, *I Dream a World* (1989)

14 We currently have a system for taking care of sickness. We do not have a system for enhancing and promoting health.

Hillary Rodham Clinton, speech (1993)

15 What we have is "sickness" care.

Maggie Kuhn, in Dieter Hessel, *Maggie Kuhn on Aging* (1977)

16 In this society, dominated as it is by the profit-seeking ventures of monopoly corporations, health has been callously transformed into a commodity—a commodity that those with means are able to afford, but that is too often entirely beyond the reach of others.

Angela Y. Davis, *Women, Culture & Politics* (1989)

17 We are fast moving toward an aristocracy of health.

Alice Tisdale Hobart, *The Serpent-Wreathed Staff* (1951)

18 France, like every other Western country except the United States, has long accepted the principle that comprehensive health care is the right of every citizen. No Frenchman need ever fear that catastrophic illness will wipe him out financially. How

long, do you suppose, will it take us, in the United States, to catch up?

> Suzanne Massie, in Robert and Suzanne Massie, *Journey* (1975)

See also Doctors, Hospitals, Nurses.

## ♦ HEART

1 My heart is like a singing bird.

> Christina Rossetti, "A Birthday" (1857), *Goblin Market* (1862)

2 Nobody has ever measured, even the poets, how much a heart can hold.

> Zelda Fitzgerald (1945), in Nancy Milford, *Zelda* (1970)

3 The heart outstrips the clumsy senses, and sees—perhaps for an instant, perhaps for long periods of bliss—an undistorted and more veritable world.

> Evelyn Underhill, *Mysticism* (1955)

4 It is only in the heart that anything really happens.

> Ellen Glasgow, *Vein of Iron* (1935)

5 I think hearts are very much like glasses—if they do not break with the first ring, they usually last a considerable time.

> L.E. Landon, *Romance and Reality* (1831)

6 It's easier to gnaw through bone / than the hide of the heart.

> Diane Glancy, "Late Winter," *Lone Dog's Winter Count* (1991)

7 It takes a long, long time for living tissue to petrify, so long that change is incomprehensible, for a tree to turn to rock. . . . It takes a long time, too, for a heart to turn to stone.

> Loretta Gage, with Nancy Gage, *If Wishes Were Horses* (1992)

8 What we have most to fear is failure of the heart.

> Sonia Johnson, *Going Out of Our Minds* (1987)

9 We are adhering to life now with our last muscle—the heart.

> Djuna Barnes, *Nightwood* (1937)

10 The heart of another is a dark forest, always, no matter how close it has been to one's own.

> Willa Cather, *The Professor's House* (1925)

11 The logic of the heart is absurd.

> Julie de Lespinasse (1774), in Katharine Prescott Wormeley, tr., *Letters of Mlle. de Lespinasse* (1903)

12 Always there remain portions of our heart into which no one is able to enter, invite them as we may.

> Mary Dixon Thayer, "Things to Live By," *Sonnets* (1933)

13 Secrets of the heart are seldom news.

> Jennifer Stone, "Beatific Blue," *Over by the Caves* (1977)

See also Broken Heart, Head and Heart, Love.

## ♦ HEARTLESSNESS

14 It was said of Moleka that he had taken his heart out of his body and hidden it in some secret place while he made love to all the women in the village. Dikeledi was the only woman who knew that. The quarrels were about where he had hidden his heart.

> Bessie Head, *Maru* (1971)

See also Cruelty.

## ♦ HEAVEN

15 God stood at the head of a table, not a wooden table, but something temporary, set up only for the occasion. Heaven was everyone delighted to see everyone, everyone dressed up. And God was the most delighted.

> Mary Gordon, *The Company of Women* (1980)

16 Heaven is a near / translatable thing; / it's here, / it's there.

> H.D., "Chance Meeting," *Red Roses for Bronze* (1931)

17 Heaven is neither a place nor a time.

> Florence Nightingale, in Sir Edward Tyas, *The Life of Florence Nightingale*, vol. 2 (1913)

18 That's got to be at least one of the benefits of heaven—never having to act normal again.

> Cynthia Rylant, *Missing May* (1992)

19 I am better able to imagine hell than heaven; it is my Puritan inheritance, I suppose.

> Elinor Wylie, *The Orphan Angel* (1926)

See also Eternity, Immortality.

## ❧ HEIGHT

1 I was too tall to make the chess team in my high
school, so I tried golf.

    Carol Mann, when asked how someone her height (6′3″)
    had dared take up golf, in Janice Kaplan, *Women and Sports*
    (1979)

2 Height isn't something you can have and just let be,
like nice teeth or naturally curly hair. People have
this idea you have to put it to use, playing basketball, for example, or observing the weather up
there. If you are a girl, they feel a particular need to
point your height out to you, as if you might not
have noticed.

    Barbara Kingsolver, *Animal Dreams* (1990)

3 Why is it that if you happen to be black and over
six feet tall, everybody thinks you supposed to play
basketball or football?

    Terry McMillan, *Disappearing Acts* (1989)

4 He was a short man, well below average, and he
walked with his chin up, gazing about as though
searching for his missing inches.

    Helen Hudson, *Meyer Meyer* (1967)

5 Then she is too high, for I myself am neither too
high nor too low.

    Elizabeth I, on being told Mary Queen of Scots was taller
    than she (1568), in Katharine Anthony, *Queen Elizabeth*
    (1929)

## ❧ HELL

6 It's only a dogma that hells exists; it isn't a dogma
that there's anybody in it.

    Antonia White, *Frost in May* (1933)

7 Hell is the place where nothing ever stops and
nothing ever changes, a far more alarming conception than the old-fashioned fire and brimstone.

    Anthony Gilbert, *The Fingerprint* (1964)

See also Eternity, Immortality.

## ❧ HELPLESSNESS

8 As helpless as a cat in paper shoes.

    Nancy Boyd, *Distressing Dialogues* (1924)

See also Vulnerability.

## ❧ HEREDITY

9 Whatever might be the truth about heredity, it was
immensely disturbing to be pressed upon by two
families, to discover, in their so different qualities,
the explanation of oneself.

    Dorothy M. Richardson, *Pilgrimage: Revolving Lights* (1923)

10 The cuckoo lays her eggs in any bird's nest; it may
be hatched among blackbirds or robins or
thrushes, but it is always a cuckoo. . . . A man cannot deliver himself from his ancestors.

    Amelia E. Barr, *The Belle of Bowling Green* (1904)

11 Heredity: the thing a child gets from the other side
of the family.

    Marcelene Cox, in *Ladies' Home Journal* (1946)

See also Essence, Identity, Nature/Nurture.

## ❧ HEROES

12 Blessed is the match consumed / in kindling flame.

    Hannah Senesh, "Blessed Is the Match" (1944), *Hannah
    Senesh* (1966)

13 Heroes take journeys, confront dragons, and discover the treasure of their true selves.

    Carol Pearson, *The Hero Within* (1986)

14 There are stars whose radiance is visible on earth
though they have long been extinct. There are people whose brilliance continues to light the world
though they are no longer among the living. These
lights are particularly bright when the night is dark.

    Hannah Senesh (1940), *Hannah Senesh* (1966)

15 Even in the darkest of times we have the right to
expect some illumination. . . . Such illumination
may well come less from theories and concepts
than from the uncertain, flickering, and often weak
light that some men and women, in their lives and
their works, will kindle under almost all circumstances and shed over the time-span that was given
them on earth.

    Hannah Arendt, *Men in Dark Times* (1968)

16 We agreed that great men and women should be
forced to live as long as possible. The reverence

they enjoyed was a life sentence, which they could neither revoke nor modify.

Maya Angelou, *All God's Children Need Traveling Shoes* (1986)

1 The historian who finds the human being more interesting than what the human being has done must inevitably endow the comparatively few individuals he can identify with too great an importance in relation to their time. Even so, I prefer this overestimate to the opposite method which treats developments as though they were the massive anonymous waves of an unhuman sea or pulverizes the fallible surviving records of human life into the gray dust of statistics.

C.V. Wedgwood, *Velvet Studies* (1946)

2 I am my own heroine.

Marie Bashkirtseff (1874), *Journal* (1887)

3 The law has no power over heroes.

Charlotte Lennox, *The Female Quixote* (1752)

4 Most American heroes of the Revolutionary period are by now two men, the actual man and the romantic image. Some are even three men—the actual man, the image, and the debunked remains.

Esther Forbes, *Paul Revere and the World He Lived In* (1942)

5 When folk tell me of this great man and that great man, I think to myself. Who was stinted of joy for his glory? How many old folk and children did his coach wheels go over? What bridal lacked his song, and what mourner his tears, that he found time to climb so high?

Mary Webb, *Precious Bane* (1924)

6 No man is a hero to his valet.

Anne-Marie Bigot de Cornuel, in Mademoiselle Aïssé, *Lettres* (1728)

See also Hero-Worship, Saints.

## ♦ HERO-WORSHIP

7 There are spines to which the immobility of worship is not a strain.

Edith Wharton, "The Angel at the Grave," *Crucial Instances* (1901)

See also Admiration, Idols.

## ♦ HESITATION

8 He who hesitates is last.

Mae West, in Joseph Weintraub, ed., *The Wit and Wisdom of Mae West* (1967)

## ♦ HIDING

9 Hiding leads nowhere except to more hiding.

Margaret A. Robinson, *A Woman of Her Tribe* (1990)

10 Let us not fear the hidden. Or each other.

Muriel Rukeyser, "Letter to the Front," *Beast in View* (1944)

11 What I have found is, anything one keeps hidden should now and then be hidden somewhere else.

Elizabeth Bowen, *The Death of the Heart* (1938)

12 I wonder why we are always sort of ashamed of our best parts and try to hide them. We don't mind ridicule of our "sillinesses" but of our "sobers."

Emily Carr, *Hundreds and Thousands* (1966)

See also Concealment, Secrets.

## ♦ HIGHWAYS

13 The shortest distance between two points is under construction.

Noelie Alito, in *Omni* (1979)

14 Once you provide a super-route, you do not just speed the already stuck cars and trucks on their way, you acquire a lot of new traffic.

Ada Louise Huxtable, in *The New York Times* (1969)

15 The freeway is the last frontier. It is unsurpassed as a training ground for the sharpening of survival skills.

Sheila Ballantyne, *Norma Jean the Termite Queen* (1975)

16 The superhighway is our true sacrificial altar.

Jessamyn West, *Hide and Seek* (1973)

## ❧ HILLS

1 Green hills be walls / Forever shaping us.
   Dorothy Livesay, "Autumn in Wales," *Poems for People* (1947)

2 My hills are like great angels, / Whose wide wings sweep the stars.
   Katharine Tynan, "The Irish Hills," *Shamrocks* (1887)

3 The hills are going somewhere; / They have been on the way a long time. / They are like camels in a line / But they move more slowly.
   Hilda Conkling, "Hills," *Poems by a Little Girl* (1920)

See also Mountains.

## ❧ HINDSIGHT

4 "One might have seen it with half an eye from the beginning." Mrs. Thornbrugh had not seen it with two eyes, as we know, till it was pointed out to her; but her imagination worked with equal liveliness backwards or forwards.
   Mrs. Humphry Ward, *Robert Elsmere* (1888)

5 There is no wisdom equal to that which comes after the event.
   Geraldine Jewsbury, *Zoë*, vol. 1 (1845)

6 The wisdom of hindsight, so useful to historians and indeed to authors of memoirs, is sadly denied to practicing politicians.
   Margaret Thatcher, *The Downing Street Years* (1993)

7 We didn't know it at the time. Prouty said afterwards he did, but Prouty's a man who knows everything after the fact. That's being an undertaker I dare say.
   Dorothy Salisbury Davis, "By the Scruff of the Soul," in *Ellery Queen's Mystery Magazine* (1963)

## ❧ HISTORY

8 History is an agreed-upon fiction.
   Diane Ackerman, *A Natural History of Love* (1994)

9 History is the study of lies, anyway, because no witness ever recalls events with total accuracy, not even eyewitnesses.
   Nancy Pickard, *Bum Steer* (1990)

10 It is sometimes very hard to tell the difference between history and the smell of skunk.
   Rebecca West, *Black Lamb and Grey Falcon* (1941)

11 History is an illogical record. It hinges on nothing. It is a story that changes and has accidents and recovers with scars.
   Gretel Ehrlich, *Heart Mountain* (1988)

12 That pious fiction we call history.
   Diane Ackerman, *The Moon by Whale Light* (1991)

13 History's like a story in a way: it depends on who's telling it.
   Dorothy Salisbury Davis, "By the Scruff of the Soul," in *Ellery Queen's Mystery Magazine* (1963)

14 There is no such thing as a neutral or purely objective historian. Without an opinion a historian would be simply a ticking clock, and unreadable besides.
   Barbara W. Tuchman, "Can History Be Served Up Hot?" in *The New York Times Book Review* (1964)

15 My own varying estimates of the facts themselves, as the years passed, showed me too clearly how much of history must always rest in the eye of the beholder; our deductions are so often different it is impossible they should always be right.
   C.V. Wedgwood, *Velvet Studies* (1946)

16 History moves in contradictory waves, not in straight lines.
   Lois Beck and Nikki Keddie, *Women in the Muslim World* (1978)

17 How is one to say exactly where history begins or ends? It is all slow oscillations, curves, and waves which take so long to reveal themselves . . . like watching a tree grow.
   Gretel Ehrlich, *Heart Mountain* (1988)

18 History, like nature, has its own economy, its own balancing of forces in the final accounting. Nothing can be lost, except to awareness.
   Helen Foster Snow, *My China Years* (1984)

19 History, in spite of the occasional protest of historians, will always be used in a general way as a collection of political and moral precedents.
   C.V. Wedgwood, *Velvet Studies* (1946)

20 History is a stern judge.
   Svetlana Alliluyeva, *Twenty Letters to a Friend* (1967)

1 History . . . isn't simply what has happened. It's a judgment on what has happened.

Cynthia Ozick, *Trust* (1966)

2 Somewhere about the eighteenth century, history tacitly replaced religion as the school of public morals.

C.V. Wedgwood, *Velvet Studies* (1946)

3 All history, of course, is the history of wars.

Penelope Lively, *Moon Tiger* (1987)

4 I have noticed that as soon as you have soldiers the story is called history. Before their arrival it is called myth, folktale, legend, fairy tale, oral poetry, ethnography. After the soldiers arrive, it is called history.

Paula Gunn Allen, in Judy Grahn, *Queen of Wands* (1982)

5 History . . . it's what those bitter old men write.

Jacqueline Kennedy Onassis (1963), in Theodore H. White, *In Search of History* (1978)

6 The history of every country begins in the heart of a man or a woman.

Willa Cather, *O Pioneers!* (1913)

7 The history of one is the history of all.

Grace King, "La Grande Demoiselle," *Balcony Stories* (1892)

8 There is no life that does not contribute to history.

Dorothy West, *The Living Is Easy* (1948)

9 If every nation gets the government it deserves, every generation writes the history which corresponds with its view of the world.

Elizabeth Janeway, *Between Myth and Morning* (1974)

10 The perpetual stream of human nature is formed into ever-changing shallows, eddies, falls and pools by the land over which it passes. Perhaps the only real value of history lies in considering this endlessly varied play between the essence and the accidents.

Mary Renault, *The Mask of Apollo* (1966)

11 History, despite its wrenching pain, / Cannot be unlived, and if faced / With courage, need not be lived again.

Maya Angelou, "On the Pulse of Morning," presidential inauguration poem (1993)

12 Within the limits of the modern nation, history tends to repeat itself by a process of almost deliber-

ate imitation. We know what to expect of ourselves and, by expecting, do it.

C.V. Wedgwood, *Velvet Studies* (1946)

13 If we do not know our own history, we are doomed to live it as though it were our private fate.

Hannah Arendt, in Carolyn Heilbrun, *Writing a Woman's Life* (1988)

14 Very often history is a means of denying the past.

Jeanette Winterson, *Oranges Are Not the Only Fruit* (1985)

15 Historical research of the truly scholastic kind is not connected with human beings at all. It is a pure study, like higher mathematics.

C.V. Wedgwood, *Velvet Studies* (1946)

16 Written history is, in fact, nothing of the kind; it is the fragmentary record of the often inexplicable actions of innumerable bewildered human beings, set down and interpreted according to their own limitations by other human beings, equally bewildered. The tribunal of history judges about as fairly as an average bench of magistrates; which is exactly what it is.

C.V. Wedgwood, *Velvet Studies* (1946)

17 I learned a history not then written in books but one passed from generation to generation on the steps of moonlit porches and beside dying fires in one-room houses, a history of great-grandparents and of slavery and of the days following slavery; of those who lived still not free, yet who would not let their spirits be enslaved.

Mildred D. Taylor, *Roll of Thunder, Hear My Cry* (1976)

18 If history is really relevant in today's world, the proposition doesn't command much respect. Perhaps the past is a different country, but if so no one much wants to travel there.

Elizabeth Janeway, *Improper Behavior* (1987)

19 History is, in its essence, exciting; to present it as dull is, to my mind, stark and unforgivable misrepresentation.

Catherine Drinker Bowen, *The Writing of Biography* (1951)

20 History . . . a sort of immortality turned upside down. Her life stretched backwards through ten centuries.

Princess Marthe Bibesco, *Catherine-Paris* (1928)

21 It is the winners who write history—their way.

Elaine Pagels, *The Gnostic Gospels* (1979)

1 Not only is history *written* by the winners, it is also made by them.
   Elisabeth Schüssler Fiorenza, *In Memory of Her* (1983)

2 When I read about some important moment or era in history, I always take it for granted that the people it happened to were aware of what was going on. In my mind's eye, I see the agricultural workers of England during the Industrial Revolution feeling the pinch and saying to each other, "Eh, lad," or whatever agricultural workers would say in those days, "what dost tha expect? It's this Industrial Revolution at the bottom of it."
   Emily Hahn, *Times and Places* (1970)

3 History is not truth versus falsehoods, but a mixture of both, a mélange of tendencies, reactions, dreams, errors, and power plays. What's important is what we make of it; its moral use. By writing history, we can widen readers' thinking and deepen their sympathies in every direction. Perhaps history should show us not how to control the world, but how to enlarge, deepen, and discipline ourselves.
   Gretel Ehrlich, *Heart Mountain* (1988)

4 History as a discipline can be characterized as having a collective forgetfulness about women.
   Clarice Stasz Stoll, *Female and Male* (1974)

5 Each feminist work has tended to be received as if it emerged from nowhere; as if each one of us had lived, thought, and worked without any historical past or contextual present. This is one of the ways in which women's work and thinking has been made to seem sporadic, errant, orphaned of any tradition of its own.
   Adrienne Rich, *On Lies, Secrets, and Silence* (1979)

6 For centuries women have been saying many of the things we are saying today and which we have often thought of as new.
   Dale Spender, *Women of Ideas and What Men Have Done to Them* (1982)

7 If women, though, had written all those books, / I know that they would read quite differently, / For well do women know the blame is wrong. / The parts are not apportioned equally, / Because the strongest take the largest cut / And he who slices it can keep the best.
   Christine de Pisan, "Letter of the God of Love" (1399), in Thelma S. Fenster and Mary Carpenter Erler, eds., *Poems of Cupid, God of Love* (1990)

8 The volumes which record the history of the human race are filled with the deeds and the words of great men . . . [but] The Twentieth Century Woman . . . questions the completeness of the story.
   Mary Ritter Beard, "The Twentieth-Century Woman Looking Around and Backward," in *Young Oxford* (1900)

9 My heart turns to and fro, / In thinking what will the people say, / They who shall see my monument in after years, / And shall speak of what I have done.
   Queen Hatshepsut, "Speech of the Queen" (c. 1450 B.C.), in Margaret Busby, ed., *Daughters of Africa* (1992)

10 What his imagination is to the poet, facts are to the historian. His exercise of judgment comes in their selection, his art in their arrangement.
   Barbara W. Tuchman, "Can History Be Served Up Hot?" in *The New York Times Book Review* (1964)

11 Every historian discloses a new horizon.
   George Sand (1871), in Raphaël Ledos de Beaufort, ed., *Letters of George Sand* (1886)

12 Qualities absolutely necessary for a historian: (1) Imagination. (2) Prejudice. (3) The power of writing your own biography at the same time.
   Mary Coleridge (1893), in Theresa Whistler, ed., *The Collected Poems of Mary Coleridge* (1954)

13 A nation does not create the historians it deserves; the historians are far more likely to create the nation.
   C.V. Wedgwood, *Velvet Studies* (1946)

See also Ancestors, Anecdotes, Past.

## § HOBBIES

14 A hobby a day keeps the doldrums away.
   Phyllis McGinley, *A Pocketful of Wry* (1940)

15 It's the safety valve of middle life, and the solace of age.
   Mary Roberts Rinehart, *The Red Lamp* (1925)

16 Hobbies protect us from passions. *One* hobby becomes a passion.
   Marie von Ebner-Eschenbach, *Aphorisms* (1893)

See also Bridge, Camping, Chess, Collecting, Fishing, Gardening, Genealogy, Poker, Sewing, Sports.

## ❦ HOLINESS

1 Every day is a god, each day is a god, and holiness holds forth in time.
   Annie Dillard, *Holy the Firm* (1977)

2 What is holiness but wholeness?
   Stella Morton, *Shadow of Wings* (1941)

3 Who can order the Holy? It is like a rain forest, dripping, lush, fecund, wild. We enter its abundance at our peril, for here we are called to the wholeness for which we long, but which requires all we are and can hope to be.
   Marilyn Sewell, *Cries of the Spirit* (1991)

4 This kind of split makes me crazy, this territorializing of the holy. Here God may dwell. Here God may not dwell. It contradicts everything in my experience, which says: God dwells where I dwell. Period.
   Nancy Mairs, *Ordinary Time* (1993)

5 Holy persons draw to themselves all that is earthly.
   Hildegard of Bingen (1150), in Gabriele Uhlein, ed., *Meditations With Hildegard of Bingen* (1983)

6 True holiness consists in doing God's will with a smile.
   Mother Teresa, in Kathryn Spink, *For the Brotherhood of Man Under the Fatherhood of God* (1981)

7 Holiness is an infinite compassion for others.
   Ralph Iron, *The Story of an African Farm* (1883)

8 The root of sanctity is sanity. A man must be healthy before he can be holy. We bathe first, and then perfume.
   Anne-Sophie Swetchine, in Count de Falloux, ed., *The Writings of Madame Swetchine* (1869)

9 All our acts have sacramental possibilities.
   Freya Stark, "Greed," in *Time and Tide* (1951)

See also Divinity, God, Religion, Ritual, The Sacred, Saints, Spirituality, Theology.

## ❦ HOLLAND

10 There is not a richer or more carefully tilled garden spot in the whole world than this leaky, springy little country.
   Mary Mapes Dodge, *Hans Brinker* (1865)

11 No wonder the tulip is the patron flower of Holland. Looking at it one almost smells fresh paint laid on in generous brilliance: doors, blinds, whole houses, canal boats, pails, farm wagons—all painted in greens, blues, reds, pinks, yellows.
   Elizabeth Coatsworth, *Personal Geography* (1976)

12 The entire country is a kind of saturated sponge.
   Mary Mapes Dodge, *Hans Brinker* (1865)

See also Europe.

## ❦ HOLLYWOOD

13 Every country gets the circus it deserves. Spain gets bullfights. Italy gets the Catholic Church. America gets Hollywood.
   Erica Jong, *How to Save Your Own Life* (1977)

14 America's greatest achievement.
   Camille Paglia, in Camille Paglia and Stewart Brand, "Hollywood: America's Greatest Achievement," *The Utne Reader* (1994)

15 Hollywood—an emotional Detroit.
   Lillian Gish, in K. Madsen Roth, ed., *Hollywood Wits* (1995)

16 Where is Hollywood located? Chiefly between the ears. In that part of the American brain lately vacated by God.
   Erica Jong, *How to Save Your Own Life* (1977)

17 Hollywood isn't a place, it's a way of life.
   Helene Hanff, *Q's Legacy* (1985)

18 To survive there, you need the ambition of a Latin-American revolutionary, the ego of a grand opera tenor, and the physical stamina of a cow pony.
   Billie Burke (1931), in Leslie Halliwell, *The Filmgoer's Book of Quotes* (1973)

19 Hollywood is the only place on earth that has more vampires, more undead, more resurrections than a month of Easter Sundays.
   Roseanne Arnold, *My Lives* (1994)

20 People in the land of LaLa look like expensive wax fruit. And they work hard to achieve that look.
   Erica Jong, *Serenissima* (1987)

1 It looks, it feels, as though it had been invented by a Sixth Avenue peepshow man.

Ethel Barrymore, in Leslie Halliwell, *The Filmgoer's Book of Quotes* (1973)

2 Hollywood's a place where they'll pay you a thousand dollars for a kiss, and fifty cents for your soul.

Marilyn Monroe, in John Robert Colombo, *Popcorn in Paradise* (1979)

3 With a mental equipment which allows me to tell the difference between hot and cold, I stand out in this community like a modern day Cicero.

Anita Loos, *No Mother to Guide Her* (1961)

4 Hollywood is no place for a woman to find a husband, especially her own.

Denise Darcel, in John Robert Colombo, *Popcorn in Paradise* (1979)

5 No one has a closest friend in Hollywood.

Sheilah Graham, *The Rest of the Story* (1964)

6 The early symptoms of the disease, which break out almost on arrival in Hollywood, are a sense of exaggerated self-importance and self-centeredness which naturally alienates all old friends. Next comes a great desire for and belief in the importance of money above all else, a loss of the normal sense of humor and proportion and finally, in extreme cases, the abandonment of all previous standards of moral value.

Elinor Glyn (1922), in Anthony Glyn, *Elinor Glyn* (1955)

7 Hollywood always had a streak of the totalitarian in just about everything it did. The old moguls were essentially hard-fisted authoritarians who had created a system of linked dictatorships to control the creative people. We were supposed to be the children; mad, tempestuous, brilliant, talented, not terribly smart children.

Shirley MacLaine, *You Can Get There From Here* (1975)

8 Hollywood was like a mouse being followed by a cat called television.

Mae West, *Goodness Had Nothing to Do With It!* (1959)

9 In Hollywood, primitive magical thinking exists side by side with the most advanced technology.

Hortense Powdermaker, *Hollywood, The Dream Factory* (1950)

10 The bite of existence did not cut into one in Hollywood. . . . Life elsewhere was real and slippery and struggled in the arms like a big fish dying in air.

Mae West, *Goodness Had Nothing to Do With It!* (1959)

11 Who do I have to sleep with to get *out* of this picture?

Anonymous actor, in Carolyn Kenmore, *Mannequin* (1969)

12 Smart writers never understand why their satires on our town are never successful. What they refuse to accept is that you can't satirize a satire.

Hedda Hopper, *From Under My Hat* (1952)

13 Writers who go to Hollywood still follow the classic pattern: either you get disgusted by "them" and you leave or you want the money and you become them.

Pauline Kael, *Deeper Into Movies* (1973)

14 The convictions of Hollywood and television are made of boiled money.

Lillian Hellman, *An Unfinished Woman* (1969)

15 Sure, you make money writing on the coast . . . but that money is like so much compressed snow. It goes so fast it melts in your hand.

Dorothy Parker (1953), in John Keats, *You Might As Well Live* (1970)

16 No matter what you say about the town, and anything you say probably is true, there's never been another like it.

Hedda Hopper, *From Under My Hat* (1952)

See also Acting, California, Celebrity, Entertainment, Films, Los Angeles, Show Business.

## ♦ HOLOCAUST

17 The stench of human wreckage in which the Nazi regime finally sank down to defeat has been the most shocking fact of modern times.

Janet Flanner ("Genêt"), *Paris Journal 1944-1965* (1965)

18 O the chimneys / On the ingeniously devised habitations of death / When Israel's body drifted as smoke / Through the air.

Nelly Sachs, title poem, *O the Chimneys* (1967)

1 World, do not ask those snatched from death / where they are going, / they are always going to their graves.

> Nelly Sachs, "World, Do Not Ask Those Snatched From Death," *O the Chimneys* (1967)

## ❧ HOME

2 Home, home, / Strayed ones home, / Rabbit to burrow / Fox to earth, / Mouse to the wainscot, / Rat to the barn, / Cattle to the byre, / Dog to the hearth, / All beasts home!

> Kathleen Raine, "Spell to Bring Lost Creatures Home," *The Year One* (1953)

3 Ah! there is nothing like staying at home, for real comfort.

> Jane Austen, *Emma* (1816)

4 The ideal of happiness has always taken material form in the house, whether cottage or castle; it stands for permanence and separation from the world.

> Simone de Beauvoir, *The Second Sex* (1949)

5 There is probably no thrill in life to compare with that of turning the key in one's first house or apartment.

> Belle Livingstone, *Belle Out of Order* (1959)

6 I don't know exactly why the notion of homeownership has such a grasp on the American imagination. Perhaps as descendants of landless immigrants we turn our plots into symbols of stability.

> Ellen Goodman, *Close to Home* (1979)

7 "Home" is any four walls that enclose the right person.

> Helen Rowland, *Reflections of a Bachelor Girl* (1909)

8 A house is no home unless it contain food and fire for the mind as well as for the body.

> Margaret Fuller, *Woman in the Nineteenth Century* (1845)

9 Home. It's being new and old all rolled into one. Measuring your new against old friends, old ways, old places. Knowing that as long as the old survives, you can keep changing as much as you want without the nightmare of waking up to a total stranger.

> Gloria Naylor, *Mama Day* (1988)

10 Home can never be transferred; never repeated in the experience of an individual. The place consecrated by parental love, by the innocence and sports of childhood, by the first acquaintance with nature; by the linking of the heart to the visible creation, is the only home.

> C.M. Sedgwick, *Hope Leslie* (1827)

11 Peace—that was the other name for home.

> Kathleen Norris, *Belle-Mère* (1931)

12 One's own surroundings means so much to one, when one is feeling miserable.

> Edith Sitwell, in John Lehmann and Derek Parker, eds., *Selected Letters* (1970)

13 There are homes you run from, and homes you run to.

> Laura Cunningham, *Sleeping Arrangements* (1989)

14 I had to leave home so I could find myself, find my own intrinsic nature buried under the personality that had been imposed on me.

> Gloria Anzaldúa, *Borderlands/La Frontera* (1987)

15 Home, as far as I'm concerned, is the place you have to leave. And then, if you're like me, spend the rest of your life mourning.

> Paulette Bates Alden, in *The Hungry Mind Review* (1993)

16 Don't you know you can't go home again?

> Ella Winter, to Thomas Wolfe who asked to use the expression as a book title (1937), *And Not to Yield* (1963)

17 You can never go home again, but the truth is you can never leave home, so it's all right.

> Maya Angelou, in Jackie Kay, "The Maya Character," *Marxism Today* (1987)

18 I was convinced you can't go home again. Now I know better. Nothing is more untrue. I know you go back over and over again, seeking the self you left behind.

> Helen Bevington, *The House Was Quiet and the World Was Calm* (1971)

19 A democratic home is the foundation of a democratic state.

> Agnes E. Benedict and Adele Franklin, *The Happy Home* (1948)

20 Giving up her home had been a much greater wrench than she had expected. . . . She had a curious sense of her own roots twined around the house, as she had once seen a tree's roots around an old shrine. In time the roots had grown into

every crevice until shrine and tree were one indestructible entity.

Alice Tisdale Hobart, *The Peacock Sheds His Tail* (1945)

1 Sweet is the hour that brings us home, / Where all
will spring to meet us; / Where hands are striving,
as we come, / To be the first to greet us.

Eliza Cook, "The Welcome Back," *The Poetical Works of
Eliza Cook* (1848)

2 My prairie people are my home / Bird I return
flying to their breasts.

Meridel Le Sueur, "Offer Me Refuge," *Rites of Ancient
Ripening* (1975)

3 As I listened to my Anishinabe friends, it came to
me that "home" is a figment in the traveler's mind,
a place where one's language fits and references
make sense. I can own this place only in my imagination.

Joanne Hart, with Hazel Belvo, *Witch Tree* (1992)

4 I have no home but me.

Anne Truitt, *Daybook* (1982)

See also Familiarity, Family, "Family Values,"
Homeland, Houses, Interior Decoration, Places,
Returning, Roots.

## ❧ HOMELAND

5 Magical country, full of memories and dreams, /
My youth lies in the crevices of your hills; / Here in
the silk of your grass by the edge of the meadows, /
Every flower and leaf has its memories of you.

Katharine Tynan Hinkson, "The Old Country," *Collected
Poems* (1930)

See also Roots.

## ❧ HOMELESSNESS

6 In most of the traditional cultures of the world,
homelessness would be impossible; first because of
large protective kin systems, and second because
homes were easily constructed from materials at
hand. In America today we consider homelessness

as a lack of shelter, not as a breakdown of community.

Lynn Maria Laitala, "In the Aftermath of Empire," in *The
Finnish American Reporter* (1992)

7 People who are homeless are not social inade-
quates. They are people without houses.

Sheila McKechnie, in *The Christian Science Monitor* (1985)

8 From my family I have learned the secrets / of never
having a home.

Linda Hogan, "Heritage," *Calling Myself Home* (1978)

9 My address is like my shoes: it travels with me.

Mother Jones, in Mary Field Parton, *The Autobiography of
Mother Jones* (1925)

10 For the homeless all ways wither / like cut flowers.

Nelly Sachs, "World, Do Not Ask Those Snatched From
Death," *O the Chimneys* (1967)

See also Poverty.

## ❧ HONESTY

11 Nobody can boast of honesty till they are tried.

Susannah Centlivre, *The Perplex'd Lovers* (1712)

12 He is only honest who is not discovered.

Susannah Centlivre, *The Artifice* (1722)

13 "Honesty" without compassion and understanding
is not honesty, but subtle hostility.

Rose N. Franzblau, in *New York Post* (1966)

14 We may argue eloquently that "Honesty is the best
Policy"—unfortunately, the moment honesty is
adopted for the sake of policy it mysteriously ceases
to be honesty.

Dorothy L. Sayers, "The Other Six Deadly Sins," *Creed or
Chaos?* (1949)

15 Honesty dies in selling itself.

George Sand, *Mauprat* (1837)

16 What is more arrogant than honesty?

Ursula K. Le Guin, *The Left Hand of Darkness* (1969)

17 I liked the store detective who said he'd seen a lot
of people who were so confused that they'd stolen
things, but never one so confused that they'd paid
twice.

Baroness Phillips, in *The Sunday Telegraph* (1977)

See also Detection, Dishonesty, Frankness, Integrity, Sincerity, Truth, Virtue.

## ∮ HONG KONG

1 Hong Kong is the supermarket of Asia.
   Eleanor Coppola, *Notes* (1979)

## ∮ HONOR

2 Honor wears different coats to different eyes.
   Barbara W. Tuchman, *The Guns of August* (1962)

3 To mention honor was to suggest its opposite.
   Dorothy L. Sayers, *Gaudy Night* (1935)

See also Courage, Integrity, Reputation, Virtue.

## ∮ HOPE

4 "Hope" is the thing with feathers — / That perches in the soul — / And sings the tune without the words — / And never stops at all.
   Emily Dickinson (1861), in T.W. Higginson and Mabel Loomis Todd, eds., *Poems by Emily Dickinson*, 2nd series (1891)

5 Hope is a song in a weary throat.
   Pauli Murray, title poem, *Dark Testament* (1970)

6 Hope is a strange invention — / A Patent of the Heart — / In unremitting action / Yet never wearing out.
   Emily Dickinson (1877), in Thomas H. Johnson, ed., *The Complete Poems of Emily Dickinson* (1960)

7 Music played in the resurrection ashes.
   Nelly Sachs, "Night of Nights," *O the Chimneys* (1967)

8 And, through and over everything, / A sense of glad awakening.
   Edna St. Vincent Millay, title poem, *Renascence* (1917)

9 How many glorious structures we had raised / Upon Hope's sandy basis!
   L.E. Landon, "St. George's Hospital," *The Improvisatrice* (1824)

10 We give birth to others / by believing in that first, small spark of life / the spark we can barely see. / It is called hope. / It is immensely helpful / at birth.
   Macrina Wiederkehr, *Seasons of Your Heart* (1979)

11 A comforting acquaintance, hope, a contagious thing like spring, inebriating like lager.
   Sylvia Ashton-Warner (1942), *Myself* (1967)

12 Hope . . . is not a feeling; it is something you do.
   Katherine Paterson, in *The Horn Book* (1992)

13 Hope is a talent like any other.
   Storm Jameson, *Journey From the North*, vol. 2 (1970)

14 Hope is a very unruly emotion.
   Gloria Steinem, *Outrageous Acts and Everyday Rebellions* (1983)

15 Hope does not necessarily have to take an object.
   Gail Goodwin, *The Odd Woman* (1974)

16 Hope is the feeling we have that the feeling we have is not permanent.
   Mignon McLaughlin, *The Neurotic's Notebook* (1963)

17 The very least you can do in your life is to figure out what you hope for. And the most you can do is live inside that hope.
   Barbara Kingsolver, *Animal Dreams* (1990)

18 To hope for Paradise is to live in Paradise, a very different thing from actually getting there.
   Vita Sackville-West, *Passenger to Teheran* (1926)

19 Hope costs nothing.
   Colette, *Claudine at School* (1900)

20 There never was night that had no morn.
   Dinah Maria Mulock Craik, "The Golden Gate," *Mulock's Poems, New and Old* (1880)

21 The longest day must have its close,—the gloomiest night will wear on to a morning. An eternal, inexorable lapse of moments is ever hurrying the day of the evil to an eternal night, and the night of the just to an eternal day.
   Harriet Beecher Stowe, *Uncle Tom's Cabin* (1852)

22 Though the morning seems to linger / O'er the hill-tops far away, / Yet the shadows bear the promise / Of a brighter coming day.
   Frances Ellen Watkins Harper, *Iola Leroy* (1892)

23 Every life has a death, and every light a shadow. Be content to stand in the light, and let the shadow fall where it will.
   Mary Stewart, *The Hollow Hills* (1973)

24 Th' longest lane will have a turning.
   Elizabeth Gaskell, *Mary Barton* (1848)

1 It's a long old road, but I know I'm gonna find the end.

> Bessie Smith, "Long Old Road" (1931), in Chris Albertson, *Bessie* (1972)

2 How poor and disheartening a thing is experience compared with hope!

> Vita Sackville-West, "The Garden in October," *Country Notes* (1940)

3 We must always live in hope; without that consolation there would be no living.

> Marie de Rabutin-Chantal, Marquise de Sévigné (1671), *Letters of Madame de Sévigné to Her Daughter and Her Friends*, vol. 1 (1811)

4 When hope is taken away from a people moral degeneration follows swiftly after.

> Pearl S. Buck, in *The New York Times* (1941)

5 Take hope from the heart of man, and you make him a beast of prey.

> Ouida, *Wisdom, Wit and Pathos* (1884)

6 To eat bread without hope is still slowly to starve to death.

> Pearl S. Buck, *To My Daughters, With Love* (1967)

7 Whenever hope and illusion become the source of the will to live, all knowledge of reality becomes highly threatening, since at any time a new piece of information might remove the grounds for this hope. This is exactly the case now. When life is motivated by hope for improvement, denial of reality is necessarily renewed and fortified.

> Christina Thürmer-Rohr, *Vagabonding* (1991)

8 Hope is slowly extinguished and quickly revived.

> Sophia Lee, *The Recess* (1785)

9 Youth can never know the worst, she understood, because the worst that one can know is the end of expectancy.

> Ellen Glasgow, *Barren Ground* (1925)

10 The worst of my life is over, / I hope, / And may the best things, please, / come soon.

> Corazon C. Aquino, in Isabelo T. Crisostomo, *Cory* (1987)

11 Rage for the world as it is / but for what it may be / more love now than last year.

> Muriel Rukeyser, "This Place in the Ways," *The Green Wave* (1948)

12 We all hope for a—must I say the word—recipe, we all believe, however much we know we shouldn't, that maybe somebody's got that recipe and can show us how not to be sick, suffer and die.

> Nan Shin, *Diary of a Zen Nun* (1986)

See also Expectations, Faith, Optimism.

## ❦ HORSES

13 When Allah created the horse, he said to the wind, "I will that a creature proceed from thee. Condense thyself." And the wind condensed itself, and the result was the horse.

> Marguerite Henry, *King of the Wind* (1948)

14 Horses make a landscape look more beautiful.

> Alice Walker, book title (1979)

15 The horse, like Cary Grant, lends romance to any venture.

> Roberta Smoodin, in *The New York Times Magazine* (1993)

16 I'd kiss his glossy neck, stroke his mane and say "Darling, darling!" for he was a staid horse who allowed intimacies.

> Jean Rhys, *Smile Please* (1979)

17 They are more beautiful than anything in the world, kinetic sculptures, perfect form in motion.

> Kate Millett, *The Loony-Bin Trip* (1990)

18 I do feel that horses have faces—and feelings too.

> Alanna Knight, *Lament for Lost Lovers* (1973)

19 Our three horses are as unlike as three persons. Perhaps more so, since they don't read, listen to radio or TV. . . . They don't try to talk like Flicka, walk like Trigger, or eat like Silver.

> Jessamyn West, *To See the Dream* (1957)

20 Horses are predictably unpredictable.

> Loretta Gage, with Nancy Gage, *If Wishes Were Horses* (1992)

21 I still subscribe to the minority view that all horses are offensive weapons and not to be trusted a yard.

> M.M. Kaye, *The Sun in the Morning* (1990)

22 Charles loathed horses; which he held to be animals of an invincible stupidity, uncontrolled imagination, and faulty deduction.

> Josephine Tey, *Brat Farrar* (1950)

1 I saw him riding in the Row, clinging to his horse like a string of onions.

    Margot Asquith, *The Autobiography of Margot Asquith* (1923)

2 I was thrown off ignominiously. . . . I'm so stiff at this moment that if one wrote letters with one's legs, I couldn't write this.

    Virginia Woolf (1913), in Nigel Nicolson, ed., *The Letters of Virginia Woolf,* vol. 2 (1976)

3 I never ride horseback now because my sympathy with the under-dog is too keen. After we have a gone a few blocks, I always dismount and say to the horse: "We'll walk it together, old dear."

    Marie Dressler, *The Life Story of an Ugly Duckling* (1924)

4 No better story than a horse race has ever been written. It takes less time than the telling of it, is as irreversible as a meteor's plunge, as inevitable as death, and you can't ever know the outcome in advance.

    Shirley Abbott, *The Bookmaker's Daughter* (1991)

## ❦ HOSPITALITY

5 The feast had all the elements of perfection: good company, firelight, and appetite.

    Kathleen Norris, *Barberry Bush* (1927)

6 The test of being a good host is how well the departing guest likes himself.

    Marcelene Cox, in *Ladies' Home Journal* (1954)

7 The folks where we were stayin' were the old-fashioned hospitable kind; they didn't let you off till your jaws struck work and wouldn't wag no more.

    Laura E. Richards, *Up to Calvin's* (1910)

8 Me and my wife spent a month with friends in Tacoma . . . and honest! we hardly had our knives out of our mouths all the time we were there. They couldn't hardly let you stop eatin' to get your sleep.

    Laura E. Richards, *Up to Calvin's* (1910)

9 It is not the correct thing for the host to take advantage of the helpless position of his guests, and to retail to them all his old stories.

    Florence Howe Hall, *The Correct Thing* (1902)

10 Each time the need gripped her to give a dinner party for twelve, or an informal party for fifty, she filled a bag and took a bus to Regent's Park where, on the edge of the bird-decorated waters, she went on until her supplies ran out and her need to feed others was done.

    Doris Lessing, "A Year in Regent's Park," *Stories* (1979)

11 Denham felt the relief that follows unaccepted hospitality.

    Rose Macaulay, *Crewe Train* (1926)

See also Entertaining, Guests, Invitation, Parties, Visits.

## ❦ HOSPITALS

12 It may seem a strange principle to enunciate as the very first requirement in a Hospital that it should do the sick no harm. It is quite necessary nevertheless to lay down such a principle.

    Florence Nightingale, *Notes on Hospitals* (1859)

13 Hospitals are only an intermediate stage of civilization.

    Florence Nightingale, "Sick-Nursing and Health-Nursing" (1893), in Lucy Ridgely Seymer, *Selected Writings of Florence Nightingale* (1954)

14 It's like a convent, the hospital. You leave the world behind and take vows of poverty, chastity, obedience.

    Carolyn Wheat, "Life, for Short," in Marilyn Wallace, ed., *Sisters in Crime 4* (1991)

15 In hospitals there was no time off for good behavior.

    Josephine Tey, *The Daughter of Time* (1951)

16 A trip to the hospital is always a descent into the macabre. I have never trusted a place with shiny floors.

    Terry Tempest Williams, *Refuge* (1991)

17 Luke got up and followed him on tiptoes, trying to keep his shoes from making that unpleasant noise on the linoleum which fills the corridors of all the hospitals in the world.

    Vicki Baum, *Mortgage on Life* (1946)

1 Looking out of a hospital window is different from looking out of any other. Somehow you do not see outside.

> Carol Matthau, *Among the Porcupines* (1992)

2 Hospital rooms seem to have vastly more ceiling than any rooms people live in.

> Bertha Damon, *A Sense of Humus* (1943)

3 Hospitals, like airports and supermarkets, only pretend to be open nights and weekends.

> Molly Haskell, *Love and Other Infectious Diseases* (1990)

4 Doctors and nurses seemed to have been born and raised in the hospital, with only short punctuations of absenteeism for such things as schooling and marriage.

> Marjorie Kellogg, *Tell Me That You Love Me, Junie Moon* (1968)

5 The ultimate indignity is to be given a bedpan by a stranger who calls you by your first name.

> Maggie Kuhn, in *The Observer* (1978)

6 One of the most difficult things to contend with in a hospital is the assumption on the part of the staff that because you have lost your gall bladder you have also lost your mind.

> Jean Kerr, "Operation Operation," *Please Don't Eat the Daisies* (1957)

See also Doctors, Health Care, Illness, Medicine, Nurses, Surgery.

## ❧ HOTELS

7 Hotel life is about the same in every latitude.

> Fanny Fern, *Ruth Hall* (1854)

8 Great hotels have always been social ideas, flawless mirrors to the particular societies they service.

> Joan Didion, "In the Islands," *The White Album* (1979)

## ❧ HOUSES

9 I gave my love to the house forever. / I will come till I cannot come, I said, / And the house said, I will know.

> Louise Townsend Nicholl, "The House," *The Blood That Is Language* (1967)

10 It is a lamb of a house, a dove, a child, a dear kind woman of a house.

> Katharine Tynan, *The Wandering Years* (1922)

11 I am as susceptible to houses as some people are susceptible to other human beings. Twice in my life I have fallen in love with one. Each time it was as violent and fatal as falling in love with a human being.

> Katharine Butler Hathaway, *The Journals and Letters of the Little Locksmith* (1946)

12 A house can have integrity, just like a person.

> Ayn Rand, *The Fountainhead* (1943)

13 The house, while sound in wind and limb, was described as being of "no character." We didn't think then that it had anything but character, rather sinister perhaps, but definitely character.

> Margery Fish, *We Made a Garden* (1956)

14 A house that does not have one worn, comfy chair in it is soulless.

> May Sarton, *Journal of a Solitude* (1973)

15 Old houses, I thought, do not belong to people, ever, not really, people belong to them.

> Gladys Taber, *Stillmeadow Daybook* (1955)

16 A man builds a house in England with the expectation of living in it and leaving it to his children; while we shed our houses in America as easily as a snail does his shell.

> Harriet Beecher Stowe, in Catherine Gilbertson, *Harriet Beecher Stowe* (1937)

17 They're all made out of ticky-tacky, and they all look just the same.

> Malvina Reynolds, "Little Boxes" (1963)

18 To one of my intense inter-uterine nature there is no measuring the shock that the loss of a house can cause.

> Margaret Anderson, *My Thirty Years' War* (1930)

19 When you dwell in a house you mislike, you will look out of a window a deal more than those that are content with their dwelling.

> Mary Webb, *Precious Bane* (1924)

20 A house is not a home.

> Polly Adler, on her life as a madam, book title (1953)

See also Home, Housework, Interior Decoration, Rooms, Walls.

## & HOUSEWIFE

1 There is, I suppose, no occupation in the world which has an influence on the efficiency and happiness of the members of nearly all other occupations so continuous and so permeating as that of the working housewife and mother.

    Eleanor F. Rathbone, *The Disinherited Family* (1924)

2 To be a housewife is to be a member of a very peculiar occupation, one with characteristics like no other. The nature of the duties to be performed, the method of payment, the form of supervision, the tenure system, the "market" in which the "workers" find "jobs," and the physical hazards are all very different from the way things are in other occupations.

    Barbara Bergmann, *The Economic Emergence of Women* (1986)

3 No laborer in the world is expected to work for room, board, and love—except the housewife.

    Letty Cottin Pogrebin (1970), in Bob Chieger, *Was It Good for You, Too?* (1983)

4 I would be content being a housewife if I could find the kind of man who wouldn't treat me like one.

    Terry McMillan, *Waiting to Exhale* (1992)

5 A house does not need a wife any more than it does a husband.

    Charlotte Perkins Gilman, *The Home* (1903)

6 I . . . call myself a domestic goddess.

    Roseanne Barr, on her alternative to "housewife," in Susan Dworkin, "Roseanne Barr," *Ms.* (1987)

See also Domesticity, Housework, Wives.

## & HOUSEWORK

7 Housekeeping ain't no joke.

    Louisa May Alcott, *Little Women* (1868)

8 Of all hateful occupations, housekeeping is to my mind the most hateful.

    Hannah Whitall Smith (1905), in Logan Pearsall Smith, ed., *Philadelphia Quaker* (1950)

9 Domestic work is the most elementary form of labor. It is suitable for those with the intelligence of rabbits. All it requires is cleanliness, tidiness and quickness—not moral or intellectual qualities at all, but merely the outward and visible signs of health.

    Rebecca West, in *The Freewoman* (1912)

10 The worst thing about work in the house or home is that whatever you do it is destroyed, laid waste or eaten within twenty-four hours.

    Lady Hasluck, in Michèle Brown and Ann O'Connor, *Woman Talk*, vol. 1 (1984)

11 Few tasks are more like the torture of Sisyphus than housework, with its endless repetition: the clean becomes soiled, the soiled is made clean, over and over, day after day.

    Simone de Beauvoir, *The Second Sex* (1949)

12 Housekeeping is like being caught in a revolving door.

    Marcelene Cox, in *Ladies' Home Journal* (1944)

13 Invisible, repetitive, exhausting, unproductive, uncreative—these are the adjectives which most perfectly capture the nature of housework.

    Angela Davis, *Women, Race and Class* (1981)

14 Domestic work, is, after all, both tedious and repetitive, and it is not surprising that most women and all men avoid as much of it as possible.

    Mary Stocks, *My Commonplace Book* (1970)

15 I think housework is far more tiring and frightening than hunting is, no comparison, and yet after hunting we had eggs for tea and were made to rest for hours, but after housework people expect one to go on just as if nothing special had happened.

    Nancy Mitford, *The Pursuit of Love* (1945)

16 People can say what they like about the eternal verities, love and truth and so on, but nothing's as eternal as the dishes.

    Margaret Mahy, *The Catalogue of the Universe* (1985)

17 Damn all kitchens. May they burn to cinders, / the kitchens that steal our dreams, drain / our lives, eat our days. . . / For our children's sakes, / Let us destroy these lonely kitchens.

    Vimala, "The Kitchen," in Susie Tharu and K. Lalita, eds., *Women Writing in India* (1991)

18 The American home is getting dirtier. People have better things to do with their time than clean.

    Mary Ellen Pinkham, in *The New York Times* (1993)

1 Hatred of domestic work is a natural and admirable result of civilization. . . . The first thing a woman does when she gets a little money into her hands is to hire some other poor wretch to do her housework.

> Rebecca West, in *The Freewoman* (1912)

2 The ladies here probably exchanged looks which meant, "Men never know when things are dirty or not"; and the gentlemen perhaps thought each to himself, "Women will have their little nonsenses and needless cares."

> Jane Austen, *Emma* (1816)

3 They shared the chores of living as some couples do—she did most of the work and he appreciated it.

> Paula Gosling, *Backlash* (1989)

4 Housework's the hardest work in the world. That's why men won't do it.

> Edna Ferber, *So Big* (1924)

5 The average man has a carefully cultivated ignorance about household matters—from what to do with the crumbs to the grocer's telephone number—a sort of cheerful inefficiency which protects him.

> Crystal Eastman (1920), in Blanche Wiesen Cook, *Crystal Eastman on Women and Revolution* (1978)

6 A man's home is his castle, and his wife is the janitor.

> Lucille Kallen, *Out There, Somewhere* (1964)

7 A woman's work, from the time she gets up to the time she goes to bed, is as hard as a day at war, worse than a man's working day. . . . To men, women's work was like the rain-bringing clouds, or the rain itself. The task involved was carried out every day as regularly as sleep. So men were happy—men in the Middle Ages, men at the time of the Revolution, and men in 1986: everything in the garden was lovely.

> Marguerite Duras, *Practicalities* (1987)

8 Housework hassles go on, are never resolved, and will probably extend into the afterlife ("Why am I the one who takes the clouds to the dry cleaners?").

> Marni Jackson, *The Mother Zone* (1992)

9 Upstairs she lay awake and planned a new, heroic role for herself. She would expiate all her sins by sinking into domesticity. . . . She would put her lily hand down into sewerages and save him the trouble of lifting up the ooze and hairs and gray slime that resulted from their daily lives.

> Edna O'Brien, *Girls in Their Married Bliss* (1964)

10 The important thing about women today is, as they get older, they still keep house. It's one reason they don't die, but men die when they retire. Women just polish the teacups.

> Margaret Mead, in Elizabeth Fishel, *Sisters* (1979)

11 The labor of women in the house, certainly, enables men to produce more wealth than they otherwise could; and in this way women are economic factors in society. But so are horses.

> Charlotte Perkins Gilman, *Women and Economics* (1900)

12 The unwaged condition of housework has been the most powerful weapon in reinforcing the common assumption that *housework is not work*, thus preventing women from struggling against it, except in the privatized kitchen-bedroom quarrel that all society agrees to ridicule, thereby further reducing the protagonist of a struggle. We are seen as nagging bitches, not workers in struggle.

> Silvia Federici, "Wages Against Housework" (1975), in Evelyn Shapiro and Barry M. Shapiro, *The Women Say/The Men Say* (1979)

13 No longer will we [women] agree to protect the hearth at the price of extinguishing the fire within ourselves.

> Celia Gilbert, in Sara Ruddick and Pamela Daniels, eds., *Working It Out* (1977)

14 At the worst, a house unkept cannot be so distressing as a life unlived.

> Rose Macaulay, "Problems of a Woman's Life," *A Casual Commentary* (1926)

15 If your house is really a mess and a stranger comes to the door, greet him with, "Who could have done this? We have no enemies."

> Phyllis Diller, *Phyllis Diller's Housekeeping Hints* (1966)

16 I have a friend who *loves* housework. Honest, she loves *all* housework. All day long she moves from one chore to the next, smiling the whole time. I went over there one day and begged her to tell me her secret. It's simple, she said, right after breakfast you light up a joint.

> Gabrielle Burton, "No One Has a Corner on Depression But Housewives Are Working on It" (1976), in Gloria Kaufman and Mary Kay Blakely, eds., *Pulling Our Own Strings* (1980)

1 I will clean house when Sears comes out with a riding vacuum cleaner.

> Roseanne Barr, in Susan Dworkin, "Roseanne Barr," *Ms.* (1987)

2 I buried a lot of my ironing in the back yard.

> Phyllis Diller (1954), in Barbara McDowell and Hana Umlauf, *Woman's Almanac* (1977)

3 I'm eighteen years behind on my ironing. There's no use doing it now, it doesn't fit anybody I know!

> Phyllis Diller, in Marjorie Holmes, *Love and Laughter* (1967)

4 I would rather lie on a sofa than sweep beneath it.

> Shirley Conran, *Superwoman* (1975)

5 Have you ever taken anything out of the clothes basket because it had become, relatively, the cleaner thing?

> Katharine Whitehorn, in *The Observer* (1964)

6 Cleaning your house / While your kids are still growing / Is like shoveling the walk / Before it stops snowing.

> Phyllis Diller, *Phyllis Diller's Housekeeping Hints* (1966)

See also Dirt, Domesticity, Work.

## ❦ HOW'S THAT AGAIN?

7 Pregnancy is difficult for women but it is even more difficult for men.

> Susan Cheever, *A Woman's Life* (1994)

8 My dear old friend King George V always told me he would never have died but for that vile doctor, Lord Dawson of Penn.

> Margot Asquith, in Mark Bonham Carter, ed., *The Autobiography of Margot Asquith* (1963)

9 I like a view but I like to sit with my back turned to it.

> Alice B. Toklas, in Elizabeth Sprigge, *Gertrude Stein* (1957)

10 My anti-liberal position should not be mistaken for conservatism.

> Camille Paglia, "Junk Bonds and Corporate Raiders: Academe in the Hour of the Wolf," *Sex, Art, and American Culture* (1992)

11 If it [rape] is a totally devastating psychological experience for a woman, then she doesn't have a proper attitude toward sex. It's this whole stupid feminist thing about how we are basically nurturing, benevolent people, and sex is a wonderful thing between two equals. With that kind of attitude, then of course rape is going to be a total violation of your entire life.

> Camille Paglia, "The Rape Debate, Continued," *Sex, Art, and American Culture* (1992)

12 You know what gets me sick and tired? The battered-woman motif. It's so misinterpreted. . . . Everyone knows throughout the world that many of these working-class relationships where women get beat up have hot sex. They ask why she won't leave him? Maybe she won't leave him because the sex is very hot. I say we should start looking at the battered-wife motif in terms of sex.

> Camille Paglia, "The Rape Debate, Continued," *Sex, Art, and American Culture* (1992)

13 It's patriarchal society that has freed me as a woman.

> Camille Paglia, *Sexual Personae* (1990)

14 Feminism, arguing from the milder women's view, completely misses the blood-lust in rape, the joy of violation and destruction.

> Camille Paglia, *Sexual Personae* (1990)

## ❦ HUMAN DIFFERENCES

15 I love *different* folks.

> Eleanor H. Porter, *Pollyanna* (1912)

16 All people are made alike. / They are made of bones, flesh and dinners. / Only the dinners are different.

> Gertrude Louise Cheney, "People," in A.K. Adams, *The Home Book of Humorous Quotations* (1969)

17 The plan of this world is infinite similarity and yet infinite variety.

> Dinah Maria Mulock Craik, title story, *The Little Lame Prince* (1875)

18 Give *your* difference, welcome *my* difference, unify *all* difference in the larger whole—such is the law of growth. The unifying of difference is the eternal process of life—the creative synthesis, the highest act of creation, the at-onement.

> M.P. Follett, *The New State* (1918)

1 The fact that we are human beings is infinitely more important than all the peculiarities that distinguish human beings from one another.

Simone de Beauvoir, *The Second Sex* (1949)

2 The crucial differences which distinguish human societies and human beings are not biological. They are cultural.

Ruth Benedict (1943), in Margaret Mead, *An Anthropologist at Work* (1959)

3 Society . . . is tolerant of crimes, and long suffering with dullness, but it shows no mercy to those who are different from other people.

Geraldine Jewsbury, *Zoë*, vol. 1 (1845)

4 There is nothing I should care more to do, if it were possible, than to rouse the imagination of men and women to a vision of human claims in those races of their fellow-men who most differ from them in customs and beliefs.

George Eliot, to Harriet Beecher Stowe (1876), in J.W. Cross, ed., *George Eliot's Life As Related in Her Letters and Journals* (1884)

5 Unity, not uniformity, must be our aim. We attain unity only through variety. Differences must be integrated, not annihilated, nor absorbed.

M.P. Follett, *The New State* (1918)

6 The ignoring of differences is the most fatal mistake in politics or industry or international life: every difference that is swept up into a bigger conception feeds and enriches society; every difference which is ignored feeds *on* society and eventually corrupts it.

M.P. Follett, *The New State* (1918)

7 When those closest to us respond to events differently than we do, when they seem to see the same scene as part of a different play, when they say things that we could not imagine saying in the same circumstances, the ground on which we stand seems to tremble and our footing is suddenly unsure.

Deborah Tannen, *You Just Don't Understand* (1990)

8 I have always noticed that people only think you are stupid if you do things differently from them.

Liza Cody, *Bucket Nut* (1993)

9 People are easier to control when they are all alike.

Lynn Maria Laitala, "In the Aftermath of Empire," in *The Finnish American Reporter* (1992)

10 It is not really difference the oppressor fears so much as similarity.

Cherríe Moraga, "La Güera," in Cherríe Moraga and Gloria Anzaldúa, eds., *This Bridge Called My Back* (1983)

11 Like and equal are two entirely different things.

Madeleine L'Engle, *A Wrinkle in Time* (1962)

12 Instead of being presented with stereotypes by age, sex, color, class, or religion, children must have the opportunity to learn that within each range, some people are loathsome and some are delightful.

Margaret Mead, *Twentieth Century Faith* (1972)

13 For some strange reason, we believe that anyone who lived before we were born was in some peculiar way a different kind of human being from any we have come in contact with in our own lifetime. This concept must be changed; we must realize in our bones that almost everything in time and history has changed *except* the human being.

Uta Hagen, with Haskel Frankel, *Respect for Acting* (1973)

14 There's a difference between exotic and *foreign*, isn't there? Exotic means you know how to use your foreignness, or you make yourself a little foreign in order to appear exotic. Real foreign is a little scary, believe me.

Bharati Mukherjee, "Fighting for the Rebound," *The Middleman* (1988)

15 It is only when the distinction is one of power or superiority that it is agreeable to find yourself different from the group.

Evelyn Scott, *Escapade* (1923)

16 There is no bleaker moment in the life of the city than that one which crosses the boundary lines between those who have not slept all night and those who are going to work. It was . . . as if two races of men and women lived on earth, the night people and the day people, never meeting face to face except at this moment.

Anaïs Nin, *A Spy in the House of Love* (1954)

17 One half of the world cannot understand the pleasures of the other.

Jane Austen, *Emma* (1816)

See also Anti-Semitism, Bigotry, Class, Difference, Discrimination, Diversity, Eccentricity, Exclusion, Human Nature, Individuality, Injustice, Minorities, Oppression, Prejudice, Racism, The Rich and the Poor, Sexism, Two Kinds of People.

## ❧ HUMAN FAMILY

1 Remember that you are all people and that all people are you.

Joy Harjo, "Remember," in Joseph Bruchac, ed., *Songs From This Earth on Turtle's Back* (1983)

2 We are all bound up together in one great bundle of humanity, and society cannot trample on the weakest and feeblest of its members without receiving the curse in its own soul.

Frances Ellen Watkins Harper, "We Are All Bound Up Together," in *Proceedings of the Eleventh Woman's Rights Convention* (1866)

3 We must stand together; if we don't, there will be no victory for any one of us.

Mother Jones, in Linda Atkinson, *Mother Jones* (1978)

4 I am an uncompromising pacifist. . . . I have no sense of nationalism, only a cosmic consciousness of belonging to the human family.

Rosika Schwimmer, citizenship hearing (1926), in Lillian Schlissel, ed., *Conscience in America* (1968)

5 Every frontier is doomed to produce an opposition beyond it. Nothing short of the universal can build the unfenced peace.

Freya Stark, *Ionia* (1954)

6 Few are the giants of the soul who actually feel that the human race is their family circle.

Elizabeth Wray Taylor, "Not Without Sentiment," in Jean Beaven Abernethy, ed., *Meditations for Women* (1947)

7 The method of moral hygiene as of physical hygiene is social coöperation. We do not walk into the Kingdom of Heaven one by one.

M.P. Follett, *The New State* (1918)

8 Today, as never before, the fates of men are so intimately linked to one another that a disaster for one is a disaster for everybody.

Natalia Ginzburg, *The Little Virtues* (1962)

9 We have to face the fact that either all of us are going to die together or we are going to learn to live together and if we are to live together we have to talk.

Eleanor Roosevelt, in *The New York Times* (1960)

10 Humanity finds itself in the midst of the world. In the midst of all other creatures humanity is the most significant and yet the most dependent upon the others.

Hildegard of Bingen (1150), in Gabriele Uhlein, ed., *Meditations With Hildegard of Bingen* (1983)

11 There are no islands any more.

Edna St. Vincent Millay, poem title, *Make Bright the Arrows* (1940)

12 When half the world is still plagued by terror and distress, you stop guiltily sometimes in the midst of your house-laughter and wonder if you've a right to it. Ought *any* of us to laugh, until *all* of us can again, you ask yourself, sometimes.

Margaret Lee Runbeck, *Time for Each Other* (1944)

13 We do too little feel each others' pain; / We do relax too much the social chain / That binds us to each other.

L.E. Landon, "The Rose," *The Golden Violet* (1827)

14 If you're going to care about the fall of the sparrow you can't pick and choose who's going to be the sparrow. It's everybody.

Madeleine L'Engle, *The Arm of the Starfish* (1965)

15 Let's build bridges here and there / Or sometimes, just a spiral stair.

Georgia Douglas Johnson, "Interracial," in Langston Hughes and Arna Bontemps, eds., *The Poetry of the Negro 1746-1949* (1949)

16 When you make a world tolerable for yourself you make a world tolerable for others.

Anaïs Nin (1954), *The Diary of Anaïs Nin*, vol. 5 (1974)

17 We humans are herd animals of the monkey tribe, not natural individuals as lions are. Our individuality is partial and restless; the stream of consciousness that we call "I" is made of shifting elements that flow from our group and back to our group again. Always we seek to be ourselves and the herd together, not One against the herd.

Anna Louise Strong, *I Change Worlds* (1935)

18 We have believed—and we do believe now—that freedom is indivisible, that peace is indivisible, that economic prosperity is indivisible.

Indira Gandhi (1970), *Speeches and Writings* (1975)

19 Each person born into this world has a right to everything he needs. His right, however, is bound up with that of every other creature and gives him

no license to grab everything he can without allowing a share for others.

Dorothy Richards, with Hope Sawyer Buyukmihci,
*Beaversprite* (1977)

1 He had the uneasy manner of a man who is not among his own kind, and who has not seen enough of the world to feel that all people are in some sense his own kind.

Willa Cather, *The Song of the Lark* (1915)

2 A lady asked me why, on most occasions, I wore black. "Are you in mourning?" "Yes." "For whom are you in mourning?" "For the world."

Edith Sitwell, *Taken Care Of* (1965)

See also Civilization, Human Differences, Interdependence, Society.


## 🔊 HUMANITY

3 Behavior of such cunning cruelty that only a human being could have thought of or contrived it we call "inhuman," revealing thus some pathetic ideal standard for our species that survives all betrayals.

Rose Macaulay, "On Thinking Well of Ourselves," *A Casual Commentary* (1926)

4 The bloody Wolf, the Wolf does not pursue; / The Boar, though fierce, his Tusk will not embrue / In his own kind, Bears, not on Bears do prey: / Thou art then, Man, more savage far than they.

Anne Killigrew, "The Miseries of Man," *Poems by Mrs. Anne Killigrew* (1686)

5 Could anything be absurder than a man? The animal who knows everything about himself—except why he was born and the meaning of his unique life?

Storm Jameson, *Before the Crossing* (1947)

6 If the whole human race lay in one grave, the epitaph on its headstone might well be: "It seemed a good idea at the time."

Rebecca West, in *The New York Times* (1977)

See also Civilization, Evolution, Human Differences, Human Family, Human Nature, Interdependence, Society, Two Kinds of People.


## 🔊 HUMAN NATURE

7 Human nature is potentially aggressive and destructive and potentially orderly and constructive.

Margaret Mead, *And Keep Your Powder Dry* (1942)

8 Humans can learn to like anything, that's why we are such a successful species. You can drop humans anywhere and they'll thrive—only the rat does as well.

Jeannette Desor, in Ellen Ruppel Shell, "Chemists Whip Up a Tasty Mess of Artificial Flavors," *Smithsonian* (1986)

9 What is man, when you come to think upon him, but a minutely set, ingenious machine for turning, with infinite artfulness, the red wine of Shiraz into urine?

Isak Dinesen, "The Dreamers," *Seven Gothic Tales* (1934)

10 I liked human beings, but I did not love human nature.

Ellen Glasgow, *The Woman Within* (1954)

11 Poor human nature, what horrible crimes have been committed in thy name!

Emma Goldman, title essay, *Anarchism* (1910)

12 Human nature is largely something that has to be overcome.

Rita Rudner, *Naked Beneath My Clothes* (1992)

See also Human Differences, Humanity, Life, "Natural," Two Kinds of People.


## 🔊 HUMILIATION

13 Humiliation is a vast country of imprecise boundaries. If you think you're there, you are. The neurotic rule: when in doubt, go ahead and feel humiliated.

Mignon McLaughlin, *The Neurotic's Notebook* (1963)

14 Humiliation is a guest that only comes to those who have made ready his resting-place, and will give him a fair welcome.

Ouida, *Wisdom, Wit and Pathos* (1884)

See also Embarrassment, Shame.

## ✦ HUMILITY

1 Humility is attentive patience.
Simone Weil, *First and Last Notebooks* (1970)

2 Humility has its origin in an awareness of unworthiness, and sometimes too in a dazzled awareness of saintliness.
Colette, *Belles saisons* (1955)

3 Compassion directed to oneself is humility.
Simone Weil, *First and Last Notebooks* (1970)

4 It is easy to be humble when a greater is preferred; but when an inferior is lifted high above our heads, how can we bear it?
Constance Fenimore Woolson, *Anne* (1882)

5 Humility is like underwear, essential but indecent if it shows.
Helen Nielsen, in *Reader's Digest* (1959)

6 Humility is not my forte, and whenever I dwell for any length of time on my own shortcomings, they gradually begin to seem mild, harmless, rather engaging little things, not at all like the staring defects in other people's characters.
Margaret Halsey, *With Malice Toward Some* (1938)

7 The woman had a humble, cringing manner. Of course, she had discovered that, having neither money nor virtue, she had better be humble if she knew what was good for her.
Jean Rhys, *After Leaving Mr. Mackenzie* (1930)

8 The proud man can learn humility, but he will be proud of it.
Mignon McLaughlin, *The Neurotic's Notebook* (1963)

9 Don't be so humble—you're not that great.
Golda Meir, in Israel and Mary Shenker, eds., *As Good As Golda* (1970)

10 Humility is no substitute for a good personality.
Fran Lebowitz, *Metropolitan Life* (1978)

See also Modesty, Virtue.

## ✦ HUMOR

11 Humor is a rubber sword—it allows you to make a point without drawing blood.
Mary Hirsch, in *View From the Loft* (1994)

12 Jokes . . . are an act of assassination without a corpse, a moment of total annihilation that paradoxically makes anything possible.
Penelope Gilliatt, *To Wit* (1990)

13 Humor hardens the heart, at least to the point of sanity.
Agnes Repplier, "They Had Their Day," *Under Dispute* (1924)

14 I had thought, on starting this composition, that I should define what humor means to me. However, every time I tried to, I had to go and lie down with a cold wet cloth on my head.
Dorothy Parker, introduction to S.J. Perelman, *The Most of S.J. Perelman* (1958)

15 The thinkers of the world should by rights be guardians of the world's mirth.
Agnes Repplier, "The Gayety of Life," *Compromises* (1904)

16 Among animals, *one* has a sense of humor. / Humor saves a few steps, it saves years.
Marianne Moore, "The Pangolin," *What Are Years?* (1941)

17 Many true words are spoken in jest.
Dinah Maria Mulock Craik, *A Life for a Life* (1866)

18 The truth I do not dare to know / I muffle with a jest.
Emily Dickinson, in Mabel Loomis Todd and Millicent Todd Bingham, eds., *Bolts of Melody* (1945)

19 Humor tells you where the trouble is.
Louise Bernikow, *Alone in America* (1986)

20 Humor comes from self-confidence. There's an aggressive element to wit.
Rita Mae Brown, *Starting From Scratch* (1988)

21 There's a hell of a distance between wisecracking and wit. Wit has truth in it; wisecracking is simply calisthenics with words.
Dorothy Parker, in Malcolm Cowley, ed., *Writers at Work* (1958)

22 Don't try for wit. Settle for humor. You'll last longer.
Elsa Maxwell, *How to Do It* (1957)

23 The essence of humor is that it should be unexpected, that it should embody an element of surprise, that it should startle us out of that reasonable gravity which, after all, must be our habitual frame of mind.
Agnes Repplier, *Americans and Others* (1912)

1 Humor to me, Heaven help me, takes in many things. There must be courage; there must be no awe. There must be criticism, for humor, to my mind, is encapsulated in criticism. There must be a disciplined eye and a wild mind. There must be a magnificent disregard of your reader, for if he cannot follow you, there is nothing you can do about it.

Dorothy Parker, introduction to S.J. Perelman, *The Most of S.J. Perelman* (1958)

2 It is a difficult thing to like anybody's else ideas of being funny.

Gertrude Stein, *Everybody's Autobiography* (1937)

3 A difference of taste in jokes is a great strain on the affections.

George Eliot, *Daniel Deronda* (1874)

4 It's dreadful when two people's senses of humor are antagonistic. I don't believe there's any bridging that gulf!

Jean Webster, *Daddy-Long-Legs* (1912)

5 Ghetto humor is the social twin of fantasy; together they sustain the powerless, who accomplish miracles through illusion.

Sheila Ballantyne, *Norma Jean the Termite Queen* (1975)

6 Humor and satire are more effective techniques for expressing social statements than direct comment.

Kristin Hunter, in Claudia Tate, ed., *Black Women Writers at Work* (1983)

7 Humor distorts nothing, and only false gods are laughed off their earthly pedestals.

Agnes Repplier, *Points of View* (1891)

8 Exaggeration is the cheapest form of humor.

Elizabeth Peters, *Naked Once More* (1989)

9 Of all the band of personal traitors the sense of humor is the most dangerous.

Margery Allingham, *The Fashion in Shrouds* (1938)

10 How fatally the entire want of humor cripples the mind.

Alice James (1889), in Anna Robeson Burr, *Alice James* (1934)

11 Total absence of humor renders life impossible.

Colette, "Chance Acquaintances," *Gigi* (1952)

12 Humor is an antidote to isolation.

Elizabeth Janeway, *Improper Behavior* (1987)

13 Humor is the first of the gifts to perish in a foreign tongue.

Virginia Woolf, "On Not Knowing Greek," *The Common Reader*, 1st series (1925)

14 The announcement that you are going to tell a good story (and the chuckle that precedes it) is always a dangerous opening.

Margot Asquith, *More or Less About Myself* (1934)

15 Though her capacity for emotion was dead, some diabolical sense of humor had sprung up like fireweed from the ruins. She could laugh at everything now, but it was ironic laughter.

Ellen Glasgow, *Barren Ground* (1925)

16 She chuckled now and again at a joke, but it was the amused grim chuckle of a person who looks up to discover that they have coincided with the needs of nature in a bird.

Djuna Barnes, *Nightwood* (1937)

17 "Ha-ha," said Sir Mark. "Hum. Very good, yes, ha-ha!" Thumbs under his lapels he looked, however, rather anxiously round the room. Conversation with someone at whose joke you have heartily laughed without seeing the point is apt to become precarious.

Elizabeth Bowen, *To the North* (1933)

18 He'd never laugh at my jokes. . . . I was a woman, meaning my relationship with humor should have been as an object, not a perpetrator.

Roseanne Arnold, *My Lives* (1994)

19 God did it on purpose so that we may love you men instead of laughing at you.

Mrs. Patrick Campbell, when asked why women have no sense of humor, in Bennett Cerf, *The Laugh's on Me* (1959)

20 We are not amused!

Queen Victoria, in *Notebooks of a Spinster Lady* (1900)

See also Comedy, Irony, Laughter, Satire, Wit, Witticisms.

# ❦ HUNGER

21 The first freedom of man, I contend, is the freedom to eat.

Eleanor Roosevelt, *Tomorrow Is Now* (1963)

1 To be bound by hungers is a beautiful thing but to be bound by physical hungers only is too low a state for man.

Meridel Le Sueur, "Evening in a Lumber Town" (1926), *Harvest Song* (1990)

2 The decision to feed the world / is the real decision.

Adrienne Rich, "Hunger," *The Dream of a Common Language* (1978)

3 There will not cease to be ferment in the world unless people are sure of their food.

Pearl S. Buck, *God's Men* (1951)

4 A hungry man is an angry one.

Buchi Emecheta, *The Joys of Motherhood* (1979)

5 A poor man defended himself when charged with stealing food to appease the cravings of hunger, saying, the cries of the stomach silenced those of the conscience.

Lady Marguerite Blessington, in R.R. Madden, *The Literary Life and Correspondence of the Countess of Blessington*, vol. 1 (1855)

6 Hunger makes a thief of any man.

Pearl S. Buck, *The Good Earth* (1931)

7 A starving man can't see right or wrong. He just sees food.

Pearl S. Buck, *God's Men* (1951)

8 Hungry people cannot be good at learning or producing anything, except perhaps violence.

Pearl Bailey, *Pearl's Kitchen* (1973)

9 No man can be wise on an empty stomach.

George Eliot, *Adam Bede* (1859)

10 Hunger steals the memory.

Louise Erdrich, *Tracks* (1988)

11 What good is school when you're hungry?

Leila Abouzeid, "Divorce," in Elizabeth Warnock Fernea, *Women and the Family in the Middle East* (1985)

12 Hunger also changes the world—when eating can't be a habit, then neither can seeing.

Maxine Hong Kingston, *The Woman Warrior* (1976)

13 Work went on monotonously, and our constant hunger was wrenching: rice powder and bran, which I sometimes roasted in an attempt to give it some flavor, had torn my insides to shreds. One morning I didn't have the strength to get up, and no one came to see what had happened to me.

Everyone was so used to having people just disappear.

Molyda Szymusiak, *The Stones Cry Out* (1984)

14 They were hungry enough to eat a sawmill and it a-running.

Ardyth Kennelly, *The Peaceable Kingdom* (1949)

15 Those boys could hear a meat bone being dropped into soup half a mile away. If a man brushed a crumb from his beard, there was their knock on his door.

Joanne Greenberg, "Children of Joy," *Rites of Passage* (1972)

16 His hunger was a pungent sauce which made possible a very fair play of knife and fork.

Elinor Wylie, *The Orphan Angel* (1926)

17 A man with money to pay for a meal can talk about hunger without demeaning himself. . . . But for a man with no money hunger is a disgrace.

Vicki Baum, *Martin's Summer* (1931)

18 When we are not physically starving, we have the luxury to realize psychic and emotional starvation.

Cherríe Moraga, "La Güera," in Cherríe Moraga and Gloria Anzaldúa, eds., *This Bridge Called My Back* (1983)

See also Appetite, Poverty, Privation.

## ❦ HUSBANDS

19 The World, by tend'rest proof discovers / They err, who say that husbands can't be lovers.

Anne Finch, "A Letter to Daphnis" (1685), *Miscellany Poems, Written by a Lady* (1713)

20 An easy-going husband is the one indispensable comfort of life.

Ouida, *Wisdom, Wit and Pathos* (1884)

21 A husband is indeed thought by both sexes so very valuable, that scarce a man who can keep himself clean and make a bow, but thinks he is good enough to pretend to any woman.

Mary Astell, *Some Reflections on Marriage* (1700)

22 Husbands is the most undiscovered nation of people there is.

Anonymous woman, in Dorothy Dix, *Dorothy Dix—Her Book* (1926)

1 Oh! how I long to see my dear husband, that I may quarrel with him!

Mrs. Inchbald, *Every One Has His Fault* (1793)

2 Divorce? No. Murder? Yes.

Anne Hayes, asked whether she had ever considered divorcing husband and Ohio State football coach Woody Hayes, in Lee Green, *Sportswit* (1984)

3 I was brought up among the sort of self-important woman who had a husband as one has an alibi.

Anita Brookner, in Sybil Steinberg, ed., *Writing for Your Life* (1992)

4 The quoted words of a husband were as sacred, as final and uncontradictable as a proverb or cliché. However she might regard him in private, in public each woman's husband became an absolute authority on everything.

Richard Shattuck, *The Half-Haunted Saloon* (1945)

5 One thing she has noticed about married women, and that is how many of them have to go about creating their husbands. They have to start ascribing preferences, opinions, dictatorial ways. Oh, yes, they say, my husband is very particular. He won't touch turnips. He won't eat fried meat. (Or he will only eat fried meat.) He likes me to wear blue (brown) all the time. He can't stand organ music. He hates to see a woman go out bareheaded. He would kill me if I took one puff of tobacco. This way, bewildered, sidelong-looking men are made over, made into husbands, heads of households.

Alice Munro, *Friend of My Youth* (1990)

6 The only way to make a husband over according to one's ideas . . . would be to adopt him at an early age, say four.

Mary Roberts Rinehart, *"Isn't That Just Like a Man!"* (1920)

7 Husbands are like caterpillars, they improve with keeping.

Anthony Gilbert, *After the Verdict* (1961)

8 Don't worry. If you keep him long enough, he'll come back in style.

Dorothy Parker, to a woman bragging about having kept her husband for seven years, in Dorothy Herrmann, *With Malice Toward All* (1982)

9 The compulsion to find a lover and husband in a single person has doomed more women to misery than any other illusion.

Carolyn Heilbrun, *Writing a Woman's Life* (1988)

10 A lover may be a shadowy creature, but husbands are made of flesh and blood.

Amy Levy, *Reuben Sachs* (1888)

11 The guy who used to appear at your front door every night because he was wild to see you, now appears there every night because that's where he happens to live.

Lucille Kallen, *Out There, Somewhere* (1964)

12 Husbands are like fires. They go out when unattended.

Zsa Zsa Gabor, in *Newsweek* (1960)

13 My husband will never chase another woman. He's too fine, too decent, too old.

Gracie Allen, in *The Reader's Digest Treasury of Wit and Humor* (1958)

14 No one in the whole world knows all a man's bignesses and all his littlenesses as his wife does.

Gene Stratton-Porter, *Freckles* (1904)

15 The true male never yet walked / Who liked to listen when his mate talked.

Anna Wickham, "The Affinity," *The Contemplative Quarry* (1915)

16 The *divine right* of husbands, like the divine right of kings, may, it is to be hoped, in this enlightened age, be contested without danger.

Mary Wollstonecraft, *A Vindication of the Rights of Woman* (1792)

17 Our domestic Napoleons, too many of them, give flattery, bonnets and bracelets to women, and everything else *but*—justice.

Fanny Fern, *Folly As It Flies* (1868)

18 There was no need. I have three pets at home which answer the same purpose as a husband. I have a dog which growls every morning, a parrot which swears all the afternoon, and a cat that comes home late at night.

Marie Corelli, asked why she had never married, in James Crichton-Browne, *What the Doctor Thought* (1930)

19 Bigamy is having one husband too many. Monogamy is the same.

Anonymous woman, in Erica Jong, *Fear of Flying* (1973)

20 It's a matter of opinion.

Hermione Gingold, when asked if her husband was still living, *How to Grow Old Disgracefully* (1988)

1 You mean apart from my own?

  Zsa Zsa Gabor, when asked how many husbands she had
  had, in Kenneth Edwards, *I Wish I'd Said That!* (1976)

See also Family, Lovers, Marriage, Relationships, Wives.

❦ HYPOCHONDRIA

2 The incurable ills are the imaginary ills.

  Marie von Ebner-Eschenbach, *Aphorisms* (1893)

See also Illness.

❦ HYPOCRISY

3 One face to the world, another at home makes for misery.

  Amy Vanderbilt, *New Complete Book of Etiquette* (1963)

4 Psychologically speaking, one may say that the hypocrite is too ambitious; not only does he want to appear virtuous before others, he wants to convince himself.

  Hannah Arendt, *On Revolution* (1963)

5 Hypocrisy is the vice of vices. . . . Only crime and the criminal, it is true, confront us with the perplexity of radical evil; but only the hypocrite is really rotten to the core.

  Hannah Arendt, *On Revolution* (1963)

6 A criminal is twice a criminal when he adds hypocrisy to his crime.

  Marie Corelli, "Unchristian Clerics," *Free Opinions* (1905)

7 Hypocrisy, the lie, is the true sister of evil, intolerance and cruelty.

  Raisa M. Gorbachev, *I Hope* (1991)

8 The prohibition law, written for weaklings and derelicts, has divided the nation, like Gaul, into three parts—wets, drys, and hypocrites.

  Florence Sabin, speech (1931)

9 Two things do me in: one's chocolate cake, the other's hypocrisy.

  Roseanne Arnold, *My Lives* (1994)

See also Deception, Dishonesty.

# I

## ❧ ICEBERGS

1 Are you aware an iceberg takes repose / With you, and when it wakes may pasture on your snows?
   Elizabeth Bishop, "The Imaginary Iceberg," *North and South* (1955)

2 The iceberg cuts its facets from within / Like jewelry from a grave.
   Elizabeth Bishop, "The Imaginary Iceberg," *North and South* (1955)

## ❧ IDEALISM

3 How lovely to think that no one need wait a moment, we can start now, start slowly changing the world!
   Anne Frank (1944), in Ralph Manheim and Michel Mok, tr., *Anne Frank's Tales From the Secret Annex* (1984)

4 We come to think of an idealist as one who seeks to realize what is not in fact realizable. But, it is necessary to insist, *to have ideals* is not the same as *to have impracticable ideals*, however often it may be the case that our ideals are impracticable.
   L. Susan Stebbing, *Ideas and Illusions* (1941)

5 She had told them nothing, given them the stone of her abstract, colorless idealism while they sat there, open-mouthed for sentimental bread.
   Elizabeth Bowen, "Daffodils," *Early Stories* (1951)

6 Idealism, that gaudy coloring matter of passion, fades when it is brought beneath the trenchant white light of knowledge. Ideals, like mountains, are best at a distance.
   Ellen Glasgow, *The Descendant* (1897)

See also Altruism, Beliefs, Convictions, Ideologies.

## ❧ IDEAS

7 There are no new ideas. There are only new ways of making them felt.
   Audre Lorde, "Poetry Is Not a Luxury," in *Chrysalis* (1977)

8 Ideas move rapidly when their time comes.
   Carolyn Heilbrun, *Toward a Recognition of Androgyny* (1973)

9 The only people in the whole world who can change things are those who can sell ideas.
   Lois Wyse, *The Rosemary Touch* (1974)

10 No matter how brilliantly an idea is stated, we will not really be moved unless we have already half-thought of it ourselves.
   Mignon McLaughlin, *The Neurotic's Notebook* (1963)

11 Beware of people carrying ideas. Beware of ideas carrying people.
   Barbara Grizzuti Harrison, *Foreign Bodies* (1984)

12 You can imprison a man, but not an idea. You can exile a man, but not an idea. You can kill a man, but not an idea.
   Benazir Bhutto, *Daughter of Destiny* (1989)

13 If you have one good idea, people will lend you twenty.
   Marie von Ebner-Eschenbach, *Aphorisms* (1893)

14 Talk uses up ideas. . . . Once I have spoken them aloud, they are lost to me, dissipated into the noisy air like smoke. Only if I bury them, like bulbs, in the rich soil of silence do they grow.
   Doris Grumbach, *Fifty Days of Solitude* (1994)

15 It is a very dangerous thing to have an idea that you will not practice.
   Phyllis Bottome, *The Mortal Storm* (1938)

1 One can live in the shadow of an idea without grasping it.

Elizabeth Bowen, *The Heat of the Day* (1949)

2 Every new truth has its birth-place in a manger, lives thirty years, is crucified, and then deified.

Lucy Stone (1856), in Elizabeth Cady Stanton, Susan B. Anthony, and Matilda J. Gage, eds., *History of Woman Suffrage*, vol. 1 (1881)

3 We are so placid that the smallest tremor of objection to anything at all is taken as a full-scale revolution. Should any soul speak up in favor of the obvious, it is taken as a symptom of the influence of the left, the right, the pink, the black, the dangerous. An idea for its own sake—especially an obvious idea—has no respectability.

Cynthia Ozick, "Women and Creativity," in *Motive* (1969)

4 General notions are generally wrong.

Lady Mary Wortley Montagu (1710), in Octave Thanet, ed., *The Best Letters of Lady Mary Wortley Montagu* (1901)

5 I had never been as resigned to ready-made ideas as I was to ready-made clothes, perhaps because, although I couldn't sew, I could think.

Jane Rule, *Lesbian Images* (1975)

6 A writer didn't need "an" idea for a book; she needed at least forty. And "get" was the wrong word, implying that you received an idea as you would a gift. You didn't get ideas. You smelled them out, tracked them down, wrestled them into submission; you pursued them with forks and hope, and if you were lucky enough to catch one you impaled it, with the forks, before the sneaky little devil could get away.

Elizabeth Peters, *Naked Once More* (1989)

7 Now some people when they sit down to write and nothing special comes, no good ideas, are so frightened that they drink a lot of strong coffee to hurry them up, or smoke packages of cigarettes, or take drugs or get drunk. They do not know that ideas come slowly, and that the more clear, tranquil and unstimulated you are, the slower the ideas come, but the better they are.

Brenda Ueland, *If You Want to Write* (1938)

8 These people who are always briskly doing something and as busy as waltzing mice, they have little, sharp, staccato ideas, such as: "I see where I can make an annual cut of $3.47 in my meat budget." But they have no slow, big ideas.

Brenda Ueland, *If You Want to Write* (1938)

9 He arrived at ideas the slow way, never skating over the clear, hard ice of logic, nor soaring on the slipstreams of imagination, but slogging, plodding along on the heavy ground of existence.

Ursula K. Le Guin, *The Lathe of Heaven* (1971)

10 Like an enormous walnut in feeble, jittery squirrel hands, an idea, bigger and closer than any idea he had ever known, had been revolving in his mind for several days.

Patricia Highsmith, *Strangers on a Train* (1950)

11 The idea was fragrant with possibilities.

Jean Ferris, *Invincible Summer* (1987)

See also Concepts, Theories, Thoughts.

## ❦ IDENTITY

12 A strong sense of identity gives man an idea he can do no wrong; too little accomplishes the same.

Djuna Barnes, *Nightwood* (1937)

13 I am aware of myself as a four-hundred-year-old woman, born in the captivity of a colonial, pre-industrial oral culture and living now as a contemporary New Yorker.

Bharati Mukherjee, in Janet Sternburg, ed., *The Writer on Her Work*, vol. 2 (1991)

14 There is no place on earth, no day or night, no hour or minute, when one is not a Jew or a woman.

Andrea Dworkin, "First Love," in Julia Wolf Mazow, ed., *The Woman Who Lost Her Names* (1980)

15 Split at the root, neither Gentile nor Jew, / Yankee nor Rebel.

Adrienne Rich, "Readings of History," *Snapshots of a Daughter-in-Law* (1963)

16 To speak as black, female, *and* commercial lawyer has rendered me simultaneously universal, trendy, and marginal.

Patricia J. Williams, *The Alchemy of Race and Rights* (1991)

17 It takes a while to walk on two feet / each one going the other way.

Diane Glancy, title poem, *Iron Woman* (1990)

18 Thea was still under the belief that . . . if you clucked often enough, the hens would mistake you for one of themselves.

Willa Cather, *The Song of the Lark* (1915)

1 I am I because my little dog knows me.

Gertrude Stein, *The Geographical History of America* (1936)

See also Character, Essence, Self.

## ✿ IDEOLOGIES

2 Ideologies—isms which to the satisfaction of their adherents can explain everything and every occurrence by deducing it from a single premise—are a very recent phenomenon. . . . Not before Hitler and Stalin were the great political potentialities of the ideologies discovered.

Hannah Arendt, *Origins of Totalitarianism* (1951)

See also Communism, Conservatives, Feminism, Idealism, Liberals, Marxism.

## ✿ IDLENESS

3 Idleness, simon-pure, from which all manner of good springs like seed from a fallow soil, is sure to be misnamed and misconstrued.

Louise Imogen Guiney, *Goose-Quill Papers* (1885)

4 We owe most of our great inventions and most of the achievements of genius to idleness—either enforced or voluntary. The human mind prefers to be spoon-fed with the thoughts of others, but deprived of such nourishment it will, reluctantly, begin to think for itself—and such thinking, remember, is original thinking and may have valuable results.

Agatha Christie, *The Moving Finger* (1942)

5 To do anything, it is first necessary to be doing nothing.

Nancy Hale, *Heaven and Hardpan Farm* (1957)

6 It is in our idleness, in our dreams, that the submerged truth sometimes comes to the top.

Virginia Woolf, *A Room of One's Own* (1929)

7 What am I doing? Nothing. I am letting life rain upon me.

Rahel Varnhagen (1810), in Hannah Arendt, *Rahel Varnhagen* (1957)

See also Inaction, Laziness, Leisure.

## ✿ IDOLS

8 Sacred cows make very poor gladiators.

Nikki Giovanni, title essay, *Sacred Cows . . . And Other Edibles* (1988)

9 Try not to have idols: they are interchangeable and lead to a wantonness that is easily mistaken for love.

Hildegard Knef, *The Verdict* (1975)

10 Guard against idols—yes, guard against all idols, of which surely the greatest is oneself.

Alexandra David-Neel (1892), *La Lampe de Sagesse* (1986)

See also Admiration, Hero-Worship.

## ✿ IGNORANCE

11 Ignorance gives one a large range of probabilities.

George Eliot, *Daniel Deronda* (1874)

12 The most violent element in society is ignorance.

Emma Goldman, title essay, *Anarchism* (1910)

13 *Only* ignorance! only *ignorance*! how can you talk about *only* ignorance? Don't you know that it is the worst thing in the world, next to wickedness? And which does the most mischief Heaven only knows. If people can say, "Oh! I did not know, I did not mean any harm," they think it is all right.

Anna Sewell, *Black Beauty* (1877)

14 There is nothing more powerful than ignorance, not even intelligence.

Lillian Smith, *The Journey* (1954)

15 Ignorance is not bliss. Ignorance is impotence; it is fear; it is cruelty; it is all the things that make for unhappiness.

Winifred Holtby, "The Right Side of Thirty" (1930), *Pavements at Anderby* (1937)

16 The bliss that comes from ignorance should seldom be encouraged for it is likely to do one out of a more satisfying bliss.

Ruth Stout, *How to Have a Green Thumb Without an Aching Back* (1955)

17 Ignorance, if not bliss, often saves a good deal of time.

Anthony Gilbert, *The Mouse Who Wouldn't Play Ball* (1943)

1 Ignorance is no excuse—it's the real thing.

>Irene Peter, in Laurence J. Peter, *Peter's Quotations* (1977)

2 Ignorance is the mother of presumption.

>Marie de Gournay, *The Ladies' Grievance* (1626)

3 Ignorance is not innocence.

>Christina, Queen of Sweden, "Maxims" (1680), in Henry Woodhead, ed., *Memoirs of Christina, Queen of Sweden*, vol. 2 (1863)

4 Most people did not care to be taught what they did not already know; it made them feel ignorant.

>Mary McCarthy, *Birds of America* (1971)

5 The know-nothings are, unfortunately, seldom the do-nothings.

>Mignon McLaughlin, *The Neurotic's Notebook* (1963)

6 To him all that was indefinite was evil; all that was unfamiliar was horrible. It is the error of ignorance at all times.

>Ouida, *Wisdom, Wit and Pathos* (1884)

7 What the eye does not see, the heart does not rue.

>Mary Collyer, *Felicia to Charlotte* (1744)

8 I didn't know what she was talking about, so I said "I know that. Who doesn't know that?"

>Lynda Barry, *The Good Times Are Killing Me* (1988)

## ❦ ILLNESS

9 I lie all day and wait for night, / I lie all night and wait for day.

>Edith Södergran, "Days of Sickness" (1916), in Samuel Charters, tr., *We Women* (1977)

10 I have never been anywhere but sick. In a sense sickness is a place, more instructive than a long trip to Europe, and it's always a place where there's no company, where nobody can follow. Sickness before death is a very appropriate thing and I think those who don't have it miss one of God's mercies.

>Flannery O'Connor, in Sally Fitzgerald, ed., *The Habit of Being* (1979)

11 Everyone who is born holds dual citizenship, in the kingdom of the well and in the kingdom of the sick. Although we all prefer to use only the good passport, sooner or later each of us is obliged, at least for a spell, to identify ourselves as citizens of that other place.

>Susan Sontag, *Illness As Metaphor* (1978)

12 What a strange distance there is between ill people and well ones.

>Winifred Holtby, in Vera Brittain, *Testament of Friendship* (1940)

13 The sick soon come to understand that they live in a different world from that of the well and that the two cannot communicate.

>Jessamyn West, *The Woman Said Yes* (1976)

14 How impossible it is for strong healthy people to understand the way in which bodily *malaise* and suffering eats at the root of one's life! The philosophy that is true—the religion that is strength to the healthy—is constantly emptiness to one when the head is distracted and every sensation is oppressive.

>George Eliot (1863), in J.W. Cross, ed., *George Eliot's Life As Related in Her Letters and Journals* (1884)

15 That is the fearful part of having been near death. One knows how easy it is to die. The barriers that are up for everybody else are down for you, and you've only to slip through.

>Katherine Mansfield (1919), in J. Middleton Murry, ed., *The Letters of Katherine Mansfield*, vol. 1 (1928)

16 Her illness seemed to be one prolonged mistake. Her self looked, wildly smiling, out of her body: what was happening in here was too terrible to acknowledge; she had to travesty it and laugh it off. Unserene, she desperately kept her head.

>Elizabeth Bowen, *The House in Paris* (1935)

17 She seemed to lie less in weakness than in unwilling credulity as though the successive disasters that make an illness had convinced her slowly, by repetition.

>Elizabeth Bowen, *The House in Paris* (1935)

18 Apprehension, uncertainty, waiting, expectation, fear of surprise, do a patient more harm than any exertion.

>Florence Nightingale, *Notes on Nursing* (1859)

19 Being a sick man is like being a log caught in a stream, Gilles. All the straws gather around it.

>Helen Waddell, *Peter Abelard* (1933)

20 A disease and its treatment can be a series of humiliations, a chisel for humility.

>Laurel Lee, *Walking Through the Fire* (1977)

1 Sickness, like sex, demands a private room, or at the very least, a discreet curtain around the ward bed.

Violet Weingarten, *Intimations of Mortality* (1978)

2 A man's illness is his private territory and, no matter how much he loves you and how close you are, you stay an outsider. You are healthy.

Lauren Bacall, *Lauren Bacall by Myself* (1979)

3 There is, let us confess it (and illness is the great confessional), a childish outspokenness in illness; things are said, truths blurted out, which the cautious respectability of health conceals.

Virginia Woolf, "On Being Ill," *The Moment* (1947)

4 Everything but truth becomes loathed in a sickroom. . . . Let the nurse avow that the medicine is nauseous. Let the physician declare that the treatment will be painful. Let sister, or brother, or friend, tell me that I must never look to be well. When the time approaches that I am to die, let me be told that I am to die, and when.

Harriet Martineau, *Life in the Sick-Room* (1844)

5 The sad truth is that there is no point to getting sick when you're a grown-up. You know why? It's because being sick is about you and your mother. . . . Without that solicitous hand on your forehead, there is no one to confirm that you are really sick.

Adair Lara, *Welcome to Earth, Mom* (1992)

6 It is the worst humiliation and grievance of the suffering, that they cause suffering.

Harriet Martineau, *Life in the Sick-Room* (1844)

7 How quickly a person in pain whom you can't help becomes a reproach. And then, no doubt, a thorn.

Beth Gutcheon, *Still Missing* (1981)

8 Severe illness isolates those in close contact with it, because it inevitably narrows the focus of concern. To a certain extent this can lead to healing, but not if the circle of concern is so tight that it cannot be broken into, or out of.

Madeleine L'Engle, *Two-Part Invention* (1988)

9 Every invalid is a prisoner.

Marguerite Yourcenar, *Memoirs of Hadrian* (1951)

10 Disease may score a direct hit on only one member of a family, but shrapnel tears the flesh of the others.

Betty Rollin, *Last Wish* (1985)

11 Any disease that is treated as a mystery and acutely enough feared will be felt to be morally, if not literally, contagious.

Susan Sontag, *Illness As Metaphor* (1978)

12 I hereby confess / That of all I possess / I'd most gladly be minus / The sinus.

Felicia Lamport, "Lines on an Aching Brow," *Scrap Irony* (1961)

13 You don't get ulcers from what you eat. You get them from what's eating you.

Vicki Baum, in Joseph L. Baron, *A Treasury of Jewish Quotations* (1956)

14 He was just about to get a job when he got intentional flu.

Jane Ace, in Goodman Ace, *Ladies and Gentlemen, Easy Aces* (1970)

15 Illness and accidents were mysterious manifestations of the war of the spirits, fought on the battleground of the body.

Jean Auel, *Clan of the Cave Bear* (1980)

16 Sickness is a belief, which must be annihilated by the divine Mind.

Mary Baker Eddy, *Science and Health* (1875)

17 The difficulty with becoming a patient is that as soon as you get horizontal, part of your being yearns not for a mortal doctor but for a medicine man.

Shana Alexander, "An Ordeal to Choke a Sword-Swallower," in *Life* (1966)

18 No man needs curing of his individual sickness; his universal malady is what he should look to.

Djuna Barnes, *Nightwood* (1937)

19 Ever since I have been ill, I have longed and longed for some palpable disease, no matter how conventionally dreadful a label it might have, but I was always driven back to stagger alone under the monstrous mass of subjective sensations, which that sympathetic being "the medical man" had no higher inspiration than to assure me I was personally responsible for, washing his hands of me with graceful complacency under my very nose. Dr. Torrey was the only man who did not assume because I was a victim to many pains, that I was, of necessity, an arrested mental development, too.

Alice James (1891), in Anna Robeson Burr, *Alice James* (1934)

1 Remembering that Alison was not well, Leonora tried to look sickly also, as that was her notion of the proper behavior in a sickroom.

Carson McCullers, *Reflections in a Golden Eye* (1941)

2 Now I am beginning to live a little, and feel less like a sick oyster at low tide.

Louisa May Alcott, in Ednah Dow Cheney, ed., *Louisa May Alcott, Her Life, Letters, and Journals* (1890)

3 The happiest people in this world are the convalescents.

Mary Adams, *Confessions of a Wife* (1902)

4 Every body's heart is open, you know, when they have recently escaped from severe pain, or are recovering the blessing of health.

Jane Austen, *Persuasion* (1818)

5 There are no sick people in North Oxford. They are either dead or alive. It's sometimes difficult to tell the difference, that's all.

Barbara Pym, *Crampton Hodnet* (1985)

6 "Dear! Everybody is ill now, I think," said Mrs. Hale, with a little of the jealousy which one invalid is apt to feel of another.

Elizabeth Gaskell, *North and South* (1854)

See also AIDS, Alzheimer's, Cancer, Diseases, Doctors, Drugs, Health, Health Care, Hospitals, Hypochondria, Medicine, Mental Illness, Migraines, Nurses, Pain, Surgery.

## ❦ ILLUSIONS

7 Illusions are art, for the feeling person, and it is by art that we live, if we do.

Elizabeth Bowen, *The Death of the Heart* (1938)

8 One illusion is as good as another.

Zelda Fitzgerald, letter to F. Scott Fitzgerald (1930), in Nancy Milford, *Zelda* (1970)

9 Borrowed illusions are better than none.

Ellen Glasgow, *The Descendant* (1897)

10 Belief in the absence of illusions is itself an illusion.

Barbara Grizzuti Harrison, *The Astonishing World* (1992)

11 Some of my best friends are illusions. Been sustaining me for years.

Sheila Ballantyne, *Norma Jean the Termite Queen* (1975)

12 Illusions: they fit like an iron lung, and / can keep you going indefinitely. The persons / suspected of stealing them are to be considered / armed, and dangerous.

Kathleen Norris, "Memorandum / The Accountant's Notebook," *Falling Off* (1971)

13 My illusion is more real to me than reality. And so do we often build our world on an error, and cry out that the universe is falling to pieces, if any one but lift a finger to replace the error by truth.

Mary Antin, *The Promised Land* (1912)

14 It takes a lot to wound a man without illusions.

Ellis Peters, *The House of Green Turf* (1969)

15 It is far harder to kill a phantom than a reality.

Virginia Woolf, "Professions for Women," *The Death of the Moth* (1942)

16 If you ever do a survey, you'll find that people prefer illusion to reality, ten to one. Twenty, even.

Judith Guest, *Ordinary People* (1976)

See also Delusion, Disillusionment, Fantasy, Imagination.

## ❦ IMAGES

17 An image is a stop the mind makes between uncertainties.

Djuna Barnes, *Nightwood* (1937)

18 We are all of us imaginative in some form or other, for images are the brood of desire.

George Eliot, *Middlemarch* (1871)

19 No tragedy was ever comprehended that went from the mouth to the ear. It has to pass from the eye to the soul.

Mother Jones (1915), in Djuna Barnes, *Interviews* (1985)

20 An image is a bridge between evoked emotion and conscious knowledge; words are the cables that hold up the bridge. Images are more direct, more immediate than words, and closer to the unconscious. Picture language precedes thinking in words; the metaphorical mind precedes analytical consciousness.

Gloria Anzaldúa, *Borderlands/La Frontera* (1987)

1 The assumption that seeing is believing makes us susceptible to visual deception.
  Kathleen Hall Jamieson, *Dirty Politics* (1992)

2 She never wanted these pictures called up on some future hot, dry day in some other place. She squinted, closed her eyes even, 'less the pictures cling to her eyes, store in the brain, to roll out later and crush her future with the weight of this place and its troubles.
  Toni Cade Bambara, "The Organizer's Wife," *The Sea Birds Are Still Alive* (1982)

See also Photography.


## ◊ IMAGINATION

3 Imagination! who can sing thy force? / Or who describe the swiftness of thy course?
  Phillis Wheatley, "On Imagination" (1773), *Memoir and Poems of Phillis Wheatley* (1838)

4 Imagination is the highest kite that can fly.
  Lauren Bacall, *Lauren Bacall by Myself* (1979)

5 The Possible's slow fuse is lit / By the Imagination.
  Emily Dickinson, in Martha Dickinson Bianchi, ed., *The Single Hound* (1914)

6 Without imagination, there is no goodness, no wisdom.
  Marie von Ebner-Eschenbach, *Aphorisms* (1893)

7 Man's most valuable faculty is his imagination.
  Madame de Staël, *Essay on Fictions* (1795)

8 O thou, the leader of the mental train.
  Phillis Wheatley, "On Imagination" (1773), *Memoir and Poems of Phillis Wheatley* (1838)

9 Imagination has always had powers of resurrection that no science can match.
  Ingrid Bengis, "Monroe According to Mailer," in *Ms.* (1973)

10 Fantasies are more than substitutes for unpleasant reality; they are also dress rehearsals, plans. All acts performed in the world begin in the imagination.
  Barbara Grizzuti Harrison, "Talking Dirty," in *Ms.* (1973)

11 What man can imagine he may one day achieve.
  Nancy Hale, in Richard Thruelsen and John Kobler, eds., *Adventures of the Mind*, 2nd series (1961)

12 Imagination is new reality in the process of being created. It represents the part of the existing order that can still grow.
  Nancy Hale, in Richard Thruelsen and John Kobler, eds., *Adventures of the Mind*, 2nd series (1961)

13 Imagination and fiction make up more than three quarters of our real life.
  Simone Weil, *Gravity and Grace* (1947)

14 I doubt the imagination can be suppressed. If you truly eradicated it in a child, that child would grow up to be an eggplant.
  Ursula K. Le Guin, "Why Are Americans Afraid of Dragons?" (1974), *Language of the Night* (1979)

15 Imagination is to love what gas is to the balloon—that which raises it from earth.
  L.E. Landon, *Romance and Reality* (1831)

16 The old proverb, applied to fire and water, may with equal truth be applied to the imagination—it is a good servant, but a bad master.
  L.E. Landon, *Romance and Reality* (1831)

17 The imagination needs moodling,—long, inefficient, happy idling, dawdling and puttering.
  Brenda Ueland, *If You Want to Write* (1938)

18 My imagination longs to dash ahead and plan developments; but I have noticed that when things happen in one's imaginings, they never happen in one's life, so I am curbing myself.
  Dodie Smith, *I Capture the Castle* (1948)

19 The curse of human nature is imagination. When a long anticipated moment comes, we always find it pitched a note too low.
  Gertrude Atherton, *Los Cerritos* (1890)

20 Imagination is so much harder to face than reality.
  Mabel Seeley, *The Crying Sisters* (1939)

21 Imagination makes cowards of us all.
  Ethel Watts Mumford, in Oliver Herford, Ethel Watts Mumford, and Addison Mizner, *The Complete Cynic* (1902)

22 Imagination, like memory, can transform lies to truths.
  Cristina Garcia, *Dreaming in Cuban* (1992)

23 The people who are willing to talk about imagination seldom have much. Imagination is a guilty secret, usually, a possession best kept inside the privacy of one's own skull.
  Margaret Lee Runbeck, *Time for Each Other* (1944)

1 Indigo, I don't want to hear another word about it, do you understand me. I'm not setting the table with my Sunday china for fifteen dolls who got their period today.

    Ntozake Shange, *Sassafrass, Cypress & Indigo* (1982)

See also Creativity, Fantasy, Illusion.

## ❧ IMITATION

2 Most imitators attempt the inimitable.

    Marie von Ebner-Eschenbach, *Aphorisms* (1893)

3 Nature, who permits no two leaves to be exactly alike, has given a still greater diversity to human minds. Imitation, then, is a double murder; for it deprives both copy and original of their primitive existence.

    Madame de Staël, *Corinne* (1807)

See also Plagiarism.

## ❧ IMMIGRANTS

4 Emigration is easy, but immigration is something else. To flee, yes; but to be accepted?

    Victoria Wolff, *Spell of Egypt* (1943)

5 I'm one of the millions of immigrant children, children of loneliness, wandering between worlds that are at once too old and too new to live in.

    Anzia Yezierska, title story, *Children of Loneliness* (1923)

6 I do not know the speech / Of this cool land, / I cannot keep its pace.

    Else Lasker-Schüler, "Homesickness," *Hebrew Ballads* (1980)

7 I'm very lonely now, Mary, / For the poor make no new friends.

    Lady Dufferin, "Lament of the Irish Emigrant" (1894), in Sean McMahon, ed., *A Book of Irish Quotations* (1984)

8 Woe is me! Bitter is me! For what is my life? Why didn't the ship go under and drown me before I came to America?

    Anzia Yezierska, "Hunger," *Hungry Hearts* (1920)

9 As one of the dumb, voiceless ones I speak. One of the millions of immigrants beating, beating out

their hearts at your gates for a breath of understanding.

    Anzia Yezierska, "America and I," *Children of Loneliness* (1923)

10 In spite of everything, we never gave up. The more we were despised, the harder we worked. We always had hope that some day things would be better. If not for us, then for our children.

    Yoshiko Uchida, *A Jar of Dreams* (1981)

11 She was trapped in a mesh of tradition woven thousands of miles away by ancestors who had had no knowledge that someday one generation of their progeny might be raised in another culture.

    Jade Snow Wong, *Fifth Chinese Daughter* (1950)

12 A characteristic thing about the aspiring immigrant is the fact that he is not content to progress alone. Solitary success is imperfect success in his eyes. He must take his family with him as he rises.

    Mary Antin, *The Promised Land* (1912)

13 My literary agenda begins by acknowledging that America has transformed *me*. It does not end until I show how I (and the hundreds of thousands like me) have transformed America.

    Bharati Mukherjee, in Janet Sternburg, ed., *The Writer on Her Work*, vol. 2 (1991)

See also Borders, Exiles, Homeland, Refugees.

## ❧ IMMORTALITY

14 This World is not Conclusion. / A Sequel stands beyond — / Invisible, as Music — / But positive, as Sound.

    Emily Dickinson (1862), in Mabel Loomis Todd, ed., *Poems by Emily Dickinson*, 3rd series (1896)

15 I believe in the immortality of the soul because I have within me immortal longings.

    Helen Keller, *Midstream* (1930)

16 I want to go on living even after my death!

    Anne Frank, *The Diary of a Young Girl* (1952)

17 I know that we live after death and again and again, not in the memory of our children, or as a mulch for trees and flowers, however poetic that may be,

but looking passionately and egocentrically out of our eyes.

Brenda Ueland (1939), *Me* (1983)

1 Biggest affirmative argument I know in favor of "If a man die, shall he live again?" is just the way you feel inside you that nothin' can stop you from livin' on.

Bess Streeter Aldrich, *Song of Years* (1939)

2 Cut down that there maple tree outside the lean-to door, burn the trunk to ashes, and Ma'll up and leach the ashes for lye. Scatter the leaves and they'll make winter mulchin'. Seeds that have been shook off will come up. No, sir, if you can't kill that old maple you ain't goin' to be able to kill *me*. I'll be in somethin' a hundred years from now, even if it's just the prairie grass or the wind in the timber or the wild geese ridin' out the storm.

Bess Streeter Aldrich, *Song of Years* (1939)

3 The soul's fierce cry for immortality is this,—only this:—Return to me after death the thing as it was before. Leave me in the Hereafter the being I am to-day. Rob me of the thoughts, the feelings, the desires that are my life, and you have left nothing to take. Your immortality is annihilation, your Hereafter is a lie.

Ralph Iron, *The Story of an African Farm* (1883)

4 One of the strange things about living in the world is that it is only now and then one is quite sure one is going to live forever and ever and ever.

Frances Hodgson Burnett, *The Secret Garden* (1911)

5 I live now on borrowed time, waiting in the ante-room for the summons that will inevitably come. And then—I go on to the next thing, whatever it is. One doesn't luckily have to bother about that.

Agatha Christie, *An Autobiography* (1977)

6 In health, in the bustle of living, it was easy to believe in heaven and a life to come. But when the blow fell, and those you loved passed into the great Silence, where you could not get at them, or they at you, then doubts, aching doubts took possession of one.

Henry Handel Richardson, *The Fortunes of Richard Mahoney: Ultima Thule* (1929)

7 The outrage was on the scale of God. My younger brother was immortal and they hadn't noticed. Immortality had been concealed in my brother's body while he was alive, and we hadn't noticed that it

dwelt there. Now my brother's body was dead, and immortality with it. . . . And the error, the outrage, filled the whole universe.

Marguerite Duras, *The Lover* (1984)

8 If we really believed that those who are gone from us were as truly alive as ourselves, we could not invest the subject with such awful depth of gloom as we do. If we would imbue our children with distinct faith in immortality, we should never speak of people as dead, but as passed into another world. We should speak of the body as a cast-off garment, which the wearer had outgrown; consecrated indeed by the beloved being that used it for a season, but of no value within itself.

Lydia Maria Child, *Letters From New York*, 2nd series (1845)

9 We were afraid of the dead because we never could tell when they might show up again.

Jamaica Kincaid, *Annie John* (1983)

10 It's the possibility that when you're dead you might still go on hurting that bothers me.

Keri Hulme, *The Bone People* (1983)

11 Immortality is a terrible curse.

Simone de Beauvoir, *All Men Are Mortal* (1955)

12 A red-hot belief in eternal glory is probably the best antidote to human panic that there is.

Phyllis Bottome, *Survival* (1943)

13 He [Christ] even restored the severed ear of the soldier who came to arrest Him—a fact that allows us to hope the resurrection will reflect a considerable attention to detail.

Marilynne Robinson, *Housekeeping* (1980)

14 Sometimes I think the resurrection of the body, unless much improved in construction, a mistake!

Evelyn Underhill (1936), in Charles Williams, ed., *The Letters of Evelyn Underhill* (1943)

15 What's so good about a heaven where, one of these days, you're going to get your embarrassing old body back?

Marsha Norman, *The Fortune Teller* (1987)

16 It is rather depressing to think that one will still be oneself when one is dead, but I dare say one won't be so critical then.

Angela Thirkell, *Northbridge Rectory* (1941)

1 Millions long for immortality who don't know what to do with themselves on a rainy Sunday afternoon.

> Susan Ertz, *Anger in the Sky* (1943)

See also Eternity, Heaven, Hell, Purgatory.

## ❧ IMPATIENCE

2 Through the windy night something / is coming up the path / towards the house. / I have always hated to wait for things. / I think I will go / to meet whatever it is.

> Elizabeth Coatsworth, *Personal Geography* (1976)

3 Everything comes to the man who won't wait.

> Ada Leverson, *The Twelfth Hour* (1907)

4 Impatience is the mark of independence, / not of bondage.

> Marianne Moore, "Marriage," *Selected Poems* (1935)

5 I have been devoured all my life by an incurable and burning impatience: and to this day find all oratory, biography, operas, films, plays, books, and persons, too long.

> Margot Asquith, *More or Less About Myself* (1934)

6 Hedda always tells us things the first time as if it were the twentieth, and her patience quite worn out with telling us!

> Kathleen Norris, *The Black Flemings* (1926)

7 Little seedlings never flourish in the soil they have been given, be it ever so excellent, if they are continually pulled up to see if the roots are grateful yet.

> Bertha Damon, *Grandma Called It Carnal* (1938)

8 The impatience of the old is the worst impatience of all.

> L.T. Meade, *The Honorable Miss* (1900)

9 "Twenty-three and a quarter minutes past," Uncle Matthew was saying furiously, "in precisely six and three-quarter minutes the damned fella will be late."

> Nancy Mitford, *Love in a Cold Climate* (1949)

See also Waiting.

## ❧ IMPERFECTION

10 Cracked things often hold out as long as whole things; one takes so much better care of them!

> Jane Welsh Carlyle, letter (1857), in Alan and Mary McQueen Simpson, eds., *I Too Am Here* (1977)

11 What is broken is broken—and I'd rather remember it as it was at its best than mend it and see the broken places as long as I lived.

> Margaret Mitchell, *Gone With the Wind* (1936)

12 When one's outward lot is perfect, the sense of inward imperfection is the more pressing.

> George Eliot (1872), in J.W. Cross, ed., *George Eliot's Life As Related in Her Letters and Journals* (1884)

13 No honey for me, if it comes with a bee.

> Sappho (6th cent. B.C.), in C.R. Haines, *Sappho: The Poems and Fragments* (1926)

See also Faults.

## ❧ IMPERIALISM

14 Imperialism was born when the ruling class in capitalist production came up against national limits to its economic expansion.

> Hannah Arendt, *Origins of Totalitarianism* (1951)

15 There are two kinds of imperialists—imperialists and bloody imperialists.

> Rebecca West, in *The Freewoman* (1911)

See also Colonialism.

## ❧ IMPERMANENCE

16 Faith, Sir, we are here today, and gone tomorrow.

> Aphra Behn, *The Lucky Chance* (1687)

17 Impermanence is the law of the universe.

> Carlene Hatcher Polite, *The Flagellants* (1966)

18 The hardest thing for me is the sense of impermanence. All passes; nothing returns.

> Ellen Glasgow, *Letters of Ellen Glasgow* (1958)

1 The days of our lives vanish utterly, more insubstantial than if they had been invented. Fiction can seem more enduring than reality.
   Penelope Lively, *Moon Tiger* (1987)

2 Impermanence is the very essence of joy—the drop of bitterness that enables one to perceive the sweet.
   Myrtle Reed, *Master of the Vineyard* (1910)

See also Change.

## ❧ IMPOSSIBLE

3 He was by this time in that state of exaltation in which the impossible looks quite natural and commonplace.
   Ouida, "The Nürnberg Stove," in H.W. Mabie, ed., *Famous Stories Every Child Should Know* (1907)

4 The impossible talked of is less impossible from the moment words are laid to it.
   Storm Jameson, *Three Kingdoms* (1926)

5 In the age in which we live, the impossible is every day losing ground.
   Anne-Sophie Swetchine, in Count de Falloux, ed., *The Writings of Madame Swetchine* (1869)

6 Nothing is impossible, we just don't know how to do it yet.
   L.L. Larison Cudmore, *The Center of Life* (1977)

7 To some people the impossible is impossible.
   Elizabeth Bibesco, *Balloons* (1922)

## ❧ IMPRISONMENT

8 Jails and prisons are designed to break human beings, to convert the population into specimens in a zoo—obedient to our keepers, but dangerous to each other.
   Angela Davis, *An Autobiography* (1974)

9 I lost all consciousness of any cause. I had no sense of being a radical, making a protest against a government, carrying on a nonviolent revolution. . . . I lost all feeling of my own identity. I reflected on the desolation of poverty, of destitution, of sickness and sin. That I would be free after thirty days meant nothing to me. I would never be free again.
   Dorothy Day, *The Long Loneliness* (1952)

10 Not even my incarceration in a damp underground dungeon will make me give up the fight in which I am engaged for liberty and for the rights of the working people. To be shut from the sunlight is not pleasant but . . . I shall stand firm. To be in prison is no disgrace.
   Mother Jones, in Linda Atkinson, *Mother Jones* (1978)

11 You put me in here a cub, but I will go out a roaring lion, and I will make all hell howl.
   Carry Nation, *The Use and Need of the Life of Carry A. Nation* (1905)

12 Those of us on the outside do not like to think of wardens and guards as our surrogates. Yet they are, and they are intimately locked in a deadly embrace with their human captives behind the prison walls. By extension so are we.
   Jessica Mitford, *Kind and Usual Punishment* (1973)

13 The character and mentality of the keepers may be of more importance in understanding prisons than the character and mentality of the kept.
   Jessica Mitford, *Kind and Usual Punishment* (1973)

14 The Administration pinned its faith on jail—that institution of convenience to the oppressor when he is strong in power and his weapons are effective. When the oppressor miscalculates the strength of the oppressed, jail loses its convenience.
   Doris Stevens, *Jailed for Freedom* (1920)

15 It was better to be in a jail where you could bang the walls than in a jail you could not see.
   Carson McCullers, *The Member of the Wedding* (1946)

See also Internment.

## ❧ IMPROVISATION

16 Improvisation can be either a last resort or an established way of evoking creativity.
   Mary Catherine Bateson, *Composing a Life* (1989)

## &#167; IMPULSES

1   I love the abandonment to impulse, I act from impulse only, and I love to madness that others do the same by me.

> Julie de Lespinasse (1773), in Katharine Prescott Wormeley, tr., *Letters of Mlle. de Lespinasse* (1901)

2   Our impulses are our birthright. . . . The impulses that make a fool or worse of us in certain circumstances may be necessary for our happiness.

> Gertrude Atherton, *Julia France and Her Times* (1912)

3   Sometimes, I think, our impulses come not from the past, but from the future.

> Mary Stewart, *The Ivy Tree* (1961)

4   I am a woman / who understands / the necessity of an impulse whose goal or origin / still lie beyond me.

> Olga Broumas, "Artemis," *Beginning With O* (1977)

## &#167; INACTION

5   There are so many things that we wish we had done yesterday, so few that we feel like doing today.

> Mignon McLaughlin, *The Second Neurotic's Notebook* (1966)

6   Inaction, contrary to its reputation for being a refuge, is neither safe nor comfortable.

> Madeleine Kunin, *Living a Political Life* (1994)

7   the thing that destroys a person/a people / is not the knowing / but the knowing and not / doing.

> Carolyn M. Rodgers, "Food for Thought," *how i got ovah* (1975)

8   What you don't do can be a destructive force.

> Eleanor Roosevelt, *Tomorrow Is Now* (1963)

9   The most ominous of fallacies—the belief that things can be kept static by inaction.

> Freya Stark, *Dust in the Lion's Paw* (1961)

10   Perhaps it is impossible for a person who does no good not to do harm.

> Harriet Beecher Stowe, *Uncle Tom's Cabin* (1852)

11   So much attention is paid to the aggressive sins, such as violence and cruelty and greed with all their tragic effects, that too little attention is paid to the passive sins, such as apathy and laziness, which in the long run can have a more devastating and destructive effect upon society than the others.

> Eleanor Roosevelt, *You Learn by Living* (1960)

12   The biggest sin is sitting on your ass.

> Florynce R. Kennedy, in Gloria Steinem, "The Verbal Karate of Florynce R. Kennedy," *Ms.* (1973)

13   The thinkers stood aside / To let the nation act.

> Elizabeth Barrett Browning, "Napoleon III in Italy," *Poems Before Congress* (1860)

14   Activity *may* lead to evil; but inactivity *cannot* be led to good.

> Hannah More, "On the Religious Employment of Time," *Strictures on the Modern System of Female Education* (1799)

See also Idleness.

## &#167; INADEQUACY

15   Let's face it—who ever is adequate? We all create situations each other can't live up to, then break our hearts at them because they don't.

> Elizabeth Bowen, *The Death of the Heart* (1938)

16   He was one of the ones who yearned / for something his heart wasn't big enough / to handle.

> Joy Harjo, "New Orleans," in Rayna Green, ed., *That's What She Said* (1984)

17   In our deepest moments we say the most inadequate things.

> Edna O'Brien, "Sister Imelda," *Returning* (1981)

18   She posed as being more indolent than she felt, for fear of finding herself less able than she could wish.

> Elizabeth Bowen, *The Death of the Heart* (1938)

19   I couldn't ever boil potatoes over the heat of your affection. Your love would never bridge a gap; it wouldn't even fill up the hole that the mice came through.

> Djuna Barnes, "What Do You See, Madam?" (1913), *Smoke and Other Early Stories* (1982)

20   Here we are sitting in a shower of gold and nothing to hold up but a pitchfork!

> Christina Stead, *House of All Nations* (1938)

See also Faults, Incompetence, Limitations.

## ✿ INANIMATE OBJECTS

1 I believe in the total depravity of inanimate things.

 Mrs. Walker, in Kate Sanborn, *The Wit of Women* (1885)

2 Since he had first held a rattle, inanimate matter had been his foe. He was a living illustration of the theory that matter cuts across the path of life. In its crossing of Jonathan's path it was never Jonathan that came off as victor.

 Mary Webb, *Seven for a Secret* (1922)

3 There's times when the crockery seems alive, an' flies out o' your hand like a bird. It's like the glass, sometimes, 'ull crack as it stands. What is to be broke *will* be broke.

 George Eliot, *Adam Bede* (1859)

4 Inkstands and tea-cups are never as full as when one upsets them.

 Edith Wharton, *A Backward Glance* (1934)

5 Paper is always strongest at the perforations.

 Carolyn M. Corry, in *Omni* (1979)

6 There are no inanimate objects.

 Barbara Grizzuti Harrison, *Foreign Bodies* (1984)

7 Strange the affection which clings to inanimate objects—objects which cannot even know our love! But it is not return that constitutes the strength of an attachment.

 L.E. Landon, *Romance and Reality* (1831)

8 Inanimate objects were often so much nicer than people, she thought. What person, for example, could possibly be so comforting as one's bed?

 Barbara Pym, *Crampton Hodnet* (1985)

See also Machines, Things.

## ✿ INCOMPETENCE

9 The adversary she found herself forced to fight was not worth matching or beating; it was not a superior ability which she would have found honor in challenging; it was ineptitude.

 Ayn Rand, *Atlas Shrugged* (1957)

10 She was always holding God's bag of tricks upside down.

 Djuna Barnes, *Nightwood* (1937)

11 The sheriff's an eager beaver who couldn't build a dam if his life depended on it.

 Margaret Millar, *How Like an Angel* (1962)

12 Inefficiency seems to be running rampant in our world, and our only hope lies in the fact that the wicked so often share this lack of dedication to a job well done.

 Helen Hayes, with Sandford Dody, *On Reflection* (1968)

## ✿ INDECISION

13 I know not what to do; my mind is divided.

 Sappho (6th cent. B.C.), in Henry Thornton Wharton, *Sappho* (1895)

14 Ah, snug lie those that slumber / Beneath Conviction's roof. / Their floors are sturdy lumber, / Their windows, weatherproof. / But I sleep cold forever / And cold sleep all my kind, / Born nakedly to shiver / In the draft from an open mind.

 Phyllis McGinley, "Lament for a Wavering Viewpoint," *A Short Walk From the Station* (1951)

15 He dithered around like a fart in a trouser leg.

 Liza Cody, *Bucket Nut* (1993)

16 Then again, maybe I won't.

 Judy Blume, book title (1971)

17 Never mind.

 Gilda Radner, as "Emily Litella," *It's Always Something* (1989)

See also Ambivalence, Choice, Doubt.

## ✿ INDEPENDENCE

18 It is easy to be independent when you've got money. But to be independent when you haven't got a thing—that's the Lord's test.

 Mahalia Jackson, with Evan McLeod Wylie, *Movin' On Up* (1966)

19 There is no such thing as being too independent.

 Victoria Billings, *The Womansbook* (1974)

See also Self-Sufficiency.

## ❧ INDIA

1 Once you have felt the Indian dust, you will never be free of it.

  Rumer Godden, *The Peacock Spring* (1975)

2 India always changes people, and I have been no exception.

  Ruth Prawer Jhabvala, *Heat and Dust* (1975)

3 India was . . . a country filled for the most part with people who live so close to the necessities of existence that only important things are important to them.

  Santha Rama Rau, *Home to India* (1945)

4 It is in the oral traditions of the villages that the arts of India are really alive. The brief Western immortality of museums is pointless to people who have seen eternity in their earth.

  Santha Rama Rau, *Home to India* (1945)

5 To the Indian, politics are what the weather is to an Englishman. Politics are an introduction to a stranger on a train, they are the standard filler for embarrassing silences in conversation, they are the inevitable small talk at any social gathering.

  Santha Rama Rau, *Home to India* (1945)

## ❧ INDIFFERENCE

6 My dear, I don't give a damn.

  Margaret Mitchell, *Gone With the Wind* (1936)

7 One must be very strong, or very stupid, or completely exhausted to face life with indifference.

  Alexandra David-Neel (1914), *La Lampe de Sagesse* (1986)

8 People never write calmly but when they write indifferently.

  Lady Mary Wortley Montagu (1709), in Octave Thanet, ed., *The Best Letters of Lady Mary Wortley Montagu* (1901)

9 It is not opposition but indifference which separates men.

  M.P. Follett, *The New State* (1918)

10 The accomplice to the crime of corruption is frequently our own indifference.

  Bess Myerson, in Claire Safran, "Impeachment?" *Redbook* (1974)

11 I want to make people feel intensely alive. I'd rather have them against me than indifferent.

  Martha Graham, in Barbara McDowell and Hana Umlauf, *Woman's Almanac* (1977)

See also Apathy.

## ❧ INDIGNATION

12 Shahid has grown increasingly committed to the art of indignation, waking up in the morning with an expression of incipient disgust already in stock for all the affronts he will surely encounter during the course of the day.

  Sara Suleri, *Meatless Days* (1989)

13 I was so obsessed and consumed with my grievances that I could not get away from myself and think things out in the light. I was in the grip of that blinding, destructive, terrible thing—righteous indignation.

  Anzia Yezierska, "Soap and Water," *Hungry Hearts* (1920)

See also Anger, Grievances, Outrage, Righteousness.

## ❧ INDIVIDUALITY

14 The boughs of no two trees ever have the same arrangement. Nature always produces *individuals*; She never produces *classes*.

  Lydia Maria Child, *Letters From New York*, 2nd series (1845)

15 One cup poured into another makes different waters; tears shed by one eye would blind if wept into another's eye. The breast we strike in joy is not the breast we strike in pain; any man's smile would be consternation on another's mouth.

  Djuna Barnes, *Nightwood* (1937)

16 Every heart is the other heart. Every soul is the other soul. Every face is the other face. The individual is the one illusion.

  Marguerite Young, *Miss MacIntosh, My Darling* (1965)

17 The individual—stupendous and beautiful paradox—is at once infinitesimal dust and the cause of all things.

  C.V. Wedgwood, *Velvet Studies* (1946)

1 Instead of boiling up individuals into the species I would draw a chalk circle round every individuality and preach to it to keep within that, and preserve and cultivate its identity.

    Jane Welsh Carlyle, to Thomas Carlyle (1845), in James Anthony Froude, ed., *Letters and Memorials of Jane Welsh Carlyle*, vol. 1 (1883)

2 I think that virtually every human being is dramatically interesting. Not only is he dramatically interesting, he is a creature of stature whoever he is.

    Lorraine Hansberry, in Robert Nemiroff, ed., *To Be Young, Gifted and Black* (1969)

3 We all try to be alike in our youth, and individual in our middle age . . . although we sometimes mistake eccentricity for individuality.

    Mrs. Alec-Tweedie, *Behind the Footlights* (1904)

4 The thing that makes you exceptional, if you are at all, is inevitably that which must also make you lonely.

    Lorraine Hansberry, in Robert Nemiroff, ed., *To Be Young, Gifted and Black* (1969)

5 To have one's individuality completely ignored is like being pushed quite out of life. Like being blown out as one blows out a light.

    Evelyn Scott, *Escapade* (1923)

6 A child develops individuality long before he develops taste.

    Erma Bombeck, *If Life Is a Bowl of Cherries, What Am I Doing in the Pits?* (1971)

See also Character, Eccentricity, Human Differences, Self, Stereotypes, Uniqueness.

## ❦ INDULGENCE

7 Our greatest indulgence towards a man springs from our despair of him.

    Marie von Ebner-Eschenbach, *Aphorisms* (1893)

See also Self-Indulgence.

## ❦ INDUSTRIALISM

8 Industrialism is the religion with "the machine" as the god going to answer all the prayers. Communism and capitalism were just competing sects.

    Dora Russell, in Dale Spender, *There's Always Been a Women's Movement This Century* (1983)

9 One of the problems with industrialism is that it's based on the premise of more and more. . . . More and more television sets. More and more cars. More and more steel, and more and more pollution. We don't question whether we *need* any more or what we'll do with them. We just have to keep on making more and more if we are to keep going. Sooner or later it's going to collapse.

    Dora Russell, in Dale Spender, *There's Always Been a Women's Movement This Century* (1983)

10 Industrial societies can only be run successfully by dictators or oligarchs.

    Dora Russell, in Dale Spender, *There's Always Been a Women's Movement This Century* (1983)

See also Business, Business and Politics, Economy.

## ❦ INEVITABILITY

11 The most beautiful thing is inevitability of events, and the most ugly thing is trying to resist inevitability. I do not struggle.

    Katharine Butler Hathaway (1929), *The Journals and Letters of the Little Locksmith* (1946)

## ❦ INEXPERIENCE

12 Nobody ever was—or ever again will be—as green as I was the day I landed in New York. That shade has been discontinued.

    Carolyn Kenmore, *Mannequin* (1969)

See also Ignorance.

## ❦ INFATUATION

13 Infatuation is one of those slightly comic illnesses which are at once so undignified and so painful that a nice-minded world does its best to ignore their existence altogether, referring to them only under provocation and then with apology, but, like its more material brother, this boil on the neck of the spirit can hardly be forgotten either by the sufferer or anyone else in his vicinity. The malady is

ludicrous, sad, excruciating and, above all, instantly diagnosable.

Margery Allingham, *The Fashion in Shrouds* (1938)

See also Love.

# ❦ INFIDELITY

1 Physical infidelity is the signal, the notice given, that all the fidelities are undermined.

Katherine Anne Porter, "'Marriage Is Belonging,'" *The Days Before* (1952)

2 No adultery is bloodless.

Natalia Ginzburg, *The City and the House* (1985)

3 When something like this happens, you suddenly have no sense of reality at all. You have lost a piece of your past. The infidelity itself is small potatoes compared to the low-level brain damage that results when a whole chunk of your life turns out to have been completely different from what you thought it was. It becomes impossible to look back at anything that's happened . . . without wondering what was really going on.

Nora Ephron, *Heartburn* (1983)

4 He did not speak again till just before he died, when he kissed his wife's hand with singular tenderness and called her "Elizabeth." She had been christened Augusta Frederica; but then, as the doctor explained, dying men often make these mistakes.

John Oliver Hobbes, *The Sinner's Comedy* (1892)

5 All I wanted was a man / With a single heart, / . . . / Not somebody always after wriggling fish / With his big bamboo rod.

Chuo Wên-chün (2nd cent. B.C.), in Kenneth Rexroth and Ling Chung, eds., *The Orchid Boat* (1972)

6 His infidelities gave me more horns than a basketful of snails.

Anna Magnani, in Oriana Fallaci, *Limelighters* (1963)

7 People who are so dreadfully "devoted" to their wives are so apt, from mere habit, to get devoted to other people's wives as well.

Jane Welsh Carlyle (1838), in James Anthony Froude, ed., *Letters and Memorials of Jane Welsh Carlyle*, vol. 1 (1883)

8 I was growing tired of all the fussing and prevaricating, of the stolen hours and the secret rendez-

vous; of the small indignities and broad discomfort that are part and parcel of adultery.

Vicki Baum, *I Know What I'm Worth* (1964)

9 That is what adultery is, a meanness and a stealing, a taking away from someone what should be theirs, a great selfishness, and surrounded and guarded by lies lest it should be found out. And out of this meanness and this selfishness and this lying flow love and joy and peace, beyond anything that can be imagined.

Rose Macaulay, *The Towers of Trebizond* (1956)

10 When one loves in a certain way, even betrayals become unimportant.

Colette, *Claudine and Annie* (1903)

11 Never tell a loved one of an infidelity: you would be badly rewarded for your trouble. Although one dislikes being deceived, one likes even less to be undeceived.

Ninon de Lenclos (1665), in Lillian Day, *Ninon* (1957)

12 He's excused, she's named and she's accused.

Christine de Pisan, "Letter of the God of Love" (1399), in Thelma S. Fenster and Mary Carpenter Erler, eds., *Poems of Cupid, God of Love* (1990)

13 I did not say I ever had any children; I said I had *maintained* them. . . . Never did I take one of those tender infants in my arms, that the forehead of my Valet, the squint-eye of my Apothecary, or the double-chin of my Chaplain, did not stare me in the face, and damp all the fine feelings of the parent, which I had just called up.

Mrs. Inchbald, *Every One Has His Fault* (1793)

14 She was never attracted to anyone young and whole-hearted and free—she was, in fact, a congenital poacher.

Radclyffe Hall, *The Well of Loneliness* (1928)

15 Wouldn't that be like shoplifting in a secondhand store?

Jean Harlow, when asked if she would steal a husband (1930), in Irving Shulman, *Harlow* (1964)

See also Betrayal.

# ❦ INFLATION

16 Inflation is the senility of democracies.

Sylvia Townsend Warner (1973), in William Maxwell, ed., *Letters: Sylvia Townsend Warner* (1982)

1 The disease is painless; it's the cure that hurts.

Katharine Whitehorn, in *The Observer* (1966)

See also Economics.

## ❦ INFLUENCE

2 Blessed influence of one true loving human soul on another!

George Eliot, "Janet's Repentance," *Scenes of Clerical Life* (1857)

3 It is easier to influence strong than weak characters in life.

Margot Asquith, *More or Less About Myself* (1934)

4 Everybody is influenced by somebody or something. If there's an original, who is the original?

Ernestine Anderson, in Brian Lanker, *I Dream a World* (1989)

5 Influencing people . . . is so dangerous. Their acts and thoughts become your illegitimate children. You can't get away from them and Heaven knows what they mayn't grow up into.

Elizabeth Bibesco, *The Fir and the Palm* (1924)

6 Influence which is given on the side of money is usually against truth.

Harriet Martineau, "On Moral Independence," *Miscellanies*, vol. 1 (1836)

7 Jackson embezzled Laurel's life. He pretended it was still in her account, but little by little, he transferred it to his own. And finally, she was bankrupt.

Gillian Roberts, "Fury Duty," in Marilyn Wallace, ed., *Sisters in Crime 3* (1990)

See also Inspiration.

## ❦ INFORMATION

8 All the news and scandal of a large county forty years ago, and a hundred years before, and ever since, all the marriages, deaths, births, elopements, law-suits, and casualties of her own times, her father's, grandfather's, great-grandfather's, nephew's, and grand-nephew's, has she detailed with a minuteness, an accuracy, a prodigality of learning, a profuseness of proper names, a pedantry

of locality, which would excite the envy of a county historian, a king-at-arms, or even a Scotch novelist.

Mary Russell Mitford, *Our Village* (1848)

9 Everybody gets so much information all day long that they lose their common sense.

Gertrude Stein (1946), in Elizabeth Sprigge, *Gertrude Stein* (1957)

See also Data, Facts, Knowledge.

## ❦ INGRATITUDE

10 The true sin against the Holy Ghost is ingratitude.

Elizabeth I, in Frederick Chamberlin, *The Sayings of Queen Elizabeth* (1923)

11 We have all known ingratitude, ungrateful we have never been.

Diane de Poitiers (1550), in Winifred Gordon, *A Book of Days* (1910)

See also Gratitude.

## ❦ INJUSTICE

12 An unrectified case of injustice has a terrible way of lingering, restlessly, in the social atmosphere like an unfinished equation.

Mary McCarthy, "My Confession" (1953), *On the Contrary* (1961)

13 All History is current; all injustice continues on some level, somewhere in the world.

Alice Walker (1978), in Gloria T. Hull, Patricia Bell Scott, and Barbara Smith, eds., *All the Women Are White, All the Blacks Are Men, But Some of Us Are Brave* (1982)

14 In this world it rains on the Just and the Unjust alike, but the Unjusts have the Justs' umbrellas.

Lynne Alpern and Esther Blumenfeld, *Oh, Lord, I Sound Just Like Mama* (1986)

15 There must always be a remedy for wrong and injustice if we only know how to find it.

Ida B. Wells (1900), in Alfreda M. Duster, ed., *Crusade for Justice* (1970)

16 Injustice is a sixth sense, and rouses all the others.

Amelia E. Barr, *All the Days of My Life* (1913)

1 Injustice boils in men's hearts as does steel in its cauldron, ready to pour forth, white hot, in the fullness of time.

   Mother Jones, in Linda Atkinson, *Mother Jones* (1978)

2 I have come to believe that the one thing people cannot bear is a sense of injustice. Poverty, cold, even hunger, are more bearable than injustice.

   Millicent Fenwick, *Speaking Up* (1982)

3 I think if I was dying and I heard of an act of injustice, it would start me up to a moment's life again.

   Olive Schreiner (1912), in S.C. Cronwright-Schreiner, ed., *The Letters of Olive Schreiner 1876-1920* (1924)

4 One had better die fighting against injustice than to die like a dog or a rat in a trap.

   Ida B. Wells (1892), in Alfreda M. Duster, ed., *The Autobiography of Ida B. Wells* (1970)

5 It would have cost me more trouble to escape from injustice, than it does to submit to it.

   Marie-Jeanne Roland (1793), in Lydia Maria Child, *Memoirs of Madame de Staël and of Madame Roland* (1847)

6 The golf links lie so near the mill / That almost every day / The laboring children can look out / And see the men at play.

   Sarah N. Cleghorn, "The Golf Links Lie So Near the Mill," *Portraits and Protests* (1917)

7 When one has been threatened with a great injustice, one accepts a smaller as a favor.

   Jane Welsh Carlyle, journal (1855), in James Anthony Froude, ed., *Letters and Memorials of Jane Welsh Carlyle*, vol. 2 (1883)

8 If I did half of the things this sorry President [Nixon] did, they would put me under the jail and send every key to the moon. They have the little punishments for the big men and the heavy chastisement for the poor.

   Ruth Shays, in John Langston Gwaltney, *Drylongso* (1980)

See also Discrimination, Intolerance, Justice, Oppression, Persecution, Prejudice.

❧ INNER LIFE

9 If we go down into ourselves we find that we possess exactly what we desire.

   Simone Weil, *Gravity and Grace* (1947)

10 The externals are simply so many props; everything we need is within us.

   Etty Hillesum (1942), *An Interrupted Life* (1983)

11 Inside myself is a place where I live all alone and that's where you renew your springs that never dry up.

   Pearl S. Buck, in *The New York Post* (1959)

12 Some peoples' lives are affected by what happens to their person or their property; but for others fate is what happens to their feelings and their thoughts—that and nothing more.

   Willa Cather, *Lucy Gayheart* (1935)

13 My life is increasingly an inner one and the outer setting matters less and less.

   Etty Hillesum (1942), *An Interrupted Life* (1983)

14 It is those who have a deep and real inner life who are best able to deal with the "irritating details of outer life."

   Evelyn Underhill (1933), in Charles Williams, ed., *The Letters of Evelyn Underhill* (1943)

15 True inward quietness . . . is not vacancy, but stability—the steadfastness of a single purpose.

   Caroline Stephen, *Light Arising* (1908)

16 In the life of each of us, I said to myself, there is a place remote and islanded, and given to endless regret or secret happiness.

   Sarah Orne Jewett, *The Country of the Pointed Firs* (1896)

17 Suddenly many movements are going on within me, many things are happening, there is an almost unbearable sense of sprouting, of bursting encasements, of moving kernels, expanding flesh.

   Meridel Le Sueur, "Annunciation" (1927), *Salute to Spring* (1940)

18 I swear that each of us keeps, battened down inside himself, a sort of lunatic giant—impossible socially, but full-scale—and that it's the knockings and batterings we sometimes hear in each other that keeps our intercourse from utter banality.

   Elizabeth Bowen, *The Death of the Heart* (1938)

19 I see nothing to fear in inner space.

   Yeshe Tsogyel (8th cent.), in Keith Dowman, *Sky Dancer* (1984)

20 Penetrate deeply into the secret existence of anyone about you, even of the man or woman whom you count happiest, and you will come upon things

they spend all their efforts to hide. Fair as the exterior may be, if you go in, you will find bare places, heaps of rubbish that can never be taken away, cold hearths, desolate altars, and windows veiled with cobwebs.

Myrtle Reed, *A Weaver of Dreams* (1911)

1 When I first began this diary I said I would give a record of my inner life. I begin to wonder if I have said anything about my inner life. What if I have *no inner life?*

Janet Frame, *Owls Do Cry* (1960)

See also Emotions, Extroverts and Introverts, Feelings, Introspection, Self, Soul, Spirituality, Voices, Wholeness.

## ✿ INNOCENCE

2 As innocent as waking babies playing with their toes.

Grace King, "The Story of a Day," *Balcony Stories* (1892)

3 Innocence is not pure so much as pleased, / Always expectant, bright-eyed, self-enclosed.

May Sarton, "Giant in the Garden," *The Land of Silence* (1953)

4 What I call innocence is the spirit's unself-conscious state at any moment of pure devotion to any object. It is at once a receptiveness and total concentration.

Annie Dillard, *Pilgrim at Tinker Creek* (1974)

5 To be innocent is to bear the weight of the entire universe. It is to throw away the counterweight.

Simone Weil, *Gravity and Grace* (1947)

6 Innocence involves an unseeing acceptance of things at face value, an ignorance of the area below the surface. . . . One cannot have both compassion and innocence.

Eugenia W. Collier, "Marigolds," in *Negro Digest* (1969)

7 Innocence ends when one is stripped of the delusion that one likes oneself.

Joan Didion, "On Self-Respect," *Slouching Towards Bethlehem* (1968)

8 Innocence is impossible when people have never had the choice of becoming corrupt by dominating others.

Sheila Rowbotham, *Woman's Consciousness, Man's World* (1973)

9 I beg you to believe me; I have never done an act of espionage against France. Never. Never.

Mata Hari, in Russell Warren Howe, *Mata Hari* (1986)

10 I am ill at ease with people whose lives are an open book.

Ivy Compton-Burnett, *More Women Than Men* (1933)

11 The innocent are so few that two of them seldom meet—when they do meet, their victims lie strewn all round.

Elizabeth Bowen, *The Death of the Heart* (1938)

12 When lightning strikes, the mouse is sometimes burned with the farm.

Phyllis Bottome, *The Mortal Storm* (1938)

13 When a person is found less guilty than he is suspected, he is concluded more innocent than he really is.

Charlotte Lennox, *Sophia* (1762)

14 To vice, innocence must always seem only a superior kind of chicanery.

Ouida, *Wisdom, Wit and Pathos* (1884)

15 It's innocence when it charms us, ignorance when it doesn't.

Mignon McLaughlin, *The Second Neurotic's Notebook* (1966)

See also Purity, Vindication.

## ✿ INNOVATION

16 At first people refuse to believe that a strange new thing can be done, then they begin to hope it can be done, then they see it can be done—then it is done and all the world wonders why it was not done centuries ago.

Frances Hodgson Burnett, *The Secret Garden* (1911)

17 Innovators are inevitably controversial.

Eva Le Gallienne, *The Mystic in the Theater* (1965)

1 There was never a place for her [Isadora Duncan] in the ranks of the terrible, slow army of the cautious. She ran ahead, where there were no paths.

> Dorothy Parker, "Poor, Immortal Isadora," in *The New Yorker* (1928)

See also Change, Discovery, Invention, Originality, Progress.

## ❦ INSANITY

2 Insanity is doing the same thing over and over again, but expecting different results.

> Rita Mae Brown, *Sudden Death* (1983)

3 How crazy craziness makes everyone, how irrationally afraid. The madness hidden in each of us, called to, identified, aroused like a lust. And against that the jaw sets. The more I fear my own insanity the more I must punish yours.

> Kate Millett, *The Loony-Bin Trip* (1990)

4 Of all the calamities to which humanity is subject, none is so dreadful as insanity. . . . All experience shows that insanity seasonably treated is as certainly curable as a cold or a fever.

> Dorothea Dix, speech (1846), in Judith Anderson, ed., *Outspoken Women* (1984)

5 Nobody gets packed off to the insane asylum in Our Town. Dotty people are just accepted, and everybody watches them and takes care of them because everybody knows the ones who really need watching are the people who are supposed to be all right.

> Carolyn Kenmore, *Mannequin* (1969)

6 Insanity comes in two basic varieties: slow and fast. I'm not talking about onset or duration. I mean the quality of the insanity, the day-to-day business of being nuts.

> Susanna Kaysen, *Girl, Interrupted* (1993)

7 You can always trust the information given you by people who are crazy; they have an access to truth not available through regular channels.

> Sheila Ballantyne, *Norma Jean the Termite Queen* (1975)

8 Crazy people who are judged to be harmless are allowed an enormous amount of freedom ordinary people are denied.

> Katherine Paterson, *Jacob Have I Loved* (1980)

9 Frankly, goin' crazy was the *best* thing that ever happened to me. I don't say it's for everybody; some people couldn't cope.

> Jane Wagner, *The Search for Signs of Intelligent Life in the Universe* (1985)

See also Depression, Madness, Mental Illness, Psychiatry, Sanity.

## ❦ INSECTS

10 Insects have had a poor press which has emphasized their role as ravagers, disease carriers or as nuisances. There is always an uncomfortable undercurrent of opinion that insects, in some fiendish manner, are trying to inherit our planet. Insects need an articulate public relations man.

> Beatrice Trum Hunter, *Gardening Without Poisons* (1964)

11 If you see a thing that looks like a cross between a flying lobster and the figure of Abraxas on a Gnostic gem, do not pay it the least attention, never mind where it is; just keep quiet and hope it will go away—for that's your best chance; you have none in a stand-up fight with a good thorough-going African insect.

> Mary H. Kingsley, *West African Studies* (1899)

12 In the South Pacific, because of their size, mosquitoes are required to file flight plans.

> Erma Bombeck, *When You Look Like Your Passport Photo, It's Time to Go Home* (1991)

13 Seventeen times he had been attacked by those vicious insects, those aberrations of nature, and his neck, arms, and ankles were battlefields where small red bumps marked the final filling stations of dead but satisfied mosquitoes.

> Lucille Kallen, *The Tanglewood Murder* (1980)

14 The greatest mercy, I have often thought, of the Mediterranean coast lies in its mosquitoes. Did we not suffer from their unwelcome attention, we could not bear our holidays to end.

> Winifred Holtby, "The Right Side of Thirty" (1930), *Pavements at Anderby* (1937)

15 There is nothing like getting used to cockroaches early when your life is going to be spent on the Coast. . . . They have none of the modest reticence of the European variety. They are very companionable, seeking rather than shunning human society,

nestling in the bunk with you if the weather is the least chilly. . . They come out most at night, but then they distinctly like a bright light, and you can watch them in a tight packed circle round the lamp with their heads towards it, twirling their antennae at it with evident satisfaction; in fact it's the lively nights those cockroaches have that keep them abed during the day.

Mary H. Kingsley, *West African Studies* (1899)

1 Slugs are things from the edges of insanity, and I am afraid of slugs and all their attributes.

M.F.K. Fisher, *Serve It Forth* (1937)

2 Flies are the price we pay for summer.

Ann Zwinger, *Beyond the Aspen Grove* (1970)

3 Bees are Black, with Gilt Surcingles — / Buccaneers of Buzz.

Emily Dickinson (1877), in Thomas H. Johnson, ed., *The Complete Poems of Emily Dickinson* (1960)

4 Everywhere bees go racing with the hours, / For every bee becomes a drunken lover, / Standing upon his head to sup the flowers.

Vita Sackville-West, "Spring," *The Land* (1927)

5 We once had a lily here that bore *108* flowers on one stalk: it was photographed naturally for all the gardening papers. The bees came from miles and miles, and there were the most disgraceful Bacchanalian scenes: bees hardly able to find their way home.

Edith Sitwell (1943), in John Lehmann and Derek Parker, eds., *Selected Letters* (1970)

6 The blossom rifled, / With laden thighs / Further each willing / Eunuch plies: / A dull way to fertilize.

Sylvia Townsend Warner, "Honey for Tea," *The Espalier* (1925)

7 Bees are captious folk / And quick to turn against the lubber's touch.

Vita Sackville-West, "Spring," *The Land* (1927)

8 Few creatures so tiny have managed to raise such unreasoning panic.

Mary Webb, in *The Spectator* (1924)

See also Butterflies.

## ❧ INSECURITY

9 Insecurity breeds treachery: if you are kind to people who hate themselves, they will hate you as well.

Florence King, *With Charity Toward None* (1992)

10 Insecure people have a special sensitivity for anything that finally confirms their own low opinion of themselves.

Sue Grafton, *"B" Is for Burglar* (1985)

See also Anxiety, Self-Esteem.

## ❧ INSENSITIVITY

11 Three girl children did nothing to reconcile Ada Hicks to a fourth; and her husband, when he heard the ghastly news, stood mute and stricken, wondering why his wife always had to tell him things like that before tea when she knew that worry gave him indigestion.

Kylie Tennant, *Ride On Stranger* (1943)

12 People of delicate health, selfish dispositions, and coarse minds, can always bear the sufferings of others placidly.

Isabel Burton, *The Inner Life of Syria, Palestine, and the Holy Land* (1884)

13 Other people's vicissitudes are fascinating—fascinating to read about, to be told of, to witness, to do anything but share. . . . And ideally, small disagreeablenesses should happen to friends' friends, not to friends of one's own.

Elizabeth Bowen, *Collected Impressions* (1950)

14 A doctrine of endurance flows easily from our lips when we are enduring jam and our neighbors dry bread, and it is still possible for us to become resigned to the afflictions of our brother.

Ellen Glasgow, *The Descendant* (1897)

15 One can suffer a convulsion of one's entire nature, and, unless it makes some noise, no one notices. It's not just that we are incurious; we completely lack any sense of each other's existences.

Elizabeth Bowen, *The Death of the Heart* (1938)

16 One of the advantages or disadvantages of the way in which we live in these modern days is that we are ceasing to feel. That is to say we do not permit ourselves to be affected by either death or misfor-

tune, provided these natural calamities leave our own persons unscathed.

Marie Corelli, *Innocent* (1914)

1 He jests at quills who never felt their wound.

Minna Thomas Antrim, *Book of Toasts* (1902)

2 If the people have no bread, let them eat cake.

Marie Antoinette, repeating an older expression (1770)

See also Complacency.

## ♦ INSIGHT

3 I used to think there would be a blinding flash of light someday, and then I would be wise and calm and would know how to cope with everything and my kids would rise up and call me blessed. Now I see that whatever I'm like, I'm pretty well stuck with it for life. Hell of a revelation that turned out to be.

Margaret Laurence, *The Fire-Dwellers* (1969)

4 I often see through things right to the apparition itself.

Grace Paley, *Enormous Changes at the Last Minute* (1974)

See also Cleverness, Intuition, Revelation, Understanding, Visions.

## ♦ INSOMNIA

5 There are twelve hours in the day, and above fifty in the night.

Marie de Rabutin-Chantal, Marquise de Sévigné (1671), *Letters of Madame de Sévigné to Her Daughter and Her Friends*, vol. 2 (1811)

6 In its early stages, insomnia is almost an oasis in which those who have to think or suffer darkly take refuge.

Colette, *The Other One* (1929)

7 If I had slept, I should not know so well / The poets.

Eliza Boyle O'Reilly, "Insomnia: Compensations," *My Candles* (1903)

8 To wake in the night: be wide awake in an instant, with all your faculties on edge: to wake, and be under compulsion to set in, night for night, at the same point, knowing from grim experience, that the demons awaiting you have each to be grappled with in turn, no single one of them left unthrown, before you can win through to the peace that is utter exhaustion.

Henry Handel Richardson, *The Fortunes of Richard Mahoney: Ultima Thule* (1929)

9 A ruffled mind makes a restless pillow.

Charlotte Brontë, *The Professor* (1846)

10 I did not sleep. I never do when I am over-happy, over-unhappy, or in bed with a strange man.

Edna O'Brien, title story, *The Love Object* (1968)

11 Sleeplessness is a desert without vegetation or inhabitants.

Jessamyn West, *The Woman Said Yes* (1976)

12 If night comes without thee / She is more cruel than day.

Alice Meynell, "To Sleep," *Last Poems of Alice Meynell* (1923)

13 He stood up and looked down at his bed accusingly, as a man might look at his tormentor. He saw its battered pillow, its blankets slipping to the floor. Sinking to the floor, he amended, staggering to the floor. Perhaps he was the tormentor and the bed his victim.

Laura Z. Hobson, *The Other Father* (1950)

14 How do people go to sleep? I'm afraid I've lost the knack. I might try busting myself smartly over the temple with the night-light. I might repeat to myself, slowly and soothingly, a list of quotations beautiful from minds profound; if I can remember any of the damn things.

Dorothy Parker, "The Little Hours," *The Collected Stories of Dorothy Parker* (1942)

See also Sleep.

## ♦ INSPIRATION

15 Inspiration is the richest nation I know, the most powerful on earth. Sexual energy Freud calls it; the capital of desire I call it; it pays for both mental and physical expenditure.

Sylvia Ashton-Warner (1942), *Myself* (1967)

1 The most beautiful thing in the world is, precisely, the conjunction of learning and inspiration.

Wanda Landowska, in Denise Restout, ed., *Landowska on Music* (1964)

2 I could never tell where inspiration begins and impulse leaves off. . . . If your hunch proves a good one, you were inspired; if it proves bad, you are guilty of yielding to thoughtless impulse.

Beryl Markham, *West With the Night* (1942)

3 There are two ways of spreading light: to be / The candle or the mirror that reflects it.

Edith Wharton, "Vesalius in Zante," *Artemis to Actaeon* (1909)

See also Impulses, Influence.

## ❦ INSTINCT

4 Instinct is a powerful form of natural energy, perhaps comparable in humans to electricity or even atomic energy in the mechanical world.

Margaret A. Ribble, *The Rights of Infants* (1943)

5 It is only by following your deepest instinct that you can lead a rich life and if you let your fear of consequence prevent you from following your deepest instinct, then your life will be safe, expedient and thin.

Katharine Butler Hathaway, *The Journals and Letters of the Little Locksmith* (1946)

6 The point is that one's got an *instinct* to live. One doesn't live because one's *reason* assents to living. People who, as we say, "would be better dead" don't want to die! People who apparently have everything to live for just let themselves fade out of life because they haven't got the energy to fight.

Agatha Christie, *Sad Cypress* (1939)

7 I believe that we are always attracted to what we need most, an instinct leading us towards the persons who are to open new vistas in our lives and fill them with new knowledge.

Helene Iswolsky, *Light Before Dusk* (1942)

See also Intuition.

## ❦ INSTITUTIONS

8 Individuals learn faster than institutions and it is always the dinosaur's brain that is the last to get the new messages!

Hazel Henderson, *The Politics of the Solar Age* (1981)

See also Bureaucracy, Organizations.

## ❦ INSULTS

9 He received insults with a glow most people reserved for compliments.

Liza Cody, *Dupe* (1981)

10 His mind divided! Verily, that is making two bites of a cherry.

L.E. Landon, *Romance and Reality* (1831)

11 Don't be angry with the gentleman for *thinking*, whatever be the cause, for I assure you he makes no common practice of offending in that way.

Fanny Burney, *Evelina* (1778)

12 The man might have become a Power, but he preferred to remain an Ass.

H.P. Blavatsky, referring to an editor (1875), *Collected Writings*, vol. 1 (1966)

13 No, you wouldn't. I'd do it myself.

Emmeline Pankhurst, response to heckler who said, "If you were my wife I'd poison you" (1909), in David Mitchell, *The Fighting Pankhursts* (1967)

14 The reason the all-American boy prefers beauty to brains is that the all-American boy can see better than he can think.

Farrah Fawcett Majors, in Judy Allen, *Picking on Men* (1985)

15 His mother should have thrown him away and kept the stork.

Mae West, *Belle of the Nineties* (1934)

See also Criticisms, Disapproval.

## ❦ INTEGRITY

16 Integrity pays, but not in cash.

Jennifer Stone, "Lesbian Liberation," *Mind Over Media* (1988)

See also Honesty, Honor.

## ❦ INTELLECTUALS

1 I would call an intellectual one whose instrument of work—his mind—is also his major source of pleasure; a man whose entertainment is his intelligence.

  Marya Mannes, "The Lost Tribe of Television," *But Will It Sell?* (1964)

2 I don't want people running around saying Gwen Brooks's work is intellectual. That makes people think instantly about obscurity. It shouldn't have to mean that, but it often seems to.

  Gwendolyn Brooks, in Claudia Tate, ed., *Black Women Writers at Work* (1983)

3 It's no surprise to me that intellectuals commit suicide, go mad or die from drink. We feel things more than other people. We know the world is rotten and that chins are ruined by spots.

  Sue Townsend, *The Secret Diary of Adrian Mole Aged 13-3/4* (1982)

4 Ben was an intellectual, and intellectuals, say what you like, seemed to last longer than anyone else.

  Muriel Spark, "The Fathers' Daughters," *Voices at Play* (1961)

5 The decision to speak out is the vocation and life-long peril by which the intellectual must live.

  Kay Boyle, in James Vinson, ed., *Contemporary Novelists* (1976)

6 A scholar's heart is a dark well in which are buried many aborted feelings that rise to the surface as arguments.

  Natalie Clifford Barney, *Adventures of the Mind* (1929)

7 The intellectual is constantly betrayed by his own vanity. Godlike, he blandly assumes that he can express everything in words.

  Anne Morrow Lindbergh, *The Wave of the Future* (1940)

See also Anti-Intellectualism, Genius, Head and Heart, Intelligence.

## ❦ INTELLIGENCE

8 The naked intellect is an extraordinarily inaccurate instrument.

  Madeleine L'Engle, *A Wind in the Door* (1973)

9 There is nothing more misleading than sagacity if it happens to get on a wrong scent.

  George Eliot, *The Mill on the Floss* (1860)

10 Although intelligence tests are usually speed tests for the sake of convenience, it is debatable whether speed has any rightful place in the basic concept of intelligence.

  Isabel Briggs Myers, with Peter B. Myers, *Gifts Differing* (1980)

11 The only useful answer to the question "Who is smarter, a man or a woman?" is, *Which* man and *which* woman?

  Estelle Ramey, in Madeline Chinnici, "Do Human Brains Have Gender?" *Self* (1990)

12 Had I been in anything inferior to him, he would not have hated me so thoroughly, but I knew all that he knew, and, what was worse, he suspected that I kept the padlock of silence on mental wealth in which he was no sharer.

  Charlotte Brontë, *The Professor* (1846)

13 It is not true that a man's intellectual power is, like the strength of a timber beam, to be measured by its weakest point.

  George Eliot, *Impressions of Theophrastus Such* (1879)

14 Intellect does not attain its full force unless it attacks power.

  Madame de Staël, *On Literature* (1800)

15 Intelligence always had a pornographic influence on me.

  Maya Angelou, *The Heart of a Woman* (1981)

16 Scheherazade is the classical example of a woman saving her head by using it.

  Esmé Wynne-Tyson, in J.M. and M.J. Cohen, *A Dictionary of Modern Quotations* (1971)

See also Brain, Cleverness, Genius, Head and Heart, Intellectuals, Mind.

## ❦ INTENSITY

17 I long to see everything, to know everything, to learn everything!

  Marie Bashkirtseff (1878), in Mary J. Serrano, tr., *The Journal of a Young Artist* (1919)

1 Life was never life to me unless my heart stood still.

   Margaret Anderson, *The Fiery Fountains* (1953)

2 Nature formed me fierce.

   Lady Caroline Lamb, *Glenarvon* (1816)

3 I am a stranger to half measures. With life I am on the attack, restlessly ferreting out each pleasure, foraging for answers, wringing from it even the pain. I ransack life, hunt it down. I am the hungry peasants storming the palace gates. I will have my share. No matter how it tastes.

   Marita Golden, *Migrations of the Heart* (1983)

4 I'm the breathless woman / I'm the hurried woman / I'm the girl with the unquenchable thirst.

   Anne Waldman, title poem, *Fast Speaking Woman* (1975)

5 The great sins and fires break out of me like the terrible leaves from the bough in the violent spring. I am a walking fire, I am all leaves.

   Edith Sitwell, in Elizabeth Salter and Allanah Harper, eds., *Edith Sitwell* (1976)

6 I had learnt to seek intensity rather than happiness, not joys and prosperity but *more of life*, a concentrated sense of life, a strengthened feeling of existence, fullness and concentration of *pulse*, energy, growth, flowering, beyond the image of happiness or unhappiness.

   Nina Berberova, *The Italics Are Mine* (1969)

7 My candle burns at both ends; / It will not last the night; / But ah, my foes, and oh, my friends— / It gives a lovely light!

   Edna St. Vincent Millay, "First Fig," *A Few Figs From Thistles* (1920)

8 Sometime write me a little poem that *isn't* intense. A lamp turned too high might shatter its chimney. Please just *glow* sometimes.

   Olive Higgins Prouty, to Sylvia Plath (1957), in Aurelia Schober Plath, ed., *Letters Home* (1973)

9 Sometimes I felt it was almost too much for her, loving and being loved so intensely. The sword was too sharp for the scabbard.

   Rosemary Kutak, *Darkness of Slumber* (1944)

10 The higher the flame shoots the quicker it blacks out.

   Helen Hull, *Landfall* (1953)

See also Passion.

## ❧ INTENTIONS

11 People with good intentions never give up!

   Jane Smiley, *Duplicate Keys* (1984)

12 Good intentions are wicked! As far as I can see, all they lead to are lies and delusions.

   Jane Smiley, *Duplicate Keys* (1984)

13 I don't see as it matters much how well you mean if it's harm you're doin'.

   Martha Ostenso, *The Mad Carews* (1927)

See also Motives.

## ❧ INTERDEPENDENCE

14 One life stamps and influences another, which in turn stamps and influences another, on and on, until the soul of human experience breathes on in generations we'll never even meet.

   Mary Kay Blakely, *Wake Me When It's Over* (1989)

15 Whatever we do to any other thing in the great web of life, we do to ourselves, for we are one.

   Brooke Medicine Eagle, *Buffalo Woman Comes Singing* (1991)

16 There's a thread that binds all of us together, pull one end of the thread, the strain is felt all down the line.

   Rosamond Marshall, *Kitty* (1943)

17 We all act as hinges—fortuitous links between other people.

   Penelope Lively, *Moon Tiger* (1987)

18 Breath is life, and the intermingling of breaths is the purpose of good living. This is in essence the great principle on which all productive living must rest, for relationships among all the beings of the universe must be fulfilled; in this way each individual life may also be fulfilled.

   Paula Gunn Allen, *The Sacred Hoop* (1986)

19 Happy are all free peoples, too strong to be dispossessed. / But blessed are those among nations who dare to be strong for the rest!

   Elizabeth Barrett Browning, "A Court Lady," *Poems Before Congress* (1860)

1 The crocodile doesn't harm the bird that cleans his teeth for him. He eats the others but not that one.

Linda Hogan, *Mean Spirit* (1990)

2 In reality, all communication that debilitates females also debilitates males, for if any system diminishes a part of the species, it diminishes all of it.

Bobbye D. Sorrels, *The Nonsexist Communicator* (1983)

3 We should not be independent like millionaires, nor dependent like laborers. My ideal is that we all be interdependent.

Rose Pastor Stokes (1912), in Herbert Shapiro and David L. Sterling, eds., *"I Belong to the Working Class"* (1992)

4 All that is due to us will be paid, although not perhaps by those to whom we have lent.

Marie von Ebner-Eschenbach, *Aphorisms* (1893)

See also Human Family, Wholeness.

## ❦ INTERESTING

5 Generally speaking anybody is more interesting doing nothing than doing something.

Gertrude Stein, *Everybody's Autobiography* (1937)

6 Unfortunately, Genji reflected, people who do not get into scrapes are a great deal less interesting than those who do.

Lady Murasaki, *The Tale of Genji* (c. 1008)

7 It is completely unimportant. That is why it is so interesting.

Agatha Christie, *The Murder of Roger Ackroyd* (1926)

## ❦ INTERFERENCE

8 Much growth is stunted by too careful prodding, / Too eager tenderness. / The things we love we have to learn to leave alone.

Naomi Long Madgett, "Woman With Flower," *Star by Star* (1965)

9 Insistent advice may develop into interference, and interference, someone has said, is the hind hoof of the devil.

Carolyn Wells, *The Rest of My Life* (1937)

10 Great mischief comes from attempts to steady other people's altars.

Mary Baker Eddy, *Miscellaneous Writings: 1883-1896* (1896)

11 The passion for setting people right is in itself an afflictive disease.

Marianne Moore, "Snakes, Mongooses, Snake Charmers, and the Like," *Selected Poems* (1935)

12 More children suffer from interference than from non-interference.

Agatha Christie, *Crooked House* (1949)

13 For your own good. What a ghastly phrase that was. It covered the most barbarous and inhuman cruelties ever inflicted.

Margaret Millar, *It's All in the Family* (1948)

14 I always distrust people who know so much about what God wants them to do to their fellows.

Susan B. Anthony, in National American Woman Suffrage Association, *Proceedings* (1896)

15 People genuinely happy in their choices seem less often tempted to force them on other people than those who feel martyred and broken by their lives.

Jane Rule, *Lesbian Images* (1975)

16 There are plenty of people, in Avonlea and out of it, who can attend closely to their neighbors' business by dint of neglecting their own; but Mrs. Rachel Lynde was one of those capable creatures who can manage their own concerns and those of other folks into the bargain.

L.M. Montgomery, *Anne of Green Gables* (1908)

17 She had lived not merely her own life but, without restraint, as many other lives as possible, and those of her family, of course, had most tempted her.

Barbara Deming, "Death and the Old Woman," *Wash Us and Comb Us* (1972)

18 I am one of those people who are blessed, or cursed, with a nature which has to interfere. If I see a thing that needs doing I do it.

Margery Allingham, *Death of a Ghost* (1934)

19 I, who fall short in managing my own affairs, can see just how it would profit my neighbor if I managed his.

Anne Ellis, *Plain Anne Ellis* (1931)

See also Codependence, Control.

## § INTERIOR DECORATION

1  I know of nothing more significant than the awakening of men and women throughout our country to the desire to improve their houses. Call it what you will—awakening, development, American Renaissance—it is a most startling and promising condition of affairs.

> Elsie de Wolfe, *The House in Good Taste* (1913)

2  Eudora . . . was idly speculating upon the blow it must have been to the decorator of the Wagon Wheel when he learned that cash registers were not available in knotty pine.

> Lange Lewis, *Juliet Dies Twice* (1948)

3  It was a Victorian parlor maid's nightmare, marked by the kind of decor involving the word "throw." Throw pillows, throw covers, throw cloths. . . . Next to throw, the operative word was "occasional." Occasional tables, occasional chairs, occasional lamps; footstools, hassocks, stacked trays, wheeled teacarts, and enough card tables to start a gambling den.

> Florence King, *Confessions of a Failed Southern Lady* (1985)

## § INTERNMENT

4  We were made to believe / our faces betrayed us. / Our bodies were loud / with yellow / screaming flesh / needing to be silenced / behind barbed wire.

> Janice Mirikitani, "Breaking Silence," in *Braided Lives* (1991)

## § INTERRUPTIONS

5  Have you ever noticed that life consists mostly of interruptions, with occasional spells of rush work in between?

> Buwei Yang Chao, in Yuenren Chao, tr., *Autobiography of a Chinese Woman* (1947)

6  Interruption is a form of contempt.

> Lucille Kallen, *Introducing C.B. Greenfield* (1979)

7  I'm always aware that I risk being taken for a neurasthenic prima donna when I explain to someone who wants "just a little" of my time that five min-

utes of the wrong kind of distraction can ruin a working day.

> Gail Godwin, in Nancy R. Newhouse, ed., *Hers* (1986)

8  When you take my time, you take something I had meant to use.

> Marianne Moore, "People's Surroundings," *Selected Poems* (1935)

9  The fact is, both callers and work thicken—the former sadly interfering with the latter.

> George Eliot (1852), in J.W. Cross, ed., *George Eliot's Life As Related in Her Letters and Journals* (1885)

10  I was always supposed to be at home when friends and acquaintances came out to see me; it would have been unkind not to receive them. Nevertheless, I was sometimes annoyed when in the midst of a difficult [mathematical] problem someone would enter and say "I have come to spend a few hours with you."

> Mary Somerville (1815), in Margaret E. Tabor, *Pioneer Women* (1933)

11  When I have any appointment, even an afternoon one, it changes the whole quality of time. I feel overcharged. There is no space for what wells up from the subconscious; those dreams and images live in deep still water and simply submerge when the day gets scattered.

> May Sarton, *Journal of a Solitude* (1973)

12  Sometimes I would almost rather have people take away years of my life than take away a moment.

> Pearl Bailey, *Talking to Myself* (1971)

See also Busyness, Conversation, Listening, Time.

## § INTIMACY

13  Intimacy is a difficult art.

> Virginia Woolf, "Geraldine and Jane," *The Common Reader*, 2nd series (1932)

14  We commonly confuse *closeness* with *sameness* and view intimacy as the merging of two separate "I's" into one worldview.

> Harriet Lerner, *Dance of Intimacy* (1989)

See also Friendship, Love, Lovers, Marriage, Relationships.

## ◊ INTOLERANCE

1 The trouble with most people is they think there's only one right way to do anything.
   Velda Johnston, *A Howling in the Woods* (1968)

2 One man's ways may be as good as another's, but we all like our own best.
   Jane Austen, *Persuasion* (1818)

3 Traditional Anglo-Saxon intolerance is a local and temporal culture-trait like any other. . . . We have failed to understand the relativity of cultural habits, and we remain debarred from much profit and enjoyment in our human relations with people of different standards, and untrustworthy in our dealings with them.
   Ruth Benedict, *Patterns of Culture* (1934)

4 The last refuge of intolerance is in not tolerating the intolerant.
   George Eliot (1857), in J.W. Cross, ed., *George Eliot's Life As Related in Her Letters and Journals* (1884)

See also Bigotry, Narrow-Mindedness, Prejudice.

## ◊ INTROSPECTION

5 Introspection is a devouring monster.
   Anaïs Nin (1936), *The Diary of Anaïs Nin*, vol. 2 (1967)

See also Extroverts and Introverts, Inner Life.

## ◊ INTUITION

6 Intuition is a suspension of logic due to impatience.
   Rita Mae Brown, *Southern Discomfort* (1982)

7 Intuition is a spiritual faculty and does not explain, but simply points the way.
   Florence Scovel Shinn, in Mary Alice Warner and Dayna Beilenson, eds., *Women of Faith and Spirit* (1987)

8 One of the many sad results of the Industrial Revolution was that we came to depend more than ever on the intellect, and to ignore the intuition with its symbolic thinking.
   Madeleine L'Engle, *Walking on Water* (1980)

9 Trusting our intuition often saves us from disaster.
   Anne Wilson Schaef, *Meditations for Women Who Do Too Much* (1990)

10 I don't believe in intuition. When you get sudden flashes of perception, it is just the brain working faster than usual. But you've been getting ready to know it for a long time, and when it comes, you feel you've known it always.
   Katherine Anne Porter, in George Plimpton, ed., *The Writer's Chapbook* (1989)

11 Enoch never nagged his blood to tell him a thing until it was ready.
   Flannery O'Connor, *Wise Blood* (1949)

See also Insight, Instinct.

## ◊ INVENTION

12 I don't think necessity is the mother of invention—invention, in my opinion, arises directly from idleness, possibly also from laziness. To save oneself trouble.
   Agatha Christie, *An Autobiography* (1977)

13 Invention is the pleasure you give yourself when other people's stuff isn't good enough.
   Julie Newmar, in Ethlie Ann Vare and Greg Ptacek, *Mothers of Invention* (1988)

See also Creation, Discovery, Innovation.

## ◊ INVITATION

14 Invitation is the sincerest flattery.
   Carolyn Wells, "More Mixed Maxims," *Folly for the Wise* (1904)

See also Hospitality.

## ◊ IOWA

15 You are brilliant and subtle if you come from Iowa and really strange and you live as you live and you

are always very well taken care of if you come from Iowa.

Gertrude Stein, *Everybody's Autobiography* (1937)

1 Iowans know themselves and what they are doing. They are doing well.

Pearl S. Buck, *Pearl Buck's America* (1971)

# ❦ IRAN

2 My country is a kingdom of fire, a carpet of sand and stone that millions of feet have trodden.

Sattareh Farman Farmaian, *Daughter of Persia* (1992)

3 The Persian's mind, like his illuminated manuscripts, does not deal in perspective: two thousand years, if he happens to know anything about them, are as exciting as the day before yesterday.

Freya Stark, *The Valleys of the Assassins* (1934)

# ❦ IRELAND

4 Not in vain is Ireland pouring itself all over the earth. . . . The Irish, with their glowing hearts and reverent credulity, are needed in this cold age of intellect and skepticism.

Lydia Maria Child, *Letters From New York*, 1st series (1842)

5 For 'tis green, green, green, where the ruined towers are gray, / And it's green, green, green, all the happy night and day; / Green of leaf and green of sod, green of ivy on the wall, / And the blessed Irish shamrock with the fairest green of all.

Mary Elizabeth Blake, "The Dawning of the Year," in Edmund Clarence Stedman, ed., *An American Anthology 1787–1900* (1900)

6 The way with Ireland is that no sooner do you get away from her than the golden mists begin to close about her, and she lies, an Island of the Blest, something enchanted in our dreams.

Katharine Tynan, *The Middle Years* (1917)

7 Ireland is not at all a simple place, and in many ways it is spare and sad. It has no wealth, no power, no stability, no influence, no fashion, no size. Its only real arts are song and drama and poem. But

Limerick alone has two thousand ruined castles and surely that many practicing poets.

Shana Alexander, "The Nearest Faraway Place," in *Life* (1967)

8 Ireland is a wonderful place to write in. Even although the atmosphere was so Faith-laden that I was often worried that I was *not* writing a book to the glory of God, I had to admit that words flowed from my pen like all-get-out. To be honest, there is *nothing to do in Ireland but write.*

Nancy Spain, *Why I'm Not a Millionaire* (1956)

9 A typical Irish dinner would be: cream flavored with lobster, cream with bits of veal in it, green peas and cream, cream cheese, cream flavored with strawberries.

Nancy Mitford, "The Other Island," *The Water Beetle* (1962)

10 In some parts of Ireland the sleep which knows no waking is always followed by a wake which knows no sleeping.

Mary Wilson Little, *A Paragrapher's Reveries* (1904)

11 The Irish have a flair for wringing from death the last drop of emotion and they do not quite understand those who react otherwise.

Dervla Murphy, *Wheels Within Wheels* (1979)

12 Religion dies hard in the Irish.

Katharine Tynan, *The Middle Years* (1917)

13 Among the best traitors Ireland has ever had, Mother Church ranks at the very top, a massive obstacle in the path to equality and freedom.

Bernadette Devlin, *The Price of My Soul* (1969)

14 The trouble with the Irish question always has been that it was an English question.

Katharine Tynan, *The Wandering Years* (1922)

15 I am troubled, I'm dissatisfied, I'm Irish.

Marianne Moore, "Spenser's Ireland," *What Are Years?* (1941)

16 Like any Irish mother, I am scar tissue to the bone.

Jennifer Stone, "In Search of Manhood," *Stone's Throw* (1988)

17 My mother was Irish and she was superstitious, if you'll forgive the tautology.

Rosalind Russell, with Chris Chase, *Life Is a Banquet* (1977)

18 The Irish never listen / We hear everything / But we wouldn't be caught dead / Listening.

Jennifer Stone, "Ethnic Ethos," in *Sandstones* (1975)

1 The Irish always jest even though they jest with tears.

    Katharine Tynan, *The Wandering Years* (1922)

2 Strange race. . . . Don't know what they want, but want it like the devil.

    Mary Roberts Rinehart, *Dangerous Days* (1919)

3 He had the Gaelic gaiety and melancholy, like the streaks of fat and lean in Irish bacon.

    Marjorie Kinnan Rawlings, *The Sojourner* (1953)

4 Irish people have a trick of over-statement, at which one ceases to wince as one grows older.

    Katharine Tynan, *Twenty-Five Years* (1913)

5 Irish eyes make love of themselves, whenever their owner is too busy about something else to keep a tight rein on them.

    Roman Doubleday, *The Hemlock Avenue Mystery* (1908)

6 The little lawyer roused himself long enough to wonder why it was that whenever four men sing in a barroom, three of them turn out to be Irish.

    Craig Rice, *The Right Murder* (1941)

## ❧ IRONY

7 Humor brings insight and tolerance. Irony brings a deeper and less friendly understanding.

    Agnes Repplier, *In Pursuit of Laughter* (1936)

8 Irony is bitter truth / wrapped up in a little joke.

    H.D., *The Walls Do Not Fall* (1944)

9 Pleasure in irony, either in your own life or in what you read, is an ego trip. "I know what others do not."

    Jessamyn West, *The Life I Really Lived* (1979)

10 Irony is an indispensable ingredient of the critical vision; it is the safest antidote to sentimental decay.

    Ellen Glasgow, *A Certain Measure* (1943)

11 A taste for irony has kept more hearts from breaking than a sense of humor—for it takes irony to appreciate the joke which is on oneself.

    Jessamyn West, *To See the Dream* (1957)

See also Humor, Satire.

## ❧ IRRATIONALITY

12 The irrational haunts the metaphysical.

    Annie Dillard, *The Writing Life* (1989)

13 The human animal varies from class to class, culture to culture. In one way we are consistent: We are irrational.

    Rita Mae Brown, *Starting From Scratch* (1988)

## ❧ ISLAM

14 If the Koran is the soul of Islam, then perhaps the institution of the Muslim family might be described as its body.

    Elizabeth Warnock Fernea, *Women and the Family in the Middle East* (1985)

15 We learned at an early age that it was men's interpretation of our religion that restricted women's opportunities, not our religion itself. Islam in fact had been quite progressive toward women from its inception.

    Benazir Bhutto, *Daughter of Destiny* (1989)

16 Oh, to lie upon the rugs of some silent mosque, far from the noise of wanton city life, and, eyes closed, gaze turned heavenwards, listen to Islam's song for ever!

    Isabelle Eberhardt (1900), in Nina de Voogd, tr., *The Passionate Nomad* (1988)

See also Religion, Spirituality.

## ❧ ISLANDS

17 Islands are gregarious animals, they decorate the ocean in convoys.

    Stella Benson, *I Pose* (1915)

18 Ambas and Bobia Islands are perfect gems of beauty. Mondoleh I cannot say I admire. It always looks to me exactly like one of those flower-stands full of ferns and plants—the sort you come across in drawing rooms at home, with wire-work legs. I do not mean that Mondoleh has wire-work legs under water, but it looks as if it might have.

    Mary H. Kingsley, *Travels in West Africa* (1897)

1 The eternal sound of the sea on every side has a tendency to wear away the edge of human thought and perception.

Celia Thaxter, *Among the Isles of Shoals* (1899)

## ❦ ISRAEL

2 To be or not to be is not a question of compromise. Either you be or you don't be.

Golda Meir, speech (1974)

3 Why the black answer of hate / to your existence, Israel? / . . . / In the others' choir / you always sang / one note lower / or one note higher.

Nelly Sachs, "Why the black answer of hate," *O the Chimneys* (1967)

4 Israel itself is the strongest guarantee against another Holocaust.

Golda Meir, *My Life* (1975)

5 Let me tell you something that we Israelis have against Moses. He took us forty years through the desert in order to bring us to the one spot in the Middle East that has no oil!

Golda Meir, in *The New York Times* (1973)

## ❦ ITALY

6 I like every single part of Italy, unlike Italians, who only like their part and hate all the rest. They say things like, "You're going to . . . *Rome*?"

Fran Lebowitz, in *Travel & Leisure* (1994)

7 Who can ever be alone for a moment in Italy? Every stone has a voice, every grain of dust seems instinct with spirit from the Past, every step recalls some line, some legend of long-neglected lore.

Margaret Fuller, in *The New-York Daily Tribune* (1847)

8 The sunshine had the density of gold-leaf: we seemed to be driving through the landscape of a missal.

Edith Wharton, *Italian Backgrounds* (1905)

9 Nobody with a dream should come to Italy. No matter how dead and buried the dream is thought to be, in Italy it will rise and walk again.

Elizabeth Spencer, *The Light in the Piazza* (1960)

10 Italy is a country which is willing to submit itself to the worst governments. It is, as we know, a country ruled by disorder, cynicism, incompetence and confusion. Nevertheless we are aware of intelligence circulating in the streets like a vivid bloodstream.

Natalia Ginzburg, *The Little Virtues* (1962)

11 The Italians are the most civilized people. And they're very warm. Basically, they're Jews with great architecture.

Fran Lebowitz, in *Travel & Leisure* (1994)

12 There's only one institution of importance in Italian-American life and that is the family.

Aileen Riotto Sirey, in Linda Brandi Cateura, *Growing Up Italian* (1987)

13 Just give the Italians a chance for drama and they take it with both hands.

Ingrid Bergman, with Alan Burgess, *Ingrid Bergman* (1980)

14 Italians are never punctual; the café, the convenient place to wait, absolves them from that. There is no question of hanging about, no looking lost and unwanted or even disreputable, as there is in hotel lobbies or the foyers of restaurants. One just sits and enjoys the scene, and waits.

Shirley Hazzard, *The Evening of the Holiday* (1965)

15 Not all Italian men are handsome, but the percentage is alarmingly high, and their tailors cooperate with nature.

Mary Chamberlin, *Dear Friends and Darling Romans* (1959)

16 Florence—the city of tranquillity made manifest.

Katherine Cecil Thurston, *The Gambler* (1905)

17 Trieste has the atmosphere of being nowhere more than any place I know.

Mary Chamberlin, *Dear Friends and Darling Romans* (1959)

See also Europe, Rome, Venice.

# J

1 January has only one thing to be said for it: it is followed by February. Nothing so well becomes it as its passing.

    Katharine Tynan, *Twenty-Five Years* (1913)

2 January, month of empty pockets!

    Colette, "Empty Pockets" (1928), *Journey for Myself* (1972)

See also Winter.

## ❧ JAPAN

3 One must learn, if one is to see the beauty in Japan, to like an extraordinarily restrained and delicate loveliness.

    Miriam Beard, *Realism in Romantic Japan* (1930)

4 Americans are so often thrown by Japan. It looks familiar but, an inch below the surface, it isn't anything like the West at all.

    Cathy N. Davidson, *36 Views of Mount Fuji* (1993)

5 "I will do my best" is a favorite Japanese expression, and, in, Japan, one's best must be very, very good.

    Cathy N. Davidson, *36 Views of Mount Fuji* (1993)

6 Everything in Japan is hidden. Real life has an unlisted phone number.

    Fran Lebowitz, in *Travel & Leisure* (1994)

## ❧ JARGON

7 Jargon seems to be the place where right and left brains meet.

    Wendy Kaminer, *I'm Dysfunctional, You're Dysfunctional* (1992)

8 A passage is not plain English—still less is it good English—if we are obliged to read it twice to find out what it means.

    Dorothy L. Sayers, "Plain English," *Unpopular Opinions* (1946)

9 She spoke academese, a language that springs like Athene from an intellectual brow, and she spoke it with a nonregional, "good" accent.

    May Sarton, *The Small Room* (1961)

10 I'm bilingual. I speak English and I speak educationese.

    Shirley M. Hufstedler, in *Newsweek* (1980)

11 If one cannot state a matter clearly enough so that even an intelligent twelve-year-old can understand it, one should remain within the cloistered walls of the university and laboratory until one gets a better grasp of one's subject matter.

    Margaret Mead, in *Redbook* (1963)

12 I cannot speak well enough to be unintelligible.

    Jane Austen, *Northanger Abbey* (1818)

13 For my part I think the Learned, and Unlearned Blockhead pretty equal; for 'tis all one to me, whether a Man talk Nonsense, or unintelligible Sense, I am diverted and edified alike by either.

    Mary Astell, *An Essay in Defense of the Female Sex* (1697)

14 I know what an Act to make things simpler means. It means that the people who drew it up don't understand it themselves and that every one of its clauses needs a law-suit to disentangle it.

    Dorothy L. Sayers, *Unnatural Death* (1927)

15 A great many people think that polysyllables are a sign of intelligence.

    Barbara Walters, *How to Talk With Practically Anybody About Practically Anything* (1970)

1 I might not know how to use thirty-four words where three would do, but that does not mean I don't know what I'm talking about.
  Ruth Shays, in John Langston Gwaltney, *Drylongso* (1980)

2 You and I come by road or rail, but economists travel on infrastructure.
  Margaret Thatcher, in *The Observer* (1985)

3 She calls a spade a delving instrument.
  Rita Mae Brown, *Southern Discomfort* (1982)

See also Language, Words.

## ❦ JAZZ

4 Jazz is the expression of America's romantic self, its sensual potency, its lyrical force.
  Anaïs Nin (1957), *The Diary of Anaïs Nin*, vol. 6 (1976)

5 Jazz was home. It created a hunger within me.
  Dianne Reeves, in Pamela Johnson, "Dianne Reeves," *Essence* (1989)

6 Jazz is the music of the body.
  Anaïs Nin (1947), *The Diary of Anaïs Nin*, vol. 5 (1974)

7 Jazz exemplifies artistic activity that is at once individual and communal, performance that is both repetitive and innovative, each participant sometimes providing background support and sometimes flying free.
  Mary Catherine Bateson, *Composing a Life* (1989)

8 Jazz is not a game of chance. Its sonorous disorder is only an appearance. It is an organized force obeying obscure laws, conforming to a secret technique, codified or not, and we discover that no one can become a virtuoso on the spur of the moment.
  Wanda Landowska, in Denise Restout, ed., *Landowska on Music* (1964)

See also Music.

## ❦ JEALOUSY

9 Jealousy is cruel as the grave.
  The Shulamite, *Song of Songs* (c. 3rd cent. B.C.)

10 Jealousy is the grave of affection.
  Mary Baker Eddy, *Science and Health* (1875)

11 Jealousy, the old Worm that bites.
  Aphra Behn, *The Lucky Chance* (1687)

12 Jealousy is the tie that binds—and binds—and binds.
  Helen Rowland, *A Guide to Men* (1922)

13 Jealousy is no more than feeling alone against smiling enemies.
  Elizabeth Bowen, *The House in Paris* (1935)

14 Jealousy is all the fun you *think* they had.
  Erica Jong, *How to Save Your Own Life* (1977)

15 Jealousy is the most dreadfully involuntary of all sins.
  Iris Murdoch, *The Black Prince* (1973)

16 Jealousy is not born of love! It is a child of selfishness and distrust.
  Mourning Dove, *Cogewea* (1927)

17 Jealousy is the very reverse of understanding, of sympathy, and of generous feeling. Never has jealousy added to character, never does it make the individual big and fine.
  Emma Goldman, "Jealousy: Causes and a Possible Cure" (1912), in Alix Kates Shulman, ed., *Red Emma Speaks* (1983)

18 The knives of jealousy are honed on details.
  Ruth Rendell, *An Unkindness of Ravens* (1985)

19 Jealousy had a taste, all right. A bitter and tongue-stinging flavor, like a peach pit.
  Dolores Hitchens, *In a House Unknown* (1973)

20 She suspected him of infidelity, with and without reason, morning, noon, and night.
  Ada Leverson, *Bird of Paradise* (1914)

21 Her jealousy never slept.
  Mary Shelley, "The Mortal Immortal: A Tale" (1833), *Tales and Stories* (1891)

22 I believe she would be jealous of a fine day, if her husband praised it.
  Hannah More, *Coelebs in Search of a Wife* (1808)

23 Jealousy is never satisfied with anything short of an omniscience that would detect the subtlest fold of the heart.
  George Eliot, *The Mill on the Floss* (1860)

1 Jealousy is like a hot pepper. Use it mildly, and you add spice to the relationship. Use too much of it and it can burn.

   Ayala M. Pines, *Romantic Jealousy* (1992)

2 Jealousy in romance is like salt in food. A little can enhance the savor, but too much can spoil the pleasure and, under certain circumstances, can be life-threatening.

   Maya Angelou, *Wouldn't Take Nothing for My Journey Now* (1993)

3 Jealousy, he thought, was as physical as fear; the same dryness of the mouth, the thudding heart, the restlessness which destroyed appetite and peace.

   P.D. James, *Death of an Expert Witness* (1977)

4 The jealous bring down the curse they fear upon their own heads.

   Dorothy Dix, *Dorothy Dix—Her Book* (1926)

5 It is surely one of the bitterest curses of that most torturing of all passions—jealousy—that it leads the sufferer persistently to seek, with craving eyes and ears, the sights and sounds that madden most.

   Bertha H. Buxton, *Jenny of "The Prince's"* (1876)

6 Some have imagined that by arousing a baseless suspicion in the mind of the beloved we can revive a waning devotion. But this experiment is very dangerous. Those who recommend it are confident that so long as resentment is groundless one need only suffer it in silence and all will soon be well. I have observed however that this is by no means the case.

   Lady Murasaki, *The Tale of Genji* (c. 1008)

7 There are two dogs who stand guard in your stomach. Their names in English are jealousy and fear. One guardian dog is jealously fearful, the other fearfully jealous. They are medicine to protect you.

   Agnes Whistling Elk, in Lynn V. Andrews, *Medicine Woman* (1981)

8 To jealousy, nothing is more frightful than laughter.

   Françoise Sagan, *La Chamade* (1965)

9 The jealousy of the dead is lasting!

   Jean Garrigue, "The Snowfall," in Howard Moss, ed., *The Poet's Story* (1973)

See also Envy.

❧ JESUS

See Christ.

❧ JEWELS

10 Never wear second-rate jewels, wait till the really good ones come to you. . . . Rather than a wretched little diamond full of flaws, wear a simple, plainly inexpensive ring. In that case you can say, "It's a memento. I never part with it, day or night."

   Colette, "Gigi," in *Présent* (1943)

See also Diamonds.

❧ JEWS

11 To be a Jew is a destiny.

   Vicki Baum, *And Life Goes On* (1931)

12 They carried their land upon their shoulders and their sanctuary in their hearts.

   Jessie E. Sampter, *The Book of the Nations* (1917)

13 A people . . . wise-hearted with the sorrows of every land.

   Jessie E. Sampter, *The Book of the Nations* (1917)

14 His cup is gall, his meat is tears, / His passion lasts a thousand years.

   Emma Lazarus, "The Crowing of the Red Cock," *Songs of a Semite* (1882)

15 I have felt that to be a Jew was, in some ways at least, to be especially privileged.

   Edna Ferber, *A Peculiar Treasure* (1939)

16 To be a Jew in the twentieth century / Is to be offered a gift. If you refuse, / Wishing to be invisible, you choose / Death of the spirit, the stone insanity.

   Muriel Rukeyser, "Letter to the Front," *Beast in View* (1944)

17 Jews are the intensive form of any nationality whose language and customs they adopt.

   Emma Lazarus, "An Epistle to the Hebrews," in *American Hebrew* (1882)

1 The nations which have received and in any way dealt fairly and mercifully with the Jew have prospered, and the nations that have tortured and oppressed him have written out their own curse.

> Olive Schreiner, *A Letter on the Jew* (1906)

2 We Jews are alike. We have the same intensities, the sensitiveness, poetry, bitterness, sorrow, the same humor, the same memories. The memories are not those we can bring forth from our minds: they are centuries old and are written in our features, in the cells of our brains.

> Leah Morton, *I Am a Woman—and a Jew* (1926)

3 The Jews are the victims of the strongest of collective suggestions. The truth is that they are neither better nor worse than others, but what comes from them is underlined, exaggerated, made responsible for all evil. They seem to have perpetually to fulfill the function of the scapegoat.

> Adrienne Monnier (1938), in Richard McDougall, tr., *The Very Rich Hours of Adrienne Monnier* (1976)

4 let my people in / to history.

> Melanie Kaye/Kantrowitz, "Jerusalem Shadow," in Deborah Keenan and Roseann Lloyd, eds., *Looking for Home* (1990)

5 Scratch a Jew and you'll find a Wailing Wall.

> Eve Merriam, "The Wall," in Nathan and Marynn Ausubel, eds., *A Treasury of Jewish Poetry* (1957)

6 Pessimism is a luxury that a Jew can never allow himself.

> Golda Meir, in *The Observer* (1974)

7 Poverty becomes a Jew like a red ribbon on a white horse.

> Anzia Yezierska, *Red Ribbon on a White Horse* (1950)

8 The alchemy of home life went far to turn the dross of the Ghetto into gold.

> Lady Katie Magnus, *Jewish Portraits* (1905)

9 For many people—from secular feminists to observant Jews—the notion of a feminist Judaism is an oxymoron.

> Judith Plaskow, *Standing Again at Sinai* (1990)

10 I am not a Jew in the synagogue and a feminist in the world. I am a Jewish feminist and a feminist Jew in every moment of my life.

> Judith Plaskow, *Standing Again at Sinai* (1990)

11 The Jewish problem is as old as history, and assumes in each age a new form. The life or death of millions of human beings hangs upon its solution; its agitation revives the fiercest passions for good and for evil that inflame the human breast.

> Emma Lazarus, "The Jewish Problem" (1882), in H.E. Jacob, *The World of Emma Lazarus* (1949)

12 The usual attitude of Christians towards Jews is—I hardly know whether to say more impious or more stupid, when viewed in the light of their professed principles. . . . They hardly know Christ was a Jew. And I find men, educated, supposing that Christ spoke Greek. To my feeling, this deadness to the history which has prepared half our world for us, this inability to find interest in any form of life that is not clad in the same coat-tails and flounces as our own, lies very close to the worst kind of irreligion.

> George Eliot, to Harriet Beecher Stowe (1876), in J.W. Cross, ed., *George Eliot's Life As Related in Her Letters and Journals* (1884)

13 You feel oppressed by your Judaism only as long as you do not take pride in it.

> Bertha Pappenheim (1936), in Joseph L. Baron, *A Treasury of Jewish Quotations* (1956)

14 The Jewish heart has always starved unless it was fed through the Jewish intellect.

> Henrietta Szold, in Mary Alice Warner and Dayna Beilenson, eds., *Women of Faith and Spirit* (1987)

15 There is never a Jewish community without its scholars, but where Jews may not be both intellectuals and Jews, they prefer to remain Jews.

> Mary Antin, *The Promised Land* (1912)

16 The Jews have produced only three originative geniuses: Christ, Spinoza, and myself.

> Gertrude Stein (1925), in Roger McAlmon, "Portrait," *Exile* (1938)

See also Anti-Semitism, Bar Mitzvahs, Bible, Clergy, Holocaust, Israel, Kosher, Minorities, Religion, Spirituality, Torah.

## ❦ JOURNALISM

17 Journalism—an ability to meet the challenge of filling space.

> Rebecca West, in *The New York Herald Tribune* (1956)

18 The tragedy of journalism lies in its impermanence; the very topicality which gives it brilliance con-

demns it to an early death. Too often it is a process of flinging bright balloons in the path of the hurricane, a casting of priceless petals upon the rushing surface of a stream.

Vera Brittain, *Testament of Friendship* (1940)

1 News is like food; it is the cooking and serving that makes it acceptable, not the material itself.

Rose Macaulay, "Problems of a Journalist's Life," *A Casual Commentary* (1926)

2 The Press wants facts . . . viewed through the medium of imagination. . . . You take a handful of dry stones . . . and put them at the bottom of a stream and let the water run over them. . . . They're just as much facts as they were when you'd got them dry in your hand—but you're not yawning over them any more . . . the water's made them come alive. Well, that's what imagination does to facts—it makes them come alive.

Patricia Wentworth, *Nothing Venture* (1932)

3 No news is bad news.

Shelley Smith, on coverage of women's sports, in Ron Rapoport, ed., *A Kind of Grace* (1994)

4 The fact of being reported increases the apparent extent of a deplorable development by a factor of ten.

Barbara W. Tuchman, in *The Atlantic* (1973)

5 When there is good news, and it is *news*, we do report it, but usually news is a record of human failure. Those wanting to celebrate human accomplishment are, as someone said, advised to go to the sports section.

Linda Ellerbee, *"And So It Goes"* (1986)

6 The first law of journalism is to confirm existing prejudice, rather than contradict it.

Linda Ellerbee, *"And So It Goes"* (1986)

7 Fact that is fact every day is not news; it's truth. We report news, not truth.

Linda Ellerbee, *"And So It Goes"* (1986)

8 What bothers me about the journalistic tendency to reduce unmanageable reality to self-contained, movielike little dramas is not just that we falsify when we do this. It is also that we really miss the good story.

Meg Greenfield, in *Newsweek* (1991)

9 In journalism there has always been a tension between getting it first and getting it right.

Ellen Goodman, in *The Boston Globe* (1993)

10 It is grievous to read the papers in most respects, I agree. More and more I skim the headlines only, for one can be sure what is carried beneath them quite automatically, if one has long been a reader of the press journalism.

Mary Ritter Beard (1948), in Nancy F. Cott, *A Woman Making History* (1991)

11 The world is full of happy people, but no one ever hears of them. You have to fight and make a scandal to get into the papers.

Gene Stratton-Porter, *A Girl of the Limberlost* (1909)

See also Journalists, Magazines, Newspapers, The Press, Writing.

## ✦ JOURNALISTS

12 Being a reporter is as much a diagnosis as a job description.

Anna Quindlen, in *The New York Times* (1993)

13 Being a reporter seems a ticket out to the world.

Jacqueline Kennedy Onassis, in *Ms.* (1979)

14 I wouldn't be here if there were no trouble. Trouble is news, and the gathering of news is my job.

Marguerite Higgins, responding to a colonel who said "the young lady" must leave the war front because there might be trouble, *War in Korea* (1951)

15 I got around a lot, and lots of people talked to me. I salted down stories by the barrel load.

Hedda Hopper, with James Brough, *The Whole Truth and Nothing But* (1963)

16 I always warn aspiring reporters to observe three basic rules: 1. Never trust an editor. 2. Never trust an editor. 3. Never trust an editor.

Edna Buchanan, *The Corpse Had a Familiar Face* (1987)

17 They are the scavengers of society who, possessing no guts of their own, tear out the guts of celebrities. They have the sycophantic, false enthusing gush of maiden aunts: who are accustomed to being trampled on doormats.

Caitlin Thomas, *Not Quite Posthumous Letter to My Daughter* (1963)

1 Their shiny gray limousines lay around Hyde Park Corner like basking sharks.

Elizabeth Longford, *The Queen* (1983)

2 However lyingly libelous they may be: nobody can seriously hurt the reputation of a Great person. If he is hurt: he is not Great. They can but scratch at his skin with their mice nails.

Caitlin Thomas, *Not Quite Posthumous Letter to My Daughter* (1963)

3 We do not precisely enjoy *liberty* at the *Figaro*. M. de Latouche, our *worthy* director (ah! you should know the fellow), is always hanging over us, cutting, pruning, right or wrong, imposing upon us his whims, his aberrations, his fancies, and we have to write as he bids.

George Sand (1831), in Raphaël Ledos de Beaufort, ed., *Letters of George Sand*, vol. 1 (1886)

4 Some of the qualities that go into making a good reporter—aggressiveness, a certain sneakiness, a secretive nature, nosiness, the ability to find out that which someone wants hidden, the inability to take "no" with any sort of grace, a taste for gossip, rudeness, a fair disdain for what people will think of you and an occasional and calculated disregard for rules—are also qualities that go into making a very antisocial human being.

Linda Ellerbee, *"And So It Goes"* (1986)

See also Journalism, The Press.

# ✤ JOURNEYS

5 The journey is my home.

Muriel Rukeyser, "Journey," *One Life* (1957)

6 It is good to have an end to journey towards; but it is the journey that matters in the end.

Ursula K. Le Guin, *The Left Hand of Darkness* (1969)

7 I am one of those who never knows the direction of my journey until I have almost arrived.

Anna Louise Strong, *I Change Worlds* (1935)

8 The initial mystery that attends any journey is: how did the traveler reach his starting point in the first place?

Louise Bogan (1933), in Ruth Limmer, ed., *Journey Around My Room* (1980)

9 No journey carries one far unless, as it extends into the world around us, it goes an equal distance into the world within.

Lillian Smith, *The Journey* (1954)

10 We all ended up somewhere with our various uncertain lives flapping about us in tatters and our pockets full of foreign coins.

Karen Elizabeth Gordon, *The Transitive Vampire* (1984)

11 It's not good to take sentimental journeys. You see the differences instead of the samenesses.

Mary Astor, *A Life on Film* (1967)

12 There is no going alone on a journey. Whether one explores strange lands or Main Street or one's own back yard, always invisible traveling companions are close by: the giants and pygmies of memory, of belief, pulling you this way and that, not letting you see the world life-size but insisting that you measure it by their own height and weight.

Lillian Smith, *The Journey* (1954)

13 Ah, I like the look of packing crates! A household in preparation for a journey! . . . Something full of the flow of life, do you understand? Movement, progress.

Lorraine Hansberry, *A Raisin in the Sun* (1959)

See also Adventure, Tourists, Travel, Wanderlust.

# ✤ JOY

14 O world, I cannot hold thee close enough!

Edna St. Vincent Millay, "God's World," *Renascence* (1917)

15 Joy is the holy fire that keeps our purpose warm and our intelligence aglow.

Helen Keller, "To the New College Girl" (1905), *Out of the Dark* (1914)

16 Surely the strange beauty of the world must somewhere rest on pure joy!

Louise Bogan (1953), in Ruth Limmer, ed., *What the Woman Lived* (1973)

17 That's joy, it's always / a recognition, the known / appearing fully itself, and / more itself than one knew.

Denise Levertov, "Matins," *The Jacob's Ladder* (1961)

1 Joy is a net of love by which you can catch souls.

> Mother Teresa, *A Gift for God* (1975)

2 You have to sniff out joy, keep your nose to the joy-trail.

> Buffy Sainte-Marie, in Susan Braudy, "Buffy Sainte-Marie," *Ms.* (1975)

3 People need joy quite as much as clothing. Some of them need it far more.

> Margaret Collier Graham, *Gifts and Givers* (1906)

4 The more the heart is sated with joy, the more it becomes insatiable.

> Gabrielle Roy, *Where Nests the Water Hen* (1951)

5 The sharing of joy, whether physical, emotional, psychic or intellectual, forms a bridge between the sharers which can be the basis for understanding much of what is not shared between them, and lessens the threat of their difference.

> Audre Lorde, *Uses of the Erotic* (1978)

6 The joy of a spirit is the measure of its power.

> Ninon de Lenclos (1694), in Edgar H. Cohen, *Mademoiselle Libertine* (1970)

7 Birds sing after a storm; why shouldn't people feel as free to delight in whatever sunlight remains to them?

> Rose Kennedy, *Times to Remember* (1974)

8 Laughing is not the first expression of joy. . . . A person laughs in idleness, for fun, not for joy. Joy has nothing, nothing but the old way of tears.

> Mrs. Oliphant, *A House in Bloomsbury* (1894)

9 The second half of joy / Is shorter than the first.

> Emily Dickinson, in Mabel Loomis Todd and Millicent Todd Bingham, eds., *Bolts of Melody* (1945)

10 Townfolk know pleasures, country people joys.

> Minna Thomas Antrim, *At the Sign of the Golden Calf* (1905)

11 If all the people who have been hurt by the war were to exclude joy from their lives, it would almost be as if they had died. Men without joy seem like corpses.

> Käthe Kollwitz (1918), in Hans Kollwitz, ed., *The Diaries and Letters of Käthe Kollwitz* (1955)

12 The unendurable is the beginning of the curve of joy.

> Djuna Barnes, *Nightwood* (1937)

See also Contentment, Ecstasy, Gladness, Happiness, Joy and Sorrow, Pleasure.

## ❧ JOY AND SORROW

13 The source of one's joy is also often the source of one's sorrow.

> Jessamyn West, *Cress Delahanty* (1948)

14 I have been in Sorrow's kitchen and licked out all the pots. Then I have stood on the peaky mountain wrapped in rainbows, with a harp and a sword in my hands.

> Zora Neale Hurston, *Dust Tracks on a Road* (1942)

15 Words are less needful to sorrow than to joy.

> Helen Hunt Jackson, *Ramona* (1884)

16 I cannot sleep—great joy is as restless as sorrow.

> Fanny Burney, *Evelina* (1778)

17 We could never learn to be brave and patient, if there were only joy in the world.

> Helen Keller, in *The Atlantic Monthly* (1890)

18 I found more joy in sorrow / Than you could find in joy.

> Sara Teasdale, "The Answer," *Rivers to the Sea* (1915)

See also Joy, Sorrow.

## ❧ JUDAISM

See Jews.

## ❧ JUDGMENT

19 Hear everything and judge for yourself.

> George Eliot, *Middlemarch* (1871)

20 A mistake in judgment isn't fatal, but too much anxiety about judgment is.

> Pauline Kael, *I Lost It at the Movies* (1965)

21 I have heard that a man might be his own lawyer, but you can't be your own judge.

> Margaret Deland, *The Awakening of Helena Richie* (1906)

1 I wonder whether our adoption of Shrink-ese as a second language, the move from religious phrases of judgment to secular words of acceptance, hasn't also produced a moral lobotomy. In the reluctance, the aversion to being judgmental, are we disabled from making any judgments at all?

> Ellen Goodman, in *The Boston Globe* (1993)

2 There are no judgments so harsh as those of the erring, the inexperienced, and the young.

> Dinah Maria Mulock Craik, *A Life for a Life* (1866)

3 She had observed that it was from those who had never sailed stormy waters came the quickest and harshest judgments on bad seamanship in heavy seas.

> Susan Glaspell, *The Visioning* (1911)

4 Youth is the period of harsh judgments, and a man seldom learns until he reaches thirty that human nature is made up not of simples, but of compounds.

> Ellen Glasgow, *The Miller of Old Church* (1911)

5 That would be a good thing for them to cut on my tombstone: Wherever she went, including here, it was against her better judgment.

> Dorothy Parker, "But the One on the Right," in *The New Yorker* (1929)

See also Judgmental, Opinion, Taste.

## ❧ JUDGMENTAL

6 A man generally judges of the disposition of others by his own. . . . Claude, being himself a deceiver, feared deception.

> Regina Maria Roche, *Clermont* (1798)

7 Alas! we give our own coloring to the actions of others.

> L.E. Landon, *Romance and Reality* (1831)

8 I learned early in life not to judge others. We outcasts are very happy and content to leave that job to our social superiors.

> Ethel Waters, with Charles Samuels, *His Eye Is on the Sparrow* (1951)

9 Kinder the enemy who must malign us, / Than the smug friend who will define us.

> Anna Wickham, "Traducers," *The Man With a Hammer* (1916)

10 We need not be too strict in seeing / The failings of a fellow being.

> Mary Lamb, "The Rook and the Sparrows," *Poetry for Children* (1809)

11 If any have a stone to throw / It is not I, ever or now.

> Elinor Wylie, "The Pebble," in William Rose Benét, ed., *Collected Poems of Elinor Wylie* (1933)

See also Disapproval, Faultfinding.

## ❧ JUSTICE

12 No question is ever settled / Until it is settled right.

> Ella Wheeler Wilcox, "Settle the Question Right," *Poems of Pleasure* (1888)

13 There is always a time to make right / what is wrong.

> Susan Griffin, "I Like to Think of Harriet Tubman," *Like the Iris of an Eye* (1976)

14 When it comes to the cause of justice, I take no prisoners and I don't believe in compromising.

> Mary Frances Berry, in Brian Lanker, *I Dream a World* (1989)

15 Justice is not cheap. Justice is not quick. It is not ever finally achieved.

> Marian Wright Edelman, *Families in Peril* (1987)

16 Crime takes but a moment but justice an eternity.

> Ellen O'Grady, in Djuna Barnes, "Woman Police Deputy Is Writer of Poetry," *The New York Sun Magazine* (1918)

17 Justice is a terrible but necessary thing.

> Jessamyn West, *The Massacre at Fall Creek* (1975)

18 One must always be ready to change sides with justice, that fugitive from the winning camp.

> Simone Weil, in Peter Viereck, *The Unadjusted Man* (1956)

19 Someone / will take the ball / from the hands that play / the game of terror.

> Nelly Sachs, "Someone," *O the Chimneys* (1967)

20 Justice is mercy's highest self.

> Frances Hodgson Burnett, *A Lady of Quality* (1896)

1 Justice is / reason enough for anything ugly. It balances the beauty in the world.

> Diane Wakoski, "Justice Is Reason Enough," *Coins & Coffins* (1962)

2 Justice consists in seeing that no harm is done to men. Whenever a man cries inwardly: "Why am I being hurt?" harm is being done to him. He is often mistaken when he tries to define the harm, and why and by whom it is being inflicted on him. But the cry itself is infallible.

> Simone Weil, "Human Personality," *The Simone Weil Reader* (1977)

3 If my cup won't hold but a pint and yourn holds a quart, wouldn't ye be mean not to let me have my little half-measure full?

> Sojourner Truth, speech (1851), in Olive Gilbert, *Narrative of Sojourner Truth* (1878)

4 Ain't I hurt enough without you having to hurt me yet with charity? You want to give me hush money to swallow down unrightness that burns my flesh? I want justice.

> Anzia Yezierska, "The Lost Beautifulness," *Hungry Hearts* (1920)

5 Who thinks of justice unless he knows injustice?

> Diane Glancy, "Portrait of the Lone Survivor," *Lone Dog's Winter Count* (1991)

6 I never promised you a rose garden. I never promised you perfect justice.

> Hannah Green, *I Never Promised You a Rose Garden* (1964)

7 The wheels of justice . . . they're square wheels.

> Barbara Corcoran, *The Hideaway* (1987)

8 Justice and judgment lie often a world apart.

> Emmeline Pankhurst, *My Own Story* (1914)

9 "Criminal justice" was a term she found more apt than it was meant to be.

> BarbaraNeely, *Blanche on the Lam* (1992)

10 We have accumulated a wealth of historical experience which confirms our belief that the scales of American justice are out of balance.

> Angela Y. Davis, *If They Come in the Morning* (1971)

11 I decided as usual that justice lay in the middle—that is to say nowhere.

> Antonia Fraser, *Quiet As a Nun* (1977)

12 Justice waits upon the great, Interest holds the scale, and Riches turns the balance.

> Mary Delarivière Manley, "The Wife's Resentment," *The Power of Love* (1720)

13 The choice between law and justice is an easy one for courageous minds.

> Rebecca West, in *The Clarion* (1913)

14 I believe in divine justice—even in our materialistic world—but I know it works through the instrumentality of human beings sufficiently in tune with it to strive for its execution.

> Etta Shiber, *Paris—Underground* (1943)

15 I remember, we must remember / until justice be done among us.

> Rosario Castellanos, "Memorandum on Tlatelolco" (1972), in Maureen Ahern, ed., *A Rosario Castellanos Reader* (1988)

16 Justice is like the Kingdom of God—it is not without us as a fact, it is within us as a great yearning.

> George Eliot, *Romola* (1862)

17 George Bush and Ronald Reagan have insured their place in history through the legacy they have created in the Supreme Court. They have managed to appoint a misogynistic woman and an anti-civil rights African-American to the Court. They have, however, also contributed a new oxymoron to the English language: Supreme Court Justice.

> Jana Rivington, in Roz Warren, ed., *Glibquips* (1994)

18 The United States Supreme Court, once a reliable if ultimate recourse for progressive and even revolutionary grievances, has become a retrograde wellspring for enormous economic and social distress.

> June Jordan, "Where Is the Rage?" *Technical Difficulties* (1992)

19 When a just cause reaches its flood-tide . . . whatever stands in the way must fall before its overwhelming power.

> Carrie Chapman Catt, speech (1911)

20 When the sense of justice seeks to express itself quite outside the regular channels of established government, it has set forth on a dangerous journey inevitably ending in disaster.

> Jane Addams, *Twenty Years at Hull House* (1910)

21 Justice, like vengeance, is not good eaten cold.

> Elsa Triolet, *Proverbes d'Elsa* (1971)

See also Equality, Fairness, Injustice, Law, Mercy, Rights.

# K

## ❦ KINDNESS

1 So many gods, so many creeds, / So many paths that wind and wind / While just the art of being kind, / Is all the sad world needs.

    Ella Wheeler Wilcox, "The World's Need," *Custer* (1896)

2 My feeling is that there is nothing in life but refraining from hurting others, and comforting those that are sad.

    Olive Schreiner (1884), in S.C. Cronwright-Schreiner, ed., *The Letters of Olive Schreiner 1876-1920* (1924)

3 To be civilized is to be incapable of giving unnecessary offense, it is to have some quality of consideration for all who cross our path.

    Agnes Repplier, "A Question of Politeness," *Americans and Others* (1912)

4 I prefer you to make mistakes in kindness than work miracles in unkindness.

    Mother Teresa, letter to her religious (1959), in Georges Gorrée and Jean Barbier, *The Love of Christ* (1982)

5 A brave man is seldom unkind.

    Pretty-shield, in Frank Bird Linderman, *Pretty-Shield, Medicine Woman of the Crows* (1932)

6 Kindness is always fashionable.

    Amelia E. Barr, *All the Days of My Life* (1913)

7 When kindness has left people, even for a few moments, we become afraid of them, as if their reason had left them.

    Willa Cather, *My Mortal Enemy* (1926)

8 If you stop to be kind, you must swerve often from your path.

    Mary Webb, *Precious Bane* (1924)

9 Many think they have good hearts who have only weak nerves.

    Marie von Ebner-Eschenbach, *Aphorisms* (1893)

10 Hester's kindness . . . was too much like the kindness of a mother cat who will wash her kitten's face whether the kitten wishes it or no.

    Sylvia Townsend Warner, "The Democrat's Daughter," *More Joy in Heaven* (1935)

11 Nobody likes having salt rubbed into their wounds, even if it is the salt of the earth.

    Rebecca West, "The Salt of the Earth," *The Harsh Voice* (1935)

12 Some people, she would say, are so full of the milk of human kindness that it slops over and messes everything.

    Winifred Holtby, *South Riding* (1936)

13 When the milk of human kindness turns sour, it is a singularly unpalatable draught.

    Agnes Repplier, *To Think of Tea!* (1932)

14 The king has been very good to me. He promoted me from a simple maid to be a marchioness. Then he raised me to be a queen. Now he will raise me to a martyr.

    Anne Boleyn (1536), in Willis J. Abbot, *Notable Women in History* (1913)

15 Kindness. The most unkind thing of all.

    Edna O'Brien, *August Is a Wicked Month* (1965)

See also Compassion, Concern, Empathy, Friend liness, Generosity, Goodness, Graciousness, Niceness, Sympathy, Virtue.

## ❦ KISSES

16 A kiss can be a comma, a question mark or an exclamation point.

    Mistinguette, in *Theatre Arts* (1955)

1 When you kiss me, / jaguars lope through my knees; / when you kiss me, my lips quiver like bronze / violets; oh, when you kiss me.

    Diane Ackerman, "Beija-Flor," *Jaguar of Sweet Laughter* (1991)

2 Kissing was like death from lightning. If it happened, you didn't know it. And vice versa.

    Jessamyn West, *Leafy Rivers* (1967)

3 I ducked my head in time, so that he was only able to imprint a chaste salute upon my forehead, as he pressed me against himself in a way I felt quite sure was not the custom of the country, at least only in as much as it is the custom of all countries.

    Margaret Fountaine (1897), in W.F. Cater, ed., *Love Among the Butterflies* (1980)

4 Ruby wasn't particular whom she kissed. In fact she led a regular mouth-to-mouth existence.

    Lillian Day, *Kiss and Tell* (1931)

5 Some men kiss and do not tell, some kiss and tell; but George Moore told and did not kiss.

    Susan Mitchell, in Oliver St. John Gogarty, *As I Was Going Down Sackville Street* (1937)

## ❧ KNOWLEDGE

6 You who want / knowledge, / seek the Oneness / within / There you / will find / the clear mirror / already waiting.

    Hadewijch II (13th cent.), in Jane Hirshfield, ed., *Women in Praise of the Sacred* (1994)

7 I am never afraid of what I know.

    Anna Sewell, *Black Beauty* (1877)

8 I was brought up to believe that the only thing worth doing was to add to the sum of accurate information in this world.

    Margaret Mead, in *The New York Times Book Review* (1964)

9 She knows what she sees. She has her eyes in the right place.

    Johanna Spyri, *Heidi* (1915)

10 Knowledge is much like dust—it sticks to one, one does not know how.

    L.E. Landon, *Romance and Reality* (1831)

11 Peculiar scraps of knowledge were stuck to him like lint from all his jobs.

    Anne Tyler, *Searching for Caleb* (1975)

12 We have a hunger of the mind which asks for knowledge of all around us, and the more we gain, the more is our desire; the more we see, the more are we capable of seeing.

    Maria Mitchell (1878), in Phebe Mitchell Kendall, ed., *Maria Mitchell* (1896)

13 He that knew all that ever learning writ, / Knew only this—that he knew nothing yet.

    Aphra Behn, *The Emperor of the Moon* (1687)

14 I am not wise. Not knowing, and learning to be comfortable with not knowing, is a great discovery.

    Sue Bender, *Plain and Simple* (1989)

15 To appear to be on the inside and know more than others about what is going on is a great temptation for most people. It is a rare person who is willing to seem to know less than he does.

    Eleanor Roosevelt, *This I Remember* (1949)

16 If knowledge is power, clandestine knowledge is power squared; it can be withheld, exchanged, and leveraged.

    Letty Cottin Pogrebin, *Deborah, Golda, and Me* (1991)

17 It is not only by the questions we have answered that progress may be measured, but also by those we are still asking. The passionate controversies of one era are viewed as sterile preoccupations by another, for knowledge alters what we seek as well as what we find.

    Freda Adler, *Sisters in Crime* (1975)

18 Nobody knows enough, but many know too much.

    Marie von Ebner-Eschenbach, *Aphorisms* (1893)

19 In much knowledge there is also much grief.

    Queen Marie of Rumania, *Masks* (1937)

20 Once you have discovered what is happening, you can't pretend not to know, you can't abdicate responsibility.

    P.D. James, in Molly Ivins, *Nothin' But Good Times Ahead* (1993)

21 There comes a time when we aren't allowed not to know.

    Judith Viorst, *Necessary Losses* (1986)

1 Knowledge . . . always imposes responsibility.
  W.M.L. Jay, *Shiloh* (1872)

2 It is important to use all knowledge ethically, humanely, and lovingly.
  Carol Pearson, *The Hero Within* (1986)

3 A time has come in our history when what is known has little connection with what is done.
  Jennifer Stone, "*Missing* Hits the Mark," *Mind Over Media* (1988)

4 Knowledge slowly builds up what Ignorance in an hour pulls down.
  George Eliot, *Daniel Deronda* (1874)

5 How long, I wonder, will ignorance spell purity and knowledge shame?
  Rosamond Lehmann, *The Ballad and the Source* (1945)

6 The only man who knows just what he thinks at the present moment is the man who hasn't done any new thinking in the past ten years.
  Susan Glaspell, *Inheritors* (1921)

7 "I may not know much"—another form of locution often favored by her. The tone in which it was spoken utterly belied the words; the tone told you that not only did she know much, but all.
  Edna Ferber, *Show Boat* (1926)

8 She knows as much about babies as a wild cat knows about tatting.
  Margaret Deland, "An Old Chester Secret," *New Friends in Old Chester* (1924)

9 Those who know nothing must believe everything.
  Marie von Ebner-Eschenbach, *Aphorisms* (1893)

10 Only people who die very young learn all they really need to know in kindergarten.
  Wendy Kaminer, *I'm Dysfunctional, You're Dysfunctional* (1992)

11 It's what you learn after you know it all that counts.
  Judith Kelman, *Someone's Watching* (1991)

See also Common Sense, Curiosity, Data, Experience, Facts, Information, Learning, Self-Knowledge, Teaching, Understanding, Wisdom.

## ❧ KOSHER

12 If you have to ask the rabbi, it isn't kosher.
  Lynne Alpern and Esther Blumenfeld, *Oh, Lord, I Sound Just Like Mama* (1986)

# L

## § LABELS

1 New labels change nothing.
Josephine Lawrence, *Let Us Consider One Another* (1945)

See also Definitions, Names, Naming.

## § LABOR

2 Human history is work history. The heroes of the people are work heroes.
Meridel Le Sueur, *North Star Country* (1945)

3 All the laws made for the betterment of workers' lives have their origin with the workers. Hours are shortened, wages go up, condition are better—only if the workers protest.
Mary Heaton Vorse, *A Footnote to Folly* (1935)

4 The origin of the labor movement lies in self-defense.
Mary Beard, *A Short History of the American Labor Movement* (1920)

5 To me, the labor movement was never just a way of getting higher wages. . . . It is the spirit of trade unionism that is most important, the service of fellowship, the feeling that the hurt of one is the concern of all and that the work of the individual benefits all.
Rose Schneiderman, with Lucy Goldthwaite, *All for One* (1967)

6 The wage-earning class the world over are the victims of society.
Elizabeth Gurley Flynn, in Theodore Dreiser, "An East Side Joan of Arc," *Broadway Magazine* (1906)

7 I learned in the early part of my career that labor must bear the cross for others' sins, must be the vicarious sufferer for the wrongs that others do.
Mother Jones, in Mary Field Parton, *The Autobiography of Mother Jones* (1925)

8 Slowly those who create the wealth of the world are permitted to share it. The future is in labor's strong, rough hands.
Mother Jones, in Mary Field Parton, *The Autobiography of Mother Jones* (1925)

9 A labor victory must be economic and it must be revolutionizing.
Elizabeth Gurley Flynn, speech (1914), in Judith Anderson, ed., *Outspoken Women* (1984)

10 Skilled labor teaches something not to be found in books or in colleges.
Harriet H. Robinson, *Early Factory Labor in New England* (1883)

11 One should not be assigned one's identity in society by the job slot one happens to fill. If we truly believe in the dignity of labor, any task can be performed with equal pride because none can demean the basic dignity of a human being.
Judith Martin, *Common Courtesy* (1985)

12 The surprise of the fight on the long day, of the experiments with the shorter one, has been not only that the business could stand it, but that the business thrived under it. . . . It is but another of the proofs which are heaping up in American industry today that whatever is good for men and women—contributes to their health, happiness, development—is good for business.
Ida Tarbell, *New Ideals in Business* (1914)

13 The trade agreement has become a rather distinct feature of the American labor movement. . . . It is based on the idea that labor shall accept the capi-

talist system of production and make terms of peace with it.

Mary Beard, *A Short History of the American Labor Movement* (1920)

1 The workers asked only for bread and a shortening of the long hours of toil. The agitators gave them visions. The police gave them clubs.

Mother Jones, in Mary Field Parton, *The Autobiography of Mother Jones* (1925)

2 I had never before seen my friends come in beaten, their heads laid open, their noses broken, or seen them jailed for peaceably demonstrating that they wanted work. I had only known how workers lived. Now I was face to face with what our society did to workers who could get no work.

Mary Heaton Vorse, *A Footnote to Folly* (1935)

3 On their side the workers had only the Constitution. The other side had bayonets.

Mother Jones, in Linda Atkinson, *Mother Jones: The Most Dangerous Woman in America* (1978)

4 We want bread and roses too.

Slogan of Massachusetts women textile strikers (1912)

See also Business, Work.


❦ LADIES

5 I have defined Ladies as people who did not do things themselves.

Gwen Raverat, *Period Piece* (1952)

6 Ladies were ladies more by virtue of the things they didn't do than by the things they did.

Emily Hahn, *Times and Places* (1970)

7 Women are not ladies. The term connotes females who are simultaneously put on a pedestal and patronized.

Cynthia Heimel, *Get Your Tongue Out of My Mouth, I'm Kissing You Good-Bye!* (1993)

8 Any woman could act like a lady, and this behavior was interpreted as being submissive, demure, inhibited. . . . Being a lady in the Western world was like footbinding in China.

Victoria Billings, *The Womansbook* (1974)

9 Ladies are just those of us who have been silenced.

Jennifer Stone, in *Mama Bears News and Notes* (1994)

10 She was a perfect lady—just set in her seat and stared.

Eudora Welty, "Lily Daw and the Three Ladies," *A Curtain of Green* (1941)

11 Such a perfect lady! She never raises her voice, she never fidgets, she never contradicts, she never gets untidy.

Elizabeth Bibesco, *The Fir and the Palm* (1924)

12 "Little lady!" That is just such a name as one would give to an idle, useless, butterfly creature, of no value but as an amusement, a plaything of leisure hours, in time of business or care to be altogether set aside and forgotten.

Dinah Maria Mulock Craik, *A Life for a Life* (1866)

13 A young lady is a female child who has just done something dreadful.

Judith Martin, *Miss Manners' Guide to Excruciatingly Correct Behavior* (1982)

14 She was an authority on where to place monograms on linen, how to instruct working folk, and what to say in letters of condolence. The word "lady" figured largely in her conversation.

Dorothy Parker, "The Wonderful Old Gentleman," *The Collected Stories of Dorothy Parker* (1942)

15 These were American *ladies*, i.e., they were of that class who have wealth and leisure to make full use of the day, and confer benefits on others.

Margaret Fuller, *Woman in the Nineteenth Century* (1845)

16 What restricts the use of the word "lady" among the courteous is that it is intended to set a woman apart from ordinary humanity, and in the working world that is not a help, as women have discovered in many bitter ways.

Judith Martin, *Miss Manners' Guide to Excruciatingly Correct Behavior* (1982)

17 Being a lady means playing the game by somebody else's rules. Playing by those rules, too many women have lost too much for too long.

Sandra Martin, "Fasting Is Unladylike," in *Illinois Times* (1982)

18 There is a difference between women and ladies. The modern parasites made ladies, but God Almighty made women.

Mother Jones, speech (1912), in Judith Anderson, ed., *Outspoken Women* (1984)

19 Give us that grand word "woman" once again, / And let's have done with "lady"; one's a term / Full

of fine force, strong, beautiful, and firm, / Fit for the noblest use of tongue or pen; / And one's a word for lackeys.

> Ella Wheeler Wilcox, "Woman," *Poems of Pleasure* (1888)

1 This noble word ["women"], spirit-stirring as it passes over English ears, is in America banished, and "ladies" and "females" substituted: the one to English taste mawkish and vulgar; the other indistinctive and gross.

> Harriet Martineau, *Society in America*, vol. 3 (1837)

2 The Word *Lady*: Most Often Used to Describe Someone You Wouldn't Want to Talk to for Even Five Minutes.

> Fran Lebowitz, *Metropolitan Life* (1978)

See also Women.

## ❦ LAND

3 This land is the house / we have always lived in.

> Linda Hogan, title poem, *Calling Myself Home* (1978)

4 Maka ke wakan—the land is sacred. These words are at the core of our being. The land is our mother, the rivers our blood. Take our land away and we die. That is, the Indian in us dies. We'd become just suntanned white men, the jetsam and flotsam of your great melting pot.

> Mary Brave Bird, with Richard Erdoes, *Ohitika Woman* (1993)

5 It has been proved that the land can exist without the country—and be better for it; it has not been proved . . . that the country can exist without the land.

> Alice Walker, "Everything Is a Human Being," *Living by the Word* (1988)

6 My own recipe for world peace is a bit of land for everyone.

> Gladys Taber, *The Book of Stillmeadow* (1948)

7 There have been few things in my life which have had a more genial effect on my mind than the possession of a piece of land.

> Harriet Martineau (1845), *Autobiography*, vol. 2 (1877)

8 Some people talk of morality, and some of religion, but give me a little snug property.

> Maria Edgeworth, *The Absentee* (1812)

9 I think nobody owns land until their dead are in it.

> Joan Didion, *Run River* (1961)

10 When people lose their ties to the land they grow corrupt. Inevitably, they grow corrupt.

> Ruth Almog, *Death in the Rain* (1982)

11 Much agricultural land which might be growing food is being used instead to "grow" money (in the form of coffee, tea, etc.).

> Frances Moore Lappé, *Diet for a Small Planet* (1971)

See also Earth, Landscape, Nature.

## ❦ LANDSCAPE

12 Landscape shapes culture.

> Terry Tempest Williams, *Pieces of White Shell* (1984)

13 Landscape consists in the multiple, overlapping intricacies and forms that exist in a given space at a moment in time.

> Annie Dillard, *Pilgrim at Tinker Creek* (1974)

14 Landscapes have a language of their own, expressing the soul of the things, lofty or humble, which constitute them, from the mighty peaks to the smallest of the tiny flowers hidden in the meadow's grass.

> Alexandra David-Neel, *My Journey to Llasa* (1927)

15 Landscape, that vast still life, invites description, not narration. It is lyric. It has no story: it is the beloved, and asks only to be contemplated.

> Patricia Hampl, *Spillville* (1987)

See also Earth, Land, Nature.

## ❦ LANGUAGE

16 We die. That may be the meaning of life. But we do language. That may be the measure of our lives.

> Toni Morrison, Nobel Prize acceptance speech (1993)

17 Only where there is language is there world.

> Adrienne Rich, "The Demon Lover," *Leaflets* (1969)

1 Language is the road map of a culture. It tells you where its people come from and where they are going.

Rita Mae Brown, *Starting From Scratch* (1988)

2 The basic agreement between human beings, indeed what makes them human and makes them social, is language.

Monique Wittig, "On the Social Contract," *The Straight Mind* (1992)

3 Language tethers us to the world; without it we spin like atoms.

Penelope Lively, *Moon Tiger* (1987)

4 Language is memory and metaphor.

Storm Jameson, *Parthian Words* (1970)

5 Language is a mixture of statement and evocation.

Elizabeth Bowen, "Advice," *Afterthought* (1962)

6 Language is wine upon his lips.

Virginia Woolf, *Jacob's Room* (1922)

7 Language helps form the limits of our reality.

Dale Spender, *Man Made Language* (1980)

8 Language casts sheaves of reality upon the social body, stamping it and violently shaping it.

Monique Wittig, "The Mark of Gender," *The Straight Mind* (1992)

9 Language, as symbol, determines much of the nature and quality of our experience.

Sonia Johnson, *The Ship That Sailed Into the Living Room* (1991)

10 Language is, without a doubt, the most momentous and at the same time the most mysterious product of the human mind.

Susanne K. Langer, *Philosophy in a New Key* (1942)

11 Language exerts hidden power, like the moon on the tides.

Rita Mae Brown, *Starting From Scratch* (1988)

12 I have been a believer in the magic of language since, at a very early age, I discovered that some words got me into trouble and others got me out.

Katherine Dunn, in Susan Cahill, ed., *Growing Up Female* (1993)

13 Words, volumes of words, all signed, were the eloquent metaphor of my life. It was the language born of hands that was my beginning.

Ruth Sidransky, *In Silence* (1990)

14 I can remember the lush spring excitement of language in childhood. Sitting in church, rolling it around my mouth like marbles—tabernacle and pharisee and parable, trespasses and Babylon and covenant.

Penelope Lively, *Moon Tiger* (1987)

15 Language. I loved it. And for a long time I would think of myself, of my whole body, as an ear.

Maya Angelou, in *The New York Times* (1993)

16 Accuracy of language is one of the bulwarks of truth.

Anna Jameson, *A Commonplace Book* (1855)

17 Like a diaphanous nightgown, language both hides and reveals.

Karen Elizabeth Gordon, *Intimate Apparel* (1989)

18 Language is double-edged; through words a fuller view of reality emerges, but words can also serve to fragment reality.

Vera John-Steiner, *Notebooks of the Mind* (1985)

19 Language screens reality as a filter on a camera lens screens light waves.

Casey Miller and Kate Swift, *Words and Women* (1976)

20 Language uses us as much as we use language.

Robin Lakoff, *Language and Woman's Place* (1975)

21 Language is neither innocent nor neutral. Linguistic habits condition our view of the world and hinder social change.

Carmen Martínez Ten, in *España 91* (1991)

22 Language is also a place of struggle.

bell hooks, *Talking Back* (1989)

23 Language is *not* neutral. It is not merely a vehicle which carries ideas. It is itself a shaper of ideas.

Dale Spender, *Man Made Language* (1980)

24 All language is political.

Robin Tolmach Lakoff, *Talking Power* (1990)

25 Language makes culture, and we make a rotten culture when we abuse words.

Cynthia Ozick, "We Are the Crazy Lady and Other Feisty Feminist Fables," in Francine Klagsbrun, ed., *The First Ms. Reader* (1972)

26 Every language reflects the prejudices of the society in which it evolved.

Casey Miller and Kate Swift, *The Handbook of Nonsexist Writing* (1980)

1 Language conveys a certain power. It is one of the instruments of domination. It is carefully guarded by the superior people because it is one of the means through which they conserve their supremacy.

Sheila Rowbotham, *Woman's Consciousness, Man's World* (1973)

2 This monopoly over language is one of the means by which males have ensured their own primacy, and consequently have ensured the invisibility or "other" nature of females.

Dale Spender, *Man Made Language* (1980)

3 Language is power, life and the instrument of culture, the instrument of domination and liberation.

Angela Carter, "Notes From the Front Line," in Michelene Wandor, ed., *On Gender and Writing* (1983)

4 I believe the deeply rooted semantic confusion between "man" as a male and "man" as a species has been fed back into and vitiated a great deal of the speculation that goes on about the origins, development, and nature of the human race.

Elaine Morgan, *The Descent of Woman* (1972)

5 Conventional English usage, including the generic use of masculine-gender words, often obscures the actions, the contributions, and sometimes the very presence of women. Turning our backs on that insight is an option, of course, but it is an option like teaching children that the world is flat.

Casey Miller and Kate Swift, *The Handbook of Nonsexist Writing* (1980)

6 We defend ourselves with descriptions and tame the world by generalizing.

Iris Murdoch, *The Black Prince* (1973)

7 In many patriarchies, language, as well as cultural tradition, reserve the human condition for the male. With the Indo-European languages this is a nearly inescapable habit of mind, for despite all the customary pretense that "man" and "humanity" are terms which apply equally to both sexes, the fact is hardly obscured that in practice, general application favors the male far more often than the female as referent, or even sole referent, for such designations.

Kate Millett, *Sexual Politics* (1969)

8 "When you say Man," said Oedipus, "you include women / too. Everyone knows that." She said, "That's what / you think."

Muriel Rukeyser, "Myth," *Breaking Open* (1973)

9 Just as the development of computer science has necessitated an expanded technical vocabulary, so too do social changes require transformations in traditional language usage.

Francine Wattman Frank and Paula A. Treichler, *Language, Gender, and Professional Writing* (1989)

10 Few would suggest that sexual or racial inequality exists because of language use. Nor would many argue that banishing sexist and racist labeling would in itself result in a just society. At the same time, it is clear that language not only reflects social structures but, more important, sometimes serves to perpetuate existing differences in power; thus a serious concern with linguistic usage is fully warranted.

Francine Wattman Frank and Paula A. Treichler, *Language, Gender, and Professional Writing* (1989)

11 Our native language is like a second skin, so much a part of us we resist the idea that it is constantly changing, constantly being renewed.

Casey Miller and Kate Swift, *The Handbook of Nonsexist Writing* (1980)

12 Death is a dramatic accomplishment of absence; language may be almost as effective.

Janet Frame, *An Angel at My Table* (1984)

13 "Zis and zat" when uttered by the French is considered charming, but "dis and dat" as an Africanism is ridiculed as gross and ugly.

Alice Childress, in Mari E. Evans, ed., *Black Women Writers (1950-1980)* (1984)

14 What has been termed "correct" English is nothing other than the blatant legitimation of the white middle-class code.

Dale Spender, *Man Made Language* (1980)

15 A language is a map of our failures.

Adrienne Rich, "The Burning of Paper Instead of Children," *The Will to Change* (1971)

16 Don't you understand that all language is dead currency? How they keep on playing shop with it all the same.

Elizabeth Bowen, *The Heat of the Day* (1949)

17 The dictionary is . . . only a rough draft.

Monique Wittig and Sande Zeig, *Lesbian Peoples* (1976)

18 Language is decanted and shared. If only one person is left alive speaking a language—the case with

some American Indian languages—the language is dead. Language takes two and their multiples.

Rita Mae Brown, *Starting From Scratch* (1988)

1 There is no liberal education for the under-languaged.

Agnes Repplier, "A Vocabulary," *Times and Tendencies* (1931)

2 English is weak in describing emotional states or intensities of interpersonal relationships.

Rita Mae Brown, *Starting From Scratch* (1988)

3 A candidate for office can have no greater advantage than muddled syntax; no greater liability than a command of language.

Marya Mannes, *More in Anger* (1958)

4 Mechanical difficulties with language are the outcome of internal difficulties with thought.

Elizabeth Bowen, *Collected Impressions* (1950)

5 Whatever its function, / *Like*'s not a conjunction.

Margaret Fishback, "The Purist to Her Love," *I Take It Back* (1935)

6 He does not so much split his infinitives as disembowel them.

Rebecca West, in *The Clarion* (1913)

7 Correct English is the slang of prigs.

George Eliot, *Middlemarch* (1871)

8 I personally think we developed language because of our deep inner need to complain.

Jane Wagner, *The Search for Signs of Intelligent Life in the Universe* (1985)

See also Aphorisms, Clichés, Communication, Euphemisms, Jargon, Languages, Metaphor, Platitudes, "Political Correctness," Proverbs, Slogans, Speech, Words, Writing.

## ❧ LANGUAGES

9 If it is true that the violin is the most perfect of musical instruments, then Greek is the violin of human thought.

Helen Keller, *The Story of My Life* (1902)

10 I very much wish that some day or other you may have time to learn Greek, because that language is

an *idea*. Even a little of it is like manure to the soil of the mind, and makes it bear finer flowers.

Sara Coleridge (1836), *Memoir and Letters*, vol. 1 (1873)

11 I stand and listen to people speaking French in the stores and in the street. It's such a pert, crisp language, elegant as rustling taffeta.

Belva Plain, *Evergreen* (1978)

12 French was the only language we had in common, and even that was like a dialect we had picked up at a rummage sale, rusty and missing a lot of essential parts.

Patricia Hampl, in *The New York Times Book Review* (1992)

13 Dialect is the elf rather than the genius of place.

Alice Meynell, "The Little Language," *Essays* (1914)

14 Basque is one of the world's more alarming languages. Only a handful of adult foreigners, they say, have ever managed to learn it. The Devil tried once and mastered only three words—profanities, I assume.

Jan Morris, "A Separate People" (1968), *Among the Cities* (1985)

15 One may almost call it [Italian] a language that talks of itself, and always seems more witty than its speakers.

Madame de Staël, *Corinne* (1807)

See also Language, Translating.

## ❧ LAST WORDS

16 Hooray for the last grand adventure! I wish I had won but it was worthwhile anyway.

Amelia Earhart, letter to be opened after her death (1937), in Hope Stoddard, *Famous American Women* (1970)

17 Adieu, my friends, I go on to glory!

Isadora Duncan (1927), in Barnaby Conrad, *Famous Last Words* (1961)

18 I do not sleep; I wish to meet my death awake.

Maria Theresa, Empress of Germany and Queen of Hungary (1780), in Mrs. Jameson, *Memoirs of Celebrated Female Sovereigns* (1831)

19 I can die now, I've lived twice!

Edith Piaf (1963), in Simone Berteaut, *Piaf* (1969)

1 It has all been very interesting.

Lady Mary Wortley Montagu (1762), in Barnaby Conrad, *Famous Last Words* (1961)

2 This is the only stone I have left unturned.

Belle Livingstone, on the inscription she wished for her tombstone, *Belle Out of Order* (1959)

3 Is everybody happy? I want everybody to be happy. I know I'm happy.

Ethel Barrymore, last words (1959)

4 Too kind, too kind.

Florence Nightingale, upon receiving the Order of Merit on her deathbed (1910), in Cecil Woodham-Smith, *Florence Nightingale* (1950)

5 Let me go, let me go.

Clara Barton (1912), in Barnaby Conrad, *Famous Last Words* (1961)

6 How fast it comes.

Dorothea Lange, in Milton Meltzer, *Dorothea Lange: A Photographer's Life* (1978)

7 All my possessions for a moment of time.

Elizabeth I, attributed (1603), in Barnaby Conrad, *Famous Last Words* (1961)

8 Nothing but death.

Jane Austen, upon being asked if there was anything she wanted (1817), in J.E. Austen-Leigh, *A Memoir of Jane Austen* (1870)

9 We shall meet again!

Jeanne Récamier (1849), in Barnaby Conrad, *Famous Last Words* (1961)

## ❧ LAS VEGAS

10 This desert town was man's own miracle of pure purposelessness.

Jane Rule, *The Desert of the Heart* (1965)

11 I love that town. No clocks. No locks. No restrictions.

Marlene Dietrich, *Marlene Dietrich's ABC* (1962)

## ❧ LATENESS

12 Five minutes—Zounds! I have been five minutes too late all my lifetime!

Hannah Cowley, *The Belle's Stratagem* (1780)

13 Ah! "All things come to those who wait"— / . . . / They *come*, but often come *too late*!

Violet Fane, "Tout Vient à Qui Sait Attendre," *From Dawn to Noon* (1882)

14 It is always so, every pleasure comes exactly half an hour too late—Life! Life!

Emily Eden, *The Semi-Detached House* (1859)

15 Now that Fate / Has brought me what so long, I so desired, / It is too late, / I am too tired.

Laurence Hope, "To Aziz," *Stars of the Desert* (1903)

16 I suppose we are all the same, we human beings. We always learn too late.

Madeleine Brent, *Merlin's Keep* (1977)

17 For most of us the space between "dreaming on things to come" and "it is too late, it is all over" is too tiny to enter.

Iris Murdoch, *The Black Prince* (1973)

18 By the time a person has achieved years adequate for choosing a direction, the die is cast and the moment has long since passed which determined the future.

Zelda Fitzgerald, *Save Me the Waltz* (1932)

See also Procrastination, Punctuality, Time, Timeliness.

## ❧ LAUGHTER

19 Laughter is by definition healthy.

Doris Lessing, *The Summer Before the Dark* (1973)

20 There can never be enough said of the virtues, the dangers, the power of a shared laugh.

Françoise Sagan, *La Chamade* (1965)

21 Where there is laughter there is always more health than sickness.

Phyllis Bottome, *Survival* (1943)

22 A good time for laughing is when you can.

Jessamyn West, *Except for Me and Thee* (1969)

23 He who laughs, lasts!

Mary Pettibone Poole, *A Glass Eye at a Keyhole* (1938)

24 Laughter is the lightning rod of play, the eroticism of conversation.

Eva Hoffman, *Lost in Translation* (1989)

1 Laughter springs from the lawless part of our nature.

Agnes Repplier, *In Pursuit of Laughter* (1936)

2 A good laugh is as good as a prayer sometimes.

L.M. Montgomery, *Rilla of Ingleside* (1921)

3 Love cannot exorcise the gifts of hate. / Hate cannot exorcise what has no weight, / But laughter we can never over-rate.

May Sarton, "An Intruder," *A Grain of Mustard Seed* (1971)

4 We cannot really love anybody with whom we never laugh.

Agnes Repplier, *Americans and Others* (1912)

5 It's possible to forgive someone a great deal if he makes you laugh.

Caroline Llewellyn, *Life Blood* (1993)

6 There comes a time when suddenly you realize that laughter is something you remember and that *you* were the one laughing.

Marlene Dietrich, *Marlene Dietrich's ABC* (1962)

7 We have to laugh. Because laughter, we already know, is the first evidence of freedom.

Rosario Castellanos, "If Not Poetry, Then What?" (1973), in Maureen Ahern, ed., *A Rosario Castellanos Reader* (1988)

8 I have often observ'd the loudest Laughers to be the dullest Fellows in the Company.

Lady Mary Wortley Montagu, *The Nonsense of Common-Sense* (1738)

9 The laughter of adults was always very different from the laughter of children. The former indicated a recognition of the familiar, but in children it came from the shock of the new.

Elizabeth Hardwick, *The Ghostly Lover* (1945)

10 The heart / That laughs must ache.

Georgiana Goddard King, *The Way of Perfect Love* (1909)

11 It was the kind of laughter that caught like briars in her chest and felt very much like pain.

Katherine Paterson, *Lyddie* (1991)

12 There is always a secret irritation about a laugh into which we cannot join.

Agnes Repplier, *Points of View* (1891)

13 Hostility is expressed in a number of ways. One is laughter.

Kate Millett, *Sexual Politics* (1969)

14 A laugh is a terrible weapon.

Kate O'Brien, *The Last of Summer* (1943)

15 Eva gurgled like a stomach.

Jean Stafford, "Polite Conversation," *The Collected Stories of Jean Stafford* (1969)

See also Humor, Smile.

§ LAW

16 Law is no explanation of anything; law is simply a generalization, a category of facts; law is neither a cause, nor a reason, nor a power, nor a coercive force; it is nothing but a general formula, a statistical table.

Florence Nightingale (1860), in Michael D. Calabria and Janet A. Macrae, eds., *Suggestions for Thought* (1994)

17 Laws . . . are felt only when the individual comes into conflict with them.

Suzanne La Follette, "Institutional Marriage and Its Economic Aspects," *Concerning Women* (1926)

18 The law's made to take care o' raskills.

George Eliot, *The Mill on the Floss* (1860)

19 It is not possible to make a bad law. If it is bad, it is not a law.

Carry Nation, *The Use and Need of the Life of Carry A. Nation* (1905)

20 To make laws that man cannot, and will not obey, serves to bring all law into contempt.

Elizabeth Cady Stanton, speech (1861)

21 Law is a substitute for love.

Helen McCloy, *A Change of Heart* (1973)

22 Our system is not one of justice, but of law.

Edna Buchanan, *The Corpse Had a Familiar Face* (1987)

23 Justice and law are sometimes in opposition.

Mrs. Henry Wood, *East Lynne* (1861)

24 That man is a creature who needs order yet yearns for change is the creative contradiction at the heart of the laws which structure his conformity and define his deviancy.

Freda Adler, *Sisters in Crime* (1975)

25 The law is above the law, you know.

Dorothy Salisbury Davis, *The Little Brothers* (1973)

1 Petty laws breed great crimes.

Ouida, "The Marriage Plate," *Pipistrello* (1881)

2 For many persons, law appears to be black magic—an obscure domain that can be fathomed only by the professional initiated into its mysteries.

Susan C. Ross, *The Rights of Women* (1973)

3 Law to her was all Greek and turkey tracks.

Jessamyn West, *The Friendly Persuasion* (1940)

4 It takes a very long time to learn that a courtroom is the last place in the world for learning the truth.

Alice Koller, *The Stations of Solitude* (1990)

5 That's the worst of the law. They never do the sensible, straightforward thing. They have to go around corners, like a cat that always takes the longest way home.

Anthony Gilbert, *The Wrong Body* (1950)

6 The mills of God work like lightning, compared with the law.

Mary Stewart, *Touch Not the Cat* (1976)

7 [Law] is one part justice to nine parts expediency. Who needs it.

Lucille Kallen, *Introducing C.B. Greenfield* (1979)

8 If you love the law and you love good sausage, don't watch either of them being made.

Betty Talmadge, in *The Reader* (1977)

9 Gerry's friends, you see, had no confidence in the United States judicial system. They did not seem comfortable in the courtroom, and this increased their unreliability in the eyes of judge and jury. If you trust the authorities, they trust you better back, it seems.

Louise Erdrich, *Love Medicine* (1984)

10 The contempt for law and the contempt for the human consequences of lawbreaking go from the bottom to the top of American society.

Margaret Mead, in Claire Safran, "Impeachment?" *Redbook* (1974)

11 That is what is so bizarre about the American legal system. Where else in the world would stealing from a phone booth be considered more serious than polluting the earth?

Laura Nader, in Karen DeCrow, *Sexist Justice* (1974)

12 We're approaching space-age technology with Model-T statutes and cases.

Lori B. Andrews, on infertility cases and the law, in *The New York Times* (1984)

13 Law is a reflection and a source of prejudice. It both enforces and suggests forms of bias.

Diane B. Schulder, "Does the Law Oppress Women?" in Robin Morgan, ed., *Sisterhood Is Powerful* (1970)

14 If you got the sayso you want to keep it, whether you are right or wrong. That's why they have to keep changing the laws—so they don't unbenefit any of these big white men.

Ruth Shays, in John Langston Gwaltney, *Drylongso* (1980)

15 Every form of bigotry can be found in ample supply in the legal system of our country.

Florynce R. Kennedy, "Institutionalized Oppression vs. the Female," in Robin Morgan, ed., *Sisterhood Is Powerful* (1970)

16 Woman throughout the ages has been mistress to the law, as man has been its master.

Freda Adler, *Sisters in Crime* (1975)

17 Avoid the law—the first loss is generally the least.

Hannah Farnham Lee, *The Log-Cabin* (1844)

18 Those learned in the law, when they do give advice without the usual fee, and in the confidence of friendship, generally say, "Pay, pay anything rather than go to law."

Isabella Beeton, *The Book of Household Management* (1861)

19 Me care for te laws when te laws care for me.

Joanna Baillie, *The Alienated Manor* (1836)

20 Where there is a will there's a law suit.

Ethel Watts Mumford, in Oliver Herford, Ethel Watts Mumford, and Addison Mizner, *The Complete Cynic* (1902)

21 Court, in our society, is often the last resort of stubbornness.

Erica Jong, *Fear of Fifty* (1994)

See also Justice, Lawyers, Litigation.

## § LAWYERS

22 It took man thousands of years to put words down on paper, and his lawyers still wish he wouldn't.

Mignon McLaughlin, *The Second Neurotic's Notebook* (1966)

1 The lawyer hummed and hawed, not because he had any real objections but because it is a lawyer's business to consider remote contingencies, and a straightforward agreement to anything would be wildly unprofessional.

Josephine Tey, *A Shilling for Candles* (1936)

2 He produced the impression of keeping copies of everything he said.

Elizabeth von Arnim, *The Enchanted April* (1922)

3 "That is difficult to say exactly," said Mr. Kirkwood, enjoying, like all lawyers, making the reply to a simple question difficult.

Agatha Christie, *The Sittaford Mystery* (1931)

4 I do believe that half a dozen commonplace attorneys could so mystify and misconstrue the Ten Commandments, and so confuse Moses' surroundings on Mount Sinai, that the great law-giver, if he returned to this planet, would doubt his own identity, abjure every one of his deliverances, yea, even commend the very sins he so clearly forbade his people.

Elizabeth Cady Stanton (1891), in Theodore Stanton and Harriot Stanton Blatch, eds., *Elizabeth Cady Stanton As Revealed in Her Letters Diary and Reminiscences*, vol. 2 (1922)

5 His anger will not fall upon you, but upon your legal adviser. And I am not afraid that he will eat me. Lawyers are indigestible.

Amelia B. Edwards, *Half a Million of Money* (1866)

6 Lawyers' work required sharp brains, strong vocal chords, and an iron butt.

Jessamyn West, *The Massacre at Fall Creek* (1975)

7 Lawyers [are] operators of the toll bridge across which anyone in search of justice has to pass.

Jane Bryant Quinn, in *Newsweek* (1978)

8 One hires laywers as one hires plumbers, because one wants to keep one's hands off the beastly drains.

Amanda Cross, *The Question of Max* (1976)

9 Lawyers are like morticians—we all need one sooner or later, but better later than sooner.

Eileen Goudge, *Garden of Lies* (1989)

10 A lawyer's relationship to justice and wisdom . . . is on a par with a piano tuner's relationship to a concert. He neither composes the music, nor interprets it—he merely keeps the machinery running.

Lucille Kallen, *Introducing C.B. Greenfield* (1979)

11 You want the unvarnished and ungarnished truth, and I'm no hand for that. I'm a lawyer.

Mary Roberts Rinehart, *The Man in Lower Ten* (1909)

12 Lawyers enjoy a little mystery, you know. Why, if everybody came forward and told the truth, the whole truth, and nothing but the truth straight out, we should all retire to the workhouse.

Dorothy L. Sayers, *Clouds of Witness* (1926)

13 I wonder if we shall ever make a lawyer of you. Don't you know that our first duty is to make things easy for our clients, who are always right, except when they come in conflict with ourselves?

Anthony Gilbert, *The Wrong Body* (1950)

14 Let you lawyers alone for speed, when you have yourselves for clients.

Mrs. Henry Wood, *East Lynne* (1861)

15 I never saw a lawyer yet who would admit he was making money.

Mary Roberts Rinehart, *The Window at the White Cat* (1910)

16 Such poor folk as to law do go, / are driven oft to curse: / But in mean while, the Lawyer thrives / the money in his purse.

Isabella Whitney, "The 104. Flower," *A Sweet Nosegay, or Pleasant Posye: Containing a Hundred and Ten Phylosophicall Flowers* (1573)

17 Lawyers never go to law, do they? They know better.

Agatha Christie, *Murder Is Easy* (1939)

18 I've always thought there must be some reason why the French words for "attorney" and "avocado" were the same.

Katherine Neville, *A Calculated Risk* (1992)

See also Law.

# ❦ LAZINESS

19 Laziness is an art, idleness is only a craft.

Comtesse Diane, *Les Glanes de la Vie* (1898)

20 I have come to the conclusion that almost no one on earth is lazy. The truth is that the man you call lazy just doesn't want to do your kind of work; he wants to do his kind.

Bertha Damon, *A Sense of Humus* (1943)

See also Idleness.

## § LEADERSHIP

1 The speed of the leader is the speed of the gang.
   Mary Kay Ash, *Mary Kay* (1981)

2 No leader can be too far ahead of his followers.
   Eleanor Roosevelt, *This I Remember* (1949)

3 What a rope of sand we are without a leader.
   Marjorie Bowen, *The Master of Stair* (1907)

4 You take people as far as they will go, not as far as you would like them to go.
   Jeannette Rankin, in Hannah Josephson, *Jeannette Rankin* (1974)

5 The art of leadership is one which the wicked, as a rule, learn more quickly than the virtuous.
   Agnes E. Meyer, *Out of These Roots* (1953)

6 Trust me, there are as many ways of living as there are men, and one is no more fit to lead another, than a bird to lead a fish, or a fish a quadruped.
   Frances Wright, *A Few Days in Athens* (1822)

7 It is high time that we had lights that are not incendiary torches.
   George Sand (1863), in Raphaël Ledos de Beaufort, ed., *Letters of George Sand*, vol. 2 (1886)

8 Would the world ever be run by anything better than personal passion, and the scoring off each other of amoral schoolboys?
   Kate O'Brien, *That Lady* (1946)

9 Reformers must expect to be disowned by those who are only too happy to enjoy what has been won for them.
   Doris Lessing, 1971 preface, *Golden Notebook* (1962)

10 A leader who doesn't hesitate before he sends his nation into battle is not fit to be a leader.
   Golda Meir, in Israel and Mary Shenker, eds., *As Good As Golda* (1970)

11 You philosophers are lucky men. You write on paper and paper is patient. Unfortunate Empress that I am, I write on the susceptible skins of living beings.
   Catherine the Great, letter to Diderot (1775), in Dominique Maroger, ed., *The Memoirs of Catherine the Great* (1955)

See also Activism, Dictators, Government, Pioneers, Politicians, Presidents, Royalty, Tyranny.

## § LEARNING

12 The ability to learn is older—as it is also more widespread—than is the ability to teach.
   Margaret Mead, *Continuities in Cultural Evolution* (1964)

13 That is what learning is. You suddenly understand something you've understood all your life, but in a new way.
   Doris Lessing, *The Four-Gated City* (1969)

14 That's the way things come clear. All of a sudden. And then you realize how obvious they've been all along.
   Madeleine L'Engle, *The Arm of the Starfish* (1965)

15 How we learn is what we learn.
   Bonnie Friedman, *Writing Past Dark* (1993)

16 Learning is always rebellion. . . . Every bit of new truth discovered is revolutionary to what was believed before.
   Margaret Lee Runbeck, *The Year of Love* (1956)

17 The world of learning is so broad, and the human soul is so limited in power! We reach forth and strain every nerve, but we seize only a bit of the curtain that hides the infinite from us.
   Maria Mitchell (1854), in Phebe Mitchell Kendall, ed., *Maria Mitchell, Life, Letters, and Journals* (1896)

18 The joy of learning is as indispensable in study as breathing is in running. Where it is lacking there are no real students, but only poor caricatures of apprentices who, at the end of their apprenticeship, will not even have a trade.
   Simone Weil, *Waiting for God* (1950)

19 There are two ways to approach a subject that frightens you and makes you feel stupid: you can embrace it with humility and an open mind, or you can ridicule it mercilessly.
   Judith Stone, *Light Elements* (1991)

20 One can learn, at least. One can go on learning until the day one is cut off.
   Fay Weldon, *Down Among the Women* (1971)

21 The excitement of learning separates youth from old age. As long as you're learning you're not old.
   Rosalyn S. Yalow, in Barbara Shiels, *Women and the Nobel Prize* (1985)

1 If you can learn from hard knocks, you can also learn from soft touches.

Carolyn Kenmore, *Mannequin* (1969)

2 There are some things you learn best in calm, and some in storm.

Willa Cather, *The Song of the Lark* (1915)

3 Too much rigidity on the part of teachers should be followed by a brisk spirit of insubordination on the part of the taught.

Agnes Repplier, *Points of View* (1891)

4 The only language men ever speak perfectly is the one they learn in babyhood, when no one can teach them anything!

Maria Montessori, *The Absorbent Mind* (1949)

5 Music lessons—or lessons in anything—can be dangerous to us, for the weekly guilt can become addictive. We can come to believe that we deserve scorn, and that we really can profit from being told repeatedly how to do it, from being given "right " answers. Gradually we lose our child-like enthusiasm for music or tennis or roller-skating or tightrope walking and substitute an intense yearning to do it "right" for the teacher.

Eloise Ristad, *A Soprano on Her Head* (1982)

6 I think you should learn, of course, and some days you must learn a great deal. But you should also have days when you allow what is already in you to swell up inside of you until it touches everything. And you can feel it inside you. If you never take time out to let that happen, then you just accumulate facts, and they begin to rattle around inside of you. You can make noise with them, but never really feel anything with them.

E.L. Konigsburg, *From the Mixed-Up Files of Mrs. Basil E. Frankweiler* (1967)

See also Education, Research, Teaching, Understanding.

## ❧ LEGENDS

7 Facts are fine, fer as they go . . . but they're like water bugs skittering atop the water. Legends, now—they go deep down and bring up the heart of a story.

Marguerite Henry, *Misty of Chincoteague* (1947)

8 Legends die hard. They survive as truth rarely does.

Helen Hayes, with Sanford Dody, *On Reflection* (1968)

9 No truth is strong enough to defeat a well-established legend.

Winifred Holtby, "The Murder of Madame Mollard" (1930), *Pavements at Anderby* (1937)

10 These are the stories that never, never die, that are carried like seed into a new country, are told to you and me and make in us new and lasting strengths.

Meridel Le Sueur, *Nancy Hanks of Wilderness Road* (1949)

11 Legends have always played a powerful role in the making of history. . . . Without ever relating facts reliably, yet always expressing their true significance, they offered a truth beyond realities, a remembrance beyond memories.

Hannah Arendt, *Origins of Totalitarianism* (1951)

12 Like all very handsome men who die tragically, he left not so much a character behind him as a legend. Youth and death shed a halo through which it is difficult to see a real face.

Virginia Woolf, "A Sketch of the Past" (1940), *Moments of Being* (1976)

13 I, personally, liked the legend.

Marlene Dietrich, on her life (1959), in Steven Bach, *Marlene Dietrich* (1992)

See also Heroes, Myth, Stories.

## ❧ LEISURE

14 Leisure requires the evidence of our own feelings, because it is not so much a quality of time as a peculiar state of mind. . . . What being at leisure means is more easily felt than defined.

Vernon Lee, "About Leisure," *Limbo* (1908)

15 It is in his pleasure that a man really lives; it is from his leisure that he constructs the true fabric of self.

Agnes Repplier, *Essays in Idleness* (1893)

16 Leisure, some degree of it, is necessary to the health of every man's spirit.

Harriet Martineau, *Society in America*, vol. 3 (1837)

17 Leisure and the cultivation of human capacities are inextricably interdependent.

Margaret Mead, in *Redbook* (1963)

1 No country can reach a high stage of civilization without a leisure class.

   Gertrude Atherton, *Can Women Be Gentlemen?* (1938)

2 People who know how to employ themselves, always find leisure moments, while those who do nothing are forever in a hurry.

   Marie-Jeanne Roland (1792), in Lydia Maria Child, *Memoirs of Madame de Staël and of Madame Roland* (1847)

3 What we lack is not so much leisure to *do* as time to reflect and time to feel. What we seldom "take" is time to experience the things that have happened, the things that are happening, the things that are still ahead of us.

   Margaret Mead and Rhoda Metraux, *A Way of Seeing* (1970)

4 People would have more leisure time if it weren't for all the leisure-time activities that use it up.

   Peg Bracken, *But I Wouldn't Have Missed It for the World!* (1973)

5 There is no pleasure in having nothing to do; the fun is in having lots to do—and not doing it.

   Mary Wilson Little, *A Paragrapher's Reveries* (1904)

6 Leisure is gone—gone where the spinning-wheels are gone, and the pack-horses, and the slow wagons, and the peddlers who brought bargains to the door on sunny afternoons.

   George Eliot, *Adam Bede* (1859)

7 The multi-billion-dollar entertainment and leisure industries notwithstanding, Americans have not learned how to use large amounts of leisure in noncompulsive, personally satisfying ways.

   Janet Saltzman Chafetz, *Masculine/Feminine or Human?* (1974)

8 Leisure's like a mirage. Lovely when it ain't there. When you are, it's a desert. Right?

   Anthony Gilbert, *A Case for Mr. Crook* (1952)

9 There is always time for a nap.

   Suzy Becker, *All I Need to Know I Learned From My Cat* (1990)

See also Busyness, Idleness, Retirement, Vacation.

# ❧ LESBIANS

10 If Lesbians were purple, none would be admitted to respected places. But if all Lesbians suddenly turned purple today, society would be surprised at the number of purple people in high places.

   Sidney Abbott and Barbara Love, *Sappho Was a Right-On Woman* (1972)

11 The Lesbian is one of the least known members of our culture. Less is known about her—and less accurately—than about the Newfoundland dog.

   Sidney Abbott and Barbara Love, *Sappho Was a Right-On Woman* (1972)

12 One of the first things a typical lesbian learns is that there is no such thing as a typical lesbian.

   Yvonne Zipter, *Diamonds Are a Dyke's Best Friend* (1988)

13 Historically, this culture has come to identify lesbians as women who over time, engage in a range and variety of sexual-emotional relationships with women. I, for one, identify a woman as a lesbian who says she is.

   Cheryl Clarke, "Lesbianism: An Act of Resistance," in Cherríe Moraga and Gloria Anzaldúa, eds., *This Bridge Called My Back* (1983)

14 A lesbian is the rage of all women condensed to the point of explosion.

   Radicalesbians, "The Woman Identified Woman," in Anne Koedt, Ellen Levine, and Anita Rapone, eds., *Radical Feminism* (1973)

15 Feminism is a theory, lesbianism is a practice.

   Ti-Grace Atkinson, speech (1970), in Sidney Abbott and Barbara Love, *Sappho Was a Right-On Woman* (1972)

16 All women are lesbians except those who don't know it.

   Jill Johnston, *Lesbian Nation* (1973)

17 Lesbian is the word, the label, the condition that holds women in line. When a woman hears this word tossed her way, she knows she is stepping out of line.

   Radicalesbians, "The Woman Identified Woman," in Anne Koedt, Ellen Levine, and Anita Rapone, eds., *Radical Feminism* (1973)

18 A lesbian who does not reinvent the world is a lesbian in the process of disappearing.

   Nicole Brossard, in Marlene Wildeman, tr., *The Aerial Letter* (1988)

19 A lesbian is a *radical* or she is not a lesbian.

   Nicole Brossard, in Marlene Wildeman, tr., *The Aerial Letter* (1988)

20 Once a woman is known as a Lesbian, both she and society often feel that no other fact about her can

rival the sexual identification. . . . No matter what a Lesbian achieves, her sexuality will remain her *primary* identity.

Sidney Abbott and Barbara Love, *Sappho Was a Right-On Woman* (1972)

1 I will be quiet, be still, and know that it is God who put the love for women in my heart.

Brigitte M. Roberts, "Be Still and Know," in Naomi Holoch and Joan Nestle, eds., *Women on Women 2* (1993)

2 Two women, eye to eye / measuring each other's spirit, each other's / limitless desire, / a whole new poetry beginning here.

Adrienne Rich, "Transcendental Etude," *The Dream of a Common Language* (1978)

3 Are there many things in this cool-hearted world so utterly exquisite as the pure love of one woman for another woman?

Mary MacLane, *The Story of Mary MacLane* (1902)

4 I felt the unordinary romance of / women who love women for the first time.

Dionne Brand, "Hard Against the Soul," *No Language Is Neutral* (1990)

5 A woman / who loves a woman / is forever young.

Anne Sexton, "Rapunzel," *Transformations* (1971)

6 In these days, when any capable and careful woman can honorably earn her own support, there is no village that has not its examples of "two hearts in counsel," both of which are feminine.

Frances E. Willard, *Glimpses of Fifty Years* (1889)

7 The suppressed lesbian I had been carrying in me since adolescence began to stretch her limbs.

Adrienne Rich, "Split at the Root," *Blood, Bread, and Poetry* (1986)

8 I resent like hell that I was maybe eighteen before I ever heard the "L" word. It would have made all the difference for me had I grown up knowing that the reason I didn't fit in was because they hadn't told me there were more categories to fit into.

Michelle Shocked, in Leigh W. Rutledge, *The Gay Decades* (1992)

9 Of course it is extremely difficult to like oneself in a culture which thinks you are a disease.

Chrystos, "I Don't Understand Those Who Have Turned Away From Me," in Cherríe Moraga and Gloria Anzaldúa, eds., *This Bridge Called My Back* (1983)

10 For a woman to be a lesbian in a male-supremacist, capitalist, misogynist, racist, homophobic, imperialist culture, such as that of North America, is an act of resistance.

Cheryl Clarke, "Lesbianism: An Act of Resistance," in Cherríe Moraga and Gloria Anzaldúa, eds., *This Bridge Called My Back* (1983)

11 Our very strength as lesbians lies in the fact that we are outside of patriarchy; our existence challenges its life.

Charlotte Bunch, "Not for Lesbians Only" (1975), *Passionate Politics* (1987)

12 The lesbian is a threatening *reality* for reality.

Nicole Brossard, in Marlene Wildeman, tr., *The Aerial Letter* (1988)

13 I became a lesbian out of devout Christian charity. All those women out there are praying for a man and I gave them my share.

Rita Mae Brown, *Venus Envy* (1993)

14 I was so excited to be able to say that I was a lesbian that I would shake hands with strangers on the street and say, "Hi! I'm Sally Gearhart and I'm a lesbian." Once, appearing on a panel program, I began, "I'm Sally Lesbian and I'm a gearhart!" I realized then that I had put too much of my identity into being lesbian.

Sally Gearhart, in Leigh W. Rutledge, *Unnatural Quotations* (1988)

15 Many lesbians were so far in the closet they were in danger of being mistaken for garment bags.

Rita Mae Brown, in *Ms.* (1995)

16 Are you still the alternative?

Martina Navratilova, responding to a reporter's question, "Are you still a lesbian?" in *Newsweek* (1994)

See also Gay Men, Lesbians and Gay Men.

# ♦ LESBIANS AND GAY MEN

17 It's funny how heterosexuals have lives and the rest of us have "lifestyles."

Sonia Johnson, *Going Out of Our Minds* (1987)

18 Deviance is whatever is condemned by the community. Most societies try to get rid of their deviants. Most cultures have burned and beaten their homosexuals and others who deviate from the sex-

ual common. The queer are the mirror reflecting the heterosexual tribe's fear: being different, being other and therefore lesser, therefore sub-human, in-human, non-human.

Gloria Anzaldúa, *Borderlands/La Frontera* (1987)

1 They're despised and rejected of their fellow-men today. What they suffer in a world not yet ready to admit their right to existence, their right to love, no normal person can realize; but I believe that the time is not so far distant when we shall recognize in the best of our intermediate types the leaders and masters of the race.

A.T. Fitzroy, *Despised and Rejected* (1918)

2 You're neither unnatural, nor abominable, nor mad; you're as much a part of what people call nature as anyone else; only you're unexplained as yet—you've not got your niche in creation.

Radclyffe Hall, *The Well of Loneliness* (1928)

3 Gay culture is far from "marginal," being rather "intersectional," the conduits between unlike beings.

Judy Grahn, *Another Mother Tongue* (1984)

4 The tribal attitude said, and continues to say, that Gay people are especially empowered because we are able to identify with both sexes and can see into more than one world at once, having the capacity to see from more than one point of view at a time. And that is also an Indian way of seeing.

Judy Grahn, *Another Mother Tongue* (1984)

5 Within any society men and women develop differently and have, each, a subculture of their own that is overbalanced in the importance it places on particular jobs, attitudes, amount of aggressiveness, roles it plays, amounts of expressed physicality and tenderness. . . . One of the major homosexual/shamanic functions in any society is to *cross over* between these two essentially different worlds and reveal them to each other.

Judy Grahn, *Another Mother Tongue* (1984)

6 It is so true that a woman may be in love with a woman, and a man with a man. It is pleasant to be sure of it, because it is undoubtedly the same love that we shall feel when we are angels.

Margaret Fuller, in Mason Wade, *Margaret Fuller, Whetstone of Genius* (1940)

7 The walls of the closet are guarded by the dogs of terror, and the inside of the closet is a house of mirrors.

Judy Grahn, *Another Mother Tongue* (1984)

8 They are a very extensive minority who have suffered discrimination and who have the same right to participation in the promise and fruits of society as every other individual.

Bella Abzug, press conference (1975)

9 No government has the right to tell its citizens when or whom to love. The only queer people are those who don't love anybody.

Rita Mae Brown, at the Gay Olympics (1982)

10 Love is love. . . . Gender is merely spare parts.

Wendy Wasserstein, *The Sisters Rosensweig* (1993)

11 If you removed all of the homosexuals and homosexual influence from what is generally regarded as American culture, you would be pretty much left with *Let's Make a Deal*.

Fran Lebowitz, in Leigh W. Rutledge, *Unnatural Quotations* (1988)

12 If homosexuality is a disease, let's all call in queer to work. "Hello, can't work today, still queer."

Robin Tyler, in Rosemary Silva, ed., *Lesbian Quotations* (1993)

See also Gay Men, Lesbians.

## ❧ LETTERS

13 Life would split asunder without them.

Virginia Woolf, *Jacob's Room* (1922)

14 Our correspondences have wings—paper birds that fly from my house to yours—flocks of ideas crisscrossing the country.

Terry Tempest Williams, *Refuge* (1991)

15 A Letter is a joy of Earth — / It is denied the Gods.

Emily Dickinson (1885), in Thomas H. Johnson, ed., *The Complete Poems of Emily Dickinson* (1960)

16 Letters . . . have souls.

Héloïse, letter to Abelard (12th cent.), in M. Lincoln Schuster, *The World's Great Letters* (1940)

1 Why is it that you can sometimes feel the reality of people more keenly through a letter than face to face?

Anne Morrow Lindbergh, *Bring Me a Unicorn* (1971)

2 A letter always feels to me like Immortality because it is the mind alone without corporeal friend.

Emily Dickinson (1868), in Mabel Loomis Todd, ed., *Letters of Emily Dickinson*, vol. 2 (1894)

3 There is a side of friendship that develops better and stronger by correspondence than contact. . . . The absence of the flesh in writing perhaps brings souls nearer.

Emily Carr (1935), *Hundreds and Thousands* (1966)

4 Letters are the stories of our souls.

Macrina Wiederkehr, *A Tree Full of Angels* (1988)

5 Letters are expectation packed in an envelope.

Shana Alexander, "The Surprises of the Mail," in *Life* (1967)

6 Letters were first invented for consoling such solitary wretches as myself. Having lost the substantial pleasures of seeing and possessing you, I shall in some measure compensate this loss by the satisfaction I shall find in your writing.

Héloïse, to Abelard (12th cent.), in M. Lincoln Schuster, *The World's Great Letters* (1940)

7 The one good thing about not seeing you is that I can write you letters.

Svetlana Alliluyeva, *Twenty Letters to a Friend* (1967)

8 That letter of hers came upon me like a kiss, so short, so sudden, and so affectionate.

Mary Russell Mitford (1819), in Henry Chorley, ed., *Letters of Mary Russell Mitford*, 2nd series, vol. 1 (1872)

9 Your letters are always to me fresher than flowers, without their fading so soon.

Sydney, Lady Morgan (1859), *Lady Morgan's Memoir*, vol. 2 (1862)

10 There's no finer caress than a love letter, because it makes the world very small, and the writer and reader, the only rulers.

Cecilia Capuzzi, in Octavia Capuzzi Locke, *Johns Hopkins Magazine* (1987)

11 Our first love-letter . . . the dread of saying too much is so nicely balanced by the fear of saying too little. Hope borders on presumption, and fear on reproach.

L.E. Landon, *Romance and Reality* (1831)

12 A real love letter is absolutely ridiculous to everyone except the writer and the recipient.

Myrtle Reed, *The Spinster Book* (1901)

13 Letters form a by-path of literature.

Agnes Repplier, "The Luxury of Conversation," *Compromises* (1904)

14 All letters, methinks, should be free and easy as one's discourse, not studied, as an oration, nor made up of hard words like a charm; 'tis an admirable thing to see how some people will labor to find out terms that may obscure a plain sense.

Dorothy Osborne (1653), in G.C. Moore Smith, *Letters of Dorothy Osborne to William Temple* (1928)

15 It is well enough when one is talking to a friend to hedge in an odd word by way of counsel now and then, but there is something mighty irksome, in its staring upon one in a letter where one ought only to see kind words and friendly remembrances.

Mary Lamb (1806), in *The Letters of Charles and Mary Anne Lamb*, vol. 2 (1976)

16 When it comes to bombshells, there are few that can be more effective than that small, flat, frail thing, a letter.

Margaret Deland, "The Harvest of Fear," *Around Old Chester* (1915)

17 A letter is a risky thing; the writer gambles on the reader's frame of mind.

Margaret Deland, *The Iron Woman* (1911)

18 Letter-writing on the part of a busy man or woman is the quintessence of generosity.

Agnes Repplier, in Grace Guiney, ed., *Letters of Louise Imogen Guiney* (1926)

19 A handwritten, personal letter has become a genuine modern-day luxury, like a child's pony ride.

Shana Alexander, "The Surprises of the Mail," in *Life* (1967)

20 He who gives quickly gives twice / in nothing so much as in a letter.

Marianne Moore, "Bowls," *Selected Poems* (1935)

21 Always serve letters with a cup of tea and a footstool. Celebrate "the reading" slowly. It is irreverent to read a letter fast.

Macrina Wiederkehr, *A Tree Full of Angels* (1988)

22 It takes two to write a letter as much as it takes two to make a quarrel.

Elizabeth Drew, *The Literature of Gossip* (1964)

1 The best letters of our time are precisely those that can never be published.

> Virginia Woolf, "Modern Letters," *The Captain's Death Bed* (1950)

2 I for one appreciate a good form letter, having worked on Capitol Hill and learned several dozen cordial ways to say nothing.

> Carrie Johnson, "Judging American Business by Its Writing Habits," in *The New York Times* (1984)

3 We always feel some difficulty in addressing those whom we are not in the habit of addressing frequently; we feel that the letter which is to make up for long silence, and epitomize the goings on of a good many months, ought to be three times as kind, satisfactory, and newsful as if two others had preceded it.

> Sara Coleridge (1837), *Memoir and Letters*, vol. 1 (1873)

4 In a letter (no matter how quickly it is written or honestly or freely or lovingly) it is more possible to be loving and lovable, more possible to reach out and to take in. . . . I feel I have somehow deceived you into thinking this is really a human relationship. It is a letter relationship between humans.

> Anne Sexton (1963), in Linda Gray Sexton and Lois Ames, eds., *Anne Sexton: A Self-Portrait in Letters* (1977)

5 The single drawback to being a good correspondent is that when finally you see the person to whom you've written for quite some time, he may find you rather less enchanting in person than you seemed on the printed page.

> Mrs. Falk Feeley, *A Swarm of Wasps* (1983)

6 A letter is not a dialogue or even an omniscient exposition. It is a fabric of surfaces, a mask, a form as well suited to affectations as to the affections.

> Elizabeth Hardwick, title essay, *Seduction and Betrayal* (1974)

7 You deserve a longer letter than this; but it is my unhappy fate seldom to treat people so well as they deserve.

> Jane Austen, to her sister Cassandra (1798), in R.W. Chapman, ed., *Jane Austen's Letters*, vol. 1 (1932)

8 I am much fonder of receiving letters, than writing them: but I believe this is no very uncommon case.

> Mary Lamb (1802), in *The Letters of Charles and Mary Anne Lamb*, vol. 2 (1976)

9 Letters are the real *curse* of my existence. I hate to write them: I have to. If I don't, there they are—the great guilty gates barring my way.

> Katherine Mansfield (1922), *Journal of Katherine Mansfield* (1927)

10 Letters are false really—they are expressions of the way you wish you were instead of the way you are.

> Anne Sexton (1961), in Linda Gray Sexton and Lois Ames, eds., *Anne Sexton: A Self-Portrait in Letters* (1977)

11 In letters we can reform without practice, beg without humiliation, snip and shape embarrassing experiences to the measure of our own desires.

> Elizabeth Hardwick, "Anderson, Millay and Crane in Their Letters" (1953), *A View of My Own* (1962)

12 Some persons' letters seem almost framed to afford a series of *alibis* for their personality.

> Vernon Lee, "Receiving Letters," *Hortus Vitae* (1904)

13 The letter is, by its natural shape, self-justifying; it is one's own evidence, deposition, a self-serving testimony. In a letter the writer holds all the cards, controls everything about himself and about those assertions he wishes to make concerning events or the worth of others. For completely self-centered characters, the letter form is a complex and rewarding activity.

> Elizabeth Hardwick, title essay, *Seduction and Betrayal* (1974)

14 I find that in letters you can make things whatever you wish them to be.

> Sandra Scofield, "Writing From Love and Grief and Fear," in Neil Baldwin and Diane Osen, eds., *The Writing Life* (1995)

15 A letter is a barrier, a reprieve, a charm against the world, an almost infallible method of acting at a distance.

> Iris Murdoch, *The Black Prince* (1973)

16 You love writing; I hate it; and if I had a lover who expected a note from me every morning, I should certainly break with him. Let me beg you then not to measure my friendship by my writing.

> Marie Madeleine de la Fayette (1673), in Marie de Rabutin-Chantal, Marquise de Sévigné, *The Letters of Madame de Sévigné*, vol. 2 (1927)

17 I wish there were some photographic process by which one's mind could be struck off and transferred to that of the friend we wish to know it,

without the medium of this confounded letter-writing!

Geraldine Jewsbury (1841), in A. Ireland, ed., *Selections From the Letters of Geraldine E. Jewsbury to Jane Welsh Carlyle* (1892)

1 She is probably by this time as tired of me, as I am of her; but as she is too polite and I am too civil to say so, our letters are still as frequent and affectionate as ever.

Jane Austen, *Lesley Castle* (1792)

2 I assure you I am as tired of writing long letters as you can be. What a pity that one should still be so fond of receiving them!

Jane Austen, to her sister Cassandra (1808), in R.W. Chapman, ed., *Jane Austen's Letters*, vol. 1 (1932)

3 Why it should be such an effort to write to the people one loves I can't imagine. It's none at all to write to those who don't really count.

Katherine Mansfield (1922), *Journal of Katherine Mansfield* (1927)

4 Yes, letter writing is antiquated—though there remain a few renegades who still so treasure the luxury of contemplating their lives in letters that they would rather write than call.

Joan Frank, "What Comes Around," in *The Utne Reader* (1993)

5 There were people whose only interest in life was writing letters. To the newspapers, to authors, to strangers, to City Councils, to the police. It did not much matter to whom; the satisfaction of writing seemed to be all.

Josephine Tey, *The Singing Sands* (1952)

6 There was no escape from the letter-writer who, a hundred or a hundred and twenty-five years ago, captured a coveted correspondent. It would have been as easy to shake off an octopus or a boa-constrictor.

Agnes Repplier, "The Correspondent," *A Happy Half-Century* (1908)

7 [Mary Wortley Montagu] wrote more letters, with fewer punctuation marks, than any Englishwoman of her day; and her nephew, the fourth Baron Rokeby, nearly blinded himself in deciphering the two volumes of undated correspondence which were printed in 1810. Two more followed in 1813, after which the gallant Baron either died at his post or was smitten with despair; for sixty-eight cases of letters lay undisturbed. . . . "Les morts n'écrivent

point," said Madame de Maintenon hopefully; but of what benefit is this inactivity, when we still continue to receive their letters?

Agnes Repplier, "The Correspondent," *A Happy Half-Century* (1908)

8 I am writing you because I have nothing to do; and I'm quitting here because I have nothing to tell you.

Anonymous Frenchwoman, quoted by Madame du Deffand (1789), in W.S. Lewis, ed., *Horace Walpole's Correspondence*, vol. 11 (1944)

See also Communication, Writing.

## ⸱ LETTING GO

9 If I can let you go as trees let go / . . . Lose what I lose to keep what I can keep, / The strong root still alive under the snow, / Love will endure—if I can let you go.

May Sarton, "The Autumn Sonnets," *A Durable Fire* (1972)

## ⸱ LIBERALS

10 Every adult should be able to make as many effective decisions without fear or favor about as many aspects of her or his life as is compatible with the like freedom of every other adult. That belief is the original and only defensible meaning of liberalism.

Judith H. Shklar, "The Liberalism of Fear," in Nancy Rosenblum, ed., *Liberalism and the Moral Life* (1989)

11 Long ago, there was a noble word, *liberal*, which derives from the word *free*. Now a strange thing happened to that word. A man named Hitler made it a term of abuse, a matter of suspicion, because those who were not with him were against him, and liberals had no use for Hitler. And then another man named McCarthy cast the same opprobrium on the word. . . . We must cherish and honor the word *free* or it will cease to apply to us.

Eleanor Roosevelt, *Tomorrow Is Now* (1963)

## ⸱ LIBERATION

12 It's as if we think liberation a fixed quantity, that there is only so much to go around. That an individual or community is liberated at the expense of another. When we view liberation as a scarce re-

source, something only a precious few of us can have, we stifle our potential, our creativity, our genius for living, learning and growing.

Andrea Canaan, "Brownness," in Cherríe Moraga and Gloria Anzaldúa, eds., *This Bridge Called My Back* (1983)

1 When I liberate myself, I'm liberating other people.

Fannie Lou Hamer, speech (1971)

See also Freedom, Liberty.

## ✦ LIBERTY

2 O Liberty! O Liberty! How many crimes are committed in thy name!

Marie-Jeanne Roland (1793), on her way to the guillotine, in Alphonse de Lamartine, *Histoire des Girondins* (1847)

3 If we do not die for liberty, we shall soon have nothing left to do but weep for her.

Marie-Jeanne Roland (1791), in Lydia Maria Child, *Memoirs of Madame de Staël and of Madame Roland* (1847)

4 There is a word sweeter than Mother, Home, or Heaven—that word is Liberty.

Matilda Joslyn Gage, in Elizabeth Cady Stanton, *Eighty Years and More* (1898)

5 I had reasoned this out in my mind; there was one of two things I had a *right* to, liberty, or death; if I could not have one, I would have the other; for no man should take me alive.

Harriet Tubman, in Sarah H. Bradford, *Harriet, The Moses of Her People* (1869)

6 Liberty . . . consists in the ability to choose.

Simone Weil, *The Need for Roots* (1949)

7 Liberty is not less a blessing, because oppression has so long darkened the mind that it can not appreciate it.

Lucretia Mott (1849), in Dana Greene, ed., *Lucretia Mott* (1980)

8 Liberty is the one thing no man can have unless he grants it to others.

Ruth Benedict (1942), in Margaret Mead, *An Anthropologist at Work* (1959)

9 It is not the fact of liberty but the way in which liberty is exercised that ultimately determines whether liberty itself survives.

Dorothy Thompson, "What Price Liberty?" in *Ladies' Home Journal* (1958)

10 Liberty, as it is conceived by current opinion, has nothing inherent about it; it is a sort of gift or trust bestowed on the individual by the state pending *good behavior.*

Mary McCarthy, "The Contagion of Ideas" (1952), *On the Contrary* (1961)

11 Absolute liberty . . . tends to corrupt absolutely.

Gertrude Himmelfarb, "Liberty: 'One Very Simple Principle'?" *On Looking Into the Abyss* (1994)

See also Liberation, Freedom.

## ✦ LIBRARIES

12 To make a library / It takes two volumes / And a fire. / Two volumes and a fire, / And interest. / The interest alone will do / If logs are few.

Carolyn Wells, with thanks to Emily Dickinson, *The Rest of My Life* (1937)

13 As a child, my number one best friend was the librarian in my grade school. I actually believed all those books belonged to her.

Erma Bombeck, letter to the American Library Association (1994)

14 Nothing sickens me more than the closed door of a library.

Barbara W. Tuchman, in *The New Yorker* (1986)

15 Invaders always destroy libraries.

Storm Jameson, *The Moment of Truth* (1949)

See also Books, Reading.

## ✦ LIFE

16 This is the urgency: Live! / and have your blooming in the noise of the whirlwind.

Gwendolyn Brooks, "The Second Sermon on the Warpland," *In the Mecca* (1968)

17 Life does not accommodate you, it shatters you. It is meant to, and it couldn't do it better. Every seed destroys its container or else there would be no fruition.

Florida Scott-Maxwell, *The Measure of My Days* (1968)

1 Life is a verb, not a noun.

Charlotte Perkins Gilman, *Human Work* (1904)

2 Your life is the one place you have to spend yourself fully—wild, generous, *drastic*—in an unrationed profligacy of self. . . . And in that split second when you understand you finally are about to die—to uncreate the world no time to do it over no more chances—that instant when you realize your conscious existence is truly flaring nova, won't you want to have used up all—*all*—the splendor that you are?

Robin Morgan, *The Anatomy of Freedom* (1982)

3 I do not want to arrive at the end of life and then be asked what I made of it and have to answer: "I acted." I want to be able to say: "I loved and I was mystified. It was a joy sometimes, and I knew grief. And I would like to do it all again."

Liv Ullmann, *Choices* (1984)

4 I don't want to get to the end of my life and find that I lived just the length of it. I want to have lived the width of it as well.

Diane Ackerman, in *Newsweek* (1986)

5 I have always had a dread of becoming a passenger in life.

Princess Margrethe of Denmark, in Peter Dragadze, "Heiress to a Friendly Throne," *Life* (1968)

6 I don't believe that life is supposed to make you feel good, or to make you feel miserable either. Life is just supposed to make you feel.

Gloria Naylor, *Bailey's Cafe* (1992)

7 To live fully, outwardly and inwardly, not to ignore external reality for the sake of the inner life, or the reverse—that's quite a task.

Etty Hillesum (1941), *An Interrupted Life* (1983)

8 Life is a succession / of moments / to live each one / is to succeed.

Corita Kent, *Moments of 1984* (1983)

9 I asked myself the question, "What do you want of your life?" and I realized with a start of recognition and terror, "Exactly what I have—but to be commensurate, to handle it all better."

May Sarton, *Journal of a Solitude* (1973)

10 I want to live faster, faster, faster! . . . I fear that this desire to live always at high pressure is the presage of a short existence. Who knows?

Marie Bashkirtseff (1874), who died at age twenty-three, in Mary J. Serrano, tr., *The Journal of a Young Artist* (1919)

11 Such a fitful fever life is!

May Christie, *Hearts Afire* (1926)

12 I warn you, / I am living for the last time.

Anna Akhmatova, "In 1940" (1940), in D.M. Thomas, tr., *You Will Hear Thunder* (1985)

13 It's not that I'm afraid to die, but I'm terribly, terribly afraid not to live.

Frances Noyes Hart, *The Crooked Lane* (1933)

14 Life is either a daring adventure or nothing. To keep our faces toward change and behave like free spirits in the presence of fate is strength undefeatable.

Helen Keller, *Let Us Have Faith* (1940)

15 To live is so startling, it leaves but little room for other occupations.

Emily Dickinson (1871), in Mabel Loomis Todd, ed., *Letters of Emily Dickinson*, vol. 2 (1894)

16 Life is creation. Self and circumstances the raw material.

Dorothy M. Richardson, *Pilgrimage: The Trap* (1925)

17 The real trick is to stay alive as long as you live.

Ann Landers, *Since You Ask Me* (1961)

18 Men for the sake of getting a living forget to live.

Margaret Fuller, *Summer on the Lakes* (1844)

19 Life was meant to be lived and curiosity must be kept alive. One must never, for whatever reason, turn one's back on life.

Eleanor Roosevelt, *The Autobiography of Eleanor Roosevelt* (1961)

20 Life seems to love the liver of it.

Maya Angelou, *Wouldn't Take Nothing for My Journey Now* (1993)

21 There is no living creature, though the whims of eons had put its eyes on boggling stalks and clamped it in a carapace, diminished it to a pinpoint and given it a taste for mud and stuck it down a well or hid it under a stone, but that creature will live on if it can.

Marilynne Robinson, *Housekeeping* (1980)

22 Life is a gamble, a chance, a mere guess. Cast a line and reel in a splendid rainbow trout or a slippery eel.

Mourning Dove, *Cogewea* (1927)

1 If you take what you want in this world you will also have to take what you get.

Louise Redfield Peattie, *The Californians* (1940)

2 We can never catch up with life. . . . We shall always be eating the soft part of our melting ice and meanwhile the nice hard part is rapidly melting too.

M.P. Follett, *Creative Experience* (1924)

3 Life itself is the proper binge.

Julia Child, in *Time* (1980)

4 What if—what if Life itself were the sweetheart?

Willa Cather, *Lucy Gayheart* (1935)

5 For me, nothing is so exciting as to imagine that *life* is my lover—and is *always* courting me. To relate to life in that way is a challenge and a surrender that invites me deeper into being alive in every moment that I can manage it.

Julie Henderson, *The Lover Within* (1986)

6 If logic tells you that life is a meaningless accident, don't give up on life. Give up on logic.

Shira Milgrom (1988), in Ellen M. Umansky and Dianne Ashton, eds., *Four Centuries of Jewish Women's Spirituality* (1992)

7 Life is change: growth is optional.

Karen Kaiser Clark, book title (1994)

8 Life need not be easy, provided only that it is not empty.

Lise Meitner (1892), in Sharon Bertsch McGrayne, *Nobel Prize Women in Science* (1993)

9 Life is easier than you'd think; all that is necessary is to accept the impossible, do without the indispensable, and bear the intolerable.

Kathleen Norris, in Dorothy Sarnoff, *Speech Can Change Your Life* (1970)

10 Existence is no more than the precarious attainment of relevance in an intensely mobile flux of past, present, and future.

Susan Sontag, "'Thinking Against Oneself': Reflections on Cioran," *Styles of Radical Will* (1966)

11 Sacredness of human life! The world has never believed it! It has been with life that we settled our quarrels, won wives, gold and land, defended ideas, imposed religions. We have held that a death toll was a necessary part of every human achievement, whether sport, war, or industry. A moment's rage over the horror of it, and we have sunk into indifference.

Ida Tarbell, *New Ideals in Business* (1914)

12 Even without wars / life is dangerous.

Anne Sexton, "Hurry Up Please It's Time," *The Death Notebooks* (1974)

13 Life seems to be a choice between two wrong answers.

Sharyn McCrumb, *If Ever I Return, Pretty Peggy-O* (1990)

14 Life is a publicity stunt. A shill. You've been had.

Kate Millett, *Flying* (1974)

15 Life itself is a party: you join after it's started and you leave before it's finished.

Elsa Maxwell, *How to Do It* (1957)

16 Life is something to do when you can't get to sleep.

Fran Lebowitz, in *The Observer* (1979)

17 Life is but a collection of habits.

Ida Tarbell, *New Ideals in Business* (1914)

18 Life is a succession of readjustments.

Elizabeth Bowen, *To the North* (1933)

19 Life is something that happens to you while you're making other plans.

Margaret Millar, *Beyond This Point Are Monsters* (1970)

20 Nothing happens, and nothing happens, and then everything happens.

Fay Weldon, *Life Force* (1992)

21 There are times when life surprises one, and anything may happen, even what one had hoped for.

Ellen Glasgow, *Vein of Iron* (1935)

22 Frog or pearl, life hid something at the bottom of the cup.

Mary Butts, *Ashe of Rings* (1925)

23 It's always something.

Gilda Radner, as "Roseanne Roseannadanna," *It's Always Something* (1989)

24 Life goes on, having nowhere else to go.

Diane Ackerman, *The Moon by Whale Light* (1991)

25 It has begun to occur to me that life is a stage I'm going through.

Ellen Goodman, *Close to Home* (1979)

1 Life was a fool's errand, carrying news to the worms.

    Kylie Tennant, *Lost Haven* (1946)

2 It is so hard for us little human beings to accept this deal that we get. It's really crazy, isn't it? We get to live, then we have to die. What we put into every moment is all we have. . . . What spirit human beings have! It *is* a pretty cheesy deal—all the pleasures of life, and then death.

    Gilda Radner, *It's Always Something* (1989)

3 Life's bare as bone.

    Virginia Woolf, "An Unwritten Novel," *Monday or Tuesday* (1921)

4 Our lives are written in disappearing ink.

    Michelle Cliff, "Monster," in *The American Voice* (1991)

5 Life is an illusion.

    Mata Hari, as she prepared to meet the firing squad (1917), in Barbara McDowell and Hana Umlauf, *Woman's Almanac* (1977)

6 I've looked at life from both sides now, / From win and lose, and still somehow. . . / It's life's illusions I recall . . . / I really don't know life at all!

    Joni Mitchell, title song (1967), *Both Sides Now* (1992)

7 All is pattern, all life, but we can't always see the pattern when we're part of it.

    Belva Plain, *Crescent City* (1984)

8 If I have learnt anything it is that life forms no logical patterns. It is haphazard and full of beauties which I try to catch as they fly by, for who knows whether any of them will ever return?

    Margot Fonteyn, *Margot Fonteyn* (1975)

9 The strangest thing about life is not its frightful cruelty, but that it can be gentle.

    Storm Jameson, *The Journal of Mary Hervey Russell* (1945)

10 Life justified itself. It might be cruel, treacherous, ironic, but it was life, and pain was as much a part of it as joy.

    Sheila Kaye-Smith, *A Challenge to Sirius* (1917)

11 It began in mystery, and it will end in mystery, but what a savage and beautiful country lies in between.

    Diane Ackerman, *A Natural History of the Senses* (1990)

12 Life is a tragic mystery. We are pierced and driven by laws we only half understand, we find that the lesson we learn again and again is that of accepting heroic helplessness.

    Florida Scott-Maxwell, *The Measure of My Days* (1968)

13 There is something all life has in common, and when I know what it is I shall know myself.

    Jean Craighead George, *The Summer of the Falcon* (1962)

14 I began to have an idea of my life, not as the slow shaping of achievement to fit my preconceived purposes, but as the gradual discovery and growth of a purpose which I did not know.

    Joanna Field, *A Life of One's Own* (1934)

15 At the moment you are most in awe of all there is about life that you don't understand, you are closer to understanding it all than at any other time.

    Jane Wagner, *The Search for Signs of Intelligent Life in the Universe* (1985)

16 When I left the stage door and sought my orientation among real people I was in a wilderness of unpredictables in an unchoreographed world.

    Margot Fonteyn, *Margot Fonteyn* (1975)

17 How we spend our days is, of course, how we spend our lives.

    Annie Dillard, *The Writing Life* (1989)

18 You don't get to choose how you're going to die. Or when. You can only decide how you're going to live. Now.

    Joan Baez, *Daybreak* (1968)

19 If you wish to live, you must first attend your own funeral.

    Katherine Mansfield, in Antony Alpers, *Katherine Mansfield* (1954)

20 I postpone death by living, by suffering, by error, by risking, by giving, by losing.

    Anaïs Nin (1933), *The Diary of Anaïs Nin*, vol. 1 (1966)

21 Naked were we born and naked must we depart. . . . No matter what you may lose, be patient for nothing belongs; it is only lent.

    Glückel of Hameln, *Memoirs of Glückel of Hameln* (1724)

22 Life is painful, nasty and short . . . in my case it has only been painful and nasty.

    Djuna Barnes, in Hank O'Neal, *Life Is Painful, Nasty and Short . . .* (1991)

23 Life is the saddest thing there is, next to death.

    Edith Wharton, *A Backward Glance* (1934)

1 All life is nothing but a brief reprieve from death.
Simone de Beauvoir, *The Prime of Life* (1960)

2 Life is a death-defying experience.
Edna Buchanan, *Miami, It's Murder* (1994)

3 For Lou Ann, life itself was a life-threatening enterprise.
Barbara Kingsolver, *The Bean Trees* (1989)

4 Life is a frail moth flying / Caught in the web of the years that pass.
Sara Teasdale, "Come," *Rivers to the Sea* (1915)

5 Sometimes it seemed to him that his life was delicate as a dandelion. One little puff from any direction, and it was blown to bits.
Katherine Paterson, *Bridge to Terabithia* (1977)

6 Life begins when a person first realizes how soon it ends.
Marcelene Cox, in *Ladies' Home Journal* (1949)

7 It's only when we truly know and understand that we have a limited time on earth—and that we have no way of knowing when our time is up—that we will begin to live each day to the fullest, as if it was the only one we had.
Elisabeth Kübler-Ross, in *Parade* (1991)

8 Life is like a great jazz riff. You sense the end the very moment you were wanting it to go on forever.
Sheila Ballantyne, title story, *Life on Earth* (1988)

9 The life . . . that she had complained against, had murmured at, had raged at and defied—none the less she had loved it so, joyed in it so, both in good days and evil, that not one day had there been when 'twould not have seemed hard to give it back to God, nor one grief that she could have forgone without regret.
Sigrid Undset, *Kristin Lavransdatter: The Cross* (1922)

10 Life is like a camel: you can make it do anything except back up.
Marcelene Cox, in *Ladies' Home Journal* (1945)

11 It seems a silly kind o' business to bring us into the world at all for no special reason 'cept to take us out of it again just as folks 'ave learned to know us a bit and find us useful.
Marie Corelli, *Innocent* (1914)

12 You live and learn and then you die and forget it all.
Lynne Alpern and Esther Blumenfeld, *Oh, Lord, I Sound Just Like Mama* (1986)

13 How short is human life! the very breath! / Which frames my words, accelerates my death.
Hannah More, "Reflections of King Hezekiah," *Sacred Dramas* (1782)

14 Never, my heart, is there enough of living.
Léonie Adams, "Never Enough of Living," *Those Not Elect* (1925)

15 Why haven't we seventy lives? One is no use.
Winifred Holtby, in Vera Brittain, *Testament of Friendship* (1940)

16 The great question of all choosers and adventurers is "Was it worth while?"—and whatever else you may expect of life, don't expect an answer to that.
Sheila Kaye-Smith, *A Challenge to Sirius* (1917)

17 I took one Draught of Life — / I'll tell you what I paid — / Precisely an existence — / The market price, they said.
Emily Dickinson, in Martha Dickinson Bianchi and Alfred Leete Hampson, eds., *Further Poems of Emily Dickinson* (1929)

18 If the payment has sometimes been excessive, it was after all the payment *for life*, and there cannot be and is no excessive payment for life.
Nina Berberova, *The Italics Are Mine* (1969)

19 When I can look Life in the eyes, / Grown calm and very coldly wise, / Life will have given me the Truth, / And taken in exchange—my youth.
Sara Teasdale, "Wisdom," *Love Songs* (1917)

20 That it will never come again / Is what makes life so sweet.
Emily Dickinson, in Mabel Loomis Todd and Millicent Todd Bingham, eds., *Bolts of Melody* (1945)

21 It is the brevity of life which makes it tolerable; its experiences have value because they have an end.
Winifred Holtby, "Sentence of Life," *Truth Is Not Sober* (1934)

22 Your life feels different on you, once you greet death and understand your heart's position. You wear your life like a garment from the mission bundle sale ever after—lightly because you realize you never paid nothing for it, cherishing because

you know you won't ever come by such a bargain again.

Louise Erdrich, *Love Medicine* (1984)

1 A short life in the saddle, Lord! / Not long life by the fire.

Louise Imogen Guiney, "The Knight Errant," *A Roadside Harp* (1893)

2 I look back on my life like a good day's work, it was done and I feel satisfied with it.

Grandma Moses, in Otto Kallir, ed., *My Life's History* (1952)

3 What an interesting life I had. And how I wish I had realized it sooner!

Colette, after seeing a film based on her life, in Helen Bevington, *When Found, Make a Verse Of* (1961)

4 You are dipped up from the great river of consciousness, and death only pours you back.

Dorothy Canfield Fisher, *The Bent Twig* (1915)

5 Living, you stand under a waterfall. . . . What a racket in your ears, what a scattershot pummeling! It is time pounding at you, time. Knowing you are alive is watching on every side your generation's short time falling away as fast as rivers drop through air.

Annie Dillard, *An American Childhood* (1987)

6 How meager one's life becomes when it is reduced to its basic facts. . . . And the last, most complete, reduction is on one's tombstone: a name, two dates.

Helen MacInnes, *The Venetian Affair* (1963)

7 There must be more to life than just eating and getting bigger.

Trina Paulus, *Hope for the Flowers* (1972)

8 I was merely a disinterested spectator at the Banquet of Life.

Elaine Dundy, *The Dud Avocado* (1958)

9 It seems to me you can be awfully happy in this life if you stand aside and watch and mind your own business, and let other people do as they like about damaging themselves and one another. You go on kidding yourself that you're impartial and tolerant and all that, then all of a sudden you realize you're dead, and you've never been alive at all.

Mary Stewart, *This Rough Magic* (1964)

10 People do not live nowadays—they get about ten percent out of life.

Isadora Duncan, "Memoirs," in *This Quarter* (1929)

11 Life after life after life goes by / without poetry, / without seemliness, / without love.

Denise Levertov, "The Mutes," *The Sorrow Dance* (1967)

12 People permit life to slide past them like a deft pickpocket, their purse—not yet missed and now too late—in his hand.

Edna Ferber, *A Kind of Magic* (1963)

13 They are committing murder who merely live.

May Sarton, "Summary," *Inner Landscape* (1938)

14 When one's young . . . everything is a rehearsal. To be repeated ad lib, to be put right when the curtain goes up in earnest. One day you know that the curtain was up all the time. That *was* the performance.

Sybille Bedford, *A Compass Error* (1968)

15 A young Apollo, golden-haired, / Stands dreaming on the verge of strife / Magnificently unprepared / For the long littleness of life.

Frances Cornford, "Youth," *Poems* (1910)

16 I had not loved enough. I'd been busy, busy, so busy, preparing for life, while life floated by me, quiet and swift as a regatta.

Lorene Cary, *Black Ice* (1991)

17 If we get used to life that is the crime.

Jean Garrigue, "Some Serious Nonsense for the Cats and Wolves," *The Monument Rose* (1953)

18 She dragged her life after her. It was fastened to her like a heavy cloak, stifling at times to wear, but then she was accustomed to it.

Mary Borden, *Flamingo* (1927)

19 It was not . . . that she was unaware of the frayed and ragged edges of life. She would merely iron them out with a firm hand and neatly hem them down.

P.D. James, *Death of an Expert Witness* (1977)

20 You took what you wanted from life, if you could get it, and you did without the rest.

Zelda Fitzgerald, *Save Me the Waltz* (1932)

21 I am one of those people who just can't help getting a kick out of life—even when it's a kick in the teeth.

Polly Adler, *A House Is Not a Home* (1953)

1 Life gives us what we need when we need it. Receiving what it gives us is a whole other thing.

Pam Houston, "In My Next Life," *Cowboys Are My Weakness* (1992)

2 It's just as possible to live to the full in a narrow corner as it is in bigness.

Sylvia Ashton-Warner, *Teacher* (1963)

3 Love and life cannot help but marry and stay married with an exhausting violence of fidelity.

Kate O'Brien, *Mary Lavelle* (1936)

4 I was, being human, born alone; / I am, being woman, hard beset; / I live by squeezing from a stone / The little nourishment I get. / In masks outrageous and austere / The years go by in single file; / But none has merited my fear, / And none has quite escaped my smile.

Elinor Wylie, "Let No Charitable Hope," *Black Armour* (1923)

5 When you consider something like death, after which (there being no news flash to the contrary) we may well go out like a candle flame, then it probably doesn't matter if we try too hard, are awkward sometimes, care for one another too deeply, are excessively curious about nature, are too open to experience, enjoy a nonstop expense of the senses in an effort to know life intimately and lovingly.

Diane Ackerman, *A Natural History of the Senses* (1990)

6 A man without ambition is dead. A man with ambition but no love is dead. A man with ambition and love for his blessings here on earth is ever so alive. Having been alive, it won't be hard in the end to lie down and rest.

Pearl Bailey, *Talking to Myself* (1971)

7 You make what seems a simple choice: choose a man or a job or a neighborhood—and what you have chosen is not a man or a job or a neighborhood, but a life.

Jessamyn West, *The Life I Really Lived* (1979)

8 Not everyone's life is what they make it. Some people's life is what other people make it.

Alice Walker, *You Can't Keep a Good Woman Down* (1981)

9 [Ade Bethune's] life itself stands as her major work of art, her great design, lovingly worked out over the years.

Judith Stoughton, *Proud Donkey of Schaerbeek* (1988)

10 Notwithstanding the poverty of my outside experience, I have always had a significance for myself, and every chance to stumble along my straight and narrow little path, and to worship at the feet of my Deity, and what more can a human soul ask for?

Alice James (1892), in Leon Edel, ed., *The Diary of Alice James* (1964)

11 Except for our higher order of minds we are like the little moles under the earth carrying out blindly the work of digging, thinking our own dark passage-ways constitute all there is to the world.

Bess Streeter Aldrich, *Spring Came on Forever* (1935)

12 Sometimes it feels like God has reached down and touched me, blessed me a thousand times over, and sometimes it all feels like a mean joke, like God's advisers are Muammar Qaddafi and Phyllis Schlafly.

Anne Lamott, *Operating Instructions* (1993)

13 It's not true that life is one damn thing after another—it's one damn thing over and over.

Edna St. Vincent Millay (1930), in Allan Ross Macdougall, ed., *Letters of Edna St. Vincent Millay* (1952)

14 Her life was like running on a treadmill or riding on a stationary bike; it was aerobic, it was healthy, but she wasn't going anywhere.

Julia Phillips, *You'll Never Eat Lunch in This Town Again* (1991)

15 Life has taught me that the greatest tragedy is not to die too soon but to live too long.

Ellen Glasgow, *Letters of Ellen Glasgow* (1958)

16 Life goes on forever like the gnawing of a mouse.

Edna St. Vincent Millay, "Ashes of Life," *Renascence* (1917)

17 Life cannot be captured in a few axioms. And that is just what I keep trying to do. But it won't work, for life is full of endless nuances and cannot be captured in just a few formulae.

Etty Hillesum (1941), *An Interrupted Life* (1983)

See also Experience, Human Nature, Life and Death, Lifelessness.

## ❦ LIFE AND DEATH

18 Life and Death are two locked caskets, each of which contains the key to the other.

Isak Dinesen, "A Consolatory Tale," *Winter's Tales* (1942)

1 Dying is a short horse and soon curried. Living is a horse of another color and bigger.

    Jessamyn West, *The Woman Said Yes* (1976)

2 The hard thing about death is that nothing ever changes. The hard thing about life is that nothing stays the same.

    Sue Grafton, *"J" Is for Judgment* (1993)

3 Life, although it takes us many years and many tears to discover it, life is only another name for death; they cannot exist independently.

    Kathleen Norris, "Beauty in Letters," *These I Like Best* (1941)

4 It is not that death comes, but that life leaves.

    Marjorie Kinnan Rawlings (1949), *Selected Letters of Marjorie Kinnan Rawlings* (1982)

5 It is not death that kills us, but life. We are done to death by life.

    Marjorie Kinnan Rawlings (1949), *Selected Letters of Marjorie Kinnan Rawlings* (1982)

6 Life is real, and death is the illusion.

    Mary Baker Eddy, *Science and Health* (1875)

7 Life is better than death, I believe, if only because it is less boring, and because it has fresh peaches in it.

    Alice Walker, "Only Justice Can Stop a Curse," *In Search of Our Mothers' Gardens* (1983)

See also Death, Life.

## ❦ LIFELESSNESS

8 I been through living for years. I just ain't dead yet.

    Zora Neale Hurston, *Moses: Man of the Mountain* (1939)

9 Listen, Fred, don't feel badly when I die, because I've been dead for a long time.

    Dorothy Parker (1967), in Marion Meade, *Dorothy Parker: What Fresh Hell Is This?* (1988)

10 People, I had by this time found, all stopped living at one time or another, however many years longer they continued to be alive.

    Edith Wharton, "The Spark," *Old New York* (1924)

11 This alone is to be feared—the closed mind, the sleeping imagination, the death of the spirit. The death of the body is to that, I think, a little thing.

    Winifred Holtby (1925), in Vera Brittain, *Testament of Friendship* (1940)

12 There ain't no use in dyin' 'fore yer time. Lots of folks is walkin' 'round jes' as dead as they'll ever be.

    Alice Caldwell Rice, *Mrs. Wiggs of the Cabbage Patch* (1901)

See also Depression, Despair.

## ❦ LIFESTYLE

13 *Lifestyle.* Not a word at all, really—rather a wordette. A genuine case of more is less. . . . The word *life* and the word *style* are, except in rare cases (and chances are that *you're* not of them), mutually exclusive.

    Fran Lebowitz, in *Interview Magazine* (1975)

14 Alternative Lifestyles, the emotional fly-drive packages of our times, come equipped with a set of clothes, a choice of authors, a limited menu of sports and a discount coupon book of clichés.

    Ellen Goodman, *Close to Home* (1979)

15 Like everything else, Preppiness begins in the home.

    Lisa Birnbach, *The Official Preppy Handbook* (1980)

## ❦ LIMITATIONS

16 Learning too soon our limitations, we never learn our powers.

    Mignon McLaughlin, *The Neurotic's Notebook* (1963)

17 I think knowing what you can *not* do is more important than knowing what you can do.

    Lucille Ball, in Eleanor Harris, *The Real Story of Lucille Ball* (1954)

18 I could never work with great spirit in any material unless I knew that the amount of it was limited—I had to be hedged in by a boundary of either space or material, in order to awaken the feeling of creative excitement.

    Katharine Butler Hathaway, *The Little Locksmith* (1942)

See also Inadequacy, Weakness.

## ❦ LINES

19 The other line moves faster. This applies to all lines—bank, supermarket, tollbooth, customs, and so on. And don't try to change lines. The other

one—the one you were in originally—will then move faster.

Barbara Ettore, in *Harper's Magazine* (1974)

1 A line is an involuntary combination of people who are simultaneously irritated with one another and focused on a single, common circle of interests and goals. This leads to a mixture of rivalry, hostility, and collective sentiment, a constant readiness to close ranks against a common enemy—anyone who breaks the rules.

Lidia Ginzburg, "The Siege of Leningrad," in *Soviet Women Writing* (1990)

2 He had been born under a dark star that always landed him behind people like that—women ahead of him in public phone booths called up relatives they hadn't seen in twenty years, men at ticket windows before him wanted a breakdown of different-class fares between Chicago and Santa Fe.

Ursula Curtiss, *The Face of the Tiger* (1958)

See also Waiting.

## ❧ LISTENING

3 Before linguistics, before the literal link of language, there was listening.

Hannah Merker, *Listening* (1994)

4 Listening is a magnetic and strange thing, a creative force. You can see that when you think how the friends that really listen to us are the ones we move toward, and we want to sit in their radius as though it did us good, like ultraviolet rays.

Brenda Ueland, *Strength to Your Sword Arm* (1993)

5 As anyone with a speech or hearing disability can tell you, listening is not always auditory communication.

Hannah Merker, *Listening* (1994)

6 Blessed / are those who listen / when no one is left to speak.

Linda Hogan, "Blessing," *Calling Myself Home* (1978)

7 With the gift of listening comes the gift of healing.

Catherine de Hueck Doherty, *Poustinia* (1975)

8 The words a man speaks are always more comforting than the words he hears.

Jessamyn West, *The Massacre at Fall Creek* (1975)

9 Someone to tell it to is one of the fundamental needs of human beings.

Miles Franklin, *Childhood at Brindabella* (1963)

10 The only listening that counts is that of the talker who alternately absorbs and expresses ideas.

Agnes Repplier, *Compromises* (1904)

11 [He] stood listening in that peculiar state of tension which everyone feels when they call and are not answered.

Mary O'Hara, *Thunderhead* (1943)

12 It seemed rather incongruous that in a society of supersophisticated communication, we often suffer from a shortage of listeners.

Erma Bombeck, *If Life Is a Bowl of Cherries, What Am I Doing in the Pits?* (1971)

13 You seldom listen to me, and when you do you don't hear, and when you do hear you hear wrong, and even when you hear right you change it so fast that it's never the same.

Marjorie Kellogg, *Tell Me That You Love Me, Junie Moon* (1968)

14 I looked for a sounding-board and I found none. / The hearts that I called out to, remained stone.

Henriette Roland-Holst, "I Looked for a Sounding-Board," in Joanna Bankier and Deirdre Lashgari, eds., *Women Poets of the World* (1983)

15 He began to realize the deep truth that no one, broadly speaking, ever wishes to hear what you have been doing.

Angela Thirkell, *The Old Bank House* (1949)

16 No one really listens to anyone else, and if you try it for a while you'll see why.

Mignon McLaughlin, *The Second Neurotic's Notebook* (1966)

17 The opposite of talking isn't listening. The opposite of talking is waiting.

Fran Lebowitz, *Social Studies* (1977)

See also Attention, Conversation, Interruptions, Talking.

## ❧ LITERATURE

18 Literature is the last banquet between minds.

Edna O'Brien, in *The New York Times* (1993)

1 That sunlight of the dead which is called literature.

    Princess Marthe Bibesco, *Catherine-Paris* (1928)

2 Literature is my Utopia. Here I am not disfranchised. No barrier of the senses shuts me out from the sweet, gracious discourse of my book-friends. They talk to me without embarrassment or awkwardness.

    Helen Keller, *The Story of My Life* (1902)

3 The test of literature is, I suppose, whether we ourselves live more intensely for the reading of it.

    Elizabeth Drew, *The Modern Novel* (1926)

4 Literature is the lie that tells the truth.

    Dorothy Allison, "The Exile's Return," in *The New York Times Book Review* (1994)

5 Don't ask to live in tranquil times. Literature doesn't grow there.

    Rita Mae Brown, *Starting From Scratch* (1988)

6 Literature is born when something in life goes slightly adrift.

    Simone de Beauvoir, *The Prime of Life* (1960)

7 When literature becomes deliberately indifferent to the opposition of good and evil it betrays its function and forfeits all claim to excellence.

    Simone Weil, *On Science, Necessity, and the Love of God* (1968)

8 The greatest literature is *moral.*

    Dorothy Thompson, *The Courage to Be Happy* (1957)

9 It is not the office of a novelist to show us how to behave ourselves; it is not the business of fiction to teach us anything.

    Agnes Repplier, "Fiction in the Pulpit," *Points of View* (1891)

10 The secret of literature, which conventional people don't guess, is that writers are forever looking for the *surprising revelation*—not for reinforcement of collective wisdom.

    Carol Bly, *The Passionate, Accurate Story* (1990)

11 Literature is an instrument of a culture, not a summary of it.

    Cynthia Ozick, "Toward a New Yiddish," *Art and Ardor* (1983)

12 A people's literature is the great text-book for real knowledge of them.

    Edith Hamilton, *The Roman Way* (1932)

13 Literature is the record of our discontent.

    Virginia Woolf, "The Evening Party" (1918), in Susan Dick, ed., *The Complete Shorter Fiction of Virginia Woolf* (1985)

14 Perversity is the muse of modern literature.

    Susan Sontag, "Camus' Notebooks" (1963), *Against Interpretation* (1966)

15 I believe all literature started as gossip.

    Rita Mae Brown, *Starting From Scratch* (1988)

16 The illusion of art is to make one believe that great literature is very close to life, but exactly the opposite is true. Life is amorphous, literature is formal.

    Françoise Sagan, in Malcolm Cowley, ed., *Writers at Work* (1958)

17 Literature is a peculiarly public product of a particularly private endeavor.

    Valerie Miner, *Rumors From the Cauldron* (1991)

18 The body of literature, with its limits and edges, exists outside some people and inside others. Only after the writer lets literature shape her can she perhaps shape literature.

    Annie Dillard, *The Writing Life* (1989)

19 Coroners' inquests by learned societies can't make Shakespeare a dead man.

    Ellen Terry, *The Story of My Life* (1908)

20 Besides Shakespeare and me, who do you think there is?

    Gertrude Stein, to someone she thought knew little about literature, in James R. Mellow, *Charmed Circle* (1974)

21 Remarks are not literature.

    Gertrude Stein, to Ernest Hemingway, *The Autobiography of Alice B. Toklas* (1933)

See also Books, Children's Literature, Essays, Fiction, Nonfiction, Novels, Plot, Poetry, Poetry and Prose, Stories, Writing.

## ❦ LITIGATION

22 In the strange heat all litigation brings to bear on things, the very process of litigation fosters the most profound misunderstandings in the world.

    Renata Adler, *Reckless Disregard* (1986)

23 You were wise not to waste years in a lawsuit. . . . He who commences a suit resembles him who

plants a palm-tree which he will not live to see flourish.

Lady Marguerite Blessington (1841), in R.R. Madden, *The Literary Life and Correspondence of the Countess of Blessington*, vol. 2 (1855)

1 We hear of those to whom a lawsuit is an agreeable relaxation, a gentle excitement. One of this class, when remonstrated with, retorted, that while one friend kept dogs, and another horses, he, as he had a right to do, kept a lawyer; and no one had a right to dispute his taste.

Isabella Beeton, *The Book of Household Management* (1861)

See also Law, Lawyers.

## ❧ LOBSTERS

2 A shoe with legs, / a stone dropped from heaven.

Anne Sexton, "Lobster," *45 Mercy Street* (1976)

3 The proper place to eat lobster . . . is in a lobster shack as close to the sea as possible. There is no menu card because there is nothing else to eat except boiled lobster with melted butter.

Pearl S. Buck, *Pearl Buck's America* (1971)

## ❧ LODGERS

4 Another expedient, towards the making of my fortune, was letting three several rooms to as many different persons, but in principle were all alike, and conjunctive in the perpetration of my destruction. . . . They had taken violent fancies to my very candlesticks and sauce-pans, my pewter terribly shrunk, and my coals daily diminished, from the same opportunity they had in conveying off my beer; and, as I kept an eating-house also, there was very often a hue and cry after an imaginary dog, that had run away with three parts of a joint of meat.

Charlotte Charke, *A Narrative of the Life of Mrs. Charlotte Charke* (1755)

## ❧ LOGIC

5 Logic is the key to an all-inclusive spiritual well-being.

Marlene Dietrich, *Marlene* (1989)

6 Nothing is as depressing as absolute logic. Look at the maze of French politics perpetrated by a logical people.

Rae Foley, *The Hundredth Door* (1950)

7 If the world were a logical place, men would ride side-saddle.

Rita Mae Brown, *Sudden Death* (1983)

See also Rationality, Reason.

## ❧ LONDON

8 London, how could one ever be tired of it?

Margaret Drabble, *The Middle Ground* (1980)

9 The London streets are paths of loveliness; the very omnibuses look like colored archangels, their laps filled full of little trustful souls.

Evelyn Underhill, *Mysticism* (1955)

10 London is the best place in the world for the happy and the unhappy, there is a floating capital of sympathy for every human good or evil.

Sydney, Lady Morgan (1844), *Lady Morgan's Memoir*, vol. 2 (1862)

11 It took no sharp eye to see at a glance that the Londoner was a different breed from the country Englishman. He was arrogant with the knowledge of his power, for he was the kingdom and he knew it.

Kathleen Winsor, *Forever Amber* (1944)

12 Nobody is healthy in London, nobody can be.

Jane Austen, *Emma* (1816)

See also England.

## ❧ LONELINESS

13 There have been weeks when no one / calls me by name.

Leah Goldberg, "Nameless Journey," *Selected Poems* (1976)

14 I've been so lonely for long periods of my life that if a rat walked in I would have welcomed it.

Louise Nevelson, *Dawns + Dusks* (1976)

1 We have all known the long loneliness and we have learned that the only solution is love and that love comes with community.

    Dorothy Day, *The Long Loneliness* (1952)

2 Birth is the start / of loneliness / & loneliness the start / of poetry.

    Erica Jong, "Dear Marys, Dear Mother, Dear Daughter," *Loveroot* (1975)

3 *Loneliness* is dangerous. It's bad for you to be alone, to be lonely, because if aloneness does not lead to God, it leads to the devil. It leads to self.

    Joyce Carol Oates, "Shame," *The Wheel of Love* (1969)

4 Loneliness and the feeling of being unwanted is the most terrible poverty.

    Mother Teresa, in "Saints Among Us," *Time* (1975)

5 Who hasn't slept in an empty bed sometimes, longing for the embrace of another person on the achingly short trip to the grave?

    Leonore Fleischer, *The Rose* (1979)

6 She had encountered one of the more devastating kinds of loneliness in existence: that of being in close contact with someone to whom she was a nonperson, and who thereby rendered her invisible and of no consequence.

    Dorothy Gilman, *Mrs. Pollifax and the Whirling Dervish* (1990)

7 Loneliness is never more cruel than when it is felt in close propinquity with someone who has ceased to communicate.

    Germaine Greer, *The Female Eunuch* (1971)

8 I have known no loneliness like this, / Locked in your arms and bent beneath your kiss.

    Babette Deutsch, "Solitude," *Banners* (1919)

9 Lonely people talking to each other can make each other lonelier. They should be careful because lonely people can't afford to cry.

    Lillian Hellman, *The Autumn Garden* (1951)

10 A person can be lonely even if he is loved by many people, because he is still not the "One and Only" to anyone.

    Anne Frank, *The Diary of a Young Girl* (1952)

11 The loneliness persisted like incessant rain.

    Ann Allen Shockley, "Spring Into Autumn," *The Black and White of It* (1980)

12 Life may be brimming over with experiences, but somewhere, deep inside, all of us carry a vast and fruitful loneliness.

    Etty Hillesum (1942), *An Interrupted Life* (1983)

13 Women especially are social beings, who are not content with just husband and family, but must have a community, a group, an exchange with others. A child is not enough. A husband and children, no matter how busy one may be kept by them, are not enough. Young and old, even in the busiest years of our lives, we women especially are victims of the long loneliness.

    Dorothy Day, *The Long Loneliness* (1952)

14 Loneliness is black coffee and late-night television; solitude is herb tea and soft music.

    Pearl Cleage, "In My Solitude," *Deals With the Devil* (1993)

15 Solitude is one thing and loneliness is another.

    May Sarton, *I Knew a Phoenix* (1959)

16 At any moment solitude may put on the face of loneliness.

    May Sarton, *Plant Dreaming Deep* (1968)

17 Loneliness is the poverty of self; solitude is the richness of self.

    May Sarton, *Mrs. Stevens Hears the Mermaids Singing* (1965)

18 Solitude is that human situation in which I keep myself company. Loneliness comes about when I am alone without being able to split up into the two-in-one, without being able to keep myself company.

    Hannah Arendt, *The Life of the Mind*, vol. 1 (1978)

19 A cat and a Bible, and nobody needs to be lonely.

    Mary Roberts Rinehart, title story, *The Frightened Wife* (1953)

20 It is better to be lonely than to wish to be alone.

    Margaret Deland, *The Story of a Child* (1892)

See also Alone, Solitude.

## ❦ LONGING

21 Longing is all that lasts.

    Jennifer Stone, *Telegraph Avenue Then* (1992)

1 It seems to me we can never give up longing and wishing while we are thoroughly alive. There are certain things we feel to be beautiful and good, and we *must* hunger after them.

    George Eliot, *The Mill on the Floss* (1860)

2 Of one thing alone I am very sure: it is a law of our nature that the memory of longing should survive the more fugitive memory of fulfillment.

    Ellen Glasgow, *The Woman Within* (1954)

3 The force behind the movement of time is a mourning that will not be comforted. That is why the first event is known to have been an expulsion, and the last is hoped to be a reconciliation and return. So memory pulls us forward, so prophecy is only brilliant memory—there will be a garden where all of us as one child will sleep in our mother Eve, hooped in her ribs and staved by her spine.

    Marilynne Robinson, *Housekeeping* (1980)

See also Desire, Hope.

## ❧ LOS ANGELES

4 Los Angeles is a sophisticated city; it has no eccentricities and no heart.

    Stella Benson, *The Little World* (1925)

5 It takes a certain kind of innocence to like L.A.

    Eve Babitz, *Eve's Hollywood* (1974)

6 Visitors to Los Angeles, then and now, were put out because the residents of Los Angeles had the inhospitable idea of building a city comfortable to live in, rather than a monument to astonish the eye of jaded travelers.

    Jessamyn West, *Hide and Seek* (1973)

7 In a foreign country people don't expect you to be just like them, but in Los Angeles, which is infiltrating the world, they don't consider that you might be different because they don't recognize any values except their own. And soon there may not be any others.

    Pauline Kael, *I Lost It at the Movies* (1965)

8 This city is a hundred years old but try and find some trace of its history. Every culture is swallowed up and spat out as a franchise. Taco Bell. Benihana of Tokyo. Numero Uno Pizza. Pup 'N' Taco. Kentucky Fried Chicken. Fast food sushi. Teriyaki Bowl.

    Anne Finger, *Past Due* (1990)

9 Los Angeles is a very transient town. It's the only place I know where you can actually rent a dog.

    Rita Rudner, *Naked Beneath My Clothes* (1992)

10 We live in Los Angeles, where you are expected to move every two to four years, so people can see how well your career is going.

    Rita Rudner, *Naked Beneath My Clothes* (1992)

See also California, Hollywood.

## ❧ LOSS

11 The longed-for ships / Come empty home or founder on the deep, / And eyes first lose their tears and then their sleep.

    Edith Wharton, "Non Dolet!" *Artemis to Actaeon* (1909)

12 We have lost so many leaves / in loss, loss, loss / Out of the sky, / What shall we do for shelter to live by?

    Josephine Miles, "Autumnal," *Prefabrications* (1955)

13 Loss grew as you did, without your consent; your losses mounted beside you like earthworm castings.

    Annie Dillard, *An American Childhood* (1987)

14 Our losses include not only our separations and departures from those we love, but our conscious and unconscious losses of romantic dreams, impossible expectations, illusions of freedom and power, illusions of safety—and the loss of our own younger self, the self that thought it would always be unwrinkled and invulnerable and immortal.

    Judith Viorst, *Necessary Losses* (1986)

15 I cannot say what loves have come and gone, / I only know that summer sang in me / A little while, that in me sings no more.

    Edna St. Vincent Millay, "What Lips My Lips Have Kissed, and Where, and Why," *The Harp-Weaver* (1923)

16 It is the private deaths of the mind / That matter— the endless burial / And the long atonement of survival.

    Minna Gellert, "Morning Is a Broken Clock," *Flesh of the Furies* (1947)

1 It is better to be drunk with loss and to beat the ground, than to let the deeper things gradually escape.

> Ivy Compton-Burnett (1969), in Hilary Spurling, *Ivy* (1984)

2 Losing is the price we pay for living. It is also the source of much of our growth and gain.

> Judith Viorst, *Necessary Losses* (1986)

3 For the first time, I was pierced by the little panic and tristesse occasioned by small things passing irrevocably from view.

> Faith Sullivan, *The Cape Ann* (1988)

4 I still miss those I loved who are no longer with me but I find I am grateful for having loved them. The gratitude has finally conquered the loss.

> Rita Mae Brown, *Starting From Scratch* (1988)

5 We never know the full value of a thing until we lose it.

> Mrs. Henry Wood, *East Lynne* (1861)

6 We never discover the value of things till we have lost them.

> Dinah Maria Mulock Craik, *A Life for a Life* (1866)

7 It is harder to lose what you never had.

> Eleanore Griffin, "My Name Is Ruth," in *Woman's Home Companion* (1943)

8 We only keep what we lose.

> May Sarton, "O Saisons! O Châteaux!" *The Lion and the Rose* (1948)

9 One knows what one has lost, but not what one may find.

> George Sand, *The Haunted Pool* (1851)

10 It was on Good Friday that Miss Bendix lost her faith. She had really lost it before then, but, as is often the case with losses, she did not notice that anything was missing for some time after it had gone.

> Naomi Royde-Smith, *Miss Bendix* (1938)

11 When I am dead and opened, you shall find Calais lying in my heart.

> Mary I, in Raphael Holinshed, *Chronicles*, vol. 3 (1577)

12 First I lost weight, then I lost my voice, and now I've lost Onassis.

> Maria Callas, in Barbara McDowell and Hana Umlauf, *Woman's Almanac* (1977)

See also Bereavement, Death, Failure, Grief, Miscarriage, Mourning, Privation, Suffering.

## ❧ LOTTERIES

13 It is a bad business, dealing in lottery tickets. Riches got in such a hasty manner never wear well.

> Mrs. Sarah J. Hale, *Traits of American Life* (1835)

14 Lotteries . . . are not native productions of my country, but introduced into our "heathen" land by so-called Christians, from a Christian nation.

> Lydia Kamekeha Liliuokalani, *Hawaii's Story by Hawaii's Queen* (1898)

See also Gambling.

## ❧ LOVE

15 Everyone admits that love is wonderful and necessary, yet no one can agree on what it is.

> Diane Ackerman, *A Natural History of Love* (1994)

16 Love is the white light of emotion.

> Diane Ackerman, *A Natural History of Love* (1994)

17 Love is the extremely difficult realization that something other than oneself is real.

> Iris Murdoch, "The Sublime and the Good," in *Chicago Review* (1959)

18 Love — is anterior to Life — / Posterior — to Death.

> Emily Dickinson (1864), in Mabel Loomis Todd, ed., *Poems by Emily Dickinson*, 3rd series (1896)

19 Love, first begotten of all created things.

> Georgiana Goddard King, *The Way of Perfect Love* (1909)

20 Love . . . is . . . the only effective counter to death.

> Maureen Duffy, *Wounds* (1969)

21 Love is a fruit in season at all times.

> Mother Teresa, *A Gift for God* (1975)

1 Love much. Earth has enough of bitter in it.
Ella Wheeler Wilcox, "Love Much," *Poems of Pleasure* (1888)

2 Love, like truth, is the unassailable defense.
Diane Ackerman, *A Natural History of Love* (1994)

3 We love because it's the only true adventure.
Nikki Giovanni, in *Reader's Digest* (1982)

4 Love is the wild card of existence.
Rita Mae Brown, *In Her Day* (1976)

5 Love is an act of sedition, a revolt against reason, an uprising in the body politic, a private mutiny.
Diane Ackerman, *A Natural History of Love* (1994)

6 Love alone matters.
St. Thérèse of Lisieux (1897), in Dorothy Day, *Therese* (1960)

7 The beginning of my history is—love. It is the beginning of every man and every woman's history, if they are only frank enough to admit it.
Marie Corelli, *Wormwood* (1890)

8 Love is the only thing that keeps me sane.
Sue Townsend, *The Secret Diary of Adrian Mole Aged 13-3/4* (1982)

9 That love is all there is, / Is all we know of Love.
Emily Dickinson, in Martha Dickinson Bianchi, ed., *The Single Hound* (1914)

10 The song may be now gay, now plaintive, but it is deathless.
Mary Johnston, *To Have and to Hold* (1900)

11 Love is the vital essence that pervades and permeates, from the center to the circumference, the graduating circles of all thought and action. Love is the talisman of human weal and woe—the open sesame to every soul.
Elizabeth Cady Stanton, speech (1860)

12 Love, like poetry, is a kind of homesickness, / the kind which made medieval monks / sleep in their coffins.
Jennifer Stone, "Nostalgia," in *Sandstones* (1975)

13 We love as soon as we learn to distinguish a separate "you" and "me." Love is our attempt to assuage the terror and isolation of that separateness.
Judith Viorst, *Necessary Losses* (1986)

14 The night was dark / and love was a burning fence / about my house.
Audre Lorde, "Gemini" (1956), *Undersong* (1992)

15 Soft are the hands of Love, / soft, soft are his feet.
H.D., "Demeter," *Collected Poems* (1925)

16 Love is repaid by love alone.
St. Thérèse of Lisieux (1897), in John Clarke, tr., *Story of a Soul* (1972)

17 'Till I loved / I never lived — Enough.
Emily Dickinson (1862), in Mabel Loomis Todd and T.W. Higginson, eds., *Poems by Emily Dickinson* (1890)

18 Till it has loved, no man or woman can become itself.
Emily Dickinson (1879), in Mabel Loomis Todd, ed., *Letters of Emily Dickinson*, vol. 2 (1894)

19 Perhaps loving something is the only starting place there is for making your life your own.
Alice Koller, *An Unknown Woman* (1982)

20 Love opens the doors into everything, as far as I can see, including and perhaps most of all, the door into one's own secret, and often terrible and frightening, real self.
May Sarton, *Mrs. Stevens Hears the Mermaids Singing* (1965)

21 I don't want to live—I want to love first, and live incidentally.
Zelda Fitzgerald (1919), in Nancy Milford, *Zelda* (1970)

22 While it is a misfortune to a woman never to be loved, it is a tragedy to her never to love.
Dorothy Dix, *Dorothy Dix* (1926)

23 It is the loving, not the loved, woman who feels lovable.
Jessamyn West, *Love Is Not What You Think* (1959)

24 It doesn't so much matter what one loves. To love is the transfiguring thing.
The Gardener, *The Garden of a Commuter's Wife* (1905)

25 Perhaps it does not matter so very much what it is one loves in this world. But love something one must.
Katherine Mansfield, "The Canary," *The Doves' Nest* (1923)

26 The story of a love is not important—what is important is that one is capable of love. It is perhaps the only glimpse we are permitted of eternity.
Helen Hayes, in *Guideposts* (1960)

27 Love, I find is like singing. Everybody can do enough to satisfy themselves, though it may not impress the neighbors as being very much.
Zora Neale Hurston, *Dust Tracks on a Road* (1942)

1 What we have once enjoyed we can never lose. All that we love deeply becomes a part of us.

Helen Keller, *We Bereaved* (1929)

2 It is impossible to repent of love. The sin of love does not exist.

Muriel Spark, *The Mandelbaum Gate* (1965)

3 Where there is no longer love, there is no longer anything.

George Sand, *Impressions et Souvenirs* (1873)

4 There is always something left to love. And if you ain't learned that, you ain't learned nothing.

Lorraine Hansberry, *A Raisin in the Sun* (1959)

5 In the arithmetic of love, one plus one equals everything, and two minus one equals nothing.

Mignon McLaughlin, *The Second Neurotic's Notebook* (1966)

6 A great love is an absolute isolation and an absolute absorption.

Ouida, *Wisdom, Wit and Pathos* (1884)

7 I go where I love and where I am loved.

H.D., *The Flowering of the Rod* (1946)

8 All places are alike to love.

Lady Mary Wroth, "Pamphilia to Amphilanthus" (1621), in Josephine A. Roberts, ed., *The Poems of Lady Mary Wroth* (1983)

9 I was in love with the whole world and all that lived in its rainy arms.

Louise Erdrich, *Love Medicine* (1984)

10 I always want to be in love, always. It's like being a tuning fork.

Edna O'Brien, "Diary of an Unfaithful Wife," in *Cosmopolitan* (1966)

11 Love is the same as like except you feel sexier.

Judith Viorst, *Love and Guilt and the Meaning of Life, Etc.* (1979)

12 Whoever has loved knows all that life contains of sorrow and of joy.

George Sand (c. 1830), in *French Wit and Wisdom* (1950)

13 To care passionately for another human creature brings always more sorrow than joy; but all the same . . . one would not be without that experience.

Agatha Christie, *Sad Cypress* (1939)

14 Love all the people you can. The sufferings from love are not to be compared to the sorrows of loneliness.

Susan Hale (1868), in Caroline P. Atkinson, ed., *Letters of Susan Hale* (1918)

15 I believe in the curative powers of love as the English believe in tea or Catholics believe in the Miracle of Lourdes.

Joyce Johnson, *Minor Characters* (1983)

16 Whoso loves / Believes the impossible.

Elizabeth Barrett Browning, *Aurora Leigh* (1857)

17 People talk about love as though it were something you could give, like an armful of flowers. And a lot of people give love like that—just dump it down on top of you, a useless strong-scented burden.

Anne Morrow Lindbergh, *Locked Rooms and Open Doors* (1974)

18 Love doesn't just sit there, like a stone, it has to be made, like bread; re-made all the time, made new.

Ursula K. Le Guin, *The Lathe of Heaven* (1971)

19 Love requires peace, love will dream; it cannot live upon the remnants of our time and our personality.

Ellen Key, in Marie Stopes, *Married Love* (1918)

20 Two persons love in one another the future good which they aid one another to unfold.

Margaret Fuller, *Woman in the Nineteenth Century* (1845)

21 Love lights more fires than hate extinguishes.

Ella Wheeler Wilcox, "Optimism," *Poems of Pleasure* (1888)

22 Love is a context, not a behavior.

Marilyn Ferguson, *The Aquarian Conspiracy* (1980)

23 Love is so very subtle an essence, such an indefinable metaphysical marvel, that its due force, though very cruelly felt by the sufferer himself, is never clearly understood by those who look on at its torments and wonder why he takes the common fever so badly.

Mary Elizabeth Braddon, *Lady Audley's Secret* (1862)

24 Love was a great disturbance.

Naomi Royde-Smith, *The Bridge* (1933)

25 Love—that arbitrary and inexorable tyrant.

Harriet E. Wilson, *Our Nig* (1859)

26 Love is a dangerous angel. . . . Especially nowadays.

Francesca Lia Block, *Weetzie Bat* (1989)

1 Love is not an emergency.

> Anonymous operator to a would-be caller during a telephone strike in France, in Simone de Beauvoir, *Force of Circumstance* (1963)

2 Love is like a card trick. After you know how it works, it's no fun any more.

> Fanny Brice, in Norman Katkov, *The Fabulous Fanny* (1952)

3 Love's a thin Diet, nor will keep out Cold.

> Aphra Behn, *The Lucky Chance* (1687)

4 Love is not enough. It must be the foundation, the cornerstone—but not the complete structure. It is much too pliable, too yielding.

> Bette Davis, *The Lonely Life* (1962)

5 Love is not all: it is not meat nor drink / Nor slumber nor a roof against the rain; / Nor yet a floating spar to men that sink.

> Edna St. Vincent Millay, "Love Is Not All," *Fatal Interview* (1931)

6 Love is not everything. . . . It is only when we are young that we think it is.

> Agatha Christie, *Death on the Nile* (1937)

7 I wonder why love is so often equated with joy when it is everything else as well. Devastation, balm, obsession, granting and receiving excessive value, and losing it again. It is recognition, often of what you are not but might be. It sears and it heals. It is beyond pity and above law. It can seem like truth.

> Florida Scott-Maxwell, *The Measure of My Days* (1968)

. 8 Love, from its very nature, must be transitory.

> Mary Wollstonecraft, *A Vindication of the Rights of Woman* (1833)

9 Love so seldom means happiness.

> Margery Allingham, *Death of a Ghost* (1934)

10 All policy's allowed in war and love.

> Susannah Centlivre, *Love at a Venture* (1706)

11 It is easier to win love than to keep it.

> Diane de Poitiers (1550), in Winifred Gordon, *A Book of Days* (1910)

12 When first we fall in love, we feel that we know all there is to know about life, and perhaps we are right.

> Mignon McLaughlin, *The Neurotic's Notebook* (1963)

13 Each one of us thinks our experience of love is different from everybody else's.

> Vibhavari Shirurkar (1935), in Susie Tharu and K. Lalita, eds., *Women Writing in India* (1991)

14 The hardest-learned lesson: that people have only their kind of love to give, not our kind.

> Mignon McLaughlin, *The Neurotic's Notebook* (1963)

15 True love isn't the kind that endures through long years of absence, but the kind that endures through long years of propinquity.

> Helen Rowland, *A Guide to Men* (1922)

16 "Love" is finding the familiar dear. / "In love" is to be taken by surprise.

> Mona Van Duyn, "Late Loving," *Near Changes* (1990)

17 I'm glad it cannot happen twice, the fever of first love.

> Daphne du Maurier, *Rebecca* (1938)

18 It was first love. There's no love like that. I don't wish it on a soul. I don't hate anyone enough.

> Carol Matthau, *Among the Porcupines* (1992)

19 First love is an astounding experience and if the object happens to be totally unworthy and the love not really love at all, it makes little difference to the intensity or the pain.

> Angela Thirkell, *Cheerfulness Breaks In* (1941)

20 It was the kind of desperate, headlong, adolescent calf love that he should have experienced years ago and got over.

> Agatha Christie, *Remembered Death* (1945)

21 Many of us are done with adolescence before we are done with adolescent love.

> Judith Viorst, *Necessary Losses* (1986)

22 Oh, what is young love! The urge of the race. A blaze that ends in babies or ashes.

> Gertrude Atherton, *Black Oxen* (1923)

23 Reason to the lovesick was fire to the feverish. It sent them clean out of their minds.

> Jessamyn West, *The Massacre at Fall Creek* (1975)

24 To see coming toward you the face that will mean an end of oneness is—far more than birth itself— the beginning of life.

> Holly Roth, *The Content Assignment* (1953)

1 I am my beloved's, and my beloved is mine.

The Shulamite, *Song of Songs* (c. 3rd cent. B.C.)

2 How do I love thee? Let me count the ways. / I love thee to the depth and breadth and height / My soul can reach.

Elizabeth Barrett Browning, *Sonnets From the Portuguese* (1850)

3 I love thee with a love I seemed to lose / With my lost saints,—I love thee with the breath, / Smiles, tears, of all my life!—and, if God choose, / I shall but love thee better after death.

Elizabeth Barrett Browning, *Sonnets From the Portuguese* (1850)

4 Though nought of me remains save smoke drawn out across the windless sky, yet shall I drift to thee unerringly amid the trackless fields of space.

Lady Murasaki, *The Tale of Genji* (c. 1008)

5 There is no question for which / you are not the answer.

Bonnie Zucker Goldsmith, "Credo," in *The Spoon River Poetry Review* (1993)

6 with each touch of you / i am fresh bread / warm and rising.

Pat Parker, "I Have," *Movement in Black* (1978)

7 Love is . . . the bite into bread again.

May Swenson, "Love Is," *To Mix With Time* (1963)

8 Clea was a woman who adored love. Hormones had always been her recreational drug of choice.

Lisa Alther, *Bedrock* (1990)

9 My love for you is more / Athletic than a verb.

Sylvia Plath, "Verbal Calisthenics" (1953), in Aurelia Schober Plath, ed., *Letters Home* (1973)

10 He said he would love me like a revolution, like a religion.

Sandra Cisneros, "One Holy Night," *Woman Hollering Creek* (1991)

11 It was a great holiness, a religion, as all great loves must be.

Elsie de Wolfe, *After All* (1935)

12 If I had never met him I would have dreamed him into being.

Anzia Yezierska, *Red Ribbon on a White Horse* (1950)

13 Love—bittersweet, irrepressible— / loosens my limbs and I tremble.

Sappho, "To Atthis" (6th cent. B.C.), in Willis Barnstone, *Sappho* (1965)

14 Pale hands I loved beside the Shalimar, / Where are you now? Who lies beneath your spell?

Laurence Hope, "Pale Hands I Loved," *Songs From the Garden of Kama* (1901)

15 More than anything in this transitory life mine eyes desire the sight of you.

Catherine of Aragon, deathbed letter to Henry VIII (1536), in Margaret Barnes, *Brief Gaudy Hour* (1949)

16 Whatever our souls are made of, his and mine are the same.

Emily Brontë, *Wuthering Heights* (1847)

17 No riches from his scanty store / My lover could impart; / He gave a boon I valued more— / He gave me all his heart!

Helen Maria Williams, "A Song," *Poems* (1786)

18 My love for Heathcliff resembles the eternal rocks beneath—a source of little visible delight, but necessary. Nelly, I *am* Heathcliff—he's always, always in my mind—not as a pleasure, any more than I am always a pleasure to myself—but as my own being.

Emily Brontë, *Wuthering Heights* (1847)

19 My love for you is the sole image / Of God a human is allowed.

Else Lasker-Schüler, "To My Child" (1920), *Hebrew Ballads* (1980)

20 To say that Ansiau . . . was in love would not be accurate—he was an idolater who had found his idol.

Zoë Oldenbourg, *The World Is Not Enough* (1948)

21 I love you more than my own skin.

Frida Kahlo, letter to Diego Rivera (1935), in Hayden Herrera, *Frida* (1983)

22 We never leave each other. / When does your mouth / say goodbye to your heart?

Mary TallMountain, "There Is No Word for Goodbye," in Joseph Bruchac, ed., *Songs From This Earth on Turtle's Back* (1983)

23 In short I will part with anything for you but you.

Lady Mary Wortley Montagu, to her future husband (1712), in Octave Thanet, ed., *The Best Letters of Lady Mary Wortley Montagu* (1901)

1 My love for you's so strong / That no one could kill it—not even you.

> Anna Akhmatova, "You Are So Heavy Now," *The Plantain* (1921)

2 It was a love like a chord from Bach, / of such pure gravity.

> Nina Cassian, "It was a love" (1963), *Call Yourself Alive?* (1988)

3 The world has little to bestow / Where two fond hearts in equal love are joined.

> Anna Laetitia Barbauld, "Delia" (1773), *The Works of Anna Laetitia Barbauld*, vol. 1 (1825)

4 I have drunk of the wine of life at last, I have known the thing best worth knowing, I have been warmed through and through, never to grow quite cold again till the end.

> Edith Wharton (1908), in Gloria C. Erlich, *The Sexual Education of Edith Wharton* (1992)

5 Love me in full being.

> Elizabeth Barrett Browning, "A Man's Requirements," in *Blackwood's Magazine* (1846)

6 There is a stage with people we love when we are no longer separate from them, but so close in sympathy that we live through them as directly as through ourselves. . . . We push back our hair because theirs is in their eyes.

> Nan Fairbrother, *An English Year* (1954)

7 There is a love that begins in the head, and goes down to the heart, and grows slowly; but it lasts till death, and asks less than it gives. There is another love, that blots out wisdom, that is sweet with the sweetness of life and bitter with the bitterness of death, lasting for an hour; but it is worth having lived a whole life for that hour.

> Ralph Iron, *The Story of an African Farm* (1883)

8 Him that I love, I wish to be / Free— / Even from me.

> Anne Morrow Lindbergh, "Even," *The Unicorn* (1956)

9 When the right man smiled it would be / music skittering up her calf / like a chuckle.

> Rita Dove, "Summit Beach, 1921," *Grace Notes* (1989)

10 She's got most of the symptoms—is twittery and cross, doesn't eat, lies awake, and mopes in corners.

> Louisa May Alcott, *Little Women* (1868)

11 The first minute I sot my grey eye onto Josiah Allen I knew my fate. My heart was a pray to feelin's it had heretofore been a stranger to. . . . And that love has been like a Becon in our pathway ever sense. Its pure light, though it has sputtered some, and in tryin' times such as washin' days and cleanin' house times has burnt down pretty low,—has never gone out.

> Josiah Allen's Wife, *My Opinions and Betsey Bobbet's* (1872)

12 Romantic love has always seemed to me unaccountable, unassailable, unforgettable, and nearly always unattainable.

> Margaret Anderson, *The Fiery Fountains* (1953)

13 In real love you want the other person's good. In romantic love you want the other person.

> Margaret Anderson, *The Fiery Fountains* (1953)

14 I used to think romantic love was a neurosis shared by two, a supreme foolishness. I no longer thought that. There's nothing foolish in loving anyone. Thinking you'll be loved in return is what's foolish.

> Rita Mae Brown, *Bingo* (1988)

15 Let us now bask under the spreading trees said Bernard in a passionate tone. Oh yes lets said Ethel and she opened her dainty parasole and sank down upon the long grass. She closed her eyes but she was far from asleep.

> Daisy Ashford (aged 9), *The Young Visiters* (1919)

16 Bernard placed one arm tightly round her. When will you marry me Ethel he uttered you must be my wife it has come to that I love you so intensly that if you say no I shall perforce dash my body to the brink of yon muddy river he panted wildly. O don't do that implored Ethel breathing rather hard.

> Daisy Ashford (aged 9), *The Young Visiters* (1919)

17 Taking the bull by both horns he kissed her violently on her dainty face. My bride to be he murmered several times.

> Daisy Ashford (aged 9), *The Young Visiters* (1919)

18 He would have fallen in love with me, I think, if I had been built like Brünhilde and had a mustache and the mind of an Easter chick.

> Anne Rivers Siddons, *Hill Towns* (1993)

19 By the time you swear you're his, / Shivering and sighing, / And he vows his passion is / Infinite, undying— / Lady, make a note of this: / One of you is lying.

> Dorothy Parker, "Unfortunate Coincidence," *Enough Rope* (1926)

1 A man falls in love through his eyes, a woman through her imagination, and then they both speak of it as an affair of "the heart."

　　Helen Rowland, *A Guide to Men* (1922)

2 Before we love with our heart, we already love with our imagination.

　　Louise Colet, in Marilyn Gaddis Rose, tr., *Lui, A View of Him* (1859)

3 Gertrude loved with all the delusion of romance, and, like many a young enthusiast, had mistaken her imagination for her mind.

　　Susan Ferrier, *The Inheritance*, vol. 2 (1824)

4 I loved my images far more than you.

　　Jean Garrigue, "Broken-Nosed Gods," *The Ego and the Centaur* (1947)

5 I know I am but summer to your heart, / And not the full four seasons of the year.

　　Edna St. Vincent Millay, "I Know I Am But Summer," *The Harp-Weaver* (1923)

6 To love somebody / Who doesn't love you / Is like going to a temple / And worshiping the behind / Of a wooden statue / Of a hungry devil.

　　Lady Kasa (8th cent.), in Joanna Bankier and Deirdre Lashgari, eds., *Women Poets of the World* (1983)

7 How do you know that love is gone? If you said you would be there at seven, you get there by nine and he or she has not called the police yet—it's gone.

　　Marlene Dietrich, *Marlene Dietrich's ABC* (1962)

8 My life will be sour grapes and ashes without you.

　　Daisy Ashford (aged 9), *The Young Visiters* (1919)

9 When love is out of your life, you're through in a way. Because while it is there it's like a motor that's going, you have such vitality to do things, big things, because love is goosing you all the time.

　　Fanny Brice, in Norman Katkov, *The Fabulous Fanny* (1952)

10 I never liked the men I loved, and never loved the men I liked.

　　Fanny Brice, in Norman Katkov, *The Fabulous Fanny* (1952)

11 There was no passion in her feeling for him, and no relief from its daily pressure. It was like being loved by a large moist sponge.

　　Phyllis Bottome, "The Other Island," *Strange Fruit* (1928)

12 A man when he is making up to anybody can be cordial and gallant and full of little attentions and altogether charming. But when a man is really in love he can't help looking like a sheep.

　　Agatha Christie, *The Mystery of the Blue Train* (1928)

13 Indeed, the sole criticism of him was that he prolonged beyond the point of decency, his look of nuptial rapture and the vagueness which rendered him, in conversation, slightly stupid.

　　Jean Stafford, *Boston Adventure* (1944)

14 A woman has got to love a bad man once or twice in her life, to be thankful for a good one.

　　Marjorie Kinnan Rawlings, *The Yearling* (1938)

15 Love never dies quite suddenly. He complains a great deal before expiring.

　　Minna Thomas Antrim, *Sweethearts and Beaux* (1905)

16 After all, my erstwhile dear, / My no longer cherished, / Need we say it was not love, / Just because it perished?

　　Edna St. Vincent Millay, "Passer Mortuus Est," *Second April* (1921)

17 Love will not always linger longest / With those who hold it in too clenched a fist.

　　Alice Duer Miller, *Forsaking All Others* (1931)

18 Take me or leave me; or, as is the usual order of things, both.

　　Dorothy Parker, "A Good Novel, and a Great Story," in *The New Yorker* (1928)

19 All discarded lovers should be given a second chance, but with somebody else.

　　Mae West, in Joseph Weintraub, ed., *The Wit and Wisdom of Mae West* (1967)

20 Every love's the love before / In a duller dress.

　　Dorothy Parker, "Summary," *Death and Taxes* (1931)

21 Love is banality to all outsiders.

　　Mae West, *Goodness Had Nothing to Do With It!* (1959)

22 She did observe, with some dismay, that, far from conquering all, love lazily sidestepped practical problems.

　　Jean Stafford, "The Liberation," *The Collected Stories of Jean Stafford* (1969)

23 Whoever said love conquers all was a fool. Because almost everything conquers love—or tries to.

　　Edna Ferber, *Giant* (1952)

1 I am not sure at all / if love is salve / or just / a deeper kind of wound. / I do not think it matters.

    Erica Jong, "The Evidence," *Half-Lives* (1971)

2 The pain of love is the pain of being alive. It's a perpetual wound.

    Maureen Duffy, *Wounds* (1969)

3 Mortal love is but the licking of honey from thorns.

    Anonymous woman at the court of Eleanor of Aquitaine (1198), in Helen Lawrenson, *Whistling Girl* (1978)

4 You see I thought love got easier over the years so it didn't hurt so bad when it hurt, or feel so good when it felt good. I thought it smoothed out and old people hardly noticed it. I thought it curled up and died, I guess. Now I saw it rear up like a whip and lash.

    Louise Erdrich, *Love Medicine* (1984)

5 The truth is simple: / you do not die / from love. / You only wish / you did.

    Erica Jong, "There Is Only One Story," *Ordinary Miracles* (1983)

6 Love has seven names, / Which, as you know, are appropriate to her; / Chain, light, live coal, and fire— / . . . dew, living spring, and hell.

    Hadewijch, "Love's Seven Names," in Mother Columba Hart, O.S.B., *Hadewijch* (1980)

7 Great loves were almost always great tragedies. Perhaps it was because love was never truly great until the element of sacrifice entered into it.

    Mary Roberts Rinehart, *Dangerous Days* (1919)

8 Great loves too must be endured.

    Coco Chanel, in Marcel Haedrich, *Coco Chanel* (1972)

9 Intense love is often akin to intense suffering.

    Frances Ellen Watkins Harper, "The Two Offers," in *Anglo-African Magazine* (1859)

10 I have found the paradox that if I love until it hurts, then there is no hurt, but only more love.

    Daphne Rae, *Love Until It Hurts* (1980)

11 The fate of love is, that it always sees too little or too much.

    Amelia E. Barr, *The Belle of Bowling Green* (1904)

12 Love is purely a creation of the human imagination . . . perhaps the most important of all the examples of how the imagination continually outruns the creature it inhabits.

    Katherine Anne Porter, "Orpheus in Purgatory," *The Days Before* (1952)

13 Because it corresponds to a vital need, love is overvalued in our culture. It becomes a phantom—like success—carrying with it the illusion that it is a solution for all problems.

    Karen Horney, *The Neurotic Personality of Our Time* (1937)

14 O Love, how thou art tired out with rhyme! / Thou art a tree whereon all poets clime.

    Margaret Cavendish, Duchess of Newcastle, "Love and Poetry," *Poems and Fancies* (1653)

15 Shall I tell you what makes love so dangerous? 'Tis the too high idea we are apt to form of it.

    Ninon de Lenclos (c. 1695), in M. Lincoln Schuster, *The World's Great Letters* (1940)

16 The more you love someone the more he wants from you and the less you have to give since you've already given him your love.

    Nikki Giovanni, *Gemini* (1971)

17 Love says, mine. Love says, I could eat you up. Love says, stay as you are, be my own private thing, don't you dare have ideas I don't share. Love has just got to gobble the other, bones and all, crunch. I don't want to do that. I sure don't want it done to me!

    Marge Piercy, *Braided Lives* (1982)

18 I dream that love without tyranny is possible.

    Andrea Dworkin, "First Love," in Julia Wolf Mazow, ed., *The Woman Who Lost Her Names* (1980)

19 Perhaps that is what love is—the momentary or prolonged refusal to think of another person in terms of power.

    Phyllis Rose, *Parallel Lives* (1983)

20 I'd always rather be with people who loved me too little rather than with people who loved me too much.

    Katherine Mansfield (1919), *Journal of Katherine Mansfield* (1927)

21 Being always overavid, I demand from those I love a love equal to mine, which, being balanced people, they cannot supply.

    Sylvia Ashton-Warner (1942), *Myself* (1967)

1 I love you so passionately, that I hide a great part of my love, not to oppress you with it.

> Marie de Rabutin-Chantal, Marquise de Sévigné (1671), *Letters of Madame de Sévigné to Her Daughter and Her Friends*, vol. 1 (1811)

2 Love never dies of starvation, but often of indigestion.

> Ninon de Lenclos (c. 1660), *Lettres de Ninon de Lenclos* (1870)

3 I will never love, for I should never be loved as I desire to be loved.

> Marie Bashkirtseff (1874), in Mary J. Serrano, tr., *The Journal of a Young Artist* (1919)

4 It is better not to be loved than to be ill-loved or half-loved.

> Louise Colet, in Marilyn Gaddis Rose, tr., *Lui, A View of Him* (1859)

5 Never, never have I been loved as I love others!

> Madame de Staël (1786), in Lydia Maria Child, *Memoirs of Madame de Staël and of Madame Roland* (1847)

6 No one has ever loved anyone the way everyone wants to be loved.

> Mignon McLaughlin, *The Neurotic's Notebook* (1963)

7 I like not only to be loved, but also to be told that I am loved. I am not sure that you are of the same mind. But the realm of silence is large enough beyond the grave. This is the world of light and speech, and I shall take leave to tell you that you are very dear.

> George Eliot (1875), in J.W. Cross, ed., *George Eliot's Life As Related in Her Letters and Journals* (1885)

8 If I'm not loved when I love, the lack can't be repaired by any action of mine or repented by the person who doesn't love me.

> Alice Koller, *An Unknown Woman* (1982)

9 You need somebody to love you while you're looking for someone to love.

> Shelagh Delaney, *A Taste of Honey* (1958)

10 Most of us love from our need to love not / because we find someone deserving.

> Nikki Giovanni, "The Women Gather," *The Women and the Men* (1975)

11 'Tis said, woman loves not her lover / So much as she loves his love of her; / Then loves she her lover / For love of her lover, / Or love of her love of her lover?

> Carolyn Wells, "Love," *Folly for the Wise* (1904)

12 To love deeply in one direction makes us more loving in all others.

> Anne-Sophie Swetchine, in Count de Falloux, ed., *The Writings of Madame Swetchine* (1869)

13 In the capacities of loving, as in all other capacities, there be diversities of gifts.

> C.M. Sedgwick, *The Linwoods* (1835)

14 I bless / all knowledge of love, all ways of publishing it.

> Mona Van Duyn, "Open Letter From a Constant Reader," *To See, To Take* (1970)

15 They who live without Love are dead. / But the worst of all deaths is this— / That the loving soul be cowardly toward Love; / For perfect Love is never cowardly.

> Hadewijch, "The Need of All Needs" (13th cent.), in Mother Columba Hart, O.S.B., *Hadewijch* (1980)

16 Love needs to be proved by action.

> St. Thérèse of Lisieux (1897), in Ronald Knox, tr., *Story of a Soul* (1958)

17 Love demands expression. It will not stay still, stay silent, be good, be modest, be seen and not heard, no. It will break out in tongues of praise, the high note that smashes the glass and spills the liquid.

> Jeanette Winterson, *Written on the Body* (1992)

18 Love is that which exists to *do* good, not merely to *get* good.

> Victoria Woodhull, in *Woodhull and Claflin's Weekly* (1873)

19 Love has nothing to do with what you are expecting to get—only with what you are expecting to give—which is everything.

> Katharine Hepburn, *Me* (1991)

20 The important thing is not to think much but to love much; do, then, whatever most arouses you to love.

> St. Teresa of Avila (1577), in E. Allison Peers, tr., *Interior Castle* (1961)

21 I do not think reading the mystics would hurt you myself. You say you must avoid books which deal with "feelings"—but the mystics don't deal with *feelings* but with *love* which is a very different thing.

You have too many "feelings," but not nearly enough love.

> Evelyn Underhill (1909), in Charles Williams, ed., *The Letters of Evelyn Underhill* (1943)

1 Love is the image of ourself until ourself destroys us.

> Jean Garrigue, "The Snowfall," in Howard Moss, ed., *The Poet's Story* (1973)

2 He that shuns love doth love him self the less.

> Lady Mary Wroth, "Pamphilia to Amphilanthus" (1621), in Josephine A. Roberts, ed., *The Poems of Lady Mary Wroth* (1983)

3 Grumbling is the death of love.

> Marlene Dietrich, *Marlene Dietrich's ABC* (1962)

4 I love you no matter what you do, but do you have to do so much of it?

> Jean Illsley Clarke, *Self-Esteem* (1978)

5 Love, love love—all the wretched cant of it, masking egotism, lust, masochism, fantasy under a mythology of sentimental postures, a welter of self-induced miseries and joys, blinding and masking the essential personalities in the frozen gestures of courtship, in the kissing and the dating and the desire, the compliments and the quarrels which vivify its barrenness.

> Germaine Greer, *The Female Eunuch* (1970)

6 Love, for both of them, had ceased to be a journey, an adventure, an essay of hope. It had become an infection, a ritual, a drama with a bloody last act, and they could both foresee the final carnage.

> Margaret Drabble, *The Middle Ground* (1980)

7 Love was a terrible thing. You poisoned it and stabbed at it and knocked it down into the mud—well down—and it got up and staggered on, bleeding and muddy and awful. Like—like Rasputin.

> Jean Rhys, *Quartet* (1928)

8 Love cannot survive if you just give it scraps of yourself, scraps of your time, scraps of your thoughts.

> Mary O'Hara, *Green Grass of Wyoming* (1946)

9 When success comes in the door, it seems, love often goes out the window.

> Joyce Brothers, *The Brothers System for Liberated Love and Marriage* (1972)

10 There is no mortal art / Can overcome Time's deep, corroding rust. / Let Love's beginning expiate Love's end.

> Helene Johnson, "Remember Not," in Langston Hughes and Arna Bontemps, eds., *The Poetry of the Negro 1746-1949* (1949)

11 Love has a hem to her garment that reaches the very dust. It sweeps the stains from the streets and lanes, and because it can, it must.

> Mother Teresa, in Georges Gorrée and Jean Barbier, *The Love of Christ* (1982)

12 Love is a choice—not simply, or necessarily, a rational choice, but rather a willingness to be present to others without pretense or guile.

> Carter Heyward, *Our Passion for Justice* (1984)

13 Every love has a poetic relevance of its own; each love brings to light only what to it is relevant. Outside lies the junk-yard of what does not matter.

> Elizabeth Bowen, *The Heat of the Day* (1949)

14 Love has the quality of informing almost everything—even one's work.

> Sylvia Ashton-Warner, *Myself* (1967)

15 If it is your time love will track you like a cruise missile. If you say "No! I don't want it right now," that's when you'll get it for sure. Love will make a way out of no way. Love is an exploding cigar which we willingly smoke.

> Lynda Barry, *Big Ideas* (1983)

16 There is nothing better for the spirit or body than a love affair. It elevates thoughts and flattens stomachs.

> Barbara Howar, *Laughing All the Way* (1973)

17 Free love is too expensive.

> Bernadette Devlin, *The Price of My Soul* (1969)

18 The end / of passion / may refashion / a friend.

> Mona Van Duyn, "The Beginning," *Firefall* (1993)

19 I have always sworn to my lovers to love them eternally, but for me eternity is a quarter of an hour.

> Ninon de Lenclos (1658), in Edgar H. Cohen, *Mademoiselle Libertine* (1970)

20 Love is a boaster at heart, who cannot hide the stolen horse without giving a glimpse of the bridle.

> Mary Renault, *The Last of the Wine* (1956)

1 Absurdity is the one thing love can't stand; it can overlook anything else,—coldness, or weakness, or viciousness,—but just be ridiculous and that's the end of it!

Margaret Deland, *Philip and His Wife* (1894)

2 How absurd and delicious it is to be in love with somebody younger than yourself! Everybody should try it.

Barbara Pym (1938), in Hazel Holt, *A Lot to Ask* (1990)

3 Nothing moves a woman so deeply as the boyhood of the man she loves.

Annie Dillard, *The Living* (1992)

4 It requires infinitely a greater genius to make love, than to make war.

Ninon de Lenclos, in Mrs. Griffith, tr., *The Memoirs of Ninon de L'Enclos*, vol. 1 (1778)

5 The memories of long love gather like drifting snow, poignant as the mandarin ducks who float side by side in sleep.

Lady Murasaki, *The Tale of Genji* (c. 1008)

6 When love comes it comes without effort, like perfect weather.

Helen Yglesias, *Family Feeling* (1976)

7 And what do all the great words come to in the end, but that?—I love you—I am at rest with you—I have come home.

Dorothy L. Sayers, *Busman's Honeymoon* (1937)

8 It is about time that soft meaningless word: Love; was taken out of the dictionary. So that instead of saying: I will love you for ever; it would be a much more convincing proof to say: I will endure you for ever.

Caitlin Thomas, *Not Quite Posthumous Letter to My Daughter* (1963)

9 Why is it that the most unoriginal thing we can say to one another is still the thing we long to hear? "I love you" is always a quotation.

Jeanette Winterson, *Written on the Body* (1992)

10 Love built on dreams / of the forgotten first unsatisfied embrace, / is satisfied.

H.D., "Winter Love" (1959), *Hermetic Definition* (1972)

11 The verb "to love" in Persian is "to have a friend." "I love you" translated literally is "I have you as a friend," and "I don't like you" simply means "I don't have you as a friend."

Shusha Guppy, *The Blindfold Horse* (1988)

12 Habit, of which passion must be wary, may all the same be the sweetest part of love.

Elizabeth Bowen, *The Heat of the Day* (1949)

13 Love is like the measles. The older you get it, the worse the attack.

Mary Roberts Rinehart, *The Man in Lower Ten* (1909)

14 We don't believe in rheumatism or true love until we have been attacked by them.

Marie von Ebner-Eschenbach, *Aphorisms* (1893)

15 Everyone wants Love to follow them / down their road; / where is it that Love wants to go?

Judy Grahn, *The Queen of Swords* (1987)

16 Art is the accomplice of love.

Jane Stanton Hitchcock, *Trick of the Eye* (1992)

17 We love what we should scorn if we were wiser.

Marie de France (12th cent.), in Jeanette Beer, tr., *Medieval Fables of Marie de France* (1981)

18 Maybe love can kill better than hate.

Maia Wojciechowska, *A Single Light* (1968)

19 Liszt said to me to-day that God alone deserves to be loved. It may be true, but when one has loved a man it is very difficult to love God. It is so different.

George Sand (1834), in Marie Jenny Howe, ed., *The Intimate Journal of George Sand* (1929)

20 Love clamors far more incessantly and passionately at a closed gate than an open one!

Marie Corelli, *The Master Christian* (1900)

21 In love, gallantry is necessary. Even when the first wild desire is gone, especially then, there is an inherent need for good manners and consideration, for the putting forth of effort. Two courteous and civilized human beings out of the loneliness of their souls owe that to each other.

Ilka Chase, *In Bed We Cry* (1943)

22 The next greatest pleasure to love is to talk of love.

Louise Labé (c. 1550), in Jehanne d'Orliac, *The Moon Mistress* (1930)

1 The final word is love.
   Dorothy Day, *The Long Loneliness* (1952)

See also Affection, Broken Heart, Courtship, Dating, Desire, Devotion, Heart, Infatuation, Intimacy, Love and Hate, Love and Sex, Lovers, Marriage, Passion, Peace and Love, Relationships, Romance, Sex, Tenderness, Weddings.

## ❧ LOVE AND HATE

2 Hate generalizes, love specifies.
   Robin Morgan, *The Anatomy of Freedom* (1982)

3 If we say I love you, it may be received with doubt, for there are times when it is hard to believe. Say I hate you, and the one spoken to believes it instantly, once for all. . . . Love must be learned, and learned again and again; there is no end to it. Hate needs no instruction, but waits only to be provoked.
   Katherine Anne Porter, "The Necessary Enemy" (1948), *The Days Before* (1952)

4 Love commingled with hate is more powerful than love. Or hate.
   Joyce Carol Oates, *On Boxing* (1987)

5 Love is a great glue, but there is no cement like mutual hate.
   Lois Wyse, *The Rosemary Touch* (1974)

6 Hate is funny. Love isn't. Love can kill you. Hate can keep you alive.
   Carol Matthau, *Among the Porcupines* (1992)

7 Hate doesn't last. Love does.
   Agatha Christie, *The Moving Finger* (1942)

See also Ambiguity, Ambivalence, Hate, Love.

## ❧ LOVE AND SEX

8 Love lay like a mirage through the golden gates of sex.
   Doris Lessing, *Children of Violence: A Proper Marriage* (1954)

9 The only door into her bedroom led through the church.
   Frances Parkinson Keyes, *Dinner at Antoine's* (1948)

10 The human need for love and sex is made to bear the burden of all our bodily starvation for contact and sensation, all our creative starvation, all our need for social contact, and even our need to find meaning in our lives.
   Deirdre English and Barbara Ehrenreich, in Evelyn Shapiro and Barry M. Shapiro, *The Women Say/The Men Say* (1979)

11 Nobody dies from lack of sex. It's lack of love we die from.
   Margaret Atwood, *The Handmaid's Tale* (1985)

12 You mustn't force sex to do the work of love or love to do the work of sex.
   Mary McCarthy, *The Group* (1954)

See also Love, Sex.

## ❧ LOVERS

13 Lovers re-create the world.
   Carter Heyward, *Our Passion for Justice* (1984)

14 It is not so much true that all the world loves a lover as that a lover loves all the world.
   Ruth Rendell, *A Judgment in Stone* (1977)

15 It is the illusion of all lovers to think themselves unique and their words immortal.
   Han Suyin, *A Many-Splendored Thing* (1952)

16 The absolute yearning of one human body for another particular one and its indifference to substitutes is one of life's major mysteries.
   Iris Murdoch, *The Black Prince* (1973)

17 Each will have two lives, a doubled state; / Each in himself will live, and in his mate.
   Louise Labé, "Sonnet XVIII" (c. 1545), in Joanna Bankier and Deirdre Lashgari, eds., *Women Poets of the World* (1983)

18 In a great romance, each person basically plays a part that the other really likes.
   Elizabeth Ashley, in *The San Francisco Chronicle* (1982)

19 Secretly, we wish anyone we love will think exactly the way we do.
   Kim Chernin, *In My Mother's House* (1983)

1 It is the way of lovers to think that none can bless or succor their love but their own selves. And there is a touch of truth in it, maybe more than a touch.

Mary Webb, *Precious Bane* (1924)

2 To be together is for us to be at once as free as in solitude, as gay as in company. We talk, I believe, all day long: to talk to each other is but a more animated and an audible thinking.

Charlotte Brontë, *Jane Eyre* (1847)

3 Sometimes idiosyncrasies which used to be irritating become endearing, part of the complexity of a partner who has become woven deep into our own selves.

Madeleine L'Engle, *Two-Part Invention* (1988)

4 Anyone can be passionate, but it takes real lovers to be silly.

Rose Franken, *Another Claudia* (1943)

5 No partner in a love relationship (whether homo- or heterosexual) should feel that he has to give up an essential part of himself to make it viable.

May Sarton, *Journal of a Solitude* (1973)

6 There is probably nothing like living together for blinding people to each other.

Ivy Compton-Burnett, *Mother and Son* (1955)

7 It is better to know as little as possible of the defects of the person with whom you are to pass your life.

Jane Austen, *Pride and Prejudice* (1813)

8 This was life, that two people, no matter how carefully chosen, could not be everything to each other.

Doris Lessing, "To Room Nineteen," *A Man and Two Women* (1963)

See also Friendship, Love, Marriage, Relationships.

## ❧ LOYALTY

9 I am come amongst you, as you see, at this time, not for my recreation and disport, but being resolved, in the midst and heat of the battle, to live or die amongst you all; to lay down for my God, and for my kingdom, and my people, my honor and my blood, even in the dust.

Elizabeth I, speech to the troops at Tilbury (1588)

10 Oh, Charlie is my darling, / My darling, my darling; / Oh, Charlie is my darling, / The young Chevalier.

Baroness Nairne, on Bonnie Prince Charlie, "Charlie Is My Darling," in Rev. Charles Rogers, ed., *Life and Songs of the Baroness Nairne* (1896)

11 Loyalty is a verbal switch-blade used by little and big bosses to force us quickly to accept a questionable situation which our intelligence and conscience should reject.

Lillian Smith, *The Journey* (1954)

12 Loyal? As loyal as anyone who plays second fiddle ever is.

Willa Cather, *Lucy Gayheart* (1935)

See also Devotion, Faithfulness.

## ❧ LUCK

13 Luck is not chance — / It's Toil — / Fortune's expensive smile / Is earned.

Emily Dickinson (1875), in Mabel Loomis Todd and Millicent Todd Bingham, eds., *Bolts of Melody* (1945)

14 How can you say luck and chance are the same thing? Chance is the first step you take, luck is what comes afterwards.

Amy Tan, *The Kitchen God's Wife* (1991)

15 There's good chances and bad chances, and nobody's luck is pulled only by one string.

George Eliot, *Felix Holt, the Radical* (1866)

16 That's the way the system works. Sometimes you get the bear, sometimes the bear gets you.

Sue Grafton, *"H" Is for Homicide* (1991)

17 If Paul . . . had tar on the seat of his breeches, and sat down in a bushel of doubloons, not one of 'em would stick to him!

Margaret Deland, "The Third Volume," *Around Old Chester* (1915)

18 Occasionally the impossible happens; this is a truism that accounts for much of what we call good luck; and also, bad.

Faith Baldwin, *Thursday's Child* (1976)

19 Luck enters into every contingency. You are a fool if you forget it—and a greater fool if you count upon it.

Phyllis Bottome, *Against Whom?* (1954)

1 People always call it luck when you've acted more sensibly than they have.

Anne Tyler, *Celestial Navigation* (1974)

2 I've always thought you've got to believe in luck to get it.

Victoria Holt, *The Pride of the Peacock* (1976)

3 It is so difficult not to become vain about one's own good luck.

Simone de Beauvoir, *Force of Circumstance* (1963)

4 Fortune is proverbially called changeful, yet her caprice often takes the form of repeating again and again a similar stroke of luck in the same quarter.

Charlotte Brontë, *Shirley* (1849)

5 I shall die young though many my years are— / For I was born under a kind star.

Katharine Tynan Hinkson, *Collected Poems* (1930)

6 You is born lucky, and it's better to be born lucky than born rich, cause if you is lucky you can git rich, but if you is born rich and you ain't lucky you is liables to lose all you got.

Margaret Walker, *Jubilee* (1966)

See also Coincidence, Destiny, Fate.

### ✦ LUXURY

7 Luxury / Is the fat worm, to be destroyed in the bud / If we would see the fruit perfect and sound.

Harriet Monroe, title poem, *The Difference* (1925)

8 Luxury that baneful poison has unstrung and enfeebled her [America's] sons . . . the Benevolent wish of general good is swallowed up by a Narrow selfish Spirit, by a spirit of oppression and extortion.

Abigail Adams, to her husband, John Adams (1779), in L.H. Butterfield et al., eds., *The Book of Abigail and John* (1975)

9 Luxuries unfit us for returning to hardships easily endured before.

Mary Mapes Dodge, *Hans Brinker* (1865)

10 In a socialist country you can get rich by providing necessities, while in a capitalist country you can get rich by providing luxuries.

Nora Ephron, *Heartburn* (1983)

11 A private railroad car is not an acquired taste. One takes to it immediately.

Eleanor Robson Belmont, *The Fabric of Memory* (1957)

See also Excess, Extravagance, Rich, Wealth.

### ✦ LYING

12 Lying is an occupation, / Used by all who mean to rise; / Politicians owe their station / But to well concerted lies.

Letitia Pilkington, "A Song," *Memoirs of Mrs. Letitia Pilkington Written by Herself* (1754)

13 The last sin, the sin against the Holy Ghost—to lie to oneself. Lying to other people—that's a small thing in comparison.

Rose Macaulay, *Crewe Train* (1926)

14 Cowards are not invariably liars, but liars are invariably cowards.

Minna Thomas Antrim, *Knocks* (1905)

15 Lying is done with words, and also with silence.

Adrienne Rich, "Women and Honor: Some Notes on Lying," *On Lies, Secrets, and Silence* (1979)

16 Once admit the idea that it is good to lie for religion's sake, and the lie may grow to any dimensions. A little lie may serve a man, but it is hard to calculate how big an one may be wanted to serve God.

Frances B. Cobbe, *Italics* (1864)

17 The liar leads an existence of unutterable loneliness.

Adrienne Rich, "Women and Honor: Some Notes on Lying," *On Lies, Secrets, and Silence* (1979)

18 Truth is no man's slave—but lies—what magnificent servants they make.

Phyllis Bottome, *The Life Line* (1946)

19 You can lock up from a thief, but you can't from a liar.

Flora Thompson, *Lark Rise* (1939)

20 Never to lie is to have no lock to your door.

Elizabeth Bowen, *The House in Paris* (1935)

21 I believe in the dull lie—make your story boring enough and no one will question it.

Sara Paretsky, *Blood Shot* (1988)

1 Maybe half a lie is worse than a real lie.
   Lillian Hellman, *Another Part of the Forest* (1947)

2 Particular lies may speak a general truth.
   George Eliot, *The Spanish Gypsy* (1868)

3 She lied with fluency, ease and artistic fervor.
   Agatha Christie, *They Came to Baghdad* (1951)

4 Elvira always lied first to herself before she lied to anybody else, since this gave her a conviction of moral honesty.
   Phyllis Bottome, *Under the Skin* (1950)

5 A liar did ought to have a good memory.
   Flora Thompson, *Lark Rise* (1939)

6 I am in perfect health, and hear it said I look better than ever I did in my life, which is one of those lies one is always glad to hear.
   Lady Mary Wortley Montagu (1747), in Octave Thanet, ed., *The Best Letters of Lady Mary Wortley Montagu* (1901)

See also Deception, Dishonesty, Flattery.

# M

## ❦ MACHINES

1 Machines seem to sense that I am afraid of them. It makes them hostile.

    Sharyn McCrumb, *The Windsor Knot* (1990)

2 Nothing is less reliable than [a machine]. . . . It is difficult not to wonder whether that combination of elements which produces a machine for labor does not create also a soul of sorts, a dull resentful metallic will, which can rebel at times.

    Pearl S. Buck, *My Several Worlds* (1954)

See also Inanimate Objects, Technology.

## ❦ MACHO

3 In the old days all the boys were men, and all the men were tough as saddle leather.

    Dorothy M. Johnson, "Prairie Kid," *Indian Country* (1953)

4 Macho: The genetic defect that makes men want to teach toddlers to box.

    Joyce Armor, *The Dictionary According to Mommy* (1990)

5 The tragedy of machismo is that a man is never quite man enough.

    Germaine Greer, "My Mailer Problem" (1971), in Bob Chieger, *Was It Good for You, Too?* (1983)

6 Macho does not prove mucho.

    Zsa Zsa Gabor, in Judy Allen, *Picking on Men* (1985)

See also Men.

## ❦ MADNESS

7 Madness . . . seems most easily explained to me as poetry in action. A life of symbol rather than reality. On paper one can understand Gulliver, or Kafka, or Dante. But let a man go about *behaving* as if he were a giant or a midget, or caught in a cosmic plot directed at himself, or in heaven or hell, and we feel horror—we want to disavow him to proclaim him as far removed as possible from ourselves.

    Helen Eustis, *The Horizontal Man* (1962)

8 Did the hospital specialize in poets and singers, or was it that poets and singers specialized in madness? . . . What is it about meter and cadence and rhythm that makes their makers mad?

    Susanna Kaysen, *Girl, Interrupted* (1993)

9 Madness might sometimes give access to a kind of knowledge. But was not a guarantee.

    Shirley Hazzard, *The Transit of Venus* (1980)

10 A touch of madness is, I think, almost always necessary for constructing a destiny.

    Marguerite Yourcenar, *With Open Eyes* (1980)

11 Mystical state, madness, how it frightens people. How utterly crazy *they* become, remote, rude; peculiar, cruel, taunting, farouche as wild beasts who have smelled danger, the unthinkable.

    Kate Millett, *The Loony-Bin Trip* (1990)

12 Madness is always fascinating, for it reveals the ungluing we all secretly fear: the mind taking off from the body, the possibility that the magnet that attaches us to a context in the world can lose its grip.

    Molly Haskell, *Love and Other Infectious Diseases* (1990)

1 Madness to us means reversion; to such people as Una and Lena it meant progression. Now their uncle had entered into a land beyond them, the land of fancy. For fifty years he had been as they were, silent, hard-working, unimaginative. Then all of a sudden, like a scholar passing his degree, he had gone up into another form.

Djuna Barnes, "The Earth" (1916), *Smoke* (1982)

2 If only no one had told them I was mad. Then I wouldn't be.

Kate Millett, *The Loony-Bin Trip* (1990)

See also Depression, Insanity, Mental Illness, Psychiatry, Psychology.

## ❧ MAGAZINES

3 Popular magazines multiply while the library shelves remain undisturbed.

Elisabeth Marbury, *My Crystal Ball* (1923)

4 The more lurid type of popular magazine with its pages that shine like shoulders after massage and its illustrations of ladies in evening dresses which remind us that in the sight of God we are all mammals.

Rebecca West, "Gallions Reach," *The Strange Necessity* (1928)

5 Magazines all too frequently lead to books and should be regarded by the prudent as the heavy petting of literature.

Fran Lebowitz, *Metropolitan Life* (1978)

6 If you're a little mouseburger, come with me. I was a mouseburger and I will help you. You're so much more wonderful than you think. *Cosmopolitan* is shot full of this stuff although outsiders don't realize it. It is, in its way, an inspiration magazine.

Helen Gurley Brown, in Nora Ephron, *Wallflower at the Orgy* (1970)

7 The fashion pages of magazines such as *Cosmopolitan* now seem to specialize in telling the career girl what to wear to charm the particular wrong type of man who reads *Playboy*, while the editorial pages tell her how to cope with the resulting psychic damage.

Alison Lurie, *The Language of Clothes* (1981)

8 If there is one specific time during the year that my spirits and coincidentally my bosoms are at their lowest, it is the day the *Sports Illustrated* swimsuit issue comes out. (By the way, wearing swimsuits is a sport like ketchup is a vegetable.)

Rita Rudner, *Naked Beneath My Clothes* (1992)

9 If he has done nothing else for American culture, he has given it two of the great lies of the twentieth century: "I buy it for the fiction" and "I buy it for the interviews."

Nora Ephron, on Hugh Hefner, in Celebrity Research Group, *The Bedside Book of Celebrity Gossip* (1984)

See also Journalism, Media.

## ❧ MAGIC

10 I am sure there is Magic in everything, only we have not sense enough to get hold of it and make it do things for us.

Frances Hodgson Burnett, *The Secret Garden* (1911)

11 Faced with unmeasurables, people steer their way by magic.

Denise Scott Brown, "Room at the Top" (1975), in Ellen Perry Berkeley and Matilda McQuaid, eds., *Architecture: A Place for Women* (1989)

12 Magic is the craft of shaping, the craft of the wise, exhilarating, dangerous—the ultimate adventure. The power of magic should not be underestimated. It works, often in ways that are unexpected and difficult to control.

Starhawk, *The Spiral Dance* (1979)

13 We were not for underestimating magic—a life-conductor like the sap between the tree-stem and the bark. We know that it keeps dullness out of religion and poetry. It is probable that without it we might die.

Freya Stark, *The Lycian Shore* (1956)

See also Miracles, Mystery.

## ❧ MAINE

14 In this state there are more different kinds of religion than in any other, I believe. These long cold solitudes incline one to meditation.

Katharine Butler Hathaway (1936), *The Journals and Letters of the Little Locksmith* (1946)

See also New England.

## ✒ MANAGEMENT

1 I learned that in dealing with things, you spent much more time and energy in dealing with people than in dealing with things.

Buwei Yang Chao, in Yuenren Chao, tr., *Autobiography of a Chinese Woman* (1947)

2 Administrative purpose usually outruns the facts. Indeed the administrative official's ardor for facts usually begins when he wants to change the facts!

M.P. Follett, *Creative Experience* (1924)

3 Her talent lay exclusively in seeing that other people employed theirs.

Josephine Tey, *Miss Pym Disposes* (1947)

See also Delegating.

## ✒ MANNERS

4 The idea that people can behave naturally, without resorting to an artificial code tacitly agreed upon by their society, is as silly as the idea that they can communicate by a spoken language without commonly accepted semantic and grammatical rules.

Judith Martin, *Common Courtesy* (1985)

5 Good manners—the longer I live the more convinced I am of it—are a priceless insurance against failure and loneliness. And anyone can have them.

Elsa Maxwell, *Elsa Maxwell's Etiquette Book* (1951)

6 What we need in the world is manners. . . . I think that if, instead of preaching brotherly love, we preached good manners, we might get a little further. It sounds less righteous and more practical.

Eleanor Roosevelt, *My Days* (1938)

7 Manners indeed are like the cypher in arithmetic— they may not be much in themselves, but they are capable of adding a great deal to the value of everything else.

Freya Stark, *East Is West* (1945)

8 Good manners have much to do with the emotions. To make them ring true, one must feel them, not merely exhibit them.

Amy Vanderbilt, *New Complete Book of Etiquette* (1963)

9 Good manners spring from just one thing—kind impulses.

Elsa Maxwell, *Elsa Maxwell's Etiquette Book* (1951)

10 Manners and morals are twin shoots from the same root.

Agnes H. Morton, *Etiquette* (1892)

11 Morals refine manners, as manners refine morals.

Marie von Ebner-Eschenbach, *Aphorisms* (1893)

12 Like language, a code of manners can be used with more or less skill, for laudable or for evil purposes, to express a great variety of ideas and emotions. In itself, it carries no moral value, but ignorance in use of this tool is not a sign of virtue.

Judith Martin, *Common Courtesy* (1985)

13 Only a great fool or a great genius is likely to flout all social grace with impunity, and neither one, doing so, makes the most comfortable companion.

Amy Vanderbilt, *New Complete Book of Etiquette* (1963)

14 The challenge of manners is not so much to be nice to someone whose favor and/or person you covet (although more people need to be reminded of that necessity than one would suppose) as to be exposed to the bad manners of others without imitating them.

Judith Martin, *Miss Manners' Guide for the Turn-of-the-Millennium* (1989)

15 Much of good manners is about knowing when to pretend that what's happening isn't happening.

Mrs. Falk Feeley, *A Swarm of Wasps* (1983)

16 Manners are about making other people reasonably comfortable. If etiquette is, in part, about how to eat that artichoke, manners is knowing not to serve them if you suspect that someone at supper is going to be uncomfortable about being confronted with one.

Mrs. Falk Feeley, *A Swarm of Wasps* (1983)

17 Eating is aggressive by nature, and the implements required for it could quickly become weapons; table manners are, most basically, a system of taboos designed to ensure that violence remains out of the question.

Margaret Visser, *The Rituals of Dinner* (1991)

18 There is no place in the world where courtesy is so necessary as in the home.

Helen Hathaway, *Manners* (1928)

1 Good general-purpose manners nowadays may be said to consist in knowing how much you can get away with.

> Elizabeth Bowen, *Collected Impressions* (1950)

2 It is bad manners to contradict a guest. You must never insult people in your own house—always go to theirs.

> Myrtle Reed, *The Book of Clever Beasts* (1904)

See also Etiquette, Politeness, Protocol, Rudeness.

## ❧ MARRIAGE

3 Reader, I married him.

> Charlotte Brontë, *Jane Eyre* (1847)

4 Nothing in life is as good as the marriage of true minds between man and woman. As good? It is life itself.

> Pearl S. Buck, *To My Daughters, With Love* (1967)

5 Marriage is the most delightful of the impermanencies of life.

> Anthony Gilbert, *Death Knocks Three Times* (1949)

6 If kissing and being engaged were this inflammatory, marriage must burn clear to the bone. I wondered how flesh and blood could endure the ecstasy. How did married couples manage to look so calm and unexcited?

> Jessamyn West, *The Life I Really Lived* (1979)

7 There is nothing more lovely in life than the union of two people whose love for one another has grown through the years from the small acorn of passion to a great rooted tree. Surviving all vicissitudes, and rich with its manifold branches, every leaf holding its own significance.

> Vita Sackville-West, *No Signposts in the Sea* (1961)

8 A successful marriage requires falling in love many times, always with the same person.

> Mignon McLaughlin, *The Second Neurotic's Notebook* (1966)

9 Any marriage worth the name is no better than a series of beginnings—many of them abortive.

> Storm Jameson, *Journey From the North*, vol. 1 (1969)

10 It takes a long time to be really married. One marries many times at many levels within a marriage. If you have more marriages than you have divorces

within the marriage, you're lucky and you stick it out.

> Ruby Dee, in Brian Lanker, *I Dream a World* (1989)

11 Marriage is a very long process.

> Elizabeth Goudge, *Green Dolphin Street* (1944)

12 The sign of a good marriage is that everything is debatable and challenged; nothing is turned into law or policy. The rules, if any, are known only to the two players, who seek no public trophies.

> Carolyn Heilbrun, *Writing a Woman's Life* (1988)

13 In the true marriage relation, the independence of the husband and wife is equal, the dependence mutual and their obligations reciprocal.

> Lucretia Mott (1880), in Theodore Stanton and Harriot Stanton Blatch, eds., *Elizabeth Cady Stanton As Revealed in Her Letters Diary and Reminiscences*, vol. 2 (1922)

14 A great marriage is not so much finding the right person as *being* the right person.

> Marabel Morgan, *The Total Woman* (1973)

15 No human being can destroy the structure of a marriage except the two who made it. It is the one human edifice that is impregnable except from within.

> Gwen Bristow, *Tomorrow Is Forever* (1943)

16 I used to believe that marriage would diminish me, reduce my options. That you had to be someone less to live with someone else when, of course, you have to be someone more.

> Candice Bergen, *Knock Wood* (1984)

17 A happy marriage is the union of two forgivers.

> Ruth Bell Graham, in Julie Nixon Eisenhower, *Special People* (1977)

18 A good marriage is one which allows for change and growth in the individuals and in the way they express their love.

> Pearl S. Buck, *To My Daughters, With Love* (1967)

19 Maybe being married is talking to oneself with one's other self listening.

> Ruth Rendell, *A Sleeping Life* (1978)

20 Take each other for better or worse but not for granted.

> Arlene Dahl, *Always Ask a Man: Arlene Dahl's Key to Femininity* (1965)

21 One advantage of marriage, it seems to me, is that when you fall out of love with him, or he falls out

of love with you, it keeps you together until you maybe fall in again.

Judith Viorst, *Love and Guilt and the Meaning of Life, Etc.* (1979)

1 I suspect that in every good marriage there are times when love seems to be over.

Madeleine L'Engle, *Two-Part Invention* (1988)

2 The best marriages, like the best lives, were both happy and unhappy. There was even a kind of necessary tension, a certain tautness between the partners that gave the marriage strength, like the tautness of a full sail. You went forward on it.

Anne Morrow Lindbergh, *Dearly Beloved* (1962)

3 A revolutionary marriage . . . [is] one in which both partners have work at the center of their lives and must find a delicate balance that can support both together and each individually.

Carolyn Heilbrun, *Writing a Woman's Life* (1988)

4 I have yet to hear a man ask for advice on how to combine marriage and a career.

Gloria Steinem, speech (1975)

5 A simple enough pleasure, surely, to have breakfast alone with one's husband, but how seldom married people in the midst of life achieve it.

Anne Morrow Lindbergh, *Gift From the Sea* (1955)

6 A long-term marriage has to move beyond chemistry to compatibility, to friendship, to companionship. It is certainly not that passion disappears, but that it is conjoined with other ways of love.

Madeleine L'Engle, *Two-Part Invention* (1988)

7 Perhaps this is in the end what most marriages are—gentleness, memory, and habit.

Storm Jameson, *That Was Yesterday* (1932)

8 I begin to see what marriage is for. It's to keep people away from each other. Sometimes I think that two people who love each other can be saved from madness only by the things that come between them—children, duties, visits, bores, relations—the things that protect married people from each other.

Edith Wharton, "Souls Related," *The Greater Inclination* (1899)

9 Monotony is not to be worshiped as a virtue; nor the marriage bed treated as a coffin for security rather than a couch from which to rise refreshed.

Freya Stark, *Perseus in the Wind* (1948)

10 It was only long after the ceremony / That we learned / Why we got married / In the first place.

Lois Wyse, "The Grand Ballroom of the Plaza Hotel," *Love Poems for the Very Married* (1967)

11 The deep, deep peace of the double-bed after the hurly-burly of the chaise longue.

Mrs. Patrick Campbell, on her recent marriage, in Alexander Woollcott, *While Rome Burns* (1934)

12 Those who have made unhappy marriages walk on stilts, while the happy ones are on a level with the crowd. No one sees 'em!

John Oliver Hobbes, *The Ambassador* (1898)

13 Monogamous heterosexual love is probably one of the most difficult, complex and demanding of human relationships.

Margaret Mead, *Male and Female* (1949)

14 Marriage is like twirling a baton, turning a handspring or eating with chopsticks; it looks so easy until you try it.

Helen Rowland, *Reflections of a Bachelor Girl* (1909)

15 The trouble with some women is they get all excited about nothing—and then marry him.

Cher, in Bob Chieger, *Was It Good for You, Too?* (1983)

16 If the right man does not come along, there are many fates far worse. One is to have the wrong man come along.

Letitia Baldrige, *Of Diamonds and Diplomats* (1968)

17 It is true that I never should have married, but I didn't want to live without a man. Brought up to respect the conventions, love had to end in marriage. I'm afraid it did.

Bette Davis, *The Lonely Life* (1962)

18 A girl must marry for love, and keep on marrying until she finds it.

Zsa Zsa Gabor, in John Robert Colombo, *Popcorn in Paradise* (1979)

19 I married twice. The first time was to show my mother I could.

Meredith Tax, "What Good Is a Smart Girl?" in Faye Moskowitz, ed., *Her Face in the Mirror* (1994)

20 I have had a couple of marriages, but like every other woman I had a perfect right to them.

Marie Dressler, *The Life Story of an Ugly Duckling* (1924)

1 What do you expect me to do? Sleep alone?

Elizabeth Taylor, on her marriages, in John Robert
Colombo, *Popcorn in Paradise* (1979)

2 I've married a few people I shouldn't have, but
haven't we all?

Mamie Van Doren, in Autumn Stephens, *Wild Women*
(1992)

3 It is ridiculous to think you can spend your entire
life with just one person. Three is about the right
number. Yes, I imagine three husbands would do
it.

Clare Boothe Luce, in *The Observer* (1981)

4 Those wishing to enter the marriage state had better not come to me for advice, for I disapprove of
it altogether.

Charlotte-Elisabeth, Duchesse d'Orléans (1697), *Life and
Letters of Charlotte Elizabeth* (1889)

5 I have not laughed since I married.

Mrs. Inchbald, *Every One Has His Fault* (1793)

6 One who no longer wishes to laugh had best marry.
. . . They will soon find that it is no laughing matter.

Charlotte-Elisabeth, Duchesse d'Orléans (1699), *Life and
Letters of Charlotte Elizabeth* (1889)

7 It is just as well not to be married, for marriage is
but another name for suffering.

Sydney, Lady Morgan (1828), *Lady Morgan's Memoir*, vol. 2
(1862)

8 I would rather be a beggar and single than a queen
and married.

Elizabeth I, in Frederick Chamberlin, *The Sayings of Queen
Elizabeth* (1923)

9 Other things titillate me more keenly than the pale
pleasures of marriage.

Christina, Queen of Sweden (1654), in Edgar H. Cohen,
*Mademoiselle Libertine* (1970)

10 O, girls! set your affections on cats, poodles, par-
rots or lap-dogs; but let matrimony alone.

Fanny Fern, *Fern Leaves*, 1st series (1853)

11 I do not choose that my grave should be dug while
I am still alive.

Elizabeth I, on being urged to marry, in Frederick
Chamberlin, *The Sayings of Queen Elizabeth* (1923)

12 I would not marry God.

Maxine Elliott (1911), on a rumored engagement, in Diana
Forbes Robertson, *My Aunt Maxine* (1964)

13 Marriage is usually considered the grave, and not
the cradle of love.

Mary Shelley, *The Last Man* (1826)

14 Personally I know nothing about sex because I've
always been married.

Zsa Zsa Gabor, in *The Observer* (1987)

15 As far as I am concerned I would rather spend the
rest of my life in prison than marry again.

George Sand (1837), in Marie Jenny Howe, ed., *The Intimate
Journal of George Sand* (1929)

16 Matrimony is a very dangerous disorder; *I had
rather drink.*

Marie de Rabutin-Chantal, Marquise de Sévigné (1689),
*Letters of Madame de Sévigné to Her Daughter and Her
Friends*, vol. 8 (1811)

17 Our people say a bad marriage kills the soul. Mine
is fit for burial.

Ama Ata Aidoo, title story, *No Sweetness Here* (1970)

18 It may be said of happy marriages as of the phoenix—there is but one a century.

Charlotte-Elisabeth, Duchesse d'Orléans (1696), *Life and
Letters of Charlotte Elizabeth* (1889)

19 Being married was like having a hippopotamus sitting on my face, Mrs. Brown. No matter how hard
I pushed or which way I turned, I couldn't get up.
I couldn't even breathe. . . . Hippopotamuses
aren't all bad. They are what they are. But I wasn't
meant to have one sitting on my face.

Faith Sullivan, *The Cape Ann* (1988)

20 Marriage! . . . Why, it is like living in a thimble with
a hippopotamus!

Phyllis Bottome, *Old Wine* (1925)

21 Conjugality made me think of a three-legged race,
where two people cannot go fast and keep tripping
each other because their two legs are tied together.

Brenda Ueland (1938), *Me* (1983)

22 The matrimonial shoe pinches me.

Amelia E. Barr, *Jan Vedder's Wife* (1885)

23 The blessings of matrimony, like those of poverty,
belong rather to philosophy than reality.

L.E. Landon, *Romance and Reality* (1831)

24 I married beneath me, all women do.

Nancy Astor, in E.T. Williams and C.S. Nicholls, eds., *The
Dictionary of National Biography 1961-1970* (1981)

1 A man is very revealed by his wife, just as a woman is revealed by her husband. People never marry beneath or above themselves, I assure you.

Carol Matthau, *Among the Porcupines* (1992)

2 Happiness in marriage is entirely a matter of chance.

Jane Austen, *Pride and Prejudice* (1813)

3 I know our marriage has just as good a chance of being wonderful as it does of missing the mark.

Whitney Otto, *How to Make an American Quilt* (1991)

4 Having once embarked on your marital voyage, it is impossible not to be aware that you make no way and that the sea is not within sight—that, in fact, you are exploring an enclosed basin.

George Eliot, *Middlemarch* (1871)

5 In marriage, as in chemistry, opposites have often an attraction.

L.E. Landon, *Romance and Reality* (1831)

6 Love-matches are made by people who are content, for a month of honey, to condemn themselves to a life of vinegar.

Lady Marguerite Blessington, in R.R. Madden, *The Literary Life and Correspondence of the Countess of Blessington*, vol. 1 (1855)

7 If men and wimmen think they are marryin' angels, they'll find out they'll have to settle down and keep house with human critters. I never see a year yet, that didn't have more or less winter in it.

Josiah Allen's Wife, *My Opinions and Betsey Bobbet's* (1872)

8 After forty years of marriage we still stood with broken swords in our hands.

Enid Bagnold, *Enid Bagnold's Autobiography* (1969)

9 The unhappily married realize something of the awfulness of the word "eternity."

Minna Thomas Antrim, *Sweethearts and Beaux* (1905)

10 Then begins / the terrible charity of marriage, / husband and wife / climbing the green hill in gold light / until there is no hill, / only a flat plain stopped by the sky.

Louise Glück, "Epithalamium," *Descending Figure* (1980)

11 Given two tempers and the time, the ordinary marriage produces anarchy.

Ellen Glasgow, *The Descendant* (1897)

12 Marriage, to him, was an institution for producing children and eliminating small talk.

Helen Hudson, *Tell the Time to None* (1966)

13 A good marriage shuts out a very great deal.

May Sarton, *A Reckoning* (1978)

14 Marriage is a great strain upon love.

Myrtle Reed, *Master of the Vineyard* (1910)

15 It's not that marriage itself is bad; it's the people we marry who give it a bad name.

Terry McMillan, *Waiting to Exhale* (1992)

16 Marriage . . . did not change people fundamentally. It only changed their habits.

Mary Roberts Rinehart, *Dangerous Days* (1919)

17 After marriage, all things change. And one of them better be you.

Elizabeth Hawes, *Anything But Love* (1948)

18 She worked so hard at making a go of their marriage that finally Dennis went.

Craig Rice, *My Kingdom for a Hearse* (1957)

19 One doesn't have to get anywhere in a marriage. It's not a public conveyance.

Iris Murdoch, *A Severed Head* (1961)

20 Marriage is not a reform school.

Ann Landers, *Since You Ask Me* (1961)

21 "Marriage is a great improver," / Wrote Miss Jane Austen, who was moved / By the connubial bliss about her / To stay forever unimproved.

Helen Bevington, "A Few More Oddities," *When Found, Make a Verse Of* (1961)

22 As so often happens in marriage, roles that had begun almost playfully, to give line and shape to our lives, had hardened like suits of armor and taken us prisoner.

Molly Haskell, *Love and Other Infectious Diseases* (1990)

23 After marriage, a woman's sight becomes so keen that she can see right through her husband without looking at him, and a man's so dull that he can look right through his wife without seeing her.

Helen Rowland, *A Guide to Men* (1922)

24 Before marriage, a man will go home and lie awake all night thinking about something you said; after

marriage, he'll go to sleep before you finish saying it.

Helen Rowland, *A Guide to Men* (1922)

1 Marriage is the tomb of friendship.

Hannah Foster, *The Coquette* (1797)

2 There is not one in a hundred of either sex, who is not taken in when they marry. . . . It is, of all transactions, the one in which people expect most from others, and are least honest themselves.

Jane Austen, *Mansfield Park* (1814)

3 Marriage always demands the greatest understanding of the art of insincerity possible between two human beings.

Vicki Baum, *And Life Goes On* (1931)

4 Any good marriage involves a certain amount of play-acting.

Margaret Millar, *A Stranger in My Grave* (1960)

5 Harold and I didn't get along badly for married people, but the trouble was I didn't misunderstand him. No marriage can be completely successful without a reasonable amount of misunderstanding.

Lillian Day, *Kiss and Tell* (1931)

6 Marriage is mostly puttin' up with things, I reckon, when it ain't makin' believe.

Ellen Glasgow, *The Miller of Old Church* (1911)

7 The reason that husbands and wives do not understand each other is because they belong to different sexes.

Dorothy Dix, in Martha Lupton, *The Speaker's Desk Book* (1937)

8 Evidently, whatever else marriage might prevent, it was not a remedy for isolation of spirit.

Ellen Glasgow, *Barren Ground* (1925)

9 Married was the loneliest I got—being without the one you're with.

Jennifer Stone, "Angst," in Dena Taylor and Amber Coverdale Sumrall, eds., *The Time of Our Lives* (1992)

10 Two by two in the ark of / the ache of it.

Denise Levertov, "The Ache of Marriage," *O Taste and See* (1964)

11 Frank had his work; I had my nothing.

Alix Kates Shulman, *Memoirs of an Ex-Prom Queen* (1972)

12 If you want to sacrifice the admiration of many men for the criticism of one, go ahead, get married.

Katharine Houghton Hepburn, to daughter Katharine (1928), in Anne Edwards, *A Remarkable Woman* (1985)

13 I don't think it's natural for two people to swear to be together for the rest of their lives.

Jane Fonda (1961), in Thomas Kiernan, *Jane Fonda* (1982)

14 I don't know why togetherness was ever held up as an ideal of marriage. Away from home for both, then together, that's much *better*.

Amanda Cross, *Death in a Tenured Position* (1981)

15 I cannot abide the Mr. and Mrs. Noah attitude towards marriage; the animals went in two by two, forever stuck together with glue.

Vita Sackville-West, *No Signposts in the Sea* (1961)

16 I took a small flat for myself and the children. . . . My husband took a room in a clean rooming house within easy walking distance of his office. . . . It is wonderful sometimes to be alone in the night and just know that someone loves you. In other moods you must have that lover in your arms. Marriage under two roofs makes room for moods.

Crystal Eastman, "Marriage Under Two Roofs," in *Cosmopolitan* (1923)

17 A man loves a woman so much, he asks her to marry—to change her name, quit her job, have and raise his babies, be home when he gets there, move where his job is. You can hardly imagine what he might ask if he didn't love her.

Gabrielle Burton, "No One Has a Corner on Depression, But Housewives Are Working on It," in Mary Kay Blakely, *The New York Times* (1981)

18 It is not an accident that most men start thinking of getting married as soon as they get their first job. This is not only because now they can afford it, but because having somebody at home who takes care of you is the only condition not to go crazy after a day spent on an assembly line or at a desk.

Silvia Federici, "Wages Against Housework" (1975), in Evelyn Shapiro and Barry M. Shapiro, *The Women Say/The Men Say* (1979)

19 Love is moral even without legal marriage, but marriage is immoral without love.

Ellen Key, title essay, *The Morality of Women* (1911)

20 Love, the strongest and deepest element in all life, the harbinger of hope, of joy, of ecstasy; love, the defier of all laws, of all conventions; love, the freest, the most powerful molder of human destiny; how

can such an all-compelling force be synonymous with that poor little State- and Church-begotten weed, marriage?

Emma Goldman, "Marriage and Love," *Anarchism* (1910)

1 The name of marriage is the bane of pleasure / And love should have no tie but Love to bind it.

Letitia Pilkington, "The Roman Father," *Memoirs of Mrs. Letitia Pilkington Written by Herself*, vol. 2 (1754)

2 *All* which *is* good and commendable, now existing, would *continue* to exist if all marriage laws were repealed to-morrow. . . . I have an *inalienable, constitutional* and *natural* right to love whom I may, to love as *long* or as *short* a period as I can; to *change* that love *every day* if I please.

Victoria Woodhull (1871), in *Woodhull and Claflin's Weekly* (1873)

3 Any one must see at a glance that if men and women marry those whom they do not love, they must love those whom they do not marry.

Harriet Martineau, *Society in America*, vol. 3 (1837)

4 All these reverend gentlemen who insist on the word "obey" in the marriage service should be removed for a clear violation of the Thirteenth Amendment to the Federal Constitution, which says there shall be neither slavery nor involuntary servitude within the United States.

Elizabeth Cady Stanton, *Eighty Years and More* (1898)

5 The Law has made the man and wife one person, and that one person the husband!

Lucretia Mott (1853), in Dana Greene, ed., *Lucretia Mott* (1980)

6 It is but the name of wife I hate.

Lady Caroline Lamb, *Glenarvon* (1816)

7 Marriage, to women as to men, must be a luxury, not a necessity; an incident of life, not all of it.

Susan B. Anthony, speech (1875)

8 With children no longer the universally accepted reason for marriage, marriages are going to have to exist on their own merits.

Eleanor Holmes Norton, "For Sadie and Maude," in Robin Morgan, ed., *Sisterhood Is Powerful* (1970)

9 Were marriage no more than a convenient screen for sexuality, some less cumbersome and costly protection must have been found by this time to replace it. One concludes therefore that people do not marry to cohabit; they cohabit to marry.

Virgilia Peterson, *A Matter of Life and Death* (1961)

10 The very fact that we make such a to-do over golden weddings indicates our amazement at human endurance. The celebration is more in the nature of a reward for stamina.

Ilka Chase, *Free Admission* (1948)

11 Marriage with love is entering heaven with one's eyes shut, but marriage without love is entering hell with them open.

Mrs. Alec-Tweedie, *Behind the Footlights* (1904)

12 When you speak of other people's marriages, you are, of course, saying something about your own.

Carol Matthau, *Among the Porcupines* (1992)

13 When any two young people take it into their heads to marry, they are pretty sure by perseverance to carry their point, be they ever so poor, or ever so imprudent, or ever so little likely to be necessary to each other's ultimate comfort.

Jane Austen, *Persuasion* (1818)

14 The real killer was when you married the wrong person but had the right children.

Ann Beattie, *Falling in Place* (1980)

15 The room was filled with people who hadn't talked to each other in years, including the bride and bridegroom.

Dorothy Parker, on her remarriage to Alan Campbell, in Lillian Hellman, *An Unfinished Woman* (1969)

16 In marriage, one cannot do anything alone—not even suffer.

Mary Adams, *Confessions of a Wife* (1902)

17 I can't speak for any other marriage, but the secret of our marriage is that we have absolutely nothing in common.

Mamie Eisenhower, in Barbara Walters, *How to Talk With Practically Anybody About Practically Anything* (1970)

18 Marrying a man is like buying something you've been admiring for a long time in a shop window. You may love it when you get it home, but it doesn't always go with everything else in the house.

Jean Kerr, "The Ten Worst Things About a Man," in *McCall's* (1960)

1 Marriage is an extraordinary thing—and I doubt if any outsider—even a child of the marriage—has the right to judge.

Agatha Christie, *Hercule Poirot's Christmas* (1938)

2 There is one thing I can't get in my head— / Why *do* people marry the people they wed?

Carolyn Wells, "The Mystery," in Carolyn Wells, ed., *The World's Best Humor* (1923)

3 This book is dedicated to my own lawful pardner, Josiah, whom (although I have been his consort for a little upwards of fourteen years) I still love with a cast-iron devotedness.

Josiah Allen's Wife, *My Opinions and Betsey Bobbet's* (1872)

4 My uncle . . . had the misfortune to be ever touched in his brain, and, as a convincing proof, married his maid, at an age when he and she both had more occasion for a nurse than a parson.

Charlotte Charke, *A Narrative of the Life of Mrs. Charlotte Charke* (1755)

5 What a holler would ensue if people had to pay the minister as much to marry them as they have to pay a lawyer to get them a divorce.

Claire Trevor, in *The New York Journal-American* (1960)

6 If you feel like getting a divorce, you are no exception to the general rule.

Elizabeth Hawes, *Anything But Love* (1948)

7 I don't think marriages break up because of what you do to each other. They break up because of what you must become in order to stay in them.

Carol Matthau, *Among the Porcupines* (1992)

8 If you made a list of the reasons why any couple got married, and another list of the reasons for their divorce, you'd have a hell of a lot of overlapping.

Mignon McLaughlin, *The Neurotic's Notebook* (1963)

9 Love, the quest; marriage, the conquest; divorce, the inquest.

Helen Rowland, *A Guide to Men* (1922)

10 In the rush of complex modern living, we have a tendency to laugh at the "bring-Papa-his-pipe-and-slippers" approach to marriage—but most men are more than a little wistful at its demise. A man dreams of home as a haven and his wife as a romantic, fragrant creature whose most important goal in life is making him comfortable.

Arlene Dahl, *Always Ask a Man: Arlene Dahl's Key to Femininity* (1965)

See also Divorce, Intimacy, Love, Lovers, Monogamy, Relationships, Weddings.

## ❧ MARXISM

11 To be a Marxist does not mean that one becomes a Communist party member. There are as many varieties of Marxists as there are of Protestants.

Helen Foster Snow, "Women and Kuomintang," *Women in Modern China* (1967)

12 [Marx's] most explosive and indeed most original contribution to the cause of revolution was that he interpreted the compelling needs of mass poverty in political terms as an uprising, not for the sake of bread or wealth, but for the sake of freedom as well.

Hannah Arendt, *On Revolution* (1963)

## ❧ MATERIALISM

13 False values begin with the worship of things.

Susan Sontag, *The Benefactor* (1963)

14 A commercial society urges its citizens to be responsible for things, but not for people. It is the unquestioned assumption of a mercantile culture that things need and deserve attention, but that people can take care of themselves.

Margaret Halsey, *The Folks at Home* (1952)

15 Democracy always makes for materialism, because the only kind of equality that you can guarantee to a whole people is, broadly speaking, physical.

Katharine Fullerton Gerould, *Modes and Morals* (1920)

16 Destitution and excessive luxury develop apparently the same ideals, the same marauding attitude towards mankind, the intensity of struggle for material goods,—surely showing how perfect is the meeting of extremes.

Alice James (1889), in Anna Robeson Burr, *Alice James* (1934)

1 A high standard of living is usually accompanied by a low standard of thinking.

   Marya Mannes, *Message From a Stranger* (1948)

2 The luxuries of the few were becoming necessities of the many.

   Flora Thompson, *Candleford Green* (1943)

See also Business, Consumerism, Possessions, Things.

## ❧ MATHEMATICS

3 I see a certain order in the universe and math is one way of making it visible.

   May Sarton, *As We Are Now* (1973)

4 Mathematics provides an invisible framework that molds the more visible surface features of daily life.

   Sheila Tobias, *Succeed With Math* (1987)

5 Mathematical expressions give us a way of thinking about relationships that would otherwise be unavailable to us.

   Sheila Tobias, *Succeed With Math* (1987)

6 The paradox of our times is that as mathematics becomes increasingly powerful, only the powerful seem to benefit from it.

   Sheila Tobias, *Succeed With Math* (1987)

7 People who don't know what math is don't know what math isn't. Therefore, fear of math may lead them to avoid all manner of data and to feel uncomfortable working with things. Any mathematician will tell you that you don't need mathematics to work the F stops on a camera, or to fix the car, or even to start your own business.

   Sheila Tobias, *Overcoming Math Anxiety* (1978)

8 Fear of mathematics is the result and not the cause of . . . negative experiences with mathematics.

   Sheila Tobias, *Overcoming Math Anxiety* (1978)

9 Until I was thirty years old, I never even dated a scientist, an engineer, or a math major. My math avoidance extended even to my social life.

   Sheila Tobias, *Overcoming Math Anxiety* (1978)

10 Although I am not stupid, the mathematical side of my brain is like dumb notes upon a damaged piano.

   Margot Asquith, *More or Less About Myself* (1934)

11 Stand firm in your refusal to remain conscious during algebra. In real life, I assure you, there is no such thing as algebra.

   Fran Lebowitz, *Social Studies* (1977)

12 I am now going to tell you about the horible and wretched plaege that my multiplication gives me you cant conceive it—the most Devilish thing is 8 times 8 & 7 times 7 it is what nature itselfe cant endure.

   Marjorie Fleming, age 7 (1810), in Frank Sidgwick, *The Complete Marjory Fleming* (1934)

## ❧ MATURITY

13 To mature is in part to realize that while complete intimacy and omniscience and power cannot be had, self-transcendence, growth, and closeness to others are nevertheless within one's reach.

   Sissela Bok, *Secrets* (1983)

14 Maturity . . . is letting things happen.

   Amanda Cross, *No Word From Winifred* (1986)

15 You grow up the day you have your first real laugh—at yourself.

   Ethel Barrymore, in Adela Rogers St. Johns, "Ethel Barrymore, Queen Once More," *Reader's Digest* (1943)

16 It's when you stop doing the stuff you have to make excuses for and when you stop making excuses for the stuff you have to do.

   Marilyn vos Savant, in *Parade* (1993)

17 From a timid, shy girl I had become a woman of resolute character, who could no longer be frightened by the struggle with troubles.

   Anna Dostoevsky, in S.S. Koteliansky, ed., *Dostoevsky Portrayed by His Wife, The Diary and Reminiscences of Mme. Dostoevsky* (1926)

18 That's maturity—when you realize that you've finally arrived at a state of ignorance as profound as that of your parents.

   Elizabeth Peters, *The Night of Four Hundred Rabbits* (1971)

See also Adulthood, Growth.

## ❦ MAY

1 May is like the first rising of the curtain before the play, the first measures of the orchestral overture. No moment afterward comes up to that.

> Bertha Damon, *A Sense of Humus* (1943)

2 It was one of those beautiful, lengthening days, when May was pressing back with both hands the shades of the morning and the evening.

> Amelia E. Barr, *The Bow of Orange Ribbon* (1886)

3 Now comes the May time, the wild hawks' play-time, / With long blithe daytime and warm night showers.

> Georgiana Goddard King, *The Way of Perfect Love* (1909)

See also Spring.

## ❦ MEANING

4 Where shall we seek for meaning? / In wisdom's court / Or in a life of sorrow?

> Sajida Zaidi, "New Angles" (1972) in Susie Tharu and K. Lalita, eds., *Women Writing in India* (1991)

5 The need to find meaning in the universe is as real as the need for trust and for love, for relations with other human beings.

> Margaret Mead, *Twentieth Century Faith* (1972)

6 One needs something to believe in, something for which one can have whole-hearted enthusiasm. One needs to feel that one's life has meaning, that one is needed in this world.

> Hannah Senesh (1938), *Hannah Senesh* (1966)

7 Life could not defeat her if she were working for something bigger than herself and her personal sorrows.

> Katharine Susannah Prichard, *Winged Seeds* (1950)

8 We who are alive at this moment are only an infinitesimal part of something that has existed for eternity and will continue when there is no longer anything to show that earth existed. Still, we must feel and believe that we are all.

> Liv Ullmann, *Changing* (1976)

See also Purpose.

## ❦ MEANS

9 Methods and means cannot be separated from the ultimate aim.

> Emma Goldman, afterword, *My Disillusionment in Russia* (1923)

10 There are many trails up the mountain, but in time they all reach the top.

> Anya Seton, *The Turquoise* (1946)

11 It is not *what* I do, it is the *way* I do it, that will get me in the end.

> Anne Wilson Schaef, *Meditations for Women Who Do Too Much* (1990)

See also Goals, Journeys.

## ❦ MEDIA

12 He had the familiar defense of all those who wield great power in a popular medium: "We only give the public what it wants—." It is the most useful, and least valid, reason for having no convictions that I know of.

> Marya Mannes, *Message From a Stranger* (1948)

13 We are given in our newspapers and on TV and radio exactly what we, the public, insist on having, and this very frequently is mediocre information and mediocre entertainment.

> Eleanor Roosevelt (1959), *My Day*, vol. 3 (1991)

14 It is hard to tell which is worst; the wide diffusion of things that are not true, or the suppression of things that are true.

> Harriet Martineau, *Society in America*, vol. 1 (1837)

See also Advertising, Films, Journalism, Magazines, Newspapers, Radio, Television.

## ❦ MEDICINE

15 Medication without explanation is obscene.

> Toni Cade Bambara, "Christmas Eve at Johnson's Drugs N Goods," *The Sea Birds Are Still Alive* (1982)

1 In medicine as in statecraft and propaganda, words are sometimes the most powerful drugs we can use.

Sara Murray Jordan, in *The New York Times* (1959)

2 Time was when medicine could do very little for critically ill or dying patients. Now it can do too much.

Lisa Belkin, *First, Do No Harm* (1993)

3 She said they [injections of morphine] didn't kill the pain but locked her up inside it.

Shirley Abbott, *Womenfolks: Growing Up Down South* (1983)

4 Harry was extremely liberal with free pills, diagnoses and advice. On occasion, he was more effective than a regular doctor, since he was unhampered by training, medical ethics or caution, and some of his cures were miraculously quick. These were the ones his friends remembered.

Margaret Millar, *The Soft Talkers* (1957)

5 Healthy people are always prejudiced against medicine.

C.M. Sedgwick, *Hope Leslie* (1827)

See also Health, Illness.

## ❧ MEDIOCRITY

6 The only sin is mediocrity.

Martha Graham, in "Martha Graham Reflects on Her Art and a Life in Dance," *The New York Times* (1985)

7 Most of the men or women who have contributed to our civilization or our culture have been vilified in their day. . . . As we denounce the rebellious, the nonconformists, so we reward mediocrity so long as it mirrors herd standards.

Tallulah Bankhead, *Tallulah* (1952)

8 Over and over again mediocrity is promoted because real worth isn't to be found.

Kathleen Norris, *Hands Full of Living* (1931)

9 "Mediocrity" does not mean an average intelligence; it means an average intelligence that resents and envies its betters.

Ayn Rand, *The New Left* (1971)

10 There is nothing upon the face of the earth so insipid as a medium. Give me love or hate! a friend that will go to jail for me, or an enemy that will run me through the body!

Fanny Burney, *Camilla* (1796)

11 We cling to a bourgeois mediocrity which would make it appear we are all Americans, made in the image and likeness of George Washington, all of a pattern, all prospering if we are good, and going down in the world if we are bad.

Dorothy Day, *The Long Loneliness* (1952)

12 A person may be totally unimaginative and have the social vision of a mole, and we still call him a decent man.

Margaret Halsey, *No Laughing Matter* (1977)

13 When Negroes are average, *they fail*, unless they are very, very lucky. Now, if you're average and *white*, honey, you can go far. Just look at Dan Quayle. If that boy was colored he'd be washing dishes somewhere.

Bessie Delany, in Sarah and A. Elizabeth Delany with Amy Hill Hearth, *Having Our Say* (1993)

14 He seems like an average type of man. He's not, like, smart. I'm not trying to bag on him or anything, but he has the same mentality I have—and I'm in the eighth grade.

Vanessa Martinez, on Vice President Dan Quayle, in *The Los Angeles Times* (1992)

15 None of us wants to be average. That we are so is a melancholy fact borne in upon us in middle life, and we do not always relish it.

Margaret Benson, *The Venture of Rational Faith* (1908)

16 I shouldn't mind it if I saw the admirable sweep on to success, or immortality, but always it seems to be the ordinary, the vulgar, and the average, or the lower average, that triumphs.

Ellen Glasgow, *Letters of Ellen Glasgow* (1958)

17 What depresses me is the inevitable way the second rate forges ahead and the deserving is left behind.

Ellen Glasgow, *Letters of Ellen Glasgow* (1958)

18 There's only one real sin, and that is to persuade oneself that the second-best is anything but the second-best.

Doris Lessing, *Golden Notebook* (1962)

19 Do you know the hallmark of the second-rater? It's resentment of another man's achievement.

Ayn Rand, *Atlas Shrugged* (1957)

1 Mediocrity is safe.

> Nikki Giovanni, in Claudia Tate, ed., *Black Women Writers at Work* (1983)

See also Conformity, Conventionality, Second-Rate.

## ❦ MEETINGS

2 The length of a meeting rises with the number of people present and the productiveness of a meeting falls with the square of the number of people present.

> Eileen Shanahan, in *Times Talk* (1963)

3 Committee meetings are always held at inconvenient times and usually take place in dark, dusty rooms the temperatures of which are unsuited to the human body.

> Virginia Graham, *Say Please* (1949)

4 If enough meetings are held, the meetings become more important than the problem.

> Susan Ohanian, *Ask Ms. Class* (1996)

5 Meetings that do not come off keep a character of their own. They stay as they were projected.

> Elizabeth Bowen, *The House in Paris* (1935)

6 Meetings . . . are rather like cocktail parties. You don't want to go, but you're cross not to be asked.

> Jilly Cooper, *How to Survive From Nine to Five* (1970)

See also Committees, Groups.

## ❦ MELANCHOLY

7 Gaiety is forgetfulness of the self, melancholy is memory of the self: in that state the soul feels all the power of its roots, nothing distracts it from its profound homeland and the look that it casts upon the outer world is gently dismayed.

> Adrienne Monnier (1942), in Richard McDougall, tr., *The Very Rich Hours of Adrienne Monnier* (1976)

8 Oh dear—Oh dear—where are my people? With whom have I been happiest? With nobody in particular. It has all been mush of a mushness.

> Katherine Mansfield (1918), *Journal of Katherine Mansfield* (1927)

9 I was not always free from melancholy; but even melancholy had its charms.

> Marie-Jeanne Roland (1791), in Lydia Maria Child, *Memoirs of Madame de Staël and of Madame Roland* (1847)

10 He is as melancholy as an unbraced drum.

> Susannah Centlivre, *The Wonder* (1714)

See also Depression, Despair, Unhappiness.

## ❦ MEMORY

11 I am rampant with memory.

> Margaret Laurence, *The Stone Angel* (1964)

12 Memory—the very skin of life.

> Elizabeth Hardwick, "Living in Italy: Reflections on Bernard Berenson," *A View of My Own* (1962)

13 Some memories are realities, and are better than anything that can ever happen to one again.

> Willa Cather, *My Antonia* (1918)

14 Memory is more indelible than ink.

> Anita Loos, *Kiss Hollywood Goodbye* (1974)

15 Memory, that library of the soul from which I will draw knowledge and experience for the rest of my life.

> Tove Ditlevsen (1967), in Tiina Nunnally, tr., *Early Spring* (1985)

16 I wear the key of memory, and can open every door in the house of my life.

> Amelia E. Barr, *All the Days of My Life* (1913)

17 His memory could work like the slinging of a noose to catch a wild pony.

> Eudora Welty, "First Love," *The Wide Net* (1943)

18 As a life's work, I would remember everything—everything, against loss. I would go through life like a plankton net.

> Annie Dillard, *An American Childhood* (1987)

19 Memories stretch and pull around me— / Bark drying on a new canoe.

> Mary TallMountain, "Ts'eekkaayah," in Joseph Bruchac, ed., *Songs From This Earth on Turtle's Back* (1983)

20 Memory is a magnet. It will pull to it and hold only material nature has designed it to attract.

> Jessamyn West, *The Life I Really Lived* (1979)

1 I can understand that memory must be selective, else it would choke on the glut of experience. What I cannot understand is why it selects what it does.

    Virgilia Peterson, *A Matter of Life and Death* (1961)

2 There seems something more speakingly incomprehensible in the powers, the failures, the inequalities of memory, than in any other of our intelligences. The memory is sometimes so retentive, so serviceable, so obedient—at others, so bewildered and so weak—and at others again, so tyrannic, so beyond control!

    Jane Austen, *Mansfield Park* (1814)

3 My memory is a card shark, reshuffling the deck to hide what I fear to know, unable to keep from fingering the ace at the bottom of the deck when I'm doing nothing more than playing Fish in the daylight with children.

    Lorene Cary, *Black Ice* (1991)

4 I remember what was missing instead of what was there. I am a chronicler of absence.

    Carrie Fisher, *Delusions of Grandma* (1994)

5 In memory each of us is an artist: each of us creates.

    Patricia Hampl, *A Romantic Education* (1981)

6 There can be no harm / In just remembering—that is all.

    Katherine Mansfield, "The Arabian Shawl," *Poems* (1930)

7 Here, in memory, we live *and* die.

    Patricia Hampl, *A Romantic Education* (1981)

8 Back on its golden hinges / The gate of Memory swings, / And my heart goes into the garden / And walks with the olden things.

    Ella Wheeler Wilcox, "Memory's Garden," *Shells* (1873)

9 The heart holds, like remembered music, / a landscape grown too dark to see.

    Gwen Harwood, "Alla Siciliana," *Poems, Volume Two* (1968)

10 There will be stars over the place forever.

    Sara Teasdale, "'There Will Be Stars'," *Dark of the Moon* (1926)

11 Years flowed in and flowed out of his mind like tides, leaving pools of memories full of small living things.

    Margaret Millar, *Ask for Me Tomorrow* (1976)

12 Memories began swarming in, vivid and impatient, like a litter of little mice.

    Simone Berteaut, *Piaf* (1969)

13 Memory walked through old men's minds like a choir boy swinging a censer.

    Maud Hart Lovelace, *Early Candlelight* (1929)

14 The charm, one might say the genius, of memory is that it is choosy, chancy and temperamental; it rejects the edifying cathedral and indelibly photographs the small boy outside, chewing a hunk of melon in the dust.

    Elizabeth Bowen, in *Vogue* (1955)

15 How we remember, what we remember, and why we remember form the most personal map of our individuality.

    Christina Baldwin, *One to One* (1977)

16 When we live with a memory we live with a corpse; the impact of the experience has changed us once but can never change us again.

    Dorothy Gilman, *A New Kind of Country* (1978)

17 Memory is a skilled seducer.

    Cristina Garcia, *Dreaming in Cuban* (1992)

18 The hills of one's youth are all mountains.

    Mari Sandoz, *The Story Catcher* (1963)

19 Memories are like corks left out of bottles. They swell. They no longer fit.

    Harriet Doerr, *Stones for Ibarra* (1978)

20 Memory's a freakish bank / where embarrassing treasures / still draw interest.

    Marge Piercy, "Lapsed," *Breaking Camp* (1968)

21 It is memory that provides the heart with impetus, fuels the brain, and propels the corn plant from seed to fruit.

    Joy Harjo, conference (1991)

22 Memory is a complicated thing, a relative to truth but not its twin.

    Barbara Kingsolver, *Animal Dreams* (1990)

23 As to memory, it is known that this frail faculty naturally lets drop the facts which are less flattering to our self-love—when it does not retain them carefully as subjects not to be approached, marshy spots with a warning flag over them.

    George Eliot, *Impressions of Theophrastus Such* (1879)

1 Pictures of my life stretch back into what must have been my very earliest childhood. . . . They are not movies, then, nor are they talkies, but they are quite distinctly feelies.

Sheila Kaye-Smith, *Three Ways Home* (1937)

2 What I remember / hardly happened; / what they say happened / I hardly remember.

Linda Pastan, "The One-Way Mirror Back," *PM/AM* (1982)

3 I can never remember things I didn't understand in the first place.

Amy Tan, *The Joy Luck Club* (1989)

4 they ask me to remember / but they want me to remember / their memories / and I keep on remembering / mine.

Lucille Clifton, "Why Some People Be Mad at Me Sometimes," *Next* (1987)

5 Sometimes what we call "memory" and what we call "imagination" are not so easily distinguished.

Leslie Marmon Silko, *Storyteller* (1981)

6 Imagination is memory's chief instrument—the person who remembers only what has actually happened has little joy in reminiscence.

Richard Shattuck, *The Half-Haunted Saloon* (1945)

7 The irony of life is not that you cannot forget but that you can.

Gertrude Atherton, *Can Women Be Gentlemen?* (1938)

8 I have a terrible memory; I never forget a thing.

Edith Konecky, *Allegra Maud Goldman* (1976)

9 Just remember enough never to be vulnerable again: total forgetting could be as self-destructive as complete remembering.

Helen MacInnes, *The Venetian Affair* (1963)

10 We more quickly forget kindnesses than offenses: caresses leave fewer traces than bites.

Comtesse Diane, *Les Glanes de la Vie* (1898)

11 I think, myself, that one's memories represent those moments which, insignificant as they may seem, nevertheless represent the inner self and oneself as most really oneself.

Agatha Christie, *An Autobiography* (1977)

12 Memory seldom fails when its office is to show us the tombs of our buried hopes.

Lady Marguerite Blessington, in R.R. Madden, *The Literary Life and Correspondence of the Countess of Blessington*, vol. 1 (1855)

13 Memory is earth's retribution for man's sins.

Augusta J. Evans, *St. Elmo* (1866)

14 It is less difficult to look beyond . . . and foretell the future, than to look back and remember what has already gone before.

Craig Rice, *Telefair* (1942)

15 What a strange thing is memory, and hope; one looks backward, the other forward. The one is of today, the other is the tomorrow. Memory is history recorded in our brain, memory is a painter, it paints pictures of the past and of the day.

Grandma Moses, in Otto Kallir, ed., *My Life's History* (1952)

16 Looking repeatedly into the past, you do not necessarily become fascinated with your own life, but rather with the phenomenon of memory.

Patricia Hampl, *A Romantic Education* (1981)

17 Memory is to love what the saucer is to the cup.

Elizabeth Bowen, *The House in Paris* (1935)

18 A person without a memory is either a child or an amnesiac. A country without a memory is neither a child nor an amnesiac, but neither is it a country.

Mary Astor, *A Life on Film* (1967)

19 One form of loneliness is to have a memory and no one to share it with.

Phyllis Rose, in Nancy R. Newhouse, ed., *Hers* (1986)

20 Isn't it funny, she thought, that it takes two generations to kill off a man? . . . First him, and then his memory.

Shirley Ann Grau, *The Keepers of the House* (1964)

21 I fear / the place I have / in the memory of others. / They remind me of things / I myself have forgot.

Tove Ditlevsen, "Self Portrait 4," in Joanna Bankier and Deirdre Lashgari, eds., *Women Poets of the World* (1983)

22 Proust's tea cake has nothing on one hour in a college dorm.

Gloria Steinem, *Outrageous Acts and Everyday Rebellions* (1983)

23 She has lost her memory. Each sentence she speaks is in the present tense. She is letting the past slip from her hand, a fish into dark water.

Mary Gordon, "My Mother Is Speaking From the Desert," in *The New York Times Magazine* (1995)

See also Forgetting, Nostalgia, Past, Remembrance.

## ♦ MEN

1 Personally, I like two types of men—domestic and foreign.

> Mae West, in Joseph Weintraub, ed., *The Wit and Wisdom of Mae West* (1967)

2 A woman who has known but one man is like a person who has heard only one composer.

> Isadora Duncan, *My Life* (1927)

3 A man in the house is worth two in the street.

> Mae West, in *Belle of the Nineties* (1934)

4 Of all the labor-saving devices ever invented for women, none has ever been so popular as the devoted male.

> Editors of *Ladies' Home Journal,* in Elizabeth Hawes, *Anything But Love* (1948)

5 It's not the men in my life that counts, it's the life in my men.

> Mae West, in *I'm No Angel* (1933)

6 There are far too many men in politics and not enough elsewhere.

> Hermione Gingold, *How to Grow Old Disgracefully* (1988)

7 I always did like a man in uniform. And that one fits you grand. Why don't you come up sometime and see me?

> Mae West, in *Diamond Lil* (1932)

8 I require only three things of a man. He must be handsome, ruthless, and stupid.

> Dorothy Parker, in John Keats, *You Might As Well Live* (1970)

9 "Boyfriends" weren't friends at all; they were prizes, escorts, symbols of achievement, fascinating strangers, the Other.

> Susan Allen Toth, *Blooming* (1978)

10 We all marry strangers. All men are strangers to all women.

> Mary Heaton Vorse, "The Pink Fence," in *McCall's* (1920)

11 As Vida is wont to say: *Men aren't like other people.*

> Mary Daheim, *The Alpine Decoy* (1994)

12 There are men I could spend eternity with. But not this life.

> Kathleen Norris, "Blue Mountain," *The Middle of the World* (1981)

13 There are really no men at all. There are grown-up boys, and middle-aged boys, and elderly boys, and even sometimes very old boys. But the essential difference is simply exterior. Your man is always a boy.

> Mary Roberts Rinehart, *"Isn't That Just Like a Man!"* (1920)

14 The material for this book was collected directly from nature at great personal risk by the author.

> Helen Rowland, *Guide to Men* (1922)

15 Give a man a free hand and he'll try to put it all over you.

> Mae West, *Klondike Annie* (1936)

16 "A man is as old as he feels, a woman is as old as she looks." . . . Mrs. McKay tossed her head. "Some man made that one up, I'll bet. They're always dealing to themselves from the bottom of the deck."

> Richard Shattuck, *The Half-Haunted Saloon* (1945)

17 Testosterone does not have to be toxic.

> Anna Quindlen, in *The New York Times* (1993)

18 Men weren't really the enemy—they were fellow victims suffering from an outmoded masculine mystique that made them feel unnecessarily inadequate when there were no bears to kill.

> Betty Friedan, in *The Christian Science Monitor* (1974)

19 Men are not amusing during the shooting season; but, after all, my dear, men were not especially designed to amuse women.

> Gertrude Atherton, *Transplanted* (1919)

20 You have to be very fond of men. Very, very fond. You have to be very fond of them to love them. Otherwise they're simply unbearable.

> Marguerite Duras, *Practicalities* (1987)

21 A man . . . is *so* in the way in the house!

> Elizabeth Gaskell, *Cranford* (1853)

22 Can you imagine a world without men? No crime and lots of happy, fat women.

> Nicole Hollander, syndicated comic strip "Sylvia" (1981)

23 Men don't live well by themselves. They don't even live like people. They live like bears with furniture.

> Rita Rudner, in Anna Quindlen, "Bears With Furniture," *Thinking Out Loud* (1993)

1 What's with you men? Would hair stop growing on your chest if you asked directions somewhere?

   Erma Bombeck, *When You Look Like Your Passport Photo, It's Time to Go Home* (1991)

2 My ancestors wandered lost in the wilderness for forty years because even in biblical times, men would not stop to ask for directions.

   Elayne Boosler, in *Time* (1990)

3 Estimated from a wife's experience, the average man spends fully one-quarter of his life in looking for his shoes.

   Helen Rowland, *A Guide to Men* (1922)

4 I'd like somebody to breed a male, genus homo, who could go and fetch a 12" x 8" black suède purse lying in the middle of a white bedspread and not come back looking baffled and saying he couldn't find it.

   Margaret Halsey, *Some of My Best Friends Are Soldiers* (1944)

5 I want to know why, if men rule the world, they don't stop wearing neckties.

   Linda Ellerbee, *Move On* (1991)

6 Dr. Ruth says we women should tell our lovers how to make love to us. My boyfriend goes nuts if I tell him how to *drive*!

   Pam Stone, in Roz Warren, ed., *Glibquips* (1994)

7 "Why do men resist putting gas in their cars until the last minute?" . . . "There's not much left in life for men to gamble about. They can gamble about the gas."

   Jessamyn West, *Hide and Seek* (1973)

8 Most men are reasonably useful in a crisis. The difficulty lies in convincing them that the situation has reached a critical point.

   Elizabeth Peters, *Curse of the Pharaohs* (1981)

9 The only time a woman really succeeds in changing a man is when he's a baby.

   Natalie Wood, in Bob Chieger, *Was It Good for You, Too?* (1983)

10 Gentlemen prefer doormats.

   Ruth Herschberger, *Adam's Rib* (1948)

11 Men often marry their mothers.

   Edna Ferber, *Saratoga Trunk* (1941)

12 The average man is more interested in a woman who is interested in him than he is in a woman—any woman—with beautiful legs.

   Marlene Dietrich (1954), in James Beasley Simpson, *Best Quotes of '54, '55, '56* (1957)

13 A fox is a wolf who sends flowers.

   Ruth Weston, in *The New York Post* (1955)

14 Every other inch a gentleman.

   Rebecca West, of Michael Arlen, in Victoria Glendinning (1928), *Rebecca West* (1987)

15 Men would always rather be made love to than talked at.

   Dorothy M. Richardson, *Pilgrimage: Revolving Lights* (1923)

16 How can the world progress if women don't consider men . . . the Man . . . first?

   Arlene Dahl, *Always Ask a Man: Arlene Dahl's Key to Femininity* (1965)

See also Brothers, Fathers, Husbands, Macho, Sons, Uncles, Women and Men.

## § MENTAL ILLNESS

17 Volumes are now written and spoken about the effect of the mind upon the body. Much of it is true. But I wish a little more was thought of the effect of the body on the mind.

   Florence Nightingale, *Notes on Nursing* (1859)

18 Every morning I woke in dread, waiting for the day nurse to go on her rounds and announce from the list of names in her hand whether or not I was for shock treatment, the new and fashionable means of quieting people and of making them realize that orders are to be obeyed and floors are to be polished without anyone protesting and faces are made to be fixed into smiles and weeping is a crime.

   Janet Frame, *Faces in the Water* (1961)

19 Lunatics are similar to designated hitters. Often an entire family is crazy, but since an entire family can't go into the hospital, one person is designated as crazy and goes inside.

   Susanna Kaysen, *Girl, Interrupted* (1993)

20 "The sooner you 'settle' the sooner you'll be allowed home" was the ruling logic; and "if you can't

adapt yourself to living in a mental hospital how do you expect to be able to live 'out in the world'?" How indeed?

Janet Frame, *Faces in the Water* (1961)

1 For nearly a century the psychoanalysts have been writing op-ed pieces about the workings of a country they've never traveled to, a place that, like China, has been off-limits. Suddenly, the country has opened its borders and is crawling with foreign correspondents, neurobiologists are filing ten stories a week, filled with new data. These two groups of writers, however, don't seem to read each other's work. That's because the analysts are writing about a country they call Mind and the neuroscientists are reporting from a country they call Brain.

Susanna Kaysen, *Girl, Interrupted* (1993)

See also Depression, Insanity, Madness, Nerves, Neurotics, Psychiatry, Psychology.


## ✑ MERCY

2 We all need the waters of the Mercy River. Though they don't run deep, there's usually enough, just enough, for the extravagance of our lives.

Jonis Agee, *Sweet Eyes* (1991)

3 We hand folks over to God's mercy, and show none ourselves.

George Eliot, *Adam Bede* (1859)

4 Too much mercy . . . often resulted in further crimes which were fatal to innocent victims who need not have been victims if justice had been put first and mercy second.

Agatha Christie, *The Halloween Party* (1969)

See also Compassion, Forgiveness, Graciousness, Kindness, Virtue.


## ✑ METAPHOR

5 Metaphor is the energy charge that leaps between images, revealing their connections.

Robin Morgan, *The Anatomy of Freedom* (1982)

6 The golden light of metaphor, which is the intelligence of poetry, was implicit in alchemical study.

To change, magically, one substance into another, more valuable one is the ancient function of metaphor, as it was of alchemy.

Patricia Hampl, *A Romantic Education* (1981)

7 Dead metaphors make strong idols.

Marcia Falk, "Notes on Composing New Blessings," in Judith Plaskow and Carol P. Christ, eds., *Weaving the Visions* (1989)


## ✑ MEXICO

8 Mexico. Melancholy, profoundly right and wrong, it embraces as it strangulates.

Ana Castillo, *The Mixquiahuala Letters* (1986)


## ✑ MIDDLE AGE

9 It's hard to feel middle-aged, because how can you tell how long you are going to live?

Mignon McLaughlin, *The Neurotic's Notebook* (1963)

10 Shall I not bless the middle years? / Not I for youth repine.

Sarah N. Cleghorn, "Contented at Forty," *Portraits and Protests* (1917)

11 Is it not possible that middle age can be looked upon as a period of second flowering, second growth, even a kind of second adolescence? It is true that society in general does not help one accept this interpretation of the second half of life.

Anne Morrow Lindbergh, *Gift From the Sea* (1955)

12 The middle-aged, who have lived through their strongest emotions, but are yet in the time when memory is still half passionate and not merely contemplative, should surely be a sort of natural priesthood, whom life has disciplined and consecrated to be the refuge and rescue of early stumblers and victims of self-despair.

George Eliot, *The Mill on the Floss* (1860)

13 The signs that presage growth, so similar, it seems to me, to those in early adolescence: discontent, restlessness, doubt, despair, longing, are interpreted falsely as signs of decay. In youth one does not as often misinterpret the signs; one accepts them, quite rightly, as growing pains. . . . But in the

middle age, because of the false assumption that it is a period of decline, one interprets these life-signs, paradoxically, as signs of approaching death.

Anne Morrow Lindbergh, *Gift From the Sea* (1955)

1 Youth was gone, but night had not fully arrived,— and some of the glow of afternoon still lingered in his blood.

Rosemary Kutak, *Darkness of Slumber* (1944)

2 Few women, I fear, have had such reason as I have to think the long sad years of youth were worth living for the sake of middle age.

George Eliot (1857), in J.W. Cross, ed., *George Eliot's Life As Related in Her Letters and Journals* (1884)

3 These years are still the years of my prime. It is important to recognize the years of one's prime, always remember that.... One's prime is elusive.

Muriel Spark, *The Prime of Miss Jean Brodie* (1962)

4 We Americans, with our terrific emphasis on youth, action, and material success, certainly tend to belittle the afternoon of life and even to pretend it never comes. We push the clock back and try to prolong the morning, over-reaching and over-straining ourselves in the unnatural effort.... In our breathless attempts we often miss the flowering that waits for afternoon.

Anne Morrow Lindbergh, *Gift From the Sea* (1955)

5 Summer days are over! / O my one true lover, / Sit we now alone together / In the early autumn weather! / From our nest the birds have flown / To fair dreamlands of their own, / And we see the days go by, / In silence—thou and I!

Julia C.R. Dorr, "Thou and I," *Poems* (1892)

6 The first impulse of many women as the current bears them toward middle age is to turn back toward youth or at least to try to remain stationary, treading water. But wise women perceive how pleasant the new scene is ... they do not struggle and they enjoy all their voyage, for they feel that evening air has a good quality of its own.

Bertha Damon, *A Sense of Humus* (1943)

7 I am a woman of a certain age / becoming invisible. / I walk the street unseen.

Suzanne Laberge, "The Metaphysics of Menopause," in Dena Taylor and Amber Coverdale Sumrall, *Women of the Fourteenth Moon* (1991)

8 The change of life is the time when you meet yourself at a crossroads and you decide whether to be honest or not before you die.

Katharine Butler Hathaway, *The Journals and Letters of the Little Locksmith* (1946)

9 We in middle age require adventure.

Amanda Cross, *Sweet Death, Kind Death* (1984)

10 We middle-aged folk have the education of life, truly; we know the multiplication table of anxieties and sorrows, the subtraction table of loss, the division table of responsibility.

Margaret Deland, "Miss Maria," *Old Chester Tales* (1898)

11 The young were always theoretical; only the middle-aged could realize the deadliness of principles.

Dorothy L. Sayers, *Gaudy Night* (1935)

12 Perhaps middle age is, or should be, a period of shedding shells; the shell of ambition, the shell of material accumulations and possessions, the shell of the ego.

Anne Morrow Lindbergh, *Gift From the Sea* (1955)

13 The middle years, caught between children and parents, free of neither: the past stretches back too densely, it is too thickly populated, the future has not yet thinned out.

Margaret Drabble, *The Middle Ground* (1980)

14 In middle age we are apt to reach the horrifying conclusion that all sorrow, all pain, all passionate regret and loss and bitter disillusionment are self-made.

Kathleen Norris, *Hands Full of Living* (1931)

15 Shipwreck in youth is sorrowful enough, but one looks for storms at the spring equinox. Yet it is the September equinox that drowns.

Helen Waddell, *Peter Abelard* (1933)

16 Middle age is when you get in the car and immediately change the radio station.

Patricia Penton Leimbach, *All My Meadows* (1977)

17 Middle age is when you find out where the action is so you can go someplace else.

Patricia Penton Leimbach, *All My Meadows* (1977)

18 "Your only aim in life seems to be to keep out of trouble." "Yes. That is the beginning of middle age."

Gordon Daviot, *The Laughing Woman* (1934)

See also Age.

## ❦ MIDWIFERY

1 I don't need a permit to deliver no babies. . . . I know they cain't stop a daddy from deliverin his own baby. I wouldn't be a bit surprised if I was asked to he'p a daddy.

> Onnie Lee Logan, after Alabama failed to renew midwife licenses, in Onnie Lee Logan, with Katherine Clark, *Motherwit: An Alabama Midwife's Story* (1989)

## ❦ MIGRAINES

2 That no one dies of migraine seems, to someone deep into an attack, an ambiguous blessing.

> Joan Didion, "In Bed" (1968), *The White Album* (1979)

3 I have learned now to live with it, learned when to expect it, how to outwit it, even how to regard it, when it does come, as more friend than lodger. We have reached a certain understanding, my migraine and I.

> Joan Didion, "In Bed" (1968), *The White Album* (1979)

4 Now I am in for it, with one of my unappeasable headaches. Don't talk to me of doctors; it is incurable as a love-fit.

> Fanny Fern, *Fresh Leaves* (1857)

See also Illness, Pain.

## ❦ MILITARISM

5 The Pentagon is the greatest power on earth today. . . . There it sits, a terrible mass of concrete, on our minds, on our hearts, squat on top of our lives. Its power penetrates into every single life. It is in the very air we breathe. The water we drink. Because of its insatiable demands we are drained and we are polluted.

> Josephine W. Johnson, *The Inland Island* (1969)

6 The function of militarism is to kill. It cannot live except through murder.

> Emma Goldman, "Preparedness: The Road to Universal Slaughter," in *Mother Earth* (1915)

7 Any society that is spending a third of its national budget on the military is a militaristic society.

> Polly Mann, in *The St. Paul Pioneer Press* (1993)

8 Militarism consumes the strongest and most productive elements of each nation.

> Emma Goldman, "Preparedness: The Road to Universal Slaughter," in *Mother Earth* (1915)

9 Militarism is the most energy-intensive, entropic activity of humans, since it converts stored energy and materials directly into waste and destruction without any useful intervening fulfillment of basic human needs. Ironically, the net effect of military, as opposed to civilian, expenditures is to increase unemployment *and* inflation.

> Hazel Henderson, *The Politics of the Solar Age* (1981)

10 We should refuse to become partners with a militarism which is still stalking unchecked under the pretense of national needs and of international justice.

> Elisabeth Marbury, *My Crystal Ball* (1923)

11 I am not being facetious when I say that the real enemies in this country are the Pentagon and its pals in big business.

> Bella Abzug, *Bella!* (1972)

12 If we pursue the arms race no other problem will be solved.

> Helen Gahagan Douglas, in Lee Israel, "Helen Gahagan Douglas," *Ms.* (1973)

13 No one can claim to be Christian who gives money for the building of warships and arsenals.

> Belva Lockwood, speech (1886)

14 The pathos of it all is that the America which is to be protected by a huge military force is not the America of the people, but that of the privileged class.

> Emma Goldman, "Preparedness: The Road to Universal Slaughter," in *Mother Earth* (1915)

15 Militarism . . . is one of the chief bulwarks of capitalism, and the day that militarism is undermined, capitalism will fail.

> Helen Keller, *The Story of My Life* (1902)

16 "Readiness," far from assuring peace, has at all times and in all countries been instrumental in precipitating armed conflicts.

> Emma Goldman, *Living My Life* (1931)

17 The insight that peace is the end of war, and that therefore a war is the preparation for peace, is at least as old as Aristotle, and the pretense that the aim of an armament race is to guard the peace is

even older, namely as old as the discovery of propaganda lies.

Hannah Arendt, *On Revolution* (1963)

1 You cannot build up a standing army and then throw it back into a box like tin soldiers. Armies equipped to the teeth with weapons, with highly developed instruments of murder and backed by their military interests, have their own dynamic functions.

Emma Goldman, "Preparedness: The Road to Universal Slaughter," in *Mother Earth* (1915)

2 The contention that a standing army and navy is the best security of peace is about as logical as the claim that the most peaceful citizen is he who goes about heavily armed.

Emma Goldman, "Patriotism," *Anarchism* (1910)

3 Those who prepare for war get it.

Winifred Holtby, in Vera Brittain, *Testament of Friendship* (1940)

See also Nuclear Weapons, War.

# § MIND

4 The mind, of course, is just what the brain does for a living.

Sharon Begley, in *Newsweek* (1995)

5 If a mind is just a few pounds of blood, dream, and electric, how does it manage to contemplate itself, worry about its soul, do time-and-motion studies, admire the shy hooves of a goat, know that it will die, enjoy all the grand and lesser mayhems of the heart?

Diane Ackerman, *The Moon by Whale Light* (1991)

6 The mind is an astonishing, long-living, erotic thing.

Grace Paley, *Enormous Changes at the Last Minute* (1974)

7 The mind is like a richly woven tapestry in which the colors are distilled from the experiences of the senses, and the design drawn from the convolutions of the intellect.

Carson McCullers, *Reflections in a Golden Eye* (1941)

8 Wit is the lightning of the mind, reason the sunshine, and reflection the moonlight.

Countess of Blessington, *Desultory Thoughts and Reflections* (1839)

9 It is in our minds that we live much of our life.

Ivy Compton-Burnett, *A Heritage and Its History* (1959)

10 The mind's pleasures are made to calm the tempests of the heart.

Madame de Staël, preface to 1814 edition, *Letters on Rousseau* (1788)

11 Such a cultivated mind doesn't really attract me. . . . No, no, the mind I love must still have wild places, a tangled orchard where dark damsons drop in the heavy grass, an overgrown little wood, the chance of a snake or two (real snakes), a pool that nobody's fathomed the depth of—and paths threaded with those little flowers planted by the mind.

Katherine Mansfield (1920), *Journal of Katherine Mansfield* (1927)

12 Sparks electric only strike / On souls electrical alike; / The flash of intellect expires, / Unless it meet congenial fires.

Hannah More, "The Bas Bleu; or Conversation" (1782), *The Works of Hannah More*, vol. 1 (1841)

13 It's as if tendencies that seem most deeply rooted in our minds, most private and singular, have come in as spores on the prevailing wind, looking for any likely place to land, any welcome.

Alice Munro, *Friend of My Youth* (1990)

14 The different faculties [of the mind] divide themselves in the main into two classifications, which I call *hot* (the creative) and *cold* (the critical).

Mary O'Hara, *Novel-in-the-Making* (1954)

15 The intellect . . . often, alas, acts the cannibal among the other faculties so that often, where the Mind is biggest, the Heart, the Senses, Magnanimity, Charity, Tolerance, Kindliness, and the rest of them scarcely have room to breathe.

Virginia Woolf, *Orlando* (1928)

16 It was seldom an idea found entrance into his head, and when once there it was no easy matter to dislodge it; it became not the mere furniture of the head, to be turned or changed at will, but seemed actually to become a part of the head itself, which

it required a sort of mental scalping or trepanning to remove.

Susan Ferrier, *The Inheritance*, vol. 1 (1824)

1  When the mind is most empty / It is most full.

Susan Fromberg Schaeffer, "Fortune Cookies," *Granite Lady* (1974)

2  A closed mind is a dying mind.

Edna Ferber, radio broadcast (1947)

3  His mind had been receptive up to a certain age, and then had snapped shut on what it possessed, like a replete crustacean never reached by another high tide.

Edith Wharton, "The Spark," *Old New York* (1924)

4  Some minds remain open long enough for the truth not only to enter but to pass on through by way of a ready exit without pausing anywhere along the route.

Elizabeth Kenny, with Martha Ostenso, *And They Shall Walk* (1943)

5  The mind is more vulnerable than the stomach, because it can be poisoned without feeling immediate pain.

Helen MacInnes, *Assignment in Brittany* (1942)

6  The mind has no sex.

George Sand (1848), in Raphaël Ledos de Beaufort, ed., *Letters of George Sand*, vol. 2 (1886)

7  She rode her mind like a bitted horse.

Storm Jameson, *The Clash* (1922)

8  All I can say about my mind is that, like a fire carefully laid by a good housemaid, it is one that any match will light.

Margot Asquith, *More or Less About Myself* (1934)

9  Mrs. Benson and I certainly did not belong in the same cage, but so fascinating was her mind that I could have groped about in it for ever.

Ethel Smyth (1893), *As Time Went On. . .* (1936)

10  His mind was an intricate, multigeared machine, or perhaps some little animal with skittery paws.

Anne Tyler, *Searching for Caleb* (1975)

11  Her mind traveled crooked streets and aimless goat paths, arriving sometimes at profundity, other times at the revelations of a three-year-old.

Toni Morrison, *Song of Solomon* (1977)

12  No point in asking Greenfield what he was up to; he had pulled up his mental drawbridge and there was no way over the moat.

Lucille Kallen, *The Tanglewood Murder* (1980)

13  The original owner had highlighted the entire book—literally. Every line on every page had been drawn through with a bright green Magic Marker. It was a terrifying example of a mind that had lost all power of discrimination.

Florence King, *Reflections in a Jaundiced Eye* (1989)

14  His mind is furnished as hotels are, with everything for occasional and transient use.

George Eliot, *Impressions of Theophrastus Such* (1879)

15  You're a perfect child, a stubborn child! Your mind's in pigtails, like your hair.

Mary Roberts Rinehart, "The Family Friend," *Affinities* (1920)

16  I was an excellent student until ten, and then my mind began to wander.

Grace Paley, in Harriet Shapiro, "Art Is on the Side of the Underdog," *Ms.* (1974)

17  The mind's cross-indexing puts the best librarian to shame.

Sharon Begley et al., "Memory," in *Newsweek* (1986)

18  The mind can store an estimated 100 trillion bits of information—compared with which a computer's mere billions are virtually amnesiac.

Sharon Begley et al., "Memory," in *Newsweek* (1986)

19  There was something she had meant to remember or to think about that was troubling her aged mind like a rat in a wall.

Jean Stafford, "The Hope Chest," *The Collected Stories of Jean Stafford* (1969)

20  I finally reconciled myself to the fact that she had partly lost her reason. . . . The death of the mind is infinitely more terrible than the death of the body and I mourned my mother that day as I was never to mourn afterwards.

Dervla Murphy, *Wheels Within Wheels* (1979)

See also Alzheimer's, Brain, Head and Heart, Intelligence, Thinking, Thoughts, The Unconscious.

## ❦ MINING

1 The life of the miner is the same wherever coal is dug and capital flies its black flag.
   Mother Jones, in Mary Field Parton, *The Autobiography of Mother Jones* (1925)

2 The mining industry might make wealth and power for a few men and women, but the many would always be smashed and battered beneath its giant treads.
   Katharine Susannah Prichard, *The Roaring Nineties* (1946)

See also Labor.

## ❦ MINORITIES

3 It frequently happens that when the dominant culture loses a vision or actively suppresses it, this lost knowledge arises again among those excluded from that culture.
   Kim Chernin, *The Obsession* (1981)

4 Every effort for progress, for enlightenment, for science, for religious, political, and economic liberty, emanates from the minority, and not from the mass.
   Emma Goldman, "Minorities Versus Majorities," *Anarchism* (1910)

5 Being a minority in both caste and class, we moved about anyway on the hem of life, struggling to consolidate our weaknesses and hang on, or to creep singly up into the major folds of the garment.
   Toni Morrison, *The Bluest Eye* (1970)

6 It is the curse of minorities in this power-worshiping world that either from fear or from an uncertain policy of expedience they distrust their own standards and hesitate to give voice to their deeper convictions, submitting supinely to estimates and characterizations of themselves as handed down by a not unprejudiced dominant majority.
   Anna Julia Cooper, *A Voice From the South* (1892)

7 Do you see any majority, anywhere, in this imperfect and irreligious world, admitting that the minority is precious?
   Katharine Fullerton Gerould, *Modes and Morals* (1920)

See also Bigotry, Discrimination, Oppression, Prejudice, Racism, Sexism.

## ❦ MIRACLES

8 Miracles come after a lot of hard work.
   Sue Bender, *Plain and Simple* (1989)

9 One of the pleasantest things those of us who write or paint do is to have the daily miracle. It does come.
   Gertrude Stein, *Paris France* (1940)

10 Every life holds that which only a miracle can cure. To prove that there have never been, that there can never be, miracles does not alter the matter. So long as there is something hoped for,—that does not come in the legitimate channel of possible events,—just so long will the miracle be prayed for.
   Grace King, "The Miracle Chapel," *Balcony Stories* (1892)

11 Miracles are God's *coups d'état.*
   Anne-Sophie Swetchine, in Count de Falloux, ed., *The Writings of Madame Swetchine* (1869)

12 It was a miracle; it was all a miracle: and one ought to have known, from the sufferings of saints, that miracles are horror.
   Nadine Gordimer, *July's People* (1981)

13 There's nothing harder to stop than somebody who wants to believe a miracle.
   Leslie Ford, *Washington Whispers Murder* (1952)

See also Magic, Wonder.

## ❦ MIRRORS

14 No mirror keeps its glances.
   Alice Meynell, "Your Own Fair Youth," *Preludes* (1875)

15 My mirror is the cemetery of smiles.
   Tada Chimako, "Mirror," in Aliki Barnstone and Willis Barnstone, eds., *A Book of Women Poets From Antiquity to Now* (1980)

16 She went over to the mirror . . . glancing at herself sidelong, as women do who think they have lost their beauty; repudiating a complete reflection.
   Rosamond Lehmann, *The Ballad and the Source* (1945)

17 My dressing mirror is a humpbacked cat. / Continuously my image changes.
   Jung Tzu, "My Dressing Mirror Is a Humpbacked Cat," in Kenneth Rexroth and Ling Chung, eds., *The Orchid Boat* (1972)

1 I often think if mirrors could give up their dead how wonderful it would be.

> Bessie Parkes Belloc, in Marie Belloc Lowndes, *"I, Too, Have Lived in Arcadia"* (1942)

2 What dynamite we handle when we lift a mirror or bend towards one! I seldom do.

> Elizabeth Coatsworth, *Personal Geography* (1976)

3 It is eleven years since I have seen my figure in a glass. The last reflection I saw there was so disagreeable, I resolved to spare myself such mortifications for the future.

> Lady Mary Wortley Montagu (1757), in Robert Halsband, ed., *The Complete Letters of Lady Mary Wortley Montagu* (1965)

## ❧ MISANTHROPY

4 My object is to live in a place that does not call itself "the community with a heart." I want one of those godforsaken towns where all the young people leave and the rest sit on the porch with a rifle across their knees.

> Florence King, *With Charity Toward None* (1992)

5 If you ever meet someone who cannot understand why solitary confinement is considered punishment, you have met a misanthrope.

> Florence King, *With Charity Toward None* (1992)

6 She usually liked everybody most when they weren't there.

> Elizabeth von Arnim, *The Enchanted April* (1922)

7 I do not want people to be very agreeable, as it saves me the trouble of liking them a great deal.

> Jane Austen, to her sister Cassandra (1798), in R.W. Chapman, ed., *Jane Austen's Letters*, vol. 1 (1932)

8 If people were not wicked I should not mind their being stupid; but, to our misfortune, they are both.

> George Sand (1831), in Raphaël Ledos de Beaufort, ed., *Letters of George Sand*, vol. 1 (1886)

9 As is the case of many misanthropes, his disdain for people led him into a profession designed to serve them.

> Toni Morrison, *The Bluest Eye* (1970)

10 An examination of misanthropy has value for Americans who do not necessarily hate everybody, but are tired of compulsory gregariousness, fevered friendliness, we-never-close compassion, goo-goo humanitarianism, sensitivity that never sleeps, and politicians paralyzed by a hunger to be loved.

> Florence King, *With Charity Toward None* (1992)

11 Misanthropy is a realistic attitude toward human nature that falls short of the incontinent emotional dependency expressed by Barbra Streisand's anthem to insecurity, "Peepul who need peepul are the luckiest peepul in the world."

> Florence King, *With Charity Toward None* (1992)

See also Distrust, Hate.

## ❧ MISCARRIAGE

12 A miscarriage is a natural and common event. All told, probably more women have lost a child from this world than haven't. Most don't mention it, and they go on from day to day as if it hadn't happened, and so people imagine that a woman in this situation never really knew or loved what she had. But ask her sometime: how old would your child be now? And she'll know.

> Barbara Kingsolver, *Animal Dreams* (1990)

## ❧ MISCHIEF

13 Between frivolity and intentional mischief there is little difference, none in the results.

> Ilka Chase, *I Love Miss Tilli Bean* (1946)

14 I can sometimes resist temptation, but never mischief.

> Joyce Rebeta-Burditt, *The Cracker Factory* (1977)

## ❧ MISERLINESS

15 "It is impossible to help all," says the miser, and—helps none.

> Marie von Ebner-Eschenbach, *Aphorisms* (1893)

16 Miserliness is the one vice that grows stronger with increasing years. It yields its sordid pleasures to the end.

> Agnes Repplier, *In Pursuit of Laughter* (1936)

1 Miserliness is a capital quality to run in families; it's the safe side for madness to dip on.

George Eliot, *Middlemarch* (1871)

2 Meanness inherits a set of silverware and keeps it in the bank. Economy uses it only on important occasions, for fear of loss. Thrift sets the table with it every night for pure pleasure, but counts the butter spreaders before they are put away.

Phyllis McGinley, *Sixpence in Her Shoe* (1964)

3 He was as tight as the paper on the wall.

Mary Roberts Rinehart, *Miss Pinkerton* (1932)

4 I never knew a man who got so hurt in his pocketbook.

Dorothy West, *The Living Is Easy* (1948)

5 You remind me of people who bring along a little box of cakes and leave it in the hall, saying to themselves: "There'll be plenty of time to produce these later," and then pick them up again when they go.

Colette, *The Last of Cheri* (1926)

6 It was said of Miss Letitia that when money came into her possession it went out of circulation.

Mary Roberts Rinehart, *The Window at the White Cat* (1910)

See also Avarice, Greed, Selfishness, Thrift.

## § MISERY

7 Youth is a blunder, manhood a struggle, old age is one long regret!

Mary Boykin Chesnut (1862), *A Diary From Dixie* (1905)

8 If you feel depressed you shouldn't go out on the street because it will show on your face and you'll give it to others. Misery is a communicable disease.

Martha Graham, in John Heilpern, "The Amazing Martha," *The Observer Magazine* (1979)

9 Real misery cuts off all paths to itself.

Iris Murdoch, *The Black Prince* (1973)

10 There is a stage in any misery when the victim begins to find a deep satisfaction in it.

Storm Jameson, *That Was Yesterday* (1932)

11 Take away the miseries and you take away some folks' reason for living. Their conversation piece anyway.

Toni Cade Bambara, *The Salt Eaters* (1980)

See also Grief, Misfortune, Sorrow, Suffering, Unhappiness.

## § MISFORTUNE

12 Ah! the difference, whether the hearse stands before one's own door, or one's neighbor's.

Fanny Fern, *Folly As It Flies* (1868)

13 Misfortune, and recited misfortune in especial, may be prolonged to that point where it ceases to excite pity and arouses only irritation.

Dorothy Parker, "No More Fun," in *The New Yorker* (1931)

14 Whatever misfortune came, he was always able to meet it by refusing to recognize it for what it was.

Martha Ostenso, *The Waters Under the Earth* (1930)

15 Those who are happy and successful themselves are too apt to make light of the misfortunes of others.

Elizabeth Gaskell, *North and South* (1854)

16 When a man has calamity upon calamity the world generally concludes that he must be a very wicked man to deserve them. Perhaps the world is right; but it is also just possible that the world . . . may be wrong.

Amelia E. Barr, *Jan Vedder's Wife* (1885)

17 This is how Americans think. You believe that if something terrible happens to someone, they must have deserved it.

Barbara Kingsolver, *The Bean Trees* (1989)

18 If you think that you are where you are just because you worked hard, it is easy to become self-righteous and make classist moral judgments about others.

Coletta Reid and Charlotte Bunch, *Class and Feminism* (1979)

19 Many things would be changed for Americans if they would only admit that there is ill-luck in this world and that misfortune is not *a priori* a crime.

Simone de Beauvoir, *America Day by Day* (1948)

See also Adversity, Disaster, Grief, Misery, Poverty, Sorrow, Tragedy, Trouble, Unhappiness.

## ⸙ MISQUOTATIONS

1 Oh, my son's my son till he gets him a wife, / But my daughter's my daughter all her life.

> Dinah Maria Mulock Craik (Craik was born in 1826; this proverb appeared in Ray's *English Proverbs* in 1670 and in Fuller's *Gnomologia* in 1732.)

2 The role of the retired person is no longer to possess one.

> Simone de Beauvoir (The origin of this misattribution is probably a misreading of de Beauvoir's *Coming of Age*, p. 266: "'The role of the retired person,' says Burgess, 'is no longer to possess one.'")

3 The Jews are among the aristocracy of every land— if a literature is called rich in the possession of a few classic tragedies, what shall we say to a National Tragedy lasting for fifteen hundred years, in which the poets and actors were also the heroes.

> George Eliot (Eliot herself cites Leopold Zunz for this quotation, which serves as the epigraph to chapter 42 of *Daniel Deronda*.)

4 When shall we live if not now?

> M.F.K. Fisher (This misattribution is probably due to a misreading of p. 40 of *The Art of Eating*: "'When shall we live, if not now?' asked Seneca before a table laid for his pleasure and his friends'.")

5 If I can't dance I don't want to be in your revolution. Or: It's not my revolution if I can't dance. Or: If I can't dance to it, it's not my revolution.

> Emma Goldman (According to Goldman biographer Alix Kates Shulman, "Dances With Feminists," *The Women's Review of Books*, December 1991, p. 13, Emma Goldman never said it. In her 1931 autobiography, *Living My Life*, p. 56, Goldman describes being accused of frivolity at a dance—a passage that Shulman recommended to an anarchist group making Goldman T-shirts for a 1973 New York City festival celebrating the end of the Vietnam War. The T-shirts duly appeared, but with the now-famous abridgement and despite the fact that the word "revolution" never appeared in the Goldman passage. The closest Goldman came to expressing the idea was "I was tired of having the Cause constantly thrown into my face. I did not believe that a Cause which stood for a beautiful ideal, for anarchism, for release and freedom from conventions and prejudice, should demand the denial of life and joy. I insisted that our Cause could not expect me to become a nun and that the movement should not be turned into a cloister. If it meant that, I did not want it.")

6 I do wish he [Calvin Coolidge] did not look as if he had been weaned on a pickle.

> Alice Roosevelt Longworth (On p. 337 of her 1933 book *Crowded Hours*, Longworth explains that her doctor told her she'd enjoy a remark just made by another patient of his. She did enjoy it and repeated it to friends. It became associated with her although she always insisted it wasn't hers.)

7 In the midst of life we are in debt.
God gives us our relatives—thank God we can choose our friends.
O wad some power the giftie gie us / to see some people before they see us.

> Ethel Watts Mumford (In 1902, Ethel Watts Mumford, Oliver Herford, and Addison Mizner published *The Complete Cynic*. Each of them contributed one-liners, for which they indicated authorship by means of initials. All three of these lines are actually Mizner's.)

8 If you bring forth what is within you, what you bring forth will save you. If you do not bring forth what is within you, what you do not bring forth will destroy you.

> Elaine Pagels (Although generally attributed correctly to Jesus Christ, these words have also been attributed incorrectly to Elaine Pagels, who quoted them as part of the Gospel of Thomas in her 1979 book, *The Gnostic Gospels*.)

9 Some say life is the thing, but I prefer reading.

> Ruth Rendell (In her 1977 book, *A Judgement in Stone*, Rendell indicates this line is someone else's, but it is still often attributed to her. Logan Pearsall Smith said it in his 1931 *Afterthoughts*.)

10 When two people love each other, they don't look at each other, they look in the same direction.

> Ginger Rogers (Although this has been attributed to Rogers, she always correctly credited it to Antoine de Saint Exupéry's *Wind, Sand, and Stars*, as she does on p. 37 of *Ginger: My Story*.)

11 It's better to light a candle than to curse the darkness.

> Eleanor Roosevelt (More familiarly known as the motto for The Christophers, this expression was originally a Chinese proverb, according to Ralph Keyes, *Nice Guys Finish Seventh*, p. 76. It's not clear how it became associated with Roosevelt, although in the third volume of *My Day*, p. 83, she says, "Even a candle is better than no light at all.")

12 The trouble with the rat race is that even if you win, you're still a rat.

> Lily Tomlin (Although this is always attributed to Tomlin, she says the line was written by Jane Wagner. In addition, the Reverend William Sloane Coffin said, "Even if you win the rat-race, you're still a rat" in the 1950s or 1960s when he was chaplain either at Williams College or at Yale University. As far as he knows, he originated it. See Margaret Halsey's similar remark under "Competition.")

1 Ginger Rogers did everything that Fred Astaire did. She just did it backwards and in high heels.

> Linda Ellerbee, Ann Richards, or Faith Whittlesey (Widely quoted and most often attributed to Ann Richards, although she has always disclaimed authorship, this remark apparently first appeared in a comic strip by Bob Thaves. In *Ginger: My Story*, p. 137, Ginger Rogers says: "A friend sent me a cartoon called 'Frank 'n Ernest' from a LA newspaper. It showed Fred on a sandwich board announcing a 'Fred Astaire Festival.' A woman was standing near the sandwich board, talking to Frank and Ernest. The balloon coming from her mouth said, 'Sure he was great, but don't forget Ginger Rogers did everything he did backwards . . . and in high heels!'" The cartoon was copyrighted 1982.)

2 A day away from Tallulah is like a month in the country.

> Ilka Chase or Dorothy Parker; also attributed to Goodman Ace, George S. Kaufman, Alexander Woollcott, and Robert Benchley. (In her autobiography, Tallulah Bankhead says, "Howard Dietz once remarked, 'A day away from Tallulah is like a month in the country.' Ever since he's enjoyed the reputation of a great wit.")

## ❧ MISTAKES

3 Just because you *made* a mistake doesn't mean you *are* a mistake.

> Georgette Mosbacher, *Feminine Force* (1993)

4 If you have to make mistakes, make them good and big, don't be middling in anything if you can help it.

> Hildegard Knef, *The Verdict* (1975)

5 If I had to live my life again I'd make all the same mistakes—only sooner.

> Tallulah Bankhead, in John Robert Colombo, *Popcorn in Paradise* (1979)

6 About mistakes it's funny. You got to make your own; and not only that, if you try to keep people from making theirs they get mad.

> Edna Ferber, *So Big* (1924)

7 Men don't make different mistakes at different periods of their lives. They make the same mistake over and over again and they pay a bigger and bigger price for it.

> Vicki Baum, *Written on Water* (1956)

8 Every great mistake has a halfway moment, a split second when it can be recalled and perhaps remedied.

> Pearl S. Buck, *What America Means to Me* (1943)

9 There's nothing final about a mistake, except its being taken as final.

> Phyllis Bottome, "The Plain Case," *Strange Fruit* (1928)

10 Mistakes are a fact of life / It is the response to error that counts.

> Nikki Giovanni, "Of Liberation," *Black Judgement* (1968)

11 If we do not always see our own mistakes and omissions we can always see those of our neighbors.

> Kathleen Norris, *Hands Full of Living* (1931)

See also Error, Flaws, Sin.

## ❧ MODELING

12 Models are supposed to be dumb. Sometimes it helps to be as numb and dumb as I was at the beginning. If you knew what was really going on, you might be too embarrassed to breathe.

> Carolyn Kenmore, *Mannequin* (1969)

## ❧ MODERATION

13 I have changed my ministers, but I have not changed my measures; I am still for moderation and will govern by it.

> Queen Anne, speech (1711)

See also Compromise, Neutrality.

## ❧ MODERNITY

14 The past is discredited because it is not modern. . . . But every one has, in his day, been modern. And surely even modernity is a poor thing beside immortality. Since we must all die, is it not perhaps better to be a dead lion than a living dog?

> Katharine Fullerton Gerould, *Modes and Morals* (1920)

## ❧ MODESTY

1 Modesty is a valuable merit . . . in people who have no other, and the appearance of it is extremely useful to those who have.

Ada Leverson, *The Limit* (1911)

2 At heart a truly modest man, he had nevertheless the modest man's pride in his modesty in the face of achievement.

Pearl S. Buck, *God's Men* (1951)

3 I have often wished I had time to cultivate modesty. . . . But I am too busy thinking about myself.

Edith Sitwell, in *The Observer* (1950)

See also Humility.

## ❧ MONDAY

4 I should think you could be gladder on Monday mornin' than any other day in the week, because 'twould be a whole *week* before you'd have another one!

Eleanor H. Porter, *Pollyanna* (1912)

## ❧ MONEY

5 Anyone pretending he has no interest in money is either a fool or a knave.

Leslie Ford, *Invitation to Murder* (1954)

6 Money is always dull, except when you haven't got any, and then it's terrifying.

Sheila Bishop, *The House With Two Faces* (1960)

7 The only way not to think about money is to have a great deal of it.

Edith Wharton, *The House of Mirth* (1905)

8 Those who never think of money need a great deal of it.

Agatha Christie, "The Second Gong," *Witness for the Prosecution* (1948)

9 "You think money the universal solvent?" "I think the lack of it the universal *in*solvent."

Julie M. Lippmann, *Martha By-the-Day* (1912)

10 I must say I hate money, but it's the lack of it I hate most.

Katherine Mansfield, in Antony Alpers, *Katherine Mansfield* (1954)

11 I believe only in money, not in love or tenderness. Love and tenderness meant only pain and suffering and defeat. I would not let it ruin me as it ruined others! I would speak only with money, hard money.

Agnes Smedley, *Daughter of Earth* (1929)

12 He knew now, more than ever, that money was everything, the wall that stood between all he loathed and all he wanted.

Willa Cather, "Paul's Case," *Youth and the Bright Medusa* (1920)

13 People who think money can do anything may very well be suspected of doing anything for money.

Mary Pettibone Poole, *A Glass Eye at a Keyhole* (1938)

14 Some people think they are worth a lot of money just because they have it.

Fannie Hurst (1952), in Joseph L. Baron, *A Treasury of Jewish Quotations* (1956)

15 There are a handful of people whom money won't spoil, and we all count ourselves among them.

Mignon McLaughlin, *The Second Neurotic's Notebook* (1966)

16 Money may not be your best friend, but it's the quickest to act, and seems to be favorably recognized in more places than most friends are.

Myrtle Reed, *Master of the Vineyard* (1910)

17 Money is everything in this world to some people, and more than the next to other poor souls.

Augusta J. Evans, *Beulah* (1859)

18 What I know about money, I learned the hard way—by having had it.

Margaret Halsey, *The Folks at Home* (1952)

19 To me, money is alive. It is almost human. If you treat it with real sympathy and kindness and consideration, it will be a good servant and work hard for you, and stay with you and take care of you. If you treat it arrogantly and contemptuously, as if it were not human, as if it were only a slave and could work without limit, it will turn on you with a great revenge and leave you to look after yourself alone.

Katharine Butler Hathaway (1932), *Journals and Letters of the Little Locksmith* (1946)

1 Money's queer. It goes where it's wanted.
Agatha Christie, *Endless Night* (1968)

2 As a cousin of mine once said about money, money is always there but the pockets change; it is not in the same pockets after a change, and that is all there is to say about money.
Gertrude Stein, in Charles P. Curtis, Jr. and Ferris Greenslet, *The Practical Cogitator* (1945)

3 No one would remember the Good Samaritan if he'd only had good intentions. He had money as well.
Margaret Thatcher, in *The London Times* (1986)

4 Money speaks sense in a language all nations understand.
Aphra Behn, *The Rover*, part 2 (1681)

5 To money: The finest linguist in the world.
Minna Thomas Antrim, *Book of Toasts* (1902)

6 The most powerful book in the world . . . is the check-book.
Mrs. Alec-Tweedie, *Behind the Footlights* (1904)

7 We can tell our values by looking at our checkbook stubs.
Gloria Steinem, speech (1978)

8 For the size of it, a check book is about the greatest convenience I know of.
Myrtle Reed, *Master of the Vineyard* (1910)

9 The two most beautiful words in the English language are "check enclosed."
Dorothy Parker, in *The New York Herald Tribune* (1932)

10 More and more I am certain that the only difference between man and animals is that men can count and animals cannot and if they count they mostly do count money.
Gertrude Stein, *Everybody's Autobiography* (1937)

11 Money is the barometer of a society's virtue.
Ayn Rand, *Atlas Shrugged* (1957)

12 The dollar sign is the only sign in which the modern man appears to have any real faith.
Helen Rowland, *Reflections of a Bachelor Girl* (1909)

13 The war [World War II], which destroyed so much of everything, was also constructive, in a way. It established clearly the cold, and finally unhypocrit- ical fact that the most important thing on earth to men today is money.
Janet Flanner ("Genêt"), *Paris Journal 1944-1965* (1965)

14 In America, money takes the place of God.
Anzia Yezierska, *Red Ribbon on a White Horse* (1950)

15 This is a speculating and selfish age; and to think "money will answer all things," is too much the characteristic of Americans.
Mrs. Sarah J. Hale, *Traits of American Life* (1835)

16 What I have here is a complete indictment of our present-day society, our whole world. What's wrong with it is money, honey, money.
Margaret Walker, in Claudia Tate, ed., *Black Women Writers at Work* (1983)

17 I have a prejudice against people with money. I have known so many, and none have escaped the corruption of power. In this I am a purist. I love people motivated by love and not by power. If you have money and power, and are motivated by love, you give it all away.
Anaïs Nin (1945), *The Diary of Anaïs Nin*, vol. 4 (1971)

18 Money destroys human roots wherever it is able to penetrate, by turning desire for gain into the sole motive. It easily manages to outweigh all other mo- tives, because the effort it demands of the mind is so very much less. Nothing is *so* clear *and so* simple as a row of figures.
Simone Weil, *The Need for Roots* (1949)

19 Money-making is like a god possessing a priest. He never will leave you, until he has occupied you, wholly changed the order of your being, and seared you through and up and down. Then only would he eventually leave you, but nothing of you except an exhausted wreck, lying prone and wondering who are you.
Ama Ata Aidoo, *Anowa* (1970)

20 So you think that money is the root of all evil? Have you ever asked what is the root of money?
Ayn Rand, *Atlas Shrugged* (1957)

21 Money can be more of a barrier between people than language or race or religion.
Vera Caspary, *A Chosen Sparrow* (1964)

22 They are the kind of people who are embarrassed by money, a dead middle-class giveaway. Poor peo-

ple are not embarrassed by money and are contemptuous of those who are.

Rosellen Brown, *Civil Wars* (1984)

1 Being moderate with oneself and generous with others; this is what is meant by having a just relationship with money, by being free as far as money is concerned.

Natalia Ginzburg, *The Little Virtues* (1962)

2 Though money is a fine servant, as a god, it does seem to develop all the evil qualities of the slave seated between the cherubim.

J.E. Buckrose, "The Sacred Million," *What I Have Gathered* (1923)

3 If money had been the way to save the world, Christ Himself would have been rich.

Phyllis Bottome, "Brother Leo," *Innocence and Experience* (1934)

4 Money does not corrupt people. What corrupts people is lack of affection. . . . Money is simply the bandage which wounded people put over their wounds.

Margaret Halsey, *The Folks at Home* (1952)

5 Money isn't everything, your health is the other ten per cent.

Lillian Day, *Kiss and Tell* (1931)

6 Friends and good manners will carry you where money won't go.

Margaret Walker, *Jubilee* (1966)

7 The best way to attract money, she had discovered, was to give the appearance of having it.

Gail Sheehy, *Hustling* (1973)

8 It is true that money attracts; but much money repels.

Cynthia Ozick, *Trust* (1966)

9 Americans want action for their money. They are fascinated by its self-reproducing qualities.

Paula Nelson, *The Joy of Money* (1975)

10 Every time a man expects, as he says, his money to work for him, he is expecting other people to work for him.

Dorothy L. Sayers, "The Other Six Deadly Sins," *Creed or Chaos?* (1949)

11 Regiments are joining in the Master Charge / That's blowing up the G.N.P. / Hardly anybody now remains at large / Who lacks creditability.

Felicia Lamport, "Wild Cards," *Light Metres* (1982)

12 Money that may never be spent is nothing but a miser's toy. Saving as an exercise in self-denial is an invalid goal, a sick use of money.

Catherine Crook de Camp, *The Money Tree* (1972)

13 Money is of value for what it buys, and in love it buys time, place, intimacy, comfort, and a private corner alone.

Mae West, *Goodness Had Nothing to Do With It!* (1959)

14 Money creates taste.

Jenny Holzer, *Truisms* (1991)

15 There are many to whom money has no personal appeal, but who can be tempted by the power it confers.

Agatha Christie, *Crooked House* (1949)

16 There are only two ways to make a lot [of money] while you're young: One is to entertain the public; and the other is to cheat it.

Kathleen Winsor, *Star Money* (1950)

17 I make money using my brains and lose money listening to my heart. But in the long run my books balance pretty well.

Kate Seredy, *The Singing Tree* (1939)

18 Money demands that you sell, not your weakness to men's stupidity, but your talent to their reason.

Ayn Rand, *Atlas Shrugged* (1957)

19 Money can be translated into the beauty of living, a support in misfortune, an education, or future security. It also can be translated into a source of bitterness.

Sylvia Porter, *Sylvia Porter's Money Book* (1975)

20 Where there is money, there is fighting.

Marian Anderson, in Kosti Vehanen, *Marian Anderson* (1941)

21 As soon as you bring up money, I notice, conversation gets sociological, then political, then moral.

Jane Smiley, *Good Will* (1989)

22 Money is only money, beans tonight and steak tomorrow. So long as you can look yourself in the eye.

Meridel Le Sueur, *Crusaders* (1955)

1 Does anybody who gave up smoking to save a pound a week *have* a pound at the end of the week? Not on your life.

> Katharine Whitehorn, *Roundabout* (1962)

2 Need of money, dear.

> Dorothy Parker, when asked what was the inspiration for most of her work, in Malcolm Cowley, ed., *Writers at Work* (1958)

3 Indeed, I thought, slipping the silver into my purse, it is remarkable, remembering the bitterness of those days, what a change of temper a fixed income will bring about.

> Virginia Woolf, *A Room of One's Own* (1929)

4 Money dignifies what is frivolous if unpaid for.

> Virginia Woolf, *A Room of One's Own* (1929)

5 In youth money is a convenience, an aid to pleasure. In age it is an absolute necessity, for when we are old we have to buy even consideration and politeness from those about us.

> Dorothy Dix, *Dorothy Dix—Her Book* (1926)

6 I have enough money to last me the rest of my life, unless I buy something.

> Anonymous woman, quoted by Hanna Holborn Gray, in *The Christian Science Monitor* (1986)

7 I can't take it with me I know / But will it last until I go?

> Martha F. Newmeyer, "Simultaneous Departure," in Frank S. Pepper, *The Wit and Wisdom of the 20th Century* (1987)

8 Gone today, here tomorrow.

> Catherine Crook de Camp, on retirement savings, *The Money Tree* (1972)

See also Bargains, Business, Consumerism, Debts, Gold, The Poor, Profit, The Rich, The Rich and the Poor, Taxes, Wealth.

## ⚘ MONOGAMY

9 Monogamy is contrary to nature but necessary for the greater social good.

> Rita Mae Brown, *Starting From Scratch* (1988)

10 Lifelong monogamy is a maniacal idea.

> Germaine Greer, *The Female Eunuch* (1970)

See also Faithfulness.

## ⚘ MOON

11 The moon is at her crystal window / Spinning and weaving.

> Hilda Conkling, "Moon in October," *Shoes of the Wind* (1922)

12 The moon / waning or waxing / a sliver set / like a cradle / a thin suggestion, / the lit edge / of porcelain.

> Yvette Nelson, *We'll Come When It Rains* (1982)

13 Moon, worn thin to the width of a quill, / In the dawn clouds flying, / How good to go, light into light, and still / Giving light, dying.

> Sara Teasdale, "Moon's Ending," *Strange Victory* (1933)

14 Stars veil their beauty soon / Beside the glorious moon, / When her full silver light / Doth make the whole earth bright.

> Sappho (6th cent. B.C.), in C.R. Haines, ed., *Sappho: The Poems and Fragments* (1926)

15 The moon came up, yellow as a prairie cowslip.

> Bess Streeter Aldrich, *Song of Years* (1939)

16 The moon / Will develop in the sky / Like a pearl.

> Susan Fromberg Schaeffer, "Sleeping in the Country," *Granite Lady* (1974)

17 The moon develops the imagination, as chemicals develop photographic images.

> Sheila Ballantyne, *Norma Jean the Termite Queen* (1975)

18 The moon is a fish that swims underwater in the daytime.

> Barbara Brooks, "Summer in Sydney," *Leaving Queensland* (1983)

19 I love old moons. There is something humanized about them; they are dulled a little, and rich in color. One can stare all night at an old moon.

> Anne Bosworth Greene, *The Lone Winter* (1923)

20 The moon had the old moon in her arms.

> Dorothy Wordsworth (1802), in William Knight, ed., *Journals of Dorothy Wordsworth*, vol. 1 (1897)

21 Moonlight lined the windowsills like a fall of snow.

> Beryl Bainbridge, *Another Part of the Wood* (1968)

22 You Moon! Have you done something wrong in heaven, / That God has hidden your face?

> Jean Ingelow, "Seven Times One," *Songs of Seven* (1885)

1 I consulted the moon / like a crystal ball.

Diane Ackerman, *The Planets* (1976)

2 The moon lives in all the alone places / all alone.

Paula Gunn Allen, "What the Moon Said," *Skins and Bones* (1988)

3 The astronomers tell us that other planets are gifted with two—four—even nine lavish moons. Imagine the romantic possibilities of nine moons.

Edna Ferber, *A Kind of Magic* (1963)

See also Sky, Stars.

## ❦ MORALITY

4 Morality is the Science of harmonious relations between intelligent beings.

Annie Besant, *Theosophy and Life's Deeper Problems* (1916)

5 Morality, like language, is an invented structure for conserving and communicating order.

Jane Rule, *Lesbian Images* (1975)

6 A moral choice in its basic terms appears to be a choice that favors survival: a choice made in favor of life.

Ursula K. Le Guin, *Dancing at the Edge of the World* (1989)

7 Morality did not keep well; it required stable conditions; it was costly; it was subject to variations, and the market for it was uncertain.

Mary McCarthy, *The Oasis* (1949)

8 One of the most marked characteristics of our day is a reckless neglect of principles, and a rigid adherence to their semblance.

Countess of Blessington, *Desultory Thoughts and Reflections* (1839)

9 Morality is a test of our conformity rather than our integrity.

Jane Rule, in Alan Twigg, *For Openers* (1981)

10 A straight line is the shortest in morals as in geometry.

Rachel [Elizabeth Felix], in Joseph L. Baron, *A Treasury of Jewish Quotations* (1956)

11 I am still sure of absolute wrong but much less certain of absolute right.

Jill Tweedie, "Strange Places," in Michelene Wandor, ed., *On Gender and Writing* (1983)

12 Is it really so difficult to tell a good action from a bad one? I think one usually knows right away or a moment afterward, in a horrid flash of regret.

Mary McCarthy, "My Confession" (1953), *On the Contrary* (1961)

13 Whoever gives the common people food to eat is a good person whoever lets the common people starve is a bad person.

Hualing Nieh, *Mulberry and Peach* (1981)

14 Perhaps the straight and narrow path would be wider if more people used it.

Kay Ingram, in *The Saturday Evening Post* (1950)

15 No morals are better than bad ones.

Minna Thomas Antrim, *At the Sign of the Golden Calf* (1905)

16 Morality is observance of the laws of wholesome living. . . . In matters of morals we can hold certain assumptions: that there are some things better or worse in human affairs; that we ought to discover the better ways; that human beings are of great worth; that good should be done and evil avoided.

Angela M. Raimo, in *Christopher News Notes* (1991)

17 Morals are a matter of private agreement; decency is of public concern.

Marguerite Yourcenar, *Memoirs of Hadrian* (1951)

18 When a new idea assaults the power of established authority, authority always screams out that morality has been affronted. It makes no difference if this idea is that the world is round or that women should vote or that the workers should control industry.

Mary Heaton Vorse, *A Footnote to Folly* (1935)

19 Government can be moral—and it must be moral—without adopting a religion. Leaders can be moral—and they should be moral—without imposing their morality on others.

Geraldine A. Ferraro, with Linda Bird Francke, *Ferraro* (1985)

20 We make a great fuss about national conscience, but it consists mainly in insisting upon everyone ascribing our national policy to highly moral motives, rather than in examining what our motives really are.

Joan Robinson, "What Are the Rules of the Game?" *Economic Philosophy* (1962)

1 When morality comes up against profit, it is seldom that profit loses.

    Shirley Chisholm, *Unbought and Unbossed* (1970)

2 The more immoral we become in big ways, the more puritanical we become in little ways.

    Florence King, *Lump It or Leave It* (1990)

3 It cannot surely be questioned but that we want a System of Morals better than any of those which are current amongst us.

    Frances B. Cobbe, "Theory of Intuitive Morals" (1855), *Life of Frances Power Cobbe*, vol. 1 (1894)

4 Life itself, however, flows and is sequential and punishes those who try to compartmentalize it. Thus if, for any reason whatsoever, moral standards are conspicuously and unprecedentedly breached in one area of society, such as the political, it will follow as the night the day that those standards will start collapsing all down the line—in sports, entertainment, education, the armed forces, business and government.

    Margaret Halsey, *No Laughing Matter* (1977)

5 The morals of to-day are the immorals of yesterday, the creeds of tomorrow.

    Minna Thomas Antrim, *At the Sign of the Golden Calf* (1905)

6 Where there is no freedom there can be no morality.

    Alison Neilans, "Changes in Sex Morality," in Ray Strachey, ed., *Our Freedom and Its Results* (1936)

7 To attain individual morality in an age demanding social morality, to pride one's self on the results of personal effort when the time demands social adjustment, is utterly to fail to apprehend the situation.

    Jane Addams, title essay, *Democracy and Social Ethics* (1902)

8 Among the educated, morality tends to mean social consciousness.

    Pauline Kael, *I Lost It at the Movies* (1965)

9 People want to be amused, not preached at, you know. Morals don't sell nowadays.

    Louisa May Alcott, *Little Women* (1868)

10 Scientific progress makes moral progress a necessity; for if man's power is increased, the checks that restrain him from abusing it must be strengthened.

    Madame de Staël (1800), in J. Christopher Herold, *Mistress to an Age* (1958)

11 Between God and love, I recognize no mediator but my conscience.

    Madame de Staël, *Delphine* (1803)

12 Morality is not tied to divine bookkeeping. God and humanity are not business partners checking out each other's claims.

    Christina Thürmer-Rohr, *Vagabonding* (1991)

13 Conventionality is not morality. Self-righteousness is not religion. To attack the first is not to assail the last.

    Charlotte Brontë, *Jane Eyre* (1847)

14 You are so afraid of losing your moral sense that you are not willing to take it through anything more dangerous than a mud-puddle.

    Gertrude Stein, "Q.E.D." (1903), *Fernhurst, Q.E.D., and Other Early Writings* (1971)

15 Your morals are like roads through the Alps. They make these hairpin turns all the time.

    Erica Jong, *Fear of Flying* (1973)

16 Her morality often changed color against the stronger color schemes of her wishes.

    Phyllis Bottome, *Danger Signal* (1939)

17 When we start deceiving ourselves into thinking not that we want something or need something, not that it is a pragmatic necessity for us to have it, but that it is a *moral imperative* that we have it, then is when we join the fashionable madmen, and then is when the thin whine of hysteria is heard in the land, and then is when we are in bad trouble. And I suspect we are already there.

    Joan Didion, "On Morality," *Slouching Towards Bethlehem* (1968)

18 The reason I left my husband was because he believed in the triple standard of morality, one for me and two for himself.

    Lillian Day, *Kiss and Tell* (1931)

See also Conscience, Ethics, Evil, Good, Principles, Taboos, Values, Virtue.

# ❦ MORNING

19 Morning has broken / Like the first morning, / Blackbird has spoken / Like the first bird.

    Eleanor Farjeon, "A Morning Song (For the First Day of Spring)," *The Children's Bells* (1960)

1 How beautiful, how buoyant, and glad is morning!

L.E. Landon, "Rebecca," *The Book of Beauty* (1833)

2 Mine is the sunlight! / Mine is the morning.

Eleanor Farjeon, "A Morning Song (For the First Day of Spring)," *The Children's Bells* (1960)

3 The moment when first you wake up in the morning is the most wonderful of the twenty-four hours. No matter how weary or dreary you may feel, you possess the certainty that . . . absolutely anything may happen. And the fact that it practically always *doesn't,* matters not one jot. The possibility is always there.

Monica Baldwin, *I Leap Over the Wall* (1950)

4 There is no doubt that running away on a fresh, blue morning can be exhilarating.

Jean Rhys, *The Left Bank* (1927)

5 I like breakfast-time better than any other moment in the day. No dust has settled on one's mind then, and it presents a clear mirror to the rays of things.

George Eliot, *Adam Bede* (1859)

6 To have a reason to get up in the morning, it is necessary to possess a guiding principle. A belief of some kind. A bumper sticker if you will.

Judith Guest, *Ordinary People* (1976)

7 The average, healthy, well-adjusted adult gets up at seven-thirty in the morning feeling just plain terrible.

Jean Kerr, "Where Did You Put the Aspirin?" *Please Don't Eat the Daisies* (1957)

8 My general attitude toward life when I first get up is of deep suspicion. . . . I am simply basted together until after breakfast.

Gladys Taber, *The Book of Stillmeadow* (1948)

9 I don't grasp things this early in the day. I mean, I hear voices, all right, but I can't pick out the verbs.

Jean Kerr, *Mary, Mary* (1963)

10 He instantly despised his guests for being still asleep, in a rush of that superiority which afflicts all those who are astir earlier than other people.

Vita Sackville-West, *The Edwardians* (1930)

11 Early risers are conceited in the morning, and stupid in the afternoon.

Rose Henniker Heaton, *The Perfect Hostess* (1931)

12 Statistically speaking, the Cheerful Early Riser is rejected more completely than a member of any other subculture, save those with boot odor.

Ellen Goodman, *Close to Home* (1979)

13 I like to wake up feeling a new man.

Jean Harlow, when asked how she liked to wake up in the morning (1930), in Irving Shulman, *Harlow* (1964)

See also Dawn.

## ❦ MOTHERHOOD

14 A mother's love for her child is like nothing else in the world. It knows no law, no pity, it dares all things and crushes down remorselessly all that stands in its path.

Agatha Christie, "The Last Séance," *The Hound of Death* (1933)

15 There is no other closeness in human life like the closeness between a mother and her baby— chronologically, physically, and spiritually they are just a few heartbeats away from being the same person.

Susan Cheever, *A Woman's Life* (1994)

16 A mother is not a person to lean upon, but a person to make leaning unnecessary.

Dorothy Canfield, *Her Son's Wife* (1926)

17 The most important thing she'd learned over the years was that there was no way to be a perfect mother and a million ways to be a good one.

Jill Churchill, *Grime and Punishment* (1989)

18 Biology is the least of what makes someone a mother.

Oprah Winfrey, in *Woman's Day* (1988)

19 Mothers . . . are basically a patient lot. They have to be or they would devour their offspring early on, like guppies.

Mary Daheim, *The Alpine Advocate* (1992)

20 Mothers had a thousand thoughts to get through with in a day, and . . . most of these were about avoiding disaster.

Natalie Kusz, *Road Song* (1990)

21 There is only one image in this culture of the "good mother." . . . She is quietly strong, selflessly giving,

undemanding, unambitious; she is receptive and intelligent in only a moderate, concrete way; she is of even temperament, almost always in control of her emotions. She loves her children completely and unambivalently. Most of us are not like her.

Jane Lazarre, *The Mother Knot* (1976)

1 You might not have thought it possible to give birth to others before one has given birth to one-self, but I assure you it is quite possible, it has been done; I offer myself in evidence as Exhibit A.

Sheila Ballantyne, *Norma Jean the Termite Queen* (1975)

2 Over the years I have learned that motherhood is much like an austere religious order, the joining of which obligates one to relinquish all claims to personal possessions.

Nancy Stahl, *If It's Raining This Must Be the Weekend* (1979)

3 Motherhood is like Albania—you can't trust the descriptions in the books, you have to go there.

Marni Jackson, *The Mother Zone* (1992)

4 A mother is never cocky or proud, because she knows the school principal may call at any minute to report that her child has just driven a motorcycle through the gymnasium.

Mary Kay Blakely, "The Pros and Cons of Motherhood," in Gloria Kaufman and Mary Kay Blakely, eds., *Pulling Our Own Strings* (1980)

5 Trivial things and important things wound into and against one another, all warring for her attention. Changing the goldfish water wasn't vital, but it couldn't wait; teaching the children their Bible was vital, but it could wait. Listening to them, growing with them, that was vital; but the bills had to be paid now, the dinner was burning right now.

Joanne Greenberg, "Children of Joy," *Rites of Passage* (1972)

6 The only thing which seems to me to be eternal and natural in motherhood is ambivalence.

Jane Lazarre, *The Mother Knot* (1976)

7 Nothing else ever will make you as happy or as sad, as proud or as tired, for nothing is quite as hard as helping a person develop his own individuality—especially while you struggle to keep your own.

Marguerite Kelly and Elia Parsons, *The Mother's Almanac* (1975)

8 Pregnancy doubled her, birth halved her, and motherhood turned her into Everywoman.

Erica Jong, *Parachutes & Kisses* (1984)

9 it was good for the virgin mary / its good enough for me.

Nikki Giovanni, "Poem for Unwed Mothers," *Re:Creation* (1970)

10 I figure when my husband comes home from work, if the kids are still alive, then I've done my job.

Roseanne Barr, in Susan Dworkin, "Roseanne Barr," *Ms.* (1987)

11 Being a housewife and a mother is the biggest job in the world, but if it doesn't interest you, don't do it. It didn't interest me, so I didn't do it. Anyway, I would have made a terrible parent. The first time my child didn't do what I wanted, I'd kill him.

Katharine Hepburn, in Liz Smith, *The Mother Book* (1978)

12 When her biographer says of an Italian woman poet, "during some years her Muse was intermitted," we do not wonder at the fact when he casually mentions her ten children.

Anna Garlin Spencer, *Woman's Share in Social Culture* (1912)

13 You think, dear Johannes, that because I occasionally lay something aside I am giving too many concerts. But think of my responsibilities—seven children still dependent on me, five who have yet to be educated.

Clara Schumann, after Robert Schumann's death (1861), in Berthold Litzmann, ed., *Letters of Clara Schumann and Johannes Brahms*, vol. 1 (1927)

14 Being asked to decide between your passion for work and your passion for children was like being asked by your doctor whether you preferred him to remove your brain or your heart.

Mary Kay Blakely, *American Mom* (1994)

15 Why was I born beneath two curses, / To bear children and to write verses? / Either one fecundity / Were heavy enough destiny. / But all my life is penalty / From the two sides of me.

Anna Wickham, "New Eve" (1915), in R.D. Smith, ed., *The Writings of Anna Wickham* (1984)

16 When I had my daughter, I learned what the sound of one hand clapping is—it's a woman holding an infant in one arm and a pen in the other.

Kate Braverman, in Judith Pierce Rosenberg, "Creative Tension," *Ms.* (1994)

17 At work, you think of the children you've left at home. At home, you think of the work you've left unfinished. Such a struggle is unleashed within yourself: your heart is rent.

Golda Meir, in Oriana Fallaci, *L'Europeo* (1973)

1 Most mothers entering the labor market outside the home are naive. They stagger home each evening, holding mail in their teeth, the cleaning over their arm, a lamb chop defrosting under each armpit, balancing two gallons of frozen milk between their knees, and expect one of the kids to get the door.

> Erma Bombeck, syndicated column "At Wit's End," (1982)

2 Reminds me of what one of mine wrote in a third-grade piece on how her mother spent her time. She reported "one half time on home, one half time on outside things, one half time writing."

> Charlotte Montgomery, in *Good Housekeeping* (1959)

3 Why not have your first baby at sixty, when your husband is already dead and your career is over? Then you can *really* devote yourself to it.

> Fran Lebowitz, in *Redbook* (1990)

4 Civilization, stretching up to recognize that every child is a portion of State wealth, may presently make some movement to recognize maternity as a business or office needing time and strength, not as a mere passing detail thrown in among mountains of other slavery.

> Miles Franklin, *Some Everyday Folk and Dawn* (1909)

5 On one thing professionals and amateurs agree: mothers can't win.

> Margaret Drabble, *The Middle Ground* (1980)

See also Mothers, Parenthood.

# ❦ MOTHERS

6 Who ran to help me when I fell, / And would some pretty story tell, / Or kiss the place to make it well? / My Mother.

> Ann Taylor, "My Mother," in Jane Taylor and Her Sisters, *Original Poems for Infant Minds* (1804)

7 My mother is a poem I'll never be able to write / though everything I write is a poem to my mother.

> Sharon Doubiago, in Tillie Olsen, *Mother to Daughter, Daughter to Mother* (1984)

8 No song or poem will bear my mother's name. Yet so many of the stories that I write, that we all write, are my mother's stories.

> Alice Walker, title essay (1974), *In Search of Our Mothers' Gardens* (1983)

9 My mother, religious-negro, proud of / having waded through a storm, is very obviously, / a sturdy Black bridge that I / crossed over, on.

> Carolyn M. Rodgers, "It Is Deep (don't never forget the bridge that you crossed over on)," *how i got ovah* (1975)

10 I cannot forget my mother. Though not as sturdy as others, she is my bridge. When I needed to get across, she steadied herself long enough for me to run across safely.

> Renita Weems, "'Hush, Mama's Gotta Go Bye-Bye,'" in Patricia Bell-Scott et al., eds., *Double Stitch* (1991)

11 Most of all the other beautiful things in life come by twos and threes, by dozens and hundreds. Plenty of roses, stars, sunsets, rainbows, brothers and sisters, aunts and cousins, comrades and friends—but only one mother in the whole world.

> Kate Douglas Wiggin, in Charles L. Wallis, ed., *The Treasure Chest* (1965)

12 I wonder why you care so much about me—no, I don't wonder. I only accept it as the thing at the back of all one's life that makes everything bearable and possible.

> Gertrude Bell (1892), in Elsa Richmond, ed., *The Earlier Letters of Gertrude Bell* (1937)

13 If you've ever had a mother and if she's given you and meant to you all the things you care for most, you never get over it.

> Anne Douglas Sedgwick, *Dark Hester* (1929)

14 To her whose heart is my heart's quiet home, / To my first Love, my Mother, on whose knee / I learnt love-lore that is not troublesome.

> Christina Rossetti, "Sonnets Are Full of Love," *A Pageant* (1881)

15 I learned your walk, talk, gestures and nurturing laughter. At that time, Mama, had you swung from bars, I would, to this day, be hopelessly, imitatively, hung up.

> SDiane Bogus, "Mom de Plume" (1977), in Patricia Bell-Scott et al., eds., *Double Stitch* (1991)

16 I had the most satisfactory of childhoods because Mother, small, delicate-boned, witty, and articulate, turned out to be exactly my age.

> Kay Boyle, in Robert McAlmon, *Being Geniuses Together* (1968)

17 I know her face by heart. Sometimes I think nothing will break her spell.

> Daphne Merkin, *Enchantment* (1986)

1 treetalk and windsong are / the language of my mother / her music does not leave me.

Barbara Mahone, title poem, *Sugarfield* (1970)

2 I am all the time talking about you, and bragging, to one person or another. I am like the Ancient Mariner, who had a tale in his heart he must unfold to all. I am always button-holing somebody and saying, "Someday you must meet my mother." And then I am off. And nothing stops me till the waiters close up the café. I do love you so much, my mother. . . . If I didn't keep calling you mother, anybody reading this would think I was writing to my sweetheart. And he would be quite right.

Edna St. Vincent Millay (1921), in Allan Ross Macdougall, ed., *Letters of Edna St. Vincent Millay* (1952)

3 There are those people who love their mothers, just so; and there are those who, out of whatever accident of temperament have to be *in love* with them.

Judith Grossmann, *Her Own Terms* (1988)

4 My mother was my first jealous lover.

Barbara Grizzuti Harrison, *Foreign Bodies* (1984)

5 You never get over bein' a child long's you have a mother to go to.

Sarah Orne Jewett, *The Country of the Pointed Firs* (1896)

6 I want to lean into her the way wheat leans into wind.

Louise Erdrich, *The Beet Queen* (1986)

7 Mother, in ways neither of us can ever understand, / I have come home.

Robin Morgan, "Matrilineal Descent," *Monster* (1972)

8 And it came to me, and I knew what I had to have before my soul would rest. I wanted to belong—to belong to my mother. And in return—I wanted my mother to belong to me.

Gloria Vanderbilt, *Once Upon a Time* (1985)

9 I sharpen more and more to your / Likeness every year.

Michele Wolf, "For My Mother," in Sandra Martz, ed., *When I Am an Old Woman I Shall Wear Purple* (1987)

10 I am a reflection of my mother's secret poetry as well as of her hidden angers.

Audre Lorde, *Zami: A New Spelling of My Name* (1982)

11 A woman *is* her mother. / That's the main thing.

Anne Sexton, "Housewife," *All My Pretty Ones* (1961)

12 i am not you anymore / i am my own collection of / gifts and errors.

Saundra Sharp, "Double Exposure," in Patricia Bell-Scott et al., eds., *Double Stitch* (1991)

13 In search of my mother's garden, I found my own.

Alice Walker, title essay (1974), *In Search of Our Mothers' Gardens* (1983)

14 Yes, Mother. . . . I can see you are flawed. You have not hidden it. That is your greatest gift to me.

Alice Walker, *Possessing the Secret of Joy* (1992)

15 I . . . have another cup of coffee with my mother. We get along very well, veterans of a guerrilla war we never understood.

Joan Didion, "On Going Home," *Slouching Towards Bethlehem* (1968)

16 Mother who gave me life / I think of women bearing / women. Forgive me the wisdom / I would not learn from you.

Gwen Harwood, "Mother Who Gave Me Life," *The Lion's Bride* (1981)

17 My mother is a good woman—a very good woman—and I am, I think, not quite all criminality, but we do not pull together. I am a piece of machinery which, not understanding, my mother winds up the wrong way, setting all the wheels of my composition going in creaking discord.

Miles Franklin, *My Brilliant Career* (1901)

18 My mother never listens to me.

Marjorie Weinman Sharmat, children's picture book title (1984)

19 What I object to in Mother is that she wants me to think her thoughts. Apart from the question of hypocrisy, I prefer my own.

Margaret Deland, *The Rising Tide* (1916)

20 My mother and I could always look out the same window without ever seeing the same thing.

Gloria Swanson, *Swanson on Swanson* (1980)

21 Whenever I'm with my mother, I feel as though I have to spend the whole time avoiding land mines.

Amy Tan, *The Kitchen God's Wife* (1991)

22 Now that I am in my forties, she tells me I'm beautiful; now that I am in my forties, she sends me presents and we have the long, personal and even remarkably honest phone calls I always wanted so intensely I forbade myself to imagine them. How strange. Perhaps Shaw was correct and if we lived

to be several hundred years old, we would finally work it all out. I am deeply grateful. With my poems, I finally won even my mother. The longest wooing of my life.

Marge Piercy, *Braided Lives* (1982)

1 No matter how old a mother is she watches her middle-aged children for signs of improvement.

Florida Scott-Maxwell, *The Measure of My Days* (1968)

2 Always that tyrannical love reaches out. Soft words shrivel me like quicklime. She will not allow me to be cold, hungry. She will insist that I take her own coat, her own food.

Elizabeth Smart, "Dig a Grave and Let Us Bury Our Mother" (1939), *In the Meantime* (1984)

3 A mother's hardest to forgive. / Life is the fruit she longs to hand you, / Ripe on a plate. And while you live, / Relentlessly she understands you.

Phyllis McGinley, "The Adversary," *Times Three* (1960)

4 Nothing would have satisfied Amelia but complete possession of her son, to all intents and purposes returning him to the dark slyness of her womb.

Marjorie Kinnan Rawlings, *The Sojourner* (1953)

5 I fear, as any daughter would, losing myself back into the mother.

Kim Chernin, *In My Mother's House* (1983)

6 Oh! mothers aren't fair—I mean it's not fair of nature to weigh us down with them and yet expect us to be our own true selves. The handicap's too great. All those months, when the same blood's running through two sets of veins—there's no getting away from that, ever after.

Henry Handel Richardson, "Two Hanged Women," *The End of a Childhood* (1934)

7 My mother phones daily to ask, "Did you just try to reach me?" When I reply, "No," she adds, "So, if you're not too busy, call me while I'm still alive," and hangs up.

Erma Bombeck, *The 1992 Erma Bombeck Calendar* (1992)

8 Did you ever meet a mother who's complained that her child phoned her too often? Me neither.

Maureen Lipman, *Thank You for Having Me* (1990)

9 Why should I be reasonable? I'm your mother.

Lynne Alpern and Esther Blumenfeld, *Oh, Lord, I Sound Just Like Mama* (1986)

10 Out of the corner of one eye, I could see my mother. Out of the corner of the other eye, I could see her shadow on the wall, cast there by the lamplight. It was a big and solid shadow, and it looked so much like my mother that I became frightened. For I could not be sure whether for the rest of my life I would be able to tell when it was really my mother and when it was really her shadow standing between me and the rest of the world.

Jamaica Kincaid, *Annie John* (1983)

11 She was the archetypal selfless mother: living only for her children, sheltering them from the consequences of their actions—and in the end doing them irreparable harm.

Marcia Muller, "Benny's Space," in Sara Paretsky, ed., *A Woman's Eye* (1991)

12 In the final analysis, each of us is responsible for what we are. We cannot blame it on our mothers, who, thanks to Freud, have replaced money as the root of all evil.

Helen Lawrenson, *Stranger at the Party* (1975)

13 "Mother" is the first word that occurs to politicians and columnists and popes when they raise the question, "Why isn't life turning out the way we wanted it?"

Mary Kay Blakely, *American Mom* (1994)

14 Blaming mother is just a negative way of clinging to her still.

Nancy Friday, *My Mother/My Self* (1977)

15 My mother is a woman who speaks with her life as much as with her tongue.

Kesaya E. Noda, "Growing Up Asian in America," in Asian Women United of California, eds., *Making Waves* (1989)

16 My mother wasn't what the world would call a good woman. She never said she was. And many people, including the police, said she was a bad woman. But she never agreed with them, and she had a way of lifting up her head when she talked back to them that made me know she was right.

Box-Car Bertha, *Sister of the Road* (1937)

17 The woman / I needed to call my mother / was silenced before I was born.

Adrienne Rich, "Re-forming the Crystal" (1973), *The Fact of a Doorframe* (1984)

18 She knew how to make virtues out of necessities.

Audre Lorde, *Zami: A New Spelling of My Name* (1982)

1 To describe my mother would be to write about a hurricane in its perfect power.

  Maya Angelou, *I Know Why the Caged Bird Sings* (1970)

2 When the strongest words for what I have to offer come out of me sounding like words I remember from my mother's mouth, then I either have to reassess the meaning of everything I have to say now, or re-examine the worth of her old words.

  Audre Lorde, *Zami: A New Spelling of My Name* (1982)

3 At that moment, I missed my mother more than I had ever imagined possible and wanted only to live somewhere quiet and beautiful with her alone, but also at that moment I wanted only to see her lying dead, all withered and in a coffin at my feet.

  Jamaica Kincaid, *Annie John* (1983)

4 She said that if I listened to her, later I would know what she knew: where true words came from, always from up high, above everything else. And if I didn't listen to her, she said my ear would bend too easily to other people, all saying words that had no lasting meaning, because they came from the bottom of their hearts, where their own desires lived, a place where I could not belong.

  Amy Tan, *The Joy Luck Club* (1989)

5 A mother . . . is forever surprised and even faintly wronged that her sons and daughters are just people, for many mothers hope and half expect that their newborn child will make the world better, will somehow be a redeemer. Perhaps they are right, and they can believe that the rare quality they glimpsed in the child is active in the burdened adult.

  Florida Scott-Maxwell, *The Measure of My Days* (1968)

6 She had risen and was walking about the room, her fat, worn face sharpening with a sort of animal alertness into power and protection. The claws that hide in every maternal creature slipped out of the fur of good manners.

  Margaret Deland, *The Rising Tide* (1916)

7 Our parents merged into the one / totemic creature: / *Come,* she said. *Come to Mother.*

  Louise Glück, "Tango," *Descending Figure* (1980)

8 The students of history know that while many mothers of great men have been virtuous, none have been commonplace, and few have been happy.

  Gertrude Atherton, *The Conqueror* (1902)

9 She did not understand how her father could have reached such age and such eminence without learning that all mothers are as infallible as any pope and more righteous than any saint.

  Frances Newman, *The Hard-Boiled Virgin* (1926)

10 I feel about mothers the way I feel about dimples: because I do not have one myself, I notice everyone who does.

  Letty Cottin Pogrebin, *Deborah, Golda, and Me* (1991)

11 My mother had died when I was seven. For many years I lived primarily to search for her.

  Jane Lazarre, *The Mother Knot* (1976)

12 The longer one lives in this hard world motherless, the more a mother's loss makes itself felt.

  Jane Welsh Carlyle, to Thomas Carlyle (1858), in James Anthony Froude, ed., *Letters and Memorials of Jane Welsh Carlyle*, vol. 2 (1883)

13 I grow old, old / without you, Mother, landscape / of my heart.

  Olga Broumas, "Little Red Riding Hood," *Beginning With O* (1977)

14 Lennie, suffering not alone for her who was dying, but for that in her which never lived (for that which in him might never live). From him too, unspoken words: *good-bye Mother who taught me to mother myself.*

  Tillie Olsen, title story, *Tell Me a Riddle* (1956)

15 We buried her . . . this mother with whom I fought so desperately, whom I loved so dearly, and of whose presence I grow daily more and more conscious.

  Ethel Smyth, *Impressions That Remained* (1919)

16 Inside my mother's death / I lay and could not breathe.

  May Sarton, "Dream," *The Silence Now* (1988)

17 The death of my mother permanently affects my happiness, more even than I should have anticipated. . . . I did not apprehend, during her life, to what a degree she prevented me from feeling heart-solitude.

  Sara Coleridge (1845), *Memoir and Letters*, vol. 1 (1873)

18 My mother was dead for five years before I knew that I had loved her very much.

  Lillian Hellman, *An Unfinished Woman* (1969)

1 The woman who bore me is no longer alive, but I seem to be her daughter in increasingly profound ways.

> Johnnetta B. Cole, in Patricia Bell-Scott et al., eds., *Double Stitch* (1991)

2 You are here, Mother, and you are / Dead, and here is your gift: my life which is my home.

> Muriel Rukeyser, "On the Death of Her Mother," *Body of Waking* (1958)

3 Time is the only comforter for the loss of a mother.

> Jane Welsh Carlyle, to Thomas Carlyle on the death of his mother (1853), in James Anthony Froude, ed., *Letters and Memorials of Jane Welsh Carlyle*, vol. 2 (1883)

4 I acknowledge the cold truth of her death for perhaps the first time. She is truly gone, forever out of reach, and I have become my own judge.

> Sheila Ballantyne, *Imaginary Crimes* (1982)

5 My mother always found me out. Always. She's been dead for thirty-five years, but I have this feeling that even now she's watching.

> Natalie Babbitt, in *The Horn Book* (1993)

6 My life now is only mine.

> Toby Talbot, on her mother's death, in Tillie Olsen, *Mother to Daughter, Daughter to Mother* (1984)

7 Were my smile not submerged in my countenance, / I should suspend it over her grave.

> Else Lasker-Schüler, "My Mother" (1925), *Hebrew Ballads* (1980)

See also Motherhood, Parents.

## ♦ MOTIVES

8 Too great a preoccupation with motives (especially one's own motives) is liable to lead to too little concern for consequences.

> Katharine Whitehorn, *Roundabout* (1962)

9 We must not inquire too curiously into motives. . . . They are apt to become feeble in the utterance: the aroma is mixed with the grosser air. We must keep the germinating grain away from the light.

> George Eliot, *Middlemarch* (1871)

See also Intentions, Purpose.

## ♦ MOUNTAIN CLIMBING

10 You never conquer a mountain. / You stand on the summit a few moments, / Then the wind blows your footprints away.

> Arlene Blum, *Annapurna* (1980)

11 Everest is a symbol of excellence, of the barely attainable. It is the mightiest challenge: a brutal struggle with rock, ice, altitude, and self. The satisfaction . . . comes from enduring the struggle, from doing more than you thought you could do, from rising—however briefly—above your everyday world, and from coming, momentarily, closer to the stars.

> Sue Cobb, *The Edge of Everest* (1989)

12 Everest wasn't like any other mountain. Only one of ten climbers who attempt the mountain stands on the summit. And for every three climbers who do scale the mountain, one dies trying. The facts aren't welcoming. But you don't plan a trip to Everest believing those facts will apply to you.

> Stacy Allison, with Peter Carlin, *Beyond the Limits* (1993)

13 When life gets tangled there's something so reassuring about climbing a mountain. The challenge is unambiguous.

> Stacy Allison, with Peter Carlin, *Beyond the Limits* (1993)

14 For those moments when it's just you and the rock and the ice and the snow, life always makes sense.

> Stacy Allison, with Peter Carlin, *Beyond the Limits* (1993)

15 That's exactly what climbing is to me. . . . *Expression*. What a painter does on a canvas, what a writer can do with the twenty-six letters in the alphabet. It's the key that unlocks my spirit, the clearest representation of who I am.

> Stacy Allison, with Peter Carlin, *Beyond the Limits* (1993)

16 Climbing is almost an unconscious act for me. I don't have to drive myself, I'm already driven.

> Stacy Allison, with Peter Carlin, *Beyond the Limits* (1993)

See also Mountains.

## ♦ MOUNTAINS

17 The heights of granite and the grassy steep / My spirit in a magic fortress keep / Where in the silence, singing waters start.

> Ann Bridge, *Singing Waters* (1946)

1 My help is in the mountain / Where I take myself to heal / The earthly wounds / That people give to me.

>  Nancy Wood, "My Help Is in the Mountain," *Hollering Sun* (1972)

2 Mountains are the altars of the gods.

>  Evelyn Scott, *Escapade* (1923)

3 There came without warning a flowing into me of that which I have come to associate with the gods. I went to the open door and looked up at the mountains with something akin to awe. It forced me out into the open where I could look up to the sacred high places on which humans do not dwell. Then it left me—perhaps to return to those sacred places.

>  Edith Warner, in Peggy Pond Church, *The House at Otowi Bridge* (1959)

4 Mountains define you. You cannot define / Them.

>  May Sarton, "Colorado Mountains," *The Lion and the Rose* (1948)

5 When God gave men tongues, he never dreamed that they would want to talk about the Himalayas; there are consequently no words in the world to do it with.

>  Sara Jeannette Duncan, *The Simple Adventures of a Memsahib* (1893)

6 Nothing puts things in perspective as quickly as a mountain.

>  Josephine Tey, *The Daughter of Time* (1951)

7 Mountains had taken the place of religion, had satisfied her religious sense, her need for adoration and worship as no service in any Cathedral, however sublime, had been able to do.

>  Ann Bridge, *Singing Waters* (1946)

8 If you grow up where a snow mountain lifts its proud crown on the home horizon, in some strange way it becomes a member of the family.

>  Margaret Craven, *Walk Gently This Good Earth* (1977)

9 When you are a child of the mountains yourself, you really belong to them. You need them. They become the faithful guardians of your life. If you cannot dwell on their lofty heights all your life, if you are in trouble, you want at least to look at them.

>  Maria Augusta Trapp, *The Story of the Trapp Family Singers* (1949)

10 Like a human being, the mountain is a composite creature, only to be known after many a view from many a different point, and repaying this loving study, if it is anything of a mountain at all, by a gradual revelation of personality.

>  Freya Stark, *The Valleys of the Assassins* (1934)

11 To rise above treeline is to go above thought, and after, the descent back into bird song, bog orchids, willows, and firs is to sink into the preliterate parts of ourselves.

>  Gretel Ehrlich, *Islands, the Universe, Home* (1991)

12 All mountain streets have streams to thread them, or deep grooves where a stream might run. You would do well to avoid that range uncomforted by singing floods. You will find it forsaken of most things but beauty and madness and death and God.

>  Mary Austin, *The Land of Little Rain* (1904)

13 The mountains were getting ready for winter, too. They were very sly about it and tried to look summery and casual but I could tell by their contours that they had slipped on an extra layer of snow—that the misty scarf blowing about that one's head would soon be lying whitely around her neck.

>  Betty MacDonald, *The Egg and I* (1945)

14 The low-lying mountains sleep at the edge of the world.

>  Harriet Monroe, "The Blue Ridge," *The Difference* (1925)

15 Since I have lost the mountains, I / Look for them in the waste of sky, / And think to see at the street's close / The lovely line of blue and rose.

>  Katharine Tynan Hinkson, "The Exile," *Collected Poems* (1930)

See also Hills, Mountain Climbing.

## ❧ MOURNING

16 Life, since thou hast left it, has been misery to me.

>  Cleopatra, at Marc Antony's tomb (30 B.C.), in Mrs. Jameson, *Memoirs of Celebrated Female Sovereigns* (1831)

17 The grass is waking in the ground, / Soon it will rise and blow in waves— / How can it have the heart to sway / Over the graves, / New graves?

>  Sara Teasdale, "Spring in War Time," *Rivers to the Sea* (1915)

1 To mourn, perhaps, is simply to prolong a posture of astonishment.

    Sara Suleri, *Meatless Days* (1989)

2 The distance that the dead have gone / Does not at first appear — / Their coming back seems possible / For many an ardent year.

    Emily Dickinson, in Mabel Loomis Todd, ed., *Poems by Emily Dickinson*, 3rd series (1896)

3 To mourn is to be extraordinarily vulnerable. It is to be at the mercy of inside feelings and outside events in a way most of us have not been since early childhood.

    Christian McEwen, "The Color of the Water, the Yellow of the Field," in Christian McEwen and Sue O'Sullivan, eds., *Out the Other Side* (1988)

4 To everyone else, the death of that being you love for his own sake, for her own sake, is an event that occurs on a certain day. For you, the death only begins that day. It is not an event: it is only the first moment in a process that lives in you, springing up into the present, engulfing you years, decades, later, as though it were the first moment again.

    Alice Koller, *The Stations of Solitude* (1990)

5 Mourning is not forgetting. It is an undoing. Every minute tie has to be untied and something permanent and valuable recovered and assimilated from the knot.

    Margery Allingham, *The Tiger in the Smoke* (1952)

6 One must go through periods of numbness that are harder to bear than grief.

    Anne Morrow Lindbergh, *Hour of Gold, Hour of Lead* (1973)

7 These talkings and comfortings lasted two or three weeks; after that no one knew me. . . . After the first thirty days of mourning, no brother, no sister, no relative came to ask: "How are you? and how are things?"

    Glückel of Hameln, *Memoirs of Glückel of Hameln* (1724)

8 Mourning has become unfashionable in the United States. The bereaved are supposed to pull themselves together as quickly as possible and to re-weave the torn fabric of life. . . . We do not allow . . . for the weeks and months during which a loss is realized—a beautiful word that suggests the transmutation of the strange into something that is one's own.

    Margaret Mead and Rhoda Metraux, *A Way of Seeing* (1970)

9 In coming to terms with the newly dead, I seem to have agitated the spirits of the long dead. They were stirring uneasily in their graves, demanding to be mourned as I had not mourned them when they were buried. I was plunged into retroactive grief for my father, and could no longer deny, though I still tried, the loss I'd suffered at the death of my mother. . . . Was it possible . . . that one could mourn over losses that had occurred more than half a century earlier?

    Eileen Simpson, *Orphans* (1990)

10 A mourner is, perforce, a person with a story. The pity is, how very rarely it gets told.

    Christian McEwen, "The Color of the Water, the Yellow of the Field," in Christian McEwen and Sue O'Sullivan, eds., *Out the Other Side* (1988)

11 The time at length arrives, when grief is rather an indulgence than a necessity and the smile that plays upon the lips, although it may be deemed a sacrilege, is not banished.

    Mary Shelley, *Frankenstein* (1818)

12 We met . . . Dr. Hall in such very deep mourning that either his mother, his wife, or himself must be dead.

    Jane Austen, to her sister Cassandra (1799), in R.W. Chapman, ed., *Jane Austen's Letters*, vol. 1 (1932)

See also Bereavement, Death, Grief, Loss, Pain, Sorrow.

## ❧ MOUTH

13 In every person's face, there is one place that seems to express them most accurately. With my grandmother you always looked at her mouth.

    Mona Simpson, *Anywhere But Here* (1986)

14 She had a plump little mouth like a buttonhole worked with a heavy satin stitch.

    Jessamyn West, *The Massacre at Fall Creek* (1975)

15 Froody lifted his lip, and it was like a small fat mouse sneering.

    Lange Lewis, *Juliet Dies Twice* (1948)

See also Appearance, Face, Speech, Talking, Teeth.

## ❧ MOVEMENTS

1 A movement is more polite than a revolution, and a lot slower.

　　Linda Ellerbee, *Move On* (1991)

2 Unity in a movement situation can be overrated. If you were the Establishment, which would you rather see coming in the door: one lion or five hundred mice?

　　Florynce R. Kennedy, in Gloria Steinem, "The Verbal Karate of Florynce R. Kennedy," *Ms.* (1973)

3 Social movements are frequently characterized by gaps between the lives of the theorists who lead the movements and those of the followers who try to practice the theorists' ideas.

　　Arlene Rossen Cardozo, *Sequencing* (1986)

4 It takes six simpletons and one zealot to start a movement.

　　Anzia Yezierska, "One Thousand Pages of Research," *Commentary* (1963)

See also Activism, Protest, Revolution, Social Change, Women's Movement.

## ❧ MOVING

5 It is impossible to create a stable society if something like a third of our people are constantly moving about. We cannot grow fine human beings, any more than we can grow fine trees, if they are constantly torn up by the roots and transplanted.

　　Agnes E. Meyer, *Out of These Roots* (1953)

6 He moves a great deal. So often . . . that every time he comes out into his backyard the chickens lie down and cross their legs, ready to be tied up again.

　　Zora Neale Hurston, "The Eatonville Anthology," in Alice Walker, ed., *I Love Myself When I Am Laughing . . . And Then Again When I Am Looking Mean and Impressive* (1979)

See also Change, Places.

## ❧ MURDER

7 Murder is the apex of megalomania, the ultimate in control.

　　Lucy Freeman, *Before I Kill More* (1955)

8 Every murderer is probably somebody's old friend.

　　Agatha Christie, *The Mysterious Affair at Styles* (1920)

9 The fashion of poisoning people is getting too common.

　　Charlotte-Elisabeth, Duchesse d'Orléans, referring to three deaths by poison at court (1690), *Life and Letters of Charlotte Elizabeth* (1889)

## ❧ MUSIC

10 Music, that vast and inevitable structure.

　　Edith Sitwell, *Taken Care Of* (1965)

11 Music my rampart, and my only one.

　　Edna St. Vincent Millay, "On Hearing a Symphony of Beethoven," *The Buck in the Snow* (1928)

12 Good music is wine turned to sound.

　　Ella Wheeler Wilcox, "The Choosing of Esther," *Poems of Progress* (1909)

13 Without music I should wish to die.

　　Edna St. Vincent Millay (1920), in Allan Ross Macdougall, ed., *Letters of Edna St. Vincent Millay* (1952)

14 I get way down in the music / Down inside the music.

　　Eloise Greenfield, "Way Down in the Music," *Honey, I Love* (1978)

15 Music gives access to regions in the subconscious that can be reached in no other way.

　　Sophie Drinker, *Music and Women* (1948)

16 Music has been my playmate, my lover, and my crying towel.

　　Buffy Sainte-Marie, in Susan Braudy, "Buffy Sainte-Marie," *Ms.* (1975)

17 Music was my refuge. I could crawl into the spaces between the notes and curl my back to loneliness.

　　Maya Angelou, *Singin' and Swingin' and Gettin' Merry Like Christmas* (1976)

18 Music, my joy, my full-scale God.

　　Gwen Harwood, "A Scattering of Ashes," *The Lion's Bride* (1981)

19 Music melts all the separate parts of our bodies together.

　　Anaïs Nin, *Winter of Artifice* (1945)

1 If God exists / then music is his love for me.
   Gwen Harwood, "A Music Lesson," *The Lion's Bride* (1981)

2 They made heaven right when they made it all music.
   Ralph Iron, *The Story of an African Farm* (1883)

3 Like the brushing of swallows' wings against the willows—sweet, sweet music!
   Louise Crane, *The Magic Spear and Other Stories of China's Famous Heroes* (1938)

4 I think I should have no other mortal wants, if I could always have plenty of music. It seems to infuse strength into my limbs and ideas into my brain. Life seems to go on without effort, when I am filled with music.
   George Eliot, *The Mill on the Floss* (1860)

5 What can wake / The soul's strong instinct of another world, / Like music?
   L.E. Landon, "Erinna," *The Golden Violet* (1827)

6 Music is not technique and melody, but the meaning of life itself, infinitely sorrowful and unbearably beautiful.
   Pearl S. Buck, *The Exile* (1936)

7 The one universal form of art is music.
   Faith Baldwin, "Communication," *Face Toward the Spring* (1956)

8 Music sets up ladders, / it makes us invisible, / it sets us apart, / it lets us escape.
   H.D., *Tribute to the Angels* (1945)

9 Nothing recalls the past like music.
   Madame de Staël, *Corinne* (1807)

10 The memories which come to us through music are not accompanied by any regrets; for a moment music gives us back the pleasures it retraces, and we feel them again rather than recollect them.
   Madame de Staël, *Letters on Rousseau* (1788)

11 People always remember the tune they fell in love to.
   Ruth Wolff, *A Crack in the Sidewalk* (1965)

12 Music revives the recollections it would appease.
   Madame de Staël, *Corinne* (1807)

13 All music, even if its occasion be a gay one, renders us pensive.
   Madame de Staël, *Corinne* (1807)

14 The music was my friend, my lover, my family.
   Maya Angelou, *Gather Together in My Name* (1974)

15 La la la, Oh music swims back to me.
   Anne Sexton, "Music Swims Back to Me," *To Bedlam and Part Way Back* (1960)

16 Sweet sounds, oh, beautiful music, do not cease!
   Edna St. Vincent Millay, "On Hearing a Symphony of Beethoven," *The Buck in the Snow* (1928)

17 Writing more and more to the sound of music, writing more and more like music. Sitting in my studio tonight, playing record after record, writing, music a stimulant of the highest order, far more potent than wine.
   Anaïs Nin (1935), *The Diary of Anaïs Nin*, vol. 2 (1967)

18 Music relates sound and time and so pictures the ultimate edges of human communications.
   Iris Murdoch, *The Black Prince* (1973)

19 I am speech / beyond words' lettered reach.
   Sister M. Madeleva, "Music," *Collected Poems* (1947)

20 Notes fly so much farther than words. There is no other way to reach the infinite.
   Anaïs Nin (1976), *The Diary of Anaïs Nin*, vol. 7 (1980)

21 Words are wearisome and worn, while the arabesques of music are forever new.
   Colette, *My Apprenticeships* (1936)

22 The power and magic of music lie in its intangibility and its limitlessness. It suggests images, but leaves us free to choose them and to accommodate them to our pleasure.
   Wanda Landowska, in Denise Restout, ed., *Landowska on Music* (1964)

23 It is our job only to make the music. The audience that should hear it will be brought to our music at the right time.
   Margueritte Harmon Bro, *Sarah* (1949)

24 There is a magic burning in it, / Cutting its facets diamond clear, / And it alone calms me in minutes / When others do not dare come near.
   Anna Akhmatova, "Music" (1958), *Poems* (1988)

25 What good is music? None . . . and that is the point. To the world and its states and armies and factories and Leaders, music says, "You are irrelevant"; and, arrogant and gentle as a god, to the suffering man it says only, "Listen." For being saved is not the point. Music saves nothing. Merci-

ful, uncaring, it denies and breaks down all the shelters, the houses men build for themselves, that they may see the sky.

Ursula K. Le Guin, "An die Musik," in *Western Humanities Review* (1961)

1 Listening to music feels like a triumphant expedition into the Future; but into a Future which is happening now.

C. Anstruther-Thomson, *Art and Man* (1923)

2 Music is a missionary effort to colonize earth for imperialistic heaven.

Rebecca West, *This Real Night* (1985)

3 Great music has always been rooted in religion— when religion is understood as an *attitude* toward superhuman power and the mysteries of the universe.

Sophie Drinker, *Music and Women* (1948)

4 While I listened, music was to my soul what the atmosphere is to my body; it was the breath of my inward life. I felt, more deeply than ever, that music is the highest symbol of the infinite and holy. . . . With renewed force I felt what I have often said, that the secret of creation lay in music. "A *voice* to light gave being." Sound led the stars into their places.

Lydia Maria Child, *Letters From New York*, 2nd series (1845)

5 It had never occurred to me before that music and thinking are so much alike. In fact you could say music is another way of thinking, or maybe thinking is another kind of music.

Ursula K. Le Guin, *Very Far Away From Anywhere Else* (1976)

6 Music is our myth of the inner life.

Susanne K. Langer, *Philosophy in a New Key* (1942)

7 Music is the most absorbing of all the arts. It absorbs the mind of the artist, whether creator or executant, to the exclusion of every other consideration outside his own immediate necessities or desires.

Baroness Orczy, *Links in the Chain of Life* (1947)

8 Music stays in the air. / It travels at the speed of breath / at the sound of light. / It is never not heard. / It can wait centuries if it has to.

Alexis De Veaux, *Don't Explain: A Song of Billie Holiday* (1980)

9 The god of music dwelleth out of doors.

Edith M. Thomas, "Music," *Lyrics and Sonnets* (1887)

10 Music comes first from my heart, and then goes upstairs to my head where I check it out.

Roberta Flack, in Terri L. Jewell, ed., *The Black Woman's Gumbo Ya-Ya* (1993)

11 The new modern music puzzled her. It made her think but it did not make her feel.

Mary Roberts Rinehart, *This Strange Adventure* (1929)

12 He's a *professional* musician. I mean, he can do it even when he's not in the mood.

Joyce Grenfell, "Shirley's Girl Friend," *"Stately As a Galleon"* (1978)

13 Musicians are divided into two classes—those who like to hear themselves play and those who like to hear themselves sing.

Mary Wilson Little, *A Paragrapher's Reveries* (1904)

14 Almost anything is enough to keep alive someone who wishes nothing for himself but time to write music.

Dorothy Canfield, "An Unprejudiced Mind," *Fables for Parents* (1937)

15 Musical genius, the least sane of all gifts, put her in touch with the greater mysteries of the Universe.

Gertrude Atherton, *The Conqueror* (1902)

16 The judgment of music, like the inspiration for it, must come slow and measured, if it comes with truth.

Lillian Hellman, *Another Part of the Forest* (1947)

17 The music sounded flat—it had the kind of depth that comes from bitterness, not wonder.

Gretel Ehrlich, *Heart Mountain* (1988)

18 In the evenings the art of building gave way to that of music, which is architecture, too, though invisible.

Marguerite Yourcenar, *Memoirs of Hadrian* (1951)

19 False notes can be forgiven, false music cannot.

Nadia Boulanger, in Don G. Campbell, *Reflections of Boulanger* (1982)

20 I am always thirsting for beautiful, beautiful, beautiful music. I wish I could make it. Perhaps there isn't any music on earth like what I picture to myself.

Olive Schreiner, *The Letters of Olive Schreiner, 1876-1920* (1976)

1 Music was not invented by the composer, but found.

Nadia Boulanger, in Don G. Campbell, *Reflections of Boulanger* (1982)

2 Composing gives me great pleasure. . . . There is nothing which surpasses the joy of creation, if only because through it one wins hours of self-forgetfulness, when one lives in a world of sound.

Clara Schumann (1853), in Berthold Litzmann, *Clara Schumann*, vol. 2 (1913)

3 To study music, we must learn the rules. To create music, we must forget them.

Nadia Boulanger, in Aaron Copland and Vivian Perris, *Copland* (1984)

4 No one really understood music unless he was a scientist, her father had declared, and not just a scientist, either, oh, no, only the real ones, the theoreticians, whose language was mathematics.

Pearl S. Buck, *The Goddess Abides* (1972)

5 Rhythm is one of the principal translators between dream and reality. Rhythm might be described as, to the world of sound, what light is to the world of sight.

Edith Sitwell, *Taken Care Of* (1965)

6 As far as the execution is concerned . . . the most frequent and most serious mistake is to follow the music instead of preceding it.

Nadia Boulanger, in Alan Kendall, *The Tender Tyrant* (1976)

7 I hate the word *practice*. Practice breeds inurement. Instead of discovering, of distinguishing traits that are deeply hidden or merely veiled, one ends seeing nothing anymore. One ceases to be aware.

Wanda Landowska, in Denise Restout, ed., *Landowska on Music* (1964)

8 I never practice, I always play.

Wanda Landowska, in *Time* (1952)

9 You should never listen to someone practice. That is their work and theirs alone.

Nadia Boulanger, in Don G. Campbell, *Reflections of Boulanger* (1982)

10 Your concert-goer, though he feed upon symphony as a lamb upon milk, is no true lover if he play no instrument. Your true lover does more than admire the muse; he sweats a little in her service.

Catherine Drinker Bowen, *Friends and Fiddlers* (1935)

11 Miss Beevor had made her playing at once much better and much worse, by giving her resolute fingers greater power to express her misunderstanding of sound.

Rebecca West, *The Fountain Overflows* (1956)

12 Of course I like music, too. Very much. It's so pleasant of an evening, especially when made by your friends at home. I often say I like it better than cards. Though I must say I do like a good game of bridge.

Dorothy Canfield, *Her Son's Wife* (1926)

13 I was no more musical than a muskrat.

Jessamyn West, *The Life I Really Lived* (1979)

14 We were none of us musical, though Miss Jenkyns beat time, out of time, by way of appearing to be so.

Elizabeth Gaskell, *Cranford* (1853)

15 People always sound so proud when they announce they know nothing of music.

Lillian Hellman, *Another Part of the Forest* (1947)

16 Three armies might have been brought to combat with half the encouragement it took to bring the timid Matilda to the harp.

L.E. Landon, *Romance and Reality* (1831)

17 Miss Eckhart worshiped her metronome. She kept it, like the most precious secret in the teaching of music, in a wall safe.

Eudora Welty, "June Recital," *The Golden Apples* (1949)

18 The conductor obeyed all too literally the proverbial mandate. His right hand rarely knew what his left hand did.

Winifred Holtby, *South Riding* (1936)

19 All the other arts are lonely. We paint alone—*my* picture, *my* interpretation of the sky. *My* poem, *my* novel. But in music—ensemble music, not soloism—we share. No altruism this, for we receive tenfold what we give.

Catherine Drinker Bowen, *Friends and Fiddlers* (1935)

20 Chamber music—a conversation between friends.

Catherine Drinker Bowen, in Kathleen Kimball, Robin Petersen, and Kathleen Johnson, eds., *The Music Lover's Quotation Book* (1990)

21 How pleasant it is to be ignorant! Not to know exactly who Mozart was, to ignore his origin, his

influence, the details of his technique! To just let him lead one by the hand.

Maria-Luisa Bombal, "The Tree," in Zoila Nelken and Rosalie Torres-Rioseco, eds., *Short Stories of Latin America* (1963)

1 Mozart eliminates the idea of haste from life. His airs . . . never rush, they are never headlong or helter-skelter, they splash no mud, they raise no dust.

Rebecca West, *Black Lamb and Grey Falcon* (1941)

2 I want Bach's Toccata and Fugue in D played at my funeral. If it isn't I shall jolly well want to know why.

Sybil Thorndike, in *English Digest* (1965)

3 I find that I never lose Bach. I don't know why I have always loved him so. Except that he is so pure, so relentless and incorruptible, like a principle of geometry.

Edna St. Vincent Millay (1920), in Allan Ross Macdougall, ed., *Letters of Edna St. Vincent Millay* (1952)

4 The one Bach piece I learnt made me feel I was being repeatedly hit on the head with a teaspoon.

Dodie Smith, *I Capture the Castle* (1948)

5 There are some composers—at the head of whom stands Beethoven—who not only do not know when to stop but appear to stop many times before they actually do.

Virginia Graham, *Say Please* (1949)

6 Seated one day at the Organ, / I was weary and ill at ease, / And my fingers wandered idly / Over the noisy keys. / . . . / But I struck one chord of music, / Like the sound of a great Amen.

Adelaide Anne Procter, "A Lost Chord," *Legends and Lyrics* (1858)

7 To play pianissimo / is to carry sweet words / to the old woman in the last dark row / who cannot hear anything else, / and to lay them across her lap like a shawl.

Lola Haskins, "To Play Pianissimo," in Emilie Buchwald and Ruth Roston, eds., *Mixed Voices* (1991)

8 Inside the piano there are a thousand irregularities: 'tis the nature of the beast. Despite it all, we continue to think we are hearing something beautiful, and so we are. Our ears, our hearts, forgive. Music could even be defined by what we happen to be forgiving at a particular time in history.

Anita T. Sullivan, *The Seventh Dragon* (1985)

9 He would dream / of his piano as if it were flesh.

Lola Haskins, "The Prodigy," in Emilie Buchwald and Ruth Roston, eds., *Mixed Voices* (1991)

10 The piano and I were now bound for life, partners, companions, mates. Nothing and no one would ever be quite that important again, not husband, not home, not family, not good reviews, not bad reviews.

Ruth Slenczynska, with Louis Biancolli, *Forbidden Childhood* (1957)

11 Jean turned the piano into a human voice, waking them out of sodden sleep. Just listening was living. Life filtered through tired bodies, bent backs. Heads lifted. Fear and worry fled from their eyes. For an instant, they breathed in a fullness of life denied them in life.

Anzia Yezierska, *Arrogant Beggar* (1927)

12 A piano is full of suppressed desires, recalcitrance, inhibition, conflict.

Anita T. Sullivan, *The Seventh Dragon* (1985)

13 I wish the Government would put a tax on pianos for the incompetent.

Edith Sitwell (1943), in John Lehmann and Derek Parker, eds., *Selected Letters* (1970)

14 To Jack, his violin is comfort and relaxation. To his inky wife, it's time to put her head down the waste-disposal unit again.

Maureen Lipman, *How Was It for You?* (1985)

15 Everything you ever had, everything you ever lost. It's all there in the trumpet—pain and hate and trouble and peace and quiet and love.

Ann Petry, "Solo on the Drums," in *'47 Magazine of the Year* (1947)

16 I'm the saxophone / that wails all night / outside your bedroom window.

Grace Bauer, "So You Want to Hear the Blues," in Emilie Buchwald and Ruth Roston, eds., *Mixed Voices* (1991)

17 I stole everything I ever heard, but mostly I stole from the horns.

Ella Fitzgerald, in Barbara McDowell and Hana Umlauf, *Woman's Almanac* (1977)

18 If morning-glories had come out of the horn instead of those sounds, Josie would not have felt a more astonished delight. She was pierced with pleasure.

Eudora Welty, "The Winds," *The Wide Net* (1943)

1 A Tutor who tooted the flute, / Tried to teach two young tooters to toot; / Said the two to the tutor, / "Is it harder to toot or / To tutor two tooters to toot?"

Carolyn Wells, "The Tutor," *Folly for the Wise* (1904)

2 All riddles are blues, / And all blues are sad, / And I'm only mentioning / Some blues I've had.

Maya Angelou, "A Good Woman Feeling Bad," *Shaker, Why Don't You Sing?* (1983)

3 The blues records of each decade explain something about the philosophical basis of our lives as black people. . . . Blues is a basis of historical continuity for black people. It is a ritualized way of talking about ourselves and passing it on.

Sherley Anne Williams, in Claudia Tate, ed., *Black Women Writers at Work* (1983)

4 Audiences like their blues singers to be miserable.

Janis Joplin, in Barbara McDowell and Hana Umlauf, *Woman's Almanac* (1977)

5 The person who sings only the blues is like someone in a deep pit yelling for help.

Mahalia Jackson, with Evan McLeod Wylie, *Movin' On Up* (1966)

6 Nobody can teach you how to sing the blues, you have to feel the blues.

Ernestine Anderson, in Brian Lanker, *I Dream a World* (1989)

7 "What do blues do for you?" "It helps me to explain what I can't explain."

Gayl Jones, *Corregidora* (1975)

8 When the white kids started to dance to it.

Ruth Brown, asked when rhythm and blues started becoming rock and roll, in *Rolling Stone* (1990)

9 Blues are the songs of despair, but gospel songs are the songs of hope.

Mahalia Jackson, with Evan McLeod Wylie, *Movin' On Up* (1966)

10 Gospel music in those days of the early 1930s was really taking wing. It was the kind of music colored people had left behind them down South and they liked it because it was just like a letter from home.

Mahalia Jackson, with Evan McLeod Wylie, *Movin' On Up* (1966)

11 Gospel singing . . . is the rawest, sweetest, uninhibited and exquisite sounds a person can make or hear. It isn't music, it's an entire experience you feel and live. A sound to rise you up again.

Lynda Barry, *The Good Times Are Killing Me* (1988)

12 The Hawaiian people have been from time immemorial lovers of poetry and music, and have been apt in improvising historic poems, songs of love, and chants of worship, so that praises of the living or wails over the dead were with them but the natural expression of their feelings.

Lydia Kamekeha Liliuokalani, *Hawaii's Story by Hawaii's Queen* (1898)

13 Only dead people need loud music, you know.

Alice Walker, *Temple of My Familiar* (1989)

See also Art, Jazz, Opera, Singing, Song.

## ♪ MYSTERIES

14 What is the modern detective story but an extension of the medieval morality play?

Catherine Aird, "The Devout Benefit of Clergy," in Dilys Winn, *Murder Ink* (1977)

15 Where there's a will there's a detective story.

Carolyn Wells, "The Turnings of a Bookworm," *Folly for the Wise* (1904)

16 Do you solemnly swear never to conceal a vital clue from the reader? Do you promise to observe seemly moderation in the use of gangs, conspiracies, Super Criminals and Lunatics and utterly and forever to forswear Mysterious Poisons unknown to science? . . . If you fail to keep your promise, may other writers steal your plots and your pages swarm with misprints.

Dorothy L. Sayers, "The Oath of Initiation Into the Detection Club of London," in Elaine Budd, *Thirteen Mistresses of Murder* (1986)

17 He [Dashiell Hammett] is so hard-boiled you could roll him on the White House lawn.

Dorothy Parker, "Oh, Look—a Good Book!" in *The New Yorker* (1931)

## ♪ MYSTERY

18 No object is mysterious. The mystery is your eye.

Elizabeth Bowen, *The House in Paris* (1936)

See also Magic, The Unknown.

## · MYSTICISM

1 The worst danger of the mystic is as always a quest of spiritual privilege leading to aloofness from the common lot.

   Vida Dutton Scudder, *The Privilege of Age* (1939)

2 Mysticism and creativity have this in common: they require a person to live truthfully at every level of being.

   Marilyn Whiteside, in *Journal of Creative Behavior* (1981)

See also Shamans, Spirituality, Visions.

## · MYTH

3 Myths are early science, the result of men's first trying to explain what they saw around them.

   Edith Hamilton, *Mythology* (1942)

4 Myths hook and bind the mind because at the same time they set the mind free: they explain the universe while allowing the universe to go on being unexplained.

   Jeanette Winterson, *Boating for Beginners* (1985)

5 A myth is far truer than a history, for a history only gives a story of the shadows, whereas a myth gives a story of the substances that cast the shadows.

   Annie Besant, *Esoteric Christianity* (1901)

6 Mythology is much better stuff than history. It has form; logic; a message.

   Penelope Lively, *Moon Tiger* (1987)

7 Mythology is the mother of religions, and grandmother of history.

   Zsuzsanna E. Budapest, "Herstory," in *Sister* (1974)

8 The test of a true myth is that each time you return to it, new insights and interpretations arise.

   Starhawk, *The Spiral Dance* (1989)

9 When the genuine myth rises into consciousness, that is always its message. You must change your life.

   Ursula K. Le Guin, "Myth and Archetype in Science Fiction" (1976), *Language of the Night* (1979)

10 Myth is someone else's religion.

   Caroline Llewellyn, *The Lady of the Labyrinth* (1990)

11 One of the great inventions of the twentieth century was the studied, methodical engineering of myth for political ends.

   Caryl Rivers, "Mythogony," in *Quill* (1985)

See also Legends.

# N

## § NAGGING

1 Nagging is the repetition of unpalatable truths.
   Edith Summerskill, speech (1960)

See also Disapproval.


## § NAMES

2 A name is a road.
   Iris Murdoch, *The Sea, The Sea* (1978)

3 A name is a solemn thing.
   L.T. Meade, *The Honorable Miss* (1900)

4 Names govern the world.
   Hannah More, *Hints Towards Forming the Character of a Young Princess* (1805)

5 Picking the right name for the baby is beset with difficulties. . . . Whatever name you choose, the baby, some years hence, will hate it anyway, and decide to have his friends call him Slats or Rocky.
   Elinor Goulding Smith, *The Complete Book of Absolutely Perfect Baby and Child Care* (1957)

6 I am the one whose love / overcomes you, already with you / when you think to call my name.
   Jane Kenyon, "Briefly It Enters, and Briefly Speaks," *The Boat of Quiet Hours* (1986)

7 Say / who I am. Set / our two fires climbing.
   Mary Virginia Micka, "Greeting," *All Rounds Returning* (1986)

8 Writing my name I raise an edifice / Whose size and shape appear to me / As homelike as the hexagon the bee / Builds for his own and honey's use.
   Jessamyn West, *Hide and Seek* (1973)

9 It would have saved trouble had I remained Perkins from the first, this changing of women's names is a nuisance we are now happily outgrowing.
   Charlotte Perkins Gilman, *The Living of Charlotte Perkins Gilman* (1935)

10 Both legally and familiarly, as well as in my books, I now have only one name, which is my own.
   Colette, *La Naissance du jour* (1928)

11 Hoary idea, in any case, expecting a woman to surrender her name to her husband's in exchange for his. Why? Would any man submerge his identity and heritage to the woman he wed?
   Marya Mannes, *Out of My Time* (1968)

12 No, no, Jean. The *t* is silent, as in *Harlow*.
   Margot Asquith, to Jean Harlow, who repeatedly mispronounced her first name, in T.S. Matthews, *Great Tom* (1974)

13 Listen how they say your name. If they can't say that right, there's no way they're going to know how to treat you proper, neither.
   Rita Dove, *Through the Ivory Gate* (1992)

See also Naming.


## § NAMING

14 Naming is a difficult and time-consuming process; it concerns essences, and it means power. But on the wild nights who can call you home? Only the one who knows your name.
   Jeanette Winterson, *Oranges Are Not the Only Fruit* (1985)

1 The name we give to something shapes our attitude toward it.

   Katherine Paterson, *Gates of Excellence* (1981)

2 From antiquity, people have recognized the connection between naming and power.

   Casey Miller and Kate Swift, *Words and Women* (1976)

3 I understand why one wants to know the names of what he loves. . . . Naming is a kind of possessing, of caressing and fondling.

   Jessamyn West, *Hide and Seek* (1973)

4 What we name must answer to us; we can shape it if not control it.

   Starhawk, *Dreaming the Dark* (1982)

5 To name oneself is the first act of both the poet and the revolutionary. When we take away the right to an individual name, we symbolically take away the right to be an individual.

   Erica Jong, *How to Save Your Own Life* (1977)

6 Naming can limit as well as empower.

   Loraine Hutchins, in Loraine Hutchins and Lani Kaahumanu, eds., *Bi Any Other Name* (1991)

7 Nature is intricately and infinitely connected. The minute I name something and begin to regard it as a separate entity, I break this unbreakable unity. So that which makes it possible for us to seek truths about the universe and about ourselves has within itself the guarantee that we will never be able to find the Truth. Our knowledge must be forever fragmented, because that is the nature of systematic knowledge.

   Katherine Paterson, *Gates of Excellence* (1981)

8 Human names for natural things are superfluous. Nature herself does not name them. The important thing is to *know* this flower, look at its color until the blueness becomes as real as a keynote of music.

   Sally Carrighar, *Home to the Wilderness* (1973)

9 It is frustrating to name someone or something when in / the *real* world all is in motion, in a state of change. / That's why there is a danger when you try to name with / one name what is many, has no sides and is round.

   Joy Harjo, in Joseph Bruchac, ed., *Songs From This Earth on Turtle's Back* (1983)

See also Definitions, Labels, Names.

## ✿ NARROW-MINDEDNESS

10 Narrow-minded people are like narrow-necked bottles. . . . The less they have in them, the more noise they make pouring it out.

   Lynne Alpern and Esther Blumenfeld, *Oh, Lord, I Sound Just Like Mama* (1986)

11 I despise a person of little mind—one might as well not have any.

   Emma Dunham Kelley, *Megda* (1891)

12 We are pledged to be blind / By a totality of mind / Which has said: we shall learn what we already believe, / Study what we like, / Behoove what we approve, / Read our own creed.

   Josephine Miles, "A Foreign Country," *Poems* (1960)

13 There is no cure for narrowness of mind.

   Andre Norton, *Wraiths of Time* (1976)

14 You may call a person vain, and they will smile; you may call them immoral, and they may even feel flattered—but call them narrow-minded and they have done with you.

   J.E. Buckrose, "The Charm of Middle Age," *What I Have Gathered* (1923)

See also Intolerance.

## ✿ NATIONS

15 Nations decay from within more often than they surrender to outward assault.

   Ellen Glasgow, *A Certain Measure* (1943)

16 It ought to be possible for individuals to become spiritually rich, to grow profound in their souls, without suffering, but ordinarily they do not, and I think it is so with countries.

   Virginia Moore, *Virginia Is a State of Mind* (1942)

See also Canada, China, Denmark, Egypt, England, France, Government, Greece, Holland, India, Ireland, Israel, Italy, Japan, Mexico, the Philippines, Portugal, Russia, Turkey, United States.

## ✿ NATIVE AMERICANS

See American Indians.

## ❧ "NATURAL"

1 At times there is nothing so unnatural as nature.
    Carolyn Wells, "Wiseacreage," *Folly for the Wise* (1904)

2 Often, when the "natural" is invoked, we are left in the dark as to whether it is meant as an explanation, a recommendation, a claim for determinism, or simply a desperate appeal, as if the "natural" were some sort of metaphysical glue that could hold our claims or values together.
    Christine Pierce, "Natural Law Language and Women," in Vivian Gornick and Barbara K. Moran, eds., *Woman in Sexist Society* (1971)

3 Humans are by nature unnatural. We do not yet walk "naturally" on our hind legs, for example: such ills as fallen arches, lower back pain, and hernias testify that the body has not adapted itself completely to the upright posture. Yet this unnatural posture . . . is precisely what has made possible the development of important aspects of our "nature": the hand and the brain, and the complex system of skills, language, and social arrangements which were both effects and causes of hand and brain.
    Dorothy Dinnerstein, *The Mermaid and the Minotaur* (1976)

4 Many "natural" events—like early death, disease, hardship—are neither desirable nor necessary.
    Phyllis Chesler, *Women and Madness* (1972)

5 The "natural" is not necessarily a "human" value.
    Shulamith Firestone, *The Dialectic of Sex* (1970)

6 Nature has her language, and she is not unveracious; but we don't know all the intricacies of her syntax just yet, and in a hasty reading we may happen to extract the very opposite of her real meaning.
    George Eliot, *Adam Bede* (1859)

7 Natural law is only whatever happens in your lifetime within fifty miles of you.
    Anonymous woman, in Jane O'Reilly, *The Girl I Left Behind* (1980)

8 For centuries the word "nature" has been used to bolster prejudices or to express, not reality, but a state of affairs that the user would wish to see.
    Eva Figes, *Patriarchal Attitudes* (1970)

See also Essence, Human Nature.

## ❧ NATURE

9 We are nature. We are nature seeing nature. We are nature with a concept of nature. Nature weeping. Nature speaking of nature to nature.
    Susan Griffin, *Woman and Nature* (1978)

10 Nature has been for me, for as long as I can remember, a source of solace, inspiration, adventure, and delight; a home, a teacher, a companion.
    Lorraine Anderson, *Sisters of the Earth* (1991)

11 To grow up in intimate association with nature—animal and vegetable—is an irreplaceable form of wealth and culture.
    Miles Franklin, *Childhood at Brindabella* (1963)

12 They are much to be pitied who have not been . . . given a taste for nature in early life.
    Jane Austen, *Mansfield Park* (1814)

13 The love of nature is a passion for those in whom it once lodges. It can never be quenched. It cannot change. It is a furious, burning, physical greed, as well as a state of mystical exaltation. It will have its own.
    Mary Webb, *The House in Dormer Forest* (1920)

14 Those who dwell, as scientists or laymen, among the beauties and mysteries of the earth are never alone or weary of life. . . . Those who contemplate the beauty of the earth find reserves of strength that will endure as long as life lasts.
    Rachel Carson, *The Sense of Wonder* (1965)

15 Meanings, moods, the whole scale of our inner experience, finds in nature the "correspondences" through which we may know our boundless selves.
    Kathleen Raine, *Selected Poems* (1988)

16 i keep knowing / the language of other nations. / i keep hearing / tree talk / water words / and i keep knowing what they mean.
    Lucille Clifton, "Breaklight," *An Ordinary Woman* (1974)

17 Nature is the common, universal language, understood by all.
    Kathleen Raine, *Selected Poems* (1988)

18 That is the stimulus of nature; it is never, never old, and always developing. Even the scarred, wrinkled earth herself is a mere infant among the old ladies and gentlemen that tread foot-paths in the sky.
    The Gardener, *The Garden of a Commuter's Wife* (1905)

1 Nature's silence is its one remark, and every flake of world is a chip off that old mute and immutable block.

Annie Dillard, *Teaching a Stone to Talk* (1982)

2 Nature's music is never over; her silences are pauses, not conclusions.

Mary Webb, *The Spring of Joy* (1917)

3 There is nothing in nature that can't be taken as a sign of both mortality and invigoration.

Gretel Ehrlich, *The Solace of Open Spaces* (1985)

4 There is no shame when one is foolish with a tree No bird ever called me crazy No rock scorns me as a whore The earth means exactly what it says.

Chrystos, "No Rock Scorns Me As Whore," in Cherríe Moraga and Gloria Anzaldúa, eds., *This Bridge Called My Back* (1983)

5 I have stopped sleeping inside. A house is too small, too confining. I want the whole world, and the stars too.

Sue Hubbell, *A Country Year* (1986)

6 Yesterday I sat in a field of violets for a long time perfectly still, until I really sank into it—into the rhythm of the place, I mean—then when I got up to go home I couldn't walk quickly or evenly because I was still in time with the field.

Anne Morrow Lindbergh, *Bring Me a Unicorn* (1971)

7 Valleys are the sunken places of the earth, cañons are scored out by the glacier plows of God.

Mary Austin, *The Land of Little Rain* (1904)

8 The land around San Juan Capistrano is the pocket where the Creator keeps all his treasures. Anything will grow there.

Frances Marion, *Westward the Dream* (1948)

9 The natural world is dynamic. From the expanding universe to the hair on a baby's head, nothing is the same from now to the next moment.

Helen Hoover, "The Waiting Hills," *The Long-Shadowed Forest* (1963)

10 Nature operates by profusion. Think of the nearly infinite number of seeds that fall to earth, only a fraction of which take root to become trees; of those five thousand or so drones that exist solely to ensure the fertilization of one queen bee; of the millions of sperm competing so fiercely to fertilize one egg.

Gabriele Lusser Rico, *Writing the Natural Way* (1973)

11 The power that makes grass grow, fruit ripen, and guides the bird in flight is in us all.

Anzia Yezierska, *Red Ribbon on a White Horse* (1950)

12 There are dangers in sentimentalizing nature. Most sentimental ideas imply, at bottom, a deep if unacknowledged disrespect. It is no accident that we Americans, probably the world's champion sentimentalizers about nature, are at one and the same time probably the world's most voracious and disrespectful destroyers of wild and rural countryside.

Jane Jacobs, *The Death and Life of Great American Cities* (1961)

13 If I have learned nothing else in all these months in the woods, I have thoroughly learned to keep hands off the processes of nature.

Laura Lee Davidson, *A Winter of Content* (1922)

14 It is the nature of human beings not to be able to leave nature alone.

Margaret Visser, *The Rituals of Dinner* (1991)

15 We have for too long accepted a traditional way of looking at nature, at nature's creatures, which has blinded us to their incredible essence, and which has made us incomparably lonely. It is our loneliness as much as our greed which can destroy us.

Joan McIntyre, *Mind in the Waters* (1974)

16 Teach the legal rights of trees, the nobility of hills; respect the beauty of singularity, the value of solitude.

Josephine W. Johnson, "On a Winter Morning," in *Ohio* (1990)

17 Nature is just enough; but men and women must comprehend and accept her suggestions.

Antoinette Brown Blackwell, *The Sexes Throughout Nature* (1875)

18 Nature doesn't move in a straight line, and as part of nature, neither do we.

Gloria Steinem, *Revolution From Within* (1993)

19 Now, nature, as I am only too well aware, has her enthusiasts, but on the whole, I am not to be counted among them. To put it rather bluntly, I am not the type who wants to go back to the land—I am the type who wants to go back to the hotel.

Fran Lebowitz, *Social Studies* (1977)

See also Animals, The Country, Desert, Earth, Flowers, Gardening, Human Nature, Land, "Natural," Plants, Trees, Wilderness, Wildlife.

## ❧ NATURE/NURTURE

1 Breed is stronger than pasture.

  George Eliot, *Silas Marner* (1861)

2 *Environment* is undoubtedly a *secondary* factor in the phenomena of life; it can modify in that it can help or hinder, but it can never *create*.

  Maria Montessori, *The Montessori Method* (1912)

3 All good qualities in a child are the result of environment, while all the bad ones are the result of poor heredity on the side of the other parent.

  Elinor Goulding Smith, *The Complete Book of Absolutely Perfect Baby and Child Care* (1957)

See also Heredity.


## ❧ NEBRASKA

4 The only thing very noticeable about Nebraska was that it was still, all day long, Nebraska.

  Willa Cather, *My Antonia* (1918)


## ❧ NECESSITY

5 Necessity is God's veil.

  Simone Weil, *Gravity and Grace* (1947)

6 Necessity does the work of courage.

  George Eliot, *Romola* (1862)

7 The contradictions the mind comes up against, these are the only realities, the criterion of the real. There is no contradiction in what is imaginary. Contradiction is the test of necessity.

  Simone Weil, *Gravity and Grace* (1947)

See also Need.


## ❧ NEED

8 It is inevitable that when one has a great need of something one finds it. What you need you attract like a lover.

  Gertrude Stein, in Elizabeth Sprigge, *Gertrude Stein* (1957)

9 God forgives those who invent what they need.

  Lillian Hellman, *The Little Foxes* (1939)

10 There wasn't enough for Indigo in the world she'd been born to, so she made up what she needed. What she thought the black people needed.

  Ntozake Shange, *Sassafrass, Cypress & Indigo* (1982)

11 In my life's chain of events nothing was accidental. Everything happened according to an inner need.

  Hannah Senesh (1943), *Hannah Senesh* (1966)

12 The least a person can ask out of life is to be needed by someone.

  Maia Wojciechowska, *A Single Light* (1968)

See also Necessity.


## ❧ NEGLECT

13 After the door of a woman's heart has once swung on its silent hinges, a man thinks he can prop it open with a brick and go away and leave it.

  Myrtle Reed, *The Spinster Book* (1901)


## ❧ NERVES

14 For me it's always midnight with the phone out of order and a murderer on the fire escape. What I suffer from nerves could be a technicolor spectacle.

  Helen Hudson, "The Strange Testament of Michael Cassidy," *The Listener* (1968)

15 But nerves! Be glad you have a nice little cirrhosis, Mrs. Munniman. Not like me with a husband silent as a stuffed sausage. I could drop dead asking him how many lumps in his tea.

  Helen Hudson, "The Strange Testament of Michael Cassidy," *The Listener* (1968)

16 He was as easy to live with as an alarm clock set to ring at regular intervals.

  Maia Wojciechowska, *A Single Light* (1968)

17 I feel so agitated all the time, like a hamster in search of a wheel.

  Carrie Fisher, *Postcards From the Edge* (1987)

18 Linda began to feel even more sharply that she was going insane. She wondered if she had already had

a nervous breakdown and just didn't have time to notice it.

Susan Cheever, *A Woman's Life* (1994)

1 No class of human creatures get so little sympathy as those who carry in their life-luggage a bundle of nerves.

Frances Willard (1860), in Ray Strachey, *Frances Willard* (1912)

See also Anxiety, Neurotics, Stress, Worry.

## ✥ NEUROTICS

2 Most of the worthwhile, the beautiful, the progressive and the useful achievements of *homo sapiens* had been produced by introverted neurotics.

Anne Blaisdell, *Nightmare* (1961)

3 Neurotics would like to sleep all the time, and to be awakened only when there is good news.

Mignon McLaughlin, *The Neurotic's Notebook* (1963)

4 At night, neurotics may toil not, but oh how they spin!

Mignon McLaughlin, *The Neurotic's Notebook* (1963)

5 The neurotic would like to trust his analyst—if only because he's paying him so much money. But he can't—because if the analyst really cared, he'd be doing it for nothing.

Mignon McLaughlin, *The Neurotic's Notebook* (1963)

6 When the pressures really mount, the neurotic must choose: Shall he have a good cry, or set fire to his neighbor's house?

Mignon McLaughlin, *The Neurotic's Notebook* (1963)

7 Neurotic quarrels always have the same theme-song: Hate me and get it over with.

Mignon McLaughlin, *The Neurotic's Notebook* (1963)

8 The neurotic longs to touch bottom, so at least he won't have *that* to worry about any more.

Mignon McLaughlin, *The Neurotic's Notebook* (1963)

See also Anxiety, Mental Illness, Nerves, Panic.

## ✥ NEUTRALITY

9 One longs for a voice in the middle . . . able to see a little right and a little wrong on both sides of many questions.

Millicent Fenwick (1976), *Speaking Up* (1982)

10 There are two sides to every issue: one side is right and the other is wrong, but the middle is always evil.

Ayn Rand, *Atlas Shrugged* (1957)

11 Intellectual neutrality is not possible in a historical world of exploitation and oppression.

Elisabeth Schüssler Fiorenza, *Bread Not Stone* (1984)

12 There is no politically neutral art.

bell hooks, in *The Other Side* (1994)

13 The worst and best are both inclined / To snap like vixens at the truth; / But, O, beware the middle mind / That purrs and never shows a tooth!

Elinor Wylie, "Nonsense Rhyme," *Angels and Earthly Creatures* (1929)

See also Compromise, Moderation.

## ✥ NEW ENGLAND

14 The New Englander landed on a stony, barren tract, and a large share of his strength during two centuries has gone to force a living out of it. Hence he has come to regard economy—a necessary unpleasant quality at best—as the chief of virtues. He has cultivated habits which verge on closeness in dealing with food, and with the expression of feeling, and even—his enemies think—with feeling itself.

Rebecca Harding Davis, *Bits of Gossip* (1904)

15 History . . . with its long, leisurely, gentlemanly labors, the books arriving by post, the cards to be kept and filed, the sections to be copied, the documents to be checked, is the ideal pursuit for the New England mind.

Elizabeth Hardwick, "Boston" (1959), *A View of My Own* (1962)

16 One person is as good as another in New England, and better, too.

Fanny Fern, *Folly As It Flies* (1868)

See also Boston, Maine, Vermont.

## ❦ NEWNESS

1 Novelty, the subtlest spring of all passion.

Gertrude Atherton, *Julia France and Her Times* (1912)

2 We tend to think things are new because we've just discovered them.

Madeleine L'Engle, *A Wind in the Door* (1973)

3 What the world, social and political, concrete and mental, really needs is not new things, but the old things made new.

Ethel M. Dell, *The Unknown Quantity* (1924)

4 New things are always ugly.

Willa Cather, in Phyllis C. Robinson, *Willa* (1983)

5 In trying to make something new, half the undertaking lies in discovering whether it can be done. Once it has been established that it can, duplication is inevitable.

Helen Gahagan Douglas, *A Full Life* (1982)

See also Adventure, Change, Discovery, Originality, The Unknown.

## ❦ NEWSPAPERS

6 If newspapers were written by people whose sole object in writing was to tell the truth about politics and the truth about art we should not believe in war, and we should believe in art.

Virginia Woolf, *Three Guineas* (1938)

7 Perhaps in the last ten years newspapers have become back fences for people now that so many of the old back fences are gone.

Anna Quindlen, *Thinking Out Loud* (1993)

8 I suppose you know where this country would be, where the *world* would be, if everyone who got depressed by the papers stopped reading them.

Sue Kaufman, *Diary of a Mad Housewife* (1967)

9 You should always believe all you read in newspapers, as this makes them more interesting.

Rose Macaulay, "Problems of a Reader's Life," *A Casual Commentary* (1926)

10 There are some things the general public does not need to know, and shouldn't. I believe the democracy flourishes when the government can take legitimate steps to keep its secrets and when the press can decide whether to print what it knows.

Katharine Graham, in Doug Henwood, "The Washington Post: The Establishment's Paper," *Extra* (1990)

11 The power is to set the agenda. What we print and what we don't print matter a lot.

Katharine Graham, in Carol Felsenthal, *Power, Privilege, and The Post* (1993)

12 Dead news like dead love has no phoenix in its ashes.

Enid Bagnold, *National Velvet* (1935)

13 Breakfast is the one meal at which it is permissible to read the paper.

Amy Vanderbilt, *New Complete Book of Etiquette* (1963)

14 Lady Middleton . . . exerted herself to ask Mr. Palmer if there was any news in the paper. "No, none at all," he replied, and read on.

Jane Austen, *Sense and Sensibility* (1811)

See also Journalism, Media, The Press.

## ❦ NEW YEAR'S EVE

15 O darkest Year! O brightest Year! / O changeful Year of joy 'and woe, / To-day we stand beside thy bier, / Still loth to let thee go!

Julia C.R. Dorr, "1865," *Poems* (1892)

16 Another year, another year,— / Alas! and must it be / That Time's most dark and weary wheel / Must turn again for me?

L.E. Landon, "New Year's Eve," *The Venetian Bracelet* (1829)

17 Celebratin' New Year's Eve is like eatin' oranges. You got to let go your dignity t' really enjoy 'em.

Edna Ferber, *Buttered Side Down* (1912)

18 The etiquette question that troubles so many fastidious people New Year's Day is: How am I ever going to face those people again?

Judith Martin, *Miss Manners' Guide to Excruciatingly Correct Behavior* (1982)

## ❦ NEW YORK

19 A city rose before me. It was narrow and tall like a gothic temple, surrounded by water, and . . . it sud-

denly appeared, as if with a slight push it detached itself out of the invisible into the visible.

Nina Berberova, *The Italics Are Mine* (1969)

1 Its sharp towers shoot up out of the rock like scissors, cutting the sky into ribbons.

Mary Borden, *Flamingo* (1927)

2 Situated on an island, which I think it will one day cover, it rises like Venice, from the sea, and like the fairest of cities in the days of her glory, receives into its lap tribute of all the riches of the earth.

Mrs. Trollope, *Domestic Manners of the Americans* (1832)

3 New York rose out of the water like a great wave that found it impossible to return again and so remained there in horror, peering out of the million windows men had caged it with.

Djuna Barnes, "The Hem of Manhattan," in *New York Morning Telegraph Sunday Magazine* (1917)

4 New York was an idea . . . an idea held simultaneously by thirteen million people.

Nancy Pickard, *But I Wouldn't Want to Die There* (1993)

5 If you *must* live in a city, New York is the only city in the world.

Katherine Neville, *A Calculated Risk* (1992)

6 The world is grand, awfully big and astonishingly beautiful, frequently thrilling. But I love New York.

Dorothy Kilgallen, after completing first round-the-world trip by a woman, *Girl Around the World* (1936)

7 Ah! some love Paris, / And some Purdue. / But love is an archer with a low I.Q. / A bold, bad bowman, and innocent of pity. / So I'm in love with / New York City.

Phyllis McGinley, "A Kind of Love Letter to New York," *The Love Letters of Phyllis McGinley* (1954)

8 There are so many New Yorks that you can always find the special one that fits your special pattern.

Lucy Sprague Mitchell, *Two Lives* (1953)

9 The New York voice reflects its diversity, its foreignness, and, inevitably, the sense of superiority New Yorkers feel or come to feel. It says, without saying, We Know.

Marya Mannes, *The New York I Know* (1961)

10 They were New Yorkers. They knew everything.

Katharine Brush, *Red-Headed Woman* (1930)

11 New York, forever the port of em- and de-barkation *en route* to Adventure.

Cornelia Stratton Parker, *Wanderer's Circle* (1934)

12 New York is the perfect town for getting over a disappointment, a loss, or a broken heart.

Shirley MacLaine, *You Can Get There From Here* (1975)

13 New York is not like London, a now-and-then place to many people. You can either not live in New York or not live anyplace else. One is either a lover or hater.

Amanda Cross, *A Trap for Fools* (1989)

14 No place has delicatessen like New York.

Judy Blume, *Are You There, God? It's Me, Margaret* (1970)

15 New York City is like the appetizer table at a Jewish wedding, loaded with salt and spice and cholesterol and flavor, with a waiter holding out pleasure in his right hand and indigestion in his left.

Leonore Fleischer, *The Fisher King* (1991)

16 The New York waiter . . . knows more than you do about everything. He disapproves of your taste in food and clothing, your gauche manners, your miserliness, and sometimes, it seems, of your very existence, which he tries to ignore.

Kate Simon, *New York Places and Pleasures* (1959)

17 The best way to get around in New York is to be both rich and patient.

Kate Simon, *New York Places and Pleasures* (1959)

18 It is often said that New York is a city of only the very rich and the very poor. It is less often said that New York is also, at least for those of us who came there from somewhere else, a city for only the very young.

Joan Didion, "Goodbye to All That," *Slouching Towards Bethlehem* (1968)

19 Like most people New Yorkers like to be thought a bit crazy.

Jan Morris, "The Islanders" (1979), *Among the Cities* (1985)

20 New York seems conducted by jazz, animated by it. It is essentially a city of rhythm.

Anaïs Nin (1934), *The Diary of Anaïs Nin*, vol. 2 (1967)

21 New York is like a disco, but without the music.

Elaine Stritch, in *The Observer* (1980)

22 Nothing is more likely to start me screaming like a madwoman than New York in February with its

piles of blackened snow full of yellow holes drilled by dogs.

> Florence King, *Southern Ladies and Gentlemen* (1975)

1 New York's the lonesomest place in the world if you don't know anybody.

> Nella Larsen, "Quicksand" (1928), *An Intimation of Things Distant* (1992)

2 New York is the meeting place of the peoples, the only city where you can hardly find a typical American.

> Djuna Barnes, "Greenwich Village As It Is," in *Pearson's Magazine* (1916)

3 I miss the animal buoyancy of New York, the animal vitality. I did not mind that it had no meaning and no depth.

> Anaïs Nin (1935), *The Diary of Anaïs Nin*, vol. 2 (1967)

4 There's something hypocritical about a city that keeps half of its population underground half of the time; you can start believing that there's much more space than there really is—to live, to work.

> Gloria Naylor, *Mama Day* (1988)

5 It is ridiculous to set a detective story in New York City. New York City is itself a detective story.

> Agatha Christie, in *Life* (1956)

6 A car is useless in New York, essential everywhere else. The same with good manners.

> Mignon McLaughlin, *The Second Neurotic's Notebook* (1966)

7 It seems to me, correct me if I'm wrong, that there are an awful lot of people in Manhattan. And it's getting worse.

> Cynthia Heimel, *But Enough About You* (1986)

## ⑧ NICENESS

8 This is a very nice day; and we are taking a very nice walk; and you are two very nice young ladies. Oh! it is a very nice word, indeed! it does for everything.

> Jane Austen, *Northanger Abbey* (1818)

9 You've been brought up to be nice—and that's a dangerous profession.

> Phyllis Bottome, "The Battle-Field," *Innocence and Experience* (1934)

10 Nice is a pallid virtue. Not like honesty or courage or perseverance. On the other hand, in a nation

notably lacking in civility, there is much to be said for nice.

> Molly Ivins, in *The Fort Worth Star-Telegram* (1994)

See also Kindness.

## ⑧ NIGHT

11 Night is the first skin around me.

> Roberta Hill Whiteman, "The Recognition," *Star Quilt* (1984)

12 The earth rests, and remembers.

> Helen Hoover, "The Waiting Hills," *The Long-Shadowed Forest* (1963)

13 Wild Nights — Wild Nights! / Were I with thee / Wild Nights should be / Our luxury!

> Emily Dickinson (1861), in T.W. Higginson and Mabel Loomis Todd, eds., *Poems by Emily Dickinson*, 2nd series (1891)

14 For the night was not impartial. No, the night loved some more than others, served some more than others.

> Eudora Welty, "Moon Lake," *The Golden Apples* (1949)

15 Tropical nights are hammocks for lovers.

> Anaïs Nin (1940), *The Diary of Anaïs Nin*, vol. 3 (1969)

16 It was one of those nights when the air is blood-temperature and it's impossible to tell where you leave off and it begins.

> Elaine Dundy, *The Dud Avocado* (1958)

17 It was the sort of night when you think you could lie in the snow until morning and never get cold.

> Faith Sullivan, *The Cape Ann* (1988)

18 This dead of midnight is the noon of thought, / And Wisdom mounts her zenith with the stars. / At this still hour the self-collected soul / Turns inward, and beholds a stranger there / Of high descent, and more than mortal rank; / An embryo God; a spark of fire divine.

> Anna Laetitia Barbauld, "A Summer Evening's Meditation" (1773), *The Works of Anna Laetitia Barbauld*, vol. 1 (1825)

19 Things that live by night live outside the realm of "normal" time and so suggest living outside the realm of good and evil, since we have moralistic feelings about time. Chauvinistic about our human need to wake by day and sleep by night, we come

to associate night dwellers with people up to no good at a time when they have the jump on the rest of us and are defying nature, defying their circadian rhythms.

Diane Ackerman, *The Moon by Whale Light* (1991)

1 My day-mind can endure / Upright, in hope, all it must undergo. / But O, afraid, unsure, / My night-mind waking lies too low, too low.

Alice Meynell, "To Sleep," *Last Poems of Alice Meynell* (1923)

2 In the evening your vision widens / looks out beyond midnight— / . . . / We are in a sickroom. / But the night belongs to the angels.

Nelly Sachs, "In the Evening Your Vision Widens," *O the Chimneys* (1967)

3 Well, this is the end of a perfect day, / Near the end of a journey, too.

Carrie Jacobs-Bond, "The End of a Perfect Day" (1910), *The Roads of Melody* (1927)

4 The night will slip away / Like sorrow or a tune.

Eleanor Farjeon, "The Night Will Never Stay," *Gypsy and Ginger* (1920)

See also Darkness, Evening, Sleep, Sunset, Twilight.

## ❧ NOISE

5 We like no noise unless we make it ourselves.

Marie de Rabutin-Chantal, Marquise de Sévigné (1674), *Letters of Madame de Sévigné to Her Daughter and Her Friends*, vol. 2 (1811)

6 If we don't sit down and shut up once in a while we'll lose our minds even earlier than we had expected. Noise is an imposition on sanity, and we live in very noisy times.

Joan Baez, *Daybreak* (1968)

7 When he mounted the stairs to his father's office he mounted them three at a time. You heard him crashing down again, whistling as he came. Except for the whistling, if someone had thrown him it would have sounded the same way.

Katharine Brush, *Red-Headed Woman* (1930)

See also Sound.

## ❧ NONFICTION

8 The challenge of nonfiction is to marry art and truth.

Phyllis Rose, in *Ms.* (1993)

See also Writing.

## ❧ NORMALCY

9 A normal human being . . . does not exist.

Karen Horney, *The Neurotic Personality of Our Time* (1937)

10 The conception of what is normal varies not only with the culture but also within the same culture, in the course of time.

Karen Horney, *The Neurotic Personality of Our Time* (1937)

11 She always says she dislikes the abnormal, it is so obvious. She says the normal is so much more simply complicated and interesting.

Gertrude Stein, *The Autobiography of Alice B. Toklas* (1933)

12 If civilization ever achieves a higher standard of what constitutes normality, it will have been the neurotic who led the way.

Nancy Hale, *Heaven and Hardpan Farm* (1957)

13 As we do at such times, I turned on my automatic pilot and went through the motions of normalcy on the outside, so that I could concentrate all my powers on surviving the near-mortal wound inside.

Sonia Johnson, *From Housewife to Heretic* (1981)

14 Normal day, let me be aware of the treasure you are. Let me learn from you, love you, savor you, bless you before you depart. Let me not pass you by in quest of some rare and perfect tomorrow. Let me hold you while I may, for it will not always be so. One day I shall dig my nails into the earth, or bury my face in the pillow, or stretch myself taut, or raise my hands to the sky, and want more than all the world your return.

Mary Jean Irion, *Yes, World* (1970)

See also Conventionality, Ordinariness, Routine.

## ❧ THE NORTH

15 The Yankees aren't fiends. They haven't horns and hoofs, as you seem to think. They are pretty much

like Southerners—except with worse manners, of course, and terrible accents.

Margaret Mitchell, *Gone With the Wind* (1936)

See also The South.

## ✶ NOSINESS

1 Some of 'em so expert on mindin' folks' business dat dey kin look at de smoke comin' out yo' chimbley and tell yuh what yuh cookin'.

Zora Neale Hurston, *Jonah's Gourd Vine* (1934)

2 There are inquiries which are a sort of moral burglary.

Katharine Fullerton Gerould, *Modes and Morals* (1920)

3 There were too many ears that listened for others besides themselves, and too many tongues that wagged to those they shouldn't.

Mildred D. Taylor, *Roll of Thunder, Hear My Cry* (1976)

See also Gossip, Interference, Small Towns.

## ✶ NOSTALGIA

4 I cannot sing the old songs / I sang long years ago, / For heart and voice would fail me, / And foolish tears would flow.

Charlotte Alington Barnard, "The Old Songs" (1860)

5 There is no remedy for this: / Good days that will not come again.

Dorothy L. Sayers, *Op. I.* (1916)

6 We have the bad habit, some of us, of looking back to a time . . . when society was stable and orderly, family ties stronger and deeper, love more lasting and faithful, and so on. Let me be your Cassandra prophesying after the fact, and a long study of the documents in the case: it was never true, that is, no truer than it is now.

Katherine Anne Porter, "'Marriage Is Belonging,'" *The Days Before* (1952)

7 I cannot think of a thing that was better in those good old days.

Rose Schneiderman, with Lucy Goldthwaite, *All for One* (1967)

8 Few cultures have not produced the idea that in some past era the world ran better than it does now.

Elizabeth Janeway, *Man's World, Woman's Place* (1971)

9 The nostalgia— / not of memories / But of what has never been!

Zoë Akins, "The Tomorrows," *The Hills Grow Smaller* (1937)

10 Some people will tell you that the old live in the past . . . old ladies feeding like docile rabbits on the lettuce leaves of other times, other manners.

Margaret Laurence, *The Stone Angel* (1964)

11 It is better to remember our love as it was in the springtime.

Bess Streeter Aldrich, *Spring Came on Forever* (1935)

12 A mark was on him from the day's delight, so that all his life, when April was a thin green and the flavor of rain was on his tongue, an old wound would throb and a nostalgia would fill him for something he could not quite remember.

Marjorie Kinnan Rawlings, *The Yearling* (1938)

13 The sudden nostalgia was as much of the body as of the spirit. Her very veins seemed full of tears.

Gertrude Atherton, *Transplanted* (1919)

See also Memory, Past, Remembrance, Sentimentality.

## ✶ NOTORIETY

14 I never claimed to be famous. Notorious I have always been.

Lola Montez (c. 1856), in Edward B. Marks, *They All Had Glamour* (1944)

## ✶ NOVELS

15 Only a novel! . . . only some work in which the greatest powers of the mind are displayed, in which the most thorough knowledge of human nature, the happiest delineation of its varieties, the liveliest effusions of wit and humor, are conveyed to the world in the best-chosen language.

Jane Austen, *Northanger Abbey* (1818)

1 A great novel is a kind of conversion experience. We come away from it changed.

Katherine Paterson, *Gates of Excellence* (1981)

2 Each sentence must have, at its heart, a little spark of fire, and this, whatever the risk, the novelist must pluck with his own hands from the blaze.

Virginia Woolf, "Life and the Novelist," *The Common Reader*, 1st series (1925)

3 The artist deals with what cannot be said in words. The artist whose medium is fiction does this *in words*. The novelist says in words what cannot be said in words.

Ursula K. Le Guin, *The Left Hand of Darkness* (1969)

4 The novel does not simply recount experience, it adds to experience.

Elizabeth Bowen, "Truth and Fiction" (1956), *Afterthought* (1962)

5 For me, the novel is experience illumined by imagination.

Ellen Glasgow, 1933 preface, *Barren Ground* (1925)

6 The novel is an art form and when you use it for anything other than art, you pervert it.

Flannery O'Connor, in Sally Fitzgerald, ed., *The Habit of Being* (1979)

7 Surely the novel should be a form of art—but art was not enough. It must contain not only the perfection of art, but the imperfection of nature.

Ellen Glasgow, *The Woman Within* (1954)

8 Novels, like human beings, usually have their beginnings in the dark.

Rita Mae Brown, *High Hearts* (1986)

9 One doesn't "get" an "idea" for a novel. The "idea" more or less "gets" you. It uses you as a kind of culture, the way a pearl uses an oyster.

Diana Chang, "Woolgathering, Ventriloquism and the Double Life," in Dexter Fisher, ed., *The Third Woman* (1980)

10 A novel is not born of a single idea. . . . For me, novels have invariably come from a complex of ideas that in the beginning seemed to bear no relation to each other, but in the unconscious began mysteriously to merge and grow. Ideas for a novel are like the strong guy lines of a spider web. Without them the silken web cannot be spun.

Katherine Paterson, in *The Writer* (1990)

11 Among the many problems which beset the novelist, not the least weighty is the choice of the moment at which to begin his novel.

Vita Sackville-West, *The Edwardians* (1930)

12 One should be able to return to the first sentence of a novel and find the resonances of the entire work.

Gloria Naylor, in *The New York Times Book Review* (1985)

13 Preeminently the novelist's gift is that of access to the collective mind.

Mary Austin, "The American Form of the Novel," in *New Republic Magazine* (1922)

14 I suppose I am a born novelist, for the things I imagine are more vital and vivid to me than the things I remember.

Ellen Glasgow, *Letters of Ellen Glasgow* (1958)

15 Novelists should never allow themselves to weary of the study of real life.

Charlotte Brontë, *The Professor* (1846)

16 The story is a piece of work. The novel is a way of life.

Toni Cade Bambara, in Janet Sternburg, ed., *The Writer on Her Work*, vol. 1 (1980)

17 Novel writing is a kind of private pleasure, even if nothing comes of it in worldly terms.

Barbara Pym (1976), in Hazel Holt, *A Lot to Ask* (1990)

18 Nearly all novels are too long.

Rose Macaulay, *Potterism* (1920)

19 I don't think you should write something as long as a novel around anything that is not of the gravest concern to you and everybody else and for me this is always the conflict between an attraction for the Holy and the disbelief in it that we breathe in with the air of the times.

Flannery O'Connor, in Sally Fitzgerald, ed., *The Habit of Being* (1979)

20 The only difficulty is to know what bits to choose and what to leave out. Novel-writing is not creation, it is selection.

Winifred Holtby (1926), in Alice Holtby and Jean McWilliam, eds., *Letters to a Friend* (1937)

21 The dead hand of research lies heavy on too many novels.

Nancy Hale, in Richard Thruelsen and John Kobler, eds., *Adventures of the Mind*, 2nd series (1961)

1 A novelist's chief desire is to be as unconscious as possible. He has to induce in himself a state of perpetual lethargy. He wants life to proceed with the utmost quiet and regularity. He wants to see the same faces, to read the same books, to do the same things day after day, month after month, while he is writing, so that nothing may break the illusion in which he is living—so that nothing may disturb or disquiet the mysterious noisings about, feelings around, darts, dashes, and sudden discoveries of that very shy and illusive spirit, the imagination.

Virginia Woolf, "Professions for Women," *The Death of the Moth* (1942)

2 In any work that is truly creative, I believe, the writer cannot be omniscient in advance about the effects that he proposes to produce. The suspense of a novel is not only in the reader, but in the novelist himself, who is intensely curious too about what will happen to the hero.

Mary McCarthy, "Settling the Colonel's Hash" (1954), *On the Contrary* (1961)

3 The novelist, afraid his ideas may be foolish, slyly puts them in the mouth of some other fool, and reserves the right to disavow them.

Diane Johnson, in *The New York Times Book Review* (1979)

4 In this genre, perfection may require the greatest genius, but mediocrity is well within everyone's grasp.

Madame de Staël, *Essay on Fictions* (1795)

5 Who are those ever multiplying authors that with unparalleled fecundity are overstocking the world with their quick succeeding progeny? They are *novel-writers*.

Hannah More, *Strictures on the Modern System of Female Education* (1799)

See also Fiction, Fictional Characters, Literature, Writing.

## ❦ NOVEMBER

6 Here's November, / The year's sad daughter.

Eleanor Farjeon, "Enter November," *The Children's Bells* (1960)

7 November is the most disagreeable month in the whole year.

Louisa May Alcott, *Little Women* (1868)

8 November's night is dark and drear, / The dullest month of all the year.

L.E. Landon, "Frances Beaumont," *Traits and Trials of Early Life* (1837)

9 In November you begin to know how long the winter will be.

Martha Gellhorn, "November Afternoon," *The Heart of Another* (1941)

10 Let others deck them as they please / In frill and furbelow. / She scorns alike the fripperies / Of flowers and of snow.

Phyllis McGinley, "November," *One More Manhattan* (1937)

11 Why has no one written a November rhapsody with plenty of lilt and swing? The poets who are moved at all by this month seem only stirred to lamentation, giving us year end and "melancholy days" remarks, thereby showing that theory is stronger than observation among the rhyming brotherhood, or else that they have chronic indigestion and no gardens to stimulate them.

The Gardener, *The Garden of a Commuter's Wife* (1905)

12 Some of the days in November carry the whole memory of summer as a fire opal carries the color of moonrise.

Gladys Taber, *Stillmeadow Daybook* (1955)

See also Autumn.

## ❦ NUCLEAR WEAPONS

13 The nihilistic conviction that human beings are meaningless, that life itself is meaningless, had taken on material form. Nuclear self-destruction was its logical expression, evidence of the absurdity of believing that human existence had meaning and purpose.

Christina Thürmer-Rohr, *Vagabonding* (1991)

14 The term "clean bombs" provides the perfect metaphor for defense analysts and arms controllers. This sort of language shields us from the emotional reaction that would result if it were clear that one was talking about plans for mass murder, for mangled bodies.

Carol Cohn, "'Clean Bombs' and Clean Language," in Jean Bethke Elshtain and Sheila Tobias, eds., *Women, Militarism, and War* (1990)

1 Cogito ergo boom.

> Susan Sontag, "'Thinking Against Oneself': Reflections on Cioran," *Styles of Radical Will* (1966)

See also Militarism, War.

## ❧ NUDITY

2 Nudists are fond of saying that when you come right down to it everyone is alike, and, again, that when you come right down to it everyone is different.

> Diane Arbus, "Notes on the Nudist Camp," *Magazine Work* (1984)

3 There are certain people who should know what you look like naked. I just don't think your high-school algebra teacher should be one of them.

> Julia Roberts, on refusing to do nude movie scenes, in *Vogue* (1994)

4 I'm wise enough to know what I didn't know when I did my first nude scene: it's all commercial bananas and nothing to do with what is valuable to the script.

> Susan Hampshire, in David Bailey and Peter Evans, *Goodbye Baby and Amen* (1969)

5 Nudity on stage? I think it's disgusting. But if I were twenty-two with a great body, it would be artistic, tasteful, patriotic and a progressive religious experience.

> Shelley Winters (1965), in Michèle Brown and Ann O'Connor, *Hammer and Tongues* (1986)

6 I had the radio on.

> Marilyn Monroe, when asked if she really had nothing on in the calendar photograph, in *Time* (1952)

## ❧ NURSERY RHYMES

7 Twinkle, twinkle, little star, / How I wonder what you are! / Up above the world so high, / Like a diamond in the sky.

> Jane Taylor, "The Star," *Rhymes for the Nursery* (1806)

8 "Will you walk into my parlor?" said the Spider to the Fly, / "'Tis the prettiest little parlor that ever you did spy."

> Mary Howitt, "The Spider and the Fly," *Ballads and Other Poems* (1847)

9 Mary had a little lamb, / Its fleece was white as snow; / And everywhere that Mary went / The lamb was sure to go.

> Sarah Josepha Hale, "Mary's Little Lamb," *Poems for Our Children* (1830)

## ❧ NURSES

10 There is no human relationship more intimate than that of nurse and patient, one in which the essentials of character are more rawly revealed.

> Dorothy Canfield, *Her Son's Wife* (1926)

11 Sick people need immediate help, understanding and humanity almost as much as they need highly standardized and efficient practice.

> S. Josephine Baker, *Fighting for Life* (1939)

12 No man, not even a doctor, ever gives any definition of what a nurse should be than this—"devoted and obedient." This definition would do just as well for a porter. It might even do for a horse. It will not do [for a nurse].

> Florence Nightingale (1860), in Victor Cohn, *Sister Kenny* (1975)

13 Nursing was regarded as simply an extension of the unpaid services performed by the housewife—a characteristic attitude that haunts the profession to this day.

> Gerda Lerner, "The Lady and the Mill Girl," in *Midcontinent American Studies Journal* (1969)

14 A good nurse is of more importance than a physician.

> Hannah Farnham Lee, *The Log-Cabin* (1844)

15 Nurses do whatever doctors and janitors won't do.

> Peggy Anderson, *Nurse* (1978)

16 A nurse is caught between the doctor's invincibility and the patient's vulnerability.

> Lynne Alpern and Esther Blumenfeld, *Oh, Lord, I Sound Just Like Mama* (1986)

17 She had no equal in sickness, and knew how to brew every old-fashioned dose and to make every variety of herb-tea, and when her nursing was put to an end by her patient's death, she was commander-in-chief at the funeral.

> Sarah Orne Jewett, *Deephaven* (1877)

1 Nature alone cures. . . . What nursing has to do . . . is to put the patient in the best condition for nature to act upon him.

Florence Nightingale, *Notes on Nursing* (1859)

2 Never to allow a patient to be waked, intentionally or accidentally, is a *sine qua non* of all good nursing.

Florence Nightingale, *Notes on Nursing* (1859)

3 Nursing is not only a natural vocation for a woman, but an occupation which increases her matrimonial chances about eighty per cent.

Gertrude Atherton, *The Living Present* (1917)

4 They ain't no feelin' in the world like takin' on somebody wilted and near bout gone, and you do what you can, and then all a-sudden the pore thang starts to put out new growth and git well.

Olive Ann Burns, *Cold Sassy Tree* (1984)

See also Health, Health Care, Hospitals, Illness.

## ❦ NUTRITION

5 I certainly feel that the time is not far distant when a knowledge of the principles of diet will be an essential part of one's education.

Fannie Merritt Farmer, *The Boston Cooking-School Cook Book* (1896)

6 What you eat today walks and talks tomorrow.

Lynne Alpern and Esther Blumenfeld, *Oh, Lord, I Sound Just Like Mama* (1986)

7 We are indeed much more than what we eat, but what we eat can nevertheless help us to be much more than what we are.

Adelle Davis, *Let's Get Well* (1965)

8 Eat breakfast like a king, lunch like a prince, and dinner like a pauper.

Adelle Davis, *Let's Eat Right to Keep Fit* (1954)

See also Dieting, Eating, Food.

## § OBJECTIVITY

1 I make no pretensions to "objectivity," a fraudulent concept in an era of industrialized and politicized science in which intellectual mercenaries too often serve power and greed, the ambitions of competing nation-states, or the requirements of commerce.

    Hazel Henderson, *The Politics of the Solar Age* (1981)

See also Detachment, Point of View, Subjectivity.

## § OBSCENITY

2 When irritated her vocabulary would . . . take the feathers off a hoody crow.

    Lillian Beckwith, *Lightly Poached* (1973)

3 The nowadays ruling that no word is unprintable has, I think, done nothing whatever for beautiful letters. . . . Obscenity is too valuable a commodity to chuck around all over the place; it should be taken out of the safe on special occasions only.

    Dorothy Parker, in *Esquire* (1957)

See also Swearing, Words.

## § OBSOLESCENCE

4 By operating on the principle of human and material obsolescence, America eats her history alive.

    Gail Sheehy, *Speed Is of the Essence* (1971)

## § OBSTINACY

5 There is no independence and pertinacity of opinion like that of these seemingly soft, quiet creatures, whom it is so easy to silence, and so difficult to convince.

    Harriet Beecher Stowe, *The Pearl of Orr's Island* (1862)

6 It's only by being obstinate that anything is got, or done.

    Rumer Godden, *China Court* (1961)

7 Obstinacy in children is like a kite; it is kept up just as long as we pull against it.

    Marcelene Cox, in *Ladies' Home Journal* (1945)

8 She had the bulging forehead of obstinacy.

    Elizabeth Daly, *Death and Letters* (1950)

See also Perseverance, Stubbornness.

## § OCEAN

9 It has always been to me, the ocean, overwhelming, monstrous, deep, dark, green and black, so foreign that it requires respect, silence, humility. . . . All of the life in it is menacing, compelling, exquisite, with nothing consoling.

    Andrea Dworkin, "First Love," in Julia Wolf Mazow, ed., *The Woman Who Lost Her Names* (1980)

10 I never liked the landsman's life, / The earth is aye the same; / Gi'e me the ocean for my dower, / My vessel for my hame. / Gi'e me the fields that no man ploughs, / The farm that pays no fee.

    Miss Corbett, "We'll Go to Sea No More," in Mary Russell Mitford, *Recollections of a Literary Life*, vol. 2 (1852)

1 Always nights I feel the ocean / Biting at my life.

    Louise Glück, "The Egg," *Firstborn* (1968)

2 The waves chewed at the sand / with white teeth.

    Nancy Mairs, "Mother, Because We Do Not Speak of Such Things, I Have Written You a Poem," *In All the Rooms of the Yellow House* (1984)

3 The vast Pacific ocean would always remain the islanders' great solace, escape and nourishment, the amniotic fluid that would keep them hedonistic and aloof, guarded, gentle and mysterious.

    Francine du Plessix Gray, *Hawaii* (1972)

See also Sea.

## ❧ OCTOBER

4 What of October, that ambiguous month, the month of tension, the unendurable month?

    Doris Lessing, *Children of Violence: Martha Quest* (1952)

5 October is a symphony of permanence and change.

    Bonaro W. Overstreet, "Mists and Mellow Fruitfulness," in Jean Beaven Abernethy, *Meditations for Women* (1947)

6 The forest's afire! / The forest's afire! / The maple is burning, / The sycamore's turning / The beech is alight!

    Eleanor Farjeon, "October's Song," *The Children's Bells* (1960)

7 As golden, as mature, as voluptuous as a Roman matron fresh from the bath, the October morning swept with indolent dignity across the land.

    Mazo de la Roche, *Jalna* (1927)

8 Winter had stretched / Long chill fingers into the brown, streaming hair / Of fleeing October.

    Alice Dunbar-Nelson, "Snow in October," in Countee Cullen, ed., *Caroling Dusk* (1927)

See also Autumn.

## ❧ OFFENSIVENESS

9 If a person begins by telling you, "Do not be offended at what I am going to say," prepare yourself for something that she knows will certainly offend you.

    Eliza Leslie, *Miss Leslie's Behavior Book* (1859)

10 Unhappily the habit of being offensive "without meaning it" leads usually to a way of making amends which the injured person cannot but regard as being amiable without meaning it.

    George Eliot, *Impressions of Theophrastus Such* (1879)

11 Lack of education is an extraordinary handicap when one is being offensive.

    Josephine Tey, *The Franchise Affair* (1948)

12 You can say the nastiest things about yourself without offending anyone.

    Phyllis Diller, in Barbara McDowell and Hana Umlauf, *Woman's Almanac* (1977)

See also Rudeness, Shocking.

## ❧ OKLAHOMA

13 Anything can have happened in Oklahoma. Practically everything has.

    Edna Ferber, *Cimarron* (1930)

## ❧ OLD AGE

See Age.

## ❧ OPERA

14 An opera begins long before the curtain goes up and ends long after it has come down. It starts in my imagination, it becomes my life, and it stays part of my life long after I've left the opera house. The audience sees only an excerpt.

    Maria Callas, in Arianna Stassinopoulos, *Maria Callas* (1981)

15 Cathedrals are built with pennies of the faithful. A great opera house also is a spiritual center, a temple of sorts, where many gather together for recreation, education, and inspiration—a blessed trinity worthy of public support.

    Eleanor Robson Belmont, *The Fabric of Memory* (1957)

1 An unalterable and unquestioned law of the musical world required that the German text of French operas sung by Swedish artists should be translated into Italian for the clearer understanding of English-speaking audiences.

    Edith Wharton, *The Age of Innocence* (1920)

2 If anything can be invented more excruciating than an English Opera, such as was the fashion at the time I was in London, I am sure no sin of mine deserves the punishment of bearing it.

    Margaret Fuller, in *The New-York Daily Tribune* (1847)

3 Going to the opera, like getting drunk, is a sin that carries its own punishment with it, and that a very severe one.

    Hannah More (1775), in William Roberts, ed., *Memoirs of the Life and Correspondence of Mrs. Hannah More,* vol. 1 (1834)

4 Buloz sleeps at the opera as comfortably as in his own bed. People tread on his coat-tails, they step on his hat, on his feet. He awakes long enough to exclaim, "Good Lord!" then goes back to sleep again.

    George Sand (1834), in Marie Jenny Howe, ed., *The Intimate Journal of George Sand* (1929)

See also Music, Performance, Singing.

## ❧ OPINION

5 The world is not run by thought, nor by imagination, but by opinion.

    Elizabeth Drew, *The Modern Novel* (1926)

6 An opinion, right or wrong, can never constitute a moral offense, nor be in itself a moral obligation. It may be mistaken; it may involve an absurdity, or a contradiction. It is a truth; or it is an error; it can never be a crime or a virtue.

    Frances Wright, *A Few Days in Athens* (1822)

7 What is asserted by a man is an opinion; what is asserted by a woman is opinionated.

    Marya Mannes, "The Singular Woman," *But Will It Sell?* (1964)

8 Instant opinion is an oxymoron. You don't get real opinions in an instant. You get reactions.

    Ellen Goodman, in *The Boston Globe* (1993)

See also Beliefs, Ideas, Judgment, Point of View, Polls, Public Opinion, Thoughts.

## ❧ OPPORTUNITY

9 One can present people with opportunities. One cannot make them equal to them.

    Rosamond Lehmann, *The Ballad and the Source* (1945)

10 Nothing is so often irretrievably missed as an opportunity we encounter every day.

    Marie von Ebner-Eschenbach, *Aphorisms* (1893)

11 When one misses an opportunity one is apt to fancy that another will never present itself.

    Marie Bashkirtseff (1884), in Mary J. Serrano, tr., *Letters of Marie Bashkirtseff* (1891)

12 The doors of Opportunity are marked "Push" and Pull."

    Ethel Watts Mumford, in Oliver Herford, Ethel Watts Mumford, and Addison Mizner, *The Complete Cynic* (1902)

13 I could never tell if it was Opportunity or the Wolf knocking.

    Anne Ellis, *The Life of an Ordinary Woman* (1929)

See also Challenge.

## ❧ OPPOSITION

14 Openly questioning the way the world works and challenging the power of the powerful is not an activity customarily rewarded.

    Dale Spender, *Women of Ideas and What Men Have Done to Them* (1982)

15 I always cheer up immensely if an attack is particularly wounding because I think, well, if they attack one personally, it means they have not a single political argument left.

    Margaret Thatcher, in *The London Daily Telegraph* (1986)

16 Uproar against a new idea, and laws to prevent anybody's accepting it, nearly always can be regarded as a signal that the new idea is just about to be taken for granted. . . . They didn't start making laws to prohibit the teaching of evolution until everybody was about to take it for granted.

    Gwen Bristow, *Tomorrow Is Forever* (1943)

1 The likelihood of one individual being right increases in direct ratio to the intensity with which others try to prove him wrong.

    Leonore Fleischer, *Heaven Can Wait* (1978)

2 I have spent many years of my life in opposition, and I rather like the role.

    Eleanor Roosevelt, letter to Bernard Baruch (1952), in Joseph P. Lash, *Eleanor: The Years Alone* (1972)

3 Opposition may become sweet to a man when he has christened it persecution.

    George Eliot, "Janet's Repentance," *Scenes of Clerical Life* (1857)

4 All external opposition, in whatever form it may appear, is harmless, compared to internal sedition.

    Maria W. Chapman, *Right and Wrong in Massachusetts* (1839)

5 To oppose something is to maintain it.

    Ursula K. Le Guin, *The Left Hand of Darkness* (1969)

See also Conflict, Contrariness, Enemies, Resistance, Troublemakers.

## ♦ OPPRESSION

6 It is natural anywhere that people like their own kind, but it is not necessarily natural that their fondness for their own kind should lead them to the subjection of whole groups of other people not like them.

    Pearl S. Buck, *What America Means to Me* (1943)

7 Class supremacy, male supremacy, white supremacy—it's all the same game. If you're on top of someone, the society tells you that you are better. It gives you access to its privileges and security, and it works both to keep you on top and to keep you thinking that you deserve to be there.

    Coletta Reid and Charlotte Bunch, *Class and Feminism* (1979)

8 God . . . hath made all men free and equal. Then why should one worm say to another, "Keep you down there, while I sit up yonder; for I am better than thou?"

    Maria W. Stewart, *Religion and the Pure Principles of Morality* (1831)

9 We first crush people to the earth, and then claim the right of trampling on them for ever, because they are prostrate.

    Lydia Maria Child, *An Appeal in Favor of That Class of Americans Called Africans* (1833)

10 When an individual (or a group of individuals) is kept in a situation of inferiority, the fact is that he *is* inferior. But the significance of the verb *to be* must be rightly understood here; it is in bad faith to give it a static value when it really has the dynamic Hegelian sense of "to have become."

    Simone de Beauvoir, *The Second Sex* (1949)

11 Personal accomplishment is almost impossible in the human categories that are maintained collectively in an inferior situation.

    Simone de Beauvoir, *The Second Sex* (1949)

12 Whatever a "superior" group has will be used to justify its superiority, and whatever an "inferior" group has will be used to justify its plight.

    Gloria Steinem, *Outrageous Acts and Everyday Rebellions* (1983)

13 When once a social order is well established, no matter what injustice it involves, those who occupy a position of advantage are not long in coming to believe that it is the only possible and reasonable order.

    Suzanne La Follette, "The Beginnings of Emancipation," *Concerning Women* (1926)

14 If you're going to hold someone down you're going to have to hold onto the other end of the chain. You are confined by your own system of repression.

    Toni Morrison, in Brian Lanker, *I Dream a World* (1989)

15 As long as you keep a person down, some part of you has to be down there to hold him down, so it means you cannot soar as you otherwise might.

    Marian Anderson, television interview (1957)

16 If given a choice, I would have certainly selected to be what I am: one of the oppressed instead of one of the oppressors.

    Miriam Makeba, with James Hall, *Makeba* (1987)

17 All oppression creates a state of war.

    Simone de Beauvoir, *The Second Sex* (1949)

18 In order to perpetuate itself, every oppression must corrupt or distort those various sources of power

within the culture of the oppressed that can provide energy for change.

Audre Lorde, *Uses of the Erotic* (1978)

1 It is precisely because certain groups have no representation in a number of recognized political structures that their position tends to be so stable, their oppression so continuous.

Kate Millett, *Sexual Politics* (1969)

2 Where a system of oppression has become institutionalized it is unnecessary for individuals to be oppressive.

Florynce R. Kennedy, "Institutionalized Oppression vs. the Female," in Robin Morgan, ed., *Sisterhood Is Powerful* (1970)

3 Tell a man what he may not sing and he is still half free; even all free, if he never wanted to sing it. But tell him what he must sing, take up his time with it so that his true voice cannot sound even in secret— there, I have seen is slavery.

Mary Renault, *The Praise Singer* (1978)

4 The oppressed without hope are mysteriously quiet. When the conception of change is beyond the limits of the possible, there are no words to articulate discontent. . . . We can only grasp silence in the moment in which it is breaking.

Sheila Rowbotham, *Woman's Consciousness, Man's World* (1973)

5 The horse on the treadmill may be very discontented, but he is not disposed to tell his troubles, for he cannot stop to talk.

Nellie L. McClung, *In Times Like These* (1915)

6 In order to survive, those of us for whom oppression is as american as apple pie have always had to be watchers, to become familiar with the language and manners of the oppressor, even sometimes adopting them for some illusion of protection. Whenever the need for some pretense of communication arises, those who profit from our oppression call upon us to share our knowledge with them. In other words, it is the responsibility of the oppressed to teach the oppressors their mistakes.

Audre Lorde, "Age, Race, Class, and Sex" (1980), *Sister Outsider* (1984)

7 If the majority culture know so little about us, it must be *our* problem, they seem to be telling us; the burden of teaching is on us.

Mitsuye Yamada, "Asian Pacific American Women and Feminism," in Cherríe Moraga and Gloria Anzaldúa, eds., *This Bridge Called My Back* (1983)

8 In many regions water turns rock-hard! That is how it is with us! Falling helpless victims of oppression again and again, our hearts grow hardened one day.

Binodini Dasi (1924), in Susie Tharu and K. Lalita, eds., *Women Writing in India* (1991)

9 He had cursed the Nordic superiority complex which could feel pity for the victims only of other types of culture, but none for the victims of its own.

Winifred Holtby, "Episode in West Kensington" (1932), *Pavements at Anderby* (1937)

10 When a man curls his lip, when he uses ridicule, when he grows angry, you have touched a raw nerve in domination.

Sheila Rowbotham, *Woman's Consciousness, Man's World* (1973)

11 If one would discern the centers of dominance in any society, one need only look to its definitions of "virtue" and "vice" or "legal" and "criminal," for in the strength to set standards resides the strength to maintain control.

Freda Adler, *Sisters in Crime* (1975)

12 What is surprising is not that oppression should make its appearance only after higher forms of economy have been reached, but that it should always accompany them.

Simone Weil (1934), *Oppression and Liberty* (1955)

13 The history of an oppressed people is hidden in the lies and the agreed-upon myth of its conquerors.

Meridel Le Sueur, *Crusaders* (1955)

14 One pets what one degrades; and one has to support what one has enfeebled.

Phyllis Bottome, *The Mortal Storm* (1938)

15 In order to create an alternative an oppressed group must at once shatter the self-reflecting world which encircles it and, at the same time, project its own image onto history.

Sheila Rowbotham, *Woman's Consciousness, Man's World* (1973)

16 These my two hands / quick to slap my face / before others could slap it.

Gloria Anzaldúa, "The Woman Who Lived Forever," in Cherríe Moraga and Gloria Anzaldúa, eds., *This Bridge Called My Back* (1983)

17 Strong nations fight, oppressed nations sing.

Lady Wilde, "Thomas Moore," *Notes on Men, Women, and Books* (1891)

1 Oppression does not remain static. It carries the seed of its own destruction.

Ann Fairbairn, *Five Smooth Stones* (1966)

2 Now I say that with cruelty and oppression it is everybody's business to interfere when they see it.

Anna Sewell, *Black Beauty* (1877)

3 The revolt against any oppression usually goes to an opposite extreme for a time.

Tennessee Claflin, in *Woodhull and Claflin's Weekly* (1871)

4 Oppressed people are frequently very oppressive when first liberated. And why wouldn't they be? They know best two positions. Somebody's foot on their neck or their foot on somebody's neck.

Florynce R. Kennedy, "Institutionalized Oppression vs. the Female," in Robin Morgan, ed., *Sisterhood Is Powerful* (1970)

5 Within our society there are hierarchies of need because there have been hierarchies of oppression.

Martha P. Cotera, *The Chicana Feminist* (1977)

6 Obviously the most oppressed of any oppressed group will be its women.

Lorraine Hansberry (1959), in Adrienne Rich, "The Problem of Lorraine Hansberry," *Blood, Bread, and Poetry* (1986)

7 In this country, lesbianism is a poverty—as is being brown, as is being a woman, as is being just plain poor. The danger lies in ranking the oppressions.

Cherríe Moraga, "La Güera," in Cherríe Moraga and Gloria Anzaldúa, eds., *This Bridge Called My Back* (1983)

8 It is critical for both more privileged and relatively more oppressed groups to listen to each other's pain without playing the who-is-more-oppressed game.

Carol Pearson, *The Hero Within* (1986)

9 Capitalist society and the racism and sexism it institutionalizes are strengthened by antagonisms.

Gloria I. Joseph and Jill Lewis, *Common Differences* (1981)

10 All of us would do well to stop fighting each other for our space at the bottom, because there ain't no more room.

Cheryl Clarke, "Lesbianism: An Act of Resistance," in Cherríe Moraga and Gloria Anzaldúa, eds., *This Bridge Called My Back* (1983)

See also Bigotry, Discrimination, Exclusion, Minorities, Persecution, Power, Powerlessness, Prejudice, Racism, Revolution, Sexism, Sexual Harassment, Superiority, Tyranny.

## ❦ OPTIMISM

11 Grab your coat, and get your hat / Leave your worry on the doorstep / Just direct your feet / To the sunny side of the street.

Dorothy Fields, "On the Sunny Side of the Street" (1930)

12 Rose-colored spectacles the hopeful wear.

Sor Juana Inés de la Cruz (1690), in Irene Nicholson, *A Guide to Mexican Poetry* (1968)

13 From every scrap you make a blanket.

Rose Chernin, in Kim Chernin, *In My Mother's House* (1983)

14 An optimist is the human personification of spring.

Susan J. Bissonette, in *Reader's Digest* (1979)

15 Nothing is ever quite as bad as it *could* be.

Amy Hempel, *At the Gates of the Animal Kingdom* (1990)

16 Some folks are natural born kickers. They can always find a way to turn disaster into butter.

Katherine Paterson, *Lyddie* (1991)

17 In spite of everything I still believe that people are really good at heart.

Anne Frank, *The Diary of a Young Girl* (1952)

18 The optimism of a healthy mind is indefatigable.

Margery Allingham, *Death of a Ghost* (1934)

19 Please understand that there is no one depressed in *this* house:—we are not interested in the possibilities of defeat;—they do not exist.

Queen Victoria, letter to A.J. Balfour during the "Black Week" of the Boer War (1900), in Lady Gwendolyn Cecil, *Life of Robert, Marquis of Salisbury*, vol. 3 (1931)

20 People who talk of new lives believe there will be no new troubles.

Phyllis Bottome, *Old Wine* (1925)

21 I do not believe that true optimism can come about except through tragedy.

Madeleine L'Engle, *Two-Part Invention* (1988)

22 There is a dangerous optimism of ignorance and indifference.

Helen Keller, *Optimism* (1903)

23 Am I like the optimist who, while falling ten stories from a building, says at each story, "I'm all right so far"?

Gretel Ehrlich, *Heart Mountain* (1988)

See also Cheerfulness, Gladness, Hope.

## ❦ ORDER

1 There should be a place for everything, and everything in its place.

Isabella Beeton, *The Book of Household Management* (1861)

2 Order is a lovely thing; / On disarray it lays its wing, / Teaching simplicity to sing.

Anna Hempstead Branch, "The Monk in the Kitchen," *Rose of the Wind* (1910)

3 Order is life to me. I could, if necessary, live in dirt but never in disorder.

Margaret Anderson, *The Fiery Fountains* (1953)

4 Order is the shape upon which beauty depends.

Pearl S. Buck, *To My Daughters, With Love* (1967)

5 Order is a lovely thing; / . . . / It has a meek and lowly grace, / Quiet as a nun's face.

Anna Hempstead Branch, "The Monk in the Kitchen," *Rose of the Wind* (1910)

6 The greatest of mythologies divided its gods into creators, preservers and destroyers. Tidiness obviously belongs to the second category, which mitigates the terrific impact of the other two.

Freya Stark, "Tidiness," in *Time and Tide* (1949)

7 When I cannot bear outer pressures any more, I begin to put order in my belongings. . . . As if unable to organize and control my life, I seek to exert this on the world of objects.

Anaïs Nin (1954), *The Diary of Anaïs Nin*, vol. 5 (1974)

8 Tidied all my papers. Tore up and ruthlessly destroyed much. This is always a great satisfaction.

Katherine Mansfield (1922), *Journal of Katherine Mansfield* (1927)

9 A life lived in chaos is an impossibility for the artist. No matter how unstructured may seem the painter's garret in Paris or the poet's pad in Greenwich Village, the artist must have some kind of order or he will produce a very small body of work. To create a *work* of art, great or small, is *work*, hard work, and work requires discipline and order.

Madeleine L'Engle, *Walking on Water* (1980)

10 A schedule defends from chaos and whim. It is a net for catching days. It is a scaffolding on which a worker can stand and labor with both hands at sections of time. A schedule is a mock-up of reason and order—willed, faked, and so brought into being.

Annie Dillard, *The Writing Life* (1989)

11 My tidiness, and my untidiness, are full of regret and remorse and complex feelings.

Natalia Ginzburg, "He and I," in Raleigh Trevelyan, ed., *Italian Writing Today* (1967)

12 Trehane operated on a basis of thoroughness: do everything, do it properly, follow up, check. If he had ever had a moment of intuition, he had slept it off.

Holly Roth, *Too Many Doctors* (1962)

13 What would happen to my illusion that I am a force for order in the home if I wasn't married to the only man north of the Tiber who is even untidier than I am?

Katharine Whitehorn, "Husband-Swapping," *Sunday Best* (1976)

14 One person's mess is merely another person's filing system.

Margo Kaufman, *1-800-Am-I-Nuts?* (1992)

See also Chaos, Control, Organizations, Shape.

## ❦ ORDINARINESS

15 Ordinary is a word that has no meaning.

Robin Morgan, "The Pedestrian Woman," *Lady of the Beasts* (1975)

16 in our ordinaryness we are most bizarre.

Ntozake Shange, *a photograph: lovers in motion* (1977)

17 The incredible gift of the ordinary! Glory comes streaming from the table of daily life.

Macrina Wiederkehr, *A Tree Full of Angels* (1988)

18 Freshness trembles beneath the surface of Everyday, a joy perpetual to all who catch its opal lights beneath the dust of habit.

Freya Stark, *Letters From Syria* (1942)

See also Conventionality, Familiarity, Normalcy.

## ❦ ORGANIZATIONS

19 The things we fear most in organizations—fluctuations, disturbances, imbalances—need not be

signs of an impending disorder that will destroy us. Instead, fluctuations are the primary source of creativity.

Margaret J. Wheatley, *Leadership and the New Science* (1992)

1 We have created trouble for ourselves in organizations by confusing control with order.

Margaret J. Wheatley, *Leadership and the New Science* (1992)

2 The trouble with organizing a thing is that pretty soon folks get to paying more attention to the organization than to what they're organized for.

Laura Ingalls Wilder, *Little Town on the Prairie* (1941)

See also Bureaucracy, Business, Committees, Groups, Institutions, Welfare.

## ❧ ORIGINALITY

3 True originality consists not in a new manner but in a new vision.

Edith Wharton, *The Writing of Fiction* (1925)

4 Originality is . . . a by-product of sincerity.

Marianne Moore, "Marianne Moore Speaks," in *Vogue* (1963)

5 It is wiser to be conventionally immoral than unconventionally moral. It isn't the immorality they object to, but the originality.

Ellen Glasgow, *The Descendant* (1897)

6 What passes for an original opinion is, generally, merely an original phrase. Old lamps for new—yes; but it is always the same oil in the lamp.

Katharine Fullerton Gerould, *Modes and Morals* (1920)

7 There are no original ideas. There are only original people.

Barbara Grizzuti Harrison, *Foreign Bodies* (1984)

8 Originality usually amounts only to plagiarizing something unfamiliar.

Katharine Fullerton Gerould, *Modes and Morals* (1920)

9 Original thought is like original sin: both happened before you were born to people you could not possibly have met.

Fran Lebowitz, *Social Studies* (1977)

See also Eccentricity, Individuality, Innovation, Newness, Uniqueness.

## ❧ ORPHANS

10 Psychic orphanhood is not new. . . . For hundreds of years, the word "orphan" had been vividly associated with massive asylums and the pale, undersized inmates in institutional garb incarcerated within their walls. It was necessary for these associations to fade, as fade they did with the sharp decline in the number of orphans, before the word could be used as a simile: I felt *like* an orphan.

Eileen Simpson, *Orphans: Real and Imaginary* (1990)

11 If you cannot trust your father and mother to love you and accept you and protect you, then you are an orphan, although your parents are upstairs asleep in their bed.

Elizabeth Feuer, *Paper Doll* (1990)

## ❧ "OUGHT"

12 Most people are so busy knocking themselves out trying to do everything they think they should do, they never get around to what they want to do.

Kathleen Winsor, *Star Money* (1950)

13 Miss Ophelia was the absolute bond-slave of the "*ought.*"

Harriet Beecher Stowe, *Uncle Tom's Cabin* (1852)

14 "Ought"! What an ugly word *that* is!

Phyllis Bottome, *The Mortal Storm* (1938)

See also Duty.

## ❧ OUTRAGE

15 Outrage, combining as it does shock, anger, reproach, and helplessness, is perhaps the most unmanageable, the most demoralizing of all the emotions.

Margery Allingham, *Death of a Ghost* (1934)

See also Anger, Indignation.

## ❧ OUTSIDERS

16 Society decides which of its segments are going to be outside its borders. Society says, "These are the

legitimate channels to my rewards. They are closed to you forever." So then the outlawed segments must seek rewards through illegitimate channels. In other words, once my Great White Father declared me illegitimate, I had to be a bastard.

Kristin Hunter, *The Landlord* (1966)

1 The world was one of great contrasts, she thought, and if the richest part of it was to be fenced off so that people like herself could only get look at it with no expectation of ever being able to get inside it, then it would be better to have been born blind so you couldn't see it, born deaf so you couldn't hear it, born with no sense of touch so you couldn't feel it. Better still, born with no brain so that you would be completely unaware of anything, so that you would never know there were places that were filled with sunlight and good food and where children were safe.

Ann Petry, *The Street* (1946)

2 You can tell by looking at most people that the world remains a stone to them and a closed door.

Meridel Le Sueur, "Annunciation" (1927), *Salute to Spring* (1940)

3 Do you know what it's like to feel *wrong* twenty-four hours a day? Do you know what it's like to be disapproved of, not only for what you do and say and think but for what you *are*?

Joyce Rebeta-Burditt, *The Cracker Factory* (1977)

4 Be nobody's darling; / Be an outcast. / Qualified to live / Among your dead.

Alice Walker, "Be Nobody's Darling," *Revolutionary Petunias* (1971)

5 I'm fundamentally, I think, an outsider. I do my best work and feel most braced with my back to the wall. It's an odd feeling though, writing against the current: difficult entirely to disregard the current. Yet of course I shall.

Virginia Woolf (1938), in Leonard Woolf, ed., *A Writer's Diary* (1953)

6 It is easy to slip into a parallel universe. There are so many of them: worlds of the insane, the criminal, the crippled, the dying, perhaps of the dead as well. These worlds exist alongside this world and resemble it, but are not in it.

Susanna Kaysen, *Girl, Interrupted* (1993)

7 When you are a member of an out-group, and you challenge others with whom you share this outsider position to examine some aspect of their lives that distorts differences between you, then there can be a great deal of pain.

Audre Lorde, in Claudia Tate, ed., *Black Women Writers at Work* (1983)

8 Untrained minds have always been a nuisance to the military police of orthodoxy. God-intoxicated mystics and untidy saints with only a white blaze of divine love where their minds should have been, are perpetually creating almost as much disorder within the law as outside it.

Katherine Anne Porter, "On a Criticism of Thomas Hardy" (1940), *The Days Before* (1952)

9 I was like a cat always climbing the wrong tree.

Carson McCullers, *Clock Without Hands* (1961)

See also Alienation, Exclusion, Minorities, Pariahs, Strangers.

# & OVERPOPULATION

10 Self-restraint may be alien to the human temperament, but humanity without restraint will dig its own grave.

Marya Mannes, "The Singular Woman," *But Will It Sell?* (1964)

# & OYSTERS

11 An oyster leads a dreadful but exciting life. Indeed, his chance to live at all is slim, and if he should survive the arrows of his own outrageous fortune and in the two weeks of his carefree youth find a clean smooth place to fix on, the years afterwards are full of stress, passion, and danger.

M.F.K. Fisher, *Consider the Oyster* (1941)

12 Almost any normal oyster never knows from one year to the next whether he is he or she, and may start at any moment, after the first year, to lay eggs where before he spent his sexual energies in being exceptionally masculine.

M.F.K. Fisher, *Consider the Oyster* (1941)

13 Music or the color of the sea are easier to describe than the taste of one of these Armoricaines.

Eleanor Clark, *The Oysters of Locmariaquer* (1964)

1 There is a shock of freshness to it. Intimations of the ages of man, some piercing intuition of the sea and all its weeds and breezes shiver you a split second from that little stimulus on the palate. You are eating the sea.

Eleanor Clark, *The Oysters of Locmariaquer* (1964)

2 A flaccid, moping, debauched mollusk, tired from too much love and loose-nerved from general world conditions, can be a shameful thing served raw upon the shell.

M.F.K. Fisher, *Consider the Oyster* (1941)

3 What could be moister / Than tears from an oyster.

Felicia Lamport, "Shell Gain," *Scrap Irony* (1961)

See also Food.

# P

## ❦ PACIFISM

1 The quietly pacifist peaceful / always die / to make room for men / who shout.

Alice Walker, "The QPP," *Revolutionary Petunias* (1971)

2 Pacifism simply is not a matter of calm looking on; it is work, hard work.

Käthe Kollwitz (1944), in Hans Kollwitz, ed., *The Diaries and Letters of Käthe Kollwitz* (1955)

3 Pacifists lead a lonely life. Not even gathering together can take the place of that vast, warm sun of approval that is shed on motherhood, on law-abiding, on killing, and on making money. Someday will we come into our own? Well, motherhood may move into the shade. Law-abiding is going through a trauma. But killing and making money are good for a long, long time.

Josephine W. Johnson, *The Inland Island* (1969)

4 The only thing for a pacifist to do is to find a *substitute* for war: mountains and seafaring are the only ones I know. But it must be something sufficiently serious not to be a game and sufficiently dangerous to exercise those virtues which otherwise get no chance.

Freya Stark, *The Coast of Incense* (1953)

See also Peace.

## ❦ PAIN

5 In the country of pain we are each alone.

May Sarton, "The Country of Pain," *Halfway to Silence* (1980)

6 My soul is a broken field / Ploughed by pain.

Sara Teasdale, "The Broken Field," *Flame and Shadow* (1920)

7 Ironshod horses rage back and forth over every nerve.

Audre Lorde, *The Cancer Journals* (1980)

8 I rock my pain to sleep like a mother her child / or I take refuge in it like a child in his mother / alternately possessor and possessed.

Rosario Castellanos, "Second Elegy," in Julian Palley, tr., *Meditation on the Threshold* (1988)

9 Pain heightens every sense. More powerfully than any drug, it intensifies colors, sounds, sight, feelings. Pain is like a glass wall. It is impossible to climb it, but you must, and, somehow, you do. Then there is an explosion of brilliance and the world is more apparent in its complexity and beauty.

Suzanne Massie, in Robert and Suzanne Massie, *Journey* (1975)

10 Even pain / Pricks to livelier living.

Amy Lowell, "Happiness," *Sword Blades and Poppy Seed* (1914)

11 Pain gives us everything we need— / . . . / She gives us our strange souls and our peculiar thoughts, / she gives us all of life's highest winnings: / love, solitude, and the face of death.

Edith Södergran, "Pain" (1916), in Samuel Charters, tr., *We Women* (1977)

12 Once you get beyond the crust of the first pang it is all the same and you can easily bear it. It is just the transition from painlessness to pain that is so terrible.

Anne Morrow Lindbergh, *Bring Me a Unicorn* (1971)

1 Pain is a new room in your house.
  Willa Gibbs, *Seed of Mischief* (1953)

2 Pain — has an Element of Blank — / It cannot recollect / When it begun — or if there were / A time when it was not.
  Emily Dickinson (1862), in Mabel Loomis Todd and T.W. Higgins, eds., *Poems by Emily Dickinson* (1890)

3 I could not recall how much time had passed for somehow or other pain is timeless, absolute. It has removed itself from space. It always has been and always will be for it exists independent of relations. I feel it as myself, and when it ceases I will cease.
  Evelyn Scott, *Escapade* (1923)

4 There was no reality to pain when it left one, though while it held one fast all other realities faded.
  Rachel Field, *All This and Heaven Too* (1939)

5 Life's sharpest rapture is surcease of pain.
  Emma Lazarus, "In Exile," *Songs of a Semite* (1882)

6 Where does the pain go when it goes away?
  Gloria I. Joseph, in Andre Lorde, *Sister Outsider* (1984)

7 Sometimes pain was a crutch to hold on to when the only alternative was nothing at all.
  Sylvie Sommerfield, *Bittersweet* (1991)

8 It's odd that you can get so anesthetized by your own pain or your own problem that you don't quite fully share the hell of someone close to you.
  Lady Bird Johnson, *A White House Diary* (1970)

9 There is much pain that is quite noiseless; and vibrations that make human agonies are often a mere whisper in the roar of hurrying existence.
  George Eliot, *Felix Holt, the Radical* (1866)

10 Isn't the fear of pain next brother to pain itself?
  Enid Bagnold, *A Diary Without Dates* (1918)

11 One does not die from pain unless one chooses to.
  Wakako Yamauchi, "Makapuu Bay," in Asian Women United of California, eds., *Making Waves* (1989)

12 Both Grace and I "took on" when in pain. We were Irish. We didn't wait for the wake to wail. We wailed while we were still hurting, not leaving all the work for others after we were past helping.
  Jessamyn West, *The Woman Said Yes* (1976)

See also Illness, Migraines, Suffering.

## ♦ PAINTING

13 He exhales paint we need / to / breathe.
  Diana Chang, "What Matisse Is After," in Dexter Fisher, ed., *The Third Woman* (1980)

14 You take a painting, you have a white, virginal piece of canvas that is the world of purity, and then you put your imagery on it, and you try to bring it back to the original purity.
  Louise Nevelson, in Arnold B. Glimcher, *Louise Nevelson* (1972)

15 Sometimes I could quit paint and take to charring. It must be fine to clean perfectly, to shine and polish and *know* that it could not be done better. In painting that never occurs.
  Emily Carr (1933), *Hundreds and Thousands* (1966)

16 I see no reason for painting anything that can be put into any other form as well.
  Georgia O'Keeffe, in Laurie Lisle, *Portrait of an Artist* (1980)

17 I like to paint something that leads me on and on into the unknown, something that I want to see away on beyond.
  Grandma Moses, in Otto Kallir, ed., *My Life's History* (1952)

18 The meaning of a word—to me—is not as exact as the meaning of a color. Colors and shapes make a more definite statement than words.
  Georgia O'Keeffe, *Georgia O'Keeffe* (1976)

19 I said to myself—I'll paint what I see—what the flower is to me but I'll paint it big and they will be surprised into taking time to look at it—I will make even busy New Yorkers take time to see what I see of flowers.
  Georgia O'Keeffe, *Georgia O'Keeffe* (1976)

20 The biggest part of painting perhaps is faith, and waiting receptively, content to go any way, not planning or forcing. The fear, though, is laziness. It is so easy to drift and finally be tossed up on the beach, derelict.
  Emily Carr (1935), *Hundreds and Thousands* (1966)

21 They thought I was Surrealist, but I wasn't. I never painted dreams. I painted my own reality.
  Frida Kahlo, in Hayden Herrera, *Frida* (1983)

22 My painting is so biographical, if anyone can take the trouble to read it.
  Lee Krasner, in Eleanor Munro, *Originals: American Women Artists* (1979)

1 I have painted portraits that to me are almost photographic. I remember hesitating to show the paintings, they looked so real to me. But they have passed into the world as abstractions—no one seeing what they are.

Georgia O'Keeffe, *Georgia O'Keeffe* (1976)

2 Soul is as necessary in a painting as body.

Marie Bashkirtseff (1881), in Mary J. Serrano, tr., *The Journal of a Young Artist* (1919)

3 There is no right and wrong way to paint except honestly or dishonestly. Honestly is trying for the bigger thing. Dishonestly is bluffing and getting through a smattering of surface representation with no meaning.

Emily Carr (1934), *Hundreds and Thousands* (1966)

4 Certainly we have bad paintings. We have only the "greatest" bad paintings.

Françoise Cachin, Director of the Musée d'Orsay in Paris, in *Time* (1986)

5 A painting is like a man. If you can live without it, then there isn't much point in having it.

Lila Acheson Wallace, in *The New York Times* (1984)

6 During the Renaissance, women were not allowed to attend art school. Everyone asks, where are the great women painters of the Renaissance?

Karen DeCrow, *Sexist Justice* (1974)

7 If I didn't start painting, I would have raised chickens.

Grandma Moses, in Otto Kallir, ed., *My Life's History* (1952)

See also Art, Artists.

## ❦ PALMISTRY

8 Palmistry is a toy left over from the childhood of our race, which we shamefacedly hide whenever anyone is looking. Although we may despise it with our superior minds, it is older and nearer to us than our minds are, like sleep or tears.

Katharine Butler Hathaway, *The Journals and Letters of the Little Locksmith* (1946)

## ❦ PANIC

9 Panic is not an effective long-term organizing strategy.

Starhawk, preface to 1988 edition, *Dreaming the Dark* (1982)

See also Anxiety, Fear, Nerves.

## ❦ PARADOX

10 I learned to make my mind large, as the universe is large, so that there is room for paradoxes.

Maxine Hong Kingston, *The Woman Warrior* (1976)

11 The world of science lives fairly comfortably with paradox. We know that light is a wave, and also that light is a particle. The discoveries made in the infinitely small world of particle physics indicate randomness and chance, and I do not find it any more difficult to live with the paradox of a universe of randomness and chance and a universe of pattern and purpose than I do with light as a wave and light as a particle. Living with contradiction is nothing new to the human being.

Madeleine L'Engle, *Two-Part Invention* (1988)

12 Play not with paradoxes. . . . 'Tis difficult enough to see our way and keep our torch steady in this dim labyrinth: to whirl the torch and dazzle the eyes of our fellow-seekers is a poor daring, and may end in total darkness.

George Eliot, *Felix Holt, the Radical* (1866)

13 I have learned since that sometimes the things we want most are impossible for us. You may long to come home, yet wander forever.

Nadine Gordimer, *The Lying Days* (1953)

14 She saw now that the strong impulses which had once wrecked her happiness were the forces that had enabled her to rebuild her life out of the ruins.

Ellen Glasgow, *Barren Ground* (1925)

15 It was to her faults that she turned to save herself now.

Madeleine L'Engle, *A Wrinkle in Time* (1962)

16 Sometimes / you can touch a star / by reaching down.

Aili Jarvenpa, "By Reaching Down," *Half Immersed* (1978)

1 To light a candle is to cast a shadow.

> Ursula K. Le Guin, *A Wizard of Earthsea* (1968)

See also Contradiction.

## ❧ PARANOIA

2 A healthy touch of paranoia makes it that much more difficult for your enemies to get to you.

> Patricia Wallace, *Dark Intent* (1995)

## ❧ PARENTHOOD

3 I cannot have a more pleasing task than taking care of my precious Child—It is an amusement to me preferable to all others.

> Nancy Shippen Livingston (1783), in Ethel Armes, ed., *Nancy Shippen* (1935)

4 Each child has one extra line to your heart, which no other child can replace.

> Marguerite Kelly and Elia Parsons, *The Mother's Almanac* (1975)

5 To have children is a double living, the earthly fountain of youth, a continual fresh delight, a volcano as well as a fountain, and also a source of weariness beyond description.

> Josephine W. Johnson, "A Time for Everything," in Jean Beaven Abernethy, *Meditations for Women* (1947)

6 To raise good human beings it is not only necessary to be a good mother and a good father, but to have *had* a good mother and father.

> Marcelene Cox, in *Ladies' Home Journal* (1959)

7 Parents teach in the toughest school in the world—The School for Making People. You are the board of education, the principal, the classroom teacher, and the janitor.

> Virginia Satir, *Peoplemaking* (1972)

8 It takes hard work and hard thinking to rear good people. The job is interesting, although the hours are bad, starting from the first day.

> Marguerite Kelly and Elia Parsons, *The Mother's Almanac* (1975)

9 If only we could have them back as babies today, now that we have some idea what to do with them.

> Nancy Mairs, *Ordinary Time* (1993)

10 If you bungle raising your children, nothing else much matters in life.

> Jacqueline Kennedy Onassis, in David Lester, *Jacqueline Kennedy Onassis* (1994)

11 Although we consider parents the king and queen of a family, we think they must respect their subjects now, if only to avoid the guillotine later.

> Marguerite Kelly and Elia Parsons, *The Mother's Almanac* (1975)

12 If you are a parent it helps if you are a grown-up.

> Eda J. LeShan, *How to Survive Parenthood* (1965)

13 Most of us become parents long before we have stopped being children.

> Mignon McLaughlin, *The Second Neurotic's Notebook* (1966)

14 An atmosphere of trust, love, and humor can nourish extraordinary human capacity. One key is authenticity: parents acting as people, not as roles.

> Marilyn Ferguson, *The Aquarian Conspiracy* (1980)

15 All the successful parents I have observed seem to possess one common quality: that of being able to visit with their children.

> Marcelene Cox, in *Ladies' Home Journal* (1952)

16 The mark of a good parent is that he can have fun while being one.

> Marcelene Cox, in *Ladies' Home Journal* (1954)

17 There are so many disciplines in being a parent besides the obvious ones like getting up in the night and putting up with the noise in the day. And almost the hardest of all is learning to be a well of affection and not a fountain, to show them we love them, not when *we* feel like it, but when *they* do.

> Nan Fairbrother, *An English Year* (1954)

18 Raising children is like baking bread: it has to be a slow process or you end up with an overdone crust and an underdone interior.

> Marcelene Cox, in *Ladies' Home Journal* (1945)

19 If from infancy you treat children as gods they are liable in adulthood to act as devils.

> P.D. James, *The Children of Men* (1992)

20 Like most other parents I see my child through an atmosphere which illuminates, magnifies, and at

the same time refines the object to a degree that amounts to a delusion.

Sara Coleridge (1833), *Memoir and Letters*, vol. 1 (1873)

1 I discovered when I had a child of my own that I had become a biased observer of small children. Instead of looking at them with affectionate but nonpartisan eyes, I saw each of them as older or younger, bigger or smaller, more or less graceful, intelligent, or skilled than my own child.

Margaret Mead, *Blackberry Winter* (1972)

2 There are only two kinds of parents. Those who think their offspring can do nothing wrong, and those who think they can do nothing right.

Miles Franklin, *My Career Goes Bung* (1946)

3 Children are so afraid of us because they know we may try to keep them from making their biggest and most important mistakes.

Brenda Ueland (1939), *Me* (1983)

4 We often experience parental anger as a horrifying encounter with our worst selves. I never even knew I had a temper until I had children.

Nancy Samalin, with Catherine Whitney, *Love and Anger* (1991)

5 If you have never been hated by your child, you have never been a parent.

Bette Davis, *The Lonely Life* (1962)

6 Successful parenting was like log rolling, and she'd often landed in the drink.

Lisa Alther, *Bedrock* (1990)

7 Kids don't stay with you if you do it right. It's one job where, the better you are, the more surely you won't be needed in the long run.

Barbara Kingsolver, *Pigs in Heaven* (1993)

8 Three stages in a parent's life: nutrition, dentition, tuition.

Marcelene Cox, in *Ladies' Home Journal* (1945)

9 When she had been a child, children were expected to defer to their parents in everything, to wait on them and help around the house and so on; but when she became a parent and was ready to enjoy her turn at being deferred to, the winds of fashion in child rearing had changed, and parents were expected to defer to their children in hopes of not squelching their imagination and creativity. She had missed out all the way around.

Lisa Alther, *Kinflicks* (1975)

10 Parents have become so convinced that educators know what is best for children that they forget that they themselves are really the experts.

Marian Wright Edelman, in Margie Casady, "Society's Pushed-Out Children," *Psychology Today* (1975)

11 Parents learn a lot from their children about coping with life.

Muriel Spark, *The Comforters* (1957)

12 We all of us wanted babies—but did we want children?

Eda J. LeShan, *How to Survive Parenthood* (1965)

13 The real menace in dealing with a five-year-old is that in no time at all you begin to sound like a five-year-old.

Jean Kerr, "How to Get the Best of Your Children," *Please Don't Eat the Daisies* (1957)

14 Most parents feel keenly the embarrassment of having the infant misbehave . . . and they are apt to offer a tacit apology and a vague self-defense by sharply reprimanding the child in words that are meant to give the visitor the idea that they—the parents—never *heard* or *saw* such conduct before, and are now frozen with amazement.

Agnes H. Morton, *Etiquette* (1892)

15 Wherever there's trouble—that's where Billy is! Sometimes . . . I say to myself, "Lillian, you should have stayed a virgin."

Lillian Carter, in Bob Chieger, *Was It Good for You, Too?* (1983)

16 The birth of a child is in many ways the end of a marriage—marriage including a child has to be reinvented, and reinvented at a time when both husband and wife are under unprecedented stress.

Susan Cheever, *A Woman's Life* (1994)

17 Parenthood: that state of being better chaperoned than you were before marriage.

Marcelene Cox, in *Ladies' Home Journal* (1944)

18 There are days and weeks, as we all have learned, when only sex and good manners hold a marriage together. With a child there is only good manners.

Marguerite Kelly and Elia Parsons, *The Mother's Almanac* (1975)

19 Intimacy between stepchildren and stepparents is indeed proverbially difficult.

Lady Murasaki, *The Tale of Genji* (c. 1008)

1 Bringing up children is not a real occupation, because children come up just the same, brought or
not.

  Germaine Greer, *The Female Eunuch* (1971)

2 The best way to raise a child is to LAY OFF..

  Shulamith Firestone, *The Dialectic of Sex* (1970)

3 Defining child care primarily as women's sphere
reinforces the devaluing of women and prevents
their equal access to power.

  Mary Frances Berry, *The Politics of Parenthood* (1993)

4 "You almost died," a nurse told her. But that was
nonsense. Of course she wouldn't have died; she
had children. When you have children, you're ob-
ligated to live.

  Anne Tyler, *Dinner at the Homesick Restaurant* (1982)

See also Children, Discipline, Generations, Parents.

## ❦ PARENTS

5 Are anybody's parents typical?

  Madeleine L'Engle, *Two-Part Invention* (1988)

6 Do they know they're old, / These two who are my
father and my mother / Whose fire from which I
came has now grown cold?

  Elizabeth Jennings, "One Flesh," *Selected Poems* (1979)

7 We all carry the Houses of our Youth inside, and
our Parents, too, grown small enough to fit within
our Hearts.

  Erica Jong, *Fanny: Being the True History of the Adventures
  of Fanny Hackabout-Jones* (1980)

8 i, woman, i / can no longer claim / a mother of flesh
/ a father of marrow / I, Woman must be / the child
of myself.

  Pat Parker, *Movement in Black* (1978)

9 The death of any loved parent is an incalculable
lasting blow. Because no one ever loves you again
like that.

  Brenda Ueland (1938), *Me* (1983)

10 One reason you are stricken when your parents die
is that the audience you've been aiming at all your
life—shocking it, pleasing it—has suddenly left the
theater.

  Katharine Whitehorn, in *The Observer* (1983)

11 When parents die, all of the partings of the past are
reevoked with the realization that this time they
will not return.

  Mary Catherine Bateson, *With a Daughter's Eye* (1984)

12 We are never done with thinking about our parents, I suppose, and come to know them better
long after they are dead than we ever did when they
were alive.

  May Sarton, *At Seventy* (1982)

13 Years cannot move / nor death's disorienting scale
/ distort those lamplit presences.

  Gwen Harwood, "The Violets," *Collected Poems* (1991)

14 Compassion for our parents is the true sign of maturity.

  Anaïs Nin (1954), *The Diary of Anaïs Nin*, vol. 5 (1974)

15 If you harbor ill-will toward your parents, I think
you have disowned part of yourself.

  Adelaide Bry, *Friendship* (1979)

16 Our sword in the stone grows straight down
through our parents. They are right to regard us
with alarm.

  Bonnie Friedman, *Writing Past Dark* (1993)

17 They were always reading the law to her at home,
which might not have been so bad if her father and
mother had read from the same book.

  Jessamyn West, *Leafy Rivers* (1967)

18 I had not stopped to think, when boys started paying attention to me, that the cup might be dashed
from my lips, though experience should have
taught me that dashing cups from lips was the way
Victorian parents got most of their exercise.

  Margaret Halsey, *No Laughing Matter* (1977)

19 They shared decisions and the making of all policy,
both in their business and in the family. . . . They
spoke all through my childhood with one unfrag-
mentable and unappealable voice.

  Audre Lorde, *Zami: A New Spelling of My Name* (1983)

20 Before we can leave our parents, they stuff our
heads like the suitcases which they jam-pack with
homemade underwear.

  Maxine Hong Kingston, *The Woman Warrior* (1976)

21 Being an adult child was an awkward, inevitable
position. You went about your business in the
world: tooling around, giving orders, being taken
seriously, but there were still these two people lurk-

ing somewhere who in a split second could reduce you to *nothing*. In their presence, you were a big-headed baby again, crawling instead of walking.

Meg Wolitzer, *This Is My Life* (1988)

1 What parent ever thought that a child had arrived at maturity?

Mrs. Mary Clavers, *A New Home* (1839)

2 Parents are untamed, excessive, potentially troublesome creatures; charming to be with for a time, in the main they must lead their own lives, independent and self-employed, with companions of their own age and selection.

Rose Macaulay, *My World My Wilderness* (1950)

3 The debt of gratitude we owe our mother and father goes forward, not backward. What we owe our parents is the bill presented to us by our children.

Nancy Friday, *My Mother/My Self* (1977)

See also Children, Family, Fathers, Generations, Mothers, Parenthood.

## ♦ PARIAHS

4 [A pariah is] something like a martyr with more suffering and less class.

Rita Mae Brown, *Bingo* (1988)

See also Outsiders.

## ♦ PARIS

5 Everything begins in Paris.

Nancy Spain, *A Funny Thing Happened on the Way* (1964)

6 Life, that is Paris! Paris, that is life!

Marie Bashkirtseff (1873), in Mary J. Serrano, tr., *The Journal of a Young Artist* (1919)

7 The perfect classroom is Paris.

Letitia Baldrige, *Of Diamonds and Diplomats* (1968)

8 The city of love, loveliness, liberty and light.

Margaret Anderson, *The Fiery Fountains* (1953)

9 Paris, France is exciting and peaceful.

Gertrude Stein, *Paris France* (1940)

10 The pearl-grey city, the opal that is Paris.

Anaïs Nin (1933), *The Diary of Anaïs Nin*, vol. 1 (1966)

11 It should always be seen, the first time, with the eyes of childhood or of love.

M.F.K. Fisher, *The Gastronomical Me* (1943)

12 Only Paris can supply the unknown force which is the very essence of love—novelty. She would grow old in other places, and twice a year she would return to Paris to be rejuvenated, like those miraculous trees of the Champs-Élysées which bear new leaves in autumn.

Princess Marthe Bibesco, *Catherine-Paris* (1928)

13 Every human activity, whether it be love, philosophy, art, or revolution, is carried on with a special intensity in Paris.

Rebecca West, *The Birds Fall Down* (1966)

14 One's emotions are intensified in Paris—one can be more happy and also more unhappy here than in any other place.

Nancy Mitford, *The Pursuit of Love* (1945)

15 People come to Paris, to the capital, to give their lives a sense of belonging, of an almost mythical participation in society.

Marguerite Duras, *Practicalities* (1987)

16 In Paris there are few changes; one always finds one's niche there when one returns—no matter how long one may have been away.

Janet Scudder, *Modeling My Life* (1925)

17 I always return to Paris, taking my selves along— past self, customary self, the self I never had.

Helen Bevington, *The Journey Is Everything* (1983)

18 We have traversed Paris in every direction, have taken daily walks of three and four hours, and that without my feeling any fatigue, without even remembering that I was walking. One has no body, one has only a soul to see and admire.

Eugénie de Guérin (1838), in Guillaume S. Trébutien, ed., *Letters of Eugénie de Guérin* (1865)

19 A walk through the Paris streets was always like the unrolling of a vast tapestry from which countless stored fragrances were shaken out.

Edith Wharton, *The Reef* (1912)

20 Whenever you are in Paris at twilight in the early summer, return to the Seine and watch the evening

sky close slowly on a last strand of daylight fading quietly, like a sigh.

Kate Simon, *Paris* (1967)

1 In Paris one should have everything or nothing. We had often had nothing, and that had had a special charm, because Paris more than any other city has pleasures available to the poor.

Eleanor Perényi, *More Was Lost* (1946)

2 Paris in the early morning has a cheerful, bustling aspect, a promise of delicious things to come, a positive smell of coffee and croissants, quite peculiar to itself. The people welcome a new day as if they were certain of liking it, the shopkeepers pull up their blinds serene in the expectation of good trade, the workers go happily to their work, the people who have sat up all night in night-clubs go happily to their rest, the orchestra of motor-car horns, of clanking trams, of whistling policemen tunes up for the daily symphony, and everywhere is joy.

Nancy Mitford, *The Pursuit of Love* (1945)

3 Paris is the loveliest city in the world. Until she opens her mouth. Should the French go forth to battle armed only with their taxi horns, they would drive all before them.

Nancy Boyd, *Distressing Dialogues* (1924)

4 I'm sure that all the drivers and motorcycle police had once been racing drivers and were eager to get back to that profession.

Eleanor Roosevelt, *On My Own* (1958)

5 If I were to choose one single thing that would restore Paris to the senses, it would be that strangely sweet, unhealthy smell of the Métro, so very unlike the dank cold or the stuffy heat of subways in New York.

May Sarton, *I Knew a Phoenix* (1959)

6 The Left Bank called me and even now it does not cease to call me and to keep me. I cannot imagine that I could ever leave it, any more than an organ can leave the place that is assigned to it in the body.

Adrienne Monnier, in Richard McDougall, tr., *The Very Rich Hours of Adrienne Monnier* (1976)

7 Food is still what Parisians buy if they can. It is a nervous means of getting satisfaction, a holdover from the lean years of the Occupation.

Janet Flanner ("Genêt"), *Paris Journal 1944-1965* (1965)

8 Trade is art, and art's philosophy, / In Paris.

Elizabeth Barrett Browning, *Aurora Leigh* (1857)

9 All the other cities of the world are simply branches of Paris.

Elsa Triolet, "Notebooks Buried," *A Fine of Two Hundred Francs* (1947)

## ❦ PARTIES

10 One cannot have too large a party.

Jane Austen, *Emma* (1816)

11 A balanced guest list of mixed elements is to a successful party what the seasoning is to a culinary triumph.

Letitia Baldrige, *Of Diamonds and Diplomats* (1968)

12 "The guest who does not dance" is one of the unfortunate things the hostess has to put up with at every one of her dances.

Lillian Eichler, *Book of Etiquette* (1921)

13 Parties are always full of people who hate parties.

Lillian Day, *Kiss and Tell* (1931)

14 I know the dying process begins the minute we are born, but sometimes it accelerates during dinner parties.

Carol Matthau, *Among the Porcupines* (1992)

15 For some unexplained reason, it's always the other end of the table that's wild and raucous, with screaming laughter and a fella who plays "Holiday for Strings" on water glasses.

Erma Bombeck, *I Lost Everything in the Post-Natal Depression* (1970)

16 If Ruby intended her party to be a *salon* it was a typographical error.

Lillian Day, *Kiss and Tell* (1931)

17 I misremember who first was cruel enough to nurture the cocktail party into life. But perhaps it would be not too much to say, in fact it would be not enough to say, that it was not worth the trouble.

Dorothy Parker, in *Esquire* (1964)

1 Cocktail parties . . . are usually not parties at all but mass ceremonials designed to clear up at one great stroke a wealth of obligations.

    Phyllis McGinley, *Sixpence in Her Shoe* (1964)

2 The fact is, the cocktail party has much in its favor. Going to one is a good way of indicating that you're still alive and about, if such is the case, and that you're glad other people are, without having to spend an entire evening proving it.

    Peg Bracken, *I Try to Behave Myself* (1963)

3 Cocktail party? . . . It's a new idea—don't you have them at Oxford? You will soon, mark my words. I rather like them. You're not obliged to talk to anybody and when you get home, it's bedtime.

    Nancy Mitford, *Don't Tell Alfred* (1960)

4 Without peanuts, it isn't a cocktail party.

    Julia Child, *Julia Child & Company* (1978)

See also Entertaining, Gaiety, Guests, Hospitality, Social Skills.

## ✿ PARTING

5 Parting is all we know of heaven, / And all we need of hell.

    Emily Dickinson, in Mabel Loomis Todd, ed., *Poems by Emily Dickinson*, 3rd series (1896)

6 In every parting there is an image of death.

    George Eliot, "The Sad Fortunes of the Rev. Amos Barton," *Scenes of Clerical Life* (1857)

7 Every time one leaves anywhere, something precious, which ought not to be killed, is left to die.

    Katherine Mansfield (1922), *Journal of Katherine Mansfield* (1927)

8 Somehow, the real moment of parting always precedes the physical act of separation.

    Princess Marthe Bibesco, *Catherine-Paris* (1928)

9 Time manages the most painful partings for us. One has only to set the date, buy the ticket, and let the earth, sun, and moon make their passages through the sky, until inexorable time carries us with it to the moment of parting.

    Jill Ker Conway, *The Road From Coorain* (1989)

10 If you must leave a place that you have lived in and loved and where all your yesterdays are buried deep—leave it any way except a slow way, leave it the fastest way you can. Never turn back and never believe that an hour you remember is a better hour because it is dead.

    Beryl Markham, *West With the Night* (1942)

11 How shall we know it is the last good-by?

    Louise Chandler Moulton, "The Last Good-by," in Edmund Clarence Stedman, ed., *An American Anthology 1787-1900* (1900)

12 Leaving can sometimes be the best way to never go away.

    Cathy N. Davidson, *36 Views of Mount Fuji* (1993)

See also Absence, Desertion, Farewells.

## ✿ PASSION

13 We must have a passion in life.

    George Sand (1831), in Raphaël Ledos de Beaufort, ed., *Letters of George Sand*, vol. 1 (1886)

14 Passion is our ground, our island—do others exist?

    Eudora Welty, "Circe," *The Bride of the Innisfallen* (1955)

15 It is the soul's duty to be loyal to its own desires. It must abandon itself to its master passion.

    Rebecca West, in Alfred Leslie Rowse, *Glimpses of the Great* (1985)

16 Passion is always a search for the ideal.

    Dorothy Graham, *The French Wife* (1928)

17 Passion, that thing of beauty, that flowering without roots, has to be born, live and die without reason.

    Georgette Leblanc (1898), in Janet Flanner, tr., *Souvenirs* (1932)

18 The fiery moments of passionate experience are the moments of wholeness and totality of the personality.

    Anaïs Nin, *The Novel of the Future* (1968)

19 Experience teaches us in a millennium what passion teaches us in an hour.

    Ralph Iron, *The Story of an African Farm* (1883)

20 How little do they know human nature, who think they can say to passion, so far shalt thou go, and no farther!

    Sarah Scott, *The History of Cornelia* (1750)

1 Passion alone could destroy passion. All the thinking in the world could not make so much as a dent in its surface.
  Ellen Glasgow, *In This Our Life* (1941)

2 The capacity for passion is both cruel and divine.
  George Sand (1834), in Marie Jenny Howe, ed., *The Intimate Journal of George Sand* (1929)

3 Passion is more important than justice.
  Carson McCullers, *Clock Without Hands* (1961)

4 There's plenty of fire in the coldest flint!
  Rachel Field, *All This and Heaven Too* (1939)

5 The worst sin—perhaps the only sin—passion can commit, is to be joyless.
  Dorothy L. Sayers, *Gaudy Night* (1935)

6 There's no blameless life / Save for the passionless.
  George Eliot, *The Spanish Gypsy* (1868)

7 Passion is what the sun feels for the earth / When harvests ripen into golden birth.
  Ella Wheeler Wilcox, "The Difference," *Poems of Pleasure* (1888)

8 Great passions, my dear, don't exist: they're liars' fantasies. What do exist are little loves that may last for a short or a longer while.
  Anna Magnani, in Oriana Fallaci, *Limelighters* (1963)

9 Jump out of the window if you are the object of passion. Flee it, if you feel it . . . passion goes, boredom remains.
  Coco Chanel, in Joseph Barry, "An Interview With Chanel," *McCall's* (1965)

10 She takes viper-broth, which has recovered her strength and spirits perceptibly: she thinks it the best thing you can possibly take. The head and tail of the viper are cut off; it is gutted and skinned; yet, even two hours after, it moves. We could not help comparing this tenacity of life to old passions.
  Marie de Rabutin-Chantal, Marquise de Sévigné (1679), *Letters of Madame de Sévigné to Her Daughter and Her Friends*, vol. 5 (1811)

11 A continual atmosphere of hectic passion is very trying if you haven't got any of your own.
  Dorothy L. Sayers, *The Unpleasantness at the Bellona Club* (1928)

See also Desire, Enthusiasm, Intensity, Longing, Love.

## ❧ PAST

12 The past is perpetual youth to the heart.
  L.E. Landon, title poem, *The Vow of the Peacock* (1829)

13 I am drunk on yesterday. / Its murmuring is preserved with every pounding of my blood, / preserved its joys, its sorrows, / lasting within me, within me.
  Anda Amir, "Lot's Wife," in Ellen M. Umansky and Dianne Ashton, eds., *Four Centuries of Jewish Women's Spirituality* (1992)

14 It is not that I belong to the past, but that the past belongs to me.
  Mary Antin, *The Promised Land* (1912)

15 The past can seldom be recalled without sadness, for it was either better or worse than the present.
  Leonora Christina, *Memory of Sorrow* (1689)

16 The past is the tense of memory and art and wisdom.
  Blanche H. Dow, "Roads and Vistas," in Jean Beaven Abernethy, ed., *Meditations for Women* (1947)

17 All normal human beings are interested in their past. Only when the interest becomes an obsession, overshadowing present and future conduct, is it a danger. In much the same way healthy nations are interested in their history, but a morbid preoccupation with past glories is a sign that something is wrong with the constitution of the State.
  C.V. Wedgwood, *Velvet Studies* (1946)

18 I sometimes think it's a mistake to have been happy when one was a child. One should always want to go on, not back.
  Mary Stewart, *The Stormy Petrel* (1991)

19 Each had his past shut in him like the leaves of a book known to him by heart; and his friends could only read the title.
  Virginia Woolf, *Jacob's Room* (1922)

20 Like camels, we lived on our past.
  Alice B. Toklas, *The Alice B. Toklas Cook Book* (1954)

21 The only thing most people regret about their past is its length.
  Kay Ingram, in *The Saturday Evening Post* (1950)

22 We are pushed forward by the social forces, reluctant and stumbling, our faces over our shoulders, clutching at every relic of the past as we are forced

along; still adoring whatever is behind us. We insist upon worshiping "the God of our fathers." Why not the God of our children? Does eternity only stretch one way?

> Charlotte Perkins Gilman, *The Home* (1903)

1 Time past is not time gone, it is time accumulated with the host resembling the character in the fairytale who was joined along the route by more and more characters none of whom could be separated from one another or from the host, with some stuck so fast that their presence caused physical pain.

> Janet Frame, *An Angel at My Table* (1984)

2 The past is strapped to our backs. We do not have to see it; we can always feel it.

> Mignon McLaughlin, *The Neurotic's Notebook* (1963)

3 Even though you've given up a past it hasn't given you up. It comes uninvited—and sometimes half welcome.

> Susan Glaspell, *The Morning Is Near Us* (1939)

4 *Yesterday* is never over. Yesterday endures eternally.

> Jehanne d'Orliac, *The Moon Mistress* (1930)

5 There is, I have learned, no permanent escape from the past. It may be an unrecognized law of our nature that we should be drawn back, inevitably, to the place where we have suffered most.

> Ellen Glasgow, *The Woman Within* (1954)

6 Sometimes a person has to go back, really back—to have a sense, an understanding of all that's gone to make them—before they can go forward.

> Paule Marshall, *The Chosen Place, The Timeless People* (1969)

7 The road was new to me, as roads always are, going back.

> Sarah Orne Jewett, *The Country of the Pointed Firs* (1896)

8 She stayed bound to a gone moment, like a stopped clock with hands silently pointing an hour it cannot be.

> Elizabeth Bowen, *The House in Paris* (1935)

9 A long past vividly remembered is like a heavy garment that clings to your limbs when you would run.

> Mary Antin, *The Promised Land* (1912)

10 I fling my past behind me like a robe / Worn threadbare in the seams, and out of date. / I have outgrown it.

> Ella Wheeler Wilcox, "The Past," *The Collected Poems of Ella Wheeler Wilcox* (1917)

11 His past was no more to him than the eggshell is to the eagle.

> Margaret Deland, *The Wisdom of Fools* (1897)

12 The past is never where you think you left it.

> Katherine Anne Porter, *Ship of Fools* (1962)

13 In the West the past is like a dead animal. It is a carcass picked at by the flies that call themselves historians and biographers.

> Miriam Makeba, with James Hall, *Makeba* (1987)

14 Living in the past is a dull and lonely business; and looking back, if persisted in, strains the neck-muscles, causes you to bump into people not going your way.

> Edna Ferber, *A Kind of Magic* (1963)

15 The mill cannot grind with the water that is past.

> Josephine Daskam, "The Sailor's Song," *Poems* (1903)

16 How swiftly the locks rust, the hinges grow stiff on doors that close behind us!

> Lady Murasaki, *The Tale of Genji* (c. 1008)

17 Waves, once they land on the beach, are not reversible.

> Grace Paley, in *Ms.* (1992)

18 The past is a sorry country.

> Barbara Grizzuti Harrison, *Foreign Bodies* (1984)

19 The farther behind I leave the past, the closer I am to forging my own character.

> Isabelle Eberhardt (1900), in Nina de Voogd, tr., *The Passionate Nomad* (1988)

20 The destruction of the past is perhaps the greatest of all crimes.

> Simone Weil, *The Need for Roots* (1949)

21 The past is part of the present which becomes part of the future.

> Lee Krasner, in Eleanor Munro, *Originals: American Women Artists* (1979)

22 The past isn't useful until its place in the present is found.

> Judith Rossner, *August* (1983)

1 One faces the future with one's past.

    Pearl S. Buck, *What America Means to Me* (1943)

2 We cannot live in the past, nor can we re-create it. Yet as we unravel the past, the future also unfolds before us, as though they are mirrors without which neither can be seen or happen.

    Judy Grahn, *Another Mother Tongue* (1984)

3 The mind must move. When there is nothing to go forward to, it explores the past. The past is really almost as much a work of the imagination as the future.

    Jessamyn West, *A Matter of Time* (1966)

4 You cannot see the past that did not happen any more than you can foresee the future.

    Madeleine L'Engle, *The Arm of the Starfish* (1965)

See also Eras, Future, History, Memory, Nostalgia, Present, Remembrance, Time.

## ॐ PATHOS

5 The pathos of life is worse than the tragedy.

    Ellen Glasgow, *Barren Ground* (1925)

See also Pity, Tragedy.

## ॐ PATIENCE

6 All fruits do not ripen in one season.

    Laure Junot, Duchesse de Abrantès, *Mémoires Historiques* (1835)

7 What is your need to eat the seed, / When growth might be so sweet?

    Anna Wickham, "Amourette," *The Contemplative Quarry* (1915)

8 Patience is bitter, but its fruit is sweet.

    Lida Clarkson, "Brush Studies," in *Ladies' Home Journal* (1884)

9 What is so certain of victory as patience?

    Selma Lagerlöf, *The Story of Gösta Berling* (1891)

10 He was resigned and on the whole patient, like a man with a very old illness.

    Margery Allingham, *The Mind Readers* (1965)

11 I am extraordinarily patient, provided I get my own way in the end.

    Margaret Thatcher, in *The Observer* (1989)

12 Patience! Patience! Patience is the invention of dullards and sluggards. In a well-regulated world there should be no need of such a thing as patience.

    Grace King, *Balcony Stories* (1892)

See also Endurance, Perseverance, Stubbornness, Virtue.

## ॐ PATRIARCHY

13 Benevolent patriarchy is still patriarchy.

    Elizabeth A. Johnson, *She Who Is* (1993)

14 If patriarchy can take what exists and make it not, surely we can take what exists and make it be.

    Nicole Brossard, in Marlene Wildeman, tr., *The Aerial Letter* (1988)

See also Sexism.

## ॐ PATRIOTISM

15 My love for my country is my religion.

    Queen Marie of Rumania (1914), in Hannah Pakula, *The Last Romantic* (1984)

16 The more I see of other countries, the more I love my own.

    Madame de Staël, *Corinne* (1807)

17 What is love of one's country; is it hate of one's uncountry? Then it's not a good thing.

    Ursula K. Le Guin, *The Left Hand of Darkness* (1969)

18 That kind of patriotism which consists in hating all other nations.

    Elizabeth Gaskell, *Sylvia's Lovers* (1863)

19 True patriotism doesn't exclude an understanding of the patriotism of others.

    Queen Elizabeth II, in Michèle Brown and Ann O'Connor, *Woman Talk*, vol. 1 (1984)

20 The development of the national spirit in its present form leads into blind alleys. Some condition

*must* be found which preserves the life of the nation, but rules out the fatal rivalry among nations.

Käthe Kollwitz (1917), in Hans Kollwitz, ed., *The Diaries and Letters of Käthe Kollwitz* (1955)

1 If you wish to understand me at all (and to write an autobiography is only to open a window into one's heart) you must understand first and foremost, that I am an Australian.

Nellie Melba, *Melodies and Memories* (1925)

2 American patriotism is generally something that amuses Europeans, I suppose because children look idiotic saluting the flag and because the constitution contains so many cracks through which the lawyers may creep.

Katharine Whitehorn, *Roundabout* (1962)

3 You can't prove you're an American by waving Old Glory.

Helen Gahagan Douglas, *A Full Life* (1982)

4 A patriot is one who wrestles for the / soul of her country / as she wrestles for her own being.

Adrienne Rich, title poem, *An Atlas of the Difficult World* (1991)

5 Question everyone in authority, and see that you get sensible answers to your questions. . . . Questioning does not mean the end of loving, and loving does not mean the abnegation of intelligence. Vow as much love to your country as you like . . . but, I implore you, do not forget to question.

Winifred Holtby, *South Riding* (1936)

6 I'm a universal patriot, if you could understand me rightly: my country is the world.

Charlotte Brontë, *The Professor* (1846)

See also Chauvinism.

## ❧ PATRONIZING

7 A patronizing disposition always has its meaner side.

George Eliot, *Adam Bede* (1859)

8 Don't Preach. Don't Patronize.

Slogan of the woman-run Americanization Committee that helped immigrants adjust to American life, in *Woman Citizen* (1917)

See also Pity.

## ❧ PEACE

9 Everyone speaks of peace; no one knows what peace is. We know at best a poisoned peace. No one has lived on an earth without weapons, without war and the threat of war on a large and small scale.

Christina Thürmer-Rohr, *Vagabonding* (1991)

10 Peace the great meaning has not been defined. / When we say peace as a word, war / As a flare of fire leaps across our eyes.

Muriel Rukeyser, "The Double Death," *One Life* (1957)

11 We have thought of peace as the passive and war as the active way of living. The opposite is true. War is not the most strenuous life. It is a kind of rest-cure compared to the task of reconciling our differences.

M.P. Follett, *The New State* (1918)

12 Peace is not a passive but an active condition, not a negation but an affirmation. It is a gesture as strong as war.

Mary Roberts Rinehart (1918), in Julia Edwards, *Women of the World* (1988)

13 They have not wanted *Peace* at all; they have wanted to be spared war—as though the absence of war was the same as peace.

Dorothy Thompson, syndicated column "On the Record" (1958)

14 The struggle to maintain peace is immeasurably more difficult than any military operation.

Anne O'Hare McCormick, in Julia Edwards, *Women of the World* (1988)

15 You cannot shake hands with a clenched fist.

Indira Gandhi, in *The Christian Science Monitor* (1972)

16 It isn't enough to talk about peace. One must believe in it. And it isn't enough to believe in it. One must work at it.

Eleanor Roosevelt, radio broadcast (1951), in Joseph P. Lash, *Eleanor: The Years Alone* (1972)

17 Peace is achieved one person at a time, through a series of friendships.

Fatma Reda, in *The Minnesota Women's Press* (1991)

18 It seems to me that there are two great enemies of peace—fear and selfishness.

Katherine Paterson, in *The Horn Book* (1991)

1 By its existence, the Peace Movement denies that governments know best; it stands for a different order of priorities: the human race comes first.
   Martha Gellhorn, "Conclusion," *The Face of War* (1959)

2 Did St. Francis preach to the birds? Whatever for? If he really liked birds he would have done better to preach to cats.
   Rebecca West, *This Real Night* (1985)

3 High above hate I dwell: / O storms! farewell.
   Louise Imogen Guiney, "The Sanctuary," *The Martyrs' Idyl* (1899)

4 Ultimately, we have just one moral duty: to reclaim large areas of peace in ourselves, more and more peace, and to reflect it towards others. And the more peace there is in us, the more peace there will also be in our troubled world.
   Etty Hillesum (1942), *An Interrupted Life* (1983)

5 Acquire inner peace and a multitude will find their salvation near you.
   Catherine de Hueck Doherty, *Poustinia* (1975)

6 Whatever peace I know rests in the natural world, in feeling myself a part of it, even in a small way.
   May Sarton, *Journal of a Solitude* (1973)

7 Peace is when time doesn't matter as it passes by.
   Maria Schell, in *Time* (1958)

8 There is no such thing as inner peace. There is only nervousness or death.
   Fran Lebowitz, *Metropolitan Life* (1978)

See also Calm, Human Family, Pacifism, Peace and Love, War.

## ❧ PEACE AND LOVE

9 Love is not a doctrine. Peace is not an international agreement. Love and Peace are beings who live as possibilities in us.
   Mary Caroline Richards, *Centering* (1964)

10 Peace and love are always in us, existing and working, but we are not always in peace and in love.
   Julian of Norwich, *Revelations of Divine Love* (1373)

See also Love, Peace.

## ❧ PENNSYLVANIA

11 Nowhere in this country, from sea to sea, does nature comfort us with such assurance of plenty, such rich and tranquil beauty as in those unsung, unpainted hills of Pennsylvania.
   Rebecca Harding Davis, *Bits of Gossip* (1904)

12 Steel wasn't the only major industry in Pittsburgh. We just had to think to recall the others.
   Annie Dillard, *An American Childhood* (1987)

## ❧ PERFECTIONISM

13 I think perfectionism is based on the obsessive belief that if you run carefully enough, hitting each stepping-stone just right, you won't have to die. The truth is that you will die anyway and that a lot of people who aren't even looking at their feet are going to do a whole lot better than you, and have a lot more fun while they're doing it.
   Anne Lamott, *Bird by Bird* (1994)

14 We know of our own knowledge that we are human beings, and, as such, imperfect. But we are bathed by the communications industry in a ceaseless tide of inhuman, impossible perfection.
   Margaret Halsey, *The Folks at Home* (1952)

15 Perfectionism is the voice of the oppressor.
   Anne Lamott, *Bird by Bird* (1994)

16 In order to go on living one must try to escape the death involved in perfection.
   Hannah Arendt, *Rahel Varnhagen* (1957)

17 Perfection bores me, in art, in music; most of all, in people. Luckily, perfection is rare.
   Vicki Baum, *I Know What I'm Worth* (1964)

See also Excellence.

## ❧ PERFORMANCE

18 Performance is an act of faith.
   Marya Mannes, *The New York I Know* (1961)

19 When you perform . . . you are out of yourself—larger and more potent, more beautiful. You are

for minutes heroic. This is power. This is glory on earth. And it is yours, nightly.

Agnes de Mille, in *The New York Times* (1963)

1 Once you get on stage, everything is right. I feel the most beautiful, complete, fulfilled. I think that's why, in the case of noncompromising career women, parts of our personal lives don't work out. One person can't give you the feeling that thousands of people give you.

Leontyne Price, in Brian Lanker, *I Dream a World* (1989)

2 I come out before an audience and maybe my house burned down an hour ago, maybe my husband stayed out all night, but I stand there. . . . I got them with me, right there in my hand and comfortable. That's my job, to make them comfortable, because if they wanted to be nervous they could have stayed home and added up their bills.

Fanny Brice, in Norman Katkov, *The Fabulous Fanny* (1952)

3 Every now and then, when you're on stage, you hear the best sound a player can hear. It is a sound you can't get in movies or in television. It is the sound of a wonderful, deep silence that means you've hit them where they live.

Shelley Winters, "That Wonderful, Deep Silence," in *Theatre Arts* (1956)

4 There were times when I was more at home in front of millions of people than I was at *home.*

Carol Burnett, *One More Time* (1986)

5 On stage I make love to twenty-five thousand people, then I go home alone.

Janis Joplin, in Bob Chieger, *Was It Good for You, Too?* (1983)

6 Maybe my audiences can enjoy my music more if they think I'm destroying myself.

Janis Joplin, interview with Mary Campbell, in Gillian G. Gaar, *She's a Rebel* (1992)

7 The awful consciousness that one is the sole object of attention to that immense space, lined as it were with human intellect from top to bottom, and on all side round, may perhaps be imagined but can not be described.

Sarah Siddons, *The Reminiscences of Sarah Kemble Siddons 1773-1785* (1942)

8 My stage fright gets worse at every performance. During the overture I hope for a theater fire, typhoon, revolution in the Pentagon.

Hildegard Knef, *The Gift Horse* (1970)

9 It is in performance that the sudden panic hits, that we beg for release from our destiny and at the same time court the very experience that terrifies us. . . . A well-meaning friend says, "There's nothing to get nervous about," and it almost helps, because the desire to strangle distracts us for the moment.

Eloise Ristad, *A Soprano on Her Head* (1982)

10 When it's all over and the ON THE AIR signs go off there isn't a more lost feeling in the world. The wonderful, exciting, even glamorous, studio is now just a room dirty with coffee cartons and cigarette butts.

Gertrude Berg, *Molly and Me* (1961)

See also Acting, Audience, Comedy, Opera, Singing, Spectators, Theater.

## ♦ PERSECUTION

11 All persecution is a sign of fear; for if we did not fear the power of an opinion different from our own, we should not mind others holding it.

Phyllis Bottome, *The Mortal Storm* (1938)

12 When there is violence against any person in society, because he or she is different, it threatens us all. Only by speaking out are any of us safe.

Madeleine Kunin, *Living a Political Life* (1994)

See also Bigotry, Discrimination, Injustice, Oppression, Prejudice.

## ♦ PERSEVERANCE

13 Diamonds are only chunks of coal, / That stuck to their jobs, you see.

Minnie Richard Smith, "Stick to Your Job," in C.F. Kleinknecht, *Poor Richard's Anthology of Thoughts on Success* (1947)

14 The great thing and the hard thing is to stick to things when you have outlived the first interest and not yet got the second which comes with a sort of mastery.

Janet Erskine Stuart, in Maud Monahan, *Life and Letters of Janet Erskine Stuart* (1922)

1 I must keep on rowing, not until I reach port but until I reach my grave.

> Madame de Staël, letter (1814), in J. Christopher Herold, *Mistress to an Age* (1958)

2 When you get in a tight place and everything goes against you till it seems as though you could not hold on a minute longer, never give up then, for that is just the time and the place the tide will turn.

> Harriet Beecher Stowe, in C.F. Kleinknecht, *Poor Richard's Anthology of Thoughts on Success* (1947)

3 Any road is bound to arrive somewhere if you follow it far enough.

> Patricia Wentworth, *Run!* (1938)

4 You went on and on at it, you wouldn't leave it alone. When one thought the thing was safely thrown out of doors you reappeared at the window with the thing in your mouth.

> Rebecca West, *Sunflower* (1925)

5 You can eat an elephant one bite at a time.

> Mary Kay Ash, *Mary Kay* (1981)

See also Determination, Obstinacy, Patience, Stubbornness.

## ᛞ PERSONALITY

6 We do not accept ourselves for what we are, we retreat from our real selves, and then we erect a personality to bridge the gap.

> Susan Sontag, *The Benefactor* (1963)

7 She had to confess inexperience; her personality was still too much for her, like a punt-pole.

> Elizabeth Bowen, *Friends and Relations* (1931)

8 What's the matter with this country is the matter with the lot of us individually—our sense of personality is a sense of outrage.

> Elizabeth Bowen, *The Last September* (1929)

9 Her personality was a little tarnished: she was in want of social renovation. She had been doing and saying the same things for too long a time.

> Edith Wharton, "The Last Asset," *The Hermit and the Wild Woman* (1908)

10 She [Ethel Waters] is one of the strangest bundles of people that I have ever met. You can just see the different folks wrapped up in her if you associate with her long. Just like watching an open fire—the color and shape of her personality is never the same twice.

> Zora Neale Hurston, *Dust Tracks on a Road* (1942)

11 It was a little like living with a cross between Martha Graham and Groucho Marx: dancing with a wisecrack.

> Jessamyn West, *Cress Delahanty* (1948)

See also Behavior, Character, Self, Temperament.

## ᛞ PERSUASION

12 She leaned toward me the way people do when they want an idea to penetrate your resistance. As though the closer they get their own brain to your brain, the easier it will be for the idea to leap across.

> Mildred Davis, *They Buried a Man* (1953)

13 We are always on the side of those who speak last.

> Marie de Rabutin-Chantal, Marquise de Sévigné (1671), *Letters of Madame de Sévigné to Her Daughter and Her Friends*, vol. 1 (1811)

14 It is easy to convince a man who already thinks as you do.

> Ellen Glasgow, *The Battle-Ground* (1902)

15 There is nothing that you may not get people to believe in if you will only tell it them loud enough and often enough, till the welkin rings with it.

> Ouida, *Wisdom, Wit and Pathos* (1884)

See also Advertising, Sales Ability.

## ᛞ PESSIMISM

16 Nothing is too bad to be true, Mr. Douglas, and nothing is true that is not bad.

> Emily Eden, *The Semi-Attached Couple* (1860)

17 Got to see it, hear it, touch it, smell it, know it by our own senses to believe it—if it's good. But if it's bad—it's true.

> Ann Fairbairn, *Five Smooth Stones* (1966)

18 "On our father's side we live till eighty or ninety, but on our mother's side we die early." Perhaps this

is the trouble with so many of us—on one side we die early.

Anne Shannon Monroe, *The Hearth of Happiness* (1929)

1 [He] has learnt to expect the skinny leg of the chicken.

Margaret Kennedy, *Lucy Carmichael* (1951)

2 What goes up must come down. But don't expect it to come down where you can find it.

Jane Wagner, *The Search for Signs of Intelligent Life in the Universe* (1985)

3 It doesn't pay well to fight for what we believe in.

Lillian Hellman, *Watch on the Rhine* (1941)

4 People who "view with alarm" never build anything.

Eleanor Roosevelt, *Tomorrow Is Now* (1963)

5 No pessimist ever discovered the secrets of the stars, or sailed to an uncharted land, or opened a new heaven to the human spirit.

Helen Keller, *Optimism* (1903)

6 One thing we know beyond all doubt: Nothing has ever been achieved by the person who says, "It can't be done."

Eleanor Roosevelt, *You Learn by Living* (1960)

7 Dwelling on the negative simply contributes to its power.

Shirley MacLaine, *Out on a Limb* (1983)

8 The pessimist . . . is seldom an agitating individual. His creed breeds indifference to others, and he does not trouble himself to thrust his views upon the unconvinced.

Agnes Repplier, "Some Aspects of Pessimism," *Books and Men* (1888)

9 Pessimism is the affectation of youth, the reality of age.

Ellen Glasgow, *The Descendant* (1897)

10 The most common type of pessimism is neither philosophical nor religious: it is the pessimism of thwarted desire. . . . It is the cynical sneer of the man who, seeking roses, finds only ashes.

Georgia Harkness, *Conflicts in Religious Thought* (1929)

11 How happy are the pessimists! What joy is theirs when they have proved that there is no joy.

Marie von Ebner-Eschenbach, *Aphorisms* (1893)

12 O, merry is the Optimist, / With the troops of courage leaguing. / But a dour trend / In any friend / Is somehow less fatiguing.

Phyllis McGinley, "Song Against Sweetness and Light," *A Pocketful of Wry* (1940)

See also Cynicism, Despair.

## ❦ PETS

13 You enter into a certain amount of madness when you marry a person with pets.

Nora Ephron, *Heartburn* (1983)

14 We are pretty sure that we and our pets share the same reality, until one day we come home to find that our wistful, intelligent friend who reminds us of our better self has decided a good way to spend the day is to open a box of Brillo pads, unravel a few, distribute some throughout the house, and eat or wear all the rest. And we shake our heads in an inability to comprehend what went wrong here.

Merrill Markoe, *What the Dogs Have Taught Me* (1992)

15 Healthy parakeets have the nervous energy of tennis players.

Mignon McLaughlin, *The Second Neurotic's Notebook* (1966)

16 He [pet goat] followed me like an unpaid bill.

Myrtle Reed, *The Book of Clever Beasts* (1904)

See also Animals, Birds, Cats, Cats and Dogs, Dogs, Wildlife.

## ❦ THE PHILIPPINES

17 Eighty dialects and languages are spoken; we are a fragmented nation of loyal believers, divided by blood feuds and controlled by the Church.

Jessica Hagedorn, *Dogeaters* (1990)

## ❦ PHILOSOPHY

18 Philosophizing is a process of making sense out of experience.

Susanne K. Langer, *Philosophical Sketches* (1962)

1 A philosophy is characterized more by the *formulation* of its problems than by its solution of them.

  Susanne K. Langer, *Philosophy in a New Key* (1942)

2 Philosophy is called upon to compensate for the frustrations of politics and, more generally, of life itself.

  Hannah Arendt, *The Life of the Mind*, vol. 1 (1978)

3 My definition [of a philosopher] is of a man up in a balloon, with his family and friends holding the ropes which confine him to earth and trying to haul him down.

  Louisa May Alcott, in Ednah Dow Cheney, ed., *Louisa May Alcott, Her Life, Letters, and Journals* (1890)

4 As a human being, you have no choice about the fact that you need a philosophy. Your only choice is whether you define your philosophy by a conscious, rational, disciplined process of thought and scrupulously logical deliberation—or let your subconscious accumulate a junk heap of unwarranted conclusions, false generalizations, undefined contradictions, undigested slogans, unidentified wishes, doubts and fears, thrown together by chance, but integrated by your subconscious into a kind of mongrel philosophy and fused into a single, solid weight: *self-doubt*, like a ball and chain in the place where your mind's wings should have grown.

  Ayn Rand, *Philosophy: Who Needs It?* (1982)

5 Metaphysical speculation is about as pointless as a discussion on the meaning of one's lungs. They're for breathing.

  P.D. James, *Death of an Expert Witness* (1977)

6 [Theorists who] tell themselves that they are not doing philosophy, while they are in fact reflecting upon the foundations of the theory of [their subject], suppose that the alternative to doing philosophy in such matters is not-doing-philosophy, whereas the alternative is merely doing-philosophy-badly.

  Alice Koller, *A Hornbook of Hazards for Linguists* (1967)

7 I sometimes call my new system "Italian pagan Catholicism," but it could more accurately be called "pragmatic liberalism," with roots in Enlightenment political philosophy. It is a synthesis of the enduring dual elements in our culture, pagan and Judeo-Christian, Romantic and Classic.

  Camille Paglia, *Sex, Art, and American Culture* (1992)

8 First, I was an idealist (that was early—fools are born, not made, you know); next I was a realist; now I am a pessimist, and, by Jove! if things get much worse I'll become a humorist.

  Ellen Glasgow, *The Descendant* (1897)

9 I have a simple philosophy. Fill what's empty, empty what's full, and scratch where it itches.

  Alice Roosevelt Longworth, in Peter Passell and Leonard Ross, *The Best* (1974)

10 I make the most of all that comes, / The least of all that goes.

  Sara Teasdale, "The Philosopher," in A.L. Alexander, ed., *Poems That Touch the Heart* (1941)

11 I am open to conviction on all points except dinner and debts. I hold that the one must be eaten and the other paid. Those are my only prejudices.

  George Eliot (1857), in J.W. Cross, ed., *George Eliot's Life As Related in Her Letters and Journals* (1884)

12 Philosophical disputes don't often affect the price of fish or wine.

  Elizabeth Janeway, *Improper Behavior* (1987)

See also Belief, Ideologies, Morality, Principles.

## ❧ PHOBIAS

13 I have three phobias which, could I mute them, would make my life as slick as a sonnet, but as dull as ditch water: I hate to go to bed, I hate to get up, and I hate to be alone.

  Tallulah Bankhead, *Tallulah* (1952)

14 Agoraphobia was my quirky armor against a gregarious America.

  Florence King, *When Sisterhood Was in Flower* (1982)

See also Fear.

## ❧ PHOTOGRAPHY

15 What the human eye observes casually and incuriously, the eye of the camera . . . notes with relentless fidelity.

  Berenice Abbott, *A Guide to Better Photography* (1941)

1 Photographs alter and enlarge our notions of what is worth looking at and what we have a right to observe. They are a grammar and, even more importantly, an ethics of seeing.

  Susan Sontag, *On Photography* (1977)

2 A photograph is a secret about a secret. The more it tells you the less you know.

  Diane Arbus, in Diane Tucker, ed., *The Woman's Eye* (1973)

3 A photograph is not only an image (as a painting is an image), an interpretation of the real; it is also a trace, something directly stenciled off the real, like a footprint or a death mask.

  Susan Sontag, *On Photography* (1977)

4 Photography is not only drawing with light, though light is the indispensable agent of its being. . . . It is painting with light.

  Berenice Abbott, *A Guide to Better Photography* (1941)

5 Life is not about significant details, illuminated a flash, fixed forever. Photographs are.

  Susan Sontag, *On Photography* (1977)

6 The lens freezes time and space in what may be an optical slavery or, contrarily, the crystallization of meaning. The limits of the lens' vision are esthetically often a virtue.

  Berenice Abbott, *A Guide to Better Photography* (1941)

7 By furnishing this already crowded world with a duplicate one of images, photography makes us feel that the world is more available than it really is.

  Susan Sontag, *On Photography* (1977)

8 One never / Gets so close to anyone within experience.

  Louise Glück, "Pictures of the People in the War," *Firstborn* (1968)

9 An event known through photographs certainly becomes more real than it would have been if one had never seen the photographs. . . . But after repeated exposure to images it also becomes less real. . . . "Concerned" photography has done at least as much to deaden conscience as to arouse it.

  Susan Sontag, *On Photography* (1977)

10 Instead of just recording reality, photographs have become the norm for the way things appear to us, thereby changing the very idea of reality and of realism.

  Susan Sontag, *On Photography* (1977)

11 The camera makes everyone a tourist in other people's reality, and eventually in one's own.

  Susan Sontag, "Shooting America," in *The New York Review of Books* (1974)

12 I have always taken pictures the way people keep journals and diaries. It's a way of ordering my reactions to the world, of placing my ideas and feelings in a concrete form outside myself, of breaking my isolation.

  Diana Michener, in Sara Ruddick and Pamela Daniels, eds., *Working It Out* (1977)

13 I really believe there are things which nobody would see unless I photographed them.

  Diane Arbus, *Diane Arbus* (1972)

14 My best pictures are always taken when I succeed in establishing a bond of sympathy with my sitter. When there is the slightest suggestion of antagonism, then my best efforts are of no avail.

  Doris Ulmann, in Dale Warren, "Doris Ulmann: Photographer-in-Waiting," *The Bookman* (1930)

15 It is the unexpected, hit-or-miss, instant impulse, these strange accidents, this surrealistic serendipity, out of which great photographs are born.

  Carolyn Kenmore, *Mannequin* (1969)

16 If anyone gets in my way when I am making a picture, I become irrational. I'm never sure what I am going to do, or sometimes even aware of what I do—only that I want that picture.

  Margaret Bourke-White, in Anne Tucker, ed., *The Woman's Eye* (1973)

17 Photography can never grow up if it imitates some other medium. It has to walk alone; it has to be itself.

  Berenice Abbott, "It Has to Walk Alone," in *Infinity* (1951)

18 What to me is anathema—a corpse-like, outmoded hangover—is for photography to be a bad excuse for another medium. . . . Is not photography good enough in itself, that it must be made to look like something else, supposedly superior?

  Berenice Abbott, *A Guide to Better Photography* (1941)

19 Cameras have arisen in our midst like a new race of mechanical ghouls.

  Edith Sitwell, "Twentieth Century Justice Through a Camera Lens" (1935), in Elizabeth Salter and Allanah Harper, eds., *Edith Sitwell* (1976)

20 We have become a nation of Kodachrome, Nikon, Instamatic addicts. But we haven't yet developed a

clear idea of the ethics of picture-taking. . . . Where do we get the right to bring other people home in a canister? Where did we lose the right to control our image?

Ellen Goodman, *Close to Home* (1979)

1 There is an aggression implicit in every use of the camera.

Susan Sontag, *On Photography* (1977)

2 The photographer both loots and preserves, denounces and consecrates.

Susan Sontag, "Shooting America," in *The New York Review of Books* (1974)

3 It came to me that what I had to do was to take pictures and concentrate upon people, only people, all kinds of people, people who paid me and people who didn't.

Dorothea Lange, in Milton Meltzer, *Dorothea Lange: Life Through the Camera* (1985)

4 We know by now how to photograph poor people. What we don't know is how to photograph affluence—whose other face is poverty.

Dorothea Lange, in Milton Meltzer, *Dorothea Lange: A Photographer's Life* (1978)

5 My mother is not smiling; Chinese do not smile for photographs. Their faces command relatives in foreign lands—"Send money"—and posterity forever—"Put food in front of the picture."

Maxine Hong Kingston, *The Woman Warrior* (1976)

6 Very few people, thank God, look like the pictures of them which are published in the papers and the weekly magazines.

Ilka Chase, *Free Admission* (1948)

7 What most of us are after, when we have a picture taken, is a good natural-looking picture that doesn't resemble us.

Peg Bracken, *The I Hate to Housekeep Book* (1962)

See also Art, Images.

## § PIETY

8 From foolish devotions may God deliver us!

St. Teresa of Avila, *Life* (1565)

9 Piety is like garlic: a little goes a long way.

Rita Mae Brown, *Bingo* (1988)

See also Religion, Spirituality.

## § PIONEERS

10 Pioneering is the work of individuals.

Susanne K. Langer, *Philosophical Sketches* (1962)

11 Pioneers may be picturesque figures, but they are often rather lonely ones.

Nancy Astor, *My Two Countries* (1923)

12 She was the true pioneer type—the one who is destined never to eat the fruits of the vineyards she has planted.

Loula Grace Erdman, *The Edge of Time* (1950)

13 The sunbonnet as well as the sombrero has helped to settle this glorious land of ours.

Edna Ferber, *Cimarron* (1930)

See also Leadership.

## § PITY

14 Pity is a corroding thing.

Martha Graham, in *The Daily Telegraph* (1979)

15 Nothing is so binding as pity.

Alice Tisdale Hobart, *The Peacock Sheds His Tail* (1945)

16 Pity is love in undress.

Marie von Ebner-Eschenbach, *Aphorisms* (1893)

17 There is always an element of pity in love.

John Stephen Strange, *Unquiet Grave* (1949)

18 Pity and love know little severance. One attends the other.

Harriet E. Wilson, *Our Nig* (1859)

19 Pity is the least of the emotions.

Tallulah Bankhead, *Tallulah* (1952)

20 Pity is exhaustible. What a terrible discovery!

Enid Bagnold, *A Diary Without Dates* (1918)

21 More helpful than all wisdom is one draft of simple human pity that will not forsake us.

George Eliot, *The Mill on the Floss* (1860)

22 I seem to be the only person in the world who doesn't mind being pitied. If you love me, pity me. The human state is pitiable: born to die, capable of so much, accomplishing so little; killing instead of

creating, destroying instead of building, hating instead of loving. Pitiful, pitiful.

Jessamyn West, *Hide and Seek* (1973)

See also Compassion, Empathy, Kindness, Pathos, Patronizing, Self-Pity, Sympathy.

## ❧ PLACES

1 Places I love come back to me like music, / Hush me and heal me when I am very tired.

Sara Teasdale, "Places," *Flame and Shadow* (1920)

2 If a place is in your blood, you leave it at your peril. You will never be happy anywhere else.

Caroline Llewellyn, *Life Blood* (1993)

3 How hard it is to escape from places. However carefully one goes they hold you—you leave little bits of yourself fluttering on the fences—little rags and shreds of your very life.

Katherine Mansfield, in Leslie Moore, *Katherine Mansfield* (1971)

4 It is typical, in America, that a person's hometown is not the place where he is living now but is the place he left behind.

Margaret Mead and Rhoda Metraux, *A Way of Seeing* (1970)

5 One should never go back to a place one has loved; for, however rough the going forward is, it is better than the snuffing out-of-love return.

Caitlin Thomas, *Not Quite Posthumous Letter to My Daughter* (1963)

6 One does not love a place the less for having suffered in it, unless it has been all suffering, nothing but suffering.

Jane Austen, *Persuasion* (1818)

7 Old Magic, Old Ways, the Old Ones themselves often seem powerless in a new place.

Anne Cameron, *Daughters of Copper Woman* (1981)

See also Cities, The Country, Home, Moving, Roots, Travel.

## ❧ PLAGIARISM

8 Some persons are so constituted that the very excellence of an idea seems to them a convincing reason that it must be, if not solely, yet especially theirs. It fits in so beautifully with their general wisdom, it lies implicitly in so many of their manifested opinions, that if they have not yet expressed it (because of preoccupation), it is clearly a part of their indigenous produce, and is proved by their immediate eloquent promulgation of it to belong more naturally and appropriately to them than to the person who seemed first to have alighted on it.

George Eliot, *Impressions of Theophrastus Such* (1879)

9 Other writers have often put a thing more brilliantly, more subtly than even a very cunning artist in words can hope to emulate. . . . And inasmuch as the condiments and secret travail of human nature are always the same, and that certain psychological moments must ever and ever recur, what more tempting than to pin down such a moment with the blow of a borrowed hammer?

Ethel Smyth, *Streaks of Life* (1922)

10 On reading aloud his daily pages he said, "I steal from you, don't I?" He laughed and continued reading. . . . I asked, "When you quote me in *The Treasure of the Humble* why have you put each time, 'an old philosopher said. . .' or else 'an old friend said. . .' or 'I do not know what sage has said. . .' or merely quotation marks?" Astonished, he lifted his head. "But don't you see it would be ridiculous to mention you. You're on the stage, a singer, nobody would believe me. It would be ridiculous."

Georgette Leblanc (1898), on Maurice Maeterlinck, in Janet Flanner, tr., *Souvenirs: My Life With Maeterlinck* (1932)

11 Mr. Fitzgerald . . . seems to believe that plagiarism begins at home.

Zelda Fitzgerald, on husband F. Scott Fitzgerald's use of material from her diary and letters, in Nancy Milford, *Zelda* (1970)

12 It is an old error of man to forget to put quotation marks where he borrows from a woman's brain!

Anna Garlin Spencer, *Woman's Share in Social Culture* (1912)

13 I doubt whether that hateful person I often mention to you would have the audacity to attribute it to himself, like my other works—that would be too much, the portrait of my mother!

Camille Claudel (c. 1930), on sculptor Auguste Rodin, in Anne Delbée, *Camille Claudel* (1982)

14 Authors from whom others steal should not complain, but rejoice. Where there is no game there are no poachers.

Marie von Ebner-Eschenbach, *Aphorisms* (1893)

See also Imitation.

## ❧ PLANETS

1 The Planets / are nine dice rolling in the dark.
   Diane Ackerman, *The Planets* (1976)

See also Earth.

## ❧ PLANTS

2 We are prone, most of us, to be inaccurate as well as unobservant; and I know of no better antidote to inaccuracy than a faithful study of plants.
   Mrs. William Starr Dana, *According to Season* (1894)

3 Once a century, all of a certain kind of bamboo flower on the same day. Whether they are in Malaysia or in a greenhouse in Minnesota makes no difference, nor does the age or size of the plant. They flower. Some current of an inner language passes between them, through space and separation, in ways we cannot explain in our language. They are all, somehow, one plant, each with a share of communal knowledge.
   Linda Hogan, in Lorraine Anderson, ed., *Sisters of the Earth* (1991)

4 The skin of moss / holds the footprints of / star-footed birds.
   Nancy Willard, "Moss," *A Nancy Willard Reader* (1991)

See also Flowers, Gardening, Nature.

## ❧ PLASTIC

5 I have witnessed the takeover of my world by plastic.
   Helen Caldicott, *If You Love This Planet* (1992)

## ❧ PLATITUDES

6 It is strange how long we rebel against a platitude until suddenly in a different lingo it looms up again as the only verity.
   Ruth Benedict (1912), in Margaret Mead, *An Anthropologist at Work* (1959)

7 Platitudes? Yes, there are platitudes. Platitudes are there because they are true.
   Margaret Thatcher, in *The London Times* (1984)

See also Clichés.

## ❧ PLAYWRIGHTS

8 If there's a spirit world why don't the ghosts of dead artists get together and inhibit bad playwrights from tormenting first-nighters?
   Gertrude Atherton, *Black Oxen* (1923)

See also Artists, Theater, Writers.

## ❧ PLEASURE

9 We should lay in a store of food, but never of pleasures; these should be gathered day by day.
   Ninon de Lenclos (1665), in Lillian Day, *Ninon* (1957)

10 It isn't the great big pleasures that count the most; it's making a great deal out of the little ones.
   Jean Webster, *Daddy-Long-Legs* (1912)

11 Few pleasures there are indeed without an after-touch of pain, but that is the preservation which keeps them sweet.
   Helen Keller, *Helen Keller's Journal* (1938)

12 A fool bolts pleasure, then complains of moral indigestion.
   Minna Thomas Antrim, *Naked Truth and Veiled Illusions* (1901)

13 I suspect anyone self-satisfied enough to refuse lawful pleasures: we are not sufficiently rich in our separate resources to reject the graces of the universe when offered.
   Freya Stark, *Beyond Euphrates* (1951)

See also Ecstasy, Happiness, Joy.

## ❧ PLOT

14 Plot is the knowing of destination.
   Elizabeth Bowen, *Collected Impressions* (1950)

1 For my part, the good novel of character is the novel I can always pick up; but the good novel of incident is the novel I can never lay down.

Agnes Repplier, "The Novel of Incident," *Essays in Miniature* (1892)

See also Literature, Writing.

## ❦ POETRY

2 If not poetry, then what?

Rosario Castellanos, essay title (1973), in Maureen Ahern, ed., *A Rosario Castellanos Reader* (1988)

3 Since flesh can't stay, / we pass the words along.

Erica Jong, "Dear Keats," *Loveroot* (1975)

4 With my singing I can make / A refuge for my spirit's sake, / A house of shining words, to be / My fragile immortality.

Sara Teasdale, "Refuge," *Love Songs* (1917)

5 The words loved me and I loved them in return.

Sonia Sanchez, *Under a Soprano Sky* (1987)

6 A poem is like a wine glass in which you can hold up a little bit of reality and taste it.

Gwen Harwood, in Jennifer Straus, *Boundary Conditions* (1992)

7 Poetry is, indeed, the deification of reality.

Edith Sitwell, *The Outcasts* (1962)

8 Poetry . . . is another way to be hurled straight into the heart of God.

Marjorie Holmes, *How Can I Find You, God?* (1975)

9 It is not by telling us *about* life that poetry enriches it; it is by *being* life.

Elizabeth Drew, *Discovering Poetry* (1933)

10 Poetry is the sung voice of accurate perception.

Patricia Hampl, in Kate Green, *If the World Is Running Out* (1983)

11 One of the unconscious functions of poetry, and the chief conscious function of the interpreter of poetry, is to waken the dead.

Elizabeth Drew, *Discovering Poetry* (1933)

12 Poetry . . . shows with a sudden intense clarity what is already there.

Helen Bevington, *When Found, Make a Verse Of* (1961)

13 Poetry has been able to function quite directly as human interpretation of the raw, loose universe. It is a mixture, if you will, of journalism and metaphysics, or of science and religion.

Annie Dillard, *Living by Fiction* (1983)

14 [Poems are] imaginary gardens with real toads in them.

Marianne Moore, in Helen Bevington, *When Found, Make a Verse Of* (1961)

15 Poetry's object is truth.

Christine de Pisan (1405), in Charity Cannon Willard, *Christine de Pizan* (1984)

16 In poetry you can leave out everything but the truth.

Deborah Keenan, in *The Grand Gazette* (1995)

17 I often think of a poem as a door that opens / into a room where I want to go.

Minnie Bruce Pratt, "All the Women Caught in Flaring Light," *Crime Against Nature* (1990)

18 Reading [poetry], you know, is rather like opening the door to a horde of rebels who swarm out attacking one in twenty places at once—hit, roused, scraped, bared, swung through the air, so that life seems to flash by; then again blinded, knocked on the head—all of which are agreeable sensations for a reader (since nothing is more dismal than to open the door and get no response).

Virginia Woolf, *Letter to a Young Poet* (1932)

19 Poetry is the alchemy which teaches us to convert ordinary materials into gold.

Anaïs Nin, *The Novel of the Future* (1968)

20 There is no architect / Can build as the muse can; / . . . / She lays her beams in music, / In music every one.

Susan Glaspell, *Alison's House* (1930)

21 Poetry is not only dream and vision; it is the skeleton architecture of our lives. It lays the foundations for a future of change, a bridge across our fears of what has never been before.

Audre Lorde, "Poetry Is Not a Luxury," in *Chrysalis* (1977)

22 Poems come from incomplete knowledge.

Diane Wakoski, "With Words," *The Motorcycle Betrayal Poems* (1971)

1 Poetry is an act of distillation. It takes contingency samples, is selective. It telescopes time. It focuses what most often floods past us in a polite blur.
   Diane Ackerman, in Janet Sternburg, ed., *The Writer on Her Work*, vol. 2 (1991)

2 Poetry is life distilled.
   Gwendolyn Brooks, in Brian Lanker, *I Dream a World* (1989)

3 Poetry cannot be explained, it must be lived.
   Anne Hébert, "Poetry Broken Solitude," *Poems* (1960)

4 I talk in riddles. I'd rather speak plainly. / But some ways are still unmapped.
   Elizabeth Smart, "All I Know About Why I Write," *In the Meantime* (1984)

5 Surely everyone who writes poetry would agree that this is part of it—a doomed but urgent wish to express the inexpressible.
   Rosemary Dobson, *Selected Poems* (1973)

6 This chain of enigmas / hung on the neck of night.
   Nelly Sachs, "This Chain of Enigmas," *O the Chimneys* (1967)

7 Poetry is a string of words that parades without a permit.
   Linda Hogan, in Janet Sternburg, ed., *The Writer on Her Work*, vol. 2 (1991)

8 Poetry is where the language is renewed.
   Margaret Atwood, in Alan Twigg, *For Openers* (1981)

9 Poetry can work with the / language, manipulate it so that it can embrace those / concepts, visions, times and places that the language / in and of itself can't do.
   Joy Harjo, in Joseph Bruchac, ed., *Songs From This Earth on Turtle's Back* (1983)

10 A poem records emotions and moods that lie beyond normal language, that can only be patched together and hinted at metaphorically.
   Diane Ackerman, in Janet Sternburg, ed., *The Writer on Her Work*, vol. 2 (1991)

11 Poetry is the most concentrated form of literature; it is the most emotionalized and powerful way in which thought can be presented.
   Amy Lowell, *Tendencies in Modern American Poetry* (1917)

12 When a poem says something that could not have been said in any other way, in music, prose, sculpture, movement or paint, then it is poetry.
   Sybil Marshall, *An Experiment in Education* (1963)

13 If food is poetry is not poetry also food?
   Joyce Carol Oates, "Writers' Hunger: Food As Metaphor," in *The New York Times* (1986)

14 Poetry is a dangerous gift.
   Grace Aguilar, *Home Influence* (1893)

15 If I read a book and it makes my whole body so cold no fire can ever warm me, I know that is poetry. If I feel physically as if the top of my head were taken off, I know that is poetry. These are the only ways I know it. Is there any other way?
   Emily Dickinson (1870), in Mabel Loomis Todd, ed., *Letters of Emily Dickinson*, vol. 2 (1894)

16 Poetry can only be judged by the standard of the personality that is judging it. We cannot escape our own limitations. Each reader gets the poetry he deserves.
   Elizabeth Drew, *Discovering Poetry* (1933)

17 Poetry is a dangerous profession between conflict and resolution, between feeling and thought, between becoming and being, between the ultra-personal and the universal—and these balances are shifting all the time.
   May Sarton, "On Growth and Change," *Sarton Selected* (1991)

18 What is poetry? Do not enquire. The secret dies by prying. How does the heart beat? I fainted when I saw it on the screen, opening and closing like a flower. . . . Poetry is like this, it is life moving, terrible, vivid. Look the other way when you write, or you might faint.
   Elizabeth Smart, "Dig a Grave and Let Us Bury Our Mother" (1939), *In the Meantime* (1984)

19 Poetry to me is prayer.
   Anne Sexton (1966), in Linda Gray Sexton and Lois Ames, eds., *Anne Sexton: A Self-Portrait in Letters* (1977)

20 Poetry is . . . / a sort of answer I feel compelled to give / to my own life.
   Furugh Farrukhzad, in Elizabeth Warnock Fernea and Basima Qattan Bezirgan, eds., *Middle Eastern Muslim Women Speak* (1977)

1 It will have to be enough / to build a congregation of poems / from what is shrouded from view.

Diane Ackerman, "Lady Canute," *Jaguar of Sweet Laughter* (1991)

2 Poetry is a dumb Buddha who thinks a donkey is as important as a diamond.

Natalie Goldberg, *Wild Mind* (1990)

3 Poetry [is] "The Cinderella of the Arts."

Harriet Monroe (1912), in Hope Stoddard, *Famous American Women* (1970)

4 The advantage of poetry over life is that poetry, if it is sharp enough, may last.

Louise Glück, in *The American Poetry Review* (1993)

5 Poetry is not a luxury.

Audre Lorde, article title, in *Chrysalis* (1977)

6 I am subjective, intimate, private, particular, / confessional. / All that happens, / happens to me. / . . . / If you're interested / in birds, trees, rivers, / try reference books. / Don't read my poems.

Nina Cassian, "Ars poetica—a polemic," *Cheerleader for a Funeral* (1992)

7 Writing poems is my way of celebrating with the world that I have not committed suicide the evening before.

Alice Walker (1973), *In Search of Our Mothers' Gardens* (1983)

8 This is my letter to the World / That never write to Me.

Emily Dickinson (1862), in Mabel Loomis Todd and T.W. Higginson, eds., *Poems by Emily Dickinson* (1890)

9 This poem isn't for you / but for me / after all.

Joy Harjo, "Your Phone Call at Eight A.M.," in Rayna Green, ed., *That's What She Said* (1984)

10 Writing poetry is like always being in love. What masochism! What luxury!

Jennifer Stone, KPFA Pacifica Public Radio show (1989)

11 Poetry exists to break through to below the level of reason where the angels and monsters that the amenities keep in the cellar may come out to dance, to rove and roar, growling and singing, to bring life back to the enclosed rooms where too often we are only "living and partly living."

May Sarton, "On Growth and Change," *Sarton Selected* (1991)

12 Poetry is the inner life of a culture, its nervous system, its deepest way of imagining the world. A culture that ignores its poets chokes off its nervous system and becomes mortally ill.

Erica Jong, *Fear of Fifty* (1994)

13 If there were no poetry on any day in the world, poetry would be invented that day. For there would be an intolerable hunger.

Muriel Rukeyser, *The Life of Poetry* (1949)

14 Breathe-in experience, breathe-out poetry.

Muriel Rukeyser, "Poem Out of Childhood," *Theory of Flight* (1935)

15 My soul, / At poetry's divine first finger-touch, / Let go conventions and sprang up surprised.

Elizabeth Barrett Browning, *Aurora Leigh* (1857)

16 I feel a poem in my heart to-night, / A still thing growing,— / As if the darkness to the outer light / A song were owing.

Mary Ashley Townsend, "Embryo," in Edmund Clarence Stedman, ed., *An American Anthology 1787-1900* (1900)

17 When in the night hour I await her coming / It seems to me my life hangs by a thread. / Youth, honors, liberty all shrink to nothing / When my dear visitor pipes by my bed.

Anna Akhmatova, "The Muse" (1924), *From Six Books* (1940)

18 The poem will not be denied; to refuse to write it would be a greater torture. It tears its way out of the brain, splintering and breaking its passage, and leaves that organ in the state of a jelly-fish when the task is done.

Amy Lowell, in Louis Untermeyer, "A Memoir," *The Complete Poetical Works of Amy Lowell* (1955)

19 How poetry comes to the poet is a mystery.

Elizabeth Drew, *Discovering Poetry* (1933)

20 I was most incorrigibly devoted to versifying. . . . I believe this scribbling itch is an incurable disease.

Letitia Pilkington, *Memoirs of Mrs. Letitia Pilkington Written by Herself*, vol. 1 (1754)

21 For me a true poem is on the way when I begin to be haunted, when it seems as if I were being asked an inescapable question by an angel with whom I must wrestle to get at the answer.

May Sarton, "Revision As Creation," *Sarton Selected* (1991)

22 Your poems will happen when no one is there.

May Sarton, "A Last Word," *A Grain of Mustard Seed* (1971)

1 I don't go get a poem. It calls me and I accept it.

   Lucille Clifton, in Christine A. Sikorski, "An Interview
   With Lucille Clifton," *A View From the Loft* (1994)

2 We ask the poet: "What subject have you chosen?"
   instead of: "What subject has chosen you?"

   Marie von Ebner-Eschenbach, *Aphorisms* (1893)

3 Try making a poem as if it were a table, clear and
   solid, standing there outside you.

   May Sarton, *Mrs. Stevens Hears the Mermaids Singing* (1965)

4 The lavish words we write / Need a base on level
   stone. / . . . / Oh Poetry-To-Come / Lay what is
   most exact / For the door-sill of your home.

   Genevieve Taggard, "Platform for Poets," *Calling Western
   Union* (1936)

5 Knowledge and diligence / Are required to versify,
   / To conjoin and diversify / Many subjects various.

   Christine de Pisan (1404), in Thelma S. Fenster and Nadia
   Margolis, tr., *The Book of the Duke of True Lovers* (1991)

6 All longed-for poems have the opaque glow / Of
   unrubbed quartz half hidden under snow.

   Louise Townsend Nicholl, "Crystal," *Collected Poems* (1953)

7 The truth of a poem is its form and its content, its
   music and its meaning are the same.

   Muriel Rukeyser, *The Life of Poetry* (1949)

8 The poet should try to give his poem the quiet
   swiftness of flame, so that the reader will feel and
   not think while he is reading. But the thinking will
   come afterwards.

   Sara Teasdale, in Marguerite Wilkinson, *New Voices* (1924)

9 I wanted to choose words that even you / would
   have to be changed by.

   Adrienne Rich, "Implosions," *Leaflets* (1969)

10 Poems reveal secrets when they are analyzed. The
   poet's pleasure in finding ingenious ways to enclose
   her secrets should be matched by the reader's
   pleasure in unlocking and revealing these secrets.

   Diane Wakoski, in *Writer's Digest* (1991)

11 I tell poets that when a line just floats into your
   head, don't pay attention 'cause it probably has
   floated into somebody else's head.

   Gwendolyn Brooks, in Brian Lanker, *I Dream a World*
   (1989)

12 Do not repeat what someone else has said, / Use
   your own words and your imagination. / But it may
   be that poetry itself / Is simply one magnificent
   quotation.

   Anna Akhmatova, "Do Not Repeat" (1956), *Poems* (1988)

13 The beautiful feeling after writing a poem is on the
   whole better even than after sex, and that's saying
   a lot.

   Anne Sexton, in William Packard, ed., *The Craft of Poetry*
   (1974)

14 As honey sweetens / the mouth readily / a poem
   should make sense / right away.

   Atakuri Molla, "As Honey Sweetens" (16th cent.), in Susie
   Tharu and K. Lalita, eds., *Women Writing in India* (1991)

15 I would like a simple life / yet all night I am laying
   / poems away in a long box.

   Anne Sexton, "The Ambition Bird," *The Book of Folly* (1972)

16 My verses are my diary. My poetry is a poetry of
   proper names.

   Marina Tsvetaeva (1922), in Claudia Roth Pierpont, "The
   Rage of Aphrodite," *The New Yorker* (1994)

17 All poets / understand the final uselessness of
   words. We are chords to / other chords to other
   chords, if we're lucky, to melody.

   Joy Harjo, "Bird," *In Mad Love and War* (1990)

18 The materials of true poetry are always humble,
   absolutely idiosyncratic, the autobiographical tatters that, in gifted hands, are made into the memoir
   that fits us all.

   Patricia Hampl, in Kate Green, *If the World Is Running Out*
   (1983)

19 Outrage and possibility are in all the poems we
   know.

   Muriel Rukeyser, *The Life of Poetry* (1949)

20 To write about the monstrous sense of alienation
   the poet feels in this culture of polarized hatreds is
   a way of staying sane. With the poem, I reach out
   to an audience equally at odds with official policy,
   and I celebrate our mutual humanness in an inhuman world.

   Maxine Kumin, "A Way of Staying Sane," in Marilyn
   Sewell, ed., *Cries of the Spirit* (1991)

21 I did not come here to talk poetry and discontent,
   some people think them synonymous.

   Emily Eden, *The Semi-Detached House* (1859)

22 All poets chew cuds.

   Sister M. Madeleva, *My First Seventy Years* (1959)

1 Poetry has a small audience, but a large influence.
  Genevieve Taggard, *Calling Western Union* (1936)

2 Poetry is often generations in advance of the thought of its time.
  Louise Bogan, "European Poetry" (1941), *A Poet's Alphabet* (1970)

3 We are far too used to the assumption that poetry and poets will be *there* when we want them, no matter how long they have been ignored, taken for granted, misused. After all, isn't poetry a form of prophecy, and aren't prophets known for their talent for flourishing in inhospitable deserts and other bleak surroundings? Maybe. But maybe not indefinitely.
  Jan Clausen, *A Movement of Poets* (1982)

4 I have yet to know the use of a poem the way I know the use of a hammer. Yet I feel a poem is surely a tool.
  Karen Brodine, "Politics of Women Writing," in *The Second Wave* (1979)

5 What was the function of poetry if not to improve the petty, cautious minds of evasive children?
  Bharati Mukherjee, "Buried Lives," *The Middleman* (1988)

6 The attempt to control poetry, to subordinate it to extra-poetic ends, constitutes misuse.
  Jan Clausen, *A Movement of Poets* (1982)

7 Poetry is the most mistaught subject in any school because we teach poetry by form and not by content.
  Nikki Giovanni, in Claudia Tate, ed., *Black Women Writers at Work* (1983)

8 We have let rhetoric do the job of poetry.
  Cherríe Moraga, "La Güera," in Cherríe Moraga and Gloria Anzaldúa, eds., *This Bridge Called My Back* (1983)

9 What form is best for poems? Let me think / Of forms less, and the external. Trust the spirit. . . . / Keep up the fire, / And leave the generous flames to shape themselves.
  Elizabeth Barrett Browning, *Aurora Leigh* (1857)

10 It was as fit for one man's thoughts to trot in iambs, as it is for me, / Who live not in the horse-age, but in the day of aeroplanes, to write my rhythms free.
  Anna Wickham, "The Egoist," *The Contemplative Quarry* (1915)

11 How can I pour the liquor of new days / In the old pipes of Rhyme?
  Anna Wickham, "Formalist," *The Man With a Hammer* (1916)

12 I, too, dislike it: there are things that are important beyond all this fiddle. / Reading it, however, with a perfect contempt for it, one discovers in / it after all, a place for the genuine.
  Marianne Moore, "Poetry" (1921), *Selected Poems* (1935)

13 It is as unseeing to ask what is the *use* of poetry as it would be to ask what is the use of religion.
  Edith Sitwell, *The Outcasts* (1962)

14 Poetry has a way of teaching one what one needs to know . . . if one is honest.
  May Sarton, *Mrs. Stevens Hears the Mermaids Singing* (1965)

15 Poetry does not necessarily have to be beautiful to stick in the depths of our memory.
  Colette, *The Blue Lantern* (1949)

16 Any time is the time to make a poem.
  Gertrude Stein, *Everybody's Autobiography* (1937)

17 Making verses is almost as common as taking snuff, and God can tell what miserable stuff people carry about in their pockets, and offer to all their acquaintances, and you know one cannot refuse reading and taking a pinch.
  Lady Mary Wortley Montagu (1747), in Octave Thanet, ed., *The Best Letters of Lady Mary Wortley Montagu* (1901)

18 I always say that one's poetry is a solace to oneself and a nuisance to one's friends.
  Hortense Calisher, "Little Did I Know," *Extreme Magic* (1964)

19 The fear of poetry is an indication that we are cut off from our own reality.
  Muriel Rukeyser, *The Life of Poetry* (1949)

20 Who, except the poets, reads poetry?
  Babette Deutsch, in Helen Hull, ed., *The Writer's Book* (1950)

21 Poem me no poems.
  Rose Macaulay, in *Poetry Review* (1963)

See also Literature, Nursery Rhymes, Poetry and Prose, Poets, Verse, Writing.

## ❦ POETRY AND PROSE

1 The borderline between prose and poetry is one of those fog-shrouded literary minefields where the wary explorer gets blown to bits before ever seeing anything clearly. It is full of barbed wire and the stumps of dead opinions.

    Ursula K. Le Guin, *Dancing at the Edge of the World* (1989)

2 Prose is the respectable, grown-up form of written communication. Poetry is reserved for children and others brave or foolish enough to refuse the mainstream's ability to stipulate what color cows must be, which notes girls may sing, who can make love with whom.

    Toni McNaron, *I Dwell in Possibility* (1992)

3 Mediocre prose might be read as an escape, might be spoken on television by actors, or mouthed in movies. But mediocre poetry did not exist at all. If poetry wasn't good, it wasn't poetry. It was that simple.

    Erica Jong, *How to Save Your Own Life* (1977)

4 It seems to me that this is the true test for poetry:— that it should go beneath experience, as prose can never do, and awaken an apprehension of things we have never, and can never, know in the actuality.

    Ellen Glasgow, *Letters of Ellen Glasgow* (1958)

5 The poet gives us his essence, but prose takes the mold of the body and mind entire.

    Virginia Woolf, "Reading," *The Captain's Death Bed* (1950)

6 Novelists have to love humanity to write anything worthwhile. Poets have to love themselves.

    Marita Golden, *A Woman's Place* (1986)

See also Literature, Poetry, Verse, Writing.

## ❦ POETS

7 He would be a poet, a keeper of other people's dreams.

    Maia Wojciechowska, *A Single Light* (1968)

8 Poets are those who know how to give shape to my dreams.

    Comtesse Diane, *Les Glanes de la Vie* (1898)

9 It is the gift of all poets to find the commonplace astonishing, and the astonishing quite natural.

    Margery Sharp, *The Rescuers* (1959)

10 Thou'rt a poet, crazed with finding words / May stick to things and seem like qualities. / No pebble is a pebble in thy hands: / 'T is a moon out of work, a barren egg, / Or twenty things that no man sees but thee.

    George Eliot, *The Spanish Gypsy* (1868)

11 poets, / these species, these sepias / whose self defense / is splashing ink.

    Nina Cassian, "Poets," *Cheerleader for a Funeral* (1992)

12 A poet perceives and gives whole-hearted expression to that which our sensibilities, not less lively but less musicanly, keep stored inside.

    Colette, *Paris From My Window* (1944)

13 The poet's mission: to forget reality, to promise the world wonders, to celebrate victories and deny death.

    Colette, "Journal à rebours" (1941), *Looking Backwards* (1975)

14 My poems covered the bare places in my childhood like the fine, new skin under a scab that hasn't yet fallen off completely.

    Tove Ditlevsen (1967), in Tiina Nunnally, tr., *Early Spring* (1985)

15 The poet . . . like the lover . . . is a person unable to reconcile what he knows with what he feels. His peculiarity is that he is under a certain compulsion to do so.

    Babette Deutsch, in Helen Hull, ed., *The Writer's Book* (1950)

16 My verse, / I can't get away from it, / I've tried to.

    H.D., "Red Rose and a Beggar" (1960), *Hermetic Definition* (1972)

17 For me, a poet is someone who is "in contact." Someone through whom a current is passing.

    Marguerite Yourcenar, *With Open Eyes* (1980)

18 Like Midas, I guess / everything we touch turns / to a poem— / when the spell is on.

    Linda Pastan, "Voices," *The Five Stages of Grief* (1978)

19 God makes many poets, but he only gives utterance to a few.

    Dinah Maria Mulock Craik, *The Ogilvies* (1898)

1 Poets are privileged to utter more than they can always quite explain, bringing up from the mind's unplumbed depths tokens of the nature of the world we carry within us.

Vernon Lee, in C. Anstruther-Thomson, *Art and Man* (1923)

2 If you know much about your work—why you work, how you work, your aims—you are probably not a poet.

Mary Webb, in *The Bookman* (1926)

3 The fact is that I have lived with the belief that power, any kind of power, was the one thing forbidden to poets. . . . Power requires that the inner person never be unmasked. No, we poets have to go naked. And since this is so, it is better that we stay private people; a naked public person would be rather ridiculous, what?

May Sarton, *Mrs. Stevens Hears the Mermaids Singing* (1965)

4 Poets ever fail in reading their own verses to their worth, / For the echo in you breaks upon the words which you are speaking, / And the chariot wheels jar in the gate through which you drive them forth.

Elizabeth Barrett Browning, "Lady Geraldine's Courtship," *Poems* (1844)

5 A poet *never* feels useful.

May Sarton, *Mrs. Stevens Hears the Mermaids Singing* (1965)

6 There's always a job for an engineer / (But nobody wants a poet).

Marya Mannes, "Help Wanted," *Subverse* (1959)

7 If there's room for poets in this world / A little overgrown (I think there is), / Their sole work is to represent the age, / Their age, not Charlemagne's.

Elizabeth Barrett Browning, *Aurora Leigh* (1857)

8 The poet is always our contemporary.

Virginia Woolf, "How Should One Read a Book?" *The Common Reader*, 2nd series (1932)

9 To me the Muses truly gave / An envied and a happy lot: / E'en when I lie within the grave, / I cannot, shall not, be forgot.

Sappho (6th cent. B.C.), in C.R. Haines, ed., *Sappho: The Poems and Fragments* (1926)

10 The people must grant a hearing to the best poets they have else they will never have better.

Harriet Monroe (1911), in Hope Stoddard, *Famous American Women* (1970)

11 A poet will even face death when he sees his people oppressed.

Carolina Maria de Jesus, *Child of the Dark* (1962)

12 He who draws noble delights from the sentiment of poetry is a true poet, though he has never written a line in all his life.

George Sand, *The Haunted Pool* (1851)

13 People wish to be poets more than they wish to write poetry, and that's a mistake. One should wish to celebrate more than one wishes to be celebrated.

Lucille Clifton, in *Poets & Writers* (1992)

14 She loved poetry / sometimes I thought that she would take the words / and eat them carefully as filaments of saffron.

June Jordan, "Three for Kimako," *Living Room* (1965)

15 Of all the art forms, poetry is the most economical . . . the one which can most easily be done between shifts at the plant, in the hospital pantry, on the crowded subway, and on scraps of surplus paper. . . . Poetry has become the major voice of poor, working-class, and Third World women. A room of one's own may be a necessity for writing prose, but so are reams of paper, a working typewriter, and plenty of time.

Audre Lorde, *Age, Race, Class and Sexuality* (1980)

16 I feel that women of my kind are a profound mistake. There have been few women poets of distinction, and, if we count only the suicides of Sappho, Laurence Hope and Charlotte Mew, their despair rate has been very high.

Anna Wickham (1935), in R.D. Smith, ed., *The Writings of Anna Wickham* (1984)

17 Nobody alive or dead deserves to be called a poetess.

Helen Bevington, *When Found, Make a Verse Of* (1961)

18 I notice that many great poets emerge from motherless childhoods. They are either early orphans or their mothers are not mentioned at all. It is not so amazing that many of these same artists turned out to be hounded by depression, drugs, and insanity, but did being motherless also drive them to creativity?

Liz Smith, *The Mother Book* (1978)

19 In this most Christian of all worlds / The poet's a Jew.

Marina Tsvetaeva, "Poem of the End" (1924), in David McDuff, ed., *Selected Poems* (1987)

1 Herman has taken to writing poetry. You need not tell anyone, for you know how such things get around.

    Elizabeth Shaw Melville (1860), in Muriel Rukeyser, *The Life of Poetry* (1949)

2 Ned was sowing his wild oats. "Poetry," she whispered, filling the word with night-club implications.

    Elizabeth Bibesco, *The Fir and the Palm* (1924)

3 Byron and Shelley and Keats / Were a trio of lyrical treats.

    Dorothy Parker, "A Pig's-Eye View of Literature," *Sunset Gun* (1928)

4 And I'll stay off Verlaine too; he was always chasing Rimbauds.

    Dorothy Parker, "The Little Hours," *The Collected Stories of Dorothy Parker* (1942)

See also Artists, Poetry, Poetry and Prose, Writers.

## ❦ POINT OF VIEW

5 Nothing that God ever made is the same thing to more than one person.

    Zora Neale Hurston, *Dust Tracks on a Road* (1942)

6 What one reads, or rather all that comes to us, is surely only of interest and value in proportion as we find ourselves therein,—form given to what was vague, what slumbered stirred to life.

    Alice James (1889), in Anna Robeson Burr, *Alice James* (1934)

7 No man ever looks at the world with pristine eyes. He sees it edited by a definite set of customs and institutions and ways of thinking.

    Ruth Benedict, *Patterns of Culture* (1934)

8 Creatures of a very particular making, we need to know the cultural blinders that narrow our world view as well as the psychological blinders that narrow our view of our personal experience.

    Christina Baldwin, *One to One* (1977)

9 Most people see what they want to, or at least what they expect to.

    Martha Grimes, *I Am the Only Running Footman* (1986)

10 Colors seen by candle-light / Will not look the same by day.

    Elizabeth Barrett Browning, "The Lady's 'Yes,'" *Poems* (1844)

11 The transcendental point of view, the habit of thought bred by communion with earth and sky, had refined the grain while it had roughened the husk.

    Ellen Glasgow, *Barren Ground* (1925)

12 I've tried to picture my world and the people in it as seen through the distorting lens of a bell jar.

    Sylvia Plath, conversation with her mother, Aurelia Plath (1962)

13 To the person in the bell jar, blank and stopped as a dead baby, the world itself is the bad dream.

    Sylvia Plath, *The Bell Jar* (1963)

14 We live what we know. If we believe the universe and ourselves to be mechanical, we will live mechanically. On the other hand, if we know that we are part of an open universe, and that our minds are a matrix of reality, we will live more creatively and powerfully.

    Marilyn Ferguson, *The Aquarian Conspiracy* (1980)

15 The temper of mind that sees tragedy in life has not for its opposite the temper that sees joy. The opposite pole to the tragic view of life is the sordid view.

    Edith Hamilton, *The Greek Way* (1930)

16 To work in the world lovingly means that we are defining what we will be *for*, rather than reacting to what we are against.

    Christina Baldwin, *Life's Companion* (1990)

17 There is a law which decrees that two objects may not occupy the same place at the same time—result: two people cannot see things from the same point of view, and the slightest difference in angle changes the thing seen.

    Mildred Aldrich, *A Hilltop on the Marne* (1915)

18 We might as well give up the fiction / That we can argue any view. / For what in me is pure Conviction / Is simple Prejudice in you.

    Phyllis McGinley, "Note to My Neighbor," *A Short Walk From the Station* (1951)

19 I am firm. You are obstinate. He is a pig-headed fool.

    Katharine Whitehorn, in *The Observer* (1974)

1 I've never known a man to be beaten fairly, nor one to be elected, unfairly.

    Anne Ellis, *Plain Anne Ellis* (1931)

2 Watch out fer these fellers around here. It ain't safe fer a pretty girl. Why, I had one just now tell me I looked like a breath of spring. Well, he didn't use them words, exactly. He said I looked like the end of a hard winter.

    Minnie Pearl (1940), *Minnie Pearl* (1980)

3 When a small thing upset someone my grandmother used to say, "Nonsense! That would never be noticed from a trotting horse."

    Emily Kimbrough, "On Seeing Clearly," in William Nichols, ed., *Words to Live By* (1962)

See also Beliefs, Egocentrism, Opinion, Philosophy.

## ✿ POISE

4 Poise and indifference so often look the same.

    Sue Grafton, *"J" Is for Judgment* (1993)

5 As we went out the door, instead of saying, "Have a good time," Mother would say, "Have poise!" as though it were optional.

    Irene Mayer Selznick, *A Private View* (1983)

See also Elegance, Self-Possession.

## ✿ POKER

6 I'd rather play poker with five or six experts than eat.

    "Poker Alice" Tubbs (c. 1900), in Autumn Stephens, *Wild Women* (1992)

7 It's what you do with what you've got; in every encounter with pure, immutable kings and queens and their rough and tumble shuffle with luck, you get the chance to make it work for you.

    Isabel Huggan, *The Elizabeth Stories* (1987)

## ✿ POLICE

8 There's really no such thing as an "ex-cop" or a cop who's "off-duty" or "retired." Once trained, once indoctrinated, a cop is always alert, assessing reality in terms of its potential for illegal acts.

    Sue Grafton, *"H" Is for Homicide* (1991)

See also Crime.

## ✿ POLITENESS

9 Politeness is sometimes a great tax upon sincerity.

    Charlotte Lennox, *Henrietta* (1758)

10 Politeness may be nothing but veneering, but a veneered slab has the advantage of being without splinters.

    Mary Wilson Little, *A Paragrapher's Reveries* (1904)

11 Civility costs nothing, and buys everything.

    Lady Mary Wortley Montagu (1756), in Robert Halsband, ed., *The Complete Letters of Lady Mary Wortley Montagu* (1965)

12 Such is the effect of true politeness, that it banishes all restraint and embarrassment.

    Fanny Burney, *Evelina* (1778)

13 True politeness is to social life what oil is to machinery, a thing to oil the ruts and grooves of existence.

    Frances Ellen Watkins Harper, "True and False Politeness," in *African Methodist Episcopal Church Review* (1898)

14 I come from people who have always been polite enough to feel that nothing has ever happened to them.

    Patricia Hampl, *A Romantic Education* (1981)

15 Perhaps among the more simple causes of domestic infelicity, lack of ordinary politeness stands at the head.

    Dr. (Mrs.) F.L.S. Aldrich, *The One Man* (1910)

16 There is a politeness so terrible, that rage beside it is balm.

    Minna Thomas Antrim, *At the Sign of the Golden Calf* (1905)

17 Be polite. Perhaps your family won't mind if you practice on them.

    Minna Thomas Antrim, *Knocks* (1905)

See also Etiquette, Graciousness, Manners, Protocol, Rudeness, Tact.

## § POLITICAL CAMPAIGNS

1 Increasingly, campaigns have become narcotics that blur our awareness of problems long enough to elect the lawmakers who must deal with them.

Kathleen Hall Jamieson, *Dirty Politics* (1992)

2 A theme is always necessary, a plain, simple, unadorned theme to confuse the ignorant.

Lillian Hellman, *Scoundrel Time* (1976)

3 A candidate has to be either a surprise or a habit.

Naomi Mitchison, *We Have Been Warned* (1936)

4 Everyone seems to be running against a liar, but nobody seems to be one. Odd—I mean, the math doesn't work out.

Meg Greenfield, in *Newsweek* (1994)

5 Politics can be an ugly game, and in a national election the stakes get higher while the tactics get lower.

Geraldine A. Ferraro, with Linda Bird Francke, *Ferraro* (1985)

6 The systematic abuse with which the newspapers of one side assail every candidate coming forward on the other, is the cause of many honorable men, who have a regard to their reputation, being deterred from entering public life; and of the people being thus deprived of some better servants than any they have.

Harriet Martineau, *Society in America*, vol. 1 (1837)

7 Television has accustomed us to brief, intimate, telegraphic, visual, narrative messages. Candidates are learning to act, speak, and think in television's terms. In the process they are transforming speeches, debates, and their appearances in news into ads.

Kathleen Hall Jamieson, *Dirty Politics* (1992)

8 In America, where the electoral process is drowning in commercial techniques of fund-raising and image-making, we may have completed a circle back to a selection process as unconcerned with qualifications as that which made Darius King of Persia. . . . He whose horse was the first to neigh at sunrise should be King.

Barbara W. Tuchman, *The March of Folly* (1984)

9 What can the people think when, thanks to disclosure, the slimy trail from the contribution to the vote can be so easily traced?

Millicent Fenwick, in *The Washington Post* (1976)

See also Elections.

## § "POLITICAL CORRECTNESS"

10 There are few things more wearisome in a fairly fatiguing life than the monotonous repetition of a phrase which catches and holds the public fancy by virtue of its total lack of significance.

Agnes Repplier, "The Eternal Feminine," *Varia* (1897)

11 People who pin their faith to a catchword never feel the necessity of understanding anything.

Agnes Repplier, "Women and War," *Counter-Currents* (1916)

See also Repetition.

## § POLITICAL PARTIES

12 In the early days of our Republic the questions asked of each office seeker were, "Is he honest? Is he capable? Is he faithful to the constitution?" In our present diseased state, the one question asked of an office seeker is, "Is he faithful to the party?"

Leonora O'Reilly, speech (1901), in Judith Anderson, ed., *Outspoken Women* (1984)

13 At every political convention all matters of right, of justice, of the eternal verities themselves, are swallowed up in the one all-important question, "Will it bring party success?"

Susan B. Anthony and Ida Husted Harper, eds., *The History of Woman Suffrage*, vol. 4 (1902)

14 The two major parties too often present us with a choice of the evil of two lessers.

Patricia Ireland, in *Ms.* (1992)

15 In the United States, as elsewhere, there are, and have always been, two parties in politics. . . . It is remarkable how nearly their positive statements of political doctrine agree, while they differ in almost

every possible application of their common principles.

Harriet Martineau, *Society in America*, vol. 1 (1837)

1 Just so soon as a party loses sight of the good of the whole and works for "party" right or wrong, it becomes a menace to the community.

Leonora O'Reilly, speech (1901), in Judith Anderson, ed., *Outspoken Women* (1984)

2 Party politics is now a real farce.

George Sand (1875), in Raphaël Ledos de Beaufort, ed., *Letters of George Sand*, vol. 3 (1886)

3 For a few political turncoats there is real excuse. One can hardly blame those whom one ministry has seen fit to throw overboard for having the strength to swim to the other side.

Dorothy Nevill, *Under Five Reigns* (1910)

4 He was popular with the party. He had plenty of money to contribute to campaign expenses, and he contributed with a lavish hand. . . . Eventually he just got tired of making an asset of himself.

Craig Rice, *Trial by Fury* (1941)

5 The Republicans love to say that the Democratic Party is ruled by "special interests." But when pressed to name these "special interests," the usual reply is women, blacks, teachers, and unions. Those are "special interests" to be proud of—because together they comprise the majority of Americans. What about the "special interests" that dominate the Republican Party—the oil companies, the banks, the gun lobby, and the apostles of religious intolerance?

Geraldine A. Ferraro, with Linda Bird Francke, *Ferraro* (1985)

6 The overwhelming majority of people who are engaged in the processes of thought and expression are Democrats because the essence of thought is exploration and diversity and change.

Marya Mannes, *More in Anger* (1958)

7 Republicans seems to me to be chiefly concerned with holding on to what they have: in society, it's position, or respectability, or what you will; in business, of course, it's profit.

Marya Mannes, *More in Anger* (1958)

8 The Republicans *think* they have a corner on morality.

Marya Mannes, *More in Anger* (1958)

9 I don't think it's possible to write a good play or paint a good picture and be a good Republican.

Marya Mannes, *More in Anger* (1958)

10 When any one tells you that he belongs to no party, you may at any rate be sure that he does not belong to yours.

Anne-Sophie Swetchine, in Count de Falloux, ed., *The Writings of Madame Swetchine* (1869)

See also Conservatives, Liberals, Politicians, Politics.

## ❧ POLITICIANS

11 All politicians are alligators; they are *all* alligators.

Billie Carr, in Molly Ivins, "Cisnero's Cross," *Mother Jones* (1993)

12 Politicians are the source of all disillusionment.

Shirley Abbott, *Womenfolks: Growing Up Down South* (1983)

13 A politician is required to listen to humbug, talk humbug, condone humbug. The most we can hope for is that we don't actually believe it.

P.D. James, *A Taste for Death* (1986)

14 Politicians aren't any more wicked than other citizens but the situation in which they are placed warps their judgment.

Helen Gahagan Douglas, *A Full Life* (1982)

15 There are no such things as good politicians and bad politicians. There are only politicians, which is to say, they all have personal axes to grind, and all too rarely are they honed for the public good.

Barbara Howar, *Laughing All the Way* (1973)

16 God is a politician; so is the devil.

Carry Nation, *The Use and Need of the Life of Carry A. Nation* (1905)

17 The mistake a lot of politicians make is in forgetting they've been appointed and thinking they've been anointed.

Mrs. Claude Pepper, in Reader's Digest Editors, *The Reader's Digest Dictionary of Quotations* (1968)

18 A politician is a fellow who will lay down your life for his country.

Texas Guinan, nightclub act (1923), in Dorothy Herrmann, *With Malice Toward All* (1982)

1 He had grown up in a country run by politicians who sent the pilots to man the bombers to kill the babies to make the world safe for children to grow up in.

    Ursula K. Le Guin, *The Lathe of Heaven* (1971)

2 The politicians were talking themselves red, white, and blue in the face.

    Clare Boothe Luce, speech (1960)

3 I'm the candidate who forgot to take off her hat before she threw it in the ring.

    Gracie Allen, *How to Become President* (1940)

4 A valuable qualification of a modern politician seems to be a capacity for concealing or explaining away the truth.

    Dorothy Nevill, *My Own Times* (1912)

5 I never saw the man yet that came out of politics as clean as he went into 'em.

    Ellen Glasgow, *The Miller of Old Church* (1911)

6 You will do very well to refuse offices; for a man seldom fails to give offense in them. It ought to weary you simply to hear them mentioned.

    St. Catherine of Siena (1376), in Vida D. Scudder, ed., *St. Catherine of Siena As Seen in Her Letters* (1905)

7 There is little place in the political scheme of things for an independent, creative personality, for a fighter. Anyone who takes that role must pay a price.

    Shirley Chisholm, *Unbought and Unbossed* (1970)

8 Brains, integrity, and force may be all very well, but what you need today is Charm. Go ahead and work on your old economic programs if you want to, I'll develop my radio personality.

    Gracie Allen, *How to Become President* (1940)

9 I must say acting was good training for the political life which lay ahead for us.

    Nancy Reagan, with Bill Libby, *Nancy* (1980)

10 What troubles me is not that movie stars run for office, but that they find it easy to get elected. It should be difficult. It should be difficult for millionaires, too.

    Shana Alexander, "It's the Idea That Offends," in *Life* (1966)

11 He had the misleading air of open-hearted simplicity that people have come to demand of their politicians.

    Rae Foley, *The Hundredth Door* (1950)

12 A politician ought to be born a foundling and remain a bachelor.

    Lady Bird Johnson, in Myra MacPherson, *The Power Lovers* (1975)

13 I would feel sorry for her if she did.

    Pat Nixon, on whether she would want daughter Tricia to marry a politician, in Barbara McDowell and Hana Umlauf, *Woman's Almanac* (1977)

14 A desire to succeed in politics is propelled by these two seemingly contradictory forces, which frequently change places and sometimes coexist: to save others and to save oneself.

    Madeleine Kunin, *Living a Political Life* (1994)

15 Every man who takes a part in politics, especially in times when parties run high, must expect to be abused; they must bear it; and their friends must learn to bear it for them.

    Maria Edgeworth, *Ormond* (1817)

16 No one asks public men to be strictly moral, but they must *seem* to be well-behaved.

    Storm Jameson, *The Early Life of Stephen Hind* (1966)

17 Convictions no doubt have to be modified or expanded to meet changing conditions but . . . to be a reliable political leader sooner or later your anchors must hold fast where other men's drag.

    Margot Asquith, *More or Less About Myself* (1934)

18 A successful politician does not have convictions; he has emotions.

    Ellen Glasgow, *The Voice of the People* (1900)

19 After a sudden religious conversion / The shrewd politician can get off the hook / By answering any who cast an aspersion / "The Lord is my shepherd and I am His crook."

    Felicia Lamport, "Sprung Lamb," *Light Metres* (1982)

See also Government, Leadership, Political Parties, Politics.

## ❧ POLITICS

20 The pursuit of politics is religion, morality, and poetry all in one.

    Madame de Staël (1790), in J. Christopher Herold, *Mistress to an Age* (1958)

1 The optimistic illusion that one can change the world is difficult to resist, especially when from time to time that illusion is sustained by even a hint of reality. Change does happen in the political process.

Madeleine Kunin, *Living a Political Life* (1994)

2 Like art, political action gives shape and expression to the things we fear as well as to those we desire. It is a creative process, drawing on the power to imagine as well as to act.

Madeleine Kunin, *Living a Political Life* (1994)

3 Politics creates an almost endless time horizon into the future. . . . As governor I had the incredible luxury of being able to dream on a grand scale. And this sense of infinite possibility gives politics its romance.

Madeleine Kunin, *Living a Political Life* (1994)

4 Anyone who can see as far as tomorrow in politics arouses the wrath of people who can see no farther than today.

Madame de Staël, *Considerations* (1818)

5 I confess to feeling continued ambivalence about political life, aware of its shortcomings and disappointments, but drawn back to it again and again because of its infinite promise. Justice can triumph, wrongs can be righted, and pain can be alleviated, if the right fix is found.

Madeleine Kunin, *Living a Political Life* (1994)

6 There aren't many idealists in politics.

Evelyn Anthony, *The Avenue of the Dead* (1982)

7 I was well on the way to forming my present attitude toward politics as it is practiced in the United States: it is a beautiful fraud that has been imposed on the people for years, whose practitioners exchange gilded promises for the most valuable thing their victims own, their votes.

Shirley Chisholm, *Unbought and Unbossed* (1970)

8 Politics are usually the executive expression of human immaturity.

Vera Brittain, *The Rebel Passion* (1964)

9 Truthfulness has never been counted among the political virtues, and lies have always been regarded as justifiable tools in political dealings.

Hannah Arendt, "Lying in Politics," *Crises of the Republic* (1972)

10 Policy and politics generally go contrary to principle.

Flannery O'Connor, in Sally Fitzgerald, ed., *The Habit of Being* (1979)

11 Politics is not really politics any more. It is run, for the most part, by Madison Avenue advertising firms, who sell politicians to the public the way they sell bars of soap or cans of beer.

Helen Caldicott, *If You Love This Planet* (1992)

12 The great science and duty of politics is lowered by the petty leaven of small and personal advantage.

L.E. Landon, *Ethel Churchill* (1837)

13 Money was the manure of politics.

Barbara Michaels, *Smoke and Mirrors* (1989)

14 We cannot cure the evils of politics with politics.

Anaïs Nin (1955), *The Diary of Anaïs Nin*, vol. 5 (1974)

15 The political arena leaves one no alternative, one must either be a dunce or a rogue.

Emma Goldman, title essay, *Anarchism* (1910)

16 The politics of character tend to drive out the politics of substance.

Judith Lichtenberg, in *The New York Times* (1990)

17 Our political scene is more volatile and given to sudden switches and memory lapses bordering on soap-opera-type amnesia (epidemic, total and terminal) than any other I know of. We are fickle and we are insatiable in our appetite for new news, new issues, new biases, new clichés. . . . It's not just (as another cliché, lifted from Andy Warhol, has it) that individuals all seem to get their fifteen minutes of celebrity in this country; everything gets only fifteen minutes.

Meg Greenfield, in *Newsweek* (1991)

18 It will be impossible to establish a higher political life than the people themselves crave.

Jane Addams, speech (1892), *Twenty Years at Hull House* (1910)

19 The apathy and inattention of the average citizen is beyond comprehension.

Abigail McCarthy, *Private Faces/Public Places* (1972)

20 People often say, with pride, "I'm not interested in politics." They might as well say, "I'm not interested in my standard of living, my health, my job, my rights, my freedoms, my future or any future."

. . . If we mean to keep any control over our world and lives, we must be interested in politics.

Martha Gellhorn, "White Into Black," in *Granta* (1984)

1 I believe that everything is political, and as such it should concern all of us. Authors who claim they don't deal with politics in their work are being naive, because even that is a political stance.

Elena Poniatowska, in Marie-Lise Gazarian-Gautiez, *Interviews With Latin American Writers* (1989)

2 The personal is political.

Slogan, women's movement (1970s)

3 The political is personal.

Gloria Steinem, *Revolution From Within* (1993)

4 In politics, guts is all.

Barbara Castle, *The Castle Diaries 1974-1976* (1980)

5 When men in politics are together, testosterone poisoning makes them insane.

Peggy Noonan, *What I Saw at the Revolution* (1990)

6 Women are young at politics, but they are old at suffering; soon they will learn that through politics they can prevent some kinds of suffering.

Nancy Astor, *My Two Countries* (1923)

7 If you're going to play the game properly, you'd better know every rule.

Barbara Jordan, in Charles L. Saunders, "Barbara Jordan," *Ebony* (1975)

8 Never lose your temper with the Press or the public is a major rule of political life.

Christabel Pankhurst, *Unshackled* (1959)

9 International politics, by and large, are a depressing study.

C.V. Wedgwood, *Velvet Studies* (1946)

10 All politicians know that every "temporary" political initiative promised as a short-term poultice stays on the books forever.

Cynthia Ozick, "Literature and the Politics of Sex: A Dissent," *Art and Ardor* (1983)

11 Haven't you ever noticed how highways always get beautiful near the state capital?

Shirley Ann Grau, *The Wind Shifting West* (1973)

See also Democracy, Elections, Foreign Affairs, Government, Political Campaigns, Political Parties, Politicians, Politics and Business, Politics and Religion, Suffrage.

## ✿ POLITICS AND BUSINESS

12 Big Business and Politics are twins, they are the monsters who kill everything, corrupt everything.

Anaïs Nin (1957), *The Diary of Anaïs Nin*, vol. 6 (1976)

13 The conduct of these two groups of men, the politicians and the businessmen, shows how absolutely interchangeable the terms "business" and "politics" are in the capitalistic world.

Sarah Tarleton Colvin, *A Rebel in Thought* (1944)

14 Politics is only the servant of industry.

Mother Jones, in Mary Field Parton, *The Autobiography of Mother Jones* (1925)

15 Business is really more powerful than politics. . . . Its power to confuse an issue by insisting upon acceptance of such clichés as "free enterprise" in a world where nothing is free from interrelationships, and its absolute refusal to meet the practical issue of needs of human beings for such simple things as food, clothing, and shelter, are the real obstruction in clearing the path for permanent prosperity and peace.

Sarah Tarleton Colvin, *A Rebel in Thought* (1944)

16 In the era of imperialism, businessmen became politicians and were acclaimed as statesmen, while statesmen were taken seriously only if they talked the language of successful businessmen.

Hannah Arendt, *Origins of Totalitarianism* (1951)

See also Business, Industrialism, Politics.

## ✿ POLITICS AND RELIGION

17 Politics and religion mixed is the headiest cocktail ever invented. That it *is* a mixture cannot, I fear, be controverted. It is very, very old.

Norah Bentinck, *My Wanderings and Memories* (1924)

18 That was one of the things he deplored about the loss of religion, it meant that people elevated politics into a religious faith and that was dangerous.

P.D. James, *A Taste for Death* (1986)

See also Politics, Religion.

## ❦ POLLS

1 The worship of Opinion is, at this day, the established religion of the United States.

  Harriet Martineau, *Society in America*, vol. 3 (1837)

2 If Rosa Parks had taken a poll before she sat down in the bus in Montgomery, she'd still be standing.

  Mary Frances Berry, in Brian Lanker, *I Dream a World* (1989)

3 We tend to tell strangers what we think will make us sound good. I myself, to my utter amazement, informed a telephone pollster that I exercised regularly, a bare-faced lie.

  Katha Pollitt, *Reasonable Creatures* (1994)

See also Public Opinion.

## ❦ THE POOR

4 We were so poor we envied everyone we ever heard of.

  Sally Stanford, *The Lady of the House* (1966)

5 The poor have been sent to the front lines of a federal budget deficit reduction war that few other groups were drafted to fight.

  Marian Wright Edelman, *Families in Peril* (1987)

6 The Great Society's War on Poverty was also a war on alternative values. In reality it became a war on the poor, not on poverty.

  Lynn Maria Laitala, in *The Finnish American Reporter* (1992)

7 As the misery of poor people increased, so did the cacophony of private interests competing for government contracts, foundation grants, donations by individuals and corporations, and tax advantages for the donations to "correct" their version of the problem. The only people who did not cash in, the only ones absent from the debate in any public way, as ever, were poor.

  Theresa Funiciello, *Tyranny of Kindness* (1993)

See also Charity, Poverty, The Rich and the Poor, Welfare.

## ❦ POPULARITY

8 Being popular is important. Otherwise people might not like you.

  Mimi Pond, *The Valley Girls' Guide to Life* (1982)

See also Charisma, Charm.

## ❦ PORNOGRAPHY

9 Pornography is the undiluted essence of anti-female propaganda.

  Susan Brownmiller, *Against Our Will* (1975)

10 For many feminists, pornography is the theory and rape is the practice.

  Cheris Kramarae and Paula A. Treichler, *A Feminist Dictionary* (1985)

11 Pornography is a direct denial of the power of the erotic, for it represents the suppression of true feeling. Pornography emphasizes sensation without feeling.

  Audre Lorde, *Uses of the Erotic* (1978)

12 Pornography is not about sex. It's about an imbalance of male-female power that allows and even requires sex to be used as a form of aggression. . . . But until we finally untangle sexuality and aggression, there will be more pornography and less erotica. There will be little murders in our beds—and very little love.

  Gloria Steinem, *Outrageous Acts and Everyday Rebellions* (1983)

13 What pornographic literature does is precisely to drive a wedge between one's existence as a full human being and one's existence as a sexual being— while in ordinary life a healthy person is one who prevents such a gap from opening up.

  Susan Sontag, "The Pornographic Imagination," *Styles of Radical Will* (1966)

14 Mind and body are not to be taken lightly. Their connection is intimate and mysterious, and better mapped by poets than pornographers.

  Shana Alexander, *Talking Woman* (1976)

15 There are laws against discrimination; laws against sexual harassment; laws against doing violence to children; against lynching; against mutilating animals. These are not issues of speech. None of these

are protected acts, even if they provide someone with sexual thrills. But do any of these to a woman in print or on a screen and we say it is speech and it is protected. In effect, protecting and defending pornography is the official state position.

Susan J. Berkson, in *The Minneapolis Star Tribune* (1994)

1 The flood of literary pornography loosed on us is dulling our reactions of surprise or shock. Its writers are forced to raise the ante, to provide stronger and stronger stimulants. Or try to provide them, since both the manner, the naming of parts and the few inexpressive four-letter words, and the matter, are narrowly limited.

Storm Jameson, *Parthian Words* (1970)

2 The sex even in serious pornography has less singularity than the mating of squirrels.

Storm Jameson, *Parthian Words* (1970)

3 Pornography is essentially reductive, an exercise in the nothing-but mode, a depersonalizing of the human beings involved, a showing-up of human lust as nothing but an affair of the genitals.

Storm Jameson, *Parthian Words* (1970)

4 All pornography becomes repetitive.

Joyce Haber, *The Users* (1976)

5 The real weakness of all porn, it seems to me, is its necessary repetition. . . . The pornographer must continually invent new sauces for old meats.

Shana Alexander, *Talking Woman* (1976)

6 I'm someone who is on the record as being pro-pornography—all the way through kiddie porn and snuff films.

Camille Paglia, "Crisis in the American Universities," *Sex, Art, and American Culture* (1992)

7 Sick and perverted always appeals to me.

Madonna, in Paul Zollo, *Songwriters on Songwriting* (1991)

8 From so much of this seriously-intended pornography there rises, even when it is lewdly or boisterously comic, the acrid smell, unmistakable, of self-dislike.

Storm Jameson, *Parthian Words* (1970)

9 Pornography exists for the lonesome, the ugly, the fearful. . . . It's made for the losers.

Rita Mae Brown, in *Ms.* (1994)

## ❧ PORTUGAL

10 Any sizable Portuguese town looks like a superstitious bride's finery—something old, something new, something borrowed, and something blue.

Mary McCarthy, "Letter From Portugal" (1955), *On the Contrary* (1961)

## ❧ POSING

11 Sometimes I pose, but sometimes I pose as posing.

Stella Benson, *I Pose* (1915)

12 Let the world know you as you are, not as you think you should be, because sooner or later, if you are posing, you will forget the pose, and then where are you?

Fanny Brice, in Norman Katkov, *The Fabulous Fanny* (1952)

## ❧ POSSESSIONS

13 All things that a man owns hold him far more than he holds them.

Sigrid Undset, *Kristin Lavransdatter: The Mistress of Husaby* (1921)

14 We possess nothing in the world—a mere chance can strip us of everything—except the power to say "I."

Simone Weil, *Gravity and Grace* (1947)

15 Mine! There isn't any such thing as mine. The world slips slithering through my fingers.

Nancy Hale, *Prodigal Women* (1942)

16 The things that are ours cannot be given away, or taken away, or lost. We break our hearts, all of us, trying to keep things that do not belong to us—and to which we have no right.

Myrtle Reed, *A Weaver of Dreams* (1911)

17 He greatly valued his possessions, chiefly because they were his, and derived genuine pleasure from contemplating a painting, a statuette, a rare lace curtain—no matter what—after he had bought it and placed it among his household gods.

Kate Chopin, *The Awakening* (1899)

1 Possessions, for the terminally frightened, bring peace of mind.

> Cynthia Heimel, *But Enough About You* (1986)

2 Spoiled. That's all it's about—can't live without this, can't live without that. You can live without anything you weren't born with, and you can make it through on even half of that.

> Gloria Naylor, *Mama Day* (1988)

3 There is, of course, a difference between what one seizes and what one really possesses.

> Pearl S. Buck, *What America Means to Me* (1943)

4 The pleasure of possession, whether we possess trinkets, or offspring—or possibly books, or prints, or chessmen, or postage stamps—lies in showing these things to friends who are experiencing no immediate urge to look at them.

> Agnes Repplier, "The Pleasure of Possession," *Times and Tendencies* (1931)

5 Through the years I have found it wonderful to acquire, but it is also wonderful to divest. It's rather like exhaling.

> Helen Hayes, with Sanford Dody, *On Reflection* (1968)

6 No one has a right to hoard things which he cannot use.

> Carrie Jacobs-Bond, *The Roads of Melody* (1927)

7 We are all more blind to what we have than to what we have not.

> Audre Lorde, "Trip to Russia," *Sister Outsider* (1984)

8 Until you make peace with who you are, you'll never be content with what you have.

> Doris Mortman, *Circles* (1984)

9 I do not own an inch of land, / But all I see is mine,— / The orchard and the mowing-fields, / The lawns and gardens fine. / The winds my tax-collectors are, / They bring me tithes divine.

> Lucy Larcom, "A Strip of Blue," in Edmund Clarence Stedman, ed., *An American Anthology 1787–1900* (1900)

See also Consumerism, Materialism, Things.

## ❧ POSSIBILITIES

10 I dwell in Possibility — / A fairer House than Prose — / More numerous of Windows — / Superior — for Doors.

> Emily Dickinson (1862), in Martha Dickinson Bianchi and Alfred Leete Hampson, eds., *Further Poems of Emily Dickinson* (1929)

11 I do not live alone. / I live in a house of many doors.

> Holly Near, "Doors" (1984), with Derk Richardson, *Fire in the Rain . . . Singer in the Storm* (1990)

12 The world is full of hopeful analogies and handsome, dubious eggs, called possibilities.

> George Eliot, *Middlemarch* (1871)

13 It is the possibilities which are the most terrible things in life.

> Phyllis Bottome, "The Vocation," *Innocence and Experience* (1934)

14 Possibilities swung from the ropes of his life like charms on a watch chain, golden.

> Susan Moody, *Mosaic* (1991)

15 What is important is not what someone is but what he is waiting for. Not the events of life but its possibilities.

> Dorothee Sölle, *The Truth Is Concrete* (1967)

16 Don't be obsessed with the idea that there is only one possibility. If you think so, there is only one.

> Katharine Butler Hathaway (1929), *The Journals and Letters of the Little Locksmith* (1946)

17 Who can choose between the worst possibility / and the last.

> June Jordan, "Roman Poem Number Thirteen," *Things That I Do in the Dark* (1981)

18 If a thing can be done why do it.

> Gertrude Stein, in Elizabeth Sprigge, *Gertrude Stein* (1957)

See also Choice, Future, Opportunities.

## ❧ POSTAL SERVICE

19 The post-office is a wonderful establishment! The regularity and dispatch of it! If one thinks of all that it has to do, and all that it does so well, it is really astonishing!

> Jane Austen, *Emma* (1816)

20 Being a postman . . . is not a congenial profession for anyone who is at all sensitive, for people visit upon the postman all their first annoyance at receiving a couple of bills when they looked for a love-letter, and if a packet is insufficiently stamped they hand over the pennies as though to a despica-

ble bandit, too outrageous to be denied, too groveling to be feared.

Sylvia Townsend Warner, "The Property of a Lady," *More Joy in Heaven* (1935)

## & POUTING

1　I believe she keeps on being queenly in her own room, with the door shut.

Edith Wharton, *The House of Mirth* (1905)

2　One should know the value of Life better than to *pout* any part of it away.

Hester Lynch Piozzi (1789), in Oswald G. Knapp, *The Intimate Letters of Hester Piozzi and Penelope Pennington 1788-1821* (1914)

## & POVERTY

3　We must talk about poverty, because people insulated by their own comfort lose sight of it.

Dorothy Day (1952), in Robert Ellsberg, ed., *By Little and by Little* (1983)

4　I don't believe that it's true that the poor will always be with us. I think that kind of pious fatalism is just an excuse for keeping things the way they are.

Margaret Culkin Banning, *The Quality of Mercy* (1963)

5　It's going to take an act of Congress to deal with poverty. . . . We have the resources but we don't have the will.

Coretta Scott King, in Alice Walker, *In Search of Our Mothers' Gardens* (1983)

6　We do not want them to have less. / But it is only natural that we should think we have not enough. / We drive on, we drive on.

Gwendolyn Brooks, "Beverly Hills, Chicago," *Annen Allen* (1949)

7　We live in the richest country in the world. There's plenty and to spare for no man, woman, or child to be in want. And in addition to this our country was founded on what should have been a great, true principle—the freedom, equality, and rights of each individual. Huh! And what has come of that start? There are corporations worth billions of dol-

lars—and hundreds of thousands of people who don't get to eat.

Carson McCullers, *The Heart Is a Lonely Hunter* (1940)

8　The rioting was a total enigma to most people—in the wake of all the anti-poverty legislative gifts. But poor people were neither receiving the money directly nor truly influencing how it would be spent. . . . Monies said to be *for them* . . . for the most part were getting nowhere near actual poor people.

Theresa Funiciello, *Tyranny of Kindness* (1993)

9　The poverty industry has become a veritable fifth estate. Acting as stand-ins for actual poor people, they mediate the politics of poverty with government officials. The fifth estate is a large and evergrowing power bloc that routinely and by whatever means necessary trades off the interests of poor people to advance its own parochial agenda. From the charities fleecing the state and the public, to the champagne fund-raisers charged off to Uncle Sam . . . the fix is in.

Theresa Funiciello, *Tyranny of Kindness* (1993)

10　Poverty has no causes. Only prosperity has causes. Analogically, heat is a result of active processes; it has causes. But cold is not the result of any processes; it is only the absence of heat. Just so, the great cold of poverty and economic stagnation is merely the absence of economic development.

Jane Jacobs, *The Economy of Cities* (1969)

11　We think of poverty as a condition simply meaning a lack of funds, no money, but when one sees fifth, sixth, and seventh generation poor, it is clear that poverty is as complicated as high finance.

Alice Childress, *A Hero Ain't Nothin' But a Sandwich* (1973)

12　The poverty of the West is far more difficult to solve than the poverty of India.

Mother Teresa, in Kathryn Spink, *For the Brotherhood of Man Under the Fatherhood of God* (1981)

13　The wealthy white western minority of the world could not hope to prosper if most of the rest of mankind were foundering in hopeless poverty. Islands of plenty in a vast ocean of misery never have been a good recipe for commercial success.

Barbara Ward, in Richard Thruelsen and John Kobler, eds., *Adventures of the Mind*, 2nd series (1961)

14　Poverty is the number-one killer of children in the United States. Doctors don't say so, at least not in so many words, because poverty isn't a medical affliction—it's an economic and social one. It kills all the same.

Theresa Funiciello, *Tyranny of Kindness* (1993)

1 Few save the poor feel for the poor.

L.E. Landon, "The Widow's Mite," *The Easter Gift* (1832)

2 I'm proud to be a hillbilly. . . . Some of the proudest people in this country are poor people.

Donna, in Kathy Kahn, ed., *Hillbilly Women* (1973)

3 It's expensive keeping people poor.

Theresa Funiciello, *Tyranny of Kindness* (1993)

4 Poverty is an expensive luxury. We cannot afford it.

Eleanor Roosevelt, *Tomorrow Is Now* (1963)

5 Except to poor people themselves, poverty is megabusiness.

Theresa Funiciello, interview (1994)

6 There is something about poverty that smells like death. Dead dreams dropping off the heart like leaves in a dry season and rotting around the feet; impulses smothered too long in the fetid air of underground caves.

Zora Neale Hurston, *Dust Tracks on a Road* (1942)

7 Abstractions hardened into the concrete: even death is a purchase. One of Bam's senior partners could afford his at the cost of a private plane—in which he crashed. July's old mother . . . would crawl, as Maureen was watching her now, coming home with wood, and grass for her brooms on her head, bent lower and lower towards the earth until finally she sank to it—the only death she could afford.

Nadine Gordimer, *July's People* (1981)

8 How many times we have picked up in the streets human beings who had been living like animals and were longing to die like angels!

Mother Teresa (1976), *Heart of Joy* (1987)

9 One day I have chicken to eat and the next day the feathers.

Calamity Jane (1890), in Karen Payne, ed., *Between Ourselves* (1983)

10 A peculiarity of the American historical sensibility allows us to be proud of great-grandfathers (or even grandfathers) who lived in crushing poverty, while the poverty of a father is too close for comfort.

Patricia Hampl, *Spillville* (1987)

11 Poverty and contempt generally go hand-in-hand in this world.

Susan Ferrier, *The Inheritance*, vol. 2 (1824)

12 By assigning his political rights to the state the individual also delegates his social responsibilities to it: he asks the state to relieve him of the burden of caring for the poor precisely as he asks for protection against criminals. The difference between pauper and criminal disappears—both stand outside society.

Hannah Arendt, *Origins of Totalitarianism* (1951)

13 Poverty made me feel weak, as if I were coming down with an awful, debilitating, communicable disease—the disease of being without money. Instead of going to the hospital, you went to the poor farm. The difference was, you never got well at the poor farm.

Faith Sullivan, *The Cape Ann* (1988)

14 Every problem born of our poverty brought with it a sense of impotence: No escape, no help, anywhere!

Rose Pastor Stokes (1899), in Herbert Shapiro and David L. Sterling, eds., *"I Belong to the Working Class"* (1992)

15 A poverty that is universal may be cheerfully borne; it is an individual poverty that is painful and humiliating.

Amelia E. Barr, *All the Days of My Life* (1913)

16 Poverty . . . is very bad for the formation of a personality. . . . Not until I knew for certain where my next meal would come from could I give myself up to ignoring that next meal; I could think of other things.

Helen Westley (1917), in Djuna Barnes, *I Could Never Be Lonely Without a Husband* (1985)

17 That's the definition of poverty. The less choice you have, the poorer you are.

Carrie Saxon Perry, in Brian Lanker, *I Dream a World* (1989)

18 Poor people who had escaped from poverty as I had, feared it, hated it and fled from it all their lives. Those born rich could afford to be touched by it.

Anzia Yezierska, *Red Ribbon on a White Horse* (1950)

19 For those who have lived on the edge of poverty all their lives, the semblance of poverty affected by the affluent is both incomprehensible and insulting.

Lillian Breslow Rubin, *Worlds of Pain* (1976)

1 We always come back to the same vicious circle—
an extreme degree of material or intellectual poverty does away with the means of alleviating it.

   Simone de Beauvoir, *The Coming of Age* (1970)

2 Bread, bread, bread! No more preachers, no more
politicians, no more lawyers, no more gods, no
more heavens, no more promises! Bread!

   Voltairine de Cleyre, in Paul Avrich, *An American Anarchist*
(1978)

See also Class, Ghetto, Homelessness, Hunger,
Misfortune, The Poor, The Rich and the Poor,
Welfare.

## ❧ POWER

3 I am more and more convinced that man is a dangerous creature; and that power, whether vested in
many or a few, is ever grasping, and, like the grave,
cries "Give, give."

   Abigail Adams, to her husband, John Adams (1775), *Letters
of Mrs. Adams* (1848)

4 "Must power always be for destruction?" said
Anna. "That has so far been largely the experience."

   Sybille Bedford, *A Favorite of the Gods* (1963)

5 Power, when invested in the hands of knaves or
fools, generally is the source of tyranny.

   Charlotte Charke, *A Narrative of the Life of Mrs. Charlotte
Charke* (1755)

6 The doctrine of blind obedience and unqualified
submission to *any human power,* whether civil or
ecclesiastical, is the doctrine of despotism.

   Angelina Grimké, "Appeal to the Christian Women of the
South," in *The Anti-Slavery Examiner* (1836)

7 You see what power is—holding someone else's
fear in your hand and showing it to them!

   Amy Tan, *The Kitchen God's Wife* (1991)

8 Power consists to a large extent in deciding what
stories will be told.

   Carolyn Heilbrun, *Writing a Woman's Life* (1988)

9 Powerful people get away with things. That's one
way to demonstrate their difference from the rest
of us.

   Elizabeth Janeway, *Improper Behavior* (1987)

10 Power in the hands of particular groups and classes
serves like a prism to refract reality through their
own perspective.

   Sheila Rowbotham, *Woman's Consciousness, Man's World*
(1973)

11 Power . . . is not an end in itself, but is an instrument that must be used toward an end.

   Jeane J. Kirkpatrick, speech (1981)

12 Our sources and uses of power set our boundaries,
give form to our relationships, even determine how
much we let ourselves liberate and express aspects
of the self. More than party registration, more than
our purported philosophy or ideology, personal
power defines our politics.

   Marilyn Ferguson, *The Aquarian Conspiracy* (1980)

13 Power can be taken, but not given. The process of
the taking is empowerment in itself.

   Gloria Steinem, *Outrageous Acts and Everyday Rebellions*
(1983)

14 In this world, all power rests upon force.

   Marie von Ebner-Eschenbach, *Aphorisms* (1893)

15 Fortune is always on the side of the big battalions.

   Marie de Rabutin-Chantal, Marquise de Sévigné (1673), in
M. Monmerqué, ed., *Lettres de Madame de Sévigné de sa
famille et de ses amis*, vol. 3 (1862)

16 Power, like fear, had a taste. But power tasted better.

   Lois Wyse, *Far From Innocence* (1979)

17 Genuine power is power-with, pseudo power,
power-over.

   M.P. Follett, *Creative Experience* (1924)

18 To get power over is to defile. To possess is to
defile.

   Simone Weil, *First and Last Notebooks* (1970)

19 Coercive power is the curse of the universe; coac-
tive power, the enrichment and advancement of
every human soul.

   M.P. Follett, *Creative Experience* (1924)

20 Power should not be concentrated in the hands of
so few, and powerlessness in the hands of so many.

   Maggie Kuhn, in "How to Fight Age Bias," *Ms.* (1975)

21 Abuse of power comes as no surprise.

   Jenny Holzer, *Truisms* (1983)

1 I have noticed this about ambitious men, or men in power—they fear even the slightest and least likely threat to it.

Mary Stewart, *The Crystal Cave* (1970)

2 Nowhere does power give itself up willingly.

Nan Levinson, "The Speech We Hate," in *Odyssey* (1993)

3 Bodies in power tend to stay in power, unless external forces disturb them.

Catharine Stimpson, "The Power to Name," in E.J. Sherman and E. Beck, eds., *The Prism of Sex* (1979)

4 Power, however it has evolved, whatever its origins, will not be given up without a struggle.

Shulamith Firestone, *The Dialectic of Sex* (1970)

5 Power can be thought of as the never-ending, self-feeding motor of all political action that corresponds to the legendary unending accumulation of money that begets money.

Hannah Arendt, *Origins of Totalitarianism* (1951)

6 Differences of power are always manifested in asymmetrical access. The President of the United States has access to almost everybody for almost anything he might want of them, and almost nobody has access to him. The super-rich have access to almost everybody; almost nobody has access to them. . . . The creation and manipulation of power is constituted of the manipulation and control of access.

Marilyn Frye, *The Politics of Reality* (1983)

7 The idea of power as a possession, whose asset can be banked and drawn on when needed, comes easy to a society whose rules grow out of the methods of finance capitalism.

Elizabeth Janeway, *Improper Behavior* (1987)

8 The instruments of power—arms, gold, machines, magical or technical secrets—always exist independently of him who disposes of them, and can be taken up by others. Consequently all power is unstable.

Simone Weil (1934), *Oppression and Liberty* (1955)

9 Most power is illusionary and perceptual. You have to create an environment in which people perceive you as having some power.

Carrie Saxon Perry, in Brian Lanker, *I Dream a World* (1989)

10 Nobody is as powerful as we make them out to be.

Alice Walker, *In Search of Our Mothers' Gardens* (1983)

11 Love of power more frequently originates in vanity than pride (two qualities, by the way, which are often confounded) and is, consequently, yet more peculiarly the sin of little than of great minds.

Frances Wright, *Views of Society and Manners in America* (1821)

12 My mother used to say when we were children, "When a boy gets a stick in his hand, his brains run out the other end of it." Power is a stick in the hand, and I have never heard of anybody who wielded a very big stick of power whose brains did not run out the other end.

Jane Jacobs, in Elizabeth Janeway, ed., *The Writer's World* (1969)

13 Power is the test. Some, once they have it, are content to buy the show of liking, and punish those who withhold it; then you have a despot. But some keep a true eye for how they seem to others, and care about it, which holds them back from much mischief.

Mary Renault, *The Praise Singer* (1978)

14 You have gathered the many powers, / You have clasped them now / Like necklaces unto your breast.

Enheduanna, "The Hymn to Inanna" (c. 2350 B.C.), in Jane Hirschfield, ed., *Women in Praise of the Sacred* (1994)

15 Before me, no Assyrian had seen the great sea: I beheld with my own eyes four seas, and their shores acknowledged my power. I constrained the mighty rivers to flow according to my will, and I led their waters to fertilize lands that had been before barren and without inhabitants.

Semiramis, Queen of Assyria, in Mrs. Jameson, *Memoirs of Celebrated Female Sovereigns* (1831)

16 Surely a King who loves pleasure is less dangerous than one who loves glory?

Nancy Mitford, "In Defense of Louis XV" (1956), *The Water Beetle* (1962)

17 The less powerful group usually knows the powerful one much better than vice versa—blacks have had to understand whites in order to survive, women have had to know men—yet the powerful group can afford to regard the less powerful one as a mystery.

Gloria Steinem, *Outrageous Acts and Everyday Rebellions* (1983)

1 Ironically, women who acquire power are more likely to be criticized for it than are the men who have always had it.

  Carolyn Heilbrun, *Writing a Woman's Life* (1988)

2 Power travels in the bloodlines, handed out before birth.

  Louise Erdrich, *Tracks* (1988)

3 Power's twin is responsibility.

  Willa Gibbs, *The Twelfth Physician* (1954)

4 Power is a companion it is not easy to part with, when it goes, the zest of life goes with it. With dry eyes and clenched fist, one stares after it, jealous of the next one it will single out.

  Queen Marie of Rumania (1926), in Hannah Pakula, *The Last Romantic* (1984)

See also Authority, Control, Oppression, Powerlessness.


## ❦ POWERLESSNESS

5 At times it is strangely sedative to know the extent of your own powerlessness.

  Erica Jong, *Fear of Flying* (1973)

6 Silence and invisibility go hand in hand with powerlessness.

  Audre Lorde, *The Cancer Journals* (1980)

7 The one power a man has that cannot be stripped from him is the power to do nothing.

  Morgan Llywelyn, *Bard* (1984)

See also Vulnerability.


## ❦ PRAISE

8 A little praise is not only merest justice but is beyond the purse of no one.

  Emily Post, *Etiquette* (1922)

9 I can eat it with a spoon or with a soup ladle or anything and I like it.

  Gertrude Stein, on praise for her work, in Elizabeth Sprigge, *Gertrude Stein* (1957)

10 It gives me no joy to be praised at the expense of a better artist, by someone who does not know the difference or who thinks me too vain to be aware of it myself.

  Mary Renault, *The Mask of Apollo* (1966)

11 There's nothing like undeserved credit to make you feel shabby.

  Charlene Weir, *The Winter Widow* (1992)

12 Commending a right thing is a cheap substitute for doing it, with which we are too apt to satisfy ourselves.

  Hannah More, *Coelebs in Search of a Wife* (1808)

13 Too much praise makes you feel you must be doing something terribly wrong.

  Dorothy Day, in Robert Ellsberg, ed., *By Little and by Little* (1983)

14 Praise out of season, or tactlessly bestowed, can freeze the heart as much as blame.

  Pearl S. Buck, *To My Daughters, With Love* (1967)

15 It is usually in better taste to praise an isolated action or a production of genius, than a man's character as a whole.

  Elizabeth Wordsworth, "Flattery," *Essays Old and New* (1919)

16 Praise requires constant renewal and expansion.

  Doris Grumbach, *Coming Into the End Zone* (1991)

See also Compliments, Flattery.


## ❦ PRAYER

17 Prayer is a long rope with a strong hold.

  Harriet Beecher Stowe, *The Pearl of Orr's Island* (1862)

18 Prayer oneth the soul to God.

  Julian of Norwich, *Revelations of Divine Love* (1373)

19 Prayer enlarges the heart until it is capable of containing God's gift of himself.

  Mother Teresa, *A Gift for God* (1975)

20 Prayer is nothing more than thought. It is a yearning of the heart.

  Sophy Burnham, *A Book of Angels* (1990)

21 Prayer is naught else but a yearning of soul. . . . It draws down the great God into the little heart; it

drives the hungry soul up to the plenitude of God; it brings together these two lovers, God and the soul, in a wondrous place where they speak much of love.

> Mechthild of Magdeburg (c. 1250), in Lucy Menzies, ed., *Mirror of the Holy* (1928)

1 I strain toward God; God strains toward me. I ache for God; God aches for me. Prayer is mutual yearning, mutual straining, mutual aching.

> Macrina Wiederkehr, *A Tree Full of Angels* (1988)

2 Prayer . . . is more than meditation. . . . In meditation the source of strength is one's self. When one prays he goes to a source of strength greater than his own.

> Madame Chiang Kai-shek, *I Confess My Faith* (1943)

3 Prayer is a law of the universe, like gravity. You don't even have to believe in God to ask.

> Sophy Burnham, *A Book of Angels* (1990)

4 Absolutely unmixed attention is prayer.

> Simone Weil, *Gravity and Grace* (1947)

5 Sometimes I think that just not thinking of oneself is a form of prayer.

> Barbara Grizzuti Harrison, *The Astonishing World* (1992)

6 Prayer is the language of the heart.

> Grace Aguilar, *The Spirit of Judaism* (1842)

7 Prayer is the natural language of love.

> Joan Brown Campbell, in Jim Castelli, ed., *How I Pray* (1994)

8 True prayer is not asking God for love; it is learning to love, and to include all mankind in one affection.

> Mary Baker Eddy, *No and Yes* (1909)

9 Prayer is essentially a process by which ideals are enabled to become operative in our lives. It may be more than this, but it is at least this.

> Georgia Harkness, *The Recovery of Ideals* (1937)

10 Prayer is an exercise of the spirit, as thought is of the mind.

> Mary F. Smith, "The Place of Prayer in Life," in Gerald K. Hibbert, ed., *Studies in Quaker Thought and Practice* (1936)

11 Prayer must be, in its own nature, absurd and impertinent.

> Mary Collyer, *Felicia to Charlotte* (1744)

12 The life of prayer is so great and various there is something in it for everyone. It is like a garden which grows everything, from alpines to potatoes.

> Evelyn Underhill, in Lucy Menzies, ed., *Collected Papers of Evelyn Underhill* (1946)

13 Is prayer your steering wheel or your spare tire?

> Corrie ten Boom, *Don't Wrestle, Just Nestle* (1978)

14 Pray inwardly, even if you do not enjoy it. It does good, though you feel nothing. Yes, even though you think you are doing nothing.

> Julian of Norwich, *Revelations of Divine Love* (1373)

15 You can do more than praying after you have prayed. You can never do more than praying before you have prayed.

> Corrie ten Boom, *Not Good If Detached* (1957)

16 To pray only when in peril is to use safety belts only in heavy traffic.

> Corrie ten Boom, *Don't Wrestle, Just Nestle* (1978)

17 He prayed as he breathed, forming no words and making no specific requests, only holding in his heart, like broken birds in cupped hands, all those people who were in stress or grief.

> Ellis Peters, *A Morbid Taste for Bones* (1977)

18 God answers sharp and sudden on some prayers, / And thrusts the thing we have prayed for in our face, / A gauntlet with a gift in 't.

> Elizabeth Barrett Browning, *Aurora Leigh* (1857)

19 Did not God / Sometimes withhold in mercy what we ask, / We should be ruin'd at our own request.

> Hannah More, "Moses in the Bulrushes," *Sacred Dramas* (1782)

20 Of Course — I prayed — / And did God Care?

> Emily Dickinson (1862), in Martha Dickinson Bianchi and Alfred Leete Hampson, eds., *Further Poems of Emily Dickinson* (1929)

21 If prayers worked, Hitler would have been stopped at the border of Poland by angels with swords of fire.

> Nancy Willard, *Things Invisible to See* (1984)

22 A desire to kneel down sometimes pulses through my body, or rather it is as if my body had been meant and made for the act of kneeling. Sometimes, in moments of deep gratitude, kneeling down becomes an overwhelming urge, head deeply bowed, hands before my face.

> Etty Hillesum (1942), *An Interrupted Life* (1983)

1 In saying my prayers, I discovered the voice of an innermost self, the raw nerve of my identity.

Gelsey Kirkland, *Dancing on My Grave* (1986)

2 Prayer does not use up artificial energy, doesn't burn up any fossil fuel, doesn't pollute. Neither does song, neither does love, neither does the dance.

Margaret Mead, in Jane Howard, *Margaret Mead* (1984)

3 She makes long, long prayers, they say—so long that she has been found in the morning fainting on the cold floor of the convent church. . . . They all say she will have a very high place in heaven; but it seems to me, unless there is a very great difference between the highest and lowest places in heaven, it is a great deal of trouble to take.

Elizabeth Rundle Charles, *Chronicles of the Schönberg-Cotta Family* (1863)

4 He didn't know exactly what he wanted to pray for; in which he was like most other people. For our real prayer, if we had the wits or the courage to formulate it, would be a general plea for everything to be all right for ever.

Angela Thirkell, *The Duke's Daughter* (1951)

5 This morning I stood on the river bank to pray. I knew then that the ancient ones were wise to pray for peace and beauty and not for specific gifts except fertility which is continued life. And I saw that if one has even a small degree of the ability to take into and unto himself the peace and beauty the gods surround him with, it is not necessary to ask for more.

Edith Warner, in Peggy Pond Church, *The House at Otowi Bridge* (1959)

6 I believe the old cliché, "God helps those who help themselves," is not only misleading but often dead wrong. My most spectacular answers to prayers have come when I was so helpless, so out of control as to be able to do nothing at all for myself.

Catherine Marshall, *Adventures in Prayer* (1975)

7 We seem to be much more comfortable talking about our sex lives than we are sharing information with each other about how we pray. Perhaps this is because praying may be the most personal and intimate thing we do.

Sherry Ruth Anderson and Patricia Hopkins, *The Feminine Face of God* (1991)

8 If a care is too small to be turned into a prayer, it is too small to be made into a burden.

Corrie ten Boom, *Each New Day* (1977)

9 Prayer is like money—it has no smell.

Simone Berteaut, *Piaf* (1969)

10 Worry is the antithesis of prayer. Prayer is an acknowledgment of faith; worry is a denial of faith.

Ethel P.S. Hoyt, *Spirit* (1921)

11 We often pray to be better, when in truth we only want to feel better.

Mignon McLaughlin, *The Neurotic's Notebook* (1963)

See also God, Spirituality.

## ❧ PRECOCITY

12 For precocity some great price is always demanded sooner or later in life.

Margaret Fuller, in Thomas Wentworth Higginson, *Margaret Fuller Ossoli* (1884)

13 In the career of a prodigy there invariably comes a time when it is compelled to relinquish being very clever for a child, and has to enter the business of life in competition with adults.

Miles Franklin, *Some Everyday Folk and Dawn* (1909)

See also Genius, Intelligence, Talent.

## ❧ PREFACES

14 Preface. Excuse me. None this time. There have already been too many big porticos before little buildings.

Fanny Fern, *Caper Sauce* (1872)

15 It would appear, from the best examples, that the proper way of beginning a preface to one's work is with a humble apology for having written at all.

Ellen Glasgow, *A Certain Measure* (1943)

16 A preface is a species of literary luxury, where an author, like a lover, is privileged to be egotistical.

L.E. Landon, *Romance and Reality* (1831)

17 I ought to have put this in the preface, but I never read prefaces, and it is not much good writing

things just for people to skip. I wonder other authors have never thought of this.

Edith Nesbitt, *The Bastable Children* (1928)

See also Books.

## ◊ PREGNANCY

1 Getting company inside one's skin.

Maggie Scarf, *Unfinished Business* (1980)

2 Let the earth look at me, and bless me, for now I am fecund and sacred, like the palms and the furrows.

Gabriela Mistral, "The Sacred Law," *Desolación* (1922)

3 Little fish, / you kick and dart and glide / beneath my ribs / as if they were your private reef.

Ethna McKiernan, "For Naoise Unborn," *Caravan* (1989)

4 In the dark / Defiant even now, it tugs and moans / To be untangled from these mother's bones.

Genevieve Taggard, "With Child" (1921), *Collected Poems* (1938)

5 Now I am nothing but a veil; all my body is a veil beneath which a child sleeps.

Gabriela Mistral, "To My Husband," in Langston Hughes, tr., *Selected Poems of Gabriela Mistral* (1957)

6 There were, in the beginning, seven children, each rising out of my great-grandmother's darkness every twelve or thirteen months like little full moons, following, even in birth, the quirky Jewish calendar. . . . My great-grandmother conceived and bore them, I am told, with bemused passivity, as tolerant as the moon must be of her own swellings and thinnings and equally unconscious.

Harriet Rosenstein, "The Fraychie Story," in *Ms.* (1974)

7 Lie in the sun with the child in your flesh shining like a jewel. Dream and sing, pagan, wise in your vitals. Stand still like a fat budding tree, like a stalk of corn athrob and aglisten in the heat. Lie like a mare panting with the dancing feet of colts against her sides. Sleep at night as the spring earth. Walk heavily as a wheat stalk at its full time bending towards the earth waiting for the reaper. Let your life swell downward so you become like a vase, a vessel. Let the unknown child knock and knock against you and rise like a dolphin within.

Meridel Le Sueur, "Annunciation" (1927), *Salute to Spring* (1940)

8 Carry yourself safely through your pregnancy; after that, if M. de Grignan really loves you, and is resolved not to kill you outright, I know what he will do, or rather what he will not do.

Marie de Rabutin-Chantal, Marquise de Sévigné (1671), to her daughter on her frequent pregnancies, *Letters of Madame de Sévigné to Her Daughter and Her Friends*, vol. 1 (1811)

9 Every pregnant woman should be surrounded with every possible comfort.

Dr. Flora L.S. Aldrich, *The Boudoir Companion* (1901)

10 The trouble with getting introspective when you're pregnant is that you never know who you might run into.

Carrie Fisher, *Delusions of Grandma* (1994)

11 When I had almost reached my term, I looked like a rat dragging a stolen egg.

Colette, *The Evening Star* (1946)

12 I was slowly taking on the dimensions of a chest of drawers.

Maria Augusta Trapp, *The Story of the Trapp Family Singers* (1949)

13 Envy the kangaroo. That pouch setup is extraordinary; the baby crawls out of the womb when it is about two inches long, gets into the pouch, and proceeds to mature. I'd have a baby if it would develop in my handbag.

Rita Rudner, *Naked Beneath My Clothes* (1992)

14 Now I was someone who ate like a wolf, napped like a cat, and dreamed like a madwoman.

Marni Jackson, *The Mother Zone* (1992)

15 I feel like a man building a boat in his basement which he may not be able to get out through the door. Trapped, frantic and trapped.

Abigail Lewis, *An Interesting Condition* (1950)

16 Her child was like a load that held her down, and yet like a hand that pulled her to her feet.

Edith Wharton, *Summer* (1918)

17 If pregnancy were a book, they would cut the last two chapters.

Nora Ephron, *Heartburn* (1983)

See also Childbirth.

## ♦ PREJUDICE

1 I was climbing up a mountain-path / With many things to do, / Important business of my own, / And other people's too, / When I ran against a Prejudice / That quite cut off the view.

    Charlotte Perkins Gilman, "An Obstacle," *In This Our World* (1893)

2 Beneath incrusted silences, a seething Etna lies, / The fire of whose furnaces may sleep—*but never dies!*

    Georgia Douglas Johnson, "Prejudice," *Bronze* (1922)

3 Prejudices are the chains forged by ignorance to keep men apart.

    Countess of Blessington, *Desultory Thoughts and Reflections* (1839)

4 Beware how you contradict prejudices, even knowing them to be such, for the generality of people are much more tenacious of their prejudices than of anything belonging to them.

    Susan Ferrier, *The Inheritance*, vol. 1 (1824)

5 If prejudices belonged to the vegetable world they would be described under the general heading of: "Hardy Perennials; will grow in any soil, and bloom without ceasing; require no cultivation; will do better when left alone."

    Nellie L. McClung, *In Times Like These* (1915)

6 Most people wish to be consoled, confirmed. They want their prejudices reinforced and their structured belief systems validated. After all, it hurts to think, and it's absolute agony to think twice.

    Jennifer Stone, "Epilogue," *Mind Over Media* (1988)

7 Prejudices are the refuge of those who cannot think for themselves.

    Comtesse Diane, *Les Glanes de la Vie* (1898)

8 Prejudice squints when it looks, and lies when it talks.

    Laure Junot, Duchesse de Abrantès, *Memoirs of Madame Junot*, vol. 1 (1883)

9 The mind that doggedly insists on prejudice often has not intelligence enough to change.

    Pearl S. Buck, *What America Means to Me* (1943)

10 Prejudices of all kinds have their strongest holds in the minds of the vulgar and the ignorant.

    Lydia Maria Child, *An Appeal in Favor of That Class of Americans Called Africans* (1833)

11 Prejudices, it is well known, are most difficult to eradicate from the heart whose soil has never been loosened or fertilized by education; they grow there, firm as weeds among stones.

    Charlotte Brontë, *Jane Eyre* (1847)

12 No man can see his own prejudices.

    Frances Wright, *A Few Days in Athens* (1822)

13 Truth is too weak to combat prejudice.

    Charlotte Lennox, *Henrietta* (1758)

14 Drive out prejudice with a pitch-fork it will ever return.

    H.P. Blavatsky, in *The Theosophist* (1883)

15 Laws will not eliminate prejudice from the hearts of human beings. But that is no reason to allow prejudice to continue to be enshrined in our laws to perpetuate injustice through inaction.

    Shirley Chisholm, in *The Congressional Record* (1970)

16 Given the ethnic and racial hierarchies of American life, there are those who dish it out and those who have to take it. Some get to dish it out without ever having to take it, some take it from those above and dish it out to those below, and some find themselves in the position of always having to take it. Such a position is, psychologically and emotionally speaking, almost unbearable. Rage and despair accumulate with no place to go.

    Elizabeth Stone, *Black Sheep and Kissing Cousins* (1988)

17 Prejudice is a seeping, dark stain, I think, more difficult to fight than hatred—which is powerful and violent and somehow more honest.

    Josephine Lawrence, *Let Us Consider One Another* (1945)

18 It's like a hair across your cheek. You can't see it, you can't find it with your fingers, but you keep brushing at it because the feel of it is irritating.

    Marian Anderson, with Emily Kimbrough, "My Life in a White World," in *Ladies' Home Journal* (1960)

19 You understand / That personally I feel / Indeed, I'd just as soon shake hands / Why, lots of them are just as / Why / As you and I.

    Eve Merriam, "Restricted," *Jewish Life* (1947)

20 Prejudices such as sexism and the deeply related homophobia, racism, and classism are not just personal problems, sets of peculiar and troubling beliefs. Exclusions and devaluations of whole groups of people on the scale and of the range, tenacity, and depth of racism and sexism and classism are

systemic and shape the world within which we all struggle to live and find meaning.

Elizabeth Kamarck Minnick, *Transforming Knowledge* (1990)

1 Whenever someone speaks with prejudice against a group—Catholics, Jews, Italians, Negroes—someone else usually comes up with a classic line of defense: "Look at Einstein!" "Look at Carver!" "Look at Toscanini!" So, of course, Catholics (or Jews, or Italians, or Negroes) must be all right. They mean well, these defenders. But their approach is wrong. It is even bad. What a minority group wants is not the right to have geniuses among them but the right to have fools and scoundrels without being condemned as a group.

Agnes E. Benedict (1940), in Joseph Telushkin, *Uncommon Sense* (1987)

2 The uncandid censurer always picks out the worst man of a class, and then confidently produces him as being a fair specimen of it.

Hannah More, *Coelebs in Search of a Wife* (1808)

3 Just as a child is born without fear, so is it born without prejudice. Prejudice, like fear, is acquired.

Marie Killilea, *Karen* (1952)

4 That is the way with people. . . . If they do you wrong, they invent a bad name for you, a good name for their acts and then destroy you in the name of virtue.

Zora Neale Hurston, *Moses: Man of the Mountain* (1939)

See also Anti-Semitism, Bigotry, Chauvinism, Discrimination, Injustice, Minorities, Oppression, Persecution, Race, Racism, Sexism.

# ❧ PREPAREDNESS

5 She had the loaded handbag of someone who camps out and seldom goes home, or who imagines life must be full of emergencies.

Mavis Gallant, *A Fairly Good Time* (1970)

6 I always knew I would turn a corner and run into this day, but I ain't prepared for it nohow.

Louise Meriwether, *Daddy Was a Number Runner* (1970)

See also Foresight.

# ❧ PRESENT

7 That was then, this is now.

S.E. Hinton, book title (1971)

8 No time like the present.

Mary Delarivière Manley, *The Lost Lover* (1696)

9 The present is the point of power.

Kate Green, *Night Angel* (1989)

10 My last defense / Is the present tense.

Gwendolyn Brooks, "Old Mary," *The Bean Eaters* (1960)

11 To those leaning on the sustaining infinite, today is big with blessings.

Mary Baker Eddy, *Science and Health* (1875)

12 The present was an egg laid by the past that had the future inside its shell.

Zora Neale Hurston, *Moses: Man of the Mountain* (1939)

13 Moments / of sinking my teeth / into now like a hungry fox: / never otherwise / am I so cruel; / never otherwise / so happy.

Marge Piercy, "Apologies," *The Moon Is Always Female* (1980)

14 To-morrow, yes, those songs will break my heart, / But I am only very glad to-night.

Dorothy L. Sayers, "Going-Down Play," *Op. I.* (1916)

15 Love the moment / and the energy / of that moment / will spread / beyond all / boundaries.

Corita Kent, *Moments* (1982)

16 The present was his; he would arrange the past to suit it.

Nadine Gordimer, *July's People* (1981)

17 I have learned to live each day as it comes, and not to borrow trouble by dreading tomorrow. It is the dark menace of the future that makes cowards of us.

Dorothy Dix, *Dorothy Dix—Her Book* (1926)

18 To live exhilaratingly in and for the moment is deadly serious work, fun of the most exhausting sort.

Barbara Grizzuti Harrison, "Oh, How We Worshiped the Gods of the Fifties!" *Off Center* (1980)

19 She was learning to love moments. To love moments for themselves.

Gwendolyn Brooks, *Maud Martha* (1953)

1 If you let yourself be absorbed completely, if you surrender completely to the moments as they pass, you live more richly those moments.

Anne Morrow Lindbergh, *Bring Me a Unicorn* (1971)

2 She seems to have had the ability to stand firmly on the rock of her past while living completely and unregretfully in the present.

Madeleine L'Engle, *The Summer of the Great-Grandmother* (1974)

3 The older one gets the more one feels that the present must be enjoyed: it is a precious gift, comparable to a state of grace.

Marie Curie (1928), in Eve Curie, *Madame Curie* (1938)

4 I take a sun bath and listen to the hours, formulating, and disintegrating under the pines, and smell the resiny hardihood of the high noon hours. The world is lost in a blue haze of distances, and the immediate sleeps in a thin and finite sun.

Zelda Fitzgerald (1938), in Nancy Milford, *Zelda* (1970)

5 The future has become uninhabitable. Such hopelessness can arise, I think, only from an inability to face the present, to live in the present, to live as a responsible being among other beings in this sacred world here and now, which is all we have, and all we need, to found our hope upon.

Ursula K. Le Guin, *Dancing at the Edge of the World* (1989)

6 We are tomorrow's past.

Mary Webb, *Precious Bane* (1924)

7 Every age, / Through being beheld too close, is ill-discerned / By those who have not lived past it.

Elizabeth Barrett Browning, *Aurora Leigh* (1856)

8 There is something about the present which we would not exchange, though we were offered a choice of all past ages to live in.

Virginia Woolf, "How It Strikes a Contemporary," *The Common Reader*, 1st series (1925)

See also Future, Past, Time.

## ✿ PRESIDENTS

9 Once a President gets to the White House, the only audience that is left that really matters is history.

Doris Kearns Goodwin, in *The New York Times* (1985)

10 Now he is a legend when he would have preferred to be a man.

Jacqueline Kennedy, on John F. Kennedy, "A Memoir," in *Look Magazine* (1964)

11 George Bush reminds every woman of her first husband.

Jane O'Reilly, in *GQ* (1984)

12 There is a character issue for Mr. Bush in this campaign. The clothes have no emperor.

Anna Quindlen, "No There There," *Thinking Out Loud* (1993)

13 Americans began with a president who couldn't tell a lie and now they have one who can't tell the truth.

Benazir Bhutto, on Richard M. Nixon, *Daughter of Destiny* (1989)

14 I am much more political than Jimmy and was more concerned about popularity and winning reelection, but I have to say that he had the courage to tackle the important issues, no matter how controversial—or politically damaging—they might be. . . . Often during his term, we used to sit around and try to think of something he was doing that was popular!

Rosalynn Carter, *First Lady From Plains* (1984)

15 In the habit of a political lifetime, Ronald Reagan innocently squirrels away tidbits of misinformation and then, sometimes years later, casually drops them into his public discourse, like gum balls in a quiche.

Lucy Howard, in *Newsweek* (1985)

16 I was cooking breakfast this morning for my kids, and I thought, "He's just like a Teflon frying pan: Nothing sticks to him."

Patricia Schroeder, on Ronald Reagan, in *The Boston Globe* (1984)

17 Reagan's genius as a communicator lies in his use of ambiguity. . . . Ambiguity is the mother of Teflon.

Robin Tolmach Lakoff, *Talking Power* (1990)

18 Ronald Reagan can't resist an appeal from defense contractors down on their luck. They ask him to spare a dime for a cup of coffee, and he gives them seven thousand dollars for a coffee maker. There wasn't a dry eye in the White House when the forgotten wealthy asked for a handout.

Geraldine A. Ferraro, with Linda Bird Francke, *Ferraro* (1985)

1 The charm of Ronald Reagan is not just that he kept telling us screwy things, it was that he believed them all. No wonder we trusted him, he never lied to us. . . . His stubbornness, even defiance, in the face of facts ("stupid things," he once called them in a memorable slip) was nothing short of splendid. . . . This is the man who proved that ignorance is no handicap to the presidency.

Molly Ivins, "Don't Worry, They're Happy," in *Savvy* (1989)

2 He'll outgrow it.

June Allyson, comforting Jane Wyman on then-husband Ronald Reagan's obsession with politics, in Celebrity Research Group, *The Bedside Book of Celebrity Gossip* (1984)

See also First Lady, Leadership.

## ❧ THE PRESS

3 The press is too often a distorting mirror, which deforms the people and events it represents, making them seem bigger or smaller than they really are.

Marguerite Yourcenar, *With Open Eyes* (1980)

4 Mother . . . considered a press conference on a par with a visit to a cage full of cobras.

Margaret Truman, *Bess W. Truman* (1986)

5 Minimum information given with maximum politeness.

Jacqueline Kennedy, guidelines for dealing with the press, in Ralph G. Martin, *A Hero for Our Time* (1983)

6 Never joke with the press. Irony does not translate into newsprint.

Erica Jong, *Serenissima* (1987)

7 In Czechoslovakia there is no such thing as freedom of the press. In the United States there is no such thing as freedom from the press.

Martina Navratilova, in Lee Green, *Sportswit* (1984)

See also Journalism, Journalists, Media, Newspapers, Publicity.

## ❧ PREVENTION

8 It is a good sanitary principle, that what is curative is preventive.

Anna Jameson, *A Commonplace Book* (1855)

## ❧ PRIDE

9 Pride is a tricky, glorious, double-edged feeling.

Adrienne Rich, "If Not With Others, How?" *Blood, Bread, and Poetry* (1986)

10 The best of all good friends is pride.

Gertrude Atherton, *Julia France and Her Times* (1912)

11 Pride never sleeps. The principle at least is always awake. An intemperate man is sometimes sober, but a proud man is never humble.

Hannah More, *Practical Piety* (1811)

12 Pride is never sinful when it is Justice.

Barbara Chase-Riboud, *Echo of Lions* (1989)

13 Wounded vanity knows when it is mortally hurt; and limps off the field, piteous, all disguises thrown away. But pride carries its banner to the last; and fast as it is driven from one field unfurls it in another.

Helen Hunt Jackson, *Ramona* (1884)

14 Supreme pride is supreme / renunciation.

Rosario Castellanos, "Foreign Woman," in Joanna Bankier and Deirdre Lashgari, eds., *Women Poets of the World* (1983)

15 He blinked his near-sighted eyes at us with the pleased and self-congratulatory air of a hen who has just laid a particularly fine egg.

E.S. Liddon, *The Riddle of the Florentine Folio* (1935)

See also Self-Esteem, Vanity.

## ❧ PRIGS

16 A prig is a fellow who is always making you a present of his opinions.

George Eliot, *Middlemarch* (1871)

## ❧ PRINCIPLES

17 If you don't stand for something, you will stand for anything.

Ginger Rogers, in *Parade* (1978)

1 Whenever two good people argue about principles, both are always right.

  Marie von Ebner-Eschenbach, *Aphorisms* (1893)

2 There is nothing as dangerous as an unembodied principle: no matter what blood flows, the principle comes first. The First Amendment absolutists operate precisely on unembodied principle.

  Andrea Dworkin, *Letters From a War Zone* (1988)

3 The first thing a principle does is to kill somebody.

  Dorothy L. Sayers, *Gaudy Night* (1935)

4 Too much principle is often more harmful than too little.

  Ellen Glasgow, *The Descendant* (1897)

See also Conscience, Convictions, Morality, Values.

## ❧ PRIORITIES

5 Every hour has its immediate duty, its special injunction which dominates all others.

  Marguerite Yourcenar, *Memoirs of Hadrian* (1951)

6 New battleships are readily ordered, when clinics, school meals, and ante-natal provision are counted as "extravagance."

  Winifred Holtby, *Women and a Changing Civilization* (1935)

See also Choice, Values.

## ❧ PRIVACY

7 Privacy—like eating and breathing—is one of life's basic requirements.

  Katherine Neville, *A Calculated Risk* (1992)

8 The human animal needs a freedom seldom mentioned, freedom from intrusion. He needs a little privacy quite as much as he wants understanding or vitamins or exercise or praise.

  Phyllis McGinley, "A Lost Privilege," *The Province of the Heart* (1959)

9 Privacy is granted to you by others, by their decency, by their understanding, by their compassionate behavior, by the laws of the land. It exists only when others let you have it—privacy is an accorded right.

  Alida Brill, *Nobody's Business* (1990)

10 All violations of essential privacy are brutalizing.

  Katharine Fullerton Gerould, *Modes and Morals* (1920)

11 Privacy is a privilege not granted to the aged or the young.

  Margaret Laurence, *The Stone Angel* (1964)

See also Rooms, Secrets, Solitude.

## ❧ PRIVATION

12 Privation is the source of appetite.

  Sor Juana Inés de la Cruz (1691), in Margaret Sayers Peden, tr., *A Woman of Genius* (1982)

13 All sorts of spiritual gifts come through privations, if they are accepted.

  Janet Erskine Stuart, in Maud Monahan, *Life and Letters of Janet Erskine Stuart* (1922)

14 The best thing to do with the best things in life is to give them up.

  Dorothy Day, in "Saints Among Us," *Time* (1975)

See also Frugality, Hunger, Poverty, Suffering.

## ❧ PRIVILEGE

15 Privilege is the greatest enemy of right.

  Marie von Ebner-Eschenbach, *Aphorisms* (1893)

16 To acknowledge privilege is the first step in making it available for wider use.

  Audre Lorde, title essay, *A Burst of Light* (1988)

17 No privileged order ever did see the wrongs of its own victims.

  Elizabeth Cady Stanton, speech (1867), in Elizabeth Cady Stanton, Susan B. Anthony, and Matilda J. Gage, eds., *The History of Woman Suffrage*, vol. 2 (1881)

18 There is no denying that there are "royal roads" through existence for the upper classes; for them, at least, the highways are macadamized, swept, and watered.

  L.E. Landon, *Ethel Churchill* (1837)

1 Privilege, almost by definition, requires that someone else pay the price for its enjoyment.

> Paula Ross, "Women, Oppression, Privilege, and Competition," in Valerie Miner and Helen E. Longino, eds., *Competition* (1987)

See also Oppression.

## ❦ PROBLEMS

2 Serious difficulties don't vanish by themselves, they are standing around your bed when you open the eyes the next morning.

> Vicki Baum, *I Know What I'm Worth* (1964)

3 Problems, unfortunately, can be addicting. Like it or not, we take a certain amount of pride in the very problems that distress us.

> Eloise Ristad, *A Soprano on Her Head* (1982)

4 A problem that presents itself as a dilemma carries an unfortunate prescription: to argue instead of act.

> Elizabeth Janeway, *Improper Behavior* (1987)

5 When one's own problems are unsolvable, and all best efforts frustrated, it is life-saving to listen to other people's problems.

> Suzanne Massie, in Robert and Suzanne Massie, *Journey* (1975)

6 Some people always assume that if you mention a problem, you caused it.

> Sonia Johnson, *Going Out of Our Minds* (1987)

See also Crises, Trouble.

## ❦ PROCRASTINATION

7 The path of duty I clearly trace, / I stand with conscience face to face, / And all her pleas allow; / Calling and crying the while for grace,— / "Some other time, and some other place; / Oh, not to-day; not now!"

> Alice Cary, "Not Now," *The Poetical Works of Alice and Phoebe Cary* (1876)

8 That which is always within our reach, is always the last thing we take; and the chances are, that what we can do every day, we never do at all.

> L.E. Landon, *Romance and Reality* (1831)

9 What may be done at any time, is never done.

> Mrs. Henry Wood, *East Lynne* (1861)

10 If you have a deadly fruit to give, it will not grow sweeter by keeping.

> Ralph Iron, *The Story of an African Farm* (1883)

11 Delay breeds fear.

> Jessamyn West, *The Life I Really Lived* (1979)

12 I . . . practiced all the arts of apology, evasion, and invisibility, to which procrastinators must sooner or later be reduced.

> Maria Edgeworth, "To-Morrow," *Popular Tales* (1804)

13 Why not seize the pleasure at once? - How often is happiness destroyed by preparation, foolish preparation!

> Jane Austen, *Emma* (1816)

## ❦ PROFIT

14 No mass appeal. Ergo no profit. Ergo no use. The current World Credo.

> Lucille Kallen, *The Tanglewood Murder* (1980)

15 Society cares for the individual only in so far as he is profitable.

> Simone de Beauvoir, *The Coming of Age* (1970)

16 The suppression of civil liberties is to many less a matter of horror than the curtailment of the freedom to profit.

> Marya Mannes, *But Will It Sell?* (1964)

17 A hobby is, of course, an abomination, as are all consuming interests and passions that do not lead directly to large, personal gain.

> Fran Lebowitz, *Metropolitan Life* (1978)

18 What most people don't seem to realize is that there is just as much money to be made out of the wreckage of a civilization as from the upbuilding of one.

> Margaret Mitchell, *Gone With the Wind* (1936)

See also Business, Money, Surplus.

## ✿ PROGRESS

1 Progress. There's a good deal too much o' this progress about nowadays, an', what's more, it'll have to stop.

> Winifred Holtby, "The Apostate" (1925), *Truth Is Not Sober* (1934)

2 Progress—progress is the dirtiest word in the language—who ever told us— / And made us believe it—that to take a step forward was necessarily, was always / A good idea?

> Edna St. Vincent Millay, "We Have Gone Too Far," *Collected Poems* (1949)

3 People tend to think that life really does progress for everyone eventually, that people progress, but actually only *some* people progress. The rest of the people don't.

> Alice Walker, in Claudia Tate, ed., *Black Women Writers at Work* (1983)

4 "Progress" affects few. Only revolution can affect many.

> Alice Walker (1978), in Gloria T. Hull, Patricia Bell Scott, and Barbara Smith, eds., *All the Women Are White, All the Blacks Are Men, But Some of Us Are Brave* (1982)

5 If a man has lived in a tradition which tells him that nothing can be done about his human condition, to believe that progress is possible may well be the greatest revolution of all.

> Barbara Ward, *The Unity of the Free World* (1961)

6 There is an unlucky tendency . . . to allow every new invention to add to life's complications, and every new power to increase life's hustling; so that, unless we can dominate the mischief, we are really the worse off instead of the better.

> Vernon Lee, "My Bicycle and I," *Hortus Vitae* (1904)

7 Whoever said progress was a positive thing has never been to Florida or California.

> Rita Mae Brown, *Bingo* (1988)

8 *Why* do progress and beauty have to be so opposed?

> Anne Morrow Lindbergh (1929), *Hour of Gold, Hour of Lead* (1973)

9 Things that don't get better, get worse.

> Ellen Sue Stern, *The Indispensable Woman* (1988)

10 This seems to be the law of progress in everything we do; it moves along a spiral rather than a perpen-dicular; we seem to be actually going out of the way, and yet it turns out that we were really moving upward all the time.

> Frances E. Willard, *A Wheel Within a Wheel* (1895)

11 Even the "worst blizzard of the century" accumulates one flake at a time.

> Mary Kay Blakely, *American Mom* (1994)

12 Perhaps all human progress stems from the tension between two basic drives: to have just what everyone else has and to have what no one has.

> Judith Stone, *Light Elements* (1991)

13 We have not crawled so very far / up our individual grass-blade / toward our individual star.

> H.D., *The Walls Do Not Fall* (1944)

See also Change, Growth, Success.

## ✿ PROHIBITION

14 Prohibition is a hard sounding word, worthless as a rallying cry, hard as a locked door or going to bed without your supper.

> Nellie L. McClung, *The Stream Runs Fast* (1945)

See also Temperance.

## ✿ PROMISCUITY

15 Boredom is often the cause of promiscuity, and always its result.

> Mignon McLaughlin, *The Neurotic's Notebook* (1963)

16 Promiscuous . . . was a word I had never applied to myself. Possibly no one ever does, for it is a sordid word, reducing many valuable moments to nothing more than doglike copulation.

> Marya Mannes, *Message From a Stranger* (1948)

See also Sex.

## ✿ PROMISES

17 Promises are the uniquely human way of ordering the future.

> Hannah Arendt, "Civil Disobedience," *Crises of the Republic* (1972)

1 Every organization of men, be it social or political, ultimately relies on man's capacity for making promises and keeping them.

Hannah Arendt, "Civil Disobedience," *Crises of the Republic* (1972)

2 Promises that you make to yourself are often like the Japanese plum tree—they bear no fruit.

Frances Marion, *Off With Their Heads* (1972)

3 I know how much you promises mean. Promisin talk don' cook rice.

Julia Peterkin, *Scarlet Sister Mary* (1928)

4 No vows are less sincere than those made in anger.

Sarah Scott, *The History of Cornelia* (1750)

## ❧ PROPHECY

5 Among all forms of mistake, prophecy is the most gratuitous.

George Eliot, *Middlemarch* (1872)

6 You can trust a crystal ball about as far as you can throw it.

Faith Popcorn, *The Popcorn Report* (1991)

7 To be a prophet it is sufficient to be a pessimist.

Elsa Triolet, *Proverbes d'Elsa* (1971)

See also Visions.

## ❧ PROSTITUTION

8 I am white and middle-class and ambitious, and I have no trouble identifying with either the call girl or the street hustler, and I can explain why in one sentence: I've been working to support myself in the city for fifteen years, and I've had more offers to sell my body for money than I have had to be an executive.

Susan Brownmiller (1971), in Anne Koedt, Ellen Levine, and Anita Rapone, eds., *Radical Feminism* (1973)

9 A call girl is simply someone who hates poverty more than she hates sin.

Sydney Biddle Barrows, *Mayflower Madam* (1986)

10 Prostitution means sexual intercourse between a man and a woman aimed at satisfying the man's sexual and the woman's economic needs. It is obvious that sexual needs, even in a male dominated system, are not as urgent and important as economic needs which, if not satisfied, lead to disease and death. Yet society considers the woman's economic need as less vital than the man's sexual one.

Nawal El Saadawi, *The Hidden Face of Eve* (1980)

11 Whether our reformers admit it or not, the economic and social inferiority of woman is responsible for prostitution.

Emma Goldman, "The Traffic in Women," *Anarchism* (1910)

12 There are *scores of thousands* of *women* who are denominated prostitutes, and who are supported by *hundreds of thousands* of *men* who should, for like reasons, also be denominated prostitutes, since what will change a woman into a prostitute must also necessarily change a man into the same.

Victoria Woodhull (1871), in *Woodhull and Claflin's Weekly* (1873)

13 The contempt which men feel for the prostitute, and the fact that they have always regarded themselves as far superior to her, even when they made use of her, suggests an attempt to rationalize the situation; it might be explained as an unconscious transference to the woman of the shame they feel for themselves in these relations.

Alison Neilans, "Changes in Sex Morality," in Ray Strachey, ed., *Our Freedom and Its Results* (1936)

14 On some level, almost every client wanted to believe that the girl was spending time with him not for money, but because she found him irresistible.

Sydney Biddle Barrows, *Mayflower Madam* (1986)

15 The grocer, the butcher, the baker, the merchant, the landlord, the druggist, the liquor dealer, the policeman, the doctor, the city father and the politician—these are the people who make money out of prostitution.

Polly Adler, *A House Is Not a Home* (1953)

16 The one thing prostitution is *not* is a "victimless crime." It attracts a wide species of preying criminals and generates a long line of victims, beginning with the most obvious and least understood—the prostitute herself.

Gail Sheehy, *Hustling* (1973)

17 There's a Book that says we're all sinners and I at least chose a sin that's made quite a few people happier than they were before they met me, a sin

that's left me with very little time to consider other extremely popular moral misdemeanors, like usury, intolerance, bearing false tales, extortion, racial bigotry, and the casting of that first stone.

> Sally Stanford, *The Lady of the House* (1966)

1 I may be good for nothing, but I'm never bad for nothing.

> Ginny, in Sydney Biddle Barrows, *Mayflower Madam* (1986)

2 Why is it immoral to be paid for an act that is perfectly legal if done for free?

> Gloria Allred and Lisa Bloom, Los Angeles Times-Washington Post News Services (1994)

3 I've made so many movies playing a hooker that they don't pay me in the regular way any more. They leave it on the dresser.

> Shirley MacLaine, *Out on a Limb* (1983)

## ❦ PROTEST

4 If I cannot air this pain and alter it, I will surely die of it. That's the beginning of social protest.

> Audre Lorde, in Claudia Tate, ed., *Black Women Writers at Work* (1983)

5 If one is going to change things, one has to make a fuss and catch the eye of the world.

> Elizabeth Janeway, in Barbaralee Diamonstein, *Open Secrets* (1972)

6 Don't agonize. Organize.

> Florynce R. Kennedy, in Gloria Steinem, "The Verbal Karate of Florynce R. Kennedy," *Ms.* (1973)

7 Responsible dissent is the essence of democracy.

> Abigail McCarthy, *Private Faces/Public Places* (1972)

8 All demonstrations . . . say, "You are rich and therefore powerful, we are very numerous and therefore potentially powerful. If we unite, our weakness and your power may cease."

> Mary Heaton Vorse (1932), in Dee Garrison, ed., *Rebel Pen* (1985)

9 The argument of the broken window pane is the most valuable argument in modern politics.

> Emmeline Pankhurst, in George Dangerfield, *The Strange Death of Liberal England* (1935)

10 The condition of our sex is so deplorable that it is our duty even to break the law in order to call attention to the reasons why we do so.

> Emmeline Pankhurst, speech (1908)

11 The human race / Has climbed on protest.

> Ella Wheeler Wilcox, "Protest," *Poems of Problems* (1914)

See also Movements, Opposition, Resistance, Revolution, Social Change.

## ❦ PROTOCOL

12 Protocol is etiquette with a government expense account.

> Judith Martin, *Gilbert* (1982)

13 Can't we do a couple of things halfway around here?

> Princess Grace of Monaco, to Prince Rainier III, in Steven Englund, *Grace of Monaco* (1984)

See also Etiquette, Manners.

## ❦ PROVERBS

14 Proverbs . . . are short sayings made out of long experience.

> Zora Neale Hurston, *Moses: Man of the Mountain* (1939)

See also Aphorisms, Quotations

## ❦ PROVIDENCE

15 The well of Providence is deep. It is the buckets we bring to it that are small.

> Mary Webb, in *Ladies' Home Journal* (1946)

16 When we reckon without Providence, we must frequently reckon twice.

> Marie de Rabutin-Chantal, Marquise de Sévigné (1672), *Letters of Madame de Sévigné to Her Daughter and Her Friends*, vol. 2 (1811)

See also God.

## ❧ PROXIMITY

1 Proximity was their support; like walls after an earthquake they could fall no further for they had fallen against each other.

Elizabeth Bowen, *Friends and Relations* (1931)

2 The longest absence is less perilous to love than the terrible trials of incessant proximity.

Ouida, *Wisdom, Wit and Pathos* (1884)

3 Love at a distance may be poignant; it is also idealized. Contact, more than separation, is the test of attachment.

Ilka Chase, *Free Admission* (1948)

See also Relationships.

## ❧ PSYCHIATRY

4 In psychoanalysis as in art, God resided in the details, the discovery of which required enormous patience, unyielding seriousness, and the skill of an acrobat—walking a tightrope over memory and speculation, instinct and theory, feeling and denial.

Judith Rossner, *August* (1983)

5 All the art of analysis consists in saying a truth only when the other person is ready for it, has been prepared for it by an organic process of gradation and evolution.

Anaïs Nin (1932), *The Diary of Anaïs Nin*, vol. 1 (1966)

6 Is it sufficient that you have learned to drive the car, or shall we look and see what is under the hood? Most people go through life without ever knowing.

June Singer, *Boundaries of the Soul* (1972)

7 If analysis works, you find out that the awful truths about yourself are not so awful. At the very least, you find out they're not original.

Betty Rollin, *First, You Cry* (1976)

8 Analysts keep having to pick away at the scab that the patient tries to form between himself and the analyst to cover over his wound. . . . The analyst . . . keeps the surface raw, so that the wound will heal properly.

Janet Malcolm, *Psychoanalysis* (1981)

9 Fortunately analysis is not the only way to resolve inner conflicts. Life itself still remains a very effective therapist.

Karen Horney, *Our Inner Conflicts* (1945)

10 Freud is the father of psychoanalysis. It had no mother.

Germaine Greer, *The Female Eunuch* (1970)

11 Freud's sexism as much as his sex shaped the patriarchal and phallocentric bias of his theory and therapy.

Janet Sayers, *Mothers of Psychoanalysis* (1991)

12 It's my profession to bring people from various outlying districts of the mind to the normal. There seems to be a general feeling it's the place where they ought to be. Sometimes I don't see the urgency myself.

Rebecca West, *The Return of the Soldier* (1918)

13 She turned, as always, to analysis, being a twentieth-century woman and so subject to the superstition that what the mind could understand couldn't any longer hurt the heart, that what the tongue could utter was in the hand's control.

Marilyn French, *The Bleeding Heart* (1980)

14 Miracles occur in psychoanalysis as seldom as anywhere else.

Karen Horney, *Self-Analysis* (1942)

15 Psychiatry is a dirty mirror.

Anne Sexton (1961), in Linda Gray Sexton and Lois Ames, eds., *Anne Sexton: A Self-Portrait in Letters* (1977)

16 When mental sickness increases until it reaches the danger point, do not exhaust yourself by efforts to trace back to original causes. Better accept them as inevitable and save your strength to fight against the effects.

George Sand (1837), in Marie Jenny Howe, ed., *The Intimate Journal of George Sand* (1929)

17 I'm devoting my life to being a psychiatric patient. It's a vocation, like being a nun, only a lot more expensive.

Joyce Rebeta-Burditt, *The Cracker Factory* (1977)

18 He discovered therapy, and psychoanalysis became the great drama of his life. He absorbed its language and its insights in much the same way that he read great literature: he became wise in a vacuum.

Vivian Gornick, *Fierce Attachments* (1987)

1 People coming away from a session with Dr. S. usually looked as if they had had fifty minutes on the anvil with an apprentice blacksmith.

Margaret Halsey, *No Laughing Matter* (1977)

2 He would let me tell my dreams. That's the main difference between a husband and a psychoanalyst.

Lillian Day, *Kiss and Tell* (1931)

3 "You seem to be reacting to your boyfriend as if he were your father," your shrink may say stonily (unless she is a strict Freudian, in which case she'll shut up and wait until you think of it yourself, a process that usually takes ten years. This is why strict Freudians have such lovely summer houses).

Cynthia Heimel, *Sex Tips for Girls* (1983)

4 I think people who go to a psychiatrist ought to have their heads examined.

Jane Ace (1940), in Goodman Ace, *Ladies and Gentlemen, Easy Aces* (1970)

See also Insanity, Madness, Mental Illness, Psychology, Therapy, The Unconscious.

## ❧ PSYCHOLOGY

5 It is easier to study the "behavior" of rats than people, because rats are smaller and have fewer outside commitments. So modern psychology is mostly about rats.

Celia Green, *The Decline and Fall of Science* (1976)

6 Psychology which explains everything / explains nothing, / and we are still in doubt.

Marianne Moore, "Marriage," *Selected Poems* (1935)

7 The phenomenal success of the recovery movement reflects two simple truths that emerge in adolescence: all people love to talk about themselves, and most people are mad at their parents. You don't have to be in denial to doubt that truths like these will set us free.

Wendy Kaminer, *I'm Dysfunctional, You're Dysfunctional* (1992)

8 What might once have been called whining is now exalted as a process of asserting selfhood; self-absorption is regarded as a form of self-expression.

Wendy Kaminer, *I'm Dysfunctional, You're Dysfunctional* (1992)

See also Mental Illness, Psychiatry, Self-Help Books, Therapy.

## ❧ THE PUBLIC

9 Since there is no such entity as "the public," since the public is merely a number of individuals, any claimed or implied conflict of "the public interest" with private interests means that the interests of some men are to be sacrificed to the interests and wishes of others. Since the concept is so conveniently undefinable, its use rests only on any given gang's ability to proclaim that "The public, *c'est moi*."

Ayn Rand, *The Virtue of Selfishness* (1964)

10 People on the whole are very simple-minded, in whatever country one finds them. They are so simple as to take literally, more often than not, the things their leaders tell them.

Pearl S. Buck, *What America Means to Me* (1943)

11 The public is more easily swayed by persons than by principles.

Rachel Field, *All This and Heaven Too* (1939)

12 Only when human sorrows are turned into a toy with glaring colors will baby people become interested—for a while at least. The people are a very fickle baby that must have new toys every day.

Emma Goldman, "The Traffic in Women," *Anarchism* (1910)

13 The "public"—a term often used in America to indicate the great metropolitan newspapers.

Mary Beard, *A Short History of the American Labor Movement* (1920)

14 Great bodies of people are never responsible for what they do.

Virginia Woolf, *A Room of One's Own* (1929)

See also Public Opinion.

## ❧ PUBLICITY

15 Press agent—a man who hitches his braggin' to a star.

Hedda Hopper, in *Reader's Digest* editors, *Fun Fare* (1949)

16 Where would anyone in publicity be if they allowed sensitivity, restraint, breeding or good taste to stand in their way?

Isabelle Holland, *Moncrief* (1975)

1 In the press, my sex life was something else again. I was Lady Bountiful of the Sheets. Some of the best fiction of the Sixties was written about my amorous adventures with an assortment of lovers who could have only been chosen by a berserk random sampler.

　　Doris Day, in A.E. Hotchner, *Doris Day* (1975)

2 Here I am, one of the most colorful women of my time—if not of my block—being made to sound positively legumelike in printed interviews.

　　Bette Midler, *A View From a Broad* (1980)

3 Almost anyone who has ever attained any kind of public stature in his or her profession can expect sometimes to see a reflection in a cracked mirror.

　　Louella Parsons, *The Gay Illiterate* (1944)

4 If some people are right, artists are put into this world not to practice their art, but to talk about it. And judging by the flattering invitations many a humble climber will receive to pontificate from the lowest rung but one of the ladder, humanity is in a dangerously receptive frame of mind, and artists a race devoid of either modesty or sense of humor.

　　Ethel Smyth, *Streaks of Life* (1922)

5 Small talents have gone very far in this age. Just as the microphone gave volume to voices that had none, so does the science of press-agentry magnify limited skills into highly saleable properties.

　　Marya Mannes, *More in Anger* (1958)

6 Talent may not be for sale, but the best way to package and display your gift is.

　　Helen Hayes, with Sandford Dody, *On Reflection* (1968)

7 You've got to win in sports—that's talent—but you've also got to learn how to remind everybody how you did win, and how often. That comes with experience.

　　Billie Jean King, with Frank Deford, *Billie Jean* (1982)

8 I don't care what is written about me—so long as it isn't true.

　　Katharine Hepburn, news item (1954)

9 Don't read your publicity—weigh it.

　　Kathleen Winsor, *Star Money* (1950)

See also Advertising, Attention.

## ❧ PUBLIC OPINION

10 In America, public opinion is the leader.

　　Frances Perkins, *People at Work* (1934)

11 Public Opinion, this invisible, intangible, omnipresent, despotic tyrant; this thousand-headed Hydra—the more dangerous for being composed of individual mediocrities.

　　H.P. Blavatsky, in *Spiritual Scientist* (1875)

12 Public opinion,—a tyrant, sitting in the dark, wrapt up in mystification and vague terrors of obscurity; deriving power no one knows from whom. . . ,—but irresistible in its power to quell thought, to repress action, to silence conviction.

　　Harriet Martineau, *Society in America*, vol. 3 (1837)

13 I've seen public opinion shift like a wind and put out the very fire it lighted.

　　Rachel Field, *All This and Heaven Too* (1939)

See also Opinion, Polls.

## ❧ PUBLISHING

14 It may be said of me by Harper & Brothers, that although I reject their proposals, I welcome their advances.

　　Edna St. Vincent Millay (1948), in Allan Ross Macdougall, ed., *Letters of Edna St. Vincent Millay* (1952)

15 I don't believe in publishers who wish to butter their bannocks on both sides while they'll hardly allow an author to smell treacle. I consider they are too grabby altogether and like Methodists they love to keep the Sabbath and everything else they can lay hands upon.

　　Amanda McKittrick Ros, letter (1910), in Frank Ormsby, ed., *Thine in Storm and Calm* (1988)

16 Writers are always a great nuisance to publishers. If they could do without them, they would.

　　Fay Weldon, in Sybil Steinberg, ed., *Writing for Your Life* (1992)

17 Either you run your publishing business far away, where your writer can't get at it, or you publish right alongside of him—and have much more fun—and much more expense.

　　Sylvia Beach, on publishing James Joyce, *Shakespeare and Company* (1956)

1 Publishers, theatrical managers, and critics ask not for the quality inherent in creative art, but will it meet with a good sale, will it suit the palate of the people? Alas, this palate is like a dumping ground; it relishes anything that needs no mental mastication.

    Emma Goldman, "Minorities Versus Majorities," *Anarchism* (1910)

2 The publishing business is an amoral industry.

    Carol Ehrlich, "The Woman Book Industry," in Joan Huber, ed., *Changing Women in a Changing Society* (1973)

3 The writer—more especially the novelist—who has not, at one moment or another, considered his publisher unworthy of him, has still to be conceived.

    Storm Jameson, *Journey From the North*, vol. 1 (1969)

4 The share of the sympathetic publisher in the author's success—the true success so different from the ephemeral—is apt to be overlooked in these blatant days, so it is just as well that some of us should keep it in mind.

    Ellen Glasgow, *Letters of Ellen Glasgow* (1958)

5 The publishing firmament pales / When the firms that once shone as its stars / become Jonahs / En-Gulfed by conglomerate whales.

    Felicia Lamport, "Brief History of Publishing—From Start to. . . ," *Light Metres* (1982)

6 Most publishers, like most writers, are ruined by their successes.

    Willa Cather, "My First Novels" (1931), *On Writing* (1949)

See also Books, Editors, Magazines, Writing.

## ✸ PUNCTUALITY

7 I am a member of a small, nearly extinct minority group, a kind of urban lost tribe who insist, in the face of all evidence to the contrary, on the sanctity of being on time. Which is to say that we On-timers are compulsively, unfashionably prompt, that there are only handfuls of us in any given city and, unfortunately, we never seem to have appointments with each other.

    Ellen Goodman, *Close to Home* (1979)

8 Punctuality comes high on my list of unforgivable sins.

    Dorothy Cannell, *The Thin Woman* (1984)

9 Punctuality is the thief of time.

    Sara Jeannette Duncan, *A Voyage of Consolation* (1898)

10 Punctuality is a praiseworthy virtue enough, but as the years went on, Mrs. Todd blew her breakfast horn at so early an hour that the neighbors were in some doubt as to whether it might not herald the supper of the day before. They also predicted that she would have her funeral before she was fairly dead.

    Kate Douglas Wiggin, "The Midnight Cry," *The Village Watch-Tower* (1895)

See also Lateness, Timeliness.

## ✸ PUNCTUATION

11 Punctuation has its own philosophy, just as style does, although not as language does. Style is a good understanding of language, punctuation is a good understanding of style.

    George Sand, *Impressions et Souvenirs* (1873)

12 Punctuation is biological. It is the physical indication of the body-rhythms which the reader is to acknowledge.

    Muriel Rukeyser, *The Life of Poetry* (1949)

13 A comma by helping you along holding your coat for you and putting on your shoes keeps you from living your life as actively as you should live it.

    Gertrude Stein (1946), in Elizabeth Sprigge, *Gertrude Stein* (1957)

14 I like to use as few commas as possible so that sentences will go down in one swallow without touching the sides.

    Florence King, *Reflections in a Jaundiced Eye* (1989)

15 Hyphens, like cats, are capable of arousing tenderness or shudders.

    Pamela Frankau, *Pen to Paper* (1961)

16 I will use a form of punctuation of my own, which will be something like this—when one is beginning he takes a long breath, for this use a capital. When he stops for breath, a comma, and when it is all gone, a period. Don't know the use of a semi-colon, but expect it is when one thinks he is out of breath and isn't.

    Anne Ellis, *The Life of an Ordinary Woman* (1929)

## ❦ PUNISHMENT

1 We are generally punished by where we have sinned.

> Charlotte-Elisabeth, Duchesse d'Orléans (1718), *Life and Letters of Charlotte Elizabeth* (1889)

2 Corporal punishment is as humiliating for him who gives it as for him who receives it; it is ineffective besides. Neither shame nor physical pain have any other effect than a hardening one.

> Ellen Key, *The Century of the Child* (1909)

See also Abuse, Discipline, Violence.

## ❦ PURGATORY

3 I see no reason why I should not live on indefinitely just as I have done, and on the whole I am more comfortable here than in Purgatory, a place that I imagine to be like the suburbs of London.

> Mary Borden, *Jane—Our Stranger* (1923)

## ❦ PURITY

4 Purity strikes me as the most mysterious of the virtues and the more I think about it the less I know about it.

> Flannery O'Connor, in Sally Fitzgerald, ed., *The Habit of Being* (1979)

See also Innocence, Virtue.

## ❦ PURPOSE

5 Nothing contributes so much to tranquilize the mind as a steady purpose—a point on which the soul may fix its intellectual eye.

> Mary Shelley, *Frankenstein* (1818)

6 There are days when I am envious of my hens: / when I hunger for a purpose as perfect and sure / as a single daily egg.

> Barbara Kingsolver, "Apotheosis," *Another America* (1992)

7 To want to be what one *can* be is purpose in life.

> Cynthia Ozick, *Trust* (1966)

8 I am in the world / to change the world.

> Muriel Rukeyser, "Käthe Kollwitz," *The Speed of Darkness* (1968)

See also Function, Goals, Incentive, Meaning, Motives.

## ❦ PUZZLEMENT

9 Miss Doggett again looked puzzled; it was as if she had heard that men only wanted one thing, but had forgotten for the moment what it was.

> Barbara Pym, *Jane and Prudence* (1953)

See also Confusion, Uncertainty.

## Q

### ❧ QUANTITY

1 There are six of the one and half-a-dozen of the other.
   L.E. Landon, *Romance and Reality* (1831)

2 The lure of quantity is the most dangerous of all.
   Simone Weil, *First and Last Notebooks* (1970)

3 Counting is the religion of this generation it is its hope and its salvation.
   Gertrude Stein, *Everybody's Autobiography* (1937)

4 Every true American likes to think in terms of thousands and millions. The word "million" is probably the most pleasure-giving vocable in the language.
   Agnes Repplier, "The Unconscious Humor of the Movies," *Times and Tendencies* (1931)

5 Too few is as many as too many.
   Gertrude Stein, *Everybody's Autobiography* (1937)

See also Size, Surplus.

### ❧ QUARRELS

6 The quarrel between them was a terrible treadmill they mounted together and tramped round and round until they were wearied out or in despair.
   Katherine Anne Porter, *Ship of Fools* (1962)

7 For forty-seven years they had been married. How deep back the stubborn, gnarled roots of the quarrel reached, no one could say—but only now, when tending to the needs of others no longer shackled them together, the roots swelled up visible, split the earth between them, and the tearing shook even to the children, long since grown.
   Tillie Olsen, title story, *Tell Me a Riddle* (1956)

8 They had quarreled about this single, solitary sore point: their life.
   Annie Dillard, *The Living* (1992)

9 Never go to bed mad—stay up and fight.
   Phyllis Diller, *Phyllis Diller's Housekeeping Hints* (1966)

10 I don't even remember what Mother and I quarreled about: it is a continual quarrel that began when I reached puberty.
   Marge Piercy, *Braided Lives* (1982)

11 In time they quarreled, of course, and about an abstraction—as young people often do, as mature people almost never do.
   Willa Cather, "Coming, Aphrodite!" *Youth and the Bright Medusa* (1920)

12 It is very often astonishing to each one quarreling to find out what the other one was remembering for quarreling. Mostly in quarreling not any one is finding out what the other one is remembering for quarreling, what the other one is remembering from quarreling.
   Gertrude Stein, *The Making of Americans* (1925)

13 During a quarrel, to have said too little may be mended; to have said too much, not always.
   Minna Thomas Antrim, *Sweethearts and Beaux* (1905)

14 Bad quarrels come when two people are wrong. Worse quarrels come when two people are right.
   Betty Smith, *Tomorrow Will Be Better* (1948)

15 To talk over a quarrel, with its inevitable accompaniment of self-justification, is too much like handling cobwebs to be very successful.
   Margaret Deland, *Philip and His Wife* (1894)

1 They buried the hatchet, but in a shallow, well-marked grave.

Dorothy Walworth, in *The Reader's Digest Dictionary of Quotations* (1968)

See also Arguments, Conflict.


## ❧ QUESTIONS

2 The impulse to ask questions is among the more primitive human lusts.

Rose Macaulay, "Into Questions and Answers," *A Casual Commentary* (1926)

3 The power to question is the basis of all human progress.

Indira Gandhi (1970), *Speeches and Writings* (1975)

4 If we would have new knowledge, we must get us a whole world of new questions.

Susanne K. Langer, *Philosophy in a New Key* (1942)

5 The only questions that really matter are the ones you ask yourself.

Ursula K. Le Guin, in *The Writer* (1992)

6 Time does not dispose of a question—it only presents it anew in a different guise.

Agatha Christie, *The Mysterious Mr. Quin* (1930)

7 Once you start asking questions, innocence is gone.

Mary Astor, *A Life on Film* (1967)

8 Questions which cannot be freed by words find it easy to slip into the blood stream, changing the body's chemistry, changing a whole life, sometimes.

Lillian Smith, *The Journey* (1954)

9 Bromidic though it may sound, some questions *don't* have answers, which is a terribly difficult lesson to learn.

Katharine Graham, in Jane Howard, "The Power That Didn't Corrupt," *Ms.* (1974)

10 Asking questions in therapy would be so helpful if anyone ever answered them accurately. But no one ever does.

Virginia M. Axline, *Dibs: In Search of Self* (1964)

11 The art of clinical diagnosis lies in the ability to ask the right questions.

Harriet B. Braiker, *The Type E* Woman* (1986)

12 The way a question is asked limits and disposes the ways in which any answer to it—right or wrong—may be given.

Susanne K. Langer, *Philosophy in a New Key* (1942)

13 You never answer a question nobody does.

Gertrude Stein, *The Geographical History of America* (1936)

14 Hypothetical questions get hypothetical answers.

Joan Baez, *Daybreak* (1968)

15 There are no right answers to wrong questions.

Ursula K. Le Guin, *Planet of Exile* (1975)

16 She was the kind of woman who liked to ask questions to which she already knew the answers. It gave her a sense of security.

Margaret Millar, *The Soft Talkers* (1957)

17 Never, never, never, on cross-examination ask a witness a question you don't already know the answer to, was a tenet I absorbed with my baby-food. Do it, and you'll often get an answer you don't want.

Harper Lee, *To Kill a Mockingbird* (1960)

18 She had the habit into which your poor conversationalists usually fall, namely, asking questions. I know nothing more disagreeable . . . than to be subjected to the society of a questioner.

Mrs. Sarah J. Hale, *Sketches of American Character* (1829)

19 It is not the correct thing to scold children for asking questions: this is about as reasonable as to scold them for breathing or thinking.

Florence Howe Hall, *The Correct Thing* (1902)

20 Children ask better questions than do adults. "May I have a cookie?" "Why is the sky blue?" and "What does a cow say?" are far more likely to elicit a cheerful response than "Where's your manuscript?" "Why haven't you called?" and "Who's your lawyer?"

Fran Lebowitz, *Metropolitan Life* (1974)

See also Answers, Curiosity, Nosiness, Why.


## ❧ QUICK THINKING

21* Never mind, Mary. Just take this turkey back to the kitchen and bring in the other one.

Mrs. Calvin Coolidge, to the maid who dropped the turkey on the floor, in Bennett Cerf, *The Laugh's on Me* (1959)

## ❧ QUILTS

1 knotted with love / the quilts sing on.

> Teresa Palma Acosta, "My Mother Pieced Quilts," in
> Joanna Bankier and Deirdre Lashgari, eds., *Women Poets of
> the World* (1983)

2 What my mother teaches me are the essential lessons of the quilt: that people and actions do move in multiple directions at once.

> Elsa Barkley Brown, "African-American Women's
> Quilting," in *SIGNS* (1989)

3 My focus on silence is to be understood as an intrinsic part of the body's search for meaning amongst the noisy assaults of everyday life. . . . What quilts have brought to the viewing of art generally is this intervening layer of silence, of collected thought and concerted attention.

> Radka Donnell, *Quilts As Women's Art* (1990)

## ❧ QUITTING

4 There comes a time when every scientist, even God, has to write off an experiment.

> P.D. James, *Devices and Desires* (1989)

5 Some things are best mended by a break.

> Edith Wharton, *The Custom of the Country* (1913)

6 The more you kick something that's dead, the worse it smells.

> Barbara Stanwyck (1941), in Al DiOrio, *Barbara Stanwyck*
> (1984)

See also Desertion, Running Away.

## ❧ QUOTATIONS

7 The next best thing to being clever is being able to quote some one who is.

> Mary Pettibone Poole, *A Glass Eye at a Keyhole* (1938)

8 I always have a quotation for everything—it saves original thinking.

> Dorothy L. Sayers, *Have His Carcase* (1932)

9 An apt quotation is like a lamp which flings its light over the whole sentence.

> L.E. Landon, *Romance and Reality* (1831)

10 Quotations can be valuable, like raisins in the rice pudding, for adding iron as well as eye appeal.

> Peg Bracken, *I Didn't Come Here to Argue* (1969)

11 When a thing has been said so well that it could not be said better, why paraphrase it? Hence my writing, is, if not a cabinet of fossils, a kind of collection of flies in amber.

> Marianne Moore, *A Marianne Moore Reader* (1961)

12 I love them because it is a joy to find thoughts one might have, beautifully expressed with much authority by someone recognizedly wiser than oneself.

> Marlene Dietrich, *Marlene Dietrich's ABC* (1962)

13 Sometimes it seems the only accomplishment my education ever bestowed on me, the ability to think in quotations.

> Margaret Drabble, *A Summer Bird-Cage* (1962)

14 Those quotations were really quite obscure. Anyone can see that he is a very well-read man.

> Barbara Pym, *Crampton Hodnet* (1985)

15 The everlasting quotation-lover dotes on the husks of learning.

> Maria Edgeworth, *Thoughts on Bores* (1826)

16 He lik'd those literary cooks / Who skim the cream of others' books, / And ruin half an author's graces, / By plucking bon-mots from their places.

> Hannah More, "Florio" (1786), *The Works of Hannah More*,
> vol. 1 (1841)

17 The most disheartening tendency common among readers is to tear out one sentence from a work, as a criterion of the writer's ideas or personality.

> Emma Goldman, introduction, *Anarchism* (1910)

18 The writer must resist this temptation [to quote] and do his best with his own tools. It would be most convenient for us musicians if, arrived at a given emotional crisis in our work, we could simply stick in a few bars of Brahms or Schubert. Indeed many composers have no hesitation in so doing. But I have never heard the practice defended; possibly because that hideous symbol of petty larceny, the inverted comma, cannot well be worked into a musical score.

> Ethel Smyth, "The Quotation-Fiend," *Streaks of Life* (1922)

See also Aphorisms, Proverbs, Slogans.

# R

## ❧ RABBITS

1 Once upon a time there were four little Rabbits, and their names were—Flopsy, Mopsy, Cottontail, and Peter.

Beatrix Potter, *The Tale of Peter Rabbit* (1901)

2 Rabbits are a foolish people. They do not fight except with their own kind, nor use their paws except for feet, and appear to have no reason for existence but to furnish meals for meat-eaters. In flight they seem to rebound from the earth of their own elasticity, but keep a sober pace going to the spring. It is the young watercress that tempts them and the pleasures of society, for they seldom drink.

Mary Austin, *The Land of Little Rain* (1904)

3 A bunny's a delightful habit / No home's complete without a rabbit.

Clare Turlay Newberry, *Marshmallow* (1942)

4 When raising rabbits, it doesn't take long to get double your bunny back.

Marcelene Cox, in *Ladies' Home Journal* (1959)

See also Animals.

## ❧ RACE

5 No matter what learned scientists may say, race is, politically speaking, not the beginning of humanity but its end, not the origin of peoples but their decay, not the natural birth of man but his unnatural death.

Hannah Arendt, *Origins of Totalitarianism* (1951)

6 Race, what is that? Race is a competition, somebody winning and somebody losing. . . . Blood doesn't run in races! Come on!

Beah Richards, in Brian Lanker, *I Dream a World* (1989)

7 Light came to me when I realized that I did not have to consider any racial group as a whole. God made them duck by duck and that was the only way I could see them.

Zora Neale Hurston, *Dust Tracks on a Road* (1942)

See also Racism.

## ❧ RACISM

8 Racism is alive and doing too well in America.

Johnnetta B. Cole, *Conversations* (1993)

9 Racism is so universal in this country, so widespread and deep-seated, that it is invisible because it is so normal.

Shirley Chisholm, *Unbought and Unbossed* (1970)

10 Racism is so extreme and so pervasive in our American society that no black individual lives in an atmosphere of freedom.

Margaret Walker, in Janet Sternburg, ed., *The Writer on Her Work*, vol. 1 (1980)

11 Racial oppression of black people in America has done what neither class oppression or sexual oppression, with all their perniciousness, has ever done: destroyed an entire people and their culture.

Eleanor Holmes Norton, "For Sadie and Maude," in Robin Morgan, ed., *Sisterhood Is Powerful* (1970)

1 I believe racism has killed more people than speed, heroin, or cancer, and will continue to kill until it is no more.

   Alice Childress, in *Stagebill* (1972)

2 None but those who experience it can know what it is—this constant, galling sense of cruel injustice and wrong. I cannot help feeling it very often,—it intrudes upon my happiest moments, and spreads a dark, deep gloom over everything.

   Charlotte L. Forten (1854), in Ray Allen Billington, ed., *The Journal of Charlotte Forten* (1953)

3 Every day I am deluged with reminders / that this is not / my land / and this is my land. / I do not believe in the war between races / but in this country / there is war.

   Lorna Dee Cervantes, "Poem for the Young White Man Who Asked Me How I, an Intelligent Well-Read Person, Could Believe in the War Between Races," *Emplumada* (1981)

4 They have stabbed themselves for freedom— jumped into the waves for freedom—starved for freedom—fought like very tigers for freedom! But they have been hung, and burned, and shot—and their tyrants have been their historians!

   Lydia Maria Child, *An Appeal in Favor of That Class of Americans Called Africans* (1833)

5 Would it please you if I strung my tears / In pearls for you to wear?

   Naomi Long Madgett, "The Race Question," *Star by Star* (1965)

6 Anger is an appropriate reaction to racist attitudes, as is fury when the actions arising from those attitudes do not change.

   Audre Lorde, "The Uses of Anger" (1981), *Sister Outsider* (1984)

7 O we are all racist we are all sexist some of us only some of us are the targets of racism of sexism of homophobia of class denigration but we all all breathe in racism with the dust in the streets with the words we read and we struggle those of us who struggle we struggle endlessly endlessly to think and be and act differently from all that.

   Rosario Morales, "We're All in the Same Boat," in Cherríe Moraga and Gloria Anzaldúa, eds., *This Bridge Called My Back* (1983)

8 SISTER! your foot's smaller / but it's still on my neck.

   Pat Parker, *Movement in Black* (1978)

9 Race prejudice is not only a shadow over the colored—it is a shadow over all of us, and the shadow is darkest over those who feel it least and allow its evil effects to go on.

   Pearl S. Buck, *What America Means to Me* (1943)

10 As surely as night follows day our country will fail in its democracy because of race prejudice unless we root it out. We cannot grow in strength and leadership for democracy so long as we carry deep in our being that fatal fault.

   Pearl S. Buck, *What America Means to Me* (1943)

11 Can you imagine if this country were not so afflicted with racism? Can you imagine what it would be like if the vitality, humor, and resilience of the black American were infused throughout this country?

   Maya Angelou, in Brian Lanker, *I Dream a World* (1989)

12 Racism is used *both* to create false differences among us *and* to mask very significant ones.

   Mirtha Quintanales, "I Paid Very Hard for My Immigrant Ignorance," in Cherríe Moraga and Gloria Anzaldúa, eds., *This Bridge Called My Back* (1983)

13 In the last few years, race relations in America have entered upon a period of intensified craziness wherein fear of being *called* a racist has so thoroughly overwhelmed fear of *being* a racist that we are in danger of losing sight of the distinction.

   Florence King, *Lump It or Leave It* (1990)

14 If some folks have buried their racial prejudices, the chances are that they've got the graves marked and will have no trouble disinterring their pet hates.

   Josephine Lawrence, *Let Us Consider One Another* (1945)

15 The white-supremacy boys are spoiled children. "I want MY way," they scream, and like all spoiled children, they advance no justification for it except that it is their way.

   Margaret Halsey, *Some of My Best Friends Are Soldiers* (1944)

16 There's nothing you can do about the race problem . . . that's safe. We've let it go too long for that. The only choice we have left is between perilous courses that are democratic and perilous courses that aren't democratic.

   Margaret Halsey, *Some of My Best Friends Are Soldiers* (1944)

17 The only way not to worry about the race problem is to be doing something about it yourself. When

you are, natural human vanity makes you feel that now the thing is in good hands.

> Margaret Halsey, *Some of My Best Friends Are Soldiers* (1944)

1 Which one of my brother's children are you?

> Mary McLeod Bethune, to the White House guard who addressed her as "Auntie," in Paula Giddings, *When and Where I Enter* (1984)

2 The main barrier between East and West today is that the white man is not willing to give up his superiority and the colored man is no longer willing to endure his inferiority.

> Pearl S. Buck, *What America Means to Me* (1943)

3 When a white man in Africa by accident looks into the eyes of a native and sees the human being (which it is his chief preoccupation to avoid), his sense of guilt, which he denies, fumes up in resentment and he brings down the whip.

> Doris Lessing, *The Grass Is Singing* (1950)

4 And who shall separate the dust / Which later we shall be: / . . . / Will mankind lie apart, / When life has settled back again / The same as from the start?

> Georgia Douglas Johnson, "The Common Dust," in Arnold Adoff, ed., *The Poetry of Black America* (1973)

See also Bigotry, Blacks, Blacks and Whites, Discrimination, Exclusion, Oppression, Prejudice, Segregation, Slavery.

## ❦ RADIO

5 A discovery that makes it possible for a man to deliver a speech and not only bore those nearby, but others hundreds of miles away.

> Agnes Repplier, in Emma Repplier, *Agnes Repplier* (1957)

6 Dorothy looked at me and looked at me and she really said she thought my brains were a miracle. I mean she said my brains reminded her of a radio because you listen to it for days and days and you get discouradged and just when you are getting ready to smash it, something comes out that is a masterpiece.

> Anita Loos, *Gentlemen Prefer Blondes* (1925)

7 The power of radio is not that it speaks to millions, but that it speaks intimately and privately to each one of those millions.

> Hallie Flanagan, *Dynamo* (1943)

8 From talk radio to insult radio wasn't really that much of a leap.

> Leonore Fleischer, *The Fisher King* (1991)

9 The ruder lecturers are, and the louder their voices, the more converts they make to their opinions.

> Winifred Holtby, "The Murder of Madame Mollard" (1930), *Pavements at Anderby* (1937)

10 The polemics of right-wing radio are putting nothing less than hate onto the airwaves, into the marketplace, electing it to office, teaching it in schools, and exalting it as freedom.

> Patricia J. Williams, "Hate Radio," in *Ms.* (1994)

See also Cranks, Media.

## ❦ RAIN

11 Rain knows the earth and loves it well, for rain is the passion of the earth.

> Estela Portillo Trambley, "Pay the Criers," *Rain of Scorpions* (1975)

12 Surround of rainbows / Listen / The rain comes upon us / Restore us.

> Meridel Le Sueur, "Surround of Rainbows," *Rites of Ancient Ripening* (1975)

13 The smell of rain is rich with life.

> Estela Portillo Trambley, "Pay the Criers," *Rain of Scorpions* (1975)

14 A rain as fine as silk spills was weaving over the lake.

> Martha Ostenso, *The Stone Field* (1937)

15 Rain fell in ropes and wind shuttled through them, webbing the city in its ephemeral weave.

> Julia O'Faolain, *No Country for Young Men* (1980)

16 He heard sound coming. Rain, like hundreds of mice running through corn.

> Virginia Hamilton, *M.C. Higgins, the Great* (1974)

17 Like a tall woman walking across the hayfield, / The rain came slowly, dressed in crystal and the sun.

> Elizabeth Coatsworth, "July Storm," *Down Half the World* (1968)

18 The pavements looked washed and sticky, like pieces of half-sucked toffee.

> Margery Allingham, *Traitor's Purse* (1941)

1 In the country they say, "We'll come when it rains." When the soft rains come soaking through the day and into the night, they go visiting, they sit around the kitchen table in a dry place and talk of children and crops.

    Yvette Nelson, *We'll Come When It Rains* (1982)

2 We prayed to see the racing clouds at bay / Rumpled like sheets after a night of joy, / To stand quite still and let the deluged day / Of rain's releasing, surge up and destroy.

    Dorothy Livesay, "The Outrider," *Day and Night* (1944)

3 Down it came, the blessed deluge. The music of rain splashing on tents and tin sheds drove men to an ecstasy of rejoicing. They turned out to cheer; lifted up their faces and opened their mouths to drink the bright drops; danced round, hallooing and shouting, getting drenched in the downpour. . . . Rain filled all the dams and banks and potholes. Every gully was a rushing torrent: water lay flashing and shining in depressions on the flat land and away through the bush.

    Katharine Susannah Prichard, *The Roaring Nineties* (1946)

4 It's raining fish-hooks and hammer handles!

    Laura Ingalls Wilder, *On the Banks of Plum Creek* (1937)

5 I began to forget when it hadn't been raining and became as one with all the characters in all of the novels about rainy seasons, who rush around banging their heads against the walls, drinking water glasses of straight whiskey and moaning, "The rain! The rain! My God, the rain!"

    Betty MacDonald, *The Egg and I* (1945)

## ♦ RAPE

6 Rape is not aggressive sexuality, it is sexualized aggression.

    Audre Lorde, "Age, Race, Class, and Sex" (1980), *Sister Outsider* (1984)

7 The attack between the thighs is only an extension of the bullet between the eyes.

    Aljean Harmetz, in Shana Alexander, *Talking Woman* (1976)

8 No zoologist, as far as I know, has ever observed that animals rape in their natural habitat, the wild.

    Susan Brownmiller, *Against Our Will* (1975)

9 Rape is . . . nothing more or less than a conscious process of intimidation by which *all men* keep *all women* in a state of fear.

    Susan Brownmiller, *Against Our Will* (1975)

10 Rapists perform for sexist males the same function that the Ku Klux Klan performed for racist whites; they keep women in their "place" through fear.

    Jo-Ann Evans Gardner (1972), in Karen DeCrow, *Sexist Justice* (1974)

11 Rape is a culturally fostered means of suppressing women. Legally we say we deplore it, but mythically we romanticize and perpetuate it, and privately we excuse and overlook it.

    Victoria Billings, *The Womansbook* (1974)

12 Perhaps it is the only crime in which the victim becomes the accused.

    Freda Adler, *Sisters in Crime* (1975)

13 Bad judgment and carelessness are not punishable by rape.

    Pearl Cleage, "The Other Facts of Life," *Deals With the Devil* (1993)

14 Disarm rapists.

    Slogan on button, in Toni Carabillo, Judith Meuli, and June Bundy Csida, *Feminist Chronicles 1953-1993* (1993)

15 A black man walking through certain white neighborhoods or a white man walking though certain black neighborhoods can understand the fear of unprovoked attack. It is the same fear a woman has when she walks down the street at night—any street, even her own. Women are always in someone else's territory.

    Andra Medea and Kathleen Thompson, *Against Rape* (1974)

16 Fear of rape is a cold wind blowing / all of the time on a woman's hunched back.

    Marge Piercy, "Rape Poem," *Living in the Open* (1976)

See also Violence.

## ♦ RATIONALITY

17 A rational process is a *moral* process.

    Ayn Rand, *Atlas Shrugged* (1957)

18 There are times when to be reasonable is to be cowardly.

    Marie von Ebner-Eschenbach, *Aphorisms* (1893)

See also Irrationality, Logic, Reason.

## ❦ RATIONALIZATION

1 *If* and *but*, life's great impediments!

    Eugénie de Guérin, letter (1834), in Guillaume S. Trébutien, ed., *Letters of Eugénie de Guérin* (1865)

2 What you wish to do you are apt to think you ought to do.

    Marie von Ebner-Eschenbach, *Aphorisms* (1893)

3 How quick come the reasons for approving what we like!

    Jane Austen, *Persuasion* (1818)

4 It is so easy to believe in pleasant impossibilities.

    Amelia B. Edwards, *Half a Million of Money* (1866)

5 He was of that pleasant temperament which believes whatever it is comfortable to believe; he was always able to explain facts to suit his mental necessities.

    Margaret Deland, "The Third Volume," *Around Old Chester* (1915)

See also Excuses, Self-Deception.

## ❦ READING

6 No entertainment is so cheap as reading, nor any pleasure so lasting.

    Lady Mary Wortley Montagu (1753), in Octave Thanet, ed., *The Best Letters of Lady Mary Wortley Montagu* (1901)

7 The greatest gift is the passion for reading. It is cheap, it consoles, it distracts, it excites, it gives you knowledge of the world and experience of a wide kind. It is a moral illumination.

    Elizabeth Hardwick, in George Plimpton, ed., *The Writer's Chapbook* (1989)

8 I pity those who have no taste for reading.

    Marie de Rabutin-Chantal, Marquise de Sévigné (1689), *Letters of Madame de Sévigné to Her Daughter and Her Friends*, vol. 8 (1811)

9 When the Day of Judgment dawns and the great conquerors and lawyers and statesmen come to receive their rewards—their crowns, their laurels, their names carved indelibly upon imperishable marble—the Almighty will turn to Peter and will say, not without a certain envy when He sees us coming with our books under our arms, "Look, these need no reward. We have nothing to give them here. They have loved reading."

    Virginia Woolf, "How Should One Read a Book?" *The Common Reader*, 2nd series (1932)

10 Those who are happy enough to have a taste for reading, need never be at a loss for amusement.

    Marie de Rabutin-Chantal, Marquise de Sévigné (1684), *Letters of Madame de Sévigné to Her Daughter and Her Friends*, vol. 6 (1811)

11 When I only begin to read, I forget I'm on this world. It lifts me on wings with high thoughts.

    Anzia Yezierska, "Wings," *Hungry Hearts* (1920)

12 I easily sink into mere absorption of what other minds have done, and should like a whole life for that alone.

    George Eliot (1872), in J.W. Cross, ed., *George Eliot's Life As Related in Her Letters and Journals* (1884)

13 Only one hour in the normal day is more pleasurable than the hour spent in bed with a book before going to sleep, and that is the hour spent in bed with a book after being called in the morning.

    Rose Macaulay, "Problems of a Reader's Life," *A Casual Commentary* (1926)

14 If, at the end of the saddest, the most disappointing and hurtful day, each one of us may come to a quiet room somewhere, and that room his own, if there is a light burning above white pillows, and a pile of books waiting under the light, then indeed we may still praise Allah, that He has not terminated all the Delights.

    Kathleen Norris, "Beauty in Letters," *These I Like Best* (1941)

15 We get no good / By being ungenerous, even to a book, / And calculating profits,—so much help / By so much reading. It is rather when / We gloriously forget ourselves and plunge / Soul-forward, headlong, into a book's profound, / Impassioned for its beauty and salt of truth— / 'T is then we get the right good from a book.

    Elizabeth Barrett Browning, *Aurora Leigh* (1857)

16 She read Dickens in the spirit in which she would have eloped with him.

    Eudora Welty, "Listening," *One Writer's Beginnings* (1984)

17 Captain Littlepage had overset his mind with too much reading.

    Sarah Orne Jewett, *The Country of the Pointed Firs* (1896)

1 She would read anything from a dictionary to a treatise on turnips. Print fascinated her, dazed her, made her good for nothing.
  Kylie Tennant, *Ride On Stranger* (1943)

2 Whatever the theologians might say about Heaven being a state of union with God, I knew it consisted of an infinite library; and eternity . . . was simply what enabled one to read uninterruptedly forever.
  Dervla Murphy, *Wheels Within Wheels* (1979)

3 The pleasure of all reading is doubled when one lives with another who shares the same books.
  Katherine Mansfield, in John Middleton Murry, ed., *The Letters of Katherine Mansfield* (1928)

4 The greatest pleasures of reading consist in re-reading.
  Vernon Lee, "Reading Books," *Hortus Vitae* (1904)

5 Most people like reading about what they already know—there is even a public for yesterday's weather.
  Nancy Mitford, "Reading for Pleasure," *The Water Beetle* (1962)

6 Though there never was so much reading matter put before the public, there was never less actual "reading" in the truest and highest sense of the term than there is at present.
  Marie Corelli, "A Vital Point of Education," *Free Opinions* (1905)

7 People read every thing nowadays, except books.
  Anne-Sophie Swetchine, in Count de Falloux, ed., *The Writings of Madame Swetchine* (1869)

8 We need the slower and more lasting stimulus of solitary reading as a relief from the pressure on eye, ear and nerves of the torrent of information and entertainment pouring from ever-open electronic jaws. It could end by stupefying us.
  Storm Jameson, *Parthian Words* (1970)

9 Children are made readers on the laps of their parents.
  Emilie Buchwald, speech (1994)

10 I learned from the age of two or three that any room in our house, at any time of day, was there to read in, or to be read to.
  Eudora Welty, "Listening," *One Writer's Beginnings* (1984)

11 Ever since I was first read to, then started reading to myself, there has never been a line read that I didn't *hear*. As my eyes followed the sentence, a voice was saying it silently to me. It isn't my mother's voice, or the voice of any person I can identify, certainly not my own. It is human, but inward, and it is inwardly that I listen to it. It is to me the voice of the story or the poem itself.
  Eudora Welty, "Listening," *One Writer's Beginnings* (1984)

12 I only read what I am hungry for at the moment when I have an appetite for it, and then I do not read, I *eat*.
  Simone Weil, *Waiting for God* (1950)

13 I read what I feel, and not what I see.
  Julie de Lespinasse (1773), in Katharine Prescott Wormeley, tr., *Letters of Mlle. de Lespinasse* (1901)

14 I think reading a novel is almost next best to having something to do.
  Margaret Oliphant, *The Days of My Life* (1857)

15 Exciting literature after supper is not the best digestive.
  Charlotte Perkins Gilman, *The Living of Charlotte Perkins Gilman* (1935)

16 A bit of trash now and then is good for the severest reader. It provides that necessary roughage in the literary diet.
  Phyllis McGinley, "New Year and No Resolutions," *Merry Christmas, Happy New Year* (1959)

17 I have only ever read one book in my life, and that is *White Fang*. It's so frightfully good I've never bothered to read another.
  Nancy Mitford, *The Pursuit of Love* (1945)

See also Books, Libraries, Literature.

## 🔊 REAL

18 The Real [is] the sole foundation of the Ideal.
  Grace Aguilar, "Amête and Yafèh," *The Vale of Cedars* (1850)

19 Nothing's real unless you want it to be, and anything can be real if you want it to enough; so real doesn't really mean anything.
  Zilpha Keatley Snyder, *Season of Ponies* (1964)

20 The longer you wear pearls, the realer they become.
  Colette, *Cheri* (1920)

1 The real thing creates its own poetry.

    Anzia Yezierska, *Red Ribbon on a White Horse* (1950)

2 Generally, by the time you are Real, most of your hair has been loved off, and your eyes drop out and you get loose in the joints and very shabby. But these things don't matter at all, because once you are Real you can't be ugly, except to people who don't understand.

    Margery Williams, *The Velveteen Rabbit* (1926)

See also Realistic, Reality, Truth.

## ❧ REALISTIC

3 Wisdom never kicks at the iron walls it can't bring down.

    Ralph Iron, *The Story of an African Farm* (1883)

4 Whenever people say, "We mustn't be sentimental," you can take it they are about to do something cruel. And if they add, "We must be realistic," they mean they are going to make money out of it.

    Brigid Brophy, in Ingrid Newkirk, *Save the Animals!* (1990)

5 If someone tells you he is going to make "a realistic decision," you immediately understand that he has resolved to do something bad.

    Mary McCarthy, "The American Realist Playwrights," *On the Contrary* (1961)

6 The adjuration to "Be realistic" merely means "Agree with me, and think the way I think."

    Margaret Halsey, *The Pseudo-Ethic* (1963)

7 I've always wondered why if people want to be happy they're escapists, but if they go around looking for trouble they're realists.

    Richard Shattuck, *The Half-Haunted Saloon* (1945)

## ❧ REALITY

8 What we call reality is an agreement that people have arrived at to make life more livable.

    Louise Nevelson, *Dawns + Dusks* (1976)

9 Reality is above all else a variable, and nobody is qualified to say that he or she knows exactly what it is. As a matter of fact, with a firm enough commit-

ment, you can sometimes create a reality which did not exist before.

    Margaret Halsey, *No Laughing Matter* (1977)

10 Reality has changed chameleonlike before my eyes so many times that I have learned, or am learning, to trust almost anything except what appears to be so.

    Maya Angelou, in Mari E. Evans, ed., *Black Women Writers (1950-1980)* (1984)

11 The world comes second hand—fifth hand—to us and the illusion that it is fresh because it is shown as a picture of an actual place or is given as a "true account" by some reporter who claims to have been "there" divides man into incalculable parts without any true center.

    Josephine Herbst, *New Green World* (1954)

12 The paradox of reality is that no image is as compelling as the one which exists only in the mind's eye.

    Shana Alexander, *Talking Woman* (1976)

13 We live in a fantasy world, a world of illusion. The great task in life is to find reality.

    Iris Murdoch, in Rachel Billington, "Profile: Iris Murdoch," *The London Times* (1983)

14 Little children do not distinguish as we do between an inner fantasy and an outer "reality." For them, experience of both kinds has the same quality of actual event.

    Miriam Lindstrom, *Children's Art* (1962)

15 Reality can easily become the current fantasy.

    Judith Rossner, *August* (1983)

16 My greatest enemy is reality. I have fought it successfully for thirty years.

    Margaret Anderson, *My Thirty Years' War* (1930)

17 Reality is a crutch for people who can't cope with drugs.

    Jane Wagner, *Appearing Nitely* (1977)

18 The people who say you are not facing reality actually mean that you are not facing *their idea* of reality.

    Margaret Halsey, *No Laughing Matter* (1977)

19 What is reality anyway? Nothin' but a collective hunch.

    Jane Wagner, *The Search for Signs of Intelligent Life in the Universe* (1985)

1 Reality was such a jungle—with no signposts, land-marks, or boundaries.

   Helen Hayes, with Sandford Dody, *On Reflection* (1968)

2 Reality is unbelievably terrifying after one has done nothing but dream.

   Katharine Butler Hathaway, *The Little Locksmith* (1942)

3 Dismounted from her dream, she could not find footing again on solid ground. Her realities re-pelled her.

   Mary O'Hara, *Thunderhead* (1943)

4 A test of what is real is that it is hard and rough. Joys are found in it, not pleasure. What is pleasant belongs to dreams.

   Simone Weil, *Gravity and Grace* (1947)

5 The dream is real, my friends. The failure to realize it is the only unreality.

   Toni Cade Bambara, *The Salt Eaters* (1980)

6 It is useless to evade reality, because it only makes it more virulent in the end. But instead, look stead-fastly into the slit, pin-pointed, malignant eyes of reality: as an old-hand trainer dominates his wild beasts. Take it by the scruff of the neck, and shake the evil intent out of it; till it rattles out harmlessly, like gall bladder stones, fossilized on the floor.

   Caitlin Thomas, *Not Quite Posthumous Letter to My Daughter* (1963)

7 Fearful as reality is: it is less fearful than evasions of reality.

   Caitlin Thomas, *Not Quite Posthumous Letter to My Daughter* (1963)

8 He knew that in so far as one denies what is, one is possessed by what is not, the compulsions, the fan-tasies, the terrors that flock to fill the void.

   Ursula K. Le Guin, *The Lathe of Heaven* (1971)

9 My nightmares have become news stories.

   Jenny Holzer, *Truisms* (1991)

10 Nothing became real for her until she had had time to live it over again. An actual occurrence was nothing but the blankness of a shock, then the knowledge that something had happened; after-wards one could creep back and look into one's mind and find new things in it, clear and solid. It was like waiting outside the hen-house until the hen came off the nest and then going in to look for the egg.

   Elizabeth Bowen, "Coming Home," *Early Stories* (1951)

11 I made some studies, and reality is the leading cause of stress amongst those in touch with it. I can take it in small doses, but as a lifestyle I found it too confining.

   Jane Wagner, *The Search for Signs of Intelligent Life in the Universe* (1985)

See also Real, Truth.

## ❧ REASON

12 Reason cannot remain a bare intellectual faculty; it must become a faculty of judgment dealing with the question of values.

   Margaret Benson, *The Venture of Rational Faith* (1908)

13 The sign of an intelligent people is their ability to control emotions by the application of reason.

   Marya Mannes, *More in Anger* (1958)

14 Reason dissipates the illusions of life, but does not console us for their departure.

   Countess of Blessington, *Desultory Thoughts and Reflections* (1839)

15 I'll not listen to reason. . . . Reason always means what some one else has got to say.

   Elizabeth Gaskell, *Cranford* (1853)

16 There was always a real reason for everything—why spoons tarnished, and jam furred, and people declined into God, or drink, or card games.

   Edna O'Brien, "A Woman by the Seaside," *Mrs. Reinhardt* (1978)

See also Explanations, Logic, Rationality.

## ❧ REBELLION

17 In the rotation of crops there was a recognized season for wild oats; but they were not to be sown more than once.

   Edith Wharton, *The Age of Innocence* (1920)

18 I hold it blasphemy to say that a man ought not to fight against authority: there is no great religion and no great freedom that has not done it, in the beginning.

   George Eliot, *Felix Holt, the Radical* (1866)

See also Resistance, Revolution, Troublemakers.

## ♠ RECEIVING

1 Giving is not at all interesting; but receiving is, there is no doubt about it, delightful.

Rose Macaulay, "Christmas Presents," *A Casual Commentary* (1926)

2 In my belief, a harvest is also a legacy, for very often what you reap is, in the way of small miracles, more than you consciously know you have sown.

Faith Baldwin, *Harvest of Hope* (1962)

See also Gifts, Giving, Gratitude.

## ♠ RECOGNITION

3 It is sometimes the man who opens the door who is the last to enter the room.

Elizabeth Bibesco, *The Fir and the Palm* (1924)

## ♠ REFORM

4 Every reformation ruins somebody.

Amelia B. Edwards, *Half a Million of Money* (1866)

5 One of the persistent ironies of reform is the impossibility of predicting the full consequences of change.

Diane Ravitch, *The Great School Wars* (1974)

6 It is better to inspire a reform than to enforce it.

Catherine the Great (c. 1780), in Dominique Maroger, ed., *The Memoirs of Catherine the Great* (1955)

7 Nothing is easier than to overdo a reformation.

Agnes Repplier, "What Children Read," *Books and Men* (1888)

8 A reform often advances most rapidly by indirection.

Frances E. Willard, *A Wheel Within a Wheel* (1895)

9 I suppose that the party or sect which is to do any work in the world must breathe its own peculiar atmosphere, speak its own little patois, and see but one side of the question on which it fights.

Rebecca Harding Davis, *Bits of Gossip* (1904)

10 [Reformers] might be classified as a distinct species having eyes in the back of their heads.

Ellen Glasgow, *The Descendant* (1897)

11 The history of the reformer, whether man or woman, on any line of action, is but this: When he sees it all alone he is a fanatic; when a good many see it with him they are enthusiasts; when all see it he is a hero.

Frances E. Willard, in Anna A. Gordon, ed., *What Frances E. Willard Said* (1905)

See also Leadership, Social Change.

## ♠ REFUGEES

12 The sudden violent dispossession accompanying a refugee flight is much more than the loss of a permanent home and a traditional occupation, or than the parting from close friends and familiar places. It is also the death of the person one has become in a particular context, and every refugee must be his or her own midwife at the painful process of rebirth.

Dervla Murphy, *Tibetan Foothold* (1966)

13 A refugee is as helpless as a new born child—but not so appealing.

Phyllis Bottome, *Against Whom?* (1954)

14 All refugees carry with them a small burden of guilt.

P.D. James, *Devices and Desires* (1989)

15 The distance between refugees / and those who plot their course / is not fixed.

Bonnie Zucker Goldsmith, "Refugees," in *The Spoon River Poetry Review* (1993)

See also Borders, Immigrants.

## ♠ REGRET

16 We might have been!—these are but common words, / And yet they make the sum of life's bewailing.

L.E. Landon, *Ethel Churchill* (1837)

1 It isn't the thing you do, Dear / It's the thing you leave undone / Which gives you a bit of a heartache / At the setting of the sun.

Margaret E. Sangster, *Winsome Womanhood* (1900)

2 The bitterest tears shed over graves are for words left unsaid and deeds left undone.

Christopher Crowfield, *Little Foxes* (1865)

3 I have such plenty, yet am poor; / I pay my roof with tears / Shed for the time when I was young, / And unaware of years.

Lizette Woodworth Reese, "Growth," *A Quiet Road* (1896)

4 That was the best time of my life, and only now that it has gone from me forever—only now do I realize it.

Natalia Ginzburg, *The Little Virtues* (1962)

5 If eternal life can be given / let me have it again as a child / among those whom I did not love / enough, while they lived.

Gwen Harwood, "Resurrection," *Bone Scan* (1988)

6 This is the bitterest of all,—to wear the yoke of our own wrong-doing.

George Eliot, *Daniel Deronda* (1874)

7 I have made it a rule of my life never to regret and never to look back. Regret is an appalling waste of energy. . . . You can't build on it; it's only good for wallowing in.

Katherine Mansfield, "Je Ne Parle Pas Français," *Bliss* (1920)

8 Never regret. If it's good, it's wonderful. If it's bad, it's experience.

Victoria Holt, *The Black Opal* (1993)

9 To weep over a folly is to double it.

Minna Thomas Antrim, *Naked Truth and Veiled Illusions* (1901)

10 Were it not better to forget, / Than but remember and regret?

L.E. Landon, *Ethel Churchill* (1837)

11 Regrets are as personal as fingerprints.

Margaret Culkin Banning, in *Reader's Digest* (1958)

See also Apologies, Remorse, Repentance.

## ❦ REJECTION

12 From this haunting feeling of being not wanted, which remained a recurrent haunt through life, I found two ways of escape, both of which in changing form also persisted. One was the invention of gods, the other was personal efficiency in work.

Anna Louise Strong, *I Change Worlds* (1935)

13 I think all great innovations are built on rejections.

Louise Nevelson, *Dawns + Dusks* (1976)

See also Unwanted.

## ❦ RELATIONSHIPS

14 Having someone wonder where you are when you don't come home at night is a very old human need.

Margaret Mead, speech (1975), in Michèle Brown and Ann O'Connor, *Woman Talk*, vol. 1 (1984)

15 What greater thing is there for two human souls, than to feel that they are joined for life—to strengthen each other in all labor, to rest on each other in all sorrow, to minister to each other in all pain, to be one with each other in silent unspeakable memories at the moment of the last parting?

George Eliot, *Adam Bede* (1859)

16 All tragedies deal with fated meetings; how else could there be a play? Fate deals its stroke; sorrow is purged, or turned to rejoicing; there is death, or triumph; there has been a meeting, and a change. No one will ever make a tragedy—and that is as well, for one could not bear it—whose grief is that the principals never met.

Mary Renault, *The Mask of Apollo* (1966)

17 Intimate relationships cannot substitute for a life plan. But to have any meaning or viability at all, a life plan must include intimate relationships.

Harriet Lerner, *Dance of Intimacy* (1989)

18 Union is only possible to those who are units. To be fit for relations in time, souls, whether of man or woman, must be able to do without them in the spirit.

Margaret Fuller, *Woman in the Nineteenth Century* (1845)

1 We shared everything all our lives, the important ones and the trivial ones, and it's the trivial ones that build ties between people.

Rae Foley, *The Sleeping Wolf* (1952)

2 We can only love a person who eats what we eat.

Rigoberta Menchú, in Elisabeth Burgos-Debray, ed., *I, Rigoberta Menchú* (1983)

3 Human relations just are not fixed in their orbits like the planets—they're more like galaxies, changing all the time, exploding into light for years, then dying away.

May Sarton, *Crucial Conversations* (1975)

4 Most real relationships are involuntary.

Iris Murdoch, *The Sea, The Sea* (1978)

5 I have noticed before that there is a category of acquaintanceship that is not friendship or business or romance, but speculation, fascination.

Jane Smiley, *Good Will* (1989)

6 She felt the natural ties of affinity rather than the conventional blind ties of the blood.

Nadine Gordimer, "La Vie Boheme," *Face to Face* (1949)

7 One hardly dares to say that love is the core of the relationship, though love is sought for and created in relationship; love is rather the marvel when it is there, but it is not always there, and to know another and to be known by another—that is everything.

Florida Scott-Maxwell, *Women, and Sometimes Men* (1957)

8 Can I ever know you / Or you know me?

Sara Teasdale, "The Mystery," *Flame and Shadow* (1920)

9 Do we really know anybody? Who does not wear one face to hide another?

Frances Marion, *Westward the Dream* (1948)

10 Seven years would be insufficient to make some people acquainted with each other, and seven days are more than enough for others.

Jane Austen, *Sense and Sensibility* (1811)

11 When you hug someone, you learn something else about them. An important something else.

E.L. Konigsburg, *From the Mixed-Up Files of Mrs. Basil E. Frankweiler* (1967)

12 If one is out of touch with oneself, then one cannot touch others.

Anne Morrow Lindbergh, *Gift From the Sea* (1955)

13 A relationship isn't meant to be an insurance policy, a life preserver or a security blanket.

Diane Crowley, syndicated column (1992)

14 I am the wind that wavers, / You are the certain land; / I am the shadow that passes / Over the sand.

Zoë Akins, "I Am the Wind," *Interpretations* (1912)

15 "If only you were you and yet not you!" / There is no peace with you / Nor ever any rest!

Jessie Redmond Fauset, "Enigma," in Langston Hughes and Arna Bontemps, eds., *The Poetry of the Negro 1746-1949* (1949)

16 Ah, how much I like you, how well we get on, when you're asleep and I'm awake.

Colette, *The Cat* (1933)

17 What if you leave and never return, / and worse, what if you return and never leave. / I fear being alone, but what if I tell you that / even more I fear never being alone.

Carol Connolly, "What If," *Payments Due* (1985)

18 Oh, it's closeness that does you in. Never get too close to people, son—did I tell you that when you were young?

Anne Tyler, *Dinner at the Homesick Restaurant* (1982)

19 She felt ill-suited to the mystery of being in a relationship. Relationship—that silk purse turned sow's ear. . . . Ensnared in a relentless beam of scrutiny, the only motion you could achieve was coming up short.

Carrie Fisher, *Delusions of Grandma* (1994)

20 Ah, the relationships we get into just to get out of the ones we are not brave enough to say are over.

Julia Phillips, *You'll Never Eat Lunch in This Town Again* (1991)

21 We didn't have a relationship, we had a personality clash.

Alice Molloy, *In Other Words* (1973)

22 I am not a cold woman, Henry, / But I do not feel for you, / What I feel for the elephants and the miasmas / And the general view.

Stevie Smith, "Lady 'Rogue' Singleton," *Mother, What Is Man?* (1942)

23 The message about sex and relationships that she had gotten as a child . . . was confused, contradictory. Sex was for men, and marriage, like lifeboats, was for women and children.

Carrie Fisher, *Surrender the Pink* (1990)

1 My hand is not at home in yours. / Your hand is lust— / my hand is longing.

>    Edith Södergran, "Discovery" (1916), in Stina Katchadourian, tr., *Love and Solitude* (1981)

2 The long-term accommodation that protects marriage and other such relationships is . . . forgetfulness.

>    Alice Walker, *You Can't Keep a Good Woman Down* (1981)

3 When a couple turns domestic, for the first while having to talk about the need for aluminum eaves troughing and other matters only gets in the way of the relationship. Then, magically, these negotiations take the place of the relationship.

>    Marni Jackson, *The Mother Zone* (1992)

4 When passion and habit long lie in company it is only slowly and with incredulity that habit awakens to finds its companion fled, itself alone.

>    Ouida, *Wisdom, Wit and Pathos* (1884)

5 A man'll seem like a person to a woman, year in, year out. She'll put up and she'll put up. Then one day he'll do something maybe no worse than what he's been a-doing all his life. She'll look at him. And without no warning he'll look like a varmint.

>    Marjorie Kinnan Rawlings, "Varmints," *When the Whippoorwill—* (1940)

6 Living with Steve is a bit like being on a roller coaster—luckily it's one of my favorite rides.

>    Janet Ahles Hays, letter (1992)

7 I have no-fail chemistry. A guy turns me on, he's the wrong one for me.

>    Linda Barnes, *Snapshot* (1993)

8 We had a lot in common, I loved him and he loved him.

>    Shelley Winters (1954), in Susan Strasberg, *Bittersweet* (1980)

9 I know a lot of people didn't expect our relationship to last—but we've just celebrated our two months' anniversary.

>    Britt Ekland, in Jilly Cooper and Tom Hartman, *Violets and Vinegar* (1980)

10 He's got tired of her now, has Martin. He said she took so much worshiping she made his knees sore.

>    Storm Jameson, *Three Kingdoms* (1926)

11 What is missing in him is probably necessary for what is missing in you. Let us not to the marriage of true impediments admit minds.

>    Jean Kerr, *Mary, Mary* (1963)

12 Underground issues from one relationship or context invariably fuel our fires in another.

>    Harriet Lerner, *The Dance of Anger* (1985)

13 Relationships that do not end peacefully, do not end at all.

>    Merrit Malloy, in Merrit Malloy and Shauna Sorensen, *The Quotable Quote Book* (1990)

See also Broken Heart, Courtship, Dating, Divorce, Estrangement, Family, Flirtation, Friendship, Intimacy, Love, Lovers, Marriage, Romance, Sex.

# ❦ RELIGION

14 You think religion is what's inside a little building filled with pretty lights from stained glass windows! But it's not. It's wings! *Wings!*

>    Dorothy Canfield Fisher, *Bonfire* (1933)

15 Religion is made up of unrestrained wishes.

>    Dorothee Sölle, *Death by Bread Alone* (1975)

16 Religion was her theater, her dance, her wine, her song.

>    Meridel Le Sueur, "Corn Village," *Salute to Spring* (1940)

17 Religion was their meat and their excitement, their mental food and their emotional pleasure.

>    Pearl S. Buck, *Fighting Angel* (1936)

18 Religion is a temper, not a pursuit. It is the moral atmosphere in which human beings are to live and move. Men do not live to breathe: they breathe to live.

>    Harriet Martineau, *Society in America*, vol. 3 (1837)

19 There is no reality on this earth except religion and the power of love; all the rest is even more fugitive than life itself.

>    Madame de Staël (1808), in J. Christopher Herold, *Mistress to an Age* (1958)

20 A religious awakening which does not awaken the sleeper to love has roused him in vain.

>    Jessamyn West, *The Quaker Reader* (1962)

1 There is no religion without love, and people may talk as much as they like about their religion, but if it does not teach them to be good and kind to man and beast, it is all a sham.

Anna Sewell, *Black Beauty* (1877)

2 To this very day, common sense in religion is rare, and we are too often trying to be heroic instead of just ordinarily good and kind.

Dorothy Day (1958), in William D. Miller, *Dorothy Day* (1982)

3 What is religion, you might ask. It's a technology of living.

Toni Cade Bambara, *The Salt Eaters* (1980)

4 Religion is love; in no case is it logic.

Beatrice Potter Webb, *My Apprenticeship* (1926)

5 Reason does not get one far toward religion, but as far as it goes, it is indispensable.

Georgia Harkness, *The Resources of Religion* (1936)

6 Religion is the most widely debated and least agreed upon phenomenon of human history.

Georgia Harkness, *Conflicts in Religious Thought* (1929)

7 When I am alone in the forest I always say my prayers; and that occasional solitary communion with God is surely the only true religion for intelligent beings.

Gertrude Atherton, *The Aristocrats* (1901)

8 Some keep the Sabbath going to Church — / I keep it, staying at Home — / With a Bobolink for a Chorister — / And an Orchard, for a Dome.

Emily Dickinson (1860), in Thomas H. Johnson, ed., *The Complete Poems of Emily Dickinson* (1960)

9 Religion, like beauty, cannot be experienced in cold blood.

Evelyn Underhill, *Mixed Pasture* (1933)

10 Religion controls inner space; inner space controls outer space.

Zsuzsanna E. Budapest, "Self-Blessing Ritual," in Carol P. Christ and Judith Plaskow, eds., *Womanspirit Rising* (1979)

11 Workers need poetry more than bread. They need that their life should be a poem. They need some light from eternity. Religion alone can be the source of such poetry.

Simone Weil, *Gravity and Grace* (1947)

12 Out of the attempt to harmonize our actual life with our aspirations, our experience with our faith, we make poetry,—or, it may be, religion.

Anna Jameson, *A Commonplace Book* (1855)

13 Religion is poetry,—poetry is religion.

Marie Corelli, *Wormwood* (1890)

14 Religion is a bridge to the spiritual, but the spiritual lies beyond religion.

Rachel Naomi Remen, in Joan Borysenko, *Guilt Is the Teacher, Love Is the Lesson* (1990)

15 Religion is different from everything else; *because in religion seeking is finding.*

Willa Cather, *My Mortal Enemy* (1926)

16 Religion is probably, after sex, the second oldest resource which human beings have available to them for blowing their minds.

Susan Sontag, "The Pornographic Imagination," *Styles of Radical Will* (1966)

17 Whilst you live a very little religion seems enough; but believe me, it requires a great deal when you come to die.

Geraldine Jewsbury, *Zoë*, vol. 2 (1845)

18 I am not yet religious: I am only disillusioned with the irreligious.

Mary Adams, *Confessions of a Wife* (1902)

19 We are afraid of religion because it interprets rather than just observes. Religion does not confirm that there are hungry people in the world; it interprets the hungry to be our brethren whom we allow to starve.

Dorothee Sölle, *Death by Bread Alone* (1975)

20 To this day I do not know whether the power which has inspired my works is something related to religion, or is indeed religion itself.

Käthe Kollwitz, in Hans Kollwitz, ed., *The Diaries and Letters of Käthe Kollwitz* (1955)

21 The religion of our fathers overhung us children like the shadow of a mighty tree against the trunk of which we rested, while we looked up in wonder through the great boughs that half hid and half revealed the sky. Some of the boughs were already decaying, so that perhaps we began to see a little more of the sky than our elders; but the tree was sound at its heart.

Lucy Larcom, *A New England Girlhood* (1889)

1 While analyzing so many people I realized the constant need of a mother, or a father, or a god (the same thing) is really immaturity. It is a childish need, a human need, but so universal that I can see how it gave birth to all religions.

Anaïs Nin (1935), *The Diary of Anaïs Nin*, vol. 2 (1967)

2 [Religion is a] primitive insurance against disaster. . . . Offer sacrifices to the gods and save your crops. And even Christianity, after all, insures heavily against the flaws in this life by belief in another.

Rose Macaulay, *Told by an Idiot* (1923)

3 In religion is much tiredness of people, a giving over of their doing to Someone Else.

Laura Riding Jackson, *The Telling* (1972)

4 Unhappiness often leads to religion.

Virginia Moore, *Virginia Is a State of Mind* (1942)

5 Extreme happiness invites religion almost as much as extreme misery.

Dodie Smith, *I Capture the Castle* (1948)

6 One has to be very religious to change one's religion.

Comtesse Diane, *Les Glanes de la Vie* (1898)

7 Governments may change, and opinions, and the very appearance of lands themselves, but the slowest thing to change is religion. What has once been associated with worship becomes holy in itself, and self-perpetuating.

Elizabeth Coatsworth, *Personal Geography* (1976)

8 An organized religion is made up of fractions of personal religion and each person must make his own contribution to the spiritual possessions which will form the inheritance for succeeding ages.

Lily H. Montagu (1928), in Ellen M. Umansky and Dianne Ashton, eds., *Four Centuries of Jewish Women's Spirituality* (1992)

9 What is *your* religion? I mean—not what you know about religion but the belief that helps you most?

George Eliot, *Middlemarch* (1871)

10 Religion is like music, one must have an ear for it. Some people have none at all.

Charlotte Mew, in Penelope Fitzgerald, *Charlotte Mew and Her Friends* (1984)

11 My own view is that one cannot be religious in general any more than one can speak language in general; at any given moment one speaks French or English or Swahili or Japanese, but not "language."

Susan Sontag, "Piety Without Content" (1961), *Against Interpretation* (1966)

12 I b'lieve in religion, and one of these days, when I've got matters tight and snug, I calculates to tend to my soul.

Harriet Beecher Stowe, *Uncle Tom's Cabin* (1852)

13 Horace Dinsmore was, like his father, an upright, moral man, who paid an outward respect to the forms of religion, but cared nothing for the vital power of godliness.

Martha Finley, *Elsie Dinsmore* (1868)

14 All outward forms of religion are almost useless, and are the cause of endless strife. . . . Believe there is a great power silently working all things for good, behave yourself and never mind the rest.

Beatrix Potter (1884), in Leslie Linder, ed., *The Journal of Beatrix Potter* (1966)

15 She wondered why it was that saving one's soul was always made so dreary and unattractive, whereas the way to Hell was always so utterly delightful.

Mae West, *Diamond Lil* (1932)

16 Alas! when will "good people" learn that the devil is never better pleased than when they try to make "religion" a gloomy thing.

Fanny Fern, *Ginger-Snaps* (1870)

17 Religion, to be a factor in experience, must be pleasurable.

Mary Austin, *Earth Horizon* (1932)

18 Religion is perhaps its own worst enemy. For religion, masquerading under the guise of archaic creeds, and impossible literalisms, and ecclesiasticism indifferent to human needs, has brought about an inevitable and in many respects wholesome revulsion.

Georgia Harkness, *Conflicts in Religious Thought* (1929)

19 [The] tendency to turn human judgments into divine commands makes religion one of the most dangerous forces in the world.

Georgia Harkness, *The Recovery of Ideals* (1937)

20 Many are called impious, not for having a worse, but a different religion from their neighbors; and many atheistical, not for the denying of God, but for thinking somewhat peculiarly concerning him.

Frances Wright, *A Few Days in Athens* (1822)

1 The perpetual danger which besets religion is that it may substitute gentility and aestheticism for prophetic insight and power.

Georgia Harkness, *The Resources of Religion* (1936)

2 A *little* knowledge and an over-abundance of zeal always tends to be harmful. In the area involving religious truths, it can be disastrous.

Kathryn Kuhlman, *I Believe in Miracles* (1962)

3 It is hard for many people today to make the distinction between religion and religiosity, the latter a dangerous parody of the former.

Abigail McCarthy, *Private Faces/Public Places* (1972)

4 Rosie is the latest and most successful of the television performers who sell salvation and do very well out of a commodity which is always in demand and which costs them nothing to supply.

P.D. James, *The Children of Men* (1992)

5 The devil makes a great deal of the religion we see.

Elizabeth Rundle Charles, *Chronicles of the Schönberg-Cotta Family* (1863)

6 The leading error of the human mind,—the bane of human happiness—the perverter of human virtue . . . is Religion—that dark coinage of trembling ignorance! It is Religion—that poisoner of human felicity! It is Religion—that blind guide of human reason! It is Religion—that dethroner of human virtue! which lies at the root of all the evil and all the misery that pervade the world!

Frances Wright, *A Few Days in Athens* (1822)

7 Religion is a superstition that originated in man's mental inability to solve natural phenomena. The Church is an organized institution that has always been a stumbling block to progress.

Emma Goldman, "What I Believe," in *The New York World* (1908)

8 It is not that religion is merely useless, it is mischievous. It is mischievous by its idle terrors; it is mischievous by its false morality; it is mischievous by its hypocrisy; by its fanaticism; by its dogmatism; by its threats; by its hopes; by its promises.

Frances Wright, *A Few Days in Athens* (1822)

9 Religion and morality are a much better whip to keep people in submission than even the club and the gun.

Emma Goldman, "Victims of Morality," in *Mother Earth* (1913)

10 So long as you believe that man is essentially evil in nature, and a more vicious doctrine was never promulgated, it follows that he is often going to need to have his ears slapped back, and who should do this but the clergy?

Anne Roe, *The Making of a Scientist* (1952)

11 It is an open question whether any behavior based on fear of eternal punishment can be regarded as ethical or should be regarded as merely cowardly.

Margaret Mead, in *Redbook* (1971)

12 While religion is ethical, it by no means follows that ethics is religion.

Georgia Harkness, *Conflicts in Religious Thought* (1929)

13 The world is full of religion, and full of misery and crime.

Frances Wright, *A Few Days in Athens* (1822)

14 Parsons always seem to be specially horrified about things like sunbathing and naked bodies. They don't mind poverty and misery and cruelty to animals nearly so much.

Susan Ertz, *The Story of Julian* (1931)

15 You've got to have something to eat and a little love in your life before you can hold still for any damn body's sermon on how to behave.

Billie Holiday, with William Dufty, *Lady Sings the Blues* (1956)

16 Unless a religion springs from within the people themselves, it is a weapon of the system.

Rigoberta Menchú, in Elisabeth Burgos-Debray, ed., *I, Rigoberta Menchú* (1983)

17 Religion supports and perpetuates the social organization it reflects.

Riane Eisler, *The Chalice and the Blade* (1987)

18 Once divested of missionary virus, the cult of our gods gives no offense. It would be a peaceful age if this were recognized, and religion, Christian, communist or any other, were to rely on practice and not on conversion for her growth.

Freya Stark, *Ionia* (1954)

19 On this earth there are many roads to heaven; and each traveler supposes his own to be the best. But they must all unite in one road at the last. It is only Omniscience that can decide. And it will then be found that no sect is excluded because of its faith.

Eliza Leslie, *Miss Leslie's Behavior Book* (1859)

1 The curse, canker, rust, and blight of the religious life, have been that we theorized instead of practiced, and that we antagonized those who differed from us as to our theories.

Frances E. Willard, in Anna A. Gordon, ed., *What Frances E. Willard Said* (1905)

2 Men who would persecute others for religious opinions, prove the errors of their own.

Lady Marguerite Blessington, in R.R. Madden, *The Literary Life and Correspondence of the Countess of Blessington*, vol. 1 (1855)

3 Religion . . . has hardened their hearts and made it impossible for them to see, except through the dark glass of their own creed, what life is or ought to be.

Pearl S. Buck, *Fighting Angel* (1936)

4 The spirit of religious totalitarianism is abroad in the world; it is in the very air we breathe today in this land. Everywhere are those who claim to have a corner on righteousness, on direct access to God. . . . The bigots of the world are having a heyday.

Sonia Johnson, *From Housewife to Heretic* (1981)

5 Each drew his sword / On the side of the Lord.

Phyllis McGinley, "How to Start a War," *Times Three* (1960)

6 We contrive to make revenge itself look like religion. We call down thunder on many a head under pretense, that those on whom we invoke it are God's enemies, when perhaps we invoke it because they are ours.

Hannah More, *Practical Piety* (1811)

7 Is religion impossible without fanaticism?

Gertrude Atherton, *Los Cerritos* (1890)

8 Under the rubric of religious freedom, we respect the right to worship differently much more than the right to worship not at all.

Wendy Kaminer, *I'm Dysfunctional, You're Dysfunctional* (1992)

9 I would no more quarrel with a man because of his religion than I would because of his art.

Mary Baker Eddy, in *The Independent* (1906)

10 How strange that some people cannot believe in both the Book of Nature and the Book of God.

Maria Mitchell (1874), in Phebe Mitchell Kendall, ed., *Maria Mitchell, Life, Letters, and Journals* (1896)

11 Science and religion, religion and science, put it as I may, they are two sides of the same glass, through which we see darkly until these two, focusing together, reveal the truth.

Pearl S. Buck, *A Bridge for Passing* (1962)

12 "There is no doubt, I suppose," retorted our grandmother, "about heaven repaying you; but there seems to be a good deal of doubt whether it will be in current coin."

Elizabeth Rundle Charles, *Chronicles of the Schönberg-Cotta Family* (1863)

13 That's what I call twaddle!

Queen Victoria, to the bishop who suggested the widowed queen now consider herself "married to Christ" (1861), in Timothy B. Benford, *The Royal Family Quiz and Fact Book* (1987)

14 "Put down enthusiasm!" . . . That is a pet saying of mine—the Church of England in a nutshell.

Mrs. Humphry Ward, *Robert Elsmere* (1888)

15 It would be easier to peel off a three-day-old Band-Aid from a hairy kneecap than to remove the patina of Baptist upbringing that coats my psyche.

Mary Ellen Snodgrass, "Growing Up Baptist," in *Ms.* (1989)

16 What a flurry of preparation for the Passover feast! What a chopping of fish and a simmering of soup and a baking of *tsimmes* and a roasting of capon and an assembling of *taigloch*! Grandma was in her element, humming Russian tunes, a beaming earth mother with her sleeves rolled up and her eyes shining. I did love Passover. And Grandma's observance of it was devout, but it was the domestic, the kitchen side of religion.

Edith Konecky, *Allegra Maud Goldman* (1976)

17 The form of religion was always a trivial matter to me. . . . The pageantry of the Roman Church that first mothered and nurtured me touches me to this day. I love the Protestant prayers of the English Church. And I love the stern and knotty argument, the sermon with heads and sequences, of the New England Congregationalist. For this catholicity Catholics have upbraided me, churchmen rebuked me, and dissenters denied that I had any religion at all.

Mary Catherwood, *Lazarre* (1901)

18 Mine was a Catholic girlhood spent gorging on metaphor. . . . Maybe we had too much meaning too early. It was like having too much money. The quirkiness of life was betrayed, given inflated significance by our rich symbology. We powered around our ordinary lives in the Cadillac language

of Catholic spirituality, looking on with pity as the Protestants pedaled their stripped-down bicycles.

Patricia Hampl, *Virgin Time* (1992)

1 Catholicism isn't a religion, it's a nationality.

Antonia White, *Frost in May* (1933)

2 Irish Catholicism is very much founded on the stone of fear and of punishment.

Edna O'Brien, in Joseph McCulloch, *Under Bow Bells* (1974)

3 He always looked up and took notice when religion was mentioned; to this family the word was like "rats" to a dog, owing, perhaps, to their many clerical ancestors, perhaps to the fact that they were latish Victorians.

Rose Macaulay, *Told by an Idiot* (1923)

4 Why do we people in churches seem like cheerful, brainless tourists on a packaged tour of the Absolute?

Annie Dillard, *Teaching a Stone to Talk* (1982)

5 It must in candor be said that his religion sat upon him lightly.

Ilka Chase, *I Love Miss Tilli Bean* (1946)

6 He had vowed long ago, and renewed his vow frequently, that if holding hands in a circle and singing hymns, as it were, was what it took to make life endurable, he would rather die.

Annie Dillard, *The Living* (1992)

7 It may be that religion is dead, and if it is, we had better know it and set ourselves to try to discover other sources of moral strength before it is too late.

Pearl S. Buck, *What America Means to Me* (1943)

8 No body can deny but religion is a comfort to the distressed, a cordial to the sick, and sometimes a restraint on the wicked; therefore whoever would argue or laugh it out of the world without giving some equivalent for it ought to be treated as a common enemy.

Lady Mary Wortley Montagu (1754), in Robert Halsband, ed., *The Complete Letters of Lady Mary Wortley Montagu* (1965)

See also Atheism, Bible, Christianity, Church, Clergy, Conversion, Cults, Doctrine, Dogma, Episcopalians, Ethics, God, Islam, Jews, Mysticism, Piety, Religious, The Sacred, Salvation, Sex and Religion, Spirituality, Theology, Torah, Worship.

## ❦ RELIGIOUS

9 I doubt if we nuns are really as self-sacrificing as we must seem to be to you who live in the world. We don't give everything for nothing, you know. The mystery plays fair.

Elizabeth Goudge, *Green Dolphin Street* (1944)

10 A woman who has been a nun is never anything else.

Phyllis Bottome, "The Vocation," *Innocence and Experience* (1934)

11 My love has made a room for me / That looks upon eternity.

Sister M. Madeleva, "Song for a Nun's Cell," *Collected Poems* (1947)

12 The life of a religious might be compared to the building of a cathedral. Day by day the stones are laid, in the beginning one hardly distinguishable from another. . . . Once a firm foundation has been laid, the building rises slowly.

Margaret Wyvill Ecclesine, *A Touch of Radiance* (1966)

See also Clergy, Spirituality.

## ❦ REMEDIES

13 Desperate ills need desperate remedies.

Agatha Christie, *The Mystery of the Blue Train* (1928)

## ❦ REMEMBRANCE

14 I'll be forgotten? That is really nothing. / I have forgotten been a hundred times, / A hundred times I have lain in my coffin, / I may be dead and buried even now.

Anna Akhmatova, "I'll Be Forgotten" (1957), *Poems* (1988)

15 Someone, I tell you / will remember us. / We are oppressed by / fears of oblivion.

Sappho, "Someone, I Tell You" (6th cent. B.C.), in Willis Barnstone, *Sappho* (1965)

16 Remember me when I am gone away, / Gone far away into the silent land.

Christina Rossetti, "Remember" (1849), *Goblin Market* (1862)

1 One remembers different persons differently, some by the impact they have made on our emotions, and others by the impression they leave in our minds.

Hallie Burnett, *The Brain Pickers* (1957)

2 Nothing is more consuming, or more illogical, than the desire for remembrance.

Ellen Glasgow, *The Woman Within* (1954)

3 O may I join the choir invisible / Of those immortal dead who live again / In minds made better by their presence.

George Eliot, "O May I Join the Choir Invisible," *The Legend of Jubal and Other Poems, Old and New* (1867)

4 Better by far you should forget and smile / Than that you should remember and be sad.

Christina Rossetti, "Remember" (1849), *Goblin Market* (1862)

See also Memory, Nostalgia.

## ❧ REMORSE

5 Remorse is the poison of life.

Charlotte Brontë, *Jane Eyre* (1847)

6 Remorse is the worst thing to bear & I am afraid that I will fall a marter to it. . . . I will tell you why it is that I have thrown away many advantages that athers have not.

Marjorie Fleming, age 7 (1810), in Frank Sidgwick, *The Complete Marjory Fleming* (1934)

7 Nothing may be more selfish than remorse.

Margaret Deland, *Philip and His Wife* (1894)

8 Remorse . . . is one of the many afflictions for which time finds a cure.

Winifred Holtby, "The Murder of Madame Mollard" (1930), *Pavements at Anderby* (1937)

See also Regret, Repentance.

## ❧ RENO

9 Reno! The land of the free and the grave of the home!

Helen Rowland, *A Guide to Men* (1922)

10 Reno with its brilliant, sordid truths fascinated me. . . . I had some difficulty in going to bed in this town where hope and despair never sleep.

Simone de Beauvoir, *America Day by Day* (1948)

## ❧ RENUNCIATION

11 Renunciation is submission to time.

Simone Weil, *The Notebooks of Simone Weil* (1951)

12 We only possess what we renounce; what we do not renounce escapes from us.

Simone Weil, *Gravity and Grace* (1947)

## ❧ REPENTANCE

13 The danger with *feelings* of penitence is that we allow them to take the place of those actions that are its true manifestation.

Elizabeth Cullinan, "The Power of Prayer," *The Time of Adam* (1971)

14 O, we all acknowledge our faults, now; 'tis the mode of the day: but the acknowledgment passes for current payment; and therefore we never amend them.

Fanny Burney, *Camilla* (1796)

15 Repentance is a one-faced Janus, ever looking to the past.

L.E. Landon, *Romance and Reality* (1831)

See also Apologies, Regret, Remorse.

## ❧ REPETITION

16 Repeating is the whole of living and by repeating comes understanding, and understanding is to some the most important part of living.

Gertrude Stein, *The Making of Americans* (1925)

17 She says the same thing over and over again thinking repetition will substitute for proof.

Rita Mae Brown, *In Her Day* (1976)

1 A meaningless phrase repeated again and again begins to resemble truth.

Barbara Kingsolver, *Animal Dreams* (1990)

2 The mind naturally accommodates itself, even to
the most ridiculous improprieties, if they occur
frequently.

Fanny Burney, *Evelina* (1778)

## ❧ REPRESSION

3 What you try to bury just ends up burying you.

Jane Wagner, *Edith Ann, My Life, So Far* (1994)

4 He had had experience with suppression; whatever
it was didn't stay suppressed, but wandered around
in the body and the mind looking for a place to
hurt.

Mary Astor, *A Place Called Saturday* (1968)

See also Concealment, Secrets.

## ❧ REPUTATION

5 Until you've lost your reputation, you never realize
what a burden it was or what freedom really is.

Margaret Mitchell, *Gone With the Wind* (1936)

6 I couldn't live my reputation down—all right then,
I'd live up to it.

Polly Adler, *A House Is Not a Home* (1953)

7 Good repute is water carried in a sieve. / Only if
you can grasp the wind in your fist / or hold an
elephant chained secure with a hair / will you
maybe succeed in keeping your good name clear.

Lalleswari (14th cent.), in Joanna Bankier and Deirdre
Lashgari, eds., *Women Poets of the World* (1983)

See also Honor.

## ❧ RESEARCH

8 Research is formalized curiosity. It is poking and
prying with a purpose.

Zora Neale Hurston, *Dust Tracks on a Road* (1942)

9 Research is a way of taking calculated risks to bring
about incalculable consequences.

Celia Green, *The Decline and Fall of Science* (1976)

10 The way to do research is to attack the facts at the
point of greatest astonishment.

Celia Green, *The Decline and Fall of Science* (1977)

11 Research is a passion with me; it drives me; it is my
relentless master.

Margaret Morse Nice (1919), *Research Is a Passion With Me*
(1970)

12 Research is the live heart of the scientific life. . . .
Greatness of position, respect for past accomplishments, the Nobel Prize itself—none of these can
compensate for the loss of vitality only research
provides.

Vivian Gornick, *Women in Science* (1983)

13 I most carefully confined myself to facts and arranged those facts on as thin a line of connecting
opinion as possible.

Mary H. Kingsley, *West African Studies* (1899)

See also Learning, Science.

## ❧ RESENTMENT

14 Resentment opens no door and breeds no courage.

Susan Glaspell, *The Morning Is Near Us* (1939)

15 Resentment is a communicable disease and should
be quarantined.

Cynthia Ozick, *Trust* (1966)

16 Resentment is an evil so costly to our peace that we
should find it more cheap to forgive even were it
not more right.

Hannah More, "Thoughts on the Importance of the
Manners of the Great, to General Society," *The Works of
Hannah More*, vol. 1 (1841)

17 He was a man who grew fat on resentment as others did on happiness.

Edith Wharton, *The Gods Arrive* (1932)

18 People don't resent having nothing nearly as much
as too little.

Ivy Compton-Burnett, *A Family and a Fortune* (1939)

1 Resentment was a justice she owed to herself. There are some offenses which it is an unworthy weakness to forget.

L.E. Landon, *Francesca Carrara* (1834)

2 Resentment isn't a magnetic personal style.

Peggy Noonan, *What I Saw at the Revolution* (1990)

See also Anger, Bitterness.

## ❦ RESIGNATION

3 I am not resigned: I am not sure life is long enough to learn that lesson.

George Eliot, *The Mill on the Floss* (1860)

4 Resignation, perhaps the most stifling word in the language.

Caitlin Thomas, *Leftover Life to Kill* (1957)

See also Acceptance.

## ❦ RESILIENCE

5 You may trod me in the very dirt / But still, like dust, I'll rise.

Maya Angelou, "Still I Rise," *And Still I Rise* (1978)

6 After the earthquake and the fire comes the still small voice.

Dorothy Thompson, *Let the Record Speak* (1939)

See also Adaptability, Comebacks, Survival.

## ❦ RESISTANCE

7 Wolf's wool is the best of wool, / but it cannot be sheared because / the wolf will not comply.

Marianne Moore, "The Student," *What Are Years?* (1941)

8 *Resistance* is the secret of joy!

Alice Walker, *Possessing the Secret of Joy* (1992)

9 What we resist persists.

Sonia Johnson, *Going Out of Our Minds* (1987)

See also Movements, Rebellion, Revolution, Troublemakers.

## ❦ RESPECT

10 True self-respect, being very different from false pride, leads inevitably to respecting others.

Virginia Moore, *Virginia Is a State of Mind* (1942)

11 The respect that is only bought by gold is not worth much.

Frances Ellen Watkins Harper, "Our Greatest Want," in *Anglo-African Magazine* (1859)

See also Admiration, Appreciation, Self-Respect.

## ❦ RESPONSIBILITY

12 Responsibility is the price every man must pay for freedom. It is to be had on no other terms.

Edith Hamilton (1961), in Doris Fielding Reid, *Edith Hamilton* (1967)

13 Nothing strengthens the judgment and quickens the conscience like individual responsibility.

Elizabeth Cady Stanton, "The Solitude of Self," in *The Woman's Column* (1892)

14 The one with the primary responsibility to the individual's future is that individual.

Dorcas Hardy, in Deborah Churchman, "Dorcas Hardy's Stamp on Social Security," *Christian Science Monitor* (1987)

15 Parents can only give good advice or put them on the right paths, but the final forming of a person's character lies in their own hands.

Anne Frank, *The Diary of a Young Girl* (1952)

16 I was thinking of my patients, and how the worst moment for them was when they discovered they were masters of their own fate. It was not a matter of bad or good luck. When they could no longer blame fate, they were in despair.

Anaïs Nin (1935), *The Diary of Anaïs Nin*, vol. 2 (1967)

17 If experience teaches anything, it is that what the community undertakes to do is usually done badly. This is due in part to the temptation to corruption that such enterprises involve, but even more, perhaps, to the lack of personal interest on the part of those engaged in them.

Suzanne La Follette, "Woman and Marriage," *Concerning Women* (1926)

18 Everybody's business is nobody's business.

Florence Warden, *A Sensational Case* (1894)

1 Some shrugged their shoulders as if to shake off whatever chips of responsibility might have lodged there.

Helen Hudson, *Meyer Meyer* (1967)

2 Who, I ask you, can take, dare take on himself the rights, the duties, the responsibilities of another human soul?

Elizabeth Cady Stanton, "The Solitude of Self," in *The Woman's Column* (1892)

3 Everybody's suffering is mine but not everybody's murdering. . . . I do not distinguish for one moment whether my child is in danger or a child in central Asia. But I will not accept responsibility for what other people do because I happen to belong to that nation or that race or that religion. I do not believe in guilt by association.

Margaret Mead, with James Baldwin, *A Rap on Race* (1971)

4 I notice that when people have no sense of responsibility, you call them either criminals or geniuses.

Margaret Deland, *The Awakening of Helena Richie* (1906)

5 Only lies and evil come from letting people off.

Iris Murdoch, *A Severed Head* (1961)

6 There's no difference between one's killing and making decisions that will send others to kill. It's exactly the same thing, or even worse.

Golda Meir, in Oriana Fallaci, *L'Europeo* (1973)

7 People tend to forget their duties but remember their rights.

Indira Gandhi, *Last Words* (1984)

8 The first rule in opera is the first rule of life . . . see to everything yourself.

Nellie Melba, *Melodies and Memories* (1925)

See also Blame, Duty, "Ought."

## ❦ RESTLESSNESS

9 I am a restlessness inside a stillness inside a restlessness.

Dodie Smith, *I Capture the Castle* (1948)

10 Now more than ever do I realize that I shall never be content with a sedentary life, and that I shall always be haunted by thoughts of a sun-drenched *elsewhere.*

Isabelle Eberhardt (1901), in Nina de Voogd, tr., *The Passionate Nomad* (1988)

See also Discontent, Wanderlust.

## ❦ RETICENCE

11 Reticences are as revealing as avowals.

Elizabeth Bibesco, *The Fir and the Palm* (1924)

12 The well-ordered mind knows the value, no less than the charm, of reticence. The fruit of the tree of knowledge . . . falls ripe from its stem; but those who have eaten with sobriety find no need to discuss the processes of digestion.

Agnes Repplier, "The Repeal of Reticence," *Counter-Currents* (1916)

See also Discretion, Silence.

## ❦ RETIREMENT

13 Retirement . . . may be looked upon either as a prolonged holiday or as a rejection, a being thrown on to the scrap-heap.

Simone de Beauvoir, *The Coming of Age* (1970)

14 Retirement revives the sorrow of parting, the feeling of abandonment, solitude and uselessness that is caused by the loss of some beloved person.

Simone de Beauvoir, *The Coming of Age* (1970)

15 In retirement, the passage of time seems accelerated. Nothing warns us of its flight. It is a wave which never murmurs, because there is no obstacle to its flow.

Anne-Sophie Swetchine, in Count de Falloux, ed., *The Writings of Madame Swetchine* (1869)

16 For millions, the retirement dream is in reality an economic nightmare . . . growing poor, being sick, living in substandard housing, and having to scrimp merely to subsist.

Sylvia Porter, *Sylvia Porter's Money Book* (1975)

17 My voice had a long, nonstop career. It deserves to be put to bed with quiet and dignity, not yanked

out every once in a while to see if it can still do what it used to do. It can't.

Beverly Sills, in *Time* (1983)

1 Like many other women who claim to live in retirement, Leonilla Leopolska was in active correspondence with all the habitable earth.

Princess Marthe Bibesco, *Catherine-Paris* (1928)

2 I married him for better or for worse, but not for lunch.

Hazel Weiss (1960), on husband George Weiss's retirement as general manager of the New York Yankees, in Lee Green, *Sportswit* (1984)

See also Age, Leisure, Unemployment.

## ❧ RETRIBUTION

3 There is a law of retribution in all things, direct or indirect, visible or invisible.

Miles Franklin, *Some Everyday Folk and Dawn* (1909)

See also Destiny, Fate, Revenge, Vengeance.

## ❧ RETURNING

4 The way back is always shorter.

Maya Deren, "The Artist As God in Haiti," in *The Tiger's Eye* (1948)

5 As roads go, the road home is as good as any.

Ellis Peters, *The Summer of the Danes* (1991)

6 Miss Froy loved her home with that intense perverted passion which causes ardent patriots to desert their native lands and makes men faithless to their wives. Like them, she left what she loved most—for the joy of the return.

Ethel Lina White, *The Wheel Spins* (1936)

7 Tom was feeling more and more like the Prodigal Son and did not like it, as indeed we daresay the Prodigal Son himself did not like it either. For to have to eat fatted calf when you are thoroughly ashamed of yourself and only want to slink in and not be noticed must be a severe trial; not to speak of one's Good Brother.

Angela Thirkell, *The Duke's Daughter* (1951)

See also Home.

## ❧ REUNIONS

8 Reunions are always fraught with awkward tensions—the necessity to account for oneself; the attempt to find, through memories, an ember of the old emotions.

Anita Shreve, *Eden Close* (1989)

See also Absence, Meetings.

## ❧ REVELATION

9 Revelation is the marriage of knowing and feeling.

Marya Mannes, *They* (1968)

See also Insight, Visions.

## ❧ REVENGE

10 If you sit long enough by the crack of the door, you'll see your enemy go by in a hearse.

Sally Stanford, *The Lady of the House* (1966)

11 Revenge leads to an empty fullness, like eating dirt.

Mignon McLaughlin, *The Neurotic's Notebook* (1963)

12 How many are the pains of those who hunger for revenge! . . . They have killed themselves even before they kill their enemies.

St. Catherine of Siena, in Suzanne Noffke, tr., *Dialogue* (1378)

13 In history it's never a tooth for a tooth, but a thousand, a hundred thousand for one.

Sybille Bedford, *A Favorite of the Gods* (1963)

14 Revenge may not be a particularly higher consciousness-oriented activity.

Carrie Fisher, *Postcards From the Edge* (1987)

See also Vengeance.

## ❧ REVOLUTION

15 Revolution is but thought carried into action.

Emma Goldman, title essay, *Anarchism* (1910)

1 Evolution when blocked and suppressed becomes revolution.

Nellie L. McClung, *In Times Like These* (1915)

2 No real social change has ever come about without a revolution.

Emma Goldman, title essay, *Anarchism* (1910)

3 All revolutions are treason until they are accomplished.

Amelia E. Barr, *The Bow of Orange Ribbon* (1886)

4 Revolution is the festival of the oppressed.

Germaine Greer, *The Female Eunuch* (1971)

5 The reason for revolution is so the good things in life circulate.

Rita Mae Brown, *In Her Day* (1976)

6 Revolution is man's normal activity, and if he is wise he will grade it slowly so that it may be almost imperceptible—otherwise it will jerk in fits and starts and cause discomfort.

Freya Stark, "Time," *The Arch of the Zodiac* (1968)

7 It is impossible to rise to freedom, from the midst of corruptions, without strong convulsions. They are the salutary crises of a serious disease. We are in want of a terrible political fever, to carry off our foul humors.

Marie-Jeanne Roland (1791), in Lydia Maria Child, *Memoirs of Madame de Staël and of Madame Roland* (1847)

8 Was revolution much more than one fast kick forward in the long process called evolution? We condemned the "cost" of revolution; but was it higher than the cost over centuries in backward, underdeveloped communities, which still covered two-thirds of the earth and which still could not guarantee their populations daily bread?

Ella Winter, *And Not to Yield* (1963)

9 Revolution always unfolds inside an atmosphere of rising expectations.

June Jordan, "America in Confrontation With Democracy," *Technical Difficulties* (1992)

10 By definition, revolutions are not linear, one step at a time, event A leading to event B, and so on. Many causes operate on each other at once. Revolutions shift into place suddenly, like the pattern in a kaleidoscope. They do not so much proceed as crystallize.

Marilyn Ferguson, *The Aquarian Conspiracy* (1980)

11 People never move towards revolution; they are pushed towards it by intolerable injustices in the economic and social order under which they live.

Suzanne La Follette, "Institutional Marriage and Its Economic Aspects," *Concerning Women* (1926)

12 Revolutionaries do not make revolutions! The revolutionaries are those who know when power is lying in the street and when they can pick it up.

Hannah Arendt, "Thoughts on Politics and Revolution," *Crises of the Republic* (1972)

13 Every revolution has its counter-revolution.

Mary Ritter Beard, "Mothercraft," in *The Woman Voter* (1912)

14 When you talk of revolution, you never talk of the day after.

Storm Jameson, *The Clash* (1922)

15 The most radical revolutionary will become a conservative on the day after the revolution.

Hannah Arendt, "Civil Disobedience," *Crises of the Republic* (1972)

16 The optimism of politics before a revolution is exceeded only by the pessimism of politics after one.

Catharine Stimpson, "'Thy Neighbor's Wife, Thy Neighbor's Servants': Women's Liberation and Black Civil Rights," in Vivian Gornick and Barbara K. Moran, eds., *Woman in Sexist Society* (1971)

17 Revolution devours its own parents as well as its own children.

Helen Foster Snow, *My China Years* (1984)

18 Revolution should never be ashamed of itself.

Teresa Billington-Greig, *The Militant Suffrage Movement* (1911)

19 The word "revolution" is a word for which you kill, for which you die, for which you send the laboring masses to their death, but which does not possess any content.

Simone Weil (1934), *Oppression and Liberty* (1955)

20 In America the word revolutionary is used to sell pantyhose.

Rita Mae Brown, *In Her Day* (1976)

21 It is better to die on your feet than to live on your knees!

Dolores Ibárruri, speech (1936), *They Shall Not Pass* (1966)

22 It is easier to die for a cause than to live for it.

Diane de Poitiers (1550), in Winifred Gordon, *A Book of Days* (1910)

1 To die for the revolution is a one-shot deal; to live for the revolution means taking on the more difficult commitment of changing our day-to-day life patterns.

> Frances M. Beal, "Double Jeopardy: To Be Black and Female," in Robin Morgan, ed., *Sisterhood Is Powerful* (1970)

2 Revolution is not a one-time event.

> Audre Lorde, "Learning From the '60s," *Sister Outsider* (1984)

3 The revolution begins at home.

> Cherríe Moraga and Gloria Anzaldùa, *This Bridge Called My Back* (1983)

4 let uh revolution come. / couldn't be no action like what / i dun already seen.

> Carolyn M. Rodgers, "U Name This One," *how i got ovah* (1975)

5 The classic trap for any revolutionary is always, "What's your alternative?"

> Shulamith Firestone, *The Dialectic of Sex* (1970)

6 If misery spelled revolt, we should have had nothing but revolt from the beginning of time. On the contrary, it is quite rare.

> Christina Stead, *House of All Nations* (1938)

7 Mercy, it's the revolution, and I'm in my bathrobe!

> Nicole Hollander, book title (1982)

See also Change, Rebellion, Social Change, War.

## ✤ REWARD

8 Every kind of reward constitutes a degradation of energy.

> Simone Weil, *Gravity and Grace* (1947)

9 Reward is its own virtue.

> Carolyn Wells, "Maxioms," *Folly for the Wise* (1904)

See also Recognition.

## ✤ THE RICH

10 The old Eskimo hunters she had known in her childhood thought the riches of life were intelligence, fearlessness, and love. A man with these gifts was rich.

> Jean Craighead George, *Julie of the Wolves* (1972)

11 If you are rich, you have lovely cars, and jars full of flowers, and books in rows, and a wireless, and the best sort of gramophone and meringues for supper.

> Winifred Holtby (1923), in Alice Holtby and Jean McWilliam, eds., *Letters to a Friend* (1937)

12 Though the worship of riches is an old religion, there has never before been a danger that it might become the *sole* religion. And yet that is what is surely going to happen to the world.

> J.E. Buckrose, "The Sacred Million," *What I Have Gathered* (1923)

13 I do want to get rich but I never want to do what there is to do to get rich.

> Gertrude Stein, *Everybody's Autobiography* (1937)

14 "You are rich," he cried; "are you therefore worthless?"

> Fanny Burney, *Cecilia* (1782)

15 Now that he was rich he was not thought ignorant any more, but simply eccentric.

> Mavis Gallant, *The Pegnitz Junction* (1973)

16 If all the rich men in the world divided up their money amongst themselves, there wouldn't be enough to go round.

> Christina Stead, *House of All Nations* (1938)

17 Rich folks always talks hard times.

> Lillian Smith, *Strange Fruit* (1944)

18 How often the rich like to play at being poor. A rather nasty game, I've always thought.

> Lillian Hellman, *Toys in the Attic* (1960)

19 The richer your friends, the more they will cost you.

> Elisabeth Marbury, *My Crystal Ball* (1923)

20 When you say fiscal responsibility, it seems to me that you really mean rich people keeping their money.

> Alice Adams, *Listening to Billie* (1978)

1 The very rich and the very social are, often, the very stuffy.

    Edna Ferber, *A Peculiar Treasure* (1939)

See also Aristocracy, Class, Luxury, Money, The Rich and the Poor, Wealth.

## ✺ THE RICH AND THE POOR

2 You and I, the rich and the poor of this world, are two locked caskets, of which each contains the key to the other.

    Isak Dinesen "A Consolatory Tale," *Winter's Tales* (1942)

3 Between prosperity and adversity there can be little real fellowship.

    Amelia B. Edwards, *Half a Million of Money* (1866)

4 It is hard to interest those who have everything in those who have nothing.

    Helen Keller, *Helen Keller's Journal* (1938)

5 The rich are never threatened by the poor—they do not notice them.

    Marie de France (12th cent.), in Jeanette Beer, tr., *Medieval Fables of Marie de France* (1981)

6 I see no present solution of a great and intricate problem but that the rich should realize their duty to the poor.

    Gertrude Atherton, *Los Cerritos* (1890)

7 I have two enemies in all the world, / Two twins, inseparably pooled: / The hunger of the hungry and the fullness of the full.

    Marina Tsvetaeva, "If the Soul Was Born With Pinions," *Swans' Encampment* (1957)

8 Riches may not bring happiness, but neither does poverty.

    Sophie Irene Loeb, *Epigrams of Eve* (1913)

9 I've been rich and I've been poor. Rich is better.

    Sophie Tucker (1940s), attributed (also attributed to Joe E. Lewis), in Ralph Keyes, *"Nice Guys Finish Last"* (1992)

10 A poor person who is unhappy is in a better position than a rich person who is unhappy. Because the poor person has hope. He thinks money would help.

    Jean Kerr, *Poor Richard* (1965)

11 Wouldn't you think some sociologist would have done a comparative study by now to prove, as I have always suspected, that there is a higher proportion of Undeserving Rich than Undeserving Poor?

    Molly Ivins, in *The Fort Worth Star-Telegram* (1992)

12 'Tis the superfluity of one man which makes the poverty of the other.

    Vernon Lee, "About Leisure," *Limbo* (1908)

13 It is easier to give all your goods to feed the poor, or not to have any goods—only your virtues, to boast of—than it is to judge the rich with charity.

    Corra Harris, in Martha Bensley Bruère and Mary Ritter Beard, *Laughing Their Way* (1934)

14 The poor never estimate as a virtue the generosity of the rich.

    Marie von Ebner-Eschenbach, *Aphorisms* (1893)

15 The poor man wishes to conceal his poverty, and the rich man his wealth: the former fears lest he be despised, the latter lest he be plundered.

    Marie von Ebner-Eschenbach, *Aphorisms* (1893)

16 The vices of the rich and great are mistaken for errors; and those of the poor and lowly, for crimes.

    Countess of Blessington, *Desultory Thoughts and Reflections* (1839)

17 Errors look so very ugly in persons of small means—one feels they are taking quite a liberty in going astray; whereas people of fortune may naturally indulge in a few delinquencies. "They've got the money for it," as the girl said of her mistress who had made herself ill with pickled salmon.

    George Eliot, "Janet's Repentance," *Scenes of Clerical Life* (1857)

18 To put it quite crudely . . . the poor don't really know how the rich live, and the rich don't know how the poor live, and to find out is really enchanting to both of them.

    Agatha Christie, *Endless Night* (1968)

19 We must be careful that the people who make $5,000 a year are not pitted against those that make $25,000 a year by those who make $900,000.

    Barbara A. Mikulski, speech (1974)

20 The difference between rich and poor is that the poor do everything with their own hands and the rich hire hands to do things.

    Betty Smith, *A Tree Grows in Brooklyn* (1943)

1 I am weary seeing our laboring classes so wretchedly housed, fed, and clothed, while thousands of
dollars are wasted every year over unsightly statues.
If these great men must have outdoor memorials
let them be in the form of handsome blocks of
buildings for the poor.

> Elizabeth Cady Stanton (1886), in Theodore Stanton and
> Harriot Stanton Blatch, eds., *Elizabeth Cady Stanton As
> Revealed in Her Letters Diary and Reminiscences*, vol. 2 (1922)

2 The rich rob the poor, and the poor rob one another.

> Sojourner Truth, in Olive Gilbert, *Narrative of Sojourner
> Truth* (1878)

3 It is very much easier for a rich man to invest and
grow richer than for the poor man to begin invest-
ing at all. And this is also true of nations.

> Barbara Ward, *The Rich Nations and the Poor Nations* (1962)

See also Class, The Poor, The Rich, Wealth.

## ❧ RIDICULE

4 It is easier for some to stand before a bullet than
before a laugh.

> S. Elizabeth Sisson, *Richard Newcomb* (1900)

5 Love can bear anything better than ridicule.

> Caitlin Thomas, *Leftover Life to Kill* (1957)

6 There is hardly any mental misery worse than that
of having our own serious phrases, our own rooted
beliefs, caricatured by a charlatan or a hireling.

> George Eliot, *Felix Holt, the Radical* (1866)

7 Ridicule may be a shield, but it is not a weapon.

> Dorothy Parker (1937), in John Keats, *You Might As Well
> Live* (1970)

8 Ridicule is like a wolf: it only destroys those who
fear it.

> Comtesse Diane, *Les Glanes de la Vie* (1898)

See also Criticism, Sarcasm, Satire, Sneers.

## ❧ RIGHTEOUSNESS

9 "I told you how it would be." Strange mode of
comforting; but such is the satisfaction which vanity tastes at the expense of misfortune.

> Madame de Staël, *Corinne* (1807)

10 Most of us have to be self-righteous before we can
be righteous.

> Vera Brittain, *Testament of Youth* (1933)

11 A man of lofty ideas is an uncomfortable neighbor.

> Marie von Ebner-Eschenbach, *Aphorisms* (1893)

12 Beware of people whose halos are on too tight.

> Sally Stanford, in Bob Chieger, *Was It Good for You, Too?*
> (1983)

13 There is no robbery so terrible as the robbery committed by those who think they are doing right.

> Mary Catherwood, *Lazarre* (1901)

14 To be in the right is often an expensive business.

> Phyllis Bottome, *Danger Signal* (1939)

15 There's one thing that always interests me about
you good people, not your certainty that the rest of
us are swine,—no doubt we are,—but your certainty that your opinions are pearls.

> Margaret Deland, *Philip and His Wife* (1894)

See also Indignation, Self-Satisfaction.

## ❧ RIGHTS

16 There is but one honest limit to the rights of a
sentient being; it is where they touch the rights of
another sentient being.

> Frances Wright, "Of Free Enquiry," *Course of Popular
> Lectures* (1829)

17 Where no individual in a community is denied his
rights, the mass are the more perfectly protected in
theirs; for whenever any class is subject to fraud or
injustice, it shows that the spirit of tyranny is at
work, and no one can tell where or how or when
the infection will spread.

> Elizabeth Cady Stanton, in *The Liberator* (1860)

18 Individual rights are not subject to a public vote; a
majority has no right to vote away the rights of a
minority.

> Ayn Rand, *The Virtue of Selfishness* (1964)

19 Once the state is looked upon as the *source* of
rights, rather than their bound protector, freedom
becomes conditional on the pleasure of the state.

> Mary McCarthy, "The Contagion of Ideas" (1952), *On the
> Contrary* (1961)

1 The notion of obligations comes before that of rights, which is subordinate and relative to the former. A right is not effectual by itself, but only in relation to the obligation to which it corresponds.

Simone Weil, *The Need for Roots* (1949)

2 There's no question in my mind but that rights are never won unless people are willing to fight for them.

Eleanor Smeal, speech (1985)

3 A right which goes unrecognized by anybody is not worth very much.

Simone Weil, *The Need for Roots* (1949)

4 Dis morning I was walking out, and . . . I saw de wheat a holding up its head, looking very big. I goes up and takes holt ob it. You b'lieve it, dere was *no* wheat dare? I says, God, what *is* de matter wid *dis* wheat? and he says to me, "Sojourner, dere is a little weasel in it." Now I hears talkin' about de Constitution and de rights of man. I comes up and I takes hold of dis Constitution. It looks *mighty big*, and I feels for *my* rights, but der aint any dare. Den I says, God, what *ails* dis Constitution? He says to me, "Sojourner, dere is a little *weasel* in it."

Sojourner Truth, in Olive Gilbert, *Narrative of Sojourner Truth* (1878)

5 I recognize no rights but *human* rights—I know nothing of men's rights and women's rights.

Angelina E. Grimké (1837), *Letters to Catherine E. Beecher* (1969)

6 Men their rights and nothing more; women their rights and nothing less.

Susan B. Anthony and Elizabeth Cady Stanton, motto of newspaper, *The Revolution* (1868)

7 My greatest disappointment in all the projects I worked on during the White House years was the failure of the Equal Rights Amendment to be ratified. . . . Why all the controversy and why such difficulty in giving women the protection of the Constitution that should have been theirs long ago?

Rosalynn Carter, *First Lady From Plains* (1984)

8 It must become a right of every person to die of old age. And if we secure this right for ourselves, we can, coincidentally, assure it for the planet.

Alice Walker, "Longing to Die of Old Age," *Living by the Word* (1988)

## ❦ RISK

9 Risk! Risk anything! Care no more for the opinions of others, for those voices. Do the hardest thing on earth for you. Act for yourself. Face the truth.

Katherine Mansfield (1922), *The Journal of Katherine Mansfield* (1927)

10 The fullness of life is in the hazards of life.

Edith Hamilton, *The Greek Way* (1930)

11 A ship in port is safe, but that's not what ships are built for.

Grace Murray Hopper, in Roger von Oech, "The Judge," *A Kick in the Seat of the Pants* (1986)

12 Leaps over walls—especially when taken late in life—can be extremely perilous. To leap successfully, you need a sense of humor, the spirit of adventure and an unshakable conviction that what you are leaping over is an obstacle upon which you would otherwise fall down.

Monica Baldwin, *I Leap Over the Wall* (1950)

13 The human soul has need of security and also of risk. The fear of violence or of hunger or of any other extreme evil is a sickness of the soul. The boredom produced by a complete absence of risk is also a sickness of the soul.

Simone Weil, *Selected Essays 1934-1943* (1962)

14 If you risk nothing, then you risk everything.

Geena Davis, in Kevin Sessums, "Geena's Sheen," *Vanity Fair* (1992)

15 If you don't risk anything, you risk even *more*.

Erica Jong, *How to Save Your Own Life* (1977)

16 I would not creep along the coast, but steer / Out in mid-sea, by guidance of the stars.

George Eliot, *Middlemarch* (1871)

17 All my life I have gone out on a limb, but I have turned the limb into a bridge, and there is cool, clear water flowing under.

Holly Near, with Derk Richardson, *Fire in the Rain . . . Singer in the Storm* (1990)

18 Please know I am quite aware of the hazards. I want to do it because I want to do it. Women must try to do things as men have tried. When they fail, their failure must be but a challenge to others.

Amelia Earhart, letter to husband George P. Putnam before a risky flight, *Last Flight* (1937)

1 What you risk reveals what you value.
  Jeanette Winterson, *Written on the Body* (1992)

2 Sometimes I think we can tell how important it is to risk by how dangerous it would be to do so.
  Sonia Johnson, *Going Out of Our Minds* (1987)

3 If you're never scared or embarrassed or hurt, it means you never take any chances.
  Julia Sorel, *See How She Runs* (1978)

4 Our whole way of life today is dedicated to the *removal of risk*. Cradle to grave we are supported, insulated, and isolated from the risks of life—and if we fall, our government stands ready with band-aids of every size.
  Shirley Temple Black, in Rodney G. Minott, *The Sinking of the Lollipop* (1968)

See also Adventure, Courage, Danger, Daring, Security.

❧ RITUAL

5 Rituals are the formulas by which harmony is restored.
  Terry Tempest Williams, *Pieces of White Shell* (1984)

6 Ritual is rooted in earth, / ancient and blest.
  H.D., "Choros Translations," *Red Roses for Bronze* (1931)

7 Ritual is the way we carry the presence of the sacred. Ritual is the spark that must not go out.
  Christina Baldwin, *Life's Companion* (1990)

8 Rituals are a good signal to your unconscious that it is time to kick in.
  Anne Lamott, *Bird by Bird* (1994)

9 Ritual is the most primitive reflection of serious thought, a slow deposit, as it were, of people's imaginative insight into life.
  Susanne K. Langer, *Philosophy in a New Key* (1942)

10 Ritual is one of the ways in which humans put their lives in perspective, whether it be Purim, Advent, or drawing down the moon. Ritual calls together the shades and specters in people's lives, sorts them out, puts them to rest.
  Clarissa Pinkola Estés, *Women Who Run With the Wolves* (1992)

11 Ritual is the bridge by which man passes, the ladder by which he climbs from earth to heaven. . . . We must not pull down the ladder till we are sure the last angel has climbed.
  Jane Harrison, *Ancient Art and Ritual* (1913)

12 Art is not the handmaid of Religion, but . . . Art in some sense springs out of Religion, and . . . between them is a connecting link, a bridge, and that bridge is Ritual.
  Jane Harrison, *Reminiscences of a Student's Life* (1925)

13 Ritual is the act of sanctifying action—even ordinary actions—so that it has meaning: I can light a candle because I need the light or because the candle represents the light I need.
  Christina Baldwin, *Life's Companion* (1990)

14 Ritual and myth are like seed crystals of new patterns that can eventually reshape culture around them.
  Starhawk, *Truth or Dare* (1987)

15 I believe that we often disguise pain through ritual and it may be the only solace we have.
  Rita Mae Brown, *Starting From Scratch* (1988)

16 The preparation for the ritual *is* the ritual.
  Kate Green, *Shattered Moon* (1986)

See also Habit, Religion, Spirituality, Traditions, Worship.

❧ RIVERS

17 A river seems a magic thing. A magic, moving, living part of the very earth itself—for it is from the soil, both from its depth and from its surface, that a river has its beginning.
  Laura Gilpin, *The Rio Grande* (1949)

18 When there is a river in your growing up, you probably always hear it.
  Ann Zwinger, *Run, River, Run* (1975)

19 People who live / by rivers  dream / they are immortal.
  Audre Lorde, "St. Louis a City Out of Time" (1971), *Undersong* (1992)

1 The brook that does go by our house is always bringing songs from the hills.

> Opal Whiteley (1920), in Benjamin Hoff, ed., *The Singing Creek Where the Willows Grow* (1986)

2 O travelers swift / From secrets to oblivion! Waters wild / That pass in act to bend a flower, or lift / The bright limbs of a child!

> Alice Meynell, "'Rivers Unknown to Song'," *Last Poems of Alice Meynell* (1923)

3 Rivers perhaps are the only physical features of the world that are at their best from the air.

> Anne Morrow Lindbergh, *North to the Orient* (1935)

4 That river—it was full of good and evil together. It would water the fields when it was curbed and checked, but then if an inch were allowed it, it crashed through like a roaring dragon.

> Pearl S. Buck, *The Old Demon* (1939)

5 As we were in the midst of the dry season, the river at Vat Thmey was now only a big snake of mud.

> Molyda Szymusiak, *The Stones Cry Out* (1984)

6 The Rhone is pale and tragic as the empty sleeve of an amputee.

> Laurent Daniel, *The Lovers of Avignon* (1943)

## ❦ ROMANCE

7 A fine romance! with no kisses! / A fine romance, my friend, this is!

> Dorothy Fields, "A Fine Romance" (1930)

8 Romance is unsatisfactory as a religion. It is no use looking for the infinite in the eyes of another.

> Jennifer Stone, "Eros: The Imperative of Intimacy," *Stone's Throw* (1988)

See also Courtship, Dating, Flirtation, Love, Relationships.

## ❦ ROME

9 Rome is everybody's memory.

> Eleanor Clark, *Rome and a Villa* (1952)

10 [Rome is] an impossible compounding of time, in which no century has respect for any other and all hit you in a jumble at every turn.

> Eleanor Clark, *Rome and a Villa* (1952)

11 Rome's riches are in too immediate juxtaposition. Under the lid of awful August heat, one moves dizzily from church to palace to fountain to ruin, a single fly at a banquet, not knowing where to light.

> Shana Alexander, "The Roman Astonishment," in *Life* (1967)

12 In Rome people seem to love with more zest, murder with more imagination, submit to creative urges more often, and lose the sense of logic more easily than in any other place.

> Letitia Baldrige, *Of Diamonds and Diplomats* (1968)

13 What is one to make of this marble rubble, this milk of wolves, this blood of Caesars, this sunrise of Renaissance, this baroquery of blown stone, this warm hive of Italians, this antipasto of civilization?

> Shana Alexander, "The Roman Astonishment," in *Life* (1967)

14 It is like a party all the time; nobody has to worry about giving one or being invited; it is going on every day in the street and you can go down or be part of it from your window.

> Eleanor Clark, *Rome and a Villa* (1952)

15 Even a tourist can tell in a Roman street that he is in something and not outside of something as he would be in most cities. In Rome to go out is to go home.

> Eleanor Clark, *Rome and a Villa* (1952)

16 The Roman form of serenade is to race a motorcycle motor under the girl's window, but mufflers are not common in any situation; the only things as dearly loved as a good noise are breakneck speed and eye-splitting lights, preferably neon—all expressions of well-being, like a huge belly-laugh.

> Eleanor Clark, *Rome and a Villa* (1952)

17 I was shocked numb to discover that Rome is *full* of Italians. The Rome I had had in mind was a solemn museum, maintained by just enough native personnel to keep it functioning for the tourist trade.

> Mary Chamberlin, *Dear Friends and Darling Romans* (1959)

18 In Rome people spend most of their time having lunch. And they do it very well—Rome is unquestionably the lunch capital of the world.

> Fran Lebowitz, *Metropolitan Life* (1978)

1　Royalty is as common here as ravioli.

　　Cindy Adams, in Joey Adams, *Cindy and I* (1957)

2　Faithful to custom, I watched the sun set on my first day in Rome from the Pincio terrace in the Villa Borghese. . . . I hadn't known until then that the sun saves all the leftover gold from the day to pour over Rome.

　　Mary Chamberlin, *Dear Friends and Darling Romans* (1959)

3　Night doesn't fall in Rome; it rises from the city's heart, from the gloomy little alleys and courtyards where the sun never gets much more than a brief look-in, and then, like the mist from the Tiber, it creeps over the rooftops and spreads up into the hills.

　　Caroline Llewellyn, *The Masks of Rome* (1988)

See also Italy.

## ❧ ROOMS

4　What a haven of rest and security is one's own room!

　　The Duchess, *Molly Bawn* (1878)

5　A room is a place where you hide from the wolves outside and that's all any room is.

　　Jean Rhys, *Good Morning, Midnight* (1939)

6　I have at last got the little room I have wanted so long, and am very happy about it. It does me good to be alone.

　　Louisa May Alcott, *Journals* (1868)

7　A woman must have money and a room of her own if she is to write fiction.

　　Virginia Woolf, *A Room of One's Own* (1929)

8　Most women still need a room of their own and the only way to find it may be outside their own homes.

　　Germaine Greer, *The Female Eunuch* (1971)

9　A room of one's own isn't nearly enough. A house, or, best, an island of one's own.

　　Lillian Hellman, *Another Part of the Forest* (1947)

See also Houses, Space, Walls.

## ❧ ROOTS

10　To be rooted is perhaps the most important and least recognized need of the human soul.

　　Simone Weil, *The Need for Roots* (1949)

11　If you go away from your own place and people— the place you spent your childhood in, all your life you'll be sick with homesickness and you'll never have a home. You can find a better place, perhaps, a way of life you like better, but the *home* is gone out of your heart, and you'll be hunting it all your life long.

　　Mary O'Hara, *Thunderhead* (1943)

12　There were years when, in search of what I thought were better, nobler things I denied these, my people, and my family. I forgot the songs they sung— and most of those songs are now dead; I erased their dialect from my tongue; I was ashamed of them and their ways of life. But now—yes, I love them; they are a part of my blood; they, with all their virtues and their faults, played a great part in forming my way of looking at life.

　　Agnes Smedley, *Daughter of Earth* (1929)

13　Whoever is uprooted himself uproots others. Whoever is rooted himself doesn't uproot others.

　　Simone Weil, *The Need for Roots* (1949)

14　Far away from my country I would be like those trees they chop down at Christmastime, those poor rootless pines that last a little while and then die.

　　Isabel Allende, *The House of Spirits* (1982)

15　To separate from my culture (as from my family) I had to feel competent enough on the outside and secure enough inside to live life on my own. Yet in leaving home I did not lose touch with my origins because *lo mexicano* is in my system. I am a turtle, wherever I go I carry "home" on my back.

　　Gloria Anzaldúa, *Borderlands/La Frontera* (1987)

16　The Gringo, locked into the fiction of white superiority, seized complete political power, stripping Indians and Mexicans of their land while their feet were still rooted in it. *Con el destierro y el exilo fuimos desuñados, destroncados, destripados*—we were jerked out by the roots, truncated, disemboweled, dispossessed, and separated from our identity and our history.

　　Gloria Anzaldúa, *Borderlands/La Frontera* (1987)

[ 593 ]ception

1 I have not seen my birthplace, / where my mother deposited the heavy load of her inside.

    Tahereh Saffir-Zadeh, "My Birthplace," *Resonance in the Bay* (1971)

2 That I can live long enough / To obtain one and only one desire— / That someday I can see again / The mulberry and catalpa trees of home.

    Ts'ai Yen, "Eighteen Verses Sung to a Tatar Reed Whistle" (c. 200), in Joanna Bankier and Deirdre Lashgari, eds., *Women Poets of the World* (1983)

See also Ancestors, Family, Home, Homeland.

## &#x266A; ROUTINE

3 The final result of too much routine is death in life.

    Gertrude Atherton, *Can Women Be Gentlemen?* (1938)

See also Habit, Normalcy, Ordinariness.

## &#x266A; ROYALTY

4 Lo, the god knows me well, / . . . / No one rebels against me in all lands. / All foreign lands are my subjects, / He placed my border at the limits of heaven.

    Queen Hatshepsut, "Speech of the Queen" (c. 1450 B.C.), in Margaret Busby, ed., *Daughters of Africa* (1992)

5 Though God hath raised me high, yet this I count the glory of my crown: That I have reigned with your loves.

    Elizabeth I, "The Golden Speech" (1601), in Frederick Chamberlin, *The Sayings of Queen Elizabeth* (1923)

6 My seat has been the seat of kings, and I will have no rascal to succeed me.

    Elizabeth I (1603), apparently said on her deathbed when pressed about a successor, in Mrs. Jameson, *Memoirs of Celebrated Female Sovereigns* (1831)

7 To be a king and wear a crown is more glorious to them that see it than it is pleasure to them that bear it.

    Elizabeth I, "The Golden Speech" (1601), in Frederick Chamberlin, *The Sayings of Queen Elizabeth* (1923)

8 There are few prisoners more closely guarded than princes.

    Christina, Queen of Sweden, "Maxims" (1680), in Henry Woodhead, *Memoirs of Christina, Queen of Sweden*, vol. 2 (1863)

9 We Princes are set as it were upon stages, in the sight and view of all the world. The least spot is soon spied in our garments, a blemish quickly noticed in our doings.

    Queen Elizabeth I (1581), in Frederick Chamberlin, *The Sayings of Queen Elizabeth* (1923)

10 You are a member of the British royal family. We are *never* tired, and we all *love* hospitals.

    Queen Mary, to a complaining young royal, in John Pearson, *The Selling of the Royal Family* (1986)

11 I am not your "love." I am Your Royal Highness!

    Princess Anne, to photographer who said, "Look this way, love," in Timothy B. Benford, *The Royal Family Quiz and Fact Book* (1987)

12 People felt they needed a [Princess] Diana to help them through difficult times. If Diana had not existed they would have had to invent her.

    Elizabeth Longford, *The Queen* (1983)

13 We'll go quietly.

    Queen Elizabeth II, at the suggestion that Great Britain might someday want a republic, in Ann Morrow, *The Queen* (1983)

## &#x266A; RUDENESS

14 Please don't think me negligent or rude. I am both, in effect, of course, but please don't think me either.

    Edna St. Vincent Millay (1920), in Allan Ross Macdougall, ed., *Letters of Edna St. Vincent Millay* (1952)

15 You can't be truly rude until you understand good manners.

    Rita Mae Brown, *Starting From Scratch* (1988)

16 Rudeness to Mrs. Dosely was like dropping a pat of butter on to a hot plate—it slid and melted away.

    Elizabeth Bowen, "Maria," *The Cat Jumps* (1934)

17 It is little consolation, and no compensation, to the person who is hurt that the offender pleads he did not mean to say or do any thing rude: a rude thing

is a rude thing—the intention is nothing—all we are to judge of is the fact.

Maria Edgeworth, *Harrington* (1833)

1 Be arrogant. . . . They won't respect you unless you're rude.

Martha Graham (1942), advice to Agnes de Mille, in Agnes de Mille, *Dance to the Piper* (1952)

2 Everybody suspects an eager desire to curry favor, but rudeness, for some reason, is always accepted as a guarantee of good faith.

Dorothy L. Sayers, *Murder Must Advertise* (1933)

See also Etiquette, Manners, Offensiveness, Politeness.


## ✿ RULES

3 Rules are like flagpoles in a slalom race: you observe their presence religiously, skirt around them as closely as possible, and never let them cut your speed.

Katherine Neville, *A Calculated Risk* (1992)

4 It seems to me there are no rules, only instances; but perhaps that is because I learned no rules, and am only an instance myself.

Eleanor Farjeon, *Portrait of a Family* (1936)

5 General rules will bear hard on particular cases.

Harriet Beecher Stowe, *Uncle Tom's Cabin* (1852)

6 General rules are dangerous of application in particular instances.

Charlotte M. Yonge, *The Pillars of the House*, vol. 2 (1889)

7 There is all the difference in the world between departure from recognized rules by one who has learned to obey them, and neglect of them through want of training or want of skill or want of understanding. Before you can be eccentric you must know where the circle is.

Ellen Terry, *The Story of My Life* (1908)

8 There's no rule so wise but what it's a pity for somebody or other.

George Eliot, *Adam Bede* (1859)

See also Exceptions, Law.


## ✿ RUMOR

9 A cruel story runs on wheels, and every hand oils the wheels as they run.

Ouida, *Wisdom, Wit and Pathos* (1884)

10 Rumor is untraceable, incalculable, and infectious.

Margot Asquith, *More or Less About Myself* (1934)

11 We must be careful what we say. No bird resumes its egg.

Emily Dickinson (1874), in Mabel Loomis Todd, ed., *Letters of Emily Dickinson*, vol. 2 (1894)

12 It starts as an inflection of the voice, a question asked in a certain tone and not answered with "no"; a prolonged little silence, a twinkle in the eye, a long-drawn "w-e-e-ell—I don't know." These are the fine roots of the tree whose poisonous fruits are gossip and slander.

Maria Augusta Trapp, *The Story of the Trapp Family Singers* (1949)

13 It is harder to kill a whisper than even a shouted calumny.

Mary Stewart, *The Last Enchantment* (1979)

14 There is a vital force in rumor. Though crushed to earth, to all intents and purposes buried, it can rise again without apparent effort.

Eleanor Robson Belmont, *The Fabric of Memory* (1957)

15 There is no fire without smoke but there is often smoke without fire.

Christine de Pisan (1404), in Thelma S. Fenster and Nadia Margolis, tr., *The Book of the Duke of True Lovers* (1991)

16 The rumor [that we were to marry] came along, growing closer all the time. In June we turned around together and looked at it. It did not seem so bad that way, so we took it into the family and changed its name to fact.

Sonja Henie, *Wings on My Feet* (1940)

17 She was always in good rumor.

Marcelene Cox, in *Ladies' Home Journal* (1942)

18 I thought you were only a rumor.

Louise Tracy, widow of Spencer Tracy, to Katharine Hepburn, in Katharine Hepburn, *Me* (1991)

See also Calumny, Gossip, "They."

## ❦ RUNNING AWAY

1 Each time that I have run away—and from a habit it quickly became an illness—I have betrayed someone. Myself, but not always only myself.

   Storm Jameson, *The Journal of Mary Hervey Russell* (1945)

See also Desertion.

## ❦ RUSSIA

2 There is something gigantic about this people . . . their imaginativeness knows no bounds. With them everything is colossal rather than well-proportioned, audacious rather than well-considered, and if they do not attain their goals, it is because they exceed them.

   Madame de Staël (1812), in J. Christopher Herold, *Mistress to an Age* (1958)

3 Moscow seethes and bubbles and gasps for air. It's always thirsting for something new, the newest events, the latest sensation. Everyone wants to be the first to know.

   Svetlana Alliluyeva, *Twenty Letters to a Friend* (1967)

4 In this city of wonder / this peaceful city / I shall be joyful, even / when I am dead.

   Marina Tsvetaeva, "Verses About Moscow," in Elaine Feinstein, ed., *Selected Poems* (1971)

5 Leningrad . . . is a city with the gift of timelessness.

   Jan Morris, "The Winter Queen" (1957), *Among the Cities* (1985)

6 Keeping your coat on indoors in Russia, no matter how public the place, is far worse than keeping your hat on as the flag goes by. It is worse than going into a Catholic church in Spain with your upper arms bare. It is worse than telling a mother her baby bores you.

   Ilka Chase, *Worlds Apart* (1972)

7 Our country is on such a low socioeconomic level that at the moment we cannot afford to divide ourselves into "us women" and "us men." We share a common struggle for democracy, a struggle to feed the country.

   Elena Bonner, speech (1990)

## ❦ RUTHLESSNESS

8 How ruthless we are when we live on the surface of life!

   Mabel Dodge Luhan, *Lorenzo in Taos* (1932)

See also Cruelty.

# S

## ♪ THE SACRED

1 Each being is sacred—meaning that each has inherent value that cannot be ranked in a hierarchy or compared to the value of another being.
> Starhawk, *Truth or Dare* (1987)

2 There is nothing so secular that it cannot be sacred, and that is one of the deepest messages of the Incarnation.
> Madeleine L'Engle, *Walking on Water* (1980)

3 To survive we must begin to know sacredness  The pace which most of us live prevents this.
> Chrystos, "No Rock Scorns Me As Whore," in Cherríe Moraga and Gloria Anzaldúa, eds., *This Bridge Called My Back* (1983)

4 There are many, many gates to the sacred and they are as wide as we need them to be.
> Sherry Ruth Anderson and Patricia Hopkins, *The Feminine Face of God* (1991)

See also Divinity, God, Holiness, Spirituality.

## ♪ SAINTS

5 A saint is simply a human being whose soul has . . . grown up to its full stature, by full and generous response to its environment, God. He has achieved a deeper, bigger life than the rest of us, a more wonderful contact with the mysteries of the Universe; a life of infinite possibility, the term of which he never feels that he has reached.
> Evelyn Underhill, *Concerning the Inner Life* (1926)

6 Saints are non-conformists.
> Eleanor Ross Taylor, title poem, *Welcome Eumenides* (1972)

7 I don't believe in God, but I do believe in His Saints.
> Edith Wharton, in Percy Lubbock, *Portrait of Edith Wharton* (1947)

8 The world needs saints who have genius, just as a plague-stricken town needs doctors.
> Simone Weil, *Oppression and Liberty* (1955)

9 The wonderful thing about saints is that they were *human*. They lost their tempers, got hungry, scolded God, were egotistical or testy or impatient in their turns, made mistakes and regretted them. Still they went on doggedly blundering toward heaven.
> Phyllis McGinley, "Running to Paradise," *Saint-Watching* (1969)

10 Don't call me a saint. I don't want to be dismissed that easily.
> Dorothy Day, in Robert Ellsberg, ed., *By Little and by Little* (1983)

See also Goodness, Holiness.

## ♪ SALES ABILITY

11 Here was a born salesman. Every time he spoke, he convinced himself.
> Emma Lathen, *Pick Up Sticks* (1970)

12 Sell, he can. He can sell last week's bait for tomorrow's halibut.
> Christina Stead, *House of All Nations* (1938)

## ♪ SALVATION

13 There is an easiness in salvation which is more difficult to us than all our efforts.
> Simone Weil, *Waiting for God* (1950)

## SANITY

1 In every society, the definitions of sanity and madness are arbitrary—are, in the largest sense, political.

Susan Sontag, "Approaching Artaud," in *The New Yorker* (1973)

2 What is sanity, after all, except the *control* of madness?

Josephine W. Johnson, *Now in November* (1934)

3 That's the truest sign of insanity—insane people are always sure they're just fine. It's only the sane people who are willing to admit they're crazy.

Nora Ephron, *Heartburn* (1983)

4 Sane people did what their neighbors did, so that if any lunatics were at large, one might know and avoid them.

George Eliot, *Middlemarch* (1871)

See also Insanity, Madness, Mental Illness.

## SARCASM

5 Her sarcasm was so quick, so fine at the point—it was like being touched by a metal so cold that one doesn't know whether one is burned or chilled.

Willa Cather, *My Mortal Enemy* (1926)

6 Many men have withstood an argument who fell before a sarcasm.

Elizabeth Elton Smith, *The Three Eras of Woman's Life* (1836)

See also Criticism, Ridicule, Satire, Wit.

## SATIRE

7 Satire should, like a polish'd razor keen, / Wound with a touch, that's scarcely felt or seen.

Lady Mary Wortley Montagu, "Verses Address'd to the Imitator of Horace" (1733), *The Works of the Right Honorable Lady Mary Wortley Montagu*, vol. 5 (1803)

8 A fondness for satire indicates a mind pleased with irritating others; for myself, I never could find amusement in killing flies.

Marie-Jeanne Roland (1776), in Lydia Maria Child, *Memoirs of Madame de Staël and of Madame Roland* (1847)

9 Satyre . . . is a sort of Glass wherein Beholders do gen'rally discover ev'rybody's Face but their own.

Erica Jong, *Fanny: Being the True History of the Adventures of Fanny Hackabout-Jones* (1980)

10 Satire, like conscience, reminds us of what we often wish to forget.

Countess of Blessington, *Desultory Thoughts and Reflections* (1839)

11 Oh, life is a glorious cycle of song, / A medley of extemporanea; / And love is a thing that can never go wrong; / and I am Marie of Roumania.

Dorothy Parker, "Comment," *Enough Rope* (1926)

See also Humor, Sarcasm.

## SATISFACTION

12 There is no state of satisfaction, because to himself no man is a success.

Ellen Glasgow, *The Descendant* (1897)

13 Nobody's ever satisfied until they've been dead a good week.

Lucille Kallen, *Out There, Somewhere* (1964)

14 A man is never more satisfied than when he is confirming a favorite theory.

Mrs. Sarah J. Hale, *Traits of American Life* (1835)

15 Satisfaction is the enemy of creativity.

Jane Lazarre, *The Mother Knot* (1976)

16 Her satisfaction rose to the surface like the thick golden cream on the milk pans.

Marjorie Kinnan Rawlings, *The Sojourner* (1953)

See also Comfort, Complacency, Contentment, Enough, Gratification, Happiness, Self-Satisfaction.

## SCANDINAVIANS

17 There were tons of bronzed Scandinavian types at the Sorbonne. Marvelously blond and healthy and

shining white teeth. Funny thing though, because someone told me that if you actually go to Scandinavia none of the people who actually live there look like that. It's just a front they put up when they're abroad.

Charlotte Bingham, *Coronet Among the Weeds* (1963)

## ❧ SCARCITY

1 It is in the best interests of those in power to continue to feed the scarcity myth, that there is not enough to go around: not enough food, housing, medical care, child care, grants, contracts, jobs.

Paula Ross, "Women, Oppression, Privilege, and Competition," in Valerie Miner and Helen E. Longino, eds., *Competition* (1987)

2 Poverty on both a personal and worldwide level is supported by our collective belief in scarcity.

Shakti Gawain, *Reflections in the Light* (1988)

See also Advertising, Business.

## ❧ SCHOOL

3 I went to kindergarten as if into daily battle. There was only one respite: nap time, when we stretched out in rows of cots, like Civil War wounded.

Laura Cunningham, *Sleeping Arrangements* (1989)

4 Neat as a freshly peeled Easter egg, / Just six years old, he sat, *comme il faut*, / In the French Lycée in Berlin.

Else Lasker-Schüler, "Hans Jacob," *Hebrew Ballads* (1980)

5 School was a worry to her. She was not glib or quick in a world where glibness and quickness were easily confused with ability to learn.

Tillie Olsen, "I Stand Here Ironing," *Tell Me A Riddle* (1956)

See also Education, Learning, Students, Teaching.

## ❧ SCIENCE

6 The true definition of science is this: the study of the beauty of the world.

Simone Weil, *The Need for Roots* (1949)

7 Science, like art, religion, political theory, or psychoanalysis—is work that holds out the promise of philosophic understanding, excites in us the belief that we can "make sense of it all."

Vivian Gornick, *Women in Science* (1983)

8 If you do something once, people will call it an accident. If you do it twice, they call it a coincidence. But do it a third time and you've just proven a natural law.

Grace Murray Hopper, in Ethlie Ann Vare and Greg Ptacek, *Mothers of Invention* (1988)

9 There is one quality that characterizes all of us who deal with the sciences of the earth and its life—we are never bored.

Rachel Carson (1963), in Paul Brooks, *The House of Life* (1972)

10 To do science today is to experience a dimension unique in contemporary working lives; the work promises something incomparable: the sense of living both personally and historically. That is why science now draws to itself all kinds of people—charlatans, mediocrities, geniuses—everyone who wants to touch the flame, feel alive to the time.

Vivian Gornick, *Women in Science* (1983)

11 Almost anyone can do science; almost no one can do good science.

L.L. Larison Cudmore, *The Center of Life* (1977)

12 We especially need imagination in science. It is not all mathematics, nor all logic, but it is somewhat beauty and poetry.

Maria Mitchell (1866), in Phebe Mitchell Kendall, ed., *Maria Mitchell, Life, Letters, and Journals* (1896)

13 Real progress in understanding nature is rarely incremental. All important advances are sudden intuitions, new principles, new ways of seeing. We have not fully recognized this process of leaping ahead, however, in part because textbooks tend to tame revolutions, whether cultural or scientific. They describe the advances as if they had been logical in their day, not at all shocking.

Marilyn Ferguson, *The Aquarian Conspiracy* (1980)

14 Good science is almost always so very simple. *After* it has been done by someone else, of course.

L.L. Larison Cudmore, *The Center of Life* (1977)

15 It is only when science asks why, instead of simply describing how, that it becomes more than technology. When it asks why, it discovers Relativity.

When it only shows how, it invents the atomic bomb.

Ursula K. Le Guin, "The Stalin in the Soul," *Language of the Night* (1979)

1 We assume that knowledge of science is the prerogative of only a small number of human beings, isolated and priestlike in their laboratories. This is not true. The materials of science are the materials of life itself. Science is part of the reality of living; it is the what, the how, and the why of everything in our experience.

Rachel Carson (1952), in Paul Brooks, *The House of Life* (1972)

2 The phrase "popular science" has in itself a touch of absurdity. That knowledge which is popular is not scientific.

Maria Mitchell (1866), in Phebe Mitchell Kendall, ed., *Maria Mitchell, Life, Letters, and Journals* (1896)

3 Science has now been for a long time—and to an ever-increasing extent—a collective enterprise. Actually, new results are always, in fact, the work of specific individuals; but, save perhaps for rare exceptions, the value of any result depends on such a complex set of interrelations with past discoveries and possible future researches that even the mind of the inventor cannot embrace the whole.

Simone Weil (1934), *Oppression and Liberty* (1955)

4 Science is not neutral in its judgments, nor dispassionate, nor detached.

Kim Chernin, *The Obsession* (1981)

5 Our science is like a store filled with the most subtle intellectual devices for solving the most complex problems, and yet we are almost incapable of applying the elementary principles of rational thought.

Simone Weil, "The Power of Words," *The Simone Weil Reader* (1977)

6 Science is essentially international, and it is only through lack of the historical sense that national qualities have been attributed to it.

Marie Curie, "Intellectual Cooperation," *Memorandum* (1926)

7 Alas! the scientific conscience had got into the debasing company of money obligation and selfish respects.

George Eliot, *Middlemarch* (1871)

See also Biology, Research, Scientists.

## ⸎ SCIENCE FICTION

8 Science fiction is not predictive; it is descriptive.

Ursula K. Le Guin, *The Left Hand of Darkness* (1969)

9 Science fiction properly conceived, like all serious fiction, however funny, is a way of trying to describe what is in fact going on, what people actually do and feel, how people relate to everything else in this vast sack, this belly of the universe, this womb of things to be and tomb of things that were, this unending story.

Ursula K. Le Guin, *Dancing at the Edge of the World* (1989)

## ⸎ SCIENTISTS

10 Science is voiceless; it is the scientists who talk.

Simone Weil, *On Science, Necessity, and the Love of God* (1968)

11 Whatever a scientist is doing—reading, cooking, talking, playing—science thoughts are always there at the edge of the mind. They are the way the world is taken in; all that is seen is filtered through an everpresent scientific musing.

Vivian Gornick, *Women in Science* (1983)

12 A scientist in his laboratory is not only a technician: he is also a child placed before natural phenomena which impress him like a fairy tale.

Marie Curie (1993), in Eve Curie, *Madame Curie* (1938)

13 The villagers seldom leave the village; many scientists have limited and poorly cultivated minds apart from their specialty.

Simone Weil, *On Science, Necessity, and the Love of God* (1968)

14 One could count on one's fingers the number of scientists throughout the world with a general idea of the history and development of their particular science: there is none who is really competent as regards sciences other than his own. As science forms an indivisible whole, one may say that there are no longer, strictly speaking, scientists, but only drudges doing scientific work.

Simone Weil, *Oppression and Liberty* (1955)

15 Scientists do what writers do. They also live with an active interiority, only the ongoing speculation in

their heads is about relations in the physical world rather than the psychological one.

Vivian Gornick, *Women in Science* (1983)

1 A scientist or a writer is one who ruminates continuously on the nature of physical or imaginative life, experiences repeated relief and excitement when the insight comes, and is endlessly attracted to working out the idea.

Vivian Gornick, *Women in Science* (1983)

2 Women have been more systematically excluded from doing serious science than from performing any other social activity except, perhaps, frontline warfare.

Sandra Harding, *The Science Question in Feminism* (1986)

3 Do not undertake a scientific career in quest of fame or money. There are easier and better ways to reach them. Undertake it only if nothing else will satisfy you; for nothing is probably what you will receive. Your reward will be the widening of the horizon as you climb. And if you achieve that reward you will ask no other.

Cecilia Payne Gaposchkin, *An Autobiography and Other Recollections* (1984)

See also Science.

## ❦ SCULPTURE

4 Sculpture may be almost anything: a monument, a statue, an old coin, a bas-relief, a portrait bust, a lifelong struggle against heavy odds.

Malvina Hoffman, *Sculpture Inside and Out* (1939)

5 Sculpture is a parable in three dimensions, a symbol of a spiritual experience, and a means of conveying truth by concentrating its essence into visible form. . . . It must be the reflection of the artist who creates it and of the era in which he lives, not an echo or a memory of other days and other ways.

Malvina Hoffman, *Sculpture Inside and Out* (1939)

6 I love my blocks of marble, always piling up in the yard like a flock of sheep.

Barbara Hepworth, *A Pictorial Autobiography* (1985)

7 It's very inconvenient being a sculptor. It's like playing the double-bass; one's so handicapped by one's baggage.

Dorothy L. Sayers, *The Unpleasantness at the Bellona Club* (1928)

8 All my early memories are of forms and shapes and textures. Moving through and over the West Riding landscape with my father in his car, the hills were sculptures; the roads defined the form. Above all, there was the sensation of moving physically over the contours of fullnessess and concavities, through hollows and over peaks—feeling, touching, seeing, through mind and hand and eye. This sensation has never left me. I, the sculptor, *am* the landscape.

Barbara Hepworth, *A Pictorial Autobiography* (1985)

9 If one of God's children finds he cannot see or feel life in other terms than those of form, if he tries to escape and live outside of this obsession and fails, he generally calls himself a sculptor.

Malvina Hoffman, *Sculpture Inside and Out* (1939)

10 The most breadless art of our day.

Martha Albrand, *The Mask of Alexander* (1955)

11 I think our civilization is minimal enough without underlining it. Sculpture as a created object in space should enrich, not reflect. . . . Beauty is its function.

Barbara Chase-Riboud, in Colin Naylor and Genesis P-Orridge, eds., *Contemporary Artists* (1977)

12 He's been a waiten there in th wood you might say since before I was born. I jist brung him out a little—but one a these days, jist you wait an see, we'll find th time an a face fer him an bring him out a that block.

Harriette Arnow, *The Dollmaker* (1954)

See also Art, Artists.

## ❦ SEA

13 The voice of the sea speaks to the soul. The touch of the sea is sensuous, enfolding the body in its soft, close embrace.

Kate Chopin, *The Awakening* (1899)

14 I was born by the sea, and I have noticed that all the great events of my life have taken place by the sea. My first idea of movement, of the dance, certainly came from the rhythm of the waves.

Isadora Duncan, *My Life* (1927)

15 Only the sea is like a human being; the sky is not, nor the earth. But the sea is always moving, always

something deep in itself is stirring it. It never rests;
it is always wanting, wanting, wanting.

Ralph Iron, *The Story of an African Farm* (1883)

1 In the biting honesty of salt, the sea makes her
secrets known to those who care to listen.

Sandra Benítez, *A Place Where the Sea Remembers* (1993)

2 The sea makes no promises and breaks none.

Lillian Beckwith, *Lightly Poached* (1973)

3 If you want to know all about the sea . . . and ask
the sea itself, what does it say? Grumble grumble
swish swish. It is too busy being itself to know
anything about itself.

Ursula K. Le Guin, "Talking About Writing," *Language of
the Night* (1979)

4 The wind walks on the sea, / printing the water's
face with charity.

Gwen Harwood, "At the Sea's Edge," *Poems* (1963)

5 The lunging waves shook froth from their mouths
like runaway horses.

Diane Ackerman, *The Moon by Whale Light* (1991)

6 The sea is a collector, quick to return a rapacious
look.

Marianne Moore, "A Grave" (1924), *Selected Poems* (1935)

7 O mother, mother, hear the sea! / it calls across the
sands; / I saw it tossing up the spray, like white, /
imploring hands.

Mary Artemisia Lathbury, "A Deep Sea Dream," *Poems of
Mary Artemisia Lathbury* (1915)

8 But, visiting Sea, your love doth press / And reach
in further than you know, / And fills all these; and,
when you go, / There's loneliness in loneliness.

Alice Meynell, "The Visiting Sea," *Preludes* (1875)

9 Afraid? Of you, strong proxy lover, you, God's sea?
/ I give you my small self ecstatically, / To be
caught, held, or buffeted; to rest / Heart to your
heart, and breast to breathing breast.

Sister M. Madeleva, "The Swimmer," *Collected Poems* (1947)

10 It is a curious situation that the sea, from which life
first arose, should now be threatened by the activities of one form of that life. But the sea, though
changed in a sinister way, will continue to exist; the
threat is rather to life itself.

Rachel Carson, preface to 1961 edition, *The Sea Around Us*
(1950)

11 If the sea is sick, we'll feel it. If it dies, we die. Our
future and the state of the oceans are one.

Sylvia A. Earle, *Sea Change* (1995)

12 The mysterious human bond with the great seas
that poets write about has a physiological base in
our veins and in every living thing, where runs fluid
of the same saline proportions as ocean water.

Anne W. Simon, *The Thin Edge* (1978)

13 It doesn't matter where on Earth you live, everyone
is utterly dependent on the existence of that lovely,
living saltwater soup. There's plenty of water in the
universe without life, but nowhere is there life
without water.

Sylvia A. Earle, *Sea Change* (1995)

14 All at last return to the sea—to Oceanus, the ocean
river, like the ever-flowing stream of time, the beginning and the end.

Rachel Carson, *The Sea Around Us* (1950)

See also Ocean.

## ❧ SEARCHING

15 We seek him here, we seek him there, / Those
Frenchies seek him everywhere. / Is he in
heaven?—Is he in hell? / That demmed, elusive
Pimpernel?

Baroness Orczy, *The Scarlet Pimpernel* (1905)

16 What we seek we do not find—that would be too
trim and tidy for so reckless and opulent a thing as
life. It is something else we find.

Susan Glaspell, *The Morning Is Near Us* (1939)

17 We find what we search for—or, if we don't find it,
we become it.

Jessamyn West, *Love Is Not What You Think* (1959)

18 When you stop looking for something, you see it
right in front of you.

Eleanor Coppola, *Notes* (1979)

19 Often the search proves more profitable than the
goal.

E.L. Konigsburg, *From the Mixed-Up Files of Mrs. Basil E.
Frankweiler* (1967)

## ❧ SEASONS

1 To stay in one place and watch the seasons come and go is tantamount to constant travel: one is traveling with the earth.

Marguerite Yourcenar, *With Open Eyes* (1980)

2 Spring is the season of hope, and autumn is that of memory.

Countess of Blessington, *Desultory Thoughts and Reflections* (1839)

3 Spring never comes abruptly; it makes promises in a longer twilight or a day of warmer sunshine, and then takes them back in a dark week of storm. It gives presages—a thaw, a swelling of maple buds, a greening of grass, a flash of bird wing; then snow falls and winter returns. Again and again spring is here and not here. But fall comes in one day, and stays.

Bertha Damon, *A Sense of Humus* (1943)

4 The seasons pitched and heaved a man from rail to rail, from weather side to lee side and back, and a lunatic hogged the helm. Shall these bones remember?

Annie Dillard, *The Living* (1992)

See also Autumn, Spring, Summer, Winter.

## ❧ SECOND-RATE

5 It is an infallible sign of the second-rate in nature and intellect to make use of everything and every one. The genius is incapable of making use of people. It is for the second-rate clever people to make use of him.

Ada Leverson, *The Limit* (1911)

6 What's terrible is to pretend that the second-rate is first-rate. To pretend that you don't need love when you do; or you like your work when you know quite well you're capable of better.

Doris Lessing, *Golden Notebook* (1962)

7 A list of our authors who have made themselves most beloved and, therefore, most comfortable financially, shows that it is our national joy to mistake for the first-rate, the fecund rate.

Dorothy Parker, "And Again, Mr. Sinclair Lewis," in *The New Yorker* (1929)

See also Mediocrity.

## ❧ SECRETS

8 Secrecy is as indispensable to human beings as fire, and as greatly feared.

Sissela Bok, *Secrets* (1983)

9 A person who has no secrets is a liar. We always fold ourselves away from others just enough to preserve a secret or two, something that we cannot share without destroying our inner landscape.

Anne Roiphe, *Lovingkindness* (1987)

10 I was seduced by secrets, which are to true love as artificial sweetener is to sugar, calorie-free but in the long run carcinogenic, not the real thing, and only a peculiar aftertaste in the mouth to tell you so, to warn you.

Fay Weldon, *Life Force* (1992)

11 I don't think secrets agree with me; I feel rumpled up in my mind since you told me that.

Louisa May Alcott, *Little Women* (1868)

12 In the mind and nature of a man a secret is an ugly thing, like a hidden physical defect.

Isak Dinesen, "Of Hidden Thoughts and of Heaven," *Last Tales* (1957)

13 In the Chinese world, nothing could be kept secret, the very word for secret also meant unlawful.

Pearl S. Buck, *My Several Worlds* (1954)

14 After a time having a secret and nobody knowing you have a secret is no fun. And although you don't want others to know what the secret is, you want them to at least know you have one.

E.L. Konigsburg, *From the Mixed-Up Files of Mrs. Basil E. Frankweiler* (1967)

15 Sometimes you just gotta trust that your secret's been kept long enough.

Anne Cameron, *Daughters of Copper Woman* (1981)

16 When she knew a secret it no longer was.

Marcelene Cox, in *Ladies' Home Journal* (1948)

17 Secrets are rarely betrayed or discovered according to any program our fear has sketched out.

George Eliot, *The Mill on the Floss* (1860)

18 One ought to have the right to have a secret and to spring it as a surprise. But if you live inside a family you have neither.

Tove Jansson, *Tales From Moominvalley* (1963)

1 Secrets are kept from children, a lid on top of the soup kettle, so they do not boil over with too much truth.

    Amy Tan, *The Joy Luck Club* (1989)

2 I will have no locked cupboards in my life.

    Gertrude Bell, in Janet E. Courtney, *An Oxford Portrait Gallery* (1931)

See also Concealment, Confidences, Hiding, Privacy, Repression.

## § SECURITY

3 Cocooning: The need to protect oneself from the harsh, unpredictable realities of the outside world.

    Faith Popcorn, *The Popcorn Report* (1991)

4 Security is when everything is settled, when nothing can happen to you; security is the denial of life.

    Germaine Greer, *The Female Eunuch* (1971)

5 Only in growth, reform, and change, paradoxically enough, is true security to be found.

    Anne Morrow Lindbergh, *The Wave of the Future* (1940)

6 The only real security is not insurance or money or a job, not a house and furniture paid for, or a retirement fund, and never is it another person. It is the skill and humor and courage within, the ability to build your own fires and find your own peace.

    Audrey Sutherland, *Paddling My Own Canoe* (1978)

7 To multiply the harbors does not reduce the sea.

    Emily Dickinson (c. 1870), in Mabel Loomis Todd, ed., *Letters of Emily Dickinson*, vol. 2 (1894)

8 Too much safety is abhorrent to the nature of a human being.

    Agatha Christie, *Curtain* (1975)

See also Contentment, Danger, Risk.

## § SEDUCTION

9 In Jacqueline's experience, charming out-of-the-way restaurants were frequently attached to out-of-the-way motels.

    Elizabeth Peters, *Naked Once More* (1989)

10 The seduction emanating from a person of uncertain or dissimulated sex is powerful.

    Colette, *The Pure and the Impure* (1932)

11 All the delusive seduction of martial music.

    Fanny Burney (1802), in Charlotte Barrett, ed., *Diary and Letters of Madame D'Arblay*, vol. 6 (1842)

See also Flirtation, Sex.

## § SEGREGATION

12 The doors of churches, hotels, concert halls and reading rooms are alike closed against the Negro as a man, but every place is open to him as a servant.

    Ida B. Wells (1893), in Alfreda M. Duster, ed., *Crusade for Justice* (1970)

See also Exclusion, Racism.

## § SELF

13 What am I? Nothing. What would I be? Everything.

    Marie Bashkirtseff (1876), in Simone de Beauvoir, *The Second Sex* (1949)

14 An "I" without a body is a possibility. But a body without an "I" is utterly impossible.

    Edith Stein, *On the Problem of Empathy* (1917)

15 First, there is the person one thinks he is and the appearance one thinks he has. Then there is the thing one actually is, and there is that which the others think, and here a myriad-faced being arose in her thought, but the second came back as being more difficult to know, for what eyes would see it and where would it stay?

    Elizabeth Madox Roberts, *Black Is My Truelove's Hair* (1938)

16 If what I am watching evaporated before my eyes, I would remain.

    Anne Truitt, *Daybook* (1982)

17 It was on that road and at that hour that I first became aware of my own self, experienced an inexpressible state of grace, and felt one with the first breath of air that stirred, the first bird, and the sun so newly born that it still looked not quite round.

    Colette, *Sido* (1930)

1 Unless I am what I am and feel what I feel—as hard as I can and as honestly and truly as I can—then I am nothing. Let me feel guilty . . . don't try to educate me . . . don't protect me.

Elizabeth Janeway, *Leaving Home* (1953)

2 It is either the beginning or the end / of the world, and the choice is ourselves / or nothing.

Carolyn Forché, "Ourselves or Nothing," *The Country Between Us* (1981)

3 I'll walk where my own nature would be leading: / It vexes me to choose another guide.

Emily Brontë, in Charlotte Brontë, ed., "Selections From the Literary Remains of Ellis and Acton Bell," memorial edition of *Wuthering Heights* and *Agnes Grey* (1850)

4 Let's dare to be ourselves, for we do that better than anyone else can.

Shirley Briggs, in Sue Patton Thoele, *The Courage to Be Yourself* (1988)

5 Free to be . . . you and me.

Marlo Thomas, book title (1974)

6 I am not at home in myself. I am my own stranger.

Anne Sexton (1964), in Linda Gray Sexton and Lois Ames, eds., *Anne Sexton: A Self-Portrait in Letters* (1977)

7 Maybe being oneself is always an acquired taste.

Patricia Hampl, in Janet Sternburg, ed., *The Writer on Her Work*, vol. 2 (1991)

8 Nothing, nothing am I but a small, loving watercourse.

Rosario Castellanos, in Irene Nicholson, *A Guide to Mexican Poetry* (1968)

9 I'm Calamity Jane. Get to hell out of here and let me alone.

Calamity Jane (1873), in Duncan Aikman, *Calamity Jane and the Lady Wildcats* (1927)

10 We is terrific.

The Supremes, in Mary Wilson, *Dreamgirl* (1986)

11 I warn you . . . I am only really myself when I'm somebody else whom I have endowed with these wonderful qualities from my imagination.

Zelda Fitzgerald, *Save Me the Waltz* (1932)

12 I am not at all the sort of person you and I took me for.

Jane Welsh Carlyle, letter to Thomas Carlyle (1822), in Alan and Mary McQueen Simpson, eds., *I Too Am Here* (1977)

13 She lives on the reflections of herself in the eyes of others.

Anaïs Nin (1931), *The Diary of Anaïs Nin*, vol. 1 (1966)

14 Part of having a strong sense of self is to be accountable for one's actions. No matter how much we explore motives or lack of motives, we are what we do.

Janet Geringer Woititz, *Adult Children of Alcoholics* (1983)

15 You need only claim the events of your life to make yourself yours. When you truly possess all you have been and done, which may take some time, you are fierce with reality.

Florida Scott-Maxwell, *The Measure of My Days* (1968)

16 What we have not has made us what we are. / . . . / What we are not drives us to consummation.

May Sarton, "Mud Season," *Cloud, Stone, Sun, Vine* (1961)

17 I am the box / within a box / within a box. / Open me and be deafened / by my shadow.

Marnie Walsh, "Poets/Poems," *A Taste of the Knife* (1976)

18 No sooner do we think we have assembled a comfortable life than we find a piece of ourselves that has no place to fit in.

Gail Sheehy, *Passages* (1976)

19 I'm not really sure which parts of myself are real and which parts are things I've gotten from books.

Anonymous, *Go Ask Alice* (1971)

20 We are not always even what we are most.

Marie von Ebner-Eschenbach, *Aphorisms* (1893)

21 The possibilities of being different from what one is are infinite. Once one has negated oneself, however, there are no longer any particular choices.

Hannah Arendt, *Rahel Varnhagen* (1957)

22 I did not lose myself all at once. I rubbed out my face over the years washing away my pain, the same way carvings on stone are worn down by water.

Amy Tan, *The Joy Luck Club* (1989)

23 The self is every person's true enemy.

Ding Ling, "Miss Sophia's Diary" (1927), *I Myself Am a Woman* (1989)

24 Who sees the other half of Self, sees Truth.

Anne Cameron, *Daughters of Copper Woman* (1981)

25 I change myself, I change the world.

Gloria Anzaldúa, *Borderlands/La Frontera* (1987)

1 People do not desire so much to appear better, as to appear different from what they really are.

　　L.E. Landon, *Romance and Reality* (1831)

2 It so often happens that others are measuring us by our past self while we are looking back on that self with a mixture of disgust and sorrow.

　　George Eliot (1861), in J.W. Cross, ed., *George Eliot's Life As Related in Her Letters and Journals* (1884)

3 We are well advised to keep on nodding terms with the people we used to be, whether we find them attractive company or not. Otherwise they run up unannounced and surprise us, come hammering on the mind's door at 4 a.m. of a bad night and demand to know who deserted them, who betrayed them, who is going to make amends.

　　Joan Didion, "On Keeping a Notebook," *Slouching Towards Bethlehem* (1968)

4 What you have become is the price you paid to get what you used to want.

　　Mignon McLaughlin, *The Neurotic's Notebook* (1963)

5 Everybody must learn this lesson somewhere— that it costs something to be what you are.

　　Shirley Abbott, *Womenfolks: Growing Up Down South* (1983)

6 When my daughter looks at me, she sees a small old lady. That is because she sees only with her outside eyes. She has no *chuming*, no inside knowing of things. If she had *chuming*, she would see a tiger lady. And she would have careful fear.

　　Amy Tan, *The Joy Luck Club* (1989)

7 "You certainly are not yourself to-day." "I so seldom am," said Cecilia.

　　Elizabeth Bowen, *To the North* (1933)

8 "He's not himself at all today," Mr. Somerset told me. People say that about Jeremy quite often, but what they mean is that he is not like other people. He is *always* himself. That's what's wrong with him.

　　Anne Tyler, *Celestial Navigation* (1974)

9 I'm the kind of woman that likes to enjoy herselves in peace.

　　Alice Walker, *The Temple of My Familiar* (1989)

10 Perhaps it was not to be wondered at if Mr. Rickman had not yet found himself. There were, as he sorrowfully reflected, so many Mr. Rickmans.

　　May Sinclair, *The Divine Fire* (1904)

11 You insult me / When you say I'm schizophrenic. / *My* divisions are / Infinite.

　　Bernice Zamora, "So Not to Be Mottled," *Restless Serpents* (1976)

See also Character, Identity, Individuality, Personality, Uniqueness, Wholeness.

## ✿ SELF-ACCEPTANCE

12 *What* a desire! . . . To live in peace with that word: Myself.

　　Sylvia Ashton-Warner (1945), *Myself* (1967)

13 When I'm trusting and being myself as fully as possible, everything in my life reflects this by falling into place easily, often miraculously.

　　Shakti Gawain, *Living in the Light* (1986)

See also Acceptance.

## ✿ SELF-ACTUALIZATION

14 I do not want to die . . . until I have faithfully made the most of my talent and cultivated the seed that was placed in me until the last small twig has grown.

　　Käthe Kollwitz (1915), in Hans Kollwitz, ed., *The Diaries and Letters of Käthe Kollwitz* (1955)

15 If you have got a living force and you're not using it, nature kicks you back. The blood boils just like you put it in a pot.

　　Louise Nevelson, *Dawns + Dusks* (1976)

16 One can never consent to creep when one feels an impulse to soar.

　　Helen Keller, *The Story of My Life* (1902)

17 The idea of a finished human product not only appears presumptuous but even, in my opinion, lacks any strong appeal. Life is struggle and striving, development and growth—and analysis is one of the means that can help in this process. Certainly its positive accomplishments are important, but also the striving itself is of intrinsic value.

　　Karen Horney, *Self-Analysis* (1942)

1 So all that is in her will not bloom—but in how many does it?

> Tillie Olsen, "I Stand Here Ironing," *Tell Me A Riddle* (1956)

See also Growth.

## ❧ SELF-APPRAISAL

2 Get rid of the tendency / to judge yourself / above, below, or / equal to others.

> Abhirupa-Nanda (6th cent. B.C.), in Susan Murcott, *The First Buddhist Women* (1991)

3 The world is terribly apt to take people at their own valuation.

> Amelia B. Edwards, *Half a Million of Money* (1866)

4 The world never puts a price on you higher than the one you put on yourself.

> Sonja Henie, *Wings on My Feet* (1940)

5 I wish I could buy you for what you are really worth and sell you for what you think you're worth. I sure would make money on the deal.

> Zora Neale Hurston, *Moses: Man of the Mountain* (1939)

See also Self-Deprecation, Self-Esteem.

## ❧ SELF-DECEPTION

6 The ingenuity of self-deception is inexhaustible.

> Hannah More, "Self-Love," *Practical Piety* (1811)

7 I lie to myself all the time. But I never believe me.

> S.E. Hinton, *The Outsiders* (1967)

8 There is, happily, no limit to the faith of human nature in believing what it wants to believe.

> Caitlin Thomas, *Leftover Life to Kill* (1957)

9 Wishful thinking dies harder than true love.

> Louise W. King, *The Day We Were Mostly Butterflies* (1963)

10 Someone will always tell you what you want to hear.

> Delia Ephron, *Funny Sauce* (1986)

11 We all have our little illusions about our own mental abilities.

> Cornelia Otis Skinner, "The Sea-Tossed Muse," *Bottoms Up!* (1955)

12 Most of our platitudes notwithstanding, self-deception remains the most difficult deception. The tricks that work on others count for nothing in that very well-lit back alley where one keeps assignations with oneself.

> Joan Didion, "On Self-Respect," *Slouching Towards Bethlehem* (1968)

See also Rationalization, Self-Indulgence, Self-Knowledge.

## ❧ SELF-DEPRECATION

13 The man who doesn't love me / I love twice: / once for his beauty, again / for his sound sense.

> Nancy Mairs, "Wise," *In All the Rooms of the Yellow House* (1984)

14 People incline to doubt the superiority of a person who will associate with them.

> Mary Catherwood, *Lazarre* (1901)

15 There is as much vanity in self-scourgings as in self-justification.

> Storm Jameson, *The Journal of Mary Hervey Russell* (1945)

16 Though humility and acknowledgement of one's *real* failings is good, the gratuitous eating of worms *not* put before us by God does not nourish our souls a bit—-merely in fact upsets the spiritual tummy.

> Evelyn Underhill (1935), in Charles Williams, ed., *The Letters of Evelyn Underhill* (1943)

17 Some women wait for themselves / around the next corner / and call the empty spot peace.

> Audre Lorde, "Stations," *Our Dead Behind Us* (1986)

18 Each of us only feels the torn lining of his own coat and sees the wholeness of the other person's.

> Erica Jong, *How to Save Your Own Life* (1977)

19 She had developed a passionate longing for making other people comfortable at her own expense. . . . She succeeded in getting other people into armchairs, without their knowing she was doing it, and

with nothing left for herself but something small and spiky in a corner.

Phyllis Bottome, "The Angel of the Darker Drink," *Innocence and Experience* (1934)

1 I am very strong & robust & not of the delicate sex nor of the fair but of the deficent in look.

Marjorie Fleming, age 7 (1810), in Frank Sidgwick, ed., *The Complete Marjory Fleming* (1934)

2 I have the perfect face for radio.

Virginia Graham, with Jean Libman Block, *There Goes What's Her Name* (1965)

3 If the souls of lives were voiced in music, there are some that none but a great organ could express, others the clash of a full orchestra, a few to which nought but the refined and exquisite sadness of a violin could do justice. Many might be likened unto common pianos, jangling and out of tune, and some to the feeble piping of a penny whistle, and mine could be told with a couple of nails in a rusty tin-pot.

Miles Franklin, *My Brilliant Career* (1901)

4 Anyone who picks up a Compton-Burnett finds it hard not to put it down.

Ivy Compton-Burnett, in Elizabeth Sprigge, *The Life of Ivy Compton-Burnett* (1973)

5 I'm Nobody! Who are you? / Are you — Nobody — Too? / Then there's a pair of us! / Don't tell! they'd advertise — you know.

Emily Dickinson (1861), in T.W. Higginson and Mabel Loomis Todd, eds., *Poems by Emily Dickinson*, 2nd series (1891)

See also Codependence.

## § SELF-DESTRUCTION

6 Give him enough rope and he will hang himself.

Charlotte Brontë, *Shirley* (1849)

7 When we consistently suppress and distrust our intuitive knowingness, looking instead for authority, validation, and approval from others, we give our personal power away.

Shakti Gawain, *Living in the Light* (1986)

8 All human beings hold the tools of their own destruction.

Barbara Gordon, *I'm Dancing As Fast As I Can* (1979)

9 I was right not to be afraid of any thief but myself, who will end by leaving me nothing.

Katherine Anne Porter, "Theft," *The Flowering Judas* (1936)

10 Neither the devil nor anyone else can ever kill me except with my own sword.

St. Catherine of Siena (1375), in Suzanne Noffke, tr., *The Letters of St. Catherine of Siena* (1988)

11 No man was ever ruined from *without*; the final ruin comes from *within*.

Amelia E. Barr, *All the Days of My Life* (1913)

12 Man is trampled by the same forces he had created.

Juana Frances, in Colin Naylor and Genesis P-Orridge, eds., *Contemporary Artists* (1977)

13 It is the loose ends with which men hang themselves.

Zelda Fitzgerald, in *Reader's Digest* (1983)

See also Suicide.

## § SELF-DETERMINATION

14 We make ourselves up as we go.

Kate Green, "Possible Love, Possible Sky," *If the World Is Running Out* (1983)

15 If it is to be, it is up to me.

Shirley Hutton, in *The Minneapolis Star Tribune* (1994)

16 Of my own spirit let me be / in sole though feeble mastery.

Sara Teasdale, "Mastery," *Love Songs* (1917)

17 If you are not your own agent, you are some one else's.

Alice Molloy, *In Other Words* (1973)

18 Can't nothin' make your life work if you ain't the architect.

Terry McMillan, *Disappearing Acts* (1989)

19 Such creatures of accident are we, liable to a thousand deaths before we are born. But once we are here, we may create our own world, if we choose.

Mary Antin, *The Promised Land* (1912)

20 They wish to dissuade me / From all that the forces of Love urge me to. / They do not understand it, and I cannot explain it to them. / I must then live

out what I am; / What Love counsels my spirit, / In this is my being: for this reason I will do my best.

Hadewijch, "To Live Out What I Am" (13th cent.), in Mother Columba Hart, O.S.B., *Hadewijch* (1980)

1 We are not born all at once, but by bits. The body first, and the spirit later; and the birth and growth of the spirit, in those who are attentive to their own inner life, are slow and exceedingly painful. Our mothers are racked with the pains of our physical birth; we ourselves suffer the longer pains of our spiritual growth.

Mary Antin, *The Promised Land* (1912)

2 Like any art, the creation of self is both natural and seemingly impossible. It requires training as well as magic.

Holly Near, with Derk Richardson, *Fire in the Rain . . . Singer in the Storm* (1990)

3 The greater part of our happiness or misery depends on our dispositions, and not on our circumstances. We carry the seeds of the one or the other about with us in our minds wherever we go.

Martha Washington (1789), in Samuel Griswold Goodrich, *Lives of Celebrated Women* (1844)

4 We make ourselves our own distress, / We are ourselves our happiness.

L.E. Landon, title poem, *The Troubadour* (1825)

5 No star is ever lost we once have seen, / We always may be what we might have been.

Adelaide Anne Procter, "A Legend of Provence," *Legends and Lyrics* (1858)

6 It was completely fruitless to quarrel with the world, whereas the quarrel with oneself was occasionally fruitful, and always, she had to admit, interesting.

May Sarton, *Mrs. Stevens Hears the Mermaids Singing* (1965)

7 Early in school, they called me "the artist." When teachers wanted things painted, they called upon me, they called upon "the artist." I am not saying that I learned my name, animals can learn their names, I am saying that they learned it.

Louise Nevelson, in Arnold B. Glimcher, *Louise Nevelson* (1972)

8 Neither woman nor man lives by work, or love, alone. . . . The human self defines itself and grows through love *and* work: all psychology before and after Freud boils down to that.

Betty Friedan, *The Second Stage* (1981)

9 Human beings are not so constituted that they can live without expansion. If they do not get it one way, they must another, or perish.

Margaret Fuller, *Woman in the Nineteenth Century* (1845)

10 Human beings have an inalienable right to invent themselves; when that right is pre-empted it is called brain-washing.

Germaine Greer, in *The London Times* (1986)

11 Every time you don't follow your inner guidance, you feel a loss of energy, loss of power, a sense of spiritual deadness.

Shakti Gawain, *Living in the Light* (1986)

12 I want the freedom to carve and chisel my own face, to staunch the bleeding with ashes, to fashion my own gods out of my entrails.

Gloria Anzaldúa, *Borderlands/La Frontera* (1987)

13 A watermelon that breaks open by itself tastes better than one cut with a knife.

Hualing Nieh, *Mulberry and Peach* (1981)

14 The compulsion to rescue willy-nilly those who are drowning strikes to the heart of our freedoms. I am all for fishing out of the water those who fall in, but let us respect those who have thrown themselves in.

Comtesse Diane, *Les Glanes de la Vie* (1898)

15 This above all, to refuse to be a victim.

Margaret Atwood, *Surfacing* (1972)

16 I have left all my business and all my husbands; I have taken with me only fair weather and my children, which is as much as I want.

Marie Madeleine de la Fayette (1673), in Marie de Rabutin-Chantal, Marquise de Sévigné, *The Letters of Madame de Sévigné*, vol. 2 (1927)

See also Self-Actualization, Identity, Self.

# § SELF-DISCIPLINE

17 The success of life, the formation of character, is in proportion to the courage one has to say to one's ownself: "Thou shalt not."

Carry Nation, *The Use and Need of the Life of Carry A. Nation* (1905)

18 As far as your self-control goes, as far goes your freedom.

Marie von Ebner-Eschenbach, *Aphorisms* (1893)

1 The worst effect of tutelage is that it negates self-discipline, and therefore people suddenly released from it are almost bound to make fools of themselves.

> Suzanne La Follette, "Woman and Marriage," *Concerning Women* (1926)

See also Willpower.

## ♪ SELF-ESTEEM

2 Miss Owen and Miss Burney asked me if I had never been in love; "with myself," said I, "and most passionately." When any man likes me I never am surprised, for I think how should he help it? When any man does *not* like me, I think him a blockhead.

> Hester Lynch Piozzi (1781), *Thraliana* (1942)

3 The brother that gets me is going to get one hell of a fabulous woman.

> Aretha Franklin, in *Vanity Fair* (1993)

4 I am said to be the most beautiful woman in Europe. About that, of course, I cannot judge because I cannot know. But about the other queens, I know. I am the most beautiful queen in Europe.

> Queen Marie of Rumania (1919), in Hannah Pakula, *The Last Romantic* (1984)

5 I'm five-feet-four, but I always feel six-foot-one, tall and strong.

> Yvette Mimieux, in John Robert Colombo, *Popcorn in Paradise* (1979)

6 If I may venture to be frank I would say about myself that I was every inch a gentleman.

> Catherine the Great (1759), in Dominique Maroger, ed., *The Memoirs of Catherine the Great* (1955)

7 I think I'm just as good as anyone. That's the way I was brought up. I'll tell you a secret: I think I'm *better*! Ha! I remember being aware that colored people were supposed to feel inferior. I knew I was a smart little thing, a personality, an individual—a human being! I couldn't understand how people could look at me and not see that, because it sure was obvious to me.

> Bessie Delany, in Sarah and A. Elizabeth Delany, with Amy Hill Hearth, *Having Our Say* (1993)

8 and he said: you pretty full of yourself ain't chu / so she replied: show me someone not full of herself / and i'll show you a hungry person.

> Nikki Giovanni, "Poem for a Lady Whose Voice I Like," *Re:Creation* (1970)

9 Beneath the surface of our daily life, in the personal history of many of us, there runs a continuous controversy between an Ego that affirms and an Ego that denies.

> Beatrice Webb, *My Apprenticeship* (1926)

10 To say something nice about themselves, this is the hardest thing in the world for people to do. They'd rather take their clothes off.

> Nancy Friday, *My Mother/My Self* (1977)

11 You can be pleased with nothing when you are not pleased with yourself.

> Lady Mary Wortley Montagu (1712), in Octave Thanet, ed., *The Best Letters of Lady Mary Wortley Montagu* (1901)

12 We are all apt to believe what the world believes about us.

> George Eliot, *The Mill on the Floss* (1860)

13 We cease loving ourselves when no one loves us.

> Madame de Staël, in C.A. Sainte-Beuve, "Madame de Staël" (1835), *Portraits of Women* (1891)

14 Those who believe they are ugly / objectify the rest of us.

> Judy Grahn, *The Queen of Swords* (1987)

15 Women who set a low value on themselves make life hard for all women.

> Nellie L. McClung, *In Times Like These* (1915)

16 He who despises himself esteems himself as a self-despiser.

> Susan Sontag, *Death Kit* (1967)

17 She'd been so programmed by Julian to think of herself as inferior material that if a man threw himself at her feet, her immediate reaction would be to call an ambulance.

> Lucille Kallen, *Introducing C.B. Greenfield* (1979)

18 No one can make you feel inferior without your consent.

> Eleanor Roosevelt, in *Catholic Digest* (1960)

19 All men seek esteem; the best by lifting themselves, which is hard to do, the rest by shoving others down, which is much easier.

> Mary Renault, *The Praise Singer* (1978)

1 Self-esteem isn't everything; it's just that there's nothing without it.

> Gloria Steinem, *Revolution From Within* (1993)

See also Confidence, Insecurity, Pride, Self-Respect.

## ❧ SELF-EVIDENT

2 Be the first to say what is self-evident, and you are immortal.

> Marie von Ebner-Eschenbach, *Aphorisms* (1893)

3 He always settled on the obvious like a hen on a porcelain egg.

> Gertrude Atherton, *Black Oxen* (1923)

4 The hardest thing to explain is the glaringly evident which everybody had decided not to see.

> Ayn Rand, *The Fountainhead* (1943)

See also Common Sense.

## ❧ SELF-HELP BOOKS

5 The buying of a self-help book is the most desperate of all human acts. It means you've lost your mind completely: You've entrusted your mental health to a self-aggrandizing twit with a psychology degree and a yen for a yacht.

> Cynthia Heimel, *Get Your Tongue Out of My Mouth, I'm Kissing You Good-Bye!* (1993)

6 Self-help books for women are part of a multibillion-dollar industry, sensitively attuned to our insecurities and our purses.

> Harriet Lerner, "When Bad Books Happen to Good People," in *Ms.* (1993)

7 The new self-help books for women . . . suggest that individual relationships between men and women can be changed solely by women making the right choices.

> bell hooks, *Talking Back* (1989)

See also Psychology, Psychiatry.

## ❧ SELF-IMPORTANCE

8 After us, the deluge.

> Madame de Pompadour (1757), in Monsieur Després, "Essay on the Marquise de Pompadour," in Madame du Hausset, *Mémoires du Madame de Hausset* (1824)

9 Interested in himself, he believed himself a subject of interest.

> Gish Jen, *Typical American* (1991)

10 Self-admiration giveth much consolation.

> Gertrude Atherton, *Julia France and Her Times* (1912)

11 Nine-tenths of our suffering is caused by others not thinking so much of us as we think they ought.

> Mary Lyon (1918), in Van Wyck Brooks, ed., *The Journal of Gamaliel Bradford* (1933)

12 We are so fond of hearing ourselves spoken of, that, be it good or ill, it is still pleasing.

> Marie de Rabutin-Chantal, Marquise de Sévigné (1671), *Letters of Madame de Sévigné to Her Daughter and Her Friends*, vol. 1 (1811)

13 Will not a tiny speck very close to our vision blot out the glory of the world and leave only a margin by which we see the blot? I know no speck so troublesome as self.

> George Eliot, *Middlemarch* (1871)

14 He was like a cock who thought the sun had risen to hear him crow.

> George Eliot, *Adam Bede* (1859)

15 He thinks he's finer than frog hair.

> Jessamyn West, *The Massacre at Fall Creek* (1975)

16 Although he was ambitious at this time to become a great writer, he saw himself rather as a literary figure than as a man at work.

> Elizabeth Taylor, *A Game of Hide-and-Seek* (1951)

17 His sense of his desserts had grown. Now he was sure that what he desired, he deserved, and anyone who denied it merited punishment.

> Mary Renault, *The Praise Singer* (1978)

18 She invents dramas in which she always stars.

> Anaïs Nin (1931), *The Diary of Anaïs Nin*, vol. 1 (1966)

19 She had no tolerance for scenes which were not of her own making.

> Edith Wharton, *The House of Mirth* (1905)

1 There were some initial difficulties when the director first told me the disappointing news that if the film was to have any semblance of reality at all there would have to be moments when other people were on screen at the same time I was.

Bette Midler, *A View From a Broad* (1980)

2 There are characters which are continually creating collisions and nodes for themselves in dramas which nobody is prepared to act with them.

George Eliot, *Middlemarch* (1871)

3 When someone sings his own praises, he always gets the tune too high.

Mary H. Waldrip, in *Reader's Digest* (1978)

4 Remember to negotiate thickness as well as height on the lettering of your name.

Julia Phillips, *You'll Never Eat Lunch in This Town Again* (1991)

5 All people interested in their work are liable to overrate their vocation. There may be makers of dolls' eyes who wonder how society would go on without them.

Harriet Martineau, *Autobiography*, vol. 1 (1877)

6 This photographer felt deeply the stab of professional insult common to people who have lived in a foreign country for a few years and *still* find their opinions not asked for at home.

Elizabeth Hardwick, "A Florentine Conference" (1951), *A View of My Own* (1962)

7 To be a professional anything in the United States is to think of oneself as an expert and one's ideas as semisacred.

Marge Piercy, "The Grand Coolie Damn," in Robin Morgan, ed., *Sisterhood Is Powerful* (1970)

8 Too much self-regard has never struck me as dignified: trying to twist over my shoulder to view my own behind.

Marge Piercy, *Braided Lives* (1982)

9 She had learnt . . . that it was impossible to discuss issues civilly with a person who insisted on referring to himself as "we."

Lisa Alther, *Kinflicks* (1975)

10 Lives there a man with soul so dead that never to himself has said, "My life would make a book."

Sophie Irene Loeb, *Epigrams of Eve* (1913)

11 She was one of the most unimportantly wicked women of her time—because she could not let her time alone, and yet could never be a part of it. She wanted to be the reason for everything and so was the cause of nothing.

Djuna Barnes, *Nightwood* (1937)

12 Oh, yes, he thinks he is God.

Lady Carina Frost, when asked whether David Frost was religious, in Michèle Brown and Ann O'Connor, *Hammer and Tongues* (1986)

13 Mrs. Morton was a lady who liked to feel that the burdens of life lay heavily upon her, far more heavily than upon anyone else.

Madeleine Brent, *Tregaron's Daughter* (1971)

14 Nobody has done anything to develop the English language since Shakespeare, except myself, and Henry James perhaps a little.

Gertrude Stein (1925), in Roger McAlmon, "Portrait," *Exile* (1938)

15 Before feminism was, Paglia was!

Camille Paglia, "Crisis in the American Universities," *Sex, Art, and American Culture* (1992)

16 Father wanted to be the corpse at every funeral, the bride at every wedding, and the baby at every christening.

Alice Roosevelt Longworth, on Theodore Roosevelt, in Dorothy Herrmann, *With Malice Toward All* (1982)

17 Someone was telling me that no more applications were being accepted for the position of God.

Jan Burke, *Sweet Dreams, Irene* (1994)

See also Arrogance, Conceit, Egocentrism, Point of View, Superiority, Vanity.

## ❦ SELF-INDULGENCE

18 People who are always making allowances for themselves soon go bankrupt.

Mary Pettibone Poole, *A Glass Eye at a Keyhole* (1938)

19 This body of ours has one fault: the more you indulge it, the more things it discovers to be essential to it. It is extraordinary how it likes being indulged.

St. Teresa of Avila, *The Way of Perfection* (1579)

See also Egocentrism, Extravagance, Self-Importance, Selfishness.

## ᔐ SELF-INTEREST

1 One speaks on behalf of others, one acts on behalf of oneself.
Comtesse Diane, *Les Glanes de la Vie* (1898)

2 Nothing's done well when it's done out of self-interest.
St. Thérèse of Lisieux (1897), in Ronald Knox, tr., *Story of a Soul* (1958)

3 Self-interest usually brings injustice with it.
Catherine the Great (c. 1780), in Dominique Maroger, ed., *The Memoirs of Catherine the Great* (1955)

4 The best thing for everyone concerned . . . is what people always say when they have arranged something exclusively to suit themselves.
Shirley Hazzard, *The Bay of Noon* (1970)

5 Nobody is a good judge in his own cause.
St. Thérèse of Lisieux (1897), in Ronald Knox, tr., *Story of a Soul* (1958)

See also Expedience.

## ᔐ SELFISHNESS

6 Selfishness is not living as one wishes to live, it is asking others to live as one wishes to live.
Ruth Rendell, *A Judgement in Stone* (1977)

7 No people complain so much of selfishness as the selfish.
Hannah Farnham Lee, *The Log-Cabin* (1844)

8 Selfishness must always be forgiven you know, because there is no hope of a cure.
Jane Austen, *Mansfield Park* (1814)

9 I have been a selfish being all my life, in practice, though not in principle.
Jane Austen, *Pride and Prejudice* (1813)

10 You are discontented with the world because you can't get just the small things that suit your pleasure, not because it's a world where myriads of men and women are ground by wrong and misery, and tainted with pollution.
George Eliot, *Felix Holt, the Radical* (1866)

11 Once you are thought selfish, not only are you forgiven a life designed mainly to suit yourself . . . but if an impulse to generosity should by chance overpower you, you will get five times the credit of some poor selfless soul who has been oozing kindness for years.
Amanda Cross, *The Question of Max* (1976)

See also Avarice, Egocentrism, Greed, Miserliness, Self-Indulgence.

## ᔐ SELF-KNOWLEDGE

12 A child should be allowed to take as long as she needs for knowing everything about herself, which is the same as learning to be herself. Even twenty-five years if necessary, or even forever. And it wouldn't matter if doing things got delayed, because nothing is really important but being oneself.
Laura Riding, *Four Unposted Letters to Catherine* (1993)

13 I'd discovered you never know yourself until you're tested and that you don't even know you're being tested until afterwards, and that in fact there isn't anyone giving the test except yourself.
Marilyn French, *The Bleeding Heart* (1980)

14 The knowledge of ourselves is a difficult study, and we must be willing to borrow the eyes of our enemies to assist the investigation.
Hannah Farnham Lee, *The Log-Cabin* (1844)

15 One way to confront the self is through analysis. One way to approach God is through prayerful contemplation. I am not so sure that in their essentials these two ways are so fundamentally different.
June Singer, *Boundaries of the Soul* (1972)

16 There's a period of life when we swallow a knowledge of ourselves, and it becomes either good or sour inside.
Pearl Bailey, *The Raw Pearl* (1968)

17 It's a sad day when you find out that it's not accident or time or fortune but just yourself that kept things from you.
Lillian Hellman, *Pentimento* (1973)

18 You can live a lifetime and, at the end of it, know more about other people than you know about yourself.
Beryl Markham, *West With the Night* (1942)

1 When one is a stranger to oneself then one is estranged from others too.

   Anne Morrow Lindbergh, *Gift From the Sea* (1955)

2 It is a fault to wish to be understood before we have made ourselves clear to ourselves.

   Simone Weil, *Gravity and Grace* (1947)

3 Nobody knows what I am trying to do but I do and I know when I succeed.

   Gertrude Stein, in John Malcolm Brinnin, *The Third Rose* (1959)

4 People are prone to build a statue of the kind of person that it pleases them to be. And few people want to be forced to ask themselves, "What if there is no me like my statue?"

   Zora Neale Hurston, *Dust Tracks on a Road* (1942)

5 I have met a thousand scamps; but I never met one who considered himself so. Self-knowledge isn't so common.

   Ouida, *Wisdom, Wit and Pathos* (1884)

6 We neither knew nor liked the people we had become.

   Barbara Howar, *Laughing All the Way* (1973)

See also Awareness, Knowledge, Psychiatry, Psychology, Understanding.

## & SELF-PITY

7 Self-pity in its early stage is as snug as a feather mattress. Only when it hardens does it become uncomfortable.

   Maya Angelou, *Gather Together in My Name* (1974)

8 Self-pity is the simplest luxury.

   Rita Mae Brown, *Bingo* (1988)

9 The teeth of self-pity had gnawed away her essential self.

   Willa Gibbs, *Seed of Mischief* (1953)

10 Self-pity had always been her sincerest emotion.

   Vera Caspary, *A Chosen Sparrow* (1964)

11 Sometimes I go about in pity for myself, and all the while, a great wind is bearing me across the sky.

   Ellen Gilchrist, title story, *Light Can Be Both Wave and Particle* (1989)

See also Pity.

## & SELF-POSSESSION

12 The greatest possession is Self-possession.

   Ethel Watts Mumford, in Oliver Herford, Ethel Watts Mumford, and Addison Mizner, *The Complete Cynic* (1902)

See also Poise.

## & SELF-RESPECT

13 There is an applause superior to that of the multitude—one's own.

   Elizabeth Elton Smith, *The Three Eras of Woman's Life* (1836)

14 To have that sense of one's intrinsic worth which constitutes self-respect is potentially to have everything: the ability to discriminate, to love and to remain indifferent. To lack it is to be locked within oneself, paradoxically incapable of either love or indifference.

   Joan Didion, "On Self-Respect," *Slouching Towards Bethlehem* (1968)

15 Character—the willingness to accept responsibility for one's own life—is the source from which self-respect springs.

   Joan Didion, "On Self-Respect," *Slouching Towards Bethlehem* (1968)

16 When asked, most folks will gladly tell us about ourselves, who we are, what we're feeling, and where we should be heading. And if we don't honor ourselves by listening to our lives, we'll believe them.

   Susan L. Taylor, in Gloria Wade-Gayles, ed., *My Soul Is a Witness* (1995)

17 Self respect . . . is a question of recognizing that anything worth having has its price.

   Joan Didion, "On Self-Respect," *Slouching Towards Bethlehem* (1968)

See also Self-Esteem.

## & SELF-SACRIFICE

18 I never know why self-sacrifice is noble. Why is it better to sacrifice oneself than someone else?

   Ivy Compton-Burnett, *Mother and Son* (1955)

1 In all proper relationships there is no sacrifice of anyone to anyone.

Ayn Rand, *The Fountainhead* (1943)

2 Taking somebody's sacrifices is like taking counterfeit money. You're only the poorer.

Dorothy Canfield Fisher, *Bonfire* (1933)

3 Some people are capable of making great sacrifices, but few are capable of concealing how much the effort has cost them.

Countess of Blessington, *Desultory Thoughts and Reflections* (1839)

4 Sacrificers . . . are not the ones to pity. The ones to pity are those that they sacrifice. Oh, the sacrificers, they get it both ways. A person knows themselves that they're able to do without.

Elizabeth Bowen, *The Death of the Heart* (1938)

5 Self-sacrifice which denies common sense isn't virtue; it's spiritual dissipation!

Margaret Deland, *The Rising Tide* (1916)

6 Is devotion to others a cover for the hungers and the needs of the self, of which one is ashamed? I was always ashamed to take. So I gave. It was not a virtue. It was a disguise.

Anaïs Nin (1946), *The Diary of Anaïs Nin*, vol. 4 (1971)

7 The capacity to sacrifice, like any skill, always needs some fine tuning. It is one thing to sacrifice briefly one's sleep to comfort a child with a bad dream; it is quite another for a mother to sacrifice her whole career for a child. It is one thing for a father to sacrifice his desire to go fishing today because he needs to go to work to feed the family; it is quite another to work for forty years at a job he hates. . . . Often such massive sacrifice, if not a result of cowardice, comes from an inability to discriminate between giving that is necessary and life-giving and giving that brings death to the Martyr and hence to those around him or her.

Carol Pearson, *The Hero Within* (1986)

8 She was a spasmodic selfless torrent like the fizz from her own cider bottles.

Kate Cruise O'Brien, "Trespasses," *A Gift Horse* (1978)

9 She had continued to sacrifice her inclinations in a manner which had rendered unendurable the lives around her. Her parents had succumbed to it; her husband had died of it; her children had resigned themselves to it or rebelled against it according to the quality of their moral fiber. All her life she had labored to make people happy, and the result of this exalted determination was a cowed and resentful family.

Ellen Glasgow, *The Miller of Old Church* (1911)

See also Codependence, Duty, Self-Deprecation.

## ❧ SELF-SATISFACTION

10 He's at the age when a man knows everything on earth an' generally knows it wrong.

Ellen Glasgow, *The Miller of Old Church* (1911)

11 Self-satisfaction, if as buoyant as gas, has an ugly trick of collapsing when full-blown.

Agnes Repplier, "Some Aspects of Pessimism," *Books and Men* (1888)

12 One's self-satisfaction is an untaxed kind of property which it is very unpleasant to find depreciated.

George Eliot, *Middlemarch* (1871)

See also Complacency, Righteousness.

## ❧ SELF-SUFFICIENCY

13 There are no magics or elves / Or timely godmothers to guide us. We are lost, must / Wizard a track through our own screaming weed.

Gwendolyn Brooks, "intermission," *Annie Allen* (1949)

14 She listens to her own tales, / Laughs at her own jokes and / Follows her own advice.

Ama Ata Aidoo, *Anowa* (1970)

15 I plant geraniums. / I tie up my hair into loose braids, / and trust only what I have built / with my own hands.

Lorna Dee Cervantes, "Beneath the Shadow of the Freeway," *Emplumada* (1981)

16 Let them think I love them more than I do, / Let them think I care, though I go alone, / If it lifts their pride, what is it to me / Who am self-complete as a flower or a stone.

Sara Teasdale, "The Solitary," *Dark of the Moon* (1926)

1 She is always optimistic and resourceful, a woman who, if cast ashore alone on a desert island, would build a house with a guest room.

Edna Buchanan, *Contents Under Pressure* (1992)

2 I read and walked for miles at night along the beach, writing bad blank verse and searching endlessly for someone wonderful who would step out of the darkness and change my life. It never crossed my mind that that person could be me.

Anna Quindlen, "At the Beach," *Living Out Loud* (1988)

3 I looked always outside of myself to see what I could make the world give me instead of looking within myself to see what was there.

Belle Livingstone, *Belle of Bohemia* (1927)

4 My mind is a world in itself, which I have peopled with my own creatures.

Lady Caroline Lamb, *Glenarvon* (1816)

5 One is never got out of the cave, one comes out of it.

Simone Weil, *First and Last Notebooks* (1970)

6 How can a rational being be ennobled by anything that is not obtained by its *own* exertions?

Mary Wollstonecraft, *A Vindication of the Rights of Woman* (1792)

7 If you would have your son to walk honorably through the world, you must not attempt to clear the stones from his path, but teach him to walk firmly over them.

Anne Brontë, *The Tenant of Wildfell Hall* (1848)

8 Those days are over / When it was expedient for two deer / To walk together, / Since anyone can see and remove / The beam in his eye with a mirror.

Ama Ata Aidoo, *Dilemma of a Ghost* (1965)

See also Independence.

## ❧ SENSES

9 We live on the leash of our senses.

Diane Ackerman, *A Natural History of the Senses* (1990)

10 There is no way in which to understand the world without first detecting it through the radar-net of our senses.

Diane Ackerman, *A Natural History of the Senses* (1990)

11 For all of my patients sensuality is a giving in to "the low side of their nature." Puritanism is powerful and distorts their life with a total anesthesia of the senses. If you atrophy one sense you also atrophy all the others, a sensuous and physical connection with nature, with art, with food, with other human beings.

Anaïs Nin (1935), *The Diary of Anaïs Nin*, vol. 2 (1967)

12 The life of sensation is the life of greed; it requires more and more. The life of the spirit requires less and less; time is ample and its passage sweet.

Annie Dillard, *The Writing Life* (1989)

13 It is immediately apparent . . . that this sense-world, this seemingly real external universe, though it may be useful and valid in other respects, cannot be *the* external world, but only the self's projected picture of it. . . . The evidence of the senses cannot be accepted as evidence of the nature of ultimate reality.

Evelyn Underhill, *Mysticism* (1955)

See also Sensuality, Smell, Touch.

## ❧ SENSIBLE

14 People miss a great deal by being sensible.

Martha Gellhorn, "Monkeys on the Roof," in *Ladies' Home Journal* (1964)

15 It's sensible people who do the most foolish things.

Richard Shattuck, *The Half-Haunted Saloon* (1945)

See also Common Sense.

## ❧ SENSITIVITY

16 I wonder if anyone else has an ear so tuned and sharpened as I have, to detect the music, not of the spheres, but of earth, subtleties of major and minor chord that the wind strikes upon the tree branches. Have you ever heard the earth breathe . . . ?

Kate Chopin, "Mrs. Mobry's Reason" (1900), *The Storm* (1974)

17 If we had a keen vision and feeling of all ordinary human life, it would be like hearing the grass grow and the squirrel's heart beat, and we should die of

...which lies on the other side of silence. As ...s, the quickest of us walk about well wadded with stupidity.

George Eliot, *Middlemarch* (1871)

1 Tender hearts as well were hearts of stone, / If what they feel is for themselves alone.

Jane Taylor, "Egotism," *Essays in Rhyme* (1816)

See also Awareness.

## ♦ SENSUALITY

2 Sensuality, wanting a religion, invented Love.

Natalie Clifford Barney, in *Adam International Review* (1962)

See also Senses, Sex.

## ♦ SENTIMENTALITY

3 Sentimentality comes from an inability, for whatever reason, to look reality in the face.

Marilyn Sewell, *Cries of the Spirit* (1991)

4 I revolted from sentimentality, less because it was false than because it was cruel.

Ellen Glasgow, *The Woman Within* (1954)

## ♦ SEPTEMBER

5 How smartly September comes in, like a racing gig, all style, no confusion.

Eleanor Clark, *Eyes, Etc.* (1977)

6 September is the time to begin again. In the country, when I could smell the wood-smoke in the forest, and the curtains could be drawn when the tea came in, on the first autumn evening, I always felt that my season of good luck had come.

Eleanor Perényi, *More Was Lost* (1946)

See also Autumn.

## ♦ SERIOUSNESS

7 The one important thing I have learnt over the years is the difference between taking one's work seriously and taking oneself seriously. The first is imperative and the second disastrous.

Margot Fonteyn, *Margot Fonteyn* (1975)

8 Seriousness is the refuge of the shallow. There are events and personal experiences that call forth seriousness but they are fewer than most of us think.

Rita Mae Brown, *Starting From Scratch* (1988)

9 Just as we are often moved to merriment for no other reason than that the occasion calls for seriousness, so we are correspondingly serious when invited too freely to be amused.

Agnes Repplier, "The American Laughs," *Under Dispute* (1924)

10 You're the unfortunate contradiction in terms—a serious good person.

Wendy Wasserstein, *The Heidi Chronicles* (1988)

## ♦ SERMONS

11 I'd as soon hear a bird-clapper preach as him— theer'd be more sense an less noise!

Mrs. Humphry Ward, *The History of David Grieve* (1891)

12 He always talks of eternity till he forgets time.

C.M. Sedgwick, *Hope Leslie* (1827)

13 I want a *human* sermon. I don't care what Melchisedek, or Zerubbabel, or Kerenhappuk did, ages ago; I want to know what *I* am to do, and I want somebody besides a theological bookworm to tell me; somebody who is sometimes tempted and tried, and is not too dignified to own it; somebody like me, who is always sinning and repenting; somebody who is glad and sorry, and cries and laughs, and eats and drinks, and *wants* to fight when they are trodden on, and *don't*!

Fanny Fern, *Ginger-Snaps* (1870)

14 That's all one asks of a sermon. No possible relevance to anything but itself.

P.D. James, *The Skull Beneath the Skin* (1982)

See also Church.

## ❧ SERVANTS

1 I felt ridiculous and almost guilty about having someone in to clean my tiny flat . . . [but] Z'mira was a "find." She only takes when you have two of something.

Gloria Goldreich, "Z'mira," in *Midstream* (1962)

2 A butler in an English household should, however, be English, and as much like an archbishop as possible.

Ada Leverson, in *Referee* (1903)

3 I realized immediately that it wasn't a servant because they don't slam doors.

Queen Elizabeth II, on the 1982 intruder into her bedroom, in Ann Morrow, *The Queen* (1983)

## ❧ SERVICE

4 Oh I am a cat that likes to / Gallop about doing good.

Stevie Smith, "The Galloping Cat," *Scorpion* (1972)

5 If I can stop one Heart from breaking / I shall not live in vain / If I can ease one Life the Aching / Or cool one Pain / Or help one fainting Robin / Unto his Nest again / I shall not live in Vain.

Emily Dickinson (1864), in Mabel Loomis Todd and T.W. Higginson, eds., *Poems by Emily Dickinson* (1890)

6 One act of beneficence, one act of real usefulness, is worth all the abstract sentiment in the world.

Ann Radcliffe, *The Mysteries of Udolpho* (1794)

7 I don't think you're much good, unless you're doing good to someone.

Rose Kennedy (1911), in Laurence Leamer, *The Kennedy Women* (1994)

8 When you cease to make a contribution you begin to die.

Eleanor Roosevelt (1960), in Joseph P. Lash, *Eleanor: The Years Alone* (1972)

9 Spiritual warrior's pledge: Not for myself alone, but that all the people may live.

Brooke Medicine Eagle, *Buffalo Woman Comes Singing* (1991)

10 God has no other hands than ours.

Dorothee Sölle, *Suffering* (1973)

11 It's so nice to be a spoke in the wheel, one that helps to turn, not one that hinders.

Gertrude Bell (1916), in Florence Bell, ed., *The Letters of Gertrude Bell*, vol. 1 (1927)

12 If we all tried to make other people's paths easy, our own feet would have a smooth even place to walk on.

Myrtle Reed, *A Weaver of Dreams* (1911)

13 A single hand's turn given heartily to the world's great work helps one amazingly with one's own small tasks.

Louisa M. Alcott, *An Old-Fashioned Girl* (1870)

14 I believe that the only possible reason for our being here is to serve in some form or another but that the form is not always readily found or recognized. And I've noticed that those who refuse to serve often wind up as slaves.

Hildegard Knef, *The Verdict* (1975)

15 Usefulness, whatever form it may take, is the price we should pay for the air we breathe and the food we eat and the privilege of being alive.

Eleanor Roosevelt, *You Learn by Living* (1960)

16 Service is the rent that you pay for room on this earth.

Shirley Chisholm, in Brian Lanker, *I Dream a World* (1989)

17 Service is the rent we pay for living.

Marian Wright Edelman, *The Measure of Our Success* (1992)

18 What do we live for, if it is not to make life less difficult to each other?

George Eliot, *Middlemarch* (1871)

19 The laws of our being are such that we must perform some degree of use in the world, whether we intend it, or not; but we can deprive ourselves of its indwelling joy, by acting entirely from the love of self.

Lydia Maria Child, *Letters From New York*, 2nd series (1845)

20 There is nothing to make you like other human beings so much as doing things for them.

Zora Neale Hurston, *Dust Tracks on a Road* (1942)

21 Public work brings a vicarious but assured sense of immortality. We may be poor, weak, timid, in debt to our landlady, bullied by our nieces, stiff in the

joints, shortsighted and distressed; we shall perish, but the cause endures; the cause is great.

Winifred Holtby, "The Right Side of Thirty" (1930), *Pavements at Anderby* (1937)

1 I have a rage for being useful, for devoting myself to somebody or something.

Eugénie de Guérin (1840), in Guillaume S. Trébutien, ed., *Letters of Eugénie de Guérin* (1865)

2 Pray for the dead and fight like hell for the living!

Mother Jones, in Mary Field Parton, *The Autobiography of Mother Jones* (1925)

3 "Can I help you?" she enquired, in a manner that said she hoped she wouldn't have to.

Liza Cody, *Dupe* (1981)

4 The things I do for England.

Diana, Princess of Wales, in Andrew Morton, *Diana* (1992)

See also Activism, Altruism, Giving, Volunteers.

## ❧ SEWING

5 Between threading a needle and raving insanity is the smallest eye in creation.

Caitlin Thomas, *Not Quite Posthumous Letter to My Daughter* (1963)

6 Half-a-day's sewing would give me such a fit of depression and *ennui* as a week's idleness would not repair. . . . I had rather wear a hair shirt than make a linen one.

Geraldine Jewsbury (1841), in Mrs. Alexander Ireland, ed., *Selections From the Letters of Geraldine Endsor Jewsbury to Jane Welsh Carlyle* (1892)

7 Remember, measure twice, cut once.

Whitney Otto, *How to Make an American Quilt* (1991)

8 I sewed good wishes and thoughts into my garments, especially so if they were wedding or graduation dresses.

Anne Ellis, *Plain Anne Ellis* (1931)

See also Quilts.

## ❧ SEX

9 Truly, a little love-making is a very pleasant thing.

L.E. Landon, *Romance and Reality* (1831)

10 Rowing in Eden — / Ah, the Sea! / Might I but moor — Tonight — / In Thee!

Emily Dickinson (1861), in T.W. Higginson and Mabel Loomis Todd, eds., *Poems by Emily Dickinson*, 2nd series (1891)

11 Even a notary would notarize our bed / as you knead me and I rise like bread.

Anne Sexton, "Song for a Lady," *Love Poems* (1969)

12 Sex is an emotion in motion.

Mae West, in Diane Arbus, "Mae West: Emotion in Motion," *Show* (1965)

13 Sexuality is a sacrament.

Starhawk, *The Spiral Dance* (1979)

14 Sex itself must always, it seems to me, come to us as a sacrament and be so used or it is meaningless. The flesh is suffused by the spirit, and it is forgetting this in the act of love-making that creates cynicism and despair.

May Sarton, *Recovering* (1980)

15 Sex is a game, a weapon, a toy, a joy, a trance, an enlightenment, a loss, a hope.

Sallie Tisdale, *Talk Dirty to Me* (1994)

16 The zipless fuck is absolutely pure. It is free of ulterior motives. There is no power game. The man is not "taking" and the woman is not "giving." No one is attempting to cuckold a husband or humiliate a wife. No one is trying to prove anything or get anything out of anyone. The zipless fuck is the purest thing there is. And it is rarer than the unicorn.

Erica Jong, *Fear of Flying* (1973)

17 Of all the things that human beings did together, the sexual act was the one with the most various of reasons.

P.D. James, *The Skull Beneath the Skin* (1982)

18 That pathetic short-cut suggested by Nature the supreme joker as a remedy for our loneliness, that ephemeral communion which we persuade ourselves to be of the spirit when it is in fact only of the body—durable not even in memory!

Vita Sackville-West, *No Signposts in the Sea* (1961)

19 'Tis better to have loved and lust than never to have loved at all.

Craig Rice, *Trial by Fury* (1941)

1 The total deprivation of it produces irritability.

Elizabeth Blackwell, *The Human Element in Sex* (1894)

2 Sex is hardly ever just about sex.

Shirley MacLaine, *Dancing in the Light* (1985)

3 Sex divorced from love is the thief of personal dignity.

Caitlin Thomas, *Not Quite Posthumous Letter to My Daughter* (1963)

4 Making love, we are all more alike than we are when we are talking or acting.

Mary McCarthy, "Characters in Fiction," *On the Contrary* (1961)

5 Sexuality is the great field of battle between biology and society.

Nancy Friday, *My Mother/My Self* (1977)

6 It's pitch, sex is. Once you touch it, it clings to you.

Margery Allingham, *The Fashion in Shrouds* (1938)

7 You cannot escape sex. It will track you to the ends of the earth.

Jan Clausen, "Depending," *Mother, Sister, Daughter, Lover* (1980)

8 People talk about "sex" as though it hopped about by itself, like a frog!

Anne Morrow Lindbergh, *Locked Rooms and Open Doors* (1974)

9 Everyone lies about sex, more or less, to themselves if not to others, to others if not to themselves, exaggerating its importance or minimizing its pull.

Daphne Merkin, in Christina Büchmann and Celina Spiegel, eds., *Out of the Garden* (1994)

10 One could plausibly argue that it is for quite sound reasons that the whole capacity for sexual ecstasy is inaccessible to most people—given that sexuality is something, like nuclear energy, which may prove amenable to domestication through scruple, but then again may not.

Susan Sontag, "The Pornographic Imagination," *Styles of Radical Will* (1966)

11 She knew, even though she was too young to know the reason, that indiscriminate desire and unselective sex were possible only to those who regarded sex and themselves as evil.

Ayn Rand, *Atlas Shrugged* (1957)

12 I don't know what I am, darling. I've tried several varieties of sex. The conventional position makes

me claustrophobic. And the others give me either stiff neck or lockjaw.

Tallulah Bankhead, in Lee Israel, *Miss Tallulah Bankhead* (1972)

13 It doesn't matter what you do in the bedroom as long as you don't do it in the street and frighten the horses.

Mrs. Patrick Campbell, in Daphne Fielding, *The Duchess of Jermyn Street* (1964)

14 Sex, unlike justice, should not be seen to be done.

Evelyn Laye, in Michèle Brown and Ann O'Connor, *Hammer and Tongues* (1986)

15 The important thing in acting is to be able to laugh and cry. If I have to cry, I think of my sex life. If I have to laugh, I think of my sex life.

Glenda Jackson, in L.M. Boyd, syndicated column (1980)

16 Sex is God's joke on the human race, Isadora thinks: if we didn't have sex to make us ridiculous, She would have had to think up something else instead.

Erica Jong, *Parachutes & Kisses* (1984)

17 If sex isn't a joke, what is it?

Nella Larsen, "Passing" (1929), *An Intimation of Things Distant* (1992)

18 Whatever else can be said about sex, it cannot be called a dignified performance.

Helen Lawrenson, *Whistling Girl* (1978)

19 What *isn't* funny about sex?

Roz Warren, in *Ms.* (1994)

20 I think it's terribly difficult to take sex seriously if you've got a sense of humor.

Charlotte Bingham, *Coronet Among the Weeds* (1963)

21 Sex and laughter do go very well together, and I wondered—and still do—which is the more important.

Hermione Gingold, *How to Grow Old Disgracefully* (1988)

22 I do not know, I am only sixty-five.

Princess Metternich, when asked at what age a woman ceases to feel the torments of the flesh, in Simone de Beauvoir, *The Second Sex* (1949)

23 I love sex as much as I love music, and I think it's as hard to do.

Linda Ronstadt, in Mark Bego, *Linda Ronstadt* (1990)

1 I consider promiscuity immoral. Not because sex is evil, but because sex is too good and too important.

Ayn Rand, in *Playboy* (1964)

2 Sex as something beautiful may soon disappear. Once it was a knife so finely honed the edge was invisible until it was touched and then it cut deep. Now it is so blunt that it merely bruises and leaves ugly marks.

Mary Astor, *A Life on Film* (1967)

3 Sex is the tabasco sauce which an adolescent national palate sprinkles on every course in the menu.

Mary Day Winn, *Adam's Rib* (1931)

4 We are on a sexual binge in this country. . . . One consequence of this binge is that while people now get into bed more readily and a lot more naturally than they once did, what happens there often seems less important.

Shana Alexander, *Talking Woman* (1976)

5 Sex: In America an obsession. In other parts of the world a fact.

Marlene Dietrich, *Marlene Dietrich's ABC* (1962)

6 It *is* something big and cosmic. What else do we have? There's only birth and death and the union of two people—and sex is the only one that happens to us more than once.

Kathleen Winsor, *Star Money* (1950)

7 In an age in which greed and lust stalk the land like some Biblical plague, it is easy to view sex as just one more thing *to be had*. It is the mythos of moderns.

Jennifer Stone, "The Revisionist Imperative," *Stone's Throw* (1988)

8 We've surrounded the most vital and commonplace human function with a vast morass of taboos, convention, hypocrisy, and plain claptrap.

Ilka Chase, *In Bed We Cry* (1943)

9 The sex that is presented to us in everyday culture feels strange to me; its images are fragments, lifeless, removed from normal experience. Real sex, the sex in our cells and in the space between our neurons, leaks out and gets into things and stains our vision and colors our lives.

Sallie Tisdale, *Talk Dirty to Me* (1994)

10 [Swingers] have gone from Puritanism into promiscuity without passing through sensuality.

Molly Haskell, in *Village Voice* (1971)

11 All the Freudian system is impregnated with the prejudice which it makes it its mission to fight— the prejudice that everything sexual is vile.

Simone Weil, *Gravity and Grace* (1947)

12 I am happy now that Charles calls on my bedchamber less frequently than of old. As it is, I endure but two calls a week and when I hear his steps outside my door I lie down on my bed, close my eyes, open my legs and think of England.

Lady Alice Hillingdon, journal (1912), in Eric Partridge, *Dictionary of Catch Phrases* (1977)

13 I think that in the sexual act, as delightful as it can be, the very physical part of it is, yes, a hammering away. So it has a certain brutality.

Louise Nevelson, *Dawns + Dusks* (1976)

14 I didn't want it like that. Not against the bricks or hunkering in somebody's car. I wanted it come undone like gold thread, like a tent full of birds.

Sandra Cisneros, "One Holy Night," *Woman Hollering Creek* (1991)

15 If our sex life were determined by our first youthful experiments, most of the world would be doomed to celibacy. In no area of human experience are human beings more convinced that something better can be had if only they persevere.

P.D. James, *The Children of Men* (1992)

16 Sex annihilates identity, and the space given to sex in contemporary novels is an avowal of the absence of character.

Mary McCarthy, "Characters in Fiction," *On the Contrary* (1961)

17 The price of shallow sex may be a corresponding loss of capacity for deep love.

Shana Alexander, *Talking Woman* (1976)

18 If sex is a war, I am a conscientious objector: I will not play.

Marge Piercy, *Braided Lives* (1982)

19 Sex gets people killed, put in jail, beaten up, bankrupted, and disgraced, to say nothing of ruined— personally, politically, and professionally. Looking for sex can lead to misfortune, and if you get lucky and find it, it can leave you maimed, infected, or dead. Other than that, it's swell: the great American pastime. . . . You probably won't see it on a bumper sticker, but sex kills.

Edna Buchanan, *The Corpse Had a Familiar Face* (1987)

1 Aren't women prudes if they don't and prostitutes if they do?

> Kate Millett, speech (1975)

2 The fact is that heterosexual sex for most people is in no way free of the power relations between men and women.

> Deirdre English and Barbara Ehrenreich, in Evelyn Shapiro and Barry M. Shapiro, *The Women Say/The Men Say* (1979)

3 More divorces start in the bedroom than in any other room in the house.

> Ann Landers, *Since You Ask Me* (1961)

4 You cannot decree women to be sexually free when they are not economically free.

> Shere Hite, *The Hite Report* (1976)

5 As I grew to adolescence, I imagined, from closely observing the boredom and vexations of matrimony, that the act my parents committed and the one I so longed to commit must be two different things.

> Shirley Abbott, *Womenfolks: Growing Up Down South* (1983)

6 I found myself thinking it was a bit like my disappointment when I was confirmed. This may be blasphemous but I think not. For expecting to achieve union with God is similar to expecting to achieve it with man. Only I minded much more as regards man.

> Dodie Smith, *The Town in Bloom* (1965)

7 There is nothing that impairs a man's sexual performance quicker than any suggestion that he's not doing it right ("Not *there*, you idiot!").

> Helen Lawrenson, *Whistling Girl* (1978)

8 This was a very racy remark for Gladys, whose idea of wild sex was Fred Astaire loosening his tie.

> Susan Isaacs, *Shining Through* (1988)

9 Henry's idea of sex is to slow the car down to thirty miles an hour when he drops you off at the door.

> Barbara Howar, on Henry Kissinger, in Bob Chieger, *Was It Good for You, Too?* (1983)

10 Archie had been no good as a dancer. He had trundled her about. She ought to have been warned by that; for dancing and sex were linked . . . and Archie, she had soon discovered, trundled through sex.

> Elizabeth Taylor, *The Wedding Group* (1968)

11 It was an old quandary for them. He needed sex in order to feel connected to her, and she needed to feel connected to him in order to enjoy sex.

> Lisa Alther, *Bedrock* (1990)

12 The largess / Of all our love is a down-curving arc / That ends in sleeping, lest we rouse to mark / How all our fires go out in nothingness.

> Ruth Benedict, "For the Hour After Love," in Margaret Mead, *An Anthropologist at Work* (1959)

13 Hickeys are like PG-13 movies. You think they're pretty hot stuff after being limited to G and PG, but you never bother with them once you're seriously into R.

> Judy Markey, *You Only Get Married for the First Time Once* (1988)

14 I read recently in an article by G.K. Chesterton, that sex without gestation and parturition is like blowing the trumpets and waving the flags without doing any of the fighting. From a woman such words, though displaying inexperience, might come with dignity; from a man they are an unforgivable, intolerable insult. What is man's part in sex but a perpetual waving of flags and blowing of trumpets and avoidance of the fighting?

> Dora Russell, *Hypatia* (1925)

15 Consumerism is what physical lust is really about.

> Carole Stewart McDonnell, in Patricia Bell-Scott, *Life Notes* (1994)

16 Sex is never an emergency.

> Elaine Pierson, book title (1970)

See also Bisexuals, The Erotic, Love, Love and Sex, Lovers, Passion, Pornography, Promiscuity, Prostitution, Seduction, Sex and Religion.

## ❧ SEX AND RELIGION

17 Sex and religion are bordering states. They use the same vocabulary, share like ecstasies, and often serve as a substitute for one another.

> Jessamyn West, *Hide and Seek* (1973)

See also Religion, Sex.

## ❦ SEX APPEAL

1 Sex appeal is fifty per cent what you've got and fifty per cent what people think you've got.

  Sophia Loren, in Leslie Halliwell, *The Filmgoer's Book of Quotes* (1973)

2 He had that nameless charm, with a strong magnetism, which can only be called "It."

  Elinor Glyn, title story, *"It"* (1927)

3 He was the kind of guy who could kiss you behind your ear and make you feel like you'd just had kinky sex.

  Julia Alvarez, *How the Garcia Girls Lost Their Accents* (1991)

4 To have "It," the fortunate possessor must have that strange magnetism which attracts both sexes. He or she must be entirely unself-conscious and full of self-confidence, indifferent to the effect he or she is producing, and uninfluenced by others. There must be physical attraction, but beauty is unnecessary.

  Elinor Glyn, title story, *"It"* (1927)

5 No matter what he does, one always forgives him. It does not depend upon looks either—although this actual person is abominably good-looking—it does not depend upon intelligence or character or—anything—as you say, it is just "it."

  Elinor Glyn, *The Man and the Moment* (1915)

See also Appearance, Charisma.

## ❦ SEX EDUCATION

6 Let a child start right in with the laws of Nature before he's old enough to be surprised at them.

  Phyllis Bottome, "The Plain Case," *Strange Fruit* (1928)

7 It is far easier to explain to a three-year-old how babies are made than to explain the processes whereby bread or sugar appear on the table.

  Dervla Murphy, *Wheels Within Wheels* (1979)

8 Before the child ever gets to school it will have received crucial, almost irrevocable sex education and this will have been taught by the parents, who are not aware of what they are doing.

  Mary S. Calderone, in *People* (1980)

9 Our teacher had given the impression that the body from waist to groin was occupied only by a neatly drawn pelvic girdle, though organs abounded elsewhere.

  Jessica Anderson, *Tirra Lirra by the River* (1978)

10 Most mothers think that to keep young people away from lovemaking, it is enough never to mention it in front of them.

  Marie Madeleine de la Fayette, *The Princess of Clèves* (1678)

## ❦ SEXISM

11 I ask no favors for my sex. All I ask of our brethren is, that they will take their feet from off our necks.

  Sarah M. Grimké, *Letters on the Equality of the Sexes and the Condition of Woman* (1838)

12 The canon and civil law; church and state; priests and legislators; all political parties and religious denominations have alike taught that woman was made after man, of man, and for man, an inferior being, subject to man. Creeds, codes, Scriptures and statutes, are all based on this idea. The fashions, forms, ceremonies and customs of society, church ordinances and discipline all grow out of this idea.

  Elizabeth Cady Stanton, *The Woman's Bible* (1895)

13 Our culture thrusts woman into the condition of the lesser, the secondary, the subspecies, the atypical, the abnormal, the adjunct. It subordinates her to the male, who is portrayed as the superior, the species, the typical, the norm, the standard. It reflects the assumption that all people are male until proven female.

  Bobbye D. Sorrels, *The Nonsexist Communicator* (1983)

14 The first problem for all of us, men and woman, is not to learn, but to unlearn.

  Gloria Steinem, in *The New York Times* (1971)

15 Historically our own culture has relied for the creation of rich and contrasting values upon many artificial distinctions, the most striking of which is sex. . . . If we are to achieve a richer culture, rich in contrasting values, we must recognize the whole gamut of human potentialities, and so weave a less arbitrary social fabric, one in which each diverse human gift will find a fitting place.

  Margaret Mead, *Sex and Temperament in Three Primitive Societies* (1963)

1 What! still retaining your Utopian visions of female felicity? To talk of our happiness!—ours, the ill-used and oppressed! You remind me of the ancient tyrant, who, seeing his slaves sink under the weight of their chains, said, "Do look at the indolent repose of those people!"

L.E. Landon, *Romance and Reality* (1831)

2 It's just as hard for man to break the habit of thinking of himself as central to the species as it was to break the habit of thinking of himself as central to the universe. He sees himself quite unconsciously as the main line of evolution, with a female satellite revolving around him as the moon revolves around the earth. This not only causes him to overlook valuable clues to our ancestry, but sometimes leads him into making statements that are arrant and demonstrable nonsense.

Elaine Morgan, *The Descent of Woman* (1972)

3 Whatever class and race divergences exist, top cats are tom cats.

Elizabeth Janeway, *Improper Behavior* (1987)

4 Women's chains have been forged by men, not by anatomy.

Estelle Ramey, "Men's Monthly Cycles," in *Ms.* (1972)

5 The man of today did not establish this patriarchal regime, but he profits by it, even when he criticizes it. And he has made it very much a part of his own thinking.

Simone de Beauvoir, in Alice Schwarzer, "The Radicalization of Simone de Beauvoir," *Ms.* (1972)

6 Men have always got so many "good reasons" for keeping their privileges. If we had left it to the men *toilets* would have been the greatest obstacle to human progress. *Toilets* was always the reason women couldn't become engineers, or pilots, or even members of parliament. They didn't have women's toilets.

Hazel Hunkins Hallinan, in Dale Spender, *There's Always Been a Women's Movement This Century* (1983)

7 My stories had nothing to do with my banishment. I was being thrown out . . . because I was a female and because "there are no facilities for ladies at the front."

Marguerite Higgins, *War in Korea* (1951)

8 The ceiling isn't glass; it's a very dense layer of men.

Anne Jardim, in *The New Yorker* (1996)

9 No one is more arrogant toward women, more aggressive or scornful, than the man who is anxious about his virility.

Simone de Beauvoir, *The Second Sex* (1949)

10 There are times when a woman reading *Playboy* feels a little like a Jew reading a Nazi manual.

Gloria Steinem, "What 'Playboy' Doesn't Know About Women Could Fill a Book," in *McCall's* (1970)

11 That seems to be the haunting fear of mankind—that the advancement of women will sometime, someway, someplace, interfere with some man's comfort.

Nellie L. McClung, *In Times Like These* (1915)

12 If people are worried about unfair advancement, they should look at the sons-in-law of the world running companies. They've truly slept their way to the top.

Mary E. Cunningham (1980), in Bob Chieger, *Was It Good for You, Too?* (1983)

13 Whenever I hear a man talking of the advantages of our ill-used sex, I look upon it as the prelude to some new act of authority.

L.E. Landon, *Romance and Reality* (1831)

14 In our steady insistence on proclaiming sex-distinction we have grown to consider most human attributes as masculine attributes, for the simple reason that they were allowed to men and forbidden to women.

Charlotte Perkins Gilman, *Women and Economics* (1900)

15 You have not a boat of your own, that is just it; that is what women always suffer from; they have to steer, but the craft is some one else's, and the haul too.

Ouida, *Wisdom, Wit and Pathos* (1884)

16 Women are from their very infancy debarred those advantages with the want of which they are afterwards reproached. . . . So partial are men as to expect bricks when they afford no straw.

Mary Astell, *A Serious Proposal to the Ladies* (1694)

17 What a wretched circle this poor way of reasoning among the Men draws them insensibly into. Why is learning useless to us? Because we have no share in public offices. And why have we no share in public offices? Because we have no learning.

Sophia, A Person of Quality, *Woman Not Inferior to Man* (1739)

1 Man has always liked to have some woman, especially one about eight feet high and of earnest aspect, to represent his ideas or inventions. At the same time, of course, he anxiously thwarted her attempts to utilize the inventions or pursue the theories he held. Thus, he wanted women to be illiterate, but to represent the Spirit of Education. . . . He wanted some smiling damsel to typify Architecture for him, but never to build his houses. And, much as he insisted on having his women folk meek and shy, he was always portraying them blowing trumpets and leading his armies to war.

> Miriam Beard, "Woman Springs From Allegory to Life," in *The New York Times* (1927)

2 The world has never yet seen a truly great and virtuous nation, because in the degradation of woman the very fountains of life are poisoned at their source.

> Elizabeth Cady Stanton (1848), *Address Delivered at Seneca Falls and Rochester* (1870)

3 To the extent that either sex is disadvantaged, the whole culture is poorer, and the sex that, superficially, inherits the earth, inherits only a very partial legacy. The more whole the culture, the more whole each member, each man, each woman, each child will be.

> Margaret Mead, *Male and Female* (1949)

4 Surely, if life is good, it is good throughout its substance; we cannot separate men's activities from women's and say, these are worthy of praise and these unworthy.

> Winifred Holtby, "Nurse to the Archbishop," *Truth Is Not Sober* (1934)

5 Sexism goes so deep that at first it's hard to see; you think it's just reality.

> Alix Kates Shulman, *Burning Questions* (1978)

6 No one sex can govern alone. I believe that one of the reasons why civilization has failed so lamentably is that it has had one-sided government.

> Nancy Astor, *My Two Countries* (1923)

7 Men alone are not capable of making laws for men and women.

> Nellie McClung (1915), in Linda Rasmussen et al., *A Harvest Yet to Reap* (1976)

8 Men have been in charge of according value to literature, and . . . they have found the contributions of their own sex immeasurably superior.

> Dale Spender, *The Writing or the Sex? or Why You Don't Have to Read Women's Writing to Know It's No Good* (1989)

9 She didn't write it. She wrote it, but she shouldn't have. She wrote it, but look what she wrote about. She wrote it, but "she" isn't really an artist and "it" isn't really serious, of the right genre—i.e., really art. She wrote it, but she wrote only one of it. She wrote it, but it's only interesting/included in the canon for one, limited reason. She wrote it, but there are very few of her.

> Joanna Russ, on devaluing women's writing, *How to Suppress Women's Writing* (1983)

10 He told me that it only seemed reasonable that if there were female studies programs there should be something for men. My answer was that we already had men's studies—it was called education.

> Arlene Voski Avakian, *Lion Woman's Legacy* (1992)

11 It was hard to speed the male child up the stony heights of erudition, but it was harder still to check the female child at the crucial point, and keep her tottering decorously behind her brother.

> Agnes Repplier, in Emma Repplier, *Agnes Repplier* (1957)

12 My idea of success was to be a boy—possibly because my brothers, Leon and Arthur, were my father's pride and joy, whereas he had to be introduced to me several times before he got it firmly planted in his mind that I was part of the family.

> Lucille Kallen, *Out There, Somewhere* (1964)

13 It is a pity that so often the only way to treat girls like people seems to be to treat them like boys.

> Katharine Whitehorn, *Roundabout* (1962)

14 The flour-merchant, the house-builder, and the postman charge us no less on account of our sex; but when we endeavor to earn money to pay all these, then, indeed, we find the difference.

> Lucy Stone (1855), in Elizabeth Cady Stanton, Susan B. Anthony, and Matilda J. Gage, eds., *History of Woman Suffrage*, vol. 1 (1881)

15 Tremendous amounts of talent are being lost to our society just because that talent wears a skirt.

> Shirley Chisholm, *Unbought and Unbossed* (1970)

16 An occupation that has no basis in sex-determined gifts can now recruit its ranks from twice as many potential artists.

> Margaret Mead, *Sex and Temperament in Three Primitive Societies* (1935)

17 The test for whether or not you can hold a job should not be the arrangement of your chromosomes.

> Bella Abzug, *Bella!* (1972)

1 Just as the difference in height between males is no longer a realistic issue, now that lawsuits have been substituted for hand-to-hand encounters, so is the difference in strength between men and women no longer worth elaboration in cultural institutions.

    Margaret Mead, *Sex and Temperament in Three Primitive Societies* (1963)

2 There's only one woman I know of who could never be a symphony conductor, and that's the Venus de Milo.

    Margaret Hillis, in *The New York Times* (1979)

3 If I had ever learned to type, I never would have made brigadier general.

    Elizabeth P. Hoisington, in *The New York Times* (1970)

4 I can't change my sex. But you can change your policy.

    Helen Kirkpatrick (1940), on being told a newspaper didn't have women on its foreign affairs staff, in Julia Edwards, *Women of the World* (1988)

5 There are very few jobs that actually require a penis or vagina. All other jobs should be open to everybody.

    Florynce R. Kennedy, in Gloria Steinem, "The Verbal Karate of Florynce R. Kennedy, Esq.," *Ms.* (1973)

6 Can anybody tell me why reporters, in making mention of lady speakers, always consider it to be necessary to report, fully and *firstly*, the dresses worn by them? When John Jones or Senator Rouser frees his mind in public, we are left in painful ignorance of the color and fit of his pants, coat, necktie and vest—and worse still, the shape of his boots. This seems to me a great omission.

    Fanny Fern, *Ginger-Snaps* (1870)

7 Of my two "handicaps," being female put many more obstacles in my path than being black.

    Shirley Chisholm, *Unbought and Unbossed* (1970)

8 Black women, historically, have been doubly victimized by the twin immoralities of Jim Crow and Jane Crow. . . . Black women, faced with these dual barriers, have often found that sex bias is more formidable than racial bias.

    Pauli Murray, in Mary Lou Thompson, ed., *Voices of the New Feminism* (1970)

9 It is interesting that many women do not recognize themselves as discriminated against; no better proof could be found of the totality of their conditioning.

    Kate Millett, *Sexual Politics* (1969)

10 A woman can do anything she wants as long as she doesn't do anything she wants! She can go anywhere she likes as long as she stays put!

    Lucille Kallen, *Out There, Somewhere* (1964)

11 We haven't come a long way, we've come a short way. If we hadn't come a short way, no one would be calling us "baby."

    Elizabeth Janeway, in Evelyn L. Beilenson and Sharon Melnick, *Words on Women* (1987)

See also Chivalry, Discrimination, Equality, Feminism, Oppression, Patriarchy, Prejudice, Sex Roles, Stereotypes, Women and Men.

## ❦ SEX ROLES

12 There is no such thing as a sphere for sex. Every man has a different sphere, in which he may or may not shine, and it is the same with every woman, and the same woman may have a different sphere at different times.

    Elizabeth Cady Stanton (1848), in Theodore Stanton and Harriot Stanton Blatch, eds., *Elizabeth Cady Stanton As Revealed in Her Letters Diary and Reminiscences*, vol. 2 (1922)

13 Biology is destiny only for girls.

    Elizabeth Hardwick, title essay, *Seduction and Betrayal* (1974)

See also "Femininity," Men, Sexism, Women, Women and Men.

## ❦ SEXUAL HARASSMENT

14 Dear me no dears, Sir.

    Aphra Behn, *The Lucky Chance* (1687)

15 All your fine officials debauch the young girls who are afraid to lose their jobs: that's as old as Washington.

    Christina Stead, *The Man Who Loved Children* (1940)

16 We need to turn the question around to look at the harasser, not the target. We need to be sure that we can go out and look anyone who is a victim of

harassment in the eye and say, "You do not have to remain silent anymore."

Anita Hill, in *The New York Times* (1992)

1 The only women who don't believe that sexual harassment is a real problem in this country are women who have never been in the workplace.

Cynthia Heimel, *Get Your Tongue Out of My Mouth, I'm Kissing You Good-Bye!* (1993)

See also Oppression, Sexism.

## ❧ SHADOWS

2 Morning: such long shadows / Like low-bellied cats / Creep under parked cars / And out again, stealthily / Flattening the grasses.

Rosemary Dobson, "Canberra Morning," *Selected Poems* (1973)

3 Through the tall window by her cot she saw two blue shadows slide down Chuckanut Ridge quick as otters, but she could not see the clouds that made them.

Annie Dillard, *The Living* (1992)

4 Overhead some white puffed clouds sped, and threw their blue shadows up the leafy stumps where the hops grew, and threw the shadows down the stumps' other sides and into the woods fast as snakes.

Annie Dillard, *The Living* (1992)

5 Shadows lie late, their long, drowsy limbs / Spread on the grass.

Babette Deutsch, "September," *The Collected Poems of Babette Deutsch* (1969)

6 Treasure the shadow. . . . There are no shadows save from substance cast.

Edith M. Thomas, "Mirage," *The Dancers* (1903)

7 Never fear shadows. They simply mean there's a light shining somewhere nearby.

Ruth E. Renkel, in *Reader's Digest* (1983)

8 There is a time, when passing through a light, that you walk in your own shadow.

Keri Hulme, *The Bone People* (1983)

9 Marred pleasure's best, shadow makes the sun strong.

Stevie Smith, "The Queen and the Young Princess," *Selected Poems* (1964)

10 The shadows cannot speak.

Paula Gunn Allen, "Shadows," *The Blind Lion* (1974)

11 It's harder to shake off shadows than realities sometimes.

Rachel Field, *And Now Tomorrow* (1942)

## ❧ SHAMANS

12 I am a medicine woman. I live in the beyond and come back.

Agnes Whistling Elk, in Lynn V. Andrews, *Medicine Woman* (1981)

13 True shamans live in a world that is alive with what is to rationalist sight unseen, a world pulsing with intelligence.

Paula Gunn Allen, *Grandmothers of the Light* (1991)

14 Medicine people are truly citizens of two worlds, and those who continue to walk the path of medicine power learn to keep their balance in both the ordinary and the non-ordinary worlds.

Paula Gunn Allen, *Grandmothers of the Light* (1991)

15 There are no medicine men, without medicine women. A medicine man is given power by a woman, and it has always been that way. A medicine man stands in the place of the dog. He is merely an instrument of woman. It doesn't look that way anymore, but it is true.

Agnes Whistling Elk, in Lynn V. Andrews, *Medicine Woman* (1981)

16 Sorcerers never kill anybody. They make people kill themselves.

Agnes Whistling Elk, in Lynn V. Andrews, *Medicine Woman* (1981)

See also Magic, Spirituality.

## ❧ SHAME

17 A woman who could bend to grief, / But would not bow to shame.

Frances Ellen Watkins Harper, "Vashti," in *The New National Era* (1870)

See also Guilt, Remorse.

## ❧ SHAPE

1 I like shape very much. A novel has to have shape, and life doesn't have any.

Jean Rhys, *Smile Please* (1979)

See also Order.

## ❧ SHARING

2 Sharing is sometimes more demanding than giving.

Mary Catherine Bateson, *Composing a Life* (1989)

3 When the animals entered the Ark in pairs, one may imagine that allied species made much private remark on each other, and were tempted to think that so many forms feeding on the same store of fodder were eminently superfluous, as tending to diminish the rations.

George Eliot, *Middlemarch* (1871)

4 Old memories are so empty when they can not be shared.

Jewelle Gomez, "No Day Too Long," in Elly Bulkin, ed., *Lesbian Fiction* (1981)

See also Generosity, Giving.

## ❧ SHIPS

5 A ship is a beauty and a mystery wherever we see it.

Harriet Beecher Stowe, *The Pearl of Orr's Island* (1862)

6 There's no place where one can breathe as freely as on the deck of a ship.

Elsa Triolet, "Notebooks Buried," *A Fine of Two Hundred Francs* (1947)

7 It's especially fitting that they call a cruise ship "she," for she is pregnant with a thousand adult embryos who long to stay forever warm and sheltered in this great white womb.

Helen Van Slyke, *A Necessary Woman* (1979)

8 In the shortest sea voyage there is no sense of time. You have been down in the cabin for hours or days or years. Nobody knows or cares. You know all the people to the point of indifference. You do not believe in dry land any more—you are caught in the pendulum itself, and left there, idly swinging.

Katherine Mansfield, "The Journey to Bruges" (1910), *Something Childish* (1924)

9 Little children never know that they feel seasick, till they are.

Katharine Brush, "Things I Have Learned in My Travels," *This Is On Me* (1940)

10 I always say that a girl never really looks as well as she does on board a steamship, or even a yacht.

Anita Loos, *Gentlemen Prefer Blondes* (1925)

11 [The transatlantic crossing was] so rough that the only thing I could keep on my stomach was the first mate.

Dorothy Parker (1935), in Marion Meade, *Dorothy Parker: What Fresh Hell Is This?* (1988)

12 Another important point regarding yachting parties; the host must supply a gig or rowboat to carry his guests to and from the shore.

Lillian Eichler, *Book of Etiquette* (1921)

See also Boats.

## ❧ SHOCKING

13 Monstrous behavior is the order of the day. I'll tell you when to be shocked. When something human and decent happens!

Lucille Kallen, *Introducing C.B. Greenfield* (1979)

14 Many people who imagine they are live wires are only shocking.

Mary Pettibone Poole, *A Glass Eye at a Keyhole* (1938)

See also Offensiveness, Unexpected.

## ❧ SHOES

15 If I had my life to live over, I would start barefoot earlier in the spring and stay that way later in the fall.

Nadine Stair, title essay, in Sandra Haldeman Martz, ed., *If I Had My Life to Live Over* (1992)

1 If high heels were so wonderful, men would be wearing them.
Sue Grafton, *"I" Is for Innocence* (1992)

2 I did not have three thousand pairs of shoes, I had one thousand and sixty.
Imelda Marcos, news item (1987)

## ❦ SHOUTING

3 Anything difficult to say must be shouted from the rooftops.
Natalie Clifford Barney, *Adventures of the Mind* (1929)

4 Shouting has never made me understand anything.
Susan Sontag, *The Benefactor* (1963)

5 So many pleasing episodes of one's life are spoiled by shouting. You never heard of an unhappy marriage unless the neighbors have heard it first.
Lillian Russell, title essay (1914), in Djuna Barnes, *I Could Never Be Lonely Without a Husband* (1985)

## ❦ SHOW BUSINESS

6 In show business there's not much point in asking yourself if someone really likes you or if he just thinks you can be useful to him, because there's no difference.
Pauline Kael, *Kiss Kiss Bang Bang* (1968)

7 In this business, nice is just another word for stupid. Nice and a nickel will buy you a phone call.
Eileen Goudge, *Such Devoted Sisters* (1992)

8 That's how it always is in the entertainment industry, your feet are always treading Jello.
Hedy Lamarr, *Ecstasy and Me* (1966)

See also Entertainment, Films, Hollywood, Stage and Screen, Theater.

## ❦ SIBLINGS

9 Fraternal love, sometimes almost every thing, is at others worse than nothing.
Jane Austen, *Mansfield Park* (1814)

10 Even the conjugal tie is beneath the fraternal. Children of the same family, the same blood, with the same first associations and habits, have some means of enjoyment in their power, which no subsequent connections can supply.
Jane Austen, *Mansfield Park* (1814)

11 We know one another's faults, virtues, catastrophes, mortifications, triumphs, rivalries, desires, and how long we can each hang by our hands to a bar. We have been banded together under pack codes and tribal laws.
Rose Macaulay, *Personal Pleasures* (1936)

12 We were like ill-assorted animals tied to a common tethering post.
Jessica Mitford, *Daughters and Rebels* (1960)

13 Comparison is a death knell to sibling harmony.
Elizabeth Fishel, in *People* (1980)

See also Brothers, Sisters.

## ❦ SIGHING

14 It made him easier to be pitiful, / And sighing was his gift.
Elizabeth Barrett Browning, *Aurora Leigh* (1857)

15 Sighing was, he believed, simply the act of taking in more oxygen to help the brain cope with an unusual or difficult set of circumstances.
Margaret Millar, *Spider Webs* (1986)

## ❦ SILENCE

16 Then silence happened: / the silence that is born of water, foaming, / Suddenly it curdles in a looking glass. / So we grow quiet. We do / the same as lakes to see the sky.
Rosario Castellanos, in Irene Nicholson, *A Guide to Mexican Poetry* (1968)

17 Who . . . tells a finer tale than any of us? Silence does.
Isak Dinesen, "The Blank Page," *Last Tales* (1957)

18 True silence is a garden enclosed, where alone the soul can meet its God.
Catherine de Hueck Doherty, *Poustinia* (1975)

1 Silence is not a thing we make; it is something into which we enter. It is always there. . . . All we can make is noise.

Mother Maribel of Wantage, in Sister Janet, *Mother Maribel of Wantage* (1972)

2 I work out of silence, because silence makes up for my actual lack of working space. Silence substitutes for actual space, for psychological distance, for a sense of privacy and intactness. In this sense silence is absolutely necessary.

Radka Donnell, *Quilts As Women's Art* (1990)

3 All artists dream of a silence which they must enter, as some creatures return to the sea to spawn.

Iris Murdoch, *The Black Prince* (1973)

4 To a poet, silence is an acceptable response, even a flattering one.

Colette, *Paris From My Window* (1944)

5 These be / Three silent things: / The falling snow . . the hour / Before the dawn . . the mouth of one / Just dead.

Adelaide Crapsey, "Triad" (1911), in Susan Sutton Smith, ed., *The Complete Poems and Collected Letters of Adelaide Crapsey* (1977)

6 Silence was the first prayer I learned to trust.

Patricia Hampl, *Virgin Time* (1992)

7 God is the friend of silence. See how nature—trees, flowers, grass—grows in silence; see the stars, the moon, and the sun, how they move in silence.

Mother Teresa, *A Gift for God* (1975)

8 Silence is another form of sound.

Jane Hollister Wheelwright, *The Ranch Papers* (1988)

9 Silence more musical than any song.

Christina Rossetti, "Rest" (1849), *Goblin Market* (1862)

10 The modes of speech are scarcely more variable than the modes of silence.

Hannah More, "Thoughts on Conversation," *Essays on Various Subjects* (1777)

11 Silences can be as different as sounds.

Elizabeth Bowen, *Collected Impressions* (1950)

12 Silence may be as variously shaded as speech.

Edith Wharton, *The Reef* (1912)

13 Silence, that inspired dealer, takes the day's deck, the life, all in a crazy heap, lays it out, and plays its flawless hand of solitaire, every card in place. Scoops them up, and does it all over again.

Patricia Hampl, *Virgin Time* (1992)

14 I'm a woman sitting here with all my words intact / like a basket of green fruit.

Rosario Castellanos, "Silence Near an Ancient Stone" (1952), in Maureen Ahern, ed., *A Rosario Castellanos Reader* (1988)

15 We perceive silence where, in fact, there is a muffler.

Louise Bernikow, *Among Women* (1980)

16 Oblivion has been noticed as the offspring of silence.

Hannah More, *Practical Piety* (1811)

17 Silence is all the genius a fool has.

Zora Neale Hurston, *Moses: Man of the Mountain* (1939)

18 Speech is often barren; but silence also does not necessarily brood over a full nest.

George Eliot, *Felix Holt, the Radical* (1866)

19 Silence isn't always golden, you know. Sometimes it's just plain yellow.

Jan Kemp, in Sherry Ruth Anderson and Patricia Hopkins, *The Feminine Face of God* (1991)

20 When great principles are involved, I deem silence criminal.

Sara G. Stanley (1864), in Dorothy Sterling, ed., *We Are Your Sisters* (1984)

21 While we wait in silence for that final luxury of fearlessness, the weight of that silence will choke us.

Audre Lorde, "The Transformation of Silence Into Language and Action," in *Sinister Wisdom* (1978)

22 Silence is where the victims dwell.

Nelly Sachs, "Glowing Enigma III," *O the Chimneys* (1967)

23 'Tis not the noisiest things that announce the direst calamities. The awful is often voiceless.

Minna Thomas Antrim, *Naked Truth and Veiled Illusions* (1901)

24 Every day silence harvests its victims. Silence is a mortal illness.

Natalia Ginzburg, *The Little Virtues* (1962)

25 Silence has a suffocating, deadening effect. And the thing that dies first is hope.

Katie Sherrod, in *The Witness* (1993)

1 Silence gives consent.
    Mrs. E.D.E.N. Southworth, *Her Love or Her Life* (1877)

2 People who know the truth have no business to allow the powers of darkness to silence them on any point that matters.
    Marie Stopes, *Married Love* (1918)

3 The moment we begin to fear the opinions of others and hesitate to tell the truth that is in us, and from motives of policy are silent when we should speak, the divine floods of light and life flow no longer into our souls.
    Elizabeth Cady Stanton, speech to the National American Woman Suffrage Association (1890)

4 Sticks and stones are hard on bones. / Aimed with angry art, / Words can sting like anything. / But silence breaks the heart.
    Phyllis McGinley, "A Choice of Weapons," *The Love Letters of Phyllis McGinley* (1954)

5 Silence is the bluntest of blunt instruments. It seems to hammer you into the ground. It drives you deeper and deeper into your own guilt. It makes the voices inside your head accuse you more viciously than any outside voices ever could.
    Erica Jong, *Fear of Flying* (1973)

6 Silences have a climax, when you have got to speak.
    Elizabeth Bowen, *The House in Paris* (1935)

7 One must learn to be silent just as one must learn to talk.
    Victoria Wolff, *Spell of Egypt* (1943)

8 Sometimes I feel that every word spoken and every gesture made merely serve to exacerbate misunderstandings. Then what I would really like is to escape into a great silence and impose that silence on everyone else.
    Etty Hillesum (1941), *An Interrupted Life* (1983)

9 When you choose to write using yourself as the source of the story, you are choosing to confront all the silences in which your story has been protectively wrapped. Your job as a writer is to respectfully, determinedly, free the story from the silences and free yourself from both.
    Christina Baldwin, lecture (1990)

10 If you listen long enough—or is it deep enough?—the silence of a lover can speak plainer than any words! Only you must know how to listen. Pain must have taught you how.
    Phyllis Bottome, "The Gate," *Innocence and Experience* (1934)

11 Silence settled on the courtroom like snow.
    Margaret Millar, *Rose's Last Summer* (1952)

12 A comfortable quiet had settled between them. A silence that was like newly fallen snow.
    Carrie Fisher, *Delusions of Grandma* (1994)

13 An audience of twenty thousand, sitting on its hands, could not have produced such an echoing silence.
    Mary Renault, *The Mask of Apollo* (1966)

14 A small silence came between us, as precise as a picture hanging on the wall.
    Jean Stafford, *Boston Adventure* (1944)

15 His silences had not proceeded from the unplumbed depths of his knowledge. He merely had nothing to say.
    Edna Ferber, "The Sudden Sixties," *Gigolo* (1922)

See also Calm, Discretion, Reticence, Solitude.

## ❧ SIMPLICITY

16 It is the sweet, simple things of life which are the real ones after all.
    Laura Ingalls Wilder (1917), in Stephen W. Hines, ed., *Little House in the Ozarks* (1991)

17 Simplicity is the peak of civilization.
    Jessie Sampter, *The Emek* (1927)

18 Simplicity is an acquired taste. Mankind, left free, instinctively complicates life.
    Katharine Fullerton Gerould, *Modes and Morals* (1920)

19 The real drawback to "the simple life" is that it is not simple. If you are living it, you positively can do nothing else. There is not time.
    Katharine Fullerton Gerould, *Modes and Morals* (1920)

20 The path to simplicity is littered with complexities.
    Susan Ohanian, *Who's in Charge?* (1994)

21 Yes, to become simple and live simply, not only within yourself but also in your everyday dealings. Don't make ripples all around you, don't try so

hard to be interesting, keep your distance, be honest, fight the desire to be thought fascinating by the outside world.

Etty Hillesum (1942), *An Interrupted Life* (1983)

1 Such words as "God" and "Death" and "Suffering" and "Eternity" are best forgotten. We have to become as simple and as wordless as the growing corn or the falling rain. We must just be.

Etty Hillesum (1942), *An Interrupted Life* (1983)

2 In the end, what affect your life most deeply are things too simple to talk about.

Nell Blaine, in Eleanor Munro, *Originals: American Women Artists* (1979)

3 I like to go to Marshall Field's in Chicago just to see how many things there are in the world that I do not want.

Mother M. Madeleva, *My First Seventy Years* (1959)

See also Simplification, Small Things.


# ❦ SIMPLIFICATION

4 It's dishonest to simplify anything that isn't simple.

Florence Sabin, in Elinor Bluemel, *Florence Sabin* (1959)

5 A little simplification would be the first step toward rational living, I think.

Eleanor Roosevelt, *My Days* (1938)

See also Simplicity.


# ❦ SIN

6 Alas, that ever I did sin! It is full merry in Heaven.

Margery Kempe, *The Book of Margery Kempe* (c. 1431)

7 All sins are attempts to fill voids.

Simone Weil, *Gravity and Grace* (1947)

8 I saw not till now what sin brings with it—that we must tread others underfoot.

Sigrid Undset, *Kristin Lavransdatter: The Bridal Wreath* (1920)

9 Sin recognized - but that - may keep us humble, / But oh, it keeps us nasty.

Stevie Smith, "Recognition Not Enough," *Poems* (1962)

10 It is a human thing to sin, but perseverance in sin is a thing of the devil.

St. Catherine of Siena (1378), in Vida D. Scudder, ed., *St. Catherine of Siena As Seen in Her Letters* (1905)

11 Sin has always been an ugly word, but it has been made so in a new sense over the last half-century. It has been made not only ugly but passé. People are no longer sinful, they are only immature or underprivileged or frightened or, more particularly, sick.

Phyllis McGinley, "In Defense of Sin," *The Province of the Heart* (1959)

12 We don't call it sin today, we call it self-expression.

Baroness Stocks, in Jonathon Green, *The Cynic's Lexicon* (1984)

13 Fashions in sin change.

Lillian Hellman, *Watch on the Rhine* (1941)

14 You see so much of the sin of human nature that you get to thinking human nature has got to sin. You are mistaken, sir; it has got to be decent.

Margaret Deland, *Dr. Lavendar's People* (1903)

15 Sin looks much more terrible to those who look at it than to those who do it.

Ralph Iron, *The Story of an African Farm* (1883)

16 Sins of commission are far more productive of happiness than the sins of omission.

Myrtle Reed, *The Spinster Book* (1901)

17 *Sins* cut boldly up through every class in society, but mere misdemeanors show a certain level in life.

Elizabeth Bowen, *The Death of the Heart* (1938)

18 The great danger is that in the confession of any collective sin, one shall confess the sins of others and forget our own.

Georgia Harkness, *The Resources of Religion* (1936)

19 Many are saved from sin by being so inept at it.

Mignon McLaughlin, *The Neurotic's Notebook* (1963)

20 Somewhere, and I can't find where, I read about an Eskimo hunter who asked the local missionary priest, "If I did not know about god and sin, would I go to hell?" "No," said the priest, "not if you did

not know." "Then why," asked the Eskimo earnestly, "did you tell me?"

Annie Dillard, *Pilgrim at Tinker Creek* (1974)

1 Mankind thinks either too much or too little of sin.

Mary Baker Eddy, *Miscellaneous Writings: 1883-1896* (1896)

See also Crime, Devil, Error, Evil, Mistakes, Slippery Slope, Vice.

## ♪ SINCERITY

2 She was so sincere that she would think only one thought at a time; and her whole nature would be behind her thought.

Phyllis Bottome, "The Wild Bird," *Innocence and Experience* (1934)

3 Sincerity is not a spontaneous flower, nor is modesty either.

Colette, *The Pure and the Impure* (1932)

4 There is such a mistaken notion abroad in this country that the individual who makes sharp remarks must be sincere, while the one who says pleasant things must be more or less a humbug.

J.E. Buckrose, "Flattery," *What I Have Gathered* (1923)

5 The most exhausting thing in life, I have discovered, is being insincere.

Anne Morrow Lindbergh, *Gift From the Sea* (1955)

6 He was declaring the ardor of his passion in such terms as but too often make vehemence pass for sincerity.

Ann Radcliffe, *The Romance of the Forest* (1791)

See also Frankness, Honesty, Truth.

## ♪ SINGING

7 Let your soul do the singin'.

Ma Rainey, to Bessie Smith, in Studs Terkel, *Giants of Jazz* (1957)

8 The songs of the singer / Are tones that repeat / The cry of the heart / 'Till it ceases to beat.

Georgia Douglas Johnson, "The Dreams of the Dream," *The Heart of a Woman* (1918)

9 Singing . . . gives right joy to speech.

Genevieve Taggard, "Definition of Song," *Calling Western Union* (1936)

10 To sing is an expression of your being, a being which is becoming.

Maria Callas, in Arianna Stassinopoulos, *Maria Callas* (1981)

11 I do like to sing to God!

Jenny Lind (1850), in Edward B. Marks, *They All Had Glamour* (1944)

12 I do not know who sings my songs / Before they are sung by me.

Mary Austin, "Whence," in *Poetry, A Magazine of Verse* (1921)

13 Of all musical instruments the human voice is the most beautiful, for it is made by God.

Shusha Guppy, *The Blindfold Horse* (1988)

14 My voice is my instrument. . . . It is not in the throat, from where it appears to come. It is in my feet and how they touch the floor, in my legs and how they lift and sink with the rhythm of the song. It is in my hips and belly and lower back.

Holly Near, with Derk Richardson, *Fire in the Rain . . . Singer in the Storm* (1990)

15 To sing is to love and to affirm, to fly and soar, to coast into the hearts of the people who listen, to tell them that life is to live, that love is there, that nothing is a promise, but that beauty exists, and must be hunted for and found. That death is a luxury, better to be romanticized and sung about than dwelt upon in the face of life.

Joan Baez, *Daybreak* (1968)

16 I am all for singing. If I had had children I should have HOUNDED them into choirs and choral societies, and if they weren't good enough for that, I would have sent them out, to sing in the streets.

Sylvia Townsend Warner (1960), in William Maxwell, ed., *Letters: Sylvia Townsend Warner* (1982)

17 A tune's like a staircase—walk up on it.

Ma Rainey, to Bessie Smith, in Studs Terkel, *Giants of Jazz* (1957)

18 Once you begin to phrase finely, you will feel more joy in the beautiful finish of a beautiful phrase than that caused by the loudest applause of an immense

audience. The latter excites for a moment; the former endures forever.

Nellie Melba, in Kathleen Kimball, Robin Petersen, Kathleen Johnson, eds., *The Music Lover's Quotation Book* (1990)

1 I can hold a note as long as the Chase Manhattan Bank.

Ethel Merman, in Fred Metcalf, *The Penguin Dictionary of Modern Humorous Quotations* (1986)

2 I have never given all of myself, even vocally, to anyone. I was taught to sing on your interest, not your capital.

Leontyne Price, in Brian Lanker, *I Dream a World* (1989)

3 I can't stand to sing the same song the same way two nights in succession, let alone two years or ten years. If you can, then it ain't music, it's close-order drill or exercise or yodeling or something, not music.

Billie Holiday, with William Dufty, *Lady Sings the Blues* (1956)

4 i wanna go see her and ask her if she will teach us how to use our voices like she used hers on that old 78 record.

hattie gossett, "billie lives! billie lives!" in Cherríe Moraga and Gloria Anzaldúa, eds., *This Bridge Called My Back* (1983)

5 She sings like she's got a secret, and if you listen long enough, she'll tell it to you—and only you.

Linda Barnes, *Steel Guitar* (1991)

6 All my life I have hated and despised alto! . . . That's why I hate Sunday. People will sing alto on Sunday that would never dream of singing it any other time.

Josephine Daskam, *The Memoirs of a Baby* (1904)

7 All the intelligence and talent in the world can't make a singer. The voice is a wild thing. It can't be bred in captivity.

Willa Cather, *The Song of the Lark* (1915)

8 I couldn't help thinkin' if she was as far out o' town as she was out o' tune, she wouldn't get back in a day.

Sarah Orne Jewett, *The Country of the Pointed Firs* (1896)

See also Music, Opera, Performance, Song.

## ✿ SINGLE

9 When my bed is empty, / Makes me feel awful mean and blue. / My springs are getting rusty, / Living single like I do.

Bessie Smith, "Empty Bed Blues," in William Harmon, ed., *The Oxford Book of American Light Verse* (1979)

10 Unmarried but happy.

Leonora Eyles, book title (1947)

11 There are a lot of great things about not being married. But one of the worst things is no one believes that.

Stephanie Brush, in *McCall's* (1993)

12 Being an old maid is like death by drowning, a really delightful sensation after you cease to struggle.

Edna Ferber, *A Peculiar Treasure* (1939)

13 Of all the benefits of spinsterhood, the greatest is carte blanche. Once a woman is called "that crazy old maid" she can get away with anything.

Florence King, *Reflections in a Jaundiced Eye* (1989)

14 There is a natural tribal hostility between the married and the unmarried. I cannot stand the shows so often quite instinctively put on by married people to insinuate that they are not only more fortunate but in some way more moral than you are.

Iris Murdoch, *The Black Prince* (1973)

15 I'm single because I was born that way.

Mae West, in Joseph Weintraub, ed., *The Wit and Wisdom of Mae West* (1967)

See also Alone, Bachelors, Dating.

## ✿ SINGLE-MINDEDNESS

16 Everybody has a *theme*. You talk to somebody awhile, and you realize they have one particular thing that rules them. The best you can do is a variation on the theme.

Meg Wolitzer, *This Is My Life* (1988)

17 All Hannah Berry's thoughts slid, as it were, in well-greased grooves; only give one a starting push and it went on indefinitely and left all others behind.

Mary E. Wilkins, *Pembroke* (1894)

## ❧ SISTERHOOD

1 We are thy sisters. . . . / Our skins may differ, but from thee we claim / A sister's privilege and a sister's name.

> Sarah L. Forten (1837), in Dorothy Sterling, ed., *We Are Your Sisters* (1984)

2 Beautiful sisters, come high up to the strongest rocks, / we are all fighting women, heroines, horsewomen.

> Edith Södergran, "Violet Twilights" (1916), in Stina Katchadourian, tr., *Love and Solitude* (1981)

3 I am the Chicana / the abandoned sister.

> Sylvia Alicia Gonzales, "Chicana Evolution," in Dexter Fisher, ed., *The Third Woman* (1980)

See also Women.

## ❧ SISTERS

4 There is no friend like a sister / In calm or stormy weather; / To cheer one on the tedious way, / To fetch one if one goes astray, / To lift one if one totters down, / To strengthen whilst one stands.

> Christina Rossetti, title poem (1859), *Goblin Market* (1862)

5 Is solace anywhere / more comforting / than in the arms / of sisters?

> Alice Walker, "Telling," *Her Blue Body Everything We Know* (1991)

6 There can be no situation in life in which the conversation of my dear sister will not administer some comfort to me.

> Lady Mary Wortley Montagu (1747), in Octave Thanet, ed., *The Best Letters of Lady Mary Wortley Montagu* (1901)

7 By now we know and anticipate one another so easily, so deeply, we unthinkingly finish each other's sentences, and often speak in code. No one else knows what I mean so exquisitely, painfully well; no one else knows so exactly what to say, to fix me.

> Joan Frank, "Womb Mates," *Desperate Women Need to Talk to You* (1994)

8 We are each other's reference point at our turning points.

> Elizabeth Fishel, *Sisters* (1979)

9 You know full as well as I do the value of sisters' affections to each other; there is nothing like it in this world.

> Charlotte Brontë, in Clement Shorter, ed., *The Brontës: Life and Letters*, vol. 1 (1969)

10 My sister taught me everything I really need to know, and she was only in sixth grade at the time.

> Linda Sunshine, *"Mom Loves Me Best" (And Other Lies You Told Your Sister)* (1990)

11 We were a club, a society, a civilization all our own.

> Annette, Cécile, Marie, and Yvonne Dionne, with James Brough, *"We Were Five"* (1965)

12 Hallie and I . . . were all there was. The image in the mirror that proves you are still here. We had exactly one sister apiece. We grew up knowing the simple arithmetic of scarcity: A sister is more precious than an eye.

> Barbara Kingsolver, *Animal Dreams* (1990)

13 My sister four years older simply existed for me because I had to sleep in the same room with her. Besides, it is natural not to care about a sister, certainly not when she is four years older and grinds her teeth at night.

> Gertrude Stein, *Everybody's Autobiography* (1937)

14 A baby sister is nicer than a goat. You'll get used to her.

> Lynne Alpern and Esther Blumenfeld, *Oh, Lord, I Sound Just Like Mama* (1986)

15 What surprised me was that within a family, the voices of sisters as they're talking are virtually always the same.

> Elizabeth Fishel, *Sisters* (1979)

16 Often, in old age, they become each other's chosen and most happy companions. In addition to their shared memories of childhood and of their relationship to each other's children, they share memories of the same home, the same homemaking style, and the same small prejudices about housekeeping that carry the echoes of their mother's voice.

> Margaret Mead, *Blackberry Winter* (1972)

17 Your sister is the only creature on earth who shares your heritage, history, environment, DNA, bone structure, and contempt for stupid Aunt Gertie.

> Linda Sunshine, *"Mom Loves Me Best" (And Other Lies You Told Your Sister)* (1990)

1 Between sisters, often, the child's cry never dies down. "Never leave me," it says; "do not abandon me."

Louise Bernikow, *Among Women* (1980)

2 Elder sisters never can do younger ones justice!

Charlotte M. Yonge, *The Pillars of the House*, vol. 2 (1889)

3 My sister and I may have been crafted of the same genetic clay, baked in the same uterine kiln, but we were disparate species, doomed never to love each other except blindly.

Judith Kelman, *Where Shadows Fall* (1987)

4 Of two sisters / one is always the watcher, / one the dancer.

Louise Glück, "Tango," *Descending Figure* (1980)

5 Sisters is probably *the* most competitive relationship within the family, but once the sisters are grown, it becomes the strongest relationship.

Margaret Mead, in Elizabeth Fishel, *Sisters* (1979)

6 If you don't understand how a woman could both love her sister dearly and want to wring her neck at the same time, then you were probably an only child.

Linda Sunshine, *"Mom Loves Me Best" (And Other Lies You Told Your Sister)* (1990)

7 Sisters define their rivalry in terms of competition for the gold cup of parental love. It is never perceived as a cup which runneth over, rather a finite vessel from which the more one sister drinks, the less is left for the others.

Elizabeth Fishel, *Sisters* (1979)

8 Near or far, there are burdens and terrors in sisterhood.

Helen Yglesias, *Family Feeling* (1976)

9 Sister, dear sister, come home and help me die.

Jessamyn West, *The Woman Said Yes* (1976)

10 The desire to be and have a sister is a primitive and profound one that may have everything or nothing to do with the family a woman is born to. It is a desire to know and be known by someone who shares blood and body, history and dreams, common ground and the unknown adventures of the future, darkest secrets and the glassiest beads of truth.

Elizabeth Fishel, *Sisters* (1979)

11 Both within the family and without, our sisters hold up our mirrors: our images of who we are and of who we can dare to become.

Elizabeth Fishel, *Sisters* (1979)

12 More than Santa Claus, your sister knows when you've been bad and good.

Linda Sunshine, *"Mom Loves Me Best" (And Other Lies You Told Your Sister)* (1990)

13 If sisters were free to express how they really feel, parents would hear this: "Give me all the attention and all the toys and send Rebecca to live with Grandma."

Linda Sunshine, *"Mom Loves Me Best" (And Other Lies You Told Your Sister)* (1990)

See also Family, Siblings.

## ❧ THE SIXTIES

14 The rules were changing. We were all soon to be marooned on a kind of moral polar ice pack that was shifting and breaking apart even as we walked across it.

Susan Cheever, *A Woman's Life* (1994)

15 The neglected legacy of the Sixties is just this: unabashed moral certitude, and the purity—the incredibly outgoing energy—of righteous rage.

June Jordan, "Where Is the Rage?" *Technical Difficulties* (1992)

## ❧ SIZE

16 At Stoke Poges the inn at which we stopped was so small that it might have been spelled "in."

Mary Anderson, *A Few Memories* (1896)

17 Do get over the idea that *size* has any value or merit. It is the enemy of most of the best things in the world—it is the enemy of the good life.

Ann Bridge, *Singing Waters* (1946)

18 Big doesn't necessarily mean better. Sunflowers aren't better than violets.

Edna Ferber, *Giant* (1952)

See also Advertising, Height, Quantity, Texas, Weight.

## ❧ SKATING

1 It's a feeling of ice miles running under your blades, the wind splitting open to let you through, the earth whirling around you at the touch of your toe, and speed lifting you off the ice far from all things that can hold you down.

> Sonja Henie, *Wings on My Feet* (1940)

See also Sports.


## ❧ SKIING

2 Off the packed trail we experience the miracle of corn snow, skiing atop the crust, like skiing on an eggshell that has been sprinkled with sugar.

> Susan Minot, "Skiing in Austria's Arlberg," in *The New York Times* (1991)

3 I hated skiing or any other sport where there was an ambulance waiting at the bottom of the hill.

> Erma Bombeck, *Aunt Erma's Cope Book* (1979)

See also Sports.


## ❧ SKY

4 Terrestrial scenery is much, but it is not all. Men go in search of it; but the celestial scenery journeys to them; it goes its way round the world. It has no nation, it costs no weariness, it knows no bonds.

> Alice Meynell, "Cloud," *Essays* (1914)

5 The sky hung over the valley, from hill to hill, like a slack white sheet.

> Elizabeth Bowen, "The Working Party," *Joining Charles* (1929)

6 Flat country seems to give the sky such a chance.

> Dodie Smith, *I Capture the Castle* (1948)

7 Elsewhere the sky is the roof of the world; but here the earth was the floor of the sky.

> Willa Cather, *Death Comes for the Archbishop* (1927)

8 The sky is reduced, / A narrow blue ribbon banding the lake. / Someone is wrapping things up.

> Susan Fromberg Schaeffer, "Post Mortem," *The Witch and the Weather Report* (1972)

9 He wondered whether the peculiar solemnity of looking at the sky comes, not from what one contemplates, but from that uplift of one's head.

> Ayn Rand, *The Fountainhead* (1943)

See also Clouds, Moon, Planets, Stars, Sun, Sunrise, Sunset.


## ❧ SLAVERY

10 Slavery's crime against humanity did not begin when one people defeated and enslaved its enemies (though of course this was bad enough), but when slavery became an institution in which some men were "born" free and others slave, when it was forgotten that it was man who had deprived his fellow-men of freedom, and when the sanction for the crime was attributed to nature.

> Hannah Arendt, *Origins of Totalitarianism* (1951)

11 The degradation, the wrongs, the vices, that grow out of slavery, are more than I can describe. They are greater than you would willingly believe.

> Harriet A. Jacobs, *Incidents in the Life of a Slave Girl, Written by Herself* (1861)

12 "Oh, slavery, slavery," my Daddy would say. "It ain't something in a book, Lue. Even the good parts was awful."

> Lucille Clifton, *Generations* (1976)

13 Oh, could slavery exist long if it did not sit on a commercial throne?

> Frances Ellen Watkins Harper (1854), in William Still, *The Underground Railroad* (1872)

14 Was it not strangely inconsistent that men fresh, so fresh, from the baptism of the Revolution should make such concessions to the foul spirit of Despotism! that, when fresh from gaining their own liberty, they could permit the African slave trade— could let their national flag hang a sign of death on Guinea's coast and Congo's shore!

> Frances Ellen Watkins Harper, "Miss Watkins and the Constitution," in *The National Anti-Slavery Standard* (1859)

15 Notwithstanding my grandmother's long and faithful service to her owners, not one of her children escaped the auction block. These God-breathing machines are no more, in the sight of their

masters, than the cotton they plant, or the horses they tend.

> Harriet A. Jacobs, *Incidents in the Life of a Slave Girl, Written by Herself* (1861)

1 I was ordered to go for flowers, that my mistress's house might be decorated for an evening party. I spent the day gathering flowers and weaving them into festoons, while the dead body of my father was lying within a mile of me. What cared my owners for that? he was merely a piece of property. Moreover, they thought he had spoiled his children, by teaching them to feel that they were human beings. This was blasphemous doctrine for a slave to teach; presumptuous in him, and dangerous to the masters.

> Harriet A. Jacobs, *Incidents in the Life of a Slave Girl, Written by Herself* (1861)

2 It is difficult for the American mind to adjust to the realization that the Rhetts and Scarletts were as much monsters as the keepers of Buchenwald— they just dressed more attractively.

> Lorraine Hansberry, speech (1964)

3 Could you have seen that mother clinging to her child, when they fastened the irons upon his wrists; could you have heard her heart-rending groans, and seen her bloodshot eyes wander wildly from face to face, vainly pleading for mercy; could you have witnessed that scene as I saw it, you would exclaim, *Slavery is damnable!*

> Harriet A. Jacobs, *Incidents in the Life of a Slave Girl, Written by Herself* (1861)

4 Slavery is a curse to the whites as well as to the blacks. It makes the white fathers cruel and sensual; the sons violent and licentious; it contaminates the daughters, and makes the wives wretched. And as for the colored race, it needs an abler pen than mine to describe the extremity of their sufferings, the depth of their degradation.

> Harriet A. Jacobs, *Incidents in the Life of a Slave Girl, Written by Herself* (1861)

5 No pen can give an adequate description of the all-pervading corruption produced by slavery.

> Harriet A. Jacobs, *Incidents in the Life of a Slave Girl, Written by Herself* (1861)

6 This is what I hold against slavery. May come a time when I for*give*—cause I don't think I'm set up to for*get*—the beatings, the selling, the killings, but I don't think I ever forgive the ignorance they kept us in.

> Sherley Anne Williams, *Dessa Rose* (1986)

7 Them white people made hate. They made hate just like they had a formula for it and followed that formula down to the last exact gallon of misery put in.

> J. California Cooper, *Family* (1991)

8 Slavery always has, and always will, produce insurrections wherever it exists, because it is a violation of the natural order of things.

> Angelina Grimké, "Appeal to the Christian Women of the South," in *The Anti-Slavery Examiner* (1836)

See also Oppression.


## ✿ SLEEP

9 Rocked in the cradle of the deep, / I lay me down in peace to sleep.

> Emma Hart Willard, *The Cradle of the Deep* (1831)

10 Blessed be sleep! We are all young then; we are all happy. *Then* our dead are living.

> Fanny Fern, *Ginger-Snaps* (1870)

11 When action grows unprofitable, gather information; when information grows unprofitable, sleep.

> Ursula K. Le Guin, *The Left Hand of Darkness* (1969)

12 Sleep is a thin white hand laid along me in the darkness.

> Evelyn Scott, *Escapade* (1923)

13 To sleep is an act of faith.

> Barbara Grizzuti Harrison, *Foreign Bodies* (1984)

14 Sleep was her fetish, panacea and art.

> Mary Webb, *Gone to Earth* (1917)

15 His sleep was a sensuous gluttony of oblivion.

> P.D. James, *Death of an Expert Witness* (1977)

16 Hers was the pleasant fatigue that comes of work well done. When at night in bed she went over the events of the day, it was with a modest yet certain satisfaction at this misunderstanding disentangled, that problem solved, some other help given in time of need. Her good deeds smoothed her pillow.

> Winifred Holtby, *South Riding* (1936)

1  I pillowed myself in goodness and slept righteously.

    Maya Angelou, *All God's Children Need Traveling Shoes* (1986)

2  I reached for sleep and drew it round me like a blanket muffling pain and thought together in the merciful dark.

    Mary Stewart, *The Hollow Hills* (1973)

3  Most people spend their lives going to bed when they're not sleepy and getting up when they are!

    Cindy Adams, in Joey Adams, *Cindy and I* (1957)

4  There is no innocent sleep so innocent as sleep shared between a woman and a child, the little breath hurrying beside the longer, as a child's foot runs.

    Alice Meynell, "Solitude," *Essays* (1914)

5  Sleeping alone, except under doctor's orders, does much harm. Children will tell you how lonely it is sleeping alone. If possible you should always sleep with someone you love. You both recharge your mutual batteries free of charge.

    Marlene Dietrich, *Marlene Dietrich's ABC* (1962)

6  Daytime sleep is a cursed slumber from which one wakes in despair.

    Iris Murdoch, *Under the Net* (1954)

7  Others may woo thee, Sleep; so will not I. / Dear is each minute of my conscious breath, / Hard fate, that, ere the time be come to die, / Myself, to live, must nightly mimic death.

    Mary Coleridge, "Sleep" (1890), in Theresa Whistler, ed., *The Collected Poems of Mary Coleridge* (1954)

8  Sleep is death without the responsibility.

    Fran Lebowitz, *Metropolitan Life* (1978)

See also Dreams, Fatigue, Insomnia, Snoring.

## § SLIPPERY SLOPE

9  The camel's nose was in the tent.

    Margaret Landon, *Anna and the King of Siam* (1944)

10  It's darn today, damn tomorrow, and next week it'll be goddamn.

    Louise Meriwether, *Daddy Was a Number Runner* (1970)

11  Heed the spark or you may dread the fire.

    Miles Franklin, *Some Everyday Folk and Dawn* (1909)

12  I was like many another who starts an intrigue timidly. Once into it, I had to go on, and therefore I had to harden my sensibilities.

    Elizabeth Borton de Treviño, *I, Juan de Pareja* (1965)

13  The first step is what I like to be sure of . . . to the second step it often binds you.

    Amelia E. Barr, *The Bow of Orange Ribbon* (1886)

14  Sometimes, when one's behaved like a rather second-rate person . . . in a kind of self-destructive shock one goes and does something *really* second-rate. Almost as if to prove it.

    Alison Lurie, *Real People* (1969)

15  When one kicks over a tea table and smashes everything but the sugar bowl, one may as well pick that up and drop it on the bricks, don't you think?

    Margery Allingham, *Dancers in Mourning* (1937)

16  Once you begin being naughty, it is easier to go on and on, and sooner or later something dreadful happens.

    Laura Ingalls Wilder, *On the Banks of Plum Creek* (1937)

17  If you are perfectly willing to shock an individual verbally, the next thing you will be doing is to shock him practically.

    Katharine Fullerton Gerould, *Modes and Morals* (1920)

18  A little misgiving in the beginning of things, means much regret in the end of them.

    Amelia E. Barr, *All the Days of My Life* (1913)

19  Anything that happens gradually is always irrevocable.

    Madame de Staël, *Letters on Rousseau* (1788)

20  This downhill path is easy, but there's no turning back.

    Christina Rossetti, "Amor Mundi" (1865), *The Poetical Works of Christina Georgina Rossetti* (1906)

See also Beginning, Sin, Small Things.

## § SLOGANS

21  Slogans let the ignorant think they understand what's going on.

    Lynne Alpern and Esther Blumenfeld, *Oh, Lord, I Sound Just Like Mama* (1986)

1 Old saws have no teeth.

> Cynthia Ozick, *Trust* (1966)

See also "Political Correctness."

## ❧ SMALL THINGS

2 There *are* no little things. "Little things," so called, are the hinges of the universe.

> Fanny Fern, *Ginger-Snaps* (1870)

3 Little drops of water, / Little grains of sand, / Make the mighty ocean / And the pleasant land. / Thus the little minutes, / Humble though they be, / Make the mighty ages / Of eternity.

> Julia A. Fletcher, "Little Things" (1845), in Hazel Felleman, ed., *The Best Loved Poems of the American People* (1936)

4 One can get just as much exultation in losing oneself in a little thing as in a big thing. It is nice to think how one can be recklessly lost in a daisy!

> Anne Morrow Lindbergh, *Bring Me a Unicorn* (1971)

5 I wait for a chance to confer a great favor, and let the small ones slip; but they tell best in the end, I fancy.

> Louisa May Alcott, *Little Women* (1868)

6 The great sacrifices are seldom called for, but the minor ones are in daily requisition; and the making them with cheerfulness and grace enhances their value.

> Countess of Blessington, *Journal of Conversations With Lord Byron* (1834)

7 We can do no great things—only small things with great love.

> Mother Teresa, in Kathryn Spink, ed., *In the Silence of the Heart* (1983)

8 I long to accomplish a great and noble task, but it is my chief duty to accomplish humble tasks as though they were great and noble. The world is moved along, not only by the mighty shoves of its heroes, but also by the aggregate of the tiny pushes of each honest worker.

> Helen Keller, in Charles L. Wallis, *The Treasure Chest* (1983)

9 We must not, in trying to think about how we can make a big difference, ignore the small daily differences we can make which, over time, add up to big differences that we often cannot foresee.

> Marian Wright Edelman, *Families in Peril* (1987)

10 To be really great in little things, to be truly noble and heroic in the insipid details of every-day life, is a virtue so rare as to be worthy of canonization.

> Harriet Beecher Stowe (1860), in Mary Alice Warner and Dayna Beilenson, eds., *Women of Faith and Spirit* (1987)

11 As often as not our whole self turns its back contemptuously on the so-called great moments and emotions and engages itself in the most trivial of things, the shape of a particular hill, a road in the town in which we lived as children, the movement of wind in grass. The things we shall take with us when we die will nearly all be small things.

> Storm Jameson, *That Was Yesterday* (1932)

12 One of the secrets of a happy life is continuous small treats.

> Iris Murdoch, *The Sea, The Sea* (1978)

13 I find you in all small and lovely things; in the little fishes like flames in the green water, in the furred and stupid softness of bumble-bees fat as laughter, in all the chiming radiance of warmth and light and scent in the summer garden.

> Winifred Holtby (1925), in Vera Brittain, *Testament of Friendship* (1940)

14 Jar one chord, the harp is silent; move one stone, the arch is shattered; / . . . / One dark cloud can hide the sunlight; loose one string, the pearls are scattered; / Think one thought, a soul may perish; say one word, a heart may break!

> Adelaide Anne Procter, "Philip and Mildred," *Legends and Lyrics* (1858)

15 Neglecting small things because one wishes to do great things is the excuse of the faint-hearted.

> Alexandra David-Neel (1889), *La Lampe de Sagesse* (1986)

16 To keep a lamp burning we have to keep putting oil in it.

> Mother Teresa, in "Saints Among Us," *Time* (1975)

17 Only those who know the supremacy of the intellectual life—the life which has a seed of ennobling thought and purpose within it—can understand the grief of one who falls from that serene activity into the absorbing soul-wasting struggle with worldly annoyances.

> George Eliot, *Middlemarch* (1871)

1 It's not the tragedies that kill us, it's the messes.

> Dorothy Parker, in Malcolm Cowley, ed., *Writers at Work* (1958)

2 Petty ills try the temper worse than great ones.

> Mrs. Henry Wood, *East Lynne* (1861)

3 It is a lot easier to forgive an occasional big fault than it is to put up with never-ending petty irritations. The big sinners at least take a day off from their vices now and then, but the little sinners who sin against our habits and ideals and conventions are always on the job.

> Dorothy Dix, *Dorothy Dix—Her Book* (1926)

4 The Atlantic's too big for me. A creek's got more of the sea in it, for people who want to turn it into poetry.

> Edith Wharton, *The Gods Arrive* (1932)

See also Simplicity, Slippery Slope, Things.

## &sect; SMALL TOWNS

5 This is a dream as old as America itself: give me a piece of land to call my own, a little town where everyone knows my name.

> Faith Popcorn, *The Popcorn Report* (1991)

6 Nobody knows *anything* about America who does not know its little towns.

> Dorothy Thompson, *The Courage to Be Happy* (1957)

7 In little towns, lives roll along so close to one another; loves and hates beat about, their wings almost touching.

> Willa Cather, *Lucy Gayheart* (1935)

8 Any deviation from the ordinary course of life in this quiet town was enough to stop all progress in it.

> Mary E. Wilkins Freeman, "The Revolt of 'Mother'," *A New England Nun* (1891)

9 In this town, you have to putter over a thing, even the slightest, a month. The powers that evolved the cabbage apple-pie in the morning, and executed it in the evening, are here unknown quantities.

> Susan Hale (1868), in Caroline P. Atkinson, ed., *Letters of Susan Hale* (1918)

10 It's a mystery to me how anyone ever gets any nourishment in this place. They must eat their meals standing up by the window so as to be sure of not missing anything.

> Agatha Christie, *Murder at the Vicarage* (1930)

11 What is its [the town's] chief business? . . . What business would the people here have but to be minding one another's business?

> Lady Gregory, "Spreading the News," *Seven Short Plays* (1909)

12 Where else on earth . . . could people know as little and yet know it so fluently?

> Ellen Glasgow, *The Romantic Comedians* (1926)

13 The small town smart set is deadly serious about its smartness.

> Edna Ferber, *Buttered Side Down* (1912)

14 There is a strange depression that hangs over every little town that is no longer in the mainstream of life.

> Margaret Craven, *Walk Gently This Good Earth* (1977)

See also Cities, Gossip, Nosiness.

## &sect; SMALL WORLD

15 There really are only five hundred people in the whole world. You just keep running into them over and over.

> Beverly Hastings, *Don't Look Back* (1991)

## &sect; SMELL

16 Smell is a potent wizard that transports us across thousands of miles and all the years we have lived.

> Helen Keller, in Diane Ackerman, *A Natural History of the Senses* (1990)

17 The sense of smell has the strongest memory of all the senses.

> Jane Seymour, *Guide to Romantic Living* (1986)

18 For the sense of smell, almost more than any other, has the power to recall memories and it is a pity that we use it so little.

> Rachel Carson, *The Sense of Wonder* (1965)

1 Smell remembers and tells the future. . . . Smell is home or loneliness. Confidence or betrayal.

> Cherríe Moraga, "La Ofrenda," *The Last Generation* (1993)

2 Smell is the closest thing human beings have to a time machine.

> Caryl Rivers, "Growing Up Catholic in Midcentury America," in *The New York Times Magazine* (1971)

3 Smell is the mute sense, the one without words.

> Diane Ackerman, *A Natural History of the Senses* (1990)

4 He smelled like something that spent the winter in a cave.

> Sue Grafton, *"B" Is for Burglar* (1985)

5 The man either burned incense, used cologne, or else a musk deer had been loose in the small office.

> Holly Roth, *Too Many Doctors* (1962)

6 The smell of lilacs crept poignantly into the room like a remembered spring.

> Margaret Millar, *Vanish in an Instant* (1952)

7 Fragrance is the voice of inanimate things.

> Mary Webb, *The Spring of Joy* (1917)

See also Senses.

## ❧ SMILE

8 Smiles are the soul's kisses.

> Minna Thomas Antrim, *Naked Truth and Veiled Illusions* (1901)

9 Let us always meet each other with a smile, for the smile is the beginning of love.

> Mother Teresa, in Barbara Shiels, *Women and the Nobel Prize* (1985)

10 Good-fellowship, unflagging, is the prime requisite for success in our society, and the man or woman who smiles only for reasons of humor or pleasure is a deviate.

> Marya Mannes, *More in Anger* (1958)

11 People who keep stiff upper lips find that it's damn hard to smile.

> Judith Guest, *Ordinary People* (1976)

12 It was a cold ray of a smile, that made you think of pale-flanked little fish swimming snugly under ice.

> Fannie Hurst, *Lummox* (1923)

13 All his life Toselli's smile had been stretched across his rage, like a tight-rope spanning a chasm.

> Josephine Tey, *A Shilling for Candles* (1936)

14 Harry smiled rather loudly.

> Ada Leverson, *The Limit* (1911)

15 She smiled quickly, brightly, all manners and no meaning.

> Dorothy M. Johnson, *Beulah Bunny Tells All* (1942)

16 She set an attentive smile on her face, like a sentinel, behind which she could cultivate her own thoughts.

> Doris Lessing, *The Summer Before the Dark* (1973)

17 He stands, smiling encouragement, like a clumsy dentist.

> Katherine Mansfield, "Bank Holiday," *The Garden Party* (1922)

18 She had long since forgotten the meaning of a smile, but the physical ability to make the gesture remained.

> Beryl Markham, *West With the Night* (1942)

19 She wore a fixed smile that wa'n't a smile; there wa'n't no light behind it, same's a lamp can't shine if it ain't lit.

> Willa Cather, "The Foreigner," in *The Atlantic Monthly* (1900)

20 Her smile reminded me of the way a child will open its mouth all right, but not let out the cry till it sees the right person.

> Eudora Welty, "The Whole World Knows," *The Golden Apples* (1949)

21 When she smiled the smile was only in the mouth and a little bitter: the face of an incurable yet to be stricken with its malady.

> Djuna Barnes, *Nightwood* (1937)

22 She had one of those frequent, but not spontaneous smiles that did for her face what artificial flowers do for some rooms. Smiles, somehow, were more *used* in those days; they were instruments, weapons, what not.

> Bertha Damon, *Grandma Called It Carnal* (1938)

23 That grin! She could have taken it off her face and put it on the table.

> Jean Stafford, title story, *Bad Characters* (1954)

24 Sometimes I not only stand there and take it, I even smile at them and say I'm sorry. When I feel that

smile coming onto my face, I wish I could take my face off and stamp on it.

Ursula K. Le Guin, *Very Far Away From Anywhere Else* (1976)

See also Face, Laughter.

## ❧ SMOKING

1 The same people who tell us that smoking doesn't cause cancer are now telling us that advertising cigarettes doesn't cause smoking.

Ellen Goodman, in *The Boston Globe* (1986)

2 *Nobody* should smoke cigarettes—and smoking with an ulcer is like pouring gasoline on a burning house.

Sara Murray Jordan, in Eleanor Harris, "First Lady of the Lahey Clinic," *Reader's Digest* (1958)

3 What a shame for a man to dress like a saint and smell like a devil!

Carry Nation, to a priest who smoked, *The Use and Need of the Life of Carry A. Nation* (1905)

4 *I* gave up smoking four years, two weeks, and five days ago. But who misses it?

Sandra Scoppettone, *Everything You Have Is Mine* (1991)

5 Now we've got smokism. It's one of the reasons I became a writer: to be able to smoke in peace.

Susanna Kaysen, *Girl, Interrupted* (1993)

See also Tobacco.

## ❧ SNAKES

6 Python carries his loneliness in him as if he had eaten clay.

Barbara Chase-Riboud, *Echo of Lions* (1989)

7 Have you ever studied a snake's face?—how optimistic they look. They have an eternal smile.

Tasha Tudor, with Richard Brown, *The Private World of Tasha Tudor* (1992)

## ❧ SNEERS

8 A sneer is like a flame; it may occasionally be curative because it cauterizes, but it leaves a bitter scar.

Margaret Deland, *The Awakening of Helena Richie* (1906)

See also Ridicule, Sarcasm.

## ❧ SNOBBERY

9 Curious, isn't it, that "talking with the right people" means something so very different from "talking with the right person"?

Margaret Barnes, *Years of Grace* (1930)

## ❧ SNORING

10 Father's snoring grows to sound increasingly like a vacuum cleaner in heat.

Margaret Halsey, *Some of My Best Friends Are Soldiers* (1944)

11 On his side of the bed Mr. Judson began to conduct a full-scale orchestra, and every instrument had sat out in the rain.

Dorothy West, *The Living Is Easy* (1948)

12 Laugh and the world laughs with you, snore and you sleep alone.

Mrs. Patrick Campbell, letter to George Bernard Shaw (1912), in Alan Dent, ed., *Bernard Shaw and Mrs. Patrick Campbell* (1952)

## ❧ SNOW

13 It is shovel, shovel, shovel snow, / Shovel everywhere you go, / Shovel high and shovel low, / Shovel, shovel, shovel snow.

Mary Dodge Woodward (1887), *The Checkered Years* (1937)

14 O transient voyager of heaven! / O silent sign of winter skies!

Emily Brontë (1837), in Clement Shorter, ed., *The Complete Poems of Emily Brontë* (1910)

15 There is salvation in snow.

Elizabeth Weber, "Winter," in *Iowa Woman* (1992)

1 The ground has on its clothes. / The trees poke out of sheets / and each branch wears the sock of God.

    Anne Sexton, "Snow," *The Awful Rowing Toward God* (1975)

2 In shaping the snow into blossoms— / The north wind is tender after all.

    Ping Hsin, "The Spring Waters" (c. 1920), in Joanna Bankier and Deirdre Lashgari, eds., *Women Poets of the World* (1983)

3 The large white snow-flakes as they flutter down, softly, one by one, whisper soothingly, "Rest, poor heart, rest!" It is as though our mother smoothed our hair, and we are comforted.

    Ralph Iron, *The Story of an African Farm* (1883)

4 Keep vigil my heart, the snow sets us on saddled racers of white foam.

    Anne Hébert, "Snow," *Poems* (1960)

5 You believe it's cold, but if you build yourself a snowhouse it's warm. You think it's white, but at times it looks pink, and another time it's blue. It can be softer than anything, and then again harder than stone. Nothing is certain.

    Tove Jansson, *Moominland Midwinter* (1958)

6 I am younger each year at the first snow. When I see it, suddenly, in the air, all little and white and moving; then I am in love again and very young and I believe everything.

    Anne Sexton (1958), in Linda Gray Sexton and Lois Ames, eds., *Anne Sexton: A Self-Portrait in Letters* (1977)

See also Weather, Winter.

## ❧ SOBRIETY

7 I was rather drunk with what I had done. And I am always one to prefer being sober. I must be sober. It is so much more exciting to be sober, to be exact and concentrated and sober.

    Gertrude Stein, in John Malcolm Brinnin, *The Third Rose* (1959)

See also Addiction, Alcohol, Alcoholism.

## ❧ SOCIAL CHANGE

8 Nearly all great civilizations that perished did so because they had crystallized, because they were incapable of adapting themselves to new conditions, new methods, new points of view. It is as though people would literally rather die than change.

    Eleanor Roosevelt, *Tomorrow Is Now* (1963)

9 Individual advances turn into social change *when enough of them occur.*

    Elizabeth Janeway, *Powers of the Weak* (1980)

10 Whenever you take a step forward you are bound to disturb something. You disturb the air as you go forward, you disturb the dust, the ground. You trample upon things. When a whole society moves forward this tramping is on a much bigger scale and each thing that you disturb, each vested interest which you want to remove, stands as an obstacle.

    Indira Gandhi (1967), *Speeches and Writings* (1975)

11 Leaders are indispensable, but to produce a major social change many ordinary people must also be involved.

    Anne Firor Scott, "The 'New Woman' in the New South," in *South Atlantic Quarterly* (1962)

12 Most people are not for or against anything; the first object of getting people together is to make them respond somehow, to overcome inertia.

    M.P. Follett, *The New State* (1918)

13 All reformations seem formidable before they are attempted.

    Hannah More, "Thoughts on the Importance of the Manners of the Great, to General Society," *The Works of Hannah More*, vol. 1 (1841)

14 When a social order is in revolution half the world is necessarily part of the new day and half of the old.

    Florence Guy Seabury, "The Sheltered Sex," *The Delicatessen Husband* (1926)

15 Thinking about profound social change, conservatives always expect disaster, while revolutionaries confidently anticipate utopia. Both are wrong.

    Carolyn Heilbrun, *Toward a Recognition of Androgyny* (1973)

16 Those interested in perpetuating present conditions are always in tears about the marvelous past that is about to disappear, without having so much as a smile for the young future.

    Simone de Beauvoir, *The Second Sex* (1949)

1 Characteristically, major social movements are spawned in obscurity at the periphery of public awareness, seem to burst suddenly and dramatically into public view, and eventually fade into the landscape not because they have diminished but because they have become a permanent part of our perceptions and experience.

　　Freda Adler, *Sisters in Crime* (1975)

2 Cultural transformation announces itself in sputtering fits and starts, sparked here and there by minor incidents, warmed by new ideas that may smolder for decades. In many different places, at different times, the kindling is laid for the real conflagration—the one that will consume the old landmarks and alter the landscape forever.

　　Marilyn Ferguson, *The Aquarian Conspiracy* (1980)

3 It is an escape for persons to cry, when this question of the equality of peoples is raised in India or in our own South, "Ah, but the situation is not so simple." . . . No great stride forward is ever made for the individual or for the human race unless the complex situation is reduced to one simple question and its simple answer.

　　Pearl S. Buck, *What America Means to Me* (1943)

4 It is a fact of history that those who seek to withdraw from its [society's] great experiments usually end by being overwhelmed by them.

　　Barbara Ward, in Richard Thruelsen and John Kobler, eds., *Adventures of the Mind*, 2nd series (1961)

5 The keys to any social reform lie in the acceptance of the need for correction and the commitment to finding ways to make that correction.

　　Bobbye D. Sorrels, *The Nonsexist Communicator* (1983)

6 Myth, legend, and ritual . . . function to maintain a status quo. That makes them singularly bad in coping with change, indeed counterproductive, for change is the enemy of myth.

　　Elizabeth Janeway, *Powers of the Weak* (1980)

7 The process of empowerment cannot be simplistically defined in accordance with our own particular class interests. We must learn to lift as we climb.

　　Angela Y. Davis, *Women, Culture & Politics* (1989)

8 If you are trying to transform a brutalized society into one where people can live in dignity and hope, you begin with the empowering of the most powerless. You build from the ground up.

　　Adrienne Rich, "'Going There' and Being Here," *Blood, Bread, and Poetry* (1986)

9 It is our duty to create a social milieu in which the young and the socially weak feel that the present and future belong to them.

　　Indira Gandhi, *Freedom Is the Starting Point* (1976)

10 When we think of what it is that politicizes people, it is not so much books or ideas, but experience.

　　Irene Peslikis, in *The Wisdom of Women* (1971)

11 Although the connections are not always obvious, personal change is inseparable from social and political change.

　　Harriet Lerner, *Dance of Intimacy* (1989)

12 Use what is dominant in a culture to change it quickly.

　　Jenny Holzer, *Truisms* (1979)

13 The history of human growth is at the same time the history of every new idea heralding the approach of a brighter dawn, and the brighter dawn has always been considered illegal, outside of the law.

　　Emma Goldman, "Address to the Jury" (1917), in Alix Kates Shulman, ed., *Red Emma Speaks* (1983)

14 It is important to recognize the limited ability of the legal system to prescribe and enforce the quality of social arrangements.

　　Hillary Rodham Clinton (1973), in Judith Warner, *Hillary Clinton* (1993)

15 The master's tools will never dismantle the master's house.

　　Audre Lorde, essay title (1979), *Sister Outsider* (1984)

See also Activism, Change, Leadership, Movements, Reform, Revolution.

## ❦ SOCIAL CLIMBING

16 Everything that goes up must come down.

　　Maxine Cheshire, in *Life* (1969)

## ❦ SOCIAL SECURITY

17 They should stop calling it "Social Security." It's as secure as a cardboard raft.

　　Katharine Whitehorn, in *The Observer* (1973)

## ❧ SOCIAL SKILLS

1 She was barely civil to them, and evidently better pleased to say "goodbye," than "how do you do."
     Anne Brontë, *The Tenant of Wildfell Hall* (1848)

2 My father was never very friendly. When I was growing up, I thought the doorbell ringing was a signal to pretend you weren't home.
     Rita Rudner, *Naked Beneath My Clothes* (1992)

3 Father G. was often obliged to enter houses where people were on the point of death or had already died; indeed he preferred this type of situation to normal parish visiting, with its awkward conversation and the inevitable cups of tea and sweet biscuits.
     Barbara Pym, *Quartet in Autumn* (1977)

4 After careful observation, Gilbert concluded that it is more effective socially to be tall and barely civil than short and eagerly sociable. This did not affect his height, but it taught him when to shut up.
     Judith Martin, *Gilbert* (1982)

5 It has lately been drawn to your correspondent's attention that, at social gatherings, she is not the human magnet she would be. Indeed, it turns out that as a source of entertainment, conviviality, and good fun, she ranks somewhere between a sprig of parsley and a single ice-skate.
     Dorothy Parker, "Wallflower's Lament" (1928), *The Portable Dorothy Parker*, rev. ed. (1973)

See also Extroverts and Introverts, Parties.

## ❧ SOCIETY

6 Snowflakes, leaves, humans, plants, raindrops, stars, molecules, microscopic entities all come in communities. The singular cannot in reality exist.
     Paula Gunn Allen, *Grandmothers of the Light* (1991)

7 Man is not made for society, but society is made for man. No institution can be good which does not tend to improve the individual.
     Margaret Fuller, *Memoirs* (1840)

8 Society in its full sense . . . is never an entity separable from the individuals who compose it. No individual can arrive even at the threshold of his potentialities without a culture in which he participates. Conversely, no civilization has in it any element which in the last analysis is not the contribution of an individual.
     Ruth Benedict, *Patterns of Culture* (1934)

9 Society, that first of blessings, brings with it evils death only can cure.
     Sophia Lee, *The Recess* (1785)

10 A well ordered society would be one where the State only had a negative action, comparable to that of a rudder: a light pressure at the right moment to counteract the first suggestion of any loss of equilibrium.
     Simone Weil, *Gravity and Grace* (1947)

11 We want a society where people are free to make choices, to make mistakes, to be generous and compassionate. This is what we mean by a moral society; not a society where the state is responsible for everything, and no one is responsible for the state.
     Margaret Thatcher, speech (1977)

12 We live in a true chaos of contradicting authorities, an age of conformism without community, of proximity without communication.
     Germaine Greer, *The Female Eunuch* (1971)

13 Because our civilization is woven of so many diverse strands, the ideas which any one group accepts will be found to contain numerous contradictions.
     Margaret Mead, *Coming of Age in Samoa* (1928)

14 A sick society, unlike a sick individual, fares best under the ministration of many doctors.
     Georgia Harkness, *The Resources of Religion* (1936)

15 Sometimes . . . the world is so much sicker than the inmates of its institutions.
     Hannah Green, *I Never Promised You a Rose Garden* (1964)

16 The trilogy composed of politics, religion and sex is the most sensitive of all issues in any society.
     Nawal El Saadawi, *The Hidden Face of Eve* (1980)

17 The person and society are yoked, like mind and body. Arguing which is more important is like debating whether oxygen or hydrogen is the more essential property of water.
     Marilyn Ferguson, *The Aquarian Conspiracy* (1980)

1 The public and the private worlds are inseparably connected . . . the tyrannies and servilities of the one are the tyrannies and servilities of the other.

Virginia Woolf, *Three Guineas* (1938)

2 The peace and stability of a nation depend upon the proper relationships established in the home.

Jade Snow Wong, *Fifth Chinese Daughter* (1950)

3 Cannibalism and human sacrifice are uncivilized. Yet our Western materialistic culture condones social cannibalism as a necessary sacrifice to society's collective appetite which, spurred by ambition and fear, demands that we devour whatever is proffered, even human dignity, in the sacred name of "the standard of living" or the so-called "national good."

Judith Groch, *The Right to Create* (1969)

4 We have become morally confused as a people, and possess neither the human sympathy nor the corporate will to put our inner convictions into practice. We are split personalities.

Agnes E. Meyer, *Journey Through Chaos* (1944)

5 I'm not interested in pursuing a society that uses analysis, research, and experimentation to concretize their vision of cruel destinies for those who are not bastards of the Pilgrims; a society with arrogance rising, moon in oppression, and sun in destruction.

Barbara Cameron, in Cherríe Moraga and Gloria Anzaldúa, eds., *This Bridge Called My Back* (1983)

6 Societies who do not care for their young people and old people are decadent, decaying societies.

Suzan Shown Harjo, in *Rethinking Schools* (1991)

7 There are people who eat the earth and eat all the people on it like in the Bible with the locusts. And other people who stand around and watch them eat it.

Lillian Hellman, *The Little Foxes* (1939)

8 Miss Manners refuses to allow society to seek its own level. Having peered through her lorgnette into the abyss, she can guess how low that level will be.

Judith Martin, *Miss Manners' Guide for the Turn-of-the-Millennium* (1989)

See also Civilization, Community, Culture, Human Family.

## ✿ SOFTBALL

9 Anyone who says that softball is a boring game to watch isn't looking at the right things.

Yvonne Zipter, *Diamonds Are a Dyke's Best Friend* (1988)

10 When I was fifteen I believed that sex was nearly the same thing as softball.

Lucy Jane Bledsoe, "State of Grace," in Naomi Holoch and Joan Nestle, eds., *Women on Women 2* (1993)

See also Athletes, Baseball, Sports.

## ✿ SOLITUDE

11 Alone, alone, oh! We have been warned about solitary vices. Have solitary pleasures ever been adequately praised? Do many people know that they exist?

Jessamyn West, *Hide and Seek* (1973)

12 Being solitary is being alone well: being alone luxuriously immersed in doings of your own choice, aware of the fullness of your own presence rather than of the absence of others.

Alice Koller, *The Stations of Solitude* (1990)

13 The true solitary . . . will feel that he is himself only when he is alone; when he is in company he will feel that he perjures himself, prostitutes himself to the exactions of others; he will feel that time spent in company is time lost; he will be conscious only of his impatience to get back to his true life.

Vita Sackville-West, *Passenger to Teheran* (1926)

14 Solitude is my element, and the reason is that extreme awareness of other people (all naturally solitary people must feel this) precludes awareness of one's self, so after a while the self no longer knows that it exists.

May Sarton, *At Seventy* (1984)

15 If any individual live too much in relations, so that he becomes a stranger to the resources of his own nature, he falls, after a while, into a distraction, or imbecility, from which he can only be cured by a time of isolation, which gives the renovating fountains time to rise up.

Margaret Fuller, *Woman in the Nineteenth Century* (1845)

1 Not to be alone—ever—is one of my ideas of hell, and a day when I have had no solitude at all in which "to catch up with myself" I find mentally, physically and spiritually exhausting.

Miss Read, *Village Diary* (1957)

2 She would not exchange her solitude for anything. *Never again to be forced to move to the rhythms of others.*

Tillie Olsen, title story, *Tell Me a Riddle* (1956)

3 The prohibition against solitude is forever. A Carry Nation rises in every person when he thinks he sees someone sneaking off to be alone. It is not easy to be solitary unless you are also born ruthless. Every solitary repudiates someone.

Jessamyn West, *Hide and Seek* (1973)

4 What others regard as retreat from them or rejection of them is not those things at all but instead a breeding ground for greater friendship, a culture for deeper involvement, eventually, with them.

Doris Grumbach, *Fifty Days of Solitude* (1994)

5 Do not allow yourself to be imprisoned by any affection. Keep your solitude. The day, if it ever comes, when you are given true affection there will be no opposition between interior solitude and friendship, quite the reverse. It is even by this infallible sign that you will recognize it.

Simone Weil, *Gravity and Grace* (1947)

6 What a commentary on our civilization, when being alone is considered suspect; when one has to apologize for it, make excuses, hide the fact that one practices it—like a secret vice!

Anne Morrow Lindbergh, *Gift From the Sea* (1955)

7 I understand hermits, but not people who can't understand hermits.

Jessamyn West, *To See the Dream* (1957)

8 Solitude is un-American.

Erica Jong, *Fear of Flying* (1973)

9 For every five well-adjusted and smoothly functioning Americans, there are two who never had the chance to discover themselves. It may well be because they have never been alone with themselves. The great omission in American life is solitude.

Marya Mannes, "To Save the Life of 'I'," in *Vogue* (1964)

10 I believe in solitude broken like bread by poetry.

Anne Hébert, "Poetry Broken Solitude," *Poems* (1960)

11 Solitude swells the inner space / Like a balloon. / We are wafted hither and thither / On the air currents. / How to land it?

May Sarton, "Gestalt at Sixty," *Selected Poems of May Sarton* (1978)

12 Was Thoreau never lonely? Certainly. Where do you think writing like his comes from? Camaraderie?

Jessamyn West, *Hide and Seek* (1973)

13 I am an incorrigible devotee to solitude, and am never so cheerful, I believe, or so unruffled by small difficulties as when I'm alone. There's a sort of obligation to be polite and pleasant to yourself when nobody else is round.

Susan Hale (1907), in Caroline P. Atkinson, ed., *Letters of Susan Hale* (1918)

14 I love to walk in lonely solitude & leave the bustel of the nosey town behind me & while I look on nothing but what strikes the eye with sights of bliss & then I think myself transported far beyond the reach of the wicked sons of men where their is nothing but strife & envying pilefring & murder where neither contentment nor retirement dweels but there dwels drunkenness.

Marjorie Fleming, age 7 (1810), in Frank Sidgwick, *The Complete Marjory Fleming* (1934)

15 The best would be to have friends who came and went away; but if I had to choose between their never coming or never going away, I think I would choose that they do not come.

Rumer Godden, *Thus Far and No Further* (1946)

16 Solitude / Is not all exaltation, inner space / Where the soul breathes and work can be done. / Solitude exposes the nerve, / Raises up ghosts. / The past, never at rest, flows through it.

May Sarton, "Gestalt at Sixty," *Selected Poems of May Sarton* (1978)

17 There are days when solitude, for someone my age, is a heady wine that intoxicates you with freedom, others when it is a bitter tonic, and still others when it is a poison that makes you beat your head against the wall.

Colette, *Les Vrilles de la vigne* (1908)

18 No doubt about it, solitude is improved by being voluntary.

Barbara Holland, *One's Company* (1992)

1 To a heart formed for friendship and affection the charms of solitude are very short-lived.

  Fanny Burney, *Cecilia* (1782)

2 There is nothing like the bootless solitude of those who are caged together.

  Iris Murdoch, *The Black Prince* (1973)

3 She was not accustomed to taste the joys of solitude except in company.

  Edith Wharton, *The House of Mirth* (1905)

See also Alone, Loneliness, Privacy, Self-Sufficiency, Silence.


## ❧ "SOMEBODY"

4 I always wanted to be somebody.

  Althea Gibson, book title (1958)

5 All my life I've always wanted to *be* somebody. But I see now I should have been more specific.

  Jane Wagner, *The Search for Signs of Intelligent Life in the Universe* (1985)

6 How dreary — to be — Somebody! / How public — like a Frog — / To tell one's name — the live-long June — / To an admiring Bog!

  Emily Dickinson (1861), *Poems by Emily Dickinson*, 2nd series (1891)

7 I think that in your language, who isn't somebody, is nobody.

  Susan Warner, *"What She Could"* (1871)

8 If, as the girls always said, it's never too early to think about whom to marry, then it could certainly not be too early to think about who to be. Being somebody had to come first, because, of course, somebody could get a much better husband than nobody.

  Alix Kates Shulman, *Memoirs of an Ex-Prom Queen* (1972)

See also Celebrity, Fame.


## ❧ SONG

9 There are three things I was born with in this world, and there are three things I will have until the day I die: hope, determination, and song.

  Miriam Makeba, with James Hall, *Makeba* (1987)

10 I sat on a broad stone / And sang to the birds. / The tune was God's making / But I made the words.

  Mary Carolyn Davies, "The Day Before April," *Youth Riding* (1919)

11 It is my heart that makes my songs, not I.

  Sara Teasdale, "What Do I Care?" *Flame and Shadow* (1920)

12 A song to me is a very tangible thing. I can feel it with my hands and see it with my eyes.

  Roberta Flack, in *Newsweek* (1971)

13 I hang my laundry on the line when I write.

  Joni Mitchell, in Kathleen Kimball, Robin Petersen, and Kathleen Johnson, eds., *The Music Lover's Quotation Book* (1990)

14 Where are those songs / my mother and yours / always sang / fitting rhythms / to the whole / vast span of life?

  Micere Githae Mugo, "Where Are Those Songs?" *Daughter of My People, Sing* (1976)

15 Whenever new ideas emerge, songs soon follow, and before long the songs are leading.

  Holly Near, with Derk Richardson, *Fire in the Rain . . . Singer in the Storm* (1990)

16 Oh, I used to sing a song. / An' dey said it was too long, / So I cut off de en' / To accommodate a frien' / Nex' do', nex' do'— / . . . / Oh, it didn't have no en' any mo'!

  Ruth McEnery Stuart, "The Endless Song," in William Harmon, ed., *The Oxford Book of American Light Verse* (1979)

See also Music, Singing.


## ❧ SONS

17 This is the womb that carried him, / like a stone cave / lived in by a tiger and now abandoned. / It is on the battlefield that you will find him.

  Auvaiyar (3rd cent.), in Joanna Bankier and Deirdre Lashgari, eds., *Women Poets of the World* (1983)

18 The tie is stronger than that between father and son and father and daughter. . . . The bond is also more complex than the one between mother and daughter. For a woman, a son offers the best chance to know the mysterious male existence.

  Carole Klein, in *Time* (1984)

1 I am persuaded that there is no affection of the human heart more exquisitely pure, than that which is felt by a grateful son towards a mother.

    Hannah More, *Coelebs in Search of a Wife* (1808)

See also Family.

# ❧ SORROW

2 Every sorrow suggests a thousand songs, and every song recalls a thousand sorrows, and so they are infinite in number, and all the same.

    Marilynne Robinson, *Housekeeping* (1980)

3 All things are dark to sorrow.

    Augusta J. Evans, *Inez* (1855)

4 Sorrow was like the wind. It came in gusts.

    Marjorie Kinnan Rawlings, *South Moon Under* (1933)

5 A day of bliss is quickly told, / A thousand would not make us old / As one of sorrow doth— / It is by cares, by woes and tears, / We round the sum of human years—.

    Mrs. Sarah J. Hale, *Sketches of American Character* (1829)

6 To speak of sorrow / works upon it / moves it from its / crouched place barring / the way to and from the soul's hall.

    Denise Levertov, "To Speak," *The Sorrow Dance* (1967)

7 Sorrow fully accepted brings its own gifts. For there is an alchemy in sorrow. It can be transmuted into wisdom, which, if it does not bring joy, can yet bring happiness.

    Pearl S. Buck, *The Child Who Never Grew* (1950)

8 Sorrow has its reward. It never leaves us where it found us.

    Mary Baker Eddy, *Science and Health* (1875)

9 Give your sorrow all the space and shelter in yourself that is its due, for if everyone bears his grief honestly and courageously, the sorrow that now fills the world will abate. But if you do not clear a decent shelter for your sorrow, and instead reserve most of the space inside you for hatred and thoughts of revenge—from which new sorrows will be born for others—then sorrow will never cease in this world and will multiply.

    Etty Hillesum (1942), *An Interrupted Life* (1983)

10 The sorrows of humanity are no one's sorrows. . . . A thousand people drowned in floods in China are news: a solitary child drowned in a pond is tragedy.

    Josephine Tey, *The Daughter of Time* (1951)

11 The pity of living only once is that there is no way, ever, to be sure which sorrows are inevitable.

    Rosellen Brown, *Civil Wars* (1984)

12 It is better to learn early of the inevitable depths, for then sorrow and death take their proper place in life, and one is not afraid.

    Pearl S. Buck, *My Several Worlds* (1954)

13 Sorrow makes us very good or very bad.

    George Sand (1871), in *French Wit and Wisdom* (1950)

14 Grief can sometimes only be expressed in platitudes. We are original in our happy moments. Sorrow has only one voice, one cry.

    Ruth Rendell, *Shake Hands Forever* (1975)

15 She fingered the edge of his mother's sorrow like a tailor feeling the quality of a rival's well-made suit. Was it anything like the pain she had felt. . . ?

    Susan Moody, *Mosaic* (1991)

16 It was the last night before sorrow touched her life; and no life is ever quite the same again when once that cold, sanctifying touch has been laid upon it.

    L.M. Montgomery, *Anne of Green Gables* (1908)

17 Of this be sure, my dearest, whatever thy life befall, / The cross that our own hands fashion is the heaviest cross of all.

    Katherine Eleanor Conway, "The Heaviest Cross of All," in Edmund Clarence Stedman, ed., *An American Anthology 1787-1900* (1900)

18 Many people misjudge the permanent effect of sorrow, and their capacity to live in the past.

    Ivy Compton-Burnett, *Mother and Son* (1955)

19 The human heart does not stay away too long from that which hurt it most. There is a return journey to anguish that few of us are released from making.

    Lillian Smith, *The Journey* (1954)

20 A man's sorrow runs uphill; true it is difficult for him to bear, but it is also difficult for him to keep.

    Djuna Barnes, *Nightwood* (1937)

21 Sorrow is tranquility remembered in emotion.

    Dorothy Parker, "Sentiment," *The Collected Stories of Dorothy Parker* (1942)

1  A lean sorrow is hardest to bear.
> Sarah Orne Jewett, "All My Sad Captains," *The Life of Nancy* (1895)

See also Crying, Despair, Grief, Joy and Sorrow, Misery, Misfortune, Mourning, Pain, Suffering, Tears, Trouble, Unhappiness.

## ❧ SOUL

2  The soul, like the moon, / is new, and always new again.
> Lalleswari (14th cent.), in Coleman Barks, *Lalla* (1992)

3  It is not that we *have* a soul, we *are* a soul.
> Amelia E. Barr, *All the Days of My Life* (1913)

4  I began to think of the soul as if it were a castle made of a single diamond or of very clear crystal, in which there are many rooms, just as in Heaven there are many mansions.
> St. Teresa of Avila (1577), in E. Allison Peers, tr., *Interior Castle* (1961)

5  The Soul should always stand ajar.
> Emily Dickinson (1865), in Mabel Loomis Todd, ed., *Poems by Emily Dickinson*, 3rd series (1896)

6  See there within the flesh / Like a bright wick, englazed / The soul God's finger lit / To give her liberty, / And joy and power and love.
> Mechthild von Magdeburg, "Love Flows From God" (c. 1250), in Joanna Bankier and Deirdre Lashgari, eds., *Women Poets of the World* (1983)

7  For what is man's soul but a flame? It flickers in and around the body of a man as does the flame around the rough log.
> Selma Lagerlöf, *The General's Ring* (1928)

8  Mystical experiences nearly always lead one to a belief that some aspect of consciousness is imperishable. In a Buddhist metaphor the consciousness of the individual is like a flame that burns through the night. It is not the same flame over time, yet neither is it another flame.
> Marilyn Ferguson, *The Aquarian Conspiracy* (1980)

9  The soul . . . may have many symbols with which it reaches toward God.
> Anya Seton, *The Turquoise* (1946)

10  The strongest, surest way to the soul is through the flesh.
> Mabel Dodge Luhan, *Lorenzo in Taos* (1932)

11  A Soul is partly given, partly wrought.
> Erica Jong, *Fanny: Being the True History of the Adventures of Fanny Hackabout-Jones* (1980)

12  Imperial Self beyond self that I call my soul, / Climb up into the crow's-nest: / Look out over the changing ocean of my life / And shout down to me whither to change my course.
> Sarah N. Cleghorn, "The Lookout," *Portraits and Protests* (1917)

13  There is no plummet to sound another's soul.
> Virgilia Peterson, *A Matter of Life and Death* (1961)

14  She hasn't called her soul her own for so long that I guess the good Lord won't hold her responsible for it.
> Mary Roberts Rinehart, *The Window at the White Cat* (1910)

See also Inner Life, Self, Spirituality.

## ❧ SOUNDS

15  I / fall into noisy abstraction, / cling to sound as if it were the last protection / against what I cannot name.
> Paula Gunn Allen, "Shadows," *The Blind Lion* (1974)

16  "Sound" is a catch-all word which describes "all that we hear," in one lump, from music to noise. . . . We consider the kingdom of our eyes far more complex, and would not dream of trying to sum it up in a word which would mean "all that we see."
> Anita T. Sullivan, *The Seventh Dragon* (1985)

17  She had an acute ear, and tiny sounds, the shiver of grass on grass in light airs, the squeaking of bats, cries of birds in a distant field, creaking of dried roots, the trickle of rain down the walls of a house, were caught by it, and offered to memory.
> Storm Jameson, *That Was Yesterday* (1932)

18  There is something strangely determinate and fatal about a single shot in the night. It is as if someone had cried a message to you in one word, and would not repeat it.
> Isak Dinesen, *Out of Africa* (1937)

See also Noise.

## ♦ THE SOUTH

1 Southerners can never resist a losing cause.
   Margaret Mitchell, *Gone With the Wind* (1936)

2 To a Southerner it is faux pas, not sins, that matter in this world.
   Florence King, *Southern Ladies and Gentlemen* (1975)

3 Haven't you lived in the South long enough to know that nothing is ever anybody's fault?
   Lillian Hellman, *The Autumn Garden* (1951)

4 For most Southerners, storytelling is as natural as breathing.
   Alice Storey, *First Kill All the Lawyers* (1988)

5 If the production of self-serving folklore qualified as an industry, the South would have been an industrial power since colonial times.
   Shirley Abbott, *Womenfolks: Growing Up Down South* (1983)

6 Southerners have been known to stay over the Fourth and not get home before Thanksgiving. Some oldtimers take in overnight guests and keep them through three generations.
   Mary Ellen Robinson Snodgrass, *Bluff Your Way in the Deep South* (1990)

7 The crowning absurdity was Sara Ellen's tireless efforts on behalf of the committee for promoting the Democratic nominee for president. Which, in the Deep South . . . is like assisting the sun to rise.
   Genevieve Holden, *The Velvet Target* (1956)

8 The South is still the South, so don't think the old ways have gone away completely. Scarlett still clings to tradition, worships her daddy and likes to dress up and flirt. Only now she's in group therapy to help her understand why.
   Marlyn Schwartz, *New Times in the Old South* (1993)

9 To grow up female in the South is to inherit a set of directives that warp one for life, if they do not actually induce psychosis.
   Shirley Abbott, *Womenfolks: Growing Up Down South* (1983)

10 She had once been a Southern belle and she had never got over it. But that disease is a curiously inverted one. It sickens almost to death any number of persons about her, but it remains robust and incurable in the woman who possesses it.
   Pearl S. Buck, *Fighting Angel* (1936)

11 It's easy for young people to get all caught up in the New South, but for traditional Southern ladies like Miss Maybelle, it's quite a different matter. . . . She thinks ladies should be, first and foremost, ladies, and that the issue of women's rights should be approached with ladylike manners and respect. Miss Maybelle thinks it's time to kick a little *fanny*.
   Marlyn Schwartz, *New Times in the Old South* (1993)

12 In Georgia no lady was supposed to know she was a virgin until she had ceased to be one.
   Frances Newman, *The Hard-Boiled Virgin* (1926)

13 In the South, Sunday morning sex is accompanied by church bells.
   Florence King, *Confessions of a Failed Southern Lady* (1985)

14 The South may be the last place where dying is still sometimes a community project.
   Shirley Abbott, *Womenfolks: Growing Up Down South* (1983)

15 Being Southerners, it was a source of shame to some members of the family that we had no recorded ancestors on either side of the Battle of Hastings.
   Harper Lee, *To Kill a Mockingbird* (1960)

16 Anybody who grows up in the South may have to reckon, some time or another, with being born again.
   Shirley Abbott, *Womenfolks: Growing Up Down South* (1983)

17 This curious sense of separateness is one of the most stubbornly preserved Southern attitudes. The South, its historians say, stands apart from other American regions because of its peculiar history. History has been cruel to Southerners, has persistently dealt them deuces.
   Shirley Abbott, *Womenfolks: Growing Up Down South* (1983)

See also The North.

## ♦ SOUTH AFRICA

18 The immediate present belongs to the extremists, but the future belongs to the moderates.
   Helen Suzman (1964), *In No Uncertain Terms* (1993)

19 Perhaps the one comforting thought . . . was that over the years when the government was tapping my telephone, it must certainly have heard some

home truths from me about themselves, often couched in good Anglo-Saxon terms.

Helen Suzman (1979), *In No Uncertain Terms* (1993)

See also Africa.


## ❧ SPACE

1 We're smart enough to know we need to live in groups to survive, but we're still animals and we needs lots of room. In the case of the male of the species we also probably need that-guy-over-there's space. And his wife and cow, too.

Julia Phillips, *You'll Never Eat Lunch in This Town Again* (1991)

2 He [Robert Benchley] and I had an office so tiny that an inch smaller and it would have been adultery.

Dorothy Parker, in Malcolm Cowley, ed., *Writers at Work* (1958)


## ❧ SPAIN

3 No conscious traveler can pass several weeks in Spain without realizing that . . . in the soul of the Spanish people, subterraneous currents of mysticism flow.

E. Allison Peers, *Spanish Mysticism* (1947)


## ❧ SPECIALIZATION

4 The streams which would otherwise diverge to fertilize a thousand meadows, must be directed into one deep narrow channel before they can turn a mill.

Anna Jameson, "Some Thoughts on Art," in *Art Journal* (1849)

5 The whole of our civilization is founded on specialization, which implies the enslavement of those who execute to those who coordinate.

Simone Weil (1934), *Oppression and Liberty* (1955)

6 There must be bands of enthusiasts for everything on earth—fanatics who shared a vocabulary, a batch of technical skills and equipment, and, perhaps, a vision of some single slice of the beauty and mystery of things, of their complexity, fascination, and unexpectedness.

Annie Dillard, *An American Childhood* (1987)

7 People like to think that nobody else can learn what they have learned. Now, that's just not true, but you can make it true by making it hard for people who don't know how to do a thing to learn how that thing is done.

Janet McCrae, in John Langston Gwaltney, *Drylongso* (1980)

8 Like most Americans, he was a specialist, and had studied only that branch of his art necessary to his own interests.

Gertrude Atherton, *Transplanted* (1919)

9 The trouble with specialists is that they tend to think in grooves.

Elaine Morgan, *The Descent of Woman* (1972)

See also Experts.


## ❧ SPECTATORS

10 On the outskirts of every agony sits some observant fellow who points.

Virginia Woolf, *The Waves* (1931)

11 This is an age of spectators. Only they are hostile spectators.

Peggy Glanville-Hicks (1956), in Anaïs Nin, *The Diary of Anaïs Nin*, vol. 6 (1976)

12 The U.S.A. has become a nation of determined spectators, willing to watch someone else perform.

Sybil Leek, *ESP: The Magic Within You* (1971)

See also Audience, Entertainment.


## ❧ SPEECH

13 Speech was present. Everywhere. Stones could speak. Rivers spoke. Sand had words. The ocean lapped the shore and told its secrets. Speech was in everything.

Ruth Sidransky, *In Silence* (1990)

1 Speech is but broken light upon the depth / Of the unspoken.

George Eliot, *The Spanish Gypsy* (1868)

2 Speech is the mark of humanity. It is the normal terminus of thought.

Susanne K. Langer, *Philosophy in a New Key* (1942)

3 To know how to say what others only know how to think, is what makes men poets or sages; and to dare to say what others only dare to think, makes men martyrs or reformers, or both.

Elizabeth Rundle Charles, *Chronicles of the Schönberg-Cotta Family* (1863)

4 Sometimes speech is no more than a device for saying nothing—and a neater one than silence.

Simone de Beauvoir, *The Prime of Life* (1960)

5 Speech is an old torn net, through which the fish escape as one casts it over them.

Virginia Woolf, "The Evening Party" (1918), in Susan Dick, ed., *The Complete Shorter Fiction of Virginia Woolf* (1985)

6 Most of us do not use speech to express thought. We use it to express feelings.

Jennifer Stone, "The Revisionist Imperative," *Stone's Throw* (1988)

7 You kin tame a bear. You kin tame a wild-cat and you kin tame a panther. . . . You kin tame anything, son, excusin' the human tongue.

Marjorie Kinnan Rawlings, *The Yearling* (1938)

8 Violence of the tongue is very real—sharper than any knife.

Mother Teresa, in Kathryn Spink, ed., *In the Silence of the Heart* (1983)

9 Sweet words are like honey, a little may refresh, but too much gluts the stomach.

Anne Bradstreet, "Meditations Divine and Moral" (1664), in John Harvard Ellis, ed., *The Works of Anne Bradstreet in Prose and Verse* (1867)

10 I like people who refuse to speak until they are ready to speak.

Lillian Hellman, *An Unfinished Woman* (1969)

11 Blessed is the man who, having nothing to say, abstains from giving us wordy evidence of the fact.

George Eliot, *Impressions of Theophrastus Such* (1879)

12 Speech with him was a convenience, like a spoon; he did not use it oftener than was necessary. In England that is not very often, such a great deal is taken for granted there; it is a kind of cult to know how much you may leave unsaid. You inherit accumulations of silence, and Kaye belongs to a very old family.

Sara Jeannette Duncan, *Those Delightful Americans* (1902)

13 Oh, I love talking with him! He puts all these couches to lie down on in his sentences.

Karen Elizabeth Gordon, *Intimate Apparel* (1989)

14 Talking to Maurizio was like playing a slot machine. . . . Suddenly, unpredictably, he would spew out words.

Julia O'Faolain, *The Obedient Wife* (1982)

15 He went on endlessly, overcome by the facile volubility of a weak nature.

Ellen Glasgow, *Barren Ground* (1925)

16 Many a pair of curious ears had been lured by that well-timed pause.

Li Ang, *The Butcher's Wife* (1983)

17 "Mother *means* to do the right thing." Dorothy paused and let the implication go on without her, like a riderless horse.

Margaret Millar, *The Soft Talkers* (1957)

18 Down through the years certain fads of slang had come and gone, and their vestiges could be found in Janie's and Mabel's conversation, like mastodon bones in a swamp.

Dolores Hitchens, *The Bank With the Bamboo Door* (1965)

19 He speaks to me as if I was a public meeting.

Queen Victoria, in G.W.E. Russell, *Collections and Recollections* (1898)

20 I very seldom during my whole stay in the country heard a sentence elegantly turned and correctly pronounced from the lips of an American.

Mrs. Trollope, *Domestic Manners of the Americans* (1832)

21 He landed on the French word the way a hen lands on the water, skeptical, but hoping for the best.

Jessamyn West, *The Friendly Persuasion* (1940)

22 Sinden spoke the rough, slurring speech of the Sussex man, with great broad vowels like pools in which the consonants drowned.

Sheila Kaye-Smith, *Gipsy Waggon* (1933)

1 She was not a woman of many words: for, unlike people in general, she proportioned them to the number of her ideas.

> Jane Austen, *Sense and Sensibility* (1811)

See also Conversation, Discretion, Language, Speeches, Storytelling, Talking, Words.

## ✦ SPEECHES

2 Say what you will in two / Words and get through. / Long, frilly / Palaver is silly.

> Marie-Françoise-Catherine de Beauveau, "Strong Feelings," in Joanna Bankier and Deirdre Lashgari, eds., *Women Poets of the World* (1983)

3 Hubert, a speech does not need to be eternal to be immortal.

> Muriel Humphrey, to husband Hubert H. Humphrey, in Max M. Kampelman, *Entering New Worlds* (1991)

4 He then entered upon a speech, which, for intricacy of design and uselessness of purpose, might have vied with the far-famed labyrinth of Crete.

> Susan Ferrier, *The Inheritance*, vol. 1 (1824)

5 It makes a great difference to a speaker whether he has something to say, or has to say something.

> Nellie L. McClung, *The Stream Runs Fast* (1945)

6 The first duty of a lecturer—to hand you after an hour's discourse a nugget of pure truth to wrap up between the pages of your notebooks and keep on the mantelpiece for ever.

> Virginia Woolf, *A Room of One's Own* (1929)

7 The best impromptu speeches are the ones written well in advance.

> Ruth Gordon, *The Leading Lady* (1948)

8 It is always much easier, I have discovered, to make people cry or gasp than to make them think.

> Golda Meir, *My Life* (1975)

9 Audiences are always better pleased with a smart retort, some joke or epigram, than with any amount of reasoning.

> Charlotte Perkins Gilman, *The Living of Charlotte Perkins Gilman* (1935)

10 He had the Irish eye that takes the audience into its confidence at once.

> Martin Ross (1905), in Gifford Lewis, ed., *The Selected Letters of Somerville and Ross* (1989)

11 Speeches and fruit should always be fresh.

> Nikki Giovanni, "In Sympathy With Another Motherless Child," *Sacred Cows . . . And Other Edibles* (1988)

See also Forensics.

## ✦ SPEED

12 Not all speed is movement.

> Toni Cade, "On the Issue of Roles," *The Black Woman* (1970)

13 Speed is the curse of the age.

> Georgette Heyer, *Death in the Stocks* (1935)

14 Life is walking fast / It wasn't how I wanted it, but I had to take what I could.

> Véronique Tadjo, "Five Poems," *Latérite* (1984)

15 Quite a small spoke is enough to stop a wheel— even a mighty big wheel—if it's going too fast.

> Ethel M. Dell, *The Keeper of the Door* (1915)

16 Life here in America is so fervid, so fast . . . that the tendencies to nervous disease are constantly aggravated.

> Christopher Crowfield, "Irritability," *Little Foxes* (1865)

17 I'd get her off before you could say Jack Robinson.

> Maria Edgeworth, *The Absentee* (1812)

18 She moved with a slowness that was a sign of richness; cream does not pour quickly.

> Rebecca West, *Black Lamb and Grey Falcon* (1941)

19 With the only certainty in our daily existence being change, and a rate of change growing always faster in a kind of technological leapfrog game, speed helps people think they are keeping up.

> Gail Sheehy, *Speed Is of the Essence* (1971)

## ✦ SPIRITUALITY

20 Nothing in all nature is so lovely and so vigorous, so perfectly at home in its environment, as a fish in

the sea. Its surroundings give to it a beauty, quality, and power which is not its own. We take it out, and at once a poor, limp dull thing, fit for nothing, is gasping away its life. So the soul, sunk in God, living the life of prayer, is supported, filled, transformed in beauty, by a vitality and a power which are not its own.

Evelyn Underhill, *The Golden Sequence* (1932)

1 Spirituality is rooted in desire. We long for something we can neither name nor describe, but which is no less real because of our inability to capture it with words.

Mary Jo Weaver, *Springs of Water in a Dry Land* (1993)

2 You're not free / until you've been made captive by / supreme belief.

Marianne Moore, "Spenser's Ireland," *What Are Years?* (1941)

3 My soul magnifies the Lord and my spirit is joyful in God my savior.

Mary, Mother of Jesus, "The Magnificat," Luke 1:46-47 (1st cent.)

4 For me, religiosity is . . . the constant remembrance of the presence of the soul.

Gabriela Mistral (1963), in Sister Rose Aquin Caimano, *Mysticism in Gabriela Mistral* (1969)

5 We must free ourselves to be filled by God. Even God cannot fill what is full.

Mother Teresa, in "Saints Among Us," *Time* (1975)

6 The highest condition of the religious sentiment is when . . . the worshiper not only sees God every where, but sees nothing which is not full of God.

Harriet Martineau, *Miscellanies*, vol. 1 (1836)

7 All the way to heaven is heaven.

St. Catherine of Siena (1375), in Dorothy Day, *By Little and by Little* (1983)

8 If there be anywhere on earth a lover of God who is always kept safe from falling, I know nothing of it, for it was not shown me. But this was shown: that whether in falling or in rising we are always kept in the same precious love.

Julian of Norwich, *Revelations of Divine Love* (1373)

9 We are learning from the teaching and example of Jesus that life itself is a religion, that nothing is more sacred than a human being, that the end of all right institutions, whether the home or the church or an educational establishment, or a government, is the development of the human soul.

Anna Howard Shaw (1917), in Aileen S. Kraditor, *The Ideas of the Woman Suffrage Movement 1890-1920* (1965)

10 Spiritual love is a position of standing with one hand extended into the universe and one hand extended into the world, letting ourselves be a conduit for passing energy.

Christina Baldwin, *Life's Companion* (1990)

11 The divorce of our so-called spiritual life from our daily activities is a fatal dualism.

M.P. Follett, *Creative Experience* (1924)

12 Spirit and body differ not essentially, but gradually.

Anne Vicountess Conway, *The Principles of the Most Ancient and Modern Philosophy* (1692)

13 Spirituality is the sacred center out of which all life comes, including Mondays and Tuesdays and rainy Saturday afternoons in all their mundane and glorious detail. . . . The spiritual journey is the soul's life commingling with ordinary life.

Christina Baldwin, *Life's Companion* (1990)

14 Spirituality promotes passivity when the domain of spirit is defined as outside the world. When this world is the terrain of spirit, we ourselves become actors in the story, and this world becomes the realm in which the sacred must be honored and freedom created.

Starhawk, *Truth or Dare* (1987)

15 When a man, a woman, see their little daily tasks as integral portions of the one great work, they are no longer drudges but co-workers with God.

Annie Besant, *Theosophy* (1912)

16 Nobody lives well who is not spiritually well.

Joan Timmerman, in Theresa King, ed., *The Spiral Path* (1992)

17 We are not human beings learning to be spiritual; we are spiritual beings learning to be human.

Jacquelyn Small, *Awakening in Time* (1991)

18 My belief is that we did not come from God so much as that we are going towards God.

Jane Duncan, *Letter From Reachfar* (1975)

19 Spirituality is basically our relationship with reality.

Chandra Patel, in Theresa King, ed., *The Spiral Path* (1992)

1 To the true servant of God every place is the right place and every time is the right time.

St. Catherine of Siena (1378), in Vida D. Scudder, ed., *St. Catherine of Siena As Seen in Her Letters* (1905)

2 Spiritual life is like a moving sidewalk. Whether you go with it or spend your whole life running against it, you're still going to be taken along.

Bernadette Roberts, in Sherry Ruth Anderson and Patricia Hopkins, *The Feminine Face of God* (1991)

3 We cannot take a single step toward heaven. It is not in our power to travel in a vertical direction. If however we look heavenward for a long time, God comes and takes us up.

Simone Weil, *Waiting for God* (1950)

4 It is not my business to think about myself. My business is to think about God. It is for God to think about me.

Simone Weil, *Waiting for God* (1950)

5 People and societies who cannot see any purpose in their existence beyond the material and the tangible must live chartlessly, and must live in spiritual misery, because they cannot overcome the greatest fact and mystery of human life, next to birth, which is death.

Dorothy Thompson, *The Courage to Be Happy* (1957)

6 We seem to be trapped by a civilization that has accelerated many physical aspects of evolution but has forgotten that other vital part of man—his mind and his psyche.

Sybil Leek, *ESP—The Magic Within You* (1971)

7 The dramatic action that we need to create a way of life on Earth that really works will be taken not through personal, social, or political action, but through spiritual action.

Brooke Medicine Eagle, *Buffalo Woman Comes Singing* (1991)

8 The liberating encounter with God/ess is always an encounter with our authentic selves resurrected from underneath the alienated self. It is not experienced against, but in and through relationships, healing our broken relations with our bodies, with other people, with nature.

Rosemary Ruether, *Sexism and God-Talk* (1983)

9 The religious need of the human mind remains alive, never more so, but it demands a teaching which can be *understood*. Slowly an apprehension of the intimate, usable power of God is growing among us, and a growing recognition of the only worth-while application of that power—in the improvement of the world.

Charlotte Perkins Gilman, *The Living of Charlotte Perkins Gilman* (1935)

10 Spirituality leaps where science cannot yet follow, because science must always test and measure, and much of reality and human experience is immeasurable.

Starhawk, *The Spiral Dance* (1979)

11 The power to love what is purely abstract is given to few.

Margot Asquith, *More or Less About Myself* (1934)

12 Spiritual teaching must always be by symbols.

Mary Baker Eddy, *Science and Health* (1875)

13 Although I try / to hold the single thought / of Buddha's teaching in my heart, / I cannot help but hear / the many crickets' voices calling as well.

Izumi Shikibu (c. 1000), in Jane Hirshfield, with Mariko Aratani, tr., *The Ink Dark Moon* (1990)

14 O my Lord, if I worship Thee from fear of Hell, burn me in Hell, and if I worship Thee from hope of Paradise, exclude me thence, but if I worship Thee for Thine own sake then withhold not from me Thine Eternal Beauty.

Rabi'a the Mystic (8th cent.), in Margaret Smith, *Rabi'a the Mystic* (1928)

15 Let there be many windows to your soul, / . . . Not the narrow pane / Of one poor creed can catch the radiant rays / That shine from countless sources.

Ella Wheeler Wilcox, "Progress," *Poems of Passion* (1883)

16 The tension between the call to the desert and to the market place arises not from the greater presence of God in one or the other, but from our varying psychological needs to apprehend him in different ways.

Sheila Cassidy, "Praying in the Market Place," *Prayer for Pilgrims* (1980)

17 Theosophy, a doctrine which teaches that all which exists is animated or informed by the Universal Soul or Spirit, and that not an atom in our universe can be outside of this omnipresent Principles—is *pure* Spiritualism.

H.P. Blavatsky, *Theosophical Glossary* (1892)

18 The goal of feminist spirituality has never been the simple substitution of Yahweh-with-a-skirt.

Rather, it seeks, in all its diversity, to revitalize relational, body-honoring, cosmologically grounded spiritual possibilities for women and all others.

Charlene Spretnak, "Wholly Writ," in *Ms.* (1993)

1 A large part of the popularity and persuasiveness of psychology comes from its being a sublimated spiritualism: a secular, ostensibly scientific way of affirming the primacy of "spirit" over matter.

Susan Sontag, *Illness As Metaphor* (1978)

2 Better let men continue to worship a winking doll than reverence nothing in heaven or earth.

Frances B. Cobbe, *Italics* (1864)

See also Belief, Bible, Christianity, Church, Clergy, Conversion, Divinity, Eternity, Faith, God, Holiness, Inner Life, Miracles, Mysticism, Prayer, Privation, Religion, Religious, Ritual, The Sacred, Saints, Sermons, Shamans, Soul, Theology, Torah, Visions, Worship.

## ✿ SPORTS

3 The real adherent of the sporting ethic knows that when he's wet, cold, hungry, sore, exhausted, and perhaps a little frightened, he's having a marvelous time.

Mrs. Falk Feeley, *A Swarm of Wasps* (1983)

4 Sport strips away personality, letting the white bone of character shine through.

Rita Mae Brown, *Sudden Death* (1983)

5 In sports, as in love, one can never pretend.

Mariah Burton Nelson, "My Mother, My Rival," in Ron Rapoport, ed., *A Kind of Grace* (1994)

6 The great difference between sport and art is that sport, like a sonnet, forces beauty within its own system. Art, on the other hand, cyclically destroys boundaries and breaks free.

Rita Mae Brown, *Sudden Death* (1983)

7 It's time to raise a generation of participants, not another generation of fans.

Janice Kaplan, *Women and Sports* (1979)

8 The act of sport remains a human act, unrelated to gender.

Mariah Burton Nelson, *Are We Winning Yet?* (1991)

9 Like many young women, I grew up believing that (1) physical ability wasn't very important, and (2) I didn't have any.

Janice Kaplan, *Women and Sports* (1979)

10 There's something about male sports privilege that contributes to the sexual objectification and abuse of women. Given how pervasive and what cultural icons men's sports are, that's a scary thought.

Mariah Burton Nelson, *The Stronger Women Get, the More Men Love Football* (1994)

11 There are boxers possessed of such remarkable intuition, such uncanny prescience, one would think they were somehow recalling their fights, not fighting them as we watch.

Joyce Carol Oates, *On Boxing* (1987)

12 The "third man in the ring" . . . makes boxing possible.

Joyce Carol Oates, *On Boxing* (1987)

13 Power-lifting as a competitive sport is about as interesting for spectators as watching cows chew their cud.

Grace Lichtenstein, *Machisma* (1981)

See also Athletes, Baseball, Basketball, Bodybuilding, Competition, Exercise, Golf, Mountain Climbing, Skating, Skiing, Softball, Surfing, Swimming, Tennis.

## ✿ SPRING

14 Every spring is the only spring, a perpetual astonishment.

Ellis Peters, *The Summer of the Danes* (1991)

15 Praise with elation, / Praise every morning / Spring's re-creation / Of the First Day!

Eleanor Farjeon, "A Morning Song (For the First Day of Spring)," *The Children's Bells* (1960)

16 Spring is the shortest season.

Linda Pastan, "The War Between Desire and Dailiness," *PM/AM* (1982)

17 Autumn arrives in the early morning, but spring at the close of a winter day.

Elizabeth Bowen, *The Death of the Heart* (1938)

1 Winter is past, and we have a prospect of spring that is superior to spring itself.

> Marie de Rabutin-Chantal, Marquise de Sévigné (1690), *Letters of Madame de Sévigné to Her Daughter and Her Friends*, vol. 9 (1811)

2 You've got maybe four special springs in your life, all the others recall them.

> Diane Vreuls, *Are We There Yet* (1975)

3 Spring, which germinated in the earth, moved also, with a strange restlessness, in the hearts of men and women. As the weeks passed, that inextinguishable hope, which mounts always with the rising sap, looked from their faces.

> Ellen Glasgow, *The Miller of Old Church* (1911)

4 A little Madness in the Spring / Is wholesome even for the King.

> Emily Dickinson, in Martha Dickinson Bianchi, ed., *The Single Hound* (1914)

5 There is a terrible loneliness in the spring.

> Ellen Glasgow, *The Miller of Old Church* (1911)

6 Spring is shoving up the front windows and resting your elbows on the sill, the sun burning your nose a little.

> Ruth Wolff, *A Crack in the Sidewalk* (1965)

7 The day widened, pulled from both ends by the shrinking dark, as if darkness itself were a pair of hands and daylight a skein between them, a flexible membrane, and the hands that had pressed together all winter—praying, paralyzed with foreboding—now flung open wide.

> Annie Dillard, *The Living* (1992)

8 In spring, nature is like a thrifty housewife . . . taking up the white carpets and putting down the green ones.

> Mary Baker Eddy, *Miscellaneous Writings: 1883-1896* (1896)

9 Suddenly a mist of green on the trees, as quiet as thought.

> Dorothy M. Richardson, *Pilgrimage: The Trap* (1925)

10 Spring was running in a thin green flame over the Valley.

> Ellen Glasgow, *Vein of Iron* (1935)

11 Everything here is yellow and green. / Listen to its throat, its earthskin, / the bone dry voices of the peepers / as they throb like advertisements.

> Anne Sexton, "It Is a Spring Afternoon," *Love Poems* (1969)

12 Birds that cannot even sing— / Dare to come again in spring!

> Edna St. Vincent Millay, "Doubt No More That Oberon," *Second April* (1921)

13 Spring glides gradually into the farmer's consciousness, but on us city people it bursts with all the relish of a sudden surprise, compensating for much of what we lose.

> Mrs. William Starr Dana, *According to Season* (1894)

14 The air and the earth interpenetrated in the warm gusts of spring; the soil was full of sunlight, and the sunlight full of red dust. The air one breathed was saturated with earthy smells, and the grass under foot had a reflection of blue sky in it.

> Willa Cather, *Death Comes for the Archbishop* (1927)

15 The spring air is soft as pin feathers.

> Virginia Moore, *Virginia Is a State of Mind* (1942)

16 It was a perfect spring afternoon, and the air was filled with vague, roving scents, as if the earth exhaled the sweetness of hidden flowers.

> Ellen Glasgow, *The Miller of Old Church* (1911)

17 Spring comes: the flowers learn their colored shapes.

> Maria Konopnicka, "A Vision" (19th cent.), in Joanna Bankier and Deirdre Lashgari, eds., *Women Poets of the World* (1983)

18 Ye may trace my step o'er the wakening earth, / By the winds which tell of the violet's birth, / By the primrose-stars in the shadowy grass, / By the green leaves, opening as I pass.

> Felicia Hemans, "The Voice of Spring," *The Poetical Works of Felicia Dorothea Hemans* (1914)

See also April, May, Seasons.

## ◊ STAGE AND SCREEN

19 On the stage you try to act real. On the screen you try to *be* real.

> Shirley MacLaine, *Dancing in the Light* (1985)

20 Fundamentally I feel that there is as much difference between the stage and the films as between a piano and a violin. Normally you can't become a virtuoso in both.

> Ethel Barrymore, in *The New York Post* (1956)

See also Films, Theater.

## ♦ STARS

1 Myriads with beating / Hearts of fire.

Sara Teasdale, "Stars," *Flame and Shadow* (1920)

2 Stars clustered about the chimney-top like silver bees in swarm.

Marjorie Kinnan Rawlings, *South Moon Under* (1933)

3 Supposing you only saw the stars once every year. Think what you would think. The wonder of it!

Tasha Tudor, with Richard Brown, *The Private World of Tasha Tudor* (1992)

4 [The stars] are more than reflected on the water, they are doubled and tripled in brilliance as the wind stirs, as if combing them through its black hair.

Marjorie Holmes, *Love and Laughter* (1967)

5 When we are chafed and fretted by small cares, a look at the stars will show us the littleness of our own interests.

Maria Mitchell (1866), in Phebe Mitchell Kendall, ed., *Maria Mitchell, Life, Letters, and Journals* (1896)

6 It is strange that there are times when I feel the stars are not at all *solemn*: they are secretly gay.

Katherine Mansfield (1920), *Journal of Katherine Mansfield* (1927)

7 There is a star that runs very fast, / That goes pulling the moon / Through the tops of the poplars.

Hilda Conkling, "Moon Song," *Poems by a Little Girl* (1920)

8 We walk up the beach under the stars. And when we are tired of walking, we lie flat on the sand under a bowl of stars. We feel stretched, expanded to take in their compass. They pour into us until we are filled with stars, up to the brim.

Anne Morrow Lindbergh, *Gift From the Sea* (1955)

9 I love the evening star. Does that sound foolish? I used to go into the backyard, after sunset, and wait for it until it shone above the dark gum tree. I used to whisper "There you are, my darling." And just in that first moment it seemed to be shining for me alone.

Katherine Mansfield, "The Canary," *The Doves' Nest* (1923)

10 Pegasus and Andromeda faced me brilliantly when I lifted my shade, so I went down and had a friendly reunion with the constellations. . . . I get a wonder-

ful peace and the most exquisite pleasure from my friendship with the stars.

Ellen Glasgow, *Letters of Ellen Glasgow* (1958)

See also Moon, Sky.

## ♦ STATISTICS

11 To understand God's thoughts we must study statistics, for these are the measure of his purpose.

Florence Nightingale, in Karl Pearson, *The Life, Letters and Labors of Francis Galton*, vol. 2 (1924)

12 There is no more effective medicine to apply to feverish public sentiments than figures.

Ida Tarbell, *The Ways of Woman* (1915)

13 It was popularly supposed that figures couldn't lie, but they did; they lied like the dickens.

Mary Stewart Cutting, title story, *The Suburban Whirl* (1907)

14 Don't believe the statistics unless you know the statistician.

Lynne Alpern and Esther Blumenfeld, *Oh, Lord, I Sound Just Like Mama* (1986)

See also Data.

## ♦ STATUS QUO

15 To be content with the world as it is is to be dead.

Dorothee Sölle, *The Truth Is Concrete* (1967)

16 The only difference between a rut and a grave . . . is in their dimensions.

Ellen Glasgow, *The Romantic Comedians* (1926)

17 All adventuring is rash, and all innovations dangerous. But not nearly so dangerous as stagnation and dry rot. From grooves, cliques, clichés and resignation—Good Lord deliver us!

Winifred Holtby (1923), in Alice Holtby and Jean McWilliam, eds., *Letters to a Friend* (1937)

18 Life is a process of *becoming*, a combination of states we have to go through. Where people fail is that they wish to elect a state and remain in it. This is a kind of death.

Anaïs Nin, *D.H. Lawrence: An Unprofessional Study* (1932)

1 The hardest thing to believe when you're young is that people will fight to stay in a rut, but not to get out of it.

Ellen Glasgow, *Barren Ground* (1925)

2 We have had, alas, and still have, the doubtful habit of reverence. Above all, we respect things as they are.

Cynthia Ozick, "Women and Creativity," in *Motive* (1969)

3 Wasn't that what happened to Lot's Wife? A loyalty to old things, a fear of the new, a fear to change, to look ahead?

Toni Cade Bambara, *The Salt Eaters* (1980)

See also Change, Conservatives, Conventionality, Traditions.

# ❧ STEADFASTNESS

4 Even though I saw the executioner and the fire, I could not say anything but what I have said.

Joan of Arc (1431), in Jules Michelet, *Joan of Arc* (1853)

5 The lady's not for turning. I will not change just to court popularity.

Margaret Thatcher, in Penny Junor, *Margaret Thatcher* (1983)

See also Consistency.

# ❧ STEALTH

6 I've nothing to do with anybody following you about. Honestly, I haven't. I wouldn't employ a man, anyway, who'd let a bloke see that he was being followed. No. When I start huntin' you, I shall be as silent and stealthy as a gas-leak.

Dorothy L. Sayers, *The Unpleasantness at the Bellona Club* (1928)

# ❧ STEREOTYPES

7 What is repugnant to every human being is to be reckoned always as a member of a class and not as an individual person.

Dorothy L. Sayers, "Are Women Human?" (1938), *Unpopular Opinions* (1946)

8 We all know we are unique individuals, but we tend to see others as representatives of groups.

Deborah Tannen, *You Just Don't Understand* (1990)

9 It always seemed to me that white people were judged as individuals. But if a Negro did something stupid or wrong, it was held against *all* of us.

Bessie Delany, in Sarah and A. Elizabeth Delany with Amy Hill Hearth, *Having Our Say* (1993)

10 If a man does something silly, people say, "Isn't he silly?" If a woman does something silly, people say, "Aren't women silly?"

Doris Day, in *National Enquirer* (1988)

11 It is sad, very sad, that once more, for the umpteenth time, the old truth is confirmed: "What *one* Christian does is his own responsibility, what *one* Jew does is thrown back at all Jews."

Anne Frank (1944), *The Diary of a Young Girl* (1952)

12 Most of us are so dominated by the idea of a vertical dividing line between masculine and feminine characteristics that we do not notice the discrepancy between the pattern and reality.

Florence Guy Seabury, "The Masculine Dilemma," *The Delicatessen Husband* (1926)

13 It's his first exposure to Third World passion. He thought only Americans had informed political opinion—other people staged coups out of spite and misery. It's an unwelcome revelation to him that a reasonably educated and rational man like Ro would die for things that he, Brent, has never heard of and would rather laugh about.

Bharati Mukherjee, "Orbiting," *The Middleman* (1988)

14 Ethnic stereotypes are misshapen pearls, sometimes with a sandy grain of truth at their center . . . but they ignore complexity, change, and individuality.

Anna Quindlen, "Erin Go Brawl," *Thinking Out Loud* (1993)

See also Bigotry, Generalizations, Prejudice, Sexism, Sex Roles.

# ❧ STOCK MARKET

15 Wall Street owns this country. It is no longer a government of the people, by the people and for

the people, but a government of Wall Street, by Wall Street and for Wall Street.

> Mary E. Lease (1891), in Judith Anderson, ed., *Outspoken Women* (1984)

1 When he came back from the gallery of the Stock Exchange . . . [h]e said hats went out of that place every day that would never smile again.

> Sara Jeannette Duncan, *Those Delightful Americans* (1902)

2 You think I know what I'm talking about? If it works I'm a genius. If it doesn't I blame it on the market, the falling dollar, Washington jitters, the weather, anything I can think of.

> Helen Yglesias, *Family Feeling* (1976)

3 Don't mail me any more proxies, please. / Tell me, incorporated tease, / Why don't you save the stamps and send, / Once in a while, a dividend?

> Margaret Fishback, "A Truculent Stockholder Speaks Her Mind," *Out of My Head* (1933)

## ❦ STONES

4 A gray stone is naturally mournful. / It is a word from the common language of the dead. / Keep it. Someday you will understand.

> Anita Endrezze-Danielson, in Joseph Bruchac, ed., *Songs From This Earth on Turtle's Back* (1983)

## ❦ STORIES

5 Once Upon a Time, / Once Upon a Time! / Everything that happened, happened / Once Upon a Time!

> Eleanor Farjeon, "O Is for Once Upon a Time," *The Children's Bells* (1960)

6 The universe is made of stories, / not of atoms.

> Muriel Rukeyser, title poem, *The Speed of Darkness* (1968)

7 The divine art is the story.

> Isak Dinesen, "The Cardinal's First Tale," *Last Tales* (1957)

8 Story is a sacred visualization, a way of echoing experience.

> Terry Tempest Williams, *Pieces of White Shell* (1984)

9 A lie hides the truth, a story tries to find it.

> Paula Fox, *A Servant's Tale* (1984)

10 Stories operate like dreams; both veil what is to be uncovered; neither is capable of the cover-up.

> Lore Segal, "Our Dream of the Good God," in Christina Büchmann and Celina Spiegel, eds., *Out of the Garden* (1994)

11 Stories are medicine.

> Clarissa Pinkola Estés, *Women Who Run With the Wolves* (1992)

12 We tell ourselves stories in order to live.

> Joan Didion, title essay, *The White Album* (1979)

13 The story was the important thing and little changes here and there were really part of the story. There were even stories about the different versions of stories and how they imagined the differing versions came to be.

> Leslie Marmon Silko, *Storyteller* (1981)

14 The story—from *Rumplestiltskin* to *War and Peace*—is one of the basic tools invented by the human mind, for the purpose of gaining understanding. There have been great societies that did not use the wheel, but there have been no societies that did not tell stories.

> Ursula K. Le Guin, "Prophets and Mirrors," in *The Living Light* (1970)

15 The ancient people perceived the world and themselves within that world as part of an ancient continuous story composed of innumerable bundles of other stories.

> Leslie Marmon Silko, in Lorraine Anderson, ed., *Sisters of the Earth* (1991)

16 There are only two or three human stories, and they go on repeating themselves as fiercely as if they had never happened before.

> Willa Cather, *O Pioneers!* (1913)

17 How our story has been divided up among the truth-telling professions! Religion, philosophy, history, poetry, compete with each other for our ears; and science competes with all together. And for each we have a different set of ears. But, though we hear much, what we are told is as nothing: none of it gives us ourselves, rather each story-kind steals us to make its reality of us.

> Laura Riding Jackson, *The Telling* (1972)

18 Within our whole universe the story only has the authority to answer that cry of heart of its charac-

ters, that one cry of heart of each of them: "*Who am I?*"

Isak Dinesen, "The Cardinal's First Tale," *Last Tales* (1957)

1 Stories ought not to be just little bits of fantasy that are used to wile away an idle hour; from the beginning of the human race stories have been used—by priests, by bards, by medicine men—as magic instruments of healing, of teaching, as a means of helping people come to terms with the fact that they continually have to face insoluble problems and unbearable realities.

Joan Aiken, *The Way to Write for Children* (1982)

2 There is no agony like bearing an untold story inside you.

Zora Neale Hurston, *Dust Tracks on a Road* (1942)

3 Writing the short story is essentially an act of grace. It's not a matter of will so much as trust. I try to let the story do some of the work for me. It knows what it wants to do, say, be. I try not to stand in its way.

Paulette Bates Alden, conference (1990)

4 For a short-story writer, a story is the combination of what the writer *supposed* the story would likely be about—plus what actually turned up in the course of writing.

Carol Bly, *The Passionate, Accurate Story* (1990)

5 Every good story . . . must leave in the mind of the sensitive reader an intangible residuum of pleasure; a cadence, a quality of voice that is exclusively the writer's own, individual, unique.

Willa Cather, preface, *The Best Short Stories of Sarah Orne Jewett* (1925)

6 In a story, the craftsmanship is fully exposed. A novel is like charity; it covers a multitude of faults.

Thea Astley, in Valerie Miner, *Rumors From the Cauldron* (1991)

7 The short story . . . is the most democratic of all the arts; anyone may tell a story, and if it is an absorbing one someone will listen.

Hallie Burnett, *On Writing the Short Story* (1983)

8 The more original a short-story writer, the odder looking the assortment of things he or she puts together for a story.

Carol Bly, *The Passionate, Accurate Story* (1990)

9 I love the short story for being round, suggestive, insinuating, microcosmic. The story has both the

inconvenience and the fascination of new beginnings.

Luisa Valenzuela, in Janet Sternburg, ed., *The Writer on Her Work*, vol. 2 (1991)

10 A story has to have muscle as well as meaning, and the meaning has to be in the muscle.

Flannery O'Connor, in Sally Fitzgerald, ed., *The Habit of Being* (1979)

11 The difference between mad people and sane people . . . is that sane people have variety when they talk-story. Mad people have only one story that they talk over and over.

Maxine Hong Kingston, *The Woman Warrior* (1976)

See also Children's Literature, Fiction, Legends, Myth, Novels, Storytelling, Writing.

# ❦ STORMS

12 Sutures of lightning tightened the edges of the sky.

T.J. MacGregor, *Kill Flash* (1987)

13 The Lightning is a yellow Fork / From Tables in the sky / By inadvertent fingers dropt / The awful Cutlery.

Emily Dickinson (1870), in Mabel Loomis Todd and Millicent Todd Bingham, eds., *Bolts of Melody* (1945)

14 The thunder seemed to lift itself off the ground, and the lightning came in sheets, instead of in great forks that flew like flights of spears among the forest trees.

Mary H. Kingsley, *Travels in West Africa* (1897)

15 Winds are birds; snow is a feather; / Wild white swans are wind and weather.

Sister M. Madeleva, "Snow Storm," *Collected Poems* (1947)

16 Think of the storm roaming the sky uneasily / like a dog looking for a place to sleep in, / listen to it growling.

Elizabeth Bishop, "Little Exercise," *North and South* (1955)

17 He had moved off in one of those weird lulls which you get in a tornado, when for a few seconds the wild herd of hurrying winds seem to have lost themselves, and wander round crying and wailing like lost souls, until their common rage seizes them

again and they rush back to their work of destruction.

Mary H. Kingsley, *Travels in West Africa* (1897)

1 The only two good words that can be said for a hurricane are that it gives sufficient warning of its approach, and that it blows from one point of the compass at a time.

Gertrude Atherton, *The Conqueror* (1902)

2 The night is dark, the waters deep, / Yet soft the billows roll; / Alas! at every breeze I weep— / The storm is in my soul.

Helen Maria Williams, "A Song," *Poems* (1786)

See also Weather, Wind.

## ❧ STORYTELLING

3 The bearers of fables are very welcome.

Monique Wittig, *Les Guérillères* (1969)

4 She was attracted by the art of storytellers more than by any other—those Oriental storytellers who sit in marketplaces and hold beneath their words a group of people who have the faces of nurslings who are suckling. The sand of time flows away and the whole sun lies like a cloak upon the shoulders of the storyteller.

Adrienne Monnier (1936), in Richard McDougall, tr., *The Very Rich Hours of Adrienne Monnier* (1976)

5 Storytelling is the oldest form of education.

Terry Tempest Williams, *Pieces of White Shell* (1984)

6 Where the storyteller is loyal, eternally and unswervingly loyal to the story, there, in the end, silence will speak. Where the story has been betrayed, silence is but emptiness.

Isak Dinesen, "The Blank Page," *Last Tales* (1957)

7 Storytelling reveals meaning without committing the error of defining it.

Hannah Arendt, *Men in Dark Times* (1968)

8 All sorrows can be borne if you put them into a story or tell a story about them.

Isak Dinesen, in Hannah Arendt, *The Human Condition* (1959)

9 I was raised by and have raised people who regard telling one story when two would do as a sign someone is not really trying.

Linda Ellerbee, *"And So It Goes"* (1986)

See also Stories.

## ❧ STRANGENESS

10 Nothing, perhaps, is strange, once you have accepted life itself, the great strange business which includes all lesser strangenesses.

Rose Macaulay, *Crewe Train* (1926)

## ❧ STRANGERS

11 Strangers are an endangered species.

Adrienne Rich, "The Spirit of Place," *A Wild Patience Has Taken Me This Far* (1981)

12 I'm a stranger wherever I go, but I'm happy.

Hualing Nieh, *Mulberry and Peach* (1981)

13 Call no man foe, but never love a stranger.

Stella Benson, *This Is the End* (1917)

14 Strangers . . . are just your friends that you don't know yet.

Margaret Lee Runbeck, *Our Miss Boo* (1942)

See also Outsiders, The Unknown.

## ❧ STRENGTH

15 Men are like tea—the real strength and goodness are not properly drawn until they have been in hot water.

Lillie Hitchcock Coit (1862), in Helen Holdredge, *Firebelle Lillie* (1967)

16 A woman is like a teabag—only in hot water do you realize how strong she is.

Nancy Reagan, in *The Observer* (1981)

17 Strength diminishes when it seems we are spending it in vain.

Susan Glaspell, *The Morning Is Near Us* (1939)

1 I think what weakens people most is fear of wasting their strength.
> Etty Hillesum (1942), *An Interrupted Life* (1983)

2 Not to discover weakness is / The Artifice of strength.
> Emily Dickinson (1865), in Mabel Loomis Todd and Millicent Todd Bingham, eds., *Bolts of Melody* (1945)

3 Everything nourishes what is strong already.
> Jane Austen, *Pride and Prejudice* (1813)

## ❦ STRESS

4 Stress is an ignorant state. It believes that everything is an emergency.
> Natalie Goldberg, *Wild Mind* (1990)

5 The bow always strung . . . will not do.
> George Eliot, *Middlemarch* (1871)

See also Anxiety, Crises, Nerves.

## ❦ STUBBORNNESS

6 The world doesn't come to the clever folks, it comes to the stubborn, obstinate, one-idea-at-a-time people.
> Mary Roberts Rinehart, "The Family Friend," *Affinities* (1920)

7 Bulldogs have been known to fall on their swords when confronted by my superior tenacity.
> Margaret Halsey, *No Laughing Matter* (1977)

8 There was no end to a road once he had set his feet upon it.
> Pearl S. Buck, *God's Men* (1951)

9 Nina felt as if she were being tracked down by a large placid resolute elephant.
> Elizabeth Janeway, *Leaving Home* (1953)

10 In the face of an obstacle which is impossible to overcome, stubbornness is stupid.
> Simone de Beauvoir, *The Ethics of Ambiguity* (1948)

See also Determination, Obstinacy, Patience, Perseverance.

## ❦ STUDENTS

11 They were completely quiet, but toward the end of the day you really can't tell what that means. It could be awe or brain death, the symptoms are identical.
> Barbara Kingsolver, *Animal Dreams* (1990)

See also Education, School.

## ❦ STUPIDITY

12 Against stupidity the gods fight in vain.
> Katharine Tynan, *The Wandering Years* (1922)

13 When I die my death will be caused by indignation at the stupidity of human nature.
> Marie Bashkirtseff (1877), in Mary J. Serrano, tr., *The Journal of a Young Artist* (1919)

14 People who cannot recognize a palpable absurdity are very much in the way of civilization.
> Agnes Repplier, *In Pursuit of Laughter* (1936)

15 Maybe people have become so stupid as a result of having too many machines  The company we keep.
> Chrystos, "No Rock Scorns Me As Whore," in Cherríe Moraga and Gloria Anzaldúa, eds., *This Bridge Called My Back* (1983)

16 The difference between genius and stupidity is that even genius has its limits.
> Rita Mae Brown, *Bingo* (1988)

See also Anti-Intellectualism, Errors, Failure, Intelligence, Mistakes.

## ❦ STYLE

17 Styles, like everything else, change. Style doesn't.
> Linda Ellerbee, *Move On* (1991)

18 Fashion is general; style is individual.
> Edna Woolman Chase and Ilka Chase, *Always in Vogue* (1954)

1 Style is something peculiar to one person; it expresses one personality and one only; it cannot be shared.

> Freya Stark, "A Note on Style" (1942), *The Arch of the Zodiac* (1968)

2 Fashion can be bought. Style one must possess.

> Edna Woolman Chase and Ilka Chase, *Always in Vogue* (1954)

See also Appearance, Clothes, Dress, Elegance, Fashion, Taste, Trends, Writing.

## ❦ SUBJECTIVITY

3 If all issues are personalized, we lose our capacity to entertain ideas, to generalize from our own or someone else's experiences, to think abstractly. We substitute sentimentality for thought.

> Wendy Kaminer, *I'm Dysfunctional, You're Dysfunctional* (1992)

See also Objectivity.

## ❦ SUBTLETY

4 She was about as subtle as a see-through blouse.

> Helen Van Slyke, *A Necessary Woman* (1979)

## ❦ SUCCESS

5 Being Number One isn't everything to me, but for those few hours on the court it's way ahead of whatever's in second place.

> Billie Jean King, with Kim Chapin, *Billie Jean* (1974)

6 He has achieved success, who has lived well, laughed often, and loved much; who has gained the respect of intelligent men and the love of little children.

> Bessie A. Stanley, in Martha Lupton, *The Speaker's Desk Book* (1937)

7 To tend, unfailingly, unflinchingly, towards a goal, is the secret of success.

> Anna Pavlova, "Pages of My Life," in A.H. Franks, ed., *Pavlova* (1956)

8 The secret of success is concentration; wherever there has been a great life, or a great work, that has gone before. Taste everything a little, look at everything a little; but live for one thing.

> Ralph Iron, *The Story of an African Farm* (1883)

9 I do not know anyone who has got to the top without hard work. That is the recipe. It will not always get you to the top, but it should get you pretty near.

> Margaret Thatcher, in *The London Daily Telegraph* (1986)

10 You can have unbelievable intelligence, you can have connections, you can have opportunities fall out of the sky. But in the end, hard work is the true, enduring characteristic of successful people.

> Marsha Evans, in Lauren Picker, "'The Key to My Success. . .'," *Parade* (1996)

11 Success supposes endeavor.

> Jane Austen, *Emma* (1816)

12 We all must pay with the current coin of life / For the honey that we taste.

> Rachel [Rachel Blumstein], "Jonathan," in Nathan and Marynn Ausubel, eds., *A Treasury of Jewish Poetry* (1957)

13 It isn't success after all, is it, if it isn't an expression of your deepest energies?

> Marilyn French, *The Bleeding Heart* (1980)

14 Success is a great healer.

> Gertrude Atherton, *Black Oxen* (1923)

15 Success breeds confidence.

> Beryl Markham, *West With the Night* (1942)

16 Success makes you think you have principles.

> Melodie Johnson Howe, "Dirty Blonde," in Marilyn Wallace, ed., *Sisters in Crime 4* (1991)

17 I personally measure success in terms of the contributions an individual makes to her or his fellow human beings.

> Margaret Mead, in *Redbook* (1978)

18 Know the difference between success and fame. Success is Mother Teresa. Fame is Madonna.

> Erma Bombeck, in *USA Today* (1991)

19 The best thing that can come with success is the knowledge that it is nothing to long for.

> Liv Ullmann, *Changing* (1976)

1 I've never sought success in order to get fame and money: it's the talent and the passion that count in success.

>   Ingrid Bergman, in Oriana Fallaci, *Limelighters* (1963)

2 Winning the prize [1963 Nobel Prize in physics] wasn't half as exciting as doing the work itself.

>   Maria Goeppert Mayer, in Barbara Shiels, *Women and the Nobel Prize* (1985)

3 What does so-called success or failure matter if only you have succeeded in doing the thing you set out to do. The DOING is all that really counts.

>   Eva Le Gallienne, in Robert A. Schanke, *Shattered Applause* (1992)

4 Who wants to read about success? It is the early struggle which makes a good story.

>   Katherine Anne Porter, "Gertrude Stein: Three Views" (1927), *The Days Before* (1952)

5 Generally speaking, we are all happier when we are still striving for achievement than when the prize is in our hands.

>   Margot Fonteyn, *A Dancer's World* (1979)

6 The trouble with success is—it takes all your time. And you can't do the things you really *want* to do!

>   Ruth Draper, "Three Women and Mr. Clifford," *The Art of Ruth Draper* (1960)

7 I am doomed to an eternity of compulsive work. No set goal achieved satisfies. Success only breeds a new goal. The golden apple devoured has seeds. It is endless.

>   Bette Davis, *The Lonely Life* (1962)

8 The trouble with being number one in the world—at anything—is that it takes a certain mentality to attain that position in the first place, and that is something of a driving, perfectionist attitude, so that once you do achieve number one, you don't relax and enjoy it.

>   Billie Jean King, with Frank Deford, *Billie Jean* (1982)

9 Achievement brings with it its own anticlimax.

>   Agatha Christie, *They Came to Baghdad* (1951)

10 "Nothing succeeds as doth succeed Success!" / None who have known Success assent to this.

>   Laurence Hope, "Happiness," *Stars of the Desert* (1903)

11 Nothing fails like success; nothing is so defeated as yesterday's triumphant Cause.

>   Phyllis McGinley, "How to Get Along With Men," *The Province of the Heart* (1959)

12 Success is a two-bladed golden sword; it knights one and stabs one at the same time.

>   Mae West, *Goodness Had Nothing to Do With It!* (1959)

13 People seldom see the halting and painful steps by which the most insignificant success is achieved.

>   Annie Sullivan, in Helen Keller, *The Story of My Life* (1902)

14 You always feel you are not deserving. People who are successful at what they do know what kind of work goes with it, so they are surprised at the praise.

>   Virginia Hamilton, in *The Horn Book* (1993)

15 Dwells within the soul of every Artist / More than all his effort can express; / And he knows the best remains unuttered, / Sighing at what *we* call his success.

>   Adelaide Anne Procter, "Unexpressed," *Legends and Lyrics* (1858)

16 It is a mark of many famous people that they cannot part with their brightest hour: what worked once must always work.

>   Lillian Hellman, *Pentimento* (1973)

17 Success can make you go one of two ways. It can make you a prima donna, or it can smooth the edges, take away the insecurities, let the nice things come out.

>   Barbara Walters, in *Newsweek* (1974)

18 Success does not implant bad characteristics in people. It merely steps up the growth rate of the bad characteristics they already had.

>   Margaret Halsey, *No Laughing Matter* (1977)

19 She's the kind of girl who climbed the ladder of success, wrong by wrong.

>   Mae West, on her character in *I'm No Angel*, in Joseph Weintraub, ed., *The Wit and Wisdom of Mae West* (1967)

20 Nothing succeeds like address.

>   Fran Lebowitz, *Metropolitan Life* (1978)

21 Integrity is so perishable in the summer months of success.

>   Vanessa Redgrave, in David Bailey and Peter Evans, *Goodbye Baby and Amen* (1969)

22 I don't think success is harmful, as so many people say. Rather I believe it indispensable to talent: if for nothing else than to increase the talent.

>   Jeanne Moreau, in Oriana Fallaci, *Limelighters* (1963)

1 When you are young you are surprised if everything isn't a success, and when you get older you're mildly surprised if anything is.

Kathleen Norris, *Woman in Love* (1935)

2 I find it's as hard to live down an early triumph as an early indiscretion.

Edna St. Vincent Millay (1922), in Allan Ross Macdougall, ed., *Letters of Edna St. Vincent Millay* (1952)

3 I think Americans love success—but hate the people who have it.

Kathleen Winsor, *Star Money* (1950)

4 The penalty of success is to be bored by the attentions of people who formerly snubbed you.

Mary Wilson Little, *A Paragrapher's Reveries* (1904)

5 It was the first operatic mountain I climbed, and the view from it was astounding, exhilarating, stupefying.

Leontyne Price, in *Life* (1966)

6 It's a little depressing to become number one because the only place you can go from there is down.

Doris Day, in A.E. Hotchner, *Doris Day* (1975)

7 The top is not forever. Either you walk down, or you are going to be kicked down.

Janet Collins, in Brian Lanker, *I Dream a World* (1989)

8 Like most people who have reached the top, I think she finds that the staying is harder than the climb.

Ilka Chase, *Free Admission* (1948)

9 Success has killed more men than bullets.

Texas Guinan, nightclub act (1920)

10 Success has made failures of many men.

Cindy Adams, in Joey Adams, *Cindy and I* (1957)

11 What is generally regarded as success—acquisition of wealth, the capture of power or social prestige— I consider the most dismal failures. I hold when it is said of a man that he has arrived, it means that he is finished—his development has stopped at that point.

Emma Goldman, "Was My Life Worth Living?" in *Harper's Magazine* (1934)

12 Success is counted sweetest / By those who ne'er succeed.

Emily Dickinson (1859), in Mabel Loomis Todd and T.W. Higginson, eds., *Poems by Emily Dickinson* (1890)

13 It's them that take advantage that get advantage i' this world.

George Eliot, *Adam Bede* (1859)

14 To be successful, a woman has to be much better at her job than a man.

Golda Meir, in Oriana Fallaci, *L'Europeo* (1973)

15 Even a stopped clock is right twice every day. After some years, it can boast of a long series of successes.

Marie von Ebner-Eschenbach, *Aphorisms* (1893)

16 For you to be successful, sacrifices must be made. It's better that they are made by others but failing that, you'll have to make them yourself.

Rita Mae Brown, *Starting From Scratch* (1988)

See also Accomplishment, Celebrity, Failure, Fame, Happiness, Success and Failure, Winning.

## ❧ SUCCESS AND FAILURE

17 It is nothing to succeed if one has not taken great trouble, and it is nothing to fail if one has done the best one could.

Nadia Boulanger, in Don G. Campbell, *Reflections of Boulanger* (1982)

18 O in success there often lurks a failure / That feeds upon the soul in hidden shame, / And in defeat there sometimes rests a triumph / Greater than fame.

Eliza Boyle O'Reilly, "Henri de la Rochejacquelin," *My Candles* (1903)

19 Success and failure are not true opposites, and they're not even in the same class. I mean, they're not even a couch and a chair.

Lillian Hellman, in *The Listener* (1979)

20 Most successes are unhappy. That's why they are successes—they have to reassure themselves about themselves by achieving something that the world will notice. . . . The happy people are failures because they are on such good terms with themselves that they don't give a damn.

Agatha Christie, *Sparkling Cyanide* (1945)

1 The success or failure of a life, as far as posterity goes, seems to lie in the more or less luck of seizing the right moment of escape.

> Alice James (1891), in Anna Robeson Burr, *Alice James* (1934)

2 Success is a public affair. Failure is a private funeral.

> Rosalind Russell, in John Robert Colombo, *Popcorn in Paradise* (1979)

See also Failure, Success.

# ❧ SUFFERING

3 Suffering has always been with us, does it really matter in what form it comes? All that matters is how we bear it and how we fit it into our lives.

> Etty Hillesum (1942), *An Interrupted Life* (1983)

4 We do not die of anguish, we live on. We continue to suffer. We drink the cup drop by drop.

> George Sand (1834), in Marie Jenny Howe, ed., *The Intimate Journal of George Sand* (1929)

5 Suffering belongs to no language.

> Adélia Prado, "Denouement," in Ellen Watson, tr., *The Alphabet in the Park* (1990)

6 True knowledge comes only through suffering.

> Elizabeth Barrett Browning (1844), in Charlotte Porter and Helen A. Clarke, eds., *The Complete Works of Elizabeth Barrett Browning* (1900)

7 I do not believe that sheer suffering teaches. If suffering alone taught, all the world would be wise, since everyone suffers. To suffering must be added mourning, understanding, patience, love, openness, and the willingness to remain vulnerable.

> Anne Morrow Lindbergh, *Hour of Gold, Hour of Lead* (1973)

8 That there should be a purpose to suffering, that a person should be chosen for it, special—these are houses of the mind, in which whole peoples have found shelter.

> Gish Jen, *Typical American* (1991)

9 The hardest thing we are asked to do in this world is to remain aware of suffering, suffering about which we can do nothing.

> May Sarton, *At Seventy* (1984)

10 Suffering is also one of the ways of knowing you're alive.

> Jessamyn West, *To See the Dream* (1957)

11 The sight or sound of perfect things causes a certain suffering.

> Adrienne Monnier (1940), in Richard McDougall, tr., *The Very Rich Hours of Adrienne Monnier* (1976)

12 Although the world is full of suffering, it is full also of the overcoming of it.

> Helen Keller, *Optimism* (1903)

13 Pain is inevitable. Suffering is optional.

> M. Kathleen Casey, in Karen Casey and Martha Vanceburg, *The Promise of a New Day* (1985)

14 Pain is an event. . . . Suffering, on the other hand, is the nightmare reliving of unscrutinized and unmetabolized pain.

> Audre Lorde, "Eye to Eye," *Sister Outsider* (1984)

15 Suffering raises up those souls that are truly great; it is only small souls that are made mean-spirited by it.

> Alexandra David-Neel (1889), *La Lampe de Sagesse* (1986)

16 A *Wounded* Deer — leaps highest.

> Emily Dickinson (1860), in Mabel Loomis Todd and T.W. Higginson, eds., *Poems by Emily Dickinson* (1890)

17 So much that was beautiful and so much that was hard to bear. Yet whenever I showed myself ready to bear it, the hard was directly transformed into the beautiful.

> Etty Hillesum (1942), *An Interrupted Life* (1983)

18 The world has been forced to its knees. Unhappily we seldom find our way there without being beaten to it by suffering.

> Anne Morrow Lindbergh, *The Wave of the Future* (1940)

19 So long as one is able to pose one has still much to learn about suffering.

> Ellen Glasgow, *Letters of Ellen Glasgow* (1958)

20 The capacity to suffer varies more than anything that I have observed in human nature.

> Margot Asquith, *More or Less About Myself* (1934)

See also Grief, Pain, Sorrow.

## ❦ SUFFRAGE

1 The vote is a power, a weapon of offense and defense, a prayer.

> Carrie Chapman Catt (1920), in Mary Gray Peck, *Carrie Chapman Catt* (1948)

2 There were some Labourists saying that other things must be dealt with before women got the vote. It was humanly natural that they, as men, should say so. Our business as women was to recognize this and act accordingly.

> Christabel Pankhurst, *Unshackled* (1959)

3 For two generations groups of women have given their lives and their fortunes to secure the vote for the sex and hundreds of thousands of other women are now giving all the time at their command. No class of men in our own or any other country has made one-tenth the effort nor sacrificed one-tenth as much for the vote.

> Carrie Chapman Catt, *Woman Suffrage by Federal Constitutional Amendment* (1917)

4 To get that word, male, out of the Constitution, cost the women of this country fifty-two years of pauseless campaign; fifty-six state referendum campaigns; 480 legislative campaigns to get state suffrage amendments submitted; forty-seven state constitutional convention campaigns; 277 state party convention campaigns; thirty national party convention campaigns to get suffrage planks in the party platforms; nineteen campaigns with nineteen successive Congresses to get the federal amendment submitted, and the final ratification campaign.

> Carrie Chapman Catt, in Mary Gray Peck, *Carrie Chapman Catt* (1948)

5 The single most impressive fact about the attempt by American women to obtain the right to vote is how long it took.

> Alice S. Rossi, "Along the Suffrage Trail," *The Feminist Papers* (1973)

See also Democracy, Elections.

## ❦ SUICIDE

6 We cannot blot out one page of our lives, but we can throw the book in the fire.

> George Sand, *Mauprat* (1837)

7 Come Death, you know you must come when you're called / Although you're a god.

> Stevie Smith, "Dido's Farewell to Aeneas," *Not Waving But Drowning* (1957)

8 People commit suicide for only one reason—to escape torment.

> Li Ang, *The Butcher's Wife* (1983)

9 There were certain hours in every life, she told herself, when the soul judged the body. Judged and forgave, or judged and condemned.

> Katherine Cecil Thurston, *The Gambler* (1905)

10 [I] have fantasies of killing myself and thus being the powerful one not the powerless one.

> Anne Sexton (1964), in Linda Gray Sexton and Lois Ames, eds., *Anne Sexton: A Self-Portrait in Letters* (1977)

11 I know of a cure for everything: salt water. . . . Sweat, or tears, or the salt sea.

> Isak Dinesen, "The Deluge at Norderney," *Seven Gothic Tales* (1934)

12 Suicides have a special language. / Like carpenters they want to know *which tools.* / They never ask *why build.*

> Anne Sexton, "Wanting to Die," *Live or Die* (1966)

13 Suicide is the ultimate "one-up," as it were, the accusation that brooks no defense, the argument won at last.

> Joanne Greenberg, "They Live," *High Crimes and Misdemeanors* (1979)

14 Killing herself was the ultimate conversation stopper, the final saying, "No backs."

> Jane Rule, "In the Attic of the House," *Christopher Street* (1979)

15 The right to choose death when life no longer holds meaning is not only the next liberation but the last human right.

> Marya Mannes, *Last Rights* (1974)

16 Nothing is so horrifying as the possibility of existing simply because we do not know how to die.

> Madame de Staël, "On Philosophy," *The Influence of the Passions* (1796)

17 I don't see why people consider suicide cowardice. I think it has a certain dignity—like leaving before you're fired.

> Rosemary Kutak, *I Am the Cat* (1948)

1 Some people say that suicide is a sin, but I have never believed that. I say it's God's way of calling certain folks home early. It's much nicer than an awful accident, where the rest of us are left wondering if the person really wanted to go.

> Faith Sullivan, *The Cape Ann* (1988)

2 Human life consists in mutual service. No grief, pain, misfortune, or "broken heart" is excuse for cutting off one's life while any power of service remains. But when all usefulness is over, when one is assured of an unavoidable and imminent death, it is the simplest of human rights to choose a quick and easy death in place of a slow and horrible one.

> Charlotte Perkins Gilman, suicide note (1935)

3 Razors pain you; / Rivers are damp; / Acids stain you; / And drugs cause cramp. / Guns aren't lawful; / Nooses give; / Gas smells awful; / You might as well live.

> Dorothy Parker, "Résumé," *Enough Rope* (1926)

See also Death, Dying, Self-Destruction, Self-Determination.

## ❦ SUMMER

4 Winter is cold-hearted, / Spring is yea and nay, / Autumn is a weather-cock / Blown every way. / Summer days for me / When every leaf is on its tree.

> Christina Rossetti, "Summer" (1845), *Goblin Market* (1862)

5 Summertime is the time of sharpest memory.

> Ruth Sidransky, *In Silence* (1990)

6 The softness of the summer day [was] like an ermine paw.

> Anaïs Nin (1937), *The Diary of Anaïs Nin*, vol. 2 (1967)

7 Summer, shrewd doctor, treats the eye before all else, / sends in the season's tray of soft foods, pollen and rose.

> Patricia Hampl, title poem, *Resort* (1983)

8 July was the month when summer, like bread in the oven, might change color, but it would rise no higher. It was at its height.

> Jessamyn West, *Leafy Rivers* (1967)

9 Summer is delicately made. / While it is, it is ceasing.

> Genevieve Taggard, "Flute in Later Summer," *Calling Western Union* (1936)

10 The months between the cherries and the peaches / Are brimming cornucopias which spill / Fruits red and purple.

> Elinor Wylie, "Wild Peaches," *Nets to Catch the Wind* (1921)

11 How softly summer shuts, without the creaking of a door.

> Emily Dickinson (1880), in Mabel Loomis Todd, ed., *Letters of Emily Dickinson*, vol. 2 (1894)

12 Generally speaking, the poorer person summers where he winters.

> Fran Lebowitz, *Social Studies* (1977)

See also August, Seasons.

## ❦ SUN

13 The sun was like a word written between the sea and the sky, a word that was swallowed up by the sea before any man had time to read it.

> Stella Benson, *This Is the End* (1917)

14 The sun is as dispassionate as the hand of a man who greets you with his mind on other things.

> Beryl Markham, *West With the Night* (1942)

15 The sun beating in on me gives my mind a dry feeling. I feel like dust.

> Evelyn Scott, *Escapade* (1923)

16 The sun pours out like wine.

> Lizette Woodworth Reese, "Trust," *A Quiet Road* (1896)

17 The sun lay like a friendly arm across her square shoulders.

> Marjorie Kinnan Rawlings, *When the Whippoorwill—* (1940)

18 The sun, God's own great shadow.

> Julia Peterkin, *Scarlet Sister Mary* (1928)

See also Sunrise, Sunset.

## ❦ SUNDAY

19 Sunday is sort of like a piece of bright gold brocade lying in a pile of white muslin weekdays.

> Yoshiko Uchida, *A Jar of Dreams* (1981)

1 Since her childhood it had seemed to her that the movement of all laws, even natural ones, was either suspended or accelerated on the Sabbath.

Ellen Glasgow, *Barren Ground* (1925)

2 This is Sunday, the deadliest of days for prisoners and solitaries.

Rosa Luxemburg, *Prison Letters to Sophie Liebknecht* (1917)

3 Sundays are terrible because it is clear that there is no one in charge of the world. And this knowledge leaves you drifting around, grappling with unfulfilled expectations and vague yearnings.

Sheila Ballantyne, *Norma Jean the Termite Queen* (1975)

4 I've always hated Sundays, always had to fight the gray gloom that comes over me on Sunday afternoons. . . . When I die it will be on a Sunday afternoon around four o'clock.

Barbara Gordon, *I'm Dancing As Fast As I Can* (1979)

5 The feeling of Sunday is the same everywhere, heavy, melancholy, standing still. Like when they say, "As it was in the beginning, is now, and ever shall be, world without end."

Jean Rhys, *Voyage in the Dark* (1934)

6 Sunday afternoons are the longest afternoons of all.

Carson McCullers, *Clock Without Hands* (1961)

## ❧ SUNGLASSES

7 Sunglasses are the twentieth-century equivalent of fans and veils. People use sunglasses to hide themselves. There is a particular art to taking off sunglasses, of choosing exactly the right moment to reveal yourself.

Jane Seymour, *Guide to Romantic Living* (1986)

## ❧ SUNRISE

8 I'll tell you how the Sun rose — / A Ribbon at a time.

Emily Dickinson (1860), in Mabel Loomis Todd and T.W. Higginson, eds., *Poems by Emily Dickinson* (1890)

9 A strip of pale daffodil, sharp as a razor blade, pried open the lid of the sky.

Phyllis Bottome, *Level Crossing* (1936)

10 Dawn is the child / wet with birth.

Charlotte DeClue, "Morning Song," in Joseph Bruchac, ed., *Songs From This Earth on Turtle's Back* (1983)

11 That leap up of the sun is as glad as a child's laugh; it is as a renewal of the world's youth.

Margaret Deland, *Florida Days* (1889)

12 So sudden and abrupt was the sunrise that the birds had to pretend they had been awake all the time.

Bessie Head, *When Rain Clouds Gather* (1969)

13 That is always such a forgiving time. When that first cold, bright streak comes over the water, it's as if all our sins were pardoned; as if the sky leaned over the earth and kissed it and gave it absolution.

Willa Cather, *My Mortal Enemy* (1926)

14 It was harder to drown at sunrise than in darkness.

Edith Wharton, *The House of Mirth* (1905)

15 In gold sandals / dawn like a thief / fell upon me.

Sappho (6th cent. B.C.), in Aliki Barnstone and Willis Barnstone, eds., *A Book of Women Poets From Antiquity to Now* (1980)

16 Dawn crept over the Downs like a sinister white animal, followed by the snarling cries of a wind eating its way between the black boughs of the thorns. The wind was the furious voice of this sluggish animal light that was baring the dormers and mullions and scullions of Cold Comfort Farm.

Stella Gibbons, *Cold Comfort Farm* (1932)

17 Dawn and its excesses always reminded me of heaven, a place where I have always known I would not be comfortable.

Marilynne Robinson, *Housekeeping* (1980)

18 Most people do not consider dawn to be an attractive experience—unless they are still up.

Ellen Goodman, *Close to Home* (1979)

See also Morning, Sun, Sunset.

## ❧ SUNSET

19 The sky broke like an egg into full sunset and the water caught fire.

Pamela Hansford Johnson, *The Unspeakable Skipton* (1981)

20 The sunset caught me, turned the brush to copper, / set the clouds / to one great roof of flame / above

the earth, / so that I walked through fire, beneath fire, / and all in beauty.

Elizabeth Coatsworth, "On the Hills," *Atlas and Beyond* (1924)

1 Each night the sunset surged with purple pampas-grass plumes, and shot fuchsia rockets into the pink sky, then deepened through folded layers of peacock green to all the blues of India and a black across which clouds sometimes churned like alabaster dolls. The visual opium of the sunset was what I craved.

Diane Ackerman, *A Natural History of the Senses* (1990)

2 The sun cast no rays, scarcely colored the sky around it, simply hung there on the earth's rim like the burning heart of creation.

Martha Ostenso, *The Dark Dawn* (1926)

3 The pale, cold light of the winter sunset did not beautify—it was like the light of truth itself.

Willa Cather, *My Ántonia* (1918)

4 Day is dying in the West; / Heav'n is touching the earth with rest.

Mary Artemisia Lathbury, "Evening Praise," *Poems of Mary Artemisia Lathbury* (1915)

See also Sun.

### ❧ SUPERFICIALITY

5 Deep down, I'm pretty superficial.

Ava Gardner, in John Robert Colombo, *Popcorn in Paradise* (1979)

6 Depth isn't everything: the spruce / has no taproot, but to hold on / spreads its underpinnings thin—.

Amy Clampitt, "The Spruce Has No Taproot," *What the Light Was Like* (1985)

### ❧ SUPERFLUITY

7 I . . . do not want anything else; it would be adding feet to a snake.

Han Suyin, *A Many-Splendored Thing* (1952)

See also Surplus.

### ❧ SUPERIORITY

8 When one clings to the myth of innate superiority, one must constantly overlook the virtues and abilities of others.

Anne Wilson Schaef, *Women's Reality* (1981)

9 His mistaken belief in his own superiority cut him off from reality as completely as if he were living in a colored glass jar.

Margery Allingham, *Traitor's Purse* (1941)

10 Giving up alcohol or cigarettes is a lead-pipe cinch compared to the renunciation of complacence by a former (self-appointed) elite.

Margaret Halsey, *No Laughing Matter* (1977)

11 Why do people who like to get up early look with disdain on those who like to lie in bed late? And why do people who like to work feel superior to those who prefer to dream?

Ruth Stout, *How to Have a Green Thumb Without an Aching Back* (1955)

12 What sense of superiority it gives one to escape reading some book which every one else is reading.

Alice James (1890), in Anna Robeson Burr, *Alice James* (1934)

13 You know how some people seem to think that their love for classical music makes them spiritual or at least something quite special? And others who think you are a monster if you don't "love children," however obnoxious the children may be? Well, I found out that many people who love flowers look down on those who don't.

Ruth Stout, *How to Have a Green Thumb Without an Aching Back* (1955)

14 And where does she find them?

Dorothy Parker, on hearing that Clare Boothe Luce was always kind to her inferiors, in Marion Meade, *Dorothy Parker: What Fresh Hell Is This?* (1988)

See also Discrimination, Equality, Oppression, Self-Importance.

### ❧ SUPERNATURAL

15 The supernatural is only the natural of which the laws are not yet understood.

Agatha Christie, title story, *The Hound of Death* (1933)

1 We have these instincts which defy all our wisdom and for which we never can frame any laws. . . . They are powers which are imperfectly developed in this life, but one cannot help the thought that the mystery of this world may be the commonplace of the next.

Sarah Orne Jewett, *Deephaven* (1877)

2 The science of tomorrow is the supernatural of today.

Agatha Christie, *The Pale Horse* (1961)

3 I knew in some marvelous way I had touched the hem of the unknown. And being me, I wanted to lift that hemline a little bit more.

Mae West, *Goodness Had Nothing to Do With It!* (1959)

See also Devil, Ghosts, God.

## ✣ SUPERSTITION

4 A little superstition is a good thing to keep in one's bag of precautions.

Gertrude Atherton, *Black Oxen* (1923)

5 No one is so thoroughly superstitious as the godless man.

Harriet Beecher Stowe, *Uncle Tom's Cabin* (1852)

6 There's a rule, I think. You get what you want in life, but not your second choice too.

Alison Lurie, *Real People* (1969)

7 The bad times I can handle. It's the good times that drive me crazy. When is the other shoe going to drop?

Erma Bombeck, *If Life Is a Bowl of Cherries, What Am I Doing in the Pits?* (1971)

See also Belief, Fear.

## ✣ SUPPORT

8 Those whom we support hold us up in life.

Marie von Ebner-Eschenbach, *Aphorisms* (1893)

9 There is no support so strong as the strength that enables one to stand alone.

Ellen Glasgow, "The Difference," *The Shadowy Third* (1923)

10 It was usual for the women of a household to do their own planting; but if a woman was sick, or for some reason was unable to attend to her planting, she sometimes cooked a feast, to which she invited the members of her age society and asked them to plant her field for her.

Buffalo Bird Woman, as told to Gilbert L. Wilson, *Buffalo Bird Woman's Garden* (1987)

11 I always wanted to be somebody. . . . If I've made it, it's half because I was game to take a wicked amount of punishment along the way and half because there were an awful lot of people who cared enough to help me.

Althea Gibson, *I Always Wanted to Be Somebody* (1958)

12 "Uncritical support" is a contradiction in terms.

Joanna Russ, "Power and Helplessness in the Women's Movement," in Christian McEwen and Sue O'Sullivan, eds., *Out the Other Side* (1988)

See also Friendship, Service, Sympathy.

## ✣ SURFING

13 Surfing is like that. You are either vigorously cursing or else you are idiotically pleased with yourself.

Agatha Christie, *The Man in the Brown Suit* (1924)

## ✣ SURGERY

14 Surgeons must be very careful / When they take the knife! / Underneath their fine incisions / Stirs the Culprit — *Life!*

Emily Dickinson (1859), in T.W. Higginson and Mabel Loomis Todd, eds., *Poems by Emily Dickinson*, 2nd series (1891)

15 He spoke of "going in" the way she'd heard old veterans in TV documentaries speak of assaults on enemy territory. . . . Except that what he would be going into was her body.

Margaret Atwood, "Hairball," *Wilderness Tips* (1991)

16 He just wanted to get that knife into me. He'd cut you if you had dandruff.

Fanny Brice, in Norman Katkov, *The Fabulous Fanny* (1952)

17 Fact One; Cataract surgery is simple, painless and (except with implants) risk free . . . the whole pro-

cedure is common, routine and nothing to worry about. Fact Two: Fact One applies only to cataracts on the eyes in somebody else's head.

    Helene Hanff, *Q's Legacy* (1985)

1 [I'm the] only topless octogenarian in Washington.

    Alice Roosevelt Longworth, after a double mastectomy, in Michael Teague, *Mrs. L.* (1981)

## ✦ SURPLUS

2 The world has become too full of many things, an overfurnished room.

    Freya Stark, *Ionia* (1954)

3 Any surplus is immoral.

    Jenny Holzer, *Truisms* (1979)

See also Profit, Quantity, Superfluity, Waste.

## ✦ SURPRISE

4 Surprises are like misfortunes or herrings—they rarely come single.

    L.E. Landon, *Romance and Reality* (1831)

5 Surprises are foolish things. The pleasure is not enhanced, and the inconvenience is often considerable.

    Jane Austen, *Emma* (1816)

6 I will not let another mail pass without giving you a piece of information which will, I fear, seriously disarrange your hair if you have not a very tight elastic to your net, and cause Mr. Boyce's hat to be lifted several inches above his head, if it is not a tolerably heavy one. It is neither more nor less than that I have been engaged for the last six months to Mr. Taylor.

    Rachel Henning (1865), *The Letters of Rachel Henning* (1963)

See also Shocking, Unexpected.

## ✦ SURVIVAL

7 Survival is a form of resistance.

    Gerda Lerner, chapter title, *Black Women in White America* (1972)

8 Surviving meant being born over and over.

    Erica Jong, *Fear of Flying* (1973)

9 When you get to the end of your rope—tie a knot in it and hang on.

    Eleanor Roosevelt, *You Learn by Living* (1960)

10 She endured. And survived. Marginally, perhaps, but it is not required of us that we live well.

    Anne Cameron, *Daughters of Copper Woman* (1981)

11 There is often in people to whom "the worst" has happened an almost transcendent freedom, for they have faced "the worst" and survived it.

    Carol Pearson, *The Hero Within* (1986)

12 Despite all the evils they wished to crush me with / I remain as steady as the three-legged cauldron.

    Monique Wittig, *Les Guérillères* (1969)

13 Surviving is important, but thriving is *elegant*.

    Maya Angelou, in Judith Paterson, "Interview: Maya Angelou," *Vogue* (1982)

14 I have not withdrawn into despair, I did not go mad in gathering honey, / I did not go mad, I did not go mad, I did not go mad.

    Hoda al-Namani, "I Remember I Was a Point, I Was a Circle," in Elizabeth Warnock Fernea, *Women and the Family in the Middle East* (1985)

15 Sometimes you don't know that the house you live in is glass until the stone you cast comes boomeranging back. Maybe that's the actual reason you threw it. Something in you was yelling, "I want out." The life you saved, as well as the glass you shattered, was your own.

    Jessamyn West, *A Matter of Time* (1966)

16 I survived my childhood by birthing many separate identities to stand in for one another in times of great stress and fear.

    Roseanne Arnold, *My Lives* (1994)

17 The guilt of outliving those you love is justly to be borne, she thought. Outliving is something we do to them. The fantasies of dying could be no stranger than the fantasies of living. Surviving is perhaps the strangest fantasy of them all.

    Eudora Welty, *The Optimist's Daughter* (1968)

18 Misfortune had made Lily supple instead of hardening her, and a pliable substance is less easy to break than a stiff one.

    Edith Wharton, *The House of Mirth* (1905)

1 "The unfit die: the fit both live and thrive." / Alas, who say so?—They who do survive.

> Sarah N. Cleghorn, "The Survival of the Fittest," *Portraits and Protests* (1917)

See also Endurance.


## ❧ SUSPENSE

2 I would rather feel the sword than behold it suspended.

> Regina Maria Roche, *Nocturnal Visit* (1800)


## ❧ SUSPICION

3 Once suspicion is aroused, every thing feeds it.

> Amelia E. Barr, *Jan Vedder's Wife* (1885)

4 The finger of suspicion never forgets the way it has once pointed.

> Anna Katharine Green, *The Leavenworth Case* (1878)

5 Suspicions grew in Edith's mind like little extra eyes.

> Margaret Millar, *The Iron Gates* (1945)

6 She mistakes suspicion for insight.

> Shirley Hazzard, *The Transit of Venus* (1980)

7 The china bowl which held her sanity and trust fell from its shelf in her mind and broke, and another reason for his lateness began to take shape in her thoughts with the same slow and inevitable accretion of detail as the child in her womb.

> Paule Marshall, *Praisesong for the Widow* (1983)

8 Nothing is so capable of overturning a good intention as to show a distrust of it; to be suspected for an enemy, is often sufficient to make a person become one.

> Marie de Rabutin-Chantal, Marquise de Sévigné (1670), *Letters of Madame de Sévigné to Her Daughter and Her Friends*, vol. 1 (1811)

9 Jealousy is the fear of losing the thing you love most. It's very normal. Suspicion is the thing that's abnormal.

> Jerry Hall, interview (1978)

See also Distrust, Doubt, Jealousy.


## ❧ SWEARING

10 Swearing is . . . learning to the ignorant, eloquence to the blockhead, vivacity to the stupid, and wit to the coxcomb.

> Mary Collyer, *Felicia to Charlotte* (1744)

11 Oaths and curses are a proof of a most heroic courage, at least in appearance, which answers the same end.

> Mary Collyer, *Felicia to Charlotte* (1744)

See also Obscenity.


## ❧ SWIMMING

12 This is no lake, / it's a flat blue egg. We peel / its shell and climb inside / like four spoons looking for the yolk.

> Ethna McKiernan, "One Summer's Lake," *Caravan* (1989)


## ❧ SYMBOLS

13 Symbols are the imaginative signposts of life.

> Margot Asquith, *More or Less About Myself* (1934)

14 That's the trouble, a sex symbol becomes a thing— I just hate to be a thing.

> Marilyn Monroe, in *Life* (1962)

15 Come to think of it, just about every tool was shaped like either a weenie or a pistol, depending on your point of view.

> Barbara Kingsolver, *The Bean Trees* (1989)

16 In many college English courses the words "myth" and "symbol" are given a tremendous charge of significance. You just ain't no good unless you can see a symbol hiding, like a scared gerbil, under every page. And in many creative writing courses the little beasts multiply, the place swarms with them. What does this Mean? What does that Symbolize? What is the Underlying Mythos? Kids come lurching out of such courses with a brain full of gerbils.

> Ursula K. Le Guin, "Myth and Archetype in Science Fiction" (1976), *Language of the Night* (1979)

## ❦ SYMPATHY

1 Sympathy is the charm of human life.

> Grace Aguilar, *The Mother's Recompense* (1851)

2 There are times when sympathy is as necessary as the air we breathe.

> Rose Pastor Stokes (1901), in Herbert Shapiro and David L. Sterling, eds., *"I Belong to the Working Class"* (1992)

3 The delicate and infirm go for sympathy, not to the well and buoyant, but to those who have suffered like themselves.

> Catharine Esther Beecher, "Statistics of Female Health," *Woman Suffrage and Woman's Professions* (1871)

4 Never does one feel oneself so utterly helpless as in trying to speak comfort for great bereavement.

> Jane Welsh Carlyle, letter to Thomas Carlyle on the death of his mother (1853), in James Anthony Froude, ed., *Letters and Memorials of Jane Welsh Carlyle*, vol. 2 (1883)

5 Since I heard that the mists of autumn had vanished and left desolate winter in your house, I have thought often of you as I watched the streaming sky.

> Lady Murasaki, *The Tale of Genji* (c. 1008)

See also Compassion, Consolation, Empathy, Pity, Virtue.

# T

## ❦ TABOOS

1 The type of figleaf which each culture employs to cover its social taboos offers a twofold description of its morality. It reveals that certain unacknowledged behavior exists and it suggests the form that such behavior takes.

   Freda Adler, *Sisters in Crime* (1975)

2 Our chief taboos are no longer conscious. They do not appear as themselves in our laws, and for the most part are not spoken of directly. But when we break them or even think of breaking them, our unconscious knowledge that we are violating sacred rules causes us to feel as if our lives are threatened, as if we may not be allowed to live.

   Sonia Johnson, *From Housewife to Heretic* (1981)

3 Taboos are falling across our culture like dominoes. What was unspeakable yesterday dominates talk shows today.

   Ellen Goodman, in *The Boston Globe* (1994)

See also Morality.

## ❦ TACT

4 Tact is after all a kind of mind-reading.

   Sarah Orne Jewett, *The Country of the Pointed Firs* (1896)

5 Tact is the ability to describe others as they see themselves.

   Mary Pettibone Poole, *A Glass Eye at a Keyhole* (1938)

6 There is something about conscious tact that is very irritating.

   Agatha Christie, *N or M?* (1941)

7 What a fine quality, what an absolute virtue Tact is. Lady Portmore never had a grain of it—a misfortune that fell more heavily on her friends than on herself.

   Emily Eden, *The Semi-Attached Couple* (1860)

See also Graciousness, Politeness.

## ❦ TALENT

8 Any talent that we are born with eventually surfaces as a need.

   Marsha Sinetar, *Do What You Love, the Money Will Follow* (1987)

9 Everyone has talent. What is rare is the courage to follow the talent to the dark place where it leads.

   Erica Jong, "The Artist As Housewife, The Housewife As Artist," in *Ms.* (1972)

10 We can't take any credit for our talents. It's how we use them that counts.

   Madeleine L'Engle, *A Wrinkle in Time* (1962)

11 Talent on its own sat gracefully only on the very young. After a certain age it was what you did with it that counted.

   Liza Cody, *Dupe* (1981)

12 The vocation exists, and so does the gift; but vocation and gift are seldom of equal proportions, and I suppose that the struggle to equate them is the true and secret tension.

   Mavis Gallant, in Susan Cahill, ed., *Women and Fiction 2* (1978)

13 We do not know and cannot tell when the spirit is with us. Great talent or small, it makes no difference. We are caught within our own skins, our own

sensibilities; we never know if our technique has been adequate to the vision.

Madeleine L'Engle, *Two-Part Invention* (1988)

1 He had all an artist needs, except the spark from the god.

Mary Renault, *The Mask of Apollo* (1966)

2 It is one thing to be gifted and quite another thing to be worthy of one's own gift.

Nadia Boulanger, in Don G. Campbell, *Reflections of Boulanger* (1982)

3 It all started when I was told that I had a gift. The gods are Yankee traders. There are no gifts. Everything has a price, and in bitter moments I have been tempted to cry "Usury!"

Bette Davis, *The Lonely Life* (1962)

4 In this world people have to pay an extortionate price for any exceptional gift whatever.

Willa Cather, title story, *The Old Beauty* (1948)

5 Gift, like genius, I often think, only means an infinite capacity for taking pains.

Ellice Hopkins, *Work Amongst Working Men* (1883)

6 Talent is the infinite capacity for taking pains. Genius is the infinite capacity for achievement without taking any pains at all.

Helene Hanff, *Q's Legacy* (1985)

7 Talent is like electricity. . . . Electricity makes no judgment. You can plug into it and light up a lamp, keep a heart pump going, light a cathedral, or you can electrocute a person with it. Electricity will do all that. It makes no judgment. I think talent is like that. I believe every person is born with talent.

Maya Angelou, in Claudia Tate, ed., *Black Women Writers at Work* (1983)

8 Patience is an integral part of talent.

Vicki Baum, *I Know What I'm Worth* (1964)

9 Timing and arrogance are decisive factors in the successful use of talent.

Marya Mannes, *Out of My Time* (1971)

10 The only thing that happens overnight is recognition. Not talent.

Carol Haney, in James Beasley Simpson, *Best Quotes of '54, '55, '56* (1957)

11 A career is born in public—talent in privacy.

Marilyn Monroe, in Gloria Steinem, "Marilyn: The Woman Who Died Too Soon," *Ms.* (1972)

12 Talent, like beauty, to be pardoned, must be obscure and unostentatious.

Lady Marguerite Blessington, in R.R. Madden, *The Literary Life and Correspondence of the Countess of Blessington*, vol. 1 (1855)

13 Talent is forgiven only in the dead; those who are still standing cast shadows.

Comtesse Diane, *Les Glanes de la Vie* (1898)

See also Ability, Genius, Sales Ability.

# ❦ TALKING

14 Every smart / Is eased in telling.

Georgiana Goddard King, *The Way of Perfect Love* (1909)

15 How often one talks not to hear what the other person has got to say, but to hear what one has got to say oneself!

Mary Coleridge (1891), in Theresa Whistler, ed., *The Collected Poems of Mary Coleridge* (1954)

16 To mention a loved object, a person, or a place to someone else is to invest that object with reality.

Anne Morrow Lindbergh, *North to the Orient* (1935)

17 The majority of the people who sought his advice really were hungry to be listened to and he insisted that talk was an outlet to be made available and free to all. "Mental gangrene isn't a disease of the garrulous," he liked to say.

Josephine Lawrence, *A Tower of Steel* (1943)

18 She talks with deliberation, as if pressing out a ruffle on each word.

Marcelene Cox, in *Ladies' Home Journal* (1942)

19 Why can't they ever let my wanderings alone?! Can't they understand that I'll talk it all to pieces if I have to tell about it.

Tove Jansson, *Tales From Moominvalley* (1963)

20 Sometimes too much talk / can kill a thing.

Paulette C. White, "A Black Revolutionary Poem," *Love Poem to a Black Junkie* (1975)

21 God gave you two eyes, two ears and one mouth. So you should watch and listen twice as much as you talk.

Lynne Alpern and Esther Blumenfeld, *Oh, Lord, I Sound Just Like Mama* (1986)

1 Chauncy Burr . . . talks well, possibly better than he thinks. But this is a common failing.

> Elizabeth Cady Stanton (1851), in Theodore Stanton and Harriot Stanton Blatch, eds., *Elizabeth Cady Stanton As Revealed in Her Letters Diary and Reminiscences*, vol. 2 (1922)

2 Like all talkers, she thought other people talked too much.

> Katherine Anne Porter, "Gertrude Stein: Three Views" (1927), *The Days Before* (1952)

3 Her tongue is hung in de middle and works both ways.

> Zora Neale Hurston, *Mules and Men* (1935)

4 His speech flows not from vanity or lust of praise, but from sheer necessity;—the reservoir is full, and runs over.

> Mary Russell Mitford, *Our Village* (1848)

5 Harry drowned his sorrows in talk, as other men drown theirs in wine, or in sport, or in taking some violent step. He intoxicated and soothed himself with conversation.

> Ada Leverson, *The Limit* (1911)

6 They . . . talk simply because they think sound is more manageable than silence.

> Margaret Halsey, *With Malice Toward Some* (1938)

7 He talks for the pleasure of his own voice, the way dogs bark and birds sing.

> Paulette Bates Alden, "Blue Mountains," *Feeding the Eagles* (1988)

8 Talking's just a nervous habit.

> Martha Grimes, *The Deer Leap* (1985)

9 I fear she wears herself out,—chiefly with *talking.* She cannot now moderate the habit; but I really fear she will shorten her days by it. On this account, it is well that she lives alone.

> Harriet Martineau (1841), in Valerie Sanders, ed., *Harriet Martineau: Selected Letters* (1990)

10 She probably labored under the common delusion that you made things better by talking about them.

> Rose Macaulay, *Crewe Train* (1926)

11 Which is it, I wonder, do I talk too much or does it merely seem to people that I talk too much? And which of those alternatives is the most disagreeable?

> Rebecca West, *The Birds Fall Down* (1966)

12 He was talking at the top of his ego.

> Miles Franklin, *Childhood at Brindabella* (1963)

13 "Well, Ipsie, all I can say is . . ." But she never said anything more, so perhaps that really was all she could say.

> Stella Benson, *Pipers and a Dancer* (1924)

14 "I suppose it's no use my saying anything. . ." he began, which usually meant he was going to have quite a lot to say.

> Margaret Mahy, *The Catalogue of the Universe* (1985)

15 Why is it that when anything goes without saying, it never does?

> Marcelene Cox, in *Ladies' Home Journal* (1948)

16 I know that after all is said and done, more is said than done.

> Rita Mae Brown, *In Her Day* (1976)

17 I am tempted to believe that much of the mischief . . . laid at the door of that poor unknown quantity *Thinking* is really due to its ubiquitous twin-brother *Talking.*

> Vernon Lee, "Against Talking," *Hortus Vitae* (1904)

18 Talking almost always smothers thinking.

> Margaret Deland, *Captain Archer's Daughter* (1932)

19 When a reserved person once begins to talk, nothing can stop him; and he does not want to have to listen, until he has quite finished his unfamiliar exertion.

> Phyllis Bottome, *Survival* (1943)

20 There was no way for me to understand it at the time, but the talk that filled the kitchen those afternoons was highly functional. It served as therapy, the cheapest kind available to my mother and her friends. . . . But more than therapy, that freewheeling, wide-ranging, exuberant talk functioned as an outlet for the tremendous creative energy they possessed.

> Paule Marshall, "The Making of a Writer: From the Poets in the Kitchen," in *The New York Times Book Review* (1983)

21 There are very few people who don't become more interesting when they stop talking.

> Mary Lowry, in *The Pacific Sun* (1985)

See also Conversation, Gossip, Listening, Speech, Storytelling.

## ❧ TASTE

1 Good taste is the worst vice ever invented.

> Edith Sitwell, in Elizabeth Salter, *The Last Years of a Rebel* (1967)

2 [Good taste] is a nineteenth-century concept. And good taste has never really been defined. The effort of projecting "good taste" is so studied that it offends me. No, I prefer to negate that. We have to put a period to so-called good taste.

> Louise Nevelson, *Dawns + Dusks* (1976)

3 A little bad taste is like a nice splash of paprika. We all need a splash of bad taste—it's hearty, it's healthy, it's physical. I think we could use *more* of it. *No* taste is what I'm against.

> Diana Vreeland, *D.V.* (1984)

4 Infallible taste is inconceivable; what could it be measured against?

> Pauline Kael, *I Lost It at the Movies* (1965)

5 Taste tends to develop very unevenly. It's rare that the same person has good visual taste *and* good taste in people *and* taste in ideas.

> Susan Sontag, "Notes on 'Camp'" (1964), *Against Interpretation* (1966)

6 No one ever went broke underestimating the taste of the American public.

> Liz Smith, in *Modern Maturity* (1994)

7 For those who like that sort of thing . . . that is the sort of thing they like.

> Muriel Spark, *The Prime of Miss Jean Brodie* (1961)

8 In every power of which taste is the foundation, excellence is pretty fairly divided between the sexes.

> Jane Austen, *Northanger Abbey* (1818)

9 Opinions: men's thoughts about great subjects. Taste: their thoughts about small ones: dress, behavior, amusements, ornaments.

> George Eliot, *Felix Holt, the Radical* (1866)

10 No argument can persuade me to like oysters if I do not like them. In other words, the disturbing thing about matters of taste is that they are not communicable.

> Hannah Arendt, *The Life of the Mind*, vol. 2 (1978)

11 Acquired tastes are the mark of the man of leisure.

> Margaret Kennedy, *The Ladies of Lyndon* (1925)

12 Good taste is his religion, his morality, his standard, and his test.

> L.E. Landon, *Romance and Reality* (1831)

13 The masses are still ungrateful or ignorant. They prefer murder, poisonings, and crimes generally to a literature possessed of style and feeling.

> George Sand (1863), in Raphaël Ledos de Beaufort, ed., *Letters of George Sand* (1886)

See also Judgment.

## ❧ TAXES

14 Only the little people pay taxes.

> Leona Helmsley, in *The Washington Post* (1989)

15 The Income-Tax presses more heavily on the possessors of small incomes than on the possessors of large incomes.

> Millicent Garrett Fawcett, *Political Economy for Beginners* (1870)

16 Why does a slight tax increase cost you two hundred dollars and a substantial tax cut save you thirty cents?

> Peg Bracken, *I Didn't Come Here to Argue* (1969)

17 Is there a phrase in the English language more fraught with menace than *a tax audit*?

> Erica Jong, *Parachutes & Kisses* (1984)

18 Father was the most unreconciled taxpayer I ever knew.

> Gladys Taber, *Especially Father* (1948)

19 It has been said that one man's loophole is another man's livelihood. Even if this is true, it certainly is not fair, because the loophole-livelihood of those who are reaping undeserved benefits can be the economic noose of those who are paying more than they should.

> Millicent Fenwick (1975), *Speaking Up* (1982)

See also Government.

## ❧ TEA

20 Gin is cheering and wine maketh glad the heart of man, but when you're in a real turmoil there's nothing like a good strong cup of tea.

> Anthony Gilbert, *Tenant for the Tomb* (1971)

1 Tea quenches tears and thirst.

> Jeanine Larmoth and Charlotte Turgeon, *Murder on the Menu* (1972)

2 Tea—that perfume that one drinks, that connecting hyphen.

> Natalie Clifford Barney, *Adventures of the Mind* (1929)

3 The tea-kettle is as much an English institution as aristocracy or the Prayer-Book.

> Catharine E. Beecher and Harriet Beecher Stowe, *American Woman's Home* (1869)

4 Ah, there's nothing like tea in the afternoon. When the British Empire collapses, historians will find that it had made but two invaluable contributions to civilization—this tea ritual and the detective novel.

> Ayn Rand, *The Fountainhead* (1943)

5 The tea-hour is the hour of peace. . . . Strife is lost in the hissing of the kettle—a tranquilizing sound, second only to the purring of a cat.

> Agnes Repplier, *To Think of Tea!* (1932)

6 Bernie made the kind of tea a mouse could stand on.

> Liza Cody, *Dupe* (1981)

7 [He] offered to make a cup of tea, the British specific against disaster, grief and shock.

> P.D. James, *A Taste for Death* (1986)

8 Tea to the English is really a picnic indoors.

> Alice Walker, *The Color Purple* (1982)

9 It took her a long time to prepare her tea; but when ready it was set forth with as much grace as if she had been a veritable guest to her own self.

> Mary E. Wilkins Freeman, title story, *A New England Nun* (1891)

10 I stir wild honey into my carefully prepared cedar tea / and wait for meaning to arise, / to greet and comfort me.

> Paula Gunn Allen, "Recuerdo," in Joseph Bruchac, ed., *Songs From This Earth on Turtle's Back* (1983)

11 It was the usual "zoo tea." You know, we eat—the others watch.

> Princess Margaret of England, on public receptions attended by royalty, news item (1954)

## ❦ TEACHING

12 Teaching is the royal road to learning.

> Jessamyn West, *The Life I Really Lived* (1979)

13 Teaching consists of equal parts perspiration, inspiration, and resignation.

> Susan Ohanian, *Ask Ms. Class* (1996)

14 Good teaching is one-fourth preparation and three-fourths theater.

> Gail Godwin, *The Odd Woman* (1974)

15 A teacher's day is half bureaucracy, half crisis, half monotony, and one-eightieth epiphany. Never mind the arithmetic.

> Susan Ohanian, *Ask Ms. Class* (1996)

16 If there was one eager eye, one doubting, critical mind, one lively curiosity in a whole lecture-room full of commonplace boys and girls, he was its servant. That ardor could command him.

> Willa Cather, *The Professor's House* (1925)

17 When I teach people I marry them.

> Sylvia Ashton-Warner, *Teacher* (1963)

18 What was the duty of the teacher if not to inspire?

> Bharati Mukherjee, "Buried Lives," *The Middleman* (1988)

19 The greatest sign of success for a teacher . . . is to be able to say, "The children are now working as if I did not exist."

> Maria Montessori, *The Absorbent Mind* (1949)

20 The task of a teacher is not to work for the pupil nor to oblige him to work, but to show him how to work.

> Wanda Landowska, in Denise Restout, ed., *Landowska on Music* (1964)

21 We teachers can only help the work going on, as servants wait upon a master.

> Maria Montessori, *The Absorbent Mind* (1964)

22 I am teaching. . . . It's kind of like having a love affair with a rhinoceros.

> Anne Sexton (1970), in Linda Gray Sexton and Lois Ames, eds., *Anne Sexton: A Self-Portrait in Letters* (1977)

23 Not just part of us becomes a teacher. It engages the whole self—the woman or man, wife or husband, mother or father, the lover, scholar or artist in you as well as the teacher earning money.

> Sylvia Ashton-Warner, *Myself* (1967)

1  Everybody is now so busy teaching that nobody has any time to learn.

   Agnes Repplier, "Mr. Wilde's *Intentions*," *Essays in Miniature* (1892)

2  We teach what we need to learn.

   Gloria Steinem, *Revolution From Within* (1993)

3  To teach one's self is to be forced to learn twice.

   Ellen Glasgow, *The Woman Within* (1954)

4  The only good teachers for you are those friends who love you, who think you are interesting, or very important, or wonderfully funny.

   Brenda Ueland, *If You Want to Write* (1938)

5  Do you know any other business or profession where highly-skilled specialists are required to tally numbers, alphabetize cards, put notices into mailboxes, and patrol the lunchroom?

   Bel Kaufman, *Up the Down Staircase* (1964)

See also Education, Knowledge, Learning.

## ❦ TEARS

6  Rich tears! What power lies in those falling drops.

   Mary Delarivière Manley, *The Royal Mischief* (1696)

7  Delicious tears! the heart's own dew.

   L.E. Landon, "The Guerilla Chief," *The Improvisatrice* (1824)

8  Tears are a river that take you somewhere. . . . Tears lift your boat off the rocks, off dry ground, carrying it downriver to someplace new, someplace better.

   Clarissa Pinkola Estés, *Women Who Run With the Wolves* (1992)

9  The longing to be holy makes us weep, and we trust tears since they are made of water and come from our body, a double blessing.

   Deborah Keenan, "Grace," *The Only Window That Counts* (1985)

10  How dry eyes can get when they are not allowed to cry!

   Maria Augusta Trapp, *The Story of the Trapp Family Singers* (1949)

11  Frequent tears have run / The colors from my life.

   Elizabeth Barrett Browning, *Sonnets From the Portuguese* (1850)

12  It is not always sorrow that opens the fountains of the eyes.

   Marie de Rabutin-Chantal, Marquise de Sévigné (1680), *Letters of Madame de Sévigné to Her Daughter and Her Friends*, vol. 6 (1811)

See also Crying, Sorrow.

## ❦ TECHNOLOGY

13  Technology evolves so much faster than wisdom.

   Jennifer Stone, "Sexual Politics in the Stone Age," *Mind Over Media* (1988)

14  Americans . . . attach such a fantastic importance to their baths and plumbing and gadgets of all sorts. They talk as if people could hardly be human beings without all that; we in Europe are beginning to wonder if people can be human beings *with* it.

   Ann Bridge, *Singing Waters* (1946)

15  One tends to assume that if you don't have, at least, a lavatory and perhaps something that will take you a lot faster than your own feet, or a certain number of gadgets in the house, then you must be in some way, a bit backward and defective. . . . The important thing to remember is that technology is not necessarily the same thing as civilization.

   Jacquetta Hawkes, in Joseph McCulloch, *Under Bow Bells* (1974)

16  America's technology has turned in upon itself; its corporate form makes it the servant of profits, not the servant of human needs.

   Alice Embree, "Media Images I: Madison Avenue Brainwashing—the Facts," in Robin Morgan, ed., *Sisterhood Is Powerful* (1970)

17  There is no monster more destructive than the inventive mind that has outstripped philosophy.

   Ellen Glasgow, *Letters of Ellen Glasgow* (1958)

See also Machines.

## ❦ TEETH

18  Beastly things, teeth. Give us trouble from the cradle to the grave.

   Agatha Christie, *At Bertram's Hotel* (1965)

1 Now then, with teeth or without?

> Queen Elizabeth II, before each of numerous portrait sittings, in Robert Lacey, *Majesty* (1977)

See also Dentists, Mouth.

## ❧ TELEPHONE

2 Oh, how often I wished that Thomas A. Watson had laid a restraining hand on A.G. Bell's arm and had said to him, "Let's not and say we did."

> Jean Mercier, *Whatever You Do, Don't Panic* (1961)

3 The interruptions of the telephone seem to us to waste half the life of the ordinary American engaged in public or private business; he has seldom half an hour consecutively at his own disposal—a telephone is a veritable *time scatterer*.

> Beatrice Webb (1898), in David A. Shannon, ed., *Beatrice Webb's American Diary* (1963)

4 Everybody is always after us to get a phone. We hate phones! . . . if the phone company installed a phone for free and paid for a man to stand there and answer it for us, seven days a week, we *still* wouldn't want a phone!

> Sadie Delany, in Sarah and A. Elizabeth Delany, with Amy Hill Hearth, *Having Our Say* (1993)

5 By inventing the telephone we've damaged the chances of telepathy.

> Dorothy M. Richardson, *Pilgrimage: Revolving Lights* (1923)

6 It is not rude to turn off your telephone by switching it on to an answering machine, which is cheaper and less disruptive than ripping it out of the wall. Those who are offended because they cannot always get through when they seek, at their own convenience, to barge in on people are suffering from a rude expectation.

> Judith Martin, *Miss Manners' Guide for the Turn-of-the-Millennium* (1989)

7 Hi, this is Sylvia. I'm not at home right now, so when you hear the beep . . . hang up.

> Nicole Hollander, book title (1983)

8 At the end of every year, I add up the time that I have spent on the phone on hold and subtract it from my age. I don't count that time as really liv-ing. I spend more and more time on hold each year. By the time I die, I'm going to be quite young.

> Rita Rudner, *Naked Beneath My Clothes* (1992)

9 All phone calls are obscene.

> Karen Elizabeth Gordon, *The Well-Tempered Sentence* (1983)

10 When a telephone rings, the average man settles deeper into his chair with the observation, "I wonder who that can be?"

> Marcelene Cox, in *Ladies' Home Journal* (1945)

11 Remember that as a teenager you are at the last stage in your life when you will be happy to hear that the phone is for you.

> Fran Lebowitz, *Social Studies* (1977)

12 Long distance calls also affect my vocal cords so that whoever I'm talking to thinks he has been mistakenly connected with the porch rocker.

> Betty MacDonald, *Onions in the Stew* (1955)

13 In the manner of all humans, who are convinced the one call gone unanswered must be The Call, the hot-line from the Universe, Jury weakened and plucked up the receiver.

> Martha Grimes, *The Anodyne Necklace* (1983)

14 Is this the party to whom I am speaking?

> Lily Tomlin, as "Ernestine," on Rowan and Martin's "Laugh-In" (1969)

15 E.T., phone home.

> Melissa Mathison, *E.T.* (1982)

See also Communication.

## ❧ TELEVISION

16 Plato has an analogy for the unenlightened mind: people living all their lives chained inside a cave, so that all they can see is shadows cast by the fire onto the opposite wall. "Would they not assume," asks Plato, "that the shadows they saw were real things?" He should see how we've made his comparison a literal fact of our lives.

> Alice Furlaud, *Air Fair* (1989)

17 People are growing up in the slack flicker of . . . a pale, wavering, oblong shimmer, emitting incessant noise, which is to real knowledge or discourse what the manic or weepy protestations of a drunk

are to responsible speech. Drunks do have a way of holding an audience, though, and so does the shimmery ill-focused oblong screen.

Adrienne Rich, *On Lies, Secrets, and Silence* (1979)

1 Have you noticed that screens are taking over? . . . It's as if people can't be comfortable for a minute without something flashing on a screen nearby.

Alice Furlaud, *Air Fair* (1989)

2 The illusion of companionship sits waiting in the television set. We keep our televisions on more than we watch them—an average of more than seven hours a day. For background. For company.

Louise Bernikow, *Alone in America* (1986)

3 For perhaps most Americans, TV is an appliance, not to be used selectively but to be turned on— there's always something to watch.

Pauline Kael, *Reeling* (1976)

4 The familiar patter of the television, the familiar voices saying the familiar things, the canned, familiar laughter came between her and her fears like a belt of static and reassured her that nothing changed, that everything stayed the same.

Cecil Dawkins, *Charleyhorse* (1985)

5 The box sanctified, conferred identity. The more familiar the face, the more to be trusted.

P.D. James, *Innocent Blood* (1980)

6 If it was on TV, it must be so. Calendars were tricky and church bells might fool you, but if you heard Ed Sullivan's voice you *knew* it was Sunday night.

Linda Ellerbee, *Move On* (1991)

7 Television and radio violence was considered by most experts of minimal importance as a contributory cause of youthful killing. . . . There were always enough experts to assure the public that crime and violence had nothing to do with crime and violence.

Marya Mannes, "The Conquest of Trigger Mortis," *But Will It Sell?* (1964)

8 Television emphasizes the deviant so that it becomes normal. . . . It's become more and more difficult for people to know the difference between fame and infamy.

Vicki Abt, on television talk shows, news item (1994)

9 On the news two dozen events of fantastically different importance are announced in exactly the same tone of voice. The voice doesn't discriminate between a divorce, a horse race, a war in the Middle East.

Doris Lessing, in Jonah Raskin, "Doris Lessing at Stony Brook," *New American Review 8* (1970)

10 A disturbing possibility exists that the television experience has not merely blurred the distinctions between the real and the unreal for steady viewers, but that by doing so it has dulled their sensitivities to real events. For when the reality of a situation is diminished, people are able to react to it less emotionally, more as spectators.

Marie Winn, *The Plug-In Drug* (1977)

11 TV is a language all its own, a land of one dimensional stereotypes that destroys culture, not adds to it. TV is anti-art, a reflection of consumerism that serves the power structure. TV is about demographics.

Roseanne Arnold, *My Lives* (1994)

12 In television the product is not the program; the product is the audience and the consumer of that product is the advertiser. The advertiser does not "buy" a news program. He buys an audience.

Linda Ellerbee, *"And So It Goes"* (1986)

13 Even if every program were educational and every advertisement bore the seal of approval of the American Dental Association, we would still have a critical problem. It's not just the programs but the act of watching television hour after hour after hour that's destructive.

Ellen Goodman, *Close to Home* (1979)

14 To a certain extent the child's early television experiences will serve to dehumanize, to mechanize, to make less *real* the realities and relationships he encounters in life. For him, real events will always carry subtle echoes of the television world.

Marie Winn, *The Plug-In Drug* (1977)

15 Until a child can meet reality, he must live in fantasy. But he must create his own fantasy. And it is television's primary damage that it provides ten million children with the same fantasy, ready-made and on a platter.

Marya Mannes, *More in Anger* (1958)

16 [Television viewing] is a one-way transaction that requires the taking in of particular sensory material in a particular way, no matter what the material might be. There is, indeed, no other experience in

a child's life that permits quite so much intake while demanding so little outflow.

Marie Winn, *The Plug-In Drug* (1977)

1 Educational television should be absolutely forbidden. It can only lead to unreasonable expectations and eventual disappointment when your child discovers that the letters of the alphabet do not leap up out of books and dance around the room with royal-blue chickens.

Fran Lebowitz, *Social Studies* (1977)

2 The six and one-fourth hours' television watching (the American average per day) which non-reading children do is what is called alpha-level learning. The mind needn't make any pictures since the pictures are provided, so the mind cuts current as low as it can.

Carol Bly, *The Passionate, Accurate Story* (1990)

3 In its effect on family relationships, in its facilitation of parental withdrawal from an active role in the socialization of their children, and in its replacement of family rituals and special events, television has played an important role in the disintegration of the American family.

Marie Winn, *The Plug-In Drug* (1977)

4 Television has proved that people will look at anything rather than each other.

Ann Landers, in Bob Chieger, *Was It Good for You, Too?* (1983)

5 There are days when any electrical appliance in the house, including the vacuum cleaner, seems to offer more entertainment possibilities than the TV set.

Harriet Van Horne, in *New York World-Telegram & Sun* (1957)

6 There is something spurious about the very term "a movie made for TV," because what you make for TV is a TV program.

Pauline Kael, *Reeling* (1976)

7 Television represents what happens to a medium when the artists have no power and the businessmen are in full, unquestioned control.

Pauline Kael, *Reeling* (1976)

8 TV by and large has become a dime-store business so far as creativity and talent are concerned. The half-hour and sixty-minute series rattle off the production lines like cans of beans, with an occasional dab of ham inside.

Hedda Hopper, with James Brough, *The Whole Truth and Nothing But* (1963)

9 Television as we have it isn't an art form—it's a piece of furniture that is good for a few things.

Pauline Kael, *Reeling* (1976)

10 TV has created a kind of false collectivity.

Adrienne Rich, in *The Hungry Mind Review* (1992)

11 Television has opened many doors—mostly on refrigerators.

Mary H. Waldrip, in *Reader's Digest* (1989)

12 She claimed I had something she called Star Trek Amnesia, she said I would purposely forget having seen an episode until the last ten minutes of the show, then I'd say, oh yeah, I remember this, but by then it was too late, I'd just go ahead and finish it.

Cass Nevada, "Commercial Breaks," in Naomi Holoch and Joan Nestle, eds., *Women on Women 2* (1993)

13 It was Tark's experience that TV addicts were usually addicted to something else as well. Food, booze, drugs, sex, money, take your pick.

T.J. MacGregor, *Storm Surge* (1993)

14 I asked Mr. Vann which O levels you need to write situation comedy for television. Mr. Vann said that you don't need qualifications at all, you just need to be a moron.

Sue Townsend, *The Secret Diary of Adrian Mole Aged 13-3/4* (1982)

15 When television is bad, nothing is worse. When television is good, it's not much better. Why do you think it's called a medium?

Susan Ohanian, *Ask Ms. Class* (1996)

16 I'm always amazed that people will actually choose to sit in front of the television and just be savaged by stuff that belittles their intelligence.

Alice Walker, in Brian Lanker, *I Dream a World* (1989)

17 McLuhanism and the media have broken the back of the book business; they've freed people from the shame of not reading. They've rationalized becoming stupid and watching television.

Pauline Kael, *Deeper Into Movies* (1973)

18 My dream is someday to have a bank of TVs, where all the different channels could be on and I could

be monitoring them. I would love that. The more the better. I love the tabloid stuff. The trashier the program is, the more I feel it's TV. . . . Because that's TV's mode. That's the Age of Hollywood. The idea of PBS—heavy-duty *Masterpiece Theater*, Bill Moyers—I hate all that.

> Camille Paglia, with Stewart Brand, "Hollywood: America's Greatest Achievement," in *The Utne Reader* (1994)

See also Entertainment, Hollywood, Media, Violence.

## ❦ TEMPERAMENT

1 Is there *any* other slavery and chain like that of temperament.

> Mrs. Humphry Ward, *The History of David Grieve* (1891)

2 Some time in our lives every man and woman of us, putting out our hands toward the stars, touch on either side our prison walls the immutable limitations of temperament.

> Margaret Deland, *Philip and His Wife* (1894)

3 Temperament is something that is an integral part of the artist. Not temper, temperament. There is a vast difference.

> Bette Davis, *The Lonely Life* (1962)

4 The artistic temperament . . . sometimes seems to me to be a battleground, a dark angel of destruction and a bright angel of creativity wrestling, and when the bright angel dominates, out comes a great work of art, a Michelangelo *David* or a Beethoven symphony.

> Madeleine L'Engle, *A Severed Wasp* (1982)

5 Romer's mother, looking intensely cross—it was her form of deep thought—was re-embroidering. . . . She had that decadent love of minute finish in the unessential so often seen in persons of a nervous yet persistent temperament.

> Ada Leverson, *The Limit* (1911)

6 Mrs. Bennett was restored to her usual querulous serenity.

> Jane Austen, *Pride and Prejudice* (1813)

7 She was one of those small tight-lipped neurotics who sometimes turn to religion and now and then to crime.

> Mary Roberts Rinehart, *Miss Pinkerton* (1932)

8 She had been born with the bit in her teeth. Jerry had never done anything he wanted to since he had married her, and he hadn't really wanted to do that.

> Kate Douglas Wiggin, "The Midnight Cry," *The Village Watch-Tower* (1895)

9 Gray hair, glasses, and an expression that made Sader suspect her husband gambled or drank, and that she forgave him for it.

> Dolores Hitchens, *Sleep With Slander* (1960)

10 She was a woman of mean understanding, little information, and uncertain temper.

> Jane Austen, *Pride and Prejudice* (1813)

11 His cravings and dreams were not for somebody to be devoted to, but for somebody to be devoted to him. And, like most people who possess this characteristic, he mistook it for an affectionate disposition.

> Harriet Beecher Stowe, *The Pearl of Orr's Island* (1862)

12 No temper could be more cheerful than hers, or possess, in a greater degree, that sanguine expectation of happiness which is happiness itself.

> Jane Austen, *Sense and Sensibility* (1911)

13 She is one of those impressive women who usually head committees on supervising movies, taking the entire sixth grade on a tour of one of our local factories, or outlawing slingshots, and I daresay she would be the first person everyone would think of if there should arise an occasion for the mothers to lift the school building and carry it bodily to another location.

> Shirley Jackson, *Life Among the Savages* (1953)

14 Aunt Celia is one of those persons who are born to command, and when they are thrown in contact with those who are born to be commanded all goes as merry as a marriage bell; otherwise not.

> Kate Douglas Wiggin, *A Cathedral Courtship* (1893)

15 She was a pink, flabby, irresponsible person, adjusting comfortably the physical burden of too much flesh to the spiritual repose of too little mind. . . . As the mother of children so numerous that their father could not be trusted to remember their names, she still welcomed the yearly addition to her family with the moral serenity of a rabbit.

> Ellen Glasgow, *Barren Ground* (1925)

1 He was a bit like a corkscrew. Twisted, cold and sharp.

> Kate Cruise O'Brien, "A Just Desert," *A Gift Horse* (1978)

2 Dramatic natures are not often insincere, they are only unreal.

> Margaret Deland, *The Way to Peace* (1910)

3 I have sometimes wondered also whether in people like me who come to the boil fast (*soupe au lait*, the French call this trait, like a milk soup that boils over) the tantrum is not a built-in safety valve against madness or illness.

> May Sarton, *Journal of a Solitude* (1973)

4 His movements were supremely deliberate and his pronouncements infinitely calculated; he moved through life like a man who found himself crossing a gorge on a high wire without a net.

> Lucille Kallen, *Introducing C.B. Greenfield* (1979)

5 Mad, bad and dangerous to know.

> Lady Caroline Lamb, after meeting Lord Byron, *Journal* (1812)

See also Behavior, Character, Personality.

## ✤ TEMPERANCE

6 No man who drank or smoked could ever come nearer to me than the telephone. I'd say, I won't let you—you nicotine-soaked, beer-besmeared, whiskey-greased, red-eyed devil—talk to me face to face.

> Carry Nation (1901), in Carleton Beals, *Cyclone Carry* (1962)

7 A Pittsburgh factory is making me a lot of hatchets on which will be the words: "Carry Nation's Loving Home Defenders. Smash the Saloon and build up the home."

> Carry Nation (1903), in Carleton Beals, *Cyclone Carry* (1962)

8 This appeal is made to the gentle, loving brave Christian women whose hearts are breaking with sympathy for the oppressed. . . . Bring your hatchets.

> Carry Nation, calling for volunteers for a "smashing" to protest drinking, in *The Topeka Journal* (1904)

9 Destroyer of the works of the Devil by the direct order of God.

> Carry Nation, when asked her occupation (1901), in Carleton Beals, *Cyclone Carry* (1962)

See also Prohibition.

## ✤ TEMPTATION

10 Where there is no temptation, there is no virtue.

> Agnes Repplier, "Conservative's Consolations," *Points of Friction* (1920)

11 To tempt and be tempted is much the same thing.

> Catherine the Great (1750), in Dominique Maroger, ed., *The Memoirs of Catherine the Great* (1955)

12 The most dangerous temptations are not due to the active, sudden flames of desire, "the lusts of the flesh," but to the disinclinations of the flesh, its indolence and sluggishness, our tendency to become creatures of habit.

> Sigrid Undset, *Men, Women, and Places* (1939)

13 We've all of us got to meet the devil alone. Temptation is a lonely business.

> Margaret Deland, *Dr. Lavendar's People* (1903)

14 Temptation almost always assails us at the point where we thought no defense necessary.

> Elizabeth Elton Smith, *The Three Eras of Woman's Life* (1836)

15 Let them who are temted to do wrong consider what they are about and turn away filled with horror dread and affright.

> Marjorie Fleming, age 8 (1811), in L. MacBean, *Marjorie Fleming's Book* (1903)

16 Temptations make one very censorious. If you are virtuous you condemn the wicked and if you are wicked, you condemn the virtuous.

> Elizabeth Bibesco, *The Fir and the Palm* (1924)

17 Better to enjoy and suffer than sit around with folded arms. You know the only true prayer? Please God, lead me into temptation.

> Jennie Lee, *My Life With Nye* (1980)

18 I generally avoid temptation unless I can't resist it.

> Mae West, in *My Little Chickadee* (1940)

## ❧ TENDERNESS

1 Tenderness is greater proof of love than the most passionate of vows.

Marlene Dietrich, *Marlene Dietrich's ABC* (1962)

See also Gentleness.

## ❧ TENNIS

2 Tennis . . . was founded on gentility. It is a very civil ritual.

Sue Cobb, *The Edge of Everest* (1989)

3 It is a game of moving chess. . . . It combines the exactitude of billiards, the coordination of hand and eye of lawn tennis and the generalship and quick judgment of polo.

Allison Danzig, *The Racquet Game* (1930)

4 The moment I stepped onto that crunchy red clay, felt the grit under my sneakers, felt the joy of smacking a ball over the net, I knew I was in the right place. I was probably about six years old.

Martina Navratilova, with George Vecsey, *Martina* (1985)

5 Good shot, bad luck and hell are the five basic words to be used in a game of tennis.

Virginia Graham, *Say Please* (1949)

6 My game was rushing the net, playing aggressively, playing for fun, playing to win. . . . There are times when I've played my life just like a tennis game.

Martina Navratilova, with George Vecsey, *Martina* (1985)

See also Sports.

## ❧ TERRORISM

7 Terrorism thrives on a free society. The terrorist uses the feelings in a free society to sap the will of civilization to resist. If the terrorist succeeds, he has won and the whole of free society has lost.

Margaret Thatcher, speech (1986), *In Defense of Freedom* (1986)

8 In the new world economy of terror, the currency is us.

Susan J. Berkson, in *The Minneapolis Star Tribune* (1995)

9 We must try to find ways to starve the terrorist and the hijacker of the oxygen of publicity on which they depend.

Margaret Thatcher, in *The London Times* (1985)

See also Violence.

## ❧ TEXAS

10 In Texas the lid blew off the sky a long time ago / So there's nothing to keep the wind from blowing / And it blows all the time.

May Sarton, "In Texas," *The Lion and the Rose* (1948)

11 No one has ever accused Texas of being in the vanguard of social progress. This is the most *macho* state in the U.S. of A. By lore, legend, and fact, Texas is "hell" on women and horses.

Molly Ivins, "The Women Who Run Texas," in *McCall's* (1990)

12 Texans do not talk like other Americans. . . . *Shit* is a three-syllable word with a *y* in it.

Molly Ivins, "Texas Observed" (1972), *Molly Ivins Can't Say That, Can She?* (1991)

13 Take Texas the way Texas takes bourbon. Straight. It goes down easier.

Edna Ferber, *Giant* (1952)

14 Here in Texas maybe we've got into the habit of confusing bigness with greatness.

Edna Ferber, *Giant* (1952)

## ❧ THANKSGIVING

15 Over the river, and through the wood, / To grandfather's house we go; / The horse knows the way, / To carry the sleigh, / Through the white and drifted snow.

Lydia Maria Child, "The New-England Boy's Song," *Flowers for Children* (1845)

16 Thanksgiving is a typically *American* holiday. In spite of its religious form (giving thanks to God for a good harvest), its essential, secular meaning is a *celebration of successful production*. It is a producers' holiday. The lavish meal is a symbol of the fact

that abundant consumption is the result and reward of production.

   Ayn Rand, in *The Ayn Rand Letter* (1971)

1 Many of the guests will eventually leave the table to
watch football on television, which would be a
rudeness at any other occasion but is a relief at
Thanksgiving and probably the only way to get
those people to budge.

   Judith Martin, *Miss Manners' Guide to Excruciatingly
   Correct Behavior* (1982)

See also Food.


## 𝄞 THEATER

2 Here were blood, lust, love, passion. Here were
warmth, enchantment, laughter, music. It was
Anodyne. It was Lethe. It was Escape. It was the
Theater.

   Edna Ferber, *Show Boat* (1926)

3 When God conceived the world, that was Poetry;
he formed it, and that was Sculpture; he colored it,
and that was Painting; and then, crowning work of
all, he peopled it with living beings, and that was
the grand, divine, eternal Drama.

   Charlotte Cushman, in Clara Erskine Clement, *Charlotte
   Cushman* (1882)

4 That winter two things happened that made me see
that the world, the flesh, and the devil were going
to be more powerful influences in my life after all
than the chapel bell. First, I tasted champagne; second, the theater.

   Belle Livingstone, *Belle Out of Order* (1959)

5 Theater is a verb before it is a noun, an act before
it is a place.

   Martha Graham, in Arlene Croce, *Afterimages* (1976)

6 Drama is made up of what people most fear and
deny in themselves. The taboos. The secrets. The
devils and the demons. The only reason they let us
live, I suppose, is because somebody has to confront what those things are like and tell other people about them.

   Elizabeth Ashley, with Ross Firestone, *Actress* (1978)

7 In the theater lying is looked upon as an occupational disease.

   Tallulah Bankhead, *Tallulah* (1952)

8 The theater, when it is potent enough to deserve its
ancestry, is always dangerous.

   Hallie Flanagan, *Dynamo* (1943)

9 Theater is by nature political.

   Naomi Thornton, in Sara Ruddick and Pamela Daniels,
   eds., *Working It Out* (1977)

10 It is best in the theater to act with confidence no
matter how little right you have to it.

   Lillian Hellman, *Pentimento* (1973)

11 Failure in the theater is more dramatic and uglier
than in any other form of writing. It costs so much,
you feel so guilty.

   Lillian Hellman, in George Plimpton, ed., *Writers at Work*,
   3rd series (1967)

12 Theater people are always pining and agonizing
because they're afraid that they'll be forgotten. And
in America they're quite right. They will be.

   Agnes de Mille, in Jane Howard, "The Grande Dame of
   Dance," *Life* (1963)

13 The first night is the worst possible time to make a
hard and fast criticism: the baby never looks its best
on the day it is born.

   Margot Fonteyn, *Margot Fonteyn* (1975)

14 Never has the theatrical profession been more
overcrowded than at the present moment.

   Mrs. Alec-Tweedie, *Behind the Footlights* (1904)

15 It's one of the tragic ironies of the theater that only
one man in it can count on steady work—the night
watchman.

   Tallulah Bankhead, *Tallulah* (1952)

16 The theater has fallen into the hands of real estate
men and syndicates and those who have no love or
interest in the stage or its life, but who have considered it principally as a means to make money.

   Eva Le Gallienne (1932), in Robert A. Schanke, *Shattered
   Applause* (1992)

17 On Broadway money rules. Like a host of vultures,
the ticket brokers, the speculators, the craft unions,
the agents, the backers, the real estate owners move
in on the creative body and take their bite. The
world of dreams breathes in an iron lung; and without this mechanical pumping it dies.

   Marya Mannes, *The New York I Know* (1961)

18 The theater should be free to the people just as the
Public Library is free, just as the museum is free....

I want the theater to be made accessible to the people.

Eva Le Gallienne (1926), in Robert A. Schanke, *Shattered Applause* (1992)

1  There is no better indication of what the people of any period are like than the plays they go to see.

Edith Hamilton, *The Roman Way* (1932)

2  People pay all that money to sit in a chair in the theater mainly because it is a respectable way to see and experience things they cannot see and experience in their own lives.

Elizabeth Ashley, with Ross Firestone, *Actress* (1978)

3  The theater is the only branch of art much cared for by people of wealth; like canasta, it does away with the bother of talk after dinner.

Mary McCarthy, "Up the Ladder From *Charm* to *Vogue*" (1950), *On the Contrary* (1961)

See also Acting, Applause, Audience, Criticisms, Performance, Playwrights, Stage and Screen.

## ❧ THEFT

4  She took a little picture of M. de Turenne from madame d'Elbeuf, who used to wear it on her arm. Madame d'Elbeuf asked her for it several times; she always told her, she had lost it, but we guess it is not lost to every one.

Marie de Rabutin-Chantal, Marquise de Sévigné (1675), *Letters of Madame de Sévigné to Her Daughter and Her Friends*, vol. 3 (1811)

5  I asked a man in prison once how he happened to be there and he said he had stolen a pair of shoes. I told him if he had stolen a railroad he would be a United States Senator.

Mother Jones, in Mary Field Parton, *The Autobiography of Mother Jones* (1925)

6  A man does not steal from one victim only, but from everyone who comes near to the theft.

Margaret Lee Runbeck, *The Year of Love* (1956)

See also Borrowing, Crime, Dishonesty, Plagiarism.

## ❧ THEOLOGY

7  This is the purpose of theology. By it my life becomes clearer and more conscious.

Dorothee Sölle, *The Truth Is Concrete* (1967)

8  Just as it is the province of science to find out what the facts of life are, to classify them and use them to verify or discredit whatever theory may have been advanced concerning them, so it is the province of a living theology to be constantly seeking from God the wit and wisdom that will interpret anew and more truly the parable of life.

Lily Dougall, "The Undiscovered Country," in B.H. Streeter et al., *Immortality* (1917)

9  All theology knowingly or not is by definition always engaged for or against the oppressed.

Elisabeth Schüssler Fiorenza, *Bread Not Stone* (1984)

10  I have come to believe that all theology is autobiography.

Laura Geller, "Encountering the Divine Presence" (1986), in Ellen M. Umansky and Dianne Ashton, eds., *Four Centuries of Jewish Women's Spirituality* (1992)

11  When Christian theology becomes traditionalism and men fail to hold and use it as they do a living language, it becomes an obstacle, not a help to religious conviction. To the greatest of the early Fathers and the great scholastics theology was a language which, like all language, had a grammar and a vocabulary from the past, but which they used to express all the knowledge and experience of their own time as well.

Lily Dougall, "The Undiscovered Country," in B.H. Streeter et al., *Immortality* (1917)

12  In some not altogether frivolous sense God needs to be liberated from our theology. Theology is not a tabernacle to contain the One who is Ahead, but it is a sign on the way, and thus is provisional. Thus the theologian is not only protester and prophet, if she is lucky, but also pilgrim.

Joan Arnold Romero, in Mary Alice Warner and Dayna Beilenson, eds., *Women of Faith and Spirit* (1987)

13  Dogma? Faith? These are the right and left pillars of every soul-crushing theology. Theosophists have no dogmas, exact no blind faith.

H.P. Blavatsky, in *The Spiritualist* (1878)

14  Sex is an aspect of human existence that has fallen prey in special measure to a very special form of theological science: the theological outgrowth or

offshoot known as moral theology. Its biblical foundations are meager in the sense that nothing of the kind exists in the New Testament, so it has had to achieve its ambition largely by dint of its own efforts.

Uta Ranke-Heinemann, *Eunuchs for Heaven* (1988)

1 The critical principle of feminist theology is the promotion of the full humanity of women. Whatever denies, diminishes, or distorts the full humanity of women is, therefore, appraised as not redemptive.

Rosemary Radford Ruether, *Sexism and God-Talk* (1983)

See also Doctrine, Dogma, God, Religion, Spirituality.

## ❧ THEORIES

2 Theories are like scaffolding: they are not the house, but you can not build the house without them.

Constance Fenimore Woolson, *Anne* (1882)

3 Theories have nothing to do with life.

Ellen Glasgow, *The Descendant* (1897)

4 Very dangerous things, theories.

Dorothy L. Sayers, *The Unpleasantness at the Bellona Club* (1928)

See also Concepts, Ideas, Thoughts.

## ❧ THERAPY

5 The trouble with therapy is that it makes life go backwards.

Anne Sexton (1963), in Linda Gray Sexton and Lois Ames, eds., *Anne Sexton: A Self-Portrait in Letters* (1977)

6 Men, as a general rule, shy away from therapy because there is no obvious way to keep score.

Merrill Markoe, *How to Be Hap-Hap-Happy Like Me* (1994)

7 That's the New York thing, isn't it. People who seem absolutely crazy going around telling you how crazy they used to be before they had therapy.

Judith Rossner, *Any Minute I Can Split* (1972)

See also Psychiatry.

## ❧ "THEY"

8 Have you heard of the terrible family They, / And the dreadful venomous things They say?

Ella Wheeler Wilcox, "They Say" (1890), in James Gilchrist Lawson, ed., *The World's Best-Loved Poems* (1927)

See also Gossip, Rumor.

## ❧ THINGS

9 I could never be lonely without a husband, but without my trinkets, my golden gods, I could find abysmal gloom.

Lillian Russell, title essay (1914), in Djuna Barnes, *I Could Never Be Lonely Without a Husband* (1985)

10 Only in a house where one has learnt to be lonely does one have this solicitude for *things*. One's relation to them, the daily seeing or touching, begins to become love, and to lay one open to pain.

Elizabeth Bowen, *The Death of the Heart* (1938)

11 It matters less to venerate things than to live with them on terms of good friendship.

Adrienne Monnier (1938), in Richard McDougall, tr., *The Very Rich Hours of Adrienne Monnier* (1976)

12 I love the things I never had / along with those I have no more.

Gabriela Mistral, "Things," in Langston Hughes, tr., *Selected Poems of Gabriela Mistral* (1957)

13 The things people discard tell more about them than the things they keep.

Hilda Lawrence, *The Pavilion* (1946)

14 Lost things, she felt certain, had a life of their own. They came back to their families like stray dogs.

Nancy Willard, *Things Invisible to See* (1984)

15 Life is one long struggle to disinter oneself, to keep one's head above the accumulations, the ever-deepening layers of objects . . . which attempt to cover one over, steadily, almost irresistibly, like falling snow.

Rose Macaulay, *Personal Pleasures* (1936)

16 As for *things*, how they do accumulate, how often I wish to exclaim, "Oh *don't* give me that!"

Susan Hale (1909), in Caroline P. Atkinson, ed., *Letters of Susan Hale* (1918)

1 The best things in life aren't things.
   Ann Landers, syndicated column (1996)

See also Inanimate Objects, Materialism, Possessions, Small Things.


# ❦ THINKING

2 Thinking . . . is a soundless dialogue, it is the weaving of patterns, it is a search for meaning. The activity of thought contributes to and shapes all that is specifically human.
   Vera John-Steiner, *Notebooks of the Mind* (1985)

3 Lying in bed just before going to sleep is the worst time for *organized* thinking; it is the best time for free thinking. Ideas drift like clouds in an undecided breeze, taking first this direction and then that.
   E.L. Konigsburg, *From the Mixed-Up Files of Mrs. Basil E. Frankweiler* (1967)

4 He did not arrive at this conclusion by the decent process of quiet, logical deduction, nor yet by the blinding flash of glorious intuition, but by the shoddy, untidy process halfway between the two by which one usually gets to know things.
   Margery Allingham, *Death of a Ghost* (1934)

5 To have ideas is to gather flowers. To think is to weave them into garlands.
   Anne-Sophie Swetchine, in Count de Falloux, ed., *The Writings of Madame Swetchine* (1869)

6 To think and to be fully alive are the same.
   Hannah Arendt, *The Life of the Mind*, vol. 1 (1978)

7 It is all right to say exactly what you think if you have learned to think exactly.
   Marcelene Cox, in *Ladies' Home Journal* (1945)

8 It interrupts any doing, any ordinary activities, no matter what they happen to be. All thinking demands a *stop*-and-think.
   Hannah Arendt, *The Life of the Mind*, vol. 1 (1978)

9 There are no dangerous thoughts; thinking itself is dangerous.
   Hannah Arendt, *The Life of the Mind*, vol. 1 (1978)

10 Thinking is the hardest work in the world; and most of us will go to great lengths to avoid it.
   Louise Dudley, "A New Government," in Jean Beaven Abernethy, *Meditations for Women* (1947)

11 Never be afraid to sit awhile and think.
   Lorraine Hansberry, *A Raisin in the Sun* (1959)

12 We have a reading, a talking, and a writing public. *When* shall we have a *thinking*?
   Countess of Blessington, *Desultory Thoughts and Reflections* (1839)

13 Readers are plentiful: thinkers are rare.
   Harriet Martineau, *Society in America*, vol. 3 (1837)

14 Thinking beings have an urge to speak, speaking beings have an urge to think.
   Hannah Arendt, *The Life of the Mind*, vol. 1 (1978)

15 The difference between you and me is that you think to live and I live to think.
   Dorothy M. Richardson, *Pilgrimage: Revolving Lights* (1923)

16 People get wisdom from thinking, not from learning.
   Laura Riding, *Four Unposted Letters to Catherine* (1993)

17 Absence of thought is indeed a powerful factor in human affairs, statistically speaking the most powerful, not just in the conduct of the many but in the conduct of all.
   Hannah Arendt, *The Life of the Mind*, vol. 1 (1978)

18 Those who cannot *think*, have, in my opinion, a necessity (which goes very far towards creating a right) for amusement.
   Mrs. Sarah J. Hale, *Sketches of American Character* (1829)

19 Thinking gets you nowhere. It may be a fine and noble aid in academic studies, but you can't think your way out of emotional difficulties. That takes something altogether different. You have to make yourself passive then, and just listen. Re-establish contact with a slice of eternity.
   Etty Hillesum (1941), *An Interrupted Life* (1983)

20 Any positive thinker is compelled to see everything in the light of his own convictions.
   Antoinette Brown Blackwell, *The Sexes Throughout Nature* (1875)

21 I can't see that she could have found anything nastier to say if she'd thought it out with both hands for a fortnight.
   Dorothy L. Sayers, *Busman's Honeymoon* (1937)

1 He looked as if his mind constantly shifted from one foot to the other.

> Marcelene Cox, in *Ladies' Home Journal* (1945)

2 She had lost her way in a labyrinth of conjecture where her worst dread was that she might put her hand upon the clue.

> Edith Wharton, "The Angel at the Grave," *Crucial Instances* (1901)

3 She had the fluency of tongue and action meted out by divine providence to those who cannot think for themselves.

> Djuna Barnes, *Nightwood* (1937)

4 Much of what Mr. [Vice-President Henry A.] Wallace calls his global thinking is, no matter how you slice it, still globaloney.

> Clare Boothe Luce, speech (1943)

See also Brain, Foresight, Ideas, Mind, Thoughts.

## ❧ THIRD WORLD

5 The Third World is not a reality but an ideology.

> Hannah Arendt, "On Violence," *Crises of the Republic* (1972)

## ❧ THOUGHTS

6 I hold it true that thoughts are things / Endowed with bodies, breath, and wings.

> Ella Wheeler Wilcox, "Secret Thoughts," *Poems of Pleasure* (1888)

7 Thoughts are acrobats, agile and quite often untrustworthy.

> Bess Streeter Aldrich, *Spring Came on Forever* (1935)

8 As a pale moth passes / In the April grasses, / So I come and go, / Softlier than snow.

> Mary Webb, "The Thought," in Martin Armstrong, ed., *The Essential Mary Webb* (1949)

9 Every thought vibrates through the universe.

> Dorothy M. Richardson, *Pilgrimage: Revolving Lights* (1923)

10 Thought is never free. It is bought in pain, / loneliness.

> Maureen Duffy, "For *The Freethinker* Centenary" (1980), *Collected Poems* (1985)

11 Your energies have wrought / Stout continents of thought.

> Marianne Moore, "That Harp You Play So Well," in Burton E. Stevenson, ed., *The Home Book of Modern Verse* (1925)

12 Creative thought seems prone to flower in symbols before it ripens to fruit.

> Maude Meagher, *Fantastic Traveler* (1931)

13 Borrowed thoughts, like borrowed money, only show the poverty of the borrower.

> Lady Marguerite Blessington, in R.R. Madden, *The Literary Life and Correspondence of the Countess of Blessington*, vol. 1 (1855)

14 I have no riches but my thoughts, / Yet these are wealth enough for me.

> Sara Teasdale, "Riches," *Love Songs* (1917)

15 I come from nothing; but from where / Come the undying thoughts I bear?

> Alice Meynell, "A Song of Derivations," *Poems* (1893)

16 Not a hundredth part of the thoughts in my head have ever been or ever will be spoken or written—as long as I keep my senses, at least.

> Jane Welsh Carlyle, to Thomas Carlyle (1858), in James Anthony Froude, ed., *Letters and Memorials of Jane Welsh Carlyle*, vol. 2 (1883)

17 I send you my thoughts—the air between us is laden, / My thoughts fly in at your window, a flock of wild birds.

> Sara Teasdale, "At Night," *Rivers to the Sea* (1915)

18 My thoughts are sea-gulls / Lifting out to sea.

> Mary Carolyn Davies, "Sea-Gull Song," *The Skyline Trail* (1924)

19 This morning my thoughts / Are as disordered / As my black hair.

> Lady Horikawa (12th cent.), in Aliki Barnstone and Willis Barnstone, eds., *A Book of Women Poets From Antiquity to Now* (1980)

20 My thoughts are like waffles—the first few don't look too good.

> Marilyn vos Savant, in *Parade* (1992)

21 First thoughts have tremendous energy. It is the way the mind first flashes on something. The internal censor usually squelches them, so we live in the realm of second and third thoughts, thoughts on thought, twice and three times removed from the direct connection of the first fresh flash.

> Natalie Goldberg, *Writing Down the Bones* (1986)

1 Every thought is strictly speaking an after-thought.
Hannah Arendt, *The Life of the Mind*, vol. 1 (1978)

2 There is thought, and then there is thinking about thoughts, and they don't feel the same.
Susanna Kaysen, *Girl, Interrupted* (1993)

3 I must say this in the behalf of my thoughts, that I never found them idle; for if the senses bring no work in, they will work of themselves, like silk-worms that spin out of their own bowels.
Margaret Cavendish, Duchess of Newcastle, "A True Relation of My Birth, Breeding, and Life," *Nature's Pictures Drawn by Fancies Pencil to the Life* (1656)

4 We are always in search of the redeeming formula, the crystallizing thought.
Etty Hillesum (1941), *An Interrupted Life* (1983)

5 Conversation is the legs on which thought walks; and writing, the wings by which it flies.
Countess of Blessington, *Desultory Thoughts and Reflections* (1839)

6 Anger and worry are the enemies of clear thought.
Madeleine Brent, *The Capricorn Stone* (1979)

7 There are no evil thoughts except one: the refusal to think.
Ayn Rand, *Atlas Shrugged* (1957)

8 Once you wake up thought in a man, you can never put it to sleep again.
Zora Neale Hurston, *Moses: Man of the Mountain* (1939)

9 Their thoughts moved brightly toward each other, like fireflies in the darkness.
Marjorie Kinnan Rawlings, *Jacob's Ladder* (1950)

10 His thoughts swam between us, hidden under rocks, disappearing in weeds, and I was fishing for them, dangling my own words like baits and lures.
Louise Erdrich, *Love Medicine* (1984)

11 She nibbled away at her thought like a rabbit with a piece of lettuce.
Rae Foley, *Death and Mr. Potter* (1955)

12 She resented the way in which he walked in and out of her mind as if it was his own flat.
Dorothy L. Sayers, *Gaudy Night* (1935)

13 There was hardly a wrinkle on her placid face. Dr. Lavendar had been heard to say, in this connection, that "thought made wrinkles." And the inference was obvious.
Margaret Deland, *Philip and His Wife* (1894)

See also Concepts, Ideas, Originality, Theories, Thinking.

## § THREATS

14 I will make you shorter by the head!
Queen Elizabeth I, when opposed by leaders of her Council (1572), in Frederick Chamberlin, *The Sayings of Queen Elizabeth* (1923)

15 Take heed how you proceed against me; for I know that for this you go about to do to me, God will ruin you and your posterity, and this whole state.
Anne Marbury Hutchinson (1640), in Selmar Williams, *Divine Rebel* (1981)

## § THRIFT

16 It's smart to be thrifty.
Bernice Fitz-Gibbon, Macy's famous advertising slogan, *Macy's, Gimbels, and Me* (1967)

17 Economy is the thief of time.
Ethel Watts Mumford, in Oliver Herford, Ethel Watts Mumford, and Addison Mizner, *The Complete Cynic* (1902)

18 The least practical of us have some petty thrift dear to our hearts, some one direction in which we love to scrimp.
Agnes Repplier, "Esoteric Economy," *Points of View* (1891)

19 Frugality without creativity is deprivation.
Amy Dacyczyn, "You Can Afford Your Dream," in *Parade* (1991)

See also Avarice, Finances, Miserliness, Money.

## § TIME

20 Backward, turn backward, O Time, in your flight, / Make me a child again just for to-night!
Elizabeth Akers Allen, "Rock Me to Sleep, Mother" (1860), in Edmund Clarence Stedman, ed., *An American Anthology 1787-1900* (1900)

1 Time was our banker once, and on our credit / Like an indulgent father let us draw. / Now he's turned sour, and our account does edit / And pounces on us with a usurer's claw.

Vita Sackville-West, "Three Sonnets," *King's Daughter* (1929)

2 O Time the fatal wrack of mortal things.

Anne Bradstreet, "Contemplations" (1650), in John Harvard Ellis, ed., *The Works of Anne Bradstreet in Prose and Verse* (1867)

3 Oh, time is death, / Come, cypress-candled death, / Take us before time kills our life.

Winifred Holtby, in Vera Brittain, *Testament of Friendship* (1940)

4 One wants more time, more youth. . . . Oh, to get it back! Oh, to dig one's toes in and refuse to be rushed headlong towards the brink!

Mary Borden, *Three Pilgrims and a Tinker* (1924)

5 Why is youth so short and age so long?

Ouida, "Fame," *Pipistrello* (1881)

6 The irreversibility of time. That's the hardest thing to accept at our age, that's the most violent aspect of death.

Francine du Plessix Gray, *Lovers and Tyrants* (1976)

7 Time's violence rends the soul; by the rent eternity enters.

Simone Weil, *Gravity and Grace* (1947)

8 Time does us violence; it is the only violence.

Simone Weil, *Gravity and Grace* (1947)

9 Time is terrible, / Avenging, and betraying.

L.E. Landon, *Ethel Churchill* (1837)

10 Time is the most terrible, the most discouraging, the most unconquerable of all obstacles, and one that may exist when no other does.

Marie Bashkirtseff (1878), in Mary J. Serrano, tr., *The Journal of a Young Artist* (1919)

11 Oh, time betrays us. Time is the great enemy.

Winifred Holtby, *South Riding* (1936)

12 Time is the mother and mugger of us all.

Karen Elizabeth Gordon, *Intimate Apparel* (1989)

13 The insolence of time is like a blow in the face from an unseen enemy.

Margaret Deland, *Sidney* (1890)

14 Time has told me / less than I need to know.

Gwen Harwood, "Resurrection," *Bone Scan* (1988)

15 You don't deal with time. Time deals with you.

Cecil Dawkins, *Charleyhorse* (1985)

16 I shall not tell you in this story about all the days when nothing happened. You will not catch me saying, "thus the sad days passed slowly by"—or "the years rolled on their weary course," or "time went on"—because it is silly; of course time goes on, whether you say so or not.

Edith Nesbitt, *The Bastable Children* (1928)

17 Time is a dressmaker specializing in alterations.

Faith Baldwin, "Four Seasons, Three Tenses," *Face Toward the Spring* (1956)

18 Time collapses and expands like an erratic accordion.

Bel Kaufman, *Up the Down Staircase* (1964)

19 [Time was] an accordion, all the air squeezed out of it as you grew older.

Helen Hooven Santmyer, . . . *And Ladies of the Club* (1984)

20 Time heals all things but one: Time.

Cynthia Ozick, *Trust* (1966)

21 Time . . . has very little to do with living except at its beginning or near its end.

Phyllis Bottome, *The Life Line* (1946)

22 He is invariably in a hurry—being in a hurry is one of the tributes he pays to life.

Elizabeth Bibesco, *Balloons* (1922)

23 "No hurry, no hurry," said Sir James, with that air of self-denial that conveys the urgent necessity of intense speed.

Ada Leverson, *The Twelfth Hour* (1907)

24 A watch is always too fast or too slow. I cannot be dictated to by a watch.

Jane Austen, *Mansfield Park* (1814)

25 Neither of them wore watches. On them, watches broke or lost themselves or speeded up to keep some lawless schedule of their own so you could almost see the minute hand racing around the dial.

Anne Tyler, *Searching for Caleb* (1975)

26 The clock talked loud. I threw it away, it scared me what it talked.

Tillie Olsen, "I Stand Here Ironing," *Tell Me A Riddle* (1956)

1 All the clocks were running again. Moomintroll felt less lonely after he had wound them up. As time was lost anyway, he set them at different hours. Perhaps one of them would be right, he thought.

Tove Jansson, *Moominland Midwinter* (1958)

2 I must govern the clock, not be governed by it.

Golda Meir, in Oriana Fallaci, *L'Europeo* (1973)

3 Grown-up people seem to be busy by clockwork: even when someone is not ill, when there has been no telegram, they run their unswerving course from object to object, directed by some mysterious inner needle that points all the time to what they must do next. You can only marvel at such misuse of time.

Elizabeth Bowen, *The House in Paris* (1935)

4 Louie had, with regard to time, an infant lack of stereoscopic vision. . . . To her everything seemed to be going on at once; so that she deferred, when she did, in a trouble of half-belief to either the calendar or the clock.

Elizabeth Bowen, *The Heat of the Day* (1949)

5 A woman's sense of time must be quite different from a man's. Her sense of continuity is internal and natural. . . . She connects directly to the source of time, and the moon that pulls the tides around the world also pulls the hormone tide within her; her months are marked off without need of calendar. She carries her months, her years, her spring and winter within herself.

Abigail Lewis, *An Interesting Condition* (1950)

6 I've been on a calendar, but never on time.

Marilyn Monroe, in *Look* (1962)

7 Oh! what a crowded world one moment may contain!

Felicia Hemans, "The Last Constantine," *The Poetical Works of Felicia Dorothea Hemans* (1914)

8 There are half hours that dilate to the importance of centuries.

Mary Catherwood, *Lazarre* (1901)

9 Hours stacked up like unclaimed packages.

Charlene Weir, *The Winter Widow* (1992)

10 Time, like money, is measured by our needs.

George Eliot, *Middlemarch* (1871)

11 We have as much time as we need.

Melody Beattie, *The Lessons of Love* (1994)

12 Our perception that we have "no time" is one of the distinctive marks of modern Western culture.

Margaret Visser, *The Rituals of Dinner* (1991)

13 Time, when it is left to itself and no definite demands are made on it, cannot be trusted to move at any recognized pace. Usually it loiters; but just when one has come to count upon its slowness, it may suddenly break into a wild irrational gallop.

Edith Wharton, *The House of Mirth* (1905)

14 The days ride stallions / and leave us in the dust.

Roberta Hill Whiteman, "Love, the Final Healer," *Star Quilt* (1984)

15 Time pulses from the afternoon like blood from a serious wound.

Hilma Wolitzer, *In the Palomar Arms* (1983)

16 My days ran away so fast. I simply ran after my days.

Leah Morton, *I Am a Woman—and a Jew* (1926)

17 The days slipped down like junket, leaving no taste on the tongue.

Betty MacDonald, *The Egg and I* (1945)

18 Lost time was like a run in a stocking. It always got worse.

Anne Morrow Lindbergh, *The Steep Ascent* (1944)

19 Whiskey and music, I reflected, especially when taken together, made time fly incredibly fast.

Jean Stafford, *Boston Adventure* (1944)

20 Alas! there is no casting anchor in the stream of time!

Countess of Blessington, *Country Quarters*, vol. 1 (1850)

21 Time is the thief you cannot banish.

Phyllis McGinley, "Ballade of Lost Objects," *The Love Letters of Phyllis McGinley* (1954)

22 Not losing time has been my permanent concern since I was three years old, when it dawned on me that time is the warp of life, its very fabric, something that you cannot buy, trade, steal, falsify, or obtain by begging.

Nina Berberova, *The Italics Are Mine* (1969)

23 Time by itself means nothing, no matter how fast it moves, unless we give it something to carry for us; something we value. Because it is such a precious vehicle, is time.

Ama Ata Aidoo, *Our Sister Killjoy* (1977)

1 Saving time, it seems, has a primacy that's too rarely examined.

> Ellen Goodman, *Close to Home* (1979)

2 If we take care of the moments, the years will take care of themselves.

> Maria Edgeworth, "Mademoiselle Panache," *Moral Tales* (1801)

3 Time has passed through me and become a song.

> Holly Near, with Derk Richardson, *Fire in the Rain . . . Singer in the Storm* (1990)

4 Time was not something that passed. All eternity was but a single fierce stroke of rapture. Existence was all a weaving to and fro upon the same dim loom.

> Martha Ostenso, *The Young May Moon* (1929)

5 We are so saturated with the notion that Time is a dimension accessible from one direction only, that you will at first probably be shocked by my saying that I can see truly as far in front of me as I can see exactly behind me.

> Mary Austin, *The American Rhythm* (1923)

6 Time is the continuous loop, the snakeskin with scales endlessly overlapping without beginning or end, or time is an ascending spiral if you will, like a child's toy Slinky. Of course we have no idea which arc on the loop is our time, let alone where the loop itself is, so to speak, or down whose lofty flight of stairs the Slinky so uncannily walks.

> Annie Dillard, *Pilgrim at Tinker Creek* (1974)

7 I began then to think of time as having a shape, something you could see, like a series of liquid transparencies, one laid on top of another. You don't look back along time but down through it, like water. Sometimes this comes to the surface, sometimes that, sometimes nothing. Nothing goes away.

> Margaret Atwood, *Cat's Eye* (1988)

8 Time was a river, not a log to be sawed into lengths.

> Margaret A. Robinson, *A Woman of Her Tribe* (1990)

9 Time was a hook in his mouth. Time was reeling him in jawfirst; it was reeling him in, headlong and breathless, to a shore he had not known was there.

> Annie Dillard, *The Living* (1992)

10 I felt time in full stream, and I felt consciousness in full stream joining it, like the rivers.

> Annie Dillard, *An American Childhood* (1987)

11 Time has lost its shoes here / it stood still.

> Fadwa Tuqan, "From Behind the Bars" (1917), in Joanna Bankier and Deirdre Lashgari, eds., *Women Poets of the World* (1983)

12 Everything takes a long, a very long time, in Malaya. Things get done, occasionally, but more often they don't, and the more in a hurry you are, the quicker you break down.

> Han Suyin, *. . . And the Rain My Drink* (1956)

13 There is Indian time and white man's time. Indian time means never looking at the clock. . . . There is not even a word for time in our language.

> Mary Brave Bird, with Richard Erdoes, *Ohitika Woman* (1993)

14 Indian time conveys an old grasp of time and life, perceived and experienced collectively by Indian people. . . . From the edge of Indian time overlooking infinity, there is acute perception and perspective.

> Anna Lee Walters, *Talking Indian* (1992)

15 The unseen / Trails they follow / Take time.

> Diane Glancy, "If Indians Are Coming It Won't Start on Time," *Iron Woman* (1990)

16 Years . . . should be nothing to you. Who asked you to count them or to consider them? In the world of wild Nature, time is measured by seasons only—the bird does not know how old it is—the rose-tree does not count its birthdays!

> Marie Corelli, *The Life Everlasting* (1911)

17 All conscious thought is a process in time; so that to think consciously about Time is like trying to use a foot-rule to measure its own length.

> Dorothy L. Sayers, "Strong Meat" (1939), *Creed or Chaos?* (1949)

18 Duration is not a test of true or false.

> Anne Morrow Lindbergh, *Gift From the Sea* (1955)

19 Time and space are only forms of thought.

> Edith Nesbitt, *The Story of the Amulet* (1906)

20 Time is, as you are probably aware, merely a convenient fiction. There is no such thing as time.

> Edith Nesbitt, *The Phoenix and the Carpet* (1903)

21 In this world we live in a mixture of time and eternity. Hell would be pure time.

> Simone Weil, *First and Last Notebooks* (1970)

1  Time: the one thing you take with you.

   Marcelene Cox, in *Ladies' Home Journal* (1948)

2  Time at length becomes justice.

   Cynthia Ozick, "Truman Capote Reconsidered," *Art and Ardor* (1983)

3  To be quite oneself one must first waste a little time.

   Elizabeth Bowen, *The House in Paris* (1935)

4  The one real thing that money buys. Time.

   Marita Bonner, "On Being Young—A Woman—and Colored" (1925), *Frye Street and Environs* (1987)

5  Killing time takes practice.

   Karen Elizabeth Gordon, *The Transitive Vampire* (1984)

6  You can kill time or kill yourself, it comes to the same thing in the end.

   Elsa Triolet, *Proverbes d'Elsa* (1971)

7  Time . . . is not a great healer. It is an indifferent and perfunctory one. Sometimes it does not heal at all. And sometimes when it seems to, no healing has been necessary.

   Ivy Compton-Burnett, *Darkness and Day* (1951)

8  Time is not so all-erasing as we think.

   Constance Fenimore Woolson, *Anne* (1882)

9  Time is a great traitor who teaches us to accept loss.

   Elizabeth Borton de Treviño, *I, Juan de Pareja* (1965)

10  Time is a Test of Trouble — / But not a Remedy — / If such it prove, it prove too / There was no Malady.

   Emily Dickinson (1863), in Mabel Loomis Todd, ed., *Poems by Emily Dickinson*, 3rd series (1896)

11  Time is a kind friend, he will make us old.

   Sara Teasdale, "Let It Be Forgotten," *Flame and Shadow* (1920)

12  Time wounds all heels.

   Jane Ace, in Goodman Ace, *The Fine Art of Hypochondria* (1966)

See also Busyness, Days, Eras, Eternity, Future, History, Interruptions, Lateness, Past, Present, Punctuality, Speed, Timeliness, Years.

## ❧ TIMELINESS

13  Persons who are born too soon or born too late seldom achieve the eminence of those who are born at the right time.

   Katharine Anthony, in Helen Hull, ed., *The Writer's Book* (1950)

14  Fate carries its own clock.

   Pearl Bailey, *The Raw Pearl* (1968)

15  Things come suitable to the time.

   Enid Bagnold, *National Velvet* (1935)

16  The appointed thing came at the appointed time in the appointed way.

   Myrtle Reed, *Master of the Vineyard* (1910)

17  I believe that everything has its own season, and each hour its law. If something anticipated arrives too late it finds us numb, wrung out from waiting, and we feel—nothing at all. The best things arrive on time.

   Dorothy Gilman, *A New Kind of Country* (1978)

18  It is so seldom in this world that things come just when they are wanted.

   Margaret Oliphant, *The Perpetual Curate* (1870)

19  Timeliness is an enemy to art.

   Anne Bosworth Greene, *The Lone Winter* (1923)

See also Lateness, Punctuality, Timing.

## ❧ TIMING

20  Timing: The alpha and omega of aerialists, jugglers, actors, diplomats, publicists, generals, prize-fighters, revolutionists, financiers, dictators, lovers.

   Marlene Dietrich, *Marlene Dietrich's ABC* (1962)

21  One should always act from one's inner sense of rhythm.

   Rosamond Lehmann, *The Ballad and the Source* (1945)

22  Death and taxes and childbirth! There's never any convenient time for any of them!

   Margaret Mitchell, *Gone With the Wind* (1936)

See also Timeliness.

## ❧ TITLES

1 I think Hemingway's titles should be awarded first prize in any contest. Each of them is a poem, and their mysterious power over readers contributes to Hemingway's success. His titles have a life of their own, and they have enriched the American vocabulary.

　　Sylvia Beach, *Shakespeare and Company* (1956)

2 We both [Erdrich and Michael Dorris] have title collections. I think a title is like a magnet. It begins to draw these scraps of experience or conversation or memory to it. Eventually, it collects a book.

　　Louise Erdrich, in *Writer's Digest* (1991)

See also Books.

## ❧ TOASTS

3 The United States of America, may they be perpetual.

　　Sarah Livingston Jay, toast following the signing of the Peace of Paris treaty (1783), in Richard B. Morris, ed.; *John Jay* (1980)

4 Gratitude to our Friends and Moderation to our Enemies.

　　Sarah Livingston Jay, toast following the signing of the Peace of Paris treaty (1783), in Richard B. Morris, ed., *John Jay* (1980)

## ❧ TOBACCO

5 To think there are men who dare so defile a church, a sacred sanctuary dedicated to God. We have to hold up our skirts and walk tiptoe, so covered is the floor, the aisle and pews, with the dark shower of tobacco juice.

　　Mary Boykin Chesnut (1865), *A Diary From Dixie* (1905)

6 Of tobacco and its consequences, I will say nothing but that the practice is at too bad a pass to leave hope that anything that could be said in books would work a cure. If the floors of boarding-houses, and the decks of steam-boats, and the carpets of the Capitol, do not sicken the Americans into a reform; if the warnings of physicians are of

no avail, what remains to be said? I dismiss the nauseous subject.

　　Harriet Martineau, *Society in America*, vol. 3 (1837)

7 Virginia reeks of tobacco. Its odor saturates her like the coat of a veteran smoker. The brown stain of tobacco juice is on every page of her history.

　　Virginia Moore, *Virginia Is a State of Mind* (1942)

See also Smoking.

## ❧ TOLERANCE

8 It takes a disciplined person to listen to convictions which are different from their own.

　　Dorothy Fuldheim, *A Thousand Friends* (1974)

9 Toleration is the greatest gift of the mind; it requires the same effort of the brain that it takes to balance oneself on a bicycle.

　　Helen Keller, *The Story of My Life* (1902)

10 Oh, that in religion, as in everything else, man would judge his brother man by his own heart; and as dear, as precious as his peculiar creed may be to him, believe so it is with the faith of his brother!

　　Grace Aguilar, title story, *The Vale of Cedars* (1850)

11 No emergency excuses you from exercising tolerance.

　　Phyllis Bottome, *The Mortal Storm* (1938)

12 Americans (I, I'm afraid, among them) go around carelessly assuming they're tolerant the way they go around carelessly saying, "You ought to be in pictures." But in the clinches, they turn out to be tolerant about as often as they turn out to be Clark Gable.

　　Margaret Halsey, *Some of My Best Friends Are Soldiers* (1944)

13 We should not permit tolerance to degenerate into indifference.

　　Margaret Chase Smith, in Raymond Swing, ed., *This I Believe: 2* (1954)

14 Even the word Tolerance is intolerable. No person has a right to tolerate another.

　　Amalie Taubels, letter (1839), in Joseph L. Baron, *A Treasury of Jewish Quotations* (1956)

1 Those wearing Tolerance for a label / Call other views intolerable.

> Phyllis McGinley, "In Praise of Diversity," *The Love Letters of Phyllis McGinley* (1954)

See also Acceptance, Intolerance.

## ❦ TOMORROW

2 Tomorrow is as fragile / as a sheer curtain pulled tight. / Any old dog / who comes along / can put his paw / through it.

> Carol Connolly, "No Vacancy," *Payments Due* (1985)

3 To-Morrow and To-Morrow, cheat our Youth: / In riper Age, To-Morrow still we cry, / Not thinking, that the present Day we Dye; / Unpractis'd all the Good we had Design'd; / There's No To-Morrow to a Willing Mind.

> Anne Finch, "There's No To-Morrow," *Miscellany Poems, Written by a Lady* (1713)

4 After all, tomorrow is another day.

> Margaret Mitchell, *Gone With the Wind* (1936)

See also Future.

## ❦ TOOLS

5 All tools inevitably planned, / Stout friends, with pledge / Of service; with their crotchets too / That masters understand.

> Vita Sackville-West, "Summer," *The Land* (1927)

6 Tools have their own integrity.

> Vita Sackville-West, "Summer," *The Land* (1927)

## ❦ TORAH

7 Though my father was poor and had nothing, the Torah, the poetry of prophets, was his daily bread.

> Anzia Yezierska, *Red Ribbon on a White Horse* (1950)

See also Bible.

## ❦ TOUCH

8 Touch is the meaning of being human.

> Andrea Dworkin, *Intercourse* (1987)

9 Touch is the landscape / of what is possible.

> Kate Green, "Possible Love, Possible Sky," *If the World Is Running Out* (1983)

10 We are what we are, the spirit afterwards, but first the touch.

> Charlotte Mew, in Penelope Fitzgerald, *Charlotte Mew and Her Friends* (1984)

11 Human thirsts are satisfied from time to time, but the thirst of the human skin is never satisfied so long as it lives.

> Joyce Carol Oates, "Bodies," *The Wheel of Love* (1969)

12 We are forever in the dark about what touch means to another. . . . With touch, one enters at once a private and an ambiguous world.

> Jessamyn West, *Love Is Not What You Think* (1959)

13 None of what I know is out of books. . . . I prefer tactual learning. Touching, on the quick of the sore nail, of present, mobile life. To toy, to gnaw, to tear: at the living element of pain. Like at a living drumstick.

> Caitlin Thomas, *Not Quite Posthumous Letter to My Daughter* (1963)

See also Senses.

## ❦ TOURISTS

14 Traveling is, and has always been, more popular than the traveler.

> Agnes Repplier, "The American Takes a Holiday," *Times and Tendencies* (1931)

15 I don't know how it is the most unattractive creatures of every nation seem to be the ones who travel.

> Elinor Glyn, *Elizabeth Visits America* (1909)

16 Many Americans think of the rest of the world as a kind of Disneyland, a showplace for quaint fauna, flora and artifacts. They dress for travel in cheap, comfortable, childish clothes, as if they were going

to the zoo and would not be seen by anyone except the animals.

Alison Lurie, *The Language of Clothes* (1981)

1 Abroad it is our habit to regard all other travelers in the light of personal and unpardonable grievances. They are intruders into our chosen realms of pleasure, they jar upon our sensibilities, they lessen our meager share of comforts, they are everywhere in our way, they are always an unnecessary feature in the landscape.

Agnes Repplier, "The Tourist," *Compromises* (1904)

2 One never feels such distaste for one's countrymen and countrywomen as when one meets them abroad.

Rose Macaulay, *Crewe Train* (1926)

3 Here is one of the points about this planet which should be remembered; into every penetrable corner of it, and into most of the impenetrable corners, the English will penetrate. They are like that; born invaders. They cannot stay at home.

Rose Macaulay, *Crewe Train* (1926)

4 One thing about tourists is that it is very easy to get away from them. Like ants they follow a trail and a few yards each side of that trail there are none.

Nancy Mitford, "The Tourist" (1959), *The Water Beetle* (1962)

5 Tourists moved over the piazza like drugged insects on a painted plate.

Shana Alexander, "The Roman Astonishment," in *Life* (1967)

6 The tourist travels in his own atmosphere like a snail in his shell and stands, as it were, on his own perambulating doorstep to look at the continents of the world. But if you discard all this, and sally forth with a leisurely and blank mind, there is no knowing what may not happen to you.

Freya Stark, *Baghdad Sketches* (1929)

See also Travel.

## ❧ TRADITIONS

7 Traditions are group efforts to keep the unexpected from happening.

Mignon McLaughlin, *The Neurotic's Notebook* (1963)

8 Traditions are the guideposts driven deep into our subconscious minds. The most powerful ones are those we can't even describe, aren't even aware of.

Ellen Goodman, *Turning Points* (1979)

9 Traditions that have lost their meaning are the hardest of all to destroy.

Edith Wharton, "Autre Temps...," *Xingu* (1916)

See also Conventions, Custom, Ritual.

## ❧ TRAGEDY

10 Tragedy had its compensations. Once the worst misfortune occurred, one never worried about the minor ones.

Mildred Davis, *The Invisible Boarder* (1974)

11 Tragedy, no matter how sad, becomes boring to those not caught in its addictive caress.

Maya Angelou, *All God's Children Need Traveling Shoes* (1986)

12 Everybody's tragedy is somebody's nuisance.

Winifred Holtby, in Vera Brittain, *Testament of Friendship* (1940)

See also Crises, Disaster, Misfortune, Trouble.

## ❧ TRAINS

13 The train ran like a struggling fish on an almost taut line; it jerked helplessly yet strongly from side to side; twitching and tugging, it was drawn through the rippling land towards the ruthless mountains.

Stella Benson, *Pipers and a Dancer* (1924)

## ❧ TRANSLATING

14 The translator, a lonely sort of acrobat, becomes confused in a labyrinth of paradox, or climbs a pyramid of dependent clauses and has to invent a way down from it in his own language.

Lydia Davis, in Maurice Blanchot, *The Gaze of Orpheus* (1981)

1 In some sense the text and the translator are locked in struggle—"I attacked that sentence, it resisted me, I attacked another, it eluded me"—a struggle in which, curiously, when the translator wins, the text wins too.

> Lydia Davis, in Maurice Blanchot, *The Gaze of Orpheus* (1981)

2 The translator [is a] . . . peculiar outcast, ghost in the world of literature, recreating in another form something already created, creating and not creating, writing words that are his own and not his own.

> Lydia Davis, in Maurice Blanchot, *The Gaze of Orpheus* (1981)

## ❧ TRANSSEXUALS

3 I was born with the wrong body, being feminine by gender but male by sex, and I could achieve completeness only when the one was adjusted to the other.

> Jan Morris, *Conundrum* (1974)

4 I believe the transsexual urge, at least as I have experienced it, to be far more than a social compulsion, but biological, imaginative, and essentially spiritual, too.

> Jan Morris, *Conundrum* (1974)

See also Gender, Sex.

## ❧ TRAVEL

5 The fabric of my faithful love / No power shall dim or ravel / Whilst I stay here,—but oh, my dear, / If I should ever travel!

> Edna St. Vincent Millay, "To the Not Impossible Him," *A Few Figs From Thistles* (1920)

6 Travel is as much a passion as ambition or love.

> L.E. Landon, *Romance and Reality* (1831)

7 All the earth is seamed with roads, and all the sea is furrowed with the tracks of ships, and over all the roads and all the waters a continuous stream of people passes up and down—traveling, as they say,

for their pleasure. What is it, I wonder, that they go out to see?

> Gertrude Bell, *Persian Pictures* (1894)

8 Traveling is seeing; it is the implicit that we travel by.

> Cynthia Ozick, "Enchantments at First Encounter," in *The New York Times Magazine* (1985)

9 Certainly, travel is more than the seeing of sights; it is a change that goes on, deep and permanent, in the ideas of living.

> Miriam Beard, *Realism in Romantic Japan* (1930)

10 This is what holidays, travels, vacations are about. It is not really rest or even leisure we chase. We strain to renew our capacity for wonder, to shock ourselves into astonishment once again.

> Shana Alexander, "The Roman Astonishment," in *Life* (1967)

11 To awaken quite alone in a strange town is one of the most pleasant sensations in the world. You are surrounded by adventure. You have no idea what is in store for you, but you will, if you are wise and know the art of travel, let yourself go on the stream of the unknown and accept whatever comes in the spirit in which the gods may offer it.

> Freya Stark, *Baghdad Sketches* (1929)

12 To me travel is a triple delight: anticipation, performance, and recollection.

> Ilka Chase, *The Carthaginian Rose* (1961)

13 Traveling is the ruin of all happiness! There's no looking at a building here after seeing Italy.

> Fanny Burney, *Cecelia* (1782)

14 The true fruit of travel is perhaps the feeling of being nearly everywhere at home.

> Freya Stark, *A Peak in Darien* (1976)

15 Traveling carries with it the curse of being at home everywhere and yet nowhere, for wherever one is some part of oneself remains on another continent.

> Margot Fonteyn, *Margot Fonteyn* (1975)

16 Through travel I first became aware of the outside world; it was through travel that I found my own introspective way into becoming a part of it.

> Eudora Welty, *One Writer's Beginnings* (1984)

17 When you travel your first discovery is that you do not exist.

> Elizabeth Hardwick, *Sleepless Nights* (1980)

1 I am never happier than when I am alone in a foreign city; it is as if I had become invisible.

Storm Jameson, *Journey From the North*, vol. 1 (1969)

2 This suspension of one's own reality, this being entirely alone in a strange city (at times I wondered if I had lost the power of speech) is an enriching state for a writer. Then the written word . . . takes on an intensity of its own. Nothing gets exteriorized or dissipated; all is concentrated within.

May Sarton, *I Knew a Phoenix* (1959)

3 Loving life is easy when you are abroad. Where no one knows you and you hold your life in your hands all alone, you are more master of yourself than at any other time.

Hannah Arendt, *Rahel Varnhagen* (1957)

4 She crossed borders recklessly, refusing to recognize limits, saying "*bonjour*" and "*buon giorno*" as though she owned both France and Italy and the day itself. . . . She was free to grasp it all: to bite into fruit that had ripened on other people's trees; to warm herself in the sun they had hung out.

Helen Hudson, *Meyer Meyer* (1967)

5 I have learned this strange thing, too, about travel: one may return to a place and, quite unexpectedly, meet oneself still lingering there from the last time.

Helen Bevington, *When Found, Make a Verse Of* (1961)

6 The impulse to travel is one of the hopeful symptoms of life.

Agnes Repplier, "The American Takes a Holiday," *Times and Tendencies* (1931)

7 A trip is what you take when you can't take any more of what you've been taking.

Adeline Ainsworth, in Peg Bracken, *But I Wouldn't Have Missed It for the World!* (1973)

8 People who travel are always fugitives.

Daphne du Maurier, *Frenchman's Creek* (1941)

9 We travel, some of us forever, to seek other states, other lives, other souls.

Anaïs Nin (1969), *The Diary of Anaïs Nin*, vol. 7 (1980)

10 Some travelers are drawn forward by a goal lying before them in the way iron is drawn to the magnet. Others are driven on by a force lying behind them. In such a way the bowstring makes the arrow fly.

Isak Dinesen, "Echoes," *Last Tales* (1957)

11 Travel itself is part of some longer continuity.

Eudora Welty, "Finding a Voice," *One Writer's Beginnings* (1984)

12 One should learn patience in a foreign land, for . . . this is the true measure of travel. If one does not suffer some frustration of the ordinary reflexes, how can one be sure one is really traveling?

Gertrude Diamant, *The Days of Ofelia* (1942)

13 I should like to take these things on full gallop, instead of dawdling along gaping at them . . . a very little Abbey goes a long way with me.

Susan Hale (1868), in Caroline P. Atkinson, ed., *Letters of Susan Hale* (1918)

14 Finally one tires / of so many spires.

Cynthia Ozick, "The 21st Cathedral of the Week," in *The New York Times Magazine* (1993)

15 We perfectly agreed in our ideas of traveling; we hurried from place to place as fast as horses and wheels, and curses and guineas, could carry us.

Maria Edgeworth, *Ennui* (1809)

16 Men travel faster now, but I do not know if they go to better things.

Willa Cather, *Death Comes for the Archbishop* (1927)

17 The true traveler is he who goes on foot, and even then, he sits down a lot of the time.

Colette, *Paris From My Window* (1944)

18 Is there *anything* as horrible as *starting* on a trip? Once you're off, that's all right, but the last moments are earthquake and convulsion, and the feeling that you are a snail being pulled off your rock.

Anne Morrow Lindbergh (1930), *Hour of Gold, Hour of Lead* (1973)

19 Whenever I prepare for a journey I prepare as though for death. Should I never return, all is in order. This is what life has taught me.

Katherine Mansfield (1922), *Journal of Katherine Mansfield* (1927)

20 It is such a bewildered, scared feeling to go for the first time to a place and not know where to call out to the driver to stop.

Katharine Butler Hathaway (1931), *Journals and Letters of the Little Locksmith* (1946)

21 We travel because we do not know. We know that we do not know the best before we start. That is

why we start. But we forget that we do not know the worst either. That is why we come back.

Stella Benson, *The Little World* (1925)

1 Trips do not end when you return home—usually this is the time when in a sense they really begin.

Agnes E. Benedict and Adele Franklin, *The Happy Home* (1948)

2 A pen and a notebook and a reasonable amount of discrimination will change a journey from a mere annual into a perennial, its pleasures and pains renewable at will.

Freya Stark, "On Traveling With a Notebook," in *The Cornhill Magazine* (1954)

3 Surely one advantage of traveling is that, while it removes much prejudice against foreigners and their customs, it intensifies tenfold one's appreciation of the good at home.

Isabella L. Bird, *A Lady's Life in the Rocky Mountains* (1880)

4 I think that to get under the surface and really appreciate the beauty of any country, one has to go there poor.

Grace Moore, *You're Only Human Once* (1944)

5 Like building a house, travel always costs more than you estimate.

Ilka Chase, *Elephants Arrive at Half-Past Five* (1963)

6 There are few certainties when you travel. One of them is that the moment you arrive in a foreign country, the American dollar will fall like a stone.

Erma Bombeck, *When You Look Like Your Passport Photo, It's Time to Go Home* (1991)

7 The expense of living abroad, I always supposed to be high, but my ideas were nowise adequate to the thing.

Abigail Adams (1784), *Letters of Mrs. Adams* (1848)

8 When traveling abroad if you see something you yearn for if you can afford it at all, buy it. If you don't you'll regret it all your life.

Ilka Chase, *Second Spring and Two Potatoes* (1965)

9 While armchair travelers dream of going places, traveling armchairs dream of staying put.

Anne Tyler, *The Accidental Tourist* (1985)

10 Is it lack of imagination that makes us come / to imagined places, not just stay at home?

Elizabeth Bishop, title poem, *Questions of Travel* (1965)

11 Traveling is so complicated. There are so many people everywhere. I make my best journeys on my couch.

Coco Chanel, in Marcel Haedrich, *Coco Chanel* (1972)

12 The great and recurrent question about Abroad is, is it worth the trouble of getting there?

Rose Macaulay, *Personal Pleasures* (1936)

13 Foreigners can't help living abroad because they were born there, but for an English person to go is ridiculous, especially now that the sun-tan lamps are so readily available.

Sue Townsend, *The Growing Pains of Adrian Mole* (1984)

14 I always think that the most delightful thing about traveling is to always be running into Americans and to always feel at home.

Anita Loos, *Gentlemen Prefer Blondes* (1925)

15 I had the real explorer's spirit which is both complaining and insular.

Mary Pakenham, *Brought Up and Brought Out* (1938)

16 O what can be so forlorn in its forlorn parts as this traveling? the ceaseless packing and unpacking, the heartless, uncongenial intercourses, the cheerless hotel, the many hours when you are too tired and your feelings too much dissipated to settle to any pursuit, yet you either have nothing to look at or are weary of looking.

Margaret Fuller, letter to Ralph Waldo Emerson (1843), in Perry Miller, ed., *Margaret Fuller* (1963)

17 Before one actually visits them, everyone tends to think of their favorite countries as one grand Disneyland filled with national monuments and historical treasures conveniently laid out for easy viewing, when what they really are filled with, of course, is people going to work, laundromats and places to buy rat poison.

Bette Midler, *A View From a Broad* (1980)

18 We of the third sphere are unable to look at Europe or at Asia as they may survey each other. Wherever we go, across Pacific or Atlantic, we meet, not similarity so much as "the bizarre." Things astonish us, when we travel, that surprise nobody else.

Miriam Beard, *Realism in Romantic Japan* (1930)

19 One's travel life is basically as incommunicable as his sex life.

Peg Bracken, *But I Wouldn't Have Missed It for the World!* (1973)

1 Travel is the most private of pleasures. There is no greater bore than the travel bore. We do not in the least want to hear what he has seen in Hong-Kong.

   Vita Sackville-West, *Passenger to Teheran* (1926)

2 Like love, travel makes you innocent again.

   Diane Ackerman, *The Moon by Whale Light* (1991)

3 There is no substitute for the riches gained on a lifetime basis by the young American who studies or works abroad.

   Letitia Baldrige, *Of Diamonds and Diplomats* (1968)

4 How could I go on my travels without that sweet soul waiting at home for my letters?

   Caryl Churchill, *Top Girls* (1984)

5 Mail from home was so important when you were traveling. It kept you in touch with the familiar, even the part you were running from.

   Helen Van Slyke, *A Necessary Woman* (1979)

6 Traveling together is a great test, which has damaged many friendships and even honeymoons.

   Rose Macaulay, *The Towers of Trebizond* (1956)

7 The laws all true wanderers obey are these: "Thou shalt not eat nor drink more than thy share," "Thou shalt not lie about the places thou hast visited or the distances thou hast traversed."

   Rosita Forbes, *The Secret of the Sahara* (1921)

8 Like good wine, our family does not travel well.

   Maureen Lipman, *How Was It for You?* (1985)

9 Almost all travel is lost on teen-agers. . . . The young do not discover the world. They discover themselves, and travel only interrupts their trips to the interior.

   Jessamyn West, *Hide and Seek* (1973)

10 Like a chastity belt, the package tour keeps you out of mischief but a bit restive for wondering what you missed.

   Peg Bracken, *But I Wouldn't Have Missed It for the World!* (1973)

11 Most passport pictures are good likenesses, and it is time we faced it.

   Katharine Brush, "Things I Have Learned in My Travels," *This Is On Me* (1940)

12 Suffering makes you deep. Travel makes you broad. In case I get my pick, I'd rather travel.

   Judith Viorst, *Love and Guilt and the Meaning of Life, Etc.* (1979)

See also Adventure, Change, Drivers, Flying, Hotels, Journeys, Places, Returning, Ships, Tourists, Trains, The Unknown, Vacation, Wanderlust.

## ❧ TREACHERY

13 There was no treachery too base for the world to commit; she knew that.

   Virginia Woolf, *To the Lighthouse* (1927)

See also Betrayal, Dishonesty, Evil.

## ❧ TREES

14 Together with a few human beings, dead and living, and their achievements, trees are what I most love and revere.

   Hildegard Flanner, *Brief Cherishing* (1985)

15 Trees is soul people to me, maybe not to other people, but I have watched the trees when they pray, and I've watched them shout and sometimes they give thanks slowly and quietly.

   Bessie Harvey, in Dallas Museum of Art, *Black Art—Ancestral Legacy* (1989)

16 Every time I meet a tree, if I am truly awake, I stand in awe before it. I listen to its voice, a silent sermon moving me to the depths, touching my heart, and stirring up within my soul a yearning to give my all.

   Macrina Wiederkehr, *A Tree Full of Angels* (1988)

17 She had so deep a kinship with the trees, so intuitive a sympathy with leaf and flower, that it seemed as if the blood in her veins was not slow-moving human blood, but volatile sap.

   Mary Webb, *Gone to Earth* (1917)

18 Enter into the life of the trees. . . . Answer back to them with their own dumb magnificence, soul words, earth words, the God in you responding to the God in them.

   Emily Carr (1931), *Hundreds and Thousands* (1966)

19 Go out there into the glory of the woods. See God in every particle of them expressing glory and strength and power, tenderness and protection.

Know that they are God expressing God made manifest.

> Emily Carr (1931), *Hundreds and Thousands* (1966)

1 Trees are nearly as important as men, and much better behaved.

> Winifred Holtby (1924), in Alice Holtby and Jean McWilliam, eds., *Letters to a Friend* (1937)

2 Trees are . . . the lungs of the earth. Just as we breathe oxygen into our lungs and exhale carbon dioxide, so trees breathe carbon dioxide into their leaves and exhale oxygen.

> Helen Caldicott, *If You Love This Planet* (1992)

3 I like trees because they seem more resigned to the way they have to live than other things do.

> Willa Cather, *O Pioneers!* (1913)

4 A stricken tree, a living thing, so beautiful, so dignified, so admirable in its potential longevity, is, next to man, perhaps the most touching of wounded objects.

> Edna Ferber, *A Kind of Magic* (1963)

5 When you look up from your typewriter, look at the trees, not the calendar.

> Mary Virginia Micka, *The Cazenovia Journal* (1990)

6 Leaves are verbs that conjugate the seasons.

> Gretel Ehrlich, *The Solace of Open Spaces* (1985)

7 The old trees have recorded another year, letting out their tough bark girdles to accommodate the new layer of muscle and adipose.

> Edith M. Thomas, *The Round Year* (1886)

8 It is such a comfort to nestle up to Michael Angelo Sanzio Raphael when one is in trouble. He is such a grand tree. He has an understanding soul. After I talked with him and listened unto his voice, I slipped down out of his arms.

> Opal Whiteley (1920), in Benjamin Hoff, ed., *The Singing Creek Where the Willows Grow* (1986)

9 Everybody who's anybody longs to be a tree— / or ride one, hair blown to froth. / That's why horses were invented.

> Rita Dove, "Horse and Tree," *Grace Notes* (1989)

10 Of the infinite variety of fruits which spring from the bosom of the earth, the trees of the wood are the greatest in dignity.

> Susan Fenimore Cooper, *Rural Hours* (1887)

11 Upon the highest ridge of that round hill covered with planted oaks, the shafts of the trees show in the light like the columns of a ruin.

> Dorothy Wordsworth (1798), in William Knight, ed., *Journals of Dorothy Wordsworth*, vol. 1 (1897)

12 The willows were sharp with tiny new leaves like the ears of baby field mice, transparent and infinitely frail.

> Martha Ostenso, *The Mandrake Root* (1938)

13 Willow trees are kind, Dear God. They will not bear a body on their limbs.

> Alice Dunbar-Nelson, "April Is on the Way" (1927), in Gloria T. Hull, ed., *The Works of Alice Dunbar-Nelson*, vol. 2 (1988)

14 The dead elm leaves hung like folded bats.

> Josephine W. Johnson, *Now in November* (1934)

15 The wild apple trees were one shout of joy.

> Anne Bosworth Greene, *The Lone Winter* (1923)

16 I lean against the birch-tree, / My arms around it twine, / It pulses, and leaps, and quivers, / Like a human heart to mine.

> Amy Levy, "The Birch-Tree at Loschwitz," in Nathan and Marynn Ausubel, eds., *A Treasury of Jewish Poetry* (1957)

17 The little birches haunt the hills / In silent, silver masses, / Their violet velvet shadow robes / Beside them on the grasses.

> Effie Lee Newsome, "Little Birches," in Langston Hughes and Arna Bontemps, eds., *The Poetry of the Negro 1746-1949* (1949)

18 When I stepped away from the white pine, I had the definite feeling that we had exchanged some form of life energy. . . . Clearly white pines and I are on the same wavelength. What I give back to the trees I cannot imagine. I hope they receive something, because trees are among my closest friends.

> Anne Labastille, *Woodswoman* (1976)

19 I cannot love evergreens—they are the misanthropes of nature. To them the spring brings no promise, the autumn no decline; they are cut off from the sweetest of all ties with their kind—sympathy. . . . I will have no evergreens in my garden; when the inevitable winter comes, every beloved plant and favorite tree shall drop together—no solitary fir left to triumph over the companionship of decay.

> L.E. Landon, *Francesca Carrara* (1834)

1 [The] aspen has éclat, a glorious brashness in defiance of the rules, the flapper who does the Charleston in the midst of the grand waltz.

Ann Zwinger, *Beyond the Aspen Grove* (1970)

2 The talking oak / To the ancients spoke. / But any tree / Will talk to me.

Mary Carolyn Davies, "Be Different to Trees," *The Skyline Trail* (1924)

See also Forests, Nature, Plants, Wilderness.


## ❦ TRENDS

3 My friend Cassie is the sort of trendsetter they ought to hire over at *People*. . . . She had a Cuisinart and a schefflera when everyone else had a crêpe pan and a philodendron.

Ellen Goodman, *Close to Home* (1979)

See also Fashion.


## ❦ TROUBLE

4 Laugh and the world laughs with you, / Weep and you weep alone. / For the sad old earth must borrow its mirth, / It has trouble enough of its own.

Ella Wheeler Wilcox, "Solitude," *Poems of Passion* (1883)

5 There are two kinds of trouble: The kind you have and the kind you haven't. There are but few of the first sort, but of the second there is no end.

Sophie Irene Loeb, *Epigrams of Eve* (1913)

6 Ah, trouble, trouble, there are the two different kinds . . . there's the one you give and the other you take.

Kay Boyle, *The Crazy Hunter* (1938)

7 To speak broadly, the troubles of life as we find them are mainly traceable to the heart or the purse.

Charlotte Perkins Gilman, *Women and Economics* (1898)

8 How beautiful is trouble / actively pursued.

Marge Piercy, "Flat on My Back," *Living in the Open* (1976)

9 It's a good thing to have all the props pulled out from under us occasionally. It gives us some sense of what is rock under our feet, and what is sand.

Madeleine L'Engle, *The Summer of the Great-Grandmother* (1974)

10 Flowers grow / out of the dark / moments.

Corita Kent, *Moments* (1982)

11 You know, some people fall right through the hole in their lives. It's invisible, but they come to it after time, never knowing where.

Louise Erdrich, *Love Medicine* (1984)

12 When life knocks you to your knees . . . well, that's the best position in which to pray, isn't it?

Ethel Barrymore, in Adela Rogers St. Johns, "Ethel Barrymore, Queen Once More," *Reader's Digest* (1943)

13 I think there is this about the great troubles—they teach us the art of cheerfulness; whereas the small ones cultivate the industry of discontent.

Mary Adams, *Confessions of a Wife* (1902)

14 Troubles cured you salty as a country ham, / smoky to the taste, thick skinned and tender inside.

Marge Piercy, "What you waited for," *To Be of Use* (1973)

15 The rainiest nights, like the rainiest lives, are by no means the saddest.

Elizabeth Stuart Phelps Ward, *The Silent Partner* (1871)

16 Trouble trouble and it will trouble you.

P.L. Travers, *Mary Poppins* (1934)

17 When one has an insatiable appetite for trouble all sorts will serve.

Kathleen Norris, *Hands Full of Living* (1931)

18 She would take any amount of trouble to avoid trouble.

Willa Cather, *The Song of the Lark* (1915)

19 Nobody knows the trouble you've seen—and nobody wants to.

Helen Yglesias, *Family Feeling* (1976)

20 Dr. Johnson said that telling one's troubles was asking for pity or praise. . . . But it is more than that. You ask to be met at the point of your reality.

Florida Scott-Maxwell, *The Measure of My Days* (1968)

21 Too often in ironing out trouble someone gets scorched.

Marcelene Cox, in *Ladies' Home Journal* (1948)

1 Trouble, like the hill ahead, straightens out when you advance upon it.

> Marcelene Cox, in *Ladies' Home Journal* (1953)

2 The blow you can't see coming is the blow that knocks you out.

> Joyce Carol Oates, "Golden Gloves," *Raven's Wing* (1985)

3 Life has this in common with prizefighting: if you've received a belly blow, it's likely to be followed by a right to the jaw.

> Amanda Cross, *The James Joyce Murder* (1967)

4 my trouble / is that I have the spirit of Gertrude Stein / but the personality of Alice B. Toklas.

> Diane Wakoski, "My Trouble," *Smudging* (1972)

5 Day after day she dragged her trouble over to our house like a sick animal she couldn't cure, couldn't kill.

> Margaret Millar, *Beyond This Point Are Monsters* (1970)

6 What fresh hell is this?

> Dorothy Parker, on the ringing of a doorbell or telephone, in Marion Meade, *Dorothy Parker: What Fresh Hell Is This?* (1988)

See also Adversity, Crises, Danger, Disaster, Misfortune, Problems.

## ❦ TROUBLEMAKERS

7 When I / die / I'm sure / I will have a / Big Funeral / Curiosity / seekers / coming to see / if I / am really / Dead / or just / trying to make / Trouble.

> Mari E. Evans, "The Rebel," *I Am a Black Woman* (1970)

8 Disturbers are never popular—nobody ever really loved an alarm clock in action, no matter how grateful he may have been afterwards for its kind services!

> Nellie L. McClung, *In Times Like These* (1915)

See also Contrariness, Opposition, Rebellion, Resistance.

## ❦ TRUST

9 I know / The soft wind will blow me home.

> Yü Hsüan-chi (9th cent.), "Living in the Summer Mountains," in Kenneth Rexroth and Ling Chung, eds., *The Orchid Boat* (1972)

10 I could be whatever I wanted to be if I trusted that music, that song, that vibration of God that was *inside* of me.

> Shirley MacLaine, *It's All in the Playing* (1987)

11 Be fervent in God, and let nothing grieve you, whatever you encounter.

> Hadewijch (13th cent.), in Mother Columba Hart, O.S.B., *Hadewijch* (1980)

12 Those who trust us, educate us.

> George Eliot, *Daniel Deronda* (1874)

13 How desperately we wish to maintain our trust in those we love! In the face of everything, we try to find reasons to trust. Because losing faith is worse than falling out of love.

> Sonia Johnson, *From Housewife to Heretic* (1981)

14 Trust, which is a virtue, is also a habit, like prayer. It requires exercise. And just as no one can run five miles a day and cede the cardiovascular effects to someone else, no one can trust for us.

> Sue Halpern, *Migrations to Solitude* (1993)

15 As contagion / of sickness makes sickness, / contagion of trust can make trust.

> Marianne Moore, "In Distrust of Merits," *Nevertheless* (1944)

16 He who has trusted where he ought not will surely mistrust where he ought not.

> Marie von Ebner-Eschenbach, *Aphorisms* (1893)

17 Allies never trust each other, but that doesn't spoil their effectiveness.

> Ayn Rand, *The Fountainhead* (1943)

18 Foolish are they indeed who trust to fortune!

> Lady Murasaki, *The Tale of Genji* (c. 1008)

19 How can the people trust the harvest, unless they see it sown?

> Mary Renault, *The King Must Die* (1958)

20 Where large sums of money are concerned, it is advisable to trust nobody.

> Agatha Christie, *Endless Night* (1968)

See also Belief, Distrust, Doubt, Faith.

## ❦ TRUTH

1 Truth is the only safe ground to stand upon.
   Elizabeth Cady Stanton, *The Woman's Bible* (1895)

2 There is in the end no remedy but truth. It is the one course that cannot be evil.
   Ellis Peters, *The Potter's Field* (1990)

3 Marvelous Truth, confront us / at every turn, / in every guise.
   Denise Levertov, "Matins," *The Jacob's Ladder* (1961)

4 Truth, that fair goddess who comes always with healing in her wings.
   Anne Shannon Monroe, *The Hearth of Happiness* (1929)

5 Truth, like surgery, may hurt, but it cures.
   Han Suyin, *A Many-Splendored Thing* (1952)

6 A sharp knife cuts the quickest and hurts the least.
   Katharine Hepburn, in *Look* (1958)

7 The truth is the kindest thing we can give folks in the end.
   Harriet Beecher Stowe, *The Pearl of Orr's Island* (1862)

8 Truth has beauty, power and necessity.
   Sylvia Ashton-Warner (1942), *Myself* (1967)

9 Truth is its own defense.
   Phyllis Bottome, *The Mortal Storm* (1938)

10 Truth is immortal; error is mortal.
   Mary Baker Eddy, *Science and Health* (1875)

11 Truth, like the burgeoning of a bulb under the soil, however deeply sown, will make its way to the light.
   Ellis Peters, *The Potter's Field* (1990)

12 There has never been a useful thought or a profound truth that has not found its century and admirers.
   Madame de Staël, *On Literature* (1800)

13 Truth will not be ignored. It will rise up and consume us.
   Katharine Wylde, *An Ill-Regulated Mind* (1885)

14 Much sheer effort goes into avoiding truth: left to itself, it sweeps in like the tide.
   Fay Weldon, *The Rules of Life* (1987)

15 It is useless either to hate or to love truth—but it should be noticed.
   Cynthia Ozick, *Trust* (1966)

16 Let us accept truth, even when it surprises us and alters our views.
   George Sand (1863), in Raphaël Ledos de Beaufort, ed., *Letters of George Sand* (1886)

17 Truth, however bitter, can be accepted, and woven into a design for living.
   Agatha Christie, *The Hollow* (1946)

18 Truth is simply whatever you can bring yourself to believe.
   Alice Childress, *Trouble in Mind* (1955)

19 Truth, though it has many disadvantages, is at least changeless. You can always find it where you left it.
   Phyllis Bottome, *Under the Skin* (1950)

20 Truth — is as old as God.
   Emily Dickinson (1864), in Mabel Loomis Todd, ed., *Letters of Emily Dickinson*, vol. 1 (1894)

21 Truth has no beginning.
   Mary Baker Eddy, *Science and Health* (1875)

22 Truth is like heat or light; its vibrations are endless, and are endlessly felt.
   Margaret Deland, *John Ward, Preacher* (1888)

23 There are no new truths, but only truths that have not been recognized by those who have perceived them without noticing.
   Mary McCarthy, "The *Vita Activa*" (1958), *On the Contrary* (1961)

24 Truth has divine properties, and the ability to see it is a gift that's given, not acquired.
   Katherine Neville, *A Calculated Risk* (1992)

25 Truth is the vital breath of Beauty; Beauty the outward form of Truth.
   Grace Aguilar, "Amête and Yafèh," *The Vale of Cedars* (1850)

26 I am the only real truth I know.
   Jean Rhys, in Susan Cahill, ed., *Women and Fiction 2* (1978)

27 Every new truth begins in a shocking heresy.
   Margaret Deland, *The Kays* (1924)

28 Most of the basic truths of life sound absurd at first hearing.
   Elizabeth Goudge, *Green Dolphin Street* (1944)

1 The mode of delivering a truth makes, for the most part, as much impression on the mind of the listener as the truth itself.

Frances Wright, *A Few Days in Athens* (1822)

2 Any truth creates a scandal.

Marguerite Yourcenar, *Memoirs of Hadrian* (1954)

3 Tell all the Truth but tell it slant — / Success in Circuit lies / Too bright for our infirm Delight / The Truth's superb surprise.

Emily Dickinson (1868), in Mabel Loomis Todd and Millicent Todd Bingham, eds., *Bolts of Melody* (1945)

4 The road to honor is paved with thorns; but on the path to truth, at every step you set your foot down on your own heart.

Ralph Iron, *The Story of an African Farm* (1883)

5 I tore myself away from the safe comfort of certainties through my love for the truth; and truth rewarded me.

Simone de Beauvoir, *All Said and Done* (1972)

6 Truth is a rough, honest, helter-skelter terrier, that none like to see brought into their drawing-rooms.

Ouida, *Wisdom, Wit and Pathos* (1884)

7 There are very few human beings who receive the truth, complete and staggering, by instant illumination. Most of them acquire it fragment by fragment, on a small scale, by successive developments, cellularly, like a laborious mosaic.

Anaïs Nin (1943), *The Diary of Anaïs Nin*, vol. 3 (1969)

8 The Truth must dazzle gradually / Or every man be blind.

Emily Dickinson (1868), in Mabel Loomis Todd and Millicent Todd Bingham, eds., *Bolts of Melody* (1945)

9 There is at least one thing more brutal than the truth, and that is the consequence of saying less than the truth.

Ti-Grace Atkinson, "The Older Woman," *Amazon Odyssey* (1974)

10 To be made evident, truth must be sought for; for of itself it is slow to appear, and between ourselves and God the obstacles are so many!

George Sand (1865), in Raphaël Ledos de Beaufort, ed., *Letters of George Sand*, vol. 2 (1886)

11 Not only are there as many conflicting truths as there are people to claim them; there are equally multitudinous and conflicting truths within the individual.

Virgilia Peterson, *A Matter of Life and Death* (1961)

12 Truth has as many coats as an onion . . . and each one of them hollow when you peel it off.

Helen Waddell, *Peter Abelard* (1933)

13 Truth is the hardest substance in the world to pin down. But the one certainty is the awesome penalty exacted sooner or later from a society whose reporters stop trying.

Flora Lewis, in Julia Edwards, *Women of the World: The Great Foreign Correspondents* (1988)

14 We shall know that we have begun to speak true by an increased hunger for true-speaking; we shall have the whole hunger only after we have given ourselves the first taste of it.

Laura Riding Jackson, *The Telling* (1967)

15 The simplest and most familiar truth seems new and wonderful the instant we ourselves experience it for the first time.

Marie von Ebner-Eschenbach, *Aphorisms* (1893)

16 There are so few truth-speaking traditions in this society in which the myth of "Western civilization" has claimed the allegiance of so many. We have rarely been encouraged and equipped to appreciate the fact that the truth works, that it releases the Spirit and that it is a joyous thing.

Toni Cade Bambara, in Claudia Tate, ed., *Black Women Writers at Work* (1983)

17 And if sun comes / How shall we greet him? / Shall we not dread him, / Shall we not fear him / After so lengthy a / Session with shade?

Gwendolyn Brooks, "truth," *Annie Allen* (1949)

18 Spiritual empowerment is evidenced in our lives by our willingness to tell ourselves the truth, to listen to the truth when it's told to us, and to dispense truth as lovingly as possible, when we feel compelled to talk from the heart.

Christina Baldwin, *Life's Companion* (1990)

19 My mouth is effective in its speech; I do not go back on my word.

Queen Hatshepsut, "Speech of the Queen" (c. 1450 B.C.), in Margaret Busby, ed., *Daughters of Africa* (1992)

20 I am not afraid of the pen, or the scaffold, or the sword. I will tell the truth wherever I please.

Mother Jones, in Linda Atkinson, *Mother Jones* (1978)

1 There are few nudities so objectionable as the naked truth.

  Agnes Repplier, "The Gayety of Life," *Compromises* (1904)

2 The naked truth is always better than the best-dressed lie.

  Ann Landers, syndicated column (1991)

3 Truth can be outraged by silence quite as cruelly as by speech.

  Amelia E. Barr, *The Bow of Orange Ribbon* (1886)

4 What a word is truth. Slippery, tricky, unreliable.

  Lillian Hellman, "On Reading Again," *Three* (1979)

5 Between the two poles of whole-truth and half-truth is slung the chancy hammock in which we all rock.

  Shana Alexander, *Talking Woman* (1976)

6 Seldom, very seldom, does complete truth belong to any human disclosure; seldom can it happen that something is not a little disguised, or a little mistaken.

  Jane Austen, *Emma* (1816)

7 To me the truth is something which cannot be told in a few words, and those who simplify the universe only reduce the expansion of its meaning.

  Anaïs Nin (1932), *The Diary of Anaïs Nin*, vol. 1 (1966)

8 My husband, who is a lawyer, is very careful with words and with the truth. He thinks that the truth exists, and it's something that is beyond questioning, which I think is totally absurd. I have several versions of how we met and how wonderful he was and all that. At least twenty. And I'm sure that they are all true. He has one. And I'm positive that it's not true.

  Isabel Allende, in Naomi Epel, ed., *Writers Dreaming* (1993)

9 People said they wanted the truth, but what they really wanted was the segment of truth that would frank them. The whole truth was too terrible for most people to contemplate.

  Anthony Gilbert, *A Spy for Mr. Crook* (1944)

10 Sometimes, surely, truth is closer to imagination—or to intelligence, to love—than to fact? To be accurate is not to be right.

  Shirley Hazzard, *The Evening of the Holiday* (1965)

11 People do think that if they avoid the truth, it might change to something better before they have to hear it.

  Marsha Norman, *The Fortune Teller* (1987)

12 Many people choose, early on, their own truths from the large smorgasbord available. And once they've chosen them, for good reason or no reason, they then proceed rather selectively, wisely gathering whatever will bolster them or at least carry out the color scheme.

  Peg Bracken, *I Didn't Come Here to Argue* (1969)

13 We are better deceived by having some truth told us than none.

  Charlotte Lennox, *Henrietta* (1758)

14 The great advantage about telling the truth is that nobody ever believes it.

  Dorothy L. Sayers, *Gaudy Night* (1935)

15 Tell people the truth, they laugh. The truth is so tragic they have to pretend it's a joke.

  Lucille Kallen, *Out There, Somewhere* (1964)

16 The language of truth is too simple for inexperienced ears.

  Frances Wright, *A Few Days in Athens* (1822)

17 The truth often does sound unconvincing.

  Agatha Christie, *Ordeal by Innocence* (1959)

18 Of course, it's the same old story. Truth usually is the same old story.

  Margaret Thatcher, in *Time* (1981)

19 Truth is so impossible. Something has to be done for it.

  Ivy Compton-Burnett, *Darkness and Day* (1951)

20 The truth does not change according to our ability to stomach it emotionally.

  Flannery O'Connor, in Sally Fitzgerald, ed., *The Habit of Being* (1979)

21 What a weak barrier is truth when it stands in the way of an hypothesis!

  Mary Wollstonecraft, *A Vindication of the Rights of Woman* (1792)

22 Truth . . . is the first casualty of tyranny.

  Barbara Grizzuti Harrison, "Nadia Comaneci," *The Astonishing World* (1992)

1 Truth made you a traitor as it often does in a time of scoundrels.
　　Lillian Hellman, *Scoundrel Time* (1976)

2 The truth which may not be told, is the truth which cannot be told.
　　Mary Butts, *Ashe of Rings* (1925)

3 Truth isn't in accounts but in account books.
　　Josephine Tey, *The Daughter of Time* (1951)

4 You cannot weave truth on a loom of lies.
　　Suzette Haden Elgin, *Native Tongue* (1984)

5 I never know how much of what I say is true. If I did, I'd bore myself to death.
　　Bette Midler, *A View From a Broad* (1980)

6 If you do not tell the truth about yourself you cannot tell it about other people.
　　Virginia Woolf, "The Leaning Tower," *The Moment* (1947)

7 You never find yourself until you face the truth.
　　Pearl Bailey, *The Raw Pearl* (1968)

8 I don't tell the truth any more to those who can't make use of it. I tell it mostly to myself, because it always changes me.
　　Anaïs Nin (1929), *Linotte, the Early Diary of Anaïs Nin*, vol. 4 (1985)

9 It takes two to tell the truth. . . . one to tell, one to hear. A speaker and a receiver. To tell the truth about any complex situation requires a certain attitude in the receiver.
　　Sybille Bedford, *A Compass Error* (1968)

10 It is terrible to destroy a person's picture of himself in the interests of truth or some other abstraction.
　　Doris Lessing, *The Grass Is Singing* (1950)

11 So often the truth is told with hate, and lies are told with love.
　　Rita Mae Brown, *Bingo* (1988)

12 Truthfulness so often goes with ruthlessness.
　　Dodie Smith, *I Capture the Castle* (1948)

13 Are we to go out with trumpets and tell everything we know, just because it is true? Is there not such a thing as egotistical truthfulness?
　　Constance Fenimore Woolson, *Anne* (1882)

14 The man who never tells an unpalatable truth "at the wrong time" (the right time has yet to be discovered), is the man whose success in life is fairly well assured.
　　Agnes Repplier, "Are Americans Timid?" *Under Dispute* (1924)

15 Truth is the only good and the purest pity. . . . Men lie for profit or for pity. All lies turn to poison, but a lie that is told for pity or shame breeds such a host of ills that no power on earth can compass their redemption.
　　Storm Jameson, *The Clash* (1922)

16 It is always hard to hear the buried truth from another person.
　　May Sarton, *Mrs. Stevens Hears the Mermaids Singing* (1965)

17 When an old truth ceases to be applicable, it does not become any truer by being stood on its head.
　　Hannah Arendt, *On Revolution* (1963)

18 Not everything in church is truth. And not all truth turns up in church.
　　Faith Sullivan, *The Cape Ann* (1988)

19 Truth has never been, can never be, contained in any one creed or system!
　　Mrs. Humphry Ward, *Robert Elsmere* (1888)

20 Any *truth*, no matter how valid, if emphasized to the *exclusion* of other truths of equal importance, is practical error.
　　Kathryn Kuhlman, *I Believe in Miracles* (1962)

21 Many a truth is the result of an error.
　　Marie von Ebner-Eschenbach, *Aphorisms* (1893)

22 The truth is balance, but the opposite of truth, which is unbalance, may not be a lie.
　　Susan Sontag, "Simone Weil" (1963), *Against Interpretation* (1966)

23 Nobody speaks the truth when there's something they must have.
　　Elizabeth Bowen, *The House in Paris* (1935)

24 The truth invariably arrives several years after you need it.
　　Mary Kay Blakely, *Wake Me When It's Over* (1989)

25 What would happen if one woman told the truth about her life? / The world would split open.
　　Muriel Rukeyser, "Käthe Kollwitz," *The Speed of Darkness* (1968)

1 Miriam's only fault is a habit of pushing the truth out in front of her like a wheelbarrow.

Margaret Millar, *Rose's Last Summer* (1952)

2 She died for truth, and she died of it. Some truths are mortal illnesses.

Marilyn French, *The Women's Room* (1977)

3 There are only two ways to tell the one hundred percent truth: anonymously and posthumously.

Susan Ohanian, *Ask Ms. Class* (1996)

4 He led a double life. Did that make him a liar? He did not feel a liar. He was a man of two truths.

Iris Murdoch, *The Sacred and Profane Love Machine* (1974)

See also Frankness, Honesty, Lying, Platitudes, Real, Reality, Sincerity.

## ✌ TURKEY

5 Istanbul . . . the constant beating of the wave of the East against the rock of the West.

Susan Moody, *Mosaic* (1991)

6 All the *salt* of Turkish life consists of politics and official intrigue.

Isabel Burton, *The Inner Life of Syria, Palestine, and the Holy Land* (1884)

## ✌ TWILIGHT

7 Twilight was the worst hour, because it was the hour of indecision.

Helen Eustis, *The Horizontal Man* (1962)

8 At twilight / we are all / at twilight / we are / at twilight / we are all orphans.

Elizabeth Coatsworth, "At Twilight," *Down Half the World* (1968)

9 It is in this unearthly first hour of spring twilight that earth's almost agonized livingness is most felt. This hour is so dreadful to some people that they hurry indoors and turn on the lights.

Elizabeth Bowen, *The Death of the Heart* (1938)

10 If there be one hour of the twenty-four which has the life of day without its labor, and the rest of night without its slumber, it is the lovely and languid hour of twilight.

L.E. Landon, *Francesca Carrara* (1834)

11 Sweet hour! when every anxious thought is still.

Cynthia Taggart, "Evening" (1817), *Poems* (1832)

See also Darkness, Evening, Night, Sunset.

## ✌ TWO KINDS OF PEOPLE

12 We are divided into two categories of people: those of us who are trying to escape from something, and those of us who are trying to find something.

Ileana, Princess of Rumania, in William Nichols, ed., *Words to Live By* (1962)

13 There are two kinds of people, those who live for their outsides and those who live for their insides.

Francesca Bendeke, in Brenda Ueland, *Me* (1983)

14 The world seems to be divided into two groups of people: those who say you can never get something for nothing, and those muddled but happy creatures who maintain that the best things in life are free.

Janet Gillespie, *The Joy of a Small Garden* (1963)

15 I learned to distinguish between the two kinds of people in the world: those who have known inescapable sorrow and those who have not.

Pearl S. Buck, *The Child Who Never Grew* (1950)

16 There were clearly two classes of people in the world: those for whom the world was magnified and enriched in words and those who could never find the beautiful world of their living and knowing on any sheet of paper.

Jessamyn West, *Cress Delahanty* (1948)

17 There are, broadly speaking, two kinds of workers in the world, the people who do all the work, and the people who think they do all the work. The latter class is generally the busiest, the former never has time to be busy.

Stella Benson, *I Pose* (1915)

18 The two kinds of people on earth I mean, / Are the people who lift and the people who lean.

Ella Wheeler Wilcox, "Which Are You?" *Custer* (1896)

1 There are only two kinds of people in the world that really count. One kind's wheat and the other kind's emeralds.

   Edna Ferber, *So Big* (1924)

2 There are two kinds of men and women, those who have in them resisting as their way of winning and those who have in them attacking as their way of winning.

   Gertrude Stein, *The Making of Americans* (1925)

3 Sometimes I think there are two kinds of people— the autobiographists and the biographists.

   Stella Benson, *Pipers and a Dancer* (1924)

4 There are two kinds of people in the world: those who live poor on a lot and those who live rich on a little.

   Marcelene Cox, in *Ladies' Home Journal* (1946)

5 There are, I sometimes think, only two sorts of people in this world—the settled and the nomad— and there is a natural antipathy between them, whatever the land to which they may belong.

   Freya Stark, *A Winter in Arabia* (1940)

6 There're two kinds of people—those who think there are two kinds of people and those who have more sense.

   James Tiptree, Jr., *Up the Walls of the World* (1978)

See also Human Differences.

## ❦ TYRANNY

7 None can be tyrants but cowards.

   Mary Astell, *An Essay in Defense of the Female Sex* (1697)

8 It is . . . far easier to act under conditions of tyranny than it is to think.

   Hannah Arendt, *The Human Condition* (1958)

9 Every successful revolution puts on in time the robes of the tyrant it has deposed.

   Barbara W. Tuchman, in *Reader's Digest* (1982)

10 A good deal of tyranny goes by the name of protection.

   Crystal Eastman, in *Equal Rights* (1924)

See also Dictators, Oppression.

# U

## ♮ UNCERTAINTY

1 A new beatitude I write for thee, / "Blessed are they who are not sure of things."

    Julia C.R. Dorr, "A New Beatitude," *Poems* (1892)

2 Uncertainty is the prerequisite to gaining knowledge and frequently the result as well.

    Edith Hamilton, *Spokesmen for God* (1949)

3 The only thing that makes life possible is permanent, intolerable uncertainty: not knowing what comes next.

    Ursula K. LeGuin, *The Left Hand of Darkness* (1969)

4 Uncertainty is the inner circle of hell.

    Anne Finger, *Past Due* (1990)

See also Confusion, Doubt, Puzzlement.

## ♮ UNCLES

5 I have nothing to say against uncles in general. They are usually very excellent people, and very convenient to little boys and girls.

    Dinah Maria Mulock Craik, title story, *The Little Lame Prince* (1875)

6 I've got an uncle myself. Nobody should be held responsible for their uncles. Nature's little throwbacks—that's how I look at it.

    Agatha Christie, "The Girl in the Train," *The Listerdale Mystery* (1934)

See also Family.

## ♮ THE UNCONSCIOUS

7 More than a burial ground for unacceptable ideas and wishes, the unconscious is the spawning ground of intuition and insight, the source of humor, of poetic imagery, and of scientific analogy.

    Judith Groch, *The Right to Create* (1969)

8 The unconscious is like a black dog. And psychoanalysis simply teaches the human being that his happiness and success depend upon his attitude toward the black dog—his beast, his property—his dog. It teaches that the best way is to make friends with the dog and to understand his nature, to conciliate him, not to be ashamed of him, not brutal to him, nor overindulgent to him. But most of all, to *know* him.

    Katharine Butler Hathaway, *The Journals and Letters of the Little Locksmith* (1946)

9 You're always running into people's unconscious.

    Marilyn Monroe, in Gloria Steinem, "Marilyn: The Woman Who Died Too Soon," *Ms.* (1972)

See also Mind.

## ♮ UNDERSTANDING

10 The crown of life is neither happiness nor annihilation; it is understanding.

    Winifred Holtby, in Vera Brittain, *Testament of Friendship* (1940)

11 The motto should not be: Forgive one another; rather, Understand one another.

    Emma Goldman, *Anarchism* (1910)

12 We / do not admire what / we cannot understand.

    Marianne Moore, "Poetry" (1921), *Selected Poems* (1935)

1 I want, by understanding myself, to understand others. I want to be all that I am capable of becoming.

    Katherine Mansfield (1922), *Journal of Katherine Mansfield* (1927)

2 We can sometimes love what we do not understand, but it is impossible completely to understand what we do not love.

    Anna Jameson, *A Commonplace Book* (1855)

3 You can't recover from what you do not understand.

    Lillian Hellman, *Maybe* (1980)

4 The growth of understanding follows an ascending spiral rather than a straight line.

    Joanna Field, *A Life of One's Own* (1934)

5 For the past several generations we've forgotten what the psychologists call our *archaic understanding*, a willingness to know things in their deepest, most mythic sense. We're all born with archaic understanding, and I'd guess that the loss of it goes directly along with the loss of ourselves as creators.

    Madeleine L'Engle, *Walking on Water* (1980)

6 Understanding . . . is a gift we should never offer uninvited.

    Nan Fairbrother, *An English Year* (1954)

7 More piercing, more unbearable than blame / Is to be understood.

    Frances Cornford, "The Betrayer" (1942), *Traveling Home* (1948)

8 Why do other people rob you with their understanding, stealing your discoveries and your guesses, invading the special domain of your insight?

    Elizabeth Bibesco, *The Fir and the Palm* (1924)

9 People don't want to be understood—I mean not completely. It's too destructive. Then they haven't anything left. They don't want complete sympathy or complete understanding. They want to be treated carelessly and taken for granted lots of times.

    Anne Morrow Lindbergh, *Bring Me a Unicorn* (1971)

10 I firmly believe kids don't want your understanding. They want your trust, your compassion, your blinding love and your car keys, but you try to understand them and you're in big trouble.

    Erma Bombeck, *If Life Is a Bowl of Cherries, What Am I Doing in the Pits?* (1971)

11 Young folks don't want you to understand 'em. You've got no more right to understand them than you have to play their games or wear their clothes. They belong to themselves.

    Edna Ferber, *Great Son* (1944)

12 Children from ten to twenty don't *want* to be understood. Their whole ambition is to feel strange and alien and misinterpreted so that they can live austerely in some stone tower of adolescence, their privacies unviolated.

    Phyllis McGinley, "New Year and No Resolutions," *Merry Christmas, Happy New Year* (1959)

13 Nothing's easier than believing we understand experiences we've never had.

    Gwen Bristow, *Tomorrow Is Forever* (1943)

14 I value more than I despise / My tendency to sin, / Because it helps me sympathize / With all my tempted kin.

    Ella Wheeler Wilcox, "Understood," *New Thought Pastels* (1906)

15 Real charity and a real ability never to condemn—the one real virtue—is so often the result of a waking experience that gives a glimpse of what lies beneath things.

    Ivy Compton-Burnett (1913), in Hilary Spurling, *Ivy* (1984)

16 Whatever people in general do not understand, they are always prepared to dislike; the incomprehensible is always the obnoxious.

    L.E. Landon, *Romance and Reality* (1831)

17 When we find that we are not liked, we assert that we are not understood; when probably the dislike we have excited proceeds from our being too fully comprehended.

    Countess of Blessington, *Desultory Thoughts and Reflections* (1839)

18 It is not a bad thing in a tale that you understand only half of it.

    Isak Dinesen, "The Dreamers," *Seven Gothic Tales* (1934)

19 Mabel Pettigrew thought: I can read him like a book. She had not read a book for over forty years,

could never concentrate on reading, but this nevertheless was her thought.

Muriel Spark, *Memento Mori* (1959)

1 This has been a most wonderful evening. Gertrude has said things tonight it will take her ten years to understand.

Alice B. Toklas, interview by Mortimer Adler (1976)

2 If you can keep your head when all about you are losing theirs, it's just possible you haven't grasped the situation.

Jean Kerr, *Please Don't Eat the Daisies* (1957)

See also Awareness, Empathy, Insight, Knowledge, Learning, Revelation, Self-Knowledge.

## ❦ UNEMPLOYMENT

3 In modern society, fear of unemployment remains the darkest of the shadows thrown by the past. In an industrial order, a man out of work is almost a man out of life.

Barbara Ward, *Faith and Freedom* (1954)

4 Of all the aspects of social misery nothing is so heartbreaking as unemployment.

Jane Addams, *Twenty Years at Hull House* (1910)

5 What is haunting is that people fallen off the train threaten those who remain on board.

Louise Bernikow, *Alone in America* (1986)

6 Many men . . . tell us the unemployed have always been with us, and always must be. It is the oldest reason in the world for tolerating injustice and misery.

Ida Tarbell, *New Ideals in Business* (1914)

See also Retirement, Work.

## ❦ UNEXPECTED

7 Truly nothing is to be expected but the unexpected!

Alice James (1891), in Anna Robeson Burr, *Alice James* (1934)

8 If you do nothing unexpected, nothing unexpected happens.

Fay Weldon, *Moon Over Minneapolis* (1991)

9 The cream of enjoyment in this life is always impromptu. The chance walk; the unexpected visit; the unpremeditated journey; the unsought conversation or acquaintance.

Fanny Fern, *Caper Sauce* (1872)

10 The cloud never comes in that quarter of the horizon from which we watch for it.

Elizabeth Gaskell, *North and South* (1854)

See also Expectations, Shocking, Surprise.

## ❦ UNHAPPINESS

11 Ah! Those strange people who have the courage to be unhappy! Are they unhappy, by the way?

Alice James (1889), in Anna Robeson Burr, *Alice James* (1934)

12 How do they who think they are unhappy differ from they who actually are?

Comtesse Diane, *Les Glanes de la Vie* (1898)

See also Bitterness, Depression, Despair, Disappointment, Discontent, Loneliness, Melancholy, Misery, Misfortune, Pouting, Sorrow, Suffering, Trouble.

## ❦ UNIFORMITY

13 The strongest bulwark of authority is uniformity; the least divergence from it is the greatest crime.

Emma Goldman, "The Individual, Society and the State" (1940), in Alix Kates Shulman, ed., *Red Emma Speaks* (1983)

See also Conventionality, Conventions.

## ❦ UNINHIBITED

14 I had got to the dawn of the beautiful not caring, but fully aware, stage, which degenerates so imperceptibly into the doing something unpermissible stage.

Caitlin Thomas, *Leftover Life to Kill* (1957)

1 I'm completely uninhabited.
  Jane Ace, in Goodman Ace, *Ladies and Gentlemen, Easy Aces* (1970)

## ❧ UNIQUENESS

2 Nature never repeats herself, and the possibilities of one human soul will never be found in another.
  Elizabeth Cady Stanton, "The Solitude of Self," in *The Woman's Column* (1892)

3 Since you are like no other being ever created since the beginning of Time, you are incomparable.
  Brenda Ueland, *If You Want to Write* (1938)

4 In order to be irreplaceable one must always be different.
  Coco Chanel, in Marcel Haedrich, *Coco Chanel* (1972)

5 Meeting people unlike oneself does not enlarge one's outlook; it only confirms one's idea that one is unique.
  Elizabeth Bowen, *The House in Paris* (1935)

6 Everything about her was at once vigorous and exquisite, at once strong and fine. He had a confused sense that she must have cost a great deal to make, that a great many dull and ugly people must, in some mysterious way, have been sacrificed to produce her.
  Edith Wharton, *The House of Mirth* (1905)

See also Eccentricity, Human Differences, Individuality, Originality.

## ❧ UNITED NATIONS

7 The United Nations emerged as a temple of official good intentions, a place where governments might—without abating their transgressions—go to church; a place made remote—by agreed untruth and procedural complexity, and by tedium itself—from the risk of intense public involvement.
  Shirley Hazzard, *Countenance of Truth* (1990)

8 Since the moment of the United Nations' inception, untold energies have been expended by governments not only toward the exclusion of persons of principle and distinction from the organization's leading positions, but toward the installation of men whose character and affiliations would as far as possible preclude any serious challenge to governmental sovereignty.
  Shirley Hazzard, *Countenance of Truth* (1990)

9 If the United Nations is a country unto itself, then the commodity it exports most is words.
  Esther B. Fein, in *The New York Times* (1985)

## ❧ UNITED STATES

10 America! America! / God shed His grace on thee / And crown thy good with brotherhood / From sea to shining sea!
  Katherine Lee Bates, "America the Beautiful" (1895)

11 Give me your tired, your poor, / Your huddled masses yearning to breathe free, / The wretched refuse of your teeming shore. / Send these, the homeless, tempest-tossed, to me, / I lift my lamp beside the golden door!
  Emma Lazarus, "The New Colossus," inscription on the Statue of Liberty (1883), *The Poems of Emma Lazarus*, vol. 1 (1888)

12 I fell in love with my country—its rivers, prairies, forests, mountains, cities and people. No one can take my love of country away from me! I felt then, as I do now, it's a rich, fertile, beautiful land, capable of satisfying all the needs of its people. It could be a paradise on earth if it belonged to the people, not to a small owning class.
  Elizabeth Gurley Flynn, *Rebel Girl* (1973)

13 In the United States there is more space where nobody is than where anybody is. That is what makes America what it is.
  Gertrude Stein, *The Geographical History of America* (1936)

14 Americans have two ardent passions; the love of liberty, and love of distinction.
  Mrs. Sarah J. Hale, *Traits of American Life* (1835)

15 After baseball, America's favorite pastime may be the process of reinventing itself, continuously redefining its identity and searching for its soul.
  Brenda Payton, in *The San Francisco Review of Books* (1993)

1 America, which has the most glorious present still existing in the world today, hardly stops to enjoy it, in her insatiable appetite for the future.

    Anne Morrow Lindbergh, *Gift From the Sea* (1955)

2 Every American carries in his bloodstream the heritage of the malcontent and the dreamer.

    Dorothy Fuldheim, *A Thousand Friends* (1974)

3 The melting pot's . . . purpose is to produce that "All-American" product. And that product is certainly not dark-skinned, does not speak American Sign Language or with an "ethnic accent," is not poor, is certainly not lesbian or gay, and is not old.

    Paula Ross, "Women, Oppression, Privilege, and Competition," in Valerie Miner and Helen E. Longino, eds., *Competition* (1987)

4 No other nation cherishes this illusion. An Englishman knows that a Russian Jew cannot in five years, or in twenty-five years, become English; that his standards and ideals are not convertible into English standards and ideals. A Frenchman does not see in a Bulgarian or a Czech the making of another Frenchman.

    Agnes Repplier, on the "melting pot," "The Modest Immigrant," *Counter-Currents* (1916)

5 A transplanted Irishman, German, Englishman is an American in one generation. A transplanted African is not one in five!

    Barbara Chase-Riboud, *Echo of Lions* (1989)

6 American society is very like a fish society. . . . Among certain species of fish, the only thing which determines order of dominance is length of time in the fish-bowl. The oldest resident picks on the newest resident, and if the newest resident is removed to a new bowl, he as oldest resident will pick on the newcomers.

    Margaret Mead, *And Keep Your Powder Dry* (1942)

7 America was founded on a genocide, on the unquestioned assumption of the right of white Europeans to exterminate a resident, technologically backward, colored population in order to take over the continent.

    Susan Sontag, "What's Happening in America," *Styles of Radical Will* (1966)

8 In order to be able to live at all in America I must be unafraid to live anywhere in it, and I must be able to live in the fashion and with whom I choose.

    Alice Walker (1973), *In Search of Our Mothers' Gardens* (1983)

9 I question whether I want to be integrated into America as it stands now, with its complacency and materialism, its soullessness.

    Paule Marshall, title story, *Reena* (1983)

10 In America, everybody is, but some are more than others.

    Gertrude Stein, *Everybody's Autobiography* (1937)

11 Most Americans have never seen the ignorance, degradation, hunger, sickness, and futility in which many other Americans live. . . . They won't become involved in economic or political change until something brings the seriousness of the situation home to them.

    Shirley Chisholm, *Unbought and Unbossed* (1970)

12 We cannot exist as a little island of well-being in a world where two-thirds of the people go to bed hungry every night.

    Eleanor Roosevelt (1959), in Joseph P. Lash, *Eleanor: The Years Alone* (1972)

13 [The United States] is an enormous frosted cupcake in the middle of millions of starving people.

    Gloria Steinem, *Moving Beyond Words* (1994)

14 Poor America, of what avail is all her wealth, if the individuals comprising the nation are wretchedly poor? If they live in squalor, in filth, in crime, with hope and joy gone, a homeless, soilless army of human prey.

    Emma Goldman, title essay, *Anarchism* (1910)

15 It is a spiritually impoverished nation that permits infants and children to be the poorest Americans.

    Marian Wright Edelman, *The Measure of Our Success* (1992)

16 The discrepancy between American ideals and American practice—between our aims and what we actually do—creates a moral dry rot which eats away at the foundations of our democratic faith.

    Helen Gahagan Douglas (1948), *A Full Life* (1982)

17 The "American dream" . . . means an economy in which people who work hard can get ahead and each new generation lives better than the last one. The "American dream" also means a democratic political system in which most people feel they can affect public decisions and elect officials who will speak for them. In recent years, the dream has been fading.

    Alice M. Rivlin, *Reviving the American Dream* (1992)

1 America is like an unfaithful lover who promised us more than we got.

    Charlotte Bunch, "Speaking Out, Reaching Out," *Passionate Politics* (1987)

2 What the people want is very simple. They want an America as good as its promise.

    Barbara Jordan, speech (1977)

3 I don't measure America by its achievement, but by its potential.

    Shirley Chisholm, *Unbought and Unbossed* (1970)

4 Americans ignore history, for to them everything has always seemed new under the sun. The national myth is that of creativity and progress, of a steady climbing upward into power and prosperity, both for the individual and for the country as a whole. Americans see history as a straight line and themselves standing at the cutting edge of it as representatives for all mankind.

    Frances FitzGerald, *Fire in the Lake* (1972)

5 I distrust the rash optimism in this country that cries, "Hurrah, we're all right! This is the greatest nation on earth," when there are grievances that call loudly for redress.

    Helen Keller, *Optimism* (1903)

6 We all take refuge in the optimism which is typical of this great creative nation. Every situation has found us unprepared.

    Frances Perkins, *People at Work* (1934)

7 The happy ending is our national belief.

    Mary McCarthy, "America the Beautiful: The Humanist in the Bathtub" (1947), *On the Contrary* (1961)

8 These Americans believe that everything is possible.

    Fredrika Bremer (1849), *America of the Fifties* (1924)

9 Americans . . . believe in the future as if it were a religion; they believe that there is nothing they cannot accomplish, that solutions wait somewhere for all problems, like brides.

    Frances FitzGerald, *Fire in the Lake* (1972)

10 Nothing is impossible in the United States.

    Eve Curie, *Madame Curie* (1938)

11 How hard it is for Americans, even Americans of good will, not to consider themselves the center of the universe!

    Simone de Beauvoir, *All Said and Done* (1972)

12 America has invested her religion as well as her morality in sound income-paying securities. She has adopted the unassailable position of a nation blessed because it deserves to be blessed; and her sons, whatever other theologies they may affect or disregard, subscribe unreservedly to this national creed.

    Agnes Repplier, "Condescension in Americans," *Times and Tendencies* (1931)

13 America has a history of political isolation and economic self-sufficiency; its citizens have tended to regard the rest of the world as a disaster area from which lucky or pushy people emigrate to the Promised Land.

    Alison Lurie, *The Language of Clothes* (1981)

14 Memory in America suffers amnesia.

    Meridel Le Sueur, *Crusaders* (1955)

15 We are a people who do not want to keep much of the past in our heads. It is considered unhealthy in America to remember mistakes, neurotic to think about them, psychotic to dwell upon them.

    Lillian Hellman, *Scoundrel Time* (1976)

16 Americans think that death is optional. They may not admit it, and will probably laugh if it's suggested; but it's a state of mind—a kind of national leitmotiv if you like—that colors everything they do. There's a nagging suspicion that you can delay death (or—who knows?—avoid it altogether) if you really try.

    Jane Walmsley, *Brit-Think, Ameri-Think* (1986)

17 He had never overheard Americans conversing without the word *dollar* being pronounced between them. Such unity of purpose, such sympathy of feeling, can, I believe, be found nowhere else, except, perhaps, in an ants' nest.

    Mrs. Trollope, *Domestic Manners of the Americans* (1832)

18 Americans talk a great deal about the price of things—more, I consider, than is entertaining, sometimes!

    Sara Jeannette Duncan, *An American Girl in London* (1900)

19 Americans relate all effort, all work, and all of life itself to the dollar. Their talk is of nothing but dollars.

    Nancy Mitford, *Noblesse Oblige* (1956)

1 Verily what bishops are to the English, bankers are to Americans.

> Mabel Ulrich, "A Doctor's Diary, 1904-1932," in *Scribner's Magazine* (1933)

2 What the Spanish War began the World War accomplished: America became the world's banker and ceased to be the world's pioneer!

> Anna Louise Strong, *I Change Worlds* (1935)

3 America is God equals America equals Business equals America equals God.

> Oriana Fallaci, *Penelope at War* (1966)

4 The crucial disadvantage of aggression, competitiveness and skepticism as national characteristics is that these qualities cannot be turned off at five o'clock.

> Margaret Halsey, *The Folks at Home* (1952)

5 Americans are nature-lovers: but they only admit of nature proofed and corrected by man.

> Simone de Beauvoir, *America Day by Day* (1948)

6 Americans live in a society of replacement parts— in theory anyone can become President or sanitation inspector.

> Frances FitzGerald, *Fire in the Lake* (1972)

7 I like Americans. They are so ridiculous. They are always risking their lives to save a minute. The pavement under their feet is red-hot.

> Nancy Boyd, *Distressing Dialogues* (1924)

8 We are a nation of twenty million bathrooms, with a humanist in every tub.

> Mary McCarthy, "America the Beautiful: The Humanist in the Bathtub" (1947), *On the Contrary* (1961)

9 American humor . . . is not subtle. It is something that makes you laugh the moment you hear it, you have not to think a scrap.

> Elinor Glyn, *Elizabeth Visits America* (1909)

10 Everything is "colossalized"—events, fortunes, accidents, climate, conversation, ambitions—everything is in the extreme. . . . They can't even have a tram run off a line, which in England or France might kill one or two people, without its making a holocaust of half a street full. . . . The thing which surprises me is they should still employ animals of normal size; one would expect to see elephants and mammoths drawing the hansoms and carts!

> Elinor Glyn, *Elizabeth Visits America* (1909)

11 Americans specially love superlatives. The phrases "biggest in the world," "finest in the world," are on all lips.

> Isabella L. Bird, *A Lady's Life in the Rocky Mountains* (1880)

12 America has enjoyed the doubtful blessing of a single-track mind.

> Ellen Glasgow, *The Woman Within* (1954)

13 Life for the European is a career; for the American, it is a hazard.

> Mary McCarthy, "America the Beautiful: The Humanist in the Bathtub" (1947), *On the Contrary* (1961)

14 All the freedom enjoyed in America, beyond what is enjoyed in England, is enjoyed solely by the disorderly at the expense of the orderly.

> Mrs. Trollope, *Domestic Manners of the Americans* (1832)

15 The idea of self-government is foreign to Americans. . . . Self-government is a form of self-control, self-limitation. It goes against our whole grain. We're supposed to go after what we want, not question whether we really need it.

> Judith Rossner, *Any Minute I Can Split* (1972)

16 People feel so strongly in this country that you ought to be able to fix at once anything that goes wrong. Press a button and something happens. Then they try to manage our political system or our economic system in the same way.

> Margaret Mead, with James Baldwin, *A Rap on Race* (1971)

17 They are noisy and talkative but very reserved, self-conscious and a little hypocritical, but they burn more boats and throw their bonnets over more windmills than any people on earth.

> Nancy Hoyt, *Roundabout* (1926)

See also Cities, Democracy, New England, The North, The South, The West, individual cities and states.

⟨ UNIVERSAL

18 Let me stand in my age with all its waters flowing round me. If they sometimes subdue, they must finally upbear me, for I seek the universal—and that must be the best.

> Margaret Fuller, *Summer on the Lakes* (1844)

1 Unless I am a part of everything I am nothing.

　　Penelope Lively, *Moon Tiger* (1987)

2 The personal, if it is deep enough, becomes universal, mythical, symbolic.

　　Anaïs Nin (1946), *The Diary of Anaïs Nin*, vol. 4 (1971)

## ❧ UNIVERSE

3 As I walk . . as I walk . . / The universe . . is walking with me . . / Beautifully . . it walks before me . . . . / Beautifully . . on every side . . . . / As I walk . . I walk with beauty.

　　Mary Austin, personal walking chant, *Everyman's Genius* (1925)

4 So loving is the universe, so joyful, so determined to give us everything we need and to love us and show us the way to live, too, that we are beaten to the ground, boiled by God's waves, as we play in the surf.

　　Sophy Burnham, *A Book of Angels* (1990)

5 Two forces rule the universe: light and gravity.

　　Simone Weil, *Gravity and Grace* (1947)

6 The entire universe is nothing but a great metaphor.

　　Simone Weil, *First and Last Notebooks* (1970)

7 What if the universe / is *not about* / us? Then what? / What / is it about / and what / about / *us*?

　　May Swenson, "The Universe," *To Mix With Time* (1963)

## ❧ THE UNKNOWN

8 The unknown is the largest need of the intellect.

　　Emily Dickinson (1876), in Mabel Loomis Todd, ed., *Letters of Emily Dickinson*, vol. 2 (1894)

9 There are some people who cannot get onto a train without imagining that they are about to voyage into the significant unknown; as though the notion of movement were inseparably connected with the notion of discovery, as though each displacement of the body were a displacement of the soul.

　　Margaret Drabble, "A Voyage to Cythera," in *Mademoiselle* (1967)

10 Settled things were enemies to me and soon lost their newness and color. The unknown called.

　　Agnes Smedley, *Daughter of Earth* (1929)

See also Adventure, Mystery, Newness, Strangers.

## ❧ UNSELFISHNESS

11 A person who can really be called an unselfish person has no place in life.

　　Ivy Compton-Burnett, *Elders and Betters* (1944)

See also Altruism, Codependence, Kindness.

## ❧ UNWANTED

12 The worst illness today is not leprosy or tuberculosis, but the sense of being unwanted, of not being loved, of being abandoned by all.

　　Mother Teresa, *Heart of Joy* (1987)

## ❧ USEFULNESS

13 That girl's as handy as a pocket in a shirt!

　　Mary Lasswell, *High Time* (1944)

See also Service.

## ❧ UTILITY

14 Utility is a metaphysical concept of impregnable circularity; utility is the quality in commodities that makes individuals want to buy them, and the fact that individuals want to buy commodities shows that they have utility.

　　Joan Robinson, "The Neo-Classics: Utility," *Economic Philosophy* (1962)

See also Economics.

## VACATION

1 For years, my husband and I have advocated separate vacations. But the kids keep finding us.
   Erma Bombeck, with Bil Keane, *Just Wait Til You Have Children of Your Own* (1971)

2 It has long been my belief that in times of great stress, such as a four-day vacation, the thin veneer of family unity wears off almost at once, and we are revealed in our true personalities.
   Shirley Jackson, *Raising Demons* (1956)

3 I wonder the human race has been so fond of migrations, when the young take so hardly to traveling.
   Ivy Compton-Burnett, *Parents and Children* (1941)

4 The family goes on vacation to become a family again.
   Marni Jackson, *The Mother Zone* (1992)

5 One of the fallacies of summer holidays is that you are going to get some serious reading done while you are lying on the beach.
   Nancy Stahl, *If It's Raining This Must Be the Weekend* (1979)

6 Holidays are enticing only for the first week or so. After that, it is no longer such a novelty to rise late and have little to do.
   Margaret Laurence, *A Jest of God* (1966)

See also Leisure, Travel.

## VALENTINES

7 Whoever decided that comic valentines were a good idea should have been sent away to think it over.
   Gladys Taber, *Still Cove Journal* (1981)

## VALUES

8 There is no hierarchy of values by which one culture has the right to insist on all its own values and deny those of another.
   Margaret Mead, *And Keep Your Powder Dry* (1942)

9 The essential characteristic of the first half of the twentieth century is the growing weakness, and almost the disappearance, of the idea of value.
   Simone Weil, *On Science, Necessity, and the Love of God* (1968)

10 Values linger on after the social structures which conceived them.
   Sheila Rowbotham, *Woman's Consciousness, Man's World* (1973)

See also "Family Values," Morality, Principles, Priorities.

## VANITY

11 Vanity, like murder, will out.
   Hannah Cowley, *The Belle's Stratagem* (1780)

12 All is vanity, and discovering it—the greatest vanity.
   John Oliver Hobbes, *The Sinner's Comedy* (1892)

13 Is there any vanity greater than the vanity of those who believe themselves without it?
   Amanda Cross, *The Question of Max* (1976)

14 We are so vain that we care even for the opinion of those we don't care for.
   Marie von Ebner-Eschenbach, *Aphorisms* (1893)

1 There is scarcely any fault in another which offends us more than vanity, though perhaps there is none that really injures us so little.

    Hannah More, "Self-Love," *Practical Piety* (1811)

2 Vanity is the quicksand of reason.

    George Sand, in *French Wit and Wisdom* (1950)

3 The passion of vanity has its own depths in the spirit, and is powerfully militant.

    Elizabeth Bowen, "The Apple Tree," *Look at All Those Roses* (1941)

4 Vanity has no sex.

    Fanny Fern, *Folly As It Flies* (1868)

5 Those who live on vanity must, not unreasonably, expect to die of mortification.

    Anne Ellis, in Martha Lupton, *The Speaker's Desk Book* (1937)

6 The inner vanity is generally in proportion to the outer self-deprecation.

    Edith Wharton, *The House of Mirth* (1905)

7 He didn't believe she would ever be guilty of those uncatalogued faint treacheries which vanity makes young people commit.

    Willa Cather, *Lucy Gayheart* (1935)

8 I never understand how writers can succumb to vanity—what you work the hardest on is usually the worst.

    Flannery O'Connor, in Sally Fitzgerald, ed., *The Habit of Being* (1979)

9 Pamper'd vanity is a better thing perhaps than starved pride.

    Joanna Baillie, *The Election* (1811)

See also Arrogance, Conceit, Egocentrism, Self-Importance.

## ❧ VARIETY

10 Variety is the soul of pleasure.

    Aphra Behn, *The Rover*, part 2 (1681)

See also Choice, Differences, Human Differences.

## ❧ VEGETARIANISM

11 As we talked of freedom and justice one day for all, we sat down to steaks. I am eating misery, I thought, as I took the first bite. And spit it out.

    Alice Walker, "Am I Blue," *Living by the Word* (1968)

12 Anyone who cares about the Earth—really cares—must stop eating animals.

    Linda McCartney, in Ingrid Newkirk, *Save the Animals!* (1990)

13 Our heavily meat-centered culture is at the very heart of our waste of the earth's productivity.

    Frances Moore Lappé, *Diet for a Small Planet* (1971)

14 Winners don't eat wieners.

    Ingrid Newkirk, *Save the Animals!* (1990)

15 It's the veal thing.

    Ingrid Newkirk, *Save the Animals!* (1990)

See also Animal Rights.

## ❧ VENGEANCE

16 The whole human race loses by every act of personal vengeance.

    Rae Foley, *Curtain Call* (1961)

17 Something of vengeance I had tasted for the first time; as aromatic wine it seemed, on swallowing, warm and racy; its afterflavor, metallic and corroding, gave me a sensation as if I had been poisoned.

    Charlotte Brontë, *Jane Eyre* (1847)

See also Revenge.

## ❧ VENICE

18 O! to make children of us again, nothing like Venice!

    Anna Jameson, "The House of Titian," *Studies, Stories, and Memoirs* (1838)

19 Venice is all sea and sculpture.

    Vera Brittain, *Testament of Youth* (1933)

1 A wondrous city of fairest carving, reflected in gleaming waters swirled to new patterning by every passing gondola.

> Sylvia Pankhurst, in Richard Pankhurst, *Sylvia Pankhurst* (1979)

2 It is the city of mirrors, the city of mirages, at once solid and liquid, at once air and stone.

> Erica Jong, "Venice: A City of Love and Death," in *The New York Times Magazine* (1986)

3 Venice, as a city, was a foundling, floating upon the waters like Moses in his basket among the bulrushes.

> Mary McCarthy, *Venice Observed* (1956)

4 City of plagues and brief liaisons, city of lingering deaths and incendiary loves, city of chimeras, nightmares, pigeons, bells. You are the only city in the world whose dialect has a word for the shimmer of canal water reflected on the ceiling of a room.

> Erica Jong, *Serenissima* (1987)

5 The trouble is, walking in Venice becomes compulsive once you start. Just over the next bridge, you say, and then the next one beckons.

> Daphne du Maurier, *Don't Look Now* (1971)

6 This city, with its weighty past, its small outlines, its strong odor, reveals in essence such wide perspectives that we are outside of time in it. We find here, better than elsewhere, the proof that difficulties are the best artisans of great destinies.

> Adrienne Monnier (1936), in Richard McDougall, tr., *The Very Rich Hours of Adrienne Monnier* (1976)

7 Venice astonishes more than it pleases at first sight.

> Madame de Staël, *Corinne* (1807)

8 If you read a lot, nothing is as great as you've imagined. Venice is—Venice is better.

> Fran Lebowitz, in *Travel & Leisure* (1994)

See also Italy.

## ❧ VERMONT

9 Vermont is a country unto itself.

> Pearl S. Buck, *Pearl S. Buck's America* (1971)

10 Vermonters, it seems to me, are like ethnics in their own land. They are exceedingly conscious of their difference from other Americans, and they talk a great deal about outsiders, newcomers, and people from the south.

> Jan Morris, "Vermont," *Locations* (1992)

11 Vermonters are not only charmless of manner, on the whole; they are also, as far as I can judge, utterly without pretense, and give the salutary impression that they don't care ten cents whether you are amused, affronted, intrigued, or bored stiff by them. Hardly anybody asked me how I liked Vermont. Not a soul said "Have a nice day!"

> Jan Morris, "Vermont," *Locations* (1992)

12 No Vermont town ever let anybody in it starve.

> Dorothy Canfield, "Henry and His Aunt Anna," *Four-Square* (1949)

13 Vermont is a jewel state, small but precious.

> Pearl S. Buck, *Pearl Buck's America* (1971)

See also New England.

## ❧ VERSE

14 My verses. I cannot say poems. Like everybody was then, I was following in the exquisite footsteps of Miss Millay, unhappily in my own horrible sneakers.

> Dorothy Parker, in Malcolm Cowley, ed., *Writers at Work* (1958)

15 All verse is occasional verse.

> Ellen Bryant Voigt, "The Last Class," *The Lotus Flowers* (1987)

See also Nursery Rhymes, Poetry.

## ❧ VETERINARY MEDICINE

16 We veterinarians—though trained as physicians—are, in fact, more like mechanics in many ways. Our patients are repaired only as long as their value exceeds the cost of upkeep, though often, it is true, that value is defined by emotion and love.

> Loretta Gage, with Nancy Gage, *If Wishes Were Horses* (1992)

17 The single hardest thing about being a doctor of animals [is] when the treatment isn't limited by my skill, education, or experience, or even by the state

of veterinary medicine itself, but by the depth of the client's wallet.... It's a heartbreaker when the question is medical and the answer is economic.

Loretta Gage, with Nancy Gage, *If Wishes Were Horses* (1992)

1 The poor man turned pale at lunch when his grouse was badly underdone; he hardly knew whether to eat it or cure it.

Katharine Whitehorn, "A Vet's Life," *Sunday Best* (1976)

## ❧ VICARIOUSNESS

2 Living by proxy is always a precarious expedient.

Simone de Beauvoir, *The Second Sex* (1949)

3 It is not morbidity which draws crowds to scenes of disaster or unusual joy. It is the desire to participate in a moment when life breaks through to some higher level of intensity so that one's own life might take fire from that sudden spurted flame.

Maya Deren, "The Artist As God in Haiti," in *The Tiger's Eye* (1948)

4 There is no such thing as vicarious experience.

M.P. Follett, *Creative Experience* (1924)

## ❧ VICE

5 How unjust life is, to make physical charm so immediately apparent or absent, when one can get away with vices untold for ever.

Margaret Drabble, *A Summer Bird-Cage* (1962)

6 It may be that vice, depravity, and crime are nearly always, or even perhaps always, in their essence, attempts to eat beauty, to eat what we should only look at.

Simone Weil, *Waiting for God* (1950)

See also Evil, Sin.

## ❧ VICTORY

7 More people are ruined by victory, I imagine, than by defeat.

Eleanor Roosevelt, *My Days* (1938)

8 The face of victory often resembles the face of defeat.

Jane Bowles, *Two Serious Ladies* (1943)

9 If one lives long enough, one sees that every victory sooner or later turns to defeat.

Simone de Beauvoir, *All Men Are Mortal* (1955)

See also Failure, Success, Success and Failure, Winning.

## ❧ VIETNAM WAR

10 To one people the war would appear each day, compressed between advertisements and confined to a small space in the living room; the explosion of bombs and the cries of the wounded would become the background accompaniment to dinner. For the other people the war would come one day out of a clear blue sky. In a few minutes it would be over: the bombs, released by an invisible pilot with incomprehensible intentions, would leave only the debris and the dead behind.

Frances FitzGerald, *Fire in the Lake* (1972)

11 The United States was not going into Vietnam merely for crass power objectives, but for the salvation of the Vietnamese, who like the majority of mankind, lived in poverty and ignorance.... Surely, the leader of no other nation would have made such a pledge in the midst of a war. No other leader would have expected his countrymen to take it as anything but a cynical gesture.

Frances FitzGerald, *Fire in the Lake* (1972)

12 The Vietnam war will not be over until it ends for everyone. Over four hundred thousand U.S. veterans are still recovering from wounds inflicted on their bodies and their spirit. Sixty-three million souls in Vietnam are still suffering from their "victory."

Le Ly Hayslip, with Jay Wurts, *When Heaven and Earth Changed Places* (1989)

## ❧ VILLAINS

13 As for an authentic villain, the real thing, the absolute, the artist, one rarely meets him even once in a

lifetime. The ordinary bad hat is always in part a decent fellow.

Colette, *La naissance du jour* (1928)

1  I am more and more convinced that the same energy of character which renders a man a daring villain would have rendered him useful to society, had that society been well organized.

Mary Wollstonecraft, *Letters Written During a Short Residence in Sweden, Norway, and Denmark* (1796)

See also Crime, Destruction, Evil.


## ❦ VINDICATION

2  To see men admitting that you are what you believe yourself to be, is one of the triumphs of existence.

Mary Catherwood, *Lazarre* (1901)


## ❦ VIOLENCE

3  Violence is a symptom of impotence.

Anaïs Nin (1960), *The Diary of Anaïs Nin*, vol. 6 (1976)

4  Generally speaking, violence always arises out of impotence. It is the hope of those who have no power.

Hannah Arendt (1967), in Elisabeth Young-Bruehl, *Hannah Arendt* (1982)

5  Violence is the instinctive response to fear.

Margaret Millar, *Vanish in an Instant* (1952)

6  Blows are sarcasms turned stupid.

George Eliot, *Felix Holt, The Radical* (1866)

7  Imagination is the first faculty wanting in those that do harm to their kind.

Margaret Oliphant, *Innocent: A Tale of Modern Life* (1874)

8  In violence, we forget who we are.

Mary McCarthy, "Characters in Fiction," *On the Contrary* (1961)

9  The extreme form of power is All against One, the extreme form of violence is One against All.

Hannah Arendt, "On Violence," *Crises of the Republic* (1972)

10  A violent act pierces the atmosphere, leaving a hole through which the cold, damp draft of its memory blows forever.

Jane Stanton Hitchcock, *Trick of the Eye* (1992)

11  Whipping and abuse are like laudanum; you have to double the dose as the sensibilities decline.

Harriet Beecher Stowe, *Uncle Tom's Cabin* (1852)

12  The practice of violence, like all action, changes the world, but the most probable change is to a more violent world.

Hannah Arendt, "On Violence," *Crises of the Republic* (1972)

13  Violence can destroy power; it is utterly incapable of creating it.

Hannah Arendt, "On Violence," *Crises of the Republic* (1972)

14  While violence can destroy power, it can never become a substitute for it.

Hannah Arendt, *The Human Condition* (1958)

15  Violence is its own anesthetist. The numbness it induces feels very much like calm.

Barbara Grizzuti Harrison, *Foreign Bodies* (1984)

16  America has become numb to violence because it just drowns in it, day in and day out.

Janet Reno, in *Newsweek* (1993)

17  It is organized violence on top which creates individual violence at the bottom.

Emma Goldman, "Address to the Jury" (1917), in Alix Kates Shulman, ed., *Red Emma Speaks* (1983)

18  Democracy cannot sustain itself amid a high degree of violence.

Mary Ritter Beard (1950), in Nancy F. Cott, *A Woman Making History* (1991)

19  No society that feeds its children on tales of successful violence can expect them not to believe that violence in the end is rewarded.

Margaret Mead, in *Redbook* (1972)

20  At the movies, we are gradually being conditioned to accept violence as a sensual pleasure. The directors used to say they were showing us its real face and how ugly it was in order to sensitize us to its horrors. You don't have to be very keen to see that they are now in fact desensitizing us.

Pauline Kael, *Deeper Into Movies* (1973)

21  Want of passion is, I think, a very striking characteristic of Americans, not unrelated to their predi-

lection for violence. For very few people truly have a passionate desire to achieve, and violence serves as a kind of substitute.

Marguerite Yourcenar, *With Open Eyes* (1980)

1 In our times, significantly, the three outstanding voices against violence have been silenced by murder—Mahatma Gandhi in India, Archbishop Romero in El Salvador, and Dr. Martin Luther King, here at home.

Millicent Fenwick, *Speaking Up* (1982)

2 A Queen, or a Prime Minister's secretary may be shot at in London, as we know; and probably there is no person eminent in literature or otherwise who has not been the object of some infirm brain or another. But in America the evil is sadly common.

Harriet Martineau (1836), *Autobiography*, vol. 2 (1877)

3 Violence commands both literature and life, and violence is always crude and distorted.

Ellen Glasgow, *Letters of Ellen Glasgow* (1958)

4 All history shows that the hand that cradles the rock has ruled the world, *not* the hand that rocks the cradle!

Clare Boothe Luce, *Slam the Door Softly* (1970)

5 Domestic violence is the front line of the war against women.

Pearl Cleage, "Basic Training: The Beginnings of Wisdom," *Deals With the Devil* (1993)

6 You'll ne'er mend your fortunes, nor help the just cause, / By breaking of windows, or breaking of laws.

Hannah More, speech (1817), in H. Thompson, *The Life of Hannah More* (1838)

7 The only thing that's been a worse flop than the organization of nonviolence has been the organization of violence.

Joan Baez, *Daybreak* (1968)

8 Today, together, let us repeat as our slogan that all trace of violence must disappear from this earth, then the sun will be honey-colored and music good to hear.

Monique Wittig, *Les Guérillères* (1969)

See also Abuse, Crime, Films, Rape, Television, Terrorism.

## ❧ VIRGINITY

9 In those days, young stars, male and female, were all virgins until married, and if divorced, they returned magically to that condition.

Shelley Winters, *Shelley* (1980)

10 Virginity is a state of mind, when all's said and done.

Mary Roberts Rinehart, *The Album* (1933)

See also Celibacy, Chastity.

## ❧ VIRTUE

11 Vice / Is nice / But a little virtue / Won't hurt you.

Felicia Lamport, "Axiom to Grind," *Scrap Irony* (1961)

12 Virtue is the music of the soul, the harmony of the passions; it is the order, the symmetry, the interior beauty of the mind; the source of the truest pleasures, the fountain of the sublimest and most perfect happiness.

Mary Collyer, *Felicia to Charlotte* (1744)

13 There isn't any virtue where there has never been any temptation. Virtue is just temptation, overcome.

Margaret Deland, *The Awakening of Helena Richie* (1906)

14 We shall all be perfectly virtuous when there is no longer any flesh on our bones.

Marguerite de Valois, in Kate Sanborn, *The Wit of Women* (1885)

15 I desire Virtue, though I love her not - / I have no faith in her when she is got: / I fear that she will bind and make me slave, / And send me songless to the sullen grave.

Anna Wickham, "Self Analysis," *The Contemplative Quarry* (1915)

16 Virtue has its own reward, but has no sale at the box office.

Mae West, in Joseph Weintraub, ed., *The Wit and Wisdom of Mae West* (1967)

17 You may have noted the fact that it is a person's virtues as often as his vices that make him difficult to live with.

Kate Douglas Wiggin, "The Midnight Cry," *The Village Watch-Tower* (1895)

1 I'm part of an old piety that suffers in silence and calls it virtue. And is the very devil to live with.

    Mary Virginia Micka, *The Cazenovia Journal* (1990)

2 There's a pitch of virtue about him that is exhausting.

    Margaret Deland, *John Ward, Preacher* (1888)

3 Some out of their own virtue make a god who sometimes later is a terror to them.

    Gertrude Stein, *The Making of Americans* (1925)

4 It is queer how it is always one's virtues and not one's vices that precipitate one into disaster.

    Rebecca West, "There Is No Conversation," *The Harsh Voice* (1935)

5 I am not impressed by external devices for the preservation of virtue in men or women. Marriage laws, the police, armies and navies are the mark of human incompetence.

    Dora Russell, *The Right to Be Happy* (1927)

6 Virtue can only flourish among equals.

    Mary Wollstonecraft, *A Vindication of the Rights of Men* (1790)

7 As far as the education of children is concerned I think they should be taught not the little virtues but the great ones. Not thrift but generosity and an indifference to money; not caution but courage and a contempt for danger; not shrewdness but frankness and a love of truth; not tact but love for one's neighbor and self-denial; not a desire for success but a desire to be and to know.

    Natalia Ginzburg, *The Little Virtues* (1962)

8 It is as easy for most of us to keep from stealing our dinners as it is to digest them, and there is quite as much voluntary morality involved in one process as the other.

    Jane Addams, title essay, *Democracy and Social Ethics* (1902)

9 A man hasn't got a corner on virtue just because his shoes are shined.

    Ann Petry, *The Narrows* (1953)

10 My virtue's still far too small, I don't trot it out and about yet.

    Colette, *Claudine at School* (1900)

See also Charity, Compassion, Courage, Empathy, Faithfulness, Generosity, Good and Evil, Goodness, Honesty, Humility, Kindness, Loyalty, Mercy, Patience, Purity, Simplicity, Sympathy, Thrift, Unselfishness.

## ❦ VISION

11 We will create a society where there are no rich or poor, no people without work or beauty in their lives, where money itself will disappear, where we shall all be brothers and sisters, where every one will have enough.

    Sylvia Pankhurst, speech (1921), in David Mitchell, *The Fighting Pankhursts* (1967)

12 So long as we think dugout canoes are the only possibility—all that is real or *can be* real—we will never see the ship, we will never feel the free wind blow.

    Sonia Johnson, *Going Out of Our Minds* (1987)

13 Your world is as big as you make it.

    Georgia Douglas Johnson, "Your World," in Arna Bontemps, ed., *American Negro Poetry* (1963)

14 A false vision was better than none.

    Martha Ostenso, *Wild Geese* (1925)

## ❦ VISIONS

15 Any of us can dream, but seeking vision is always done not only to heal and fulfill one's own potential, but also to learn to use that potential to serve all our relations: the two-leggeds, the four-leggeds, the wingeds, those that crawl upon the Earth, and the Mother Earth herself.

    Brooke Medicine Eagle, in Joan Halifax, *Shamanic Voices* (1979)

16 When a vision begins to form everything changes, including the air around me. I seem no longer to be in the same atmosphere. I feel a peacefulness and a love that are indescribable. I stand alone, and nothing worldly can touch me.

    Jeane Dixon, in Ruth Montgomery, *A Gift of Prophecy* (1965)

17 I have gotten back more and more to the ancient ways. This happened as I began to have visions; I was drawn back to the old ways by them. I did not choose it outwardly; it came as I released old ways of being, its irresistible call bringing me home.

    Brooke Medicine Eagle, in Joan Halifax, *Shamanic Voices* (1979)

18 Visualization, that seeing of that which is not yet, which is not actually before us, as yet, is essential

for the attainment of all the good that man may aspire to.

Tehilla Lichtenstein, "God in the Silence" (1947), in Ellen M. Umansky and Dianne Ashton, eds., *Four Centuries of Jewish Women's Spirituality* (1992)

See also Dreams, Prophecy, Voices.

## ❦ VISITS

1 It was a delightful visit; - perfect, in being much too short.

Jane Austen, *Emma* (1816)

See also Guests, Hospitality.

## ❦ VITALITY

2 Vitality . . . the one gift that no art could counterfeit, and the one the gods give least often and with least wish to be kind.

Storm Jameson, *Three Kingdoms* (1926)

See also Energy.

## ❦ VIVISECTION

3 We stand face to face with a new vice . . . the vice of scientific cruelty.

Frances Power Cobbe, *Life of Frances Power Cobbe*, vol. 2 (1894)

See also Animal Rights.

## ❦ VOICE

4 His voice was intimate as the rustle of sheets.

Dorothy Parker, "Dusk Before Fireworks," *The Collected Stories of Dorothy Parker* (1942)

5 His voice sounded like two hands rubbing together.

Veronica Black, *Last Seen Wearing* (1990)

6 Her voice went up the Major's back and around his neck like a woman's arm.

Kay Boyle, "Major Alshuster," *The White Horses of Vienna* (1936)

7 Her voice was sharp and probing, like a needle in the hands of a nervous nurse.

Ann Bannon, *Women in the Shadows* (1959)

8 Her voice had the sway of an aerialist crossing the high wire.

Eudora Welty, "Moon Lake," *The Golden Apples* (1949)

9 Her voice was heavy, throaty, expressionless. She threw it like a weapon.

Mary Roberts Rinehart, *The Window at the White Cat* (1910)

10 Her voice . . . slides over her words like cold water, as though they were stones and had no life.

Susan Moody, *Mosaic* (1991)

11 "Take it from me, nice women don't want the vote." His voice dripped fatness.

Nellie L. McClung, *The Stream Runs Fast* (1945)

12 Oh, how she loved to stand about the lobby of an afternoon, nabbing at passersby with her chronic cheerfulness, snapping her bright voice at them like a towel!

Karen Elizabeth Gordon, *Intimate Apparel* (1989)

13 When she gets excited, her voice rises to a pitch generally considered suitable only for hog-calling.

Margaret Halsey, *Some of My Best Friends Are Soldiers* (1944)

14 She had one of those high-pitched apologetic voices which seemed to make every pronouncement sound like a spirit message, inconclusive but faintly ominous.

Margery Allingham, *Safer Than Love* (1962)

## ❦ VOICES

15 I answered the voice that I was a poor girl who knew nothing of riding and warfare.

Joan of Arc (1425), in Willard Trask, tr., *Joan of Arc, A Self Portrait* (1936)

16 We have so many voices in us, how do we know which ones to obey?

Edna O'Brien, *I Hardly Knew You* (1978)

1 Might we not say to the confused voices which sometimes arise from the depths of our being, "Ladies, be so kind as to speak only four at a time"?

Anne-Sophie Swetchine, in Count de Falloux, ed., *The Writings of Madame Swetchine* (1869)

## ❧ VOLUNTEERS

2 The essence of volunteerism is not giving part of a surplus one doesn't need, but giving part of one's self. Such giving is more than a duty of the heart, but a way people help themselves by satisfying the deeper spiritual needs that represent the best that is in us.

Kathleen Kennedy Townsend, in *Christopher News Notes* (1993)

3 Volunteer activities can foster enormous leadership skills. The nonprofessional volunteer world is a laboratory for self-realization.

Madeleine Kunin, *Living a Political Life* (1994)

See also Activism, Service.

## ❧ VULGARITY

4 Vulgarity begins when imagination succumbs to the explicit.

Doris Day, in A.E. Hotchner, *Doris Day* (1975)

## ❧ VULNERABILITY

5 It is true that no one can harm the person who wears armor. But no one can help him, either.

Kristin Hunter, *The Landlord* (1966)

6 Better to be wounded, a captive, and a slave, than always to walk in armor.

Margaret Fuller, *Summer on the Lakes* (1844)

7 when i let / my defenses go / blessings came running.

Macrina Wiederkehr, *Seasons of Your Heart* (1979)

8 She has no oil on her feathers.

Josephine Tey, *Miss Pym Disposes* (1947)

9 All are / naked, none is safe.

Marianne Moore, title poem, *What Are Years?* (1941)

See also Helplessness, Powerlessness, Security.

# W

## ❧ WAITING

1  Waiting is one of the great arts.
   Margery Allingham, *The Tiger in the Smoke* (1952)

2  Everyone has their time and kind of waiting.
   Elizabeth Gaskell, *Mary Barton* (1848)

3  Waiting, done at really high speeds, will frequently look like something else.
   Carrie Fisher, *Delusions of Grandma* (1994)

4  Waiting has teeth in it.
   Margaret Hasse, "My Mother's Lullaby," *Stars Above, Stars Below* (1984)

5  Each time he dared another encounter with the clock it informed him stolidly that time was a mighty opponent to those who deliberately sought to kill it.
   Ruth Fenisong, *The Butler Died in Brooklyn* (1943)

6  We usually learn to wait only when we have no longer anything to wait for.
   Marie von Ebner-Eschenbach, *Aphorisms* (1893)

See also Impatience, Lines, Patience.

## ❧ WALKING

7  Walking is almost an ambulation of mind.
   Gretel Ehrlich, *Islands, the Universe, Home* (1991)

## ❧ WALLS

8  Walls protect and walls limit. It is in the nature of walls that they should fall. That walls should fall is the consequence of blowing your own trumpet.
   Jeanette Winterson, *Oranges Are Not the Only Fruit* (1985)

9  Constant walls and a roof do something to me at any time and when the aspens turn golden, I seethe inside until finally I revolt and leave everything.
   Edith Warner, in Peggy Pond Church, *The House at Otowi Bridge* (1959)

10  Walls turned sideways are bridges.
    Angela Davis, *An Autobiography* (1974)

11  A wall is the safeguard of simplicity.
    Alice Meynell, "The Sea Wall," *Essays* (1914)

12  Walls have an engrossing quality. If there are many of them they assert themselves and domineer. They insist on the unique importance of the contents of walls and would have you believe that the spaces above them, the slow procession of the seasons and the alternations of sunshine and rain, are accessories, pleasant or unpleasant, of walls,—indeed that they were made, and a bungling job, too, and to be disregarded as a bungling job should be, solely that walls might exist.
    Edna Brush Perkins, *The White Heart of Mojave* (1922)

See also Houses, Rooms.

## ❧ WANDERLUST

13  I desired the fate of figureheads / Which leave port early and return late / I am jealous of the return and the departure / And of the wet corals tied about their throats. . . . / Since, from the depths of danger, one returns more beautiful, / Returning with a face burning and fabled.
    Lucie Delarue-Mardrus, "Prefatory Poem," *The Figurehead* (1908)

14  I like any place that isn't here.
    Edna Ferber, "If I Should Ever Travel," *Gigolo* (1922)

1 My favorite thing is to go where I've never been.

Diane Arbus, *Diane Arbus* (1972)

2 My heart is warm with the friends I make, / And better friends I'll not be knowing; / Yet there isn't a train I wouldn't take, / No matter where it's going.

Edna St. Vincent Millay, "Travel," *Second April* (1921)

3 A nomad I will remain for life, in love with distant and uncharted places.

Isabelle Eberhardt (1902), in Nina de Voogd, tr., *The Passionate Nomad* (1988)

4 So much do I love wandering, / So much I love the sea and sky, / That it will be a piteous thing / In one small grave to lie!

Zoë Akins, "The Wanderer," *The Hills Grow Smaller* (1937)

See also Journeys, Restlessness, Travel.

## ❧ WAR

5 War has crossed out the day and replaced it with horror, and now horrors are unfolding instead of days.

Zlata Filipovic, *Zlata's Diary* (1994)

6 It was a time when only the dead / smiled.

Anna Akhmatova, "Requiem" (1935), *Poems* (1988)

7 All quiet along the Potomac to-night; / No sound save the rush of the river; / While soft falls the dew on the face of the dead— / The picket's off duty forever!

Ethel Lynn Beers, "The Picket Guard," in *Harper's Magazine* (1861)

8 War is madness.

Anaïs Nin (1939), *The Diary of Anaïs Nin*, vol. 2 (1967)

9 War will hit you hard / coming at you like lions raging.

Hind bint Utba, "Fury Against the Moslems at Uhud" (7th cent.), in Joanna Bankier and Deirdre Lashgari, eds., *Women Poets of the World* (1983)

10 War brutalizes all whom it touches; if it did not do so it could not be endured.

Agnes Newton Keith, *Three Came Home* (1947)

11 All war is insane.

Madeleine L'Engle, *A Wind in the Door* (1973)

12 War is the unfolding of miscalculations.

Barbara W. Tuchman, *The Guns of August* (1962)

13 Before a war, military science seems a real science, like astronomy. After a war it seems more like astrology.

Rebecca West, in Jonathon Green, *Morrow's International Dictionary of Contemporary Quotations* (1982)

14 The calamity of war, wherever, whenever and upon whomever it descends, is a tragedy for the whole of humanity.

Raisa M. Gorbachev, *I Hope* (1991)

15 Art transcends war. Art is the language of God and war is the barking of men. Beethoven is bigger than war.

Fannie Hurst, *Lummox* (1923)

16 You can no more win a war than you can win an earthquake.

Jeannette Rankin, in Hannah Josephson, *Jeannette Rankin* (1974)

17 I can not believe that war is the best solution. No one won the last war, and no one will win the next war.

Eleanor Roosevelt, letter to Harry S. Truman (1948), in Joseph P. Lash, *Eleanor: The Years Alone* (1972)

18 One is left with the horrible feeling now that war settles *nothing*; that to *win* a war is as disastrous as to lose one!

Agatha Christie, *An Autobiography* (1977)

19 Every war already carries within it the war which will answer it. Every war is answered by a new war, until everything, everything is smashed.

Käthe Kollwitz (1944), in Hans Kollwitz, ed., *The Diaries and Letters of Käthe Kollwitz* (1955)

20 I am sure that you will never end war with wars.

Nancy Astor, *My Two Countries* (1923)

21 The sword of murder is not the balance of justice. Blood does not wipe out dishonor nor violence indicate possession.

Julia Ward Howe, "Mother's Day Proclamation" (1870)

22 No war, not even to punish an aggressor, is a good thing. Today people must learn to take into account each others' interests, if only for the sake of their own survival. I do not believe that, in this

system of coordinates, the point where politics and simple human morality intersect is only idealism.

Raisa M. Gorbachev, *I Hope* (1991)

1 Everything you do in a war is crime in peace.

Helen McCloy, *A Change of Heart* (1973)

2 The people who are doing the work and the fighting and the dying, and those who are doing the talking, are not at all the same people.

Katherine Anne Porter, "American Statement" (1942), *The Days Before* (1952)

3 It is the people who have no say in making wars who suffer most from the consequences of them.

Philippa Carr, *The Gossamer Cord* (1992)

4 Boredom!!! Shooting!!! Shelling!!! People being killed!!! Despair!!! Hunger!!! Misery!!! Fear!!! That's my life!

Zlata Filipovic, *Zlata's Diary* (1994)

5 I do not want to see mothers and fathers digging graves for their children.

Audrey Hepburn, on her work for UNICEF, in Warren G. Harris, *Audrey Hepburn* (1994)

6 I don't believe that the big men, the politicians and the capitalists alone, are guilty of the war. Oh no, the little man is just as guilty, otherwise the peoples of the world would have risen in revolt long ago!

Anne Frank, *The Diary of a Young Girl* (1952)

7 How many are dying / from the taxes I've paid / with my tired hands?

Chrystos, "Down," *Dream On* (1991)

8 Never think that wars are irrational catastrophes: they happen when wrong ways of thinking and living bring about intolerable situations. . . . The root causes of conflict are usually to be found in some wrong way of life in which all parties have acquiesced, and for which everybody must, to some extent, bear the blame.

Dorothy L. Sayers, "Why Work?" *Creed or Chaos?* (1949)

9 If you are required to kill someone today, on the promise of a political leader that someone else shall live in peace tomorrow, believe me, you are not only a double murderer, you are a suicide, too.

Katherine Anne Porter, "The Situation in American Writing" (1939), *The Days Before* (1952)

10 War is never fatal but always lost.

Gertrude Stein, *Wars I Have Seen* (1945)

11 From the earliest wars of men to our last heartbreaking worldwide effort, all we could do was kill ourselves. Now we are able to kill the future.

Martha Gellhorn, *The Face of War* (1959)

12 Technology has allowed the world of men in our society to separate itself from the sight and the sounds of killing; from the horror of it, but not from the killing. It must be easy to kill from a roomful of fluorescent lights and wash-and-wear shirts.

Caryl Rivers, "Men and Women," in *Glamour* (1973)

13 The high stage of world-industrial development in capitalistic production finds expression in the extraordinary technical development and destructiveness of the instruments of war.

Rosa Luxemburg, *The Crisis in the German Social Democracy* (1918)

14 War is bestowed like electroshock on the depressive nation: thousands of volts jolting the system, an artificial galvanizing, one effect of which is loss of memory. War comes at the end of the twentieth century as absolute failure of imagination, scientific and political. That a war can be represented as helping a people to "feel good" about themselves, their country, is a measure of that failure.

Adrienne Rich, *What Is Found There* (1993)

15 War, which perpetuates itself under the form of preparation for war, has once and for all given the State an important role in production.

Simone Weil (1933), *Oppression and Liberty* (1955)

16 No matter what rallying cries the orators give to the idiots who fight, no matter what noble purposes they assign to wars, there is never but one reason for a war. And that is money. All wars are in reality money squabbles.

Margaret Mitchell, *Gone With the Wind* (1936)

17 One grows strangely apprehensive / When one contemplates the sense of / *Peace offensive*, / Which, aggressively commanding / That which passeth understanding / Turns the sentiment it rouses / To: "A *pax* on both your houses."

Felicia Lamport, "Embattled Oxymoron," *Cultural Slag* (1966)

1 Oh, would that men, since it would indeed please God, had not, on either side, the courage to bear arms!

> Christine de Pisan, "Lament on the Evils of the Civil War" (1410), in Josette A. Wisman, tr., *The Epistle of the Prison of Human Life* (1984)

2 War is the admission of defeat in the face of conflicting interests: by war the issue is left to chance, and the tacit assumption that the best man will win is not at all justified. It might equally be argued that the worst, the most unscrupulous man will win, although history will continue the absurd game by finding him after all the best man.

> Germaine Greer, *The Female Eunuch* (1971)

3 War may claim for itself the power to destroy and to clear the ground. It can never construct or create. It is not the means by which ideals are imposed. There is ultimately no way of combating a wrong idea but the setting forth of a right one.

> A. Maude Royden, "War and the Woman's Movement," in Charles Roden Buxton, ed., *Towards a Lasting Settlement* (1915)

4 We have war when at least one of the parties to a conflict wants something more than it wants peace.

> Jeane J. Kirkpatrick, in *Reader's Digest* (1994)

5 Only very coarse persons wanted wars.

> Pearl S. Buck, *The Old Demon* (1939)

6 I want to stand by my country, but I cannot vote for war. I vote no.

> Jeannette Rankin, casting her vote against declaration of war (1917), in Hannah Josephson, *Jeannette Rankin* (1974)

7 As a woman I can't go to war, and I refuse to send anyone else.

> Jeannette Rankin, again voting no to declaration of war (1941), in Hannah Josephson, *Jeannette Rankin* (1974)

8 I am sick of war. Every woman of my generation is sick of war. Fifty years of war. Wars rumored, wars beginning, wars fought, wars ending, wars paid for, wars endured.

> Josephine W. Johnson, *The Inland Island* (1969)

9 Arise then, women of this day! Arise, all women who have hearts, whether your baptism be that of water or of tears! Say firmly, "We will not have great questions decided by irrelevant agencies. Our husbands shall not come to us, reeking of carnage, for caresses and applause. Our sons shall not be taken from us to unlearn all that we have been able to teach them of charity, mercy and patience. We women of one country will be too tender of those of another country to allow our sons to be trained to injure theirs." From the bosom of the devastated earth a voice goes up with our own, it says, "Disarm! Disarm!"

> Julia Ward Howe, "Mother's Day Proclamation" (1870)

10 Mine eyes have seen the glory of the coming of the Lord: / He is trampling out the vintage where the grapes of wrath are stored.

> Julia Ward Howe, "Battle Hymn of the Republic," in *The Atlantic* (1862)

11 I have little faith in the theory that organized killing is the best prelude to peace.

> Ellen Glasgow, *Vein of Iron* (1935)

12 The suppression of war is not the equivalent of peace.

> Vida Dutton Scudder, *The Privilege of Age* (1939)

13 War is an old, old plant on this earth, and a natural history of it would have to tell us under what soil conditions it grows, where it plays havoc, and how it is eliminated.

> Ruth Benedict (1939), in Margaret Mead, *An Anthropologist at Work* (1959)

14 You truly point out that war is only a symptom of the whole horrid business of human behavior, and cannot be isolated, and that we shall not, even if we abolish war, abolish hate and greed. So might it have been argued about slave emancipation, that slavery was but one aspect of human disgustingness, and that to abolish it would not end the barbarity that causes it. But did the abolitionists therefore waste their breath? And do we waste ours now in protesting against war?

> Rose Macaulay, "An Open Letter" (1937), in Jane Emery, *Rose Macaulay* (1991)

15 Was that what, ultimately, war did to you? It was not the physical dangers—the mines at sea, the bombs from the air, the crisp ping of a rifle bullet as you drove over a desert track. No, it was the spiritual danger of learning how much easier life was if you ceased to think.

> Agatha Christie, *There Is a Tide* (1948)

16 Modern war, they argued, as it was plain for everyone to see, had become so diabolical, so destructive, so incompatible with ethics, Christian teaching, nineteenth-century thought or mere common sense as to be as unthinkable for men to use against one another as putting one another into a pot to

boil and eat. They also saw, being honest men, that very few people anywhere saw anything of the kind.

Sybille Bedford, *A Favorite of the Gods* (1963)

1 The worst thing about war is that so many people enjoy it.

Ellen Glasgow, *The Woman Within* (1954)

2 If we justify war, it is because all peoples always justify the traits of which they find themselves possessed, not because war will bear an objective examination of its merits.

Ruth Benedict, *Patterns of Culture* (1934)

3 All wars are sacred to those who have to fight them. If the people who started wars didn't make them sacred, who would be foolish enough to fight?

Margaret Mitchell, *Gone With the Wind* (1936)

4 Nothing so comforts the military mind as the maxim of a great but dead general.

Barbara W. Tuchman, *The Guns of August* (1962)

5 Wars may be fought by decent men, but they're not won by them.

P.D. James, *A Taste for Death* (1986)

6 Dead battles, like dead generals, hold the military mind in their dead grip.

Barbara W. Tuchman, *The Guns of August* (1962)

7 War is the supreme form of prestige.

Simone Weil, *The Notebooks of Simone Weil* (1951)

8 Since war is a convulsion that occurs when political processes fail to settle disputes among or within nations, the aftermath of war includes an upheaval of the status quo.

June A. Willenz, *Women Veterans* (1983)

9 There's a consensus out that it's OK to kill when your government decides who to kill. If you kill inside the country you get in trouble. If you kill outside the country, right time, right season, latest enemy, you get a medal.

Joan Baez, *Daybreak* (1968)

10 If it's natural to kill, why do men have to go into training to learn how?

Joan Baez, *Daybreak* (1968)

11 The least stupid question a man asks in his lifetime is not: Is there a God and is He a god or a devil? But: Brother, why are you killing me?

Storm Jameson, *The Intruder* (1956)

12 Seems nothing draws men together like killing other men.

Susan Glaspell, *Inheritors* (1921)

13 The worst barbarity of war is that it forces men collectively to commit acts against which individually they would revolt with their whole being.

Ellen Key, *War, Peace, and the Future* (1916)

14 When peace comes we will perhaps in time be able to forgive the Arabs for killing our sons, but it will be harder for us to forgive them for having forced us to kill their sons.

Golda Meir (1969), in Marie Syrkin, ed., *A Land of Our Own* (1973)

15 The sky of Beirut rained down missiles and shells and the horror isolated us in shelters and underground vaults where we spent our nights waiting for death, until morning came and then we would start to check on each other and to feel our limbs to see if they were still there.

Emily Nasrallah, "Those Memories," in Elizabeth Warnock Fernea, *Women and the Family in the Middle East* (1985)

16 Great armies are nothing but a collection of weakness.

Christina, Queen of Sweden, "Maxims" (1680), in Henry Woodhead, *Memoirs of Christina, Queen of Sweden*, vol. 2 (1863)

17 War makes its own morals.

Margaret Bourke-White, *Portrait of Myself* (1963)

18 Formerly, a nation that broke the peace did not trouble to try and prove to the world that it was done solely from higher motives. . . . *Now war has a bad conscience.* Now every nation assures us that it is bleeding for a human cause, the fate of which hangs in the balance of its victory. . . . No nation dares to admit the guilt of blood before the world.

Ellen Key, *War, Peace, and the Future* (1916)

19 War has to be nourished by lies.

Margaret Deland, *The Kays* (1924)

20 There never was a war that was / not inward; I must / fight till I have conquered in myself what / causes war.

Marianne Moore, "In Distrust of Merits," *Nevertheless* (1944)

21 All disasters stem from us. . . . Yet we could fight war and all its excrescences by releasing, each day,

the love which is shackled inside us, and giving it a chance to live.

Etty Hillesum (1942), *An Interrupted Life* (1983)

1 Our human situation no longer permits us to make armed dichotomies between those who are good and those who are evil, those who are right and those who are wrong. The first blow dealt to the enemy's children will sign the death warrant of our own.

Margaret Mead, *Continuities in Cultural Evolution* (1964)

2 All wars derive from lack of empathy: the incapacity of one to understand and accept the likeness or difference of another. Whether in nations or the encounters of race and sex, competition then replaces compassion, subjection excludes mutuality.

Marya Mannes, *Out of My Time* (1971)

3 Every victory of man over man has in itself a taste of defeat, a flavor of death; there is no essential difference between the various human groups, creatures whose bones and brains and members are the same; and every damage we do there is a form of mutilation, as if the fingers of the left hand were to be cut off by the right; there is no pleasure in it, nor any deep sense of achievement or of peace.

Freya Stark, "Travel for Solitude," in *The Spectator* (1950)

4 Is war perhaps nothing else but a need to face death, to conquer and master it, to come out of it alive—a peculiar form of denial of our own mortality?

Elisabeth Kübler-Ross, *On Death and Dying* (1969)

5 A self-respecting nation is ready for anything, including war, except for a renunciation of its option to make war. But why is it so essential to be able to make war? No one knows, any more than the Trojans knew why it was necessary for them to keep Helen.

Simone Weil, "The Power of Words," *The Simone Weil Reader* (1977)

6 When a new post-war generation has grown to puberty and to youth and to manhood and womanhood, it should read, and it should be realistically told, of the futility, the idiocy, the utter depravity of war. For that matter, this instruction could begin at the age of six with the taking of those toy guns out of those toy holsters and throwing them in the ash-cans where they belong.

Edna Ferber, *A Kind of Magic* (1963)

7 It would be impossible to explain the last war to these children, let alone preparations for another. They really know about war and what it does to life. . . . Adults could not persuade these small survivors that it is always necessary to make the world safe for democracy, but never safe for children.

Martha Gellhorn, "The Children Pay," in *The Saturday Evening Post* (1949)

8 I dream of giving birth to a child who will ask, "Mother, what was war?"

Eve Merriam, in *Peacemaking: Day by Day* (1989)

See also Conflict, Militarism, Nuclear Weapons, Pacifism, Peace, Revolution, Vietnam War.

## ✿ WASHINGTON, D.C.

9 Washington . . . is a company town. Most of the interesting people in Washington either work for the government or write about it.

Sally Quinn, *We're Going to Make You a Star* (1975)

10 It is a small village in some ways. Everybody knows everything about everyone else. If something happens to you at one o'clock, the whole town knows it by two.

Nancy Hoyt, *Roundabout* (1926)

11 A city where the Capitol Dome, perforated like a kitchen colander, is the symbol of how secrets are kept.

Leslie Ford, *Washington Whispers Murder* (1952)

12 There was no other city in the world where rumor fed upon itself so virulently. Whispers wiped out careers just as cholera destroyed its human victims.

Evelyn Anthony, *The Avenue of the Dead* (1982)

13 In Washington it is an honor to be disgraced. By that I mean you have to have *been* somebody to fall.

Meg Greenfield, in *Newsweek* (1986)

14 Washington knows that it is not safe to kick people who are down until you find out what their next stop will be.

Judith Martin, *Style and Substance* (1986)

15 Today Washington is our Hollywood, the Senate our Warner Bros., the White House our Beverly Hills. People who never read a line of a movie

magazine deal with the lives of leaders as if they were Elizabeth Taylor and Richard Burton.

Ellen Goodman, *At Large* (1981)

1 Fashion here echoes politics; skirts and hairstyles usually end up at compromise lengths designed not to offend anyone or make a statement of any kind.

Maureen Dowd, in *The New York Times* (1993)

2 Social climbing and power climbing—the two are often synonymous—are what make Washington run. . . . If there are more than two people together, if there are three, one of them is climbing.

Sally Quinn, *We're Going to Make You a Star* (1975)

3 Power . . . was the coin of the Washington realm and, without it, you might as well file for bankruptcy.

Elizabeth L. Ray, *The Washington Fringe Benefit* (1976)

4 I love Washington, but it *is* a self-important town.

Lady Bird Johnson, *A White House Diary* (1970)

5 There is a gentle absurdity about Washington, D.C., and it is easy to develop affection for the place, if you can forget that the consequences of what goes on there are real, whereas what goes on there may not be.

Linda Ellerbee, *"And So It Goes"* (1986)

6 Washington's capitol is a reproach to common decency, this government like a fish, "stinks worse at the head."

Carry Nation, *The Use and Need of the Life of Carry A. Nation* (1905)

7 Too small to be a state but too large to be an asylum for the mentally deranged.

Anne M. Burford, in *The Washington Post* (1984)

## ❧ WASTE

8 Waste is a spiritual thing and harms the soul as well as the pocketbook.

Kathleen Norris, *Hands Full of Living* (1931)

9 That, if there was any one thing she had learned of America in her forty-two years of residence, was typical of the whole country. Waste, waste, waste.

Dorothy Salisbury Davis, *Death of an Old Sinner* (1957)

See also Surplus.

## ❧ WATER

10 My old friend, water, my good companion, my beloved mother and father: I am its most natural offspring.

Doris Grumbach, *Coming Into the End Zone* (1991)

11 In all the years when I did not know what to believe in and therefore preferred to leave all beliefs alone, whenever I came to a place where living water welled up, blessedly cold and sweet and pure, from the earth's dark bosom, I felt that after all it must be wrong not to believe in anything.

Sigrid Undset, *Men, Women, and Places* (1939)

## ❧ WEAKNESS

12 Our strength is often composed of the weakness that we're damned if we're going to show.

Mignon McLaughlin, *The Second Neurotic's Notebook* (1966)

13 Weakness is a great bully without knowing it.

Margaret Deland, *Philip and His Wife* (1894)

14 How strong sometimes is weakness!

Fanny Fern, *Folly As It Flies* (1868)

15 He [Peter III] did not have a bad heart; but a weak man usually has not.

Catherine the Great, in Katharine Anthony, *Catherine the Great* (1926)

16 In our country everything is weakening. The money is weak. Democracy is weak and the politicians are very weak. Everything that is weak dies one day.

Carolina Maria de Jesus, *Child of the Dark* (1962)

17 You allers was soft, and you allers will be. If 't wa'n't for me keeping you stiffened up, I b'lieve you'd leak out o' the house into the dooryard.

Kate Douglas Wiggin, *Rebecca of Sunnybrook Farm* (1903)

See also Inadequacy, Limitations, Powerlessness.

## ❧ WEALTH

18 Wealth consists not in having great possessions but in having few wants.

Esther de Waal, *Seeking God* (1984)

1 To be content with little is difficult; to be content with much, impossible.

　　Marie von Ebner-Eschenbach, *Aphorisms* (1893)

2 Verily, affluence brings anxiety!

　　Anne Ellis, *Plain Anne Ellis* (1931)

3 The true defense against wealth is not a fear of wealth—of its fragility and of the vicious consequences that it can bring—the true defense against wealth is an indifference to money.

　　Natalia Ginzburg, *The Little Virtues* (1962)

4 Wealth means power: the power to subdue, to crush, to exploit, the power to enslave, to outrage, to degrade.

　　Emma Goldman, title essay, *Anarchism* (1910)

5 Great wealth is its own nationality.

　　Velda Johnston, *I Came to a Castle* (1969)

6 Wealth covers sin—the poor / Are naked as a pin.

　　Kassia, "Epigrams" (9th cent.), in Joanna Bankier and Deirdre Lashgari, eds., *Women Poets of the World* (1983)

7 Wealth is the product of man's capacity to think.

　　Ayn Rand, *Atlas Shrugged* (1957)

8 People who are so arrogant on account of their wealth are about equal in civilization to Laplanders, who measure a man's worth by the number of his reindeer. A man with a thousand reindeer is a very great man. The aristocracy of wealth is the lowest and commonest possible.

　　Fredrika Bremer (1850), *America of the Fifties* (1924)

9 There are many excuses for the persons who made the mistake of confounding money and wealth. Like many others they mistook the sign for the thing signified.

　　Millicent Garrett Fawcett, *Political Economy for Beginners* (1870)

10 What a ready passport wealth gives its possessor to the good opinions of this world!

　　Mrs. Sarah J. Hale, *Traits of American Life* (1835)

11 No one in the United States has the right to own millions of acres of American land, I don't care how they came by it.

　　Edna Ferber, *Giant* (1952)

12 To despise riches, may, indeed, be philosophic, but to dispense them worthily, must surely be more beneficial to mankind.

　　Fanny Burney, *Evelina* (1778)

13 Why snatch at wealth, and hoard and stock it? / Your shroud, you know, will have no pocket!

　　Betty Paoli, *Neueste Gedichte* (1870)

See also Class, Luxury, Money, The Rich, The Rich and the Poor.

## ❧ WEATHER

14 How we are all more or less creatures of Sun, Shadow, and Imagination, impressed or depressed by weather!

　　The Gardener, *The Garden of a Commuter's Wife* (1905)

15 Among famous traitors of history one might mention the weather.

　　Ilka Chase, *The Varied Airs of Spring* (1969)

16 Americans resent the vagaries of weather to a degree unknown to other peoples. . . . Weather is a force we have lost touch with. We feel entitled to dominate it, like everything else in the environment, and when we can't are more panic-stricken than primitives who know that when nature is out of control they can only pray to the gods.

　　Eleanor Perényi, *Green Thoughts* (1981)

17 On the farm the weather was the great fact, and men's affairs went on underneath it, as the streams creep under the ice.

　　Willa Cather, *My Antonia* (1918)

18 Dolly used to get almost tipsy upon sunshine. The weather is as much part of some people's lives as the minor events which happen to them.

　　Miss Thackeray, *Old Kensington*, vol. 1 (1873)

19 O! if there were a continuance of days like this, the dead would arise out of their graves; the air has resurrection in it.

　　Eugénie de Guérin (1841), in Guillaume S. Trébutien, ed., *Letters of Eugénie de Guérin* (1865)

20 Fog rested on the hills and caught on the tall bolls of the sequoias and the fronds of the date palms. Like a soaked goose-down comforter, it sagged

onto the beach, creating a charcoal-gray unity of air, wet sand, and Pacific whitecaps.

Susan Dunlap, "No Safety," in Marilyn Wallace, ed., *Sisters in Crime* (1989)

1 If the fog comes on little cat feet, then hail comes on wild pony hooves.

Patricia Penton Leimbach, *All My Meadows* (1977)

2 What dreadful hot weather we have!—It keeps one in a continual state of inelegance.

Jane Austen, to her sister Cassandra (1796), in R.W. Chapman, ed., *Jane Austen's Letters*, vol. 1 (1932)

3 I had never before seen heat, as you can see smoke or rain. But there it was, jigging and quavering above brown grasses and spiky thorn-trees and flaring erythrinas.

Elspeth Huxley, *The Flame Trees of Thika* (1959)

4 The heat was like a hand on the face all day and night.

Josephine W. Johnson, *Now in November* (1934)

5 In Chungking's summer, people could not sleep. They strolled in the night until exhaustion pushed them into stupor—a stupor abridged by the ferocious return of the despotic sun at dawn, exploding out of the river and laying its slaughtering rays upon all.

Han Suyin, *Till Morning Comes* (1982)

6 It was one of those wet, miserable evenings, gratis copies distributed by November through the year.

L.E. Landon, *Romance and Reality* (1831)

7 It was a bitter and biting iron-gray afternoon, that clanked like armor and was as cold as a frosty axe-head.

Ardyth Kennelly, *The Peaceable Kingdom* (1949)

8 Out of the sun, the cold bit like ivory fangs.

Marjorie Kinnan Rawlings, *The Sojourner* (1953)

9 It is so bitterly cold that the wine as well as water freezes in the glasses at the King's table.

Charlotte-Elisabeth, Duchesse d'Orléans (1695), *Life and Letters of Charlotte Elizabeth* (1889)

10 It is freezing fit to split a stone.

Marie de Rabutin-Chantal, Marquise de Sévigné (1689), in Leonard Tancock, tr., *Madame de Sévigné, Selected Letters* (1982)

11 It was so cold I almost got married.

Shelley Winters, in *The New York Times* (1956)

12 The cold spurred her ambition. When frost came, you had to decide things.

Ruth Suckow, "A Great Mollie," *A Ruth Suckow Omnibus* (1988)

13 The coldness had been admitted by none of the seven or eight people who, in degrees of elderly beauty, sat here full in the sun, at this sheltered edge of the lawn: they continued to master the coldness, or to deny it, as though with each it were some secret *malaise*.

Elizabeth Bowen, "Sunday Afternoon," *Ivy Gripped the Steps* (1946)

14 It's too cold to think warmly. Which gives me insight into the European. Where else would colonialism, slavery, capitalism come from except out of the icebox.

Toni Cade Bambara, "Broken Field Running," *The Sea Birds Are Still Alive* (1982)

15 It is impossible, to me at least, to be poetical in cold weather.

George Eliot (1840), in J.W. Cross, ed., *George Eliot's Life As Related in Her Letters and Journals* (1884)

16 It is only in sorrow bad weather masters us; in joy we face the storm and defy it.

Amelia E. Barr, *Jan Vedder's Wife* (1885)

17 Wild nights are my glory.

Madeleine L'Engle, *A Wrinkle in Time* (1962)

See also Rain, Snow, Storms, Summer, Wind, Winter.

## ❧ WEDDINGS

18 A wedding isn't for the bride and groom, it's for the family and friends. The B. and G. are just props, silly stick figures with no more significance than the pink and white candy figures on the top of the cake.

Susan Cheever, *Looking for Work* (1979)

19 My wedding was not mine, it was my mother's. Yours will be mine.

Lynne Alpern and Esther Blumenfeld, *Oh, Lord, I Sound Just Like Mama* (1986)

20 Our wedding plans please everybody as if we were fertilizing the earth and creating social luck.

Marge Piercy, *Braided Lives* (1982)

1 A wedding invitation is beautiful and formal notification of the desire to share a solemn and joyous occasion, sent by people who have been saying "Do we have to ask them?" to people whose first response is "How much do you think we have to spend on them?"

> Judith Martin, *Miss Manners' Guide to Rearing Perfect Children* (1984)

2 The organ pealed forth. . . . In every heart began to spring that exquisite hope, seldom if ever realized, that the bride will have had a fit, or eloped with someone else.

> Angela Thirkell, *Cheerfulness Breaks In* (1941)

3 In olden times sacrifices were made at the altar—a custom which is still continued.

> Helen Rowland, *Reflections of a Bachelor Girl* (1909)

4 O how short a time does it take to put an eternal end to a woman's liberty!

> Fanny Burney, after attending a wedding (1768), in Annie Raine Ellis, ed., *The Early Diary of Frances Burney*, vol. 1 (1889)

See also Marriage.


# ❧ WEIGHT

5 My weight is always perfect for my height—which varies.

> Nicole Hollander, book title (1982)

6 I had no intention of giving her my vital statistics. "Let me put it this way," I said. "According to my girth, I should be a ninety-foot redwood."

> Erma Bombeck, *If Life Is a Bowl of Cherries What Am I Doing in the Pits?* (1971)

7 I am also five three and in the neighborhood of one thirty. It is a neighborhood I would like to get out of.

> Flannery O'Connor, in Sally Fitzgerald, ed., *The Habit of Being* (1979)

8 When people say "chic," they mean thin.

> Carol Matthau, *Among the Porcupines* (1992)

9 Everything from television to fashion ads has made it seem wicked to cast a shadow. This wild emaciated look appeals to some women, though not to many men, who are seldom seen pinning up a *Vogue* illustration in a machine shop.

> Peg Bracken, *Appendix to the I Hate to Cook Book* (1966)

10 When women are excited about a date, they go immediately on a diet, because all women know they are hideously obese.

> Cynthia Heimel, *Get Your Tongue Out of My Mouth, I'm Kissing You Good-Bye!* (1993)

11 We know that every woman wants to be thin. Our images of womanhood are almost synonymous with thinness.

> Susie Orbach, in Kim Chernin, *The Obsession* (1981)

12 A waist is a terrible thing to mind.

> Jane Caminos, *That's Ms. Bulldyke to You, Charlie!* (1992)

13 TV cameras seem to add ten pounds to me. So I make it a policy never to eat TV cameras.

> Kitty Carlisle, in John Robert Colombo, *Popcorn in Paradise* (1979)

14 Give me a dozen such heart-breaks, if that would help me to lose a couple of pounds!

> Colette, *Cheri* (1920)

15 There's nothing on earth to do here but look at the view and eat. You can imagine the result since I do not like to look at views.

> Zelda Fitzgerald, letter to her daughter (1927), in Nancy Milford, *Zelda* (1970)

16 Lucy decided to forget her weight just this once and enjoy herself. This was a decision she made with deplorable frequency.

> Josephine Tey, *Miss Pym Disposes* (1947)

17 The older you get, the harder it is to lose weight, because your body has made friends with your fat.

> Lynne Alpern and Esther Blumenfeld, *Oh, Lord, I Sound Just Like Mama* (1986)

18 His body's taken on the weight his mind still refuses to accept.

> Toni Cade Bambara, *The Salt Eaters* (1980)

19 Little snax / Bigger slax.

> Ruth S. Schenley, in Michèle Brown and Ann O'Connor, *Hammer and Tongues* (1986)

See also Chocolate, Dieting, Fat, Food.

## ❧ WELFARE

1 Anyone who can live on welfare should be courted by Wall Street. He is a financial genius.

Joanna Clark, "Motherhood," in Toni Cade, ed., *The Black Woman* (1970)

2 Think of the worst experience you've ever had with a clerk in some government service job—motor vehicles, hospital, whatever—and add the life-threatening condition of impending starvation or homelessness to the waiting line, multiply the anxiety by an exponent of ten, and you have some idea of what it's like in a welfare center.

Theresa Funiciello, *Tyranny of Kindness* (1993)

3 It [welfare] is a crude and irrational system of income distribution, usually capricious and often downright cruel.

Theresa Funiciello, *Tyranny of Kindness* (1993)

4 Being a mother is a noble status, right? Right. So why does it change when you put "unwed" or "welfare" in front of it?

Florynce Kennedy, in Gloria Steinem, "The Verbal Karate of Florynce R. Kennedy, Esq.," *Ms.* (1973)

5 The ADC mother learns that there are two kinds of housewives, the "good" ones and the "bad" ones. The "good" ones do the same work as she does but they are still living with a man. . . . The "bad" ones are those who are not living with or being paid for by *a man* and so the state replaces him in the form of an ADC check.

André Leo, "ADC: Marriage to the State," in Anne Koedt, Ellen Levine, and Anita Rapone, eds., *Radical Feminism* (1973)

6 A.F.D.C. is like a super-sexist marriage. You trade in *a* man for *the* man. But you can't divorce him if he treats you bad. He can divorce you, of course, cut you off anytime he wants. But in that case, *he* keeps the kids, not you.

Johnnie Tillmon, "Welfare Is a Women's Issue," in *Ms.* (1972)

7 Our social welfare system suspended common sense years ago.

Theresa Funiciello, *Tyranny of Kindness* (1993)

8 The welfare system traps single mothers into remaining poverty-stricken pseudo-housewives and sentences their children to deprivation.

Barbara Bergmann, *The Economic Emergence of Women* (1986)

9 There's a group of Americans who are fully employed. They aren't very well paid or they're not paid at all. They're called mothers; and I've never heard of a mother who wasn't a working mother. And that includes the mothers on welfare.

Theresa Funiciello, speech (1994)

10 That's what a welfare check is: a certificate of blame. And it arrives every month.

Johnnie Tillmon, "Welfare Is a Women's Issue," in *Ms.* (1972)

11 [Social] workers have this attitude that the welfare is coming right out of their pockets—an outlook the hierarchy likes to cultivate.

Theresa Funiciello, *Tyranny of Kindness* (1993)

12 Most social welfare programs get their funding not for being good at what they do but for being politically connected to the sources of the money.

Theresa Funiciello, interview (1994)

13 Welfare as we know it cannot be fixed. Tinkering with it for decades has accomplished little of value. Bureaucracies within bureaucracies have bloomed, mutations of a polluted society. Too many contradictory interests compete at the public trough in the name of poor people.

Theresa Funiciello, *Tyranny of Kindness* (1993)

14 The agencies [in the welfare business] . . . were in an inherent conflict of interest with poor people. Welfare mothers, for instance, wanted an adequate guaranteed income, which would have rendered many of the activities of the social welfare professionals meaningless. The agencies wanted a guaranteed income, too: for themselves. With the money and power to lobby effectively, they got it.

Theresa Funiciello, *Tyranny of Kindness* (1993)

See also Charity, The Poor, Poverty.

## ❧ THE WEST

15 The West is color. . . . Its colors are animal rather than vegetable, the colors of earth and sunlight and ripeness. Tawny, buff, ocher, umber, tan, beige, sienna, sorrel, bay, blood-bay, chestnut, roan, palomino: the colors of objects bleached, sun-drenched, dry, aromatic, warm; the color of stubble fields, of barley, of foothills, of sage, of ocean

and desert sands; colors capable of reflecting light like a mirror.

Jessamyn West, "The West—A Place to Hang Your Dreams," in *Woman's Home Companion* (1956)

1 Billings is some lively town. It supports about fifteen hundred toughs. These are hectic days—like hell let out for noon.

Calamity Jane, letter (1893), in Karen Payne, ed., *Between Ourselves* (1983)

## ✿ WHISTLING

2 If there is whistling in the great beyond, I'll kill myself.

Jean Stafford, *The Catherine Wheel* (1951)

3 His wife had once shown him a bit in the *Mail* that said whistling was the sign of an empty mind. But it hadn't cured him.

Josephine Tey, *A Shilling for Candles* (1936)

## ✿ WHITES

4 Most of the time when "universal" is used, it is just a euphemism for "white": white themes, white significance, white culture.

Merle Woo, "Letter to Ma," in Cherríe Moraga and Gloria Anzaldúa, eds., *This Bridge Called My Back* (1983)

5 A white person was by definition somebody. Other people needed, across their hearts, one steel rib.

Gish Jen, *Typical American* (1991)

6 The psychological consequences of this spread of white culture have been out of all proportion to the materialistic. This world-wide cultural diffusion has protected us as man had never been protected before from having to take seriously the civilizations of other peoples; it has given to our culture a massive universality that we have long ceased to account for historically, and which we read off rather as necessary and inevitable.

Ruth Benedict, *Patterns of Culture* (1934)

7 The truth is that Mozart, Pascal, Boolean algebra, Shakespeare, parliamentary government, baroque churches, Newton, the emancipation of women, Kant, Marx, Balanchine ballet, *et al.*, don't redeem

what this particular civilization has wrought upon the world. The white race *is* the cancer of human history, it is the white race, and it alone—its ideologies and inventions—which eradicates autonomous civilization wherever it spreads, which has upset the ecological balance of the planet, which now threatens the very existence of life itself.

Susan Sontag, in *Partisan Review* (1967)

8 How in the hell could God take the black earth and make himself a white man out of it?

Louise Meriwether, *Daddy Was a Number Runner* (1970)

9 I know now that once I longed to be white.

Nellie Wong, "When I Was Growing Up," in Cherríe Moraga and Gloria Anzaldúa, eds., *This Bridge Called My Back* (1983)

10 He had the patient, practical, uninterested tone of the white person willing to help a native with money or authority, so long as he is not expected to listen to any human details of the predicament.

Nadine Gordimer, *The Lying Days* (1953)

See also Blacks, Blacks and Whites.

## ✿ WHOLENESS

11 I knew without a glimmer of doubt that all things in the universe were connected by a living truth that would not relent its continuing search for wholeness until every form of life was united.

Lynn V. Andrews, *Crystal Woman* (1987)

12 The most comprehensive formulation of therapeutic goals is the striving for *wholeheartedness*: to be without pretense, to be emotionally sincere, to be able to put the whole of oneself into one's feelings, one's work, one's beliefs.

Karen Horney, *Our Inner Conflicts* (1945)

13 A person who believes . . . that there is a whole of which one is a part, and that in being a part one is whole: such a person has no desire whatever, at any time, to play God. Only those who have denied their being yearn to play at it.

Ursula K. Le Guin, *The Lathe of Heaven* (1971)

14 Wholeness comes from living your life consciously during the day and then exploring your inner life or unconscious at night.

Margery Cuyler, in Jim Roginski, *Behind the Covers* (1985)

1 African tradition deals with life as an experience to be lived. . . . We live in accordance with, in a kind of correspondence with the rest of the world as a whole. And therefore living becomes an experience, rather than a problem, no matter how bad or how painful it may be.

> Audre Lorde, in Claudia Tate, ed., *Black Women Writers at Work* (1983)

See also Human Family, Inner Life, Integrity, Interdependence, Self, Universal, Universe.

## 🔊 WHY

2 There is really nothing more to say—except *why*. But since *why* is difficult to handle, one must take refuge in *how*.

> Toni Morrison, *The Bluest Eye* (1970)

3 Grown people know that they do not always know the why of things, and even if they think they know, they do not know where and how they got the proof. Hence the irritation they show when children keep on demanding to know if a thing is so and how the grown folks got the proof of it. It is so troublesome because it is disturbing to the pigeon-hole way of life.

> Zora Neale Hurston, *Dust Tracks on a Road* (1942)

4 More than likely, we will never achieve the satisfaction of knowing a single "why" of our becoming, any more than our limited, earthbound brain could ever meaningfully grasp a clear purpose behind the vastness of the universe. Any answer would necessarily include understanding the why of the why, and that would be a little like looking into one's own eyes.

> Frances Wosmek, *Acknowledge the Wonder* (1988)

See also Answers, Explanations, Questions.

## 🔊 WICKEDNESS

5 The difference between weakness and wickedness is much less than people suppose; and the consequences are nearly always the same.

> Lady Marguerite Blessington, *The Confessions of an Elderly Gentleman* (1836)

See also Evil, Mischief.

## 🔊 WIDOWHOOD

6 The final lesson of learning to be independent—widowhood . . . is the hardest lesson of all.

> Anne Morrow Lindbergh, in Julie Nixon Eisenhower, *Special People* (1977)

See also Death, Loneliness.

## 🔊 WILDERNESS

7 I go into the wilderness and rediscover the home within.

> China Galland, in Lorraine Anderson, ed., *Sisters of the Earth* (1991)

8 We use the word "wilderness," but perhaps we mean wildness. Isn't that why I've come here, to seek the wildness in myself and, in so doing, come on the wildness everywhere, because after all, I'm part of nature too.

> Gretel Ehrlich, *Islands, the Universe, Home* (1991)

See also Forests, Nature, Wildlife.

## 🔊 WILDLIFE

9 It is impossible to be among the woods animals on their own ground without a feeling of expanding one's own world, as when any foreign country is visited.

> Marjorie Kinnan Rawlings, *Cross Creek* (1942)

10 One of the things I like best about animals in the wild is that they're always off on some errand. They have appointments to keep. It's only we humans who wonder what we're here for.

> Diane Ackerman, *The Moon by Whale Light* (1991)

11 Probably we never fully credit the interdependence of wild creatures, and their cognizance of the affairs of their own kind.

> Mary Austin, *The Land of Little Rain* (1904)

12 If you look close . . . you can see that the wild critters have "No Trespassing" signs tacked up on every pine tree.

> Marguerite Henry, *Misty of Chincoteague* (1947)

1 Whatever sales people or sentimental books may state, wild animals do not make good pets. Captivity, no matter how "kind," is always cruel.

    Joan Ward-Harris, *Creature Comforts* (1979)

2 The animals of the planet are in desperate peril. . . . Without free animal life I believe we will lose the spiritual equivalent of oxygen.

    Alice Walker, "The Universe Responds," *Living by the Word* (1988)

See also Animals.

## ❦ WILLPOWER

3 It is always hard to believe that the will to change something does not produce an immediate change.

    Janet Frame, *Faces in the Water* (1961)

See also Courage, Self-Discipline.

## ❦ WIND

4 Wind / Gives speech / To trees.

    Helen Aoki Kaneko, "Wind," in Dexter Fisher, ed., *The Third Woman* (1980)

5 Wind moving through grass so that the grass quivers . . . moves me with an emotion I don't ever understand.

    Katherine Mansfield (1922), *The Journal of Katherine Mansfield* (1927)

6 In this world I shall not find / Any comforter like Wind, / . . . the Winds have brothered me.

    Margaret Widdemer, "Wind-Litany," *The Factories* (1915)

7 The wind is like a great bird tumbling over the sea with bright flashing wings.

    Katherine Mansfield (1919), in J. Middleton Murry, ed., *The Letters of Katherine Mansfield*, vol. 1 (1928)

8 To-day it has blown knives and files; a cold, rasping, savage day.

    Jane Welsh Carlyle (1855), in James Anthony Froude, ed., *Letters and Memorials of Jane Welsh Carlyle*, vol. 2 (1883)

9 The wind waited for them at the corner, striking suddenly like an assassin.

    Elizabeth Taylor, *A View of the Harbor* (1947)

10 Wise guy, he not go against wind. In Chinese we say, Come from South, blow with wind—poom!— North will follow. Strongest wind cannot be seen.

    Amy Tan, *The Joy Luck Club* (1989)

11 It is hard for people who have not lived in Los Angeles to realize how radically the Santa Ana figures in the local imagination. . . . The wind shows us how close to the edge we are.

    Joan Didion, "Los Angeles Notebook," *Slouching Towards Bethlehem* (1968)

See also Storms, Weather.

## ❦ WINE

12 Wine is earth's answer to the sun.

    Margaret Fuller, in Lydia Maria Child, *Letters From New York*, 2nd series (1845)

13 If you are not proud of your cellar, there is no thrill of satisfaction in seeing your guest hold up his wineglass to the light and look judicial.

    George Eliot, *Middlemarch* (1871)

14 In France wine is thought of as food, so necessary to life that nobody is too poor to go without it.

    Katharine Butler Hathaway, *The Journals and Letters of the Little Locksmith* (1946)

15 Most of the men regarded Europe as a wine list. In their mental geography Rheims, Rhine, Moselle, Bordeaux, Champagne, or Würzburg were not localities but libations.

    Edna Ferber, title story, *Gigolo* (1922)

16 Wine could become a place rather than a beverage.

    Morgan Llywelyn, *Bard* (1984)

17 Great people talk about ideas, average people talk about things, and small people talk about wine.

    Fran Lebowitz, *Social Studies* (1977)

See Alcohol, Drinking.

## ❦ WINNING

18 Conquer but never triumph.

    Marie von Ebner-Eschenbach, *Aphorisms* (1893)

1 In sports, you simply aren't considered a real champion until you have defended your title successfully. Winning it once can be a fluke; winning it twice proves that you are the best.

> Althea Gibson, in Ed Fitzgerald, ed., *I Always Wanted to Be Somebody* (1958)

2 Whoever said, "It's not whether you win or lose that counts," probably lost.

> Martina Navratilova, in Roz Warren, ed., *Glibquips* (1994)

3 The one who cares the most wins. . . . That's how I knew I'd end up with everyone else waving the white flags and not me. That's how I knew I'd be the last person standing when it was all over. . . . I cared the most.

> Roseanne Arnold, *My Lives* (1994)

4 The main thing is not a matter of wanting to win; the main thing is being scared to lose.

> Billie Jean King, with Frank Deford, *Billie Jean* (1982)

5 Counting both times I cheated this week / I won at solitaire twice.

> Mary Virginia Micka, *Hexameron* (1986)

6 It often doth befall, / He who conquers loses all.

> Dinah Maria Mulock Craik, "Headings of Chapters," *Mulock's Poems, New and Old* (1880)

See also Success, Victory.

## ❧ WINTER

7 A tomb of life, not death, / Life inward, true, / Where the world vanishes / And you are you.

> Vita Sackville-West, "Winter," *The Garden* (1946)

8 There is a wilder solitude in winter / When every sense is pricked alive and keen.

> May Sarton, "The House in Winter," *A Private Mythology* (1966)

9 There is a privacy about it which no other season gives you. . . . In spring, summer and fall people sort of have an open season on each other; only in the winter, in the country, can you have longer, quiet stretches when you can *savor* belonging to yourself.

> Ruth Stout, *How to Have a Green Thumb Without an Aching Back* (1955)

10 In a way winter is the real spring, the time when the inner thing happens, the resurge of nature.

> Edna O'Brien, "Clara," *Mrs. Reinhardt* (1978)

11 I shall like my battle. This sort of day puts one in mood for it. Plenty of wood in the shed, jam and potatoes and apples in the cellar, hay and oats and Cressy in the barn. Pooh—what is winter?

> Anne Bosworth Greene, *The Lone Winter* (1923)

12 The cold was our pride, the snow was our beauty. It fell and fell, lacing day and night together in a milky haze, making everything quieter as it fell, so that winter seemed to partake of religion in a way no other season did, hushed, solemn.

> Patricia Hampl, *A Romantic Education* (1981)

13 It is a pleasure to a real lover of Nature to give winter all the glory he can, for summer *will* make its own way, and speak its own praises.

> Dorothy Wordsworth (1802), in William Knight, ed., *Journals of Dorothy Wordsworth*, vol. 1 (1897)

14 The short, half-tone scale of winter weathers / is a spread pigeon's wing. / Winter lives under a pigeon's wing, a dead wing with damp feathers.

> Elizabeth Bishop, "Paris, 7 a.m.," *North and South* (1955)

15 Throughout the winter, nature's active and crescent principle seems never held wholly in abeyance. From time to time, some precocious member of a dormant family, plant or animal, may be observed awake and stirring, as one who, having much on hand to accomplish, makes an early start by candle-light.

> Edith M. Thomas, *The Round Year* (1886)

16 Blackberry winter, the time when the hoarfrost lies on the blackberry blossoms; without this frost the berries will not set. It is the forerunner of a rich harvest.

> Margaret Mead, *Blackberry Winter* (1972)

17 The summer lasted a long long time, like verse after verse of a ballad, but when it ended, it ended like a man falling dead in the street of heart trouble. One night, all in one night, severe winter came, a white horse of snow rolling over Bountiful, snorting and rolling in its meadows, its fields.

> Ardyth Kennelly, *The Peaceable Kingdom* (1949)

18 Winter could drop down out of a clear sky, sharp as an icicle, and, without a sound, pierce your heart.

> Jessamyn West, *The Massacre at Fall Creek* (1975)

1 In our part of the world winter is the normal state of affairs and seems to last about five years. This is fine for the skiers, but by the end of March all gardeners and mothers of small children have begun to go mad.

> Janet Gillespie, *The Joy of a Small Garden* (1963)

2 There seems to be so much more winter than we need this year.

> Kathleen Norris, *Bread Into Roses* (1936)

3 Hoary-headed old Winter, I have had enough of you!

> Fanny Fern, *Fresh Leaves* (1857)

4 That winter, cold settled in the bones as if it would be stored there indefinitely like ice in an icehouse.

> Esther Hautzig, *The Endless Steppe* (1968)

5 Perhaps I am a bear, or some hibernating animal, underneath, for the instinct to be half asleep all winter is so strong in me.

> Anne Morrow Lindbergh, *Bring Me a Unicorn* (1971)

6 I could almost wish myself a dormouse or a she-bear, to sleep away the rest of this cold, cold winter.

> Anna Jameson (1836), in Geraldine Macpherson, *Memoirs of the Life of Anna Jameson* (1878)

See also February, January, Seasons, Snow, Weather.

## ☙ WISDOM

7 We can be wise from goodness and good from wisdom.

> Marie von Ebner-Eschenbach, *Aphorisms* (1893)

8 Silence and reserve will give anyone a reputation for wisdom.

> Myrtle Reed, *Old Rose and Silver* (1909)

9 Wisdom is harder to *do* than it is to know.

> Yula Moses, in John Langston Gwaltney, *Drylongso* (1980)

10 Daddy knows better. . . . He has eaten more salt than I have eaten rice.

> Jade Snow Wong, *Fifth Chinese Daughter* (1950)

11 The perfection of wisdom, and the end of true philosophy, is to proportion our wants to our possessions, our ambitions to our capacities.

> Frances Wright, *A Few Days in Athens* (1822)

See also Knowledge.

## ☙ WIT

12 An epigram is a flashlight of a truth; a witticism, truth laughing at itself.

> Minna Thomas Antrim, *Naked Truth and Veiled Illusions* (1901)

13 A flash of wit, like a flash of lightning, can only be remembered, it cannot be reproduced.

> Mary Clemmer Hudson, in Kate Sanborn, *The Wit of Women* (1885)

14 He sharpened his wits on the edge of her nerves.

> Marcelene Cox, in *Ladies' Home Journal* (1942)

15 If evolution was worth its salt, by now it should've evolved something better than survival of the fittest. Yeah, I told 'em I think a better idea would be survival of the wittiest. At least, that way, the creatures that didn't survive could've died *laughing.*

> Jane Wagner, *The Search for Signs of Intelligent Life in the Universe* (1985)

16 Wit is the salt of conversation, not the food, and few things in the world are more wearying than a sarcastic attitude towards life.

> Agnes Repplier, "Wit and Humor," *Essays in Idleness* (1893)

17 Wit, wit!—I look upon it always as a draught of air; it cools indeed, but one gets a stiff neck from it.

> Catharina Elisabetha Goethe (1782), in Alfred S. Gibbs, ed., *Goethe's Mother* (1880)

18 They had not much original wit, but had inherited a stock of cheerful sayings which passed as such.

> Flora Thompson, *Over to Candleford* (1941)

19 Wit destroys eroticism and eroticism destroys wit, so women must choose between taking lovers and taking no prisoners.

> Florence King, *Reflections in a Jaundiced Eye* (1989)

See also Conversation, Humor, Irony, Laughter, Satire, Witticisms.

## ❧ WITTICISMS

1 Thou canst not serve both cod and salmon.
   Ada Leverson, in *The London Times* (1970)

2 Never darken my Dior again!
   Beatrice Lillie, to waiter who spilled soup on her, *Every Other Inch a Lady* (1972)

3 No one has called so far, but one old lady to look at a house. I directed her to the cemetery to spare expense of moving.
   Emily Dickinson (1863), in Mabel Loomis Todd, ed., *Letters of Emily Dickinson*, vol. 2 (1894)

4 You can lead a horticulture, but you can't make her think.
   Dorothy Parker, when challenged to use "horticulture" in a sentence, in John Keats, *You Might As Well Live* (1970)

5 One man's fish is another man's *poisson*.
   Carolyn Wells, "More Mixed Maxims," *Folly for the Wise* (1904)

6 Those who "cursed the day they were born" must have been infant prodigies.
   Ethel Watts Mumford, in Oliver Herford, Ethel Watts Mumford, and Addison Mizner, *The Complete Cynic* (1902)

See also Criticisms, Wit.

## ❧ WIVES

7 It is a truth universally acknowledged that a single man in possession of a good fortune, must be in want of a wife.
   Jane Austen, *Pride and Prejudice* (1813)

8 While I was ironing one evening, it suddenly occurred to me that I, too, would like to have a wife. . . . My God, who *wouldn't* want a wife?
   Judy Syfers, in *Ms.* (1972)

9 A successful woman preacher was once asked "what special obstacles have you met as a woman in the ministry?" "Not one," she answered, "except the lack of a minister's wife."
   Anna Garlin Spencer, *Woman's Share in Social Culture* (1912)

10 Wife and servant are the same, / But only differ in the name.
   Lady Mary Chudleigh, "To the Ladies," *Poems on Several Occasions* (1703)

11 If you ain't got on to it by now, that I'm no little, tremblin' wife, you never will. Those kind has nerves. I only got nerve.
   Julie M. Lippmann, *Martha By-the-Day* (1912)

See also Family, Housewife, Husbands, Lovers, Marriage.

## ❧ WOLVES

12 Wolves . . . are a balance wheel of nature.
   Lois Crisler, *Arctic Wild* (1958)

13 Wolves are brotherly. They love each other, and if you learn to speak to them, they will love you too.
   Jean Craighead George, *Julie of the Wolves* (1972)

14 The shops, the paraphernalia show that longing for connection with wolves. We embrace them on T-shirts, on cards. Everyone from three-year-olds to ninety-three-year-olds feels strongly about this. A critter like the wolf has tremendous presence in the cultural psyche.
   Renee Askins, in Karin Winegar, "War Over the Wolf," *The Minneapolis Star Tribune Sunday Magazine* (1992)

15 The things we want to kill in the wolf—freedom, unpredictability—are the things we begin to recognize we as people have lost.
   Renee Askins, in Karin Winegar, "War Over the Wolf," *The Minneapolis Star Tribune Sunday Magazine* (1992)

See also Animals, Wildlife.

## ❧ WOMEN

16 Where there is a woman there is magic.
   Ntozake Shange, *Sassafrass, Cypress & Indigo* (1982)

17 One gender to walk the wide world in / Is the feminine, / A plight that—softly to a friend— / I can recommend.
   Helen Bevington, "To Susan at Birth," *Nineteen Million Elephants* (1950)

1 I am woman, hear me roar / In numbers too big to ignore, / And I know too much / To go back and pretend.

> Helen Reddy, "I Am Woman" (1972)

2 I'm a woman / Phenomenally. / Phenomenal woman, / That's me.

> Maya Angelou, "Phenomenal Woman," *And Still I Rise* (1978)

3 A woman's place is on top.

> Slogan on T-shirts, 1978 American Women's Himalayan Expedition to Annapurna, in Arlene Blum, *Annapurna* (1980)

4 Confusion has seized us, and all things go wrong, / The women have leaped from "their spheres," / And, instead of fixed stars, shoot as comets along, / And are setting the world by the ears!

> Maria Chapman, "The Times That Try Men's Souls," in Elizabeth Cady Stanton, Susan B. Anthony, and Matilda J. Gage, eds., *The History of Woman Suffrage*, vol. 1 (1881)

5 Without a woman, he who's natural / Is sad, for she's his mother, sister, love. / And rarely is she enemy to him.

> Christine de Pisan, "Letter of the God of Love" (1399), in Thelma S. Fenster and Mary Carpenter Erler, eds., *Poems of Cupid, God of Love* (1990)

6 Let Greeks be Greeks, and women what they are.

> Anne Bradstreet, prologue to "The Tenth Muse, Lately Sprung Up in America" (1650), in John Harvard Ellis, ed., *The Works of Anne Bradstreet in Prose and Verse* (1867)

7 Women are not inherently passive or peaceful. We're not inherently anything but human.

> Robin Morgan, in Shirley Chisholm, *Unbought and Unbossed* (1970)

8 Women, ever since there have been women, have had a way of being people.

> Laura Riding, "Women As People" (1934), *The Word "Woman"* (1993)

9 One is not born, but rather becomes, a woman.

> Simone de Beauvoir, *The Second Sex* (1949)

10 Whatever women do they must do twice as well as men to be thought half as good. Luckily, this is not difficult.

> Charlotte Whitton, in *Canada Month* (1963)

11 We are becoming the men we wanted to marry.

> Gloria Steinem, in *Ms.* (1982)

12 A woman without a man is like a fish without a bicycle.

> Irina Dunn, graffito (1970)

13 We're half the people; we should be half the Congress.

> Jeannette Rankin (1966), in Hannah Josephson, *Jeannette Rankin* (1974)

14 Now that you have touched the women, you have struck a rock, you have dislodged a boulder, and you will be crushed.

> South African chant in the campaign against the pass laws (1956), in Angela Y. Davis, *Women, Culture & Politics* (1989)

15 These is old blues / and I sing em like any woman do. / These the old blues / and I sing em, sing em, sing em. Just like any woman do. / My life ain't done yet. / Naw. My song ain't through.

> Sherley Anne Williams, "Any Woman's Blues," *The Peacock Poems* (1975)

16 The heart of a woman falls back with the night, / And enters some alien cage in its plight, / And tries to forget it has dreamed of the stars / While it breaks, breaks, breaks on the sheltering bars.

> Georgia Douglas Johnson, title poem, *The Heart of a Woman* (1918)

17 Am I not a woman and a sister?

> "Ladies Department," *The Liberator* (1831), and motto, anti-slavery coin (1838)

18 And ar'n't I a woman?

> Sojourner Truth, speech (1851), in Olive Gilbert, *Narrative of Sojourner Truth* (1878)

19 When will it no longer be necessary to attach special weight to the word "woman" and raise it specially?

> Ding Ling, "Thoughts on March 8" (1942), *I Myself Am a Woman* (1989)

20 Women have no wilderness in them, / They are provident instead, / Content in the tight hot cell of their hearts / To eat dusty bread.

> Louise Bogan, "Women," *Body of This Death* (1923)

21 Oh, God, who does not exist, you hate women, otherwise you'd have made them different.

> Edna O'Brien, *Girls in Their Married Bliss* (1964)

22 The truth is, we [women] live like bats, or owls, labor like beasts, and die like worms.

> Margaret Cavendish, Duchess of Newcastle, "Female Orations," *Orations of Diverse Sorts* (1662)

1 Cows in India occupy the same position in society as women did in England before they got the vote. Woman was revered but not encouraged. Her life was one long obstacle race owing to the anxiety of man to put pedestals at her feet. While she was falling over the pedestals she was soothingly told that she must occupy a Place Apart—and indeed, so far Apart did her place prove to be that it was practically out of earshot. The cow in India finds her position equally lofty and tiresome. You practically never see a happy cow in India.

Stella Benson, *The Little World* (1925)

2 Let me not be sad because I am born a woman / In this world; many saints suffer in this way.

Janabai (c. 1340), in Susie Tharu and K. Lalita, eds., *Women Writing in India* (1991)

3 All of the women I know feel a little like outlaws.

Marilyn French, *The Women's Room* (1977)

4 Well-behaved women rarely make history.

Laurel Thatcher Ulrich, in Kay Mills, *From Pocahontas to Power Suits* (1995)

5 All women are misfits, I think; we do not fit into this world without amputations.

Marge Piercy, *Braided Lives* (1982)

6 If the shoe doesn't fit, must we change the foot?

Gloria Steinem, *Outrageous Acts and Everyday Rebellions* (1983)

7 Society, while willing to make room for women, is not willing to make changes for them.

Shirley Williams, in Joseph McCulloch, *Under Bow Bells* (1974)

8 If . . . society will not admit of woman's free development, then society must be remodeled.

Elizabeth Blackwell (1848), in Elizabeth Cady Stanton, Susan B. Anthony, and Matilda J. Gage, eds., *The History of Woman Suffrage*, vol. 1 (1881)

9 All sorts of articles and letters appear in the papers about women. Profound questions are raised concerning them. Should they smoke? Should they work? Vote? Marry? Exist? Are not their skirts too short, or their sleeves? Have they a sense of humor, of honor, of direction? Are spinsters superfluous? But how seldom similar inquiries are propounded about men.

Rose Macaulay, *Mystery at Geneva* (1923)

10 In a world not made for women, criticism and ridicule follow us all the days of our lives. Usually they are indications that we are doing something right.

Erica Jong, *Fear of Fifty* (1994)

11 Let us in through the guarded gate, / Let us in for the world's sake.

Margaret Widdemer, "The Women's Litany," *The Factories* (1915)

12 'Tis woman's strongest vindication for speaking that *the world needs to hear her voice*. It would be subversive of every human interest that the cry of one-half the human family be stifled. . . . The world has had to limp along with the wobbling gait and one-sided hesitancy of a man with one eye. Suddenly the bandage is removed from the other eye and the whole body is filled with light. It sees a circle where before it saw a segment. The darkened eye restored, every member rejoices with it.

Anna Julia Cooper, *A Voice From the South* (1892)

13 Too many women in too many countries speak the same language—silence.

Anasuya Sengupta, "Silence," news item (1995)

14 I was elected by the women of Ireland, who instead of rocking the cradle, rocked the system.

Mary Robinson, news item (1990)

15 I think being a woman is like being Irish. . . . Everyone says you're important and nice but you take second place all the same.

Iris Murdoch, *The Red and the Green* (1965)

16 This world taught woman nothing skillful and then said her work was valueless. It permitted her no opinions and said she did not know how to think. It forbade her to speak in public, and said the sex had no orators.

Carrie Chapman Catt, in Susan B. Anthony and Ida Husted Harper, eds., *The History of Woman Suffrage*, vol. 4 (1902)

17 Now we are expected to be as wise as men who have had generations of all the help there is, and we scarcely anything.

Louisa May Alcott, *Jo's Boys* (1886)

18 Woman is shut up in a kitchen or in a boudoir, and astonishment is expressed that her horizon is limited. Her wings are clipped, and it is found deplorable that she cannot fly.

Simone de Beauvoir, *The Second Sex* (1949)

19 It is not the inferiority of women that has caused their historical insignificance; it is rather their his-

torical insignificance that has doomed them to inferiority.

Simone de Beauvoir, *The Second Sex* (1949)

1 Until women assume the place in society which good sense and good feeling alike assign to them, human improvement must advance but feebly.

Frances Wright, "Of Free Enquiry," *Course of Popular Lectures* (1829)

2 Woman has been the great unpaid laborer of the world.

Elizabeth Cady Stanton, Susan B. Anthony, and Matilda J. Gage, eds., *The History of Woman Suffrage*, vol. 1 (1881)

3 By and large, mothers and housewives are the only workers who do not have regular time off. They are the great vacationless class.

Anne Morrow Lindbergh, *Gift From the Sea* (1955)

4 Women were the slave class that maintained the species in order to free the other half for the business of the world.

Shulamith Firestone, *The Dialectic of Sex* (1970)

5 Women are the true maintenance class. Society is built upon their acquiescence, and upon their small and necessary labors.

Sally Kempton, in *Esquire* (1970)

6 I am to gratify his pleasure and nurse his child, I am a piece of household furniture, I am a *woman*.

Sophia Tolstoy (1863), in O.A. Golinenko et al., eds., *The Diaries of Sophia Tolstoy* (1985)

7 The economic dependence of women is perhaps the greatest injustice that has been done to us, and has worked the greatest injury to the race.

Nellie L. McClung, *In Times Like These* (1915)

8 Woman's normal occupations in general run counter to creative life, or contemplative life, or saintly life.

Anne Morrow Lindbergh, *Gift From the Sea* (1955)

9 Most women work one shift at the office or factory and a "second shift" at home.

Arlie Hochschild, *The Second Shift* (1989)

10 Each suburban wife struggled with it alone. As she made the beds, shopped for groceries, matched slipcover material, ate peanut butter sandwiches with her children, chauffeured Cub Scouts and Brownies, lay beside her husband at night—she

was afraid to ask even of herself the silent question—"Is this all?"

Betty Friedan, *The Feminine Mystique* (1963)

11 The problem that has no name—which is simply the fact that American women are kept from growing to their full human capacities—is taking a far greater toll on the physical and mental health of our country than any known disease.

Betty Friedan, *The Feminine Mystique* (1963)

12 The feminine mystique has succeeded in burying millions of American women alive.

Betty Friedan, *The Feminine Mystique* (1963)

13 The most wasteful "brain drain" in America today is the drain in the kitchen sink.

Elizabeth Gould Davis, *The First Sex* (1971)

14 Any woman who has a career and a family automatically develops something in the way of two personalities, like two sides of a dollar bill, each different in design. . . . Her problem is to keep one from draining the life from the other.

Ivy Baker Priest, *Green Grows Ivy* (1958)

15 Giving the utmost of herself to three absorbing interests [marriage, motherhood, career] . . . was a problem for a superwoman, and a job for a superwoman, and only some such fabled being could have accomplished it with success.

Storm Jameson, *Three Kingdoms* (1926)

16 Consider the "new" woman. She's trying to be Pollyanna Borgia, clearly a conflict of interest. She's supposed to be a ruthless winner at work and a bundle of nurturing sweetness at home.

Rita Mae Brown, *In Her Day* (1976)

17 I have a brain and a uterus, and I use both.

Patricia Schroeder, in Letty Cottin Pogrebin, "Anatomy Isn't Destiny," *The New York Times* (1977)

18 If God had wanted us to think just with our wombs, why did He give us a brain?

Clare Boothe Luce, *Slam the Door Softly* (1970)

19 Womanhood is the great fact in her life; wifehood and motherhood are but incidental relations.

Elizabeth Cady Stanton, Susan B. Anthony, and Matilda J. Gage, eds., *The History of Woman Suffrage*, vol. 1 (1881)

20 In education, in marriage, in religion, in everything, disappointment is the lot of women. It shall be the business of my life to deepen this disap-

pointment in every woman's heart until she bows down to it no longer.

Lucy Stone, speech (1855), in Elizabeth Cady Stanton, Susan B. Anthony, and Matilda J. Gage, eds., *The History of Woman Suffrage*, vol. 1 (1881)

1 Woman's discontent increases in exact proportion to her development.

Elizabeth Cady Stanton, Susan B. Anthony, and Matilda J. Gage, eds., *The History of Woman Suffrage*, vol. 1 (1881)

2 Patience and endurance were not virtues in a woman; they were necessities, forced on her. Perhaps some day things would change and women would renounce them. They would rise up and say: "We are not patient. We will endure no more." Then what would happen to the world?

Mary Roberts Rinehart, *This Strange Adventure* (1929)

3 I do not wish them to have power over men; but over themselves.

Mary Wollstonecraft, *A Vindication of the Rights of Woman* (1792)

4 There is a hidden fear that somehow, if they are only given a chance, women will suddenly do as they have been done by.

Eva Figes, *Patriarchal Attitudes* (1970)

5 Women's reality has been perceived as fiction. Let us name some of those realities here: maternity, rape, prostitution, chronic fatigue, verbal, physical, and mental violence. Newspapers present these as *stories*, not fact.

Nicole Brossard, in Marlene Wildeman, tr., *The Aerial Letter* (1988)

6 Long before *Playboy*, Woman was not the sum of her parts: her parts were her sum.

Marya Mannes, *Out of My Time* (1971)

7 Everyone knew in the 1950s why a girl from a nice family left home. The meaning of her theft of herself from her parents was clear to all—as well as what she'd be up to in that room of her own.

Joyce Johnson, *Minor Characters* (1983)

8 I ran away. I hurried more than if lions had chased me. Without telling him. Without telling my mother or father. There wasn't any liberty in San Francisco for ordinary women. . . . You got married, were an old maid, or went to hell. Take your pick.

Maud Parrish, *Nine Pounds of Luggage* (1939)

9 People are just not very ambitious for women still. Your son you want to be the best he can be. Your daughter you want to be happy.

Alexa Canady, in Brian Lanker, *I Dream a World* (1989)

10 It occurred to me when I was thirteen and wearing white gloves and Mary Janes and going to dancing school, that no one should have to dance backward all their lives.

Jill Ruckelshaus, speech (1973)

11 Women never have young minds. They are born three thousand years old.

Shelagh Delaney, *A Taste of Honey* (1958)

12 little old ladies is the term they use / to make us laugh at the women who / have been fighting for sixty years.

Alta, "L.O.L.," *No Visible Means of Support* (1971)

13 Women get more radical with age.

Slogan, in Gloria Steinem, *Outrageous Acts and Everyday Rebellions* (1983)

14 Womanist is to feminist as purple to lavender.

Alice Walker, *In Search of Our Mothers' Gardens* (1983)

15 If you sing too often of woe, yours or your sisters', you may be charged with being "too personal," "too autobiographical," too much a woman who cries out, who acknowledges openly, shamelessly, the pain of living and the joy of becoming free.

Nellie Wong, "In Search of the Self As Hero: Confetti of Voices on New Year's Night," in Cherríe Moraga and Gloria Anzaldúa, eds., *This Bridge Called My Back* (1983)

16 Women are repeatedly accused of taking things personally. I cannot see any other honest way of taking them.

Marya Mannes, *More in Anger* (1958)

17 If you're going to generalize about women, you'll find yourself up to *here* in exceptions.

Dolores Hitchens, *In a House Unknown* (1973)

18 Sentences that begin with "all women" are never, never true.

Margaret Culkin Banning, *A Week in New York* (1941)

19 I'm all for women myself. I believe they're the comin' man.

Julie M. Lippmann, *Martha By-the-Day* (1912)

See also Chivalry, Equality, "Femininity," Housewife, Ladies, Sexism, Sex Roles, Sisterhood, Wives, Women and Men.

# ❧ WOMEN AND MEN

1 The first thing that strikes the careless observer is that women are unlike men. They are "the opposite sex"—(though why "opposite" I do not know; what is the "neighboring sex"?).

> Dorothy L. Sayers, "The Human-Not-Quite-Human," *Unpopular Opinions* (1946)

2 I have never in all my various travels seen but two sorts of people, and those very like one another; I mean men and women, who always have been and ever will be the same.

> Lady Mary Wortley Montagu (1747), in Octave Thanet, ed., *The Best Letters of Lady Mary Wortley Montagu* (1901)

3 The sexes in each species of beings . . . are always true equivalents—equals but not identicals.

> Antoinette Brown Blackwell, *The Sexes Throughout Nature* (1875)

4 You bore me . . . when you talk about one sex or the other, as if they were separate things. There is only one human entity and that is a man and a woman.

> Margery Allingham, *The Fashion in Shrouds* (1938)

5 There should be an end to the bitterness of feeling which has arisen between the sexes in this century.

> Charlotte Perkins Gilman, *Women and Economics* (1899)

6 On the whole, Western society is organized around the assumption that the differences between the sexes are more important than any qualities they have in common.

> Ann Oakley, *Sex, Gender, and Society* (1972)

7 There is more difference within the sexes than between them.

> Ivy Compton-Burnett, *Mother and Son* (1955)

8 What is human and the same about the males and females classified as *Homo sapiens* is much greater than the differences.

> Estelle Ramey, "Men's Monthly Cycles," in *Ms.* (1972)

9 The basic discovery about any people . . . is the discovery of the relationship between its men and women.

> Pearl S. Buck, *Of Men and Women* (1941)

10 Mr. Darwin . . . has failed to hold definitely before his mind the principle that the difference of sex, whatever it may consist in, must itself be subject to natural selection and to evolution.

> Antoinette Brown Blackwell, *The Sexes Throughout Nature* (1875)

11 A sense of deep strain between women and men has been permeating our species' life as far back into time as the study of myth and ritual permits us to trace human feeling.

> Dorothy Dinnerstein, *The Mermaid and the Minotaur* (1976)

12 War and the "war of the sexes" are neither divinely nor biologically ordained.

> Riane Eisler, *The Chalice and the Blade* (1987)

13 True emancipation . . . will have to do away with the absurd notion of the dualism of the sexes, or that man and woman represent two antagonistic worlds.

> Emma Goldman, "The Tragedy of Woman's Emancipation," *Anarchism* (1910)

14 The dogma of woman's complete historical subjection to man must be rated as one of the most fantastic myths ever created by the human mind.

> Mary Ritter Beard, *Woman As a Force in History* (1946)

15 I object to anything that divides the two sexes. My main point is this: human development has now reached a point at which sexual difference has become a thing of altogether minor importance. We make too much of it; we are men and women in the second place, human beings in the first.

> Olive Schreiner (1884), in S.C. Cronwright-Schreiner, ed., *The Letters of Olive Schreiner 1876-1920* (1924)

16 There are only two basic ways of structuring the relations between the female and male halves of humanity. All societies are patterned on either a dominator model—in which human hierarchies are ultimately backed up by force or the threat of force—or a partnership model, with variations in between.

> Riane Eisler, *The Chalice and the Blade* (1987)

17 So long as women are slaves, men will be knaves.

> Elizabeth Cady Stanton (1890), in Theodore Stanton and Harriot Stanton Blatch, eds., *Elizabeth Cady Stanton As Revealed in Her Letters Diary and Reminiscences*, vol. 2 (1922)

18 Lots of men hate women now-a-days. . . . It was a man-made world, and now we're asking to go shares in the making.

> Phyllis Bottome, *Private Worlds* (1934)

1 As women got little crumbs of power, men began to act paranoid—as if we'd disabled them utterly. Do all women have to keep silent for men to speak? Do all women have to be legless for men to walk?

　　Erica Jong, *Fear of Fifty* (1994)

2 Etiquette requires that the association of men and women in refined circles shall be frank without freedom, friendly without familiarity.

　　Agnes H. Morton, *Etiquette* (1892)

3 Grandmother belongs to the generation of women who were satisfied to have men retain their vices, if they removed their hats.

　　Margaret Deland, *The Rising Tide* (1916)

4 Women have served all these centuries as looking-glasses possessing the magic and delicious power of reflecting the figure of man at twice its natural size.

　　Virginia Woolf, *A Room of One's Own* (1929)

5 Men reflect women *half* their natural size.

　　Dell Richards, *Lesbian Lists* (1990)

6 Our culture is definitely the eighth grade. It's run by eighth-grade boys, and the way these boys show a girl they like her is by humiliating her and making her cry.

　　Merrill Markoe, *What the Dogs Have Taught Me* (1992)

7 Stupid men, who accuse / women without reason: / you've never noticed, I suppose, / it's you who taught the lesson. / If with an upsurge of desire / . . . / You wear her last defenses down, / and then you gravely tell her / she's frivolous, though it was *you* / who caused harm to befall her.

　　Sor Juana Inés de la Cruz, "Hombres Necios" (1690), in Irene Nicholson, *A Guide to Mexican Poetry* (1968)

8 My research suggests that men and women may speak different languages that they assume are the same, using similar words to encode disparate experiences of self and social relationships. Because these languages share an overlapping moral vocabulary, they contain a propensity for systematic mistranslation.

　　Carol Gilligan, *In a Different Voice* (1982)

9 The most sympathetic of men never fully comprehend woman's concrete situation.

　　Simone de Beauvoir, *The Second Sex* (1949)

10 I do not think women understand how repelled a man feels when he sees a woman wholly absorbed in what she is thinking, unless it is about her child, or her husband, or her lover. It gives one gooseflesh.

　　Rebecca West, "There Is No Conversation," *The Harsh Voice* (1935)

11 The old myths had it wrong; woman was really created first, and in her need to mother she asked for a child. The Creator then gave her man, who has ever since been her biggest, first child. For just as surely as the woman must mother, the man must be mothered.

　　Anne Shannon Monroe, *The Hearth of Happiness* (1929)

12 Sometimes I wonder if men and women really suit each other. Perhaps they should live next-door and just visit now and then.

　　Katharine Hepburn, in *Esquire* (1980)

13 Men and women, women and men. It will never work.

　　Erica Jong, *Fear of Flying* (1973)

14 If American men are obsessed with money, American women are obsessed with weight. The men talk of gain, the women talk of loss, and I do not know which talk is the more boring.

　　Marya Mannes, *More in Anger* (1958)

15 If a woman gets nervous, she'll eat or go shopping. A man will attack a country—it's a whole other way of thinking.

　　Elayne Boosler, in Gloria Kaufman, *In Stitches* (1991)

16 If a woman drinks the last glass of apple juice in the refrigerator, she'll make more apple juice. If a man drinks the last glass of apple juice, he'll just put back the empty container.

　　Rita Rudner, in *First* (1993)

17 I early became conscious that men breathe more audibly than women. Sit in a room in silence with men and women, and you can always hear the men breathing.

　　Miles Franklin, *Childhood at Brindabella* (1963)

18 Women speak because they wish to speak, whereas a man speaks only when driven to speech by something outside himself—like, for instance, he can't find any clean socks.

　　Jean Kerr, *The Snake Has All the Lines* (1960)

19 Women have one great advantage over men. It is commonly thought that if they marry they have done enough, and need career no further. If a man

marries, on the other hand, public opinion is all against him if he takes this view.

Rose Macaulay, "A Preliminary Word," *A Casual Commentary* (1926)

1 A critical, strong speech made by a man is "blunt" or "outspoken" or "pulls no punches." A speech of similar force and candor made by a woman is "waspish," "sarcastic," or "cutting." A man of strong opinions is defined as having "deep convictions." A woman so constituted is merely "opinionated," and always "aggressive."

Marya Mannes, *Out of My Time* (1971)

2 If a man wants to get it right, he's looked up to and respected. If a woman wants to get it right, she's difficult or impossible. If he acts, produces and directs, he's called multitalented. If she does the same thing, she's called vain and egotistical.

Barbra Streisand, news item (1994)

3 A man has to be Joe McCarthy to be called ruthless. All a woman has to do is put you on hold.

Marlo Thomas, in *First* (1993)

4 A man at his desk in a room with a closed door is a man at work. A woman at a desk in any room is available.

Marya Mannes, "The Singular Woman," *But Will It Sell?* (1964)

5 Men play harder than they work; women work harder than they play.

Mary Roberts Rinehart, *"Isn't That Just Like a Man!"* (1920)

6 When a woman breaks through the lines of convention she will go farther than a man.

Roman Doubleday, *The Hemlock Avenue Mystery* (1908)

7 It's surely no accident that there are horoscopes in *Vogue, Glamour, Mademoiselle, Woman, New Woman, Elle* and *Cosmo* . . . but not *Sports Illustrated, GQ, Esquire, Field & Stream* or *Guns & Ammo.*

Merrill Markoe, *What the Dogs Have Taught Me* (1992)

8 A woman reasons by telegraph, and his [a man's] stage-coach reasoning cannot keep pace with hers.

Mary Walker (1867), in Charles McCool Snyder, *Dr. Mary Walker* (1962)

9 If you want something said, ask a man. If you want something done, ask a woman.

Margaret Thatcher, speech (1965), in Penny Junor, *Margaret Thatcher* (1983)

10 "A woman is as good as a man" is as meaningless as to say, "a Kaffir is as good as a Frenchman" or "a poet is as good as an engineer" or "an elephant is as good as a racehorse"—it means nothing whatever until you add: "at doing what?"

Dorothy L. Sayers, "Are Women Human?" (1938), *Unpopular Opinions* (1946)

11 Whatever it is morally right for man to do, it is morally right for woman to do.

Angelina E. Grimké (1837), *Letters to Catherine E. Beecher* (1969)

12 What is wrong in woman's life / In man's cannot be right.

Frances Ellen Watkins Harper, "A Double Standard," *The Sparrow's Fall* (1894)

13 I'm not denyin' the women are foolish: God Almighty made 'em to match the men.

George Eliot, *Adam Bede* (1859)

See also Androgyny, Equality, Gender, Housework, Husbands, Men, Sexism, Sex Roles, Stereotypes, Wives, Women.

## ❦ WOMEN'S MOVEMENT

14 The men are much alarmed by certain speculations about women; and well they may be, for when the horse and ass begin to think and argue, adieu to riding and driving.

Adelaide Anne Procter, letter to Anna Jameson (1838), in Geraldine Macpherson, *Memoirs of the Life of Anna Jameson* (1878)

15 There's always been a women's movement this century!

Mary Stott, in Dale Spender, *There's Always Been a Women's Movement This Century* (1983)

16 The explanation of the ebb and flow of the women's movement . . . is partly psychological. During those early post-war years when successes came thick and fast and were almost thrust upon us, the nation was still under the influence of the reconstruction spirit, when everything seemed possible. . . . A few years later the nation had reached the stage which follows a drinking bout. It was feeling ruefully in its empty pockets. It did not want to part with anything to anybody. Its head

ached. Noble sentiments made it feel sick. It wanted only to be left alone.

> Eleanor F. Rathbone, "Changes in Public Life," in Ray Strachey, ed., *Our Freedom and Its Results* (1936)

1 The history of men's opposition to women's emancipation is more interesting perhaps than the story of that emancipation itself.

> Virginia Woolf, *A Room of One's Own* (1929)

2 By the way in the new Code of Laws which I suppose it will be necessary for you to make I desire you would Remember the Ladies, and be more generous and favorable to them than your ancestors. Do not put such unlimited power into the hands of the Husbands. Remember all Men would be tyrants if they could. If particular care and attention is not paid to the Ladies we are determined to foment a Rebellion, and will not hold ourselves bound by any Laws in which we have no voice, or Representation. That your Sex are Naturally Tyrannical is a Truth so thoroughly established as to admit of no dispute, but such of you as wish to be happy willingly give up the harsh title of Master for the more tender and endearing one of Friend.

> Abigail Adams, to her husband, John Adams (1776), in L.H. Butterfield et al., eds., *The Book of Abigail and John* (1975)

See also Feminism, Sisterhood, Women.

## ❧ WONDER

3 Wonder is music heard in the heart, is voiceless.

> Rosemary Dobson, "Wonder," *Selected Poems* (1973)

4 If a child is to keep alive his inborn sense of wonder . . . he needs the companionship of at least one adult who can share it, rediscovering with him the joy, excitement and mystery of the world we live in.

> Rachel Carson, *The Sense of Wonder* (1965)

5 Everything has its wonders, even darkness and silence, and I learn, whatever state I may be in, therein to be content.

> Helen Keller, *The Story of My Life* (1902)

6 If I had influence with the good fairy who is supposed to preside over the christening of all children I should ask that her gift to each child in the world be a sense of wonder so indestructible that it would last throughout life, as an unfailing antidote against the boredom and disenchantments of later years,

the sterile preoccupation with things that are artificial, the alienation from the sources of our strength.

> Rachel Carson, *The Sense of Wonder* (1965)

7 Wonder and despair are two sides of a spinning coin. When you open yourself to one, you open yourself to the other. You discover a capacity for joy that wasn't in you before. Wonder is the promise of restoration: as deeply as you dive, so may you rise.

> Christina Baldwin, *Life's Companion* (1990)

8 For the first time in her life she thought, might the same wonders never come again? Was each wonder original and alone like the falling star, and when it fell did it bury itself beyond where you hunted it?

> Eudora Welty, "The Winds," *The Wide Net* (1943)

See also Curiosity, Miracles.

## ❧ WORDS

9 The words! I collected them in all shapes and sizes, and hung them like bangles in my mind.

> Hortense Calisher, "Little Did I Know," *Extreme Magic* (1964)

10 God wove a web of loveliness, / Of clouds and stars and birds, / But made not anything at all / So beautiful as words.

> Anna Hempstead Branch, "Songs for My Mother: Her Words," *The Shoes That Danced* (1905)

11 I love smooth words, like gold-enameled fish / Which circle slowly with a silken swish.

> Elinor Wylie, "Pretty Words," in William Rose Benét, ed., *Collected Poems of Elinor Wylie* (1933)

12 Stitches / holding seams / in the clothes / that cover up / our naked souls—.

> Paulette C. White, "Words," *Love Poem to a Black Junkie* (1975)

13 Words were living things to her. She sensed them bestriding the air and charging the room with strong colors.

> Paule Marshall, *Brown Girl, Brownstones* (1959)

14 A word is no light matter. Words have with truth been called fossil poetry, each, that is, a symbol of a creative thought.

> Edith Hamilton, *The Greek Way* (1930)

1 in a ward on fire, we must / find words / or burn.

Olga Broumas, "Artemis," *Beginning With O* (1977)

2 Words set things in motion. I've seen them doing it. Words set up atmospheres, electrical fields, charges.

Toni Cade Bambara, in Janet Sternburg, ed., *The Writer on Her Work*, vol. 1 (1980)

3 A word is dead when it is said, some say. I say it just begins to live that day.

Emily Dickinson (1872), in Mabel Loomis Todd, ed., *Letters of Emily Dickinson*, vol. 2 (1894)

4 Words are anybody's / Equitable things, / . . . / All within the public domain.

Helen Bevington, "Words Are Anybody's," *Nineteen Million Elephants* (1950)

5 Her profession was words and she believed in them deeply. The articulation, interpretation, appreciation, and preservation of good words. . . . Words could incite, soothe, destroy, exorcise, redeem.

Gail Godwin, *The Odd Woman* (1974)

6 A word is the taste / our tongue has of eternity; / that's why I speak.

Rosario Castellanos, "The Splendor of Being," in Magda Bogin, tr., *The Selected Poems of Rosario Castellanos* (1988)

7 Honeyed words like bees, / Gilded and sticky, with a little sting.

Elinor Wylie, "Pretty Words," in William Rose Benét, ed., *Collected Poems of Elinor Wylie* (1933)

8 You can taste a word.

Pearl Bailey, in *Newsweek* (1967)

9 By men's words we know them.

Marie de France (12th cent.), in Jeanette Beer, tr., *Medieval Fables of Marie de France* (1981)

10 Words, living and ghostly, the quick and the dead, crowd and jostle the otherwise too empty corridors of my mind. . . . To move among this bright, strange, often fabulous herd of beings, to summon them at my will, to fasten them on to paper like flies, that they may decorate it, this is the pleasure of writing.

Rose Macaulay, *Personal Pleasures* (1936)

11 Although they are / Only breath, words / which I command / are immortal.

Sappho (6th cent. B.C.), in Mary Barnard, tr., *Sappho* (1958)

12 And now we come to the magic of words. A word, also, just like an idea, a thought, has the effect of reality upon undifferentiated minds.

Emma Jung, "On the Nature of the Animus" (1931), *Animus and Anima* (1957)

13 They say that there is no reality before it has been given shape by words rules regulations. They say that in what concerns them everything has to be remade starting from basic principles. They say that in the first place the vocabulary of every language is to be examined, modified, turned upside down, that every word must be screened.

Monique Wittig, *Les Guérillères* (1969)

14 Words, once they're printed, have a life of their own.

Carol Burnett, in *Reader's Digest* (1982)

15 I cannot remember a time when I was not enraptured or tortured by words. Always there have been words which, sometimes for their sound alone, sometimes for their sound and sense, I would not use. From a loathing of their grossness or sickliness, their weight or want of weight. Their inexactitude, their feeling of acidity or insipidity. Their action, not only on the intelligence but on the nerves, was instant.

Mary Butts, *The Crystal Cabinet* (1937)

16 Words have their genealogy, their history, their economy, their literature, their art and music, as too they have their weddings and divorces, their successes and defeats, their fevers, their undiagnosable ailments, their sudden deaths. They also have their moral and social distinctions.

Virgilia Peterson, *A Matter of Life and Death* (1961)

17 You may choose your word like a connoisseur, / And polish it up with art, / But the word that sways, and stirs, and stays, / Is the word that comes from the heart.

Ella Wheeler Wilcox, "The Word," *New Thought Pastels* (1906)

18 Words of affection, howsoe'er express'd, / The latest spoken still are deem'd the best.

Joanna Baillie, "Lines to Agnes Baillie on Her Birthday," *The Dramatic and Poetical Works of Joanna Baillie* (1853)

19 I say that words are men and when we spell / In alphabets we deal with living things; / With feet and thighs and breasts, fierce heads, strong wings; /

Maternal Powers, great Bridals, Heaven and Hell. /
There is a menace in the tales we tell.

> Anna Hempstead Branch, title poem, *Sonnets From a Lock Box* (1929)

1 Words, words, / Ye are like birds. / Would I might
fold you, / In my hands hold you / Till ye were
warm and your feathers a-flutter; / Till, in your
throats, / Tremulous notes / Foretold the songs ye
would utter.

> Josephine Preston Peabody, "Prelude," in Edmund
> Clarence Stedman, ed., *An American Anthology 1787-1900*
> (1900)

2 We think because we have words, not the other
way around. The more words we have, the better
able we are to think conceptually.

> Madeleine L'Engle, *Walking on Water* (1980)

3 What's a word, a talisman, to hold against the
world?

> Rita Dove, *The Other Side of the House* (1988)

4 For me words still possess their primitive, mystical,
incantatory powers. I am inclined to use them as
part of an attempt to make my own reality more
real for others, as part of an effort to transcend
emotional danger. For me, words are a form of
action, capable of influencing change. Their articulation represents a complete, lived experience.

> Ingrid Bengis, *Combat in the Erogenous Zone* (1972)

5 All words, anyway / are epitaphs.

> Linda Pastan, "Friday's Child," *PM/AM* (1982)

6 Words. Frail beasts of burden that crashed down to
their knees under what she wanted to say.

> Fannie Hurst, *Lummox* (1923)

7 All things tend to become specialized, except only
words. . . . The word alone grows not expert and
special, but general and inexpert. It is obliged to do
more various things, and to do them with less di-
rectness.

> Alice Meynell, title essay, *The Second Person Singular* (1921)

8 The older I grow the more sharply I mistrust
words. So few of them have any meaning left. It is
impossible to write one sentence in which every
word has the bareness and hardness of bones, the
reality of the skeleton.

> Storm Jameson, *No Time Like the Present* (1933)

9 A trite word is an overused word which has lost its
identity like an old coat in a second-hand shop.

The familiar grows dull and we no longer see, hear,
or taste it.

> Anaïs Nin (1950), *The Diary of Anaïs Nin*, vol. 5 (1974)

10 Words and eggs must be handled with care. / Once
broken they are impossible / things to repair.

> Anne Sexton, "Words," *The Awful Rowing Toward God*
> (1975)

11 Words have been used too often; touched and
turned, and left exposed to the dust of the street.
The words we seek hang close to the tree. We come
at dawn and find them sweet beneath the leaf.

> Virginia Woolf, *Jacob's Room* (1922)

12 Words are sometimes sensitive instruments of precision with which delicate operations may be performed and swift, elusive truths may be touched;
often they are clumsy tools with which we grope in
the dark toward truths more inaccessible but no
less significant.

> Helen Merrell Lynd, *On Shame and the Search for Identity*
> (1958)

13 Peoples of the earth, / do not destroy the universe
of words, / . . . / O that no one mean death when he
says life— / and not blood when he speaks cradle.

> Nelly Sachs, "Peoples of the earth," *O the Chimneys* (1967)

14 We must use words as they are used, or stand aside
from life.

> Ivy Compton-Burnett, *Mother and Son* (1955)

15 An appreciation of words is so rare that everybody
naturally thinks he possesses it, and this universal
sentiment results in the misuse of a material whose
beauty enriches the loving student beyond the
dreams of avarice.

> Agnes Repplier, "Words," *Essays in Idleness* (1893)

16 It is as dangerous for people unaccustomed to handling words and unacquainted with their technique
to tinker about with these heavily-charged nuclei of
emotional power as it would be for me to burst into
a laboratory and play about with a powerful elec-
tromagnet or other machine highly charged with
electrical force.

> Dorothy L. Sayers, "Creative Mind" (1942), *Unpopular Opinions* (1946)

17 Some words / bedevil me.

> Audre Lorde, "Coal" (1962), *Undersong* (1992)

18 Our words have wings, but fly not where we would.

> George Eliot, *The Spanish Gypsy* (1868)

1 Damn words; they're just the pots and pans of life, the pails and scrubbing-brushes. I wish I didn't have to think in words.

    Edith Wharton, *The Gods Arrive* (1932)

2 Words are name tags which save us the trouble of thinking about the objects or ideas which they represent. Here exactly lies their capacity for mischief.

    Judith Groch, *The Right to Create* (1969)

3 One must be chary of words because they turn into cages.

    Viola Spolin, in *The Los Angeles Times* (1974)

4 Words can destroy. What we call each other ultimately becomes what we think of each other, and it matters.

    Jeane J. Kirkpatrick, speech (1982)

5 A broken bone can heal, but the wound a word opens can fester forever.

    Jessamyn West, *The Life I Really Lived* (1979)

6 There are worse words than cuss words, there are words that hurt.

    Tillie Olsen, "Hey Sailor, What Ship?" *Tell Me a Riddle* (1956)

7 All books are either dreams or swords, / You can cut, or you can drug, with words.

    Amy Lowell, title poem, *Sword Blades and Poppy Seed* (1914)

8 It is not that i am playing word games, it is that the word games are there, being played, and i am calling attention to it.

    Alice Molloy, *In Other Words* (1973)

9 Mama . . . made up words from scratch, by combining words, by turning them upside down, by running them backward. She built word palaces. Structures came out of her mouth like Steinberg pictures: wobbly, made of material fabricated on the spot, and no more useful than a poem.

    Jessamyn West, *Hide and Seek* (1973)

10 Ours was a storytelling family even in pleasing times, and in those days my parents looked on words as our sustenance, rich in their flavor and wholesome for the soul.

    Natalie Kusz, *Road Song* (1990)

11 Almost all words do have color and nothing is more pleasant than to utter a pink word and see someone's eyes light up and know it is a pink word for him or her too.

    Gladys Taber, *Stillmeadow Daybook* (1955)

12 Nouns and verbs are almost pure metal; adjectives are cheaper ore.

    Marie Gilchrist, in Leonora Speyer, "On the Teaching of Poetry," in *Saturday Review of Literature* (1946)

13 Adjectives are the curse of America.

    Rita Mae Brown, *In Her Day* (1976)

14 Might, could, would—they are contemptible auxiliaries.

    George Eliot, *Middlemarch* (1871)

15 Just-in-your-own words was Mr. Gilmer's trademark. We often wondered who else's words Mr. Gilmer was afraid his witness might employ.

    Harper Lee, *To Kill a Mockingbird* (1960)

16 She might struggle like a fly in a web. He wrapped her around and around with beautiful sentences.

    Mary H. Catherwood, "The King of Beaver," *Mackinac and Lake Stories* (1899)

17 The Greeks had a word for it.

    Zoë Akins, play title (1929)

See also Actions, Clichés, Conversation, Euphemisms, Jargon, Language, Metaphor, Obscenity, Platitudes, Speech, Swearing, Talking, Writing.

## ❦ WORK

18 I am fierce for work. Without work I am nothing.

    Winifred Holtby, in Vera Brittain, *Testament of Friendship* (1940)

19 In my studio I'm as happy as a cow in her stall.

    Louise Nevelson, *Dawns + Dusks* (1976)

20 To find joy in work is to discover the fountain of youth.

    Pearl S. Buck, *The Joy of Children* (1964)

21 I believe in hard work. It keeps the wrinkles out of the mind and the spirit.

    Helena Rubinstein, *My Life for Beauty* (1966)

22 The ability to take pride in your own work is one of the hallmarks of sanity. Take away the ability to

both work and be proud of it and you can drive anyone insane.

> Nikki Giovanni, in Gloria Wade-Gayles, ed., *My Soul Is a Witness* (1995)

1 It is not hard work which is dreary; it is superficial work.

> Edith Hamilton (1959), in Doris Fielding Reid, *Edith Hamilton* (1967)

2 Work . . . has always been my favorite form of recreation.

> Anna Howard Shaw, *The Story of a Pioneer* (1915)

3 To love what you do and feel that it matters—how could anything be more fun?

> Katharine Graham, in Jane Howard, "The Power That Didn't Corrupt," *Ms.* (1974)

4 What a richly colored strong warm coat / is woven when love is the warp and work is the woof.

> Marge Piercy, "The inquisition," *The Moon Is Always Female* (1980)

5 I believe in my work and the joy of it. You have to be with the work and the work has to be with you. It absorbs you totally and you absorb it totally. Everything must fall by the wayside by comparison.

> Louise Nevelson, *Dawns + Dusks* (1976)

6 I went back to being an amateur, in the sense of somebody who loves what she is doing. If a professional loses the love of work, routine sets in, and that's the death of work and of life.

> Ade Bethune, in Judith Stoughton, *Proud Donkey of Schaerbeek* (1988)

7 I am so full of my work, I can't stop to eat or sleep, or for anything but a daily run.

> Louisa May Alcott, *Journals* (1868)

8 Work is not, primarily, a thing one does to live, but the thing one lives to do. It is, or it should be, the full expression of the worker's faculties.

> Dorothy L. Sayers, "Why Work?" *Creed or Chaos?* (1949)

9 It has been my experience that one cannot, in any shape or form, depend on human relations for lasting reward. It is only work that truly satisfies.

> Bette Davis, *The Lonely Life* (1962)

10 There can be no substitute for work, neither affection nor physical well-being can replace it.

> Maria Montessori, *The Secret of Childhood* (1936)

11 A human being *must* have occupation, if he or she is not to become a nuisance to the world.

> Dorothy L. Sayers, "Are Women Human?" (1938), *Unpopular Opinions* (1946)

12 Work in some form or other is the appointed lot of all.

> Anna Jameson, "The Communion of Labor" (1856), in *Sisters of Charity, Catholic and Protestant, and the Communion of Labor* (1859)

13 The pitcher cries for water to carry / and a person for work that is real.

> Marge Piercy, "To be of use," *Circles on the Water* (1982)

14 Work is a world apart from jobs. Work is the way you occupy your mind and hand and eye and whole body when they're informed by your imagination and wit, by your keenest perceptions, by your most profound reflections on everything you've read and seen and heard and been part of. You may or may not be paid to do your work.

> Alice Koller, *The Stations of Solitude* (1990)

15 Dedication to one's work in the world is the only possible sanctification. Religion in all its forms is dedication to Someone Else's work, not yours.

> Cynthia Ozick, *Trust* (1966)

16 Work is creativity accompanied by the comforting realization that one is bringing forth something really good and necessary, with the conviction that a sudden, arbitrary cessation would cause a sensitive void, produce a loss.

> Jenny Heynrichs, "Was Ist Arbeit?" in *Neue Bahnen, Organ des Allgemeinen Deutschen Frauenvereins* (1866)

17 Her work, I really think her work / is finding what her real work is / and doing it, / her work, her own work, / her being human, / her being in the world.

> Ursula K. Le Guin, "The Writer on, and at, Her Work," in Janet Sternburg, ed., *The Writer on Her Work*, vol. 2 (1991)

18 People are not the best because they work hard. They work hard because they are the best.

> Bette Midler, *A View From a Broad* (1980)

19 Do what you love, the money will follow.

> Marsha Sinetar, book title (1987)

20 The best careers advice given to the young . . . is "Find out what you like doing best and get someone to pay you for doing it."

> Katharine Whitehorn, "A-Work and B-Work," *Sunday Best* (1976)

1 When you're following your energy and doing what you want all the time, the distinction between work and play dissolves.

> Shakti Gawain, *Living in the Light* (1986)

2 That society exists to frustrate the individual may be seen from its attitude to work. It is only morally acceptable if you do not want to do it. If you do want to, it becomes a personal pleasure.

> Celia Green, *The Decline and Fall of Science* (1976)

3 He works so hard . . . I wish I could persuade him to take things a little more easily; but it would be like inducing a sledge hammer to loiter on the downward arc.

> Margaret Halsey, *Some of My Best Friends Are Soldiers* (1944)

4 Workaholics are energized rather than enervated by their work—their energy paradoxically expands as it is expended.

> Marilyn Machlowitz, *Workaholics* (1980)

5 I am disturbed that a natural human inclination [work] should, by some Freudian turn of phrase, be considered compulsive—perhaps even pathological. To me this is a complete misreading of the human enterprise.

> Joyce Carol Oates, in Leif Sjoberg, "An Interview With Joyce Carol Oates," *Contemporary Literature* (1982)

6 I don't think that work ever really destroyed anybody. I think that lack of work destroys them a hell of a lot more.

> Katharine Hepburn, *Me* (1991)

7 If you rest, you rust.

> Helen Hayes, with Katherine Hatch, *My Life in Three Acts* (1990)

8 The simple idea that everyone needs a reasonable amount of challenging work in his or her life, and also a personal life, complete with noncompetitive leisure, has never really taken hold.

> Judith Martin, *Common Courtesy* (1985)

9 The person who knows "how" will always have a job. The person who knows "why" will always be his boss.

> Diane Ravitch, in *Time* (1985)

10 Always be smarter than the people who hire you.

> Lena Horne, interview (1985)

11 If people are highly successful in their professions they lose their senses. Sight goes. They have no time to look at pictures. Sound goes. They have no time to listen to music. Speech goes. They have no time for conversation. They lose their sense of proportion—the relations between one thing and another. Humanity goes.

> Virginia Woolf, *Three Guineas* (1938)

12 We spend so much time in our work and in work-related activities that our awarenesses and our perceptions become narrower and narrower. We reach a point where we can't talk about anything but our work and, if the truth be known, we don't *want* to talk about anything but our work. . . . We have taken a rainbow and compressed it into a solid, uninteresting beam of light.

> Anne Wilson Schaef, *Meditations for Women Who Do Too Much* (1990)

13 For workaholics, all the eggs of self-esteem are in the basket of work.

> Judith M. Bardwick, *The Plateauing Trap* (1986)

14 I am not at all in favor of hard work for its own sake; many people who work very hard indeed produce terrible things, and should most certainly not be encouraged.

> Edna St. Vincent Millay (1927), in Allan Ross Macdougall, ed., *Letters of Edna St. Vincent Millay* (1952)

15 She had worked so hard for so many years that the habit had degenerated into a disease, and thrift had become a tyrant instead of a slave in her life.

> Ellen Glasgow, *Barren Ground* (1925)

16 What's the need of working if it doesn't get you anywhere? What's the use of boring around in the same hole like a worm? Making the hole bigger to stay in?

> Marita Bonner, "The Purple Flower" (1928), *Frye Street and Environs* (1987)

17 Six months of looking for a job had made me an expert at picking out the people who, like me, were hurrying up to wait—in somebody's outer anything for a chance to make it through their inner doors to prove that you could type two words a minute, or not drool on your blouse while answering difficult questions about your middle initial and date of birth.

> Gloria Naylor, *Mama Day* (1988)

18 The question was not how to get a job, but how to live by such jobs as I could get.

> Dorothy M. Richardson, *The Long Day* (1905)

1 There are so many ways of earning a living and most of them are failures.

    Gertrude Stein, *Ida* (1941)

2 Although we may not realize it, or want to admit it, many of us bring our personal lives, with childhood's emotional baggage, to work every day with us, with far greater intensity than we bring work home at night.

    Paula Bernstein, *Family Ties, Corporate Bonds* (1985)

3 What a denial of our humanity that at the centers of power, where decisions are made, there is no room for nurturing, for love, and children. There is more to life than the "inhuman" work place. It is terrible that many men do not know that: it is a tragedy if women follow them.

    Dora Russell, in Dale Spender, *There's Always Been a Women's Movement This Century* (1983)

4 I yield to no one in my admiration for the office as a social center, but it's no place actually to get any work done.

    Katharine Whitehorn, *Sunday Best* (1976)

See also Business, Collaboration, Housework, Interruptions, Labor, Retirement, Unemployment.

## ❧ WORLDLINESS

5 Americans ought to be the best-traveled, most cosmopolitan people on earth, not only because experience of the world is desirable in its own right, but because as a people acquires a great concentration of power, worldliness becomes a moral imperative.

    Shana Alexander, "The Real Tourist Trap," in *Life* (1968)

6 The unfortunate thing about worldliness is that its rewards are rather less than its appetites.

    Phyllis Bottome, "A Game of Skill," *Innocence and Experience* (1934)

See also Cosmopolitan.

## ❧ WORRY

7 Worry is like a rocking chair—it keeps you moving but doesn't get you anywhere.

    Corrie ten Boom, *Prison Letters* (1975)

8 A worried man could borrow a lot of trouble with practically no collateral.

    Helen Nielsen, *Borrow the Night* (1956)

9 When you borrow trouble you give your peace of mind as security.

    Myrtle Reed, *A Weaver of Dreams* (1911)

10 Worry is like racing the engine of an automobile without letting in the clutch.

    Corrie ten Boom, *Don't Wrestle, Just Nestle* (1978)

11 It ain't never no use puttin' up your umbrell' till it rains!

    Alice Caldwell Rice, *Mrs. Wiggs of the Cabbage Patch* (1901)

12 Worrying is one of my few forms of prayer.

    Joanne Greenberg, "The Jaws of the Dog," *High Crimes and Misdemeanors* (1979)

13 He would simply tell her not to worry, which was about as effective as ordering someone not to think of an elephant.

    Judith Kelman, *Someone's Watching* (1991)

14 A request not to worry . . . is perhaps the least soothing message capable of human utterance.

    Mignon G. Eberhart, *The House on the Roof* (1934)

15 Let us be of good cheer, remembering that the misfortunes hardest to bear are those which never come.

    Amy Lowell, in Charles L. Wallis, ed., *The Treasure Chest* (1965)

16 While most of the things you've worried about have never happened, it's a different story with the things you haven't worried about. They are the ones that happen.

    Ruth Rendell, *Talking to Strange Men* (1987)

17 The best course was to buy a house across a road from a cemetery and look at it every morning. Reminding yourself where it all ended anyway, you'd never get upset about anything again.

    Mildred Davis, *They Buried a Man* (1953)

18 I always feel sorry for people who think more about a rainy day ahead than sunshine today.

    Rae Foley, *Suffer a Witch* (1965)

19 We have to fight them daily, like fleas, those many small worries about the morrow, for they sap our energies.

    Etty Hillesum (1942), *An Interrupted Life* (1983)

1 Worries are the most stubborn habits in the world. Even after a poor man has won a huge lottery prize, he will still for months wake up in the night with a start, worrying about food and rent.
Vicki Baum, *And Life Goes On* (1932)

2 That was a snake that would lay eggs in my brain.
Faith Sullivan, *The Cape Ann* (1988)

See also Anxiety, Concern.

## 5 WORSHIP

3 To discover, or recover, the sense of religious certainty one must worship.
Georgia Harkness, *The Resources of Religion* (1936)

4 One can be coerced to church, but not to worship.
Georgia Harkness, *The Resources of Religion* (1936)

See also Church, God, Religion, Ritual, Spirituality.

## 5 WRITERS

5 Everybody can write; writers can't do anything else.
Mignon McLaughlin, *The Neurotic's Notebook* (1963)

6 why do you write they ask / why do you breathe i ask.
Alta, *i am not a practicing angel* (1975)

7 Authorship has never been with me a matter of choice. I have not done it for amusement, or for money, or for fame, or for any reason but because I could not help it.
Harriet Martineau, *Autobiography*, vol. 1 (1877)

8 I am not a born writer, but I was born a writer.
Enid Bagnold, *Enid Bagnold's Autobiography* (1969)

9 To me, writing is not a profession. You might as well call living a profession. Or having children. Anything you can't help doing.
Vicki Baum, *I Know What I'm Worth* (1964)

10 Perhaps few people realize that this gift is life itself. I would give up almost everything else in the world for my pen!
Ursula Bloom, *Life Is No Fairy Tale* (1976)

11 Writing is the only thing that . . . when I'm doing it, I don't feel that I should be doing something else instead.
Gloria Steinem, *Outrageous Acts and Everyday Rebellions* (1983)

12 Writers live twice.
Natalie Goldberg, *Writing Down the Bones* (1986)

13 Writers do not live one life, they live two. There is the living and then there is the writing. There is the second tasting, the delayed reaction.
Anaïs Nin (1932), *The Diary of Anaïs Nin*, vol. 1 (1966)

14 I write because I want more than one life; I insist on a wider selection. It's greed plain and simple. When my characters join the circus, I'm joining the circus. Although I'm happily married, I spend a great deal of my time mentally living with incompatible husbands.
Anne Tyler, "Because I Want More Than One Life," in *The Washington Post* (1976)

15 My writing is full of lives I might have led.
Joyce Carol Oates, in Jay Parini, "My Writing Is Full of Lives I Might Have Led," *The Boston Globe Magazine* (1987)

16 I write in the first person because I have always wanted to make my life more interesting than it was.
Diane Wakoski, *Trilogy* (1974)

17 A writer paradoxically seeks the truth and tells lies every step of the way.
Anne Lamott, *Bird by Bird* (1994)

18 My function as a writer is not story-telling but truth-telling: to make things plain.
Laura Riding Jackson, *Progress of Stories* (1935)

19 Writers are the moral purifiers of the culture. We may not be pure ourselves but we must tell the truth, which is a purifying act.
Rita Mae Brown, *Starting From Scratch* (1988)

20 Writing, as I experience it, means wringing out the heart/mind until it stops lying.
Jennifer Stone, *Telegraph Avenue Then* (1992)

21 The role of the writer is not to say what we can all say, but what we are unable to say.
Anaïs Nin (1954), *The Diary of Anaïs Nin*, vol. 5 (1974)

22 One of the obligations of the writer, and perhaps especially of the poet, is to say or sing *all* that he or

she can, to deal with as much of the world as becomes possible to him or her in language.

Denise Levertov, *The Poet in the World* (1973)

1  Becoming a writer is about becoming conscious.

Anne Lamott, *Bird by Bird* (1994)

2  wires instead of veins. that's what writers are made of. we get these electric demands & if we don't co-operate, we don't get to go to sleep. wired. coffee nerves without the coffee.

Alta, *The Shameless Hussy* (1980)

3  It's a nervous work. The state that you need to write is the state that others are paying large sums to get rid of.

Shirley Hazzard, in *The New York Times* (1980)

4  When I work I feel more alive than under any other circumstances. There's not an "I love you" in the world that can match it. I feel safe, excited, at peace, erotic, centered. Nothing can touch me.

Vivian Gornick, in Donna Perry, ed., *Backtalk* (1993)

5  I don't believe other people are ever as foolishly excited as I am while I'm working. How could they be? Writers would have to live in trees.

Katherine Mansfield (1920), in J. Middleton Murry, ed., *The Letters of Katherine Mansfield*, vol. 2 (1928)

6  I learned that you should feel when writing, not like Lord Byron on a mountain top, but like a child stringing beads in kindergarten,—happy, absorbed and quietly putting one bead on after another.

Brenda Ueland, *If You Want to Write* (1938)

7  I shall live bad if I do not write and I shall write bad if I do not live.

Françoise Sagan, in *The New York Times Book Review* (1956)

8  Writing is the passageway, the entrance, the exit, the dwelling place of the other in me.

Hélène Cixous, "Sorties," *The Newly Born Woman* (1986)

9  It's the writing, not the being read, that excites me.

Virginia Woolf (1928), in Leonard Woolf, ed., *A Writer's Diary* (1953)

10  It is for this, partly, that I write. How can I know what I think unless I see what I write?

Erica Jong, *Fear of Flying* (1973)

11  Had I been blessed with even limited access to my own mind there would have been no reason to write.

Joan Didion, in Janet Sternburg, ed., *The Writer on Her Work*, vol. 1 (1980)

12  I write entirely to find out what I'm thinking, what I'm looking at, what I see and what it means. What I want and what I fear.

Joan Didion, in Janet Sternburg, ed., *The Writer on Her Work*, vol. 1 (1980)

13  Writing has been a way of explaining to myself the things I do not understand.

Rosario Castellanos, in Irene Nicholson, *A Guide to Mexican Poetry* (1968)

14  I suppose I have written novels to find out what I *thought* about something and poems to find out what I *felt* about something.

May Sarton, *Journal of a Solitude* (1973)

15  Writing, which is my form of celebration and prayer, is also my way of inquiry.

Diane Ackerman, in Sybil Steinberg, ed., *Writing for Your Life* (1992)

16  I have never written a book that was not born out of a question I needed to answer for myself.

May Sarton, *At Seventy* (1984)

17  For me, writing something down was the only road out.

Anne Tyler, in Janet Sternburg, ed., *The Writer on Her Work*, vol. 1 (1980)

18  All writers are exiles wherever they live and their work is a lifelong journey towards the lost land.

Janet Frame, *The Envoy From Mirror City* (1985)

19  A writer is a foreign country.

Marguerite Duras, *Practicalities* (1987)

20  I write in order to belong.

Elena Poniatowska, in Janet Sternburg, ed., *The Writer on Her Work*, vol. 2 (1991)

21  When I write stories I am like someone who is in her own country, walking along streets that she has known since she was a child, between walls and trees that are hers.

Natalia Ginzburg, *The Little Virtues* (1962)

22  My scepticism long ago led me to the belief that writers write for themselves and not for their readers and that art has nothing to do with communi-

cation between person and person, only with communication between different parts of a person's mind.

Rebecca West, "The Art of Scepticism," in *Vogue* (1952)

1  I write for myself and strangers.

Gertrude Stein, *The Making of Americans* (1925)

2  No one ever found wisdom without also being a fool. Writers, alas, have to be fools in public, while the rest of the human race can cover its tracks.

Erica Jong, in Janet Sternburg, ed., *The Writer on Her Work*, vol. 1 (1980)

3  The writer must be willing, above everything else, to take chances, to risk making a fool of himself— or even to risk revealing the fact that he *is* a fool.

Jessamyn West, *To See the Dream* (1957)

4  I am dissatisfied with everything I have ever written and regard it all only as a preparation for that one work which probably I don't have it in me to write but which I hope I can go on trying for.

Ruth Prawer Jhabvala, in Susan Cahill, ed., *Women and Fiction 2* (1978)

5  I went for years not finishing anything. Because, of course, when you finish something you can be judged. . . . I had poems which were rewritten so many times that I suspect it was just a way of avoiding sending them out.

Erica Jong, in William Packard, ed., *The Craft of Poetry* (1974)

6  Writers are doubters, compulsives, self-flagellants. The torture only stops for brief moments.

Erica Jong, *Fear of Fifty* (1994)

7  Show me a writer, any writer, who hasn't suffered and I'll show you someone who writes in pastels as opposed to primary colors.

Rita Mae Brown, *Starting From Scratch* (1988)

8  There is no security, no assurance that because we wrote something good two months ago, we will do it again. Actually, every time we begin, we wonder how we ever did it before.

Natalie Goldberg, *Writing Down the Bones* (1986)

9  Every time I start on a new book, I am a beginner again. I doubt myself, I grow discouraged, all the work accomplished in the past is as though it never was, my first drafts are so shapeless that it seems impossible to go on with the attempt at all, right up

until the moment . . . when it is has become impossible not to finish it.

Simone de Beauvoir, *Force of Circumstance* (1963)

10  Elizabeth Hardwick told me once that all her first drafts sounded as if a chicken had written them. So do mine for the most part.

Flannery O'Connor, in Sally Fitzgerald, ed., *The Habit of Being* (1979)

11  Getting the first draft finished is like pushing a peanut with your nose across a very dirty floor.

Joyce Carol Oates, in Robert Compton, "Joyce Carol Oates Keeps Punching," *The Dallas Morning News* (1987)

12  I can't write five words but that I change seven.

Dorothy Parker, in Malcolm Cowley, ed., *Writers at Work* (1958)

13  I can't think why I was cursed with this inordinate desire to write, if the high gods weren't going to give me some more adequate means of expressing myself.

Winifred Holtby (1921), in Alice Holtby and Jean McWilliam, eds., *Letters to a Friend* (1937)

14  I've got a penny-ante talent, out of which I try to drum up a living for myself. And what nobody seems to realize is that it's just as difficult to get a bad idea as a good one.

Kathleen Winsor, *Star Money* (1950)

15  The strength of this inborn desire to write has always baffled me. It is understandable that the really gifted should feel an overwhelming urge to use their gift; but a strong urge with only a slight gift seems almost a genetic mistake.

Dervla Murphy, *Wheels Within Wheels* (1979)

16  The tumult of my fretted mind / Gives me expression of a kind; / But it is faulty, harsh, not plain - / My work has the incompetence of pain.

Anna Wickham, "Self Analysis," *The Contemplative Quarry* (1915)

17  I lived with the mental restlessness of wanting to write, the inner nauseas of the half-finished, the great releases of the completed poem.

Sister M. Madeleva, *My First Seventy Years* (1959)

18  I know some very great writers, writers you love who write beautifully and have made a great deal of money, and not *one* of them sits down routinely feeling wildly enthusiastic and confident. Not one of them writes elegant first drafts. All right, one of them does, but we do not like her very much. We

do not think that she has a rich inner life or that God likes her or can even stand her.

Anne Lamott, *Bird by Bird* (1994)

1 She was constitutionally unable to believe that all other writers didn't have it easy. For it was obvious that their words were hummingbirds, a bright whir of them over the typewriter, seeking only a landing strip. She alone stared at the white paper.

Peg Bracken, *I Didn't Come Here to Argue* (1969)

2 Contrary to what many of you might imagine, a career in letters is not without its drawbacks—chief among them the unpleasant fact that one is frequently called upon to actually sit down and write.

Fran Lebowitz, *Metropolitan Life* (1978)

3 Making a decision to write was a lot like deciding to jump into a frozen lake.

Maya Angelou, *The Heart of a Woman* (1981)

4 I certainly do not adore the writer's discipline. I have lost lovers, endangered friendships, and blundered into eccentricity, impelled by a concentration which usually is to be found only in the minds of people about to be executed in the next half hour.

Maya Angelou, in Mari E. Evans, ed., *Black Women Writers (1950-1980)* (1984)

5 The writer's way is rough and lonely, and who would choose it while there are vacancies in more gracious professions, such as, say, cleaning out ferryboats?

Dorothy Parker, introduction to S.J. Perelman, *The Most of S.J. Perelman* (1958)

6 I truly was neither flesh, fowl nor good red herring, for this is what a writer is, a rogue who is outside any and every group, even the "group" of writers.

Jane Duncan, *Letter From Reachfar* (1975)

7 Every day one has to *earn* the name of "writer" over again, with much wrestling.

Sylvia Plath (1956), in Aurelia Schober Plath, ed., *Letters Home* (1973)

8 An author who waits for the right "mood" will soon find that "moods" get fewer and fewer until they cease altogether.

Vera Brittain, *On Becoming a Writer* (1947)

9 I changed from an amateur to a professional . . . which is to write even when you don't want to,

don't much like what you are writing, and aren't writing particularly well.

Agatha Christie, *An Autobiography* (1977)

10 While feeling far less injured by toil than my friends took for granted I must be, I yet was always aware of the strong probability that my life would end as the lives of hard literary workers usually end,—in paralysis, with months or years of imbecility.

Harriet Martineau, *Autobiography*, vol. 1 (1877)

11 When you have a great and difficult task, something perhaps almost impossible, if you only work a little at a time, every day a little, *without faith and without hope*, suddenly the work will finish itself.

Isak Dinesen, in Glenway Wescott, *Images of Truth* (1962)

12 As for my next book, I am going to hold myself from writing till I have it impending in me: grown heavy in my mind like a ripe pear; pendant, gravid, asking to be cut or it will fall.

Virginia Woolf (1928), in Leonard Woolf, ed., *A Writer's Diary* (1954)

13 I feel within myself an immense power, but I cannot bring it out. I stand a barren vine-stalk; no grape will swell, though the richest wine is slumbering in its roots.

Margaret Fuller, in Thomas Wentworth Higginson, *Margaret Fuller Ossoli* (1890)

14 I have suffered, like other writers, from indolence, irresolution, distaste to my work, absence of "inspiration," and all that: but I have also found that sitting down, however reluctantly, with the pen in my hand, I have never worked for one quarter of an hour without finding myself in full train.

Harriet Martineau, *Autobiography*, vol. 1 (1877)

15 What release to write so that one forgets oneself, forgets one's companion, forgets where one is or what one is going to do next—to be drenched in work as one is drenched in sleep or in the sea. Pencils and pads and curling blue sheets alive with letters heap up on the desk.

Anne Morrow Lindbergh, *Gift From the Sea* (1955)

16 Writing is a good example of self-abandonment. I never completely forget myself except when I am writing and I am never more completely myself than when I am writing.

Flannery O'Connor, in Sally Fitzgerald, ed., *The Habit of Being* (1979)

1 If you are a writer you locate yourself behind a wall of silence and no matter what you are doing, driving a car or walking or doing housework . . . you can still be writing, because you have that space.

Joyce Carol Oates, in *The New York Times* (1980)

2 A writer's working hours are his waking hours. He is working as long as he is conscious and frequently when he isn't.

Edna Ferber, *A Kind of Magic* (1963)

3 A writer needs certain conditions in which to work and create art. She needs a piece of time; a peace of mind; a quiet place; and a private life.

Margaret Walker, in Janet Sternburg, ed., *The Writer on Her Work*, vol. 1 (1980)

4 You must find your own quiet center of life, and write from that to the world.

Sarah Orne Jewett, letter to Willa Cather (1908), in Elizabeth Silverthorne, *Sarah Orne Jewett* (1993)

5 I will write my books and raise the children. Anything else just fritters me away. I know this makes me seem narrow, but in fact, I *am* narrow. I like routine and rituals and I hate leaving home.

Anne Tyler, in Janet Sternburg, ed., *The Writer on Her Work*, vol. 1 (1980)

6 Volume depends precisely on the writer's having been able to sit in a room every day, year after year, alone.

Susan Sontag, in *The New York Times Book Review* (1986)

7 Successful writers are not the ones who write the best sentences. They are the ones who keep writing.

Bonnie Friedman, *Writing Past Dark* (1993)

8 There is no perfect time to write. There's only now.

Barbara Kingsolver, in *Writer's Digest* (1994)

9 When you make a decision to write according to a set schedule and really stick to it, you find yourself writing very fast. At least I do.

Françoise Sagan, in Malcolm Cowley, ed., *Writers at Work* (1958)

10 It should surprise no one that the life of the writer—such as it is—is colorless to the point of sensory deprivation. Many writers do little else but sit in small rooms recalling the real world.

Annie Dillard, *The Writing Life* (1989)

11 Appealing workplaces are to be avoided. One wants a room with no view, so imagination can meet memory in the dark.

Annie Dillard, *The Writing Life* (1989)

12 The ideal view for daily writing, hour on hour, is the blank brick wall of a cold-storage warehouse. Failing this, a stretch of sky will do, cloudless if possible.

Edna Ferber, *A Kind of Magic* (1963)

13 The writer is either a practicing recluse or a delinquent, guilt-ridden one; or both. Usually both.

Susan Sontag, in *The New York Times Book Review* (1986)

14 There are times . . . when any visitor—in person, by phone, by mail—is an intruder, a burglar, a space hogger, an oxygen taker, a chaos maker, a conflict inducer, a mood chaser, and a total drag.

Toni Cade Bambara, in Mari E. Evans, ed., *Black Women Writers (1950-1980)* (1984)

15 My closely guarded solitude causes some hurt feelings now and then. But how to explain, without wounding someone, that you want to be wholly in the world you are writing about, that it would take two days to get the visitor's voice out of the house so that you could listen to your own characters again?

Margaret Bourke-White, *Portrait of Myself* (1963)

16 Writers are always anxious, always on the run— from the telephone, from people, from responsibilities, from the distractions of this world.

Edna O'Brien, in George Plimpton, ed., *The Writer's Chapbook* (1989)

17 Writers . . . haven't time to meet one another. But then, a writer learns nothing from a writer, conversationally. If a writer has anything witty, profound or quotable to say he doesn't say it. He's no fool. He writes it.

Edna Ferber, *A Kind of Magic* (1963)

18 Lunches are just not good. They take the heart out of the day and the spaciousness from the morning's work.

May Sarton, *Journal of a Solitude* (1973)

19 Recollect that to a woman who gets her living by her pen, "time is money," as it is to an artist. Therefore, encroaching on her time is lessening her income. And yet how often is this done (either heedlessly or selfishly) by persons professing to be her

friends, and who are habitually in the practice of interrupting her in her writing hours.

Eliza Leslie, *Miss Leslie's Behavior Book* (1859)

1 I lived in the midst of an affectionate charming family, and I am sure that there is no greater obstacle to a person who is just beginning to write.

Katharine Butler Hathaway, *The Little Locksmith* (1942)

2 Writing is unsocial, solitary work and the one safety-valve sort of reaction from it is contact with people. Otherwise the writing and the writer both suffer from lack of aeration and contact with material of art.

Katharine Butler Hathaway, *The Journals and Letters of the Little Locksmith* (1946)

3 I have never been able to write with anything more than the left hand of my mind; the right hand has always been engaged in something to do with personal relationships. I don't complain, because I think my left hand's power, as much as it has, is due to its knowledge of what my right hand is doing.

Rebecca West, in A.L. Rowse, *Glimpses of the Great* (1985)

4 Every life is a tragedy, but far more the writer's life, because the more he has to see, the more deeply he understands and feels about life, the less time he has to put it down.

Gabrielle Roy, in Donald Cameron, *Conversations With Canadian Novelists* (1973)

5 As I look back on what I have written, I can see that the very persons who have taken away my time are those who have given me something to say.

Katherine Paterson, *The Spying Heart* (1989)

6 As soon as you become a writer, you lose contact with ordinary experience or tend to.... The worst fate of a writer is to become a writer.

Mary McCarthy (1966), in Carol Gelderman, *Conversations With Mary McCarthy* (1991)

7 The best time for planning a book is while you're doing the dishes.

Agatha Christie (1955), in James Beasley Simpson, *Best Quotes of '54, '55, '56* (1957)

8 My occupational hazard is that I can't help plagiarizing from real life.

Mary McCarthy (1979), in Carol Brightman, *Writing Dangerously* (1992)

9 I resent people who say writers write from experience. Writers don't write from experience, though many are hesitant to admit that they don't. I want to be clear about this. If you wrote from experience, you'd get maybe one book, maybe three poems. Writers write from empathy.

Nikki Giovanni, in Claudia Tate, ed., *Black Women Writers at Work* (1983)

10 Every secret of a writer's soul, every experience of his life, every quality of his mind is written large in his works, yet we require critics to explain the one and biographers to expound the other. That time hangs heavy on people's hands is the only explanation of the monstrous growth.

Virginia Woolf, *Orlando* (1928)

11 A person who publishes a book willfully appears before the populace with his pants down.... Kathleen is about to publish a book. If it is a good book, nothing can hurt her. If it is a bad book, nothing can help her.

Edna St. Vincent Millay (1927), in Allan Ross Macdougall, ed., *Letters of Edna St. Vincent Millay* (1952)

12 If the very thought of taking off all your clothes in the middle of the Washington Mall during a school holiday makes you blush, you haven't even begun to dream what it feels like to publish a book.

Nancy Mairs, *Voice Lessons* (1994)

13 I'm widest awake as a writer doing something new, engaged in a process I'm not sure I can finish, generating at the edge of my powers. Some people bungee jump; I write.

Barbara Kingsolver, in Mary Ann Grossmann, "Crab Clause," *St. Paul Pioneer Press* (1995)

14 What with the reviews of critics, the sarcasms of one's friends, the reproaches of one's own taste, there's precious little peace after publishing a book.

Winifred Holtby, in Vera Brittain, *Testament of Friendship* (1940)

15 If I could I would always work in silence and obscurity, and let my efforts be known by their results.

Emily Brontë (1850), in Bertha W. Smith and Virginia C. Lincoln, eds., *The Writing Art* (1931)

16 Whenever an encounter between a writer of good will and a regular person of good will happens to touch on the subject of writing, each person discovers, dismayed, that good will is of no earthly use. The conversation cannot proceed.

Annie Dillard, *The Writing Life* (1989)

1 Miserable is the fate of writers: if they are agreeable, they are offensive; and if dull, they starve.

Lady Mary Wortley Montagu (1709), in Octave Thanet, ed., *The Best Letters of Lady Mary Wortley Montagu* (1901)

2 There is no denying the fact that writers should be read but not seen. Rarely are they a winsome sight.

Edna Ferber, *A Kind of Magic* (1963)

3 Like all great writers . . . he puts his best in his books, and sometimes lacks magnetism and fresh thought in talking.

Gertrude Atherton, *The Aristocrats* (1901)

4 Any writer knows he has to pay for his compliments. As soon as he has said, Why, thank you, that's very generous of you, the other person clears his throat and dives into his own writing experiences.

Mary Jane Ward, *The Snake Pit* (1946)

5 Meeting writers is always so disappointing. . . . There is this terrific book that has changed your life, and then you meet the author, and he has shifty eyes and funny shoes and he won't talk about anything except the injustice of the United States income tax structure toward people with fluctuating income, or how to breed Black Angus cows, or something.

Ursula K. Le Guin, "Talking About Writing," *Language of the Night* (1979)

6 Writers and artists [are] to be themselves with dignity, not to be always feeling apologetic toward the normal people and trying to explain and adapt themselves.

Katharine Butler Hathaway, *The Journals and Letters of the Little Locksmith* (1946)

7 I had always envisioned the literary life or, as we used to say in East Texas, "being an arthur," as involving a lot of hanging out at Elaine's in New York City with terribly witty people. I have finally become an arthur and I find myself hanging out at obscure radio stations, trying to think of answers to questions like, "So, what *is* it about Texas?"

Molly Ivins, "Being an 'Arthur'," in *Mother Jones* (1992)

8 What really annoys me are the ones who write to say, I am doing your book for my final examinations and could you please tell me what the meaning of it is. I find it just so staggering—that you're supposed to explain the meaning of your book to some total stranger! If I knew what the meanings of my books were, I wouldn't have bothered to write them.

Margaret Drabble, in George Plimpton, ed., *The Writer's Chapbook* (1989)

9 My favorite author's question of all time—because it's so simple to answer . . . "Is your hair really like that, or do you get it done?"

Margaret Atwood, speech (1993)

10 The only real trouble that writing has ever brought me is an occasional sense of being invaded by the outside world. Why do people imagine that writers, having chosen the most private of professions, should be any good at performing in public, or should have the slightest desire to tell their secrets to interviewers.

Anne Tyler, in Janet Sternburg, ed., *The Writer on Her Work*, vol. 1 (1980)

11 The reward for writing well appears to be not to be able to do it for a long time.

Rosellen Brown, on book promotion, interview (1992)

12 Many persons erroneously suppose that an author has always on hand an unlimited number of her own books; or that the publisher will kindly give her as many as she can want for herself and friends. This is by no means the case.

Eliza Leslie, *Miss Leslie's Behavior Book* (1859)

13 For a dyed-in-the-wool author nothing is as dead as a book once it is written. . . . She is rather like a cat whose kittens have grown up. While they were a-growing she was passionately interested in them but now they seem hardly to belong to her—and probably she is involved with another batch of kittens.

Rumer Godden, in *The New York Times Book Review* (1963)

14 My books don't seem to belong to me after I have once written them; and I find myself delivering opinions about them as if I had nothing to do with them.

George Eliot (1857), in J.W. Cross, ed., *George Eliot's Life As Related in Her Letters and Journals* (1885)

15 Could anyone fail to be depressed by a book he or she has published? Don't we always outgrow them the moment the last page has been written?

Mary Ritter Beard (1943), in Nancy F. Cott, *A Woman Making History* (1991)

1 When I say "work" I only mean writing. Everything else is just odd jobs.

Margaret Laurence, in Donald Cameron, *Conversations With Canadian Novelists* (1973)

2 Writers in a profit making economy are an exploitable commodity whose works are products to be marketed, and are so judged and handled.

Tillie Olsen, *Silences* (1978)

3 I learned long ago that the only satisfaction of authorship lies in finding the very few who understand what we mean. As for outside rewards, there is not one that I have ever discovered.

Ellen Glasgow, *Letters of Ellen Glasgow* (1958)

4 One ought not to *write* for money, but I consider it a first duty after one has written to exact the highest possible price. It is not a matter which concerns only the writer, but all writers.

Gail Hamilton (1890), in Susan Coultrap-McQuin, ed., *Gail Hamilton* (1992)

5 I try to live what I consider a "poetic existence." That means I take responsibility for the air I breathe and the space I take up. I try to be immediate, to be totally present for all my work.

Maya Angelou, in Claudia Tate, ed., *Black Women Writers at Work* (1983)

6 All writers who can claim to be called "living" must be political in a sense. They must have what the Quakers call a concern to understand what is happening in the world, and must engage themselves, in their writing, to promote no comfortable lies, of the sort which people will pay well to be told rather than the truth.

Storm Jameson, in Vera Brittain, *Testament of Friendship* (1940)

7 The political writer, then, is the ultimate optimist, believing people are capable of change and using words as one way to try and penetrate the privatism of our lives.

Cherríe Moraga, in Cherríe Moraga and Gloria Anzaldúa, eds., *This Bridge Called My Back* (1983)

8 How can one not speak about war, poverty, and inequality when people who suffer from these afflictions don't have a voice to speak?

Isabel Allende, in Marie-Lise Gazarian-Gautiez, *Interviews With Latin American Writers* (1989)

9 Writers in Latin America live in a reality that is extraordinarily demanding. Surprisingly, our answer to these demands protects and develops our individuality. I feel I am not alone in trying to give their voice to those who don't have it.

Elena Poniatowska, in Janet Sternburg, ed., *The Writer on Her Work*, vol. 2 (1991)

10 That is what I work to do: to produce stories that save our lives.

Toni Cade Bambara, in Mari E. Evans, ed., *Black Women Writers (1950-1980)* (1984)

11 Not until I was seven or more, did I begin to pray every night, "O God, let me write books! Please, God, let me write books!"

Ellen Glasgow, *The Woman Within* (1954)

12 Most of the basic material a writer works with is acquired before the age of fifteen.

Willa Cather, in René Rapin, *Willa Cather* (1930)

13 Anyone who is going to be a writer knows enough at fifteen to write several novels.

May Sarton, *Mrs. Stevens Hears the Mermaids Singing* (1965)

14 Looking back, I imagine I was always writing. Twaddle it was, too. But better far write twaddle or anything, anything, than nothing at all.

Katherine Mansfield (1922), *Journal of Katherine Mansfield* (1927)

15 A young musician plays scales in his room and only bores his family. A beginning writer, on the other hand, sometimes has the misfortune of getting into print.

Marguerite Yourcenar, in *Time* (1981)

16 When people ask me what qualifies me to be a writer for children, I say I was once a child. But I was not only a child, I was, better still, a weird little kid, and though I would never choose to give my own children this particular preparation for life, there are few things, apparently, more helpful to a writer than having once been a weird little kid.

Katherine Paterson, *Gates of Excellence* (1981)

17 The child is never far to seek in the author.

Radclyffe Hall, *The Well of Loneliness* (1928)

18 All is fish that comes to the literary net. Goethe puts his joys and sorrows into poems, I turn my adventures into bread and butter.

Louisa May Alcott, *Journals* (1868)

19 My muse is a sad cow slowly chewing her cud. And her occasional profound sigh reminds me that hur-

rying my process comes only to a facile, near-sighted, unrealized writing.

Mary La Chapelle, Minnesota State Arts Board newsletter (1990)

1 Once the disease of reading has laid hold upon the system it weakens it so that it falls an easy prey to that other scourge which dwells in the ink pot and festers in the quill. The wretch takes to writing.

Virginia Woolf, *Orlando* (1928)

2 Authors before they write should read.

Fanny Burney (1779), in Charlotte Barrett, ed., *Diary and Letters of Madame D'Arblay*, vol. 1 (1842)

3 [The writer] is careful of what he reads, for that is what he will write.

Annie Dillard, *The Writing Life* (1989)

4 Read a lot and hit the streets. A writer who doesn't keep up with what's out there ain't gonna be out there.

Toni Cade Bambara, in Claudia Tate, ed., *Black Women Writers at Work* (1983)

5 Our Author . . . / Sends me with dismal voice, and lengthen'd phiz, / Humbly to own one dreadful fault of *his*: / A fault, in modern Authors not un-common, / It is,—now don't be angry—He's—*a woman.*

Mrs. Inchbald, *Every One Has His Fault* (1793)

6 The indifference of the world which Keats and Flaubert and other men of genius have found so hard to bear was in her case [the woman writer's] not indifference but hostility. The world did not say to her as it said to them, Write if you choose; it makes no difference to me. The world said with a guffaw, Write? What's the good of your writing?

Virginia Woolf, *A Room of One's Own* (1929)

7 It is through the ghost [writer] that the great gift of knowledge which the inarticulate have for the world can be made available.

Elizabeth Janeway, in Helen Hull, ed., *The Writer's Book* (1950)

8 If, as I suspected at the time, I was a one-book writer, I wanted to be the kind of one-book writer who writes only one book.

Margaret Halsey, *The Folks at Home* (1952)

9 A writer looking for subjects inquires not after what he loves best, but after what he alone loves at all.

Annie Dillard, in *The Writer* (1989)

10 It's an act of faith to be a writer in a postliterate world.

Rita Mae Brown, *Starting From Scratch* (1988)

11 Even when I cannot write, I know I am still a writer, just the way I know I am still sexual even if I have not had a lover for many months.

Olga Broumas, in Bonnie Friedman, *Writing Past Dark* (1993)

12 Writers sometimes talk as though they were the only friends of civilization. This is their conceit. But they have special powers to serve—or to corrupt—civilization, and are obliged to use them.

Storm Jameson, *The Journal of Mary Hervey Russell* (1945)

13 For years I thought my work still lay ahead, and now I find it is behind me: there was no moment when it took place.

Simone de Beauvoir, *Force of Circumstance* (1963)

14 To be any sort of competent writer one must keep one's psychological distance from the supreme art-ists.

Cynthia Ozick, "The Lesson of the Master," *Art and Ardor* (1983)

15 For writers from working-class families, the mak-ing of art is cultural disenfranchisement, for we do not belong in literary circles and our writing rarely makes it back home.

Valerie Miner, "Writing With Class" (1988), *Rumors From the Cauldron* (1991)

16 We must protect the minority writers because they are the research workers of literature. They keep it alive. It has been fashionable of late to seek out and force such writers into more popular channels, to the detriment of both writer and an unprepared public.

Anaïs Nin (1950), *The Diary of Anaïs Nin*, vol. 5 (1974)

17 I keep feeling that there isn't one poem being writ-ten by any one of us—or a book or anything like that. The whole life of us writers, the whole product I guess I mean, is the one long poem—a commu-nity effort if you will. It's all the same poem. It

doesn't belong to any one writer—it's God's poem perhaps. Or God's people's poem.

Anne Sexton, letter to Erica Jong (1974), in Linda Gray Sexton and Lois Ames, eds., *Anne Sexton: A Self-Portrait in Letters* (1977)

1 Literature is a place for generosity and affection and hunger for equals—not a prizefight ring. We are increased, confirmed in our medium, roused to do our best, by every good writer, every fine achievement. Would we want one good writer or fine book less?

Tillie Olsen, *Silences* (1978)

2 The writer of originality, unless dead, is always shocking, scandalous; novelty disturbs and repels.

Simone de Beauvoir, *The Second Sex* (1949)

3 I certainly am glad you like the stories because now I feel it's not bad that I like them so much. The truth is I like them better than anybody and I read them over and over and laugh and laugh, then get embarrassed when I remember I was the one wrote them.

Flannery O'Connor, in Sally Fitzgerald, ed., *The Habit of Being* (1979)

4 There is no greater fraud or bore than the writer who has acquired the art of saying nothing brilliantly.

Gertrude Atherton, *The Californians* (1898)

5 As a writer you are free. . . . You are in the country where *you* make up the rules, the laws. You are both dictator and obedient populace. It is a country nobody has ever explored before. It is up to you to make the maps, to build the cities. Nobody else in the world can do it, or ever could do it, or ever will be able to do it again.

Ursula K. Le Guin, *Language of the Night* (1979)

6 Your freedom as a writer is not freedom of expression in the sense of wild blurting; you may not let rip. It is life at its most free, if you are fortunate enough to be able to try it, because you select your materials, invent your task, and pace yourself.

Annie Dillard, *The Writing Life* (1989)

7 The writer's intention hasn't anything to do with what he achieves. The intent to earn money or the intent to be famous or the intent to be great doesn't matter in the end. Just what comes out.

Lillian Hellman, in George Plimpton, ed., *Writers at Work*, 3rd series (1967)

8 The work reveals the creator—and as our universe in its vastness, its orderliness, its exquisite detail, tells us something of the One who made it, so a work of fiction, for better or worse, will reveal the writer.

Katherine Paterson, *The Spying Heart* (1989)

9 Having been unpopular in high school is not just cause for book publication.

Fran Lebowitz, *Metropolitan Life* (1978)

10 It is, I confess, very possible that these my Labors may only be destined to line Trunks, or preserve roast Meat from too fierce a Fire; yet in that Shape I shall be useful to my Country.

Lady Mary Wortley Montagu, on her political writings, *The Nonsense of Common-Sense* (1738)

11 When I'm really involved or getting towards the end of a novel, I can write for up to ten hours a day. At those times, it's as though I'm writing a letter to someone I'm desperately in love with.

Joyce Carol Oates, in Rita D. Jacobs, "A Day in the Life," *T.W.A. Ambassador* (1987)

12 Painters work from the ground up. The latest version of a painting overlays earlier versions, and obliterates them. Writers, on the other hand, work from left to right. The discardable chapters are on the left.

Annie Dillard, *The Writing Life* (1989)

13 The only time I'm pleased with myself is when I'm exhausted and shaking from having written too much.

Mabel Seeley, in Carmen Nelson Richards and Genevieve Rose Breen, eds., *Minnesota Writes* (1945)

14 I write emotional algebra.

Anaïs Nin (1946), *The Diary of Anaïs Nin*, vol. 4 (1971)

15 Writing is one of the few professions in which you can psychoanalyze yourself, get rid of hostilities and frustrations in public, and get paid for it.

Octavia Butler, in "Birth of a Writer," *Essence* (1989)

16 Writing is like getting married. One should never commit oneself until one is amazed at one's luck.

Iris Murdoch, *The Black Prince* (1973)

17 If you don't keep and mature your force and above all have time and quiet to perfect your work, you will be writing things not much better than you did five years ago. . . . Otherwise, what might be strength is only crudeness, and what might be in-

sight is only observation. You will write about life, but never life itself.

Sarah Orne Jewett, to Willa Cather, *Letters of Sarah Orne Jewett* (1911)

1 Writing about why you write is a funny business, like scratching what doesn't itch. Impulses are mysterious, and explaining them must be done with mirrors, like certain cunning sleight-of-hand routines.

Patricia Hampl, in Janet Sternburg, ed., *The Writer on Her Work*, vol. 2 (1991)

2 The manuscript may go forth from the writer to return with a faithfulness passing the faithfulness of the boomerang or the homing pigeon.

Rose Macaulay, "Problems of a Writer's Life," *A Casual Commentary* (1926)

3 I didn't set out to become an unpublished writer, it just happened.

Nora Bartlett, "An Excerpt From My Unpublished Writing," in Michelene Wandor, ed., *On Gender and Writing* (1983)

4 If I stop writing my life will have been an abject failure. It is that already to other people. But it could be an abject failure to myself. I will not have earned death.

Jean Rhys, *Smile Please* (1979)

5 They're fancy talkers about themselves, writers. If I had to give young writers advice, I would say don't listen to writers talk about writing or themselves.

Lillian Hellman, in *The New York Times* (1960)

6 When the writers refer to themselves as "we" and to the reader as "you," this is two against one.

Judith Rascoe, in *The New York Times Book Review* (1984)

7 Began the second part of "Little Women." . . . Girls write to ask who the little women marry, as if that was the only end and aim of a woman's life. I *won't* marry Jo to Laurie to please any one.

Louisa May Alcott, *Journals* (1868)

8 Writing is one of the few professions left where you take all the responsibility for what you do. It's really dangerous and ultimately destroys you as a writer if you start thinking about responses to your work or what your audience needs.

Erica Jong, in William Packard, ed., *The Craft of Poetry* (1974)

9 Any writer overwhelmingly honest about pleasing himself is almost sure to please others.

Marianne Moore, "Marianne Moore Speaks," in *Vogue* (1963)

10 The transaction between a writer and the spirit of the age is one of infinite delicacy, and upon a nice arrangement between the two the whole fortune of his works depend.

Virginia Woolf, *Orlando* (1928)

11 Many a fervid man / Writes books as cold and flat as graveyard stones.

Elizabeth Barrett Browning, *Aurora Leigh* (1856)

12 There are enough women to do the childbearing and the childrearing. I know of none who can write my books.

Henry Handel Richardson, in Tillie Olsen, *Silences* (1978)

13 Did you ever stop to think that a writer will spend three years, or many more, on a book that the average reader will skim through in a few hours?

Ellen Glasgow, *Letters of Ellen Glasgow* (1958)

14 It takes years to write a book—between two and ten years. . . . Out of a human population on earth of four and a half billion, perhaps twenty people can write a book in a year. Some people lift cars, too. Some people enter week-long sled-dog races, go over Niagara Falls in barrels, fly planes through the Arc de Triomphe. Some people feel no pain in childbirth. Some people eat cars. There is no call to take human extremes as norms.

Annie Dillard, *The Writing Life* (1989)

15 Fortunately age does not affect literature. After a man is dead, he may continue in the business and often rank higher than his living competitors.

Myrtle Reed, *The Book of Clever Beasts* (1904)

See also Artists, Collaboration, Playwrights, Poets, Writing.

## ❦ WRITING

16 Writing is a kind of double living. The writer experiences everything twice. Once in reality and once in that mirror which waits always before or behind.

Catherine Drinker Bowen, in *The Atlantic* (1957)

1 We write to taste life twice, in the moment, and in retrospection.

> Anaïs Nin (1954), *The Diary of Anaïs Nin*, vol. 5 (1974)

2 Writing does not exclude the full life; it demands it.

> Katherine Anne Porter, in Hallie Burnett, *On Writing the Short Story* (1983)

3 Writing is thinking. It is more than living, for it is being conscious of living.

> Anne Morrow Lindbergh, *Locked Rooms and Open Doors* (1974)

4 Writing forces consciousness.

> Melody Beattie, *The Lessons of Love* (1994)

5 Writing is not an amusing occupation. It is a combination of ditch-digging, mountain-climbing, treadmill and childbirth. Writing may be interesting, absorbing, exhilarating, racking, relieving. But amusing? Never!

> Edna Ferber, *A Peculiar Treasure* (1939)

6 Writing has often been accompanied by terror, silences, and then wild bursts of private laughter that suddenly make all the dread seem worthwhile.

> Erica Jong, *Fear of Fifty* (1994)

7 The writer's advantage, in some respects, over those whose expression lies in other fields, is in the privilege of a double—sometimes a triple—living. Pleasure multiplied in the mirrors of words, and pain siphoned off in words.

> Josephine W. Johnson, "A Time for Everything," in Jean Beaven Abernethy, *Meditations for Women* (1947)

8 One of the few things I know about writing is this: spend it all, shoot it, play it, lose it, all, right away, every time. . . . Anything you do not give freely and abundantly becomes lost to you. You open your safe and find ashes.

> Annie Dillard, *The Writing Life* (1989)

9 It is only by expressing all that is inside that purer and purer streams come. . . . Pour out the dull things on paper too—you can tear them up afterward—for only then do the bright ones come. If you hold back the dull things, you are certain to hold back what is clear and beautiful and true and lively.

> Brenda Ueland, *Strength to Your Sword Arm* (1993)

10 I want books written out of a brain and heart and soul crowded and vital with Life, spelled with a big L. I want poetry bursting with passion. I don't care

a hang for the "verbal felicities." They'll do for the fringe, but I want the garment to warm me first.

> Gertrude Atherton, *The Aristocrats* (1901)

11 If we had to say what writing is, we would define it essentially as an act of courage.

> Cynthia Ozick, in Bill Gordon, *"How Many Books Do You Sell in Ohio?"* (1986)

12 Talent is helpful in writing, but guts are absolutely necessary.

> Jessamyn West, *The Woman Said Yes* (1976)

13 I believe one writes because one has to create a world in which one can live.

> Anaïs Nin (1954), *The Diary of Anaïs Nin*, vol. 5 (1974)

14 There are—as every one knows—two kinds of writing: one coming out of your vitals and the other from the top of your head. The first is the only sort from which any true private pleasure can be gained, for it is a way of getting something out of life which seemed to be there in childhood, when childhood is quite over.

> J.E. Buckrose, "The Fun of Being an Author," *What I Have Gathered* (1923)

15 Writing is about . . . shocking yourself. When I write, I like to make myself cry, laugh—I like to give myself an experience. I see a lot of writing out there that's very safe. But if you're not scaring yourself, why would you think that you'd be scaring anybody else? If you're not coming to a revelation about your place in the universe, why would you think anyone else would?

> Kate Braverman, in Lisa Schiffman, "Sabotage in the Writing Place," *The San Francisco Review of Books* (1993)

16 All of writing is a huge lake. There are great rivers that feed the lake, like Tolstoy and Dostoyevsky. And there are mere trickles, like Jean Rhys. All that matters is feeding the lake. I don't matter. The lake matters. You must keep feeding the lake.

> Jean Rhys, in Madeleine L'Engle, *Walking on Water* (1980)

17 Good writing is about telling the truth. We are a species that needs and wants to understand who we are. Sheep lice do not seem to share this longing, which is one reason they write so very little. But we do.

> Anne Lamott, *Bird by Bird* (1994)

18 There are more truths in a good book than its author meant to put in it.

> Marie von Ebner-Eschenbach, *Aphorisms* (1893)

1 Verbal felicity is the fruit of ardor, of diligence, and of refusing to be false.

> Marianne Moore (1951), in Patricia C. Willis, ed., *The Complete Prose of Marianne Moore* (1986)

2 No matter how true I believe what I am writing to be, if the reader cannot also participate in that truth, then I have failed.

> Madeleine L'Engle, *Walking on Water* (1980)

3 Our finest writing will certainly come from what is unregenerate in ourselves. It will come from the part that is obdurate, unbanishable, immune to education, springing up like grass.

> Bonnie Friedman, *Writing Past Dark* (1993)

4 The most egotistic of occupations, and the most gratifying while it lasts.

> Vita Sackville-West, *No Signposts in the Sea* (1961)

5 Writing is not, alas, like riding a bicycle: it does not get easier with practice.

> Nancy Mairs, *Voice Lessons* (1994)

6 We speak naturally but spend all our lives trying to write naturally.

> Margaret Wise Brown, in Leonard S. Marcus, *Margaret Wise Brown* (1992)

7 There's less skill and more plain hard work to writing than anyone except a writer thinks.

> Mabel Seeley, in Carmen Nelson Richards and Genevieve Rose Breen, eds., *Minnesota Writes* (1945)

8 Much of the activity we think of as writing is, actually, *getting ready to write.*

> Gail Godwin, "Rituals and Readiness," in Neil Baldwin and Diane Osen, eds., *The Writing Life* (1995)

9 Writing is harder than anything else; at least *starting* to write is.

> Kristin Hunter, in Claudia Tate, ed., *Black Women Writers at Work* (1983)

10 [Writing is] the art of applying the seat of the pants to the seat of the chair.

> Mary Heaton Vorse, in Bill Gordon, *"How Many Books Do You Sell in Ohio?"* (1986)

11 People who write for a living recognize only two states of being: writing and making excuses.

> Susan Ohanian, *Ask Ms. Class* (1996)

12 Writing is so difficult that I often feel that writers, having had their hell on earth, will escape all punishment hereafter.

> Jessamyn West, *To See the Dream* (1957)

13 So many people seem to imagine that because the actual tools of writing are easily accessible, it is less difficult than the other arts. This is entirely an illusion.

> Vera Brittain, *On Becoming a Writer* (1947)

14 What a difficult kind of work to choose! But of course one did not choose it. There was no choice.

> Ivy Compton-Burnett (1962), in Hilary Spurling, *Ivy* (1984)

15 Writing is probably about five percent talent and ninety-five percent hard work. And I think most people have got five percent talent.

> Joan Riley, in Donna Perry, ed., *Backtalk* (1993)

16 Writing is not hard work, it is simply an obsession.

> Hallie Burnett, *The Brain Pickers* (1957)

17 The profession of writing is nothing else but a violent, indestructible passion. When it has once entered people's heads it never leaves them.

> George Sand (1831), in Raphaël Ledos de Beaufort, ed., *Letters of George Sand,* vol. 1 (1886)

18 The way to wealth through the quill seems long.

> Elizabeth Rundle Charles, *Chronicles of the Schönberg-Cotta Family* (1863)

19 Money and writing appear to be mutually exclusive.

> Rita Mae Brown, *Starting From Scratch* (1988)

20 I have always wanted to write in such a way that will make people think, "Why, I've always thought that but never found the words for it."

> Pamela Hansford Johnson, in *The New York Times* (1981)

21 One writes in order to feel.

> Muriel Rukeyser, *The Life of Poetry* (1949)

22 In order to write really well and convincingly one must be somewhat poisoned by emotion. Dislike, displeasure, resentment, fault-finding, indignation, passionate remonstrance, a sense of injustice, are perhaps corrosive to the container but they make fine fuel.

> Edna Ferber, *A Kind of Magic* (1963)

1 In any really good subject, one has only to probe deep enough to come to tears.

  Edith Wharton, *The Writing of Fiction* (1925)

2 Whatever is clearly expressed is well wrote.

  Lady Mary Wortley Montagu (1759), in Robert Halsband, ed., *The Selected Letters of Lady Mary Wortley Montagu* (1970)

3 A writer's first duty is to be clear. Clarity is an excellent virtue. Like all virtues it can be pursued at ruinous cost. Paid, so far as I am concerned, joyfully.

  Storm Jameson, *Parthian Words* (1970)

4 There is a loving way with words and an unloving way. And it is only with the loving way that the simplicity of language becomes beautiful.

  Margaret Wise Brown, in Leonard S. Marcus, *Margaret Wise Brown* (1992)

5 No author should be blamed for obscurity, nor should any pains be grudged in the effort to understand him, provided that he has done his best to be intelligible. Difficult thoughts are quite distinct from difficult words. Difficulty of thought is the very heart of poetry.

  Alice Meynell, "Robert Browning," in *The Pen* (1880)

6 I think every creative impulse that a working writer, or artist of any sort has, comes out of that dark old country where dreams come from.

  Anne Rivers Siddons, in Naomi Epel, *Writers Dreaming* (1993)

7 You may write for the joy of it, but the act of writing is not complete in itself. It has its end in its audience.

  Flannery O'Connor, in Sally Fitzgerald, ed., *The Habit of Being* (1979)

8 If you do not breathe through writing, if you do not cry out in writing, or sing in writing, then don't write, because our culture has no use for it.

  Anaïs Nin, "The New Woman" (1971), *The White Blackbird* (1985)

9 Of two evils, had not an author better be tedious than superficial! From an overflowing vessel you may gather more, indeed, than you want, but from an empty one you can gather nothing.

  Hannah More, *Coelebs in Search of a Wife* (1808)

10 Accuracy is the basis of style. Words dress our thoughts and should fit; and should fit not only in their utterances, but in their implications, their sequences, and their silences, just as in architecture the empty spaces are as important as those that are filled.

  Freya Stark, *Perseus in the Wind* (1948)

11 A sentence is not emotional a paragraph is.

  Gertrude Stein, "Sentences and Paragraphs," *How to Write* (1931)

12 A mere chronicle of observed events will produce only journalism; combined with a sensitive memory, it can produce art.

  Hallie Burnett, *On Writing the Short Story* (1983)

13 What I really do is take real plums and put them in an imaginary cake.

  Mary McCarthy, in Elisabeth Niebuhr, "The Art of Fiction XXVII," *The Paris Review* (1962)

14 Love scenes, if genuine, are indescribable; for to those who have enacted them the most elaborate description seems tame, and to those who have not, the simplest picture seems overdone.

  Louisa May Alcott, *An Old-Fashioned Girl* (1870)

15 A favorite strategy [of poor writers] was the paragraph-terminating: Right? Followed immediately by Wrong. This linear invitation to a mugging was considered a strategy of wit.

  Renata Adler, *Speedboat* (1976)

16 Excessive literary production is a social offense.... Everyone who contributes to the "too much" of literature is doing grave social injury.

  George Eliot (1871), in J.W. Cross, ed., *George Eliot's Life As Related in Her Letters and Journals* (1884)

See also Anthologies, Art, Artists, Autobiography, Biography, Books, Children's Literature, Creativity, Diaries, Essays, Fantasy Fiction, Fiction, Fictional Characters, Ideas, Journalism, Language, Letters, Literature, Magazines, Metaphor, Mysteries, Nonfiction, Novels, Plagiarism, Plot, Poetry, Poetry and Prose, Poets, Prefaces, Punctuation, Satire, Stories, Symbols, Verse, Words, Writers.

## ❧ WRONGDOING

17 There are different kinds of wrong. The people sinned against are not always the best.

  Ivy Compton-Burnett, *The Mighty and Their Fall* (1962)

18 What he saw was that behind the new wrongs were the old ones, and that the sinners of to-day were, perhaps, the sinned against of yesterday.

  Ellen Glasgow, *The Battle-Ground* (1902)

1 We are rather apt to consider an act wrong because it is unpleasant to us.

George Eliot, *Middlemarch* (1871)

2 It is better to suffer wrong than to do wrong, because you can remain the friend of the sufferer; who would want to be the friend of and have to live together with a murderer? Not even another murderer.

Hannah Arendt, *The Life of the Mind*, vol. 1 (1978)

See also Apology, Crime, Detection, Evil, Guilt, Sin.

## ❧ WYOMING

3 If anything is endemic to Wyoming it is wind. This big room of space is swept out daily, leaving a bone yard of fossils, agates, and carcasses in every stage of decay. Though it was water that initially shaped the state, wind is the meticulous gardener, raising dust and pruning the sage.

Gretel Ehrlich, *The Solace of Open Spaces* (1985)

# Y

## ❧ YEARS

1 I could not prove the Years had feet — / Yet confident they run.

    Emily Dickinson (1862), in Mabel Loomis Todd and Millicent Todd Bingham, eds., *Bolts of Melody* (1945)

2 There are years that ask questions and years that answer.

    Zora Neale Hurston, *Their Eyes Were Watching God* (1937)

See also Age, Eras, 1492, New Year's Eve, The Sixties, Time.

## ❧ YOUTH

3 Thou blessed season of our spring, / When hopes are angels on the wing.

    L.E. Landon, "Poetical Portrait II," *The Venetian Bracelet* (1829)

4 Youth is, after all, just a moment, but it is the moment, the spark that you always carry in your heart.

    Raisa M. Gorbachev, *I Hope* (1991)

5 That's what being young is all about. You have the courage and the daring to think that you can make a difference. You're not prone to measure your energies in time. You're not likely to live by equations.

    Ruby Dee, in Brian Lanker, *I Dream a World* (1989)

6 Youth lives in an atmosphere of energy waiting to make contact.

    Hallie Flanagan, *Dynamo* (1943)

7 It is not possible for civilization to flow backwards while there is youth in the world. Youth may be headstrong, but it will advance its allotted length.

    Helen Keller, *Midstream* (1930)

8 A young girl's heart is indestructible.

    Esther Hautzig, *The Endless Steppe* (1968)

9 Who would ever think that so much can go on in the soul of a young girl?

    Anne Frank, *The Diary of a Young Girl* (1952)

10 Human nature is so well disposed towards those who are in interesting situations, that a young person, who either marries or dies, is sure to be kindly spoken of.

    Jane Austen, *Emma* (1816)

11 Why, I wonder, do people who at one time or another have all been young themselves, and who ought therefore to know better, generalize so suavely and so mendaciously about the golden hours of youth—that period of life when every sorrow seems permanent, and every set-back insuperable?

    Vera Brittain, *Testament of Youth* (1933)

12 People are always talking about the joys of youth—but, oh, how youth can suffer!

    Willa Cather, *My Mortal Enemy* (1926)

13 Youth is the season of tragedy and despair. Youth is the time when one's whole life is entangled in a web of identity, in a perpetual maze of seeking and of finding, of passion and of disillusion, of vague longings and of nameless griefs, of pity that is a blade in the heart, and of "all the little emptiness of love."

    Ellen Glasgow, *The Woman Within* (1954)

14 Youth is a mortal wound.

    Katherine Paterson, *Jacob Have I Loved* (1980)

15 We real cool. We / Left school. We / Lurk late. We / Strike straight. We / Sing sin. We / Thin gin. We / Jazz June. We / Die soon.

    Gwendolyn Brooks, "We Real Cool," *The Bean Eaters* (1960)

1 Youth, balancing itself upon hope, is forever in extremes: its expectations are continually aroused only to be baffled, and disappointment, like a summer shower, is violent in proportion to its brevity.

L.E. Landon, *Romance and Reality* (1831)

2 If youth is the season of hope, it is often so only in the sense that our elders are hopeful about us; for no age is so apt as youth to think its emotions, partings, and resolves are the last of their kind. Each crisis seems final, simply because it is new.

George Eliot, *Middlemarch* (1871)

3 All the humiliating, tragicomic, heartbreaking things happened to me in my girlhood, and nothing makes me happier than to realize I cannot possibly relive my youth.

Ilka Chase, *Past Imperfect* (1942)

4 My idea of hell is to be young again.

Marge Piercy, *Braided Lives* (1982)

5 If youth did not matter so much to itself, it would never have the heart to go on.

Willa Cather, *The Song of the Lark* (1915)

6 Youth was serious / but not entirely fatal.

Rosario Castellanos, "Monologue of a Foreign Woman" (1959), in Julian Palley, tr., *Meditation on the Threshold* (1988)

7 In youth our most bitter disappointments, our brightest hopes and ambitions, are known only to ourselves. Even our friendship and love we never fully share with another; there is something of every passion, in every situation, we conceal.

Elizabeth Cady Stanton, "The Solitude of Self," in *The Woman's Column* (1892)

8 Heroics are not easily had for the young in our times. Perhaps that is why they go to such extremes to create their own dangers.

Gail Godwin, "False Lights," *Dream Children* (1976)

9 Young people want to look like peas in a pod, and there is no use trying to make them different.

Ilka Chase, *Past Imperfect* (1942)

10 Youth has a quickness of apprehension, which it is very apt to mistake for an acuteness of penetration.

Hannah More, "On the Danger of Sentimental or Romantic Connections," *Essays on Various Subjects* (1777)

11 Your youth is like a water-wetted stone, / Bright with a beauty that is not its own.

Frances Cornford, "Susan to Diana," *Autumn Midnight* (1923)

12 He was beautifully sozzled last night, and had one breakfast before he came out and another with me at the Mitre. I do not envy the heart of youth, but only its head and stomach.

Dorothy L. Sayers, *Gaudy Night* (1935)

13 The search of the Holy Grail or the voyage towards a new continent never enlisted so much energy and so much faith as does this pursuit of youth by old age. It is a race not of the fleet but of the most credulous.

Elisabeth Marbury, *My Crystal Ball* (1923)

14 When a man of forty falls in love with a girl of twenty, it isn't her youth he is seeking but his own.

Lenore Coffee, in John Robert Colombo, *Popcorn in Paradise* (1979)

15 This is a youth-oriented society, and the joke is on them because youth is a disease from which we all recover.

Dorothy Fuldheim, *A Thousand Friends* (1974)

16 Youth is something very new: twenty years ago no one mentioned it.

Coco Chanel, in Marcel Haedrich, *Coco Chanel* (1972)

17 I shall die very young . . . maybe seventy, maybe eighty, maybe ninety. But I shall be very young.

Jeanne Moreau, in Diana Vreeland, *D.V.* (1984)

18 What is youth anyway? Nothing but a tight skin.

Frances Marion, *Off With Their Heads* (1972)

19 As long as you can still be disappointed, you are still young.

Sarah Churchill, in *The Observer* (1981)

20 The young are inclined to measure yesterday's ways by tomorrow's standards.

Madeleine Brent, *Moonraker's Bride* (1973)

21 The hatred of the youth culture for adult society is not a disinterested judgment but a terror-ridden refusal to be hooked into the . . . ecological chain of birthing, growing, and dying. It is the demand, in other words, to remain children.

Midge Decter, *The New Chastity and Other Arguments Against Women's Liberation* (1972)

22 Youth is stranger than fiction.

Marcelene Cox, in *Ladies' Home Journal* (1951)

See also Adolescence, Age, Babies, Childhood, Children, Inexperience.

# Z

## ZOOS

1 It had never occurred to him that an animal could be stripped of everything that went with it, of which its instincts were an inseparable part, and that you could have just its little body in a space of nothingness. As if looking at *that* told you anything but the nature of sorrow, which you knew anyway.

L.M. Boston, *A Stranger at Green Knowe* (1961)

2 In the false country of the zoo / Grief is well represented there.

Jean Garrigue, "False Country of the Zoo," *The Ego and the Centaur* (1947)

3 Here in their ugly, empty cages the monkeys were no more tropical than a collection of London rats or dirty park pigeons.

L.M. Boston, *A Stranger at Green Knowe* (1961)

## ZUCCHINI

4 Marrows—alas!—are arriving in a steady stream at the back door. . . . Oddly enough, the majority of people who grow them in Fairacre say, as they hand them over: "Funny thing! I don't care for them myself. In fact, none of the family likes them!" But still they plant them. It must be the fascination of seeing such a wonderful return for one small seed, that keeps marrow-growers at their dubious task.

Miss Read, *Village Diary* (1957)

5 We come back to autumn, / to zucchini that wilt like witches' shoes.

Margaret Hasse, "A Notch in the Spiral," *Stars Above, Stars Below* (1984)

See also Gardening.

# Name Index

Numbers refer to the page on which the quotation begins and the number of the quotation on the page. Pen names are in quotation marks. When a pseudonym is the principal name by which someone was known, quotation marks are not used but the real name follows in parentheses.

Abbott, Berenice (1898–1991), U.S. photographer, 516:15, 517:4, 517:6, 517:17–18

Abbott, Shirley Jean (1934– ), U.S. writer, 28:12, 75:20, 120:3, 160:8, 239:12, 247:4, 263:14, 322:4, 436:3, 531:12, 605:5, 621:5, 651:5, 651:9, 651:14, 651:16–17

Abbott, Sidney (1937– ), U.S. writer, 390:10–11, 390:20

Abhirupa-Nanda (6th c. B.C.), Indian Buddhist poet, 606:2

Abouzeid, Leila (20th c.), Moroccan writer, journalist, 332:11

Abt, Vicki (1942– ), U.S. sociologist, 684:8

Abzug, Bella Savitsky (1920– ), U.S. lawyer, politician, 59:11, 134:6, 134:9, 218:17, 293:17, 392:8, 444:11, 624:17

Ace, Jane Sherwood (1905–1974), U.S. radio actor, 339:14, 556:4, 698:12, 718:1

Ackerman, Diane (1948– ), U.S. poet, writer, 33:1, 33:6, 33:8, 34:13, 43:15, 80:11, 125:4, 163:6, 189:2, 199:4, 203:18, 219:10, 231:17, 260:19, 261:13, 303:7, 313:8, 313:12, 376:1, 397:4, 398:24, 399:11, 402:5, 409:15–16, 410:2, 410:5, 445:5, 456:1, 482:19, 520:1, 522:1, 522:10, 523:1, 601:5, 615:9–10, 641:3, 672:1, 705:2, 744:10, 764:15

Acosta, Teresa Palma. See Palma Acosta, Teresa

Adams, Abigail Smith (1744–1818), U.S. letterwriter, 7:8, 88:4, 98:14, 149:2, 181:5, 422:8, 540:3, 704:7, 756:2

Adams, Alice (1926– ), U.S. writer, 586:20

Adams, Cindy (Cynthia Heller Adams, 20th c.), U.S. comedian, 231:3, 592:1, 638:3, 667:10

Adams, Léonie Fuller (1899– ), U.S. poet, 41:8, 163:15, 400:14

Adams, Marian Sturgis Hooper (Mrs. Henry Adams, "Clover," 1843–1885), U.S. photographer, 151:10

Adams, Mary (19th c.), U.S. writer, 149:15, 242:16, 271:16, 305:13, 340:3, 432:16, 575:18, 707:13

Adams, Maude (1872–1953), U.S. actor, 281:5

Adams, Sarah Flower (1805–1848), English hymnist, 285:6

Adamson, Joy (1919–1980), Austrian wildlife expert, writer, 31:18

Addams, Jane (Laura Jane Addams, 1860–1935), U.S. humanitarian, reformer, settlement house founder, sociologist, Nobel Prize winner, 7:16, 100:9, 109:4, 183:13, 206:3, 222:1, 374:20, 457:7, 533:18, 717:4, 729:8

Adler, Freda (1934– ), U.S. educator, criminal justice specialist, writer, 21:18, 149:7, 149:9, 194:11, 222:15, 376:17, 385:24, 386:16, 493:11, 566:12, 644:1, 677:1

Adler, Polly (1900–1962), U.S. madam, 323:20, 401:21, 553:15, 581:6

Adler, Renata (1938– ), Italian-born U.S. writer, film critic, philosopher, 36:11, 78:6, 79:7, 152:3, 166:9, 255:12–13, 256:6, 276:16, 405:22, 776:15

Adnan, Etel (1925– ), Lebanese poet, 176:9

Agee, Jonis (20th c.), U.S. writer, educator, 442:2

Aguilar, Grace (1816–1847), English novelist, Jewish scholar, 522:14, 543:6, 568:18, 676:1, 699:10, 709:25

Aidoo, Ama Ata (1940– ), Ghanaian poet, playwright, writer, 164:11, 429:17, 453:19, 614:14, 615:8, 696:23

Aiken, Joan Delano (1924– ), English writer, 662:1

Ainsworth, Adeline (20th c.), U.S. writer, 703:7

Aird, Catherine (pseud., 1930– ), English writer, 472:14

Akhmatova, Anna (1889–1966), Russian poet, 17:6, 97:5, 227:8, 397:12, 414:1, 468:24, 523:17, 524:12, 579:14, 733:6

Akins, Zoë (Zoë Akins Rumbold, 1886–1958), U.S. playwright, poet, novelist, screenwriter, 266:3, 484:9, 573:14, 733:4, 759:17

Albrand, Martha (Heidi Huberta Freybe Lamon, "Katrin Holland," "Heidi Huberta," 1914–1981), German-born U.S. writer, 600:10

Alcott, Louisa May ("A.M. Barnard," 1832–1888), U.S. writer, 76:14, 116:6, 176:14, 209:14, 237:18, 238:10, 281:16, 295:7, 296:8, 300:1, 324:7, 340:2, 414:10, 457:9, 486:7, 516:3, 592:6, 602:11, 617:13, 639:5, 750:17, 760:7, 770:18, 773:7, 776:14

Alden, Paulette Bates (1947– ), U.S. writer, 14:12, 250:13, 318:15, 662:3, 679:7

Aldrich, Bess Streeter (1881–1954), U.S. writer, 58:10, 116:2, 343:1–2, 402:11, 455:15, 484:11, 693:7

Aldrich, Flora L. Southard (1859–1921), U.S. physician, educator, 120:14, 529:15, 545:9

Aldrich, Mildred (1853–1928), English writer, 528:17

Alec-Tweedie, Mrs. See Tweedie, Ethel Brilliana Harley D.

Alexander, Mrs. Cecil Frances Humphreys (1818–1895), Irish poet, hymnist, 147:7

Alexander, Shana Ager (1925– ), U.S. writer, editor, journalist, 36:15, 60:3, 87:3, 93:20, 94:6, 107:3, 137:1, 142:2, 187:4, 304:2, 339:17, 363:7, 393:5,

Hasluck, Dame Alexandra (1908– ), Australian writer, 324:10

Hasse, Margaret (1950– ), U.S. poet, 732:4, 780:5

Hastings, Beverly ("Carol Barkin," "Elizabeth Caroll," "Katherine Duval," "E. James Lloyd," "James Lloyd," "Elizabeth James," 1944– ), U.S. writer, 640:15

Hathaway, Helen Durham (1893–1932), U.S. etiquette writer, 426:18

Hathaway, Katharine Butler (1890–1942), English writer, 16:15, 54:6, 54:9, 97:6, 114:8, 121:15, 147:21, 162:23, 215:7, 235:8, 246:16, 258:2, 323:11, 349:11, 357:5, 403:18, 425:14, 443:8, 452:19, 501:8, 537:16, 570:2, 703:20, 715:8, 745:14, 768:1–2, 769:6

Hatshepsut (c. 1450 B.C.), Egyptian queen, 315:9, 593:4, 710:19

Hautzig, Esther Rudomin (1930– ), Polish-born U.S. writer, 252:1, 747:4, 778:8

Hawes, Elizabeth (20th c.), U.S. writer, 70:2, 98:9, 144:2, 205:3, 244:5, 430:17, 433:6

Hawkes, Jacquetta Hopkins (1910–1996), English archaeologist, writer, 682:15

Hawkins, Beverly J. (20th c.), U.S. writer, 183:15

Hayes, Anne (20th c.), U.S., 333:2

Hayes, Ednah Proctor Clarke (19th c.), U.S. poet, 68:19

Hayes, Helen (Helen Hayes Brown MacArthur, 1900–1993), U.S. actor, writer, 10:4, 140:18, 188:16, 188:18, 347:12, 389:8, 410:26, 537:5, 557:6, 570:1, 761:7

Hays, Janet Ahles (1943– ), U.S. educator, 574:6

Hays, Mary (1760–1843), English writer, 67:1

Hayslip, Le Ly (1949– ), Vietnamese-born U.S. writer, 726:12

Hazzard, Shirley (Shirley Hazzard Steegmuller, 1931– ), Australian-born U.S. writer, 242:14, 365:14, 424:9, 612:4, 675:6, 711:10, 718:7–8, 764:3

H.D. See Doolittle, Hilda

Head, Bessie (1937–1986), South African-born Botswana writer, 115:4, 310:14

Head, Edith Clare Posener (1898–1981), U.S. costume designer, 5:12, 122:18

Heaton, Rose Henniker (1884–1975), English writer, poet, 2:16, 458:11

Hébert, Anne (1916– ), Canadian poet, 522:3

Heilbrun, Carolyn Gold ("Amanda Cross," 1926– ), U.S. writer, social critic, educator, 20:20, 29:4–5, 85:15, 96:13, 139:3, 156:16, 261:7, 333:9, 335:8, 387:8, 427:12, 428:3, 431:14, 434:14, 443:9, 481:13, 540:8, 542:1, 708:3, 723:13

Heimel, Cynthia (1947– ), U.S. writer, humorist, 82:3, 90:7, 126:12, 143:16, 189:1, 221:6, 245:5–6, 264:7, 379:7, 482:7, 537:1, 556:3, 610:5, 626:1, 741:10

Hellman, Lillian Florence (1906–1984), U.S. playwright, writer, 30:3, 63:13, 78:2, 97:11, 105:4, 127:9, 135:4, 156:12, 235:14, 267:16, 301:17, 303:4, 317:14, 407:9, 423:1, 463:18, 469:16, 470:15, 478:9, 515:3, 530:2, 586:18, 592:9, 612:17, 631:13, 646:7, 651:3, 653:10, 666:16, 667:19, 689:10–11, 711:4, 712:1, 716:3, 720:15, 772:7, 773:5

Helmsley, Leona M. (1921– ), U.S. hotel owner, 680:14

Héloïse (1101–1164), French religious, 392:16, 393:6

Hemans, Felicia Dorothea Browne (1793–1835), English poet, 195:11, 213:12, 300:15, 658:18, 696:7

Hemingway, Mary Welsh (1908– ), U.S. writer, 67:13

Hempel, Amy (1951– ), U.S. writer, 494:15

Henderson, Hazel (1933– ), U.S. futurist, 203:10, 274:15, 357:8, 444:9, 489:1

Henderson, Julie K. (1950– ), Australian therapist, 303:3, 398:5

Henie, Sonja (1912–1969), Norwegian-born U.S. iceskater, 594:16, 606:4, 636:1

Hennig, Margaret Marie (1940– ), U.S. businesswoman, writer, 183:11

Henning, Rachel (Rachel Henning Taylor, 1826–1914), English-born Australian letterwriter, 674:6

Hennisart, Martha, and Mary Jane Latsis ("Emma Lathen," "R.B. Dominic," 20th c.), U.S. lawyer and U.S. economist, mystery writers, 596:11

Henry, Marguerite (1902– ), U.S. writer, 32:15, 91:18, 321:13, 389:7, 744:12

Hepburn, Audrey (Andrey Kathleen Ruston, 1929–1993), British-born U.S. actor, 734:5

Hepburn, Katharine Houghton (1907– ), U.S. actor, 417:19, 459:11, 557:8, 709:6, 754:12, 761:6

Hepburn, Katharine Martha Houghton (1878–1951), U.S. suffragist, birth control reform leader, 431:12

Hepworth, Dame Barbara (1903–1975), English sculptor, 600:6, 600:8

Herbst, Josephine Frey (Josephine Herrmann, 1892–1962), U.S. writer, 164:12, 181:18, 230:3, 569:11

Herschberger, Ruth (1917– ), U.S. writer, 441:10

Hershey, Laura (20th c.), U.S. journalist, 180:5

Hess, Joan (1949– ), U.S. writer, 8:10, 235:15

Heyer, Georgette (Georgette Heyer Rougier, 1902–1974), English writer, 654:13

Heynrichs, Jenny (19th c.), German editor, 760:16

Heyward, Carter (1946– ), U.S. Episcopal priest, theologian, writer, 286:10, 418:12, 420:13

Hibbert, Eleanor ("Victoria Holt," "Jean Plaidy," "Philippa Carr," "Eleanor Burford," "Elbur Ford," "Kathleen Kellow," "Ellalice Tate," 1906–1993), English writer, 422:2, 572:8, 734:3

Higgins, Marguerite (20th c.), U.S. photojournalist, war correspondent, 370:14, 623:7

Highsmith, Patricia (Mary Patricia Plangman Highsmith, "Claire Morgan," 1921–1995), U.S. writer, 336:10

Hildegard of Bingen (1098–1179), German mystic, theologian, 22:5, 185:16, 285:5, 285:9, 286:5, 316:5, 328:10

Hill, Anita Faye (1956– ), U.S. lawyer, educator, 625:16

Hill, Mildred J. (1878–1916), U.S. musician, 70:5

Hill, Patty Smith (1868–1946), U.S. educator, reformer, 70:5

Hillesum, Etty (Esther Hillesum, 1914–1943), German-Jewish diarist, Auschwitz victim, 132:11, 148:5, 148:14–15, 162:20, 162:22, 174:12, 175:3, 176:12, 224:14, 224:19, 242:17, 250:11, 297:2, 352:10, 352:13, 397:7, 402:17, 407:12, 512:4, 543:22, 630:8, 630:21, 631:1, 649:9, 664:1, 668:3, 668:17, 692:19, 694:4, 736:21, 762:19

Hillingdon, Lady Alice (1857–1940), Englishwoman, 620:12

Hillis, Margaret Eleanor (1921– ), U.S. choral director, conductor, 625:2

Himmelfarb, Gertrude (1922– ), U.S. historian, philosopher, 129:8, 396:11

# Subject and Key Line Index